State	Population (1000's in 2006)[c]	Per Capita Personal Income (2005)[d]	Obama/McCain Vote 2008 (%)[e]	Conservatism (rank)[f]
Alabama	4,599	$29,623	39/61	8
Alaska	670	$35,433	36/62	22
Arizona	6,166	$30,157	45/54	28
Arkansas	2,811	$26,641	39/59	6
California	36,458	$36,890	61/37	43
Colorado	4,753	$37,459	53/46	36
Connecticut	3,505	$47,519	62/36	47
Delaware	853	$37,084	61/38	42
Florida	18,090	$34,099	51/49	31
Georgia	9,364	$31,191	47/52	18
Hawaii	1,285	$34,468	72/27	48
Idaho	1,466	$28,398	36/62	12
Illinois	12,832	$36,264	62/37	40
Indiana	6,314	$31,150	50/49	16
Iowa	2,982	$31,795	54/45	23
Kansas	2,764	$32,948	41/57	10
Kentucky	4,206	$28,317	41/58	19
Louisiana	4,288	$24,582	40/59	7
Maine	1,322	$30,808	58/40	37
Maryland	5,616	$41,996	61/38	41
Massachusetts	6,437	$43,702	62/36	49
Michigan	10,096	$32,735	57/41	32
Minnesota	5,167	$37,322	54/44	38
Mississippi	2,911	$24,925	43/57	1
Missouri	5,843	$31,299	49/50	20
Montana	945	$28,906	47/50	17
Nebraska	1,768	$32,988	41/57	14
Nevada	2,496	$35,780	55/43	21
New Hampshire	1,315	$37,835	55/44	39
New Jersey	8,725	$43,822	57/42	45
New Mexico	1,955	$27,912	57/42	35
New York	19,306	$40,072	62/37	46
North Carolina	8,857	$31,029	50/49	15
North Dakota	636	$31,230	45/53	2
Ohio	11,478	$31,867	52/47	26
Oklahoma	3,579	$29,908	34/66	3
Oregon	3,701	$32,174	55/43	33
Pennsylvania	12,441	$34,848	55/44	30
Rhode Island	10,068	$35,219	64/35	43
South Carolina	4,321	$28,212	45/54	9
South Dakota	782	$32,642	45/53	4
Tennessee	6,039	$30,952	42/57	13
Texas	23,508	$32,604	44/55	10
Utah	2,550	$27,497	34/63	5
Vermont	624	$32,731	67/31	50
Virginia	7,643	$37,552	52/47	24
Washington	6,396	$35,234	58/41	34
West Virginia	1,818	$26,029	43/56	27
Wisconsin	5,557	$33,251	56/43	25
Wyoming	515	$37,270	33/65	29

Sources:

[c] Hovey, Kendra A., and Harold A. Hovey. 2007. *CQ's State Fact Finder 2007*. Washington, DC: CQ Press, 18.

[d] Hovey and Hovey 2007, 44.

[e] CNN Election Center 2008 website (http://www.cnn.com/election/2008/results)—as of November 15, 2008

[f] Adapted from: Erikson, Robert S., Gerald C. Wright, and John P. McIver. 2006. "Public Opinion in the States: A Quarter Century of Change and Stability." In *Public Opinion in State Politics*, ed. Jeffrey E. Cohen. Stanford, CA: Stanford University Press.

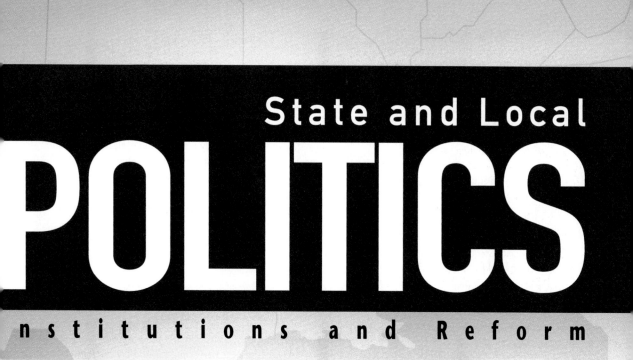

State and Local
POLITICS
nstitutions and Reform

Todd Donovan
Western Washington University

Christopher Z. Mooney
University of Illinois at Springfield

Daniel A. Smith
University of Florida

WADSWORTH
CENGAGE Learning

Australia • Brazil • Canada • Mexico • Singapore • Spain • United Kingdom • United States

WADSWORTH
CENGAGE Learning™

State and Local Politics: Institutions and Reform
Todd Donovan, Christopher Z. Mooney, Daniel A. Smith

Publisher: Suzanne Jeans
Editor in Chief: PJ Boardman
Executive Editor: Carolyn Merrill
Development Editor: Rebecca Green
Assistant Editor: Katherine Hayes
Editorial Assistant: Angela Hodge
Media Editor: Laura Hildebrand
Associate Media Editor: Caitlin Holroyd
Senior Marketing Manager: Amy Whitaker
Marketing Coordinator: Josh Hendrick
Marketing Communications Manager:
   Heather Baxley
Senior Content Project Manager:
   Josh Allen
Art Director: Linda Helcher
Print Buyer: Linda Hsu
Senior Rights Acquisition
   Account Manager, Text: Katie Huha
Senior Rights Acquisition Account
   Manager, Images: Jennifer Meyer Dare
Production Service: S4Carlisle
Cover Image: Fancy/© Jupiter Images

For product information and technology assistance, contact us at **Cengage Learning Customer & Sales Support, 1-800-354-9706**

For permission to use material from this text or product, submit all requests online at **www.cengage.com/permissions.**
Further permissions questions can be emailed to
permissionrequest@cengage.com.

Library of Congress Control Number:

Student Edition:
ISBN-13: 978-0-495-80223-5
ISBN-10: 0-495-80223-9

Wadsworth
20 Channel Center Street
Boston, MA 02210
USA

Cengage Learning is a leading provider of customized learning solutions with office locations around the globe, including Singapore, the United Kingdom, Australia, Mexico, Brazil and Japan. Locate your local office at **international.cengage.com/ region**

Cengage Learning products are represented in Canada by Nelson Education, Ltd.

For your course and learning solutions, visit **www.cengage.com.**

Purchase any of our products at your local college store or at our preferred online store **www.CengageBrain.com.**

Printed in Canada
2 3 4 5 6 7 13 12 11 10

To our families, with love: Deborah, Fiona, and Ian; Laura, Allison, and Charlie; and Brenda, Eliot, and Safi.

Studying State and Local Government

How can we best teach the politics, government, and policy of state and local government to undergraduates? As anyone teaching this course knows, American state and local governments arguably provide the single best opportunity to study political phenomena in the world. They are a manageable number of cases similar enough in social structure, economics, politics, and government to allow meaningful comparisons of them that are not overwhelmed by extraneous variation. But they are also different enough from one another in theoretically and substantively important ways to allow the exploration of a wide range of questions about political behavior and policy making that are central to our understanding of politics. What is the best way to choose our leaders? How should we make public policy? What are the impacts of our political institutions and public policies on public problems, people, businesses, the economy, or anything else? These and other fundamental political questions can not only be addressed very productively by studying the American states and communities, they can often be addressed *best* there.

The study of state and local government can be just as productive and interesting for undergraduate students as it is for working political scientists. But as we all know, an undergraduate course in state and local government is not necessarily the highlight of a student's college career. It is often taught as a large service course and required by a variety of majors—everything from education to journalism to social work—or as a social science general education course. Ironically, however, in addition to the great leverage state and local governments can provide in exploring broad political questions, these governments have a far greater practical impact on the lives of most students than almost anything else they study in a political science class. For example, most teachers and social workers will be working for these governments throughout their careers, and many journalists will at least begin their careers by covering them. As we point out throughout this book, every American is affected deeply and daily by the politics and government of the states and local communities in a wide range of ways. Most college students are already affected every day by state and local laws, ordinances, and regulations having to do with their driver's licenses and cars, the clubs and restaurants where they work and play, their relationships with their landlords, and so forth. And, of course, most of them attend large public universities that are entirely entities of these governments.

Another reason why studying state and local government can be both important for and interesting to college students is that they tend to move around more often than the average American. As they go from place to place for college, a new job, or just spring break, they are frequently exposed to the diversity of state and local laws around the country—the differing speed limits, voter registration requirements, tax structures, gambling laws, alcohol sales regulations, and so forth. For the untrained person, these variations are just confusing annoyances, but for those students taking a good state and local government class—and especially for those students who are reading this book—these are teachable moments. *As the professor of this course, you can use these students' experiences to motivate discussion of the various topics in this book* and as ways to exemplify points and train students in comparative political analysis. In the long run, these skills that you impart to students in this way will help them to both notice and understand these differences, making them more enlightened and better citizens for the rest of their lives.

Approach of this Book

We wrote this book with these teachable moments in mind, packing each chapter with lively and wide-ranging examples pulled from headlines across the nation to illuminate our points. From the outset, we have made every effort to engage, excite, and inform students about American state and local government and politics and to help them develop their critical thinking skills. Our intention was to write a book that will help you to teach an interesting and exciting course, one that both you and your students will enjoy and learn a lot from.

Themes

To accomplish this task, we have integrated the following themes throughout the book.

Institutions Matter. The central theoretical theme of this book is that institutions matter. The states and communities are especially well suited for testing and demonstrating this proposition. Furthermore, the institutions of state and local government matter a great deal, so this proposition is clearly evident to students. We want to help students understand why and how institutions affect politics, policy, and people's lives. Throughout the book, we show countless ways in which state and local government affects the lives of students, and the lives of others living in the country, every day.

Reform Can Happen. Reform is important. If institutions have consequences, then how and when they are changed is well worth considering, too. By focusing on reform, we excite

students about the possibility of change and motivate their civic engagement. If reform can happen, then political science can be a dynamic and compelling pursuit.

Comparisons Help Us Understand the Political World. This is our central methodological theme. We continually return to the questions of how politics and government differ among the states and communities and the causes and effects of this variation. To demonstrate this point and to get students accustomed to thinking comparatively, we provide dozens of maps and tables showing variation across the nation of various political, policy, and socioeconomic factors.

What Makes This Book Unique

Up-to-Date Scholarship. Since the 1990s, there has been a renaissance in political science scholarship using the states and communities to understand political processes and behavior. We have integrated the insights of this literature throughout the book so that students and instructors have access to the most current research available on the subject. *No other state and local government college textbook is as up-to-date or as thorough in its discussion of the cutting-edge literature as is this book, nor does any other textbook integrate that literature as smoothly and coherently as this one does.* We have meticulously documented our sources to assist students working on class assignments, as well as to help instructors wanting to keep abreast of this important, extensive, and fast-moving literature. Footnotes at the bottom of each page provide students and faculty with ready access to these scholarly and data sources, and our list of **Suggested Readings** and **Websites** at the end of each chapter can help direct those interested in learning more about a particular subject.

Political Science. This is a political science textbook, not just a government textbook. We very self-consciously show students how to use the variation among the states and communities to develop and test hypotheses about political behavior and policy making. Unlike other texts that simply describe how things are, we expose students to a multitude of differences among the states and communities and ask them to think critically about their causes and effects. In doing so, students will not only learn much about American states and communities, but *they will also learn how to think like political scientists*. This skill will help them in any college course they take thereafter, as well as throughout their lifetime.

Three Unique Chapters: Direct Democracy, Land Use Policy, and Morality Policy. These three subjects have been at the center of some of the most significant political battles in the country in recent years, They have recently generated a great deal of high-quality scholarship, and they are sure to engage student interest. Direct democracy—which represents one of the major institutional differences among states—has been used by citizens to pass laws cutting taxes, increasing funding for public education, banning smoking in public places, prohibiting same-sex marriage, providing funding for stem cell research, and raising the minimum wage. Land use policy, including zoning regulations and eminent domain, is central to our understanding of the historical development, and current political landscape, of many American local governments. Morality policy—from teaching sex education and evolution in the public schools, to the regulation of alcohol, gambling, and pornography, to the permissibility of abortions and same-sex marriage—has long inspired extraordinary political acts and has generated heated debate over the basic values that define our personal identities in the American states and communities.

Plan of the Book and What's New to This Edition

State and local politics have important consequences for students. The book begins with an introduction to some of the major questions asked when we study state and local politics and a discussion of some of the methods we use to answer such questions. Chapter 1 also includes a completely new opening vignette comparing the diverging public policies of two states (New Hampshire and Vermont) with similar political histories and cultures and updated data from the most recent elections. Also new to Chapter 1 is a section about state constitutions, including a table detailing some characteristic differences across the states. Chapter 2 opens with a new vignette on the protracted controversy over President Obama's federal stimulus package, and includes a new table detailing the direct aid to state and local governments under the American Recovery and Reinvestment Act of 2009. It also introduces students to how states and localities function in the American federal system, and how other models of federalism compare with "progressive federalism" under the Obama administration.

The next seven chapters introduce students to various state and local political institutions, with a particular emphasis on how different institutions, in different places, may produce different outcomes. Chapter 3 contains a new vignette about the local-level mobilization of anti-tax protesters after the election of President Obama, is completely updated to reflect the most recent elections, and examines rules that affect elections and participation. Chapter 4 covers the unique institutions of direct democracy. It highlights the latest battles over ballot initiatives, an update on initiative use and spending in the 2008 election, discussion of local recall efforts from 2009, and a new normative discussion on the impact of ballot measures on minorities. Chapter 5 covers political parties, and Chapter 6 examines interest groups. Beyond integrating the latest scholarship, both chapters have new opening vignettes, introducing students to the striking lack of interparty competition in many of the states and the efforts of state and local governments to lobby the federal government for grants, respectively. Updates to Chapter 5 include new discussions on the blanket primary system, party fusion voting, and barriers to third party access. It also contains revised 50-state party contribution data from 2008 and updated party competition strength scores. In Chapter 6, we expand our coverage of interest group contributions to state party committees and interest group power across the states, and provide new interest group scorecards evaluating the voting records of state legislators. Chapters 7, 8, and 9 examine the core institutions of American state politics: legislatures, governors (and now other offices within the executive branch), and courts, respectively. These three chapters each have completely new opening vignettes and boxed features throughout. Chapters 7 and 8 have new data and discussion of the 2007, 2008, and 2009 elections. Chapter 7 includes an enlarged discussion of bureaucratic oversight by the state legislature. Chapter 8 includes new sections on the bureaucracy and independently elected executives. Chapter 9 has three new figures.

Chapter 10 is devoted to state and local fiscal politics, and serves as a segue to a series of chapters exploring how politics affect public policy. This chapter is updated to include the most current Census of Government data on state and local finances and is re-cast to highlight the difficulty of budgeting during one of the nation's most severe economic recessions. Although all of first 10 chapters include treatments of state and local issues, Chapter 11 (municipal governments) and Chapter 12 (local land use) give particular attention to local politics and policy. Both Chapter 11 and 12 are updated to reflect the most current estimates from the U.S. Census Bureau, and the land use chapter includes new discussion of the "housing bubble" that may have caused the global financial crisis of 2008–2009. The final three chapters are devoted to specific policy areas where states and local governments are particularly influential: morality policy (Chapter 13), social welfare and health (Chapter 14), and education (Chapter 15).

For this new edition, every chapter has been completely updated, integrating the most recent scholarship on each topic, offering new extended current examples from the politics and government of states and communities around the country, and providing entirely new material in the boxed features. In addition, new for this edition are two features. First, each chapter now includes a You Decide! box. This new feature enhances the book's efforts to develop critical thinking skills in readers by adding a set of strongly normative questions for each chapter. Second, many chapters also now include a Media Resources section at the end, giving instructors and readers ideas for movies, databases, online games, and other resources to enhance readers' learning on various topics.

Special Features and Pedagogy

Boxed Features. To emphasize the themes of the book, four boxed features in each chapter highlight the effects of institutions, the comparative method, political reforms, and normative questions. These boxes provide thought-provoking, concrete examples of the kinds of problems and issues faced at the state and local level, encouraging students to understand better how institutions and political systems affect people and businesses in real-life situations.

- *Institutions Matter.* These boxes examine the way institutions influence politics, government, and policy. Examples of topics covered in these boxes include the impact that the threat of ballot initiatives has in spurring legislative action on issues; alternative views of federalism, home rule, and morality policy on decency standards in Utah and Nevada; and Alaska's use of the mixed primary system.
- *Comparisons Help Us Understand.* These boxes use comparative data from the states to test different hypotheses about the political process. For example, in Chapter 4, this

feature examines the question of whether direct democracy or representative democracy results in better outcomes for minority groups; in Chapter 5, it details the existence of factions of dissent within political parties; and in Chapter 13, it lays out variations in policies on same-sex marriage in a number of different states.

- *Reform Can Happen.* These boxes look at the different ways reforms may be implemented. In Chapter 4, for example, the feature looks at the impact of direct democracy in implementing medical marijuana legislation. Other chapters examine efforts to de-professionalize state legislatures by imposing term limits, the types of future reforms likely to inspire morality politics, and the role played by third-party candidates to place reform issues on the public agenda.

- *You Decide!* The study of politics and policy at the state and local levels is infused with normative questions, questions about what individuals or governments *ought* to do for ethical or moral reasons. Although the approach of this book in general is a descriptive and analytical one, in these *You Decide!* boxes, we raise such normative questions explicitly. For example, in Chapter 2, we ask whether concerns over homeland security should trump an individual's civil liberties when it comes to obtaining a driver's license; and in Chapter 14, we ask students to grapple with the question of whether the states or the federal government is better equipped to provide health care.

Full-Color Design. Dozens of vivid tables, maps, graphs, and photographs throughout the book provide the visual tools students need to process detailed comparative data on the states.

Endpapers. For convenient reference, the inside front cover of the book provides basic comparative reference information on state and local governments. On the back inside cover are four maps showing examples of major differences in state government institutions, a taste of the sort of variation we highlight throughout the book.

Other Pedagogical Features. Each chapter includes a full set of study aids including a chapter outline, chapter opening vignette, chapter summary, key terms, discussion questions, suggested readings, and an annotated list of websites. The chapter outlines list the major sections of the material presented so students can get a general sense of the topics to be covered. The opening vignettes introduce the chapter with a current example of an issue directly related to the material, giving students a sense of how the principles and concepts presented in the chapter play out in real-life situations. The summary provides a recap of the most important ideas of the chapter. The key terms and definitions provide an opportunity for students to check their mastery of the terminology, while the suggested readings and a list of annotated websites give students a starting point for further exploration and study.

Instructor and Student Resources

PowerLecture

ISBN-10: 1439083088 | ISBN-13: 9781439083086
This one-stop lecture, class preparation, and exam tool makes it easy for you to assemble, edit, publish, and present custom lectures for your course and prepare your examinations. The PowerPoint® lectures bring together text-specific outlines; tables, statistical charts, and graphs; and photos from the book. In addition, you can add your own materials to create an even more powerful, personalized presentation. A test bank in Microsoft® Word and ExamView® computerized testing offer a large array of well-crafted multiple-choice and essay questions, along with their answers and page

references. An Instructor's Manual includes a chapter summary, learning objectives, chapter outlines, discussion questions, and suggestions for stimulating class activities and projects.

WebTutor™ ToolBox for Blackboard®

Printed Access Card
ISBN-10: 0534274897 | ISBN-13: 9780534274894

WebTutor™ ToolBox for WebCT™

Printed Access Card
ISBN-10: 0534274889 | ISBN-13: 9780534274887
WebTutor ToolBox offers a full array of online study tools that are text specific, including learning objectives, glossary flashcards, practice quizzes, web links, and a daily news feed from NewsNow, an authoritative source for late-breaking news to keep instructors and students on the cutting edge.

Companion Website for *State and Local Politics: Institutions and Reform*

www.cengage.com/politicalscience/donovan/stateandlocalpol2e

A companion website gives students access to tutorial quizzes, learning objectives, key term flashcards, crossword puzzles, and web links.

Dozens of people have helped us with this book, both on this new edition and on previous editions. We would like to express our deepest gratitude to all those who offered countless hours of their valuable time in this way over the years.

In writing this thoroughly revised second edition, we have had help from a variety of political scientists and those working in and around state and local government nationwide. These include: Judge Tom Barber, Florida's 13th Judicial Circuit; Richard Brisbin, West Virginia University; Ben Collins, Performance Evaluation and Expenditure Review Committee, State of Mississippi; Jennifer A. Carter, University of Illinois at Springfield; Donald Haider-Markel, University of Kansas; Melinda Gann Hall, Michigan State University; Carl Klarner, Indiana State University; Beth Reingold, Emory University; Kira Sanbonmatsu, Rutgers University; STATEPOL listserv members Richard Winters, Dartmouth College; Jessica I. Monge, National Association of Latino Elected Officials; Rosalind Gold, National Association of Latino Elected Officials; Gilda Morales, Center for American Women and Politics; Patrick McConnell, University of Illinois at Springfield; Mike Snyder, University of Illinois at Springfield; Adam Brown, Brigham Young University; Janine Parry at the University of Arkansas, and John McGlennon, William and Mary College.

In addition, we continue to owe a great debt of thanks to some of the nation's other top political scientists who gave us detailed feedback on early drafts of the chapters in their areas of expertise: Thad Beyle (University of North Carolina at Chapel Hill), Chris Bonneau (University of Pittsburgh), Tom Carsey (University of North Carolina at Chapel Hill), Susan Clarke (University of Colorado-Boulder), Richard Clucas (Portland State University), Chris Cooper (Western Carolina University), Peter Eisinger (New York University), Margaret Ferguson (Indiana University at Indianapolis), Peter Francia (Eastern Carolina University), Don Haider-Markel (University of Kansas), Zoltan Hajnal (University of California, San Diego), Melinda Gann Hall (Michigan State University), Jennifer Jensen (SUNY-Binghamton), Lael Keiser (University of Missouri-Columbia), Gary Moncrief (Boise State University), Karen Mossberger (University of Illinois at Chicago), Dometrius Nelson (Texas Tech University), Adam Newmark (Appalachian State University), Steve Nicholson (University of California, Merced), Tony Nownes (University of Tennessee), Elizabeth Oldmixon (North Texas University), David Paul (Ohio State University-Newark), Marvin Overby (University of Missouri-Columbia), Eric Plutzer (Penn State University), Mark Rom (Georgetown University), Beth Rosenson (University of Florida), Richard Scher (University of Florida), Joe Soss (University of Wisconsin-Madison), Don Studlar (West Virginia University), Ray Tatalovich (Loyola University, Chicago), Bob Turner (Skidmore College), Craig Volden (Ohio State University), Carol Weissert (Florida State University), Dick Winters (Dartmouth College), Gerald Wright (Indiana University at Bloomington), and Joseph Zimmerman (SUNY-Albany).

We would also like to thank those scholars and teachers who reviewed the book for this second edition:

Matthew Beverlin, Rockhurst University
Robert E. Breckinridge, Mount Aloysius College
Frank J. Coppa, Union County College
William Cunion, Mount Union College
Alesha E. Doan, University of Kansas
Margaret Gonzalez-Perez, Southeastern Louisiana University
Janet Raup Gross, Columbus State Community College
Eric T. Kasper, University of Wisconsin-Barron County
William J. Lipkin, Kean University
Bryan McQuide, University of Idaho
Cynthia E Newton, Norwich University
Kevin Parsneau, Minnesota State University
William Pierros, Concordia University-Chicago
Sherri Thompson Raney, Oklahoma Baptist University
Jesse Richman, Old Dominion University

First edition reviewers:

Robert Alexander, Ohio Northern University
Ross C. Alexander, North Georgia College & State University
David Bartley, Indiana Wesleyan University
Jack M. Bernardo, County College of Morris
Scott E. Buchanan, Columbus State University
Thomas M. Carsey, University of North Carolina-Chapel Hill

Carolyn Cocca, SUNY-Old Westbury
Nelson Dometrius, Texas Tech University
Donald P. Haider-Markel, University of Kansas
Amy E. Hendricks, Brevard Community College
Paula M. Hoene, Walla Walla Community College
Clarkston Pressley Martin Johnson, University of California, Riverside
Andrew Karch, University of Texas at Austin
Christine Kelleher, Villanova University
Kenneth Kickham, University of Central Oklahoma
Junius Koonce, Edgecombe Community College
Adam Newmark, Appalachian State University
Anne Peterson, University of Washington, Bothell
Sherri Thompson Raney, Oklahoma Baptist University
John David Rausch, Jr., West Texas A&M University
Scott Robinson, University of Texas at Dallas
David L. Schecter
California State University-Fresno
Richard Scher, University of Florida
John A. Straayer, Colorado State University
Paul Teske, UCDHSC, Graduate School of Public Affairs
Caroline Tolbert, University of Iowa
Susan Peterson Thomas, Kansas State University
Jeff Worsham, West Virginia University

We would also like to thank those wonderful people at Cengage who have worked for years to help us turn our manuscript into this book and get it into your hands: Carolyn Merrill, Executive Editor; Rebecca Green, Development Editor; Katie Hayes, Assistant Editor; Angela Hodge, Editorial Assistant; Joshua Allen, Senior Content Project Manager; Amy Whitaker, Senior Marketing Manager; and Josh Hendrick, Marketing Coordinator. Finally, we would like to give a special thanks to Caroline Tolbert, not only for her extensive and valuable comments on the manuscript at various points in its development, but for her tremendous support, encouragement, and friendship from the beginning of this project to the end.

TODD DONOVAN (Ph.D. University of California, Riverside) is a professor of political science at Western Washington University where he teaches state and local politics, American politics, parties, campaigns and elections, comparative electoral systems, and

introductory research methods and statistics. His research interests include direct democracy, election systems and representation, political behavior, sub-national politics, and the political economy of local development. He has published extensively in academic journals, written a number of books on direct democracy, elections, institutions, and reform, and has received numerous grants and awards for his work. With Ken Hoover, he is the co-author of *The Elements of Social Scientific Thinking*, also with Wadsworth.

CHRISTOPHER Z. MOONEY (Ph.D. University of Wisconsin, Madison) is professor of political science at the University of Illinois, Springfield, and research fellow at the Institute of Government and Public Affairs

at the University of Illinois. He is the founding editor of *State Politics and Policy Quarterly*, the official journal of the State Politics and Policy section of the American Political Science Association. He has published many books and articles on legislative politics, morality policy, and research methods. He can be heard each week as a regular panelist on *State Week in Review*, an NPR radio program broadcast statewide in Illinois.

DANIEL A. SMITH (Ph.D. University of Wisconsin, Madison) is associate professor of political science at the University of Florida and Interim Director of the M.A. Political Campaigning Program. In addition to teaching graduate and under-

graduate courses on state and local politics, political parties, interest groups, campaign finance, and direct democracy, he has published widely on the politics of direct democracy, political parties, interests groups, and campaign finance. He is the author of two books on the politics and processes of ballot initiatives. Smith, a former Fulbright Scholar, serves on the Board of Directors of the Ballot Initiative Strategy Center Foundation (BISCF) and is a frequent commentator on Florida politics.

1

Introduction to State and Local Politics

A TALE OF TWO STATES

Separated only by the scenic Connecticut River, Vermont and New Hampshire are almost mirror images of one another on the map, looking like a slightly stiff yin and yang. Both lightly populated, upper New England states bordering Canada, they each have a long and rich history dating to colonial times. Vermont and New Hampshire share many geographic features—high stony mountains (the Green and White Mountains, respectively), dense forests, plenty of snow in the winter, and rural countryside dotted with quaint villages and bed-and-breakfast inns. But if we look below the surface of geology, weather, and history, we find another story. In particular, in their politics, Vermont and New Hampshire could hardly be more different.

New Hampshire's motto is "Live Free or Die," and the Granite State's long tradition of flinty, New England individualism is reflected in its state and local government. In 1776, it was the first state to declare independence from England. Today, it is the only state with neither an income tax nor a sales tax; most states have both. Instead, New Hampshire government relies heavily on "sin taxes," their so-called "beer, booze, belly, butts, and bets" revenue (i.e., liquor sales and taxes, restaurant and cigarette taxes, and the lottery). These are neither lucrative nor reliable funding sources for government services, but they do often end up being paid for by out-of-state tourists.[1] Not coincidentally, New Hampshire is one of the states with the lowest state and local government spending in almost all policy areas.

More narrowly, the New Hampshire General Court (the name of its state legislature) has wrestled with an issue that exemplifies the state's commitment to antigovernment **libertarianism**—mandatory automobile seat belt usage for adults.[2] The issue has been before New Hampshire lawmakers many times since 1995, when it became the last state in the nation without such a requirement. Every time the issue is raised, the debate surrounding it is filled with considerable angst and bitterness. At a legislative hearing on a seatbelt bill in 2009, opponents showed up in helmets, chains, and kneepads, protesting what they saw as this unnecessary intrusion into their lives. Advocates pointed to studies that showed seat belts save thousands of lives each year on the nation's highways. They also pointed to the $3.7 million annually in federal highway funds that the state would get if the law was passed. Opponents called that government blackmail and claimed that their personal liberty was worth more than $3.7 million. And it's not that New Hampshire drivers are necessarily opposed to wearing seat belts. One study showed that almost 70 percent of them do so even without the requirement.[3] What opponents objected to was the state telling them what they can and cannot do in the privacy of their personal cars.

On the other hand, consider what some people derisively call "the People's Republic of Vermont." Situated just to the west across the Connecticut River from New Hampshire, the Green Mountain State has a much more activist government and many laws that are more intrusive than simply requiring the use of seat belts. For example, Vermont has some of the nation's most restrictive laws protecting the environment and controlling land use and development. The state also has some of the most extensive social services in the country, and, in part as a result, it consistently ranks near the top of per capita state and local government spending. For example, Vermont spends 38 percent more per student educating its children than does its neighbor to the east.[4] Not surprisingly, Vermont is the more liberal of the two states, with Barack Obama winning 22 percent more votes there.

Vermont and New Hampshire were not always so different. Indeed, Vermont was every bit the Yankee its neighbor was until sometime after World War II. Even now, both states have a strong libertarian streak—witness their being among the first states to establish civil unions and same-sex marriage (see Chapter 13). While we cannot say for sure why

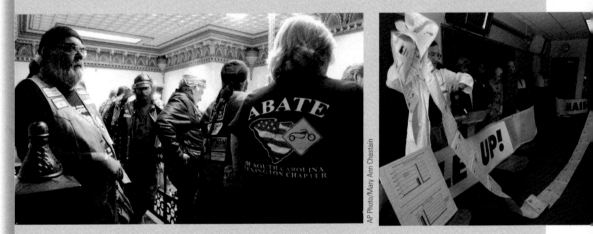

The debate over a mandatory seatbelt law in New Hampshire attracted a variety of people and arguments to the state capitol.

Vermont provides one of the most generous social service safety nets in the country.

these states diverged so much in the past half century, one theory is particularly instructive.[5] In 1931, Vermont established a state income tax both to help it struggle through the Great Depression and to help repair their many roads and bridges that had recently been damaged in catastrophic flooding.[6] As a result, during America's economic boom years in the 1950s and 1960s, this income tax caused Vermont's government revenues to increase substantially without any direct increase in tax rates. This yielded much more money for the state to provide services to its residents, and it also allowed the state to hire highly professional state workers who scoured the country for programs and policies that could be usefully applied in their state. Although these services and skilled government employees were expensive, Vermonters apparently enjoyed the services they received and put up with their tax burden, which today is the highest in the nation.[7]

New Hampshire, on the other hand, muddled through the Great Depression and beyond without adopting the income tax, although it came very close to doing so in 1949. So since then, raising state revenue typically has required politically bruising battles for less-than-lucrative revenue options, such as the 1964 establishment of the first state-run lottery. As a result, New Hampshire currently has the second lowest tax burden in the country, even though many of the state's basic demographics and public needs are much the same as those of its neighbor. This difference in government services may also have helped cause different immigration patterns in the two states. Those who enjoyed more government services "voted with their feet"[8] by moving to Vermont, while those who preferred lower taxes moved to New Hampshire.[9] Giving credence to this explanation is that some of the differences between these states have begun to fade in recent years as many out-of-staters (especially from liberal Massachusetts) have begun flocking to New Hampshire for its natural beauty and peace and quiet.

1   Richard Winters, "Political Choice and Expenditure Change in New Hampshire and Vermont," *Polity* 12(1980):598–62.
2   Jennifer Levitz, "In the Land of 'Live Free or Die,' Some Refuse to Buckle under to Pressure," *The Wall Street Journal,* 18 March 2009, online edition; Norma Love, "Seat Belt Battle Goes on in N.H.," *The Boston Globe,* 21 April 2009, online edition.
3   Kathleen O'Leary Morgan and Scott Morgan, eds., *State Rankings 2008: A Statistical View of America* (Washington, DC: CQ Press, 2008), p. 577. Mandatory seat belt advocates note that the average usage level among the states is 81 percent, so New Hampshirites use them considerably less than most.
4   Morgan and Morgan, ibid., p. 138.
5   Winters op cit.
6   Frank M. Bryan, *Yankee Politics in Rural Vermont* (Lebanon, NH: University Press of New England, 2002).
7   Morgan and Morgan, op. cit., p. 314.
8   Paul E. Peterson, *City Limits* (Chicago: University of Chicago Press, 1981).
9   Other factors undoubtedly also affected these states' differences, like New Hampshire's influential *Manchester Union Leader* and having its governor being its only statewide elected officer. See Winters, op. cit.

VERMONT

NEW HAMPSHIRE

Introduction

Welcome to the study of perhaps the most important thing you have never thought much about before—American state and local government. We start our opening chapter with this comparison of New Hampshire and Vermont because it demonstrates four key points that we hope that this book will help you appreciate about this subject and, in addition, what we hope you will also learn about politics and people, in general.

First, state and local governments are vitally important to Americans in countless ways, and not just regarding "politics" and "the economy," concepts that may seem rather vague and general to you. State and local governments have significant impacts on you, personally, in dozens of practical ways every day. Twenty-four hours a day, seven days a week, 52 weeks a year, at every stage of your life, these governments are busy affecting the quality of your life and the choices you can make. In fact, state and local governments have a far greater impact on your daily life than the federal government does—unless you are serving in the U.S. armed forces. On virtually every page of this book, you will see just how state and local governments affect you and everyone you know in a multitude of ways every day.

Our second major theme is that **political institutions** matter. Political institutions are the rules, laws, and organizations through which government functions. These are enduring mechanisms designed to translate the principles and values of public policy into reality. They often define consequences for policy makers' and citizens' choices, encouraging some and discouraging others. Vermont's income tax is an institution that is said to have had a wide range of consequences, many of them only very indirectly related to government revenue generation. This is just one of the scores of examples we will discuss in some details of how the institutions with which we organize government can have important, complex, and not always intended consequences.

Reform is the third theme of this book. Among all the forces affecting people's lives, the people and their government can change—or **reform**—its political institutions most readily. Government cannot easily alter many of the general social forces that influence peoples' lives. A state or community's partisan makeup, demography, and economy have major political and personal impacts, but the government can do little about them in the short term, even if it so desired. But virtually any political institution or policy can be reformed if the people want to do so badly enough. For example, in 1931, Vermont's leaders felt the state needed a steady stream of revenue to support the programs that the people needed, so they adopted the income tax. States and communities are constantly tinkering with their institutions and changing their policies. Throughout this book, we will discuss both the causes and effects of many such reforms.

Our final theme is that states and communities and their governments differ from one another in countless ways, and comparisons of these differences can help us understand much about general principles and patterns of politics and government. Despite the homogenizing effects of television, the internet, big box stores, and chain restaurants, this is still very much a big, diverse country. States and communities differ in their history, economy, people, and geography. State and local governments differ in how they are organized, the policies they pursue, and the institutions they establish. Even two states like New Hampshire and Vermont, which to outsiders might at first blush seem like two peas in a pod, differ in many ways. Because of these differences, it matters what state and community you live in, whether you're a student, parent, consumer, businessperson, retiree, or are filling any other role throughout your life. This diversity can be baffling and, at times, frustrating. This is especially true for governmental and political differences, because they can seem so arbitrary. For example, you may know someone who attends a public university in another state where the tuition is much higher or lower than yours—why is that the case? Other differences can be equally confusing and troubling to other people. Why are cigarette taxes so much higher in Michigan than across the border in Indiana? Why do people in Vancouver, Washington, pay no state income tax, while those just across the Columbia River in Portland, Oregon, pay no sales tax? Why does the public high school in one town have a beautiful swimming pool and a large auditorium, while the school in another town cannot afford to offer its students music or art classes? Why are the rivers cleaner and the parks nicer in some states than in others? And on and on the questions go.

The countless differences among states and communities are especially relevant for this book and the course for which you are reading it. While these differences may cause some people to scratch their heads or pound the table, political scientists see this diversity as a wonderful opportunity to extend our understanding of how people work together to survive and thrive, that is, to extend our understanding of government, politics, and policy. Because of this diversity, the study of state and local government not only raises important and interesting questions, but also offers an extraordinary way to answer them— *the comparative method.* We use the variation among the states and communities to explore the forces at work in politics and government in the United States today. For example, if we want to explain government support of higher education, we can identify states that charge different college tuition rates at their universities and compare those states on other characteristics to find clues to explain this difference. Perhaps states that charge less tuition are wealthier, have more diverse economies, or have a more liberal political culture than do other states. Perhaps these factors have subtle and complex relationships that are not obvious. With over 87,000 state and local governments in the United States,[1] political scientists

working in this field have a vast and rich laboratory. The comparative method allows us to tease out and demonstrate often quite intricate patterns of relationships.

In this chapter, we demonstrate the importance of studying American state and local government, and we explain our approach to doing so. By the time you have finished this book, we hope that you won't be able to read or hear a news story about government or politics without asking yourself:

- Why has that government dealt with that public problem in that way?
- How have other governments dealt with that problem?
- Why have these governments adopted these different approaches to solving that problem?
- Which approach to that problem is better?

In other words, you will become an amateur political scientist. But more important, you will become a better and more intellectually active citizen with the tools to understand politics and government at all levels much more deeply.

State and Local Government: At Your Service All Day, Every Day

Even though you may never have thought about it before, state and local government is intimately connected to your life every day in more ways than you can count. Just walk through your day and see how they affect you. Your alarm clock rings—the state government determines whether you will fall back and spring forward for daylight-saving time.[2]

---

[1] U.S. Census Bureau, *Census of Governments,* GC02-1(P) (Washington, DC: U.S. Government Printing Office, 2002).

[2] *Residents of Arizona and Hawaii do not change their clocks.* Daylight-saving time was a highly controversial political issue in Indiana before it was settled in 2005. See Joseph Popiolkowski, "Daylight-Savings Time Dawns in Indiana," *Stateline.org,* 20 September 2009, online edition.

State and local governments provide a wide variety of services for you, including police protection, mass transit, and water and sewer services.
David Sailors/Encyclopedia/Corbis, Kurt Rogers/San Francisco Chronicle/Corbis, MANDEL NGAN/AFP/Getty Images

Even before you're ready to get up, trash collectors bang cans in the street and the bus or mass transit train rumbles by—each of these is a local government function. You turn on the light—an extraordinarily complicated set of state and local regulations keep electricity generation safe, affordable, and not unduly damaging to the environment. You may even live in one of those communities—like Springfield, Illinois, and Orlando, Florida—where the local government actually generates and sells its own electricity. You eat breakfast—the organic milk on your cereal is regulated and inspected by state officials. You take a shower—the water is probably provided by your local public utility. You drive to school—the roads are built and maintained by state, county, and local employees, and police officers from these same governments ensure their safety. You sit down in class—if you attend a college run by a state or local government (as the vast majority of American college students do), then your entire education is controlled by employees of these governments. Your college's admissions requirements, tuition and fees, degree requirements, course catalogue and schedule, the topics that are covered in each class (even the fact that you have been assigned to read this book) are all determined by state or local government officials.[3]

Even beyond college, state and local governments affect your life and those of your family and friends in innumerable other ways. They regulate restaurants, doctors, dentists, and nurses—and even hair, fingernail, and tanning salons—to watch out for your health and safety. They regulate the insurance and banking industry to watch out for your financial well-being. Do you want to smoke a cigarette? State and local governments tax you heavily for the privilege, and then they tell you where and when you can do it. Do you want to go to a dance club? State and local laws regulate how loud the music can be, how much tax you pay on your food and beverage, who can serve you, how late the club can stay open, and how many people can enter. Do you want to build a house or start a business? Buy insurance or drive a car? Get married or get divorced? All these and many more of life's regular activities are regulated, encouraged, deterred, modified, or monitored by state and local government. They even closely regulate funeral homes and cemeteries

This may be starting to sound like some insidious plot straight out of George Orwell's *1984*, but virtually every one of these activities has been demanded by some group of citizens or businesses. Typically, people in the government are not out looking to take over more aspects of your life. Rather, we want and ask government to do many things for us—to educate us well, to build good roads, to keep

---

[3] Private colleges are also affected heavily by the governments of the states and communities in which they are located, through various laws and regulations, monetary incentives, and so forth.

us safe from crime, to ensure that the various industries and professions we rely on are safe, reliable, and honest, and so forth. In our modern, complex society, we want and need government both to encourage the things we want and to discourage those things that are unsafe or undesirable; and throughout American history, we have turned to state and local governments for help first. Washington, D.C., and the federal government are far away from most of us, both physically and psychologically. State and local governments are literally as close as the sidewalk in front of our house, the cop on the corner, and the school down the block. In fact, aside from international relations and national defense (no small things, of course), the national government has very little to do with the public services you receive every day.

These days, as has been true throughout most of U.S. history, state and local governments control virtually all domestic government policy in the country. Thus, it should be no surprise that service in these governments is extremely attractive today to high-powered individuals who are smart and want to make a difference in the world. The most obvious examples of these are Mayor Michael Bloomberg of New York City and Governor Arnold Schwarzenegger of California. Bloomberg made billions on Wall Street and in the communications industry before searching for—and finding—a greater challenge running the Big Apple. He did this so successfully that the city council repealed mayoral term limits in 2008 so he could run for his third four-year term. Schwarzenegger not only starred in dozens of box office hits, but he also ran his own very successful production company before winning the extraordinary 2003 recall election, ousting sitting Governor Gray Davis and beating 135 other candidates in the process. Schwarzenegger took on perhaps the most difficult challenge in government, running a state that some argue is "ungovernable" due to its seemingly intractable fiscal, social, and environmental problems.[4] These bigger-than-life characters,

When they brought their rock-star status to state and local government, TIME magazine dubbed Schwarzenegger and Bloomberg the "New Action Heroes."

the "New Action Heroes" as *TIME* magazine called them,[5] are just the most visible of a new generation of highly talented men and women, successful in a variety of endeavors of life, who were looking for a challenge and an opportunity to give back to their communities and found them in state and local government service. People like Bobby Jindal, governor of Louisiana, Corey Booker, mayor of Newark, New Jersey, and Jennifer Granholm, governor of Michigan, have all taken on great challenges with hard work, intelligence, and new ideas, and they have made a significant difference. When Barack Obama—who served in the Illinois State Senate longer than he served in the U.S. Senate—looked around the country to staff his first cabinet, he found almost half of them serving (or having recently served) in state and local government—four governors (Tom Vilsack, Iowa; Gary Locke, Washington; Kathleen Sebelius, Kansas; and Janet Napolitano, Arizona), two local government officials

---

[4] "The Ungovernable State," *The Economist,* 19 February 2009, online edition.

[5] Michael Grunwald, "The New Action Heroes," *TIME,* 25 June 2007, 32–38.

(Arne Duncan, CEO of the Chicago Public Schools; and Shaun Donovan, director of the New York City Department of Housing Preservation and Development), and a state agency director (Lisa Jackson, New Jersey Commissioner of Environmental Protection). Thus, state and local government not only have major influences on your life every day, but they are also where the action is for public service.

Government, Politics, and Public Policy— Definitions

To start this book, we must describe three basic concepts that are at the center of our discussion: government, politics, and public policy. Although you surely have some idea about what these are, we start with an explicit definition of each to give a clear and common understanding as we move forward.

Government

Government can be thought of as the set of authoritative institutions by which a geographically defined group of people organizes itself to achieve their common goals. As individuals, human's abilities and capacities are very limited; working together, people can do much more than they can do alone. This is something our species—and its predecessors—learned in the distant evolutionary past. Alone, no person could hunt a mastodon or even survive long in a hostile environment, much less build a dam, use stem cells to develop a cure for diabetes, or protect the environment from toxic waste dumping. Personal economic rewards can motivate people to work toward some common goals voluntarily. Microsoft was organized to make computer software and Federal Express was organized to deliver packages, and the people working together to accomplish those goals do so because they either earn a salary or a return on their investments. But it is very difficult to

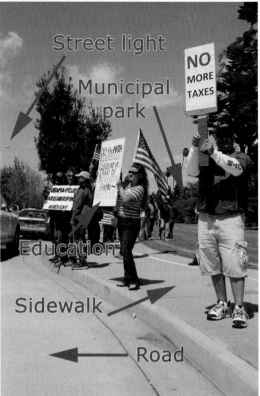

These people are holding a TEA Party on April 15, 2009—"TEA" stands for "Taxed Enough Already." But these labels demonstrate how some of their taxes were being put to work, even as they protest them. Note that the public services being highlighted here are provided by state and local governments. In addition, state and local governments provide traffic safety, police protection, and other services that allow these people to protest.

organize building a dam, studying stem cells, or monitoring the amount of waste that companies produce in such a way that an immediate profit can be made from them. Sure, towns are protected from floods, people are cured of disease, and the environment is improved. But ironically, when *everyone* benefits from the actions of a group, and when there is no way to stop those who don't help from gaining this benefit, *no one* has an incentive to contribute individually.[6]

---

[6] Mancur Olson, *The Logic of Collective Action*, rev. ed. (Cambridge, MA: Harvard University Press, 1971).

State and local elections—just like state and local government generally—bring citizens and government officials into close contact with one another.

This is what economists and political scientists call a **collective action problem**—the problem of coordinating a group of people to achieve a common goal. Think about group projects you have done for college classes; the same principle applies here. No person or company will take the initiative to complete a major project alone, no matter how meritorious, when the benefits are widely dispersed, noneconomic, and/or received over a very long period of time—the Red Cross and Doctors Without Borders notwithstanding.

So over the past 10,000 or more years, human beings have enhanced the lot of their species by developing government as a way to solve problems and complete tasks with widely dispersed, long-term benefits where the potential for short-term, private profit is limited. By paying taxes and following laws, we all help to achieve these **public goods** that benefit the community but that no one would or could accomplish alone. Government, then, consists of the people who are hired and the institutions that are established to accomplish these common tasks that help us all.

Politics

Politics is the process that a group of people uses to determine what its government ought to do. We use politics to decide which public goods our government should provide, how it should

do so, who should benefit, and how we are going to pay for them. Politics consists of elections, campaigns, lobbying, lawmaking, and much else that we see daily in the news, and each of these affects these important decisions about government action. This is most obvious in election campaigns. For example, one candidate for mayor wants to encourage economic growth in her city, while the other one focuses on preserving the environment and lowering the crime rate. In their campaigns, these candidates tell voters what they want to do and why, and then people vote for the candidate with the plan and ideas that most closely agrees with their values and beliefs. But politics is also at work, if less directly, when groups of citizens and businesses contact that winning mayor and present their arguments about what city government ought to do. The mayor then considers the values and information she hears during this lobbying, weighs it against her own knowledge and judgment, and then makes policy decisions. This aspect of politics is different than what you see in campaign commercials and debates on television, but it remains an important part of the process by which government decisions are made.

Public Policy

Public policy consists of a government's decisions and actions that are designed to accomplish the common goals identified through the political process for that **jurisdiction**. Any official or regular action of a government or its officers is a policy, including its institutions, laws, and regulations; the norms and traditions that help determine its officers' actions are also policy, if less formal and less explicitly stated. At root, every policy helps provide some public good. For example, a road's speed limit is reduced from 30 to 15 miles per hour in a school zone because it is in the city's common interests to protect young children from harm. Sometimes a government worker's action may not seem like a public policy and sometimes the public good behind a policy is hard to see. For example, professors at the University of Iowa are required to give a final exam in every undergraduate class. This is a public policy because it is a regulation established by a government official—the university's provost (who works for the state of Iowa). What is the common goal behind this final exam requirement? It is probably meant to enhance the education of Iowa students by (1) motivating them to study, (2) forcing professors to give them that motivation, and (3) encouraging professors to teach well (because poor teaching may translate into poor performance on the exams). A steady flow of well-educated college students is a public good that the university produces for the people of Iowa.

There are, then, two distinct reasons for opposing a public policy: (1) you believe that government should not pursue the common goal that the policy is meant to achieve and (2) you think that that policy will not help reach that common goal. For example, a state senator in New Jersey is pushing to legalize sports betting so that the state can beef up its sagging coffers by taxing some of the billions of dollars that are now bet illegally each year through off-shore internet sites and other ways.[7] You may oppose this policy, first, based on its efficacy in attaining its goal. That is, you may think that people would avoid the taxes by continuing to bet on sports using the illegal means they use today. But you might also argue against this policy because you don't like its goal—you just may think that the state should not be in the business of sports gambling, either for moral reasons or because you think it could lead to social problems. As any policy debate develops, different goals may be pursued and different approaches to meeting those goals may be tried. In this way, public

policy is constantly evolving through the process of political reform.

Government, politics, and public policy are all about how people work together in groups to accomplish what they cannot accomplish alone. In this book, we explore how government, politics, and policy interact with the various social and economic conditions in different parts of the United States to yield the marvelous tapestry of public life that exists today in our states and communities.

Differences in Government, Politics, and Public Policy—Three Examples

American states and communities differ in a wide range of ways, including in their governments, politics, and public policy. Not only are these differences inherently important, but also, political scientists can use them to help explain why people and groups behave as they do in the political world. You will read about dozens of these differences throughout this book, but here are three examples to whet your appetite.

Differences in Government: Choosing State Judges

All federal judges are nominated by the president and confirmed by the U.S. Senate. All governors are elected, as are all state and federal lawmakers. All secretaries of state senates are appointed by the leaders of those bodies. State judges, however, who preside over 98 percent of American court cases,[8] come to the bench in a variety of ways (see Chapter 9). In 12 states, judges for at

---

[7] Pamela M. Prah, "Sports Betting Next Target for Some States," *Stateline.org,* 7 May 2009.

[8] For data on the number of cases in federal and state courts, see the websites of the U.S. Bureau of Justice Statistics (http://www.ojp.usdoj.gov/bjs/) and the National Center for State Courts (http://www.ncsconline.org), respectively.

Figure 1.1

State Supreme Court Judicial Selection

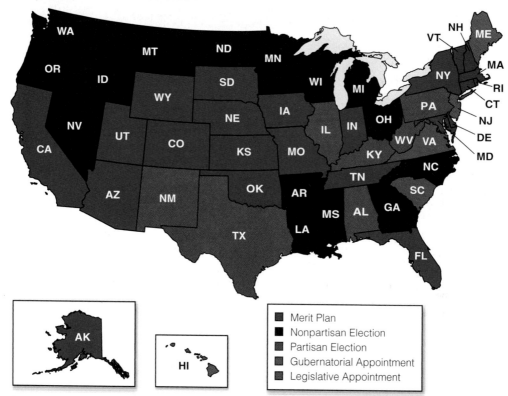

Merit Plan
Nonpartisan Election
Partisan Election
Gubernatorial Appointment
Legislative Appointment

In Ohio, party affiliations do not appear on the ballot, but candidates are chosen through partisan primaries.
**In 2010, voters in Nevada will decide whether to change from a system of nonpartisan elections for selecting their state supreme court justices to the Merit Plan.*
Source: Audrey S. Wall, *The Book of the States 2008*, vol. 40 (Lexington, KY: Council of State Governments, 2008), pp. 277–278. See the source for details.

least some courts are elected on a partisan ballot. So just like governors and state legislators, someone wanting to be a judge in these states runs for a party's nomination in a primary election or convention and then faces an opponent from the other party (or parties) in a general election. Twenty-one states use nonpartisan elections to fill at least some of their judgeships. Candidates for these judicial seats run without declaring a party label, something that is done in many local government elections. In five states, judges are simply appointed by either the legislature or the governor. Finally, 24 states use a hybrid of appointment and **retention election,**

where at the end of a judge's term, voters decide simply whether he or she should keep the job, that is, be retained.[9] Figure 1.1 shows how each of the states selects their supreme court justices.

At this point, two questions may have popped into your mind: (1) Why do states select their judges differently? and (2) What difference does it make that they do? These two questions will be discussed throughout the book regarding a wide variety of differences

[9] You may have noticed that the number of states mentioned here as having these selection methods does not add up to 50. That is because several states use different methods for selecting judges on different courts.

COMPARISONS HELP US UNDERSTAND

American states and communities vary on a multitude of factors—social, economic, political, and more. This diversity not only makes life here exciting and interesting, it can also help us understand how politics and policy work. When a political scientist sees a difference between communities or states, two big questions immediately come to mind: (1) What caused these differences? and (2) What are the effects of these differences? The cause-and-effect relationships behind the answers to these questions often both explain the narrow differences being observed at the time and enlighten us on more general processes of politics and policy making. Throughout this book, we compare and contrast states and communities and their governments to enhance our appreciation of American political life. In addition, we include a "Comparisons Help Us Understand" sidebar in each chapter highlighting how these differences can be used in this way.

among the states and communities, and we'll talk about this particular difference at greater length in Chapter 9. For now, let us say that, first, the states tend to differ from one another on judicial selection because (a) Americans have been ambivalent about exactly what they want their judges to do, and their values about this have evolved over the years; and (b) the selection method chosen by a state largely reflects the values that were in vogue about judges at the time they gained statehood or made major changes to their constitution. Second, what difference does judicial selection make? That is a tougher and, in the end, a more important question, but scholars have recently made headway in answering it. For example, one study has shown that elected judges reflect the values of the state's citizens better than appointed judges do.[10] This sounds great, but maybe not if you are convicted of a crime—another study showed that as judges approach reelection, they sentence defendants to noticeably longer sentences.[11] Perhaps more disturbing, one study

suggests that elected judges may favor defendants whose attorneys have contributed to their (the judge's) election campaign.[12] This is just one of the scores of examples we will discuss of how the institutions with which we organize government can have important, complex, and not always intended consequences.

Differences in Politics: Political Parties and Competition

American political parties are not nearly as ideological or well organized as those in most other democracies, but they still serve an essential role in our political process (see Chapter 5).[13] Among the most important functions of parties are those that they serve in the policy-making process. Almost all[14] governors and legislators are elected with a party affiliation, as are many local government policy makers. These party affiliations allow policy makers to organize themselves as to their general beliefs about policy and government action.

---

[10] Paul Brace and Brent D. Boyea, "State Public Opinion, the Death Penalty, and the Practice of Electing Judges," *American Journal of Political Science* 52(2008):360–72.

[11] Gregory A. Huber and Sanford C. Gordon, "Accountability and Coercion: Is Justice Blind When It Runs for Office?" *American Journal of Political Science* 48(2004):247–63.

[12] Damon M. Cann, "Justice for Sale? Campaign Contributions and Judicial Decisionmaking," *State Politics and Policy Quarterly* 7(2007):281–97.

[13] Malcolm E. Jewell and Sarah M. Morehouse, *Political Parties and Elections in American States*, 4th ed. (Washington, DC: CQ Press, 2001).

[14] Nebraska's lawmakers are elected on nonpartisan ballots.

By and large, this means that Republicans tend to agree more among themselves on many important issues than they do with Democrats, and vice versa. This process of sorting out and choosing up sides facilitates lawmaking, since it limits and defines the values that need to be reflected in policy and the conflicts that need to be resolved in the process. We will talk about this at length with regard to the legislative process in Chapter 7.

The states' party politics vary in a variety of ways. Some states are predominately one party or another. For example, politics in Massachusetts and Hawaii is dominated by the Democratic Party, while Republicans tend to control government in South Carolina and Idaho. States also vary on the stability of this party control. Some states have had the same partisan makeup for decades, while others have had significant changes in recent years. In particular, for over 100 years after the Civil War, the states in the southeast part of the country were known as the "Solid South" for Democrats' supremacy in the region. In the last quarter of the 20th century, however, the region, whose voters have long tended to be very conservative, began to swing toward the party that better represented its values and ideology (the Republicans) to the point where much of the South is now "solid" in the other direction—for the GOP.[15]

Another aspect of political party variation among the states that has serious implications for government and policy is the extent to which a state's legislature and governorship are controlled by the same or different parties, that is, whether the state has unified or **divided government.** Lawmaking in states where the governor and majority of both chambers of the legislature are of the same party is much different than where each party controls at least one part of these legs of the process. With divided government, a much wider range of values and opinions must be taken into account in policy making, which makes compromise and finding a balance among these values and opinions both imperative and more difficult. This is especially true when the two chambers of the legislature are divided.[16] In Figure 1.2, we show which states have divided and unified government and, of those with the latter, which are controlled by which party.

Differences in Public Policy: Capital Punishment

Since there is so much variety in government and politics around the country, it should be no surprise that public policy also varies tremendously. One of the most extreme ways in which the states' policies differ from one another is on capital punishment, that is, whether and under what conditions a state government is allowed to execute a person for committing a crime. Execution is the ultimate impact that a government can have on a person. Early in U.S. history, the states executed people for a wide variety of crimes, primarily because there was no practical alternative to punish those convicted of committing severe offenses. For example, in New York around the time of the American Revolution, 20 percent of all the sentences handed down by state courts were for hanging.[17] Over the years, as penal options expanded, public opinion changed, and the courts interpreted the U.S. Constitution differently, executions have become rare and only used as punishment for some of the most heinous murders.[18]

---

[15] Danny Hayes and Seth C. McKee, "Toward a One-Part South?" *American Politics Research* 36(2008):3–32.

[16] James R. Rogers, "The Impact of Divided Government on Legislative Production," *Public Choice* 123(2005):217–33.

[17] Walter Berns, *For Capital Punishment: Crime and the Morality of the Death Penalty* (New York: Basic Books, 1979), pp. 43–44.

[18] Christopher Z. Mooney and Mei Hsein Lee, "Morality Policy Re-Invention: State Death Penalties," *Annals of the American Academy of Political and Social Science* 566(1999):80-92. Statutes in seven states also allow for capital punishment for the rape of a child; nine states allow it for treason; and seven states allow it for various other extreme crimes. But in 2008, the U.S. Supreme Court ruled that execution for such non-murder crimes was cruel and unusual and therefore violated the 8th Amendment to the U.S. Constitution (*Kennedy v. Louisiana* 554 U.S. ___ [2008]).

Figure 1.2

Divided and Unified Party Government in the States

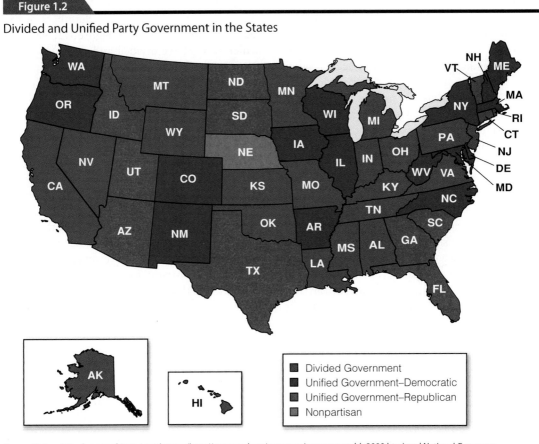

	Divided Government
	Unified Government–Democratic
	Unified Government–Republican
	Nonpartisan

Source: National Conference of State Legislatures (http://www.ncsl.org/statevote/partycomptable2009.htm) and National Governors Conference (http://www.nga.org/).

The states vary in two important ways in their capital punishment policies. First, and most obviously, 35 states allow executions for some crimes and 15 never do. And the ranks of the non–capital punishment states appear to be growing.[19] Most of the 15 non-death penalty states abolished the practice in the 19th century, but since 2007, New Jersey, New Mexico, and New York have done so, and Colorado and Maryland came close to doing so in 2009.[20] Many states have had rancorous debate on the issue for years. Religious and civil liberties groups argue that it is immoral for a government to take a life as punishment for a crime, regardless of the nature of that crime; victims' rights and law enforcement groups argue that victims deserve justice; both sides debate the deterrent effect of capital punishment. One of death penalty's opponents' more recent—and effective—arguments has been that, with all the court cases and extra costs of maintaining a death

---

[19] Every year, bills are introduced to repeal and/or reinstate the death penalty in some states. To keep up to date on legislative and executive action on this issue, see the Death Penalty Information Center's web site: http://www.deathpenaltyinfo.org.

[20] Kirk Johnson, "Death Penalty Repeal Fails in Colorado," *The New York Times,* 5 May 2009, online edition.

Figure 1.3

Capital Punishment and Executions in the States Since 1976

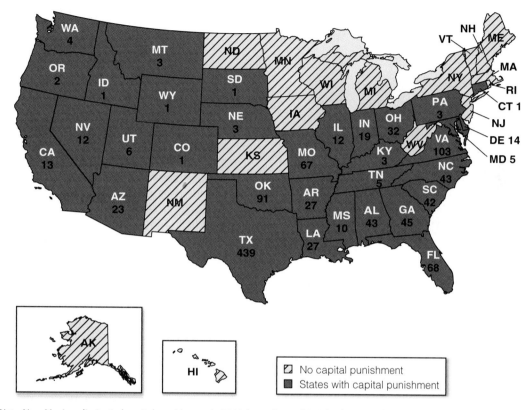

Note: New Mexico eliminated capital punishment in 2009, but prior to this, it had executed one person since 1976.
Source: The Death Penalty Information Center (http://www.deathpenaltyinfo.org/). This information is up to date as of September 10, 2009.

row, executions are actually more expensive than life imprisonment.[21]

Second, among those states that allow executions, there is great variation in how often they actually put criminals to death. Many states have capital punishment on the books more as a symbol than as a criminal justice option that is actually used much in practice. For example, Kansas and New Hampshire have executed no one since a key U.S. Supreme Court decision in 1976,[22] while Connecticut, Colorado, Idaho, South Dakota, and Wyoming have each only executed one person. On the other hand, in that same time period, Texas has executed 439 people and Virginia 103.[23] In addition, this difference is not simply a function of a state's size; Oklahoma, a state with fewer residents than Colorado and almost exactly as many as Connecticut, has executed 91 people since 1976. Figure 1.3 shows which

---

[21] John Ingold, "Death Penalty Dealt Blow," *The Denver Post,* 22 April 2009, online edition.

[22] *Gregg v. Georgia* 428 U.S. 153 (1976)
[23] For all these states, these are the numbers of executions as of September 10, 2009.

One of 86 prisoners on Oklahoma's death row, the eleventh largest in the country.

states do and do not allow capital punishment, and among those that do, the number of executions since 1976.

Diversity across the States and Communities

As anyone knows who has ever traveled more than 20 miles from home, American states and communities differ from one another in many ways besides their governments, politics, and public policy. The United States is heterogeneous in so many ways that its diversity in government, politics, and public policy is not only less noticeable but also perhaps even less significant than its diversity in other ways. In fact, the variation in the social, economic, and even geographical characteristics of this country goes a long way toward explaining some of the political and policy differences we find. We don't have space to describe the diversity of this country fully, but we can consider some of it. Much of this diversity will be familiar to you, but maybe you never thought about it systematically before or in relation to politics. As we

describe these characteristics, think about how they could help explain the diversity of policy and politics among the states and communities.

Geography and History

Some of the differences among the American states and communities are rooted in their oldest characteristics. The very geography and geology of a place can affect its politics and policy. For example, since Florida's sunshine and beaches attract so many tourists, that state can easily "export" some of its tax burden by relying heavily on the sales tax to fund its governments (Chapter 10). Likewise, Louisiana, Alaska, and Texas get outsiders to help pay for their public services by taxing oil and natural gas extraction. Indeed, any area's geography has a strong effect on its economy, which in turn has a big effect on its politics and public policy. For example, the climate and soil of the Southeast were especially suited for cotton and tobacco farming, which led to big plantations, slavery, Jim Crow laws, and conservative politics, while the flat and fertile land of the central part of the country led to independent homesteading by immigrants in the 19th century and a shift to large-scale commodity farming and the depopulation of the region with agricultural mechanization in the 20th and 21st centuries. On the other hand, New England's many rivers gave it the power needed to develop the first manufacturing economy in the country in the 19th century, which led to urban living, labor unions, and political machines. Even within a single state, geographic variation can define politics and policy.[24] For example, political conflict in Mississippi often divides those who live in its northern hills from those who live in the Delta region and those who live along the Gulf Coast. Many states' internal politics are defined by conflict between their coastal and

---

[24] James G. Gimpel and Jason E. Schuknecht, *Patchwork Nation: Sectionalism and Political Change in American Politics* (Ann Arbor, MI: University of Michigan Press, 2003).

inland areas, their mountainous and plains regions, or their rural and urban regions.[25]

Early U.S. political history can also explain much of the variation in our politics and policy that we see today. During the Civil War, 11 states seceded from the country,[26] and the politics of these states still have unique qualities that can be traced back to that war and its aftermath.[27] The residual resentment for the humiliations of Union occupation during the Reconstruction era has instilled in these states a special antagonism toward the national government, an attitude that affects federalism in these states (see Chapter 2). Politics and policy in the West still reflect traces of their years as frontier territory, such as women being more likely to be elected to office there than in most states in the East (see Chapter 7). On the frontier, everyone worked hard to survive, and so gender equality was more the norm than elsewhere in the country. In addition, these states simply needed to do whatever they could to attract women since relatively few of them wanted to endure the privations of the frontier. These two forces led to the region empowering women politically to a greater extent than elsewhere in the country. For example, women could vote in Wyoming

in 1869, 50 years before the 19th Amendment to the U.S. Constitution recognized that right for them throughout the country.

Social Forces

States and communities also differ on a wide range of social characteristics that can affect their politics and policy, a few of which are shown in Table 1.1. For example, a recent poll documented how the states vary on their residents' emotional and physical well-being—or "happiness."[28] States also vary dramatically on the extent to which their adult residents have college degrees, from 37.9 percent in Massachusetts to 17.3 in West Virginia. You might be able to conceive of many ways in which happiness and education could affect, or be affected by, politics and policy. In this section we focus on a couple of social characteristics whose political impacts scholars have explored at some length—race/ethnicity and religion. As a country of immigrants, much of these features of Americans' social heritage has been brought from elsewhere in the world in the past several generations. And just as important for understanding state and local politics in the United States, our social heritage is not evenly distributed around the country.

Historically, immigrants from the same place tended to enter the country at the same place and stay near their point of entry, at least for a few generations. As a result, big cities in the Northeast and Midwest have lots of people of eastern and southern European descent, whose ancestors arrived there in the late 19th and early 20th centuries, and the South has lots of African Americans because many of their ancestors were enslaved there until 1865. Immigrants from Latin America often came to the United States from or through Mexico and the Caribbean, so Florida, Texas, Arizona, and California have many Latino residents; immigrants from Asia often entered the country in

---

[25] Shanna Pearson-Merkowitz and John Michael McTague, "Partisan Mountains and Molehills: The Geography of U.S. State Intraparty Factionalism," *State Politics and Policy Quarterly* 8(2008):7–31; V. O. Key, Jr., *Southern Politics* (New York: Vintage, 1949).

[26] The 11 states that made up the Confederacy were Virginia, North Carolina, South Carolina, Georgia, Florida, Tennessee, Alabama, Mississippi, Louisiana, Arkansas, and Texas. Delaware, Kentucky, Maryland, and Missouri were known as Border States, since they had both slavery and significant pro-Confederacy public sympathy during the Civil War, but they never seceded from the United States. Interestingly, West Virginia began the war as a section of Virginia, but in 1863, it split off to become a separate state that supported the Union. After the war, Virginia unsuccessfully disputed the legal sleight-of-hand involved in the split (*Virginia v. West Virginia*, 78 U.S. 39 [1870]), which irritated Virginia for over 100 years. See Richard Orr Curry, *A House Divided: A Study of Statehood Politics and Copperhead Movement in West Virginia* (Pittsburgh, PA: University of Pittsburgh Press, 1964).

[27] Key, op. cit.

[28] Associated Press, "Utah, Hawaii, Wyoming Top 'Happiness' Poll," *MSNBC.com*, 11 March 2009, online edition.

Table 1.1

Social Characteristics: "Happiness," College Education, and the Importance of Religion in the States

State	"Happiness"	College Education	Importance of Religion	State	"Happiness"	College Education	Importance of Religion
AL	33	21.4	82	NE	16	27.5	67
AK	20	26.0	51	NV	38	21.8	54
AZ	10	25.3	61	NH	13	32.5	46
AR	46	19.3	78	NJ	25	33.9	60
CA	9	29.5	57	NM	17	24.8	66
CO	4	35.0	57	NY	35	31.7	56
CT	19	34.7	55	NC	34	25.6	76
DE	36	26.1	61	ND	28	25.7	68
FL	30	25.8	65	OH	47	24.1	65
GA	23	27.1	76	OK	43	22.8	75
HI	2	29.2	57	OR	18	28.3	53
ID	11	24.5	61	PA	32	25.8	65
IL	31	29.5	64	RI	37	29.8	53
IN	45	22.1	68	SC	26	23.5	80
IA	27	24.3	64	SD	39	25.0	68
KS	22	28.8	70	TN	42	21.8	79
KY	49	20.0	74	TX	21	25.2	74
LA	40	20.4	78	UT	1	28.7	69
ME	29	26.7	48	VT	14	33.6	42
MD	6	35.2	65	VA	15	33.6	68
MA	8	37.9	48	WA	7	30.3	52
MI	41	24.7	64	WV	50	17.3	71
MN	5	31.0	64	WI	24	25.4	61
MS	48	18.9	85	WY	3	23.4	58
MO	44	24.5	68	US average		27.5	65
MT	12	27.0	56				

Source:

1. *Happiness:* Ranking of the states, where 1 is the state with the most "happy" residents and 50 is the state with the least "happy" residents, where "happiness" is the 2008 Gallup-Healthways Well-Being Index. This index is based on surveys of residents using a variety of questions about their satisfaction with life, family and job, their health, and their general well-being (http://www.ahiphiwire.org/WellBeing/Display. aspx?doc_code=RWBStateRanks).

2. *College education:* The percentage of a state's population over 25 years old who had completed a bachelor's degree in 2007. U.S. Census Bureau data (http://factfinder.census.gov/servlet/GRTTable?_bm=y&-geo_id=01000US&-_box_head_nbr=R1502&-ds_ name=ACS_2007_1YR_G00_&-_lang=en&-redoLog=false&-format=US-30&-mt_name=ACS_2007_1YR_G00_R2512_US30&- CONTEXT=grt).

3. *Importance of religion:* The percentage of survey respondents in a state who responded "yes" in a 2008 Gallup poll question, "Is religion an important part of your daily life?" (http://www.gallup.com/poll/114022/State-States-Importance-Religion.aspx).

the West, so Washington, Oregon, and California have many Asian Americans.

Internal migratory patterns that developed over the years also have helped shape our current ethnic and racial makeup. For example, as political oppression and agricultural mechanization forced many African Americans to leave the South, they moved to the big cities where manufacturing jobs were plentiful, such as Los Angeles, Chicago, Detroit, and New York, especially during the two world wars. As a result, African Americans living in the Northeast, Midwest, and West tend to be concentrated in urban areas more than are those who live in the South. More recently, Latinos also have moved north in larger numbers. But even though many Latinos are also attracted to big cities (as are Americans of all racial and ethnic backgrounds), they are settling more frequently than blacks in smaller towns and rural areas, where many have found jobs in food production. Table 1.2 shows the current distribution of the major racial and ethnic groups around the country, along with the percentage of people in each state who are first-generation immigrants to this country.

A state or community's racial and ethnic composition can affect its politics and policy in a variety of important ways.[29] For example, despite the fact that they comprise a lower percentage of the population in the Midwest and Northeast than in the South, African Americans began to be elected to political office earlier in the former than the latter because their concentration in the cities more often led to their having majorities in political districts.[30] And even just the amount of racial and ethnic diversity in an area—regardless of which groups are in the majority or minority—can affect such things as public attitudes toward government and the outcomes of certain government programs.[31] One voting phenomenon that has been heavily studied (and debated) in the states and communities over the years is called "racial backlash."[32] This idea is that people in the racial majority in a place are more likely to vote against the interests of those in the minority, the larger that that minority is. This helps explain the antidemocratic phenomenon of African Americans' interests being less well represented in the South (before the changes wrought by the civil rights movement), even though they lived in the larger numbers there than in the North. And there has long been strong debate, especially in the larger and more heterogeneous states, about whether it is appropriate for small and homogenous states, such as Iowa and New Hampshire, to dominate the presidential nominating process by holding the earliest caucuses and primaries.[33]

Along with race, religion is perhaps the most important social characteristic differentiating U.S. states and communities and their politics

---

[29] Rodney E. Hero, *Faces of Inequality: Social Diversity in American Politics* (Oxford: Oxford University Press, 1998); Rodney E. Hero and Caroline J. Tolbert, "A Racial/Ethnic Diversity Interpretation of Politics and Policy in the States of the U.S.," *American Journal of Political Science* 40(1996):851–71; and Regina P. Branton and Bradford S. Jones, "Reexamining Racial Attitudes: The Conditional Relationship between Diversity and Socioeconomic Environment," *American Journal of Political Science* 49(2005):359–72.

[30] Of course, African Americans' underrepresentation in political offices in the South before the end of the 20th century was also caused by the institutionalized racism in those states that routinely denied them their political rights.

[31] Michael Rushton, "A Note on the Use and Misuse of the Racial Diversity Index," *Policy Studies Journal* 36(2008):445–59; David W. Pitts, "Diversity, Representation and Performance: Evidence about Race and Ethnicity in Public Organizations," *Journal of Public Administration and Research* 15(2005):615–31.

[32] Caroline J. Tolbert and John A. Grummel, "Revisiting the Racial Threat Hypothesis: White Voter Support for California's Proposition 209," *State Politics and Policy Quarterly* 3(2003):183–202; Michael W. Giles and Kaenan Hertz, "Racial Threat and Partisan Identification," *American Political Science Review* 88(1994):317–26.

[33] Stephen Ohlemacher, "Early Primary States among the Least Diverse," *State Journal-Register* (Springfield, IL), 17 May 2007, p. 2.

Table 1.2

State Racial and Ethnic Characteristics

State	% White	% African American	% Latino	% Asian American	% Foreign Born
AL	70.3	26.2	2.7	1.0	3.0
AK	68.1	3.8	5.9	4.8	7.2
AZ	76.4	3.5	29.6	2.4	15.6
AR	78.6	15.6	5.3	1.2	4.2
CA	60.3	6.2	36.2	12.3	27.4
CO	83.5	3.9	19.9	2.7	10.0
CT	79.6	9.4	11.5	3.4	12.8
DE	72.3	20.3	6.5	2.9	7.6
FL	76.3	15.3	20.6	2.2	18.9
GA	62.0	29.9	7.8	2.8	9.1
HI	26.6	2.2	8.2	38.8	17.3
ID	92.5	0.6	9.8	1.1	5.6
IL	70.5	14.7	14.9	4.3	13.8
IN	85.7	8.7	5.0	1.3	4.2
IA	92.6	2.3	4.0	1.6	3.9
KS	85.5	5.7	8.8	2.2	6.0
KY	89.2	7.6	2.2	0.9	2.5
LA	64.2	31.6	3.2	1.4	3.3
ME	95.2	1.1	1.2	1.0	3.4
MD	60.6	28.9	6.3	4.9	12.4
MA	82.6	6	8.2	4.8	14.2
MI	79.4	14.1	4.0	2.4	6.1
MN	87.9	4.3	4.0	3.5	6.6
MS	59.8	37.5	2.1	0.7	1.7
MO	83.9	11.3	3.0	1.4	3.5
MT	89.6	0.6	2.8	0.5	1.7
NE	89.2	4.0	7.5	1.4	5.6
NV	74.0	7.4	25.1	6.1	19.4
NH	94.8	1.0	2.5	2.0	5.1
NJ	69.5	13.7	15.9	7.5	19.9
NM	69.1	2.3	44.4	1.4	9.3
NY	66.0	15.6	16.4	6.9	21.8
NC	70.0	21.3	7.0	1.8	7.0
ND	90.7	0.8	1.9	1.0	2.4
OH	84.0	11.7	2.5	1.6	3.7
OK	74.9	7.5	7.2	1.6	5.0

Table 1.2

State Racial and Ethnic Characteristics

State	% White	% African American	% Latino	% Asian American	% Foreign Born
OR	85.8	1.7	10.6	3.6	9.8
PA	83.7	10.4	4.5	2.4	5.4
RI	82.8	5.6	11.2	2.8	12.7
SC	67.3	28.4	3.8	1.2	4.3
SD	87.4	1.1	2.3	0.8	1.8
TN	79.1	16.7	3.5	1.3	4.1
TX	70.3	11.5	36.0	3.4	16.0
UT	90.0	1.0	11.6	2.0	8.2
VT	96.1	0.6	1.3	1.1	3.4
VA	70.4	19.6	6.6	4.8	10.3
WA	80.7	3.4	9.4	6.6	12.3
WV	94.4	3.4	1.1	0.6	1.3
WI	87.3	6.0	4.9	1.9	4.5
WY	91.6	0.6	7.3	0.6	3.1
US average	73.9	12.4	15.1	4.4	12.6

Source: These are estimates of the racial and ethnic makeup of the states in 2007 (the last year these data were available at press time) made by the U.S. Census Bureau from their *2007 American Community Survey, 1-Year Estimates* (http://factfinder.census.gov/servlet/GRTSelectServlet?ds_name=ACS_2007_1YR_G00_).

and policy. There is a deep irony in the role of religion and politics in this country. While the U.S. Constitution guarantees freedom of and from religion, and while the United States was the first country to recognize such rights, today, we are probably the most religious country in the Western world.[34] Many of our earliest immigrants came here to escape religious persecution in Europe, but once they arrived, they frequently set up religiously oppressive regimes of their own.[35] People of different religions established settlements in different parts of the Eastern Seaboard. Puritans established a colony in what is now Massachusetts, Roman Catholics did so in Maryland, Quakers in Pennsylvania, French Protestants in South Carolina, and so on. American states and communities continue to vary in the proportion of different religious denominations' adherents that live in them.[36] Besides denomination, the general propensity to be religious varies from place to place. A 2008 Gallup poll of 350,000 Americans found that fully 85 percent of Mississippians agreed when asked the question, "Is religion an important part of your daily life?" while only 42 percent of Vermonters did so.[37]

Not surprisingly, such large variation on this important social force can lead to significant differences in politics and policy around the country.

[34] Pippa Norris and Ronald Inglehart, *Sacred and Secular: Religion and Politics Worldwide* (New York: Cambridge University Press, 2004).
[35] James A. Morone, *Hellfire Nation: The Politics of Sin in American History* (New Haven, CT: Yale University Press, 2003).
[36] Clifford Grammich, *Many Faiths of Many Regions: Continuities and Changes among Religious Adherents across U.S. Counties,* WR-211(Santa Monica, CA: RAND Labor and Population working paper series, 2004).
[37] Frank Newport, "State of the States: Importance of Religion" Gallup Poll Report, 28 January 2009 (http://www.gallup.com/poll/114022/State-States-Importance-Religion.aspx).

America's great economic, social, and racial diversity are reflected in the great diversity of the policy and politics of the states and communities.

Perhaps most obviously, we know that a state or community's religious makeup influences policies that have a strong moral dimension, such as abortion regulation and same-sex marriage (see Chapter 13).[38] But religion can also have unexpected effects, such as the Roman Catholic Church's strong influence on education policy in some places due to its long tradition of running parochial schools. In fact, in big cities with many Catholic residents, such as New York, Los Angeles, and Chicago, the Catholic school system can rival the public school system for students and resources. As a result, even state-level education policy can be affected.

Economic Characteristics

Certainly, the geographic, historical, and social characteristics of a state or community help shape its economy, but how people earn their living and the types of businesses and industries that exist in a place can also have significant independent effects on its government, politics, and public policy. This becomes especially obvious in a time of great economic strife, as the country experienced since the end of 2008. States that rely on manufacturing and exports, such as California, or where the real estate boom of the 1990s and 2000s was especially strong, such

as Nevada and, again, California, have been especially hard hit by the current recession, so their state and local government budgets have been decimated to an even greater extent than in other states.[39] In one month (February 2009), one in every 60 homes in Las Vegas was in some stage of foreclosure, more than seven times the national average.[40] Under those conditions, a city both has the greatest need for revenue, to help those in need, and the least ability to generate it, since local governments rely heavily on property taxes (see Chapter 10). By one estimate, all but four state governments were projected to have a budget deficit in 2010.[41] The states that are in the best fiscal shape—Alaska, Montana, North Dakota, and Wyoming—have small populations and significant mineral resources that have helped them through the recession. On the other hand, Michigan, whose economy has long been focused on the recently decimated automobile manufacturing industry (Cash-for-Clunkers, notwithstanding), continues its downward track from a rich industrial state to an impoverished state losing population and searching for a way forward. Projected state government budget deficits for 2010 are

---

[38] Raymond Tatalovich and Byron W. Daynes, eds., *Moral Controversies in American Politics*, 3rd ed. (Armonk, NY: M. E. Sharpe, 2004); Christopher Z. Mooney, ed., *The Public Clash of Private Values: The Politics of Morality Policy* (Chatham, NJ: Chatham House, 2001).

[39] Katharine Q. Seelye, "To Save Money, States Turn to Furloughs," *The New York Times*, 24 April 2009, online edition.

[40] Brian Wargo, "Las Vegas Leads Nation in Foreclosures," *Las Vegas Sun*, 11 March 2009, online edition.

[41] Iris J. Lav and Elizabeth McNichol, "State Budget Troubles Worsen," Center on Budget and Policy Priorities report, 18 May 2009 (http://www.cbpp.org/cms/?fa=view&id=711).

| Figure 1.4 |

Projected State Government Budget Deficits, 2010

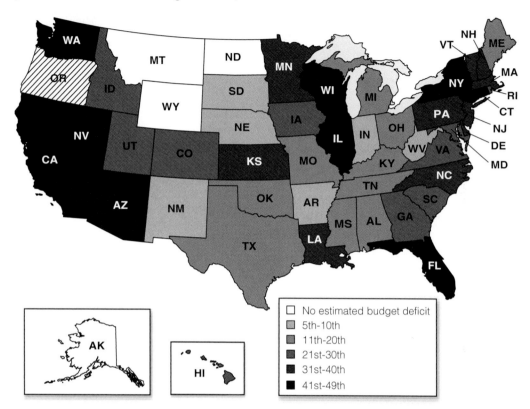

Note: A state government budget deficit is the difference between the amount of money it spends and the amount it receives in taxes and other revenue in a fiscal year. This set of estimates is from: Iris J. Lav and Elizabeth McNichol, "State Budget Troubles Worsen," Center on Budget and Policy Priorities report, 18 May 2009 (http://www.cbpp.org/cms/?fa=view&id=711). This study had no data for Oregon.

one way to assess a state government's current financial woes. Figure 1.4 shows how state deficits are distributed around the country.

Public policy is influenced in many ways by the shape of a location's economy. Everything from education funding and environmental regulation to infrastructure needs and taxation is influenced by the sort of economic activity in a state or community. One important economic characteristic that Michigan's plight suggests is the extent to which a state has moved from an economy based on the production of goods to one based on services, especially in the high-tech sector of the economy. The

"digital divide" not only distinguishes between people who use and are comfortable with technology from those who are not, it also distinguishes between states that have a strong technology sector in their economy from those that do not.[42]

Finally, a state or community's wealth can have wide-ranging political effects. Places with more money can certainly afford to provide

---

[42] Karen Mossberger, Caroline J. Tolbert, and Mary Stansbury, *Virtual Inequality: Beyond the Digital Divide* (Washington, DC: Georgetown University Press, 2003).

Table 1.3

Economic Characteristics—IT Jobs, Household Income, and Home Foreclosures in the United States

State	IT Jobs	Household Income	% Home Foreclosures	State	IT Jobs	Household Income	% Home Foreclosures
AL	1.9	$40,554	0.268	NE	2.2	$47,085	0.474
AK	1.9	$64,333	0.486	NV	1.6	$55,062	3.376
AZ	1.7	$49,889	1.516	NH	2.3	$62,369	0.212
AR	1.9	$38,134	0.513	NJ	3.3	$67,035	0.902
CA	3.1	$59,948	1.921	NM	2.0	$41,452	0.357
CO	3.5	$55,212	1.919	NY	3.2	$53,514	0.493
CT	2.7	$65,967	0.833	NC	2.0	$44,670	0.739
DE	1.8	$54,610	0.266	ND	2.1	$43,753	0.082
FL	2.4	$47,804	2.002	OH	2.0	$46,597	1.797
GA	2.9	$49,136	1.566	OK	2.3	$41,567	0.520
HI	2.1	$63,746	0.197	OR	2.1	$48,730	0.543
ID	2.1	$46,253	0.611	PA	2.2	$48,576	0.302
IL	2.4	$54,124	1.250	RI	2.1	$53,568	0.410
IN	2.0	$47,448	1.027	SC	1.8	$43,329	0.220
IA	2.2	$47,292	0.314	SD	2.1	$43,424	0.007
KS	2.9	$47,451	0.203	TN	2.0	$42,367	0.983
KY	2.1	$40,267	0.274	TX	2.4	$47,548	0.936
LA	1.8	$40,926	0.204	UT	2.6	$55,109	0.852
ME	2.1	$45,888	0.042	VT	2.3	$49,907	0.009
MD	2.8	$68,080	0.830	VA	2.7	$59,562	0.514
MA	3.0	$62,365	0.660	WA	2.8	$55,591	0.573
MI	2.0	$47,950	1.947	WV	1.7	$37,060	0.053
MN	2.3	$55,802	0.513	WI	2.1	$50,578	0.486
MS	1.6	$36,338	0.114	WY	1.5	$51,731	0.151
MO	2.4	$45,114	0.906	US average	2.5	$54,740	1.033
MT	2.0	$43,531	0.268				

Source:
1. IT Jobs: The percentage of the civilian employed population 16 years old and over in a state that is working in the information technology industry, 2007 (U.S. Census Bureau: http://factfinder.census.gov/servlet/GRTTable?_bm=y&-_box_head_nbr=R2405&-ds_name=ACS_2007_1YR_G00_&-_lang=en&-format=US-30&-CONTEXT=grt).
2. Household Income: Median household income in a state, 2007 (U.S. Census Bureau: http://factfinder.census.gov/servlet/GRTTable?_bm=y&-ds_name=ACS_2007_1YR_G00_&-_col=disp_order&-CONTEXT=grt&-mt_name=ACS_2007_1YR_G00_R1901_US30&-_source=mdr&-redoLog=false&-geo_id=01000US&-format=US-30&-_lang=en)
3. Home Foreclosures: The percentage of households in a state that have filed for bankruptcy, 2007 (From: Melinda Fulmer, "States Ranked by Foreclosure Rates," *MSN Real Estate*, n.d., online edition (http://realestate.msn.com/article.aspx?cp-documentid=13107814).

better public services to their citizens. But less obviously, and sadly, wealthy places actually need to tax their citizens at a lower rate than poorer places. This is because they have more wealth to tax, so doing so at a lower rate yields plenty of resources for government. For example, 10 percent of $100 is the same as 1 percent of $1,000. Furthermore, wealthy states and communities typically need fewer resources overall because well-off people need certain

YOU DECIDE

Discussions of politics and government often cry out for normative judgments, that is, value judgments about what is good and what is bad, what government ought to do, what it ought not to allow people to do, and so forth. Like other scientists, in their professional work, political scientists tend to avoid the normative and focus more on descriptive analysis of the world. That is, we emphasize questions of what is, rather than what ought to be. But policy makers and voters always make normative judgments about government and politics, and as active citizens who are interested in their world, political scientists can be excused for sometimes having opinions and values and hoping to see them inform policy and government. Indeed, many political scientists work as policy analysts for governments or interest groups, as advisors for candidates and parties, and even as elected officials themselves from time to time. As you read this book, you will undoubtedly feel the urge to express an opinion about a variety of the policies and government institutions we discuss—at least we hope that you do. In each chapter, we include a "You Decide" sidebar that highlights a normative question about policy or government that we hope you think about carefully and about which you come to a reasoned decision. We hope that you use some of the comparative skills you have learned to arrive at your decisions or to think about the other information you would need to do so.

expensive government services (such as social welfare programs and police and fire protection) less than poor people. This is why people find that their property taxes sometimes go down when they move to the suburbs from the city, even though their schools and other services are sometimes better. On the other hand, people with more money often demand higher-quality government services and are willing to pay for them. For instance, they may be willing to pay higher taxes for high schools that offer several foreign languages and have a swimming pool, whereas these may be luxuries that a poor community simply cannot afford, no matter how much they may want them, since they have fewer resources and a greater need for remedial reading and math classes, counselors, security, and so forth.

These are just a few of the multitude of ways in which a state or community's economy can have significant effects on its government, politics, and public policy. As you read through this book, you will see many more.

Political Values

Last, but probably most obviously, another set of potential explanations for the political differences among the states and communities is the thoughts, ideas, and values of the people who live there. Of course, in a democracy, we believe that what voters want and believe should determine the form of government they have and the policies that their government pursues. And in broad terms, scholars have found that this is indeed the case in the American states and communities.[43]

---

[43] Robert S. Erikson, Gerald C. Wright, and John P. McIver, *Statehouse Democracy: Public Opinion and Policy in the American States* (New York: Cambridge University Press, 1993); and Robert S. Erikson, Gerald C. Wright, and John P. McIver, "Public Opinion in the States: A Quarter Century of Change and Stability," in *Public Opinion in State Politics*, ed. Jeffrey E. Cohen (Stanford, CA: Stanford University Press, 2006); Charles Barrilleaux, Thomas Holbrook, and Laura Langer, "Electoral Competition, Legislative Balance, and American State Welfare Policy," *American Journal of Political Science* 46(2002):415–27.

First, consider people's most deep-seated ideas and values about politics, the proper role of government, and other people. These beliefs do not change quickly over time, either for an individual or a community, and they are not evenly distributed around the country.[44] The most common way Americans think about general political values is along a one-dimensional continuum of **political ideology**, from liberal to conservative. Although most Americans—and even political scientists—would be hard-pressed to define these terms clearly, people have a general understanding about what they mean and are willing to tell a pollster where they fall on this continuum. Those places in the United States that are more conservative tend to elect more Republicans and have policies that we associate with that ideology and that party, such as stricter abortion and gambling regulations, less spending on education and welfare, more punitive criminal laws, and tax rates that are harder on the poor.[45] There is a similar correlation between policy, party, and ideology in the more liberal and Democratic places around the country. Although this may not surprise you, only recently have scholars been able to find solid evidence that, in fact, Americans' values are translated fairly accurately through political parties into public policy.[46] Scholars were able to do this by taking advantage of the variation found on these factors among the U.S. states and communities.

Look at Figure 1.5, showing the states' political ideology, and Figure 1.6, showing how the states voted in the 2008 presidential election. Notice that you can see how ideology and partisan voting is related, even for presidential elections, where voters know much more about candidates than their party affiliation. Of course, there are some discrepancies between these two maps. What might explain these disconnects between ideology and partisan voting? As you read further in this book, you will learn that we often find complicated relationships among the characteristics of the states that can help us understand politics and policy better than if we only studied a single government.

Next, consider more specifically a place's **political culture** that is, its residents' general attitudes about what government should be like and what it ought to do. A generation ago, political scientist Daniel Elazar made an observation about state political culture that scholars still use fruitfully today. Elazar argued that the United States has three dominant political cultures based on the values and attitudes of our original European settlers and the ways in which they migrated through the country.[47] As Figure 1.7 shows, the northern tier of states was populated more by reform-minded Protestants (starting with the Pilgrims of Plymouth Rock) who began in New England and then moved across the top of the country. These descendants of the Pilgrims were met in the rural areas of the upper Midwest by later-arriving, but like-minded, Scandinavians. These two groups of people tended to view government as a valuable tool with which to improve social conditions, and they felt that all citizens should participate in the political process in order to do so. Elazar called this set of attitudes a **moralistic political culture,** and we see strong remnants of it today in places like New Hampshire, Wisconsin, and Oregon.

---

[44] Paul Brace, Kevin Arceneaux, Martin Johnson, and Stacy G. Ulbig, "Reply to 'The Measurement and Stability of State Citizen Ideology.'" *State Politics and Policy Quarterly* 7(2007):133–40.

[45] This was not always the case, since the very conservative South tended to vote Democratic for over 100 years after the Civil War out of animosity toward the party of Lincoln, which defeated the Confederacy. In the past generation, partisan politics in the South has become much more reflective of the values of the parties nationwide (see Chapter 5).

[46] Robert S. Erikson, "The Relationship between Public Opinion and State Policy: A New Look Based on Some Forgotten Data," *American Journal of Political Science* 20(1976):25–36.

---

[47] Daniel J. Elazar, *American Federalism: A View from the States,* 3rd ed., (New York: Harper and Row, 1984), Chapter 5.

Figure 1.5

Political Values: Conservatism versus Liberalism

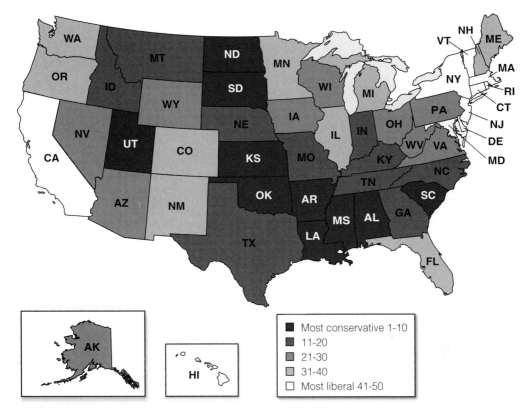

Most conservative 1-10
11-20
21-30
31-40
Most liberal 41-50

Note: These data represent the average of hundreds of public opinion polls undertaken from 1996 to 2003. In this map, the darker the state, the more conservative are its residents. The *darker* the state, the *more conservative* it is, and the *lighter* the state, the *more liberal* it is.

Source: Adapted from: Erikson, Robert S., Gerald C. Wright, and John P. McIver. 2006. "Public Opinion in the States: A Quarter Century of Change and Stability." In *Public Opinion in State Politics,* ed. Jeffrey E. Cohen. Stanford, CA: Stanford University Press.

In contrast, the southern tier of states was originally settled by wealthy planters and noblemen from England and elsewhere, along with their African slaves and many white indentured servants. The social structure that evolved for this plantation economy led to a political culture where government was viewed as something that the social and economic elites could use to maintain and preserve the status quo—with them on top. Thus, it was thought that those in the lower classes (black or white) should not get involved in politics and government and not expect to get much from them. Elazar called this a **traditionalistic politics culture,** and the politics of places like Mississippi, South Carolina, and Virginia continue to reflect this culture, more or less.

Finally, the mid-Atlantic seaboard states and the big cities of the Midwest tended to be settled by people who arrived with perhaps less money than the Southern planters, but with a nonetheless strong commercial attitude, both about life in general and about government. These industrious people sought their fortunes through business and hard work, and they did not see any problem with government helping

Figure 1.6

Voting in the 2008 Presidential Election

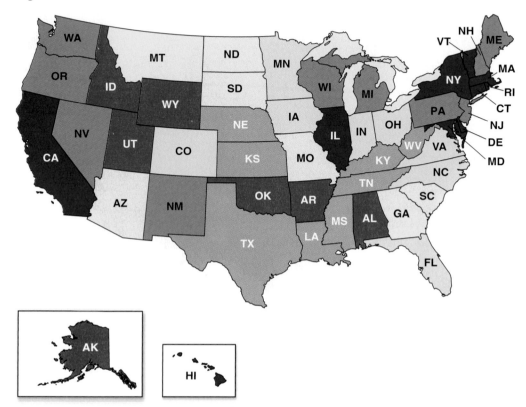

Note: In this map, the darker the color, the more lop-sided the victory for Barack Obama (if blue) or John McCain (if red).
Source: CNN Election Center 2008 website (http://www.cnn.com/election/2008/results) November 15, 2008.

a person achieve his or her own personal economic goals. As a result, political machines arose in these areas to help immigrants adjust to American life, and a little political corruption was sometimes tolerated as the price for making government work. This culture still influences politics and policy in places like New Jersey, Illinois, and Ohio, and Elazar called it an **individualistic political culture.**

According to Elazar, as Americans moved generally westward across the country in the 19th and 20th centuries, they took their political cultures with them, so that these cultures also diffused generally in an east-west

pattern across the country. The impacts of this dimension of political culture have been wide-ranging. For example, places with a moralistic political culture make it easier for people to vote, places with an individualistic political culture have stronger and more competitive political parties, and places with a tradition-alistic political culture spend less money on education and public services for their poor.[48]

---

[48] For an example of a political culture argument informed by Elazar's framework, see Joel Lieske, "Regional Subcultures of the United States," *Journal of Politics* 55(1993):888–913.

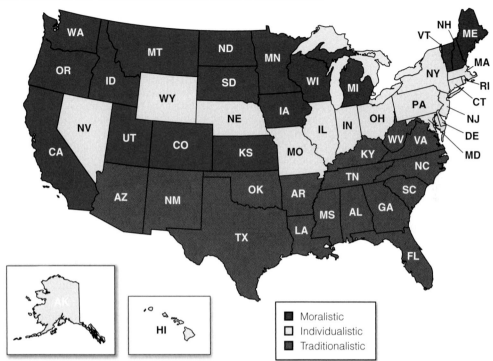

Figure 1.7

Political Culture in the United States: Daniel Elazar's Classification

■ Moralistic
□ Individualistic
■ Traditionalistic

Note: See the text for definitions of Elazar's categories of political culture.
Source: Elazar, Daniel J. 1984. *American Federalism: A View from the States.* 3rd ed. New York: Harper and Row, 136–7.

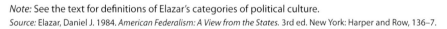

The Rules of the Game Have Consequences: Political Institutions, State Constitutions, and Reform

As you can see, even in the 21st century, the United States is a highly diverse country. Television, the internet, and Americans' penchant for peripatetic movement have homogenized the country to some degree, but Arizona is still not Ohio, and New York City is still not Los Angeles. You have already seen how some of the fundamental differences among people and places can go a long way toward explaining

some of the differences we see in politics and policy around the country. But just as people's lives are not completely determined by the circumstances into which they were born (like their race, their parents' income, and where they live), people in the states and communities make choices about their governments that affect their politics and policy for good or ill. That is, we can establish the political institutions that we want, and these institutions can affect the way we live and how our governments work. Just as important, if we want to change our policies or politics or the world we live in, we need to concentrate on the aspects of civil society that we are able to *change*. Someone who wants to ban capital punishment cannot suddenly make her state more liberal. Nor can someone who wants to spend more money on

REFORM CAN HAPPEN

A "reform" is simply a change in something, usually a policy or an institution. But the word has the connotation of being both a positive and a purposeful change. A reform doesn't just happen by accident; it is an intentional change made because a certain effect is expected. Political advocates use the word to encourage support for a proposed change. After all, who can be against a "reform"? Calling something a reform also implies a relatively broad and systematic change. Thus, "reform movements" push for a variety of related changes, and we talk about several of these in this book, such as movements to increase campaign finance regulation, change the selection of judges, and limit the terms of state legislators. In each chapter, we include a "Reform Can Happen" sidebar that focuses on a reform movement—large or small, broad or narrow—involving state or local government. These sidebars demonstrate that policy and institutions—even the oldest and most well-known—are established by people and that they can be changed when either they are found to be deficient or people's goals and values change.

state universities easily make his state wealthier. But people can reform their state's political institutions to facilitate the enactment of the policies they would like. Therefore, political institutions take on a special importance in the study and explanation of the political differences among the states and communities.

State Constitutions

When you talk about the institutions of state and local government in the United States, the first place to look is in state **constitutions.** These are the basic charters that set out the guiding principles behind, and establish the major institutions of, both state and local government.[49] In this way, state constitutions are much like the U.S. Constitution. This should not be surprising, since 32 of the 39 signers of the U.S. Constitution had served in one of the original 13 states' legislatures and were therefore intimately familiar with the governments that those states' constitutions had established.[50] Then as

new states were admitted to the union, their constitutions were usually copied in large part from one of the earlier states' charters.

State constitutions define the major institutions of state and local government, such as the powers of the governor, the functions and forms of the legislature, the organization of the court system, and many more. Many of the institutional differences among state governments are enshrined in these constitutions, as we will discuss at length throughout this book. For example, in Chapter 4, we talk about how voters in 24 states can initiate ballot measures to change a state's law or even its very constitution. In Chapter 8, we describe how seven states have no elected lieutenant governor, and in Chapter 9, we discuss how some states have intermediate courts of appeal and some do not.

In addition to these institutions, state constitutions also establish basic rights for its residents. Most state charters contain a "bill of rights," often echoing federal constitutional rights. This is often redundant, because the federal constitution sets a minimum floor for the rights that all Americans enjoy. But state constitutions frequently establish rights for their residents that are even more extensive than those guaranteed by the national document.

---

[49] George E. Connor and Christopher W. Hammons, eds., *The Constitutionalism of American States* (Columbia, MO: University of Missouri Press, 2008).

[50] Peverill Squire and Keith E. Hamm, *101 Chambers: Congress, State Legislatures, and the Future of Legislative Studies* (Columbus, OH: The Ohio State University Press, 2005), p. 19.

For example, the Hawaii Constitution has a bill of rights with 25 sections, including the right to bear arms and limitations on the quartering of soldiers, as in the federal document, but also including rights having to do with marriage, sexual assault against minors, and public access to information. And Hawaii's charter has by no means the most extensive bill of rights section. Variations in state constitutions mean that residents of different states have different rights. Even just the wording of these rights on the same topic can lead to significant differences for people in the states. Consider the South Carolina Constitution, which says that the state shall provide: "a system of free public schools open to all children [and] establish, organize and support such other public institutions of learning, as may be desirable." This defines a relatively weak right to education when compared with places like Kentucky and Ohio, whose constitutions require "thorough and efficient" education, or Florida and Virginia, whose constitutions give all students the right to a "quality" education (see Chapter 15).

In addition to these more extensive provisions of basic rights, state constitutions have other important differences from the U.S. Constitution. First, unlike the federal document, state constitutions frequently deal with specific public policy. Americans experimented with putting policy in the U.S. Constitution during the 1920s, with the 18th Amendment banning alcohol sales (i.e., "prohibition"), but this was such a disaster that it was repealed in 1933 (see Chapter 13). But the states have always zealously incorporated policy into their constitutions, largely because it was a "safe" place to do so.[51] That is, regular laws, or **statutes,** can be changed relatively easily, but constitutional provisions typically require larger majorities in the legislature and/or a vote by the people. If an interest group has the political strength

to accomplish this at a given moment in time, inserting policy into the constitution reduces the chances of it being overturned when public opinion changes at a later date. As a result, state constitutions can have a dizzying array of policy written into them, such as the Ohio Constitution mandating a bonus for Korean War veterans,[52] the Oklahoma Constitution setting the maximum level of interest a bank can charge for a loan,[53] and the Utah Constitution prohibiting children under the age of 14 from working in underground mines.[54]

Another way that state constitutions differ from the federal constitution has to do with the difference between relationship between the federal and state governments, on one hand, and a state and its local governments, on the other. As discussed in Chapter 2, while the states have considerable autonomy with respect to the federal government, local governments are entirely creatures of their state. That is, local governments only exist because state governments create them, and the ways in which local governments are established are laid out in a state's constitution. Most state constitutions have a major section describing how local governments can be founded, defining the types of local governments, and spelling out local government structure, responsibilities, and prerogatives. Each local government typically has a **local charter,** a document that acts like a constitution, outlining basic institutions and sometimes rights. But a state's constitution closely circumscribes the choices that can be made in the form and content of local charters. The U.S. Constitution, on the other hand, deals with its relationship with the states in a single provision of 28 words—the 10th Amendment—which says that the states have

---

[51] Christopher Hammons, "Was James Madison Wrong? Rethinking the American Preference for Short, Framework-Oriented Constitutions," *American Political Science Review* 93(1999):837–49.

[52] Steven H. Steinglass and Gino J. Scarselli, *The Ohio State Constitution: A Reference Guide* (Westport, CT: Praeger, 2004).

[53] Danny M. Adkison and Lisa McNair Palmer, *The Oklahoma State Constitution: A Reference Guide* (Westport, CT: Praeger, 2001).

[54] Jean Bickmore White, *The Utah State Constitution: A Reference Guide* (Westport, CT: Praeger, 1998).

the right to do whatever they want to do as long as it does not violate the federal constitution. Since the states have complete control and responsibility for their local governments, their constitutions must spend a good deal of space discussing them.

Because of their more extensive discussion of rights, policy, and local government, state constitutions are typically much longer than the U.S. Constitution, which has roughly 8,300 words. As you can see in Table 1.4, state constitutions range from New Hampshire's concise 9,200-word document to Alabama's whopping 350,000-word tome; the 50 documents average about 26,000 words.[55] Since they are so long and complicated, states tend to amend their constitutions rather frequently. While the federal constitution has been amended only 27 times since it was ratified in 1788, only Illinois (11) and Rhode Island (10) have amended their state charters less often—and their present constitutions were adopted in 1970 and 1986, respectively. Thirty states have amended their existing constitutions over 100 times each, and most states having completely rewritten their charters at least once in their history.

Reform and Institutions

A major theme of this book is that *political institutions influence politics and public policy.*[56] As anyone who has ever played volleyball, Dungeon and Dragons, or Halo knows, the rules of a game have a significant impact on who wins, and it is no different in government and politics. Political institutions are the rules that define how the game of government and politics is played, the end product of that game being public policy. But the rules of this

game are far more detailed and complicated than even those of Dungeons and Dragons. Some political institutions are at least somewhat familiar to everyone, like the governor's office, the local school board, and the state's Department of Natural Resources. These institutions have buildings and staff with official titles, some of whom even wear uniforms. These really *look* like institutions. But some political institutions exist simply as sets of rules without physical edifice. For example, there is no building you can point to and say, "That is a primary election system," but a primary election system is a political institution that is both very important and varies from state to state (Chapter 3). Direct democracy (Chapter 4), political parties (Chapter 5), and interest groups (Chapter 6) are also this type of institution.

More important than any outward trappings, a political institution consists of a more or less elaborate set of rules, some of which are laws, some official regulations, and some merely procedures and customs. Such rules determine, for example, when the governor can veto a bill, how much discretion the school board has in setting high school graduation requirements, and what a game warden must do to arrest someone for poaching. The rules that define and empower political institutions in U.S. states and communities are almost countless and incredibly diverse, even in a single state or community.

But just as important for our purposes, these institutions can be quite different among jurisdictions. For example, the mayor's offices in Indianapolis and Dallas are very different institutions because the rules that define their powers are very different. Judges in New York and California are selected in different ways, and their courts are organized differently. Rules can even vary within a single institution; for example, New Hampshire's Senate has very different powers and election rules than its House of Representatives. Such variation in political institutions can lead to a whole gamut of political and policy differences among these places.

Those who work in and around politics and government understand the importance of

---

[55] Wall, op. cit., p. 10.

[56] Douglass C. North, *Institutions, Institutional Change and Economic Performance* (New York, Cambridge University Press, 1990); Elinor Ostrom, *Governing the Commons: The Evolution of Institutions for Collective Action* (New York, Cambridge University Press, 1990).

Table 1.4

Characteristics of U.S. State Constitutions

State	Effective Date of Current Constitution	Number of Constitutions since Statehood	Number of Amendments to Current Constitution	Word Count of Current Constitution*	State	Effective Date of Current Constitution	Number of Constitutions since Statehood	Number of Amendments to Current Constitution	Word Count of Current Constitution*
AL	11/28/1901	6	799	350,000	MT	7/1/1973	2	30	13,145
AK	1/3/1959	1	29	15,988	NE	10/12/1875	2	224	34,220
AZ	2/14/1912	1	141	45,783	NV	10/31/1864	1	134	31,377
AR	10/30/1874	5	92	59,500	NH	6/2/1784	2	145	9,200
CA	7/4/1879	2	514	54,645	NJ	1/1/1948	3	42	22,956
CO	8/1/1876	1	150	74,522	NM	1/6/1912	1	155	27,200
CT	12/30/1965	4	29	17,256	NY	1/1/1895	4	217	51,700
DE	6/10/1897	4	140	19,000	NC	7/1/1971	3	34	16,532
FL	1/7/1969	6	110	51,456	ND	11/2/1889	1	149	19,130
GA	7/1/1983	10	66	39,526	OH	9/1/1851	2	163	48,521
HI	8/21/1959	1	108	20,774	OK	11/16/1907	1	175	74,075
ID	7/3/1890	1	119	24,232	OR	2/14/1859	1	238	54,083
IL	7/1/1971	4	11	16,510	PA	1/1/1968	5	30	27,711
IN	11/1/1851	2	46	10,379	RI	12/4/1986	3	10	10,908
IA	9/3/1857	2	52	11,500	SC	1/1/1896	7	492	32,541
KS	1/29/1861	1	93	12,296	SD	11/2/1889	1	213	27,675
KY	9/28/1891	4	41	23,911	TN	2/23/1870	3	38	13,300
LA	1/1/1975	11	151	54,112	TX	2/15/1876	5	456	90,000
ME	11/15/1820	1	171	16,276	UT	1/4/1896	1	107	18,037
MD	10/5/1867	4	221	44,000	VT	7/9/1793	3	53	10,286
MA	10/25/1780	1	120	36,700	VA	7/1/1971	6	43	21,601
MI	1/1/1964	4	28	34,659	WA	11/11/1889	1	101	33,564
MN	5/11/1858	1	119	11,547	WV	4/9/1872	2	71	26,000
MS	11/1/1890	4	123	24,323	WI	5/29/1848	1	144	14,749
MO	3/30/1945	4	109	42,600	WY	7/10/1890	1	97	31,800

*Word counts are estimated in some cases.

Source: Adapted from Table 1.1, "General Information on State Constitutions," *The Book of the States 2008,* vol. 40, ed. Audrey S. Wall (Lexington, KY, Council of State Governments, 2008).

institutions and institutional reform only too well. State and local governments are constantly tinkering with their rules about their officials' powers, how people vote, what is taxed, and every other government function and political activity imaginable. Changes in these institutions take up much of the time of policy makers and

those trying to influence them. Those advocating a given change call it a "reform," a word with a positive connotation. Of course, not all reforms have their intended effects. For example, in 1999, then-Governor George Ryan of Illinois issued an executive order that governors and other state-wide officials in the state could not take campaign

INSTITUTIONS MATTER

Political institutions are the rules, laws, and organizations through which, and by which, governments function. Political institutions are established by human beings for a purpose and with a permanence that goes beyond the people who established them. They require or prohibit, encourage or discourage certain behavior. They impose rights and duties, and they empower certain people or groups and limit the influence of others. Since people create institutions, they can be changed. Political institutions can be large, complex, and well known, like your state legislature and your university. They can also be relatively narrow and simple rules or laws that channel people and resources, such as the type of primary election system or judicial selection mechanism a state uses. Political institutions can be established through formal channels and backed by the force of law—like a state court system—or they can be processes and organizations developed voluntarily by people outside of government to engage in politics and influence policy making—like political parties and interest groups. Throughout this book, we discuss the various impacts that state and local political institutions have on politics and public policy, and in each chapter, we include an "Institutions Matter" sidebar that highlights an institution and its impacts.

contributions from their employees, and his successor, Governor Rod Blagojevich, followed suit with an even tighter restriction in 2008. These reforms did nothing to stop these men from being arrested and (at least one) imprisoned[57] for corruption related to campaign contributions. Throughout this book, we describe a wide range of political institutions and show how they affect who gets what from government and what happens when you change them.

The Political Science of State and Local Government: Using the Comparative Method

Another central theme of this book is that we can use the **comparative method** of political

analysis in the states and communities to help *explain how politics and public policy work*. The diversity among the states and communities often suggest propositions—or **hypotheses**—about political behavior and policy making and allows us to test them. For example, why do women comprise 30.4 percent of the New Mexico legislature, while only 16.4 percent of the West Virginia legislature is female? Are there social or economic reasons for this difference, or does it come down to difference in political values? If the latter, why do these states differ in their values? Why does New York City have such an extensive and efficient mass transit system, while Los Angeles does not? Does it have to do with history, geography, political culture, or something else? Why does Texas execute a dozen or more murderers every year, while Wisconsin didn't even execute serial killer Jeffrey Dahmer? Is this perhaps due to political ideology?

More important than just trying to explain the idiosyncratic differences we observe, political scientists use this variation among the states and communities to test many of the most general theories about political behavior and policy

---

[57] At press time, Ryan is serving a six-and-a-half-year sentence in the Federal Correctional Complex in Terre Haute, Indiana, for corruption offenses, and Blagojevich is awaiting trial on 16 charges of corruption, including actions involved in his alleged auctioning off of President Barrack Obama's former United States Senate seat.

making.[58] Science consists of developing general theories about how the world works and then observing the world to see if hypotheses derived from those theories seem to be correct. In this way, political science is no different than biology or chemistry.[59] But a significant difficulty for political scientists in this respect is that our **units of analysis** are often so diverse that a particular phenomenon may have many possible explanations. So since two pieces of iron can be assumed (or tested) to be exactly the same before placing one of them into an experimental solution, any difference in them observed later can be safely attributed to that solution.

But it is not that easy to test for cause and effect in politics and government. Suppose you wanted to understand the influences on women's representation in democratically elected legislatures. You might hypothesize that a more educated citizenry would be more likely to elect women to office because education would weaken traditional negative stereotypes and biases about women's role in society. You might think about testing this hypothesis by comparing national lawmaking bodies to one another, seeing if more educated countries tended to have more women lawmakers. But the problem with this would be that the multitude and magnitude of other differences among countries would overwhelm your ability to find any influence of education. For example, the fact that there are more women in the Norwegian Storting than the Spanish Cortes Generales might have something to do with the higher level of education in Norway than Spain, but it might also have to do with the huge differences between the two countries' other historic, social, and economic characteristics or their very different political institutions. On the other hand, while the states also differ in these ways, as we have shown, the

differences are much more constrained, so that tests of this hypothesis could be more valid and less confounded by these other factors.[60] Even New Mexico and West Virginia are much more similar to one another than are Norway and Spain, in many ways. This makes the states and communities an ideal place to test general theories about political behavior and policy making.

In this book, we focus on using the comparative method to evaluate *the effects of political institutions on politics and public policy*. Reformers who promote institutional change are essentially posing a hypothesis. For instance, as you will read in Chapter 9, the American Bar Association argues that state judges should be appointed to the bench, in part, because voters don't know enough about the law and the courts to select judges who will reflect their values and expectations well.[61] By using the comparative method, scholars have been able to test whether this and other reforms of state and local government institutions have the effects that their advocates hypothesize.[62] Just as important, this approach also allows us to see if these reforms have had any of the undesirable effects that their opponents hypothesized or even any effects that no one predicted. Thus, the comparative method not only allows us to develop and test theory about political behavior and policy making, it also helps us evaluate policies and institutions so that those with the best outcomes can be implemented in other states and communities.

---

[58] Christopher Z. Mooney, "*State Politics and Policy Quarterly* and the Study of State Politics: The Editor's Introduction," *State Politics and Policy Quarterly* 1(2001):1–4.

[59] Jon R. Bond, "The Scientification of the Study of Politics: Some Observations on the Behavioral Evolution in Political Science," *Journal of Politics* 69(2007):897–907.

[60] John F. Camobreco and Michelle A. Barnello, "Postmaterialism and Post-Industrialism: Cultural Influences on Female Representation in State Legislatures," *State Politics and Policy Quarterly* 3(2003):117–38.

[61] Kent A. Lambert, "Judicial Elections Continue under Fire," *Litigation News* (Washington, DC: American Barb Association), 27 March 2009 (http://www.abanet.org/litigation/litigationnews/top_stories/judicial-elections.html).

[62] For recent examples of this sort of analysis of government reforms, see Chris W. Bonneau and Melinda Gann Hall, *In Defense of Judicial Elections* (New York: Routledge, 2009); and Karl T. Kurtz, Bruce Cain, and Richard G. Niemi, eds., *Institutional Change in American Politics: The Case of Term Limits* (Ann Arbor, MI: University of Michigan Press, 2007).

Summary

State and local governments have a major impact on your everyday life, whether you know it or not. All day, every day, in dozens of ways, these governments affect your pocketbook, your quality of life, your family, and your future. The more you know about state and local government, the more control you can take over your own life.

American states and communities differ from one another in myriad ways, including their histories, social structures, economics, and political values. Political institutions—the rules, laws, and organizations through which and by which government functions—are enduring mechanisms designed to translate the principles and values of public policy into reality, and these also differ around the country. Political scientists use the variation of these characteristics and institutions to describe how, and understand why, we choose to organize ourselves and our governments, and what impacts these choices have. Throughout this book, we examine a variety of public policy and institutional reforms, considering why they developed and what impacts they had, both expected and unexpected.

In this chapter, we laid out the four basic themes that will guide this book:

- American states and communities *vary widely* in their politics, policy, and governments and the factors that affect those things.
- *Political institutions* can affect politics and public policy.
- Public policies and political institutions can be *reformed*.
- *Comparisons* of the states and communities provide a tremendous opportunity to understand politics and policy making.

Key Terms

Collective action problem

Comparative method

Constitution

Divided government

Hypothesis

Individualistic political culture

Jurisdiction

Libertarianism

Local charter

Moralistic political culture

Political culture

Political ideology

Political institution

Public goods

Reform

Retention election

Statute

Traditionalistic political culture

Unit of analysis

Discussion Questions

1. List six ways in which state and/or local government institutions and policies have affected you today. How and why might these six effects have been different if you were somewhere else in the country?
2. States vary widely in their policy regarding capital punishment. How do the states vary on this policy? What might explain why the states choose these different policies?

3. Briefly discuss how states' social and ethnic diversity impact public policy choices.
4. What is the comparative method of political analysis? Provide examples of how this method is useful for explaining patterns in politics and policy making.

Suggested Readings

Connor, George E., and Christopher W. Hammons, eds. 2008. *The Constitutionalism of American States.* Columbia, MO: University of Missouri Press.

Erikson, Robert S., Gerald C. Wright, and John P. McIver. 1993. *Statehouse Democracy: Public Opinion and Policy in the American States.* New York: Cambridge University Press.

Gimpel, James G., and Jason Schuknecht. 2003. *Patchwork Nation: Sectionalism and Political Change in American Politics.* Ann Arbor, MI: University of Michigan Press.

Gray, Virginia, and Russell L. Hanson, eds. 2008. *Politics in the American States: A Comparative Analysis,* 9th ed. Washington, DC: CQ Press.

Hero, Rodney E. 1998. *Faces of Inequality: Social Diversity in American Politics.* New York: Oxford University Press.

Johnson, Janet Buttolph, H. T. Reynolds, and Jason D. Mycoff. 2008. *Political Science Research Methods,* 6th ed. Washington, DC: CQ Press.

Key, V. O., Jr. 1949. *Southern Politics: In the State and Nation.* New York: Knopf.

Morgan, Kathleen O'Leary, and Scott Morgan, eds. *State Rankings 2009: A Statistical View of America.* Washington, DC: CQ Press.

Orfield, Myron. 2002. *American Metropolitics: New Suburban Reality.* Washington, DC: Brookings Institution.

Peterson, Paul E. 1981. *City Limits.* Chicago: University of Chicago Press.

Wall, Audrey S., ed. 2009. *The Book of the States 2009,* vol. 41. Lexington, KY: Council of State Governments.

Web Sites

Council of State Governments (http://www.csg.org): The CSG is a nonprofit association of state governments doing research, training, and advocacy for all branches of state government.

National League of Cities (http://www.citymayors.com/orgs/natleague.html): As the oldest organization representing municipal governments in the United States, NLC works with 49 state municipal leagues to strengthen cities.

Stateline.org (http://www.stateline.org): Staffed entirely by professional journalists, Stateline.org was founded by the Pew Research Center as a nonprofit resource for journalists covering state governments. It offers in-depth and timely news stories on public policy in the states and communities, both from a single-state and comparative perspective.

Statistical Abstract of the United States (http://www.census.gov/compendia/statab/): The U.S. government gathers an enormous amount of data about U.S. states and communities and their residents. The Statistical Abstract is the Census Bureau's consolidation report of a wide range of these data.

2

Federalism: State and Local Politics within a Federal System

STIMULATING THE STATES WITH FEDERAL STIMULUS DOLLARS

"I think we just have a fundamental disagreement here," Louisiana Governor Bobby Jindal cautioned on NBC's *Meet the Press*. If all the Obama administration does "is borrow federal money and give it to the states," the Republican continued, "all we're really doing is delaying the inevitable." Less than a week after President Barack Obama signed into law the economic stimulus package—the American Recovery and Reinvestment Act of 2009—Governor Jindal (pictured below) and several of his fellow conservative governors publicly announced that they would reject portions of Congress' $787 billion stimulus package that was earmarked to their state governments. The governors—most vocally C. L. "Butch" Otter of Idaho, Bobby Jindal of Louisiana, Haley Barbour of Mississippi, Mark Sanford of South Carolina, Rick Perry of Texas, and former governor Sarah Palin of Alaska—expressed their opposition to several provisions in the federal legislation that would require additional state spending or taxes.

From the Republican governors' perspective, accepting billions in federal stimulus dollars would compromise their ideological opposition to deficit spending. More pragmatically, some of them were upset that portions of the federal money would have to be spent on what they deemed nonurgent areas, including health care coverage for children and child support enforcement, energy-efficient vehicles for government employees, and even some transportation projects. Governor Sanford, thumbing his nose at some $700 million in federal stimulus money as well as Democrats and fellow Republicans in the state legislature, said he didn't think it was a good idea "to spend money that you don't have." For his part, Governor Jindal said his state would reject nearly $100 million in federal dollars to expand unemployment coverage because Congress attached "strings" to the stimulus money that would require the state to broaden its coverage to those currently unemployed and seeking assistance. "I never imagined," a spokesperson for Governor Otter decried, "that Congress would tell the state of Idaho that they have to spend $5.5 million on bike paths or pedestrian lanes."

That some Republican governors would turn up their collective noses at millions in federal aid earmarked for their states did not sit well with some of their constituents, many of whom would benefit directly from the federal aid. As the Democratic governor of Montana, Brian Schweitzer, noted, "You can philosophize in D.C. all you want, but we in the states have to get things done. A governor's job is to deliver for people: to create good jobs, to keep criminals in prison, to educate children, to make sure we have decent roads. This recovery package does that." Similarly aghast were multitudes of local officials, whose ailing schools, municipalities, and county governments were flowing in red ink and would have been better able to make ends meet by receiving the federal assistance. Most mayors, such as Adrian Fenty of Washington, D.C. (pictured with President Barack Obama, above), clamored for the federal stimulus dollars, expressing a commitment to steer the money to the communities that needed it the most.

A few Republican governors broke ranks with members of their own party. In supporting President Obama's plan, Florida's Charlie Crist said he was putting ideology aside to look out for the best interests of the residents of his state. Agreeing with Schweitzer and other Democratic governors, Crist said on *Meet The Press*, "I think my obligation as the CEO of the state is to do everything I can to help us get through this tough economy." The $12.2 billion in federal aid to Florida, Crist argued, would help bail the state out of its fiscal crisis. "This is going to help in our education in Florida by about $3.5 billion. It's going to help us with Medicaid—and the vulnerable among us that really need help and need it now . . . [it] will also help us with road construction and producing jobs."[1]

1   Shaila Dewan, "6 Governors May Reject Portions of Stimulus," *New York Times*, 21 February 2009. Available: http://www .nytimes.com/2009/02/21/us/21govs.html?_r=1; J. David Goodman, "Governors' Fight over Stimulus May Define G.O.P.," *New York Times*, 22 February 2009. Available: http://www.nytimes.com/2009/02/23/us/politics/23governors.html?hp; Associated Press, "S.C.'s Sanford Makes It Official, Rejects $700 Million Stimulus," *Miami Herald*, 13 April 2009.

In 2009, the Republican Governor of Louisiana, Bobby Jindal, told reporters that he wanted his state to reject the nearly $100 million in federal stimulus dollars that could be used to expand the unemployment benefits of thousands of his state's residents.

Introduction

The federal government's rapid response in 2009—providing billions of stimulus dollars to the states following the collapse of the U.S. economy—once again altered the terms of agreement between the federal government and state and local governments. By reexerting its power over the subnational governments, the federal government elevated the stature of the powerbrokers operating in the nation's capital, Washington, D.C. Such is the contemporary flow of American federalism, continual waves of ideology infused with pragmatism, devolving power to the states and recentralizing it back to the national government.

In this chapter, we examine the dynamic relationship between the federal and state governments. The ambiguity in the demarcation of state and national (or federal) institutional powers inherent in the U.S. Constitution has defined the way Americans have thought about government and politics and how we have designed our government institutions. After defining federalism and placing the American federal system in a broader comparative context, we investigate the ambiguities inherent in the U.S. Constitution. In discussing the historical trajectory and evolution of American federalism, we discuss the roles that Congress and the federal courts have played in delineating the relative powers of the national and state governments. We conclude by discussing how power has become more centralized in Washington following 9/11 and the downturn in the U.S. economy. What should become apparent in this story of American intergovernmental relations is the gradual, if at times punctuated, expansion of federal powers over the past century.

What Is Federalism?

The 50 American state governments constitute semisovereign political systems. Governmental powers in the United States are split geographically between national, state, and local governments. **Federalism** is the structural (or constitutional) relationship between a national government and its constitutive states. **Intergovernmental relations,** on the other hand, are the interactions among the federal government, state governments, and local governments. A federalist system of intergovernmental relations conjoins a national government with semiautonomous subnational governments, but allows each to retain, to some degree, its "own identity and distinctiveness."[1] Although maintaining separate and autonomous powers, each layer of government is responsible for providing for the social and economic welfare of the populations living within its jurisdiction.[2] As we discuss below, the structure of a federalist system is different from those of unitary and confederal systems of governance.

How does a federalist system work? In theory, federalism combines the unifying powers of the national government with the diversity of subnational governments. The American states are not mere administrative appendages or extensions of the national government. Rather, they have discrete powers that are derived from the federal Constitution as well as their own constitutions and laws. Each layer of government has some autonomy, but there is much overlap in the powers held by the national and state governments.[3] It may seem somewhat ironic, then, that although many countries—including Australia, Brazil, Canada, Germany, India, Italy, Mexico, Nigeria, Russia, Spain, and even Iraq—have adopted an American system of federalism, the term *federalism* is not mentioned in the U.S. Constitution.

[1] Ronald Watts, "Federalism, Federal Political Systems, and Federations," *Annual Review of Political Science* 1 (1998):117–37.

[2] Paul Peterson, *City Limits* (Chicago: University of Chicago Press, 1981), p. 67.

[3] David Walker, *The Rebirth of Federalism* (Chatham, NJ: Chatham House, 1995).

Sovereignty and State Variation in a Federalist System

In theory, under federalism states retain a broad swath of sovereign powers, subject to the will of their own citizens. "In establishing this system," writes historian Samuel Beer, "the American people authorized and empowered two sets of governments: a general government for the whole, and state governments of the parts."[4] Such is a system of dual federalism, whereby governmental functions are apportioned so that, in the words of Founding Father James Madison, the states are "no more subject within their respective spheres to the general authority than the general authority is subject to them within its own sphere"[5] (see Figure 2.1). Though sometimes pictured as a "layer cake," dual federalism does not necessarily imply that the national and state governments never encroach upon each other's territory. Rather, if a confectionary metaphor is to be used, the American system might be more aptly described as a "marble cake."[6]

Unitary Systems: Centralized Power

In contrast to a federalist system of governance, some countries have **unitary systems** of governance, with all governmental power vested in the national government. As Figure 2.2 shows, a unitary system has a strong central government that controls virtually all aspects of its constitutive subnational governments (be they regional, territorial, state, or local units). Unitary systems, such as those in France, Israel, the Philippines, Sweden, China, and Kenya, consolidate all constitutional authority in the

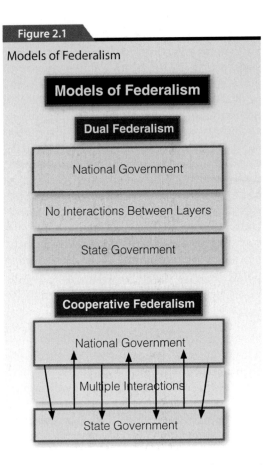

Figure 2.1

Models of Federalism

national government. In a sense, subnational divisions of the country are mere administrative appendages of the national government; that is, policy is made at the national level, and the subnational units simply carry out that policy.

There is far less regional diversity in terms of subnational electoral systems, governance structure, and public policy in countries with unitary systems of governance. The central governments in unitary systems are simply able to control the policy making that takes place at the subnational levels of government. For example, between 1952 and 1975, Sweden's national parliament moved to eliminate 90 percent of all local governments.[7] In France, the national

---

[4] Samuel Beer, *To Make a Nation: The Rediscovery of American Federalism* (Cambridge, MA: Harvard University Press, 1993), pp. 1–2.

[5] James Madison, "The Federalist No. 39: Conformity of the Plan to Republican Principles," *Independent Journal* 16 January 1788. Available: http://www.constitution.org/fed/federa39.htm.

[6] Morton Grodzins, "The American System," in Robert Goldwin, ed., *A Nation of States* (Chicago: Rand McNally, 1969); and Morton Grodzins, *The American System* (Chicago: Rand McNally and Company, 1966).

---

[7] Thomas Anton, *American Federalism and Public Policy* (New York: Random House, 1989), p. 3; and Virginia Gray and Peter Eisinger, *American States & Cities*, 2nd ed. (New York: Longman, 1997), p. 26.

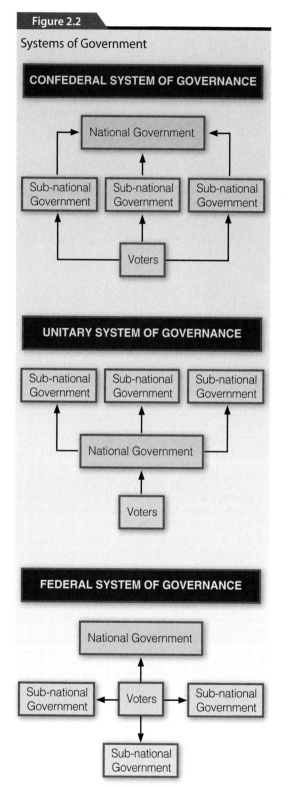

Figure 2.2

Systems of Government

government in Paris makes most laws, which are then dutifully administered by the country's 22 provincial regions. By contrast, in the United States, policy decisions concerning criminal justice, public education, social welfare, health care, and transportation are often left to the states.[8]

Over the past decade, some Western European countries with unitary systems, such as France and The Netherlands, have seen many of their national powers curtailed by the European Union (EU).[9] Driven originally by the need for economic consolidation so as to compete more effectively in the global marketplace with the United States, the EU has broadened its political powers. Although still lacking a formal constitution, across a plethora of policy domains—including health care and social welfare, workers' rights, immigration, the environment, and even foreign affairs and defense—the EU has effectively usurped some of the sovereign powers traditionally held by European governments.[10] As we shall see, in some ways the centralizing political development of the EU mirrors that of the United States.

Confederal Systems: Decentralized Power

In terms of a spectrum of the balance of power between national and subnational levels of government, a **confederal system** is located at the opposite pole from a unitary system. A confederacy, as Figure 2.2 shows, is a system of governance whereby the national government is subject to the control of subnational, autonomous governments. In a confederacy, the constituent subnational governments enter into a covenant with one another and derive the bulk of their sovereign powers not

---

[8] Mitchell Pickerill and Paul Chen, "Medical Marijuana Policy and the Virtues of Federalism," *Publius* 38(2008): 22–55.

[9] Michael Goldsmith, "Central Control over Local Government—A Western European Comparison," *Local Government Studies* 28(2002):91–112.

[10] Europa, "Activities of the European Union," June 2005. Available: http://europa.eu.int/pol/index_en.htm.

COMPARISONS HELP US UNDERSTAND

THE STRENGTHS AND WEAKNESSES OF CONFEDERAL SYSTEMS OF GOVERNANCE

Compared to both federalist and unitary systems of governance, the confederal form has come under the most criticism over the years for its apparent instability and ineffectualness. The most prominent, and for some the most infamous, confederal governance structure in the world today is headquartered in New York City—the United Nations (UN). Today, no purely confederal national government exists, although for over 500 years Switzerland operated as a confederation, with its 23 autonomous cantons holding veto power over the policy decisions of the central government until 1847.

Despite persistent critiques of the UN's confederal structure that it decentralizes too much authority, many countries with federal and unitary governments have recently decentralized power and authority to their subnational units. A study issued by the World Bank found that 76 percent of 127 countries in its study had at least some decentralized political systems (meaning they had at least one elected subnational level of government). It also found a high correlation between fiscal and political decentralization, and found that countries with high gross national products were more likely to adopt both fiscal and political decentralization reforms.[1] Many of the decentralization efforts, which the World Bank and other lending institutions often require when they provide financial assistance, have occurred in African and Latin American countries.

United Nations Headquarters, New York City

Comstock Images/Jupiter Images

Note

1. World Bank, *World Development Report*, Washington, D.C. 1999/2000. Available: http://www.worldbank.org/wdr/2000/.

from the central government, but from their own constitutions.[11] As we discuss below, in the history of the United States there have been

[11] Daniel Elazar, *American Federalism: A View from the States*, 3rd ed. (New York: Harper & Row, 1984); Daniel Elazar, "Contrasting Unitary and Federal Systems," *International Political Science Review* 18(1997):237–52.

two confederacies: the Articles of Confederation (1781–89) and the Civil War–era Confederate States of America (1861–65).

Defenders of confederal systems of shared governance argue there are several advantages when governmental powers are devolved to subnational units. First, because they are closer to and more familiar with the interests and needs of their constituents, locally elected officials are able to better represent the wishes and needs of citizens. Second, decentralized decision making encourages policy experimentation and pluralistic solutions to local problems. Third, because there are more avenues for expressing opinions, democratic participation among the citizenry increases when government is decentralized. Fourth, policy responsiveness is enhanced when political authority is dispersed among subnational units. Finally, subnational units are able to provide and manage governmental services more efficiently than if they were carried out by the central government.

Of course, the decentralization of political power can lead to asymmetrical, or uneven, relations among the states. In the United States, not all states have the same degree of power within the federalist system. Although all states are afforded the same protection and authority under the U.S. Constitution, some states have more clout within the federation because of the relative size of their economies and populations, differences in their socioeconomic and demographic makeup, and disparities in their social and cultural environments. These variations have led to differential power relations among the states, as well as between each state and the federal government.[12]

Why Federalism? America's Founding

One of the most fundamental struggles in American political history has been the turf battle for political power waged between the states and the national (or, as mentioned, federal) government. The cyclical ebb and flow of this tension between the national and state governments has been continuous for over two centuries, and is rooted in the founding of the country. As Martha Derthick writes, "American

federalism was born in ambiguity, it institutionalizes ambiguity in our form of government, and changes in it tend to be ambiguous too."[13] The inherent, ambiguous tensions of the American federalist system can be traced back to the late 18th century. In developing a federalist system, the founders had no working model on which to draw.[14] So, why did the United States end up adopting a federalist system of governance?

The Articles of Confederation

The United States has not always had a federalist system. The American colonies were originally chartered as independent settlements, under the control of European colonial powers. Settlers identified themselves not as Americans, but as subjects of a colonial power. By the late 18th century, though, citizens of several of the original 13 colonies—frustrated by the dictates of the British Parliament and the monarchy of King George III—began challenging the consolidated power of Great Britain.[15] Rebellious leaders of the colonies convened in September 1774 to establish the First Continental Congress. Proposed jointly by the Massachusetts and Virginia legislatures, 12 of the 13 colonies sent delegates to Philadelphia for the proceedings; only Georgia did not immediately send representatives. The Continental Congress was weak, though, as the states retained the authority to reject or alter its wishes.

After the signing of the Declaration of Independence in 1776, it became apparent to many leaders of the fledging states that they needed a stronger central government, albeit one that would not undermine the sovereignty of the states. In 1777, the Second Continental

---

[12] Charles Tarlton, "Symmetry and Asymmetry as Elements of Federalism: A Theoretical Speculation," *Journal of Politics* 27(1965):861–74.

[13] Martha Derthick, "American Federalism: Half-Full or Half-Empty," *The Brookings Review* 18(2000):24–27.
[14] Jack Rakove, *Original Meanings: Politics and Ideas in the Making of the Constitution* (New York: Knopf, 1997), p. 168.
[15] Over a span of a few years, a series of parliamentary acts were handed down from London, including the 1765 Stamp Act, which required the colonies to place revenue stamps on all official documents, the 1767 Townshend Acts, which placed duties on colonial imports, and the 1773 Tea Act, which granted the East India Company a monopoly over the export of tea from Britain.

Congress approved the **Articles of Confederation**, the country's first constitution, and sent it to the states for ratification.[16] As a confederal system, the document delimited the separation of powers between two layers of governments in an effort to make one nation out of 13 independent sovereign entities. Under the Articles, Congress was granted the authority to declare war and make peace, enter treaties and alliances, coin or borrow money, and regulate trade with Native Americans, but it could not levy requisite taxes or adequately enforce its commerce and trade regulations among the states. Members of the Continental Congress, who served one-year terms and were chosen by their state legislatures, acted typically as delegates of their state legislatures. Beholden to the states, the federal government—which lacked an executive branch to enforce laws passed by Congress—was wholly reliant on the states for its operating expenses.

The Federalists

Many founders were appalled by the ineffectualness of the federal government under the Articles. General George Washington, for one, was "mortified beyond expression" that the federal government under the Articles was so emasculated that it could not even defend its citizens from relatively minor internal threats.[17] Tensions between rival sovereigns—the 13 states and Congress—were mounting. In May 1787, Congress called for a Constitutional Convention to amend the U.S. Constitution. Over that summer, delegates to the Constitutional Convention would decide to scrap the Articles, replacing them with a federalist system. In addition to restructuring the federal government's institutional design, the proposed constitution would alter the relationship between the federal government and the states, having each share power and the representation of their respective constituencies.[18]

Federalists who supported the new constitution argued in favor of a strong central government. But they made it clear that the central government's authority would be checked by the separation of powers among the legislative, executive, and judicial branches, as well as through the division of sovereignty between the states and the federal government.[19] Writing in 1787 and 1789 under the pseudonym "Publius," James Madison, Alexander Hamilton, and John Jay authored a series of pamphlets that collectively became known as the Federalist Papers. As part of a public relations campaign to generate popular support for the ratification of the Constitution, the authors claimed the new constitution would provide for internal checks and balances in the fledgling nation and would structurally limit the supremacy of the national government by creating competitive (sometimes rival, sometimes cooperative) state governments.[20]

The U.S. Constitution and the Historical Development of Federalism

Following Congress' submission of the U.S. Constitution to the states in 1787 and its subsequent ratification, a vexing question continued

---

[16] The Articles effectively served for nearly 12 years as the country's first constitution, despite the fact that it was not ratified until March 1781. Merrill Jensen, *The New Nation: A History of the United States during the Confederation: 1781–1789* (New York: Vintage Books, 1950), 18–27.

[17] Letter from George Washington to David Humphreys, 22 October 1786. The George Washington Papers at the Library of Congress, 1741–1799. Available: http://lcweb2 .loc.gov/cgi-bin/query/r?ammem/mgw:@field(DOCID+@ lit(gw290023)).

[18] David Brian Robertson, "Madison's Opponents and Constitutional Design," *American Political Science Review* 99(2005):225–43.

[19] Joseph Ellis, *Founding Brothers: The Revolutionary Generation* (New York: Knopf, 2001).

[20] David Epstein, *The Political Theory of the Federalist* (Chicago: University of Chicago Press, 1984); Frederic Stimson, *The American Constitution as It Protects Private Rights* (New York: Charles Scribner's Sons, 1923).

Figure 2.3

Original Constitutional Powers of National and State Governments

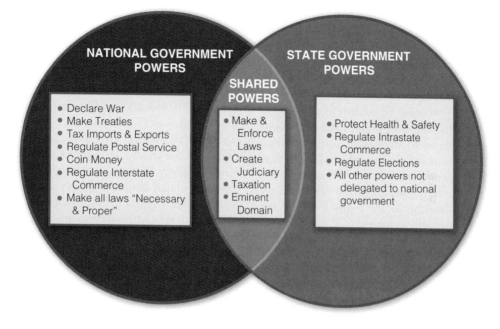

to linger: which had more authority, the Union or the states?[21] Federalist sympathizers tried to downplay the power of the federal government in the proposed constitution. Temporally and territorially, of course, the states clearly preceded the Union. Yet, compared with the failed Articles, the U.S. Constitution laid out clear powers for the federal government. Figure 2.3 displays some of the basic powers held in principle by the national and state governments when the Constitution was first adopted. As we discuss later in this chapter, the division of powers between the states and the federal government today hardly resembles the allocation in the 1790s. The continual fluctuation in the relative authority of the states and the federal government has cumulated in a slow expansion of federal power over time.

---

[21] Jack Rakove, *Original Meanings: Politics and Ideas in the Making of the Constitution* (New York: Knopf, 1997).

Federal Powers under the U.S. Constitution

There are several provisions found in the U.S. Constitution that enhance the power of the federal government, and specifically the authority of Congress. The document grants Congress, the bicameral legislative arm of the national government, several explicit powers. These include the right to declare war; provide for the common defense; lay and collect taxes, duties, imposts, and excises; regulate commerce with foreign nations, among the several states, and with the Indian tribes; establish post offices and post roads; and provide for the general welfare of the United States. These "expressed" or "enumerated" powers of Congress, found in Article I, Section 8, Clauses 1–17 of the Constitution, especially the Commerce Clause, expand Congress' reach.

The National Supremacy Clause Article VI, Section 2, known as the **National Supremacy**

Clause, stipulates that the U.S. Constitution and national laws and treaties "shall be the supreme law of the land . . . anything in the Constitution or Laws of any State to the Contrary notwithstanding." This means that the federal Constitution and federal laws trump any conflicting state constitutional provision or laws. Thus, when there is no clear delineation of which level of government is to have the dominant role in policy making, or when there is a conflict in national and state public policies, federal laws are superior to state laws, and state laws superior to local ordinances. It bears noting that there is no mention of local governments in the U.S. Constitution. Powers of local governments are largely determined by states through the creation of municipal charters.

State and local governments, for example, are not permitted to enter into treaties with American Indian tribal nations without authorization from the federal government. Indian nations, which exist in 34 states, are domestic dependent nations, a term coined by the U.S. Supreme Court in its 1831 decision *Cherokee Nation v. Georgia*. According to the high court's ruling in *Worcester v. Georgia*, which was handed down the following year, the national government has the authority to enter into agreements with sovereign Indian tribes. However, the federal government occasionally grants states the power to negotiate certain compacts with the tribes located within their boundaries.

One of the most common negotiation areas between the states and Indian tribes has to do with casino gambling. Congress in 1988 passed the Indian Gaming Regulatory Act, which requires tribes to enter compacts with their state governments specifying the types of gaming that are permitted on reservation lands and any compensation that should be made to the state governments. In 2000, for example, California voters approved a constitutional amendment allowing Nevada-style gambling on Indian reservations; in return, more than 60 Indian tribes, which generate over $5 billion in gambling revenue each year, agreed to allow unions to organize in their casinos, provide more than $1 million in aid to nongaming tribes, and make quarterly payments to the state to offset gambling addiction programs and other costs associated with the increased economic development and social pressures stemming from gaming.[22]

The Commerce Clause The **Commerce Clause** is the third clause in Article I, Section 8 of the U.S. Constitution. The clause gives Congress the power "[t]o regulate Commerce with foreign Nations, and among the several States, and with the Indian Tribes." As we discuss at length below, Congress has interpreted the 16-word clause broadly, greatly expanding its legislative power to intervene in a wide number of facets of the national economy. Beginning in 1824, with its decision *Gibbons v. Ogden*, the U.S. Supreme Court has generally granted Congress broad powers to pass laws dealing with issues only indirectly related to interstate commerce, such as civil rights, environmental regulations, possession of firearms and drugs, and internet transactions. Congress's broad definition of interstate commerce has even been used to regulate internet sales, racial segregation in restaurants and hotels, and the production of subsistence wheat crops in Kansas. Today, with the increased interconnectivity of human activity, most economic activities extend beyond a state's borders and thus may fall prey to congressional regulations.

The Necessary and Proper Clause Unlike the Articles of Confederation, the Constitution also grants Congress wide discretion in its interpretation of its powers in Article I, Section 8. Clause 18 of Article I, Section 8, known as the **Necessary and Proper Clause** or the Elastic Clause, has been a key component in the centralization of power by Congress over time. The clause enables Congress to interpret and expand upon the 17 preceding substantive

---

[22] Institute of Governmental Studies, "Indian Gaming in California," University of California at Berkeley, 2006. Available: http://igs.berkeley.edu/library/htIndianGaming.htm.

clauses in Article I, Section 8. Congress' implied powers give the national legislative body authority to make all laws that shall be "necessary and proper for carrying into execution the foregoing powers."

The Full Faith and Credit Clause Enshrined in Article IV, Section 1, the **Full Faith and Credit Clause** stipulates that the states must mutually accept one another's public acts, records, and judicial proceedings. Congress is given the authority to oversee the manner and effect of the reciprocity among the states. Today, the Full Faith and Credit Clause has regained prominence in the controversy over the legality of gay marriage in a handful of states. In 1996, Congress passed and President Bill Clinton signed into law the Defense of Marriage Act. The act gave states the power to not legally recognize marriages between gay and lesbian couples performed in another state. Still, as we shall see in Chapter 13, some social conservatives contend that if the U.S. Constitution is not amended, gay rights activists may be able to use the clause to force states that have outlawed gay marriage to recognize legal same-sex marriages sanctioned in other states.

Privileges and Immunities Clauses: Article IV and the 14th Amendment Article IV, Section 2 of the Constitution, the **Privileges and Immunities Clause**, ensures that residents of one state cannot be discriminated against by another state when it comes to fundamental matters, such as pursuing one's professional occupation, access to the courts, or equality in taxation.[23] Because of the Privileges and Immunities Clause, a state, for example, may not bar citizens from other states from practicing law in the state, assuming they pass the state's bar exam.

Section 2 of Article IV also includes a provision that was upheld by the U.S. Supreme

Court's rather infamous 1857 decision *Dred Scott v. Sanford*. Before it was stricken by the 13th Amendment in 1865, the third clause of Article IV permitted states to maintain the institution of slavery and required fugitive slaves who had fled to free states to be forcibly returned to their legal slaveholders. The clause continues to be invoked by states wishing to preserve states' rights. In 1978, the high court struck down the "Alaska Hire Law," which had restricted the occupational opportunities of nonresidents interested in working in the state's oil industry. The Court, though, continues to permit what some view as a discriminatory practice: allowing public universities to charge higher tuition for out-of-state students.

The 14th Amendment, which we discuss in greater detail below, includes its own Privileges and Immunities Clause. The provision, ratified in 1868, was intended to bar discrimination by the states against their own citizens, most notably former slaves. The U.S. Supreme Court, however, greatly weakened the provision in what are known as the Slaughterhouse Cases (1873). The Court ruled that the 14th Amendment's Privileges and Immunities Clause does not protect the privileges and immunities of a person's state citizenship, only his or her national citizenship. The decision has remained largely intact, despite the obvious fact that the post–Civil War amendments in the 1860s and 1870s were intended to end the discrimination of individuals, specifically newly freed slaves. Slavery, of course, is no longer legal. Yet states still engage in other forms of discrimination. All states, for example, only permit state residents to become governor. Some states even require their residents to be citizens of the state for several consecutive years before they become eligible to run for elective office.

State Powers under the U.S. Constitution

Federalists such as Alexander Hamilton, James Madison, and their fellow delegates who supported a strong national government during

---

[23] David Bogen, *Privileges and Immunities: A Reference Guide to the United States Constitution* (Westport, CT: Praeger, 2003).

the proceedings of the 1787 Constitutional Convention in Philadelphia did not prevail on all fronts. Anti-Federalists, as they were known, expressed their discontent over the increased powers of the federal government. The Constitution was unfinished, they contended, as it failed to enshrine the rights of the states. "The Constitution did settle many questions, and it established a lasting structure of rules and principle," writes Herbert Storing. "But it did not settle everything; it did not finish the task of making the American polity."[24] With the ratification of the U.S. Constitution, the political dialogue was just beginning, as Anti-Federalist concerns and principles became central to the ongoing debate.

The Bill of Rights Joining Thomas Jefferson and George Mason of Virginia, James Madison would eventually moderate his strong defense of the national government, insisting too that a **Bill of Rights** be appended to the Constitution upon its ratification. In December 1791, three-quarters of the states ratified the first 10 proposed amendments to the Constitution. A major goal of the Bill of Rights was to ensure the protection of individuals from the national government. But it also protects the autonomy of the states. The 9th and 10th Amendments guaranteed that states were not deprived by the federal government of any rights not explicitly expressed in the Constitution. As many people in the states quickly discovered, though, the Bill of Rights did not immediately prevent state governments from depriving their residents of rights.

The 10th Amendment The 10th Amendment explicitly limits the powers of national government vis-à-vis the states. Known also as the **Reserve Clause**, it gives the states broad authority, stipulating: "The powers not delegated to the United States by the Constitution, nor prohibited by it to the States, are reserved to the States respectively, or to the people." Because there is no mention in the U.S.

Constitution of numerous substantive issues, such as those dealing with education, public health, the environment, or criminal justice, it was widely understood by the founders that these policy domains would be left to the states. Despite the centralization of power brought about by the ratification of the U.S. Constitution in 1788, the Bill of Rights infused the states with more sovereign powers. Because of the 10th Amendment, in theory at least, the states are not administrative arms of the national government, but rather constituent parts that retain their autonomy from the central government.

Federalism Today

As discussed previously, there are numerous provisions in the U.S. Constitution granting authority to the national government. Through the various powers granted by the U.S. Constitution, Congress has often asserted its authority over the states, preempting state laws. **Federal preemption** occurs when the federal government takes regulatory action that overrides state laws. Advocates of federal preemption claim that it is necessary to create a uniformity of laws and regulations so as to avoid a confusing and inconsistent patchwork of standards across the states. But preemptive legislation by Congress has created an ongoing tussle between the federal government and the states.[25] According to one count, between 1789 and 2005, Congress passed 529 preemption statutes.[26] Since the mid-1990s alone, Congress has preempted, and thus partially or completely curtailed, state regulatory authority in numerous areas, including food safety, health care, telecommunications, international trade, and financial services. Critics of federal preemption claim that it leads to less flexibility in regulations and the delivery of public services, hurts the ability of states to experiment with

---

[24] Herbert Storing, ed. *The Anti-Federalist: Writings by the Opponents of the Constitution* (Chicago: University of Chicago Press, 1985), p. 1.

[25] Joseph Zimmerman, *Contemporary American Federalism* (Westport, CT: Praeger, 1992).
[26] Joseph Zimmerman, *Congressional Preemption: Regulatory Federalism* (Albany: State University of New York Press, 2005).

INSTITUTIONS MATTER

JOHN C. CALHOUN'S COMPACT THEORY OF FEDERALISM

States' rights under the dual federalist system were taken to their logical extreme by John C. Calhoun during the first half of the 19th century. Calhoun, who served as vice president of the United States under the administrations of Presidents John Quincy Adams and Andrew Jackson, forcefully advanced what he called a compact theory of federalism. Interpreting the U.S. Constitution in the same vein as the Articles of Confederation, Calhoun argued the Constitution was confederal, binding together informally the several sovereign states. He contended that the enumerated powers of the federal government were severely circumscribed, being derived wholly from the powers of the states. Calhoun's defense of states' rights included the concept of **nullification**, which held that a state was justified in rejecting national legislation and could render federal laws void and unenforceable if it refused to accept them. If federal laws were to be enforceable, such as a protective tariff placed on imported goods that was passed by Congress in 1828, they would need concurrent majorities, whereby the laws were consented to by a majority of citizens at both the national and state levels. If citizens in a state took a national law to be objectionable, a state had the right to nullify the law, making it invalid within the state's borders. Calhoun went so far as to declare that states had the right to secede, removing themselves from the Union.[1]

Hanfstaengl Collection/The Image Works

Note

1. Irving Bartlett, *John C. Calhoun: A Biography* (New York: Norton, 1993); and John Niven, *John C. Calhoun and the Price of the Union* (Baton Rouge, LA: Louisiana State University Press, 1988).

---

and develop best practices, limits the ability of states to coordinate their economic development priorities with their regulatory policies, and diminishes the protections that states are able to craft for their citizens.[27]

The Ebb and Flow (and Gradual Erosion) of Federalism

In 1908, future-President Woodrow Wilson wrote, "The question of the relations of the states and the federal government is the cardinal question" of the American political system.[28] The fluidity as well as the inherent tension existing between the national and subnational levels of government are defining characteristics of American federalism. The ebb and flow between the states and the national government, which were codified by the ratification of the U.S. Constitution in 1788 and the Bill of Rights in 1791, are a recurrent theme in the study of American politics. Competition or even disharmony between the national and state levels of government, then, is to be expected, with disagreements between

---

[27] Raymond Scheppach, "Federal Preemption: A Serious Threat," 17 August 2004. Available: http://www.Stateline.org.

[28] Quoted in Kenneth Vines, "The Federal Setting of State Politics," in Herbert Jacob and Kenneth Vines, eds., *Politics in the American States*, 3rd ed. (Boston: Little, Brown and Company, 1976).

the two layers of government being interpreted as a healthy sign that the division of powers is working.[29]

The Shifting Sands of Federalism

Since the country's founding, the locus of political power in the United States has flowed from the federal government to the states and back again to the federal government. These tidal shifts, though, have not been equal in force. Although at any given moment the relative level of power between the states and the national government is refreshingly and predictably fluid,[30] with each wave the federal government has slowly eroded the sovereignty of the states. Many waves of federal encroachment on state power have been the result of crises—from the Civil War, to World War I, to the Depression and the New Deal, to the War on Poverty in the 1960s, to 9/11. In the aftermath of each of these tidal storms, the states did not become mere appendages of the national government, but they did successively lose ground to the federal government.

The reason for this constant shifting and gradual expansion of the power of the federal government stems from the fact that the authority of the federal and state government is not clearly demarcated in the U.S. Constitution. Because of the ambiguities of national and state powers, logical arguments have been made equally forcibly in defense of states' rights or for more centralized power. For example, at one extreme of the spectrum, Vice President John C. Calhoun of South Carolina in the mid-19th century advocated the theory of **nullification**, arguing that the states held veto

power over the actions of the federal government, which included the right to permit slavery and reject national trade agreements. At the other extreme, Alexander Hamilton argued that the United States had the right to establish a national bank that could assist the federal government in meeting its financial obligations, and that the national government could impose tariffs and duties to protect nascent industries that were central to the national interest. Over the long haul, Hamilton's view of a stronger, more centralized federal government has largely prevailed.

Centralization and Devolution

The American federal system continually cycles through periods of centralization and devolution. **Devolution** is the decentralization of power and authority from a central government to state or local governments; **centralization** reverses the flow, empowering a national governing authority with unitary control and authority. Writing in the 1830s, the French observer Alexis de Tocqueville noted that devolution not only had positive administrative effects but also had beneficial political effects, in that it enhanced the civic values and opportunities of citizens.[31] Because the national government does not have monopoly power in the American system, the embrace of **decentralization** has at times lead to a tremendous amount of diversity across the states regarding the kinds of laws subnational governments have adopted over time.

In the American context, centralization and devolution are relative terms, denoting the distribution of power and the level of policy making responsibility taken on by the national or state governments. Besides the role of the federal courts, the level of centralization or devolution present in the American federalist system is dependent on a host of outside factors. In times of war and national crises, such as the aftermath

---

[29] Thomas Dye, *American Federalism: Competition among Governments* (Lexington, MA: Lexington Books Heath, 1990); and D. Kenyon and John Kincaid, eds., *Competition among States and Local Governments: Efficiency and Equity in American Federalism* (Washington, DC: The Urban Institute, 1991). See also, William Riker, *The Development of American Federalism* (Boston: Kluwer Academic Publishers, 1987).

[30] Zimmerman, *Contemporary American Federalism*, 1992.

[31] Alexis de Tocqueville, *Democracy in America*. Book 1, chapter 5. Available: http://xroads.virginia.edu/~HYPER/DETOC/home.html.

of 9/11, an increasing amount of power tends to become centralized in Washington, D.C. Centralization also occurs when people call to redistribute the nation's wealth in an effort to create greater equity in society, perceive a need to establish national standards or policy goals, and make efforts to create more efficiencies in the implementation of public policy. Power tends to flow back to the states when citizens clamor for public policies that are better tailored to fit their specific needs or when there is growing distrust of nationally elected officials. Although at times political power devolves to the states, rarely does it completely offset any preceding periods of centralization.

Creeping Centralization: The Political Evolution of Federal Power

Abetted by the power vested in Congress by the federal courts, the authority of the federal government relative to the states grew considerably during the late 19th and 20th centuries.[32] During the mid-19th century, Congress passed several laws that slowly expanded the power of the federal government. For example, in 1862 in the midst of the Civil War, the federal government cleared the way for westward expansion by passing the Pacific Railroad Act, giving charters to companies building a transcontinental railroad. That same year, Congress passed the Morrill Act, which provided territory to establish public schools and land grant universities, and the Homestead Act, which allowed citizens or persons intending to become citizens to acquire 160 acres of public land, and then purchase it after five years for a nominal fee.[33] Following the Civil War,

with the Union Army's defeat of the Confederate Army, advocates of states' rights were momentarily silenced, setting the foundation for a stronger federal government and the development of a national grants-in-aid system. In 1913, with the ratification of the 16th Amendment permitting the federal government to tax incomes, the powers of the federal government were dramatically enhanced.

The New Deal, World War II, and Cooperative Federalism

The relative sovereignty of the 50 states was altered during three notable high points of federal governmental power in the 20th century: the New Deal, World War II, and the Great Society programs of the 1960s.[34] Although there has been much rhetoric about the devolution of power to state and local governments, much of the political power initially grabbed by the federal government vis-à-vis the states during these time periods remains in Washington, D.C.

Although growth of national power was gradual, with its expansion originating during the period of Reconstruction,[35] the New Deal programs of the 1930s advanced by the administration of President Franklin Delano Roosevelt forcefully inserted the administration of the federal government into the national economy as never before. In 1933, in an effort to mitigate the Great Depression, Congress passed the Agricultural Adjustment Act, which created educational programs and protected farmers by providing crop subsidies. The same year, Congress created the Civil Works Administration, which created public works jobs for millions of the unemployed, and also established the Civilian Conservation Corps, which sent a quarter of a million men to work camps around

---

[32] See Stephen Skowronek, *Building a New American State: The Expansion of National Administrative Capacities, 1877–1920* (Cambridge, MA: Cambridge University Press, 1982).
[33] Daniel J. Elazar, *The American Partnership: Intergovernmental Co-operation in the Nineteenth-Century United States* (Chicago: University of Chicago Press, 1962).

[34] Martha Derthick, "Wither Federalism?" *The Urban Institute* 2(1996). Available: http://www.urban.org/UploadedPDF/derthick.pdf.
[35] Kimberley S. Johnson, *Governing the American State: Congress and the New Federalism, 1877–1929* (Princeton: Princeton University Press, 2006).

the country to help reforest and conserve the land. The Works Progress Administration, created by Congress in 1935, employed more than 8 million workers in construction and other jobs.[36] In 1936, Congress passed legislation creating a joint federal-state entitlement program, Aid to Families with Dependent Children (AFDC), which provided direct aid to families falling below the poverty line. Although these and other unprecedented incursions by Congress into policy areas previously controlled by the states were found to be constitutional, the U.S. Supreme Court struck down several other New Deal programs, including the National Recovery Administration and the Agricultural Adjustment Act, because of the congressional encroachment on the states.

The entry in 1941 of the United States into World War II gave rise to greater federal powers. In addition to asking Americans to make sacrifices for the war effort, the federal government commanded control of several aspects of the economy, rationing foodstuffs and consumer goods and even nationalizing some factories for wartime production. In addition to the dramatic increase in the number of military personnel, the number of civilian employees working in the federal bureaucracy skyrocketed, rising nearly fourfold to almost 4 million workers by 1945. At the same time, as we discuss in Chapter 10 when examining the fiscal effects of federalism, annual spending by the federal government rose tenfold during the war, from $9 billion to more than $98 billion. By the end of the war, political power rested squarely in the hands of the president and the U.S. Congress.

The efforts of the Roosevelt administration, with the blessing and support of the Democrat-controlled Congress, to insert the federal government into the economy by way of the states

are often characterized as **cooperative federalism**.[37] In such an arrangement, responsibilities for virtually all functions of government are interdependent, shared between the federal, state, and local governments. National and subnational officials act primarily as colleagues, not adversaries.[38] Although traces of such interlevel cooperation existed prior to the New Deal, the collaboration between various layers of government blossomed during the 1930s, with Congress utilizing **categorical grants** to entice the state governments to cooperate.

The Great Society and Coercive Federalism

In the 1960s, Congress further expanded the scope of the federal government by using **block grants** to spread a wide swath of programs across the nation. Following the assassination of President John F. Kennedy, President Lyndon B. Johnson urged Congress to create a "Great Society," one that would bring about many of the social and economic changes unrealized during his predecessor's truncated term in office. Many political observers questioned the ability, as well as the will, of many state officials to provide equal protection of the law and social services to all their citizens. Political scientist John Kincaid has characterized this period of expanding national growth and attendant federal programs, which some scholars date from 1960 to 1972, as **coercive federalism**.[39] With the federal government spearheading and funding several new programs in its war on poverty, some scholars have referred euphemistically to this period as creative federalism.[40] Congress sought to

[36] William E. Leuchtenberg, *Franklin D. Roosevelt and the New Deal, 1932–1940* (Princeton: Princeton University Press, 1963); and Alan Brinkley, *The End of Reform: New Deal Liberalism in Recession and War* (New York: Knopf, 1995).

[37] Elazar, *The American Partnership,* 1962.

[38] Walker, *The Rebirth of Federalism,* 1995.

[39] John Kincaid, "From Dual to Coercive Federalism in American Intergovernmental Relations," in John Jun and Deil Wright, eds., *Globalization and Decentralization* (Washington, DC: Georgetown University Press, 1996), pp. 29–47.

[40] Walker, *The Rebirth of Federalism,* 1995, p. 25.

relieve growing social pressures found across the American states by expanding social welfare programs, including those intended to reduce urban and rural poverty and eradicate public school inequalities. In many instances, the federal government completely bypassed the states, funneling grant-in-aid directly to local governments.

In the 1960s, building on the U.S. Housing Act of 1937, Congress established an array of federal programs to aid citizens in policy areas traditionally left to the states. With the approval of the Economic Opportunity Act of 1964, Congress created an Office of Economic Opportunity that was in charge of administering numerous local antipoverty programs. The following year, Congress established the Department of Housing and Urban Development, which was charged with improving public housing and urban life. In addition, Congress passed the 1964 Civil Rights Act—which enforced the right to vote, extended federal protection against discrimination in public accommodations, and outlawed job discrimination—and the 1965 Voting Rights Act, which guaranteed the right to vote to African Americans. In the mid-1960s, Congress passed legislation creating Medicare, which created a national health insurance program for the elderly, and Medicaid, a joint federal/state-funded health care program for poor people. Each and every one of these programs increased the relative power of the federal government vis-à-vis the states.

The Continued Expansion of Federal Powers during the 1970s

Although many of the programs established during the Great Society era have been either mothballed or transferred in part by Congress to the states, many still exist. The list of programs created by the federal government during the 1960s and early 1970s is impressive and expansive. In each case, state sovereignty over these policy areas was slowly eroded. Created in the 1960s, the Head Start public education program continues to prepare disadvantaged poor children for their first years of school; similarly, the Food Stamps program provides sustenance to those falling below the poverty line. Medicare and Medicaid, two of the largest domestic federal programs today, provide millions of Americans with medical insurance and health care. In addition to continuing to regulate auto emissions and the use of toxic chemicals, the Environmental Protection Agency, created by Congress in 1970, enforces the cleanup of hazardous waste, monitors the ozone layer, and enforces clean air and water laws.

In the early 1970s, the Nixon administration pushed for more block grants and changes to the way federal grants were administered. The president also pushed for **General Revenue Sharing (GRS)**, a grant-in-aid program whereby the federal government provides financial aid to subnational units, but does not prescribe how those units are to allocate the funding. Congress, however, abandoned the grant-in-aid scheme, as lawmakers were unable to claim credit for projects that the federal government paid for but were implemented by subnational officials.[41]

All of these social welfare programs have undergone restructuring since their creation. Yet, they are very much essential components of the social welfare system expanded by the federal government during the 1960s.[42] Indeed, Great Society programs have had lasting effects on reducing malnutrition, infant mortality, and inequality in obtaining medical services, as well as improving affordable housing, job training, and environmental cleanup efforts.[43]

---

[41] Timothy Conlan, *New Federalism: Intergovernmental Reform from Nixon to Reagan* (Washington, DC: Brookings, 1988).

[42] Michael Katz, *The Undeserving Poor: From the War on Poverty to the War on Welfare* (New York: Pantheon, 1989); and James Patterson, *America's Struggle Against Poverty, 1900–1980* (Cambridge, MA: Harvard University Press, 1981).

[43] John Schwarz, *America's Hidden Success: A Reassessment of Public Policy from Kennedy to Reagan*, rev. ed. (New York: W.W. Norton, 1988), pp. 68–69.

New Federalism during the Reagan Era

In the 1980s, many scholars observed how power seemed to be devolving back to the states. They pointed to the rise of entrepreneurial activities of the American states, with the state governments taking on new responsibilities to energize their economies by creating new jobs and economic opportunities.[44] The creative, self-directed activities of state and local governments conformed to the dominant political ideology of the time, decentralization, advanced most prominently by Republican President Ronald Reagan. In his first inauguration in 1981, Reagan famously pronounced, "Government is not the solution to our problem; government is the problem." To many states' rights proponents, they had a champion in the White House.

During the Reagan years (1981–1989), Congress aggressively consolidated categorical grants into block grants, cutting or eliminating entirely the funding of existing federal programs in the process. This wholesale transformation occurred despite the fact that the administration never outlined a clear set of principles regarding the proper delineation of federal and state powers. In 1982, the administration went so far as to propose what would become known as the "Big Swap," whereby the federal government would turn over to the states the responsibility to provide for education, social services, transportation, and cash public assistance programs, in exchange for taking over the provision of health services for the poor. To offset their increased costs, the states would receive a portion of the federal tax revenue. Congress rejected the proposal, as members were leery that the state and local governments would be unable to shoulder the financial costs of their new policy responsibilities.[45] As one longtime observer of American federalism noted, the Reagan administration's zeal to lessen the capacity of the federal government was not so much driven by devolution as by an "antigovernmental imperative" of "individualism."[46] Reagan and his top officials calculated that if federal dollars to states and localities were reduced, those governments would necessarily cut back on social programs. But rather than cutting programs, many state and local governments used their own funds to continue the programs. This was not the first time in American history that arguments over federalism were used to try to conceal or advance other political agendas, including the politics of race and social control.[47]

The Political Expediency of Federalism

Despite Reagan's pronouncements that power should be devolved to the states, the federal government continued to exert its authority vis-à-vis the states during the 1980s and 1990s. It is often the case that federal officials will spout the devolution line, but when push comes to shove, they usually—if not always—back off.[48] Many actions taken by Congress in the 1980s were driven by political expediency as much as any ideological commitment to the Reagan doctrine of "New Federalism." Take, for instance, the passage of the Anti-Drug

---

[44] Peter Eisinger, *The Rise of the Entrepreneurial States* (Madison: University of Wisconsin Press, 1988); and David Osborne, *Laboratories of Democracy* (Boston: Harvard Business School Press, 1988).

[45] Alice Rivlin, "The Federal Government in a Federal System: Current Intergovernmental Programs and Options for Change," Congressional Budget Office, August 1983. Available: http://www.cbo.gov/showdoc.cfm?index=5067&sequence=0.

[46] Samuel Beer, *To Make a Nation: The Rediscovery of American Federalism* (Cambridge, MA: Harvard University Press, 1993), p. xiii.

[47] Joe Soss, Richard Fording, and Sanford Schram, "The Color of Devolution: Race, Federalism and the Politics of Social Control," *American Journal of Political Science* 52(2008):536–53.

[48] Timothy Conlan, *From New Federalism to Devolution: Twenty-Five Years of Intergovernmental Reform* (Washington, DC: Brookings, 1998).

Abuse Act of 1988, which came exactly four years after the passage of the Comprehensive Crime Control Act of 1984. The bills, which created mandatory sentences for federal crimes and revised bail and forfeiture procedures, came just a few weeks prior to the 1984 and 1988 general elections, respectively. Both pieces of legislation were largely the result of Democrats and Republicans trying to outbid each other to look tough on crime at election time.

With the Anti Drug Abuse Act of 1988, Congress felt it needed to respond to the tragic death of Boston Celtics first-round draft pick Len Bias. Bias was a collegiate star at the University of Maryland who died of a cocaine overdose. Then-speaker of the U.S. House of Representatives, Democrat Tip O'Neill from Boston, worked with Republican leaders to pass mandatory five-year federal sentences for possession of small amounts of illegal drugs favored by the poor (5 grams of crack cocaine, or 10 grams of methamphetamines or PCP) and of larger amounts favored by the wealthy (500 grams of powered cocaine). The law, which required employers receiving federal aid to provide a "drug-free workplace" or risk suspension or termination of a grant or contract, was adopted without hearings, debate, or expert testimony.

Expanding National Power: Setting National Standards

In the early 1990s, Congress passed numerous laws encroaching on the power of the states. In 1990, Republican President George H. W. Bush signed into law a bill (the Gun Free School Zones Act of 1990) passed by a Democratic-controlled Congress making the possession of guns in or near schools a federal crime. In 1994, President Clinton signed into law bills making domestic violence (the Violence against Women Act of 1994) and failure to run background checks before the sale of weapons (the Brady Bill of 1994) federal crimes. (Both laws were later struck down by the U.S. Supreme Court.) By 1994, Congress had created 50 new crimes that could be prosecuted in federal court, many

with possible death sentences.[49] With its "Three Strikes You're Out" legislation, Congress federalized penalties for the possession of marijuana, created mandatory minimum sentence guidelines for federal judges, and allowed the death penalty for certain drug-related crimes. Prior to 1994, many of these crimes were prosecuted in state courts, at the discretion of state prosecutors. With all these laws, Democrats joined Republicans to ensure that their party would not be demonized come election time as being soft on crime.

The Devolution Revolution?

After Republicans took over the U.S. House and Senate in 1994, under the leadership of House Speaker Newt Gingrich, a more conservative Congress did try to tackle the centralization of power in Washington, D.C. Led by Gingrich, Republicans pushed forth their Contract with America, which, among other policy goals, called for devolution of power to the states. One of the only pieces of legislation packaged as part of the Contract with America to become law was the Unfunded Mandate Reform Act of 1995. In an effort to mitigate criticism among state and local government officials for the encroachment of the federal government on state powers, Congress agreed to restrict bills containing unfunded mandates. An **unfunded mandate** is a public policy that requires a subnational government to pay for an activity or project established by the federal government. Many state and local governments were upset with regulations handed down by Congress in the 1980s and 1990s with no money with which to implement the legislation. With its 1995 act, Congress still must include a cost estimate for any program including a mandate costing state or local governments at least $50 million. In addition, any mandate costing state or local governments

---

[49] American Bar Association Report, "The Federalization of Criminal Law," 16 February 1999. Available: http://www.abanet.org/crimjust/fedreport.html.

more than $50 million a year can be stopped by a point-of-order objection raised on either the House or Senate floor. A majority of the membership in either chamber is allowed to override the point of order and pass the mandate, but the objection affords the chamber an opportunity for debate.

Despite the flurry of rhetoric urging the decentralization of power to the states since the Republican Party took control of Congress in the mid-1990s, Congress has taken few concrete steps to actually transfer policy responsibilities to the states. As has been the case since the United States' founding, philosophical and ideological arguments over federalism have been trumped by quests for political power. Most notably, Congress passed legislation to "end welfare as we know it" by altering the long-standing joint federal-state social welfare entitlement program, AFDC. As we discuss in Chapter 14, AFDC was replaced by the Personal Responsibility and Work Opportunity Reconciliation Act

YOU DECIDE

HOMELAND SECURITY OR UNFUNDED FEDERAL MANDATE?

Notice anything different about your new driver's license? Perhaps it has a digitized photograph, a hologram, a tamperproof casing, or a barcode on the backside? In January 2005, Congress passed the National Intelligence Reform Act. In addition to several other provisions that reorganized national security agencies in response to the 9/11 terrorist attacks, the law created national standards for the issuance of state driver's licenses. With the U.S. Department of Transportation overseeing the changes of what is known as the "Real ID" law, states are now required to develop "smart" driver's licenses that have a digital photograph or some other unique biometric identifier, such as a fin-

Minnesota high-tech driver's license

gerprint or retinal-scan imprint. Although the law does not require states to immediately capture an applicant's biometrics, some critics claim that the law is an unfunded federal mandate and an intrusion of the federal government into an area traditionally regulated by the states. A handful of states, including Montana and Washington, have even passed laws refusing to comply with the new federal requirments.[1]

What do you think? Should states refuse to comply with the federal law? Is it an intrusion on states' rights? Or does the federal government have a legitimate national security interest, drawing on its powers found in the Commerce Clause, to regulate driver's licenses?

Note

1. Susan Llewelyn Leach, "A Driver's License as National ID?" *Christian Science Monitor* (January 24, 2005). Available: http://www.csmonitor.com/2005/0124/p11s02-ussc.html; Eric Kelderman, "States' Rebellion at Real ID Echoes in Congress," Stateline.org (May 9, 2007). Available: http://www.stateline.org/live/details/story?contentId=206433.

(PRWORA), which created a block grant program, Temporary Assistance for Needy Families (TANF), signed into law by President Clinton in 1996. The new law required eligible recipients to work in exchange for time-limited assistance, but gave the states wide latitude in determining both the work requirements and the levels of cash and in-kind assistance that recipients could receive.

Despite the rhetoric of devolution, the actions of Congress during the administration of George W. Bush further increased the powers of the federal government. Following the complications of the 2000 presidential election, Congress passed the Help America Vote Act of 2002, a grant-in-aid program that required the states to conform to federal standards concerning registration and voting. That same year, President Bush signed into law the No Child Left Behind Act, which mandated that public schools make "adequate yearly progress" or risk losing federal support. With each of these laws, Congress greatly expands its reach into what are traditionally the domains of state or local government.

When Does the Federal Government Become Stronger?

There has been little systematic research investigating the distribution of political power between the American states and the federal government over time. Using a measure of the level of policy centralization between 1947 and 1998, one recent study finds that the authority of the national government in the United States has gradually increased since World War II, diminishing the power of the state governments. The authors do not find, however, any patterns of stable growth in federal authority during the five-decade period. Rather, the growth in the authority of the national government has come in fits and starts. More significantly, perhaps, efforts to devolve power to the states during the presidential administrations of Republicans Richard Nixon and Ronald Reagan—contrary to their rhetoric of devolving power

to the states—did not lead to the states having increased policy-making authority.[50]

Umpiring Federalism: The U.S. Supreme Court

Given the inherent ambiguity in the interpretation and implementation of American federalism, who determines whether the state governments or the federal government has the constitutional authority to make laws? Soon after the founding of the United States, the federal courts assumed the role of adjudicating disputes between the federal and state governments. As umpire, the federal courts determine who is in the right when disputes between the national and subnational levels of government arise. In particular, the U.S. Supreme Court serves as the ultimate arbiter of the tension existing between the federal government and the states, with the highest state courts deciding the constitutionality of state laws under state constitutions. However, as we witnessed in 2001 with the Supreme Court's controversial *Bush v. Gore* decision that tipped the presidential contest, its decisions on questions of federalism are not always consistent or grounded in historical precedence.[51] In its hasty decision, the five conservative members of the Court ruled against the precedence of states' rights, overturning the Florida Supreme Court's ruling that ordered a manual recount of all undervoted ballots in the state. Table 2.1 provides a list of major U.S. Supreme Court decisions dealing with questions of federalism.

---

[50] Ann Bowman and George Krause, "Power Shift: Measuring Policy Centralization in U.S. Intergovernmental Relations, 1947–1998," *American Politics Research* 31(2005):301–25.
[51] E. J. Dionne and William Kristol, *Bush v. Gore: The Court Cases and the Commentary* (Washington, DC: Brookings Institution Press, 2001).

Table 2.1

Major U.S. Supreme Court Rulings Dealing with Issues of Federalism

McCulloch v. Maryland (1819)	Court upholds the power of Congress to incorporate the Second Bank of the United States and upholds that the State of Maryland could not tax it.
Gibbons v. Ogden (1824)	Court strikes down state licensing requirement on out-of-state steamboat operators, citing the Supremacy Clause and Commerce Clause.
Barron v. Baltimore (1833)	Court rules that the states are not limited by the Takings Clause of the 5th Amendment, and that states may seize private property for public use.
Dred Scott v. Sanford (1857)	Court upholds the institution of slavery and rules that fugitive slaves who had fled to "free" states may be forcibly returned to their legal slaveholders.
Slaughterhouse Cases (1873)	Court rules that the 14th Amendment prohibits states from infringing upon the rights of a person's national citizenship, but not his or her state citizenship.
Gitlow v. New York (1925)	Court rules that the 14th Amendment incorporates the 1st Amendment's protection of freedom of speech, making it applicable to the states.
Brown v. Board of Education of Topeka (1954)	Court rules that racial segregation in public schools violates the equal protection of the laws guaranteed by the 14th Amendment, reversing its previous decision, *Plessy v. Ferguson* (1896).
Garcia v. San Antonio Metropolitan Transit Authority (1985)	Court rules that federal wage and hour standards are applicable to employees of state and local governments.
United States v. Lopez (1995)	Court strikes down a federal law that prohibits possession of firearms near schools because it exceeds Congress's power under the Commerce Clause.
Seminole Tribe v. State of Florida (1996)	Court rules that Indian tribes are not permitted to sue states under a federal law, because Congress has only limited power to enact laws infringing upon state governmental entities.
Printz v. United States (1997)	Court strikes down federal law requiring mandatory background checks when purchasing firearms because it exceeds Congress's power under the Necessary and Proper Clause.
United States v. Morrison (2000)	Court strikes down federal Violence against Women Act because the law did not deal with an activity that substantially affected interstate commerce.
Bush v. Gore (2001)	Court rules that the 14th Amendment's Equal Protection Clause guarantees individuals that their ballots cannot be devalued later by arbitrary and disparate treatment, ending the Florida recount because different standards were applied from county to county.
University of Alabama v. Garrett (2001)	Court rules that states have sovereign immunity from lawsuits filed in U.S. District Court by their employees.
Gonzales v. Raich (2005)	Court rules that federal law enforcement officials have the authority to enforce a congressional act prohibiting the cultivation and possession of marijuana, even for physician-approved uses.
Granholm v. Heald (2005)	Court rules that states may not favor in-state wineries, as the Commerce Clause prohibits the discriminatory regulation of alcohol.
Gonzales v. Oregon (2006)	Court upholds an Oregon law allowing physician-assisted suicide and limits the federal government's effort to punish doctors prescribing a lethal dose of drugs.
Parents Involved in Community Schools v. Seattle School District No. 1 (2007)	Court strikes down a policy of the Seattle school district to assign children to public schools using racial classifications to achieve greater racial integration, on the ground that it violated the 14th Amendment's Equal Protection Clause.
District of Columbia v. Heller (2008)	Court overturns Washington, D.C.'s ban on the possession of handguns for private use and its requirement that all firearms be kept unloaded or bound by a trigger lock, citing the 2nd Amendment's right to keep and bear arms.
Northwest Austin Municipal Utility District Number One (NAMUDNO) v. Holder (2009)	Court upholds the power of Congress to extend Section 5 of the 1965 Voting Rights Act requiring states and local governments with legacies of racial discrimination to receive "preclearance" from the federal Department of Justice when proposing changes to voting systems, but allowing those jurisdictions to terminate their coverage under Section 5.

Judicial Review of the Power of the Federal Government

In 1819, 16 years after the U.S. Supreme Court ruled that it had the final word on determining whether laws were in conflict with the U.S. Constitution, the high court put the question of national government broadly usurping state power to the test in the case *McCulloch v. Maryland*. The State of Maryland had imposed a tax on transactions, including those of the Second Bank of the United States, on all banks that were not chartered in the state. The Supreme Court, under the direction of Chief Justice John Marshall, ruled that although it was not explicitly granted the right, Congress with its implied powers had the authority to establish a national bank. Under the Commerce Clause, found in Article I, Section 8 of the Constitution, the Court ruled that Congress had the power to lay and collect taxes, borrow money, and regulate commerce. Therefore, the Court ruled that the national bank was a "necessary and proper" outgrowth of the federal government's powers. Furthermore, the Court ruled that the State of Maryland had no constitutional authority to tax the national bank. The ruling, in tandem with *Gibbons v. Ogden* (1824), which permitted Congress to regulate interstate navigation, solidified the supremacy of the federal government over the state governments. In particular, the Court's rulings greatly empowered the federal government's hold over questions of dealing with interstate commerce.

The Supreme Court and Dual Federalism

For much of American history, not all individuals have been protected equally by the U.S. Constitution's Bill of Rights. Irrespective of one's race, ethnicity, or creed, a person's civil liberties largely have depended on where that person resided. Although perhaps difficult to comprehend today, the civil liberties found the first eight amendments to the U.S. Constitution did not automatically apply to all citizens. Rather, from the late 18th and into the 20th century (1789–1913), the United States was characterized by a system of dual federalism. In theory, under **dual federalism**, citizens are essentially governed by two separate legal spheres. Every eligible person is a citizen of the national government and, separately, a citizen of the state in which he or she resides.

In a series of early rulings, the U.S. Supreme Court interpreted the Bill of Rights as being applicable only to the actions of the federal government, not the states. In its 1833 decision *Barron v. Mayor and City Council of Baltimore*, the Court ruled that these federal civil liberties provided "security against the apprehended encroachments of the general government—not against those of local governments." The Court ruled that the 5th Amendment to the U.S. Constitution—which limits the taking of private property for public use without just compensation—did not apply to the states, as "each state established a constitution for itself, and in that constitution, provided such limitations and restrictions on the powers of its particular government, as its judgment dictated."[52]

Unless specifically limited by their own state constitutions, states were not bound by the restrictions that the Bill of Rights placed on the federal government. Indeed, the states were not obliged to take positive (or affirmative) action to protect their citizens from governmental actions, even those of other citizens. For example, several states in the early 19th century had established official state religions; Congregationalism, for example, was Connecticut's official religion until 1818, and until 1833 every man in Massachusetts was required by state law to belong to a church. Other states limited the freedom of their citizens to openly criticize the government.

---

[52] Harry Scheiber, "Federalism and the American Economic Order, 1789–1910," *Law & Society Review* 10(1975): 57–118.

The Civil War and National Unity

Prior to the Civil War (1861–1865), the American system of dual federalism permitted the states certain latitude to determine their own social and economic relations. In the mid-19th century, there were clear regional divisions in the United States. In addition to deep cultural differences, there were profound disagreements among the states on how to best manage and regulate the national economy, including most notably the question of slavery. Undergirding these questions of human rights and the economy, though, was the ever-present issue of federalism, namely, states' rights.

The Civil War fundamentally changed American federalism. In early 1861, following the election of Republican Abraham Lincoln, seven southern states seceded from the Union. In February, these states, led by South Carolina, created a new government, the Confederate States of America. The state governments seized property—including forts—of the federal government. Soon thereafter, in April 1861, the American Civil War began. Eventually, 11 southern states would secede from the Union; by the end of the war, over 620,000 Union and Confederate soldiers were killed. With the end of the war came the opportunity for the victorious national government to reshape the contours of American federalism.

Incorporating the 14th Amendment in the States

The end of the Civil War fundamentally altered the American system of dual federalism. Most notably, the ratification of the 14th Amendment in 1868 provided for a single national citizenship. In part, the 14th Amendment states,

> No State shall make or enforce any law which shall abridge the privileges or immunities of citizens of the US; nor shall any state deprive any person of life, liberty, or property without due process of law; nor deny to any person within its jurisdiction the equal protection of the laws.

In extending federal rights through the Due Process Clause and "Equal Protection of the Laws" Clause of the 14th Amendment, the Supreme Court has slowly incorporated the Bill of Rights into the states. The **incorporation of the Bill of Rights** has been gradual, taking place through a series of U.S. Supreme Court decisions. For example, it was not until 1925, when the Court ruled in *Gitlow v. New York*, that the 14th Amendment made the 1st Amendment's protection of freedom of speech applicable to the states. Subsequent rulings by the Court slowly began incorporating other amendments of the U.S. Constitution that protect the civil liberties of Americans into the states.[53] Although this process of incorporation was slow, many states adopted new state constitutions that provided greater rights than the federal Constitution.

Writing in the late 1800s, Lord James Bryce, a trenchant observer of American politics, was duly concerned about the system of American federalism. Bryce, the long-serving British ambassador to the United States, contended that the constitutionally prescribed dispersion of authority between the national and state governments weakened the ability of nationally elected officials to respond to internal and external threats to the nation, or changes in public opinion on domestic policy. For Bryce, the constitutional crisis over slavery that led to the Civil War was "the function of no one authority in particular to discover a remedy, as it would have been the function of a cabinet in Europe."[54]

Fortunately for Americans, Bryce noted, there were centrifugal forces that led toward increasing uniformity among the states, most notably national political parties that advanced coherent policy agendas, a transitory population, modern communications and transport,

---

[53] Carl Swidorski, "The Courts, the Labor Movement and the Struggle for Freedom of Expression and Association, 1919–1940," *Labor History* 45(2004):61–84.

[54] James Bryce, *The American Commonwealth*, vol. 2 (New York: Macmillian, 1893), pp. 358–59.

and a lack of significant physical boundaries between states. These forces, which were not bound by the federal structure, helped to homogenize differences among the states and allow for a more national trajectory in the historical development of federalism.

Establishing Minimum Standards for the States

Through a series of rulings during the 1950s and 1960s, the U.S. Supreme Court aggressively drew upon the 14th Amendment to greatly expand the scope of powers held by Congress to enforce the amendment's guarantees. Under the guidance of Chief Justice Earl Warren, a former Republican governor of California who was appointed to the Court by President Dwight D. Eisenhower in 1953, the Court ruled that state and local governments were required to affirm the equal protection of their citizens. In the landmark decision *Brown v. Board of Education* (1954), the Court overturned the long-standing practice of "separate but equal" racial segregation of public schools. The Court also invalidated discriminatory electoral practices in several states with a series of decisions anchored by *Baker v. Carr* (1962), which granted the federal courts jurisdiction to hear reapportionment cases dealing with the malapportionment of legislative seats, and required that state legislatures be apportioned on the basis of population.[55]

On the heels of the Warren Court, Chief Justice Warren Burger also enshrined a broad array of due process rights afforded to individuals under the 14th Amendment. In its 1963 decision *Gideon v. Wainwright*, the Court struck down a criminal procedural statute in Florida that criminal suspects did not have the right to consult with an attorney. In *Griswold v. Connecticut*, which the Court decided in 1965, the Warren Court struck down a Connecticut law

that forbade married couples from using contraception after Estelle Griswold was arrested and convicted for distributing birth control products from her clinic. In its majority and concurrent decisions, the Court established the "right of privacy," found in the "penumbra" of the 9th Amendment as well as that of the 14th Amendment's Due Process Clause. In *Miranda v. Arizona* (1966), the Court ruled that when arresting a person, state and local police must inform a suspect of his or her 5th and 6th Amendment rights, and that a person has the right to remain silent and must be clearly informed of his or her right to consult an attorney during a subsequent interrogation prior to being charged with a crime. In its 1973 *Roe v. Wade* decision, the Court ruled that states, such as Texas where the case unfolded, were not permitted to criminalize or wholly thwart abortions, as such actions would violate a woman's right to privacy afforded to her under the 14th Amendment, although in subsequent abortion-related decisions (as we discuss in detail in Chapter 13), such as *Webster v. Reproductive Health Services* (1989), the Court gave the states considerably more room to regulate the procedure.[56]

In each of these decisions, the high court established minimal standards—a floor—in terms of incorporating the protections of civil rights and liberties afforded by the federal Bill of Rights and 14th Amendment. In this era of "new judicial federalism," the Court did not curtail the right of the states to go beyond these minimal standards. Indeed, many states have public policies—for example, minimum or living wage laws, environmental regulations, and antidiscrimination laws—that far exceed the standards set by the federal government.[57] Most notably, in 1985, the high court ruled in

[55] Gerald Rosenberg, *The Hollow Hope: Can Courts Bring about Social Change?* (Chicago: University of Chicago Press, 1991).

[56] Jean Cohen, "Democracy, Difference and the Right of Privacy," in Seyla Benhabib, *Democracy and Difference: Contesting the Boundaries of the Political* (Princeton, NJ: Princeton University Press), pp. 187–217.

[57] John Kincaid, "The State and Federal Bills of Rights: Partners and Rivals in Liberty," *Intergovernmental Perspective* 17(1991):31–34.

Garcia v. San Antonio Metropolitan Transit Authority that federal wage and hour standards (set by Congress in 1974) were applicable to employees of state and local governments. In other words, the Court agreed that Congress had the authority over the supposedly "sovereign" states regarding how much they had to pay their workers.[58]

Expanding States' Rights

With its ever-evolving interpretations of the Constitution, the U.S. Supreme Court recently has made decisions that have tried to return some authority back to the states. Leading the charge to rein in the powers of the federal government, former Chief Justice William H. Rehnquist, who died in 2005, took a much narrower view of the scope of the 14th Amendment. With Rehnquist at the helm of a deeply divided bench, the Supreme Court began to crack down on the national encroachment on state government prerogatives, especially those enhanced by an expansive reading of the Interstate Commerce Clause. In *United States v. Lopez* (1995), the Court found that Congress had overstepped its authority when in 1990 it passed the Gun-Free School Zones Act, which made it a federal crime to carry a firearm in a designated school zone. A high school senior, Alfonso Lopez Jr., was charged by the federal government after he brought a concealed handgun to school. Lopez was subsequently found guilty and sentenced to prison for six months. In its narrow 5–4 decision, the Court ruled that Congress did not have the authority to craft a criminal statute under the guise of regulating a supposed economic activity as permitted under the jurisdiction of the Commerce Clause. Rehnquist's majority opinion reasoned that because the activity did not directly affect interstate commerce (there was no evidence that the gun in question traveled across state lines), Congress did not have the authority to criminalize the possession of

a gun in a school zone. It was the first decision in over 50 years in which the Court abrogated Congress's power to regulate an activity by using the Commerce Clause for cover.[59]

Two years later, in 1997, the high court ruled again to limit the reach of Congress. In *Printz v. United States*, the Court reaffirmed the principle that the Necessary and Proper Clause does not give Congress the power to compel local law enforcement agents, such as Montana's Ravalli County Sheriff Jay Printz, the plaintiff in the case, to conduct background checks on individuals wishing to buy a handgun. In a 5–4 decision, the Court ruled that Congress stretched the Necessary and Proper Clause too far when it passed the Brady Handgun Violence Prevention Act in 1993. The Court ruled that Congress could not use the Necessary and Proper Clause to regulate handgun sales. Then in 2000, the Court ruled in *United States v. Morrison* that the Violence against Women Act that Congress passed in 1994 was unconstitutional, as it did not deal with an activity that substantially affected interstate commerce. Time and again under the leadership of Rehnquist, the high court limited Congress's authority to invoke the Commerce Clause to regulate in areas that have only an insignificant connection with interstate commerce.[60]

Protecting the States from Lawsuits

Under Rehnquist, the Court also greatly expanded the rights of states by expanding their protection from lawsuits. According to the U.S. Constitution's 11th Amendment, ratified in 1795, the states have "sovereign immunity," meaning they have some protection from lawsuits brought by individuals.[61] In 1996, the U.S.

---

[58] John Pittenger, "Garcia and the Political Safeguards of Federalism: Is There a Better Solution to the Conundrum of the Tenth Amendment?" *Publius* 22(1992):1–19.

[59] Cornell Clayton and Howard Gillman, eds., *Supreme Court Decision-Making: New Institutional Approaches* (Chicago: University of Chicago Press, 1999).
[60] Mark Tushnet, *Taking the Constitution Away from the Courts* (Princeton, NJ: Princeton University Press, 1999).
[61] Sanford Schram and Carol Weissert, "The State of U.S. Federalism: 1998–1999," *Publius: The Journal of Federalism* 29(1999):1–34.

REFORM CAN HAPPEN

TOASTING THE U.S. SUPREME COURT

Have a thirst for a full-bodied Napa Valley Cabernet Sauvignon? How about a California-grown Pinot Noir, Merlot, or Chardonnay? Prior to 2005, if you were at least 21 years old and living in Wisconsin—or any of the other 28 states permitting direct shipments from California wine makers—your thirst could be readily quenched by ordering a bottle either by phone or over the internet. Direct mailing of wine to consumers is big business, with the more than 3,200 wineries in the country accounting for more than $18 billion in annual sales. But if you were living in Michigan, New York, Florida, or several other states banning out-of-state shipments of wine, you were out of luck. In those states, you were permitted to order wine and have it delivered to your doorstep, but only if it was produced in-state.

In May 2005, in a 5–4 decision, the U.S. Supreme Court ruled in *Granholm v. Heald* that the Constitution prohibited such discriminatory regulation, as the "state regulation of alcohol is limited by the nondiscrimination principle of the Commerce Clause." Although the 21st Amendment to the Constitution gives states tremendous leeway in regulating alcohol, "if a state chooses to allow direct shipments of wine," wrote Justice Anthony Kennedy in the majority opinion, "it must do so on evenhanded terms." The high court indicated that the states remain free to permit or ban the direct sale of wine to consumers, but it ruled that they may not give "preferential treatment" in direct sales to local wineries. Since the ruling, nearly two-thirds of the states now permit direct shipping of wine to consumers, including both Michigan and New York, but more than a dozen states have decided to completely ban all direct mail wine sales.[1]

Note

1. Linda Greenhouse, "Supreme Court Lifts Ban on Wine Shipping," *New York Times*, 17 May 2005, p. A1; Wine Institute, http://wi.shipcompliant.com/Home.aspx?SaleTypeID=1

Supreme Court ruled in *Seminole Tribe v. State of Florida* that the Seminole Indians were not permitted to sue the State of Florida for what the tribe alleged was the state's failure to negotiate in good faith new regulations for casino gaming activities as required by Congress's Indian Gaming Regulatory Act of 1988. The Court's 5–4 decision held that Congress did not have the authority under the Commerce Clause to trump the protections from lawsuits afforded the states under the 11th Amendment. In 2001, the high court gave states even greater protections when it ruled in *University of Alabama v. Garrett* that states had sovereign immunity from lawsuits filed in federal court by their employees. In its rulings, the Court has sent a message that federal powers could be limited, and that

individuals are generally not permitted to sue state and local governments in federal court unless Congress specifically enacts legislation pursuant to its power to enforce "equal protection of the laws" under the 14th Amendment.

States' Rights Legacy and the Roberts Court

Following a string of decisions granting more power to the federal government, many court-watchers asked whether the Court's federalism revolution would outlast the Rehnquist Court. Some asked whether the Court's effort to protect states' rights was more "a revolution of convenience" than driven by some deep ideological commitment to decentralized government.[62] With the appointment of John Roberts as the new chief justice in 2005, it appears that the Court's effort under Rehnquist to bolster states' rights has begun to fade.

Some cracks in the Court's bulwark to protect states' rights were already appearing in the waning days of the Rehnquist Court. Prior to retiring from the bench in 2005, Chief Justice Rehnquist was on the losing side in the case *Gonzales v. Raich*, when the Court ruled that federal law enforcement officials have the authority to enforce a congressional act prohibiting the cultivation and possession of marijuana, even for physician-approved uses. Since the mid-1990s, 10 states had passed ballot initiatives permitting physicians to prescribe medical marijuana to patients to relieve their pain and suffering. The Court's majority allowed Congress to preempt state medical marijuana laws, meaning that the more than 100,000 patients receiving the herbal doses are now subject to federal arrest and prosecution. The chief justice was one of only three justices who voted in the minority, arguing that on grounds of states' rights, California should be allowed to regulate homegrown "medical marijuana." With the decision, some Supreme Court watchers, such as Michael Greve of the conservative-leaning American Enterprise Institute, now claim that "the federalism boomlet" that devolved responsibilities to the states "has fizzled," as "the court never reached a stable equilibrium" to enable decentralization to take hold for good.[63]

Yet in 2006, the newly constituted Roberts Court ruled 6–3 to uphold an Oregon law allowing physician-assisted suicide and to strike down the federal government's effort in 2001 to punish any doctor prescribing a lethal dose of a federally controlled drug in an effort to terminate a patient's life. The Court's majority in *Gonzales v. Oregon* found that the Department of Justice did not have the authority to use the 1971 Controlled Substances Act to override the Oregon law, which was passed via a citizen initiative in 1994, and then reaffirmed in a 1997 statewide referendum.[64] Rather, the Court ruled that the states—not the federal government—were responsible for the regulation of their own medical practices. The Court's ruling, with Roberts notably joining a dissenting opinion, provided the first evidence that the new leader of the high court was ready to retreat from Rehnquist's states' rights agenda, though some of his fellow justices were perhaps not yet ready to follow.[65]

Because of the inherent ambiguity in the U.S. Constitution, the Supreme Court has a tremendous amount of power in settling interpretive differences between the federal government and the state governments. In one sense, federalism is what five judges with lifetime tenure say it is, and the Court's interpretation evolves as its members come and go. As the recent spate of rulings on federalism suggests—with the Court deciding that Congress has the power to criminalize the cultivation of marijuana for medical use even though a state allows it, but that Congress does not have the power to criminalize the possession of a handgun near a school or prevent a state from allowing certain citizens to take their own lives—there is some truth to this somewhat cynical interpretation of how federalism plays out in practice. Whether this drastic or not, the American federalist system has been undoubtedly affected by the legal reasoning, political ideology, and personal preferences of the nine justices on the high court.

[62] Linda Greenhouse, "The Rehnquist Court and Its Imperiled States' Right Legacy," *The New York Times* 13 June 2005, p. A3.

[63] Greenhouse, "The Rehnquist Court and Its Imperiled States' Right Legacy," 2005.

[64] Charles Lane, "Court Hears Case on Suicide Law," *The Washington Post* 6 October 2005, p. A4.

[65] Charles Lane, "Justices Uphold Oregon Assisted-Suicide Law," *The Washington Post* 18 January 2006, p. A1.

Federalism in an Age of Terror and Economic Crisis

As mentioned earlier, the national government's response to the terrorist attacks of September 11, 2001, as well as to subsequent threats to the security of the nation, has created a new set of challenges for the 87,000-plus local and 50 state governments. A hallmark of the "war on terror" waged by the administration of George W. Bush was the centralization of political power in Washington, D.C. Yet, much of the war on terror continues to be conducted on the ground at the state and local levels. As such, many subnational governments have been severely affected, and in some cases constrained, by the crush of new federal laws and administrative rulings stemming—however indirectly—from 9/11.

9/11 and Federal Powers

During the first term of George W. Bush, the Republican-controlled Congress passed numerous laws impinging on the authority of the states. The USA Patriot Act, passed in 2001 just 45 days after the 9/11 attacks, expanded the federal government's police powers, including the right to access medical and tax records, book purchases, and the borrowing of library books, as well as conduct secret home searches. President Bush even authorized the National Security Agency to monitor—without preclearance from a judge—phone calls and emails of U.S. citizens. In response, nearly 400 local governments and a handful of states passed resolutions denouncing the Patriot Act. Some of these nonbinding resolutions urge local law enforcement officials to refuse requests made by federal officials that may violate an individual's civil rights under the U.S. Constitution.[66]

Reverberations from 9/11 have also touched upon substantive policy areas that seem to have little to do with homeland security. Besides concerns voiced by civil libertarians that much of the new federal legislation has curtailed the civil liberties of American citizens, Congress passed legislation increasing federal control over state and local governments in a host of policy arenas. The federal crackdown on foreign threats has impinged directly on areas normally under the control of state and local governments, enabling the federal government to reign supreme over the states. Under the ever-expansive umbrella of homeland security, federal laws regulating public health care facilities, restricting the importation of prescription drugs, nationalizing K–12 education policies, and standardizing state driver's licenses have all encroached upon policy areas traditionally delegated to the states.

The War on Terror and State Militias

One of the areas greatly affected by the post-9/11 landscape concerns the National Guard. According to Article I, Section 8 of the U.S. Constitution, the National Guard is commanded directly by governors during times of peace. Unlike federal troops, which may not enforce civilian laws unless authorized by Congress, the National Guard is permitted to enforce state laws. Immediately following 9/11, many governors called up members of the National Guard to protect potentially vulnerable airports, nuclear power plants, water treatment facilities, and bridges in their states. In the past, governors have activated the National Guard to deal with natural disasters and civil unrest in their states—providing flood relief to Iowa residents in 2001 and securing South Central Los Angeles in 1992 after rioters killed 55 people and destroyed more than $1 billion worth of property following the acquittal of police officers on trial for the beating of motorist Rodney King.[67]

---

[66] Bill of Rights Defense Committee, "Resolutions Passed and Efforts Underway, By State," 2005. Available: http://www.bordc.org/index.php.

[67] Robert Preiss, "The National Guard and Homeland Defense," *Joint Forces Quarterly* 36(2005):72–78. Available: http://www.ngb.army.mil/media/transcripts/Preiss_JFQ_36_article.pdf.

National Guard helping Hurricane Katrina victims in New Orleans in 2005.

Mario Tama/Edit/Getty Images

angered by the slow response by the federal government.[69] Governor Blanco was so incensed that she initially refused a White House request to turn over control of the National Guard to President Bush. In response to the chaotic response in the aftermath of Hurricane Katrina, Congress in 2006 modified a 200-year-old law, the Insurrection Act of 1807, to empower the president to take control of National Guard troops not only to put down rebellions but also for natural disasters and other public emergencies.[70]

Due to the ongoing U.S. military presence in both Iraq and Afghanistan, there are fewer National Guard troops available stateside to help out in emergency situations here in the U.S. Since September 2001, over half-a-million National Guardsmen and -women (along with other "reservists") have been "involuntarily activated"—that is, called into federal service by the Pentagon.[68] Because these erstwhile "weekend warriors" may serve up to two years of active duty overseas, governors have fewer troops to deploy when natural disasters strike. In September 2005, when Hurricane Katrina hit the northern Gulf of Mexico coast, search-and-rescue and disaster relief efforts were hampered in Alabama, Florida, Louisiana, and Mississippi due to the lack of National Guard troops available. Louisiana Governor Kathleen Blanco and New Orleans Mayor Ray Nagin, both Democrats, as well as many residents of the Crescent City, were understandably

Crises and Opportunistic Federalism

The centralization of power in Washington, D.C., that followed 9/11 and Hurricane Katrina was not unexpected.[71] After every other national crisis—the Civil War, the Great Depression, and World War II—the federal government has asserted greater authority over states and localities. For over 200 years, in the aftermath of a national tragedy the national government has tried to usurp political power, preempting the authority of subnational state and local governments.[72]

[68] Lawrence Kapp, "Reserve Component Personnel Issues: Questions and Answers," Congressional Research Service, Library of Congress, 10 January 2005. Available: http://us.gallerywatch.com/docs/php/US/CRS/RL30802.pdf.

[69] Cherie D. Maestas, Lonna Rae Atkeson, Thomas Croom, and Lisa A. Bryant, "Shifting the Blame: Federalism, Media, and Public Assignment of Blame Following Hurricane Katrina," *Publius* 38(2008):609–32.

[70] Kavan Peterson, "Governors Lose in Power Struggle over National Guard," *Stateline* 12 January 2007. Available: http://www.stateline.org/live/details/story?contentId=170453.

[71] Carmine Scavo, Richard C. Kearney, and Richard J. Kilroy, "Challenges to Federalism: Homeland Security and Disaster Response," *Publius* 38(2008):81–110.

[72] Joseph Zimmerman, "Federal Preemption under Reagan's New Federalism," *Publius* 21(1991):7–28.

The pattern simply reasserted itself after 9/11, as wave after wave of federal power has washed away much of the authority of the American states.

Due to the shock of 9/11 and the public outcry to secure the nation's homeland, President Bush had increased the role of the federal government in the name of defending the homeland, and Congress obligingly followed his lead. Some, though, have questioned the increased role (and spending) of the federal government. For example, in 2005 the Republican-controlled Congress appropriated $825 million in Urban Area Security Initiative grants to the nation's cities. Congress decreased the total amount it spent on the program in 2006, but many of the new grants to combat terrorism were disbursed to cities not typically considered high-risk areas. Ironically, many members of Congress, who once heralded the downsizing of the federal government when President Reagan was in office, eagerly supported increasing the powers and spending of the federal government, especially if those dollars were for homeland security programs or newly created federal jobs in their own states. Indeed, after a decade of downsizing the personnel of the federal bureaucracy, with more than 350,000 federal jobs cut during the eight years of the administration of President Clinton, the federal government created more than 100,000 new public sector jobs during Bush's first term in office.[73]

Both Republicans and Democrats use centralization arguments when they advance their policy goals and political opportunism. Backlashes against centralized policy making in the nation's capital—from the abandonment of the First Bank of the United States

in 1811, to the collapse of Reconstruction in the 1870s, to the Great Society programs of the 1960s—are as predictable as the cycles of the moon. Indeed, there are growing indications that subnational resistance to contemporary federal policies and the co-optation of power by those inside the Beltway is already taking root. Somewhat hypocritically, it is now the Democrats—who since the 1930s, and especially during the Great Society years of the 1960s, called on the federal government to override states' rights—who are leading the charge to downsize the federal government's reach in many policy realms, especially in areas concerning public education and homeland security. With the American federalist system, ideological visions of federalism are readily trumped by political considerations.

Economic Crisis and Progressive Federalism

Upon assuming office in January 2009, one of President Barack Obama's first executive orders allowed the states—and specifically, California—more leeway in setting higher standards on greenhouse gas emissions and mileage standards for vehicles. With a stroke of his pen, Obama signaled that he was willing to give the states greater authority to deal with pressing environmental issues. If the states wanted to pass their own environmental standards and regulations that exceeded those of the federal government in an effort to save energy and clean up the environment, the Obama administration would not stand in their way.

For some, this early executive decision by the Democratic administration indicated a new wave of federalism infused by "a spirit of cooperative federalism." But do early executive actions mean that the Obama administration has fully embraced states' rights? Does it usher in a new type of federalism—dubbed **progressive federalism** by some—where states are given

---

[73] U.S. Office of Management and Budget, "The Budget of the United States Government, Fiscal Year 2006, Historical Tables." Available: http://www.gpoaccess.gov/usbudget/fy06/pdf/hist.pdf.

Table 2.2

2009 Federal Stimulus Package, Direct Aid to State and Local Governments

Category of Spending	Description of Spending	Amount
Health Care	Increase the federal government's contribution for Medicaid costs	$87.1 billion
Education	Increase aid for local school districts and public colleges and universities	$53.6 billion
Education	Create new tax credit bonds for construction and repair of public school facilities or to acquire land for construction of new public schools	$10.9 billion
Infrastructure	Create new tax credit bonds for investment in areas with significant poverty, unemployment, or home foreclosure	$6.5 billion
Bonds	Create a tax credit bond option for state and local governments, allowing them to sell taxable debt	$4.3 billion
Unemployment	Increase grants to states to modernize their systems to increase coverage among low-wage, part-time, and other jobless workers	$4.2 billion
Law Enforcement	Increase financing for state and local law enforcement	$4 billion
Welfare	Increase block grants for welfare program, specifically Temporary Assistance for Needy Families	$2.7 billion
Unemployment	Increase aid to provide retraining and extend unemployment benefits to workers who lost jobs due to trade or outsourcing	$1.6 billion
Energy	Authorize use of state and local renewable energy bonds and energy conservation bonds to finance state and local government projects	$1.4 billion
Welfare	Rescind federal law cutting state financing for child support enforcement	$1 billion
Housing and Employment	Increase aid to states to find housing and jobs for disabled people	$640 million
Bonds	Repeal of alternative minimum tax on private activity bonds	$555 million
Education	Increase aid to states and local school districts to track student data and improve teacher quality	$550 million
Unemployment	Increase aid to states to help unemployed workers find jobs	$500 million
Energy	Increase grants to states for energy-efficient vehicles and infrastructure	$400 million
Taxes	Delay withholding tax on any payments made for property or services	$291 million
Infrastructure	Allow states to use private activity bonds to finance high-speed rail	$288 million
Rural Assistance	Provide loans for essential facilities in rural developments, such as hospitals	$150 million
Homelessness	Provide aid to states to provide services to homeless children	$70 million
Housing	Allow state housing agencies to claim Treasury Department grants	$69 million

Source: New York Times, from Congressional Budget Office, 2009, Available: http://projects.nytimes.com/44th_president/stimulus.

the green light to supersede regulations set by the federal government? Perhaps, but more likely it's really a rehashing of cooperative (or coercive) federalism, with the federal government calling most of the shots and setting the standards.

What is clear is that when it comes to regulatory actions on issues such as environmental standards and consumer protection, the Obama administration has made a sharp break from the previous eight years of Republican efforts to use federal powers to deregulate and lower environmental standards. Some commentators have described Obama's view of intergovernmental relations as having the federal government provide a floor, not a ceiling. States must adhere to federal guidelines and regulations, but they may go beyond them if they see fit. Others more critical of the heightened regulations emerging out of Washington, D.C., see it as an open invitation for the states to become too experimental, leading to what some have called "free-for-all federalism" and a "patchwork of laws."[74]

Certainly, Congress' passage of the American Recovery and Reinvestment Act of 2009 has given the federal government even more say over a range of issue areas. With over $150 billion going to the state and local governments to help close their budget gaps, the Democratic Congress and Obama administration made sure numerous strings were attached to the money, ensuring that the federal government would have a say on how the money would be spent at the subnational level. As Table 2.2 details, the states received an infusion of federal dollars—Medicaid funding for health care, K–12 and higher education funding, unemployment assistance, renewable energy grants, aid to combat homelessness, grants for welfare assistance, and money for thousands of "shovel-ready" transportation projects.

Summary

In his landmark dissent in *New State Ice Co. v. Liebmann* (1932), Louis Brandeis, an associate justice of the U.S. Supreme Court, coined the phrase "laboratories of democracy." Brandeis wrote, "It is one of the happy incidents of the federal system that a single courageous State may, if its citizens choose, serve as a laboratory; and try novel social and economic experiments without risk to the rest of the country." Many commentators have lauded Brandeis's minority ruling, as it highlights the genius of the United States' federal system. With the premium the system places on state and local experimentation as well as competition, in theory the responsibilities for policy making are often devolved to the states.

Despite the gradual erosion of authority caused by wave after wave of federal government power crashing on their shores, the states have retained considerable policy-making discretion. The states have been at the forefront of experimentation in education, social welfare, political economy, criminal justice, and regulatory policies, and are often in competition with one another in crafting and implementing public policies. As Justice Brandeis indicated, competition among the states, as well as between the states and the federal government, encourages policy experimentation and diffusion among the states.[75] But policy experimentation is also a highly political

---

[74] John Schwartz, "Obama Seems to Be Open to a Broader Role for States," *New York Times* 30 January 2009. Available: http://www.nytimes.com/2009/01/30/us/politics/30federal.html?ref=us.

[75] Karen Mossberger, *The Politics of Ideas and the Spread of Enterprise Zones* (Washington, DC: Georgetown University Press, 2000).

process.[76] In the American system, the states not only do battle with the federal government but also perennially challenge one another over how to implement domestic public policies being handed down from Washington.

Since at least the turn of the 20th century to the present day, however, the states have had to struggle to maintain their autonomy from the federal government. In addition, states have had to go it alone when the federal government has opted not to become involved in making public policy. Recently, for example, California voters approved a $3 billion bond measure, placed on the ballot via an initiative, for stem cell research. The effort to fund such research was precipitated by cutbacks by the federal government to fund stem cell research. With the State of California functioning within a competitive market, taxpayers there are willing to finance research that will in all likelihood benefit the state's economy.

In this sense, the "quiet revolution" in the states, which Carl Van Horn observed in the 1980s, is still occurring.[77] However, as states have gradually become more powerful actors, increasing their state capacities and becoming more professionalized, so too has the federal government. State governments, with their ambiguous constitutional autonomy, continue to be relegated as semisovereign units in the system of American federalism. The following chapters compare many of the institutional differences found across the states and their localities.

Key Terms

Articles of Confederation	Devolution	National Supremacy Clause
Bill of Rights	Dual federalism	Necessary and Proper Clause
Block grants	Federalism	Nullification
Categorical grants	Federal preemption	Privileges and Immunities Clause
Centralization	Full Faith and Credit Clause	
Coercive federalism	General Revenue Sharing (GRS)	Progressive Federalism
Commerce Clause		Reserve Clause
Confederal system	Incorporation of the Bill of Rights	Unfunded mandate
Cooperative federalism	Intergovernmental relations	Unitary system
Decentralization		

---

[76] Andrew Karch, *Democratic Laboratories: Policy Diffusion among the American States* (Ann Arbor: University of Michigan Press, 2007); Charles R. Shipan and Craig Volden, "Bottom-Up Federalism: The Diffusion of Antismoking Policies from U.S. Cities to States," *American Journal of Political Science* 50(2006):825–43.

[77] Karl Van Horn, *The State of the States* (Washington, DC: CQ Press, 1989).

Discussion Questions

1. The federal government's powers expanded following the September 11, 2001, terrorist attacks. Do you think the federal government's increased powers are warranted? Has the federal government encroached too far on states' rights?
2. What are the advantages and disadvantages of a federalist system of government compared to a unitary or confederal system of government?
3. How did the powers of Congress under the Articles of Confederation compare to those of the 1787 U.S. Constitution?
4. Has President Obama's 2009 federal stimulus altered the relationship between the states and the federal government? Do you think it constitutes a new form of federalism, what some are calling "progressive federalism?"

Suggested Readings

Beer, Samuel. *To Make a Nation: The Rediscovery of American Federalism*. 1993. Cambridge, MA: Harvard University Press.

Conlan, Timothy. *New Federalism: Intergovernmental Reform from Nixon to Reagan*. 1988. Washington, DC: Brookings Institute.

Elazar, Daniel. 1984. *American Federalism: A View from the States*, 3rd ed. New York: Harper & Row, 1984.

Karch, Andrew. *Democratic Laboratories: Policy Diffusion among the American States*. 2007. Ann Arbor, MI: University of Michigan Press.

Walker, David. *The Rebirth of Federalism*. 1995. Chatham, NJ: Chatham House.

Zimmerman, Joseph. *Contemporary American Federalism*. 1992. Westport, CT: Praeger.

Web Sites

American Enterprise Institute (http://www.federalismproject.org): AEI's Federalism Project provides scholarly research on American federalism and monitors recent developments.

Brookings Institution (http://www.brookings.edu): Brookings' Governance Studies Program provides numerous scholarly reports on the developments of American federalism.

Institute of Federalism (http://www.federalism.ch): An international research center based in Switzerland that focuses on questions of culture and federalism.

Publius (http://publius.oxfordjournals.org): *Publius: The Journal of Federalism* is the leading journal devoted to federalism, with scholarly articles examining the latest developments and trends on federalism and intergovernmental relations.

Urban Institute (http://www.urban.org/center/anf/index.cfm): UI's Assessing the New Federalism project examines federal programs that affect municipalities, documents how children and families are affected by these programs, and provides national survey data on the topic.

3

AP Photo/Alden Pellett

Participation, Elections, and Representation

fewer vote in "odd year" (that is, not during the year of a presidential election) state elections and even fewer in local elections.

Scholars and democratic theorists offer us limited guidance about how much public participation can shrink before the legitimacy of a democratic government evaporates. It seems clear, however, that fewer are participating now than in previous decades and that there are growing differences between those who do participate and those who do not.[6] If participating citizens were largely similar to nonparticipating citizens, low levels of political participation might not be such a worry. As we see below, however, there is clear evidence of **participation bias**—or differences between those citizens who participate and those who do not.[7]

Participation Is Much More Than Voting

Voting involves electing representatives, and in many places that use direct democracy (see Chapter 4), voting also involves public decisions to approve or reject policy proposals. There are many other ways, in addition to voting, that Americans are engaged politically. Some of these other forms of political participation may be seen as attempts to instruct elected officials how to act after elections are held. Indeed, all of what governments do—the laws, policies, rules, and regulations they pass—takes place between elections, after we have voted. People participate by joining groups, lobbying, contacting officials, attending meetings, and writing letters, among other activities.

Why Bother? The Stakes Are High Although most Americans do not usually vote in their state and local elections, political engagement

at the local level is relatively impressive when compared with the public's engagement with national political campaigns and presidential elections. If public opinion surveys are to be believed, many (and occasionally most) adult Americans show up to vote in presidential elections once every four years, but they spend little time actively engaged working on national political issues. More Americans say that they spend their time working on issues that face their schools and their communities rather than spend time involved with high-profile presidential elections. This makes some sense, given the stakes. In the previous chapter, we discussed the scope of what state and local governments do. Most critically, state and local governments spend about 17 cents of every dollar generated by the American economy (more than that spent by the federal government). The U.S. Supreme Court has given states wide latitude over many areas of policy. Cities and counties control nearly all aspects of land use decisions, and state and local courts administer the vast majority of civil and criminal cases. Furthermore, over 95 percent of all elected positions in the United States are at the local level.

Participation at state and local levels, then, is likely to have a substantial impact on what government does. Americans are actually relatively optimistic about their ability to accomplish things at the local level. As Table 3.2 illustrates, nearly three-quarters believed that "people like you" can have a moderate or big impact in making their community a better place to live. Table 3.3 illustrates that although Americans are fairly cynical about politics generally, and many distrust government at any level, they are more trusting of their local governments and less likely to believe that they have "no say" at the local level compared to the national level.

Yet, the effect of political participation might be understood in terms of the cliché, "The squeaky wheel gets the grease." That is, if we assume that governments respond mostly to those who participate, and less to those who do not, we can understand who gets what from government, at least in part, by considering who participates.

---

[6] Stephen Macedo et al., *Democracy at Risk: How Political Choices Undermine Citizen Participation, and What We Can Do about It* (Washington, DC: Brookings Institution, 2005).

[7] See, for example, Sidney Verba, Kay Schlozman, and Henry E. Brady, *Voice and Equality: Civic Voluntarism in American Politics* (Cambridge, MA: Harvard University Press, 1995).

Table 3.2

Local Political Efficacy (N = 3,003)

Overall, How Much Impact Do You Think People Like You Can Have in Making Your Community a Better Place to Live?	%
No impact at all	4
A small impact	19
A moderate impact	42
A big impact	35

Source: Social Capital Benchmark Survey, 2000.

Table 3.3

Public Trust and Efficacy in Local and National Government (N = 3,003)

Trust Local or National Government to Do What Is Right	Local (%)	National (%)
Always or most of the time	42	29
Some of the time	46	53
Hardly ever	11	18

Source: Social Capital Benchmark Survey, 2000.

People Like Me Have No Say in What Local or National Government Does[a]	Local (%)	National (%)
Agree	35	41
Disagree	62	50

[a] Question to respondents was as follows: "Do you agree or disagree that 'people like me have no say in what the [federal] government does' and 'People running my community don't really care much about what happens to me'?"

Sources: National Election Study, 2000; and Social Capital Benchmark Survey, 2000.

Table 3.4

Levels of Local Participation in the United States (N = 3,003)

In the Last 12 Months, Did You	Overall (%)	Poor (%)	Wealthy (%)
Attend a public meeting to discuss school or town affairs?	45	31	63
Work on a community project?	38	23	60
Attend a PTA or school group meeting?	24	14	34
Participate in a neighborhood or homeowner association meeting?	22	12	41
Participate in a group that took action for local reform?	18	9	30

Note: Poor = household income is $20,000 or less; wealthy = $100,000 or more.

In the Last 12 Months, Did You	Overall (%)	Rent (%)	Own (%)
Attend a public meeting to discuss school or town affairs?	45	36	49
Work on a community project?	38	28	42
Attend a PTA or school group meeting?	24	19	26
Participate in a neighborhood or homeowner association meeting?	22	14	26
Participate in a group that took action for local reform?	18	15	19

Source: Social Capital Benchmark Survey, 2000.

Who Participates? Who Does Not?

Political participation in nearly all forms—voting, attending meetings, contacting public officials, and contributing to political candidates—is not behavior that is randomly distributed across the population. Depending upon the form of participation we are examining, there may be substantial differences between those who participate and those who do not. Consider the forms of participation listed in Table 3.4. There are striking differences across income groups. The wealthy tend to be overrepresented relative to average people and less wealthy people in several forms of local-level political participation. Most wealthy people say they go to public meetings and work on community projects. Most of the least affluent people do not. It is important to note that wealth itself and education alone are not what cause people to participate in politics. Education and wealth lower the costs of becoming engaged with politics. By costs, we mean such things as time and the difficulty of collecting and processing political information.

Voting

When we consider voting, there are clear differences between who votes and who does not. One study found that although 55 percent of all American adults earned lower- to middle-level incomes, this majority group represented only 46 percent of voters in national elections, 43 percent of campaign hours volunteered, and just 16 percent of campaign dollars provided to candidates.[8] This participation gap between the affluent and less wealthy may even be greater in state and local elections that have lower levels of citizen participation. The voting population tends to overrepresent the affluent, older voters, people from white-collar professions, people with higher levels of education, and those who have jobs.[9] This said, voters are probably more representative of the general citizenry than other types of participants, such as campaign contributors and members of organized political groups.[10]

Voter turnout in local elections is also significantly higher in cities with a higher social status population and in places with more voters who are over 65 years old.[11] Public opinion surveys suggest that homeownership may have no impact on whether someone votes in national elections,[12] but the incentives to vote that come with homeownership—being concerned about property values and property taxes—are more likely to be felt in local elections. Records of actual votes cast in a nonpartisan Atlanta mayoral race, for example, demonstrated that homeowners are more likely to vote than renters. The stimulating effect of property tax issues on voter turnout was famously seen in California in 1978, where more people voted on a property tax cut measure (Proposition 13) than voted in the gubernatorial race on the same ballot.

As Table 3.4 illustrates, homeowners are more likely than renters to report many other forms of local political participation. With lower levels of participation, renters and the less affluent might be expected to have less influence in local politics relative to their share of the population.

Contacting and Contributing

The participation gap between rich and poor is even more striking when we look at the "activists"—people who donate their time and money to candidates and who contact government officials. Sixty percent of all reported "contacts" with public officials came from the top 45 percent of income earners.[13] Studies of people who contact local officials suggest that contacting increases with social status and income, although contacts based on needing help from the government may be related to having less income.[14] It's not just income alone that causes contacting. Wealth corresponds

---

[8] Verba et al., *Voice and Equality*.

[9] Jan Leighley and Jonathan Nagler, "Socioeconomic Class Bias in Turnout, 1964–1988: The Voters Remain the Same," *American Political Science Review* 86(3)(1992):725–36; and Jan Leighley and Jonathan Nagler, "Individual and Systemic Influences on Turnout: Who Votes?" *Journal of Politics* 54(3)(1992):718–40.

[10] Verba et al., *Voice and Equality*.

[11] Zoltan Hanjal and Paul Lewis, "Municipal Institutions and Voter Turnout in Local Elections," *Urban Affairs Quarterly* 38(5)(2003):654–68.

[12] Eric Plutzer, "Voter Turnout and the Life Cycle: A Latent Growth Curve Analysis" (paper presented at the Midwest Political Science Association meeting, 1997).

[13] Verba et al., *Voice and Equality*.

[14] Elaine Sharp, "Citizen Initiated Contacting of Local Officials and Socio-Economic Status," *American Political Science Review* 76(1982):109–15; but see Rodney Hero, "Explaining Citizen-Initiated Contacting of Government Officials," *Social Science Quarterly* 67(1986):626–35; and Michael Hirlinger, "Citizen-Initiated Contacting of Local Officials," *Journal of Politics* 54(1992):553–64.

with education, with political skills, and with **efficacy**—the sense that political involvement can actually make a difference.

Attending Meetings

State and local politics differ from national politics in that the actions of government are more accessible locally. Many aspects of state and local government require open public meetings that provide for public comment. Individual citizens and people representing organized groups may attend without having to bear substantial travel costs. Mandates that government provide open meetings do not necessarily ensure that officials give full consideration to all citizen comments.

Interest Group Activity

In addition to contributing to groups, citizens join and serve on boards of homeowners' associations, school groups, and many different voluntary political and social groups that work to shape their states and communities. An influential theory of interest group activity, collective action theory, predicts that groups seeking economic benefits from governments (such as tax breaks and public subsidies) are more likely to remain organized and well funded than groups seeking "public" benefits, such as parks and consumer protections.[15] Records detailing which political groups register to lobby the federal government are consistent with this theory. Nearly two-thirds of political action committees (PACs)—including those spending the most on lobbying—are affiliated with corporations, trade groups, professional associations, and the health care industry. Only 22 percent were "nonconnected" ideological and public interest groups, and 10 percent were labor groups.[16]

At the local level, the presence of organized suburban neighborhood associations may have

an upper-status bias, reflecting that affluent suburbanites have resources to organize and work collectively to protect themselves (and their property values) from unwanted development.[17] Survey data reported in Table 3.4 also show large differences across income groups in who gets involved with local political groups. Compared to those from households in the bottom one-fifth of all incomes, people in the top fifth of all incomes were twice as likely to be involved with parent-teacher association (PTA) groups and other school groups. They were three times more likely to be involved with neighborhood groups and almost four times more likely to be involved with a local political reform group.

Group activity can have important effects on the policies that states and cities adopt. In the early part of the 20th century, the work of women's groups accelerated state adoption of "mothers' pension benefits"—a forerunner to federal Aid to Families with Dependent Children (AFDC).[18] When American women were largely shut out of the voting arena, middle-class and upper-status women formed a million-member General Federation of Women's Clubs that lobbied effectively for mothers' pensions and consumer protections.[19]

Grassroots Political Activity

Many interest groups function by collecting contributions from members to pay for the work of full-time staff. Groups with a broader base of support may rely on rank-and-file members or on the general public, to bring attention to their issue. As examples, neigh-

---

[15] Mancur Olson, *The Logic of Collective Action* (1965).

[16] As of January 2000. See Federal Elections Commission, http://www.fec.gov/press/pacchart.htm.

[17] John Logan and Gordana Rabrenovic, "Neighborhood Associations: Their Issues, Their Allies," *Urban Affairs Quarterly* (1990):2668–94.

[18] Theda Skocpol, Christopher Howard, and Susan Goodrich Lehmann, "Women's Associations and the Enactment of Mothers' Pensions in the United States," *American Political Science Review* 87(3)(1993):686–701.

[19] Ada Davis, "The Evolution of the Institutions of Mothers Pensions in the United States," *American Journal of Sociology* 35(1937):573–87.

REFORM CAN HAPPEN

THE LONG, SLOW ROAD TO VOTING RIGHTS

The 15th Amendment to the U.S. Constitution, adopted in 1870, states that the right to vote shall not be denied on the basis of race, color, or previous condition of servitude. Despite this, it took decades to eliminate most race-based barriers to voting in the United States. By 1910, virtually all blacks were unable to vote in the former Confederate states. It wasn't until 1915, when the U.S. Supreme Court struck down the **grandfather clause** in an Oklahoma law in *Guinn v. United States*, that the Court slowly began using the 15th Amendment to eliminate the major barriers that states used to disenfranchise blacks. Such clauses granted the right to vote only to men who had ancestors who could vote before the civil war. By 1944, the Court ruled that Texas could not ban blacks from primary elections (in *Smith v. Allwright*). In 1960, the Court ruled that cities could not redraw boundaries to remove blacks from a city (*Gomillion v. Lightfoot*).

The **Voting Rights Act** of 1965 was a historic piece of legislation that provided a major expansion of access to voting for millions of Americans. One key feature of the act (Section 5) was taking control of elections away from local governments and granting authority over many voter registration and election procedures to the U.S. Department of Justice. Jurisdictions covered under Section 5 could not change any rules about voting until the attorney general or a federal court "pre-cleared" the change after determining it not have a discriminatory effect.

Many barriers to voting still remained after the initial Voting Rights Act was passed. For example, the act had no provisions against the local poll tax. The U.S. Supreme Court ruled the poll tax unconstitutional in 1966 (*Harper v. Virginia Board of Elections*). Newly enfranchised blacks were denied influence in many jurisdictions by **racial gerrymandering** (that is, drawing boundaries to dilute minority vote share) and at-large elections that can dilute the influence of minority voters. The act was amended in 1975 and 1982 to address these issues and to expand protections to Hispanics, Asians, and Native Americans. Although the VRA was extended by Congress in 2006, its future is uncertain. A 2009 U.S. Supreme Court ruling *(Northwest Austin v. Holder)* made it easier for some jurisdictions covered by the act to avoid preclearance requirements, and revealed a court divided over the continued need for major parts of the act.

borhood groups may attempt to pack city council hearings with residents worried about the impact of proposed developments, or to promote neighborhood interests. Crime and environmental degradation have prompted grassroots activism at the local level. Grassroots neighborhood groups also organize to fight poverty, promote quality housing, and resist urban renewal. Prominent figures supported by grassroots neighborhood groups have been elected mayor in cities such as Boston, Cleveland, Portland, and Santa Monica, California.

Social Movements and Protest

In addition to joining formal groups, people participate in larger, broad-based social movements. Social movements may comprise many loosely affiliated groups that share a common purpose of sustained, mass-based participation throughout a large number of communities in order to mobilize public opinion and change public policy. Formal channels of participation in social movements are sometimes difficult to define but may include the forms discussed above as well as lawful

Peter Pettus/Library of Congress

Participants in the 1965 civil rights march from Selma, Alabama, to Montgomery, the state capital. This march and others brought attention to barriers that kept blacks from voting. Participants were attacked and beaten by police before they reached Montgomery.

protest, public demonstrations, and peaceful civil disobedience.

The American civil rights movement serves as a classic example of a broad, mass-based social movement working in many communities to change the nation's perceptions of racial segregation and voting rights abuses.

Rioting

Rioting is a rare, often spontaneous form of illegal action using physical violence. Rioting does not qualify as legitimate political participation, but it may reflect the failure of politics. Some consider rioting to be a political challenge to authority; others see it as an opportunistic attempt to loot and commit other crimes.[20] American cities have a history of riots fueled by racial animosity. Fatal white-on-black race

riots were common in American cities in the 19th and early 20th centuries. In 1920, more than 300 African Americans were killed by whites in a single event in Tulsa, Oklahoma.[21]

Rioting occurred in hundreds of communities throughout the urban United States during the 1960s. Although the root causes of the 1960s rioting were traced to poverty, major riots were triggered by sudden, dramatic public events (such as a conflict with police or the murder of Dr. Martin Luther King, Jr.). There is evidence that the participants in urban riots of the 1960s were fairly evenly distributed across income, educational, and occupational groups in their communities and that rioters were not simply jobless thugs and criminals.[22]

---

[20] National Advisory Commission on Civil Disorders Kerner Commission Report; and Edward Banfield, *Rioting for Fun and Profit.*

[21] There were 20 such riots in 1919 alone. Dennis R. Judd and Todd Swanstrom, *City Politics* (2004).

[22] T. David Mason and Jerry Murtagh, "Who Riots? An Empirical Examination of the 'New Urban Black' versus Social Marginality Thesis," *Political Behavior* 7(4)(2004):352–73. Also *Social Science Quarterly*, special issue (1969).

The impetus for adopting antipoverty programs in the late 1960s can be traced, in part, to elected officials responding to widespread urban rioting.

Although much less common since the 1960s, sporadic rioting occurred in U.S. cities in the 1980s (Miami) and 1990s in response to conflicts with police in minority neighborhoods. In 1992, several days of widespread rioting caused at least 45 deaths, 2,000 injuries, and $1 billion in property damages in the greater Los Angeles area. The rioting began in response to a trial court acquitting police officers who had been charged with the 1991 beating of an African American motorist (Rodney King).

How Many Citizens Participate?

Records show low levels of voting at the state and local levels, yet many American adults are politically active at the local level. Between elections, these politically active citizens try to shape policy by attending meetings and testifying at public hearings. In 2000, 45 percent of Americans reported that they had attended at least one meeting in the last 12 months to discuss affairs related to their town or schools. Another 20 percent said they attended at least two such meetings in the previous year. Significant numbers also reported working on community projects and working with groups that promoted social and political change in their communities.[23] Political participation can also take forms such as circulating petitions, attending protests, contacting elected officials, writing letters, and the like. Over 50,000,000 Americans belong to homeowners' associations, with over 1 million serving on boards and committees. Although these numbers are impressive, local political participation seems to be declining. By 1990, half as many people reported voting in local elections than did in 1967.[24]

---

[23] Social Benchmark Survey.
[24] Verba et al., *Voice and Equality*, p. 72.

Barriers to Participation at the State and Local Levels

As Figure 3.1 illustrates, there is substantial variation in voter participation across the 50 states, just as there is across American towns and cities. Minnesota and Maine led the nation in the percentage of adults over 18 who voted in the 2008 presidential election, with over 70 percent of their **voting-age population** (all people over age 18) having participated. Hawaii, Texas, and Arizona rank lowest, with less than half of the adults in these states voting. These vastly different participation rates are a result of many factors. States like Minnesota have far more people with traits known to correspond with interest in politics. A higher proportion of Minnesotans have college degrees and higher income levels than people in states like Texas. Maine and Minnesota also have far fewer noncitizens than Texas and Arizona. Only U.S. citizens can vote in presidential elections, which means we should also think of voter turnout as a percentage of a state's **voting-eligible population**—that is, the proportion of citizens who vote who are not disenfranchised by felony convictions. States differ as to the rules they use to define which citizens are eligible to participate in elections, and they use different rules about when (or if) a person must register to vote prior to an election.

Race-Based and Gender-Based Barriers

States set many rules that affect who votes and who does not. Although the 15th Amendment to the U.S. Constitution (1870) says that the right to vote cannot be denied "on account of race or color," the amendment was substantially meaningless for nearly a century. In the later half of the 19th century, many states erected substantial barriers to the voting process in order to prevent African Americans

Figure 3.1

Voter Participation in the 2008 Presidential Election, by State

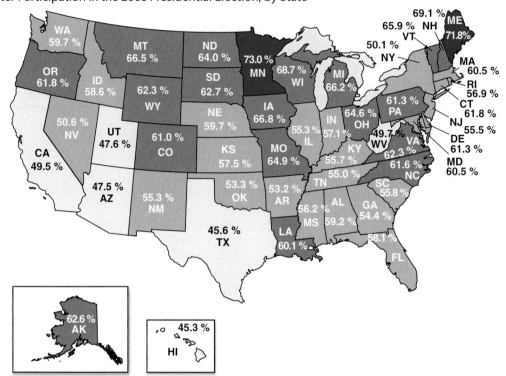

http://elections.gmu.edu/voter_turnout.htm

Percentage of all state residents 18 years of age or over voting in the November 2008 general election.

from voting. Some rules requiring that voters register far in advance of elections were often adopted in response to the perception that corrupt party machines (see Chapter 5) had their supporters "vote early, and vote often." Other barriers were racially motivated, such as racial gerrymandering, closing polling places, not allowing voters to register, implementing **literacy tests** and **poll taxes** (charging a fee to vote), and establishing grandfather clauses that allowed whites to vote regardless of whether they paid a poll tax or passed a literacy test. Such rules were used to reverse the expansion of African American voting rights that occurred after the Civil War.[25]

Prior to 1920, states could also deny women the right to vote, and most did. Utah and Washington allowed women to vote briefly in the 1880s, and the Territory of Wyoming gave women the vote in 1869. Idaho (1896), Washington (1910), and California (1911) were the first states to extend voting rights to women. After the 19th Amendment (1920) was adopted, women won the right to vote in any state, but racially motivated barriers to voting persisted.

Prior to the civil rights movement and Voting Rights Act of 1965, local election officials had the discretion to apply these barriers selectively, in order to disenfranchise blacks but not whites.[26] In some places, blacks who attempted

---

[25] See Alexander Keyssar, *The Right to Vote: The Contested History of Democracy in the United States* (New York: Basic Books, 2000).

[26] U.S. Department of Justice, http://www.usdoj.gov/crt/voting/intro/intro_c.htm.

to register faced economic reprisals, physical violence, and even death. In 1964, for example, only 7 percent of blacks in Mississippi were registered to vote, compared to 70 percent of whites. In Alabama, 19 percent of blacks were registered in 1965, compared to 70 percent of whites.[27] At the time the Voting Rights Act was adopted, several southern states required people to pass subjective literacy tests in order to register, and four southern states required voters to pay a tax to vote in state elections.[28] The Voting Rights Act applied to states, counties, and cities that had low minority voter participation. It gave the federal government the authority to enforce the right to register and vote and allowed federal observers to monitor elections. It gave federal authorities the power to review and "pre-clear" any changes to voter registration and election rules in jurisdictions covered by the act in order to restore voting rights. It also ended literacy tests in six southern states with low registration levels (Alabama, Georgia, Louisiana, Mississippi, Virginia, and much of North Carolina).

As late as 1970, 18 states still had literacy tests that prospective voters were required to pass in order to register (these were finally banned in 1975 due to their history of discriminatory application).[29] In 1972, the U.S. Supreme Court moved to end state laws requiring that a person reside in a jurisdiction at least one year prior to registering to vote. In 1975, the act was amended to apply to states and counties with low registration levels and large non-English-speaking populations (all of Alaska, Arizona, and Texas and many areas in other states). The act was also amended to give plaintiffs greater latitude to challenge election practices—including at-large plans—that can be shown to dilute minority representation.

Despite Civil War–era amendments to the U.S. Constitution extending voting rights regardless of race, it took well over a century for the U.S. Congress and the U.S. Supreme Court to strike down the most overt prohibitions on voting.[30] But the gap between white and black registration levels in southern states covered by the Voting Rights Act was nearly eliminated by 1988 as a result of the Voting Rights Act. This does not mean that all barriers were eliminated by the act. Some state and local governments responded to increased minority participation by changing how they conducted their elections in order to dilute the influence of minority voters. The act is still used to guard against such practices. In 2006, Congress voted to reauthorize the act for another 25 years. Whether racially motivated or not, state policies that made it difficult to register and vote are still more likely to be present in states with greater racial diversity.[31] Mississippi and South Carolina—which have some of the highest proportions of black residents in the United States—had the longest requirements for pre-registration before elections (30 days in 2010). Polls were open for 14 or 15 hours in Connecticut, Rhode Island, Maine, and parts of New Hampshire on Election Day 2008 but for just 12 hours in racially diverse Florida, Georgia, Mississippi, South Carolina, and Texas.

Registration Barriers

Although many of the most egregious barriers to voting are now gone, there are still important differences in registration laws across the

---

[27] Bernard Grofman, Lisa Handley, and Richard G. Niemi, *Minority Representation and the Quest for Voting Equality* (New York: Cambridge Press, 1992).

[28] Chandler Davidson, "The Evolution of Voting Rights Law," in Grofman, Handley, and Niemi, *Minority Representation*.

[29] In *Oregon v. Mitchell* (1970), the U.S. Supreme Court upheld a temporary five-year federal ban on the tests. The ban was made permanent in 1975.

[30] Chandler Davidson and Bernard Grofman, eds., *Quiet Revolution in the South: The Impact of Voting Rights Act 1965–1990* (Princeton, NJ: Princeton University Press, 1994).

[31] Kim Q. Hill and Jan Leighley, "Racial Diversity, Voter Turnout, and Mobilizing Institutions in the United States," *American Politics Quarterly* 27(3)(1999):275–95; and Shaun Bowler and Todd Donovan, "State-Level Barriers to Participation" (paper presented at the American Political Science Association meeting, September 2005).

INSTITUTIONS MATTER

DIFFERENT WAYS TO DRAW DISTRICTS

The practice of drawing electoral boundaries for a jurisdiction is known as districting, or redistricting. Because so many voters support whatever candidate their party nominates for an office, the location of boundaries for a district can have huge implications for which party wins the district. A district where 60 percent of the voters are Democrats will almost certainly elect a Democrat. Likewise, a district that is 60 percent Republican will almost certainly elect a Republican. People drawing boundaries for districts have knowledge of where each party's voters live.

This raises the question, then, about who should draw district boundaries. Although the process varies considerably from state to state, in most states, the legislature has the final say over what the boundaries for state legislative and congressional districts will look like. This means that a party having a majority in the legislature, with a sympathetic governor, can largely draw maps as it sees fit: It can maximize the number of districts that the majority party is likely to win or it can create "safe" seats for incumbents (or both). The majority party may also try to spread the opposition party's supporters thinly across as many districts as possible to dilute their power. If control of government is divided between both major parties, incumbents of both parties might see fit to agree that most districts should be safe for one or the other party.[1] These "bipartisan" plans may protect incumbents from having a serious threat in any reelection campaign. Some suggest that drawing too many districts that are "safe" will produce polarization in representation if Democratic districts only elect strong liberals, and Republican districts only elect strong conservatives.[2] Competitive districts, in contrast, may elect moderates.[3]

Several states place control of drawing district maps in the hands of an appointed commission or with the courts. Commissions and courts may have partisan interests but not as strong as the partisan interests affecting legislators. One study of state districting plans found that elections were more competitive when districting plans were produced by courts and commissions than when produced by incumbent politicians.[4]

Notes
1. Bruce Cain, "Assessing the Partisan Effects of Redistricting," *American Political Science Review* (1985):320–33.
2. Sean Theriault, *Party Polarization in Congress* (New York: Cambridge University Press) (2008).
3. There is not conclusive evidence of this. See Nolan McCarty, Keith Poole, and Howard Rosenthal, "Does Gerrymandering Cause Polarization?" *American Journal of Political Science* (2009).
4. Jamie Carson and Michael Crespin, "The Effect of State Redistricting Methods on Electoral Competition in United States House Races," *State Politics and Policy Quarterly* (2004).

states. In 1995, the National Voter Registration Act (also called the "Motor Voter" Act) went into effect, requiring that states accept mail-in registrations for federal elections if postmarked 30 days prior to an election and requiring that public agencies provide voter registration forms. States continue to have discretion to allow voter registration on the same day of the election or to have waiting periods of up to 30 days. States also have the discretion to adopt laws that make it easier (or harder) to vote by mail. States with higher proportions of African American residents continue to have more barriers to registration and easy voting.[32]

Having registration offices open for shorter hours, and having closing dates for registration further from the election, can depress turnout.[33]

[32] Bowler and Donovan, "State-Level Barriers to Participation."
[33] Leighley and Nagler (1992); Jan Leighley and Jonathan Nagler, "Individual and Systemic Influences on Turnout: Who Votes?" *Journal of Politics* 54(1992):718–41; Rosenstone and Wolfinger, "The Effect of Registration Laws on Voter Turnout," *American Political Science Review* 72(1978):22–45.

Conversely, states that allow registration on the day of the election rank highest in voter participation. As of 2010, there were 10 states where unregistered voters could nonetheless vote on election day (Idaho, Iowa, Maine, Minnesota, Montana, New Hampshire, North Carolina, Wisconsin, and Wyoming). North Dakota does not require voter registration, and Connecticut allows election day registration for presidential elections. One study estimated that turnout in the 2008 election was 7 percent higher in states with election day registration, but these states already had higher turnout so the effect of election day registration was probably lower.[34] In most states it is the citizen's responsibility to remember to register ahead of time and to seek out a public agency in order to do this. In many other nations with higher voter turnout, the government assumes the responsibility for finding citizens and making sure they are properly registered to vote (just as the U.S. Census Bureau attempts to find everyone once a decade).

Districting Barriers

A larger institutional barrier to voting may be found in the nature of American elections themselves. Elections for nearly every seat in the U.S. House of Representatives, most state legislatures, and many city and county councils are conducted in single-member districts under **winner-take-all election** rules. This means that the single candidate winning the most votes represents a specific geographical area. Winner-take-all election rules tend to produce two-party systems. That is, because there is nothing to be won for candidates from parties that always place third or fourth, people fear wasting their vote on such parties, and only the largest parties survive.[35] Winner-take-all

elections are the main reason why the U.S. Congress, every state legislature, and nearly every local partisan council are dominated by representatives of just one or two political parties.

District boundaries used to elect representatives must be redrawn on occasion, or redistricted, to account for shifts in population. Critics of the redistricting process note that incumbents can have too much influence over how their district lines are drawn, such that elected officials are picking their voters rather than voters picking the officials. Democrat incumbents have incentives to make sure that their districts' boundaries include as many loyal Democratic voters as possible, whereas Republican incumbents have incentives to pack their districts with as many Republican voters as possible.[36] In many states, partisan elected officials have near total control over how these districts are drawn. In other states, legislators pick "bipartisan" commissions to make district maps or have the courts settle the issues. Parties keep detailed records of block-by-block voting trends and use sophisticated computer mapping programs to design their preferred districts.

When elections are one sided, there is less campaign activity. When elections are contested by just one major party, there may be no campaign. Without campaigns, voters are probably less likely to notice that an election is being held. Turnout decline in American congressional elections since 1960 corresponds with a decline in competitive elections, as more districts are drawn to be safe for just one party or the other. Congressional and state legislative races are often uncontested by one of the major parties because they have no chance to win. In recent years, nearly one-third of all state legislative races have not been contested by one of the major parties.[37] When fewer races are contested, fewer candidates campaign, and

---

[34] Stuart Comstock-Gay, Steven Carbo, and Regina Eaton, "Voters with Election Day Registration." Available: demos. org. Michael Hanmer, Discount Voting: Voter Registration Reforms and their Effects (Cambridge, MA Cambridge University Press, 2009)

[35] William Riker, "The Two-Party System and Duverger's Law: An Essay on the History of Political Science," *American Political Science Review* 76(4)(1982):753–66.

[36] Rob Ritchie, *Monopoly Politics*; and Center for Voting and Democracy.

[37] NCSL report.

COMPARISONS HELP US UNDERSTAND

TAXATION WITHOUT REPRESENTATION: SHOULD NONCITIZENS VOTE?

Although the U.S. Constitution stipulates that the right to vote in federal elections extends to citizens, this clause does not apply to state and local elections. States can determine if legal immigrant noncitizens are eligible to vote. Noncitizens could previously vote in many states, but voting rights were eliminated by the 1920s when America closed its doors to immigration for several decades. Immigration was later reestablished, without state and local voting rights. An estimated 20 million legal immigrants now work in the United States and pay taxes. They may also serve in the military, but they cannot vote. Historically, granting the right to vote to immigrants was seen as a method to get people engaged with politics. Advocates of voting rights for noncitizens note that America's noncitizens could vote in colonial times and in many U.S. states until an anti-immigrant backlash in the 1920s. Until 1926, 22 states and territories allowed immigrants to vote in local elections.[1]

Many nations, including Chile, Ireland, and New Zealand, allow noncitizens to vote in local elections.[2] A few places, such as Takoma Park, Maryland, allow legal immigrants to vote in local elections. New York City and Chicago have recently allowed legal immigrants to vote in school board elections. In 2004, San Francisco voters rejected a proposal to allow noncitizens to vote in local elections, whereas voters in the Massachusetts cities of Amherst and Cambridge passed similar initiatives. Opponents, such as the New York City mayor, Michael Bloomberg, argue that if immigrants want the full rights of citizens, including voting rights, they should become citizens.

Notes
1. Alexandra Marks, "Should Noncitizens Vote?" *Christian Science Monitor,* 27 April 2004.
2. Ronald Hayduk, "Immigrant Voting Rights Receive More Attention," 2004, http://www.migrationinformation.org.

fewer citizens are likely to be engaged by the election.[38]

Who Is Ineligible?

State governments set rules about who is eligible to vote in their state and local elections. They have the power to decide if certain groups of people may or may not vote in state and local elections (federal law regulates who may vote in federal contests). Depending on the state, people found to be "mentally incompetent," convicted felons who served their time, people in prison, people on parole, and legal immigrant noncitizens may be banned from voting. Or depending on the state's laws, they may be permitted to vote.

California, New Jersey, Arizona, Texas, and Florida had more noncitizens per capita in 2008 than any other state. Noncitizens typically cannot vote. Florida, Texas, and Mississippi also have far more inmates, parolees, felons, and ex-felons than the average state and do not allow many of them to vote.[39] Felon voting bans were adopted by states in the late 1860s and 1870s as the 15th Amendment was extending voting rights to African Americans.[40] States with larger nonwhite prison populations

---

[38] Todd Donovan and Shaun Bowler, *Reforming the Republic: Democratic Institutions for the New America* (Upper Saddle River, NJ: Prentice Hall, 2004).

[39] Over 1 percent of the Texas adult population are felons or ex-felons. The U.S. average is 0.67 percent. See Michael McDonald, Voter Turnout Project, George Mason University. Ex-felons may vote in Texas but parolees, inmates, and probationers may not. Mississippi and Florida also prevent ex-felons from voting.

[40] See Jeff Manza and Christopher Uggen, *Locked Out: Felon Disenfranchisement and American Democracy* (New York: Oxford University Press, 2005).

Figure 3.2

Barriers to Voting in the U.S. States, by State

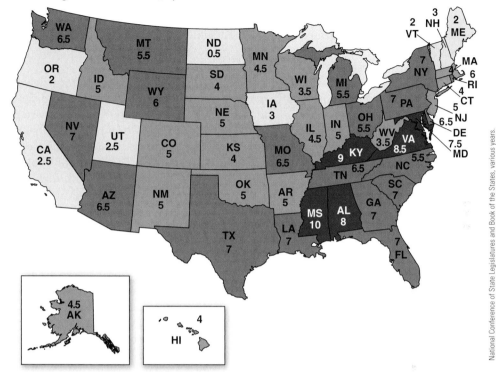

National Conference of State Legislatures and Book of the States, various years.

States are ranked on a scale of 0 to 10, with low scores representing few barriers to registration and voting and high scores representing more barriers. The index represents barriers such as long advance dates for registration, a prohibition on absentee voting, a prohibition on early voting, a restriction on parolees and felons voting, and shorter-than-average polling place hours.

were more likely to ban convicted felons from voting than states where more whites were in the prison population. States with more white prisoners in the 20th century were subsequently more likely to soften or repeal these laws than states with higher African American prison populations.[41] Southern states have been significantly less likely to repeal laws that prevent ex-felons from ever voting again. One of the largest sources in the decline in voter turnout in recent years is the steep increase in the proportion of citizens who are losing their voting rights due to felony convictions, often for drug possession.[42]

Where Are the Greatest Barriers?

Figure 3.2 illustrates which states had the most barriers to voting and registration as of 2005. We identified 10 restrictions that states may place on voting and registration and then assigned a state one point for each restriction the state maintains. Restrictions include requiring that voters register at least

[41] Angela Behrens, Christopher Uggen, and Jeff Manza, "Ballot Manipulation and the 'Menace of Negro Domination': Racial Threat and Felon Disenfranchisement in the United States, 1850–2002," *American Journal of Sociology* 109(2003):559–605.

[42] Michael P. McDonald and Sam Popkin, "The Myth of the Vanishing Voter," *American Political Science Review* 95(2000):963–74.

20 days in advance, not allowing polling place registration, not allowing parolees or felons to vote, having shorter than average polling place hours, allowing no early voting, placing restrictions on "no excuse" absentee voting, and other similar rules.

The state with the most of these restrictions on voting is Mississippi (scoring a perfect 10), followed by several other southern states, including Kentucky (9), Virginia and Alabama (8), and Maryland, Florida, Georgia, and Texas (7). Nevada, New York, and Pennsylvania also score high (7). North Dakota places the least restrictions on voting (1), followed by Vermont, Oregon, and Maine (2) as well as Utah (2.5), California (2.5), and New Hampshire (3). Other things being equal, states with more of these barriers had lower participation in the 2004 presidential election. On average, every three restrictions that a state maintains were associated with 2.4 percent less voter turnout. Rules requiring advance registration have particularly noticeable effects. Every 10 additional days that a state required for advance registration were associated with 2.5 percent less turnout in 2004.[43]

Party System Barriers

Local political party organizations traditionally played a large role in mobilizing voters and getting them to participate in politics. Local party "machines" once relied heavily on large numbers of loyal workers to get their supporters to the polls. Some party workers could be rewarded with municipal jobs in exchange for their work on behalf of the party's electoral efforts. Party workers checked the sign-in sheets at polling places to track who had not yet voted, tracked down those who had not yet voted, gave people rides to polling places, and called on neighbors to remind them to vote. It helped if local elections were contested under party labels and

held in synch with high-profile national races. Party labels and local party organizations lowered the "cost" that voters faced when voting. Party labels—usually Democrat or Republican—told voters a lot about relatively unknown candidates seeking state and local offices.

Decades of antiparty reform laws passed by state legislatures have changed the role of parties in many states.[44] Civil service reforms make it difficult—if not illegal—for parties to reward their supporters with public sector jobs. Nowadays, nearly 75 percent of local elections are nonpartisan. Nearly all local elections (95 percent) in western states are nonpartisan, whereas most local contests in the northeastern states remain partisan.[45] Turnout remains higher today in local partisan elections. Many places also have their nonpartisan local elections in "off years," out of synch with higher profile contests—further depressing turnout.

Historians demonstrate that many of these antiparty reforms were adopted at the start of the 20th century to "depoliticize" local politics and ensure that the influence of working-class people and racial and ethnic minorities would be diluted in favor of people who wanted to improve the business climate in their cities.[46] The drop in party mobilization of voters has been found to be one of the largest factors behind low turnout in the United States.[47] With the decline of parties, Americans may now be less likely to have someone knock on their door to encourage them to vote. However, experiments

---

[43] Analysis from Bowler and Donovan, "State-Level Barriers to Participation."

[44] Walter Dean Burnham, *Critical Elections and the Mainsprings of American Politics* (New York: Norton, 1970), chs. 4–5.

[45] Tari Renner, ed., "The Municipal Election Process: The Impact on Minority Representation," in *The Municipal Yearbook* (Washington, DC: International City Managers Association, 2005).

[46] Amy Bridges, *Morning Glories* (Princeton, NJ: Princeton University Press, 1999); and Burnham, *Critical Elections.*

[47] Steven Rosenstone and John Mark Hansen, *Mobilization, Participation and Democracy in America* (New York: Longman, 2003).

in cities like Columbus, Ohio, and Raleigh, North Carolina, demonstrate that face-to-face visits with voters before a local election can increase participation by about 10 percent.[48] However, few organizations have the resources to mount large-scale, door-to-door canvassing drives.

Noncompetitive Elections

Local elections may be less competitive than in previous decades. This means elections have less ability to get people's attention or provide them with information about local affairs. One study estimated that the number of candidates seeking local office dropped by 15 percent from 1974 to 1994.[49] Another study found that 17 percent of mayoral candidates ran unopposed in California in 2003 and found that seven California cities cancelled their elections that year due to lack of competition.[50]

State laws determine how local elections will be conducted. In many local elections, candidates run at large (that is, citywide). These **at-large elections** were another antiparty, Progressive era reform designed to weaken the influence of political parties and the lower-status voters, often recent immigrants, whom they relied upon for support. At-large elections were sold as a "good government" reform, in part, for their ability to get working-class ethnics, blacks, and Socialists off of city councils.[51] Because minorities and the poor are often concentrated in specific neighborhoods, and because most white voters usually vote for white

President Lyndon Johnson giving Dr. Martin Luther King, Jr., a pen used to sign the Voting Rights Act of 1965.

Hulton Archive/Getty Images

candidates,[52] racial and ethnic minority candidates often have a better chance of being elected from small districts than at large when they run for a citywide office.[53] Districted contests facilitate the election of minority candidates, but if districts are drawn to be heavily homogeneous (that is, safe for a minority group), districted elections may also limit competition.

The Effect of Place

People who live in smaller communities tend to participate more. Across a wide range of American towns and cities, people are more likely to contact public officials and attend board meetings, for example, if they live in a place with a smaller population.[54] Voter

[48] Alan S. Gerber and Donald P. Green, "The Effects of Personal Canvassing, Telephone Calls and Direct Mail on Voter Turnout: A Field Experiment," *American Political Science Review* 94(3)(1993):658.

[49] Robert Putnam, *Bowling Alone* (New York: Simon and Schuster, 2000).

[50] *The New York Times*, 21 September 2003, p. 30.

[51] Amy Bridges, *Morning Glories*; Samuel P. Hays, "The Politics of Municipal Reform in the Progressive Era," *Pacific Northwest Quarterly* (1961); and Chandler Davidson and George Korbel, "At-Large Elections and Minority Group Representation," *Journal of Politics* 43(1981): 982–1005.

[52] Paul Kleppner, *Chicago Divided: The Making of a Black Mayor* (DeKalb, IL: Northern Illinois Press, 1985). For a thorough review of the literature and critical analysis of this proposition, see Keith Reeves, *Voting Hopes or Fears: White Voters, Black Candidates and Racial Politics in America* (New York: Oxford University Press, 1997).

[53] Davidson and Grofman, *Quiet Revolution in the South* (1992); and Richard Engstrom and Michael D. McDonald, "The Election of Blacks to City Councils," *American Political Science Review* 75(1981):344–54.

[54] Eric Oliver, "City Size and Civic Involvement in Metropolitan America," *American Political Science Review* 94(2) (2000):362–63; also see Robert Dahl and Edward Tufte, *Size and Democracy* (1973).

turnout in local elections is also higher in places with a lower population, even after accounting for things such as levels of income and the racial-ethnic composition of the cities.[55] People in Vermont are more likely to attend town meetings if they live in less populous communities.[56]

A sense of place, or a sense of community, seems to increase political participation. Many people develop the social skills and networks— the **social capital**—they use in political activity by volunteering with local service clubs and social, fraternal, and religious groups.[57] For example, by organizing a bake sale for a church or an auction to raise money for a soccer team, one might build social networks and learn fundraising skills that carry over to political activity. Where there is more social capital, then there is likely to be more political participation. Social capital seems to coexist with trusting other people, and residents of smaller places tend to trust other people more than residents of larger places do.[58] A prominent investigation of social capital found that people in smaller places were much more likely to volunteer in their communities, to work on community projects, and to give to charity.[59]

Personal Barriers

When Americans are asked about the barriers to local participation, lack of information is the barrier most frequently cited as

Table 3.5	

Public Attitudes as Barriers to Participation in Local Politics

Public Attitudes	%
Lack of information or don't know how to begin	35
Feel can't make a difference	26
Work schedule (too busy)	25
Poor transportation	20
Feel unwelcome	22
Safety concerns	28

Source: Social Capital Benchmark Survey, 2000.

being a serious impediment. As Table 3.5 illustrates, over one-third of Americans agree that not knowing where to begin, or not having enough information, is a serious barrier to becoming involved in local politics. People with no education beyond high school, African Americans, and Hispanics were significantly more likely to share these sentiments.[60] People who work in congested urban areas a few miles from their neighborhood polling places may also be less likely to vote.[61]

Breaking Down Barriers to Voter Participation

One of the ironies about low rates of political participation in the United States is that for the last several decades, serious efforts have been made to remove barriers to voting and political participation—but participation remains low. Congress passed the Voting Rights Act in 1965, empowering the federal government to take control of local voter registration agencies away from racist state and local governments.

---

[55] Hanjal and Lewis, "Municipal Institutions and Voter Turnout." Also see Stephen Hansen, Thomas Palfrey, and Howard Rosenthal, "The Downsian Model of Electoral Participation: Formal Theory and Empirical Analysis of the Constituency Size Effect," *Public Choice* 52(1987):15–33.

[56] Frank Bryan, *Real Democracy: The New England Town Meeting and How It Works* (Chicago: University of Chicago Press, 2003).

[57] James Coleman, *Foundations of Social Theory* (Cambridge, MA: Belknap, 1990); and Putnam, *Bowling Alone.*

[58] Wendy Rahn and Thomas Rudolph, "A Tale of Political Trust in American Cities," *Public Opinion Quarterly* 69(2005):530–60.

[59] Putman, *Bowling Alone.*

[60] Social Capital Benchmark Survey; and author's calculations.

[61] James Gimpel and J. E. Schuknecht, "Political Participation and the Accessibility of the Ballot Box," *Political Geography* 22(2003):471–88.

Federal antipoverty "community action" programs of the 1960s also included requirements for the "maximum feasible participation" of community residents in implementing the programs.[62] The participatory elements of community action programs were soon abandoned as being ineffective, but the Voting Rights Act had the dramatic effect of bringing voter participation rates among African Americans to levels equal with those of whites.[63]

Subsequent efforts to boost participation have been less effective. In the 1980s, political parties spent millions on Get Out the Vote (GOTV) drives. In the 1990s, Congress also passed the Motor Voter Act to make registration easier. MTV's Rock the Vote encouraged young people to register and vote. These efforts may have increased registrations, but they seem to have had little effect on getting newly registered voters to actually vote. The hotly contested Bush versus Kerry 2004 presidential race, in contrast, was associated with an increase in voting.

State-Level Reform Efforts

In the past decade, several states have also attempted to make it easier for people to vote. On the West Coast and in a few states in other areas, for example, many people now take advantage of less restrictive rules about absentee voting. These rules allow them to vote permanently by mail without having to provide any reason. Oregon adopted all-mail elections in 1998, and 37 of 39 counties in Washington held all elections by mail as of 2009. Texas, Iowa, and other states implemented "early voting" and set up polling places days before elections in 2008 to make voting easier. Some states have experimented with internet voting, particularly for overseas military personnel.

Effect of Reforms on Voter Participation

Despite these efforts, participation in American elections remains low compared to most other established democracies. There is some evidence that reforms such as voting by mail might slightly increase turnout, and liberal absentee laws were found to increase turnout among students.[64] Studies suggest that the increased turnout associated with making voting more convenient might exacerbate social bias in the electorate by increasing turnout among white, wealthy, and better-educated voters at a greater rate than turnout among minorities and the less affluent.[65]

Interest Matters

It probably comes as little surprise that participation in state and local politics is largely the domain of those who are most interested in politics. It may be less obvious that having an interest in politics often has a distinct class bias and that some reforms designed to increase turnout might, ironically, magnify this bias. Efforts to increase participation by making it easier to vote can increase turnout do not make elections any more interesting. As noted above, lack of information is the primary reason that people mention when citing barriers to participation—particularly the less affluent, the less educated, and racial and ethnic minorities. Competitive elections, increased campaign activity, and active political parties may increase interest and information about

---

[62] Daniel Patrick Moynihan, *Maximum Feasible Misunderstanding: Community Action in the War on Poverty* (New York: Basic Books, 1969).

[63] When the effects of income and education on participation are accounted for, African Americans vote at higher rates than whites. Leighley and Nagler, "Individual and Systemic Influences."

[64] Jeffrey Karp and Susan Banducci, "Absentee Voting, Participation, and Mobilization," *American Politics Research* 29(2001):183–95.

[65] J. Eric Oliver, "The Effects of Eligibility Restrictions and Party Activity on Absentee Voting and Overall Turnout," *American Journal of Political Science* 40(1996):498–513; and Jeff Karp and Susan Banducci, "Going Postal: How All Mail Elections Influence Turnout," *Political Behavior* 22(2000):223–39. On internet voting, see R. Michael Alvarez and Jonathan Nagler, "The Likely Consequences of Internet Voting for Political Representation," *Loyola of Los Angeles Law Review* 34(2001):1115–52.

elections. Most current reform efforts focus on making it more convenient for people to vote. The people who take advantage of increased convenience tend to be people who already have some engagement with politics—those with education and higher incomes.[66]

Increasing Citizen Engagement with Competitive Elections

This is not to say that reforms cannot increase participation across the board. Increased electoral competition, and more information about candidates and issues, may significantly increase participation in state and local politics. Partisan local elections, multiparty politics, and even "semiproportional" nonpartisan elections have each been shown to be associated with higher levels of participation.[67]

Some observers suggest that eliminating partisan gerrymandering of electoral districts might also help boost interest in state politics by making more state legislative contests competitive.[68] In presidential, gubernatorial, congressional, and state legislative races, voter participation is greater in places where the vote gap between the winning and losing candidates narrows. People tend to participate more when elections are close than when they are uncompetitive. Some suggest that voters are more likely to calculate that their participation will be decisive in close races—causing turnout to increase.[69] We suggest

that close, competitive elections increase participation, as these races generate more campaign activity and information. Others contend that close elections force party leaders and political groups to mobilize more voters.[70] However, if every district was drawn so that either party had a chance to win, a relatively small shift in votes in each district from one party to another could result in dramatic changes in how many seats a party holds in the legislature.

Experiments with Alternative Local Election Systems

Different types of local election systems can also encourage more candidates to run, which increases campaign activity and, as a result, increases participation. Unique experiments with "semiproportional" local election systems in Texas, Alabama, and a few other states demonstrated that **cumulative voting systems** offer minority candidates more opportunities to win than standard at-large elections. There are different forms of at-large elections. Under standard at-large elections, if there are five city council seats, each seat is elected separately by all voters in the city. Cities using standard at-large elections often narrow the field of candidates with a primary contest that determines the two candidates who will contest each position in the general election. The candidate with a majority wins, and if there is a cohesive city-wide majority, it sweeps every seat. This means minority-supported candidates have little chance to win. Cumulative voting modifies the at-large system by allowing voters to cast multiple votes for one or more candidates running citywide. This allows some candidates with less than a majority to win and causes minority candidates to run active campaigns. Cumulative voting has been found to increase campaign activity by local groups and increase turnout in local elections by about 5 percent.[71]

[66] A full extension of this argument can be found in Adam Berinsky, "The Perverse Consequences of Electoral Reform in the United States," *American Politics Research* 33(4) (2005):471–91.

[67] Andre Blais and Ken Carty, "Does Proportional Representation Foster Voter Turnout?" *European Journal of Political Research* 18(1990):167–81; and Shaun Bowler, Todd Donovan, and David Brockington, *Election Reform and Minority Representation* (2003).

[68] Morris Fiorrina, S. Adams, and J. Pope, *Culture War? Myth of a Polarized America* (New York: Longman, 2006); conversely, see Nolan McCarty, Keith Pool, and Howard Rosenthal, "Does Gerrymandering Cause Polarization?" *American Journal of Political Science* 53(3)(2009):666–80.

[69] For a discussion, see Gary Cox and Michael Munger, "Closeness, Expenditures and Turnout in the 1982 US House Election," *American Political Science Review* 83(1989):217–31.

[70] V. O. Key Jr., *Southern Politics: In the State and Nation* (New York: Knopf, 1949).

[71] Bowler et al., *Election Reform*.

E-Government

City and state governments have also tried to stimulate citizen interest and participation by making it easier for people to follow government through electronic media from the convenience of their own homes. Many states and cities maintain public access cable TV stations to broadcast hearings and meetings and maintain ever-improving websites designed to make it easier to contact public officials.

Voter Choice in State and Local Elections

When people vote in partisan state and local elections, their decision-making process is somewhat similar to the process they use when voting in national elections. Voters who identify with a political party have a strong inclination to pick candidates from their party. Party labels—Democrat, Republican, Libertarian, and so on—act as a cue as to the policies the candidate might pursue. If people know nothing about a candidate except the candidate's party label—as is often the case—the inclination to vote based on party labels may even be stronger because voters have little more to guide their choices. Voters also tend to give incumbents the benefit of the doubt and may also reward or punish candidates for state offices based on the health of the economy.[72] They may also be more likely to punish a governor for the health of the state economy than the national economy.[73] Despite these factors, a voter's party affiliation is the main thing driving voter choice in partisan contests.

If candidates must run for office without party labels on the ballot, however, the voter's decision-making process is different. In nonpartisan elections, which are quite common at the local level, voters may be more likely to rely on endorsements of slating groups. These groups mimic the role of parties by recruiting and publicizing candidates sympathetic to the goals of the group. Pro-business slating groups have been found to have important influence in low-turnout local elections.[74] In smaller communities, the absence of parties and slating groups may cause voters to look for familiar-sounding names (incumbents) or look for friends and neighbors who might be running.[75] Even in **primary election** contests in California (where all candidates are from the same party), candidates for less visible "down-ballot" offices collect more votes near their hometowns, where they are better known.[76]

Effects of Voter Participation on Public Policy

Levels of participation in state and local politics are affected by state laws that regulate voter registration, polling place hours, absentee voting rules, representation, and many other factors. As we have shown above, these rules can make it easier or harder to vote and can make elections more or less interesting by limiting or increasing electoral competition, information, and representation. It is important to stress that the effects of these rules are not neutral; many of them filter out minorities and the less affluent or increase participation by the wealthy. In this section, we consider how rules might affect who participates and how this affects who gets represented and who gets what from government.

First, one must consider how different the participating electorate could be under different

---

[72] Lonna Atkeson and Randal Partin, "Economic and Referendum Voting," *American Political Science Review* 89(1995):99–107.

[73] Robert Stein, "Economic Voting for Governor and US Senator," *Journal of Politics* 52(1990):29–53.

[74] Chandler Davidson and Luis Fraga, "Slating Groups as Parties in a 'Nonpartisan' Setting," *Western Political Quarterly* 41(1988):373–90.

[75] Key, *Southern Politics*.

[76] Shaun Bowler, Todd Donovan, and Joseph Snipp, "Local Sources of Information and Voter Choice in State Elections: Micro-Level Foundations of the Friends and Neighbors Effect," *American Politics Quarterly* 21(1993):473–89.

institutional conditions, all of which can be changed by altering state laws. The first condition we describe below is a recipe for higher participation, and the second is a recipe for lower participation.

High Voter Participation Election Rules

Under one condition, state law could allow cities to have partisan local elections, with state and local contests held in conjunction with an "even year" general election. By holding state and local contests in synch with presidential contests, more people would probably vote in state and local races. New voters could be allowed to register at the polls and vote on the day of the election. If a state used highly competitive districts to elect its legislature, more candidates would campaign, further increasing interest. Ex-felons and legal immigrant noncitizens could be allowed to vote in state and local races. Some elections could also be awarded by proportional representation, further encouraging different candidates to campaign. It is unlikely these sorts of reforms would be adopted without massive public pressure, as incumbent politicians of both major parties typically resist changing the rules that existed when they were elected.[77]

Low Voter Participation Election Rules

Under a second condition, state law could require local elections to be nonpartisan—a rule that limits the information available to the voters. State and local contests could be allowed only in "odd years" when no important federal contests are on the ballot. Voters would have to register at least 30 days in advance, and only citizens without felony convictions could vote. State legislative districts could be gerrymandered to ensure that parties didn't have to compete against each other in a single district, and local council races could be by single-member districts, leaving many incumbents without opposition.

Our point is not that more voter participation is always better but that participation is, in part, a function of laws that are under state control. State legislatures can make it harder or easier for people to participate, and state laws can make elections more or less competitive. State laws affect not only who can vote but also if the elections will generate interest sufficient to stimulate the participation of a wide range of people. Rules thus shape the composition of the electorate; that is, they determine who ends up making demands on government.

The scope of the differences between participants and nonparticipants is likely to vary across states and is due to state laws as well as the demographic profile of the state's residents. In California, surveys estimate that 70 percent of likely voters in 2006 and 63 percent of likely voters in the 2008 election were white, yet whites were not a majority of the population.[78] Different turnout rates reflect lower participation among young voters and Latinos and the fact that many Latino citizens have not registered to vote. States with larger proportions of recent immigrants have similar gaps between participants and nonparticipants. An estimated 20 million legal, tax-paying immigrant noncitizens—1.3 million in New York City alone—are prohibited from voting in the United States. In a few communities, however, they are allowed to vote in local elections.[79]

Public Policy and Public Opinion

Representation means that elected officials, to some degree, produce laws and policies that their constituents want. Evidence from the 50 states

---

[77] Shaun Bowler, Todd Donovan, and Jeffrey Karp, "Why Politicians Like Electoral Institutions: Self-Interest, Values or Ideology," *Journal of Politics* 68(2)(2006):454.

[78] CNN exit poll results for 2008. See also Mark Baldassare, "California's Exclusive Electorate," Public Policy Institute of California (2006).

[79] Alexandra Marks, "Should Non Citizens Vote?" *Christian Science Monitor,* 27 April 2004.

demonstrates that citizens' preferences for public policy generally correspond with the policies that states adopt. States where more people identified themselves as liberals had more liberal public policies, and states where more people identified themselves as conservatives had more conservative policies.[80] Something must be working to connect public preferences to policy. Elected representatives may reflect the public in response to those citizens who participate in politics, and those who participate may be fairly representative of the public opinion of the state's larger population. That is, representatives may respond to pressure from voters and constituents and do what the voters want. Or politicians may simply anticipate what people want, regardless of whether people participate or not. This distinction presents an important question for democracy: does active political participation make the actions of government better represent what citizens want? Put differently, does more participation—or less social bias in participation—make state and local policy more representative of public opinion? One study of California found voters and nonvoters had substantially different attitudes about what government should do—with nonvoters much more supportive of higher taxes.[81]

Does Participation Make State and Local Policy More Representative?

It is possible for elected officials to be perfectly representative of the public, even if most people didn't participate in politics. This would require that representatives have a keen sense of what everyone wanted and strong incentives to give people what they want. More realistically, representatives may do things that reflect what the general public wants when there is more pressure on them to do so.

As examples, states with just one dominant political party (such as the U.S. South through most of the 20th century) had policies less representative of what the public probably wanted than states where two parties compete for voter support. Competition between parties is expected to force legislators to try to attract support by passing popular policies—including things that are popular with the poor.[82] Primary election systems that allow more people to participate also produce representatives who are more likely to share their constituents' opinions on policy.[83] States with direct democracy (Chapter 4) also adopt some public policies, such as death penalty laws and laws requiring parental notification for abortions, which are closer to the state's public opinion than policies adopted in states that lack the pressure of direct democracy.[84]

Participation Bias

As we illustrated earlier in this chapter, people who participate in politics are different than nonparticipants. But does this mean that nonparticipants want different things from their governments than participants do or that by responding mainly to those who participate, governments are not very representative of the general public? Scholars are divided on this question. A study of a national sample of public opinion in 1972 and another from 1988 found that voters and nonvoters had largely similar

---

[80] Robert Erikson, Gerald Wright, and John P. McIver, *Statehouse Democracy: Public Opinion and Policy in the American States* (New York: Cambridge University Press, 1993).

[81] Baldassare (2006).

[82] Key, *Southern Politics*, ch. 14, p. 307. Evidence from the contemporary era suggests the poor get more when Democrats are in power rather than when their party is losing in close competition against Republicans.

[83] Elisabeth Gerber and Rebecca Morton, "Primary Election Systems and Representation," *Journal of Law, Economics and Organizations* 14(2)(1998):304–24

[84] Elisabeth Gerber, *The Populist Paradox* (Princeton, NJ: Princeton University Press, 1999); also see John Matsusaka, *For the Many or the Few* (Chicago: University of Chicago Press, 2004).

policy preferences.[85] These results have been used to support the idea that American governments are largely representative of all citizens, even those who do not vote. If government responds only (or mostly) to those who vote or contribute, participation bias (the overrepresentation of the wealthy) might mean that state and local policies are not representative of the population. Recent studies of national opinion have found that nonvoters are more liberal on social welfare issues than voters.[86]

Participation is relatively high in national elections, however. Far fewer vote in state and local contests. Given this fact, and given the increased information demands associated with state and local elections, it is possible that there are greater gaps in policy preferences between participants and nonparticipants in local elections than in national contests. If participants are different than nonparticipants, what are the policy consequences of this participation bias?

Effects of Participation Bias

Several scholars provide evidence that the turnout decline in American elections has produced an overrepresentation of upper-middle-class and upper-class people and an underrepresentation of lower- and middle-class citizens.[87] One way to assess if participation bias matters is to look at how differences in state policies across the 50 states correspond with differences in who participates.

Effects on State Policies The magnitude of this "class bias"—the overrepresentation of the wealthy—is larger in some states and smaller in others. A study of the 1980s found the inequality in participation was highest in Kentucky, New Mexico, Texas, Georgia, and Arkansas. These are states with high minority populations—most with legacies of erecting barriers to voter participation (see Figure 3.2). States with the most balanced representation between the rich and poor were New Jersey, Minnesota, Louisiana, Illinois, and Nebraska.[88] The study found that state-level class bias in participation during the 1980s was strongly related to lower state welfare (AFDC) spending. States where the poor were underrepresented among participating voters spent less per person on welfare than states where the poor were better represented. A study of state spending from 1978 to 1990 found similar results, with welfare spending higher where there was higher lower-status-voter turnout.[89]

If bias in participation affects which candidates end up winning elections, then it may also affect what governments do. Despite claims by third-party presidential candidates Ralph Nader (in 2000) and George Wallace (in 1968) that there is no difference between the Democratic and Republican parties, there are clear policy differences at the state level related to which party has more control over the state government. Republican control at the state level means less Medicaid spending; Democrats spend more.[90] Republicans may tax less[91] and use a different mix of taxes and expenditures than Democrats[92] (see Chapter 10).

[85] Raymond Wolfinger and Steven Rosenstone, *Who Votes* (New Haven, CT: Yale University Press, 1980); and Sidney Verba, Kay Schlozman, Henry Brady, and Norman Nie, "Citizen Activity: Who Participates? What Do They Say?" *American Political Science Review* (1993):303–18.

[86] Adam Berinsky, "Silent Voices: Opinion Polls, Social Welfare Policy and Political Equality in America," *American Journal of Political Science* 46(2002):276–87.

[87] Frances Fox Piven and Richard A. Cloward, *Why Americans Don't Vote* (New York: Pantheon, 1989); and Walter Dean Burnham, "The Turnout Problem," in *Elections American Style*, ed. A. James Reichley (1987).

[88] Kim Q. Hill and Jan Leighley, "The Policy Consequences of Class Bias in State Electorates," *American Journal of Political Science* 36(2)(1992):351–65.

[89] Kim Q. Hill, Jan Leighley, and Angela Hinton-Andersson, "Lower-Class Mobilization and Policy Linkages in the U.S. States," *American Journal of Political Science* 39(1) (1998):75–86.

[90] Coleen Grogan, "Political-Economic Factors Influencing State Medicaid Policy," *Political Research Quarterly* 47(3) (1994):589–623.

[91] Brian Knight, "Supermajority Vote Requirements for Tax Increases: Evidence from the States," *Journal of Public Economics* 67(1)(2000):41–67.

[92] Rogers and Rogers (2000); and Timothy Besley and Anne Case, "Political Institutions and Policy Choices: Evidence from the United States," *Journal of Economic Literature* 41(1)(2002):7–73.

Elections and Representation

Elections can be thought of as a tool for translating votes into "seats." When a group or party has seats in a state legislature or on a city or county council, they have a form of representation. Election rules have a great effect on which parties or groups have representation. The rules used to conduct elections, like many things examined in this book, are not always (if ever) neutral. They can affect who wins and who loses, and who gets more seats—in short, who ends up being represented.

Number of Representatives per District

The number of representatives elected inside a district's boundaries can also affect who is represented in a legislature. Most states now elect their state legislators from single-member districts (SMDs)—but it hasn't always been this way. In single-member districts, the winning candidate is typically elected with a majority vote, but if three or more candidates divide up the vote enough, whoever has the most support—a simple plurality—wins. Some states have more than one representative per district (just as each U.S. state has two U.S. senators per statewide district or as Australian states elect six federal senators per statewide district). The number of representatives for a specific geographic area is referred to as **district magnitude**.

In the middle of the 20th century, about half of all American state legislative seats were elected by **multimember districts** (or MMDs), where two or more candidates are elected to represent each district.[93] Many of these older MMDs overrepresented rural areas. A series of U.S. Supreme Court rulings required that states apportion legislative districts equally according to population.[94] Since the 1950s, many states have abandoned their MMD systems, often as part of their plans to equally apportion districts by population. Those that now use MMDs can no longer give extra representation to rural areas.

There are important differences in how states use MMDs to elect their legislatures. In Washington and Idaho, lower house districts elect two representatives, but candidates run for two separate positions. These elections are largely identical to those held in SMDs because voters cannot vote for more than one candidate per position. In Arizona, however, voters cast two votes to select two representatives from a single list of candidates who will represent their district. The top two candidates win. In Vermont, if there are three representatives per district, voters cast three votes across a single list, and the top three win. Illinois used three-member districts with a semiproportional representation system known as cumulative voting for decades, ending the system in 1980. In MMD systems such as those used in Arizona, Vermont, or Illinois (until 1980), candidates can win a seat with less than a majority and even with less than a plurality. The winning candidates are the first-, second-, and third-place finishers—depending on how many seats are elected from the district. New Jersey, North Dakota, and South Dakota also use MMDs to elect their lower house.

Effects of Multimember Districts on Minority Representation MMD elections can produce different patterns of representation than SMD elections. Some suggest that MMDs hurt the chances of minority candi-dates, especially in areas where minority vote strength is geographically concentrated—places where a heavily minority SMD might be drawn.[95] Others note that evidence showing

---

[93] Maurice Klain, "A New Look at the Constituencies: The Need for a Recount and Reappraisal," *American Political Science Review* 49(1955):1105–19.

[94] *Baker v. Carr* (1962); *Reynolds v. Sims* (1964); and *Wesberry v. Sanders* (1964).

[95] Malcolm E. Jewell, *Representation in State Legislatures* (Lexington, KY: University of Kentucky Press, 1982); and Gary Moncrief and Joel Thompson, "Electoral Structure and State Legislative Representation," *Journal of Politics* 54(1992):246–56.

MMDs giving advantages to white candidates is dated. Because MMDs allow candidates to win with a relatively low vote share, MMDs might help minority candidates get elected. Recent studies suggest these systems may have produced more racial and ethnic minority representation in state legislatures from 1980 to 2003 than found under SMDs. African Americans appeared particularly advantaged but Latinos less so.[96]

There is clear evidence that traditional "at-large" MMDs disadvantage minority candidates in local elections.[97] In these systems, candidates file for one position out of several in a district, and only the first-place candidate for each position can win a seat. In *Gingles v. Thornberg* (1986), the U.S. Supreme Court ruled that local MMD at-large elections may be an unconstitutional "dilution" of minority vote influence if the minority group is geographically compact and politically cohesive and there is a history of "bloc voting" by whites that leads to the defeat of minority candidates. If these conditions exist, a judge may order the jurisdiction to switch to SMD elections or some alternative that will allow the minority group to elect a representative of their choice. However, in *Shaw v. Reno* (1993), a 5–4 Court decision also ruled that it would not tolerate district maps that maximize minority representation by drawing majority-minority districts based exclusively on where minority voters live.

District Type and Ideological Polarization

MMDs and SMDs may also create different representation of ideologies in state legislatures. Winner-take-all rules mean that just one candidate is ever elected for any position or just one representative per district (i.e., an SMD). One influential theory predicts that when only one candidate can win and most voters are centrists,

all candidates seeking the office have incentives to take positions near the "center" of the political spectrum.[98] In contrast, when two or more candidates are elected to represent the same district, candidates may have incentives to position themselves closer to one or the other end of the ideological spectrum. If they can get elected with fewer votes by placing second or even third, they don't need to appeal to most voters in order to win. This means that candidates further from the ideological center may have more chances to win under MMD elections. There is evidence of more ideological extremism in the Arizona House, which is elected by MMDs, than in the Arizona Senate, which is elected by SMDs.[99] Another study found the same thing in Illinois when its house was elected by MMDs.[100]

Campaign Spending

Politicians campaign to tell voters about themselves (and their opponents). These campaigns cost money, and politicians spend a significant amount of their time raising campaign funds.[101] Money clearly matters at all levels of American politics: Candidates who spend more in state and local races typically do better in elections than those who spend less.[102] Campaign spending may be particularly important for candidates challenging incumbents. Because

---

[96] Lilliard Richardson and Christopher Cooper, "The Mismeasure of MMD: Reassessing the Impact of Multi-Member Districts on the Representation on Descriptive Representation in the United States" (2003).

[97] Engstrom and McDonald, "The Election of Blacks to City Councils."

[98] Anthony Downs, *An Economic Theory of Democracy* (1957); and Gary Cox, "Centripetal and Centrifugal Incentives in Electoral Systems," *American Journal of Political Science* 34(1990):903–35.

[99] Lilliard Richardson, Brian Russell, and Christopher Cooper, "Legislative Representation in Single Member versus Multi Member District Systems: The Arizona State Legislature," *Political Research Quarterly* 57(2004):337–44.

[100] Greg Adams, "Legislative Effects of Single-Member vs. Multi-Member Districts," *American Journal of Political Science* 40(1996):129–44.

[101] Peter Francia and Paul Herrnson, "Begging for Bucks," *Campaigns and Elections* (April 2001).

[102] Kedron Bardwell, "Campaign Finance Laws and the Competition for Spending in Gubernatorial Elections," *Social Science Quarterly* 84(4)(2003):811–25; and Robert K. Goidel, Donald A. Gross, and Todd G. Shields, *Money Matters: Consequences of Campaign Finance Reform in U.S. House Elections* (Lanham, MD: Rowman & Littlefield, 1999).

challengers are less well known than incumbents, challenger spending may produce more "bang for the buck" than incumbent spending. Challenger spending disseminates information about a lesser-known candidate, so any dollar spent can increase information about the candidate. Incumbents may be so well known prior to an election that their spending may have less effect on their vote share.[103]

Spending on campaigns transmits information to citizens—through television, radio, direct mail, and other modes of advertising. Because the information is meant to cast candidates in a good light (and their opponents in a bad light), the quality of this information may be dubious. A survey of voters in one state found that 81 percent believed campaign advertising was "misleading." A slightly higher proportion of politicians in the state agreed.[104] Nonetheless, voters use the information they get from political ads. People are more likely to be aware of state-level elections as spending increases,[105] and spending may cause skeptical voters to seek out additional information. Spending may also cause increased media coverage. Although turnout in elections is mostly structured by larger socioeconomic and institutional forces already discussed in this chapter, higher levels of spending in state-level races can also increase voter turnout.[106] One study of spending in state legislative races concluded that for every dollar spent per eligible voter, turnout increased by 1.2 percent.[107]

Finance Regulations State laws also determine who can contribute to state and local candidates; how much individuals, groups, or political parties may give; and how contributions must be disclosed to the public. Some states, such as Massachusetts and Oregon, have a broad range of restrictions on contributions. Others, including Idaho, Texas, and Virginia, have minimal regulations.[108] Defenders of these regulations note that they give the public more information about who the candidates might be beholden to and that these rules limit the influence of money in politics. Critics argue that limits on spending might make it harder for lesser-known challengers to unseat incumbents and that spending limits may make elections less competitive. There is some evidence that these rules do reduce spending in state races and that they might also limit electoral competition if limits are set too low.[109]

Clean Money A handful of states and cities provide full or partial public financing for state candidates in exchange for candidates promising to reject all private contributions. Maine and Arizona became the first states to do this in 2000. Vermont, Connecticut, New Mexico, and North Carolina have also adopted **clean money** programs, and other states, such as Minnesota, provide partial public funding of candidate campaigns in exchange for candidates limiting the total amount that they raise from private sources. A proposal to provide public funds for elections of the Secretary of State appeared on the 2010 California ballot.

One major idea behind these clean money laws is to ensure candidates are not beholden to their donors. Advocates of publicly financed campaigns also hope it will broaden the pool of people who seek office and cut down the

---

[103] Gary Jacobson, "The Effects of Campaign Spending in House Elections: New Evidence for Old Arguments," *American Journal of Political Science* 34(1990):334–62; and Donald Philip Green and Jonathan S. Krasno, "Rebuttal to Jacobson's 'New Evidence for Old Arguments,'" *American Journal of Political Science* 34(1990):363–72.

[104] Todd Donovan, Shaun Bowler, and David McCuan, "Political Consultants and the Initiative Industrial Complex," in *Dangerous Democracy?* eds. Sabato, Ernst, and Larson (Lanham, MD: Rowman & Littlefield, 2001), 127.

[105] Shaun Bowler and Todd Donovan, *Demanding Choices* (Ann Arbor, MI: University of Michigan Press, 1998), p. 152.

[106] Robert Hogan, "Campaign and Contextual Influences on Voter Participation in State Legislative Elections," *American Politics Review* 27(4)(1999):403–33.

[107] Francia and Herrnson, "Begging for Bucks."

[108] John Pippen, Shaun Bowler, and Todd Donovan, "Election Reform and Direct Democracy: Campaign Finance Regulation in the American States," *American Politics Quarterly* 30(6)(2002):559–82.

[109] Donald Gross, Robert Goidel, and Todd Shields, "State Campaign Finance Regulations and Electoral Competition," *American Politics Research* 30(2)(2002):143–65.

AP Photo/Reed Saxon

Hundreds of members of the California Nurses Association rally in Sacramento to promote the California Clean Money and Fair Elections Act, which would establish public financing for candidates who reject private contributions.

amount of time politicians spend raising money. Jesse Ventura, a professional wrestler turned city mayor, was elected governor of Minnesota under the Reform Party banner with the help of public campaign funds. One study found that state legislative candidates do spend less time raising money in states with public financing of campaigns.[110]

Representation of Parties

Every American state is now—more or less—a two-party system: 99.9 percent of state legislativeseats are held by Democrats or Republicans. There have been brief periods of multiparty politics in a few states and long periods of one-party rule in many southern states. These are exceptions, however, and not the rule. Nearly every partisan office in the United States is elected on a winner-take-all basis. Second-, third-, and lower-place candidates win nothing. If a party rarely does better than second place in most contests, it will win few offices and

likely disappear. The near total, oligopolistic control that Democrats and Republicans have over elected offices overstates the level of support these parties have among the public.[111] Winner-take-all election rules, combined with the ballot access laws discussed above, essentially predetermine that only two parties will ever be represented.

Despite this, third-party and independent candidates have had more success in state and local elections than in congressional and federal races over the last several decades. Since 1990, a few were elected as governor (Angus King in Maine, Jesse Ventura in Minnesota, and Lowell Weicker in Connecticut).[112] As of 2010, minor parties and independent candidates held just 20 seats in state legislatures (out of 7,333 positions in the 49 states with partisan legislatures).[113] Several of these minor-party and independent candidates served in Vermont (which uses MMD elections and clean money for campaign finance). Minor-party and independent candidates have also won seats in Arizona and Massachusetts under clean money rules. Some of the remaining handful of candidates who are not affiliated with a major party are southern Democrats who defected from their party as their state's population grew more conservative.

Representation of Women

States differ substantially in terms of the number of women who are elected to office. As of 2010, 24.3 percent of state legislators

---

[110] Peter Francia and Paul S. Herrnson, "The Impact of Public Finance Laws on State Legislative Elections," *American Politics Research* 31(5)(2003):520–39.

[111] Depending on the year, about one-third of Americans fail to identify with either major party, and less than 40 percent of Americans support the idea of maintaining the two-party system (NES data, 2000–02).

[112] Howard J. Gold, "Explaining Third-Party Success in Gubernatorial Elections," *Social Science Journal* 42(2005): 523–40.

[113] Data from National Conference of State Legislatures, "2009 Partisan Composition of State Legislatures," http://www.ncsl.org/statevote/partycomptable2007.htm. Nebraska has a nonpartisan legislature.

were women—far more than in the U.S. Congress and double the levels of women in state legislatures back in 1981. Although this is still modest representation given that most of the population is female, the growth of representation of women in the past 30 years has important implications. A growing number of women in state-level posts means that the pool of women with elected experience who seek higher-level positions has grown.

In seven states (Arizona, Colorado, Hawaii, Minnesota, New Hampshire, Vermont, and Washington), one-third of all state legislators were women as of 2010. States with the lowest rates of women representation were South Carolina (10 percent), Oklahoma (11 percent), and Alabama (12 percent). Why do some states have three times more representation of women than others? Some have noted that three of the seven states with the most women in their legislatures (Arizona, Vermont, and Washington) use MMD elections.[114] One problem with this logic, however, is that Washington does not use "pure" MMD elections; candidates actually run for individual positions, where the winner takes all. Other explanations for the differences in levels of women's representation emphasize the role of political parties and regional (or cultural) effects. Some parties have made greater efforts to recruit

candidates to seek office.[115] There are clear regional differences. Women are less represented in the South and more represented in the West and New England.

Representation of Racial and Ethnic Minorities

African Americans, Latinos, Asians, and Native Americans are underrepresented in state legislatures relative to their share of U.S. population, as illustrated in Table 3.6. The pattern for minority representation at the local level is similar. Although 11 percent of all state legislative seats are held by minorities, some groups are better represented than others. Minority populations are not evenly distributed across the nation or within states such as Hawaii, California, and New Mexico, where various minority groups combine to form a majority of the state's population. This means that there are great differences across the United States in minority representation at the state and local levels.

Hawaii (67 percent "minority" legislators), California (27 percent), Texas (25 percent), Mississippi (25 percent), Alabama (25 percent), New Mexico (23 percent), and Louisiana (22 percent) had some of the highest levels of minority representation in their

Table 3.6

Minority Representation in U.S. State Legislatures

	White (%)	African American (%)	Latino (%)	Asian or Pacific Islander (%)	Native American (%)
U.S. population	66	13	15	4	1
All state legislators	86	9	3	1	1

Source: Samantha Sanchez, "Money and Diversity in State Legislatures, 2003" (Institute on Money in State Politics, 2005).

[114] Wilma Rule and Joseph F. Zimmerman, *United States Electoral Systems: Their Impact on Women and Minorities* (Westport, CT: Greenwood Press, 1992).

[115] Miki Caul, "Women's Representation in Parliament: The Role of Political Parties," *Party Politics* 5(1999):79–98.

states' legislatures. States with few minorities, not surprisingly, elect few minorities. The Iowa legislature, for example, had no African American or Latino legislators in 2009. Yet, even relatively high levels of minority representation in such places as California and New Mexico are deceptive. These states, along with Arizona, lead the nation in the gap between the proportion of state residents who are minority and the proportion of their representatives who are. In contrast, minorities in Mississippi and Alabama, although still underrepresented, are much more represented relative to their share of the population than minorities in California, Texas, and Arizona.[116]

Why are large populations of minorities better represented in some places than others? The answers, in part, are race and single-member districting. In state and local elections, African Americans benefit from the use of **majority-minority districts** drawn with boundaries that ensure the district's population is heavily African American. This guarantees that the district will elect an African American, and it has led to near proportional representation of African Americans in many local elections. It also explains relatively high levels of minority representation in Deep South states, where African Americans are the predominant minority group.[117] In western and southwestern states, however, the largest minority group is Latino. Latinos turn out at lower rates than African Americans and are not as segregated as African Americans in the South.[118] Latinos, moreover, are a less ethnically cohesive group than African Americans. All of these factors combine to make it more difficult to design districts at the state or local level that are certain to produce Latino representation.[119] At the local level, Latinos win more seats via SMDs than they do under "at-large" arrangements,[120] but they may not win as many seats as African Americans.

Majority-minority districts present a paradox. They clearly increase the numbers of minorities holding state and local offices, and they offer people **descriptive representation;** that is, the ability to see people like themselves serving as their representative. When minority candidates win seats, moreover, they are able to affect the substance of public policy in ways that benefit their constituents and affect whether minorities are hired to implement policies approved by cities and school boards.[121] Descriptive representation of minorities at the local and congressional level may also increase minority trust and participation and reduce political alienation among minority citizens.[122]

---

[116] Samantha Sanchez, *Money and Diversity in State Legislatures, 2003* (Helena, MT: Institute on Money in State Politics, 2005).

[117] Engstrom and McDonald, "The Election of Blacks to City Councils."

[118] Douglas Massey and Nancy Denton, "Trends in Residential Segregation of Blacks, Hispanics and Asians," *American Sociological Review* 52(1987):802–25.

[119] Jerry Polinard, Robert Wrinkle, and Tomas Longoria, "The Impact of District Elections on the Mexican American Community," *Social Science Quarterly* 17(3) (1991):608–14; Delbert Taebel, "Minority Representation on City Councils: The Impact of Structure on Blacks and Hispanics," *Social Science Quarterly* 59(1978):142–52; A. Velditz and C. Johnson, "Community Segregation, Electoral Structure and Minority Representation," *Social Science Quarterly* 67(1982):729–36.

[120] David Leal, Ken Meier, and Valerie Martinez–Ebers, "The Politics of Latino Education: The Biases of At-Large Elections," *Journal of Politics* 66(4)(2004):1224.

[121] J. L. Polinard, Robert Wrinkle, Tomas Longoria, and Norman Binder, *Electoral Structure and Urban Policy: The Impact of Mexican American Communities* (New York: M. E. Sharpe, 1994); and Kenneth J. Meier, Eric Gonzalez Juenke, Robert Wrinkle, and J. L. Polinard, "Structural Choices and Representation Biases: The Post-Election Color of Representation," *American Journal of Political Science* 49(4)(2005):748–49.

[122] Lawrence Bobo and Frank Gilliam Jr., "Race, Sociopolitical Participation and Black Empowerment," *American Political Science Review* (1990):377–93; Adrian Pantoja and Gary Segura, "Does Ethnicity Matter? Descriptive Representation in Legislatures," *Social Science Quarterly* 84(2003):441–60; and Susan Banducci, Todd Donovan, and Jeffrey Karp, "Minority Representation, Empowerment and Participation," *Journal of Politics* 66(2004):534.

Some suggest that there may be a trade-off between descriptive representation and the substantive representation of minority interests. By packing large proportions of a minority group into one safe district, the group may have less overall influence in a legislature than they may have had if they were a swing group electing representatives across a larger number of districts.[123] Almost 95 percent of minority state legislators were Democrats in 2005, so we might assume that people in these districts find their substantive policy interests advanced by Democrats more than Republicans. A majority-minority district can help elect a minority Democrat representative, but this may also weaken other Democrats' chances of winning in surrounding districts. The minority district gains descriptive Democratic representation locally, but Democrats may elect fewer seats statewide, making it more difficult to advance the substantive policy goals of minority voters in the majority-minority district. Another potential consequence of majority-minority districts is a loss of electoral competitiveness. Minority legislators are much more likely to run unopposed than white legislators.[124]

YOU DECIDE

SHOULD FELONS HAVE THE RIGHT TO VOTE?

State laws determine whether or not people convicted of felony crimes may vote. Five million Americans can not vote because they live in states with rules that ban felons from voting – even people who have served their time. Is this a good policy? Advocates of felon disenfranchisement argue that "a person who breaks the law should not make the law,"[1] and that people who have committed serious crimes can't be trusted with the right to vote. In Florida, nearly one million ex-felons have lost the right to vote – a right that can only be restored if the Governor grants a personal request for clemency.

Others suggest that ex-offenders' voting rights are denied arbitrarily, without much regard for the severity of a crime. Twenty-five years ago, less than 10% of prisoners were convicted of drug crimes. Since then, violent crime rates in America have dropped sharply, but felony incarcerations have increased as a result of tougher penalties, particularly for possession and sale of illegal drugs. Today, almost 40% of people in prison committed non-violent drug or property crimes.[2] Harsh drug laws, in effect, are being perpetuated by elected officials who cannot be held accountable by many of the people most adversely affected by the laws. Some judges, including Supreme Court Justice Sonia Sotomayor, argue that state felon disenfranchisement laws violate Section 2 of the federal Voting Rights Act (VRA),[3] because African Americans and Latinos are more likely to be convicted of drug crimes. The VRA prohibits voting rules that discriminate on the basis of race and ethnicity.

Notes
1. Bill McCollum. "Be Responsible About Felons' Rights," Orlando Sentinel, Apr. 1, 2007.
2. Bureau of Justice Statistics data.
3. Dissenting opinion in Hayden v. Pataki, May 4 2006.

---

[123] David Lublin, *The Paradox of Representation: Racial Gerrymandering and Minority Interests in Congress* (Princeton, NJ: Princeton University Press, 1997).

[124] Sanchez, "Money and Diversity in State Legislatures, 2003," p. 6.

Summary

A healthy democracy depends, at least in part, on having citizens who are engaged with each other and with politics. Participation in local voluntary groups is one way that people learn the skills required to be citizens. As important as local democracy is, this chapter illustrates that there are substantial barriers to participation at the state and local levels. Elections are often designed to be uncompetitive, a situation that may only serve incumbents well. Nonpartisan races, uncompetitive elections, and other barriers may depress interest in state and local politics.

But this need not be the case. One theme of this book is that institutions matter and institutions can change. Race-based barriers to voting have been reduced substantially over the last 100 years. This is evidence that the rules can change and that political participation can become more inclusive.

Key Terms

At-large elections	Literacy tests	Social capital
Clean money and public financing of campaigns	Majority-minority district	Voting-age population
Cumulative voting	Multimember district	Voting-eligible population
Descriptive representation	Participation bias	Voting Rights Act
District magnitude	Poll tax	Winner-take-all
Efficacy	Primary election	
Grandfather clause	Racial gerrymandering	

Discussion Questions

1. Which demographic groups are most likely to participate in local political activities? What effect does this have on policy making?
2. Discuss the terms and effects of voting rights legislation. What barriers have been overcome and what barriers remain?
3. How do levels of citizen participation and political efficacy in local elections compare to those in national elections?
4. Do people have more influence when participating in local or national politics?
5. Why are minorities better represented in some districts than others? What effect does this have on their influence in legislatures?

Suggested Readings

Berkman, Michael, and Eric Plutzer. 2006. *Ten Thousand Democracies: Politics and Public Opinion in America's School Districts.* Washington, DC: Georgetown University Press.

Browning, Robert, D. Rodgers, and D. Tabb. 1984. *Protest Is Not Enough: The Struggle of Blacks and Hispanics for Equality in Urban Politics.* Berkeley: University of California Press.

Erikson, Robert, Gerald Wright, and John McIver. 1994. *Statehouse Democracy: Public Opinion and the American States.* New York: Cambridge University Press.

Gimple, James, J. Celeste Lay, and Jason Schuknecht. 2003. *Cultivating Democracy: Civic Environments and Political Socialization in America.* Washington, DC: Brookings Institution Press.

Oliver, J. Eric. 2001. *Democracy in Suburbia.* Princeton, NJ: Princeton University Press.

Putnam, Robert. 2000. *Bowling Alone: The Collapse and Revival of American Community.* New York: Simon and Schuster.

Rosenthal, Alan. 1998. *The Decline of Representative Democracy: Process, Participation, and Power in State Legislatures.* Washington, DC: CQ Press.

Web Sites

The Immigrant Voting Project (http://www.immigrantvoting.org): The Immigrant Voting Project documents the practice of enfranchising noncitizens in local (municipal and school board) elections.

Center for Voting and Democracy (http://www.fairvote.org): The center promotes election systems that increase voter turnout, fair representation, inclusive policy, and meaningful choices. It conducts research, analysis, education, and organizing to ensure all Americans can exercise their right to vote and elect representatives who reflect our racial and political diversity.

Public Campaign (http://www.publicampaign.org): Public Campaign is a nonpartisan organization dedicated to reforming how elections are financed. It provides details on state and local efforts to promote publicly financed campaigns.

National Association of Secretaries of State (http://www.nass.org): The association offers information about election administration, voter participation, and electronic or e-government services administered by secretaries of state. It also has links to state-specific sites for voter registration and the location of local polling places.

Bowlingalone.com (http:www.bowlingalone.com): The site promotes a book on social capital by Robert Putnam. The site provides access to the public opinion data used in this chapter and information about how the United States can "civicly reinvent itself again."

4

State and Local Direct Democracy

GOVERNING BY THE BALLOT

Arnold Schwarzenegger might be remembered as the direct democracy governor. Schwarzenegger's first experience with statewide politics was as the public face and chief funding source behind a popular 2002 California ballot initiative that increased spending on after-school programs. His initiative, Proposition 49, was seen as an effort by the Hollywood actor to prepare for a future bid as a Republican gubernatorial candidate. Direct democracy soon paved the way to the governor's office for Schwarzenegger. Fiscal crisis and voter dissatisfaction in 2003 led to a recall of the incumbent governor, Gray Davis, and Schwarzenegger won a free-for-all special election that was part of the recall vote. As governor, he moved from campaigning for ballot initiatives to trying to govern with them. After being elected, Schwarzenegger promoted several ballot measures to advance policies that he could not push through the state legislature. At the height of his popularity, he weighed in on 10 measures on the November 2004 ballot, including some that determined the fate of his plans to deal with the budget crisis he inherited. The California Republican Party even mailed a 12-page, multi-colored brochure entitled "Governor Arnold Schwarzenegger's Ballot Proposition Voter Guide" to millions of voters. Voters sided with the governor on nine of the 10 measures on which he voiced an official position.

Schwarzenegger later discovered that it can be difficult to govern by direct democracy. In 2005, and again in 2009, he championed more ballot measures. In 2005, he asked people to support his fiscal agenda after the Democratic-controlled

Governor Arnold Schwarzenegger's voter's guide. These were mailed to thousands of homes in 2005 with instructions on how to support his positions on ballot measures. All of the governor's proposals were defeated.

legislature would not pass some of his key proposals. Schwarzenegger called a special election in November 2005 for the sole purpose of letting voters have the final say on his policies. Voters rejected all four of the governor's proposals, including a measure to weaken the legislature's control over budgeting.[1] Four years later, with the state facing a $40 billion deficit, the governor and legislature crafted a compromise budget deal. Part of the plan depended on voters approving six ballot measures, including proposals to borrow billions against lottery revenues, to raise taxes, and to change how funds from previous voter-approved initiatives could be spent. Once again, voters said no. Schwarzenegger's style of "going to the people" illustrates how places with direct democracy can have different styles of politics than places that do not. As we will see in this chapter, direct democracy can have important effects on how citizens, groups, and elected officials are able to affect what government does.

1   Elizabeth Garrett, "Democracy in the Wake of the California Recall," *University of Pennsylvania Law Review* 153(2004):239–84; Daniel A. Smith, "Initiatives and Referendums: The Effects of Direct Democracy on Candidate Elections," in *The Electoral Challenge: Theory Meets Practice,* ed. Steven Craig (Washington, DC: CQ Press, 2006); and Richard Hasen, "Rethinking the Unconstitutionality of Contribution and Expenditure Limits in Ballot Measure Campaigns," *Southern California Law Review* 78(2005):885–926.

Introduction

The link between citizens and their government can be quite different at the state and local levels than at the national level. State legislators and local governments regularly refer matters to voters for their approval; in fact, most states require that amendments to state constitutions ultimately be approved by voters. In nearly half the states, people can draft their own legislation and petition to have a public vote to approve or reject it. Additionally, many local governments, including those in states that do not allow the usage of direct democracy at the state level, permit this process. Some of our biggest cities—including Baltimore, Columbus, Dallas, Denver, Detroit, Houston, Jacksonville, Los Angeles, Miami, Milwaukee, New York, Phoenix, Portland, San Antonio, San Diego, San Francisco, Seattle, and Washington, D.C.—permit citizens to propose charter amendments to be placed on the ballot for fellow citizens to either adopt or reject. In fact, a majority of Americans reside in cities and towns where they can vote directly on matters of public policy.[1] Processes of direct democracy can leave elected representatives with limited influence over public policy. It is difficult to understand state and local politics in much of the nation without considering the effects of direct democracy.

In many American states and communities, citizens have more ability to affect what their governments do than other people in almost any other political system in the world. Apart from areas in Switzerland, no other places with such freewheeling democratic arrangements exist. In its most extreme form, direct democracy gives people outside the corridors of power the potential to cut taxes, propose tax hikes or new spending programs, veto most laws passed by elected representatives, and even remove elected officials from office. This contrasts dramatically with how American citizens participate in national politics. Although the United States is one of the few advanced democracies to have never put a question of national policy or constitutional design up for a public vote, these questions are commonly decided by voters at the state and local levels. Americans regularly decide on matters such as local school funding, land-use rules, social policy, or how much their state should borrow for specific long-term projects. The scope of direct democracy varies widely across the states and thus provides one of the key features distinguishing politics in some states and cities from that in other places.

In this chapter, we consider American direct democracy as a grand democratic experiment that allows us to consider, in effect, whether more democracy is "better." That is, does democratic politics work "better" when citizens are given more direct control over their government? As we shall see, no consensus exists among political observers, pundits, journalists, scholars, or politicians about these questions. We also illustrate that each state has a unique set of rules defining how direct democracy works, and these rules affect how much the process is used. Politics and policies can be fundamentally different in states with freewheeling forms of direct democracy.

Institutions of Direct Democracy

Three main features of direct democracy are the referendum, the initiative, and the recall. Almost every state uses some form of referendum. As Figure 4.1 reveals, 24 states have some form of a statewide initiative, 24 allow a statewide popular referendum (most of which also provide the initiative), and 18 states have provisions for the recall of state officials.

Referendum

A referendum is a public vote on a statute or a constitutional amendment that has already

---

[1] John Matsusaka, *For the Many or the Few: The Initiative, Public Policy, and American Democracy* (Chicago: University of Chicago Press, 2004).

Figure 4.1

States with Statewide Initiative, Popular Referendum, and Recall

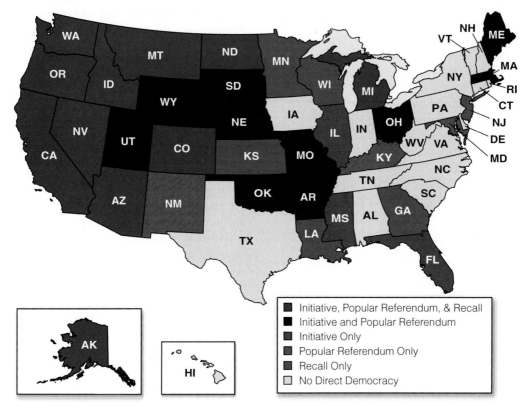

Legend:
- ■ Initiative, Popular Referendum, & Recall
- ■ Initiative and Popular Referendum
- ■ Initiative Only
- ■ Popular Referendum Only
- ■ Recall Only
- □ No Direct Democracy

Source: National Conference of State Legislatures

been considered by a state legislature or local government. The most widely used instrument of direct democracy in the American states (and localities) is the legislative referendum. In the case of the **legislative referendum**, elected officials have control over the question that voters will consider, although legislators are often bound to place certain items on state ballots. Use of legislative referendums at the national level is quite widespread, with nearly every advanced democratic nation other than the United States using the process.[2] Every American state has some provision for a legislative referendum— particularly for state constitutional matters.

Most state constitutions require that voters approve constitutional amendments via referendum, and some require that voters approve when a state issues debt. Legislators may also choose to defer to the wisdom of voters and allow them to have the final say over controversial issues, such as tax increases.

The **popular referendum**, by way of contrast, allows a person or group to file a petition to have a public vote on a bill that the legislature has already approved. Every state with the initiative process (except Florida, Illinois, and Mississippi) also allows citizens to propose popular referendums.[3] The popular

[2] David Butler and Austin Ranney, eds., *Referendums around the World: The Growing Use of Direct Democracy* (Washington, DC: AEI Press, 1994).

[3] David Magleby, *Direct Legislation: Voting on Ballot Propositions in the United States* (Baltimore, MD: Johns Hopkins University Press, 1984).

referendum is effectively a public veto of a law. Proponents may qualify popular referendums for the ballot by collecting a certain percentage of signatures in a set amount of time following the passage of the legislation in question.

Initiative

The two types of initiative process in the United States are the direct initiative and indirect initiative. The **direct initiative** allows a person or group to file a proposed bill with a state office and then collect signatures from voters to qualify the measure for a spot on the state ballot. If the initiative qualifies, voters have a direct say on approving or rejecting the proposal. If voters approve the measure, it becomes law.[4] An **indirect initiative** functions as a petition to have the legislature consider a bill proposed by citizens. This is similar to the Swiss system. If the indirect initiative qualifies by its proponents collecting enough signatures, the legislature can adopt or reject the bill. If it is rejected by the legislature, it must be placed on the ballot to give voters a chance to approve or reject the proposal.

Direct and indirect initiatives appear on the ballot if sufficient signatures are collected. Rules for qualifying initiatives vary across the states, but the number of signatures on petitions required to qualify is typically set as a fixed percentage of votes cast in a previous election, or as a fixed percentage of all registered voters. Most states with any sort of initiative process only have direct initiatives; however, a few (Alaska, Maine, Massachusetts, and Wyoming) have indirect initiatives only. Five additional states (Michigan, Nevada, Ohio, Utah, and Washington) allow both direct and indirect initiatives.

Depending on the state, a legislature may submit to voters an indirect initiative that it rejected, along with its own alternative proposal; alternatively, the legislature may simply take no action.

Recall

The **recall** allows a person or group to file a petition for a public vote to remove an elected official from office prior to when the official's term expires. The first place in the United States to adopt the recall was Los Angeles in 1903. Many cities and 18 states now have rules allowing for the recall of elected officials, although the process is rarely used at the state level. In most states that allow the recall process, the signature requirement for qualification is much greater than that required for the initiative and referendum.[5] Only two governors have been recalled: Lynn Fraiser of North Dakota in 1921 and Gray Davis of California in 2003.[6] Recall efforts against mayors, city councilpersons, and school boards are more common. There is some controversy about whether there should be narrow grounds for having a recall, or if a recall should be allowed simply because an elected official becomes unpopular. In 2009, the mayor of Toledo, Ohio, was subjected to a recall for allegedly mismanaging the budget (it failed to qualify). Dissatisfaction with economic conditions, taxes, and public services led to recall efforts that year against the mayors of Akron, Ohio, and Kansas City, Missouri.[7]

Some states require that proponents of either a state or local recall establish compelling grounds to have a vote to remove an elected official (such as criminal misconduct),

---

[4] A simple majority is usually required for approval, although some states require more. See Richard Ellis, *Democratic Delusions: The Initiative Process in America* (Lawrence, KS: University Press of Kansas, 2002).

[5] Magleby, *Direct Legislation*.

[6] Shaun Bowler and Bruce Cain, eds., *Clicker Politics: Essays on the California Recall* (Englewood Cliffs, NJ: Prentice Hall, 2005).

[7] Kevin Friedl, "Mayors Face Tough Times," *National Journal Online,* 29 June 2009. Available: http://www.nationaljournal.com/njonline/no_20090626_9048.php.

What should be grounds for a recall? Sam Adams, Portland, Oregon's first openly gay mayor, was made the target of a recall effort after it was revealed that he had lied during his election campaign. Adams had denied having a sexual relationship with an 18-year-old legislative intern, Beau Breedlove, but admitted to it soon after taking office in 2009.

whereas other states' rules are less restrictive or have no formal requirement that substantial misconduct be established in order to proceed with a recall. States also differ in how recalls are conducted. In some situations, voters are given two choices on one ballot: First, they decide if the official should be removed; then they may decide who should replace the official. This was the case with the California recall, where, after deciding on Governor Davis's fate, voters then had 135 candidates to choose from (including actor Arnold Schwarzenegger, porn publisher Larry Flint, ex–child actor Gary Coleman, and at least two adult "entertainers," Angelyne and Mary Carey; see Figure 4.2). In other cases, voters are only asked the question about the recall. In these cases, the office is left vacant until the next election, a replacement is appointed, or a special election is conducted later to fill the vacancy.

More Responsible and More Representative Government?

Part of the difficulty in assessing the merits and pitfalls of direct democracy lies in how we define what a "better" democratic system might look like. One way to consider this task is to ask if direct democracy in the states makes politics more responsible and more representative.[8] Early advocates of direct democracy claimed that it could do both.

---

[8] Todd Donovan and Shaun Bowler, "Responsible and Representative?" in *Citizens as Legislators: Direct Democracy in the United States*, ed. Shaun Bowler, Todd Donovan, and Caroline Tolbert (Columbus, OH: Ohio State University Press, 1998).

Figure 4.2

California Recall Ballot

---

003   **A**

OFFICIAL BALLOT

Statewide Special Election

Sonoma County

October 7, 2003

This ballot stub shall be removed and retained by the voter.

MARK YOUR CHOICE(S)
IN THIS MANNER ONLY: ▬
VOTING AREA

STATE	
Shall **GRAY DAVIS** be recalled (removed) from the office of Governor?	Yes
	No

Candidates to succeed **GRAY DAVIS** as Governor if he is recalled. Vote for One	
KURT E. "TACHIKAZE" RIGHTMYER, Independent Middleweight Sumo Wrestler	
DANIEL W. RICHARDS, Republican Businessman	
KEVIN RICHTER, Republican Information Technology Manager	
REVA RENEE RENZ, Republican Small Business Owner	
SHARON RUSHFORD, Independent Businesswoman	
GEORGY RUSSELL, Democratic Software Engineer	
MICHAEL J. WOZNIAK, Democratic Retired Police Officer	
DANIEL WATTS, Green College Student	
NATHAN WHITECLOUD WALTON, Independent Student	
MAURICE WALKER, Green Real Estate Appraiser	
CHUCK WALKER, Republican Business Intelligence Analyst	
LINGEL H. WINTERS, Democratic Consumer Business Attorney	
C.T. WEBER, Peace and Freedom Labor Official/Analyst	
JIM WEIR, Democratic Community College Teacher	
BRYAN QUINN, Republican Businessman	
MICHAEL JACKSON, Republican Satellite Project Manager	
JOHN "JACK" MORTENSEN, Democratic Contractor/Businessman	
DARRYL L. MOBLEY, Independent Businessman/Entrepreneur	
JEFFREY L. MOCK, Republican Business Owner	
BRUCE MARGOLIN, Democratic Marijuana Legalization Attorney	
GINO MARTORANA, Republican Restaurant Owner	
PAUL MARIANO, Democratic Attorney	

49-A007R   **CONTINUED OTHER SIDE**   **A**

I HAVE VOTED—HAVE YOU?

MARK YOUR CHOICE(S)
IN THIS MANNER ONLY: ▬
VOTING AREA

(CANDIDATES CONTINUED)	
ROBERT C. MANNHEIM, Democratic Retired Businessperson	
FRANK A. MACALUSO, JR., Democratic Physician/Medical Doctor	
PAUL "CHIP" MAILANDER, Democratic Golf Professional	
DENNIS DUGGAN MCMAHON, Republican Banker	
MIKE MCNEILLY, Republican Artist	
MIKE P. MCCARTHY, Independent Used Car Dealer	
BOB MCCLAIN, Independent Civil Engineer	
TOM MCCLINTOCK, Republican State Senator	
JONATHAN MILLER, Democratic Small Business Owner	
CARL A. MEHR, Republican Businessman	
SCOTT A. MEDNICK, Democratic Business Executive	
DORENE MUSILLI, Republican Parent/Educator/Businesswoman	
VAN VO, Republican Radio Producer/Businessman	
PAUL W. VANN, Republican Financial Planner	
JAMES M. VANDEVENTER, JR., Republican Salesman/Businessman	
BILL VAUGHN, Democratic Structural Engineer	
MARC VALDEZ, Democratic Air Pollution Scientist	
MOHAMMAD ARIF, Independent Businessman	
ANGELYNE, Independent Entertainer	
DOUGLAS ANDERSON, Republican Mortgage Broker	
IRIS ADAM, Natural Law Business Analyst	
BROOKE ADAMS, Independent Business Executive	
ALEX-ST. JAMES, Republican Public Policy Strategist	
JIM HOFFMANN, Republican Teacher	
KEN HAMIDI, Libertarian State Tax Officer	

49-A008R   **CONTINUED NEXT CARD**   **A**

Sample Ballot

The Promise of Direct Democracy

Direct democracy has its roots in the Populist and Progressive movements of the late 19th century and early 20th century, respectively. In the early 1900s, campaign contributions were largely unregulated, and bribery and graft were not uncommon in state legislatures. State and local elected officials were paid poorly, and, with few laws regulating political corruption, they were subject to influence by firms seeking favorable treatment from government. As one observer of the 1880s Oregon legislature noted, it consisted of "briefless lawyers, farmless farmers, business failures, bar-room loafers, Fourth-of July orators [and] political thugs."[9] Many elected officials had little enthusiasm for social, economic, and political reforms that may have had widespread support among the general public.

To Populist and Progressive reformers of that era, representative government alone could not be trusted to serve the public interest. Their goal was to give the public greater influence over the behavior of elected officials. Reformers were suspicious of the power that wealthy economic interests had over elected representatives. In this context, then, reformers argued that by giving people the ability to write their own laws and veto unpopular laws passed by legislators, public policy would be more representative of public opinion. Likewise, it was assumed, then, that elected officials would often work to protect powerful economic interests by doing such things as granting monopolies, giving away public resources, blocking health and safety regulations, and blocking anticorruption laws. If the public could use direct democracy as an end run around these elected officials, reformers assumed that public policy would become more responsible.

Defending Direct Democracy

Prior to being elected president in 1912, Woodrow Wilson offered a pragmatic defense of the instrumental use of the initiative. Wilson argued that if a state legislature was unable or unwilling to pass popular legislation, citizens could directly propose and adopt laws themselves to correct any legislative "sins of omission." Even indirectly, the mere threat of an initiative—the "gun behind the door," as Wilson called it—could pressure recalcitrant legislators to take action. For Wilson, direct legislation was not a radical solution; he foresaw the device being used sparingly. The initiative would serve as a stopgap mechanism—a benign tool that would "restore," not "destroy," representative government. The expedience of direct legislation, according to Wilson, could bring "our representatives back to the consciousness that what they are bound in duty and in mere policy to do is represent the sovereign people whom they profess to serve." As a prodding instrument, then, the initiative had the potential of directly or indirectly bringing forth substantive policy changes in the American states.[10]

This was, in part, the promise of direct democracy 100 years ago. In considering how direct democracy works in American states and communities today, it is important to consider the adoption of direct democracy in its historic context. We assess how it might make politics more representative of public opinion and consider whether it makes policy more responsible. The latter quality, of course, is much more difficult to assess.

---

[9] David Schuman, "The Origin of State Constitutional Direct Democracy: William Simon Uren and the Oregon System," *Temple Law Review* 67(1994):947–63, 949.

[10] Daniel A. Smith and Caroline J. Tolbert, *Educated by Initiative: The Effects of Direct Democracy on Citizens and Political Organizations in the American States* (Ann Arbor, MI: University of Michigan Press, 2004).

INSTITUTIONS MATTER

"THE GUN BEHIND THE DOOR"

In 2006, state legislatures across the country were evidently feeling the "heat" being packed by various groups, as the threat of the citizen initiative impelled them into action. According to the Ballot Initiative Strategy Center (http://www.ballot.org; see "Websites"), a nonprofit group that tracks ballot initiatives, several state legislatures took up bills they had previously ignored (or opposed) because potential ballot issues resonated strongly with citizens.

In the spring of 2006, a citizens' group in Oregon collected signatures for an initiative to rein in the runaway interest rates that payday loan companies foist on borrowers. The measure was polling like gangbusters. It was so popular that the Oregon legislature decided to convene a special session in April to pass legislation nearly identical to the initiative. Not only that, but the sponsor of the bill was also the same woman who the previous year had killed legislation that would have accomplished the same ends—and all because of the threat of an initiative. In Michigan, the Republican-controlled legislature realized in March 2006 there was a good chance a popular minimum wage initiative would be on the November ballot. The GOP leadership, fearful of having their candidates running in an election with such a popular issue, decided to push through the legislature a languishing Democratic bill to raise the state's minimum wage. Democratic governor Jennifer Granholm signed the bill into law. The initiative campaign, which was organized by organized labor, promptly shuttered its doors.

Using the initiative process as a lever to pry stubborn legislation out of the recesses of a legislature is nothing new. Woodrow Wilson argued in 1911 that it could be used by citizens to apply tacit pressure on capricious state legislatures, forcing them to abide by the will of the people. By way of analogy, Wilson understood the practice of citizen lawmaking as the "gun behind the door—for use only in case of emergency, but [a] mighty good persuader, nevertheless."[1]

Note

1. Ballot Initiative Strategy Center, "Oregon: Another Initiative 'Pays' Off," 21 April 2006, http://ballotblog.typepad.com/ballotblog/2006/04/oregon_another_.html.

Populist Origins of Direct Democracy

Although states in New England have practice with town meeting forms of local government that provide for direct citizen voting on policy questions, direct democracy did not exist at the state level prior to the late 1890s. Eighteen of the 24 states that currently have the initiative process adopted it between 1898 and 1914. Many of the early initiatives reflected the agenda of groups that agitated for the adoption of direct democracy. Issues such as women's suffrage, Prohibition, labor laws, and electoral reforms were common in the first decade that direct democracy was in use.

The initiative process at the state level was first adopted in South Dakota in 1898, but it was first used statewide in Oregon in 1904. Several political movements that included organized labor, disaffected farmers, proponents of the so-called single tax, Prohibitionists, and women's suffrage advocates pressed their states to adopt the initiative, recall, and referendum. These direct democracy tools were part of a larger set of reforms advocated by the **Populist Party** in the 1890s, including direct election of U.S. senators, direct election of the president, direct voter control candidate nominations, direct primary elections, and the income tax.[11] Recall that Figure 4.1 illustrates how direct democracy is more common in the West, in part because minority parties had greater political influence and some of these states were just forming their first constitutions when Populists and Progressives were most influential.[12]

Although short-lived on the political scene, the Populists were one of the most influential third parties in American history. Their attack on the disproportionate influence of powerful economic interests (railroads, banks, mining firms, and monopolies) had great appeal to laborers, western farmers, and miners. Democrat William Jennings Bryan, who ran for president on the Populist ticket in some states in 1896, was soundly defeated, but he ran very strong in western states, sweeping Populist and "Fusion" Democrats into Congress and state legislatures. Bryan spent part of his career in the 1890s promoting direct democracy in states where Populists had political success.[13] Even though Populists were largely dead as a political party by 1900, states where Bryan had his greatest electoral appeal, as well as states where Socialist presidential candidate Eugene Debs ran strongest early in the 20th century, were most likely to amend their state constitutions to allow some forms of direct democracy by 1914.[14] Direct democracy is more common in the West, in part because Populists and Socialists had greater political influence there and because Progressive era reformers gained

influence in these states in the first decades of the 20th century. Direct democracy was part of a broad set of **Progressive era reforms** that included attempts at weakening political parties, improving public health and working conditions, and regulating business.

Adopting Direct Democracy during the Progressive Era

Whereas the Populists set the stage for U.S. direct democracy in the 1890s, most states actually adopted institutions of direct democracy during the Progressive era of the next two decades. Populists and Progressives differed in their critiques of American representative government. As such, the Populists' saw that common people were trustworthy and competent and that elected legislators were neither. The Populists' goal was to take power away from incumbent politicians, vested interests, and party machines and give it to voters. Progressives, on the other hand, were more sympathetic to the legislative process but wanted to "liberate representative government from corrupt forces so that it might become an effective instrument for social reform."[15] The Progressive model aimed to use direct democracy to improve representative government rather than replace it. Early advocates of direct democracy envisioned a process that allowed regular citizens to resolve a particular grievance. But modern direct democracy may have evolved into a process where professional politicians and wealthy interests use initiatives and referendums to advance their own agendas.[16]

---

[11] Shaun Bowler, Todd Donovan, and Eric D. Lawrence, "Adopting Direct Democracy: Tests of Competing Explanations of Institutional Change," *American Politics Research* (forthcoming).

[12] Daniel A. Smith and Dustin Fridkin, "Delegating Direct Democracy: Interparty Legislative Competition and the Adoption of the Initiative in the American States," *American Political Science Review* 102(2008):333–50.

[13] Steven Piott, *Giving Voters a Voice: The Origins of the Initiative and Referendum in America* (Columbia, MO: University of Missouri Press, 2003).

[14] Shaun Bowler, Todd Donovan, and Eric D. Lawrence, "Introducing Direct Democracy" (paper presented at the annual meeting of the American Political Science Association, Washington, DC, August 2005).

[15] Bruce Cain and Kenneth Miller, "The Populist Legacy: Initiatives and the Undermining of Representative Government," in *Dangerous Democracy? The Battle over Ballot Initiatives in America*, ed. Larry Sabato, Bruce Larson, and Howard Ernst (Lanham, MD: Rowman & Littlefield, 2002).

[16] Daniel A. Smith, *Tax Crusaders and the Politics of Direct Democracy* (New York: Routledge, 1998); Todd Donovan, Shaun Bowler, David McCuan, and Ken Fernandez, "Contending Players and Strategies: Opposition Advantages in Initiative Elections," in Bowler, Donovan, and Tolbert, *Citizens as Legislators*.

The Ebb and Flow of Ballot Initiatives

From the 1930s to the 1960s, as legislatures became more professional and anticorruption laws took hold, direct democracy was used less. It made a comeback, however, as groups again began to use the initiative process to promote public votes on policy questions. There was a steady increase in the number of ballot measures qualified in all states since the 1960s. After a decline in the 1940s and 1950s, use of initiatives reached a new peak in the 1990s, when there were nearly 400 initiatives on statewide ballots—far more than in any other decade.[17] The annual use of initiatives remained relatively high by historic standards after 2000. It is important to remember that roughly 60 percent of all initiatives that qualify for state ballots are rejected by voters; however, measures that pass can have a powerful effect on the design of state political institutions and on the political agenda.[18]

Studies find a large degree of stability in terms of the subjects of ballot measures on which voters have been asked to decide over most of the last 100 years. The most common initiatives since 1980 have been governmental reform measures, such as term limits and campaign finance regulation (23 percent) and taxation questions (22 percent). Social and moral issues (17 percent) and environmental measures (11 percent) are the next most common questions.[19] Some attribute the revival of direct democracy in recent decades to a new generation of citizens who demand more say in politics but who are less interested in traditional forms of participation via representation by political parties.[20] Others note that the rise of initiative use in the United States corresponded with the proliferation of new interest groups[21] and with the maturation of a sophisticated industry of campaign professionals promoting the use of initiatives.[22]

Direct Democracy and National Politics

Battles over several state initiatives from the later decades of the 20th century have set the stage for major policy debates at the national level. Contemporary initiative efforts in the states sometimes become part of larger campaigns that shape the issues discussed by politicians in Washington and those trying to win election to federal office. Antitax initiatives from the late 1970s—most notably, California's Proposition 13 in 1978—foreshadowed the enthusiasm for the Reagan-era federal tax cuts of the early 1980s.[23] Initiatives in California and Washington targeting affirmative action set the tone for national debate on the policy in the late 1990s. That same decade, voters in over a dozen states decided the fate of proposals to limit state legislative terms. Popular enthusiasm for term limits may have led some aspiring candidates for Congress to take positions in favor of short tenure in office (although several years later, many of those same members had less enthusiasm for limiting how long they should serve).

---

[17] Ellis, *Democratic Delusions*.

[18] David Magleby, "Direct Legislation in America," in Butler and Ranney, *Referendums around the World*.

[19] Caroline J. Tolbert, "Cycles of Democracy: Direct Democracy and Institutional Realignment in the American States," *Political Science Quarterly* 118(2003):467–89.

[20] Russell Dalton, Wilhelm Burklin, and Andrew Drummond, "Public Attitudes toward Direct Democracy," *Journal of Democracy* 12(2001):141–53; and Ian Budge, "Political Parties in Direct Democracy," in *Referendum Democracy: Citizens, Elites and Deliberation in Referendum Campaigns*, ed. Matthew Mendelsohn and Andrew Parkin (New York: Palgrave, 2002).

[21] David Magleby, "Direct Legislation in America," in Butler and Ranney, *Referendums around the World*.

[22] David Broder, *Democracy Derailed: Initiative Campaigns and the Power of Money* (New York: Harcourt Brace, 2000); and Sabato, Larson, and Ernst, *Dangerous Democracy?*

[23] Smith, *Tax Crusaders and the Politics of Direct Democracy*.

State initiatives and referendums proposing to ban gay marriage in 2004 had effects that spilled into the presidential election. Voters were more likely to evaluate George W. Bush and John Kerry in terms of the gay marriage issue if they lived in one of the 13 states where there was a gay marriage ban measure on the state's ballot.[24] Initiative activists with an eye on the national stage have gotten their proposals on the ballot in multiple states to promote their causes and set the national agenda.[25] As a result, measures backed by national groups advocating such things as increasing the minimum wage, eminent domain, school choice, nuclear freeze, term limits, the repeal of affirmative action, and tax cuts have each gotten their measures on the ballot in several different states.

Nonetheless, most of the initiatives and referendums to reach a state's ballot are home-grown proposals. This does not mean that most initiatives are the product of the "average" citizen who rallies the grassroots to challenge an established order. The initiative process is also used by a wide array of interest groups, by business groups, and by political parties. Ballot initiatives targeting the use of public services by illegal immigrants have been used by the Republican Party in attempts to mobilize

supporters or drive a wedge through the rival party's base.[26] Democrats have made similar attempts to mobilize likely Democratic voters with minimum wage initiatives.[27] Incumbent politicians, candidates for office, and wealthy individuals also promote their pet causes with initiatives.[28] In states where expensive petition campaigns are required to qualify for the ballot, many of the same powerful interest groups that dominate legislative politics—trial lawyers, teachers' unions, nurses, insurance companies, and casinos and Indian tribes—also fund campaigns promoting and opposing initiatives.[29]

The Explosion Continues

The most initiatives in the United States in one year was 87 (in 1914 and 1996). In the 2008 general election, there were 59 statewide initiatives and two popular referendums on statewide ballots; two years earlier, there were 74 initiatives and five popular referendums.[30] In both elections there also were hundreds more local referendums and initiatives on the ballots of all 50 states. Substantively, ballot propositions cover a remarkable range of issues; some of the issues involved are complex, whereas others are relatively straightforward. Some measures make national headlines; others remain obscure in terms of public or media attention. Voters have cast ballots dealing with issues as diverse as banning gay marriage, punishing negligent doctors, prohibiting the confinement

[24] Todd Donovan, Caroline J. Tolbert, and Daniel A. Smith, "Priming Presidential Votes by Direct Democracy," *Journal of Politics* 70(2008):1217–31; David Campbell and J. Quinn Monson, "The Religion Card: Gay Marriage and the 2004 Presidential Election," *Public Opinion Quarterly* 72(3):399–419; Gregory B. Lewis, "Same-Sex Marriage and the 2004 Presidential Election," *Political Science and Politics* 38(2005):195–200; Daniel A. Smith, Matthew DeSantis, and Jason Kassel, "Same-Sex Marriage Ballot Measures and the 2004 Presidential Election," *State and Local Government Review* 38(2)(2006):77–90; Alan Abramowitz, "Terrorism, Gay Marriage, and Incumbency: Explaining the Republican Victory in the 2004 Presidential Election," *Forum* 2 (2004):art. 3, http://www.bepress.com/forum/vol2/iss4/art3; Barry Burden, "An Alternative Account of the 2004 Presidential Election," *Forum* 2 (2004):art. 2, http://www.bepress.com/forum/vol2/iss4/art2.

[25] Steven P. Nicholson, *Voting the Agenda: Candidates Elections and Ballot Propositions* (Princeton, NJ: Princeton University Press, 2005).

[26] Daniel A. Smith and Caroline Tolbert, "The Initiative to Party: Partisanship and Ballot Initiatives in California," *Party Politics* 7(2001):781–99; and Richard Hasen, "Parties Take the Initiative (and Vice Versa)," *Columbian Law Review* 100(2001):731–52.

[27] Jeanne Cummings, "Wedge Issue: Minimum Wage," *Wall Street Journal*, 1 May 2006, p. A4.

[28] Ellis, *Democratic Delusions*.

[29] Shaun Bowler and Todd Donovan, *Demanding Choices: Opinion, Voting, and Direct Democracy* (Ann Arbor, MI: University of Michigan Press, 1998).

[30] National Conference of State Legislatures, "Ballot Measure Database," 2009, http://www.ncsl.org/default.aspx?tabid=16580.

REFORM CAN HAPPEN

INITIATING MEDICAL MARIJUANA LAWS

Most Americans think that marijuana should be made legal for medical purposes, with support for general legalization growing. A 2005 Gallup poll found 78 percent of Americans favored legalizing marijuana for medical use, and a 2009 Zogby poll found 52 percent supported legal, regulated sales that could be taxed. Despite the popularity of medical marijuana, the federal government and nearly all the state legislatures have rejected the policy.[1] Not to be stymied by their elected officials, citizens in 11 states (as well as those in the District of Columbia) have used ballot initiatives to pass laws allowing physicians to prescribe marijuana to patients suffering chronic pain. Legislators passed similar measures in four other states.[1]

Those sympathetic to direct democracy often suggest that elected officials are sometimes more responsive to lobbyists than public opinion. The initiative, they say, allows citizens to vote on laws that their state legislatures refuse to enact. Although ballot campaigns may be expensive, they claim that money cannot buy a ballot initiative victory at the polls. Can money buy a public policy that the citizens of a state don't want? Critics of direct democracy suggest the legislative process is a better way to make policy because elected officials are more knowledgeable about complex issues. They claim that "special interest" money can buy public policy if issues are put to a public vote. Medical marijuana ballot initiatives are an example, they say. The successful measures do not reflect public opinion but instead are the brainchild of a few wealthy people who don't even live in their states. Some of the early marijuana initiatives in Alaska, Arizona, California, Montana, and Oregon were funded by George Soros, who earned billions in currency markets; George Zimmer, founder of the Men's Wearhouse clothing chain; and John Sperling, founder of the for-profit University of Phoenix. Defenders of initiatives counter that much of the money was spent on collecting signatures to qualify for the ballot, and that election results reflect popular opinion. Regardless of whether either interpretation is correct, direct democracy will continue to have important consequences on state politics and policy in the cities and states where it is used. Indeed, the fiscal crisis of 2008–2010 led states like California to look at taxes on marijuana sales as a new and lucrative source of state revenues—if voters approve. In 2009, a measure to tax medical marijuana was approved with 80 percent voter support in cash-strapped Oakland, California. City officials hoped the tax could generate $1 million in annual revenue.[2]

Notes

1. Only four state legislatures (Hawaii, New Mexico, Rhode Island, and Vermont) have passed legislation making it legal for doctors to prescribe marijuana to their suffering patients.
2. "Oakland Council Backs Tax on Marijuana," *The Wall Street Journal Online,* 30 April 2009. Available: http://online.wsj.com/article/SB124105239168771233.html.

of pregnant pigs, limiting the taxation and spending powers of state governments, funding stem cell research, and ending affirmative action programs and social welfare benefits to illegal immigrants. In many states, virtually no subject matter is off-limits.

Looking back at the November 2008 ballot, a dozen states had measures dealing with the conduct of elections. Three states featured initiatives targeting immigrants (two of which failed), and three had measures that proposed banning abortion (all of which were rejected). Arizona, California, and Florida voters approved same-sex marriage measures. Coloradoans rejected an anti-affirmative action proposal, while Nebraskans approved a similar measure. Arkansas voters approved an initiative that prohibited gay couples from adopting

Jeff Greenberg / Alamy

In 2004, 74 percent of Ann Arbor, Michigan, voters approved Proposal C, a ballot measure changing the city charter to allow use of marijuana for medical purposes. Voters in several states have approved similar ballot measures. Oakland voters approved taxation of medical marijuana in 2009.

children. Coloradoans had 14 measures on their ballot, and rejected several proposals that would have made it easier for the state to tax and spend. Twelve measures appeared on ballots in Oregon and California. Californians approved billions of dollars in bond sales (for hospitals, veterans, and a high-speed train), and approved an initiative prohibiting the confinement of pregnant pigs and other farm animals.[31]

Differences across Initiative States

States differ with regard to how directly democratic their direct democracy processes are in practice. In most of the United States, direct democracy is limited to legislative referendums used at both the state and local levels. Most western states that adopted the initiative early have rules that allow citizens to draft **constitutional initiatives** as well as **statutory initiatives**. Statutory initiatives are more readily amended or repealed by the legislature in some states (such as Colorado, Maine, Idaho, and Missouri), whereas others require waiting periods, supermajorities, or both before a statutory initiative may be amended. California is the only state where the legislature may neither amend nor repeal an initiative statute.

In states where rules for direct democracy were put in place when Populists and Progressives were still influential (such as Arizona, California, Colorado, and Oregon), provisions for the initiative and popular referendum are more radically democratic than what exists in states that adopted the initiative process later in the 20th century. States that adopted the direct initiative and popular referendum in the early 1900s have rules that make it relatively easy to qualify for the ballot. Most early-adopting states have a relatively low threshold of signatures required to qualify initiatives as well as other requirements to qualify ballot measures.[32]

Using the Initiative

As Figure 4.3 reveals, Oregon and California—two early adopters—lead the pack in initiative use, with both states averaging close to 6.3 initiatives per each two-year election

[31] Ballot Initiative Strategy Center, "2008 Ballot Election Results," 13 November 2008, http://www.ncsl.org.

[32] Shaun Bowler and Todd Donovan, "Measuring the Effect of Direct Democracy on State Policy: Not All Initiatives Are Created Equal," *State Politics and Policy Quarterly* 4(2004):345–63.

Figure 4.3

Historic Statewide Initiative Use (year of adoption through 2008)

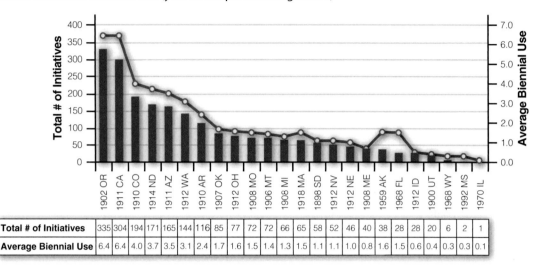

Total # of Initiatives	335	304	194	171	165	144	116	85	77	72	72	66	65	58	52	46	40	38	28	28	20	6	2	1
Average Biennial Use	6.4	6.4	4.0	3.7	3.5	3.1	2.4	1.7	1.6	1.5	1.4	1.3	1.5	1.1	1.1	1.0	0.8	1.6	1.5	0.6	0.4	0.3	0.3	0.1

Note: Bars represent the total number of initiatives that have qualified in a state since its adoption of direct democracy, with values plotted along the left-side axis. The line represents the average number of initiatives in a state every two years, with values plotted on the right-side axis.

Source: data from iandrinstitute.org, bisc.org, and ncsl.org.

cycle. Over 300 initiatives have appeared on Oregon ballots since that state adopted direct democracy, with California having nearly as many. The six states with the most frequent use of initiatives (Arizona, California, Colorado, North Dakota, Oregon, and Washington) have averaged more than three initiatives per general election since the Progressive era.[33] Roughly 60 percent of all initiative activity has taken place in these six states.[34] Few states, however, look like California or Oregon in terms of the ease of qualifying initiatives for the ballot and the difficulty that legislatures face when it comes to amending voter-approved initiatives.

The handful of states that adopted direct democracy long after the demise of the Populists

and Progressives have much more restrictive rules on how it can be used. Alaska included the initiative in its constitution when it was admitted to the union (1959), but only Florida and Wyoming (1968), Illinois (1970), and Mississippi (1992) have adopted the initiative process since that time. Three of these states (Florida, Illinois, and Mississippi) only allow constitutional initiatives. Illinois and Mississippi place severe restrictions on the subject matter that may appear on the ballot, and both states have strict provisions for qualification. As such, initiatives are rarely used in these two states—only one initiative has ever appeared on the Illinois ballot, and only two have qualified in Mississippi.[35]

---

[33] Caroline Tolbert, Daniel Lowenstein, and Todd Donovan, "Election Law and Rules for Using Initiatives," in Bowler, Donovan, and Tolbert, *Citizens as Legislators*.

[34] Ballot Initiative Strategy Center, "Election Results 2004."

[35] National Conference of State Legislatures, Initiative and Referendum in the 21st Century: Final Report and Recommendations of the NCSL I&R Task Force (Denver, CO, 2000), http://www.ncsl.org/programs/legman/irtaskfc/IandR_report.pdf.

Limits on Initiative Content

Generally speaking, any topic is a potential initiative subject. A few states, however, prohibit measures dealing with the judiciary, bills of rights, or tax questions. The major constraints on initiatives are constitutionality and single-subject laws, both of which are typically evaluated by state courts after a measure has been approved by voters. Some states allow elected officials or courts to amend or revise the language of propositions without the proponent's consent. Of the 24 states, only six have much of a preelection review at all. Four states—Colorado, Idaho, Montana, and Washington—have an advisory preelection certification process.

Half of the initiative states have rules that limit initiatives to one subject. Most state courts have been fairly tolerant of individual proposals with sweeping breadth, as long as their component parts could be seen as reasonably germane to one subject. State legislatures originally adopted the **single-subject rule** to ban egregious attempts at building coalitions of supporters by rolling many attractive features into a single measure in the hope of expanding potential support for it. One famous yet unsuccessful initiative proposal from California linked the regulation of margarine, voting rights for Native Americans, gambling, fishing, mining, and apportionment of the state senate into a single initiative question.[36] This sort of "logrolling" proposal is prohibited by single-subject laws. Only Florida's State Supreme Court has been known to regularly nullify initiatives on single-subject grounds, even after proponents have collected hundreds of thousands of valid signatures to qualify their measures for the ballot. The Florida State Supreme Court is also the only court to overtly declare that single-subject evaluations should be applied more rigorously to initiatives than legislative bills.[37] Since 2000,

however, state courts in California, Colorado, Nevada, and Oregon have become more rigid in the application of their state's single-subject rule. At times, this has meant that a single initiative must be split into several questions that are put before voters simultaneously.[38]

Qualifying for the Ballot

Initiatives and referendums, when they qualify for the ballot, are usually placed on a ballot whenever the next regularly scheduled general election occurs. This means direct democracy votes typically occur in even-numbered years. Some states (including Maine, Ohio, and Washington) have initiative votes annually in November, and a few (such as California) place initiatives and referendums on general and primary ballots every two years, so voters decide on an array of initiatives and referendums at least twice a year in even years. California and a handful of other states also allow either the governor or the legislature to schedule special statewide elections in odd years for votes on initiatives and referendums.

States that allow the initiative have considerable variation regarding how easy it is for citizens to use the process. Most states share four basic steps.[39] First, the proposal is drafted by proponents. Next, it is forwarded to a state office that issues an official title and summary of the measure. Proponents may then circulate petitions—usually within a fixed time period, often 90 or 180 days—for voters to sign. Finally, the state verifies whether a valid number of signatures were collected. If so, the proposal is placed on the ballot.

Rules for qualification vary across direct democracy states. In some states, petitioners have less time than in others. Some states also require that a certain proportion of signatures be collected in specific geographical areas, such

---

[36] Winston Crouch, *The Initiative and Referendum in California* (Los Angeles: Haynes Foundation, 1950).

[37] Daniel Lowenstein, *Election Law: Cases and Materials* (Durham, NC: Carolina Academic Press, 1995), p. 282.

[38] Ellis, *Democratic Delusions*, pp. 144–46.

[39] For a more detailed discussion of California's initiative process, see California Secretary of State, http://www.ss.ca.gov/elections/elections.htm.

as congressional districts. States also differ in the proportion of voters' signatures required to qualify for the ballot. Differences in these rules, and in the population of a state, affect how costly it is to get on a ballot. The difficulty of collecting hundreds of thousands of signatures means that many proponents hire people to collect signatures. Qualification is more difficult, and more costly (see Table 4.1), when a higher proportion of signatures must be collected in a shorter time period.[40]

Amateurs or Professionals?

In many states, it is difficult to place a measure on the ballot unless professional petition firms are paid to collect some or all the signatures required for qualification. In large states like California and Florida, where nearly 700,000 valid signatures are required to qualify a constitutional amendment initiative for 2010, few measures reach the ballot without proponents resorting to hiring firms that use paid petition gatherers to collect signatures. Some of these signature-gathering firms will have their subcontractors carry multiple petitions for the various groups that have hired them to gather signatures. For instance, in Missouri in 2006, employees of National Voter Outreach, a paid signature-gathering firm based in Carson City, Nevada, were carrying petitions for three separate measures: a measure tightening the state's eminent domain law, a measure limiting the taxing and spending authority of the state, and a measure increasing the tax on cigarettes to pay for health care costs for people receiving Medicaid. In states that have fewer voters, it is easier to collect the required signatures. In Colorado, for example, 76,000 valid signatures were needed to qualify either a statutory or constitutional amendment initiative in 2010. A hundred years ago, when there were far fewer people voting, fewer signatures were required to qualify a measure for the ballot, which may have helped to simplify the logistics of qualification.

Today, few citizen-based groups have the resources to collect signatures equal to 12, 8, or even 5 percent of a state's voting population. The use of paid signature gatherers and professional campaign staff has been part of the process in some states since early in the

Table 4.1	
Ease of Qualifying Ballot Initiatives Index	

State	Qualification Difficulty Index
Oregon	0
California	1
Colorado	1
North Dakota	1
Arkansas	2
Ohio	2
Michigan	2
South Dakota	2
Idaho	2
Arizona	3
Washington	3
Oklahoma	3
Montana	3
Missouri	3
Massachusetts	3
Utah	3
Nebraska	4
Maine	4
Nevada	4
Florida	4
Illinois	4
Alaska	5
Mississippi	5
Wyoming	6

Note: Higher scores indicate more difficulty; states with lower scores have the least burdensome rules for qualification.
Source: Shaun Bowler and Todd Donovan, "Measuring the Effect of Direct Democracy on State Policy: Not All Initiatives Are Created Equal," *State Politics and Policy Quarterly* 4 (2004): 345–63.

---

[40] Susan Banducci, "Direct Legislation: When Is It Used and When Does It Pass?" in Bowler, Donovan, and Tolbert, *Citizens as Legislators*.

20th century.[41] In the early 1900s, paid petition gatherers in some states were earning upwards of $0.03 a signature.[42] As the raw number of signatures required to qualify has increased, fewer voluntary, "grassroots" measures appear on state ballots.[43] In California, for example, volunteer petition campaigns are rarely successful. Those who wish to get a constitutional initiative amendment onto the ballot have to gather signatures equivalent to 8 percent of the number of votes for governor. This means gathering close to 1 million signatures in just 150 days, as a large percentage of signatures will surely be found to be invalid. Petition management firms in the state offer proponents a guarantee of qualification but at a price that runs close to $2 million for each initiative to be qualified. Paid signature gatherers in California have been known to earn up to $5 per valid signature, although the $1 to $2 range is more typical. In less populous states, the cost to qualify an initiative ranges anywhere between $50,000 and $400,000.

Champions of the Populist-Progressive vision of direct democracy have long argued that if the process is to combat the power of wealthy established interests, petition efforts should rely on volunteers only. In this spirit, several states passed laws banning the use of paid signature gathering. In the early 1900s, several states, including Ohio, South Dakota, and Washington, passed laws banning paid petition-gatherers. In the 1930s and 1940s, Oregon and Colorado also passed laws banning the practice, with Idaho and Nebraska following suit in the late 1980s.[44] The U.S. Supreme Court eventually overturned these laws in a 1988 decision, *Meyer v. Grant*, reasoning that the 1st Amendment protected paid petitioning, as it was a form of political speech.[45] This ruling, and the difficulties of qualifying measures, means that wealthy groups (unions, corporations, business organizations, professional associations, and trade groups) and wealthy individuals play a prominent, if not dominant, role in affecting what gets put to a public vote. Roughly a dozen states have responded by passing laws requiring circulators to disclose if they are being paid or not, and Oregon and North Dakota prohibit paid signature gathers from being compensated on a per-signature basis, requiring them instead to be paid a fixed salary or an hourly wage.[46]

Millionaires' Amusement?

Wealthy individuals, such as Microsoft co-founder Paul Allen, Hollywood actor-director Rob Reiner, billionaire financier George Soros, tech-industry businessman Ron Unz, and even actor Arnold Schwarzenegger (in his pregovernor, *Terminator* days), have all bankrolled the qualification of successful ballot initiatives. For his part, Allen convinced taxpayers to subsidize a new stadium for his then mediocre football team, the Seattle Seahawks, but Washington voters rejected the school reform initiative he funded. In 1998, Reiner sponsored an initiative to create early childhood development programs, and in 2006, he sponsored a tax on wealthy individuals to expand

---

[41] Charles Beard and Birl Shultz, eds., *Documents on the State-Wide Initiative, Referendum and Recall* (New York: Macmillan, 1912); and David McCuan, Shaun Bowler, Todd Donovan, and Ken Fernandez, "California's Political Warriors: Campaign Professionals and the Initiative Process," in Bowler, Donovan, and Tolbert, *Citizens as Legislators*.

[42] Daniel A. Smith and Joseph Lubinski, "Direct Democracy during the Progressive Era: A Crack in the Populist Veneer?" *Journal of Policy History* 14(4)(2002):349–83.

[43] Broder, *Democracy Derailed*; Peter Schrag, *Paradise Lost: California's Experience, America's Future* (New York: New Press, 1998); John Haskell, *Direct Democracy or Representative Government? Dispelling the Populist Myth* (Boulder, CO: Westview, 2001); and Ellis, *Democratic Delusions*.

[44] National Conference of State Legislatures, *Initiative and Referendum in the 21st Century*.

[45] *Meyer v. Grant* 486 U.S. 414 (1988).

[46] Todd Donovan and Daniel A. Smith, "Identifying and Preventing Signature Fraud on Ballot Measure Petitions," in Michael Alvarez, Thad E. Hall, and Susan D. Hyde, eds., *Election Fraud: Detecting and Deterring Electoral Manipulation* (Washington, DC: Brookings, 2008).

preschool education. In the 1990s, Soros, along with a couple of other wealthy individuals, helped finance nearly a dozen initiatives legalizing the medical use of marijuana. Unz used his money to bankroll measures to repeal bilingual education programs in California, Arizona, Colorado, and Massachusetts. In 2002, Schwarzenegger funded an initiative that bulked up spending on his state's after-school programs (and helped to burnish his image as a budding policy wonk).

Financing Direct Democracy Campaigns

The large sums of money spent on ballot measure campaigns gave rise to concerns about the presence of an "initiative industrial complex."[47] From this perspective, paid political consultants are seen not just as "guns for hire" but also as actors who create the demand for their services by advocating their own proposals for ballot measures. Their services include contracting petition work, polling, crafting TV ads, and purchasing airtime for the ads.

The public clearly has concerns about the campaign side of direct democracy. Despite being overwhelmingly in favor of the initiative process, people claim that initiative campaigns are misleading, that campaigns are too expensive, and that "special interests" dominate the process.[48] Longtime and persistent critic of the initiative process, *The Los Angeles Times* editorialized in 2003 that "Direct democracy is running amok" in California. Critics in other states agree, such as the former president of the Florida Senate, who has warned of the potential "Californication" of Florida resulting from the rash of expensive initiative campaigns.[49]

One critical question about direct democracy is whether the initiative process is driven by citizens, or by political consultants.[50] Some note that consulting and initiative marketing firms "sometimes test market issues for their feasibility ... and then shop for a group to back them" and that petition firms may try to drum up business after pitching issues to potential sponsors.[51] However, few examples of this have occurred in California or elsewhere. The claim is likely overreaching, as one is hard-pressed to find evidence of this type of practice, save for a single campaign professional promoting a lottery initiative in 1988.[52]

Nonetheless, the amount of money spent on initiative politics can be staggering. In 2008, over $800 million was spent nationally on state-level initiative and referendum campaigns,[53] more money than was spent on Barack Obama's presidential campaign. In 2006, nearly $525 million was spent on 73 ballot initiative campaigns in 18 states. In several states, more money was spent on ballot initiative campaigns than for all other races for political office combined. In California alone, proponents and opponents of eight initiatives on the November ballot spent more than $300 million in an effort to qualify the measures and sway voters on the merits of their arguments.

Direct Democracy Campaigns and the Supreme Court

These enormous expenditures are possible because the U.S. Supreme Court views initiative campaigns differently than candidate contests. The Court recognizes that large contributions

---

[47] Schrag, *Paradise Lost*; and David Magleby and Kelly Patterson, "Consultants and Direct Democracy," *Political Science and Politics* 31(1998):160–62.

[48] Shaun Bowler, Todd Donovan, Max Neiman, and Johnny Peel, "Institutional Threat and Partisan Outcomes: Legislative Candidates' Attitudes toward Direct Democracy," *State Politics & Policy Quarterly* 1(2001):364–79.

[49] Smith, "Initiatives and Referendums."

[50] Magleby and Patterson, "Consultants and Direct Democracy."

[51] Schrag, *Paradise Lost*, p. 16.

[52] Todd Donovan, Shaun Bowler, and Dave McCuan, "Political Consultants and the Initiative Industrial Complex," in S. Bowler, T. Donovan, and C. Tolbert, eds., *Citizens as Legislators* (Columbus, OH: Ohio State University Press, 1998).

[53] Spending data reported by www.followthemoney.org.

to candidates may create either the appearance or the actuality that a candidate for office may become corrupted.[54] This ruling has allowed Congress and state legislatures some limited ability to regulate the size of contributions given to candidates. Contributions to initiative campaigns, in contrast, are seen as attempts at direct communication with voters rather than attempts to influence elected officials. In *Bellotti v. First National Bank of Boston*, the Court reasoned in 1978 that there was no possibility of corruption or appearance of corruption because a ballot measure cannot provide illicit political favors to a donor of a campaign. In its *Bellotti* decision, the Court reasoned that states thus have no compelling reason to limit the 1st Amendment right of donors contributing to initiative campaigns.[55] The 1978 decision was also the Court's first effort to explicitly extend free speech rights to corporations.[56] Put simply, no limits exist on what sources can be used, or the amount spent, in ballot initiative campaigns.

"Special Interests" and Initiative Campaigns

As noted, one common critique of direct democracy is that well-financed campaigns trick voters into passing policies that they actually do not prefer. The argument that "special" interests dominate the initiative process is a plausible one. After all, if it can take up to $1 million to simply ensure a proposal gets on the ballot, playing initiative politics obviously requires significant resources. Ordinary citizens are likely to lack such funds, but established, well-funded groups are not so disadvantaged. Powerful special interests, the argument goes, can afford to get any issues they want onto the ballot, and once the initiative is on the ballot, they buy enough spin doctors, campaign managers, and TV ads to get voters to vote for things they do not want or for things that harm the public interest.[57]

We can assess this argument by breaking it into two questions: first, do "special" economic interests dominate the initiative process (as opposed to broad-based, citizen concerns); and second, are voters readily swayed by expensive TV campaigns? One way to assess these questions is to ask whether narrowly focused economic interests (for example, banks, trade and industry groups, corporations, and professional associations) outspend other, broader-based kinds of citizens' groups. Another way is to ask whether these economic groups tend to win the initiative contests they finance.

Which Groups Dominate Direct Democracy? One major study of the role that interest groups play in the initiative process defines economic groups as those whose members and donors are almost exclusively business firms and professional organizations rather than individual citizens. Examples include the Missouri Forest Products Association, the California Beer and Wine Wholesalers, the Washington Software Association, and businesses such as casino operators and tobacco giant Philip Morris.[58] This study of eight states found that 68 percent of campaign contributions came from such narrowly based economic groups. It also found that ballot measures with more financial backing from economic interests were more likely to fail.[59] A similar study found that wealthy economic interests in California regularly outspent broadly based "citizen" groups, and 80 percent of campaign spending by these economic groups

---

[54] *Buckley v. Valeo* 424 U.S. 1 (1976).

[55] *First National Bank of Boston v. Bellotti* 435 U.S. 765 (1978); and Daniel A. Smith, "Campaign Financing of Ballot Initiatives in the American States," in Sabato, Larson, and Ernst, *Dangerous Democracy?*

[56] Tolbert, Lowenstein, and Donovan, "Election Law and Rules for Using Initiatives."

[57] For variants of this argument, David Broder, *Democracy Derailed*; Schrag, *Paradise Lost*; and Smith, *Tax Crusaders and the Politics of Direct Democracy.*

[58] Elisabeth Gerber, *The Populist Paradox: Interest Group Influence and the Promise of Direct Legislation* (Princeton, NJ: Princeton University Press, 1999), pp. 69–71.

[59] Gerber, *The Populist Paradox*, p. 110.

was directed against citizen group proposals that threatened business interests. However, when economic interest groups spend in favor of their own initiatives, they usually lose.[60]

In short, most of the big money in direct democracy comes from "special" interests defending themselves or, as with the case of the malpractice initiatives in Florida, fighting each other. A battle over a 1988 automobile insurance regulation in California provides an extreme example: Insurance companies and trial lawyers' groups spent over $82 million promoting four competing initiatives and spending heavily against a fifth proposal placed on the ballot by Ralph Nader's consumer group. Voters rejected all four well-financed initiatives but approved the fifth insurance measure (the one endorsed by consumer activist Nader).[61]

Record Expenditures In 2008, over half of the $800 million spent on ballot measures was associated with a handful of campaigns. As Table 4.2 shows, initiative campaigns in California, Colorado, and Ohio spent over $0.5 billion to convince voters to accept or reject measures on the ballot. The most expensive campaign was an effort to convince California voters to approve a package of measures that expanded gambling (and tax revenues from gambling) on tribal lands. As in other years, spending advantages were often associated with the success of a campaign. But this is not always the case. Well-funded opponents of a same-sex marriage ban were not able to prevail in California. The "payday loan" industry outspent opponents promoting regulations on the industry by nearly 40 to 1 in Ohio, yet were defeated. That industry also outspent

---

[60] Elisabeth Gerber, "Interest Group Influence in the California Initiative Process," Public Policy Institute of California Report, November 1998, http://www.ppic.org/content/pubs/R_1198EGR.pdf.

[61] Arthur Lupia, "Shortcuts versus Encyclopedias: Information and Voting Behavior in California Insurance Reform Elections," *American Political Science Review* 88(1994):63–76.

Table 4.2

Most Expensive Ballot Initiative Campaigns, 2008

State	Ballot No.	Subject	Side	Expenditure
CA	94, 95, 96, 97	Tribal gambling compacts	**Yes** No	**$108 million** $64 million
CA	8	Ban same-sex marriage	**Yes** No	**$42 million** $64 million
OH	6	Allow state's first casino	Yes **No**	$26 million **$39 million**
CA	7	Utilities buy 20% clean energy	Yes **No**	$9 million **$30 million**
CO	47, 49	Prohibit closed shop, no paycheck deductions (antiunion)	Yes **No**	$6 million **$31 million**
CA	93	Revise term limits	Yes **No**	$17 million **$9 million**
CA	98, 99	Eminent domain	Yes **No**	$7 million **$17 million***
CA	10	Bonds for alternative fuel vehicles	Yes **No**	$23 million **$0.2 million**
OH	5	Limit payday loan businesses	**Yes** No	**$0.5 million** $21 million
CO	58	Severance tax increase	Yes **No**	$6 million **$12 million**

Bold indicates winning side.
*Groups spent across multiple campaigns to defeat a proposal while advocating alternative measure that voters approved.

opponents by 14 to 1 in Arizona, where they were also defeated.

High levels of expenditure listed in Table 4.2 reflect the high costs of campaigning in populous states like California and Ohio. When the costs of campaigns and number of voters are considered, spending on ballot measures is much higher in other states. One Alaska campaign over adding new regulations to mining saw $61 spent per vote cast in 2008. The same year, over $12 was spent per vote cast on a South Dakota abortion measure. In each case, most of the spending was on the "no" side, and the measures were defeated.

Does Money Matter in Initiative Campaigns?

Money spent to defeat initiatives can be quite effective. Some research shows that a dollar spent by the "no" campaign has almost twice as much impact on the eventual vote share than a dollar spent by the "yes" side.[62] This may explain why narrow economic groups regularly defeat initiatives such as environmental or business regulations that enjoy substantial majority support in preelection polls, but they can have trouble advancing their own interests.[63] There is some evidence that measures supported by broad-based and grassroots citizens' groups pass at rates a bit higher than average, regardless of campaign spending.[64] But wealthy interests may avoid wasting their money when defeat is certain. When this is accounted for, money spent by both the "yes" and "no" sides appear to have similar effects on support for ballot measures.[65]

Although exceptions do exist, wealthy economic interests aren't usually successful at using initiatives to "buy" public policy that directly benefits them, in part because their proposals can mobilize opposition spending by other wealthy interests. This was the case with the 2008 Ohio casino initiative listed in Table 4.2. It generated massive opposition spending from the owners of a casino in a neighboring state who feared losing customers. Most initiatives that do pass can be seen as things, for better or worse, that tap into the preferences and concerns of the broader public, such as social and moral questions.[66] Many measures that pass, such as tougher criminal-sentencing laws, animal protection laws regulating hunting, or even somewhat peculiar measures—such as a 1998 California initiative that banned the slaughter of horses for human consumption and a 2002 Florida initiative that amended the state's constitution to prohibit the confinement of gestating pigs in crates—pass despite having relatively little campaign spending by the proponents.

Dumber than Chimps? Voting on Ballot Questions

A voter's ability to make reasonably informed choices on ballot measures depends on what sort of information is available. Few suggest that voters study the details of the laws they are voting on. Rather than using exhaustive research, they decide on the basis of information shortcuts that are easily available.[67] Information about who is in favor or against a proposal may be the primary shortcut many people use.[68] Partisanship is one of the most reliable predictors of voting on ballot measures.[69] If, for example, voters see a prominent Democrat support a proposition, then loyal Democratic voters are likely to support the proposition and Republicans oppose it.

Where do voters find these cues to help them make informed decisions on ballot questions?

---

[62] Banducci, "Direct Legislation."

[63] Magleby, *Direct Legislation*; and Bowler and Donovan, *Demanding Choices*.

[64] Gerber, *The Populist Paradox*, pp. 18–19; and Donovan, Bowler, McCuan, and Fernandez, "Contending Players and Strategies," 90.

[65] Thomas Stratmann, "Is Spending More Potent for or against a Proposition?" *American Journal of Political Science* 50(2006):788–801.

[66] Bowler and Donovan, *Demanding Choices*.

[67] Arthur Lupia, "Dumber than Chimps? An Assessment of Direct Democracy Voters," in Sabato, Larson, and Ernst, *Dangerous Democracy?*

[68] Arthur Lupia and Matthew McCubbins, *The Democratic Dilemma: Can Citizens Learn What They Need to Know?* (New York: Cambridge University Press, 1998); Lupia, "Shortcuts versus Encyclopedias"; and Bowler and Donovan, *Demanding Choices*.

[69] Regina Branton, "Examining Individual-Level Voting Behavior on State Ballot Propositions," *Political Research Quarterly* 56(2003):367–77. Smith and Tolbert, "The Initiative to Party."

In many states, an official state agency mails every registered voter a pamphlet that lists each ballot proposal and includes arguments for and against the proposition. Other sources include media coverage and paid ads. The availability of information shortcuts may explain why so few examples of initiatives pass that are later found to be unpopular with the voters who approved them.

The Role of the Media in Initiative Campaigns

A survey of voters found that just 20 percent claimed to make use of TV ads. A follow-up question found that only 13 percent of this group thought the information in the ads was "very important" in affecting their decisions. In contrast, 85 percent of consultants saw TV and radio as "very important" information for voters. Consultants see TV and radio ads as the most influential, whereas voters themselves see ads as one of the least important sources of information. Similarly, consultants afford the advertising mailers produced by the campaigns a much larger degree of importance than do voters.

These differences between what voters say they use when deciding on ballot measures and what consultants think they use may come as little surprise. Most people probably have little wish to claim being dupes of advertising, whereas consultants believe in their own importance. Thus, if these responses contain bias, it is probably for voters to underestimate the effects of ads and for consultants to overestimate their effects. However disparate and inconsistent the results, they could be accurate: It may be that a relatively small group responds to information in TV ads, but these might be the voters who consultants are trying to reach with their ads.

Despite these differences in perceptions of information sources, some similarities emerge. Both consultants and voters, for example, recognize the importance of the news media. Voters see news media as more important than advertisements, and the consultants' evaluations of the importance of news are similarly high.

Consultants and voters also have similar perceptions of the state-provided voter's guide in terms of importance. The voter's guide is seen by voters and consultants as an especially important piece of campaign information provided to voters. This is consistent with our idea that it provides a convenient and easy source of endorsements.

TV ads may actually provide useful cues to voters. One study of initiative campaign TV ads from several states found the ads often provide cues, such as names of sponsors or opponents, as well as name prominent groups, newspapers, and politicians who have taken positions on the measure. High levels of spending on initiative TV ads probably increase public awareness of initiatives[70] and may increase public attention to campaign issues. This may explain higher levels of general knowledge about politics in states with prominent initiative campaigns.[71] Relatedly, another study found voters more likely to have heard about initiatives when more was spent on the campaigns and that more citizens voted on initiatives that had higher campaign spending.[72]

Direct Democracy and Electoral Politics

Initiative and referendum campaigns can alter a state's political context. Several examples of ballot measures affect the agenda and tone of candidate elections.[73] In 1998, for example, Republican Party operatives in Colorado tried

---

[70] Bowler and Donovan, "Do Voters Have a Cue?"; Stephen P. Nicholson, "The Political Environment and Ballot Proposition Awareness," *American Journal of Political Science* 47(2003):403–10.

[71] Mark Smith, "Ballot Initiatives and the Democratic Citizen," *Journal of Politics* 64(2002):892–903.

[72] Bowler and Donovan, *Demanding Choices.*

[73] Nicholson, *Voting the Agenda;* Donovan, Tolbert, and Smith, "Priming Presidential Votes by Direct Democracy"; Sunshine Hillygus and Todd Shields, "Moral Issues and Voter Decision Making in the 2004 Presidential Election," *Political Science and Politics* 38 (2005): 201–10; Burden, "An Alternative Account of the 2004 Presidential Election."

YOU DECIDE

DOES DIRECT DEMOCRACY DECEIVE VOTERS?

Because voters may not know much about the subjects of ballot initiatives and may not have partisan cues when voting, there may be room for campaign ads to determine which initiatives voters approve. It is unclear, however, how much effect paid ads have on voter choices. Most people believe that initiative campaign ads are attempts to mislead.[1] Despite the expenditure of tremendous sums of money, voters claim to discount the usefulness of political ads. One survey found people had multiple sources of information to consider when deciding on initiatives, and most reported that they didn't rely much on information from paid ads. Most voters claimed that neutral information provided by the state, and information from the news media, was most important to them when figuring out how to vote on initiatives. When campaign consultants who worked on initiative campaigns were asked about the information voters relied on, they had a different sense of which information was most important.[2] Table 4.3 displays results from surveys of voters and campaign consultants.

What do you think? Are voters able to vote their preferences when it comes to ballot measures? Is the text of a ballot measure too difficult to decipher for the average voter? Do you think voters can draw on shortcuts—cues from trusted or notorious interest groups, political parties, or political elites—to help inform themselves of their vote choice? Or are all voters susceptible to slick 30-second campaign ads and catchy sound bites? Looking at the data in Table 4.3, why do you think there is such a discrepancy between consultants and voters when it comes to which informational sources they say are the most important in ballot initiative campaigns?

Table 4.3

Importance of Sources of Information[a] for Ballot Initiative Campaigns

	Consultant's Views			Voter's Views		
	Very Important (%)	Important (%)	Not Important (%)	Very Important (%)	Important (%)	Not Important (%)
TV and radio ads	83	17	0	13	60	26
TV and radio news	72	28	0	34	56	10
Ballot pamphlet	64	31	5	69	30	1
Newspapers	41	59	0	50	47	3
Flyers and/or mailers	39	54	7	9	72	18
Word of mouth	35	37	28	34	53	13

[a]Values are the percentage responding that a source of information is very important, important, or not important at all.

Source: Shaun Bowler and Todd Donovan, "Do Voters Have a Cue? TV Ads as a Source of Information in Referendum Voting," *European Journal of Political Research* 41(2002):777–93.

Notes

1 Bowler, Donovan, Neiman, and Peel, "Institutional Threat and Partisan Outcomes," 370.
2 Shaun Bowler and Todd Donovan, "Do Voters Have a Cue? TV Ads as a Source of Information in Referendum Voting," *European Journal of Political Research* 41(2002): 777–93.

to link Democratic candidates to positions on state ballot initiatives that Republicans expected voters to find unpopular. Democrats did the same and ran campaign ads linking the Republican gubernatorial candidate to two antiabortion measures. The Republican had been trying to distance himself from the social conservative.[74] During their 2004 Florida campaign, the rival U.S. Senate candidates attempted to craft their campaign themes to fit with initiatives on the state's ballot. Republican nominee Mel Martinez, for example, worked several ballot issues into his standard campaign speech and at candidate debates.[75] In California, numerous candidates for governor, including Arnold Schwarzenegger, have sponsored initiatives to promote their candidacies.

Political party organizations also use initiatives to promote **wedge issues**—measures they hope will divide the opposing party's candidates and weaken the opposition's base of support. Two major examples of wedge issues from the past decade are affirmative action and immigration initiatives. In 1996, Republicans promoted a California initiative to restrict affirmative action and another measure restricting services to illegal immigrants, hoping that Democrats across the nation would be forced to adopt policy positions that would harm their chances for reelection. Republican governor Pete Wilson of California, as well as Democratic candidate John Van de Kamp, raised money to put several policy questions on the ballot when they sought office.[76]

Anecdotes and academic studies also suggest that different ballot measures can mobilize different elements of the electorate at different times.[77] A classic example is the 1982 California gubernatorial election. The Democratic mayor of Los Angeles, Tom Bradley, led narrowly in polls conducted immediately prior to the November vote, but Bradley ended up losing to Republican George Deukmejian. In this case, polls may have had difficulty estimating how an initiative would shape the participating electorate. The same ballot included a highly contested gun control measure, Proposition 15, which the National Rife Association (NRA) opposed. The NRA spent over $5 million against the measure and rallied pro-gun voters to the polls.[78] Deukmejian probably benefited from these voters being drawn to the polls.

Spillover Effects of Ballot Measures in Candidate Races

Direct democracy's effect on candidate races may be indirect. One prominent study found that various state and local ballot measures advocating a freeze on the development of nuclear weapons in 1982 affected how voters evaluated candidates in U.S. Senate elections, in some U.S. House races, and even in some gubernatorial contests. In places where voters were presented the nuclear freeze question, they were more likely to evaluate candidates in terms of the nuclear proliferation measure. There were similar effects with California's Proposition 187 in 1994, which restricted social services to illegal immigrants, and Proposition 209 in 1996, which ended affirmative action in the state. Both ballot questions shaped the issues voters used to evaluate candidates.[79]

One need only to point to the 2004 presidential election to understand the potential ramifications of ballot measures on candidate elections. Assessing George W. Bush's narrow victory in Ohio, which tipped the electoral college balance in his favor, journalists and political analysts were quick to credit the mobilizing effects of Issue 1, a statewide antigay marriage measure on the ballot that year.

---

[74] Smith and Tolbert, *Educated by Initiative.*

[75] Smith, "Initiatives and Referendums."

[76] Smith and Tolbert, "The Initiative to Party."

[77] Caroline J. Tolbert, John Grummel, and Daniel A. Smith, "The Effect of Ballot Initiatives on Voter Turnout in the American States," *American Politics Research* 29(2001):625–48.

[78] John Allswang, *The Initiative and Referendum in California, 1898–1998* (Stanford, CA: Stanford University Press, 2000), pp. 125–26.

[79] Nicholson, *Voting the Agenda*, pp. 111, 124.

The New York Times speculated that "state constitutional amendments banning same-sex marriage increased the turnout of socially conservative voters in many of the 11 states where the measures appeared on the ballot," with the measures appearing "to have acted like magnets for thousands of socially conservative voters in rural and suburban communities who might not otherwise have voted."[80] Although scholars have questioned the actual turnout effects of the statewide same-sex marriage ballot measures, the margin in Ohio was so close that if the initiative had even a minor effect on turning out pro-Bush voters, it may have been decisive.[81]

Direct Democracy and Turnout in Elections

As the 2004 Ohio example suggests, statewide ballot initiatives may affect politics by bringing voters to the polls. In 1978, more Californians cast votes for a critical antitax measure (**Proposition 13**) than cast votes for the governor's race on the same ballot. Studies of voting prior to the 1990s concluded that ballot measures did not affect voter turnout. Political scientist David Magleby concluded in 1984 that "turnout is not increased by direct legislation," although occasionally, a highly salient measure, such as California's Proposition 13 in 1978, "might encourage" higher turnout.[82]

Recent studies of initiative use, however, have produced evidence that initiatives can increase turnout by nearly 2 percent per initiative in midterm elections and nearly 1 percent

in presidential elections, all else being equal.[83] Initiatives receiving substantial media attention have the greatest effect on turnout, particularly in "off-year" (non–presidential election year) state elections.[84] In municipal races, evidence has shown that at the local level, cities that use the initiative process have higher voter turnout than cities that don't allow their citizens to place measures directly on the ballot.[85]

Interest Groups, Initiatives, and Elections

Interest groups may use direct democracy to force the hands of legislative candidates running for office by placing measures on ballots to force them to take a position on their issues. Interest groups also use ballot initiatives to exploit wedge issues, drain campaign resources from potential opponents, and mobilize their voters.[86] California's anti–affirmative action measure, Proposition 209, was placed on the ballot by conservative groups who hoped that if the measure generated support from white Democratic voters, they might also consider breaking away from Democratic candidates who were opposed to the measure.

Pro-business interest groups, including Americans for Tax Reform, promoted "paycheck protection" ballot measures in Oregon and California to require individual union members to give their leaders prior approval for dues to be used for political purposes. A leader of Americans for Tax Reform envisioned that the issue would force organized labor to spend millions of dollars in campaign funds on efforts to defeat the measures—money that unions would not be able to contribute

[80] Jame Dao, "Flush with Victory, Grass-Roots Crusader against Same-Sex Marriage Thinks Big," *The New York Times*, 26 November 2004, p. A28.
[81] Sunshine Hillygus and Todd Shields, "Moral Issues and Voter Decision Making in the 2004 Presidential Election," *Political Science and Politics* 38(2005):201–10; Smith, DeSantis, and Kassel, "Same-Sex Marriage Ballot Measures"; Burden, "An Alternative Account of the 2004 Presidential Election"; and Abramowitz, "Terrorism, Gay Marriage, and Incumbency."
[82] Magleby, *Direct Legislation*, p. 197.

[83] Tolbert, Grummel, and Smith, "The Effect of Ballot Initiatives on Voter Turnout in the American States."
[84] Mark Smith, "The Contingent Effects of Ballot Initiatives and Candidate Races on Turnout," *American Journal of Political Science* 45(2001):700–06.
[85] Zoltan Hajnal and Paul Lewis, "Municipal Institutions and Voter Turnout in Local Elections," *Urban Affairs Review* 35(2003):645–68.
[86] Smith and Tolbert, "The Initiative to Party."

to Democratic candidates. They turned out to be right—unions spent some $24 million to narrowly defeat the measure in California.[87]

Groups also use initiatives to pass policies that they cannot get through the legislature. Large membership interests, such as teachers' unions, have been successful in promoting initiatives designed to benefit their members. The California Teachers' Association, for example, sponsored the successful Proposition 98 in 1988, mandating that a fixed percentage of state general fund revenues support K–12 education. More recently, Washington's teachers' union also promoted two successful initiatives: Initiative 728 mandated smaller class sizes, and Initiative 732 mandated pay raises for the state's public school teachers. Interest groups also use ballot initiatives to send signals to legislators, or to force legislators to come up with an alternative.

Some research suggests that the initiative process may actually stimulate greater interest group activity, increasing the number of broad-based interest groups in a state. Interest groups in initiative states tend to have more members than those in noninitiative states, because the process provides potential groups with yet another incentive to become mobilized and engaged in the political process. States with the initiative, studies have found, have more registered citizens and nonprofit groups than those states without the process.[88]

The Effects of Direct Democracy on Citizens

Some propose that frequent voting on ballot measures may make people feel more as if they "have a say" in politics.[89] Evidence of this is mixed. Some studies show that people in states with initiatives are more likely than people in noninitiative states to think government is responsive,[90] and that initiative use corresponds with people believing they can make a difference in politics.[91] It is difficult to determine if this is due to something else about states that use initiatives, and scholars have been unable to replicate results linking initiative use to opinions about government responsiveness.[92] Others have found that people have higher levels of factual knowledge about politics in places where initiatives are used more frequently, perhaps because initiatives stimulate media attention.[93] Others have linked the use of direct democracy to happiness, at least in Switzerland.[94] Another found that people in initiative states are more likely to engage in political discussion, have greater political knowledge, and contribute to interest groups.[95] None of this means that initiatives make people more likely to trust government. Initiatives, many with antigovernment themes, may create an environment that encourages people to distrust government.[96]

---

[87] Smith and Tolbert, *Educated by Initiative*.

[88] Frederick Boehmke, "The Effect of Direct Democracy on the Size and Diversity of State Interest Group Populations," *Journal of Politics* 64(2002):827–44.

[89] Shaun Bowler and Todd Donovan, "Democracy, Institutions, and Attitudes about Citizen Influence on Government," *British Journal of Political Science* 32(2002):371–90.

[90] Bowler and Donovan, "Democracy, Institutions and Attitudes"; Smith and Tolbert, *Educated by Initiative*.

[91] Bowler and Donovan, "Democracy, Institutions and Attitudes."

[92] Joshua Dyck and Edward Lascher, Jr., "Direct Democracy and Political Efficacy Reconsidered," *Political Behavior* (2009).

[93] Mark Smith, "Ballot Initiatives and the Democratic Citizen"; Matthias Benz and Alois Stutzer, "Are Voters Better Informed When They Have a Larger Say in Politics?" *Public Choice* 119(2004):31–59.

[94] Bruno Frey and Alois Stutzer, "Happiness, Economy and Institutions," *The Economic Journal* 110(2000):918–38.

[95] Caroline J. Tolbert, Ramona McNeal, and Daniel A. Smith, "Enhancing Civic Engagement: The Effect of Direct Democracy on Political Participation and Knowledge," *State Politics and Policy Quarterly* 3(2003):23–41.

[96] Joshua Dyck, "Initiated Distrust: Direct Democracy and Trust in Government," *American Politics Research* 34(2009):539–68.

Direct Democracy and Minorities

As noted, one of the original concerns about direct democracy is the potential it has to allow a majority of voters to trample the rights of minorities. Many still worry that the process can be used to harm gays and lesbians as well as ethnic, linguistic, and religious minorities.[97] Those who worry about repressive majorities point to a series of antiminority measures approved by voters. A majority of voters have supported initiatives repealing affirmative action protections in California, Michigan, Washington, and Nebraska, but in 2008, voters in Colorado bucked the trend, and narrowly defeated an anti–affirmative action ballot initiative. The battle over illegal immigration has been a perennial issue on the ballot in Arizona. Voters have approved propositions repealing bilingual education in Arizona, California, and Massachusetts (though Coloradoans rejected such an initiative in 2002). Initiatives declaring English an "official language" have been approved in numerous states.[98] Scores of measures dealing with gay rights and gay marriage have appeared on state and local ballots,[99] and many cities have held referendums on whether to abolish low-income housing.[100] This presents a critical question: Does direct democracy harm minorities?

Recent scholarly research shows that the initiative process "is sometimes prone to produce laws that disadvantage relatively powerless minorities—and probably is more likely than legislatures to do so."[101] State and local ballot initiatives have been used to undo policies—such as school desegregation, protections against job and housing discrimination, and affirmative action—that minorities have secured from legislatures where they are included in the bargaining process. But most initiatives probably do not produce divisions between majorities of white voters and minority voters. Studies of support for ballot initiatives across different groups of voters show that minority voters were no more likely to support the losing side in an initiative contest than white voters. This may reflect that most initiatives do not pit the interests of racial and ethnic minorities against those of the majority or perhaps that minorities and whites have similar issues and concerns addressed by the initiative process. It is important to note, however, that on issues dealing with racial and ethnic matters, studies show that racial and ethnic minorities do end up more on the losing side of the popular vote.[102]

The issue of gay rights has been one of the more contentious areas of initiative politics where minority interests are frequently put to a vote. Majorities have, in some cases, voted to restrict the extension of some civil rights to gays and lesbians. Until recently, with the rash of anti same-sex marriage amendments on statewide ballots, voters in a number of states

---

[97] See, for example, Lydia Chavez, *The Color Bind: California's Battle to End Affirmative Action* (Berkeley: University of California Press, 1998); Barbara Gamble, "Putting Civil Rights to a Popular Vote," *American Journal of Political Science* 41(1998):245–69; Rodney Hero and Caroline Tolbert, "A Racial/Ethnic Diversity Interpretation of Politics and Policy in the States of the U.S.," *American Journal of Political Science* 40(1996):851–71; and Donald P. Haider-Markel, Alana Querze, and Kara Lindaman, "'Win, Lose or Draw?' A Reexamination of Direct Democracy and Minority Rights," *Political Research Quarterly* 60(2007):304–14. Conversely, see Bruno Frey and L. Goette, "Does the Popular Vote Destroy Civil Rights?" *American Journal of Political Science* 41(1998):245–69.

[98] Jack Citrin, Beth Reingold, Evelyn Walters, and Donald Green, "The 'Official English' Movement and the Symbolic Politics of Language in the United States," *Western Political Quarterly* 43(1990):535–60.

[99] Donald Haider-Markel, "AIDS and Gay Civil Rights: Politics and Policy at the Ballot Box," *American Review of Politics* 20(1999):349–75; and Todd Donovan, James Wenzel, and Shaun Bowler, "Direct Democracy Initiatives after *Romer*," in Craig Zimmerman, Ken Wald, and Clyde Wilcox, eds., *The Politics of Gay Rights* (Chicago: University of Chicago Press, 2000).

[100] Roger Caves, *Land Use Planning: The Ballot Box Revolution* (Newbury Park, CA: Sage, 1992).

[101] Cain and Miller, "The Populist Legacy," in Sabato, Larson, and Ernst, *Dangerous Democracy?* p. 52.

[102] Zoltan Hajnal, Elisabeth Gerber, and H. Louch, "Minorities and Direct Legislation: Evidence from California Ballot Proposition Elections," *Journal of Politics* 64(2002):154–77.

COMPARISONS HELP US UNDERSTAND

DEMOCRACY AND MINORITIES

Are minorities better off when policies are decided by representative democracy or directly by voters? History shows that both can produce antiminority outcomes. State legislators have approved laws allowing slavery, racial segregation, laws excluding Chinese from owning land, the internment of Japanese in concentration camps during World War II, and laws advanced by the Ku Klux Klan designed to strip Catholics of their rights. None of these discriminatory laws needed direct democracy to flourish. But representative democracy, with its opportunities for minority representatives to participate while laws are being crafted, may have a better record of advancing civil rights.

In recent years, voters and legislators have been making decisions about the nature of rights that are extended to gays and lesbians. A recent study compared minority rights decisions produced by representative democracy to those produced by direct democracy.[1] It found that most civil rights bills affecting gays and lesbians in state legislatures were "pro-gay" (for example, banning job discrimination) and that slightly more progay than antigay bills (for example, rules against being a foster parent) were approved by state legislators. With direct democracy, most civil rights proposals were antigay, and antigay measures were more likely to pass. Overall, representative democracy produced progay outcomes 44 percent of the time, compared to 39 percent for direct democracy. The difference between outcomes across these institutions is subtle, because most pro- or anti–minority rights proposals failed. But the authors note that minority rights suffer more under direct democracy, especially when the policy is antiminority in intent.

Note

1. Donald P. Haider-Markel, Alana Querze, and Kara Lindaman, "Win, Lose or Draw? A Reexamination of Direct Democracy and Minority Rights," *Political Research Quarterly* 60(2007):304–14.

AP Photo/Gary Kazanjian

52 percent of California voters approved Proposition 8 in 2008 to reverse the state's Supreme Court ruling that had legalized same-sex marriage. In 2009, voters in Maine repealed legislation legalizing same-sex marriage, while voters in Washington state approved their legislature's "everything but marriage" domestic partnership law.

had refused to pass most measures that would deny gays and lesbians protections against discrimination. A 1992 antigay measure in Colorado, Amendment 2, which changed the state constitution to expressly prohibit local laws aimed at protecting gays and lesbians against discrimination, was a major exception.[103] The Colorado measure was eventually overturned by the U.S. Supreme Court in 1996 for being an unconstitutional denial of equal protection before the law.[104] Voters, however, have been much less tolerant of granting equal rights to marriage. By 2010, citizens in at least 27 states had voted to ban same-sex marriage. About half of these proposals reached the ballot via the initiative process, but most were referred to voters by state legislatures.

The record of direct democracy for minority interests is a mixed bag then. Racial and ethnic minorities may agree with majority voters on most ballot measures, but there have been some critical initiatives where minority rights have been lost when put to a public vote. Yet, in nearly every instance where the initiative process has been used to limit minority rights to fair housing, desegregated schools, public services, and protections against discrimination, courts have stepped in to overturn initiatives and uphold minority rights.[105] But regardless of whether antiminority ballot measures pass or fail, they may still have effects on people they target. By targeting a minority group with an initiative, for example, public attitudes about the group (or about policies that benefit the group) can be changed, with mass opinion becoming less tolerant of the targeted minority group.[106]

The Effects of Direct Democracy on Public Policy

By this point, it should be clear that there are many reasons to expect that direct democracy can make a state's political environment and its public policies different than if there were no initiative process. When voters are allowed to make direct choices on policies, they sometimes make decisions that their elected representatives would not. An obvious example of this is term limits. Voters in many states have placed limits on time their representatives may serve. Absent the initiative process, elected representatives rarely, if ever, adopt such a policy.[107] But besides term limits and some forms of campaign finance reform, states that use the initiative are no more likely than states without the process to adopt other ethics and lobbying reform measures.[108] It is unclear, then, whether direct democracy systematically makes policy more representative of what people want or if it leads to "better" public policy.

Some scholars and practitioners have proposed that the mere presence of the initiative process can affect public policy by changing how legislators behave. If legislators anticipate that there is a threat that someone might pass a law by initiative, then legislators may have greater incentives to pass some version of the law so they can maintain influence over what the final law looks like.[109] Initiatives can also send signals about the sort of policies the public

---

[103] Donovan, Wenzel, and Bowler, "Direct Democracy Initiatives after Romer."

[104] *Romer v. Evans* 517 U.S. 620 (1996).

[105] Kenneth Miller, "Constraining Populism: The Real Challenge of Initiative Reform," *Santa Clara Law Review* 41(2001):1037–84; and Bowler and Donovan, *Demanding Choices.*

[106] Donovan, Wenzel, and Bowler, "Direct Democracy and Minorities."

[107] The exception is Louisiana. Caroline Tolbert, "Changing Rules for State Legislatures: Direct Democracy and Governance Policies," in Bowler, Donovan, and Tolbert, eds., *Citizens as Legislators*; and Bowler and Donovan, "Measuring the Effect of Direct Democracy on State Policy."

[108] Daniel A. Smith, "Direct Democracy and Election and Ethics Laws," in Bruce Cain, Todd Donovan, and Caroline Tolbert, eds., *Democracy in the States: Experiments in Elections Reform* (Washington, DC: Brookings, 2008).

[109] Gerber, *The Populist Paradox.*

wants.[110] Several studies show that certain public policies—including abortion regulations, death penalty laws, some civil rights policies, and spending on some state programs—more closely match public opinion in states with initiatives than in states without initiatives.[111] As an example, states with liberal public opinion and initiatives may have relatively liberal abortion rules, whereas states with conservative opinions and initiatives may have conservative policies. Absent the initiative, policies may be less likely to reflect the state's opinion climate. Studies that examine a wide range of state policies, however, find no such effects; some initiatives may make policy more reflective of public opinion with some policies but not others.[112]

The biggest effects of direct democracy on policy may be in the realm of what Caroline Tolbert calls "governance policy"—policies that set the rules about how government can function. Voters in initiative states can, and do, pass measures that amend rules that structure the political system itself. These include initiatives that may run counter to the interests of elected officials. States with the initiative process are more likely to have adopted term limits and tougher rules for adopting new taxes and increasing spending[113] and were quicker to adopt some campaign finance regulations.[114] Examples of tax limitation measures include California's Proposition 13 of 1978, Oregon's Measure 5 in 1990, and Colorado's Taxpayers Bill of Rights (TABOR) amendment of 1992. If given a chance via direct democracy, voters often place constraints on what their representatives can do, especially when it comes to fiscal matters.

Long-Term Effects of Direct Democracy

Direct democracy can alter state policy directly by providing an additional point of access for citizens and interest groups. Advocates of decriminalization of drugs, campaign finance reforms, physician-assisted suicide, and many other policies have successfully used direct democracy to do an "end run" around state legislatures that did not turn their ideas into policy. As noted, some suggest this threat of the "gun behind the door" makes state policy more representative of state opinion. But what are the major long-term consequences of direct democracy on state policy?

In addition to promoting specific policy ideas, the initiative process allows those outside of the legislature, and those outside of the traditional corridors of power, the ability to permanently change rules that define institutions of government. As examples, initiatives have been used to rewrite state rules about how judges sentence criminals, how much a state may collect via existing taxes, and how much the legislature may spend in a given year. Initiatives have been used to change rules about future tax increases and have placed limits on how often legislators may run for reelection. As we note in Chapter 10, these tax and expenditure limits (TELs) adopted by direct democracy

---

[110] Thomas Romer and Howard Rosenthal, "Bureaucrats versus Voters: On the Political Economy of Resource Allocation by Direct Democracy," *Quarterly Journal of Economics* 93(1979):563–87.

[111] Kevin Arceneaux, "Direct Democracy and the Link between Public Opinion and State Abortion Policy," *State Politics and Policy Quarterly* 2(2002):372–87; Elisabeth Gerber, "Legislative Response to the Threat of Popular Initiatives," *American Journal of Political Science* 40(1996):99–128; Gerber, *The Populist Paradox*; Matsusaka, *For the Many or the Few*; and Bowler and Donovan, "Measuring the Effect of Direct Democracy on State Policy."

[112] Michael Hagen, Edward Lascher, and John Camobreco, "Response to Matsusaka: Estimating the Effect of Ballot Initiatives on Policy Responsiveness," *Journal of Politics* 63(2001):1257–63; and John Camobreco, "Preferences, Fiscal Policies, and the Initiative Process," *Journal of Politics* 60(1998):819–29.

[113] Tolbert, "Changing Rules for State Legislatures."

[114] John Pippen, Shaun Bowler, and Todd Donovan, "Election Reform and Direct Democracy: The Case of Campaign Finance Regulations in the American States," *American Politics Research* 30(2002):559–82.

may have important long-run effects on state and local finances.

The long-term effect of policy passed by direct democracy is probably more consequential in states that allow constitutional initiatives. When initiatives constraining taxing and spending are embedded in a state's constitution, it is difficult for elected officials to amend budgeting rules. This complicates their budgeting tasks. This means that voters can place things in their constitution that limit property taxes, increase tobacco taxes, guarantee a certain share of general funds for education, or authorize teacher pay raises and smaller class sizes. Even statutory initiatives can complicate the task of crafting long-term budgets. A single ballot may present voters with choices about cutting some taxes, raising others, issuing bonds for specific projects, and increasing spending on specific programs. When legislatures pass their budgets, their choices about increasing spending or cutting taxes need not be linked to specific revenue sources and programs. Voters, deciding on individual initiatives, face no such constraints.

Despite all of this, there are reasons to expect that the long-range effects of direct democracy are not that dramatic. Once an initiative is approved by voters, proponents often do not have the resources or political clout to maintain pressure on legislators over time to ensure that their law is implemented as the proponents would like. Elected officials can eventually rewrite rules, amend what voters approved (in most states), or stall implementation. The end result may be that "the policy impact of most initiatives reflects a compromise between what electoral majorities and government actors want."[115] This means that governing is quite different in initiative states, yet direct democracy has not replaced the role of the legislature.

Majority Tyranny and Judicial Review

The potential effects of initiatives on policy are further muted when we consider judicial review.[116] Initiatives, like any other law, must be consistent with the U.S. Constitution and state constitutions and must abide by a state's regulations on the initiative process, such as subject matter constraints. State and federal courts tend to treat initiative laws just like laws passed by legislatures, regardless of how popular they may have been with voters. Courts have been very willing to strike down voter-approved initiatives.[117] One study of several states found that most state initiatives ended up being challenged in court, with 40 percent overturned in whole or in part.[118] People challenging voter-approved initiatives in court may increase their odds of success because they are able to "venue shop": They can file cases in different districts of either state or federal courts in order to find judges most likely to grant them a favorable ruling.

Assessments of Direct Democracy

When some of the most careful observers of American politics turn their attention to the process of direct democracy, their assessments of it are rather negative. Alan Rosenthal, a preeminent scholar of state legislatures, suggests that growing enthusiasm for direct democracy—in the form of growing use of opinion polls that influence representatives as well as use of initiative and referendum—has a corrosive effect on representative government. Rosenthal suggests that a demise of representative government

---

[115] Elisabeth Gerber, Arthur Lupia, Mathew McCubbins, and Roderick Kiewiet, *Stealing the Initiative* (Upper Saddle River, NJ: Prentice Hall, 2001), p. 110.

[116] Todd Donovan, "Direct Democracy as Super Precedent?" *Political Constraints of Citizen-Initiated Laws* 43(2007):191–234.

[117] Kenneth Miller, *Direct Democracy and the Courts* (Cambridge, MA: Cambridge University Press, 2009).

[118] Miller, "Constraining Populism."

has occurred in American states over recent decades, leaving legislators with less responsibility for government and leaving states more difficult to govern.[119] Some blame direct democracy for shattering the fiscal health of some states, then leaving elected officials to pick up the pieces. Initiatives are also blamed for promoting confrontational (and unconstitutional) policies that target minority groups, such as immigrants and gays and lesbians.

David Broder, an insightful U.S. journalist, echoes this sentiment. Broder spent weeks on the West Coast observing the initiative campaigns being waged in California in 1998. The nearly $200 million spent in California initiative campaigns was nearly as much as taxpayers spent on the public financing of the national presidential campaigns that year. Broder's experience in California led him to conclude that wealthy special interests and political parties were driving the process, spending millions to place their measures on ballots and then spending heavily on deceptive advertising to convince voters to approve their schemes.[120]

Public Approval of Direct Democracy

As Figure 4.4 reveals, the public remains quite supportive of the initiative process in

---

Figure 4.4

Public Opinion about Direct Democracy in California and Washington

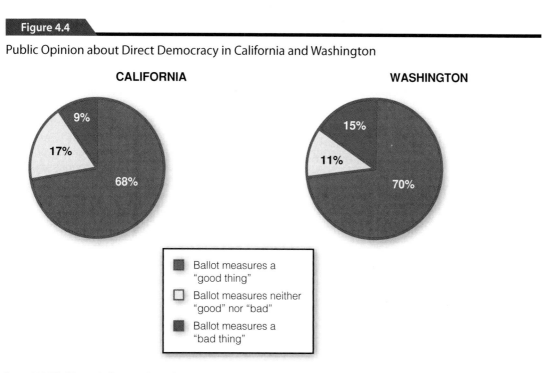

Source: 2009 Washington Poll, 2004 Field/California Poll.

---

[119] Alan Rosenthal, *The Decline of Representative Government* (Washington, DC: CQ Press, 1998).

[120] Broder, *Democracy Derailed*; also see Schrag, *Paradise Lost*.

Figure 4.5

Support for a National Referendum Process

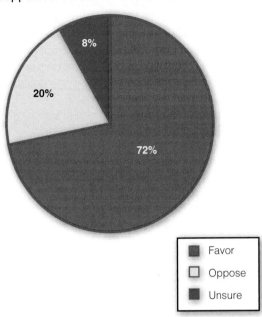

8%

20%

72%

■ Favor

□ Oppose

■ Unsure

Source: Shaun Bowler and Todd Donovan, "Reasoning about Institutional Change: Winners, Losers and Support for Electoral Reform," *British Journal of Political Science* 37(2007):455–76.

states where it is used rather frequently. The public looks at direct democracy quite differently, and more positively, than many political observers and elected officials. Even voters who have experienced California's high-stakes, high-cost ballot initiatives remain generally supportive of the process. As Figure 4.5 shows, Americans give widespread support to expanding direct democracy nationally. Over 70 percent of Americans surveyed said they favored having a national vote on important matters of policy.[121]

Surveys of elected officials find much less enthusiasm about direct democracy. For their part, legislators in direct democracy states would like to change things so that they have

more say over what ends up going to a public vote and also have more ability to amend laws after voters approve them. Voters in these states, for their part, are unwilling to let their representatives have such discretion.[122] Recent proposals for expanding initiative use to additional states appear sensitive to critics of California's process and are less sweeping than the early 20th-century models. An initiative plan considered by the New Jersey legislature in 2002, for example, would limit subject matter and only permit petitions for statutory measures that would first be evaluated by the legislature.[123] In 2006, the Minnesota and Alabama state legislatures each considered bills to create a scaled-down version of the initiative, and the governor of Rhode Island asked voters in a November advisory referendum whether they would like to have the initiative process.

The Case For and Against Direct Democracy

To its defenders, direct democracy was seen as a tool that would empower the "grassroots" and weaken the influence that special interests had over elected representatives. Direct democracy could "level the playing field" by giving more political value to individual voters, as opposed to those who finance political campaigns. Proponents of direct democracy also argued that the process can build better citizens. Participating in meaningful policy choice may lead citizens to seek out more information. Voting directly on policy might also encourage citizens to have more interest in politics and feel more engaged with their government.[124]

---

[121] Shaun Bowler and Todd Donovan, "Reasoning about Institutional Change: Winners, Losers and Support for Electoral Reform," *British Journal of Political Science* 37(2007):455–476.

[122] Bowler, Donovan, Neiman, and Peel, "Institutional Threat and Partisan Outcomes."
[123] Craig Holman, "An Assessment of New Jersey's Proposed Limited Initiative Process," Brennan Center for Justice at New York University School of Law, 2002, http://www.iandrinstitute.org/New%20IRI%20Website%20Info/I&R%20Research%20and%20History/I&R%20Studies/Holman%20-%20Review%20of%20Proposed%20NJ%20Initiative%20Process%20IRI.pdf.
[124] For a summary of these arguments, see Smith and Tolbert, *Educated by Initiative.*

From the start, critics of direct democracy raised several objections to the process. It may be difficult, they claimed, for the average voter to understand the nuances of difficult public policy questions, as many people simply pay no attention to politics. Elected officials have time to deliberate about issues and reach compromises that might accommodate rival positions. Initiative proposals, in contrast, can be framed by a proponent as an all-or-nothing choice, which is then decided upon by a relatively ill-informed electorate. A more enduring critique focuses on the potential for tyranny of the majority. American representative government involves many checks and balances and veto points. Direct democracy, in contrast, allows voters to pass laws hostile to minority interests or pass laws repealing hard-fought victories that minorities achieved via representative government.[125] A modern criticism of the process is that it now costs $1 million or more to qualify measures for the ballot in a large state—leaving the process well beyond the reach of average citizens. Peter Schrag, an astute and longtime observer of politics in the Golden State, described in his scathing book on direct democracy how the initiative process encourages the "embracing and demagoguing [of] hot-button issues" by candidates who hope to "showcase" their credentials.[126]

The Future of American Direct Democracy

As noted, many critics describe state and local direct democracy as a kind of "faux populism."[127] Instead of making politics more representative or more responsible, modern direct democracy may no longer have room for regular, grassroots citizen activists. Criticism of modern direct democracy has led to the introduction of scores of proposals to reform the process. Each year,

legislators in initiative states propose legislation to alter how the initiative process works. Few of these have been approved, but they illustrate how some elected officials view what the future of direct democracy should be.

Restricting the Use of the Initiative Process Surveys of legislators reveal support for direct democracy as a concept, coupled with a desire to get elected representatives more involved with laws that voters might approve.[128] Many reform proposals introduced by state legislatures are designed to make it more difficult to qualify measures for the ballot.[129] These include proposals to raise the number of signatures required or shorten the time period to collect signatures. Other proposals of this sort include rules requiring that a certain proportion of signatures be collected across all regions of a state (counties or congressional districts) and rules making it more difficult to pay people to collect signatures.[130] In the wake of California's recall of Governor Davis, there were also calls to make future use of recall petitions more difficult.

Even if these proposals were to enjoy majority support among legislators, barriers exist to discourage the passage of such regulations. Major structural rules governing direct democracy are embedded in state constitutions, and constitutional changes require voter approval. Politicians may be reluctant to attack the mechanisms of direct democracy, fearing a populist backlash. Public opinion surveys demonstrate that voters do not want to limit their power over the initiative process, so constitutional referendums proposing to do this are more than likely to be rejected (although Floridians in 2006 approved a legislative referendum requiring all subsequent ballot measures to receive at least

---

[125] Gamble, "Putting Civil Rights to a Popular Vote."

[126] Schrag, *Paradise Lost*, p. 226.

[127] Smith, *Tax Crusaders and the Politics of Direct Democracy.*

[128] Bowler, Donovan, Neiman, and Peel, "Institutional Threat and Partisan Outcomes."

[129] Waters, *The Battle over Citizen Lawmaking.*

[130] Daniel A. Smith, "The Legislative Regulation of the Initiative" (paper presented at the annual meeting of the State Politics & Policy Association, Philadelphia, PA, May 2008).

60 percent of the popular vote). Furthermore, federal courts have rejected overt attempts to ban the use of paying people to collect signatures and rules requiring that signatures be collected across all of a state's counties, regardless of the population of counties.[131]

The popular appeal of direct democracy remains deeply rooted. Another problem with proposals to reform the mechanisms of direct democracy is that most do nothing about campaign spending levels. Because ballot initiative campaign spending cannot be limited according to the 1978 *Bellotti* decision, gross disparities in spending between proponents and opponents of an initiative can only be mitigated if public funds were used to maintain some minimum level of funding for both sides. Tougher qualification barriers, in contrast, are likely to make it more difficult to organize volunteers to qualify measures as well as increase the costs of paying petitioners to qualify something for the ballot. Rather than increasing the influence of "grassroots" citizens' groups, reforms that make it more difficult to qualify measures will probably increase any advantages that wealthy interests may already have. Ironically, if it becomes more difficult or costly to collect signatures, the need to pay people to collect signatures is likely to increase.

Ballot Campaign Finance Reforms Recognizing the high cost of qualifying initiative and referendum petitions, and how this may exclude some groups from the process but not others, one proposal suggested California should simply skip the petition process and allow someone to qualify a measure by paying a fee similar to what it would cost the proponent to collect signatures.[132] This would generate millions of dollars per initiative for a state and perhaps limit the number of initiatives to reach the ballot. Others have suggested that the problem is

not too many initiatives—but initiative campaigns where one side has a huge spending advantage over the other.[133] Because the *Bellotti* decision means that ballot initiative campaign spending cannot be limited, gross disparities in spending between proponents and opponents of an initiative can only be mitigated if public funds were used to maintain some minimum level of funding for both sides.

Expanding the Use of Direct Democracy At the same time as many incumbent state legislators are attempting to limit use of direct democracy in their states, there have been proposals in noninitiative states to introduce the initiative and referendum. The most visible of these proposals come from governors rather than legislators. Past governors of Louisiana (Mike Foster), Minnesota (Jesse Ventura), New York (George Pataki), and Rhode Island (Donald Carcieri) have made public their support of the process. There have also been several legislative attempts by minority parties to introduce the process.[134] Legislation considered, but ultimately rejected, by the New Jersey legislature in 2002, for example, would have given citizens the power of the indirect statutory initiative. That November, voters in Rhode Island easily approved an advisory referendum placed on the ballot by the governor asking whether the state should have an initiative process; lawmakers subsequently ignored the popular vote. More recently, the Minnesota and Alabama legislatures considered bills to create a scaled-down version of the initiative, but those efforts failed. Public opinion polls also show widespread public support for expanding the use of direct democracy to the national level (recall Figure 4.5). The idea of expanding the use of direct democracy is popular in states that already have it and in states that do not.

---

[131] *Meyer v. Grant*, 486 U.S. 414 (1988); Smith, "Campaign Financing of Ballot Initiatives in the American States."
[132] National Conference of State Legislatures, *Initiative and Referendum in the 21st Century*.

[133] Elisabeth Gerber and Arthur Lupia, "Campaign Competition and Policy Responsiveness in Direct Political Behavior," *Political Behavior* 17(1995):287–306.
[134] Holman, "An Assessment of New Jersey's Proposed Limited Initiative Process."

Despite this public enthusiasm and the support of some states' governors, voters have little reason to expect that direct democracy will expand to additional states in the near future. This is due to the fact that state legislators largely control whether their state will change rules to allow direct democracy. Legislators are reluctant to adopt rules that weaken their control over the political agenda.[135]

Absent heightened interparty legislative competition and another social movement pushing for major political reform similar to the Populist and Progressive movements a century ago, elected representatives are unlikely to adopt or expand direct democracy.[136] Voters have probably even less reason to expect adoption of the initiative, referendum, or recall at the national level.

YOU DECISION DECIDE

WHAT GROUNDS FOR RECALLING ELECTED OFFICIALS?

Recall elections are rather rare at the state level, but thousands of recall elections have been held to determine the fate of members of school boards, county commissions, city councils, and mayors. Thirty-six states permit the recall of local officials. A recall is like having a snap election to remove someone from office before they complete the term they were elected to. But is this a good idea? Defenders of the process suggest the recall is the ultimate method to keep officials accountable and responsive to the public.

Critics respond that recall elections are needlessly expensive, and that they make it more difficult for elected officials to govern. When might it be legitimate to remove someone from office before their term is up? Thomas Cronin notes that many people think recalls should be limited to situations where an elected official has "clearly displayed malfeasance" in office.[1] Under such conditions, recalls might be limited to cases where someone was found to be taking bribes, stealing public funds, or being grossly incompetent in office. Others would use the recall more freely — perhaps when an elected official is seen as having lost public trust due to personal issues (sexual affairs, private business practices) that might have nothing to do with performance in office. In practice, recalls are used commonly for political reasons, and as a result of policy disputes. Supporters of defeated candidates target successful candidates for recall, and groups frequently target school board and city council majorities for recall when dissatisfied with key policy decisions.

Would frequent use of recall make government more responsive, or more chaotic and confrontational?

Note
1   Thomas E. Cronin. *Direct Democracy: The Politics of Initiative, Referendum and Recall.* Cambridge, MA: Harvard University Press, 1989, p. 151.

---

[135] Shaun Bowler, Todd Donovan, and Jeffrey Karp, "Why Politicians Like Electoral Institutions: Self-Interest, Values, or Ideology?" *Journal of Politics* 68(2006):434–46.

[136] Smith and Fridkin, "Delegating Direct Democracy."

Summary

Direct democracy is a curious American institution. It plays a large role in the politics of some states and communities but much less of a role in other places. The initiative, referendum, and recall were adopted in an era when overt corruption among state legislators and local elected officials was common. Rather than thwarting the political influence of wealthy interests, however, direct democracy may give powerful, established interests an additional tool they may use to shape public policy. It represents one of the major institutional differences between states like California and New York or between Arizona and Connecticut.

This chapter illustrates that direct democracy—specifically, the initiative process—has important effects where it is used. It can change the rules that affect how elected officials govern, and may alter participation levels and the issues voters use when evaluating candidates. There is also some evidence that direct democracy may lead state policies to be more representative of what voters in a state prefer. Furthermore, as we discuss in more detail in Chapter 10, direct democracy can affect state and local fiscal policy. In short, few similar institutions in the United States are associated with as many differences between the states. Whether direct democracy makes politics better is often left to the eye of the beholder.

Key Terms

Constitutional initiative	Popular referendum	Recall
Direct initiative	Populist Party	Single-subject rule
Indirect initiative	Progressive Era reforms	Statutory initiative
Legislative referendum	Proposition 13	Wedge issues

Discussion Questions

1. Why is the initiative process called the "gun behind the door"? Provide examples of how this process has been used effectively.
2. Discuss some of the criticism of financing ballot initiatives. How has the U.S. Supreme Court ruled when it comes to spending money on ballot initiatives?
3. What is the general public's view of direct democracy? Discuss the merits and pitfalls of the process. Would direct democracy work at the national level?
4. How have minorities been affected by direct democracy measures? What minority groups have been on the front line of initiative battles, and how have they faired?
5. What is the future of direct democracy in the states? If you live in a state that permits statewide ballot initiatives, is direct democracy under fire? If you live in a state that does not permit statewide ballot initiatives, is there a push to adopt the process? What are the politics behind the adoption, or regulation, of direct democracy?

Suggested Readings

Boehmke, Frederick. 2005. *The Indirect Effect of Direct Legislation: How Institutions Shape Interest Group Systems*. Columbus, OH: Ohio State University Press.

Bowler, Shaun, and Todd Donovan. 1998. *Demanding Choices: Opinion, Voting, and Direct Democracy*. Ann Arbor, MI: University of Michigan Press.

Broder, David S. 2000. *Democracy Derailed: Initiative Campaigns and the Power of Money*. New York: Harcourt.

Ellis, Richard. 2002. *Democratic Delusions: The Initiative Process in America*. Lawrence, KS: University of Kansas Press.

Gerber, Elisabeth R. 1999. *The Populist Paradox: Interest Group Influence and the Promise of Direct Legislation*. Princeton, NJ: Princeton University Press.

Magleby, David B. 1984. *Direct Legislation: Voting on Ballot Propositions in the United States*. Baltimore, MD: Johns Hopkins University Press.

Matsusaka, John. 2004. *For the Many or the Few: The Initiative, Public Policy and American Democracy*. Chicago: University of Chicago Press.

Nicholson, Stephen P. 2005. *Voting the Agenda: Candidates, Elections and Ballot Propositions*. Princeton, NJ: Princeton University Press.

Schrag, Peter. 1998. *Paradise Lost: California's Experience, America's Future*. New York: New Press.

Smith, Daniel A. 1998. *Tax Crusaders and the Politics of Direct Democracy*. New York: Routledge.

Smith, Daniel A., and Caroline Tolbert. 2004. *Educated by Initiative: The Effects of Direct Democracy on Citizens and Political Organizations in the American States*. Ann Arbor, MI: University of Michigan Press.

Web Sites

Ballot Initiative Strategy Center (http://www.ballot.org): In addition to coordinating a national strategy to use ballot initiatives to strengthen progressive politics across the states, BISC tracks initiatives circulating for qualification to statewide ballots.

Initiative and Referendum Institute (http://www.iandrinstitute.org): In addition to tracking initiatives and referendums on the ballot, the I&R Institute provides a historical database that dates back to 1904.

National Conference of State Legislatures (http://www.ncsl.org/programs/legman/elect/initiat.htm): Although generally critical of direct democracy, NCSL does an excellent job of tracking ballot initiatives and popular referendums and also provides a historical database.

Centre for Research on Direct Democracy (http://c2d.unige.ch): C2D, based in Geneva, Switzerland, provides an international online library and several direct democracy data sets.

5

Charles Krupa/AP Photo

Political Parties

WHERE'S THE INTERPARTY COMPETITION?

Dean Cannon represents the northern portion of Orange County, Florida, in the Florida House of Representatives. The Republican was first elected to the state legislature in 2004. In that year's general election—an open-seat contest featuring no incumbent on the ballot—the Winter Park attorney and former student body president of the University of Florida raised close to $250,000 for his campaign. His Democratic opponent raised just $3,125. Cannon won the Republican-leaning district with 57 percent of the vote. Since that time, the Democratic Party of Florida has conceded the district, as Representative Cannon has not faced another Democratic challenger. Yet in 2008, the prolific rainmaker and Speaker-designate of the Florida House of Representatives continued to call up potential donors and attend fundraisers, raking in nearly $600,000 to defend his seat. Cannon's worthy opponent in the 2008 general election? Thomas Kelly, founder of the British Reformed Sectarian Party of Florida, which Kelly personally established in 2003 to protest a federal court ruling upholding the right of major political parties in the state to require candidates to sign loyalty oaths to run in their primaries.[1]

As the last three presidential elections have made ever so clear, Florida is a battleground state. The Sunshine State has some 700,000 thousand more registered Democrats than Republicans. Yet, Republicans dominate the Florida legislature due to the overtly partisan way legislative districts are drawn in the state. As a result, there is little interparty competition when it comes to state legislative elections. In 2006, only six of Florida's 20 Senate seats that were up for election were contested by candidates from both major parties, and only 36 of the state's 120 House seats had both Republican and Democratic candidates on the ballot. In 2008, the trend continued. More than half of all legislative races were decided well before the November election, with only one major-party candidate appearing on the general election ballot. Today, less than two dozen of Florida's 140 legislative races are considered competitive due to the partisan gerrymandering.

The lack of interparty competition is not limited to Florida. Nationwide in 2008, roughly 40 percent of the 5,773 regularly scheduled partisan legislative contests had only one major party candidate on the ballot. The lack of interparty competition is particularly stark in some states. In Massachusetts, a Democratic Party stronghold, only one in four Democratic state legislative candidates faced a Republican candidate in 2008. That year, the Arkansas Republican Party failed to field candidates in 60 percent of the state legislative contests. Similarly, the state Democratic parties of Georgia, South Carolina, and Wyoming did not run candidates in nearly half of the legislative races, conceding them by default to the Republicans running for office.[2] But even these figures underestimate the lack of real interparty competition in the states.

According to campaign finance figures calculated by the National Institute on Money in State Politics, in roughly a dozen states less than 10 percent of all legislative races were competitive when looking at campaign contributions collected by major party candidates. Only 4 percent of legislative races in Georgia had competitive spending; in Arkansas, California, Florida, and South Carolina, only 7 percent of all legislative races had comparable spending by the Republican and Democratic candidates.[3] When considering interparty competition in the states, then, those ubiquitous national maps covered with red and blue states give a false impression of how vibrant competition between the parties is within the states.

AP Photo/Phil Coale

Rep. Dean Cannon, R-Winter Park, delivers remarks after being named as House Speaker Designate, Monday, March 2, 2009, in Tallahassee, Fla.

1   Richard Winger, "Three Minor Parties Have Nominees for Florida Legislature," *Ballot Access News*, 21 June 2008, http://www.ballot-access.org/2008/06/21/three-minor-parties-have-nominees-for-florida-legislature/. In 2006, 37.6 percent of state legislative elections had only one major party candidate on the general election ballot; the percentage was 38.7 in 2004, 36.9 in 2002, and 40.6 in 2000.

2   "Legislative Nominees on Ballot," *Ballot Access News*, 1 November 2008, http://www.ballot-access.org/2008/110108.html#5. Gary Robertson, "Legislative Candidates Run Unopposed," *Sacramento Bee,* 27 October 2006, http://dwb.sacbee.com/24hour/politics/election/state_local/story/3404323p-12511215c.html; Joe Follick, "Gerrymandered State Means Little Nov. Drama," *Gainesville Sun,* 26 September 2008, http://www.gainesville.com/article/20080926/news/809272288/1002/news01?title=gerrymandered_state_means_little_nov__drama.

3   National Institute on Money in State Politics, "(m)c50," http://www.followmoney.org/database/graphs/competitive/index.phtml.

Introduction

Political parties play a central role in the electoral process, governance, and policy making of the states. Two longtime observers of state politics, Sarah Morehouse and Malcolm Jewell, go so far as to say, "The single most important factor in state politics is the political party."[1] Not all parties at the state and local level, of course, are equally powerful. Parties come in all kinds of shapes, sizes, and political flavors, and their respective influence within a state varies widely. At their most rudimentary level, parties allow individuals to come together periodically to articulate a political viewpoint. Beyond aggregating and advancing citizen concerns, parties help to cultivate and nurture political leaders, mobilize citizens to vote, organize governments, and formulate public policy.[2] As rational actors, parties have a reflexive quality to their workings. Parties are shaped by other political institutions; in turn, they are able to shape and reform the political institutions under which they operate. In this chapter, we examine this dynamic, reflexive process by focusing on the functions and responsibilities of political parties.

Understanding Political Parties

Political parties serve multiple functions. Parties may be rightly understood as one of the principal agencies for "aggregating and mobilizing the interests of vast numbers of citizens, enhancing voters' capacity to hold public officials accountable, acting as agents of political socialization, and organizing the decision-making institutions of government."[3] Parties recruit candidates running for office, oversee the nominations of those candidates, and provide a durable link between citizens and their governments. Less clear is whether a party needs to be ideologically coherent or merely functional in order to truly be understood as a party.[4]

Responsible Party Model

Some scholars have viewed parties from a normative perspective, offering a prescriptive ideal of what parties ought to strive to become. According to this **responsible party model**, parties should be ideologically consistent, in that they should present to voters a clear platform and set of policies that are principled and distinctive. Voters are expected to choose a candidate based on whether or not they agree with the proposed programs and policies of that candidate's party. Once taking office, the candidate (and his or her party) is to be held responsible for implementing the party's program and policies. Edmund Burke, an Irish philosopher and a member of the British House of Commons, wrote in his 1770 political tract *Thoughts on the Present Discontents* that a "[p]arty is a body of men united, for promoting by their joint endeavors, the national interest, upon some particular principle in which they are all agreed."[5] For Burke, parties were distinguished by their unity and ideological purity (or lack thereof), their consistency, and their ability to provide for a "loyal opposition."[6]

[1] Sarah Morehouse and Malcolm Jewell, *State Politics, Parties, and Policy,* 2nd ed. (Boulder, CO: Rowman & Littlefield, 2003), p. 15.

[2] David Hedge, *Governance and the Changing American States* (Boulder, CO: Westview, 1998).

[3] John Bibby and Thomas Holbrook, "Parties and Elections," in Virginia Gray and Russell Hanson, eds., *Politics in the American States: A Comparative Analysis*, 8th ed. (Washington, DC: CQ Press, 2004).

[4] John Coleman, "Responsible, Functional, or Both? American Political Parties and the APSA Report after Fifty Years," in John Green and Rick Farmer, eds., *The State of the Parties: The Changing Role of Contemporary American Parties*, 4th ed. (Lanham, MD: Rowman & Littlefield, 2003).

[5] Edmund Burke, *Select Works of Edmund Burke: A New Imprint of the Payne Edition*, vol. 1 (Indianapolis, IN: Liberty Fund, 1999), p. 150.

[6] Richard Hofstadter, *The Idea of a Party System: The Rise of Legitimate Opposition in the United States, 1780–1840* (Berkeley: University of California Press, 1969).

Grounded in the belief that parties should promote the public's general interest, Burke's ideological definition of responsible parties seems at times far removed from the American context. Because of institutional constraints (as we discuss in Chapter 3)—such as single-member, winner-take-all elections and direct and open primaries—the two major political parties tend to operate as "big tents," allowing considerable disagreement over their principles and policies in an effort to win elections. Still, the two major parties have retained ideological distinctiveness from one another since the 1850s.[7] Over the last 30 years, the Republican and Democratic parties at the national level increasingly seem to resemble European parties in terms of their internal coherence at both the mass and elite levels.[8]

Yet, if the Republican and Democratic parties strived to be ideologically pure and responsible, they would likely be relegated to the electoral sidelines, unable to build broad coalitions and be competitive. As we shall discuss later, third (or minor) parties often have much more coherent and consistent principles and policies, but their candidates almost always fail to win office. Besides third parties, though, one would be hard-pressed to glean examples of political parties in the American states that reflect Burke's normative ideal of responsible parties.

COMPARISONS HELP US UNDERSTAND

FACTIONS WITHIN STATE PARTIES

All state parties have some internal divisions, although the internecine splits vary in degree. A few state parties are ideologically consistent and rigorous, with elected officials carrying out the party platform once they assume office. A great many state parties, though, are less ideologically coherent and have members who disagree widely on specific issues, be they social or economic. From Mississippi to Alaska, there are prochoice and prolife Democrats and Republicans who disagree fundamentally with other members of their respective parties on the issue of abortion. In socially conservative Utah, members of the Log Cabin Republicans support gay rights. Fiscally conservative "Blue Dog" Democrats in Louisiana and Mississippi support limited spending on welfare and lower taxes, and in Arkansas and Florida, "Yellow Dog Democrats" are such loyalists they will vote for a mangy yellow dog before voting for a Republican. In Colorado, California, Oregon, and Maine, there are sizeable numbers of Republicans who have colorful libertarian streaks. Registered Republicans have voted in favor of ballot measures decriminalizing the use of marijuana for medicinal purposes, even though their state parties officially opposed the policy.[1]

Note

1. Sarah Morehouse and Malcolm Jewell, *State Politics, Parties, and Policy*, 2nd ed. (Boulder, CO: Rowman & Littlefield, 2003), p. 106. See also Richard Elling, "State Party Platforms and State Legislative Performance: A Comparative Analysis," *American Journal of Political Science* 23(1979):383–405; David Colburn, *From Yellow Dog Democrats to Red State Republicans* (Gainesville: University of Florida Press, 2007).

---

[7] John Gerring, *Party Ideologies in America, 1828–1996* (Cambridge: Cambridge University Press, 2001); John Petrocik, "Issue Ownership in Presidential Elections, with a 1980 Case Study," *American Journal of Political Science* 40 (1996):825–50; Daniel Coffey, "State Party Activists and State Party Polarization," in Green, John C. and Daniel Coffey, eds. 2007. *The State of the Parties: The Changing Role of Contemporary American Parties*, 5th ed. (Boulder, CO: Rowan and Littlefield).

[8] Geoffrey C. Layman, Thomas M. Carsey, and Juliana Menasce Horowitz, "Party Polarization in American Politics: Characteristics, Causes, and Consequences," *Annual Review of Political Science* 9(June 2006):67–81; and Gary Miller and Norman Schofield, "Activists and Partisan Realignment in the United States," *American Political Science Review* 97(May 2003):245–60.

Functional Party Model

Whatever relevance Burke's ideological conception of party had for 18th-century England, it is clearly an inappropriate model for understanding the realities of American state parties. With the rarest of exceptions, American political parties (and their nominees) have not been known for their ideological purity. Although political parties have some established and agreed-upon principles and policies, these convictions may change over time. Indeed, it is sometimes the case that parties will pursue policies that run contrary to principles in order to save their principles.[9] As we shall see, this should not necessarily be interpreted as the parties being hypocritical; rather, the parties, as rational actors, are being functionally responsible.

Instead of being ideologically coherent, it is quite rational at times for parties to try to broaden their coalitions in their search for the elusive median voter. After all, parties are self-interested organizations, striving to maximize votes for their candidates in order to win elections.[10] Emphasizing the pragmatic character of American parties, political scientist Leon Epstein offered a **functional party model**, defining parties as "any group, however loosely organized, seeking to elect governmental officeholders under a given label."[11] The functional definition captures the primary goal of parties in the United States: winning and maintaining control of political office. Although a party may be ideologically consistent and coherent, these are not prerequisites. From this perspective, the foremost goal of political parties at all levels—national, state, and local—is to wield political power.[12] As such, political parties are "institutions responding to changes and searching for roles."[13]

Lingering Antiparty Sentiments

Writing over a half century ago, responsible party advocate E. E. Schattschneider argued that democratic governments could be governed by either special interests or parties, but he thought political parties were clearly superior political organizations. "Political parties created democracy," Schattschneider wrote with some hyperbole in 1942, and "democracy is unthinkable save in terms of parties."[14] Rule by parties, Schattschneider and many other political scientists still contend, allows for the public interest to prevail by encouraging the mobilization of majorities.[15]

Yet, although political parties are an essential component for democratic governance, they have been excoriated throughout American history.[16] Many of the founders, for instance, viewed parties as nothing more than large factions driven by selfish motives that were destructive of the common good. In Federalist Paper No. 10, James Madison viewed political parties as majority factions that were evil and to be avoided if possible. Parties were not likely to promote the general interest; rather, they could be expected to promote the particular interests of a specific class of citizens. President George Washington had an even starker view of parties. In his farewell address in 1796, Washington chastised the growing "spirit of

---

[9] Anson Morse, "What Is a Party?" *Political Science Quarterly* 11(1896):68–81.

[10] Anthony Downs, *An Economic Theory of Democracy* (New York: Harper, 1957), p. 25.

[11] Leon Epstein, *Political Parties in Western Democracies* (New York: Praeger, 1967).

[12] Leon Epstein, *Political Parties in the American Mold* (Madison, WI: University of Wisconsin Press, 1986), p. 25.

[13] Sandy Maisel, ed., "Political Parties at the Century's End," in *The Parties Respond*, 2nd ed. (Boulder, CO: Westview, 1994), p. 383.

[14] E. E. Schattschneider, *Party Government* (New York: Holt, Rinehart & Winston, 1942), p. 1.

[15] Walter Dean Burnham, *Critical Elections and the Mainsprings of American Politics* (New York: Norton, 1970); and Seymour Martin Lipset, "The Indispensability of Political Parties," *Journal of Democracy* 11(2000):48–55.

[16] Nancy Rosenblum, *On the Side of the Angels: An Appreciation of Parties and Partisanship* (Princeton: Princeton University Press, 2008).

party," saying it would "distract" and "enfeeble the public administration."[17]

Why Parties?

As rational actors, political parties—regardless of their degree of ideological consistency or functional capacity—are essential for the exercise of democratic governance. Parties serve multiple functions, but nearly all of them are related to the individual ambition of politicians and the broader goal of obtaining and retaining political power.[18] In this sense, parties often combine functional and responsible attributes. One of the main functions of parties is to regularize the "office-seeking ambition" of politicians. In other words, parties are essential players in the effort to increase the chances of a candidate winning office. Parties also function to help citizens overcome collective action barriers to mobilization. The American electoral system requires candidates for elective office to achieve broad-based electoral support in order to ensure they win a plurality of votes at the polls. Parties are the vehicles that can enable candidates to capture wide support. Finally, parties allow legislators to overcome collective action problems when voting on public policies. They help to routinize the decision making of governments, allowing officeholders to normalize the give-and-take of legislative policy making.

Regulating Parties as Quasi-Public Entities

Political parties are "quasi-public" entities, meaning that they not only are regulated by the states but also carry out official functions conferred upon them by the states. As such, they are more akin to public utilities than private associations.[19] Until the 1950s, for example, many Democratic parties in the South were permitted by state law to hold discriminatory "white-only" primaries that excluded blacks from participating in the party nomination process. These "Jim Crow" laws, which codified racial segregation far beyond electoral politics and were designed specifically to restrict black suffrage, included barriers to voting as poll taxes, literacy tests, and an array of complex voter registration laws.[20] In 1964, the 24th Amendment was ratified, outlawing the poll tax in federal elections. The next year, Congress enacted the Voting Rights Act, outlawing state election laws that discriminated against minorities, immigrants, and the poor.

Today, party registration, party nomination, and ballot access laws still vary greatly, including the openness of party primaries across the states and ballot access laws. Although the U.S. Constitution and federal law establish that the voting age is 18 and over, that federal elections are held on the first Tuesday after the first Monday in November, that there may be no poll taxes or literacy tests to determine voter eligibility, and that all polling places must be accessible to people with disabilities, within these broad parameters, every state is permitted to establish its own set of laws that regulate voting and political party status.[21] As such, state regulations governing political parties differ considerably.

In a series of rulings, the U.S. Supreme Court provided broad contours of what is permissible when it comes to the rights of political parties and their members as well as the kinds of regulations the states may place on political parties.[22] In general, the high Court has upheld the associational rights of the major

---

[17] George Washington, "Farewell Address," 1796, http://usinfo.state.gov/usa/infousa/facts/democrac/49htm.

[18] Joseph Schlesinger, "The New American Political Party," *American Political Science Review* 79(1985):1152–69; and John Aldrich, *Why Parties? The Origin and Transformation of Party Politics in America* (Chicago: University of Chicago Press, 1995).

[19] Epstein, *Political Parties in the American Mold*, pp. 155–99.

[20] V. O. Key, *Southern Politics in the State and Nation* (New York: Knopf, 1949).

[21] Bibby and Holbrook, "Parties and Elections."

[22] David Ryden, *The Constitution, Interest Groups, and Political Parties* (Albany: State University of New York Press, 1996).

parties, but it has also reaffirmed the rights of states to regulate state parties in the name of maintaining and preserving political stability.[23] Although hardly constitutive of a coherent jurisprudence, several important Court rulings concern the associational rights and state regulations of state political parties.[24]

Primaries and Caucuses

Parties have broad discretion in determining how candidates running on their party labels are to be nominated. By defining who may participate in their nomination process, the parties are essentially able to define who belongs as a party member. At the same time, state legislatures make the rules governing elections, including whether the state will have a primary election or a caucus in which the nominees running on party labels are determined. Primaries and caucuses are held weeks or months ahead of the general election to determine who will appear on the general election ballot. In a **direct primary** election, voters select one candidate affiliated with a political party for each elected office; the party nominees later face one another in a general election. In contrast to these partisan primaries, most local elections (as well as statewide elections in Nebraska) are nonpartisan. In these contests, every voter receives the same primary ballot, voters do not have to be registered with a party to participate, and candidates' party affiliation is not listed on the ballot. The two candidates receiving the most votes win spots on the general election ballot. As discussed at greater length below, state laws and party rules regulate who may vote in primaries. Several types of direct primary elections are used: closed, semiclosed, open, semiopen, and blanket.

Caucus A few states use a **caucus**, or even a series of caucuses, to nominate candidates. At a caucus, party members informally meet, deliberate, and then cast votes for their preferred candidates. Party members not only discuss the candidates and the pressing issues but also elect delegates to the party's county conventions. These, in turn, elect delegates to the party's congressional and state conventions, which (in presidential election years) elect national convention delegates. In Iowa, for example, a caucus participant must be registered with a party as well as a resident of the precinct in which the caucus is being held (often in a school, a town hall, or even a private home). Iowa has no absentee voting, as the citizen must attend a caucus meeting to have his or her voice heard and counted. (Iowa allows all citizens to register, update their registration, and change their party registration on the night of a caucus.) Guests are permitted to attend a caucus, but they may not participate.

Closed and Open Primaries A **closed primary** system is one in which voters must register with a political party prior to election day and can only vote for candidates of the party for which they are registered. Independent or unaffiliated voters may not vote in a party's primary. In 1984, the Connecticut Republican Party challenged the state's closed primary system by adopting a party rule allowing independents—citizens not officially registered with any party—to participate in its party's primary elections. The Republican Party subsequently challenged the state's closed primary law in federal court, claiming that it barred individuals from entering into political association with the party. In *Tashjian v. Republican Party of Connecticut* (1986), the U.S. Supreme Court in a 5–4 decision ruled that a 1955 state law requiring voters who wished to participate in a party's primary to be a registered member of that party was unconstitutional.

Striking down the state's law as excessive, the court sided with the Republican Party, opening the way for the state to adopt an open primary system. In an **open primary**, voters

---

[23] Sandy Maisel and John Bibby, "Power, Money, and Responsibility in the Major American Parties," in John Green and Paul Herrnson, eds., *Responsible Partisanship? The Evolution of American Political Parties since 1950* (Lawrence, KS: University Press of Kansas, 2002).

[24] Lisa Disch, *The Tyranny of the Two-Party System* (New York: Columbia University Press, 2002).

are not required to register their party affiliation with the state and may freely and secretly choose the ballot of any party's primary in which they wish to vote. Some states use a **semiopen primary**, which permits registered voters to vote in any party's primary, but voters must publicly declare on election day the party primary in which they choose to vote.

Despite the high Court's 1984 *Tashjian* ruling requiring open primary systems if the state parties so choose, many state parties have opted to keep their primaries closed. In 2005, the court ruled in *Clingman v. Beaver* that Oklahoma's **semiclosed primary** law, which permits voting in a primary only by those who are registered with the party or who are registered as independents, was constitutional. In other words, Oklahoma may prohibit a voter who is registered with one party from voting in another party's primary.

Today, as Figure 5.1 displays, 27 states currently have closed or semiclosed primaries, 21 have open or semiopen systems, and two (Louisiana and Washington) have variations of a **top-two blanket primary**. These categories are not definitive, as few states, including Alaska (see Figure 5.2), use a mix of open and closed primaries. In these states, the parties are permitted to choose for themselves their own type of primary election. Until 2007, for example, West Virginia's Democratic primaries were closed, but Republican primaries were semiopen, with independents allowed to cast ballots for Republican candidates. Now both parties have open primaries.

Figure 5.1

States with Closed Primaries, Open Primaries, and Top-Two Blanket Primaries

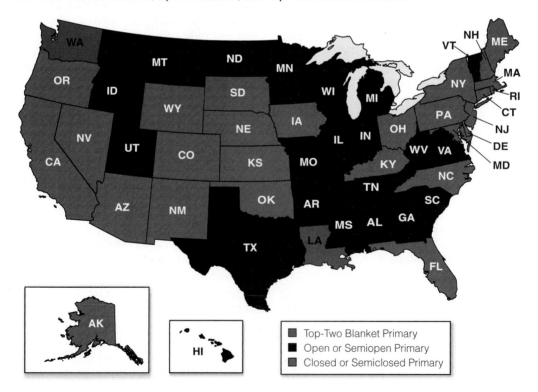

Top-Two Blanket Primaries In 2008, the U.S. Supreme Court weighed in on the side of the associational rights of the major political parties. The court handed Republican and Democratic state political parties a defeat when it ruled that a successful 2004 ballot initiative in Washington calling for a top-two blanket primary system was constitutional. In its decision, *Washington State Grange v. Washington State Republican Party,* the court ruled that the top-two blanket primary, in which the two candidates for an office—regardless of their party affiliations—who receive the most votes in the primary are to face off in the general election, did not deprive state parties of their associational rights to choose their party nominees.

The U.S. Supreme Court's ruling on Washington's top-two blanket primary took some court watchers by surprise. Eight years earlier, in *California Democratic Party v. Jones,* the court struck down as unconstitutional a top-two primary system that had been approved by California voters in a 1996 ballot initiative. Modeled after Washington's old blanket primary system, which was created in 1935, California's proposed primary would have allowed all eligible voters, irrespective of their party affiliation, to vote in the primary for any candidate running on any party ticket. The triumphant candidates from each political party, including third-party candidates, would then square off in the general election. The Republican and Democratic state parties and two other minor parties argued that under the primary system—which replaced the state's closed primary system—the parties would lose control over their own nomination processes, which they claimed violated their 1st Amendment right of freedom of association. The Court struck down the state's blanket primary, ruling that California's law was "forcing political parties to associate with those who do not share their beliefs." After the ruling, the state legislature responded in 2000 by passing a modified closed primary system, permitting unaffiliated citizens to vote in a party's primary if the party so desired.

Louisiana continues to use its own unique top-two blanket primary system. Primaries for state and local offices (but not federal offices) in the Bayou State are nonpartisan, with all candidates, regardless of their party label, facing off in a single primary. A candidate wins the election outright if he or she wins more than 50 percent of the vote in the primary election. If no candidate wins a majority of votes in the primary, the top two candidates—irrespective of their party—then run against one another in the general election. Louisiana's primary system has enabled extremist candidates to qualify for the general election, even though they have combined for substantially less than 50 percent of the primary vote. In the 1991 gubernatorial election, Louisiana's blanket primary system received national attention when David Duke, the former head of the state's Ku Klux Klan and a Republican state legislator, qualified for the runoff election after a former governor (and the eventual general election winner), Edwin Edwards, failed to win 50 percent of the vote in the primary.

Presidential Party Nominations Numerous state legislatures have established special primary elections or caucuses in presidential election years in an effort to have more sway in determining who will be the parties' presidential nominees. States establish the date of their presidential caucuses or primaries, but the national parties ultimately determine whether the party delegates selected during these elections are valid.[25] For example, in 2007, both the Florida and Michigan legislatures passed laws moving up their presidential primaries to January 2008. The earlier dates conflicted with a Democratic National Committee (DNC) rule that only four states—Iowa, New Hampshire,

---

[25] Bruce Cain and Megan Mullin, "Competing for Attention and Votes: The Role of State Parties in Setting Presidential Nomination Rules," in Maisel, ed., *The Parties Respond.*

INSTITUTIONS MATTER

ALASKA'S OPTIONAL PRIMARY SYSTEM

In 2001, the Republican-controlled state legislature in Alaska adopted a restrictive closed primary system. In 2005, however, the Alaska Supreme Court invalidated the statute, ruling that such a primary system violated the state's constitutional guarantees of associational rights. As a result of the decision, Alaska now affords parties the option of holding the primary of their choosing. Two or more political parties may decide jointly to hold a primary, whereby all the candidates that have opted in are on the same ballot. The candidate from each party who wins the most votes advances to the general election. In contrast, a party may hold a semiclosed primary if it so desires. In 2008, as Figure 5.2 shows, the Democratic, Libertarian, and Alaskan Independence parties decided to hold a combined, semiopen primary, allowing any registered voter (including even Republicans) to vote for any one of their candidates running for office. In contrast, the Alaska Republican Party opted to hold a semiclosed primary, allowing registered Republicans, as well as registered undeclared and nonpartisan voters, to cast ballots for its slate of Republican candidates.

Figure 5.2

Alaska's 2008 Primary Election Ballot Choices

2008 Primary Election Ballot Choices

There are three ballot types– you may vote ONE

Your party affiliation listed on the precinct register will determine the ballot type you are eligible to vote.

Ballot Type	Candidates on Ballot	Who Can Vote This Ballot
A-D-L Candidate and **Ballot Measures**	**Alaskan Independence Democrat Libertarian**	*Any registered voter* Party affiliation listed on register is: A – D – G – L – M – R – N – U – V
Republican Candidate with **Ballot Measures**	**Republican**	*Voters Registered as:* **Republican, Undeclared and Nonpartisan** Party affiliation listed on register is: R – U – N
Measures Only	**No Candidates** This ballot contains ballot measures only.	*Any registered voter* If you request a primary ballot type that you are not eligible to vote, you must vote a questioned ballot. If you would like to vote for just the ballot measures and not vote for any candidates, you may request the measures only ballot.

Source: Alaska lieutenant governor, http://www.elections.alaska.gov/forms/x01.pdf

South Carolina, and Nevada—could hold binding presidential nominating contests prior to February 5. As a result, the DNC ruled that it would not recognize the results of either Florida or Michigan's early primaries that Hillary Clinton easily won, and that it would strip both state Democratic parties of all their delegates to the 2008 Democratic National Convention in

Denver.[26] In the end, after Barack Obama secured the Democratic Party's presidential nomination, the national party restored all the delegates from the two states. To many observers, this kind of gamesmanship between the national parties and state legislatures is widely expected to precede the 2012 presidential election.

The Effect of Primary Systems on Representation As should be evident, primaries vary with regard to how much voters are permitted to participate in the nomination process. The most restrictive form is the closed primary, where only previously registered party members may participate. New York, for example, requires a citizen to be registered with the state as a party member for a full year before being eligible to vote in a primary election. The semiclosed primary is not quite as restrictive, as independents are permitted to participate along with registered party members. With the open primary, any registered voter may vote in any party's primary on election day, although some require voters to temporarily declare a party then. Louisiana and Washington's blanket primaries are the least restrictive system, with voters permitted to vote for any candidate running for office, irrespective of their party.

In theory, open primaries should encourage more participation among the electorate, as all voters, even independents (sometimes referred to as unaffiliateds), may cast a ballot in the election. The costs associated with voting are much less in blanket and open primary systems than in closed systems. Yet, analyses of voter turnout levels across states with open versus closed primary systems do not reveal any significant differences in rates, as the mobilization of citizens goes well beyond the particularized costs or benefits of an individual's decision to vote. Because open primaries diminish the control that parties and candidates have over who participates in the nomination process, parties

and candidates may have less incentive to bolster turnout.[27]

Party Endorsements of Candidates

The U.S. Supreme Court has ruled that individuals are able to associate with a party of their choice. In *Eu v. San Francisco Democratic Committee* (1989), the Court struck down a California law that prohibited parties from officially endorsing or opposing candidates running in primary elections and forbade candidates running in primary elections from claiming that they were officially endorsed by their parties. The law also tightly regulated the internal governance of state parties, limiting the term of office for the state party central committee chair and requiring the chair to rotate between members living in northern and southern California.

Members of the parties challenged the law in federal court on the grounds that it deprived them and the parties of their 1st Amendment rights, specifically the freedoms of speech and association. The Court agreed, saying that the state legislature had no compelling state interest to burden the constitutional rights of the parties and their members. Despite the ruling, many state parties continue to abide by state regulations, satisfied with the status quo.[28] Roughly three-quarters of the states regulate the organizational structure of state parties, including how party leaders are to be selected and how their candidates are to be replaced should the need arise.

Party Fusion

States may prohibit the names of candidates running for political office from appearing more than once on a ballot, a practice known as **party fusion.** Fusion permits two or more parties to nominate the same candidate for

---

[26] National Conference of State Legislatures, "Presidential Primaries," http://ncsl.org/programs/legman/elect/Changing-EliminatingPP.htm.

[27] Rebecca Morton, *Analyzing Elections* (New York: Norton, 2006).

[28] Morehouse and Jewell, *State Politics, Parties and Policy*, p. 113.

office. The candidate's name appears on the ballot alongside the name of each party that cross-endorses him or her.

During the late 19th century, party fusion was a regular feature of American electoral politics, especially in western and midwestern states. Issue-oriented third parties—such as the Greenback, Granger, Free Silver, and Populist parties—frequently cross-listed their candidates on the tickets of the weaker of the two major parties in the state. In the South, the Republican Party would occasionally temporarily fuse with third parties in an effort to derail the dominant Democratic Party.[29] For example, during the 1890s in North Carolina, the Populist and Republican parties used fusion to combined forces to unseat the dominant Democratic Party. Although their party platforms were incommensurable on numerous issues—including the tariff, the gold standard, and racial segregation—the two parties turned a blind eye to their differences in their successful effort in 1894 to dethrone the ruling Democrats.[30]

Of the 10 states (Arkansas, Connecticut, Delaware, Idaho, Mississippi, New York, South Carolina, South Dakota, Utah, and Vermont) that currently allow party fusion, only minor parties in Arkansas and New York continue to use it with considerable frequency. The Conservative, Independence, and Working Families parties in New York (see Figure 5.3) are usually not strong enough to have their own candidates win when running against Republican or Democratic candidates. Instead, these minor parties routinely cross-endorse Republican or Democratic candidates running for office. In 2008, for example, the state's Conservative and Independent parties both cross-endorsed Republican John McCain, and the Working Families Party cross-endorsed Democrat Barack Obama. If the cross-endorsed candidate wins, the minor party can claim that it had a hand in the victory—

Working Families Party fusion poster endorsing Barack Obama

Courtesy of Eden Schulz/Working Families

pointing to the votes cast for the candidate on its minor party label. Votes for the fused candidate also help the minor party retain its ballot access status.[31]

Party Ballot Access

States have been granted wide latitude by the U.S. Supreme Court to determine what parties and their nominees—from dog catchers to governors to the president—must do to qualify for the ballot. In some states, the rules are fairly restrictive; in others, they are less so. Democrats and Republicans are, by state law, usually given "major-party" status and are entitled to permanent space on the ballot. A minor party may have to

[29] Peter Argersinger, "A Place at the Table," *American Historical Review* 85(1980):287–306.
[30] Helen G. Edmonds, *The Negro in Fusion Politics in North Carolina, 1894–1901* (Chapel Hill: University of North Carolina Press, 1951).

[31] Joel Rodgers, "Pull the Plug," *Administrative Law Review* 52(2000):743–68; and David Dulio and James Thurber, "America's Two-Party System: Friend or Foe?" *Administrative Law Review* 52(2000):769–92.

Figure 5.3

New York Party Fusion Ballot, 2008

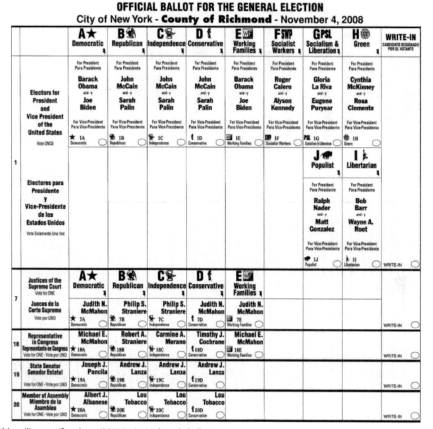

Source: http://blog.silive.com/firstglance/2008/11/1103-Sample-ballot.jpg.

collect a certain number of signatures or register some percentage of the state's voters with their minor party before being granted ballot access. Candidates wishing to run as independents in a general election or candidates running as the nominee of a new political party usually have to collect thousands of signatures in order to qualify for the ballot. In other states, candidates wishing to run for office need only pay a nominal filing fee. In Florida in 2000, 10 presidential candidates qualified for the election, which made designing the ballot layout (including Palm Beach County's infamous butterfly ballot) more complicated. In most states, parties typically retain their ballot access as long as one of

their candidates collects a minimum percentage of votes cast in a state election.

During the 1950s, in the midst of the "Red Scare," many states made their ballot access laws more restrictive for third parties, as they feared members of the Communist Party might qualify for state ballots. The Supreme Court, in its 1968 decision *Williams v. Rhodes,* ruled that ballot access laws could be stricken if they were "invidiously discriminatory" and violated the 14th Amendment's Equal Protection Clause by giving the two major parties "a decided advantage over new parties." Three years later, though, the court clarified that barriers to access for minor parties would have to be extremely high to be ruled

YOU DECIDE

SHOULD PARTY FUSION BE BANNED?

In a 1997 ballot access lawsuit, *Timmons v. Twin Cities Area New Party,* the U.S. Supreme Court upheld the regulatory power of state legislatures by affirming Minnesota's law banning fusion—the listing of a candidate on the ballot under two or more political parties. The Court ruled 6–3 that the state's antifusion law was constitutional. The Court reasoned that the ban on party fusion did not severely burden the associational rights of the members of the New Party, a recently formed third party. In the words of Chief Justice William Rehnquist, who wrote the majority decision, states should be able to avoid "voter confusion," protect the "stability of their political systems," and ensure the integrity of the ballot by prohibiting candidates to be cross-listed as two or more parties' nominee for a given elective office. In upholding the state's antifusion law, Rehnquist's majority opinion concluded that, "The Constitution permits the Minnesota legislature to decide that political stability is best served through a healthy two-party system," and that the U.S. Constitution "does not require Minnesota, and the approximately 40 other States that do not permit fusion, to allow it."

What do you think of Chief Justice Rehnquist's reasoning? Do you think party fusion leads to voter confusion and political instability? Are voters in New York—a state that permits fusion—more sophisticated than those in Minnesota? Or, do you think the majority opinion's hostility toward fusion is driven by a concern to protect the two-party system?

unconstitutional. For example, the Court upheld state laws requiring third-party candidates to collect up to 5 percent of a state's registered voters—exceeding tens of thousands of signatures—to qualify for the ballot.[32]

Many states continue to have very onerous ballot qualification standards. Until 1939, for example, a Massachusetts law required only 1,000 signatures for a third-party candidate to qualify for the ballot. But the state legislature changed the law that year to require third-party candidates to collect 3 percent of the previous gubernatorial vote—or more than 50,000 signatures. Although the legislature reduced the threshold to 2 percent of the last gubernatorial vote in 1973, only five third-party candidates have qualified for the statewide ballot since the 1930s.[33] In the 1970s, Arkansas lawmakers required minor parties to collect signatures equal

to 7 percent of votes cast in the last election to qualify for the ballot. After the U.S. Supreme Court ruled the percentage was too high, lawmakers reduced the threshold to 3 percent. But a federal judge ruled that third party candidates could petition onto the ballot under an even lower threshold (10,000 signatures). In 2008, its U.S. Senate candidate garnered 20 percent of the statewide vote, but because the party's gubernatorial and presidential candidates won less than 3 percent of votes cast, the Arkansas Greens lost their short-lived designation as a political party. In Virginia, candidates running as independents for statewide office are required to collect 10,000 signatures from registered voters to have their names placed on the ballot; at least 400 of those signatures must come from each of Virginia's congressional districts. Three states (Nebraska, Oregon, and Texas) have primary screen-out laws. Citizens who vote in a partisan primary in these states are not permitted to sign a petition to qualify an independent candidate or a new party for the ballot. And in West Virginia, registered Democrats and Republicans who sign petitions

---

[32] Richard Winger, "The Importance of Ballot Access," 1994, http://www.ballot-access.org/winger/iba.html.
[33] Richard Winger, "What Are Ballots For?" (1988), http://www.ballot-access.org/winger/wabf.html.

to qualify minor-party candidates on the ballot are prohibited from voting in their own parties' primaries. According to a leading observer, there are nearly 20 lawsuits pending around the country, filed by third parties and independent candidates, challenging ballot access laws.[34]

Defending the Two-Party Duopoly

Despite some public sentiment in favor of shaking up the two-party system,[35] efforts by state lawmakers to keep new parties and independent candidates off the ballot have more often than not been upheld by the U.S. Supreme Court. Many of the high court's rulings have been tinged with strong normative overtones, with justices going out of their way to lavish praise upon the two-party system. Paying homage to the responsible party model, Justice Lewis Powell in his 1980 dissent in *Branti v. Finkel* celebrated how "[b]road based political parties supply an essential coherence and flexibility to the American political scene." Similarly, Antonin Scalia opined in his dissent in *Rutan v. Republican Party of Illinois* (1990), "The stabilizing effects of such a [two-party] system are obvious." And in her concurring opinion, Justice Sandra Day O'Connor wrote in *Davis v. Bandemer* (1986), "There can be little doubt that the emergence of a strong and stable two party system in this country has contributed enormously to sound and effective government." Because the Court has given wide discretion to the parties to regulate themselves and to the states to preserve order, states show considerable regulatory differences—from party nominations and preprimary endorsements, to fusion, to ballot access. Each of these regulations has affected the strength of state parties and, in turn, has altered the representative nature of parties within the political process.[36]

Party-in-the-Electorate

As we shall see, parties are often understood as tripartite social structures composed of three integrated components: party-in-the-electorate, party organization, and party-in-government.[37] Although somewhat limited and overly schematic, the three-pronged framework can serve as a heuristic, allowing us to isolate and appreciate the various dimensions of political parties.[38] We begin our discussion with party-in-the-electorate, which refers to ordinary citizens—eligible voters as well as nonvoters—who identify with and share some sense of loyalty to a particular party.

Partisan Identification

The strength of an individual's attachment to a political party is measured by **party identification**, or PID. A person's PID usually forms early in adulthood, and is largely conditioned by one's family. Party identification is a genuine form of social identity that is affected in part by sociopsychological influences; a person is often initially drawn to a political party because of his or her sense of belonging and allegiance.[39] As people age, though, they often make retrospective and prospective cognitive evaluations (or running tallies) of how the parties are doing.[40] Because some people are continually adjusting their PID in response to political and economic change, evidence at the macro level reveals that the average PID in some states has been slowly changing.[41] For example, in the 1980s, many white Southerners who were ideologically

---

[34] Richard Winger, "Status of Ballot Access Lawsuits," (2009), http://www.ballot-access.org/2009/05/.

[35] Todd Donovan, Janine Parry, and Shaun Bowler, "O Other, Where Art Thou: Support for Multi-Party Politics in the US," *Social Science Quarterly* 86(2005):147–59.

[36] Elisabeth Gerber and Rebecca Morton, "Primary Election Systems and Representation," *Journal of Law, Economics, and Organization* 14(1998):304–24.

[37] Key, *Politics, Parties, and Pressure Groups*, 5th ed. (New York: Thomas Y. Crowell, 1964), pp. 163–65.

[38] J. P. Monroe, *The Political Party Matrix: The Resistance of Organization* (Albany: State University of New York Press, 2001).

[39] Donald Green, Bradley Palmquest, and Eric Schickler, *Partisan Hearts and Minds: Political Parties and the Social Identities of Voters* (New Haven, CT: Yale University Press, 2002).

[40] Morris Fiorina, *Retrospective Voting in American National Elections* (New Haven, CT: Yale University Press, 1981).

conservative but still loyal to the Democratic Party began identifying more with the Republican Party. As a result, southern states began turning redder, as the party-in-the-electorate became more aligned with the GOP.

Political Ideology

Not all Democrats and Republicans have the same political ideology or a consistent and coherent belief system concerning the principles of political rule. When individual political ideologies are aggregated, political ideologies found across the states vary considerably. Cultural, economic, demographic, and sociological dissimilarities may lead states to have more liberal or more conservative electorates. The poorer a citizen is, the more likely he or she is to vote for Democratic candidates, holding constant other factors, whereas wealthier citizens tend to vote for Republican candidates, all else equal. Yet, scholars have identified an interesting paradox: overall, wealthier states tend to elected more Democratic candidates, whereas poorer states tend to elect more Republicans, although the partisan gulf between the rich and the poor is greater in red states than blue ones.[42]

Because national public opinion polls tend not to survey a representative number of respondents from all 50 states, there are relatively few direct measures of state-level political ideology. As such, scholars have tried to derive indirect measures of a state's political ideology by using election returns and interest groups' ratings of members of Congress from each state, pooling data from national polls

and estimating state public opinion, and using data from national election surveys designed to study U.S. Senate races.[43] Regardless of the method, these studies show that southern states—such as Alabama, Arkansas, and Oklahoma—tend to be the most ideologically conservative, and northern states—such as Massachusetts, Maryland, and New York—tend to be the most liberal in the country.

Does a state's political ideology predict the kinds of public policies it adopts? Usually, but not always. If you recall from Chapter 1, state policies tend to reflect the median ideological preferences of the states' citizens. However, Democratic-controlled legislatures tend to produce policies that are more conservative than their more liberal citizens.[44] The reason for this divergence between citizen ideology and public policy is often rational; parties often pursue public policies to win future elections rather than passing public policies that are reflective of their ideology.[45]

---

[41] Robert Erikson, Michael MacKuen, and James Stimson, *The Macro Polity* (New York: Cambridge University Press, 2002); and Alan Abramowitz and Kyle Saunders, "Ideological Realignment in the U.S. Electorate," *Journal of Politics* 60(1998):634–52; Seth McKee, *Republican Ascendancy in Southern U.S. House Elections* (Boulder, CO: Westview Press, 2009).

[42] Andrew Gelman, et al. *Red State, Blue State, Rich State, Poor State: Why Americans Vote the Way They Do* (Princeton: Princeton University Press, 2008).

[43] See Jeffrey Lax and Justin Phillips, "Gay Rights in the States: Public Opinion and Policy Responsiveness," *American Political Science Review* 103(2009):367–386; William Berry et al., "Measuring Citizen and Government Ideology in the American States," *American Journal of Political Science* 42(1998):327–48; Gerald Wright, Robert Erikson, and John McIver, "Measuring State Partisanship and Ideology with Survey Data," *Journal of Politics* 47(1985):469–89; Barbara Norrander, "Measuring State Public Opinion with the Senate National Election Study," *State Politics and Policy Quarterly* 1(2001):111–25; Paul Brace et al., "Public Opinion in the American States: New Perspectives Using National Data," *American Journal of Political Science* 46(2002):173–89; and Thomas Carsey and Geoffrey Layman, "Party Polarization and 'Conflict Extension' in the American Electorate," *American Journal of Political Science* 46(2002):786–802.

[44] Wright, Erikson, and McIver, "Measuring State Partisanship and Ideology."

[45] Downs, *An Economic Theory of Democracy*; Thomas Dye, "Party and Policy in the States," *Journal of Politics* 46(1984):1097–116; Charles Barrileaux, Thomas Holbrook, and Laura Langer, "Electoral Competition, Legislative Balance, and American State Welfare Policy," *American Journal of Political Science* 46(2002):415–27.

Are a State's Partisan Identification and Political Ideology Related?

A state's partisan identification leanings and its political ideology are not always correlated, or linked together. States populated with citizens having strong Republican ties—Utah, South Dakota, Idaho, and Kansas, for example—are not inhabited solely by citizens who are ideologically conservative. Some states with heavy Republican PID are actually less ideologically conservative than states with high percentages of Democratic identifiers. Likewise, several states with strong Democratic PID are considerably more ideologically conservative than states with high proportions of Republican identifiers. Only a functional understanding of political parties can accommodate the tremendous diversity of political ideology and partisanship found across the American states.

For example, states with more ideologically liberal populations are not necessarily more Democratic, and states more ideologically conservative are not necessarily more Republican. Massachusetts, for instance, lives up to its reputation as being one of the most liberal states in the union. Yet seven states, including Oklahoma, a state ranked as one of the most conservative in the country, have stronger levels of Democratic PID than the Bay State. According to one study, two of the most conservative states—Arkansas and Alabama—do not even register in the top 30 of Republican-leaning states with respect to their PID.[46]

From an institutional perspective, there are several reasons why a state's political ideology and partisanship are not always correlated. As mentioned in Chapter 3, states have differing registration laws, making it alternatively easier or more difficult for citizens to initially register with a political party or subsequently switch their party registration. Most states require voting-age citizens to register their party affiliation with the state at least 30 days prior to an election, although under the National Voter Registration Act passed by Congress in 1993, all states must allow voters to register to vote by mail and when applying for a driver's license. Nine states (Idaho, Iowa, Maine, Minnesota, Montana, New Hampshire, North Carolina, Wisconsin, and Wyoming) have same-day registration, allowing eligible citizens to register to vote on election day. Since 1951, North Dakota has had no voter registration requirements; all voting-age citizens may cast ballots. These differences can affect partisan identification, irrespective of political ideology. Residents in states with strict registration laws, for example, might be more inclined to identify with a political party because they are required by state law to register with a party if they want to participate in the electoral process. Variations in state registration laws may also help to explain why the percentage of voters who are registered with a party in a state is not always a reliable indicator of the level of partisan identification within a state.

As we have seen, states also have different kinds of primary election laws. If a state has a closed primary, for example, only citizens who register with the state as members of the party may vote in primary elections when the party's nominee for political office is selected. In states with closed primaries, as opposed to open primaries, citizens have a strong incentive to identify closely (and indeed register) with either the Democratic or Republican Party if they want to be full participants in the electoral process. As we detail later in the chapter, states also have varying levels of party competition. In states with low interparty competition, citizens may gravitate toward the more dominant of the two major parties in the state, shunning the perennial "loser" party. Finally, party organizational strength across the states varies considerably, which leads to differences in how state parties may be able to reach out to and mobilize the electorate.

---

[46] Norrander, "Measuring State Public Opinion with the Senate National Election Study."

Does Partisanship Affect Participation?

As we discussed in Chapter 3, some states and communities have higher turnout levels than others. From a party-in-the-electorate perspective, strong partisans—regardless of whether they are Republicans or Democrats—tend to vote more frequently than nonpartisans. Since the 1970s, however, turnout across all the states has steadily declined. Some scholars argue that this is due to a partisan dealignment in the electorate, as people increasingly consider themselves to be independents.[47] Others note that lower turnout is related to a decline in interparty competition,[48] with the parties achieving their policy objectives without mobilizing voters.[49] Several observers have suggested that the withering of the party-in-the-electorate is linked to the decline of state and local party organizations, as the parties have shifted away from mobilizing a broad array of voters, targeting instead only likely voters.[50]

Party Organization

Over the years, state and local party organizations have shown their adaptability by responding to changing regulatory and electoral conditions. In the early 1970s, state and local political parties—along with their national brethren—were often given up for dead because they were seen as dinosaurs of a bygone era. Today, most state and many local political parties are vibrant organizations, carrying out essential campaign activities, such as mobilizing voters and raising campaign funds in support of their candidates. Party organization refers to the network of elected and appointed party officials; paid staffers; national, state, and local committees; and volunteer workers.[51] Some political scientists have reduced the organizational role of parties to a single function—that of electing candidates. In today's "candidate-centered era," parties are designed primarily as "party-in-service" to candidates.[52]

The level of party organization across the 50 states varies considerably. State parties are typically composed of a state central committee, congressional district committees, county committees, and ward or precinct committees. The structure of state parties, though, can be far more complex. Figure 5.4 depicts the Byzantine organizational flowchart of the California Democratic Party. Each level of the state party has members who are either elected or appointed to their positions. Almost all party officials at the local level are volunteers, although most state parties now have permanent, paid staff at the central committee level.[53] Most state parties convene annual conventions that are attended by party delegates and the party's elected officials, and many hold primaries to choose a party's nominee for the general election, although a few still use party conventions to vet and select party nominees.

At minimum, if a party organization is to be successful, it must be able to overcome barriers to collective action. The organizational

[47] Martin Wattenberg, *Where Have All the Voters Gone?* (Cambridge, MA: Harvard University Press, 2002); and Thomas Patterson, *The Vanishing Voter: Public Involvement in an Age of Uncertainty* (New York: Knopf, 2002).

[48] Kim Hill and Jan Leighley, "Party Ideology, Organization, and Competitiveness as Mobilizing Forces in American Democracy," *American Journal of Political Science* 37(1993):1158–78.

[49] Matthew Crenson and Benjamin Ginsberg, *Downsizing Democracy: How America Sidelined Its Citizens and Privatized Its Public* (Baltimore, MD: Johns Hopkins University Press, 2002); and Peter Francia et al., "The Battle for the Legislature: Party Campaigning in State House and State Senate Elections," in Green and Farmer, eds., *The State of the Parties*.

[50] Francis Fox Piven and Richard Cloward, *Why Americans Still Don't Vote: And Why Politicians Want It That Way* (Boston: Beacon Press, 2000); and Steven Schier, *By Invitation Only: The Rise of Exclusive Politics in the United States* (Pittsburgh, PA: University of Pittsburgh Press, 2000).

[51] John Bibby, "Party Networks: National-State Integration, Allied Groups, and Issue Activists," in John Green and Daniel Shea, eds., *The State of the Parties: The Changing Role of Contemporary Parties,* 3rd ed. (New York: Rowman & Littlefield, 1999).

[52] Schlesinger, "The New American Political Party."

[53] Raymond La Raja, "State Political Parties after BCRA," in Michael Malbin, ed., *Life after Reform* (Boulder, CO: Rowman & Littlefield, 2003).

Figure 5.4

Organizational Structure of the California Democratic Party

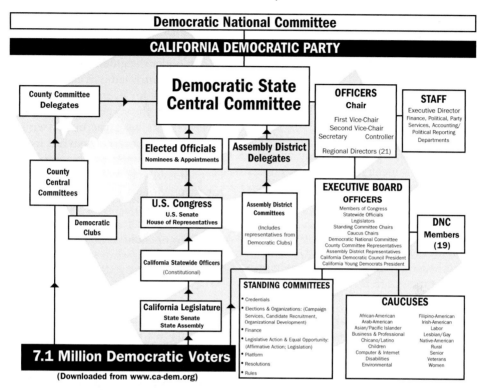

Source: California Democratic Party, http://www.kintera.org/site/pp.asp?c=fvLRK7O3E&b=33603.

configuration a party selects, though, may be tight or loose. A functional definition of a political party accommodates variation in party organizations found across the country—from urban party machines, to well-financed and professionally staffed state party committees, to the underfinanced and disorganized bands of volunteers running some local party organizations. Recall that a functional definition of parties is not concerned with a party's organizational hierarchy; rather, its preoccupation with contesting and winning elections. State, and especially local party organizations along with broader networks of "informal party organizations," may even have the effect of pushing politicians to become more partisan, moving them toward the ideological margins.[54] As rational actors, then, state and local parties—often with their candidates in tow—have adapted their organizational structures to the changing regulatory and electoral environment, thereby ensuring their continued relevance.

Although there has been a shift over time to more candidate-centered campaigns in the American states, state parties have proven themselves to be quite resilient, mutating their structures to fit with the changing times.[55] State parties in the 50 states are nominally independent of one another and the national parties, but there have been recent efforts to strengthen the ties between the national, state, and local parties as well as between the state parties.

[54] Seth E. Masket, *No Middle Ground: How Informal Party Organizations Control Nominations and Polarize Legislatures* (Ann Arbor: University of Michigan Press, 2009).

[55] J. P. Monroe, *The Political Party Matrix* (Albany: State University of New York Press, 2001).

Parties in the "Party Era"

During the mid-19th century, in the midst of the "Party era," state and local party organizations reigned supreme. They were far more powerful than the national parties. Forming coalitions to win elections, state and local parties responded to a rapidly expanding electorate. In New York in the 1820s, for example, the Democratic Party machine was known as the Albany Regency, which was controlled for a time by future U.S. President Martin Van Buren. The parties developed a **spoils system** whereby nonelective government positions were doled out to loyal supporters as **patronage appointments.** Through such appointments, state and especially local parties endeared themselves to their communities by offering jobs in the public sector in exchange for votes. The parties also garnished the pay of government workers and party supporters, requiring monthly "assessments"—akin to religious tithing—as a means for raising money for the party.[56] With such arrangements, parties helped to integrate citizens, many of them recently naturalized immigrants, into the political system. As early as the 1840s, state Democratic parties were full-fledged operations, holding annual conventions, developing their own party platforms, and mobilizing the party faithful with Get-Out-the-Vote (GOTV) rallies. On election day, the parties even printed their own ballots and distributed them at the polls.[57]

The Urban Party Machine

Working behind the scenes at the local level was the **party boss.** Bosses, such as William Marcy "Boss" Tweed of New York City, were often seen as unprincipled, self-serving, and corrupt. A chair maker and volunteer fireman,

Boss Tweed gradually worked his way up through the party as a city alderman, U.S. representative, and state senator. Eventually, he came to rule Tammany Hall, the city's moniker for the Democratic Party political machine that emerged in the 1850s. In the 1860s and 1870s, under the guidance of Tweed, the party machine controlled virtually all the party's nominations for every office in not only the city but also the state. Quid pro quo financial arrangements were the norm, with the local party machine receiving payoffs from business interests in exchange for favorable legislation. Party bosses were handsomely compensated for their "honest graft." Tweed, for instance, was appointed as a director of the Erie Railroad in exchange for having the party push through legislation benefiting the company.

The Rebirth of Party Organizations

For much of the 20th century, state and local political party organizations became a mere shadow of their former selves. During the Progressive Era, reformers intentionally weakened parties. In the late 1890s and early 1900s, non-partisan reformers pushed through legislation—including the Australian (or secret) ballot, nonpartisan local elections, direct primaries for party nominations, and commission or manager-commission forms of municipal government—in an attempt to wrest control from local and state party bosses.

Beginning in the 1950s, state and local party organizations were further weakened by the rise of candidate-centered campaigns. Aided by the rise of electronic media, first radio and then television, candidates for public office were able to circumvent party machines and take their messages directly to the voters. Image and personality, rather than organizational hierarchies, along with the rise of special interests, helped to insulate candidates from the trappings of party organizations. By the late 1960s, the relevance of political parties came under question. An increase in nonvoters in tandem with a **partisan dealignment** in the electorate led some observers to write premature obituaries for political

---

[56] Anthony Corrado, "Money and Politics: A History of Federal Campaign Finance Law," in Anthony Corrado et al., eds., *A New Campaign Finance Sourcebook* (Washington, DC: Brookings Institution, 2003).

[57] Joel Silbey, "Beyond Realignment and Realignment Theory: American Political Eras, 1789–1989," in Byron Shafer, ed., *The End of Realignment? Interpreting American Electoral Eras* (Madison, WI: University of Wisconsin Press, 1991).

Connecticut Gov. M. Jodi Rell waves to delegates as she enters the Republican state convention in New Britain, Conn., in 2006. Despite high approval ratings, Gov. Rell announced that she would not seek reelection in 2010.

Party delegates at the 2008 Texas Republican Party Convention in Houston.

programmatic capacities. Research conducted during the 1970s and 1980s highlighted the institutionalization of state parties, depicting the integration of new party professionals and the bureaucratization of what were once often parochial, unsophisticated organizations. Most state parties during the period began to establish permanent headquarters and hire specialized staff to raise contributions and direct campaigns.[60] The parties transformed themselves from provincial party machines into service vendors ready to recruit, train, and support candidates in their run for office.[61] Although the labor-intensive parties of the 19th century are in the past, state and local party organizations have reinvigorated themselves as service providers. By the turn of the millennium, scholars generally agreed that state political parties were as strong and fiscally sound as they were anytime in recent history.[62]

Measuring Party Organizational Strength

There are several comparative studies of the 50 state organizations that measure party organizational strength. Unfortunately, none of these measures fully captures the organizational strength of state parties. In the 1980s, Yale University scholar David Mayhew advanced

parties.[58] Historians have noted how parties today, when compared with their 19th-century predecessors, "can hardly be seen as the vigorous, robust, and meaningful players within the nation's political system that they once were."[59]

In the late 1970s, parties reemerged from their prolonged slumber. Many state and local party organizations—especially Republican state parties—began to strengthen themselves organizationally, expanding their bureaucratic and

---

[58] David Broder, *The Party's Over: The Failure of Politics in America* (New York: Harper & Row, 1972); and Wattenberg, *Where Have All the Voters Gone?*
[59] Joel Silbey, The American Political Nation, 1838–1893 (Stanford, CA: Stanford University Press, 1991).

[60] Cornelius Cotter, James L. Gibson, John F. Bibby, and Robert J. Huckshorn, *Party Organizations in American Politics* (New Brunswick, NJ: Eagleton Institute of Politics, Rutgers University, 1984).
[61] Paul Herrnson, "Do Parties Make a Difference? The Role of Party Organizations in Congressional Elections," *Journal of Politics* 48(1986):589–613; and Xandra Kayden and Eddie Mahe, *The Party Goes On: The Persistence of the Two Party System in the United States* (New York: Basic Books, 1985).
[62] John Aldrich et al., "Challenges to the American Two-Party System: Evidence from the 1968, 1980, 1992, and 1996 Presidential Elections," *Political Research Quarterly* 53(2000):495–522; and Morehouse and Jewell, *State Politics, Parties, and Policy.*

a measure of traditional party organization (TPO) that classified state parties as being more or less conforming to a 19th-century ideal type of party control.[63] Mayhew's measure assessed the autonomy, durability, and hierarchy of the party organization, taking into consideration the degree to which it relied on material incentives to maintain and stimulate partisan loyalty and participation and to control the nominations and campaigns of their candidates. Political scientist Sarah Morehouse argues that state party organizational strength varies considerably, but she finds states with stronger party systems tend to have greater legislative support for the agenda put forth by the governor.[64]

Unfortunately, the methodologies scholars have utilized to measure party organizational strength have varied widely, leading to some inconsistent findings.[65] Many of the studies gauging state party organization have measured the number of staff and other party assets. Party organizations, of course, are much more than their staff. They can also be understood as a complex web of political consultants and campaign specialists and elected officials in national, state, and local offices as well as their respective staff. A recent study finds that party organization strength influences the ideological tenor of the party, with more top-down, hierarchical structures being more moderate, and those with more open structures being more polarized.[66]

State Party Financing

As with any organization, the capacity and relative power of state party organizations are directly affected by their money-raising prowess. Considerable variation in state campaign finance laws exists across the states when it comes to restricting contributions and expenditures of political parties. Thirteen states (Arkansas, Florida, Georgia, Idaho, Illinois, Maine, Missouri, Nebraska, Nevada, New Mexico, Oregon, Utah, and Virginia) allow unlimited contributions from virtually any source to be made to state political parties. Roughly the same number have similarly lax contribution regulations, except that they prohibit donations from corporations and labor unions; eight other states prohibit contributions from corporate entities but allow union donations. Alabama, for instance, allows individuals, labor unions, **political action committees (PACs)**, and national party committees to contribute unlimited sums to the state political parties, but limits corporations to donations up to $500 per election. Campaign finance laws in Arizona are similar to Alabama's, except that corporations and unions may not make contributions to state parties with money drawn from their own treasuries. Montana and Oklahoma prohibit corporate contributions to state parties, but Montana allows unlimited union contributions, whereas Oklahoma limits them to $5,000 per year. Connecticut, on the other hand, allows individuals to contribute up to $5,000 per year to state parties, but completely bans corporations and unions from making contributions from their treasuries, permitting them only to make limited PAC contributions.[67]

Many of these state campaign finance regulations are new. Over the past two decades, more than 30 states have adopted campaign finance laws that directly or indirectly affect state parties. Going through state legislatures,

[63] David Mayhew, *Placing Parties in American Politics: Organization, Electoral Settings, and Government Activity in the Twentieth Century* (Princeton, NJ: Princeton University Press, 1986), pp. 19–20.

[64] Sarah Morehouse, *The Governor as Party Leader: Campaigning and Governing* (Ann Arbor: University of Michigan Press, 1998).

[65] See, for example, James Gibson et al., "Assessing Party Organizational Strength," *American Journal of Political Science* 27(1983):193–222; James Gibson, John Frendreis, and Laura Vertz, "Party Dynamics in the 1980s: Changes in County Party Organizational Strength 1980–1984," *American Journal of Political Science* 33(1989):67–90; and Robert Huckshorn et al., "Party Integration and Party Organizational Strength," *Journal of Politics* 48(1986):976–91.

[66] Daniel Coffey, "Measuring Gubernatorial Ideology: A Content Analysis of State of the State Speeches," *State Politics and Policy Quarterly* 5(2005):88–103. See also John Coleman, "Party Organizational Strength and Public Support for Parties," *American Journal of Political Science* 40(1996):805–24.

[67] Center for Responsive Government, "Contributions Limits on State Party Committees" (2002), http://www.publicintegrity.org/partylines/overview.aspx?act=cl; National Conference of State Legislatures, "Limits on Contributions to Political Parties" (2009), http://www.ncsl.org/programs/legismgt/ABOUT/contrib_pol_parties.htm.

AP Photo/Jack Plunkett

2010 Texas gubernatorial candidate Kinky Friedman, left, is joined by Willie Nelson, right, and Jesse Ventura at a Friedman fundraiser held at Nelson's ranch near Austin, Texas.

the California and New York Democratic parties, and the California, Florida, and New York Republican parties. The Republican Party of Florida topped all other state parties in total receipts, hauling in nearly $39 million. In contrast, in 2008 the Republican Party of Alaska raised $164,934, with the Alaska Democratic Party bringing in only $153,369.[69]

The Impact of the Bipartisan Campaign Reform Act of 2002 on State Party Organization

On December 10, 2003, the U.S. Supreme Court upheld the bulk of the **Bipartisan Campaign Reform Act of 2002** (BCRA), also known as the McCain-Feingold Act. In *McConnell v. Federal Election Commission*,[70] the Court let stand nearly all of BCRA's Title I, which banned parties from using soft money for "federal election activity."[71] In banning soft money—which before BCRA included six- and seven-figure contributions from individuals and the treasuries of companies and labor unions—the law not only altered the strategies and activities of the national political parties but also by extension those of state parties. With state parties no longer permitted to solicit soft money for use in federal campaigns or receive transfers of soft money from the national parties, some observers questioned whether state parties would be able to survive under BCRA.

but also circumventing politicians who were the beneficiaries of weak campaign finance restrictions, good government public interest groups placed more than two dozen initiatives on statewide ballots dealing with campaign finance issues during the decade.

The capacity of state parties to raise campaign contributions ranges tremendously. The disparity across states in party fundraising has less to do with the organizational strength of state Democratic or Republican parties and more to do with the kind of campaign finance laws that are on the books and the competitiveness of state and federal elections.[68] In 2008, the state parties in the 50 states raised more than $440 million for state elections (which excludes contributions raised by the state parties for federal elections). Overall, state Republican parties raised roughly $222 million, just a few million more than the combined total for state Democratic parties.

In Table 5.1, we provide the contributions made to the Democratic and Republican state parties for state campaigns in 2008. A handful of state parties raked in more than $20 million during the cycle, including

---

[68] Raymond La Raja, Susan Orr, and Daniel A. Smith, "Surviving BCRA: State Party Finance in 2004," in John Green and Daniel Coffey, eds., *The State of the Parties*, 5th ed. (Boulder, CO: Rowman & Littlefield, 2006).

[69] National Institute on Money in State Politics, "Total Dolars for all Party Committees" (2009), http://www.follow themoney. org/database/nationalview.phtml?l=0&f=P&y=2008&abbr=0.

[70] *McConnell v. Federal Election Commission*, 540 U.S. (2003); U.S. Lexis 9195 (2003).

[71] The term *soft money* was originally used in 1983 to describe "largely unregulated and unlimited nonfederal money raised by political parties that fall outside FECA limitations"; Diane Dwyre and Robin Kolodny, "Throwing Out the Rule Book: Party Financing of the 2000 Elections," in David B. Magleby, ed., *Financing the 2000 Election* (Washington, DC: Brookings Institution Press, 2002), p. 142.

Table 5.1

Contributions to State Parties, 2008 (in millions)

State	Democratic	Republican	State	Democratic	Republican
Alabama	$3.37	$1.37	Montana	$3.41	$0.86
Alaska	$0.15	$0.16	Nebraska	$0.03	$0.01
Arizona	$4.08	$0.81	New Hampshire	$2.79	$0.54
Arkansas	$1.59	$0.92	New Jersey[a]	$2.35	$10.56
California	$28.80	$32.13	New Mexico	$1.41	$1.72
Colorado	$1.26	$0.46	New York	$20.97	$24.77
Connecticut	$0.09	$0.31	North Carolina	$12.01	$2.84
Delaware	$2.26	$0.91	North Dakota	$1.67	$1.46
Florida	$17.05	$38.99	Ohio	$6.92	$9.16
Georgia	$2.28	$6.79	Oklahoma	$0.74	$0.86
Hawaii	$0.23	$0.36	Oregon	$3.80	$2.62
Idaho	$0.30	$0.63	Pennsylvania	$3.85	$7.26
Illinois	$7.13	$11.48	Rhode Island	$0.29	$0.23
Indiana	$4.62	$5.30	South Carolina	$2.27	$4.83
Iowa	$9.17	$4.40	South Dakota	$0.27	$1.74
Kansas	$2.26	$1.21	Tennessee	$3.97	$2.67
Kentucky	$1.48	$0.97	Texas	$7.66	$4.83
Louisiana	$3.16	$2.84	Utah	$1.91	$2.22
Maine	$2.45	$1.52	Vermont	$0.28	$0.18
Maryland	$1.95	$0.80	Virginia[a]	$6.50	$4.41
Massachusetts	$2.68	$0.39	Washington	$12.76	$5.40
Michigan	$7.48	$6.10	West Virginia	$0.25	$0.00
Minnesota	$9.38	$5.10	Wisconsin	$2.07	$1.84
Mississippi[a]	$0.45	$4.00	Wyoming	$0.66	$0.64
Missouri	$9.93	$9.83			

[a] 2004 Data (2008 Data unavailable).

Source: National Institute For Money in State Politics, http://www.followthemoney.org/database/nationalview.phtml.

Until the 2004 election cycle, many state parties were the beneficiaries of—and, in the eyes of some, dependent upon—**soft money**.[72] Under the Federal Elections Campaign Act of 1971 (FECA), the previous federal campaign finance regime, not only did state parties raise sizeable amounts of soft money for federal campaigns on their own, but they were also the beneficiaries of soft money transfers from the national parties to be used for electoral activities. In order to take advantage of financial incentives under FECA that permitted hard–soft dollar splits on coordinated spending between the national and state parties, the national parties often exchanged soft dollars that they raised for more valuable hard dollars

---

[72] Bibby and Holbrook, "Parties and Elections."

raised by state parties. With BCRA's passage, there was good reason to anticipate dire consequences for state parties. Some observers thought the national parties would be able to offset their loss of outlawed soft dollars by raising more hard dollars, and others questioned whether state parties would be able to respond in the post-BCRA era.[73] Yet, BCRA's impact on state and local parties has been minimal, as most of them have been able to adapt to the changes in federal law.[74]

Party-in-Government

Party-in-government refers to candidates running for elective office as well as officeholders at the local, state, and national levels who are elected under the party label. With the exception of Nebraska (because of its nonpartisan, unicameral legislature), Republicans and Democrats dominate the governmental structure of every state. As you will see in Chapter 7, political parties structure state government, especially state legislatures. Of course, because of winner-take-all elections and restrictive ballot access laws, the two-party dominance of state legislatures and statewide elected officials exaggerates the level of popular support for the two parties in the electorate. Due to these structural barriers, it is difficult for citizens who are displeased with the two-party system to articulate their dissatisfaction with the status quo.[75]

Party Competition in State Legislatures

Although political parties may be inevitable, their mere existence is not sufficient to guarantee a democratic form of governance. Rather, competition between the parties is said to be essential for democracies to function. Competition forces the parties to become more internally cohesive and disciplined, giving citizens a real choice at the polls.[76] "Democracy," Schattschneider once claimed, "is not to be found in parties but between the parties."[77]

Partisan control of state legislatures has ebbed and flowed over time. Between 1950 and 2000, a clear majority of legislative seats across the states were held by Democrats; by 2000, the partisan split in legislative seats had become dead-even between the parties, as Republicans gained a larger share of legislative seats. Since that time, however, Democrats have slowly regained their advantage at the aggregate level. Figure 5.5 shows the overall trend over time in the number of legislative seats held by the two major parties between 1938 and 2010. In 2010, of the 7,333 House and Senate seats in the 49 states that use partisan elections (which excludes Nebraska), Democrats controlled 4,059 (55 percent) seats, Republicans held 3,247 (44.1 percent) seats, and Independents and third-party candidates controlled only 70 (0.9 percent).[78]

States, of course, vary considerably with respect to the degree of legislative party control. As we discuss in the following section, some states historically have experienced intense two-party competition, whereas others have had a tradition of single-party dominance. Many of the social and economic conditions as well as numerous institutional rules that helped to

---

[73] Ruth Jones, "State Public Campaign Finance: Implications for Partisan Politics," *American Journal of Political Science* 25(1981):342–61; Ray La Raja, "Political Parties in the Era of Soft Money," in Maisel, ed., *The Parties Respond*; Ray La Raja, "State Parties and Soft Money: How Much Party Building?" in Green and Farmer, eds., *The State of the Parties*; and Sarah Morehouse and Malcolm Jewell, "State Parties: Independent Partners in the Money Relationship," in Green and Farmer, eds., *The State of the Parties*.

[74] Raymond La Raja, *Small Change: Money, Political Parties, and Campaign Finance Reform* (Ann Arbor: University of Michigan Press, 2008); La Raja, Orr, and Smith, "Surviving BCRA."

[75] Theodore Lowi and Joseph Romance, *A Republic of Parties? Debating the Two-Party System?* (Lanham, MD: Rowman & Littlefield, 1998).

[76] Key, *The Responsible Electorate: Rationality in Presidential Voting, 1936–1960* (Cambridge, MA: Harvard University Press, 1966).

[77] Schattschneider, *Party Government*.

[78] National Conference of State Legislatures, "2009 Partisan Composition of State Legislatures," http://www.ncsl.org/statevote/partycomptable2009.htm.

Figure 5.5

Republican and Democratic Share of Legislative Seats, 1938–2009

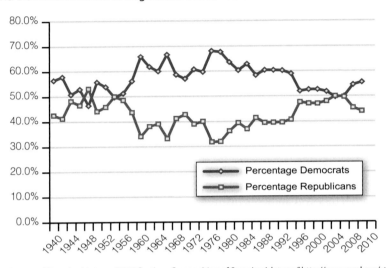

Source: National Conference of State Legislatures, "2009 Partisan Composition of State Legislatures," http://www.ncsl.org/statevote/
partycomptable2009.htm.

ensure one-party dominance have eroded or have been eliminated, making two-party competition more common throughout the country. This is particularly true in the South, as the Republican Party over the past 30 years has become more competitive, and even dominant, in some states. Today, two-party competition exists in every state, although to different degrees.

Party Control and Interparty Competition

There are numerous ways to measure the party control and interparty competition of a state's party system. One of the most popular methods was first developed by Austin Ranney and has become known as the "Ranney Index."[79] The index averages four measures

[79] Austin Ranney, "Parties in State Politics," in Herbert Jacobs and Kenneth N. Vines, eds., *The American States* (Boston: Little, Brown, 1965). See also James King, "Inter-Party Competition in the American States: An Examination of Index Components," *Western Political Quarterly* 42(1989):83–92; and Thomas Holbrook and Emily Van Dunk, "Electoral Competition in the American States," *American Political Science Review* 87(1993):955–62.

of party competition: the proportion of the gubernatorial vote won, the proportions of the state senate and state house seats won, and the proportion of time (over a given period) the governorship and the two legislative chambers are controlled by a party. The Ranney Index of state party control ranges from 0 (complete Republican control) to 100 (complete Democratic control), and the Index of interparty competition ranges from 50 (no party competition) to 100 (a perfectly competitive two-party system).

Table 5.2 compares the Ranney Index's party control and interparty competition figures over two periods, 1980–2000 and 2003–2006. The states are grouped based on their most recent party control rankings. Through the 1980s and 1990s, Democrats dominated party control in the American states, with 31 states falling under Democratic Party control and the 50-state average at 55.6, substantially higher than the midpoint. The most Democratic state during the 20-year span—in terms of control of the governor's office and the state legislature—was Maryland (with a score of 80.8), followed

Table 5.2

Ranney Indices of State Party Control and Two-Party Competition, 1980–2000, and 2003–2006

State	State Party Control, 1980–2000	State Party Control, 2003–2006	State Two-Party Competition, 1980–2000	State Two-Party Competition, 2003–2006
Republican Party Dominance				
Idaho	30.8	21.7	80.8	71.7
Utah	25.1	23.4	75.1	73.4
North Dakota	37.9	23.9	87.9	73.9
South Dakota	27.2	24.3	77.2	74.3
Alaska	46.5	29.8	96.5	74.5
Florida	57.7	30.2	92.3	79.8
Texas	60.7	31.2	89.3	80.2
South Carolina	62.6	32.3	87.4	82.3
Georgia	77.7	33.9	72.3	83.9
Missouri	62.2	34.1	87.4	84.1
Two-Party Competition				
Ohio	44.1	36.0	94.1	86.0
Kansas	33.1	38.0	83.1	88.0
Wyoming	35.0	38.7	85	88.7
Virginia	62.2	41.1	87.8	91.1
Arizona	35.2	41.9	85.2	91.9
Indiana	44.2	45.0	94.2	95.0
New Hampshire	33.5	46.1	83.5	96.1
Wisconsin	52.0	46.1	98	96.1
Michigan	48.0	47.1	98	97.1
Nevada	57.7	47.2	92.3	97.2
Montana	44.1	47.3	94.1	97.3
Delaware	51.5	47.8	98.5	97.8
Pennsylvania	43.9	49.8	93.9	99.8
Kentucky	72.9	51.4	77.1	98.6
Minnesota	59.2	52.9	90.8	97.1
Iowa	46.9	53.2	96.9	96.8
Mississippi	75.8	56.5	74.2	93.5
Oregon	54.2	57.9	95.8	92.1
Connecticut	57.7	58.1	92.3	91.9
New York	52.3	58.3	97.7	91.7
California	59.5	59.0	90.5	91.0
Colorado	40.9	59.2	94	90.8
Oklahoma	66.4	59.5	83.6	90.5

(continued)

Table 5.2

Ranney Indices of State Party Control and Two-Party Competition, 1980–2000, and 2003–2006 continued

State	State Party Control, 1980–2000	State Party Control, 2003–2006	State Two-Party Competition, 1980–2000	State Two-Party Competition, 2003–2006
Maine	54.9	61.1	95.1	88.9
Vermont	53.9	61.8	96.1	88.2
Tennessee	61.6	64.1	88.4	85.9
Democratic Party Dominance				
Washington	59.4	65.3	90.6	84.7
Alabama	72.6	65.5	77.4	84.5
Illinois	48.3	65.6	98.3	84.4
North Carolina	67.2	66.5	82.8	83.5
Hawaii	78.7	67.2	71.3	82.8
Louisiana	76.5	69.2	73.5	80.8
New Jersey	45.7	69.2	95.7	80.8
Maryland	80.8	71.5	69.2	78.5
Rhode Island	74.9	72.7	75.1	77.3
New Mexico	62.1	73.5	87.9	76.5
Arkansas	79.2	74.2	70.8	75.8
West Virginia	75.4	77.0	74.6	73.0
Massachusetts	73.4	77.6	76.6	72.4
50 state average	55.6	51.0	86.7	86.3

Source: Morehouse and Jewell (2003), Table 4.1; Thomas Holbrok and Raymond La Raja, "Parties and Elections," in Virginia Gray and Russell L. Hanson, eds., *Politics in the American States: A Comparative Analysis,* 9th ed. (Washington, DC: CQ Press), Table 3-4.
Note: State party control ranges from 0 (complete Republican control) to 100 (complete Democratic control); interparty competition ranges from 50 (no party competition) to 100 (a perfectly competitive two-party system).

closely by Arkansas and Hawaii. In the 1980s and 1990s, only 18 states were in Republican hands. Utah, with a score of 25.1, was by far the most Republican state during the period, with South Dakota and Idaho also solidly in GOP hands.

In the more recent period, Democrats have lost some ground to their Republican counterparts, as Democratic party control has weakened compared to the earlier two-decade period. Between 2003 and 2006, only 13 states fell into Democratic control according to the Ranney Index (with party control scores exceeding 65.0). Eleven states exhibited Republican Party dominance in the more recent period, up

from eight during the previous two decades. Massachusetts (with a party control score of 77.6) dethroned Maryland for the most-Democratic state, with West Virginia, Arkansas, New Mexico, and Rhode Island rounding out the top five. Idaho (with a party control score of 21.7), Utah, the Dakotas, and Nebraska were the states with the most Republican control.

Most states have remained fairly stable over the past 30 years in terms of party control (California, Connecticut, Indiana, and Michigan moved less than one point on the index over the two periods), but a few have witnessed drastic party control swings. Florida, Texas, South Carolina, Georgia, and Missouri all came under solid Republican Party control between 2003 and 2006, after averaging Democratic party control during the 1980s and 1990s. Quite fewer states moved in the other direction, although Colorado, Illinois, and New Jersey were much "bluer" in the 2000s than in the earlier period.

Ranney's second index—interparty competition—over the two time periods give us a sense of where the battles between the two major parties for control of state government have taken place. In the earlier period, from 1980 to 2000, the states with the highest two-party competition scores—Delaware (98.5), followed closely by Wisconsin, Michigan, and New York—experienced intense interparty competition over the two decades. In contrast, heavily Democratic Maryland, with an interparty competition score of 69.2, was by far the least competitive state over the time frame. Utah, with the strongest Republican Party control score of any state during the earlier time frame, interestingly had a higher interparty competition score (75.1) than seven states controlled by the Democrats. More recently, Kentucky and Pennsylvania—with 98.6 and 99.8 two-party competition scores—could hardly be any more competitive. Between 2003 and 2006, the 50-state average for interparty competition was 86.3, virtually unchanged from the 86.7 score during the early period. Red-state Idaho, with a two-party competition score of 71.7, ranks dead last in interparty competition, but Blue-state Massachusetts is a close second, with a score of 72.4.

Increasing Interparty Competition

Since the 1970s, across a range of indicators, there has been a gradual increase in interparty competition in the American states. Much of this increase has occurred in the South, where there has been a wholesale transformation of solid Democratic Party control giving way to the rise of the Republican Party. Between 1980 and 2000, Democratic Party control in the states declined as the 20th century came to a close. When comparing the averages of the last five years with the first five years of the period, 40 states shifted from being less Democratic to being more Republican, and nearly all the states that were classified as Republican became even stronger under GOP control.[80]

Why Interparty Competition Matters

State governments produce different kinds of public policies depending on the dynamics of party strength, and heightened interparty competition leads to public policies that are more representative of the whole population of a state rather than just the elites. In his classic work, *Southern Politics in the State and Nation*, V. O. Key argued that the lack of party competition in southern states from the 1880s through the 1950s enabled the "haves" in society to run roughshod over the "have-nots," as the dominant Democratic Party had no fear of reprisal at the polls. Key argues that because they were unlikely to be defeated at the next election, the majority southern Democrats did not have to respond to the concerns and needs of all the people residing in their states. Others have formally tested Key's proposition that lack of party competition leads to worse redistributive policy outcomes, finding some support.[81] More recently, as interparty competition has increased across the country, scholars have found that increased party competition in a state tends to lead to the passage by state legislatures of more liberal public policies. Specifically, Democratic-controlled legislatures in states with tough electoral competition from Republicans tend to pass more liberal public policies, whereas the reverse holds for

---

[80] Morehouse and Jewell, *State Politics, Parties, and Policy*, p. 109.

[81] James Garand, "Partisan Change and Shifting Expenditure Priorities in the American States, 1945–1978," *American Politics Quarterly* (October 1985):355–91; and Morehouse and Jewell, *State Politics, Parties, and Policy*, p. 50.

Republican-controlled state legislatures facing stiff Democratic electoral challenges.[82]

There is also scholarly evidence that heightened interparty competition leads to greater levels of participation by citizens. General election voter turnout in the 11 southern states from 1960 to 1986 averaged less than 40 percent, well below the national average. With the decline of the Democratic Party's lock on state government and the advent of greater interparty competition, average turnout among these states increased to nearly 43 percent between 1990 and 1996. Comparing the two periods, Alabama had an eight point increase, and Louisiana experienced a double-digit jump in turnout.[83]

Parties Take the Initiative

As discussed in greater length in Chapter 4, the practice of direct democracy in the American states has traditionally been used by citizen groups to challenge the power of parties. In particular, the initiative, whereby citizens collect signatures to place a measure on the ballot for fellow citizens to consider, was used by antiparty forces during the Progressive Era to weaken the organizational autonomy of parties, most notably the control of parties over their candidate nominations. In the 1980s, though, state political parties began using the initiative

process to help advance their candidates running for office. Although the mechanisms of direct democracy were originally intended to allow citizens to circumvent unresponsive state legislatures, the parties understand that placing ballot measures can help their candidates win office.[84]

Ballot measures can help candidates distinguish themselves from their rivals, exploit wedge issues, drive up turnout, and raise and spend unlimited soft money. Ballot measures can also be used to drain the resources of opposing groups or parties.[85] For example, in 1996, the California Republican Party advocated the passage of Proposition 209, the California Civil Rights Initiative. Disavowing his long-standing support for affirmative action, Republican governor Pete Wilson helped rescue the floundering ballot initiative campaign to end affirmative action. The state Republican Party provided funding to the proponents of the measure with the hope that it would splinter Democratic support for President Bill Clinton's reelection bid. In a teleconference call with Newt Gingrich, Wilson claimed that Proposition 209 was "a partisan issue . . . that works strongly to our advantage [and] has every bit the potential to make a critical difference" to defeat Clinton.[86] At Wilson's behest, the California Republican Party then contributed $997,034 to the Yes on Prop. 209 campaign, with the Senate Republican Majority Committee contributing an additional $90,000.[87]

---

[82] Holbrook and Van Dunk, "Electoral Competition in the American States"; Charles Barrilleux, "Party Strength, Party Change, and Policymaking in the American States," *Party Politics* 6(2000):61–73; Charles Barrilleux, "A Test of the Independent Influences of Inter-Party Electoral Competition and Party Strength on State Policy," *American Journal of Political Science* 41(1997):1462–66; Charles Barrilleux, Thomas Holbrook, and Laura Langer, "Electoral Competition, Legislative Balance, and American State Welfare Policy," *American Journal of Political Science* 46(2002):415–27; and James Alt and Robert Lowry, "Divided Government, Fiscal Institutions and Budget Deficits: Evidence from the States," *American Political Science Review* 88(1994):811–28.

[83] Calculations derived from Morehouse and Jewell, *State Politics, Parties, and Policy,* table 2.1.

[84] Daniel A. Smith and Caroline Tolbert, "The Instrumental and Educative Effects of Ballot Measures: Research on Direct Democracy in the American States," *State Politics and Policy Quarterly* 7(2007):417–46.

[85] Daniel A. Smith, "Initiatives and Referendums: The Effects of Direct Democracy on Candidate Elections," in Stephen Craig, ed., *The Electoral Challenge: Theory Meets Practice* (Washington, DC: CQ Press, 2006).

[86] Peter Schrag, *Paradise Lost: California's Experience, America's Future* (New York: New Press, 1998), p. 226

[87] Daniel A. Smith and Caroline J. Tolbert, "The Initiative to Party: Partisanship and Ballot Initiatives in California," *Party Politics* 7(2001):739–57.

Although party organizations are increasingly playing an important role in ballot campaigns when they have an opportunity to use an issue to their partisan advantage, parties do not ultimately control the direct democracy agenda. Compared to the amount of money contributed directly by corporations, unions, and even wealthy individuals, parties tend to be bit players. Parties rarely provide the majority of funding to campaigns for or against an initiative, and they rarely sponsor their own popular initiatives. Yet, directly and indirectly, parties have played a substantial role in funding some highly salient initiative campaigns, including ballot measures on term limits, paycheck protection, illegal immigration, affirmative action, and minimum wage.[88]

Whither Third Parties?

Nearly every state is dominated by a two-party system. As we discuss in greater length in Chapter 7, nearly all state legislative seats are held by either Democrats or Republicans, with third-party organizations in most states virtually nonexistent. Although some scholars point to the historical or cultural bias for having two dominant parties in the states, the primary reason for the two-party duopoly is institutional. There are many constraints that limit the possible success of third parties. Some of these barriers are constitutional, such as the single-member district electoral systems used in most states. Other hurdles are statutory, such as ballot access restrictions, which are often very onerous for third parties and their candidates.[89]

Third parties at the state and local levels have not always been weak. The adoption in most states of the Australian ballot (or secret ballot) in the late 19th century initially gave a boost to third parties. The Australian ballot placed governments—rather than the parties themselves—in charge of printing ballots and administrating elections, making voting a private rather than a public act. The secret ballot diminished the power of the party bosses, who could no longer directly monitor the vote choices of citizens and also made split-ticket voting possible. Furthermore, many states during this period switched from a **party-column ballot** (sometimes known as the Indiana ballot), which listed all the candidates running for separate offices by their political party and had the effect of strengthening the parties, to an **office-block ballot**, which made split-ticket voting easier, thereby weakening the major parties.[90] Today, 17 states still use party-column ballots, which encourage straight-party voting (see Figure 5.6). With the push of a single button, voters are able to support all the candidates running for office of a given party.[91]

Third parties, such as the Libertarian, Green, and Natural Law parties, have been hampered by both the direct primary system and ballot access laws adopted by the states. The direct primary system of nominating congressional and state officials has hurt the prowess of state-level third parties in the states. Because party bosses no longer overtly control the nomination processes of the two major parties, Republican and Democratic party dissidents are able to act as "outsiders" while remaining within the two parties. As such, the major parties are able to absorb dissidents and broader protest movements, which in the past often led to the rise of third parties.

---

[88] Daniel A. Smith and Carolilne J. Tolbert, *Educated by Initiative:* The Effects of Direct Democracy on Citizens and Political Organizations in the American States (Ann Arbor: University of Michigan Press, 2004).

[89] John Bibby and Sandy Maisel, *Two Parties—or More?* 2nd ed. (Boulder, CO: Westview, 2002).

[90] Richard Niemi and Paul Herrnson, "Beyond the Butterfly: The Complexity of U.S. Ballots," *Perspectives on Politics* 1(2003):317–26.

[91] David Kimball, Chris T. Owens, and Katherine M. Keeney, "Residual Votes and Political Representation," in Robert Watson, ed., *Counting Votes: Lessons from the 2000 Presidential Election in Florida* (Gainesville: University Press of Florida, 2004).

Figure 5.6

Party-Column and Office-Block Ballots

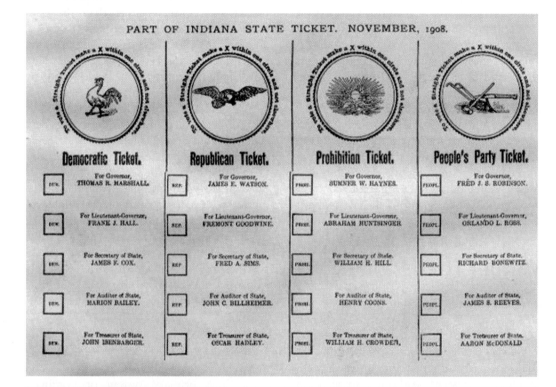

Source: Alex Peterman, *Elements of Civil Government* (New York: American Book Company, 1916). Available: http://www.gutenberg.org/files/15018/15018-h/images/img-187.jpg and http://www.gutenberg.org/files/15018/15018-h/images/img-186.jpg.

REFORM CAN HAPPEN

Jesse Ventura

AP Photo/Janet Hostetter

THIRD-PARTY GUBERNATORIAL CANDIDATES SPOILING FOR A FIGHT

Third-party candidates running for governor rarely win, but in some rare instances, they manage to spoil the two-party duopoly. In 2008, 26 third-party and independents qualified for the ballots in the 11 states that held gubernatorial races. Of the more than 16 million votes cast across the 11 states, these candidates won just 408,585 votes, less than 3 percent of the vote. Two years earlier, voters in 27 of the 36 states that held gubernatorial contests had the opportunity to cast a vote for a third-party candidate; in nine states, however, only Republican and Democratic gubernatorial candidates were on the ballot.

Third-party and independent gubernatorial candidates not only face structural barriers—such as ballot access restrictions—but they also often are excluded from public forums and debates, which can cost them valuable name recognition and fundraising opportunities. Running against mountaintop strip mining, and earning the endorsement of the Sierra Club, West Virginia's Mountain Party candidate for governor, top Jesse Johnson, won 4 percent of the vote in 2008, making it the most successful gubernatorial campaign in the country. In 2006, Garrett Michael Hayes, the Libertarian Party's long-shot candidate for governor in Georgia, was permitted to join a debate with the Republican incumbent, Governor Sonny Perdue, and his Democratic challenger, Lieutenant Governor Mark Taylor. Hayes ended up winning less than 4 percent of the vote in the general election. Yet, his tally, paltry by most standards, was the most any minor-party gubernatorial candidate running in the state had earned since 1902, when the People's Party candidate won 6.4 percent of the vote in a two-man race.

In 1998, former professional wrestler Jesse "The Body" Ventura, running as a Reform Party candidate, was invited to spar with the Democratic and Republican nominees in two televised debates. Ventura's solid performance in the debates gave his campaign a shot in the arm, especially among young voters, and he went on to win the election with 37 percent of the vote.

Ballot access laws in the states ensure that the two major parties are guaranteed a place on the ballot, whereas minor parties—if they do not win a certain percentage of the vote in a previous election—are required to circulate petitions to gather signatures in order to qualify for the ballot. In some states, this barrier to access is relatively easy to overcome. Colorado lawmakers in 1998 made it easier for minor parties to win recognition as actual political parties and not just as political organizations; all a third party needs to be recognized is to have 1,000 registrants and run at least 10 candidates for statewide or legislative seats. If a minor party fails to meet this requirement, it must either collect 10,000 signatures on petitions or have one of its candidates win at least 5 percent of a statewide vote. Other states, such as Illinois, have much more stringent ballot access requirements for minor parties. Third-party candidates have three months to collect valid signatures from 5 percent of those who voted in the last election for the office for which they are running in order to qualify for the ballot.

Third parties and their candidates face a host of psychological barriers too. At the individual level, citizens who vote regularly (likely voters) tend to have a strong allegiance to one of the two major parties. In addition, citizens who are alienated from the political system, and who therefore might be likely suspects to vote for a third-party candidate, are much less likely to vote. Because of the winner-take-all nature of most state and local elections, third parties often have a difficult time convincing contributors to give them money. Because candidates running on third-party tickets have little chance of winning, the media tend not to cover them. It becomes a self-fulfilling prophecy that because their candidates rarely win, third parties have a difficult time recruiting qualified candidates to run on their ticket.

Every blue moon, of course, third-party candidates do win elective office at the state or local level. A study of voting patterns for presidential candidates found three factors have motivated citizens to vote for third-party candidates: majority party deterioration, an influx of new voters with weak allegiance to the two major parties, and, most importantly, attractive third-party candidates who present viable alternatives to major nominees.[92]

The same factors are often in place at the state level. Since 1930, eight third-party and independent candidates have been elected governor, including four since 1990 (Alaska independent Walter J. Hickel, Connecticut independent Lowell P. Weicker Jr., Maine independent Angus S. King Jr., and Minnesota Reform Party Jesse Ventura). More recently, Vermont's Progressive Party's nominee for governor won 22 percent of the vote in 2008, and the party has five members in the Vermont House of Representatives and one in the state Senate. Bob Kiss, the mayor of Burlington (sometimes referred to as "The People's Republic of Burlington"), was elected as the nominee of the Vermont Progressive Party. Nationwide, over the past 30 years, more than 150 nominees of third parties have been elected to state legislative seats.

Summary

Regardless of whether they are understood as responsible or functional organizations, the two major political parties are essential players in state politics and governance. From primary systems to ballot access laws, parties help to structure the electoral and governing environments in states, which in turn affect the parties. The partisan identification and political ideology of a state's electorate, which are not always synonymous, help to shape the organization and the governance strategies of the parties. The strength of state parties is ever-shifting in terms of their electoral, organizational, and governance strength, with considerable differences across the states. As we shall see in the following chapter, the balance of power between political parties and interest groups varies across the states and even within states over time. Sometimes, it seems as though interest groups are subservient to parties; at other times, the relationship appears to be reversed.

---

[92] Steven Rosenstone, Roy Behr, and Edward Lazarus, *Third Parties in America: Citizen Response to Major Party Failure*, 2nd ed. (Princeton, NJ: Princeton University Press, 1996). Dean Lacey and Quinn Monson, "The Origins and Impact of Votes for Third-Party Candidates: A Case Study of the 1998 Minnesota Gubernatorial Election," *Political Research Quarterly* 55 (2002): 409–437.

Key Terms

Bipartisan Campaign Reform Act of 2002

Caucus

Closed primary

Direct primary

Functional party model

Office-block ballot

Open primary

Partisan dealignment

Party boss

Party-column ballot

Party fusion

Party identification

Patronage appointments

Political action committee (PAC)

Responsible party model

Semiclosed primary

Semiopen primary

Soft money

Spoils system

Top-two primary blanket

Discussion Questions

1. Are political parties necessary in the American system of government?
2. Discuss the differences between the responsible party model and the functional party model. Use examples from your own state to explain why parties in the United States tend to be more "functional" than "responsible."
3. What are the differences between open and closed primary systems? How have Supreme Court rulings affected primary system laws? Which kind of primary system do you think is the fairest, and why?
4. Why do candidates running on third-party tickets have such difficult time winning office? Discuss various barriers to third-party candidates, and make suggestions on how third parties might be able to garner more success at the polls in state elections.

Suggested Readings

Aldrich, John H. 1995. *Why Parties? The Origin and Transformation of Party Politics in America*. Chicago: University of Chicago Press.

Cotter, Cornelius P., James L. Gibson, John F. Bibby, and Robert J. Huckshorn. 1984. *Party Organizations in American Politics*. New Brunswick, NJ: Eagleton Institute of Politics, Rutgers University.

Gelman, Andrew, et al. 2008. Red State, Blue State, Rich State, *Poor State: Why Americans Vote the Way They Do*. Princeton: Princeton University Press.

Holbrook, Thomas M., and Raymond J. La Raja. 2008. "Parties and Elections," in Virginia Gray and Russell L. Hanson, eds., *Politics in the American States: A Comparative Analysis*, 9th ed. Washington, DC: CQ Press.

La Raja, Raymond. 2008. *Small Change: Money, Political Parties, and Campaign Finance Reform* (Ann Arbor: University of Michigan Press.

Masket, Seth E. 2009. *No Middle Ground: How Informal Party Organizations Control Nominations and Polarize Legislatures*. Ann Arbor: University of Michigan Press.

McKee, Seth. 2009. *Republican Ascendancy in Southern U.S. House Elections.* Boulder, CO: Westview Press.

Morehouse, Sarah, and Malcolm Jewell. 2003. *State Politics, Parties, and Policy,* 2nd ed. Boulder, CO: Rowman & Littlefield.

Web Sites

Ballot Access News (http://www.ballot-access.org): A treasure trove of information on state ballot access laws, primary systems, and barriers to third parties.

Politics 1 (http://www.politics1.com/parties.htm): Provides background information and links to all the political parties that are active in the United States.

Project Vote-Smart (http://www.vote-smart.org): A nonprofit organization that provides a wealth of information on all candidates running for state and federal office.

National Institute on Money in State Politics (http://www.followthemoney.org): Provides comprehensive and up-to-date campaign contribution data for state political parties and candidates.

6

AP Photo/Phil Coale

Interest Groups

LOCAL GOVERNMENTS LEARN TO LOBBY WASHINGTON, D.C.

Looking for a larger slice of the federal pie? Hire a lobbyist. That's what thousands of interest groups do every year to improve their chances of securing federal grants-in-aid in the nation's capital. But interest groups are not alone in lobbying the federal government. Increasingly, municipalities, counties, and other local governments across the country are hiring Gucci-clad lobbyists on retainers, even as these same local governments are furloughing or dismissing pubic employees during the recent economic doldrums.

Stimulated by the allure of federal stimulus dollars, local governments are finding it necessary to enlist the services of contract lobbyists in Washington, D.C. Officials in large cities and small towns are calculating the potential payoff of landing federal aid for specific projects that might offset the loss of revenue that most local governments are experiencing. For example, the city of Tracy, California, paid the D.C. firm, Patricia Jordan and Associates $10,000 in the first quarter of 2009 to lobby the Federal Emergency Management Agency and the Federal Highway Administration for stimulus dollars that would go toward much needed transit and emergency management projects. At the same time, the city—located an hour east of San Francisco—was forced to cut staff by 5 percent and furlough city workers due to budget cuts. Leon Churchill, Tracy's city manager, contended that the lobbying expenses made sense, as "the opportunity was too immense to bypass."

Similarly, the Board of Trustees of Deer Park, Illinois, a village of only 3,200 residents, voted to spend $60,000 lobbying Congress and the federal agencies designated to distribute federal funds. Scott Gifford, president of Deer Park's board, reasoned that it was worth spending the money "to potentially bring in $1.3, $1.5 million" in federal dollars. "We were looking for a way to make up some of the shortfalls we see for the next couple of years until we get out of this recession," said Gifford, defending the board's decision.

Major cities, such as Chicago, St. Louis, and Seattle, have all redoubled their lobbying efforts in the nation's capital. Many have hired former lawmakers to plead their case and insert earmarks into appropriations legislation. The city of Hartford, Connecticut, for example, hired a team of lobbyists, including Nancy Johnson, a former member of the U.S. House of Representatives, to do its bidding in Washington. Sarah Barr, director of communications for the city of Hartford, contends it's a wise investment. "That's where the money's coming from right now," she said, "and we need to get our piece of the pie." Other local governments are following suit. The erstwhile oil boom-town of Glenpool, Oklahoma, just south of Tulsa, hired former U.S. Representative Bill Brewster, and the Morgan City Harbor and Terminal District—a special district in Louisiana—hired former Speaker of the U.S. House of Representatives, Bob Livingston, to make sure its share of federal dollars keeps flowing.[1]

Scott Gifford, president of the Village of Deer Park Board of Trustees, says his community will spend about $60,000 on lobbyists this year in the hope of getting $1.3 to $1.5 million in government money for road and drainage projects.

1   Kevin Freking, "Communities Hire Lobbyists to Produce Cash," *The Washington Times*, 4 May 2009.

Introduction

Interest groups are often portrayed in the media as detriments to the common good or general welfare. "The popular perception," according to one longtime scholar of state politics, "is that interest groups are a cancer spreading unchecked throughout the body politic, making it gradually weaker, until they eventually kill it."[1] Yet, organized interests, like political parties, play an indispensable role in state politics. Documenting widespread voluntary organizations in the American states in the 1830s, French observer Alexis de Tocqueville noted, "In democratic countries knowledge of how to combine is the mother of all other forms of knowledge . . . If men are to remain civilized or become civilized, the art of association must develop and improve."[2] Not only do voluntary associations—what we today call interest groups—help protect the interests of those who join them, but also, as Tocqueville pointed out, belonging to an organization cultivated the democratic values and capacities of individuals and enriched communities.

As we shall see, interest groups are essential components of the democratic process. They serve a basic function of aggregating different points of view and pushing policy agendas in the public sphere. By linking the public to elected officials, interest groups encourage individuals to participate in state and local affairs, allowing their voices to be heard. Without a collective voice, citizens would have relatively little direct power over their elected officials. Casting ballots, after all, happens infrequently, every two years or so. Most people have limited access to their elected officials; few have the cachet to be able to pick up a phone and talk directly to their governor or state legislator. If individuals are to be heard and represented by elected officials,

they require a vehicle to collectively convey their concerns. As countervailing forces, interest groups can apply pressure on public officials, educating them about the issues. They can push for the creation of new public policies, urge the defeat of existing programs, or argue for the maintenance of the status quo. They can even serve as **governmental watchdogs**, monitoring government programs and sounding a public alarm if they uncover inefficient or mismanaged programs or corruption.

Of course, interest groups do not always promote the values and desires of the public interest; regularly, they attempt to promote their own agendas and sway public officials. Some groups have more clout—some might say too much—in state and local politics, influencing who governs.[3] It will also become apparent to you that interest groups are not randomly distributed throughout society but reflect an inherent upper-class bias, with corporate interests and wealthier individuals having greater representation in state and community interest group systems.[4]

After defining interest groups and placing them within the broader framework of a pluralist system, we investigate in this chapter how interest groups are organized and maintained, what roles they play in state politics, and why states have different types of interest group systems. How do interest groups form, and how are they able to sustain themselves? In what types of activities, besides lobbying, do interest groups engage themselves? Why do some states have larger interest group systems than other states, and why are some interest group systems more diverse? Perhaps most importantly, we assess whether the structure of the interest group system is biased, which might make state and local governments less responsive to the public interest. As political institutions, then, interest groups are able

---

[1] Jeffrey Berry, *The New Liberalism: The Rising Power of Citizen Groups* (Washington, DC: Brookings Institution Press, 1997), p. 19.
[2] Alexis de Tocqueville, *Democracy in America*, vol. 2, bk. 2 (1835–40).

[3] Robert Dahl, *Who Governs?* (New Haven, CT: Yale University Press, 1961).
[4] Peter Bachrach and Morton S. Baratz, "Two Faces of Power," *American Political Science Review* 56(1962):947–52.

to alter the political environment and public policies of states and communities.

Understanding Interest Groups

Some political observers warn that rule by special interests leads to government dominated by selfish, narrow, anti-majoritarian organizations. Others argue that interest groups represent a broad swath of interests, leading to a counterbalancing of various issues and viewpoints. Regardless of which side is correct, interest groups try to aggregate a narrow set of preferences and concentrate them as specific demands. Exploiting the cracks of our federalist system and the separation of legislative, executive, and judicial powers existing at all governmental levels, interest groups have multiple points of entry into the political system when trying to shape public policies.

Defining Interest Groups

What are interest groups, and how do they differ from merely having an interest? As you might expect, interest groups come in all shapes and sizes, advancing a seemingly infinite number of political causes. Nearly every one of you will belong to at least one—if not several—interest groups during your lifetime. An **interest group** is a formally organized body of individuals, organizations, or enterprises that shares common goals and joins in a collective attempt to influence the electoral and policy-making processes. Simply put, an interest group is any organization that attempts to influence the electoral process or governmental policy making. Unlike political parties, interest groups do not nominate or run a slate of candidates for political office and do not take over the reins of government. Many interest groups are heavily involved in the electoral process; others focus on lobbying elected officials and policy makers.

If we are to adhere strictly to this definition, "farmers," for example, would not constitute an interest group. Because different farmers have different interests, they fail to meet the definitional standard of sharing common goals. For example, dairy farmers in Wisconsin have interests that are quite dissimilar from those of alfalfa, soybean, and corn growers in Iowa and Illinois or even other dairy farmers in California and Vermont. Wisconsin dairy farmers want to keep down the cost of the feed for their herd, prevent California milk producers from expanding their agribusiness operations, and ensure a fair milk-pricing system. Some may want to increase state and federal subsidies to set aside land for conservation easements protecting wetlands; limit price supports for small, organic dairies in Vermont; and even allow the injection of bovine growth hormone into their cows to increase milk production. Indeed, there are even several competing interest groups representing milk producers in Wisconsin, including the National Milk Producers Federation, the Dairy Farmers of America, the Wisconsin Dairy Business Association, and the State Dairyman's Association. Nationally, there are hundreds of organizations representing the interests of farmers, from the American Farm Bureau, to the Grange, to the Cattlemen's Association, to the National Pork Producers Council. It is important to keep in mind that an interest is categorically different from an organization or a group. Individuals may (and often do) share common concerns with one another without ever belonging to a group.

Types of Interest Groups

The universe of interest groups is not limited to membership organizations, or groups of like-minded individuals sharing common social, economic, or political goals joining together to advance them. Membership organizations bring together individuals—such as the myriad farmer organizations mentioned above—to pursue their collective goals. Some well-known membership organizations with an active presence in the states include the Chamber of Commerce, the Sierra Club, the National Rifle Association, the American Federation of Teachers, Common Cause, and the American Association for Justice (formerly known as the Association of Trial Lawyers of America).

In addition to membership organizations, the definition also includes associations. Associations do not have individuals as members; rather, their members are composed of individual businesses, unions, or even other associations from the public and private spheres. The Oklahoma Petroleum Marketers and Convenience Store Association, the Michigan Beer and Wine Wholesalers, and the Association of Washington Business are all examples of associations, which are sometimes known as "peak associations."

Finally, under this broad definition of interest groups, enterprises—from corporate and family-owned banks to hospitals to insurance companies to colleges and universities—are also included. Enterprises are not membership-based and do not have individuals as members. Employees of an enterprise are usually not involved or even consulted when it pursues a policy or electoral outcome. Publicly traded corporations, for example, do not need to obtain shareholder approval before pursuing political and electoral goals. As such, an enterprise is permitted to support issues and candidates that may be at odds with the preferences of its employees or shareholders.

Pluralist Theory

An acceptance of minority factions—what today some might call interest groups—is central to the concept of **pluralism**. Pluralism assumes that conflict is at the heart of politics and accepts that a diversity of interests will lead to consensual outcomes through the tug-and-pull of discussion and debate. In theory, the pluralist framework suggests that broad-based, public-regarding interests seeking the expansion or preservation of the public

good are able to countervail and compete with private sector interests seeking narrow, concentrated benefits.

Writing in 1951, political scientist David Truman expanded on the writings of Founder James Madison, arguing that humans are naturally predisposed to creating and participating in groups. Once formed, some groups not only exert power over other groups, keeping each other in check, but also are able to exert power over their own members. Because individuals have many, heterogeneous interests, most people belong to several groups. A stabilizing equilibrium among the competing interests gradually emerges over time, with various interests canceling out one another. Furthermore, even if a group has yet to form, there exists a **potential interest** that may be represented by the shared attitudes among individuals. Potential interests are adequately heard by elected officials, according to Truman, because they advance views that are widely held in society and reflect the attitudes of most citizens. Perhaps somewhat unbelievably, Truman went so far as to argue that individuals with few formal groups in the 1950s—such as African Americans working on plantations owned by white Southerners in the Mississippi Delta—were afforded representation by the pluralist interest group system, as established groups would represent the workers' interests on their behalf.[5]

Critiques of Pluralism

Pluralist theory is not without its critics. Over the years, scholars have pointed out that some of the assumptions regarding the formation of interest groups under the theory of pluralism are questionable. How innate and apparent for individuals is the "knowledge of how to combine,"

---

[5] David Truman, *The Governmental Process* (New York: Alfred A. Knopf, 1951), 502–11. For a formal model showing how unorganized interests may be afforded representation, see Arthur T. Denzau and Michael C. Munger, "Legislators and Interest Groups: How Unorganized Interests Get Represented," *American Political Science Review* 80(1986):89–106.

YOU DECIDE

ARE INTEREST GROUPS A "NECESSARY EVIL"?

Interest groups are not new. Although the term did not become part of the political vernacular until the late 19th century, interest groups are rooted in the fabric of American political life and were heavily involved in the founding of the nation. Interest groups, or what Founder James Madison referred to as "minority factions" in his classic essay, *Federalist Paper No. 10*, are inevitable in a free society. The causes of factions, Madison argued, are "sown into the nature of man." Although a "necessary evil," Madison realized that factions were essential to liberty. If citizens lacked the ability to form factions, they could potentially be tyrannized by government, squandering their fundamental liberties in the process. For Madison, the solution, then, was creating an institutional framework of checks and balances to control the baneful effects of factions.[1]

Is Madison correct? Are factions a "necessary evil"? With more competitive political parties representing the interests of people living in states and communities, are interest groups even needed today? Is it possible that interest groups today even cause more "evil" than good? Some political commentators argue that the proliferation of interest groups leads to "demosclerosis," with lobbyists and corrosive campaign contributions undermining the national welfare.[2] Drawing examples from your community or state, update Madison's argument.

Notes
1. James Madison, *Federalist No. 10*, 1788, http://www.constitution.org/fed/federa10.htm.
2. Jonathan Rauch, *The Silent Killer of American Government* (New York: Times Books, 1994).

as Tocqueville observed, and is it as easy or natural as pluralists generally assume? Does everyone have an equal voice in the pluralist system? Do all potential interests eventually become heard? Do the various interests in a pluralist system really counterbalance one another?

Some critics of the Madisonian pluralist framework have focused on the transactions between interest organizations and their membership as well as government officials.[6] Among other things, these transactional theorists argue

---

[6] See David Lowery and Holly Brasher, *Organized Interests and American Government* (Boston: McGraw Hill, 2003). Lowery and Brasher argue that a neopluralist approach provides a "middle ground" and that "under specific conditions, the world of interest organization politics might appear consistent with either [of the] other two perspectives." For a classic neopluralist approach to interest groups, see John P. Heinz, Edward Laumann, Robert L. Nelson, and Robert Salisbury, *The Hollow Core* (Cambridge, MA: Harvard University Press, 1993).

that a system of interest group competition, whether or not intended so, advantages economic interests, placing their narrow interests over those of the collective good. E. E. Schattschneider, for one, argued that powerful interest groups are able to privatize conflict so that other interests are limited in their ability to become involved in the policy-making process. The pressure group system contains an inherent bias, transactionalists such as Schattschneider claim, as it only represents interests that are organized. Public interests—those that are shared by and benefit the community because of the nonexclusive nature of the benefits being sought—are at a disadvantage when they go up against private interests that are exclusive and adverse to the rights of others.

Interest groups pressing for private gain, of course, try to rationalize their interests, calling them public interests ("What's good for GM is good for the country" was a common slogan in the 1950s—though painfully ironic today), but public interests are often unorganized and cannot compete well against organized private interests. Contra Truman, Schattschneider did not think group organization is inherent, permanent, or inevitable; being an interest is not merely a stage of development in becoming a group. Rather, the pressure group system is limited to those groups that are private and that are organized. As a result, Schattschneider concluded, "The flaw in the pluralist heaven is that the heavenly chorus sings with a strong upper-class accent," in that the pluralist system has a **mobilization of bias** that benefits private, organized interests. The universe of interest groups, for Schattschneider, does not reflect all potential interests whose voices are not heard.[7]

Others have gone even further in their critiques of pluralism. Charles Lindblom contended that economic interest groups have a structural advantage in regard to politicians in market economies. For Lindblom, business has a "privileged position," in that its private decisions can hurt citizens and government officials with "automatic recoil" punishments. A business's decision to relocate or lay off workers can threaten the economic stability of a state or local government. If an automobile manufacturer in Michigan announces plans to move its operations to Mexico, the plant closing will likely increase unemployment in the community, prompt other businesses to also move, and discourage economic investment in the area. Using its threat of exit, business is able to indirectly limit the ability of governmental officials to regulate economic interests. Local and state officials are compelled to provide financial inducements—essentially, pay a ransom—to keep businesses from fleeing. Thus, for Lindblom, policy making is structurally constrained, or imprisoned, by the ability of certain interest groups to manipulate the market system.[8]

If critics such as Schattschneider and Lindblom are correct—that not all interests can be organized and some are structurally more advantaged than others—then it is questionable whether the pluralist system can effectively represent all interests equally. Interestingly, Madison himself had intimated in his *Federalist No. 10* essay that not all interests in society were equally represented nor were factions in society randomly distributed across the population. Madison noted that the "unequal distribution of property" has led to a persistent division in society: "Those who hold and those who are without property," Madison wrote, "have ever formed distinct interests in society."[9] These different classes of people would gravitate together, joining into factions to articulate their concerns. Because the distribution of interests participating in the interest group system is uneven and "far from isomorphic with the distribution of interests in society," for-profit and business organizations are likely to dominate.[10]

Interest Groups and Their Members

Why do people join interest groups, and how do they maintain themselves organizationally? Scholars have taken two very different approaches—one grounded in social dynamics and group theory and the other in micro-level economics—in an effort to gain some leverage on these questions.

How Do Interest Groups Form?

In the 1950s, Truman, who defended interest group pluralism, advanced what is known as **disturbance theory**. Focusing on macro-level

---

[7] E. E. Schattschneider, *The Semisovereign People* (New York: Holt, Rinehart & Winston, 1960).
[8] Charles Lindblom, "Market as Prison," *Journal of Politics* 44(1982):324–36.

[9] Madison, *Federalist No. 10*.
[10] David Lowery and Virginia Gray, "Bias in the Heavenly Chorus: Interests in Society and before Government," *Journal of Theoretical Politics* 16(2004):5–30.

shifts that cause groups to emerge in response to a change in the status quo, Truman argued that voluntary associations would form naturally out of the desire of humans to satisfy their needs. Various interests, including even potential interests, would galvanize collectively, according to Truman, when their common interests were marginalized or threatened. When macro-level societal or environmental disturbances in society occur—such as changes in demographic shifts, changes in the economy, advances in technology, or crises or societal disruptions, such as those resulting from plagues and disease, war, or even natural disasters like hurricanes or earthquakes—new patterns of interaction are created. With such occurrences, nascent groups will emerge in response to the change in the status quo. The resulting new groups help restore the larger "social equilibrium" of the interest group system. For Truman, then, it was rational for individuals to voluntarily join groups to further their own goals and interests.[11]

Other social scientists were not so sure about the natural proclivity of individuals to voluntarily join groups. For some, disturbance theory seemed too easy. Problematizing the logic of collective action, economist Mancur Olson turned his attention to micro-level, transactional reasons why an individual may—or may not—choose to join a group. Olson began by tackling the **free-rider problem**; that is, the assumption that individuals will try to benefit from public goods without paying for them. Contra Truman, Olson contended that there are many costs associated with an individual joining a group. If given a choice, rational actors would generally not join groups, choosing instead to benefit from the actions of the groups without bearing any of the attendant costs.[12]

Flipping many of the assumptions of pluralism on its head, Olson pointed out that individuals usually join groups for three reasons: peer pressure, coercion, or if they receive some type of **selective benefit**. By keeping itself small, a group can exert peer pressure on potential free-riders, embarrassing them to join the group. When small, it is easy for a group to determine who is benefiting from its actions without bearing the costs of membership. Individuals, too, have an easier way of calculating the costs and benefits of becoming a member when a group is small. People might also join groups when they are coerced to do so. For example, say you just graduated from law school and want to become a practicing attorney in North Carolina. You first must pass the state bar exam. Once you do, you must pay annual dues to the North Carolina State Bar and complete mandatory continuing legal education requirements every year.

For some, an important incentive to join a group is to receive a selective benefit that is only provided to members of the group. For example, some retirees join the American Association of Retired Persons (AARP) for the various benefits the association provides to its 30 million–plus members, such as discounts on group health insurance, lower rates on hotels and car rentals, or price-reduced tickets to the theater and the movies. Like Truman's macro-level perspective, Olson's rational choice micro-level framework does not provide a complete picture of group activity. Some people, of course, decide to join groups even if no overt peer pressure, coercion, or selective benefits exist. We do not necessarily think any worse of these people—call them altruistic if you will—but Olson's rational choice framework sees them largely as acting irrationally by not taking advantage of free-ridership.

How Are Interest Groups Maintained?

The theories advanced by Truman and Olson are still widely relied upon when explaining group membership, although they have been modified over the years. For example, some

[11] Truman, *The Governmental Process*.
[12] Mancur Olson, *The Logic of Collective Action* (Cambridge, MA: Harvard University Press, 1965).

scholars have attempted to flesh out Olson's rational choice framework by adding to his subcategory of selective benefits additional reasons why people may join groups. Not only do groups provide material incentives to attract and retain members, but many also offer purposive and solidarity benefits to their prospective and current members.[13] The increase in the number of interest groups may also be due to the rise of entrepreneurs, people who drive dynamic political change by making personal sacrifices in order to get a group up and running. After all, selective benefits—whatever they may consist of—cannot be given to members of a group until the organization actually comes into existence. Furthermore, it may be the case that societal disturbances do not naturally beget new organizations.[14]

Many of Truman's potential interests, especially those in the public interest, emerge and are maintained only because they are the beneficiaries of a generous patron. As government expands its reaches into various policy domains, many existing organizations, business enterprises, and foundations, and even some governmental agencies themselves, have used their wealth to create organizations to respond in kind. Rather than drawing from a membership base, private foundations such as the Ford, MacArthur, or Scaife foundations provide sustenance grants to groups that in turn advocate a progressive or conservative agenda.[15] Many of the groups that are beneficiaries of such largess do not have members. Instead, they are often centralized and oligarchic, focusing their energies on shaping the public debate in states and communities.

Who Joins Interest Groups?

As was certainly true during the founding, not all interests are equally represented in a state's interest group system. Individuals with higher incomes, those possessing more education, and those holding more professional jobs tend to belong to interest groups more than others. Drawing on survey data from more than 15,000 respondents in the late 1980s, a team of political scientists examined who was more likely to join groups. Beyond the obvious finding that not all individuals participate in interest groups at the same rates—some individuals have more resources (such as time and money) and more natural inclination to become engaged in civic life than others—they find that many people are never asked to participate in a group. Others are frequently recruited and mobilized to participate in interest groups. The study finds that an individual's education and income levels are the best predictors of who is recruited to join a group in political action. When trying to attract new members, groups tend to look to those with personal financial resources. Half of poor respondents surveyed in the study said they never receive mass mailings soliciting them to join a group. In contrast, only 12 percent of wealthy respondents say they never receive solicitations in the mail. Agreeing with Schattschneider, the authors suggest that the structure of the interest group system possesses an inherent bias, as groups systematically direct their recruitment efforts toward wealthier, more educated individuals.[16]

---

[13] James Q. Wilson, *Political Organizations* (New York: Basic Books, 1973).

[14] Robert Salisbury, "An Exchange Theory of Interest Groups," *Midwest Journal of Political Science* 13(1969): 1–32; and Robert Salisbury, "The Paradox of Interest in Washington: More Groups, Less Clout," in Anthony King, ed., *The New American Political System* (Washington, DC: American Enterprise Institute, 1978).

[15] Jack Walker, "The Origins and Maintenance of Interest Groups," *American Political Science Review* 77(1983):390–406.

[16] Kay Lehman Schlozman, Sidney Verba, and Henry Brady, "Civic Participation and the Equality Problem," in Theda Skocpol and Morris P. Fiorian, eds., *Civic Engagement in American Democracy* (Washington, DC: Brookings Institution Press, 1999); see also Lawrence Rothenberg, "Organizational Maintenance and the Retention Decision in Groups," *American Political Science Review* 82(1988): 1129–52.

REFORM CAN HAPPEN

A NONPROFIT LOBBYING SUCCESS STORY

A few years ago, the New Mexico State Legislature passed with unanimous support a bill creating the New Mexico Housing Trust Fund (HTF). Democratic Governor Bill Richardson signed the bill into law on April 4, 2005. The HTF, for which $10 million was appropriated from the state capital outlay fund, is run by the New Mexico Mortgage Finance Authority. The authority provides competitive grants to state, local, and tribal organizations that make investments in housing for persons of low and moderate income.

The establishment of the HTF was a huge victory for New Mexico's nonprofit community, which had lobbied tirelessly for the legislation. Joining forces in the Housing Trust Fund Coalition, which led the grassroots lobbying campaign, were over 150 organizations from New Mexico's nonprofit sector, including faith, labor, advocacy, and community groups. Some of the coalition members included the Community Action Agency of Southern New Mexico, the Enterprise Foundation, Jubilee Housing, the Lutheran Office of Governmental Ministry–New Mexico, the New Mexico Conference of Churches, the New Mexico Coalition to End Homelessness, the New Mexico Human Needs Coordinating Council, and the New Mexico Mortgage Finance Authority.

The coalition's field campaign included classic outsider techniques, including phone calls, signed postcards, and letters mailed to state legislators. The coalition also relied on insider techniques, such as making public presentations and providing testimony (including personal stories) at legislative committee hearings. With the passage of the New Mexico Housing Trust Fund Act, the state joined 36 others that have created their own housing trust funds.[1]

Notes
1. New Mexico Human Needs Coordinating Council, "The State Housing Trust Fund," January 2007, http://www.hncc.org/issues/display.php?ID=22.

Interest Group Techniques

In their concerted effort to represent their constituencies, interest groups use different tactics to shape public policies and elections. What do interest groups do, how do their techniques differ, and which groups are most active at the state and local levels? From classic insider techniques, such as lobbying policy makers, to outsider techniques, such as issue advocacy, electioneering, and litigation, interest groups are increasingly using multiple strategies to maximize their effectiveness.[17]

---

[17] Kay Lehman Schlozman and John Tierney, *Organized Interests and American Democracy* (New York: Harper & Row, 1986); Thomas Gais, *Improper Influence: Campaign Finance Law, Political Interest Groups, and the Problem of Equality* (Ann Arbor: University of Michigan Press, 1986); and Ken Kollman, *Outside Lobbying: Public Opinion and Interest Groups Strategies* (Princeton, NJ: Princeton University Press, 1998).

Although interest groups do not typically engage in every type of activity, there are many common patterns across the states and across interests. Table 6.1 details various insider and outsider techniques that some 301 state-level organizations surveyed in three states (California, South Carolina, and Wisconsin) use to shape public policy. Nearly all state-level interest organizations report using insider techniques, such as lobbying state legislators, testifying at legislative hearings, contacting government officials, helping to draft legislation, and meeting with government officials. Interest groups also report using several outsider tactics, including grassroots campaigns to mobilize supporters, letter-writing campaigns, and having influential constituents contact elected officials. Less than half report they contribute money to candidates, and still fewer say they work on campaigns

Table 6.1

Percentage of Interest Groups Using Insider and Outsider Techniques

Technique	Activity	%
Insider	Testifying at legislative hearings	99
Insider	Contacting government officials directly to present point of view	97
Insider	Alerting state legislators to the effects of a bill in their districts	94
Outsider	Entering into coalitions with other groups	93
Outsider	Having influential constituents contact legislator's office	92
Insider	Helping to draft legislation	88
Outsider	Mounting grassroots lobbying efforts	86
Insider	Attempting to shape implementation of policies	85
Insider	Consulting with government officials to plan legislative strategy	84
Outsider	Shaping government's agenda by raising new issues and calling attention to previously ignored problems	83
Outsider	Inspiring letter-writing or telegram campaigns	83
Insider	Helping to draft regulations, rules, or guidelines	81
Insider	Engaging in informal contacts with officials	81
Insider	Serving on advisory commissions and boards	76
Outsider	Talking to media	74
Outsider	Making monetary contributions to candidates	45
Insider	Attempting to influence appointment to public office	42
Outsider	Filing suit or otherwise engaging in litigation	40
Insider	Doing favors for officials who need assistance	36
Outsider	Working on an election campaign	29
Outsider	Endorsing candidates	24
Outsider	Running advertisements in media about position	21
Outsider	Engaging in protests or demonstrations	21

Source: Anthony Nownes and Patricia Freeman, "Interest Group Activity in the States," *Journal of Politics* 60(1998):86–112, table 2.

or endorse candidates. Two of every five organizations claim they use litigation as a strategy, but only one in five runs issue ads or engages in protest activities.[18] Although activities of interest groups operating at the local level are similar, because many community-based groups lack necessary resources, they tend to use more reactive—as opposed to proactive—strategies when trying to influence public policy.[19]

Lobbying

Lobbying is an integral part of the state and local policy-making process, as it is the

[18] Anthony Nownes and Patricia Freeman, "Interest Group Activity in the States," *Journal of Politics* 60(1998): 86–112.

[19] Christopher Cooper and Anthony Nownes, "Citizen Groups in Big City Politics," *State and Local Government Review* 35(2003):102–11. We examine local power structures and land-based growth coalitions in more detail in Chapters 11 and 12.

systematic effort to influence public policy by pressuring governmental officials to make decisions that comport with the interests of the group pursuing the desired action. The advocacy community in every state capital now consists of hundreds or even thousands of people being paid to alter public policy. The growth of the lobbying industry is indicative of its importance. As one keen observer of state legislatures notes: "Any group that can be touched by state government cannot afford to be without representation. If groups do not realize the need for a lobbyist at the outset, they soon learn their lesson."[20] This was certainly the case regarding Native American tribes. Since the passage of the Indian Gaming Regulatory Act in 1988, which opened the way for casino-style gambling on tribal lands, the lobbying efforts of Indian tribes have skyrocketed, as they have used their newfound wealth to pursue traditional insider strategies.[21] As with other groups, the lobbying efforts of the tribes have helped ensure their collective voice is heard by state and local policy makers.

It should come as no surprise to you that lobbying is big business. More than $1 billion a year is routinely spent on lobbying activities in the 42 states that require lobbying expenditure reports. In some states, lobbyists—not citizens—have become known sardonically as the "True Constituency."[22]

What Do Lobbyists Do? Lobbyists try to influence policy making by marshaling information and communicating it to policy makers.[23] Lobbyists regularly monitor pending legislation, communicating directly with policy

makers and their staff about the potential substantive and political impacts of policy choices. Lobbyists need to know not only how but also when to communicate information and to whom. In addition to meeting with policy makers, lobbyists provide information to officials about issues and give testimony before committee hearings. In states with less professional legislatures, elected officials often do not have the resources to stay informed on every issue, so they take cues from lobbyists. Lobbyists even help draft legislation.

The general lobbying strategy of most interest groups is to use professional advocates, whether employed full time by the group or on a contractual basis, to meet with policy makers, help them with their policy and political concerns, and develop relationships with them beyond the immediate issue. To be effective, lobbyists need to consider the receptivity of policy makers to the sort of information the group the lobbyist represents wants to convey. For a policy maker to accept a lobbyist's argument on an issue, the lobbyist—and the group or firm the lobbyist represents—must have not only access to but also credibility with lawmakers and policy makers. One surefire way lobbyists have traditionally enhanced the receptivity of public officials to their arguments has been by developing long-term working relationships with them. The reputation of a lobbyist is a cherished resource and is essential for the lobbyist to gain access on behalf of the group he or she represents. Developing such a relationship enhances both the access and credibility of the group, making it more likely that the policy maker will believe and act upon the group's argument when it is presented to him or her.

Types of Lobbyists Lobbying may be conducted by in-house, contract, government, or voluntary lobbyists. Roughly 40 percent of all the lobbying done in state capitals is conducted by **in-house lobbyists**, that is, with individuals who are employees of a membership group, association, or institution representing their

[20] Alan Rosenthal, *The Third House: Lobbyists and Lobbying in the States* (Washington, DC: CQ Press, 1993), p. 5.

[21] Richard Witmer and Fredrick Boehmke, "American Indian Political Incorporation in the Post–Indian Gaming Regulatory Act Era," *Social Science Journal* 44(2007): 127–45.

[22] Martin Dyckman, "It's Fla. Voters vs. the True Constituency," *St. Petersburg (Fla.) Times*, 3 April 2005.

[23] Anthony Nownes, *Pressure and Power: Organized Interests in American Politics* (Boston: Houghton Mifflin, 2001).

Lobbyists and lawmakers crowd "The Rail" outside the Illinois House of Representatives chambers at the Illinois State Capitol in Springfield, Illinois.

own organization. The Kentucky Distillers' Association, the Montana Mining Association, the Texas Association of Business, the California Nations Indian Gaming Association, the Iowa Corn Growers Association, and the Nevada State AFL-CIO all use in-house lobbyists to maintain a foot in the doors of state lawmakers and policy makers. As part of their job, executive directors, public relations officers, and lawyers often serve as in-house lobbyists for their organizations. Most in-house lawyers have extensive experience working in the area in which they are doing the lobbying. According to one survey of interest group activity in the states, roughly 75 percent of in-house lobbyists are male.[24]

In contrast, **contract lobbyists** work either independently or for a lobbying firm. They typically work for multiple clients and charge their clients an hourly fee. Many contract lobbyists—who are predominantly male—are former legislators, elected or appointed state officials, or staff. Contract lobbyist extraordinaire Frank L. "Pancho" Hays (who sold his Colorado lobbying firm Hays Hays and Wilson in 2003) was legendary in Denver for his self-effacing, ever-professional demeanor. The son of a former lieutenant governor, Hays represented business interests as diverse as the Denver Broncos professional football team, tobacco giant Philip Morris, the Wine and Spirits Wholesalers of Colorado, Colorado Ski Country USA, the Colorado Association of Realtors, and the Cherry Creek School District. Roughly 20 percent of the lobbying corps in state capitals is composed of contract

---

[24] Clive Thomas and Ronald Hrebenar, "Interest Groups in the States," in Virginia Gray and Russell Hanson, eds., *Politics in the American States: A Comparative Analysis*, 9th ed. (Washington, DC: CQ Press, 2008).

lobbyists, depending on the professionalization of the state legislature.[25]

Lobbying done by government employees, who are sometimes referred to euphemistically as governmental relations personnel or legislative liaisons, is also quite common. Roughly 30 percent of all lobbyists in the states are government lobbyists, a figure that is difficult to exactly determine, as many states do not require government personnel to register when they lobby. Municipal, county, and regional governments as well as special districts, fire and police forces, and municipal and county hospitals and agencies all have business before the state. Similarly, state agencies, public colleges and universities, and other public utilities and corporations are affected by public policies. All of these public sector entities employ governmental relations personnel to advocate their vested interests in state capitals. Many, although still not half, of government lobbyists are female, who tend to be career bureaucrats or former legislative staff with extensive experience in dealing with the governmental agency they represent.[26]

Finally, about 10 percent of state lobbying communities are composed of individuals who give their time and expertise without compensation.[27] These individuals are known as volunteers or, in some instances, as hobbyists. Volunteer lobbyists tend to assist public interest groups—retirees helping out the League of Women Voters of Ohio or the Gray Panthers of Metro Detroit, college students interning with Common Cause Kansas and Georgia Public Interest Research Group (GeorgiaPIRG), or high school students earning civic education credit that is part of a class requirement by putting in 10 hours a week working with Arizona Rock the Vote or the Maine chapter of Mothers Against Drunk Driving. Others are regular gadflies who like hanging around state legislatures and

partaking in the action. As one public interest group jokes, volunteer lobbyists are the only ones left worthy of the name lobbyists, as contract and in-house lobbyists do not need to hang out in the lobbies anymore; their campaign contributions and influence enable them to be ushered directly in the front door of legislators' offices.[28]

The Rise of the Statehouse Lobbying Corps In the 1980s, the number of firms and individuals registered to lobby state governments skyrocketed. By 1990, the average number of interest groups in a state registered to lobby a state legislature was 587, up from an average of only 196 in 1975. The total number of registered lobbyists also increased exponentially over the time period. In 1990, there were nearly 29,352 lobbyists registered in the 50 states, up from just 15,064 in 1980.[29] Today, there are nearly 40,000 registered lobbyists in the states.[30]

State lawmakers are far outnumbered by lobbyists. On average, there are roughly six lobbyists for every one state legislator. In New York, there were 6,624 lobbyists registered in Albany in 2008, enough for each lawmaker to have more than 30 lobbyists to call his or her own. There are more than 10 registered lobbyists for each Colorado, Florida, Illinois, and Ohio lawmaker. In contrast, only two states, Maine and New Hampshire, have more lawmakers than registered lobbyists.[31] Although the "old bulls"—large corporations—still tend to dominate the lobbying corps in state legislatures, much turnover occurs in the corridors of state capitols. The annual turnover of

---

[25] Nownes and Freeman, "Interest Group Activity in the States."

[26] Thomas and Hrebenar, "Interest Groups in the States."

[27] Nownes and Freeman, "Interest Group Activity in the States."

[28] Center for Lobbying in the Public Interest, "Ten Immutable Paradoxes of Public Interest Lobbying," http://clpi.org/tips_facts.html#.

[29] Jennifer Anderson et al., "Mayflies and Old Bulls: Organization Persistence in State Interest Communities," *State Politics and Policy Quarterly* 4(2004):140–60.

[30] National Institute on Money in State Politics, "Total Lobbyists for 2007," http://www.followthemoney.org/database/graphs/lobbyistlink/lobbymap.phtml?p=0&y=2007&l=0.

[31] New York State Commission on Public Integrity, *2008 Annual Report*, http://www.nyintegrity.org/pubs/2009/050709_press.html.

Figure 6.1

State Lobbying Laws, 2005

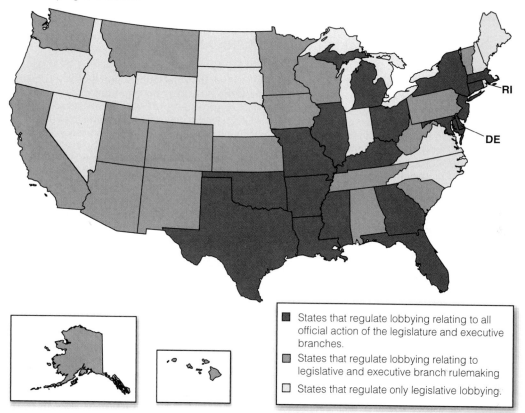

Legend:
- ■ States that regulate lobbying relating to all official action of the legislature and executive branches.
- ■ States that regulate lobbying relating to legislative and executive branch rulemaking
- □ States that regulate only legislative lobbying.

Source: State Legislatures, April 2005, http://www.ncsl.org/programs/pubs/slmag/2005/05SLApr_TandT.pdf.

registered lobbyists working for businesses is actually higher than it is for those working for membership groups and associations.[32]

Regulating Lobbyists State ethics laws and registration requirements for lobbyists have been on the books for years.[33] New York instituted the first comprehensive governmental ethics law in 1954. Since that time, states have passed a patchwork of ethics legislation, resulting in a "Byzantine array of public integrity rules and regulations that vary tremendously from state to state."[34] As Figure 6.1 reveals, 12 states regulate only legislative lobbying, 20 regulate the lobbying of both legislative and executive officials, and 18 regulate the lobbying of all government officials.

Every state requires lobbyists to register with a state regulatory agency or the state legislature, although limitations and disclosure requirements on lobbying activities vary considerably. Several states do not require a fee to register as a lobbyist. In Massachusetts, by way of contrast, the annual fee is $1,000. Thirty-seven states currently require lobbyists to report their

[32] Anderson et al., "Mayflies and Old Bulls."
[33] Rosenthal, *The Third House*; and Beth Rosenson, "Against Their Apparent Self-Interest: The Authorization of Independent State Legislative Ethics Commissions, 1973–1996," *State Politics and Policy Quarterly* 3(2003):42–66.

[34] Peggy Kerns and Ginger Sampson, "Do Ethics Laws Work?" *State Legislatures* (July/August 2003):40–43.

COMPARISONS HELP US UNDERSTAND

REPRESENTING THE AMERICAN DREAM

"We represent the American dream. That's why we win these things. It's about housing . . . [but] the other stuff helps." The "other stuff," according to Mike Toalson, the chief lobbyist and executive vice president of the Home Builders Association of Virginia, is the extensive campaign contributions and gifts his group has lavished on members of the Virginia General Assembly. Over the past decade, his association, with its 6,400 dues-paying members and its powerful political action committee (PAC) known as Build-PAC, has pumped in excess of $1 million into the coffers of the 14 Senators who sit on the Local Government Committee and the 22 members of the House of Delegates who sit on the Counties, Cities, and Towns Committee. The association has been an equal-opportunity donor, contributing roughly the same amount to Republican and Democratic committee members. Prior to his retirement in 2009, former Minority Leader, Franklin P. Hall (D-Richmond), raked in more than $145,000 from the home builders during his 30-plus-year career in the legislature. Several other members have received over $100,000 from building and construction PACs during their tenures in office. Only one member of the House committee—Republican Robert Marshall, an ardent opponent of sprawl—has never taken a penny from the association. The powerful lobby has virtually guaranteed that bills seeking to limit development or rein in sprawl will die in committee. Delegate Marshall, who regularly sponsors bipartisan slow-growth bills, refers somewhat ruefully to his own committee as "a funeral pyre for all those bills."[1]

For close observers of state lobbying laws, the influence of home builders in Virginia should not come as a surprise. Virginia has some of the weakest lobbying regulations in the country, and the laws on its books are substantially weaker than they were 20 years ago. According to a recent composite index of state lobbying regulations, Virginia is tied for third, behind North Dakota and Wyoming, for the most lax lobbying requirements in the country. On the other end of the continuum, South Carolina has the toughest laws, followed by Alaska and Maine.[2]

Notes
1. Michael Shear, "Va. Growth Bolstered by Well-Funded Voting Bloc," *The Washington Post*, 30 January 2006, p. B1.
2. Adam Newmark, "Measuring State Legislative Lobbying Regulation," *State Politics and Policy Quarterly* 5(2005):182–91.

expenditures, 24 have independent ethics commissions to launch investigations and enforce lobbying regulations, and 22 have a "cooling-off" period before government officials or legislators can become lobbyists. Another 38 states ban lobbyists from accepting payment that is contingent upon the defeat or enactment of a piece of legislation or administrative action and another four limit the practice. Several states, including Indiana, South Carolina, and Wisconsin, prohibit public employees from accepting "anything of value" that could be reasonably expected to influence a government employee's official action. In Wisconsin, this includes items as seemingly innocuous as a cup of coffee.

Many states also ban gifts from lobbyists when the legislature is in session.

The strength of state lobbying laws tends to fluctuate over time. Virginia, and to a lesser degree Indiana, which in the early 1990s had some of the most rigorous lobbying restrictions, now rank near the bottom of the spectrum.[35] For years, Alaska, California, Texas, and Washington have had some of the toughest and most comprehensive disclosure and monitoring regulations for lobbyists. Twenty years ago, South Carolina's regulations on lobbyists

---

[35] Ibid.

were among the least restrictive of any state, but now the state has among the toughest anti-lobbying laws in the country. The stringency of South Carolina's lobbying laws increased dramatically in the early 1990s. In the wake of scandals, states often shore up their lobbying regulations. Kentucky has improved from one of the weakest regulators of lobbyists to one of the strongest, in large part due to a series of scandals involving state lawmakers. After some questionable dealings involving lobbyists and state legislators, Florida now bans all gifts and travel provided by lobbyists and requires lobbyists to submit detailed disclosure accounts of all their spending. Other states have recently taken similar steps to revamp their relatively weak ethics laws.

New York, New Jersey, and Tennessee—after several lobbying scandals—have tried to tighten rules for lobbyists. The first executive order of Jon Corzine, the multimillionaire one-term Democratic governor of New Jersey first elected in 2005, required all members of state boards and commissions to file financial disclosure forms. In Tennessee, where an FBI sting ensnared four state legislators taking bribes, the governor convened a special session in 2006 to deal with "a culture of corruption in Nashville." Saying he wanted to "get out in front of the curve and be actively addressing these issues," the governor, Democrat Phil Bredesen, asked the legislature to ban most gifts from lobbyists to elected officials and government employees, require disclosure of lobbyist expenditures, and create an independent ethics commission. The New York State Lobbying Commission is taking more cautious steps to rein in lobbyists: The state's long-standing $75 limit on lobbyists' gifts to lawmakers is now interpreted to apply to an entire year, as opposed to each event or meal.[36]

The relative effectiveness of lobbyists is conditioned by institutional constraints existing within a state. State lobbying restrictions on gifts to lawmakers and prohibitions on campaign finance activities by lobbyists can diminish the clout of lobbyists. Term limits on state legislators can affect the behavior and relative influence of lobbyists.[37] Term limits tend to weaken the long-standing ties and social networks that lobbyists work tirelessly to cultivate over time with government officials. Studies have shown that states with term limits have more lobbyists who report having to work harder to do their jobs. Yet, term-limited states also seem to have worse ethical behavior among lobbyists, which might be tied to lobbyists in these term-limited states wielding more influence in the legislative process than they do in states where incumbents may keep their office interminably.[38]

Occasionally, lobbyists run afoul of the regulations. In late 2005, lobbyist Linda Kowalski entered a plea bargain with the Connecticut Office of State Ethics. She agreed to pay a $25,000 fine and follow tighter disclosure requirements for allegedly filing false lobbying reports and exceeding limits on meals and gifts to legislators. Although Kowalski admitted no wrongdoing and maintained her innocence, she agreed to pay the fine and abide by the new restrictions. From 1998 to 2002, Kowalski worked as a contract lobbyist for the state's trash agency, the Connecticut Resources Recovery Authority. At the time, she also served as a chief fundraiser for Governor John Rowland and the Republican Governors Association. In 2002, the trash agency was involved in negotiations with the now-defunct energy powerhouse Enron Corp. Kowalski allegedly exceeded lobbying expenditure limits when entertaining staffers of Rowland's office. A decade earlier, Kowalski

---

[36] Broder, "Amid Scandals, States Overhaul Lobbying Laws."

[37] John Carey, Richard Niemi, and Lynda Powell, *Term Limits in State Legislatures* (Ann Arbor: University of Michigan Press, 2000); and Marjorie Sarbaugh-Thompson et al., *The Political and Institutional Effects of Term Limits* (New York: Palgrave Macmillan, 2004).

[38] Christopher Mooney, "Lobbyists and Interest Groups," in Karl Kurtz, Bruce Cain, and Richard Niemi, *Institutional Change in American Politics: The Case of Term Limit* (Ann Arbor, Mich: University of Michigan Press, 2007).

had similarly violated Connecticut's rigorous ethics laws. She was forced to pay a $50,000 civil penalty for illegal lobbying activities on behalf of the Connecticut Retail Merchants Association, which had provided meals and gifts of alcoholic beverages, tickets to sporting events, and golf outings to lawmakers in excess of the $50 annual limit.[39]

Issue Advocacy

Rather than having their lobbyists directly press lawmakers and public officials to take action that benefits their members, some interest groups use indirect tactics to influence the making of public policy. Although fewer interest groups report regularly engaging in outsider strategies rather than insider strategies, many groups do engage in issue advocacy. **Issue advocacy** is a form of political speech that mentions issues and the positions taken on those issues by elected officials or candidates but stops short of expressly advocating the support or defeat of those elected officials or candidates. Issue ads themselves may be articulated in any type of media—TV and radio broadcasts, newspaper ads, billboards, placards, banners strung behind airplanes, handbills, and fliers—with some costing millions and other just a few dollars. Each state regulates issue advocacy differently, although most take their cues from the federal government's regulations. All are bounded by rulings handed down by the U.S. Supreme Court.

Issue Advocacy in Historical Perspective
Issue advocacy has been used by interest groups since the 19th century. At that time, party machines dominated state and local politics, and many citizen groups started to become more formally organized. Because their demands were not being fulfilled through two-party system politics,

workers, farmers, and women were among the first interests to become organized at the subnational level. Industrial workers complained about being systematically denied fair working conditions and the right to organize. Farmers and ranchers were upset with the high costs of transportation being charged by monopolistic railroad companies. Millions of women were upset with being denied the right to vote. Yet, these concerns were not making their way onto the agendas of the political parties. Tracing the development of interest organizations in California, Washington, and Wisconsin during the Progressive era, one scholar has shown how farmers, workers, and women—among other interests—were able to eventually organize themselves into interest groups, creating new political opportunities for representation.[40]

Today, a wide variety of interest groups engage in outsider issue advocacy strategies that often resemble the activities of the earliest interest groups. Although done with less frequency today than in the past, interest groups sometimes sponsor boycotts, sit-ins, rallies, mass rallies, and marches to give their issues visibility and engender public support. For example, hundreds of supporters of Georgia death-row inmate Troy Davis, who was scheduled to be executed for the 1989 murder of an off-duty police officer, regularly rallied on the steps of the Georgia state capitol in Atlanta to put pressure on the state parole board to consider granting Davis clemency. Supported by members of anti-death penalty interest groups, such as Amnesty International, as well as judges and former state prosecutors convinced of his innocence after several witnesses recanted their statements fingering Davis, members of his family and friends wore blue t-shirts proclaiming "I am Troy Davis" and carried placards during the choreographed demonstrations.

---

[39] Jon Lender, "Lobbyist Agrees to Pay Fine: Settlement Heads off Costly Ethics Case," *Hartford* (Conn.) *Courant*, 30 November 2005, p. B1.

[40] Elisabeth S. Clemens, *The People's Lobby: Organizational Innovation and the Rise of Interest Group Politics in the United States, 1890–1925* (Chicago: University of Chicago Press, 1997).

Kim Davis, center, sister of Troy Davis, a death-row inmate scheduled to die Sept. 23, 2008 is surrounded by supporters during an Amnesty International rally at the Georgia State Capitol in Atlanta, Sept. 11, 2008.

Perhaps in part due to the international attention Davis' supporters generated by their mass rallies, the U.S. Supreme Court in 2009 ordered a federal trial court to hear new testimony in the case.[41]

Earned Media When engaging in issue advocacy, interest groups try to frame issues to sway public opinion in a direction that may help place indirect pressure on policy makers. From authoring op-eds and running TV and newspaper ads pushing an issue, to blasting fax and e-mail press releases to the media, to mounting a grassroots letter-writing campaign, to engaging in more shocking protests and demonstrations, interest groups often take their influence to the proverbial (and sometimes

literal) streets. By raising an issue outside of the legislative arena, organized interests are able to use **earned media**—generating newsworthy events or stories for the press to report on for free—to help mobilize public opinion in favor of or against a public policy. Interest groups hope that by communicating information and positions on policies to citizens directly, the resulting buzz concerning the issues will be indirectly relayed to policy makers, influencing their decisions.[42]

Grassroots and Astroturf Mobilization Mobilizing support for public policies at the grassroots level is another form of issue advocacy.

---

[41] Adam Liptak, "Supreme Court Orders New Look at Death Row Case," *New York Times*, 17 August, 2009. Available: http://www.nytimes.com/2009/08/18/us/18scotus.html.

[42] Kenneth Goldstein, *Interest Groups, Lobbying, and Participation in America* (Cambridge, MA: Cambridge University Press, 1999); and Jack Walker, *Mobilizing Interest Groups in America: Patrons, Professionals, and Social Movements* (Ann Arbor: University of Michigan, 1991).

Generating ground-level support from members of an organization, or more generally from supporters of an issue, helps a group apply pressure on legislators and other elected officials. When done well, it "demonstrates vocal and tangible support (or opposition) for a measure," says Alan Rosenthal, as "constituents tell legislators how the measure will affect them, instead of the lobbyist doing it."[43] Some lobbying firms also engage in what are more derisively known as **astroturf campaigns**, where constituencies are essentially manufactured by an interest group to give legislators the appearance that the electorate is up in arms about a certain policy. Corporations are increasingly using astroturf campaigns to influence public policy, as they can help expand the scope of conflict and give them the appearance that they have broader public support for their issue position.

Although nearly all interest groups engage in issue advocacy, groups use different tactics. Not surprisingly—as the anti-Schwarzenegger protest in California makes evident—labor unions at the state and local levels often engage in protest activities, drawing on their membership base to make their collective voice heard by elected officials, the media, and the general public. Public interest groups also engage in protest activities, relying on their legions of volunteers, whereas trade and professional organizations rarely engage in such demonstrations. Corporations, and to a lesser degree governmental groups, tend to be less likely to participate in grassroots lobbying efforts and letter-writing campaigns than unions, trade associations, and nonprofit citizen organizations. Governmental groups are much less likely to use these techniques as part of their issue advocacy strategy.[44]

Other groups, most notably liberal- and conservative-leaning public interest groups, associations, and labor unions, provide their members (and the broader general public)

with information about incumbents and candidates running for office. These educational efforts—the groups do not actually endorse candidates—are nevertheless quite political. Some groups produce scorecards reporting the voting records of incumbents. For example, New Yorkers against Gun Violence is a nonprofit advocacy group that publicizes the destructive effects of gun violence in New York and advocates gun legislation. The group regularly compiles and distributes a legislative voting scorecard detailing whether members of the legislature supported or opposed key bills dealing with guns, as Figure 6.2 shows.

Ballot Measures   As we discussed in Chapter 4, in many of the two dozen states that permit the process, ballot initiative are increasingly becoming a way for interest groups to advance their causes. In these states, which tend to have more interest groups than states without the process, ballot measures serve as another issue advocacy weapon in the arsenal of politically active groups.[45] Although the costs of running a ballot campaign in some states can be substantial—in California, Florida, and even Colorado, ballot campaigns can reach more than $10 million—the resulting policy payoff may be worth it. By circumventing unresponsive legislatures, groups can take their issue directly to the citizens.

Historically, interest groups have turned to ballot measures when the usual legislative channels have been blocked by party bosses or rival interest groups. Although citizen-dominated interest groups have had more success than economic interest groups in passing favorable ballot measures, economic groups have not been shy to use the process.[46] Not always

---

[43] Rosenthal, *The Third House*, p. 155.
[44] Nownes and Freeman, "Interest Group Activity in the States."

[45] Frederick Boehmke, *The Indirect Effect of Direct Legislation: How Institutions Shape Interest Group Systems* (Columbus: Ohio State University Press, 2005).
[46] Elisabeth Gerber, *The Populist Paradox: Interest Group Influence and the Promise of Direct Legislation* (Princeton, NJ: Princeton University Press, 1999); and Daniel Smith, *Tax Crusaders and the Politics of Direct Democracy* (New York: Routledge, 1998).

Figure 6.2

Partial New York Legislative Scorecard Produced by GunFreeKids.org and New Yorkers Against Gun Violence

GUNFREEKIDS.ORG AND NEW YORKERS AGAINST GUN VIOLENCE	2008 NEW YORK LEGISLATIVE SCORECARD

About the Scorecard

This scorecard rates, and in certain instances, endorses candidates for the New York State Senate and Assembly. The criteria for compiling our ratings and endorsements focuses on three areas: 1) Responses to our Questionnaire, 2) Past Votes, and 3) Gun Lobby Endorsements and Campaign Contributions. The highest rating we give is an "A, if the candidate has returned the questionnaire, voted with us in the past and never accepted money from the gun lobby and/or received a favorable rating from the gun lobby. The lowest rating we give is an "F".

Senate Candidates by District

Candidate	District	Party	GFK/ NYAGV Rating	Endorse	Candidate	District	Party	GFK/ NYAGV Rating	Endorse
Kenneth Lavalle	1	R	F		Barbara Donno*	7	R	F	
John Flanagan	2	R	F		Craig Johnson	7	D	B+	Yes
Michael DePoll*	2	D	N/A		Carol Gordon*	8	D	B	
Caesar Trunzo	3	R	F		Charles Fuschillo	8	R	F	
Brian Foley*	3	D	B+	Yes	Roy Simon*	9	D	N/A	
John Albano*	4	WF	N/A		Dean Skelos	9	R	F	
Tanya Gilliard*	4	D	N/A		Shirley Huntley	10	D	B	
Owen Johson	4	R	F		James Gennaro*	11	D	B	
Matthew Meng*	5	D	B		Frank Padavan	11	R	B	
Carl Marcellino	5	R	F		Thomas Dooley*	12	R	N/A	
Kristen McElroy*	6	D	B		George Onorato	12	D	B	
Kemp Hannon	6	R	F		Hiram Monserrate*	13	D	N/A	

*Indicates Challenger Parties: R = Republican, D = Democrat, I = Independent, C = Conservative, WF = Working Families

INSTITUTIONS MATTER

TAKING THE INITIATIVE FOR ANIMAL PROTECTION

Why do some states prohibit the use of leghold traps, while others permit it? During the 1990s, interest groups—led by the Humane Society of the United States—placed 17 animal protection initiatives on the ballots of 11 states permitting the plebiscitary process. The measures dealt with an impressive array of animal protection issues—from prohibiting the use of steel-jaw leghold traps in Arizona, Colorado, and Massachusetts; to banning cockfighting in Arizona and Missouri; to barring the use of hounds and baiting in the hunting of bears in Colorado, Idaho, and Michigan; to ending trophy hunting of mountain lions in California and airborne hunting of wolves, foxes, lynx, and wolverines in Alaska; and to outlawing mourning dove hunting in Ohio.

As the largest animal protection membership association in the world, with more than 250 staff employed in nine regional offices, the Humane Society turned to the initiative process after having difficulty passing animal protection legislation in the states. According to Wayne Pacelle, president of the organization, many state legislatures are dominated by rural and agricultural interests. Frustrated by the unwillingness of some state legislatures to adopt animal protection laws, the interest group decided to circumvent intransigent state legislatures and use the initiative process to supplement its traditional insider lobbying approach. The decision to embark upon an outsider strategy was made easier by the fact that the group's membership was exploding. The organization was able to tap into its vast nationwide membership, which grew from roughly 1 million members in 1990 to over 7 million members in 2000. Members provided their labor as well as their financial resources during the qualifying and electoral stages of the ballot measure process. On election day, voters approved 12 and rejected five of the Humane Society's ballot measures, a 71 percent success rate.[1]

Notes

1. Daniel A. Smith, "Representation and the Spatial Bias of Direct Democracy," *University of Colorado Law Review* 78: 1395–1434.

---

successful in their endeavors, vested economic interest groups still have played a major role in ballot campaigns since the turn of the 20th century.[47] In 1910, in South Dakota, for example, 12 propositions were placed on the ballot, including one by the railroad industry seeking to overturn a law requiring electric headlights for locomotives and another seeking to topple a law regulating embalming procedures of undertakers.[48] In Oregon, in 1908, rival upstream and downstream fishing companies placed counterpropositions on the June primary ballot that tried to eradicate each other's means of fishing for salmon on the Columbia River.[49]

In the 2005 special election in California, for example, over $262 million was spent by various groups contesting eight ballot initiatives on the ballot.[50] The pharmaceutical industry's association, PhRMA, spent over $80 million in its effort to defeat a liberal

---

[47] Daniel Smith and Joseph Lubinski, "Direct Democracy during the Progressive Era: A Crack in the Populist Veneer?" *Journal of Policy History* 14(2002):349–83.

[48] Daniel Smith, "Special Interests and Direct Democracy: An Historical Glance," in M. Dane Waters, ed., *The Battle over Citizen Lawmaking: A Collection of Essays* (Durham, NC: Carolina Academic Press, 2001).

[49] Joseph G. Lapalombara and Charles B. Hagan, "Direct Legislation: An Appraisal and a Suggestion," *American Political Science Review* 45(1951):400–21; Shaun Bowler and Todd Donovan, *Demanding Choices: Opinion, Voting, and Direct Democracy* (Ann Arbor: University of Michigan Press, 1998), pp. 118–28.

[50] Kate Folmar and Aaron Davis, "Fall Ballot Campaign Set Record for Expenses," *San Jose Mercury News*, 1 February 2006.

ballot measure that would have reduced the cost of prescription drugs, as well as to promote its own counterproposition that would have preserved the status quo. Both measures ended up failing, which was a major victory for PhRMA. Other special interests poured money into the ballot issue campaigns. Using a temporary dues increase on its 300,000-plus members, the California Teachers Association spent some $58 million in its successful effort to defeat ballot initiatives backed by Governor Schwarzenegger that targeted public sector unions and teacher tenure. All told, California unions and their out-of-state allies spent more than $120 million to defeat the governor's slate of propositions on the ballot. Special interests backing the governor's reform agenda contributed over $70 million to the sponsoring committees, including some $44 million to the governor's own ballot initiative committee, the California Recovery Team.[51]

Nonprofit groups have had some success using the initiative process to advance their issues. Spurned for years due to the grip of the tobacco and business lobbies in Tallahassee, a coalition of four prominent public health organizations—the American Cancer Society, the American Heart Association, the American Lung Association, and the Campaign for Tobacco-Free Kids—joined forces to place an initiative on Florida's 2002 statewide ballot. Their proposed constitutional amendment, Amendment 6, called for the prohibition of workplace smoking. The four nonprofits contributed 99 percent of the $5.854 million raised by the ballot committee, Smoke-Free for Health, Inc.[52] With public opinion polling numbers showing the public favored the measure by a three-to-one margin, the tobacco and business associations decided not to aggressively oppose the measure. The measure passed easily,

garnering 71 percent of the statewide vote and receiving a majority of votes in all of Florida's 67 counties.

Electioneering

Interest groups not only try to shape the public policy debate through their lobbying and issue advocacy. Organized interests can also actively participate in the electoral process in a variety of ways. Many become engaged in candidate campaigns in an effort to influence who will be elected and thus have a hand in making public policy. The practice of explicitly supporting candidates or political parties is known as **electioneering**. Working on campaigns or financing candidates and parties helps to solidify the relationships that interest groups have with winning candidates and the parties in control of the state legislatures. Not all electioneering comes in the form of financial contributions. Some interest groups provide candidates and political parties with nonmonetary, in-kind contributions. Such contributions include sharing data from public opinion polls, giving out membership lists for fundraising, and lending staff and field operations for support during the campaign. Other groups will publicly endorse their support or opposition for candidates. Of course, many groups give monetary contributions directly to candidates and political parties. For these groups, state laws vary considerably with regard to what kinds of contributions they are permitted to give, how much they may give, and to whom they may give.

Regulating Campaign Contributions Rulings by the U.S. Supreme Court have consistently struck down federal and state laws banning or limiting expenditures by interest groups that are made independently of candidates and parties, which are known as independent expenditures. However, the Court has given wide latitude to state legislatures to regulate and limit the amount of money that interest groups may give directly to candidates and political

[51] Ballot Initiative Strategy Center, "PhRMA Breaks National Fundraising Record for Ballot Campaigns," 9 August 2005, http://ballot.org.
[52] Elizabeth Garrett and Daniel Smith, "Veiled Political Actors and Campaign Disclosure Laws in Direct Democracy," *Election Law Journal* 4(2005):295–328.

parties.[53] Countless municipal and county governments, and all but 13 states, have passed laws that place restrictions on the amount of campaign contributions that can be made by interest groups to candidates and political parties. The effort by states to limit spending in candidate campaigns has largely stemmed from the perception that special interests—predominantly corporations and business associations—have had undue influence in candidate races.

Similar to the regulation of elections, there exists a tremendous amount of variation across the states in the amount of regulation in the campaign finance activities of interest groups. Nineteen states prohibit corporations from making contributions to state parties and candidates from their general treasuries; another dozen states ban unions from contributing to campaigns using their general treasury funds. Eighteen states permit state parties to receive unlimited contributions from **political action committees (PACs)**, legal entities that allow like-minded individuals who belong to a corporation, labor union, or virtually any other organization to pool their money and contribute directly to candidates and political parties.

PACs operating in Tennessee, for instance, may make unlimited contributions to parties, but they are limited in how much they can contribute to candidates ($7,500 per election to those running for statewide office). The Tennessee Registry of Election Finance is the regulatory body that is charged with overseeing and enforcing campaign finance activities in the state. The requirement that interest groups funnel their contributions through PACs is not universal. Thirteen states allow interest groups to give directly from their corporate or union treasuries to candidates. Eleven states, including Florida, Illinois, and Virginia, permit any type of interest group to make unlimited contributions to state political parties.[54]

PAC Contributions PAC contributions made to candidates running for office depend largely on the type and ideology of the interest group that controls the PAC. Some interest groups give according to their principles; others have more pragmatic giving patterns. Liberal PACs affiliated with local and state chapters of unions such as the Service Employees International Union and the American Federation of Teachers as well as prochoice groups, such as NARAL and Planned Parenthood, give nearly all their contributions to Democrats. Conservative PACs affiliated with single issues, such as the National Rifle Association (NRA) and state affiliates of the National Right to Life, give nearly exclusively to Republicans. In contrast, many corporate-controlled PACs are equal-opportunity givers, writing checks to both Republican and Democratic candidates—as long as they are incumbents. Rather than ideology, these pragmatic PACs use their campaign donations as a means to purchase continued access to lawmakers and policy makers. According to one study, the energy industry—primarily oil and gas companies and their peak associations—pumped more than $134.7 million into candidate committees and state parties between 1990 and 2004. Nearly 70 percent of those contributions went to incumbents, irrespective of their political party.[55]

In 2008 alone, state-level candidates (running for governor, state legislature, and state supreme court) and other political committees raised over $2.6 billion, up $0.5 billion from 2004, but down from the $3.5 billion brought in by the same entities in 2006. (There are many more statewide and legislative elections in midterm than presidential election years.) As in previous years, most of the money flowed from

---

[53] *Nixon v. Shrink Missouri Government PAC* (2000); but see the Supreme Court's decision, Sorrell, Vermont Republican State Committee, et al. (2006), for limits on expenditures and how low states can regulate contributions to candidates.

[54] Edward Feigenbaum and James Palmer, *Campaign Finance Law 2002* (Washington, DC: Federal Election Commission, 2003).

[55] Edwin Bender, "Energy Companies Build Power Base in Statehouses," Institute on Money in State Politics, http://www.followthemoney.org/press/Reports/200410061.pdf.

Table 6.2

Top-Ten Industries Contributing to State Party Committees, 2008

Sector	Democratic	Republicans	Total
Finance, Insurance, & Real Estate	$49,710,468	$69,446,583	$119,157,051
Labor	$96,005,731	$13,612,965	$109,618,696
General Business	$31,406,111	$54,296,708	$85,702,819
Lawyers & Lobbyists	$54,993,412	$28,563,122	$83,556,534
Health	$32,052,480	$38,097,287	$70,149,767
Energy and Natural Resources	$17,931,667	$31,070,912	$49,002,579
Construction	$11,978,489	$23,354,580	$35,333,069
Communications & Electronics	$15,434,010	$18,676,308	$34,110,318
Agriculture	$6,282,341	$11,789,711	$18,072,052
Transportation	$6,981,108	$11,043,269	$18,024,377
Totals	$322,775,817	$299,951,445	$622,727,262

Source: Institute on Money in State Politics, State Elections Overview, 2009, http://www.followthemoney.org/database/IndustryTotals.phtml.

special interests in the form of PAC contributions. General business and labor organizations both gave more than $200 million to candidates running for state offices in 2008, lawyers and lobbyists greased the campaign coffers of candidates to the tune of $142 million, and the combined financial, insurance, and real estate sector contributed over $108 million. Single-issue groups, which usually are more ideological, contributed nearly $112 million to candidates running for state offices.[56]

Interest Group Contributions to State Parties Interest group contributions to Democratic and Republican party committees in 2008 reveal similar patterns, except that Democratic state parties received more contributions than their Republican counterparts. Table 6.2 details the contributions, totaling over $622 million, made by interest groups to state political parties, broken down by industry sector. The contributions (which come largely from PACs and, where permitted, direct contributions from corporate and labor treasuries) give a sense of which kinds of interest groups are contributing to which state parties. It is clear from the table that

some industries give much more to one political party, whereas others give to both equally. Not surprisingly, unions and trial lawyers and lobbyists tend to give disproportionately to Democrats. Republican state parties receive the bulk of contributions made by finance, insurance, and real estate interests, health associations, general construction interests, and energy and natural resources corporations and associations.[57] For example RPAC, the PAC for the National Association of Realtors and its state affiliates, contributed more than $22 million on state and local candidates and ballot issue committees in 2008, and typically 40 percent of its roughly 1.2 million members make voluntary PAC donations each year.[58]

[56] National Institute on Money in State Politics, "Total Dollars for Candidates and Committees," 2008, http://www.followthemoney.org/database/nationalview.phtml.

[57] National Institute on Money in State Politics, "State Elections Overview, 2004," http://www.followthemoney.org/press/Reports/200601041.pdf; Institute on Money in State Politics, "State Elections Overview, 2009," http://www.followthemoney.org/database/IndustryTotals.phtml; see also, Matt Grossmann and Casey B. K. Dominguez, "Party Coalitions and Interest Group Networks," American Politics Research 37 (2009):767–800.

[58] National Institute on Money in State Politics, "Industry Influence," 2008, http://www.followthemoney.org/database/IndustryTotals.phtml; "Make Your Voice Heard," *Realtor Magazine Online*, 1 March 2005, http://www.realtor.org/rmomag.nsf/0/c265e4d06795d2a986256fa9005ec7aa?OpenDocument.

Some single-issue, ideological organizations make extensive PAC contributions to state-level candidates and state party committees. Over three two-year election cycles (1997–2002), the NRA's PAC, the copacetic-sounding Political Victory Fund, contributed more than $3.35 million to candidates running in all but three states (Alaska, Massachusetts, and New Hampshire). In the 2002 election cycle, the NRA contributed a total of $1.1 million, with over half of the money going to state legislative candidates. The total amount of that cycle was nearly double what the NRA spent on state-level campaigns four years earlier.[59] In the 2008 election cycle, the NRA contributed more than $450,000 to state party and legislative committees, targeting hundreds of legislative races. Republican candidates and parties were the biggest beneficiaries, receiving over 80 percent of the total contributions.

Money, it is often said, is like water. It is hydraulic, leveling itself and circumventing any barriers placed in its way. It can swamp the democratic process. A survey conducted in 2002 of some 1,300 interest groups operating in 38 states found that state contribution limits affect the contribution strategies that groups make. States with laws severely restricting interest group contributions to candidates tend to increase their spending in other electioneering areas. Interest groups operating in those states tend to increase their expenditures on issue advertising and independent expenditures on behalf of candidates.[60]

Litigation

Some interest groups turn their attention to state and federal courts when doing battle. As interpreters of laws and constitutions, courts are important venues for interest groups if they

Lawyers for the NAACP (Thurgood Marshall, center) confer at the U.S. Supreme Court prior to oral arguments for *Brown v. Board of Education* (1954).

New York World-Telegram/Library of Congress

have been stymied by policy makers or administrators charged with implementing a law. One survey of state organizations finds that roughly half of all interest groups report that they either often or sometimes use litigation, or legal action, as a tactic.[61] For some groups, a lawsuit may be easier, less expensive, and more effective than paying lobbyists to advance their cause through the legislative process. This might be especially true for groups with small memberships, little political influence in the state or community, or less than stellar reputations.

When pursuing a litigation strategy, interest groups tend to use one of two tactics. Some groups will seek out laws that they view as unconstitutional and file what is known as a test case on behalf of an aggrieved individual. One of the best-known test cases is *Brown v. Board of Education of Topeka* (1954). The National Association for the Advancement of Colored People (NAACP) had filed a suit on behalf of the parents of an eight-year-old elementary student, Linda Brown, who was forced to attend an all-black school in Kansas even though an all-white elementary school was only a few blocks from her home. In 1954, the U.S. Supreme Court struck down the practice of racial segregation in public schools ("separate but equal"). The Court ruled that

---

[59] Denise Roth Barber, "Names in the News: The NRA," Institute on Money in State Politics, 13 July 2004, http://www.followthemoney.org/press/Reports/200407131.pdf; National Institute on Money in State Politics, "Industry Influence," 2008, http://www.followthemoney.org/database/IndustryTotals.phtml.

[60] Robert Hogan, "State Campaign Finance Laws and Interest Group Electioneering Activities," *Journal of Politics* 67(2005):887–906.

[61] Nownes and Freeman, "Interest Group Activity in the States."

the 14th Amendment of the U.S. Constitution prohibited states from denying equal protection of the laws to persons within their jurisdiction.[62] Following the success of *Brown,* many other liberal organizations turned to the courts in the 1950s and 1960s, as many judges were seen as more progressive on social issues than were many state and local governments. In addition to civil rights associations like the NAACP, consumer rights advocacy organizations, women's and prochoice groups, and environmental organizations all used lawsuits—especially pursued in federal courts—to advance their causes.

Beginning in the 1970s, many conservative groups started pushing lawsuits to advance their agendas, in part because they had more sympathizers sitting on the federal and state benches. Perhaps most notably, the National Right to Life Committee, founded in 1973 following the U.S. Supreme Court's *Roe v. Wade* ruling legalizing abortion, has relied on litigation as a key strategy to challenge state statutes protection a woman's right to an abortion. The increase in litigation by interest groups has been well documented: Between 1953 and 1993, the number of U.S. Supreme Court cases drawing interest group attention increased from just 13 percent to 92 percent of all cases.[63]

When an interest group is not an immediate party in a lawsuit, its lawyers may choose to file an amicus curiae brief (*amicus curiae* is Latin for "friend of the court"). These written briefs, which are usually filed on appeal of a case in either state or federal court, offer supplemental legal arguments that attempt to influence the reasoning of the court. To file an amicus, as they are often referred, an interest group must first obtain the permission of one of the parties involved in the case. It is increasingly the case that lawyers for multiple interest groups will file friend-of-the-court briefs for a single case. For instance, in 1972,

the U.S. Supreme Court case ruled in *Wisconsin v. Yoder* that children of the Old Order Amish faith were permitted to stop going to school after they turned 16 because attendance conflicted with their religious beliefs. Prior to the Court's judgment, several religious denominations filed briefs supporting the students, including the National Council of Churches of Christ in the United States, the General Conference of Seventh Day Adventists, the American Jewish Congress, the Synagogue Council of America, the National Jewish Commission on Law and Public Affairs, and the Mennonite Central Committee. Although not always prevailing, lawsuits filed by interest groups can deliver results that are otherwise unattainable in other political arenas.[64]

The Dynamics of State Interest Group Systems

How do state interest group systems evolve over time, how are they comparatively different from one another, and which groups tend to hold the upper hand in a state's system? As studies on the dynamics of state interest group systems make evident, the concern voiced by critics of pluralist theory—that the system is biased in favor of economic interests—appears to be supported by empirical data.

The Advocacy Explosion

Paralleling the trend in Washington, D.C., the number and types of interest groups in the American states greatly expanded during the 1960s and 1970s.[65] In part, the

---

[62] *Brown v. Board of Education of Topeka* 347 U.S. 483 (1954).

[63] Andrew Koshner, *Solving the Puzzle of Interest Group Litigation* (Westport, CT: Greenwood Press, 1998).

[64] Donald R. Songer and Ashlyn Kuersten, "The Success of Amici in State Supreme Courts," *Political Research Quarterly* 48(1995):31–42; Melinda Gann Hall, "Constituent Influence in State Supreme Courts: Conceptual Notes and a Case Study," *Journal of Politics* 49(1987):1117–24; and Lee Epstein and C. K. Rowland, "Debunking the Myth of Interest Group Invincibility in the Courts," *American Political Science Review* 58(1991):206–17.

[65] Nownes, *Pressure and Power.*

so-called advocacy explosion was due to the rapid increase in the number of public interest groups that grew out of the social movements for civil rights, women's rights, consumer protection, environmentalism, and protests against the Vietnam War. The rise in the number and types of interest groups was also partly in response to the increased power and involvement in the economy of federal and state governments.

Many of the emergent groups were markedly different from federated interest groups of a bygone era. The new groups relied more on members writing checks than participating in mass demonstrations.[66] There was also a marked decline in the number of members belonging to older federated civic associations, such as the Rotary Club, the Lions Club, the Kiwanis Club, the League of Women's Voters, and the National Parent-Teacher Association. These groups, like the Women's Christian Temperance Union in the 19th century, combined social and ritual activities, elected their leaders, held regular meetings of the membership, and had members who came from different economic backgrounds. Somewhat ironically, the progressive groups that emerged out of the 1960s had an upper-class bias. These new public interest groups were structurally different than those of the past, essentially "organizations without members." They were fairly oligarchic, were more centralized and professionalized, and fostered a "doing for, not doing with" mentality.[67]

The rise of public interest groups in the American states and communities in the 1970s was not limited to newfangled nonprofit public interest groups pushing postmaterialist values. The rise of liberal-leaning citizen groups in the 1960s and 1970s helped to fuel a conservative backlash. During the 1970s and 1980s, conservative public interest groups, such as the

Eagle Forum, with over 30 state chapters; the Moral Majority; and the Christian Coalition established themselves as key political actors in many of the states. As countervailing forces, these economic and social groups continue to serve as foils to the liberal and progressive groups that emerged out of the social changes begotten from the 1960s.

There was a simultaneous backlash in the business community. In response to the strengthened public interest lobby as well as to the prowess of organized labor which had reached its zenith of influence in the 1950s, businesses began forming their own peak associations.[68] Today, corporate and business interests dominate the universe of state interest group systems. According to the most recent survey of interest groups registered in the states, enterprises comprise nearly three-fifths of all registered groups, with associations accounting for an additional 22 percent. Membership-based groups only account for 19 percent of all registered interest groups, down from 31 percent of all groups in 1980.[69]

The number of professional associations registered in the states, particularly ones representing business and trade interests, also rose in the 1970s and 1980s. The sharp rise was fueled in part by the surge in the number of white-collar jobs and women entering the workforce. By one count, the number of professional associations increased from just 6,500 national organizations in 1958 to more than 23,000 by 1990, and there is evidence that policy at the federal level stimulates interest group activity in the states.[70] Whereas some of

---

[66] Darrell West, *Checkbook Democracy* (Boston: Northeastern University Press, 2000).

[67] Theda Skocpol, "Associations without Members," *American Prospect* 45(1999):66–73.

[68] Jeffrey Berry, *The Interest Group Society*, 3rd ed. (New York: Longman, 1997).

[69] Anderson et al., "Mayflies and Old Bulls."

[70] Theda Skocpol, Marshall Ganz, and Ziad Munson, "A Nation of Organizers: The Institutional Origins of Civic Voluntarism in the United States," *American Political Science Review* 94(2000):527–46; Frank Baumgartner, Virginia Gray, and David Lowery, "Federal Policy Activity and the Mobilization of State Lobbying Organizations," *Political Research Quarterly* 62 (2009): 552–67.

these professional associations are well established and have active chapters in the states, others such as the Montana Bed and Breakfast Association, the Mid-Atlantic Alpaca Association, and the Oregon State Beekeeper's Association are relatively new.

Density and Diversity of State Interest Group Systems

The explosion of interest groups has not been consistent across all states, policy domains, or types of interests represented in a state's interest group system. The states have considerable variation in terms of the composition of interest groups. Interest group power, in turn, is not distributed evenly across the systems. So, why are state interest group systems different from one another?

Following the pluralist logic that groups emerge when a disturbance in the status quo occurs, the number and types of interest groups will grow as a society becomes more complex. There are considerable differences in the size, strength, and dynamics of state economies. As a state's economy grows, so does the number of interest groups operating in that state.[71] States with the largest economies invariably have the most interest groups. In 1997, for instance, Texas and California both had over 2,000 interest groups with registered lobbyists, Illinois had over 1,500, and Pennsylvania, Minnesota, New York, Ohio, Missouri, Florida, Michigan, and Massachusetts all had more than 1,000. At the other end of the spectrum, five states— Rhode Island, Wyoming, New Hampshire, Delaware, and Hawaii—all had less than 300 interest groups with registered lobbyists.

As competition for resources among registered organizations in the states increases, however, interest group systems gradually become denser and the expansion rate of the system slows down.[72] A state's **interest group system density** refers to the number of functioning groups relative to the size of the state's economy. Wealthier states tend to have more interest groups, in part because governments are able to attract new businesses by increasing their expenditures. In states with fairly dense interest group systems, the relative power of each group is lessened. A state's **interest group system diversity**, in contrast, refers to the spread of groups across various social and economic realms. Interest group diversity is positively related to a state's economic diversity.[73]

The states show a tremendous amount of diversity in terms of the kinds of interest groups that have representation. In some states, such as New Mexico, California, Montana, and Wyoming, nearly one of every three interest groups with a registered lobbyist is a nonprofit organization. In New Jersey, by way of contrast, only 14 percent of all groups are in the nonprofit sector. The Dakotas, followed closely by Montana, lead the way with the highest percentage of membership organizations, with roughly 30 percent of their interest group systems composed of groups with individuals as members. Less than 14 percent of all groups are membership-based in Pennsylvania and New Jersey, with Texas having the fewest, at only 11.7 percent. Texas is the state with the highest percentage (71.5 percent) of interest groups that are enterprises; in Wisconsin, less than 40 percent of all groups with a registered lobbyist are enterprises. At 31.6 percent, North Carolina has the highest percentage of associations, with Idaho a close second; the percentage in Utah, by contrast, is roughly half that amount.[74]

---

[71] David Lowery and Virginia Gray, "The Density of State Interest Group Systems," *Journal of Politics* 55(1993):191–206.

[72] Virginia Gray and David Lowery, *The Population Ecology of Interest Representation: Lobbying Communities in the American States* (Ann Arbor: University of Michigan Press, 1996).

[73] Virginia Gray and David Lowery, "The Expression of Density Dependence in State Communities of Organized Interests," *American Politics Research* 29(2001):374–91.

[74] Virginia Gray and David Lowery, "The Institutionalization of State Communities of Organized Interests," *Political Research Quarterly* 54(2001):265–84.

Explaining Interest Group System Density and Diversity

Several factors seem to contribute to the density and diversity of a state's interest group system. States with more competition among the parties also tend to have denser interest group systems, as the lack of single-party rule perhaps exacerbates policy uncertainty and, thus, more intergroup competition. The legislatures of states with denser interest group systems tend to be less productive, as measured by the proportion of all bills introduced that are passed. Interestingly, states that have the initiative process also tend to have an increased number and a greater diversity of active interest groups. One study finds that states that allow the initiative process had on average 17 percent more interest groups between 1975 and 1990, after controlling for other factors that might lead to interest group growth, than states without the process.[75] A parallel study finds that actual initiative use by a state leads to a general increase in the number of membership groups, associations, and not-for-profit organizations that have registered lobbyists in the state, indicating that the institution of direct democracy can increase the aggregate size as well as the diversity of state-level interest groups.[76] Finally, states with more diverse interest group systems tend to adopt a greater number of public policies that are more distributive and progressive.[77]

In states with dense and diverse interest group systems, it is difficult for a single interest to dictate the overall policy agenda of state government. But even in these states with more diversified economies, interest groups are often able to carve space for themselves within a policy domain that is central to their policy objectives, where they become a dominant force. The number of participants in these policy niches tends to be limited in scope, with the vested interests holding considerable influence. In ensuring its survival, a successful interest group is able to stake out its own niche within a given policy domain.

The maximum size of a state's interest group system ultimately depends on the broad parameters of a state's economic and political resources. From this perspective, a state's interest group system is largely driven by its internal economic resources and is constrained by environmental factors. Interest group system stabilization, thus, is set sooner in states with smaller economic capacities.[78] As occurs with biological ecosystems, though, there appears to be a saturation point for state interest group systems. When such a saturation point is reached, the density and diversity of interest groups begin to slow. The competition among interest groups for scarce resources, in this case government grants and programs, intensifies. In turn, as the interest group system stabilizes, it becomes increasingly difficult for the system to support more groups in competition with one another. In terms of turnover of groups within state interest group systems, a recent study finds that for-profit organizations are no more persistent than nonprofit organizations, and enterprises are actually less likely to persist year-in and year-out when compared to membership groups and associations.[79]

Interest Group Competition: Who's Got Clout?

Today, most states and many communities have much more diversified economies than they did a half century ago. This economic

---

[75] Frederick Boehmke, "The Effect of Direct Democracy on the Size and Diversity of State Interest Group Populations," *Journal of Politics* 64(2002):827–44.

[76] Daniel Smith and Caroline Tolbert, *Educated by Initiative: The Effects of Direct Democracy on Citizens and Political Organizations in the American States* (Ann Arbor: University of Michigan Press, 2004).

[77] Sarah Morehouse and Malcolm Jewell, *State Politics, Parties and Policy*, 2nd ed. (New York: Rowman & Littlefield, 2003).

[78] Gray and Lowery, *The Population Ecology of Interest Representation*.

[79] Anderson et al., "Mayflies and Old Bulls."

change has led to a robust competition among a variety of private and public sector interest groups that battle over the making of public policy. Yet, as Lindblom suggested, private economic interests dominate pluralist interest group systems. For example, the oil industry remains king in Alaska and Louisiana, the agriculture lobby reins supreme in Iowa and South Dakota, ranching interests continue to be a strong force in Nebraska, and the tourism industry holds an upper hand in Florida, Nevada, and Hawaii. Although the company town, communities literally built by firms to house their employees, disappeared from the local landscape long ago,[80] some towns— Bentonville, Arkansas, the corporate headquarters of Wal-Mart, comes to mind—are still dominated by a single industry.

An interest group's clout, or relative influence, is largely determined by its own internal resources, but it is bounded by external conditions. Internal resources include a group's political, organizational, and managerial skills as well as its finances, the size and geographical distribution of its membership, its political cohesiveness, and its long-term relations with public officials. A group's policy goals are also conditioned by external factors, such as the political climate of the state or community, including partisan identification, political culture, issues and events, and public opinion. Although it is difficult, if not impossible, to precisely measure a group's "clout," these internal and external factors affect the ability of an interest organization to wield influence and power within a state or community. When lacking in clout, some groups opt to team up with other organizations to build coalitions. Rather than acting independently and going it alone, it sometimes makes strategic sense for an organization to form alliances with other like-minded

groups, especially if competition increases among groups in the system.[81]

Most Influential Interests in the 50 States

Is it possible to rank the most powerful interests in the 50 states? Based on survey responses from political scientists working in all 50 states, Table 6.3 categorizes interest organizations by their effectiveness, listing the 20 most influential interests in the states in 2007 (with comparison rankings from 1985). The table reveals how some sectors of interest organizations are influential interests across many states, whereas others are only effective in a few states.[82]

General business organizations, most notably the Chamber of Commerce, and teachers' associations, such as the American Federation of Teachers and the National Education Association, are powerful interest groups in most of the 50 states today, just as they were in 1985. Interest groups representing energy utilities, insurance companies, hospitals, lawyers, and manufacturers are also forces to be reckoned with in most states. Although liquor, wine, and beer interests are not nearly as powerful (the industry was 28th most influential according to the 2007 rankings), the lobby has a presence in all 50 states. The brewer Anheuser-Busch, for instance, employs lobbyists in all 50 states because alcohol policy is largely regulated by the states. On the other hand, groups

---

[80] John Gaventa, *Power and Powerlessness: Quiescence and Rebellion in an Appalachian Valley* (Champaign-Urbana, IL: University of Illinois Press, 1980).

[81] Clive Thomas and Ron Hrebenar, "Who's Got Clout?" *State Legislatures* (April 1999):30–34; Kevin Hula, *Lobbying Together: Interest Group Coalitions in Legislative Politics* (Washington, DC: Georgetown University Press, 1999); and Michael T. Heaney, "Outside the Issue Niche: The Multidimensionality of Interest Group Identity," *American Politics Research* 32(2004):1–41.

[82] Totals for a category interest may exceed 50, as some interest groups within a category sometimes were reported to be in separate categories by the political scientists who were surveyed. See Clive Thomas and Ronald Hrebenar, "Interest Groups in the States," in Virginia Gray and Russell Hanson, eds., *Politics in the American States: A Comparative Analysis*, 9th ed. (Washington, DC: CQ Press, 2008), pp. 117–18.

representing senior citizens, forest products, mining companies, and tobacco companies have a strong presence in only a handful of states.

Overall, the relative power of interest groups across the 50 states has remained fairly constant over time. Table 6.3 reveals little change between 1985 and 2007 in terms of the relative strength and weakness of interest organizations. In addition to the aforementioned economic interests, groups representing physicians, general farm organizations, and realtors have retained their strength through the years. Although minimal, some change has occurred across some of the sectors: hospital and nursing home associations, the insurance industry, gaming, and contractors, builders, and developers have all become relatively stronger (including the venerable NRA), whereas energy corporations and their associations, banks, and other financial enterprises have become weaker players.

Table 6.3

The 20 Most Influential Interests in the 50 States, 2007

2007 Ranking (1985 Ranking in parentheses)	Interest Organization	Number of states in 2007 in which the interest ranked among		
		Most Effective	Somewhat Effective	Less/Not Effective
1 (2)	General business organizations (state chambers of commerce, etc.)	39	14	5
2 (1)	Schoolteachers' organizations (NEA and AFT)	31	17	2
3 (6)	Utility companies and associations (electric, gas, water, telephone/telecommunications)	28	22	9
4 (4)	Manufacturers (companies and associations)	25	18	14
5 (17)	Hospital/nursing homes associations	24	18	10
6 (13)	Insurance: general and medical (companies and associations)	22	16	14
7 (11)	Physicians/state medical associations	21	16	14
8 (22)	Contractors, builders, developers	21	12	27
9 (9)	General local government organizations (municipal leagues, county organizations, elected officials)	18	18	15
10 (8)	Lawyers (predominantly trial lawyers, state bar associations)	20	13	18
11 (14)	Realtors' associations	20	10	20
12 (10)	General farm organizations (state farm bureaus, etc.)	14	17	19
13 (3)	Bankers' associations	15	14	21
14 (19)	Universities and colleges (institutions and employees)	14	14	23
15 (5)	Traditional labor associations (predominantly the AFL-CIO)	15	11	24
16 (15)	Individual labor unions (Teamsters, UAW)	13	11	26
17 (36)	Gambling Interests (race tracks, casinos and lotteries)	13	9	28
18 (7)	Individual banks and finance institutions	11	11	28
19 (29)	State agencies	10	13	30
20 (23)	Environmentalists	8	17	25

Source: Clive Thomas and Ronald Hrebenar, "Interest Groups in the States," in Virginia Gray and Russell Hanson, eds., *Politics in the American States: A Comparative Analysis*, 9th ed. (Washington, DC: CQ Press, 2008), p. 117.

Table 6.4

Classification of the 50 States According to the Overall Impact of Interest Groups in 2006–2007, Compared with Previous Classifications

Dominant (4)	Dominant/ Complementary (26)	Complementary (15)	Complementary/ Subordinate (5)
Alabama	− Alaska	Colorado	+/− Kentucky
Florida	Arizona	+/− Connecticut	− Michigan
+/− Hawaii	Arkansas	Indiana	Minnesota
+ Nevada	California	Maine	− South Dakota
	+ + Delaware	Massachusetts	Vermont [a]
	Georgia	+/− Montana	
	Idaho	New Hampshire	
	+ Illinois	New Jersey	
	+ Iowa	New York	
	+ Kansas	North Carolina	
	− Louisiana	North Dakota	
	+ Maryland	Pennsylvania	
	− Mississippi	+ Rhode Island	
	+ Missouri	− Washington	
	Nebraska	Wisconsin	
	− New Mexico		
	Ohio		
	Oklahoma		
	Oregon		
	− South Carolina		
	− Tennessee		
	Texas		
	Utah[a]		
	Virginia		
	− West Virginia		
	Wyoming		

[a] Utah and Vermont are in the same categories they occupied in 1985, but both states have moved twice since 1985—into the complementary category and then back to their original categories.

Note: The symbols +/ −, + +, and − − indicate that a state has moved across adjoining categories since the first survey in 1985. If a state has moved up and down, it is designated with a +/ −; if it has moved up only, it is designated with + +; and if it has moved down only, it is marked by − −. The symbols + and − indicate movement of one category only, up or down, since the 1985 survey.

Source: Clive Thomas and Ronald Hrebenar, "Interest Groups in the States," in Virginia Gray and Russell Hanson, eds., *Politics in the American States: A Comparative Analysis*, 9th ed. (Washington, DC: CQ Press, 2008), p. 121.

Despite some flux in the relative strength of the different sectors represented in state interest group systems, economic groups remain powerful players in most states, just as they were back in the 1950s when the first survey of interest groups was conducted.[83] This has led some observers, following the pioneering

---

[83] Belle Zeller, *American State Legislatures*, 2nd ed. (New York: Thomas Y. Crowell, 1954).

work of Schattschneider and Lindblom, to again ask whether a corporate bias in the interest group systems of the states exists. One recent study—which finds that 77 percent of the total universe of state interest groups is made up of for-profit organizations—seems to confirm Schattschneider's prediction that private interest organizations will dominate the interest group system.[84] Yet, the dominance of business interests is not hegemonic. Business interests do not control all policy niches. As state economies increase in size, business interests tend to fragment to some degree.[85] As interest group systems become more and more crowded and complex, it is possible that powerful groups—including business associations and firms—may lose their "clout."[86]

Relative Impact of Interest Groups Interest group strength can also be measured with a fivefold typology that assesses the overall impact of interest groups relative to other actors (most notably political parties) in a state's political system. A survey of the 50 states reveals that the power of interest groups compared to other actors can be considered dominant in four states, dominant/complementary in 26 states, complementary in 15 states, complementary/subordinate in five states, and subordinate in no states.[87] Table 6.4 provides the overall impact of interest groups in the 50 states. The number of states found in each category today has changed since the survey was first conducted in the early 1980s; roughly half of the states are still classified in the same category as they were in 1985, with the remainder shifting categories. Slightly more than half of the states today are categorized as dominant/complementary. Why are interest group systems in some states more dominant than others? Although it's difficult to precisely answer this question, states with less robust economies tend to have political systems with more dominant interest groups. Conversely, in states with larger economies, interest groups were weaker or more complementary relative to other actors, such as state parties.[88]

Summary

Despite some concerns over the undue influence of economic interests, voluntary associations since Madison's time have played a vital role in American states and communities. Like political parties, interest groups are political institutions that operate as rational actors. Some interest groups employ lobbyists to place pressure on public officials. Others use issue advocacy, electioneering, and litigation to advance their collective goals. Whatever their tactic, interest groups are constantly fighting to shape the political terrain, molding it to reflect their image. Although pluralist theory suggests all interests have an equal chance to be heard in the public sphere, there are many barriers to collective action. Because economic and political resources are not distributed evenly across society, some interests are more easily articulated and aggregated than others. As such, not all societal interests are equally represented in states and communities by organized interests nor are they all heard by elected officials and policy makers. It should come as no surprise, then, that in a country with a market-oriented political economy, state and local interest group systems tend to favor economic interests.

---

[84] Anderson et al., "Mayflies and Old Bulls."

[85] Lowery and Gray, "Bias in the Heavenly Chorus."

[86] Schattschneider, *The Semisovereign People*; and Schlozman and Tierney, *Organized Interests and American Democracy.*

[87] John Heinz et al., *The Hollow Core* (Cambridge, MA: Harvard University Press, 1993); and Thomas and Hrebenar, "Interest Groups in the States."

[88] Heinz et al., *The Hollow Core*; and Mark Smith, *American Business and Political Power* (Chicago: University of Chicago Press, 2000).

Key Terms

Astroturf campaign

Contract lobbyist

Disturbance theory

Earned media

Electioneering

Free-rider problem

Governmental watchdog

In-house lobbyist

Interest group

Interest group system density

Interest group system diversity

Issue advocacy

Lobbying

Mobilization of bias

Pluralism

Political action committee (PAC)

Potential interest

Selective benefit

Discussion Questions

1. James Madison, in the 1790s, and David Truman in the 1950s, understood the formation of interest groups as "necessary evils." What were their arguments, however, in favor of interest groups? What were their recommended solutions to any evils involved?
2. What are the different kinds of lobbyists, and which do you think are the most effective? Be sure to discuss the types of techniques that lobbyists use. Do all lobbyists use the same techniques?
3. How do states regulate lobbyists? Which states have the most stringent rules, and do you think they are effective? Cite recent examples of lobbyist infractions from your own state.
4. How does a state's socioeconomic makeup influence its interest group density and diversity? What factors contribute to the density and diversity of a state's interest group system?
5. How is interest group strength measured, and what are the strongest interest groups in the 50 states? What is the overall impact of interest groups in your state, compared to other states? Do you agree with the ranking? Why or why not?

Suggested Readings

Alexander, Robert. 2005. *The Classics of Interest Group Behavior*. Boston: Thomson Wadsworth.

Baumgartner, Frank, and Beth L. Leech. 1998. *Basic Interests: The Importance of Groups in Politics and in Political Science*. Princeton, NJ: Princeton University Press.

Berry, Jeffrey. 1999. *The New Liberalism: The Rising Power of Citizen Groups*. Washington, DC: Brookings Institution Press.

Gray, Virginia, and David Lowery. 1996. *The Population Ecology of Interest Representation: Lobbying Communities in the American States*. Ann Arbor, MI: University of Michigan Press.

Olson, Mancur. 1965. *The Logic of Collective Action*. Cambridge, MA: Harvard University Press.

Rosenthal, Alan. 2001. *The Third House: Lobbyists and Lobbying in the States*. Washington, DC: CQ Press.

Schattschneider, E. E. 1960. *The Semisovereign People*. New York: Holt, Rinehart & Winston.

Truman, David B. 1951. *The Governmental Process*. New York: Alfred A. Knopf.

Web Sites

American League of Lobbyists (http://www.alldc.org): The American League of Lobbyists is an association devoted to enhancing the professionalism, competence, and ethical standards of lobbyists.

Common Cause (http://www.commoncause.org): Founded in 1970 and with chapters in all 50 states, Common Cause is a nonpartisan, nonprofit advocacy organization that strives to hold elected leaders accountable to the public interest.

Political Advocacy Groups: A Directory of United States Lobbyists (http://www.vancouver.wsu.edu/fac/kfountain/): An index by issue area of over 400 interest groups in the United States, with links to their sites.

Project VoteSmart (http://www.vote-smart.org/): Project VoteSmart, a nonprofit, nonpartisan organization, provides a compilation of interest organizations that can searched by subject or by state.

7

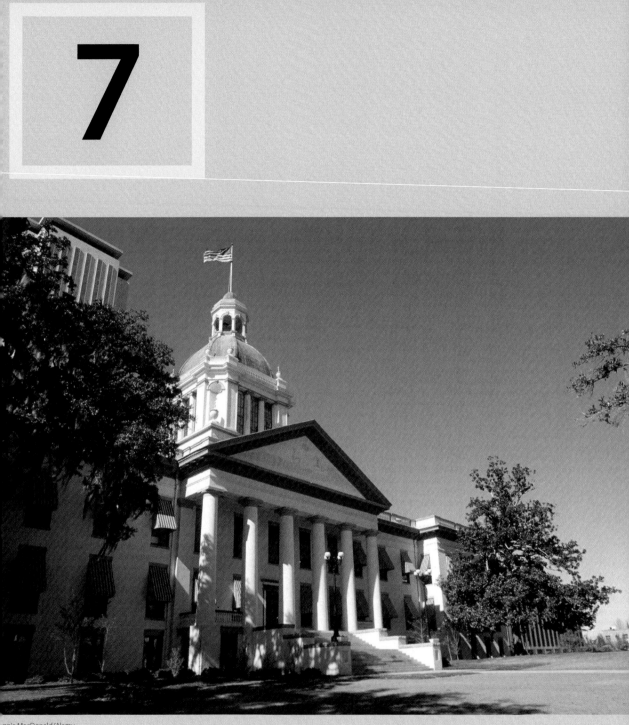

State Legislatures

TOUGH TIMES IN TALLAHASSEE

In the heart of the worst national recession since World War II, with its real estate mortgage meltdown leading Florida to the bottom of the country's economic trough, the 2009 state legislative session in Tallahassee got off to a very bad start.[1] Even before the official opening of its 60-day session on March 4, the Florida House of Representatives was embroiled in controversy and uncertainty. Its Speaker-elect, Representative Ray Sansom of Destin, was forced from his post amid investigations into (among other things) allegations that he steered $35 million in construction money to Northwest Florida State College in exchange for a high-level, unadvertised job at the school. Sansom's claim he was just helping his constituency (the school was in his district) did not calm the criticisms. As a result, Representative Larry Cretul, who had filled the largely ceremonial position of Speaker pro tempore, was thrust unexpectedly as the new Speaker of the House into the eye of the political maelstrom that characterized the Sunshine State's most difficult legislative session in memory.

Even under the best of circumstances, any state's legislative process is difficult, what with dozens of lawmakers and thousands of issue advocates converging on the capitol to help solve the state's problems with limited time and resources. As in all states in 2009, the severe recession made Florida's problems worse and its resources more limited than usual. A majority in both the 120-member House and the 40-member Senate must come to agreement to pass a bill, which is no simple task. Winning passage of any significant bill is difficult because so many people and groups have a stake in the status quo. At the beginning of the 2009 Florida session, as at the beginning of all state legislative sessions, however, there was hope for great things. In particular, many Florida legislators and advocates were working for serious tax reform, both to make taxes more fair and to generate more revenue for the state in its hour of need. And tax reform was closely linked to the one bill that simply must pass each year—the state government's budget.

The budget is the state's taxing and spending plan for the following year. If the budget does not pass, then state government shuts down—no parks, beaches, public schools, community colleges, universities, police force, prisons, National Guard, among many other services. Knowing that this simply cannot be allowed to happen, policy makers know that they must pass the budget. So the big question of every legislative session is: What will the content of the budget be? Of course, everyone—every legislator and advocate, the governor and every executive branch official, and every Floridian—has budget priorities. This means that tough choices have to be made, because even in the best of years, a state's resources are limited. And in 2009, there were far fewer resources available than usual. For example, legislators would end up cutting higher educa-tion funding drastically. Florida's 11 public universities received $62 million less than they had in the previous year, and this was on top of almost $70 million in cuts in the previous two years. Combined, these cuts represented an almost 16 percent decrease in state fund-ing to Florida's universities, which—despite tuition increases—led to programs being elimi-nated, faculty and staff being fired, and enrollments being slashed. Cuts in other areas of government service were just as deep.

Republicans controlled Florida state government handily in 2009, with large majori-ties in the House and Senate and with Republican Charlie Christ in the governor's man-sion. One might think that unified party government like this would make lawmaking easier. But when government is handing out more pain than pleasure—that is, when it is cutting more than it is increasing spending—controlling government does not give a political party credit, it gives it blame. In addition to cutting services, Republicans in the Florida legislature were also forced to do two things that they especially hated to do—raise taxes and fees, and accept federal stimulus money. Throughout the session, the two chambers battled over how to raise revenue. The Senate pushed for a cigarette tax, and the House eventually agreed. After refusing to close numerous sales tax loopholes to raise revenue, the House voted to increase a variety of fees, such as those for deer and turkey hunting licenses, drivers' licenses and plates for motor vehicles, and even an $8.94 daily fee for parolees for wearing electronic bracelet monitors. And after weeks of deriding it as "Obama bucks," legislative Republicans finally had to swallow their pride and take $5 billion in federal stimulus money.

The Sansom scandal also provoked calls for ethics reform, with a special focus on the legislative budget process. The actual budget bill is an extremely large and complicated document that has major effects on people, governments, and businesses statewide. As such, the final negotiations are often tedious, excruciating, and long. Historically, after the broad strokes of the plan had been hammered out in committee and open floor debate, top legislative leadership wrote up the "budget proviso" language in closed session. These were the documents that detailed how the legislature wanted the state funds to be spent. Working in closed session allowed lawmakers to make tough decisions and compromises without the close scrutiny of the press and interest groups. In light of the Sansom scandal, however, these closed sessions were seen more as an opportunity for corruption, so they were opened up in 2009.

Further complicating the process was the "accidental speaker," Representative Cretul, who neither sought nor prepared for this role. In a chamber accustomed to a strong leader, as are many state houses, this caused serious problems even with simply moving the leg-islative process along. Combine this with a hands-off governor who was grooming his image for a run at the U.S. Senate in 2010 and a term-limited body where few members had more than six years of experience, and you had a recipe for a bitter and difficult lawmaking session. By the time it ended on May 2, no one could blame Florida's legislators for being glad to leave Tallahassee. Hurricane season may have been just beginning, but Florida's lawmakers surely felt like they had just been through a 60-day-long Category IV storm.

AP Photo/Phil Coale

1 This vignette was developed with information from a variety of contemporary news sources, including: Alex Leary, "No Return for Sansom," *Times* (Tampa Bay, FL), 1 February 2009, online edition; Shannon Colavecchio-Van Sickler, "Colleges Could Turn Away 60,000 Report Says," *Times* (Tampa Bay, FL), 5 February 2009, online edition; Amy Hollyfield, "State Weighs Tapping into Prepaid Tuition Fund for Economic Relief," *The Miami Herald*, 8 March 2009, online edition; Alex Leary and Marc Caputo, "Florida Legislature's Stormy Session Is One for the Books," *The Miami Herald,* 3 May 2009, online edition; Mary Ellen Klas, "Legislature's Scorecard for 2009: 1 New Tax, Little Reform," *The Miami Herald*, 3 May 2009, online edition; Shannon Colavecchio-Van Sickler, "Deep Cuts Hit UF at All Levels," *Times* (Tampa Bay, FL), 5 May 2009, online edition; Associated Press, "Trustees Approve $42M in Cuts to UF Budget," *Orlando Sentinel*, 26 May 2009, online edition.

Introduction

Our opening tale of the Florida legislature's frenzied and difficult 2009 session highlights many of both the recent and the perennial features of the major lawmaking body in each state. Legislatures and legislators have the tough job of dealing with the public problems of the state with limited resources. Some years this job is harder than others, but it is never easy. The way that state legislative institutions are set up makes the job especially difficult, with the large numbers of decision makers, frequent elections, two chambers, and more. Some institutions have evolved to help make these bodies run better, like legislative committees and leadership, but they do not solve all the difficulties. Because public problems outstrip public resources, compromise is always needed in lawmaking, leading to dissatisfaction and frustration.

In the 15 states that have them, state legislative term limits have undoubtedly complicated lawmaking by reducing institutional knowledge and shifting influence to other actors in the process. The part-time nature of service in most state legislatures can exacerbate their woes since, like all of us, lawmakers are prone to certain all-too-human frailties. Since most lawmakers need an external source of income, conflicts of interest can arise, even if they rarely rise to the level of outright graft and corruption, as alleged in the Sansom case. Regardless, the recent well-publicized cases of legislative corruption in several states have shaken the public's faith in their representatives. Various ethics laws and regulations have been advocated, and sometimes adopted, but none of them is a panacea. And despite any problems with the legislative process, and no matter what its outcomes in a given state in a given year, two things are guaranteed: The legislative outputs will have important effects on all the residents of the state, and lawmakers will do it all over again next year.[1]

State legislatures provide a vital link between a state's citizens and its government—they are the "engines of democracy."[2] These lawmakers have the smallest constituencies of any type of state or federal official, and they best reflect America's diversity. It is now common for women and members of minority groups not only to serve in state legislatures but also to hold the highest leadership positions there. These bodies are richly diverse in other ways, too. For example, in the New Hampshire House of Representatives, the nation's youngest (Jeff Fontas, 21) and oldest (Angeline Kopka, 92) state lawmakers serve side by side, and some of the nation's 7,382 state lawmakers are openly gay or lesbian (e.g., Minnesota Representative Karen Clark and Utah Senator Scott McCoy).[3] Furthermore, since lawmaking is not a full-time job for most state legislators, and since they therefore live and work in and among their constituents most of the time, people are far more likely to know them than, say, their governor or member of Congress.

Serving as a state legislator is service, indeed. The pay is low, the hours are long, and the conditions are poor,[4] but their work is essential in the process of translating the wishes and needs of a state's citizens into public policy. Every law that exists in a state, every change in any state law, and every penny that a state spends must be approved by the state legislature in a long and complicated process much like that of the U.S. Congress. It is impossible to overemphasize the importance of legislatures for their states.

If state lawmaking is such a tough job under such tough conditions, why do people actively

---

[1] This is except for those five state legislatures (in Montana, Nevada, North Dakota, Oregon, and Texas) that meet biennially. These state legislatures will do it all over again in two years.

[2] Alan Rosenthal, *Engines of Democracy: Politics and Policymaking in State Legislatures* (Washington, DC: CQ Press, 2009).

[3] Donald Haider-Markel, "Gay and Lesbians in American State Legislatures," unpublished manuscript (Department of Political Science, University of Kansas); Morgan Cullen, "He's 21. She's 92," *State Legislatures* (July/August 2008):52–54.

[4] For example, see: Jennifer Mock, "Lawmakers Share Apartment during Session: Homes Away from Home Vary for Legislators with One Even Staying in a Travel Trailer, *The Oklahoman*, 28 March 2007, online edition; Nicholas K. Geranios, "Police: Legislator Target of Extortion," *The Seattle Times*, 31 October 2007.

and aggressively run for these positions? Plain ambition is one reason. Being a state legislator is excellent training for higher office, and lawmakers often move up the political ladder.[5] Almost half of those serving in Congress today are former state legislators; even President Barack Obama served in the Illinois Senate recently (from 1997 to 2004). In fact, some (including Obama himself) have argued that what the president learned in the state legislature, about the details of public policy, how to work with people of all stripes, the skills of compromise, debate, and perseverance, and much more, were even more important to his success at the national level than what he learned in the U.S. Senate.[6]

Beyond self-aggrandizement, the work of public service in state legislatures is truly important and satisfying—and it simply fascinates many people.[7] State lawmakers work to solve problems in every area of life, from helping poor people get health care to improving a state's business climate to attract jobs, from reducing city traffic to building roads and bridges, from educating preschool children to searching for a cure for Alzheimer's disease. Just ask Fred Risser. After 52 years representing Madison in the Wisconsin House and Senate, in November 2008, he was elected to another four-year term.[8]

State Legislatures: The Basics

After 250 years of constant tinkering and practice, U.S. state legislatures have evolved to the institutions we see today. As lawmaking

bodies, they are similar to one another and to the U.S. Congress. This should not be surprising, as their common ancestors were the 17th- and 18th-century legislative assemblies of the British colonies on the eastern seaboard, such as Virginia's House of Burgesses, where many of our founders served, including George Washington, Thomas Jefferson, and Patrick Henry. The writers of the U.S. Constitution did not copy the British Parliament, that "mother of Parliaments," in designing the U.S. Congress. Rather, they looked to the states, many of whom had over 100 years of legislative experience.[9] In particular, the **bicameral** arrangement that exists in 49 states (Nebraska's legislature is a **unicameral** body) arose from colonial arrangements wherein one chamber would consist of the king's appointed representatives and the other would consist of representatives of "freemen" living in the colony. In today's bicameral state legislatures, one chamber is called the Senate and the other chamber is usually called the House of Representatives, although some states use other names, such as the House of Delegates in West Virginia and the Assembly in New York. For a piece of legislation to become law, it must be approved by at least a majority of the members of each chamber in exactly the same form.

In a given state, the House has more members than the Senate, typically about two or three times as many, and so their districts are proportionally smaller. Senators are most commonly elected to four-year terms from **single-member districts (SMDs)**, that is, districts from which they are the only senator; House members are usually called representatives and elected to two-year terms from SMDs.[10] Some legislators (about 13 percent nationwide) are elected from districts with more than one member serving in them, like

---

[5] Michael B. Berkman, "State Legislators in Congress: Strategic Politicians, Professional Legislatures, and the Party Nexus," *American Journal of Political Science* 38(1994):1025–1055.
[6] Alan Ehrenhalt, "Barack's Chops," *Governing* (July 2008):7–9; Beth Fouhy, "Obama Tackles Questions about His Experience: Senator Touts Background as State Lawmaker," *State Journal-Register* (Springfield, IL), 22 April 2007, p. 63; Michael D. Shear and Cesi Connolly, "In Illinois, A Similar Fight Tested a Future President," *The Washington Post*, 9 September 2009, on-line edition.
[7] Tom Loftus, *The Art of Legislative Politics* (Washington, DC: CQ Press, 1994).
[8] Morgan Cullen, "The Long View," *State Legislatures* (May 2009):33–34.

---

[9] Peverill Squire and Keith E. Hamm, *101 Chambers: Congress, State Legislatures, and the Future of Legislative Studies* (Columbus, OH: The Ohio State University Press, 2005), pp. 22–25.
[10] In 12 states, senators have two-year terms, and in five states, representatives have four-year terms.

members of the U.S. Senate (two of whom serve each state). These are called **multi-member districts (MMDs)**. Table 7.1 shows how the different state legislatures vary on these characteristics. MMDs were once more common because they make it easier to draw districts (since fewer need to be drawn). They have been used less in recent years because of

Table 7.1

State Legislatures, Terms, Seats, and MMDs

State	Name of Both Chambers Together	Senate			Name of Chamber	House		
		Length of Term (years)	Number of Seats	% MMDs[a]		Length of Term (years)	Number of Seats	% MMDs[a]
AL	Legislature	4	35	0	House*	4	105	0
AK	Legislature	4	20	0	House*	2	40	0
AZ	Legislature	2	30	0	House*	2	60	100%
AR	General Assembly	4	35	0	House*	2	100	0
CA	Legislature	4	40	0	Assembly	2	80	0
CO	General Assembly	4	35	0	House*	2	65	0
CT	General Assembly	2	36	0	House*	2	151	0
DE	General Assembly	4	21	0	House*	2	41	0
FL	Legislature	4	40	0	House*	2	120	0
GA	General Assembly	2	56	0	House*	2	180	0
HI	Legislature	4	25	0	House*	2	51	0
ID	Legislature	2	35	0	House*	2	70	0
IL	General Assembly	4	59	0	House*	2	118	0
IN	General Assembly	4	50	0	House*	2	100	0
IA	General Assembly	4	50	0	House*	2	100	0
KS	Legislature	4	40	0	House*	2	125	0
KY	General Assembly	4	38	0	House*	2	100	0
LA	Legislature	4	39	0	House*	4	105	0
ME	Legislature	2	35	0	House*	2	151	0
MD	General Assembly	4	47	0	House of Delegates	4	141	67%
MA	General Court	2	40	0	House*	2	160	0
MI	Legislature	4	38	0	House*	2	110	0
MN	Legislature	4	67	0	House*	2	134	0
MS	Legislature	4	52	0	House*	4	122	0

State	Name of Both Chambers Together	Senate			Name of Chamber			
		Length of Term (years)	Number of Seats	% MMDs[a]		Length of Term (years)	House Number of Seats	% MMDs[a]
MO	General Assembly	4	34	0	House*	2	163	0
MT	Legislature	4	50	0	House*	2	100	0
NE	Legislature	4	49	0	**	**	**	**
NV	Legislature	4	21	11%	Assembly	2	42	0
NH	General Court	2	24	0	House*	2	400	88%
NJ	Legislature	4	40	0	General Assembly	2	80	100%
NM	Legislature	4	42	0	House*	2	70	0
NY	Legislature	2	62	0	Assembly	2	150	0
NC	General Assembly	2	50	0	House*	2	120	0
ND	Legislative Assembly	4	47	0	House*	4	94	100%
OH	General Assembly	4	33	0	House*	2	99	0
OK	Legislature	4	48	0	House*	2	101	0
OR	Legislative Assembly	4	30	0	House*	2	60	0
PA	General Assembly	4	50	0	House*	2	203	0
RI	General Assembly	2	38	0	House*	2	75	0
SC	General Assembly	4	46	0	House*	2	124	0
SD	Legislature	2	35	0	House*	2	70	100%
TN	General Assembly	4	33	0	House*	2	99	0
TX	Legislature	4	31	0	House*	2	150	0
UT	Legislature	4	29	0	House*	2	75	0
VT	General Assembly	2	30	77%	House*	2	150	39%
VA	General Assembly	4	40	0	House of Delegates	2	100	0
WA	Legislature	4	49	0	House*	2	98	100%
WV	Legislature	4	34	100%	House of Delegates	2	100	40%
WI	Legislature	4	33	0	Assembly	2	99	0
WY	Legislature	4	30	0	House*	2	60	0

[a] This is the percentage of districts that have more than one member serving in them.

* House of Representatives.

** Nebraska's unicameral legislature has only a senate.

Sources: Council of State Governments, *Book of the States 2008*, vol. 40, ed. Audrey Wall (Lexington, KY: Council of State Governments, 2008), pp. 80, 85; and the National Conference of State Legislatures' website, www.ncsl.org/programs/legismgt/about/legislator_overview.htm.

their adverse impact on the fair representation of racial minorities.[11]

Whereas state legislatures have similar structures and the same governance role in their respective states, they vary dramatically in their **legislative professionalism.** States with larger, more urban, growing, and diverse populations, such as Massachusetts, Illinois, and especially California, tend to have the most professionalized legislatures.[12] These bodies meet most of the year, are well staffed, and pay their members a wage on which they can live without the need for another job, if they so choose.[13] On the other hand, smaller, more rural, and more homogeneous states, such as New Hampshire, Wyoming, and Arkansas, have what might be called **citizen-legislatures,** where lawmaking is a part-time job, with legislatures meeting 30 to 90 days a year, earning less than $20,000 per year, and having very few staff to help them. Of course, there are many states that hold the middle ground on these characteristics and whose legislatures also take the middle ground on professionalism, such as Colorado, Missouri, and Delaware. Figure 7.1 breaks down the state legislatures into five categories according to their professionalism, based on their session length, members' salaries, and number of staff.[14] Whereas once all state lawmakers had another job to help them make a living, today one out of six of them consider lawmaking to be their only

job.[15] About the same number consider their main occupation to be an attorney, way down from even just 30 years ago. More than one in four own or work in private business, while most others are retired, farm, or are teachers or medical professionals. In addition, today's state lawmakers pursue a smattering of many other types of professional activities.

State Legislative Elections

There are 7,382 men and women serving in the 50 state legislatures, from 20 in the Alaska Senate to 400 in the New Hampshire House of Representatives, and each of these legislators was elected to his or her seat.[16] To better understand state legislatures and state legislators, you must first understand state legislative elections.

The Paradox of Competition in State Legislative Elections

A healthy representative democracy requires vigorous electoral competition. When either candidate could win a given race, each one works hard to appeal to voters. Energetic campaign activity raises voters' interest in and understanding of the race, the office being contested, and the candidates. Probably more important, elected officials who anticipate a close race in the next election will make every effort to serve and represent their constituents well. When a race is not competitive—that is, when only one candidate has a real chance of winning—neither the voters nor the candidates take much interest in it and elected officials have little electoral incentive to work hard for their constituents.

[11] Bernard Grofman and Lisa Handley, "The Impact of the Voting Rights Act on Black Representation in Southern State Legislatures," *Legislative Studies Quarterly* 16(1991):111–28.

[12] James D. King, "Changes in Professionalism in U.S. State Legislatures," *Legislative Studies Quarterly* 25(2000): 327–44; Christopher Z. Mooney, "Citizens, Structures, and Sister States: Influences on State Legislative Reform," *Legislative Studies Quarterly* 20(1995):47–68.

[13] H. W. Jerome Maddox, "Opportunity Costs and Outside Careers in U.S. State Legislatures," *Legislative Studies Quarterly* 29(2004):517–44.

[14] Peverill Squire, "Measuring Legislative Professionalism," *State Politics and Policy Quarterly* 7(2007):211–27.

[15] Anonymous, "Working Full-Time in State Legislatures," *State Legislatures*, July/August 2009, p. 6.

[16] All legislators are elected to their seats except for the few at any given time who have been appointed to serve out the remainder of a term for an elected legislator who died or resigned.

| Figure 7.1 |

State Legislative Professionalism

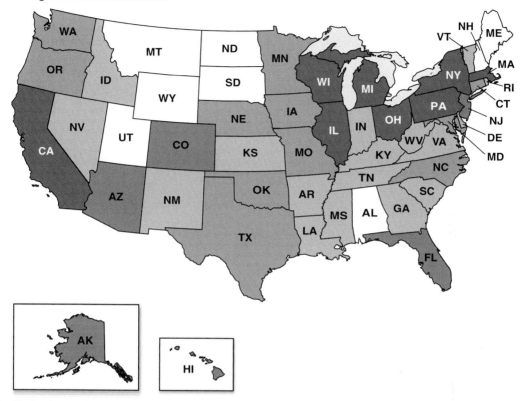

Note: This legislative professionalism scale is based on legislative salary, session length, and staffing, all compared to the U.S. Congress, using 2003 data. The states are categorized on the raw values of their legislative professionalism, not simply their percentile on the scale. Darker states have more professional legislatures.

Source: Modified from: Peverill Squire, "Measuring Legislative Professionalism," *State Politics and Policy Quarterly* 7(2007):211–27.

Of course, elected officials also serve their districts out of a sense of duty, but the fear of losing the next election is a strong institutional motivation for good representation.

Are state legislative elections competitive? The data from recent elections suggest a paradoxical answer to this question. First, considering the macro-level, or overall, picture, there seems to be relatively strong competition in state legislative elections. As described in Chapter 5, elections since 1992 have yielded remarkably similar total numbers of Democratic and Republican state legislators nationwide. For example, after the 2004 elections, there were 3,640 Republican and 3,655 Democrat state legislators in the country—a difference of about one-fifth of 1 percent of the total.[17] This reflected the very close partisan competition at the national level that year, with George Bush beating John Kerry by only a 50.7-to-48.3 percent margin. State legislative elections since then have continued to track national trends, with Democrats picking up 322 seats in 2006 and another 98 in 2008. Following a small Republican pick

---

[17] *Book of the States 2006*, op. cit. In addition to these Democrats and Republicans, there were 58 Independents, 22 vacancies, six Progressives, and one Green.

Table 7.2

Party Affiliation of State Legislators, 2010

State	Senate				House of Representatives			
	Democrat	Republican	Other	Vacant	Democrat	Republican	Other	Vacant
AL	19	13	0	3	62	43	0	0
AK	10	10	0	0	18	22	0	0
AZ	12	18	0	0	25	35	0	0
AR	27	8	0	0	71	28	1	0
CA	25	15	0	0	50	28	1	1
CO	21	14	0	0	38	27	0	0
CT	24	12	0	0	114	37	0	0
DE	16	5	0	0	24	17	0	0
FL	14	26	0	0	44	76	0	0
GA	22	34	0	0	75	105	0	0
HI	23	2	0	0	45	6	0	0
ID	7	28	0	0	18	52	0	0
IL	37	22	0	0	70	48	0	0
IN	17	33	0	0	52	48	0	0
IA	32	18	0	0	56	44	0	0
KS	9	31	0	0	48	77	0	0
KY	15	22	1	0	65	35	0	0
LA	22	15	0	2	52	50	3	0
ME	20	15	0	0	96	54	1	0
MD	33	14	0	0	104	36	1	0
MA	35	5	0	0	143	16	1	0
MI	16	22	0	0	67	43	0	0
MN	46	21	0	0	87	47	0	0
MS	27	25	0	0	74	48	0	0
MO	11	23	0	0	74	89	0	0
MT	23	27	0	0	50	50	0	0
NE	0	0	49	0	*	*	*	*
NV	12	9	0	0	28	14	0	0
NH	14	10	0	0	223	177	0	0
NJ	23	17	0	0	47	33	0	0
NM	27	15	0	0	45	25	0	0
NY	32	30	0	0	109	41	0	0
NC	30	20	0	0	68	52	0	0
ND	21	26	0	0	36	58	0	0
OH	12	21	0	0	53	46	0	0

State	Senate				House of Representatives			
	Democrat	Republican	Other	Vacant	Democrat	Republican	Other	Vacant
OK	22	26	0	0	39	62	0	0
OR	18	12	0	0	36	24	0	0
PA	20	30	0	0	104	99	0	0
RI	33	4	1	0	69	6	0	0
SC	19	27	0	0	53	71	0	0
SD	14	20	1	0	24	46	0	0
TN	14	19	0	0	48	51	0	0
TX	12	19	0	0	73	77	0	0
UT	8	21	0	0	22	53	0	0
VT	23	7	0	0	95	48	7	0
VA	21	19	0	0	39	59	2	0
WA	31	18	0	0	63	35	0	0
WV	28	6	0	0	71	29	0	0
WI	18	15	0	0	52	46	1	0
WY	7	23	0	0	18	41	0	1
US	1,022	892	52	5	3,037	2,355	18	2

*Nebraska's nonpartisan unicameral legislature has only a senate.

Note: This table shows the number of members of each chamber of each of these parties, as of January 15, 2010.

Source: National Conference of State Legislatures, "2010 (Post-Election) Partisan Composition of State Legislatures," (http://www.ncsl.org/?tabid=19051).

up in the 2009 elections, the current distribution is at 4,059 Democratic and 3,247 Republican state legislators (see Table 7.2).

Even though Democrats' current 55.4 percent is a substantial lead, history suggests that they will lose seats in 2010, as the nation swings back toward the Republicans. This occurs because Democratic gains in the past two elections have been made in the small number of legislative seats that are closely contested by the parties, the so-called **swing seats**. The fact that the Democrats gained only 98 seats in 2008 (as opposed to their 322-seat gain in 2006), a year that brought them great success nationally, demonstrates how little of the "low-hanging fruit" there was left for the party to pick at the state legislative level.[18]

Another way to look at political competition on the macro level is to think about party control of state legislative chambers. As we discuss later in this chapter, the party that has a majority of seats in a chamber has a huge advantage in pursuing its policy agenda there. Recent elections have shown that the two major parties vie closely for control of many state legislative chambers. For example, of the 84 chambers that had partisan elections in 2008,[19] 11 changed party control. In other words, 2008 saw major partisan change in 13 percent of those state legislative chambers with elections that year. And it was not only Democrats who made these gains in the year

---

[18] Michael D. McDonald and Robin Best, "Equilibria and Restoring Forces in Models of Vote Dynamics," *Political Analysis* 14(2006):369–92; Tim Storey, "The Perils of Success," *State Legislatures* (September 2008):15–18.

[19] In 2008, six states (Alabama, Louisiana, Maryland, Mississippi, New Jersey, and Virginia) did not have legislative elections, none of the senators in Minnesota or Michigan were up for reelection, and Nebraska's legislature is nonpartisan.

of Obama's victory; in fact, almost as many chambers flipped from Democratic to Republican control as the other way around. In addition, several other chambers came very close to changing their partisan control. For example, if a mere 10 people (out of over 40,000 people casting votes) had switched their votes from the Republican to the Democratic candidate in the 105th Texas House of Representatives district in Dallas, that chamber would have changed party control, too.[20] The 2008 results also suggest the potential for more change in party control in 2010, when fewer than two districts need to change party in 15 chambers for this to occur (see Table 7.2). Certainly, there are chambers with lopsided partisan distributions, such as in Hawaii, Idaho, Massachusetts, and Kansas, but these distributions reflect well the lopsided electorates in those states. In summary, even after an election cycle hyped as a big win for one party (2008), we see considerable macro-level political competition in state legislative elections.

On the other hand, if we look at these elections on the micro level, that is, if we look at individual state legislative races, then we actually find precious little political competition. This is exhibited in various ways. First, whether you measure competition as the percentage of races with more than one candidate, the percentage where the incumbent lost, or the winner's share of vote, competition has been declining in primary elections for state legislative seats at a steady pace for almost 80 years.[21] Likewise in general elections, when an **incumbent**—the current state legislator—runs, he or she wins

approximately 93 percent of the time; many state legislative races are routinely won by 10 or 20 percent or more.[22] In fact, 33 percent of the winners of state legislative general elections in 2008 did not even have an opponent (see Table 7.3). Thus, while having two candidates in a race, that is, **contestation**, is the minimum requirement for any competition at all, even this is not occurring in one-third of general election races. Even in California, where contestation is high and state legislative **term limits** have been imposed to enhance electoral competition (see Reform Can Happen box), when an incumbent state senator was defeated in a primary in 2008, it made statewide news, because she was the first senator to lose a primary there in 12 years.[23] Connecticut couldn't even encourage contestation by paying candidates to run. In 2008, when the state started a public financing program for state legislative races, contestation actually declined compared to the previous election.[24] And remember that Texas House election, where a 10-vote switch in one district would have changed the chamber's partisan control in 2008? In that same election, less than a quarter of the general election races had even as few as 20 percentage points between the winner and loser.[25] The other three-quarters of the seats were uncompetitive by anyone's definition,

---

[20] Or at least the chamber would have gone from Republican control to being tied. See: Daniel C. Vock, "Dems Take Full Control in 3 More States," *Stateline.org*, 7 November 2008; Brandon Formby, "GOP Keeps Control of Texas House after Heated Race Decided," *Dallas Morning News*, 11 November 2008, online edition.

[21] Stephen Ansolabehere, John Mark Hansen, Shigeo Hirano, and James M. Snyder, Jr., "The Decline of Competition in U.S. Primary Elections, 1908–2004," in Michael P. McDonald and John Samples, eds., *The Marketplace of Democracy: Electoral Competition and American Politics* (Washington, DC: Brookings Institution, 2006).

[22] Richard G. Niemi, Lynda W. Powell, William D. Berry, Thomas M. Carsey, and James M. Snyder Jr., "Competition in State Legislative Elections, 1992–2002," in Michael P. McDonald and John Samples, eds., *The Marketplace of Democracy* (Washington, DC: Brookings Institution, 2006); Robert E. Hogan, "Institutional and District-Level Sources of Competition in State Legislative Elections," *Social Science Quarterly* 84(2003):543–60.

[23] Aurelio Rojas, "Migden's Senate Loss Is Rare for Incumbent," *The Sacramento Bee*, 4 June 2008, online edition.

[24] Mark Pazniokas, "Despite Public Financing, More State Races Unopposed," *The Hartford (CT) Courant*, 3 June 2008, online edition. On the other hand, a recent study has shown that, more generally, setting campaign contribution limits low can increase contestation: Keith E. Hamm and Robert E. Hogan, "Campaign Finance Laws and Candidacy Decisions in State Legislative Elections," *Political Research Quarterly* 61(2008):458–67.

[25] "2008 Election Coverage: State House- Texas," *USA Today*, 5 November 2008, online edition.

Table 7.3

Partisan Contestation in State Legislative Races, 2008 (Arranged from Most to Fewest Combined Opposed Races)

State	Combined % Races Opposed*	% House Races Opposed*	% Senate Races Opposed*
MN	100.0%	100.0%	100.0%
NV	98.1%	90.0%	100.0%
UT	97.8%	93.3%	98.7%
MI	94.6%	No election	94.5%
SD	94.3%	97.1%	92.9%
ND	94.2%	95.7%	93.5%
CA	93.0%	100.0%	91.3%
ME	90.9%	100.0%	88.7%
CO	86.9%	89.5%	86.2%
IA	82.4%	80.0%	83.0%
MT	82.4%	72.0%	85.0%
OH	81.7%	87.5%	80.8%
WA	80.7%	73.1%	82.7%
AK	80.0%	80.0%	80.0%
NY	75.5%	82.3%	72.7%
NH	74.8%	100.0%	73.3%
TX	73.9%	80.0%	73.3%
DE	72.6%	60.0%	75.6%
IN	71.2%	68.0%	72.0%
CT	71.1%	83.3%	68.2%
WI	70.4%	56.3%	72.7%
AZ	70.0%	73.3%	68.3%
VT	68.9%	80.0%	66.7%
KS	67.3%	85.0%	61.6%
ID	61.9%	60.0%	62.9%
RI	61.1%	63.2%	60.0%
OR	60.5%	43.8%	65.0%
HI	60.3%	83.3%	54.9%

(continued)

Table 7.3

Partisan Contestation in State Legislative Races, 2008 (Arranged from Most to Fewest Combined Opposed Races) continued

State	Combined % Races Opposed*	% House Races Opposed*	% Senate Races Opposed*
MO	60.0%	82.4%	57.7%
NC	58.2%	60.0%	57.5%
PA	57.0%	84.0%	53.7%
OK	55.2%	45.8%	57.4%
WV	55.2%	75.0%	52.0%
FL	52.5%	42.9%	57.5%
IL	50.0%	47.5%	50.8%
TN	48.7%	68.8%	45.5%
WY	40.8%	31.3%	43.3%
NM	38.4%	28.6%	44.3%
SC	34.7%	43.5%	31.5%
KY	33.6%	57.9%	29.0%
GA	24.2%	32.1%	21.7%
AR	23.7%	11.1%	26.0%
MA	16.5%	12.5%	17.5%
US average	67.0%	71.7%	66.3%

*The percentage of those seats up for election that had both a Democrat and a Republican running in the general election.

Note: These states are arranged in order from the one with the most contested races to the one with the fewest. Alabama, Louisiana, Maryland, Mississippi, New Jersey, and Virginia held no state legislative races in 2008, nor did the Michigan state senate. Nebraska's unicameral legislature is excluded because it is nonpartisan.

Source: John McGlennon, "The Competition Gap: How Candidate Recruitment in State Legislative Elections Foreshadows Party Change." A Report from the Thomas Jefferson Program in Public Policy. (Williamsburg, VA: The College of William and Mary, 2009).

REFORM CAN HAPPEN

STATE LEGISLATIVE TERM LIMITS

The lack of micro-level competition in state legislative races and the high rate of incumbents' reelection success have not gone unnoticed. Indeed, they inspired the most significant state legislative reform movement in a generation—the drive for state legislative term limits. Term limits are specific and reasonably low ceilings on the number of times an officeholder can be reelected. In the 1990s, 21 states adopted such limits for their state lawmakers, although they were repealed or struck down in six of these states. In the 15 states that now have the reform, the restrictions on lawmakers' service range from 6 to 12 consecutive years (see Figure 7.2).[1]

Figure 7.2

State Legislative Term Limits

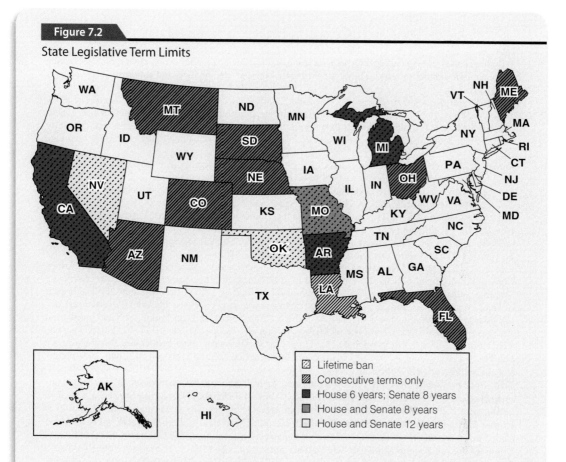

Lifetime ban
Consecutive terms only
House 6 years; Senate 8 years
House and Senate 8 years
House and Senate 12 years

Note: The states that are blank have no state legislative term limits.

Advocates thought that term limits would increase competition in state legislative elections by forcing incumbents out of office every so often,[2] and one early study suggested that this might be true.[3] But more recently, several studies have shown that state legislative term limits have neither increased competition nor decreased campaign spending.[4] In fact, the reform may even reduce competition. More incumbents seem to be running unopposed under term limits, with potential candidates simply waiting for their legislator's limit to be reached, at which time they all join in the fray for the open seat. But term limits do seem to stir the political pot generally, with termed-out lawmakers running more frequently for local offices and Congress, while local officials seek slots opened up by term limits.[5]

In addition, the reform has had a wide range of unintended consequences, including empowering the governor at the expense of the legislature and causing general mayhem in the legislative process, at least in the adjustment period.[6] Even though term limits were originally advocated by conservatives and Republicans, evidence is beginning to emerge that their political impacts have not been favorable for these groups.[7] Thus, state legislatures' experience with term limits offers a good example of an institutional reform with significant unintended consequences. While the benefits and costs of the effects of term limits can be debated, one thing is certain: They remain popular with the voters who originally put them in place. In the several initiative elections in recent years on proposals to repeal or reduce the severity of a state's legislative term limits, none have been successful.[8] The only repeals and amendments of the reform have been done by the courts and the legislatures themselves.[9]

(Continued)

Notes

[1] Term limits also vary depending on whether a lawmaker can run again after sitting out a term after serving the maximum number of terms. This is the difference between lifetime bans and consecutive service bans (see Figure 7.2).

[2] George F. Will, *Restoration: Congress, Term Limits, and the Recovery of Deliberative Democracy* (New York: Free Press, 1993); John H. Fund, "Term Limitation: An Idea Whose Time Has Come," in Gerald Benjamin and Michael J. Malbin, eds., *Limiting Legislative Terms* (Washington, DC: Congressional Quarterly Press, 1992); Mark P. Petracca, "The Poison of Professional Politics," *Policy Analysis* 151(1991), online edition.

[3] Kermit Daniel and John R. Lott Jr., "Term Limits and Electoral Competition: Evidence from California's State Legislative Races," *Public Choice* 90(1997):165–84.

[4] Marjorie Sarbaugh-Thompson, Lyke Thompson, Charles D. Elder, John Strate, and Richard C. Elling, *The Political and Institutional Effects of Term Limits* (New York: Palgrave-Macmillan, 2004); Scot Schraufnagel and Karen Halperin, "Term Limits, Electoral Competition, and Representational Diversity: The Case of Florida," *State Politics and Policy Quarterly* 6(2006):448–62; Seth Masket and Jeffrey B. Lewis, "A Return to Normalcy? Revisiting the Effects of Term Limits on Competitiveness and Spending in California Assembly Elections," *State Politics and Policy Quarterly* 7(2007):20–38.

[5] Christopher Z. Mooney, "The Effects of Term Limits in Professionalized State Legislatures," in Rick Farmer, Christopher Z. Mooney, Richard J. Powell, and John C. Green, eds., *Legislating without Experience: Case Studies in State Legislative Term Limits* (Lanham, MD: Lexington, 2007); Richard J. Powell, "The Impact of Term Limits on the Candidacy Decisions of State Legislators in U.S. House Elections," *Legislative Studies Quarterly* 25(2000):645–61; Rebecca A. Tothero, "The Impact of Term Limits on State Legislators' Ambition for Local Office: The Case of Michigan's House," *Publius* 33(2003):111–22; Jeffrey Lazarus, "Term Limits' Multiple Effects on State Legislators' Career Decisions," *State Politics and Policy Quarterly* 6(2006):357–83; Jennifer A. Steen, "The Impact of State Legislative Term Limits on the Supply of Congressional Candidates," *State Politics and Policy Quarterly* 6(2006):430–47.

[6] Thad Kousser, *Term Limits and the Dismantling of State Legislative Professionalism* (New York: Cambridge University Press, 2005); Karl T. Kurtz, Bruce Cain, and Richard G. Niemi, eds., *Institutional Change in American Politics: The Case of Term Limits* (Ann Arbor, MI: University of Michigan Press, 2007); Rick Farmer, Christopher Z. Mooney, Richard J. Powell, and John C. Green, eds., *Legislating without Experience: Case Studies in State Legislative Term Limits* (Lanham, MD: Lexington, 2007); Christopher Z. Mooney, "Term Limits as a Boon to Legislative Scholarship," *State Politics and Policy Quarterly* 9(2009):204–28.

[7] Richard J. Powell, "Minority Party Gains under State Legislative Term Limits," *State Politics and Policy Quarterly* 8(2008):32–47; Dan Walters, "Reforms Push Political Cash out of Sight," *Victorville* (CA) *Daily Press*, 24 June 2008, online edition.

[8] Carol S. Weissert and Karen Halperin, "The Paradox of Term Limit Support—To Know Them Is NOT to Love Them," *Political Research Quarterly* 60(2007):516–30; Janine Parry and Todd Donovan, "Leave the Rascals in? Explaining the Poor Prospects of Term Limit Extensions," *State Politics and Policy Quarterly* 8(2008):293–308.

[9] Daniel A. Smith, "Overturning Term Limits: The Legislature's Own Private Idaho?" *PS: Political Science and Politics* 36(2003):215–20; David W. Chen and Michael Barbaro, "Across Country, New Challenges to Term Limits," *The New York Times*, 25 September 2008, online edition; Anonymous, "Editorial: The Seductive Charms of Term Limits," *The New York Times*, 9 June 2008, online edition; Josh Goodman, "The Limits of Limits," *Governing* (April 2009):14.

with the winners getting 60 percent of the vote or more—often, a lot more. In fact, more races had no contestation at all than had its winner get less than 60 percent of the vote. The Texas House is not abnormal in this respect; it actually is above average when it comes to general election contestation.

The paradox remains: While macro-level state legislative election results reflect the close competition between the political parties seen in recent national elections, or at least they reflect the partisan balances in their states, races for most individual state legislative seats tend to be noncompetitive. What causes this odd situation? The answer has to do with how people vote for state legislators, and how our electoral institutions translate these votes into state legislative seats, especially how state legislative districts are drawn.

Party, Incumbency, and Voting Decisions in State Legislative Elections

To understand the paradox of competition in state legislative elections, we must first understand what these elections are like. First, the size of legislative districts varies dramatically from state to state based on the number of seats in a chamber and the number of people living in the state, from California Senate districts with 919,916 people in them to New Hampshire House districts with only 3,290 people.[26] The average state's House district has about 56,000 people in it, and the average state's Senate district has about 154,000. Thus, even compared to members of the U.S. House (each with about 697,000 constituents), state lawmakers have very small districts. Because Americans tend to live near those who are like themselves racially, socially, and economically, these small districts are also relatively homogeneous.[27] That is, while a congressional district may stretch hundreds of miles and encompass farms, small towns, suburbs, and urban areas, a state legislative district may cover as little as a few square miles in a heavily populated city or a dozen sparsely populated counties full of farmers and small-town folks.

The small size of these districts works against voters getting information about state legislative races. These districts usually do not include an entire **media market,** so TV and radio advertising is uneconomical, because many viewers are outside of the district where an ad would air.[28] Local TV news rarely covers state legislative elections, largely for the same reason—any given legislative race is not meaningful to very many viewers.[29] As a result, because Americans tend to get their political information from mass media advertisements and news, these races are often invisible to most voters. Furthermore, state legislative races are typically overshadowed by candidates "up the ticket" for Congress, governor, and president.[30] For people who have a limited attention span for politics, state legislative races are not nearly as relevant as other races. So, while voters may have a pretty good idea about how they will vote in these more visible races, they typically have given little thought to their vote for the state legislature.

While voters may enter the voting booth with little information about the specific state legislative candidates on their ballot, once in the booth, they always have one important piece of information on which to base their vote.[31] It is written on the ballot next to or below each candidate's name—the candidate's party affiliation. This, in conjunction with voters' own party leanings, as discussed in Chapter 5, determines most people's votes in state legislative races in general elections. When you know nothing else about a candidate, why not vote for the one from the party with which you most often agree? That person is more likely than the other candidate to have values and beliefs about politics and policy that are most in line with your own

---

[26] Based on the U.S. Census Bureau's 2008 population estimates.

[27] Matthew S. Levendusky and Jeremy C. Pope, "Measuring Aggregate-Level Ideological Heterogeneity," *Legislative Studies Quarterly* 35(2010): forthcoming; Bill Bishop, *The Big Sort: Why the Clustering of Like-Minded America Is Tearing Us Apart* (New York: Houghton Mifflin, 2008).

[28] Gary F. Moncrief, Peverill Squire, and Malcolm E. Jewell, *Who Runs for the Legislature?* (Upper Saddle River, NJ: Prentice Hall, 2001), ch. 4.

[29] Jeff Venezuela, "Midwest Local TV Newscasts Average 36 Seconds of Election Coverage in Typical 30-Minute Broadcast," press release (Madison, WI: UW NewsLab, University of Wisconsin–Madison, 2006).

[30] Richard G. Niemi and Lynda W. Powell, "Limited Citizenship? Knowing and Contacting State Legislators after Term Limits," in Rick Farmer, John David Rausch Jr., and John C. Green, eds., *The Test of Time* (Lanham, MD: Lexington, 2003).

[31] Except Nebraska, where state legislative elections are nonpartisan.

values and beliefs. Otherwise, why would you identify with that party? Such party-based voting is perfectly rational in our political system. But when it is the norm for races in small and politically homogeneous districts, like those for the state legislature, it generates limited two-party competition in general elections. If a district is full of Democratic (or Republican) voters, then the Democratic (or Republican) state legislative candidate is most likely to win.

Another effect of voters' lack of information about state legislative races is that if one simply recognizes a name on the ballot in a contest, he or she is more likely to vote for that candidate.[32] Why might a voter have heard more about one candidate than another? Incumbency is the biggest reason. The sitting state legislator has campaign experience, has appeared in newspapers for legislative accomplishments, has been visible at public events, and has mailed information to the voter. This information has probably been positive, because the incumbent controlled most if it, but even if it is negative, research shows that bad publicity can turn into positive name recognition in low-information races like those for the state legislature.[33] As time passes, people are likely to forget why they remember a candidate's name and just assume it was something good. Thus, all things being equal, the effect of name recognition tends to work to the incumbent's advantage.

Campaigns can also increase name recognition, which is their primary purpose. State legislative campaigns have traditionally been down-home affairs, run from a kitchen table and a home computer, with a small group of the candidate's friends and neighbors going door to door, distributing campaign brochures,

putting up yard signs, and so forth.[34] But even a down-home campaign can cost money for yard signs, brochures, doughnuts for volunteers, and so on. Research shows that campaign spending is generally effective; all things being equal, the more money a candidate spends on the campaign, the more votes he or she receives.[35]

The effects of incumbency and campaign spending are quite intertwined. Interest groups may try to gain access to lawmakers by giving them campaign contributions. Thus, incumbents' electoral chances are improved both by the name recognition they earn from serving in the legislature and by having more money to spend on campaigns than their challengers.

Actual state legislative election results confirm this line of thinking—incumbents who run for reelection win overwhelmingly.[36] For example, in 2008, in the 133 races for the Texas House where there was an incumbent on the general election ballot, 128 of them won. That 96.2 percent incumbent success rate is about par for state legislative general elections in recent years.[37] However, this success rate is inflated by the fact that if an incumbent foresees defeat, he or she may not run for reelection.[38] Incumbents also are occasionally challenged successfully in their party's primary.[39] In Texas in 2008, 17 general election House races had no

---

[32] Marsha Matson and Terri Susan Fine, "Gender, Ethnicity, and Ballot Information: Ballot Cues in Low-Information Elections," *State Politics and Policy Quarterly* 6(2006):49–72.

[33] Barry C. Burden, "When Bad Press Is Good News—The Surprising Benefits of Negative Campaign Coverage," *Harvard International Journal of Press-Politics* 7(2002):76–89.

[34] Loftus, op. cit.; Moncrief, Squire, and Jewell, op. cit.; Ralph G. Wright, *Inside the Statehouse: Lessons from the Speaker* (Washington, DC: CQ Press, 2005).

[35] Anthony Gierzynski and David Breaux, "Legislative Elections and the Importance of Money," *Legislative Studies Quarterly* 21(1996):337–57.

[36] Robert E. Hogan, "Challenger Emergence, Incumbent Success, and Electoral Accountability in State Legislative Elections," *Journal of Politics* 66(2004):1283–1303; David Breaux, "Specifying the Impact of Incumbency on State Legislative Elections," *American Politics Quarterly* 18(1990):270–86.

[37] Niemi et al., op. cit.

[38] Gary W. Cox and Jonathan N. Katz, *Elbridge Gerry's Salamander: The Electoral Consequences of the Reapportionment Revolution* (New York: Cambridge University Press, 2002).

[39] Robert E. Hogan, "Sources of Competition in State Legislative Primary Elections," *Legislative Studies Quarterly* 28(2003):103–26; Robert E. Hogan, "Campaign War Chests and Challenger Emergence in State Legislative Elections," *Political Research Quarterly* 54(2001):815–30.

incumbent on the ballot, and most of these were voluntary retirements. But even with all this, out of all 150 districts in the entire election season, 128 incumbents, or 85.3 percent, were reelected.

On the other hand, the fact that voters know so little about state legislative candidates—even current officeholders—can have its disadvantages for incumbents. In particular, one bad piece of information that catches voters' attention may be enough to turn even a long-term legislator out of office. For example, after Pennsylvania lawmakers voted themselves a pay raise in 2005, the state's media wrote stories about the various perks of office that they enjoyed, such as generous pension benefits and lobbyist wining, dining and providing tickets to Steelers and Eagles games, among other things. Perhaps as a result, in 2006, Pennsylvania voters threw incumbents out in record numbers, including some top legislative leaders.[40]

Incumbents can also be vulnerable to well-funded activist groups, or even wealthy individuals, who want to affect the makeup of state legislatures. Officeholders must cast many votes, and these can sometimes annoy such groups. State legislators are more vulnerable to this sort of attack than are congressional or statewide officeholders, because the costs of their campaigns are low enough that sometimes $100,000 (or even $10,000) can make a real difference. In 2008, for example, wealthy gadflies from across the political spectrum in Michigan, New York, and Montana threw millions of dollars into state legislative races with some effect.[41]

Thus, most state legislative races are usually decided by incumbency and/or the partisan alignment of the district. This goes a long way toward explaining the dearth of district-level competition in state legislative races. Another crucial part of the explanation has to do with political institutions—the processes by which state legislative districts are drawn.

State Legislative Redistricting

Each state legislator is elected from a specific, legally defined subsection of the state, his or her legislative district. A state's legislative map is written into law, with the boundaries precisely described as running down certain streets, fields, golf courses, and airports,[42] so that every square inch of the state is placed into exactly one Senate and one House district.[43] Precisely where each of these boundaries runs is determined by policy makers using various criteria, some written into law and some considered custom and preference.[44] Because of these criteria and the way people are distributed around the state, districts are not simply neat, geometric figures, nor are they shaped simply by geography (e.g., by rivers and mountain ranges) or by other political boundaries (e.g., city or county boundaries). What is more, the U.S. Supreme Court requires that legislative districts be redrawn every 10 years to reflect changes in a state's population. How these districts are drawn helps explain the lack of political competition in state legislative races.

"One Person, One Vote" Before the early 1960s, most states rarely redrew their legislative district boundaries, because **redistricting** causes great political conflict. Redrawing district boundaries means moving some of a lawmaker's old constituents to a new district and bringing in new people to take their place. You might think that legislators would appreciate gaining constituents who would vote for

[40] Alan Greenblatt, "Perks That Kill," *Governing* (July 2006):18.

[41] Nicholas Confessore, "Billionaire's Albany Reform Group Puts Its Money behind 39 Incumbent Senators," *The New York Times*, 26 August 2008, online edition; Tom Lutey, "3 Targeted, Lose Re-election Bids," *Billings* (MT) *Gazette*, 6 June 2008, online edition; Charlie Cain, "Stryker Plans Assault on Key Republicans," *Detroit News*, 16 May 2008, online edition.

[42] Those who draw political district maps like to place their boundaries on streets, fields, golf courses, and airports because no one lives in these places.

[43] MMDs might be thought of as containing more than one "district," one for each legislator elected from it.

[44] Richard Forgette, Andrew Garner, and John Winkle, "Do Redistricting Principles and Practices Affect U.S. State Legislative Electoral Competition?" *State Politics and Policy Quarterly* 9(2009):151–75; Jason Barabas and Jennifer Jerit, "Redistricting Principles and Racial Representation," *State Politics and Policy Quarterly* 4(2004):415–36.

them and losing constituents who would not, but they can never be sure which voters are which. Besides, legislators invest considerable time and effort into building favorable name recognition in their districts through campaigns, newsletters, personal favors, professional service, and the like.[45] So in this situation, as in many other aspects of elections, legislators generally favor the status quo. The current arrangements got them elected, so why would they want to change them? And before the 1960s, they didn't, sometimes for many decades.

The problem with this status quo bias was that while the legislative district boundaries remained the same, the states' populations were constantly shifting. The early- to mid-20th century was a time of great upheaval and change. In particular, people were driven from the countryside to the cities by the Great Depression, two world wars, and the mechanization of agriculture. Although most Americans lived in rural areas in 1900, by 1960, most of them lived in the cities and suburbs. Because of this migration, districts that were equal in population in 1900 were very unequal by 1960. Some states suffered from extreme legislative **malapportionment,** that is, the unequal representation of people living in different districts. For example, Connecticut's districts were so malapportioned in 1960 that a party controlling districts containing as little as 12 percent of the state's population could have had a majority of seats in its state House.[46] Ironically, the worse this situation got, the more politically difficult it was for state policy makers to do anything about it. Those lawmakers and voters who benefited from malapportionment had strong incentive to throw roadblocks in the way of any changes. Lawmakers often ignored their own state laws requiring redistricting because the political pain was just too great.[47]

In a series of landmark decisions beginning in 1962, the U.S. Supreme Court changed all this by ruling that the Equal Protection Clause of the 14th Amendment to the U.S. Constitution required that districts in the same legislative chamber[48] had to be "substantially equal" in population.[49] Thus, the Court established the principle of "one person, one vote,"[50] meaning that all votes in a state must be of equal value. With malapportioned districts, a person's vote in a smaller district is worth more than a person's vote in a larger district. For instance, a person in a district of 5,000 people would have three times the influence in an election as a person in a district of 15,000 people for the same chamber— 1/5,000 versus 1/15,000—and influence in an election equals influence in the legislature.

These Supreme Court decisions forced the states to spend the rest of the 1960s undertaking the gut-wrenching task of completely redrawing their state legislative (and congressional) districts so that they would be equal in population based on the 1960 U.S. census.[51] Most state legislatures were required to draw their own districts, which made the process particularly painful since everyone involved knew that these changes would lead to many legislators losing their next elections. Where legislatures were not able to get the job done, the courts intervened. For example, the failure of the Illinois General Assembly and governor to agree on a set of legislative districts led to the state using what was called the "Bed-Sheet Ballot" to elect lawmakers in 1964, a 33-inch piece of paper on which every voter in the state had to choose from among 236 candidates for

---

[45] Robert G. Boatright, "Static Ambition in a Changing World: Legislators' Preparations for, and Responses to, Redistricting," *State Politics and Policy Quarterly* 4(2004):436–54.

[46] Richard K. Scher, Jon L. Mills, and John J. Hotaling, *Voting Rights and Democracy* (Chicago: Nelson-Hall, 1997).

[47] C. Herman Pritchett, "Equal Protection and Urban Majority," *American Political Science Review* 58(1964):869–75.

[48] This principle applies only within a given chamber. So, for example, South Dakota House districts may have more people in them than North Dakota Senate districts, but all South Dakota House districts must be equal in population.

[49] The pivotal cases on state legislative redistricting in this period were *Baker v. Carr*, 369 U.S. 186 (1962); *Reynolds v. Sims*, 377 U.S. 533 (1964); and *Lucas v. 44th General Assembly of Colorado*, 377 U.S. 713 (1964).

[50] The principle was originally referred to as "one man, one vote," but we prefer the nonsexist phrasing.

[51] Gordon E. Baker, *The Reapportionment Revolution* (New York: Random House, 1966).

177 Illinois House seats.[52] By the end of the 1960s, however, one way or another, every state had redrawn its legislative districts to comply with the Supreme Court mandates. This eliminated the rural bias in state legislatures, shifting political power to the urban and suburban areas where most people lived.[53]

Drawing New Districts Since Americans are always on the move, districts that start off equal in population do not stay that way for long. The U.S. Supreme Court requires that states maintain the one person, one vote standard by going through the redistricting process after each national census to adjust to the population shifts that will have occurred over the previous decade. But if redistricting in the 1960s was like an 8.0 earthquake on the Richter scale, the regular decennial redistricting is generally only like a 6.0 trembler. Yes, it causes a significant political battle in every state every decade, but policy makers have developed the processes and skills required to fight those battles in a rather orderly way. The result is that the changes made each decade are not nearly as large as those that were required in the 1960s, when policy makers had to make up for generations of neglect.

Each decade in each state, new maps are adopted either through the regular legislative process or through a nonpartisan or bipartisan commission.[54] With either mechanism, decisions must be made about precisely where to draw the district lines and what criteria will be used to do so. The Supreme Court requires that every redistricting plan meet two criteria to be constitutional: (1) Each district must be geographically **contiguous,** and (2) districts in a given chamber must be "substantially equal" in population, as of the most recent census.[55] Beyond these national legal minimums, there is much variation among the states in the criteria redistricters use to draw maps, and there is much disagreement among scholars and policy makers about what criteria ought to be used. Some argue that districts should be compact, follow local government boundaries, or reflect "communities of interest," that is, groups of people with common cultural or economic values.[56] Some of these criteria are embodied in various state statutes and constitutions, while some are mere desiderata; others fall somewhere in the middle, as more or less vague goals defined by various courts.

Racial and ethnic representation is one criterion that has long been important in legislative redistricting. Multimember districts were once used to dilute minority voters' power, but this use of MMDs was banned by the national **Voting Rights Act of 1965.**[57] In the 1980s, the Supreme Court seemed to encourage drawing "majority–minority" districts where possible, that is, including enough people of a given race or ethnicity—generally, African Americans or Latinos—so that they might be able to elect one of their own.[58] However, in the 1990s, the Court appeared to change its mind, ruling that race could not be the primary consideration in drawing a district.[59] But race and ethnicity continue to be considerations for redistricters because (1) it is illegal to draw maps to disenfranchise minority voters deliberately; (2) partisanship and race are closely intertwined in the United States and it is legal to draw maps for partisan advantage; and (3) all things being equal, many people believe that representing minorities fairly is simply the right thing to do. Furthermore, since the courts continue to

---

[52] James L. McDowell, "The Orange-Ballot Election: The 1964 Illinois At-Large Vote and After," *Journal of Illinois History* 10(2007):289–314.

[53] Stephen Ansolabehere and James M. Snyder Jr., "Reapportionment and Party Realignment in the American States," *University of Pennsylvania Law Review* 153(2004):433–57.

[54] Michael P. McDonald, "A Comparative Analysis of Redistricting Institutions in the United States, 2001–02," *State Politics and Politics Quarterly* 4(2004):371–95.

[55] The U.S. Supreme Court allows the largest and smallest districts in a state legislative chamber to vary by as much as 10 percent.

[56] Barabas and Jerit, op. cit.

[57] Grofman and Handley, op. cit.

[58] *Thornburg v. Gingles*, 478 U.S. 30 (1986).

[59] *Shaw v. Reno*, 509 U.S. 630 (1993); *Miller v. Johnson*, 515 U.S. 900 (1995).

COMPARISONS HELP US UNDERSTAND

CONTRASTING REDISTRICTING PROCESSES—THE RIDICULOUS (TEXAS) AND THE SUBLIME (IOWA)

The states use different processes for legislative redistricting, as discussed in the text, but the resulting politics of redistricting vary even more dramatically among the states. These dramatic differences can tell us much about the overall politics and political culture of the states. Consider, for example, Iowa and Texas.

The 2000 U.S. census ignited what can only be called "The Redistricting Wars" in Texas.[1] Republican Congressman Tom DeLay of Sugarland was the majority leader in the U.S. House in the early 2000s, and he did not like the congressional districts drawn by the Democrat-controlled Texas legislature in 2002 (recall that a state's legislature draws its congressional districts, too). DeLay was outraged by the political gerrymander he said was responsible for giving Democrats 17 House seats from Texas as compared to the Republicans' 15 seats following the 2002 election, even though the state had given favorite son George Bush 59.3 percent of the vote in the presidential contest of 2000. So when Republicans took control of the state legislature in 2002, DeLay had a novel idea—why not *re*-redistrict? That is, he convinced the legislature to draw a new set of congressional districts that would be more favorable to Republicans. No state had ever tried to redistrict more than once a decade, and opponents of the plan fought it unsuccessfully all the way to the U.S. Supreme Court.[2] After a superheated political battle—including the spectacle of Democratic state legislators twice fleeing the state to deprive the legislature of a quorum—the Republicans succeeded in passing a districting plan that ended up giving the Republicans a 21–11 margin in Texas's U.S. House delegation following the 2004 election.

Iowa, on the other hand, has a unique redistricting system that aims to eliminate political gerrymandering and incumbent protection altogether.[3] In the Hawkeye State, nonpartisan legislative staffers are assigned to draw state legislative and congressional districts based almost solely on simple population data, with an eye toward not splitting political units (like cities and counties) between different districts, when possible. By law, these redistricters are not even allowed to consider where incumbent legislators live. As a result, the final 2001 map put 64 (of 150) incumbent state legislators in districts with at least one of their colleagues, and two of their five members of Congress were likewise paired. And there was no partisan slant to these pairings. For instance, the two members of Congress placed in the same district were both Republicans, the party that controlled both chambers of the Iowa General Assembly. While the legislature must officially approve the district maps drawn by their staffers, and legislators may ask them to redraw the plan, public and media pressure to keep the process nonpartisan usually leads the General Assembly to accept the first or second plan. The result is that Iowa has legislative and congressional districts that are more competitive than those in most other states, and there have been no lawsuits over their redistricting plans since the 1970s—another rarity.

There could be no starker difference between the Texas-sized political conflict and institutional innovation in the name of partisan advantage in the Lone Star State and Iowa's technocratic, bloodless redistricting institution assiduously designed to avoid any taint of political unfairness. This tells us quite a bit about what is acceptable political behavior in these two states, and it also shows the impacts of political institutions. In the Texas experience, we see that merely moving around district lines (an institutional change) radically changed its congressional map from an outrageous Democratic gerrymander to only a modestly bad Republican one. In Iowa, we see that its unique redistricting institution can be fairly said to enhance political competition; with only 1 percent of the U.S. population, Iowa's maps generated 10 percent of the competitive congressional races in the country in the early 2000s.[4]

Notes

1. Layla Copelin, "DeLay and His Legacy Are Both on Trial," *Austin* (TX) *American-Statesman*, 18 December 2005, p. A1; David Espo, "Top Court Rules States Free to Redistrict," *Sacramento Bee*, 28 June 2006, online edition; and Tim Storey, "Supreme Court Tackles Texas," *State Legislatures* (April 2006):22–24.
2. *League of Latin American Citizens v. Perry*, 548 U.S. 399 (2006).
3. Alan Greenblatt, "Monster Maps: Has Devious District-Making Killed Electoral Competition?" *Governing* 19(1) (2005):46–50; Paul Chesser, "Iowa Offers Redistricting Lessons," *Carolina Journal*, 23 January 2004, online edition.
4. Brian O'Neill, "The Case for Federal Anti-Gerrymandering Legislation," *University of Michigan Journal of Law Reform* 38(2005):683–96.

weigh in on the subject,[60] race will likely be a consideration in the round of redistricting that follows the 2010 census.

Three general forces shape the politics of legislative redistricting:

- Conflicts of interest among those charged with drawing the maps (in most cases, state legislators and political parties)
- The general public's lack of concern with, or knowledge of, the redistricting process
- The lack of agreed-upon criteria for redistricting

The politics that follow from these three forces yield districts that have at least two general characteristics.[61] First, they tend to be electorally safe for most incumbent legislators and their parties. A lawmaker has a strong and direct interest in precisely how his or her district is drawn, probably more so than any other single piece of legislation in a decade. Those boundaries can mean political life or death. So the price of a legislator's vote for an overall districting plan may be a favorable district for him or her. Often, the result is a plan chock-a-block with **incumbent-protection districts,** districts with lopsided partisan balances incorporating as much of an incumbent's previous district as possible. This means that incumbent legislators are even more difficult to defeat than normal and the overall partisan balance in the legislature is reinforced. This effect is strongest when both parties have a voice in the process, whether due to **divided government** or the use of a bipartisan redistricting commission. Of course, this status quo bias would be much stronger if no redistricting occurred at all, as so often happened prior to the early 1960s, but this incumbent-protection dynamic mutes the potential of this process to shake up a state's political system every 10 years.[62]

The second effect of the politics of redistricting is that when one party controls the process, whether by having unified government or by controlling the redistricting commission, political **gerrymandering** may occur. That is, the party in control may try to draw districts that improve its chances of winning more seats. A party can do this both by dispersing some of its opponent's voters so that they are less than a majority in many districts—so-called **cracking**—and by **packing** many of the others into a few seats so as to "waste" the votes they get over 50 percent. Such machinations often lead to irregular, if not downright bizarre, boundaries as district-drawers search for just the right balance of partisan votes. Gerrymandering is named after the 19th-century Massachusetts political boss and U.S. vice president, Elbridge Gerry, who attempted to maximize his party's legislative advantage by drawing such weirdly shaped districts that a famous political cartoon caricatured one of them as a salamander.

With today's detailed census and voter databases and geographic information system (GIS) software, redistricters can now easily outdo Gerry in their pursuit of political advantage (see Figure 7.3). Surprisingly, perhaps, the U.S. Supreme Court has held that it is perfectly legal for those drawing these districts to pursue partisan advantage, so long as they break no other state or federal laws in the process.[63] Stories also abound of lawmakers lobbying for other idiosyncratic edits to their maps, such as the exclusion of potential challengers or splitting up the real estate of a high-profile sports arena so it could be in three different districts. Once, a lawmaker asked for the addition of a long finger of land through a city to an area in which no people lived.[64] Staffers working on the map were puzzled by this request until they realized that the vacant place on the map that the legislator wanted in his district was a cemetery—and his mother "lived" there.

Certain forces limit the amount of blatant partisan or incumbent-protection gerrymandering

---

[60] For example, the Supreme Court just decided a new redistricting case in 2009: *Bartlett v. Strickland* 555 U.S. XXX (2009).

[61] McDonald, op. cit.

[62] John N. Friedman and Richard T. Holden, "The Rising Incumbent Reelection Rate: What's Gerrymandering Got to Do with It?" *Journal of Politics* 71(2009):593–611.

---

[63] *Easley v. Cromartie*, 532 U.S. 234 (2001).

[64] This story was told by a legislative staffer to one of the authors.

Figure 7.3

Political Gerrymandering—Then and Now

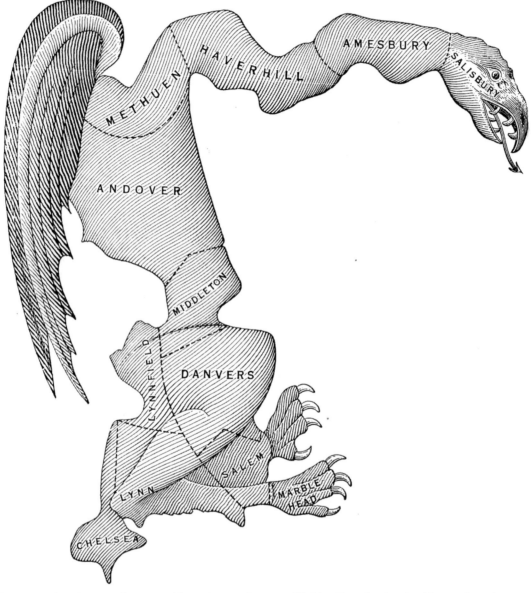

This early political cartoon lampoons Massachusetts Governor Elbridge Gerry for drawing bizarre-shaped state legislative districts to advantage his party in the early 19th century. But consider these four current Mississippi House of Representatives districts (Districts 23, 62, 80, and 95). Although they are admittedly extreme examples, they are by no means the only odd-shaped state legislative districts in use today. Why might these districts been drawn as they were? If you were a political cartoonist, what objects or animals could you make out of them?

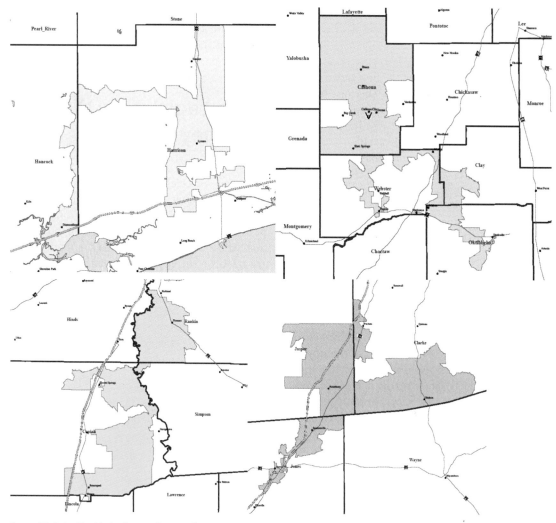

Source: Mississippi Legislative Reapportionment Committee, 2002 (Ben Collins, Coordinator).

that can occur in state legislative and congressional redistricting. First, some states have institutionalized certain redistricting criteria by putting them into law, and studies show that even the most determined "gerrymanderers" have a hard time getting around them.[65] For instance, 21 states require that county or municipal boundaries be followed, 19 require that districts be compact, and 10 require efforts to preserve old districts, all of these to the extent possible while meeting the one person, one vote mandate. Not only can such institutions increase electoral competition and reduce gerrymandering, but the U.S. Supreme Court has also recently given them strong status in law.[66] Second, the clashing interests among map makers, whether between the two political parties or between individual legislators and their parties, mitigate the mischief

[65] Barabas and Jerit, op. cit.; Forgette, Garner, and Winkle, op. cit.; Jonathon Winburn, *The Realities of Redistricting: Following the Rules and Limiting Gerrymandering in State Legislative Redistricting* (Lanham, MD: Lexington, 2008); David Butler and Bruce Cain, *Congressional Redistricting: Comparative and Theoretical Perspectives* (New York: Macmillan, 1992).

[66] *Bartlett v. Strickland.*

that they can do.[67] Finally, despite all the data and high-tech equipment at the disposal of today's redistricters, they still cannot predict the future. The census data they use is two and a half years out of date by the time even the first general election they are used in takes place.[68] Because Americans are so mobile, major demographic changes can occur in these districts over the decade in which they are used, especially in suburban areas around large cities. Thus, gerrymandering has a less significant impact on legislative elections than one might think given that lawmakers get to draw their own districts.

Revisiting the Paradox of Competition in State Legislative Elections

In the end, the way people vote and the way state legislative districts are drawn go a long way toward explaining why we find close competition between the parties in the aggregate (or at least a good reflection of the state or national electorate's partisan balance) but little of it in individual races. State legislative districts tend to be homogeneous due to their relatively small size and Americans' increasingly segregated living patterns, and they are further homogenized and manipulated during the redistricting process. This results in near certainty about which party will win each seat in the general election. For example, in California's 2004 general election, of the 153 congressional and state legislative seats up for election, none of them changed parties—and this is in a state where legislative term limits are supposed to decrease incumbents' dominance in elections.[69] On the other hand, when averaged up to the state or national level, state legislative elections do a good job of reflecting the balance between the two major political parties today.

State Legislators: Who Are They?

Those who win state legislative races barely have time to celebrate before they must meet in their respective state capitols to begin work. State legislators make big decisions about public policy and the allocation of resources that affect your life every day, so who they are makes a difference. Although any generalization about these 7,382 unique individuals glosses over many differences, looking at them in broad strokes can help us begin to understand how well the legislature represents the residents of the states.

Like most American political elites, state legislators are unrepresentative of the diversity of the country's population in many ways. The average state legislator is a 56-year-old white man, either in business or a lawyer, who is married and has lived in the same area most of his life.[70] Non-Latino whites make up only about 66 percent of Americans, a bit more than half are women, most are not lawyers or businessmen, and most tend to move every five years or so.[71] But if we look past simple averages, we find that state legislators are much more varied than any other set of state or national elected officials. In particular, the descriptive representativeness of state legislatures, that is, the extent to which these lawmakers look like the people they serve, has been improving steadily in recent years, although there is still wide variability in it among the states.

[67] Brian F. Schaffner, Michael W. Wagner, and Jonathon Winburn, "Incumbents Out, Party In? Term Limits and Partisan Redistricting in State Legislatures," *State Politics and Policy Quarterly* 4(2004):396–414.

[68] So, for example, the next redistricting process will use census data collected on 1 April 2010, to draw districts first used for a general election on 6 November 2012.

[69] Alan Greenblatt, "Monster Maps: Has Devious District-Making Killed Electoral Competition?" *Governing* (January 2006):46–50.

[70] National Conference of State Legislatures, "Legislator Demographics," http://74.125.95.132/search? q=cache:afgUnnxedKsJ:www.ncsl.org/%3Ftabid%3 D14850+%22legislator+demographics%22&cd=1&hl=e n&ct=clnk&gl=us

[71] Morgan and Morgan, op. cit., p. 466.

Figure 7.4

Progress in Women's Representation in State Legislatures

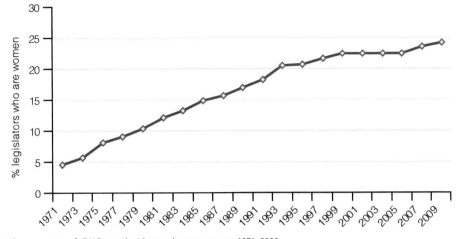

Note: Charts the percentage of all U.S. state legislators who were women, 1971–2009.

Source: Center for American Women and Politics, "Historical Information about Women in State Legislatures," http://www.cawp.rutgers.edu/fast_facts/levels_of_office/StateLeg-HistoricalInfo.php.

Women in the State Legislature

Women were the first underrepresented group to make headway in state legislatures. The first of these, Representatives Carrie Clyde Holly, Frances Klock, and Clara Cressingham, were all elected to the Colorado General Assembly in 1894, but for the next 80 years, women made little steady progress in this regard.[72] By 1971, at the beginning of the modern women's movement in this country, only 4.5 percent of state legislators were women. Since then, however, women have made solid, if not spectacular, gains. Today, 24.2 percent of state legislators are women. To put this in context,[73] only 12.0 percent of governors (see Chapter 8) and 16.8 percent of members of Congress are women, but 25.4 percent of elected statewide executive officials (such as lieutenant governors and attorneys general) are women.[74] Figure 7.4 shows that while women made steady progress in state legislatures from 1971 to 1993, that progress has slowed since then. Regardless of the speed of their recent progress, remarkably, there has never been a year since 1972 when fewer women nationally served as state legislators than in the previous year. Just as important, more women are assuming state legislative leadership positions.[75] Although it was not until the 1980s that the first women assumed the top leadership positions of House Speaker and Senate president, as of 2010, 44 women from 22 states had done so.[76]

---

[72] Kathleen A. Bratton, Kerry L. Haynie, and Beth Reingold, "Gender, Race, and Representation: The Changing Landscape of Legislative Diversity," in Audrey S. Wall, ed., *The Book of the States 2008*, vol. 40 (Lexington, KY: Council of State Governments, 2008).

[73] To put these numbers in international perspective, consider that out of 187 countries ranked in 2009 by the Inter-Parliamentary Union, women's representation in the U.S. Congress ranked 85th ("Women in National Parliaments," http://www.ipu.org/wmn-e/classif.htm#2). The states' 24.2 percent would place it 46th, between Liechtenstein and Singapore.

[74] Center for Women and American Politics, "Women in Elective Office 2009," http://www.cawp.rutgers.edu/fast_facts/levels_of_office/documents/elective.pdf.

[75] Garry Boulard, "It's Different at the Top," *State Legislatures*, July/August 2009, pp.20–22.

[76] Center for American Women and Politics, "Women State Legislators: Leadership Positions and Committee Chairs 2009," http://www.cawp.rutgers.edu/fast_facts/levels_of_office/documents/leglead.pdf.

Figure 7.5

Representation of Women in State Legislatures, 2010

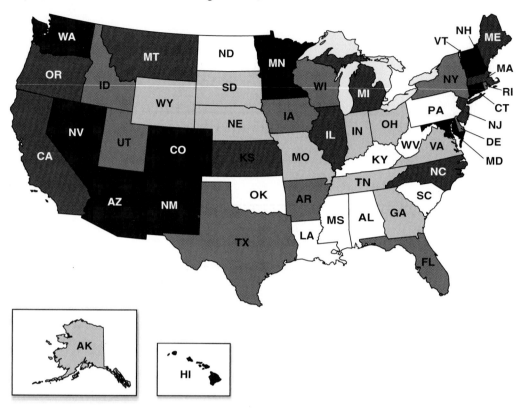

Note: These are the rankings of the states on the percentage of women in both chambers of their state legislature after the 2008 elections. The darker the state, the more representation women have in its legislature. The states range from 13.7 percent women in South Carolina to 40 percent in Colorado.

Source: National Conference of State Legislatures, "Women in State Legislatures: 2009 Legislative Session," http://www.ncsl.org/LegislaturesElections/WomensNetwork/WomeninStateLegislatures2009/tabid/15398/Default.aspx

Even though women have made steady progress nationwide in their state legislative representation, if we break the data down a bit, we see considerable variation that may help us better understand state legislatures and American politics more generally. First, women are not represented equally well in all states. At the extremes in 2010, women's representation ranges from the New Hampshire Senate, the first state legislative chamber to have a majority of women (13 of 24), to the South Carolina Senate, which, following the 2008 elections, became the first chamber since 1991 to have no women among its members. Figure 7.5

shows how women's legislative representation, combined in both chambers, varies among the states. The West and Northeast tend to have more women legislators, while the Southeast tends to have fewer.

Also notice that state legislative women are not equally well represented in the two major parties.[77] After the 2008 elections, a record 30.9 percent of Democratic state legislators were women, while they made up only

[77] Linda Fieldmann, "Why GOP Is Trending Away from Women in State Legislatures," *Politico.com*, 20 July 2009, on-line edition.

Figure 7.6

Women's State Legislative Representation, by Party

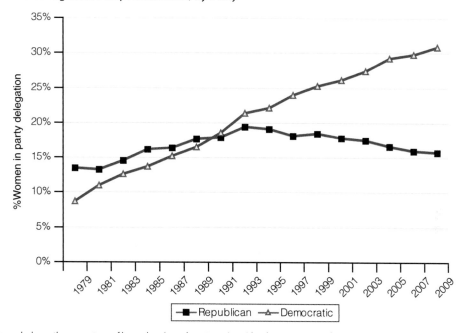

Note: This graph shows the percentage of lawmakers in each party nationwide who were women from 1979 to 2009.
Source: Center for American Women and Politics; Wall op. cit., various editions; compiled by authors.

15.8 percent of Republican lawmakers. Just as important, the proportion of women in the Republican legislative ranks has been decreasing somewhat, so that today's representation is lower than at any time in the last 20 years. This discrepancy did not always exist. Figure 7.6 shows that until 1992, the vaunted Year of the Woman, when the electoral success of women candidates across the country took a great leap,[78] proportions of women state legislators in the parties were largely equivalent; if anything, Republican women were even better represented. Starting with the 1992 election, however, women's representation among Democratic legislators has been progressively greater, while among Republicans, it has been flat or even decreasing. Today, a Democratic state legislator is almost twice as likely to be a woman as is a Republican legislator.

Why has women's representation in state legislatures increased so dramatically since the 1970s? Why is there so much variation in this representation across the states and parties? Why is it still far below a fair level of representation that would reflect women's proportion in society? Although we do not yet have complete answers to these questions, recent scholarship can give us certain insights. For example, state legislatures with lower pay and shorter sessions and those that use MMDs tend to have more women.[79] The standard explanation for

---

[78] Michelle Swers, "Whatever Happened to the Year of the Woman: Lessons from the 1992 and 2002 Elections," *PS: Political Science and Politics* 37(2004):61–62.

[79] James D. King, "Single-Member Districts and the Representation of Women in American State Legislatures: The Effects of Electoral System Change," *State Politics and Policy Quarterly* 2(2002):161–75; and Peverill Squire, "Legislative Professionalization and Membership Diversity in State Legislatures," *Legislative Studies Quarterly* 17(1992):69–79.

this has to do with the bias against women serving in elective office, a carryover from the prefeminist period. This story goes that seats in high-paying, professionalized legislatures with single-member districts appear more valuable, generating more competition for them and the tendency to fill them with men. Supporting this explanation is the finding that when a state's electorate and party leaders hold more traditional attitudes toward religion and gender roles, women are less well represented in its legislature.[80] This would also account for the upward trend in women's overall representation since 1971, a time when women began moving in large numbers into many nontraditional professions, and attitudes toward their role in society were changing. Studies show that voters are no longer especially sexist in their choice of candidates.[81] Thus, most of the remaining inequities have been attributed to residual biases in political elites[82] and attitudes of potential women candidates themselves who appear to underestimate their chances of winning and therefore are more hesitant to enter political races than men.[83] The differences between the parties have not yet been studied in depth, but they could be related to the gender gap in political ideology and policy

preferences.[84] Perhaps holding both parties to a 50 percent standard is unfair, especially if there are more women than men Democratic voters and more men than women Republican voters (see You Decide! box).

Racial and Ethnic Minorities in the State Legislature

State legislative representation for people whose racial or ethnic heritage is in the minority in the United States has also improved in recent decades, but for different reasons than that of women. For example, in 1969, there were only 172 African American state legislators (2.3 percent of all state legislators), but today there are 623 (8.4 percent).[85] One way to look at this is that since African Americans make up 12.8 percent of the U.S. population, they are now better represented in state legislatures than are women. Why has African American representation in state legislatures increased? The Voting Rights Act (VRA) of 1965 has had a lot to do with it.[86] Focusing mainly on the states of the old Confederacy, which have the highest proportions of African American residents, the VRA banned practices that discouraged blacks from voting, eliminated the MMDs that diluted their votes, and encouraged the drawing of majority-black political districts where possible. As a result, the number of African American state legislators in these states increased from only 3 in 1965, to 176 as early as 1985, and to 320 in 2010. Efforts to draw majority–minority districts in the 1980s and 1990s also helped

[80] Kevin Arseneaux, "The 'Gender Gap' in State Legislative Representation: New Data to Tackle an Old Question," *Political Research Quarterly* 54(2001):143–60; John F. Camobreco and Michelle A. Barnello, "Postmaterialism and Post-Industrialism: Cultural Influences on Female Representation in State Legislatures," *State Politics and Policy Quarterly* 3(2003):117–38.

[81] Barbara Burrell, *A Woman's Place Is in the House: Campaigning for Congress in the Feminist Era* (Ann Arbor, MI: University of Michigan Press, 1994); Robert Darcy, Susan Welch, and Janet Clark, *Women, Elections, and Representation* (Lincoln, NE: University of Nebraska Press, 1994).

[82] Kira Sanbonmatsu, *Where Women Run: Gender and Party in the American States* (Ann Arbor, MI: University of Michigan Press, 2006).

[83] Shannon Jenkins, "A Woman's Work Is Never Done? Fund-Raising Perception and Effort among Female State Legislative Candidates," *Political Research Quarterly* 60(2007):230–39; Richard L. Fox and Jennifer L. Lawless, "Entering the Arena? Gender and the Decision to Run for Office," *American Journal of Political Science* 48(2004):264–80.

[84] Barbara Norrander and Clyde Wilcox, "The Gender Gap in Ideology," *Political Behavior* 30(2008):503–23.

[85] Samantha Sanchez, *Money and Diversity in State Legislatures, 2003* (Helena, MT: Institute on Money in State Politics, 2005); updated by the authors with data from the Joint Center for Political and Economic Studies.

[86] Grofman and Handley, "The Impact of the Voting Rights Act"; Janine A. Parry and William H. Miller, "'The Great Negro State of the Country?' Black Legislators in Arkansas, 1973–2000," *Journal of Black Studies* 36(2006):833–72.

YOU DECIDE

GENDER REPRESENTATION OF DEMOCRATS AND REPUBLICANS: WHAT'S FAIR?

While the percentage of women in state legislatures has been increasing steadily for almost four decades, it is still much smaller than the percentage of women in the U.S. population (24.2 percent versus 50.7 percent in 2010). Thus, women are underrepresented in these bodies. Just as interesting to political scientists, however, is the big difference between the political parties in the percentage of state lawmakers who are women (see Figure 7.5). In 2010, nearly 30.9 percent of Democratic state legislators were women, while only 15.8 percent of Republican state legislators were. At face value then, women appear to be far better represented in the state legislatures by Democrats than by Republicans. But is it fair to hold both parties to the same standard in making this comparison? While the U.S. population is 50.7 percent female, fewer Republican voters are female than Democratic voters.

So what is the proper standard to use to compare the gender representation of the political parties in the state legislatures? If not the overall 50.7 percent that women make up in the nation as a whole, then what standard would be better and how would you actually get data to make that comparison? What normative and practical political questions are raised by the difference in the representation of women by Democratic and Republican state lawmakers?

increase African American representation in legislatures outside the South.

In addition to African Americans, there are now 178 Latinos (2.4 percent of lawmakers) serving in state legislatures, according to the National Association of Latino Elected Officials. This is disproportionate with Latinos' 15.1 percent share of the U.S. population, making them perhaps the most underrepresented major demographic group today. This is due largely to their low political participation, which stems from the abundance of children, first-generation citizens, and noncitizens among them today.[87] A recent study has shown that legislatures with greater turnover have better Latino representation, suggesting that incumbents' electoral advantage is slowing their progress here.[88] As time passes, their

political participation and state legislative representation may well increase rapidly, like that of African Americans following the enactment of the VRA. Latino political representation has already been helped somewhat by the VRA and the drawing of majority–minority districts, but the biggest reason for their recent gains in state legislatures is simply the growing number of Latinos in the population.

There are also 85 Asian American legislators (1.2 percent, as compared to 4.4 percent in the population) and 78 Native American legislators (1.1 percent, as compared to 1.0 percent in the population), according to the National Conference of State Legislatures.[89] Most Asian American state legislators serve in Hawaii and

---

[87] Rodney Hero, F. C. Garcia, J. Garcia, and H. Pachon, "Latino Participation, Partisanship, and Office Holding," *PS: Politics and Political Science* 33(2000):529–34.

[88] Jason P. Casellas, "The Institutional and Demographic Determinants of Latino Representation," *Legislative Studies Quarterly* 34(2009):399–426.

[89] National Conference of State Legislators, "Number of Native American Legislators 2009," http://www.ncsl.org/LegislaturesElections/LegislatorsLegislativeStaffData/NativeAmericanLegislators2009/tabid/14762/Default.aspx; National Conference of State Legislators, "Number of Asian American Legislators 2009," http://www.ncsl.org/LegislaturesElections/LegislatorsLegislativeStaffData/AsianAmericanLegislators2009/tabid/14762/Default.aspx.

California, states with many people of Asian heritage. For the same reason, Montana and Oklahoma have the most Native American legislators.

As with women, the percentage of racial and ethnic minorities in state legislative chambers varies dramatically across the states, but unlike with women, much of the cross-state variation in minority representation is easy to explain. The percentage of African Americans or Latinos in a state's legislature is largely a function of their presence in the state's population.[90] But these numbers alone tell us little about how well racial and ethnic minorities are represented. As discussed in Chapter 1, the proportion of people of different races and ethnicities varies widely from state to state, while gender is distributed much more evenly.[91] A better way to assess the racial and ethnic representation of a state legislature is to compare the percentage of its members who are minorities to the percentage of the state's population who are minorities. Figure 7.7 shows how the states rank in this way. A ratio of 1.00 shows that a state's percentages of minority lawmakers and residents are equal, a score below 1.00 shows the extent to which a lawmaking body is unrepresentative in this respect, and a score above 1.00 shows the extent to which minorities are overrepresented.

Figure 7.7 shows that minority legislative representation is not easy to explain at first glance. Non-Hispanic whites, or Anglos, make up the majority of Americans (66.1 percent), so those who are non-Anglo (African Americans, Hispanics, Asians, Native Americans, those of mixed heritage, and others) constitute those who are traditionally defined as "minorities" in this country. In two states, however, Anglos are actually in the minority—Hawaii

(24.8 percent Anglo) and New Mexico (42.5 percent Anglo). As it happens, the legislatures in these states are the most representative, with Hawaii's having a representation ratio of 1.05 and New Mexico's of .88. More generally, there is an imperfect tendency among the states for representation to be positively related to the percentage of racial and ethnic minorities in a state.[92] That is, the higher the proportion of non-Anglos in a state, the better they are represented in the state legislature. This is not the same as saying that there are simply more minority legislators in states where more people of those heritages live. It is saying that the higher the proportion of non-Anglos in a state, the more equal are the population and legislative proportions of race and ethnicity. It is possible, for example, for a state to have few non-Anglos in both the population and legislature and to have equal representation, but this does not tend to be the case.

This relationship between minority proportion and representation helps demonstrate the "Matthew 25:29" principle at work in political districts in the winner-take-all elections that are most common in the United States.[93] This principle derives its name from the Christian Bible, in the 25th chapter of the Gospel of Matthew, verse 29: "For everyone who has will be given more, and he will have an abundance. Whoever does not have, even what he has will be taken from him." That is, in our system, majorities—such as party, racial, ethnic, economic interest, or whatever—tend to win majorities in legislatures that are disproportionately larger than their majorities among voters.[94] For instance, suppose that Republican voters accounted for 51 percent of the voters in a state and Democrats accounted for 49 percent. If these parti-

---

[90] For example, in 2010, the simple correlation between the percentage of African Americans in states' legislatures and their populations is .96; for Latinos, it is .92.

[91] The percentage of men in a state ranges from 54 percent in Alaska to 47.5 percent in Rhode Island. See: Morgan and Morgan, op. cit., p. 464.

[92] This correlation is .70.

[93] This is as opposed to proportional representation systems, in which minorities can receive a more proportionate level of seats in a legislature.

[94] Of course, this does not explain the poor representation of women in state legislatures. This can be blamed on our cultural history of sexism, for the most part.

Figure 7.7

Minority Representation in State Legislatures

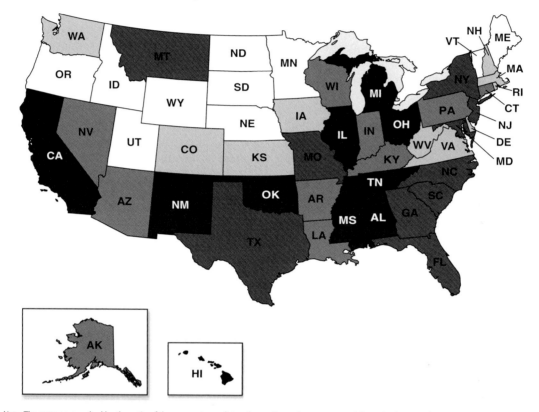

Note: The states are ranked by the ratio of the percentage of state lawmakers who are not non-Hispanic whites to the percentage of the state's population who are not non-Hispanic whites, in 2009. These ratios range from 1.05 in Hawaii and .88 in New Mexico to .07 in Idaho and .12 in Vermont. The darker the state, the more representative its legislature is of the racial and ethnic minorities in its population.

Source: Compiled and calculated by the authors from data in Morgan and Morgan op. cit., Sanchez op. cit., the National Association of Latino Elected Officials, and the Joint Center for Political and Economic Studies.

sans were distributed evenly around the state so that every legislative district had a 51–49 voter split, then the GOP would win 100 percent of the legislative seats. Such a legislature would not be representative of partisans in the state. Since voters are not distributed evenly, with likes tending to live near likes, this force toward unrepresentativeness is mitigated, but it continues to work to some degree, and the smaller a minority, the stronger this force is.

As shown in Figure 7.7, states in the South and those in the North with large urban centers have high proportions of African Americans,

and they rank high on descriptive representation. States with many Latinos, like California, Florida, and New Mexico, or Native Americans, like Montana and Oklahoma (and, again, New Mexico) also rank highly. On the other hand, highly homogenous states, including Maine, North Dakota, and West Virginia, tend be to less representative. But some states defy this trend. For example, Delaware ranks low on representation even though its minority population is similar to that of Alabama and South Carolina, and Ohio ranks high even though it has relatively fewer non-Anglos than

Oregon or Kansas. Some of this discrepancy can be explained by living patterns in these states; the more concentrated ethnic groups are among themselves, the more likely they will be to elect a person of their own heritage. Of course, all this discussion is based on the assumption that people are more likely to vote for those of their own racial and ethnic heritage than others, clearly a more questionable assumption today than in years gone by.

Finally, scholars are just beginning to study two other aspects of descriptive representation in state legislatures: the intersection of gender and racial representation, that is, the presence of women of color in state legislatures, and sexual orientation representation. First, early findings suggest that representativeness for women of color cannot be explained by simply extending theories of the representation of minority men or white women. For example, since at least 1976, gender representation has been better for African Americans and Latinos than for Anglos. One study found that in 2003, while women made up 21 percent of white legislators, 35 percent of black lawmakers were women, as were 29 percent of Latino lawmakers.[95] Equally interesting, scholars are beginning to find that the explanations for why the representation of women of color varies among the states are subtly different than those of either non-Anglo men or Anglo women.[96] And second, a recent study of openly gay state law-makers suggests that their representation may be about on par with that of this sexual minority in the population.[97] This is especially surprising because experimental research suggests that voters tend to view a generic openly gay person as less politically viable than a generic straight person.[98] This may suggest that when confronted with an actual gay person, rather than a hypothetical, Americans are more open-minded than they once were. Ongoing scholarship in both these areas holds great promise for expanding our understanding of lawmaking and representation.

The Impact of Broader Representation

Assessing racial, gender, and sexual orientation descriptive representation in state legislatures is relatively easy to do, but it is much harder to say with certainty what difference it makes. Seeing people like ourselves in political office gives us an emotional lift and a sense of attachment to the government and of political efficacy. President Obama's 2008 election spawned much discussion of this, and even being represented by a person of one's own gender or heritage in the state government can have such salutary effects.

Beyond this, does better descriptive representation make a difference in public policy and governance? Political scientists have begun to study this difficult question. The most straightforward way of doing this is to assess the degree to which women and minority lawmakers differ from their white male colleagues. The idea here is that if non-Anglo and female lawmakers are different in policy-relevant ways, then more of them serving in the statehouse will have policy impacts. If so, then better descriptive representation is positive even beyond its symbolic value, since it would mean that the

[95] Becki Scola, "Women of Color in State Legislatures: Gender, Race, Ethnicity and Legislative Office Holding," *Journal of Women, Politics & Policy* 28(2006):43–69; see also: Wendy G. Smooth, "African American Women and Electoral Politics: Journeying from the Shadows to the Spotlight," in Susan J. Carroll and Richard L. Fox, eds., *Gender and Elections: Shaping the Future of American Politics* (New York: Cambridge University Press, 2006); Robert Darcy and Charles D. Hadley, "Black Women in Politics: The Puzzle of Success," *Social Science Quarterly* 69(1988):629–45.

[96] Beth Reingold, Kathleen A. Bratton, and Kerry L. Haynie, "Descriptive Representation in State Legislatures and Intersections of Race, Ethnicity, and Gender," presented at the American Empirical Series, Stanford Institute for the Quantitative Study of Society (May 2009).

[97] Haider-Markel, op. cit.

[98] Rebekah Herrick and Sue Thomas, "Gays and Lesbians in Local Races: A Study of Electoral Viability," *Journal of Homosexuality* 42(2001):103–126.

values and preferences of those other than white men would be better reflected in policy. For example, African American male and white female legislators each tend to be more interested in education, social welfare, and health care policy,[99] with African American women lawmakers having an especially high interest in progressive legislation.[100] Latino legislators have a special interest in immigration and bilingual education.[101] These preferences are seen in the types of committees they serve on, the bills they introduce, and how they vote on legislation. Certainly some of these differences reflect the values of the constituents who send them to the statehouse, but there is evidence that lawmakers' race and gender have independent effects on their preferences.[102] Not surprisingly, scholars have also found evidence that as non-Anglos and women become better represented in state legislatures, their preferences become better reflected in public policy.[103] On the other hand, there is also disturbing evidence that there can sometimes be a backlash against

them and their interests,[104] but this effect seems to be short-lived.[105]

Because of their greater numbers in state legislatures, scholars have been able to study women lawmakers more and longer than minority lawmakers. In the 1970s and 1980s, when women were making their first inroads into public office, the differences between female and male lawmakers were fairly stark. Aside from having somewhat different policy agendas, these women tended to be older, have fewer children, be more often unmarried or divorced, be social workers or teachers rather than lawyers, and be less politically ambitious than their male colleagues.[106] In recent years, however, as women have become commonplace in legislatures, most of these demographic differences between the genders in the statehouse have vanished. On the other hand, the ideological gender gap seen among American voters is exaggerated in the statehouse, with the average female legislator being more liberal on social issues, the environment, gun control, and abortion regulation than her male colleague. Interestingly, there is far less of this sort of difference among Democratic than Republican lawmakers.[107] That is, while male and female Democrats are similarly liberal, Republican women tend to be significantly to the left of their male counterparts. In addition, women may also engage in more constituent service and be more

[99] Kerry L. Haynie, *African American Legislators in the American States* (New York: Columbia University Press, 2001); Kathleen A. Bratton and Kerry L. Haynie, "Agenda Setting and Legislative Success in State Legislatures: The Effects of Gender and Race," *Journal of Politics* 61(1999):658–79.

[100] Bryon D'Andra Orey, Wendy Smooth, Kimberly S. Adams, and Kisha Harris-Clark, "Race and Gender Matter: Refining Models of Legislative Policy Making in State Legislatures," *Journal of Women, Politics, and Policy* 28(2006):97–119.

[101] Kathleen Bratton, "The Behavior and Success of Latino Legislators: Evidence from the States," *Social Science Quarterly* 87(2006):1136–57.

[102] Sarah Poggione, "Exploring Gender Differences in State Legislators' Policy Preferences," *Political Research Quarterly* 57(2004):305–14.

[103] Jocelyn Elise Crowley, "Moving beyond Tokenism: Ratification of the Equal Rights Amendment and the Election of Women State Legislatures," *Social Science Quarterly* 87(2006):519–39; C. T. Owens, "Black Substantive Representation in State Legislatures from 1971–1994," *Social Science Quarterly* 86(2005):779–91; Robert R. Preuhs, "The Conditional Effects of Minority Descriptive Representation: Black Legislators and Policy Influence in the American States," *Journal of Politics* 68(2006):585–99.

[104] Haider-Markel, op. cit.; Matthew C. Fellowes and Gretchen Rowe, "Politics and the New American Welfare States," *American Journal of Political Science* 48(2004):362–73; Joe Soss, Sanford F. Schram, Thomas P. Vartanian, and Erin O'Brien, "Setting the Terms of Relief: Explaining State Policy Choices in the Devolution Revolution," *American Journal of Political Science* 45(2001):378–95; Caroline J. Tolbert and Gertrude A. Steuernagel, "Women Lawmakers, State Mandate, and Women's Health," *Women and Politics* 22(2001):1–39.

[105] Robert R. Preuhs, "Descriptive Representation as a Mechanism to Mitigate Policy Backlash," *Political Research Quarterly* 60(2007):277–92; Preuhs, 2006, op. cit.

[106] Anne Marie Camissa and Beth Reingold, "Women in State Legislatures and State Legislative Research: Beyond Sameness and Difference," *State Politics and Policy Quarterly* 4(2004):181–210.

[107] Poggione, op. cit.

cooperative, consensus-building, and egalitarian in the legislative process.[108]

As you will read later, legislative committees play a critical role in lawmaking. Early research on women's legislative committee membership found that they were more likely to be on "women's issues" committees, like those dealing with families and children, education, health care, and so forth, and less likely to be on "power committees," like those dealing with taxes and the budget. This effect was especially pronounced for African American and Latino legislators who were female.[109] The question was then raised whether this difference was caused by the preferences of the women lawmakers or by some bias of (presumably male) legislative leaders. The fact that these differences have diminished in recent years seemed to support the bias explanation, but a new survey of state lawmakers suggests otherwise.[110] It showed that while women are now just as likely as men to be on power committees, they frequently preferred to be on social service and education committees. This is powerful evidence of a true difference between the policy agendas of men and women lawmakers, and thus, it is strong support for the importance of gender representation.

Of course, for any underrepresented group, achieving its political goals requires more than just gaining a few seats in the legislature. In particular, as we shall see, real policy making requires developing legislative majorities. This means that even if a legislature is representative of racial and ethnic minorities, then they will still be at a disadvantage. But numerical minorities can influence lawmaking even in a process that puts a premium on majorities. First, lawmakers in committee or chamber leadership positions have disproportionate influence in their chambers, and committee chairs have been filled increasingly by women and minorities in recent years, largely in proportion to their numbers in their chambers.[111] In addition, lawmakers from these underrepresented groups have also begun to take chamber leadership positions. Forty-four women from 22 states have held the very top leadership position in a state legislative chamber, as have 12 African Americans and eight Latinos (see Table 7.4).[112] The 2009 legislative session found 10 of the 99 state legislative chambers being led by women and five by African Americans, a new record in both cases.[113] In 2008, Colleen Hanabusa became the first woman of color to preside over a state legislative chamber when she became President of the Hawaii State Senate, and later that same year, Karen Bass of California became

---

[108] Lyn Kathlene, "Power and Influence in State Legislative Policy-Making: The Interaction of Gender and Position in Committee Hearing Debates," *American Political Science Review* 88(1994):560–76.

[109] Luis Ricardo Fraga, Valerie Martinez-Ebers, Linda Lopez, and Ricardo Ramirez, "Representing Gender and Ethnicity: Strategic Intersectionality," in Beth Reingold, ed., *Legislative Women: Getting Elected and Getting Ahead* (Boulder, CO: Lynne Reinner, 2008).

[110] Susan J. Carroll, "Committee Assignments: Discrimination or Choice?" in Beth Reingold, ed., *Legislative Women: Getting Elected and Getting Ahead* (Boulder, CO: Lynne Reinner, 2008).

[111] Byron D'Andra Orey, L. Marvin Overby, and Christopher W. Larimer, "African-American Committee Chairs in U.S. State Legislatures," *Social Science Quarterly* 88(2007):619–39; Robert R. Preuhs, "Descriptive Representation, Legislative Leadership, and Direct Democracy: Latino Influence on English Only Laws in the States, 1984–2002," *State Politics and Policy Quarterly* 5(2005):203–24; and Cindy S. Rosenthal, *When Women Lead: Integrative Leadership in State Legislatures* (New York: Oxford University Press, 1998).

[112] In addition, several Latino and Asian Americans have served as the top leader in Arizona, New Mexico, and Hawaii, where people of these heritages are well represented. Center for American Women and Politics, "Women State Legislators: Leadership Positions 2009," http://www.cawp.rutgers.edu/fast_facts/levels_of_office/documents/leglead.pdf.

[113] One of these five African American leaders started, but did not finish, the 2009 session as presiding officer. Peter Groff, president of the Colorado State Senate, resigned to head up President Obama's faith-based initiative center in the U.S. Department of Education. Malcolm Smith, Majority Leader in the New York State Senate, lost his position as presiding officer temporarily in June 2009 during battle over the chamber's majority (see: Danny Hakim and Jeremy W. Peters, "Door Is Locked, and Senate Is in Gridlock," *The New York Times*, 11 June 2009, online edition).

Table 7.4

African American and Latino Leaders of Majority Parties in State Legislative Chambers

Name	State- Chamber	Party	Dates of Service
African American			
Terrance Carroll	CO-House	D	2009–present
Peter Groff	CO- Senate	D	2009
Malcolm Smith	NY- Senate	D	2009–present
Karen Bass	CA- Assembly	D	2008–11
Emil Jones, Jr.	IL- Senate	D	2003–09
Herbert Wesson	CA- Assembly	D	2002–04
Daniel T. Blue, Jr.	NC- House	D	1991–94
Willie L. Brown, Jr.	CA- Assembly	D	1981–95
K. Leroy Irvis	PA- House	D	1977–78, 1983–88
S. Howard Woodson, Jr.	NJ- Assembly	D	1974–76
Cecil A. Partee	IL- Senate	D	1971–73; 1975–77
John R. Lynch	MS- House	R	1871–73
Latino			
Pedro Espada, Jr.	NY- Senate	D	2009
Marco Rubio	FL- House	R	2007–09
Fabian Nuñez	CA- Assembly	D	2004–08
Albio Sires	NJ- House	D	2002–06
Ben Luján	NM- House	D	2001–present
Antonio Villaraigosa	CA- Assembly	D	1998–2000
Cruz Bustamante	CA- Assembly	D	1996–98
Raymond G. Sanchez	NM- House	D	1983–2000

Note: The authors compiled this list with the help of the National Conference of State Legislators, the Joint Center for Political and Economic Studies, and the National Association of Latino Elected Officials.

the first African American women to become a house speaker.[114] Another way that women and minorities have gained significant influence in state legislatures is by forming informal legislative groups, such as a Black Legislators' Caucus or a Conference of Women Legislators. Such groups provide training and mentoring for new lawmakers, a sense of group cohesion among its members, and a vehicle with which to mobilize blocs of votes that can be used to

gain support from other legislators on issues important to the group.[115]

The Job of the State Legislature

Within a few weeks of each general election, state legislators head to their respective state

---

[114] In fact, the lower chamber in California is called the Assembly.

[115] Michelle G. Briscoe, "Cohesiveness and Diversity among Black Members of the Texas State Legislature," in Charles E. Menifield and Steven D. Shaffer, eds., *Politics in the New South* (Albany, NY: SUNY Press, 2005); Tracy Osborn, "Women Representing Women: Pursuing a Women's Agenda in the States" (Ph.D. diss., Indiana University, 2004).

capitols to begin the job they were elected to do. As an institution, the state legislature has three basic jobs:

- To help make and revise the state's laws
- To oversee the executive branch's implementation of the state's laws
- To represent the interests of the state's citizens to the state government

While these jobs have some overlap, it is useful to discuss them separately.

Lawmaking

First and foremost, the state legislature's job is to deliberate on the public problems of the state and then make or modify state law to address them—a huge undertaking, to say the least. Each state's legal code consists of thousands of laws touching on every facet of life and business, and every one of these laws has been passed by the legislature over the years.[116] Everything that a state or local government official does must be authorized by the legislature. Roads, bridges and mass transit, education from preschool to the doctoral level, parks, prisons and police, hunting, haircutting, and health clubs—all these and much more may be considered in depth by a state legislature each year. Then each year in every state, all this deliberation about public problems results in thousands of **bills,** formal proposals to change state law. For example, in their 2009 legislative session, members of the Connecticut House and Senate considered 3,936 bills and passed 266 of these into law. Lawmaking is a big job for state legislators, and they take this important responsibility very seriously.

The process of making law is complex and difficult—and for a good reason. Mark Twain once said, "No man's life, liberty, or property is safe while the legislature is in session."[117] Like all jokes, this one holds a large measure of truth. Americans tend to be suspicious of government, so we make the legislative process slow and difficult to reduce the risk of unwise or dangerous state government action. In the end, only about 20 percent of the bills considered by state legislatures actually become law.[118] To do so, a bill must be approved by both chambers by at least a majority vote in exactly the same form and then be signed by the governor.[119]

The basic legislative process in the states is quite similar to that of Congress. First, someone says, "There ought to be a law!" Since this is their main business, legislators are always on the lookout for good ideas. They get many of these bill ideas from their constituents, the news, and their personal experiences, but the main source of these ideas is interest groups and their lobbyists, since their members can be affected directly—positively or negatively—by state policy. Regardless of the source of the idea, once a legislator files a bill with the clerk of the chamber, he or she becomes the **bill's sponsor,** at which point the legislative process formally begins. Next, the bill is assigned to a **standing committee** of the legislature for consideration. This committee may hold a public hearing to gather information about the bill's potential effects and its political support. The sponsor is typically the first, and sometimes the only, person to speak at the hearing, giving his or her rationale for the necessity and efficacy of the bill. Constructing a pleasing story about the bill can be critical to convincing colleagues to approve the bill. Opponents, if any, also try to tell a story about the bill that supports their position. So, for example, a bill giving in-state college tuition to the children of undocumented immigrants might be described as a way to "educate kids and promote the American dream" or

---

[116] This is true except for those relatively very few laws that are passed through the initiative process (see Chapter 4).

[117] Tommy Neal, *Learning the Game: How the Legislative Process Works* (Denver, CO: National Conference of State Legislatures, 2005), p. 33.

[118] This varies quite a bit across the states. For example, in 2007, Colorado legislators passed 73.5 percent of its bills, while Connecticut passed only 7.8 percent. See: Wall, op. cit., p. 130.

[119] Alternatively, the governor's veto may be overridden by the legislature.

as "coddling criminals."[120] In addition, a person from the state agency that would be assigned to implement the bill often weighs in. Given the bureaucrat's expertise and at least relative objectivity, this person's perspective usually carries considerable weight. Furthermore, since the committee specializes in the bill's policy area, the lawmakers that serve on it will already have at least a bit of expertise on the subject.

After hearing these arguments, the committee deliberates. If the problems raised about the bill are sufficiently worrisome, the committee may simply not report it back to the full chamber (or report it unfavorably), and it will not become law in the current legislative session. One of the central functions of standing committees is to screen out bad, weak, or politically unpalatable bills. There is no reason to waste the full chamber's time considering bills that have obvious problems. But state legislative committees tend to be weaker at screening bills than their congressional counterparts.[121] In many states, if a sponsor really wants to get a bill passed in committee, he or she can do so.

The other major function of legislative committees is to **amend** bills, if and as needed, in light of any political or policy weaknesses that might be raised in the hearings and deliberations. If the committee agrees with the general idea of a bill, such amendments may improve both its effectiveness in dealing with the policy problem and the bill's chances of becoming law. In the end, if the committee is convinced of the bill's merit, amended or not, it will vote to report the bill to the full chamber for further consideration.

At this point in the process, the majority party leader (whether the speaker of the house, president of the senate, or a person with some other title) has a critical opportunity to affect the bill's fate in most chambers, particularly if he or she opposes the bill. Standing committees report out far more bills than their full chambers can reasonably consider, creating a bottleneck in the process. One of the majority party leader's central functions is to manage the process by selecting which bills will be considered on the **chamber floor**.[122] How do they make this choice? First, legislative leaders dislike controversial bills because they consume too much of the chamber's precious floor time. Less commonly, majority party leaders will kill bills they do not want to see debated on the floor for political reasons. Perhaps the debate would expose rifts among legislators of their own party, or perhaps voting on the bill would be politically damaging for some majority party legislators facing tough reelection campaigns.[123] Less frequently, a majority party leader may have policy preferences (either personal preferences or, more commonly, those of his or her party) that would be advanced by killing or passing a particular bill, and the leader uses his or her **gatekeeping** power to do so.

Once a bill gets to the floor of the full chamber, lawmakers first consider whether to amend it. Various legislators, especially the bill's sponsor and members of the committee that reviewed it, may speak to describe its intent and political support and opposition (if any). Sometimes suggestions for changes are offered, and to reduce controversy and increase the chances of passage, sponsors tend to agree to amendments, unless they think that they go too far in changing the bill's original intent. Even though the norm in most chambers is to defer to sponsors when possible, at this stage of the process, it is the chamber's bill, and it will pass or fail on its own merits.

---

[120] Gary Reich and Alvar Ayala Mendoza, "'Educating Kids' versus 'Coddling Criminals': Framing the Debate over In-State Tuition for Undocumented Students in Kansas," *State Politics and Policy Quarterly* 8(2008):177–97.

[121] Wayne Francis, *The Legislative Committee Game: A Comparative Analysis of Fifty States* (Columbus, OH: Ohio State University Press, 1989).

[122] A few states, like Colorado, limit the majority leader's power to do this, requiring a floor vote on every bill that comes out of committee. This weakens the power of the majority leader and reduces the amount of deliberation any given bill has on the floor.

[123] John H. Aldrich and James S. Battista, "Conditional Party Government in the States," *American Journal of Political Science* 46(2002):164–72.

Finally, the chamber votes on the bill, and a majority vote passes it in that chamber.[124] Since the goal of the legislative process prior to the floor **roll call** vote is to screen out bills that are flawed or lack political support, most bills that survive to the chamber floor not only pass, but pass by a wide margin. A legislator's default floor vote is "aye"; that is, legislators typically need a reason to vote against a bill on the floor rather than for it. Usually, a legislator will only vote against a bill if it somehow hurts his or her district and, in the long run, his or her chance at reelection. Generally speaking, a lawmaker will vote against a bill if voting for it could be made to look bad in an opponent's campaign brochure. Because lawmakers vote on hundreds of varied, technical, and arcane bills every year, on most of them, they usually know only the bare minimum when they cast their roll call votes. Therefore, to avoid casting "bad" votes, legislators routinely take **voting cues** from their colleagues.[125]

Cue-taking is informal, and it can happen in a variety of ways, but it often happens like this for roll call votes. Most state legislative chambers have a large electronic "tote board" showing each lawmaker's vote during the roll call. Lawmakers with some knowledge of a bill—such as members of the reviewing committee, the bill's sponsor and co-sponsors, and key opponents (if any)—will vote immediately as the vote is called, with the aye or nay lights flashing by their names. Uninformed legislators check the votes of members of their own party and those from similar and neighboring districts. Lacking other information, voting with their colleagues who are similarly positioned helps legislators avoid casting votes that may hurt their districts (and thereby may come back to haunt them in a reelection campaign). The result of this process is that a lawmaker generates a remarkably consistent voting record that reflects his or her party ideology and is aligned with his or her district's interests.[126]

A bill that manages to overcome these difficult hurdles in its chamber of origin is then sent to the other chamber, where the entire process is repeated—introduction, committee evaluation and amendment, and floor consideration and voting. As in its chamber of origin, if the bill fails to pass any of the hurdles in the second chamber, it does not become law, at least that year. Even if the bill passes the second chamber, it may be amended there. Remember that a bill must pass both chambers in identical form before it can become law. For example, in a recent legislative session in Texas, a proposal was derailed when a house member pointed out that the bill that her chamber passed had a comma where the Senate-passed bill had a semicolon.[127] If the second chamber passes an amended bill, to become law, the different versions must be reconciled and then voted on again in each chamber. This may be done by one chamber simply accepting the other chamber's version, or if neither chamber acquiesces, a temporary **conference committee** with members of both chambers may convene to craft a bill that can pass both chambers. Typically, conference committee members are appointed by the leaders of each party in each chamber and include the bill's primary sponsor in each chamber and the leaders of the standing committees that heard the bill. If the conference committee

---

[124] Certain types of bills require a supermajority vote, such as bills for borrowing money or votes to override a governor's veto.

[125] This process is best described in the context of congressional roll call voting in: John W. Kingdon, *Congressmen's Voting Decisions*, 3rd ed. (Ann Arbor, MI: University of Michigan Press, 1989).

[126] Shannon Jenkins, "Party Influences on Roll Call Voting: A View from the U.S. States," *State Politics and Policy Quarterly* 8(2008):239–62; Gerald C. Wright, "Do Term Limits Affect Legislative Roll Call Voting? Representation, Polarization, and Participation," *State Politics and Policy Quarterly* 7(2007):256–80; but sometimes lawmakers can adapt their voting to situations, e.g., see: Thad Kousser, Jeffrey B. Lewis, and Seth E. Masket, "Ideological Adaptation: The Survival Instinct of Threatened Lawmakers," *Journal of Politics* 69(2007):828–43.

[127] Polly Ross Hughes, "Comma Kills Journalists' Shield Law in Texas House," *The Houston Chronicle*, 22 May 2007, online edition.

Figure 7.8

Simplified Version of How a Bill Becomes a Law in the Typical Bicameral State Legislature

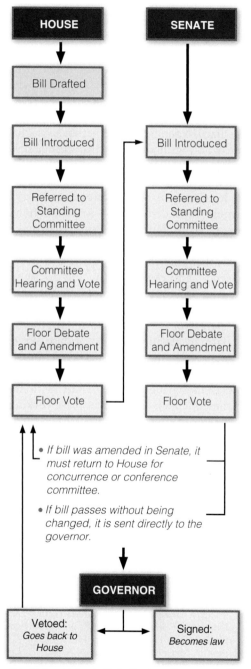

Note: A bill could also start in the Senate and then go to the House.

can reach a compromise, it reports it out to each chamber floor (if no agreement can be reached, the bill dies). There, legislators are only allowed to vote aye or nay on the compromise bill, with no amendments being allowed. In the end, even more often than regular bills, conference committee bills usually pass on the floor. By this point in the process, most concerns raised about the bill have been worked out. Besides, too much effort will have been put into it for it to fail.

Once both chambers pass the bill in identical form, it is sent to the governor for consideration. Usually, the governor approves of the bill by signing it, thus completing the process—the bill becomes state law on its effective date, as specified in the bill. Alternatively, the governor can veto the bill, sending it back to the legislature for further deliberation. As described in Chapter 8, veto powers of the governor vary significantly among the states, with most governors having a much more powerful veto than that of the president. Regardless of the type of veto used, the legislature has the opportunity to **override** it, usually through a **supermajority** vote in each chamber. But a governor's veto is very hard to override. Governors do not veto bills lightly or often, so when one does, he or she takes it seriously and uses considerable political resources to make sure not to be overridden.[128]

Overseeing the Executive Branch

Although it is neither as formal nor as well publicized nor anywhere near as time consuming as lawmaking, legislatures also oversee the state executive branch's **implementation** of laws and programs. In this way, the legislature acts like the board of directors of a large corporation, setting general policy for the organization and then checking occasionally to make sure that the agencies are executing that policy as originally intended.

---

[128] Carl E. Klarner and Andrew Karch, "Why Do Governors Issue Vetoes? The Impact of Individual and Institutional Influences," *Political Research Quarterly* 61(2008):574–84; Vicky M. Wilkins and Garry Young, "The Influence of Governors on Veto Override Attempts: A Test of Pivotal Politics," *Legislative Studies Quarterly* 27(2002):557–76.

AP Photo/Darron Cummings

State agencies' annual budgetary hearings are an important part of "police-patrol" legislative oversight of the executive branch. Here, an Indiana state agency head justifies his requests for spending, while lawmakers grill him about how his agency is implementing state law and policy.

First, and most effectively, the legislature can control policy implementation simply by stating clearly in its original legislation what an agency is supposed to do. The more detailed the legislation, the less discretion an agency has and, therefore, the more likely that **legislative intent** will be followed. For example, if the legislature passes a law that just reads, "The Board of Higher Education (BHE) shall offer high-quality postsecondary education," the BHE has tremendous leeway in determining how higher education will be offered in the state.[129] It might decide to emphasize liberal arts education, by providing resources for state colleges to hire plenty of professors of ancient Greek history, foreign languages, and philosophy, reducing class sizes, and eliminating engineering and business schools. But state legislators may have an entirely different idea in mind, perhaps thinking that technical training and practical education should be emphasized, focusing on community colleges and professional graduate degree programs. Had these legislators been more specific in their enabling legislation, the BHE probably would have given them at least much more

of what they wanted. Indeed, legislators often write specific legislative language when they want to force a recalcitrant agency or governor to implement legislation a certain way.[130]

But most of the time, lawmakers writing legislation simply cannot anticipate the many details and uncertainties involved in running an agency or enforcing a law. Therefore, they give agencies great flexibility to make the multitude of specific, but important, policy decisions needed to fill in these details. Arguably, these decisions are best made by people with specialized training and experience, such as those working in the executive agencies. For example, who would you rather see set the requirements for a medical degree, generalist state legislators or medical professionals? Furthermore, these detailed decisions can often be made only after bureaucrats and policymakers see how a new law actually works in practice.

Another way for the legislature to oversee an agency is to check occasionally to be sure the agency is following legislative intent, an action called **ex post oversight,** taking either a "fire alarm" or a "police patrol" approach.[131] Fire alarm oversight occurs in response to problems that are brought to lawmakers' attention somehow, often as a result of their helping constituents having some difficulty with state government. Such constituent **casework** can sometimes call attention to systematic problems with an agency that need to be addressed by the legislature. For example, perhaps some of a lawmaker's constituents are unable to get into the area's community college because the BHE has

---

[129] A recent study on the relationship between state legislatures and the higher education bureaucracy is: Michael K. McLendon and James C. Hearn, "The Enactment of Reforms in State Governance of Higher Education: Testing the Political Instability Hypothesis," *Journal of Higher Education* 78(2007):645–63.

[130] Sean Gailmard, "Discretion Rather than Rules: Choice of Instruments to Control Bureaucratic Policy Making," *Political Analysis* 17(2009):25–44; Jason A. McDonald, "Agency Design and Postlegislative Influence over the Bureaucracy," *Political Research Quarterly* 60(2007): 683–95; Christopher Reenock and Sarah Poggione, "Agency Design as an Ongoing Tool of Bureaucratic Influence," *Legislative Studies Quarterly* 29(2004):383–406; John D. Huber, Charles R. Shipan, and Madelaine Pfahler, "Legislatures and Statutory Control of Bureaucracy," *American Journal of Political Science* 45(2001):330–45.

[131] Mathew D. McCubbins and Thomas Schwartz, "Congressional Oversight Overlooked: Police Patrols versus Fire Alarms," *American Journal of Political Science* 28(1984):165–79.

reduced its course offerings. This could alert the lawmaker to the BHE's emphasis on liberal arts, perhaps contrary to legislative intent (or at least, perhaps, contrary to *her* legislative intent).

The most effective control, however, may result from the fact that agency officials know that the people with whom they work *could* complain to their state legislators if they have a problem. This encourages these bureaucrats to implement policy conscientiously and to provide good public service. The media provide another important source of fire alarm oversight. The dramatic reduction in state news coverage in recent years has reduced the media's importance here, thus reducing the effectiveness of legislative oversight.[132]

Other oversight techniques are more systematic and ongoing, more like police patrols than fire alarms. Perhaps the most important of these is the legislature's annual review of the proposed state budget. A chamber's budget committee typically has the most experienced and influential lawmakers sitting on it, legislators who specialize in specific agency budgets and, over time, learn the ins and outs of such agencies. Their in-depth knowledge allows them to question these agency officials in detail about what they are doing and why, with the threat of budget cuts (and the hope of budget increases) keeping them cognizant of lawmakers' needs and desires. Likewise, **administrative rules review committees,** legislative institutions that review the myriad regulations that agencies issue each year in implementing policy, can provide effective oversight.[133] In most states, the **state auditor** also works for the legislature, and when it does, this can be another powerful institution of legislative police patrol oversight.[134]

The state auditor is a high-ranking official who heads a unit that conducts financial and program evaluations of state agencies, both routinely and in response to legislative requests. Finally, legislatures can build oversight into programs they establish, such as by requiring periodic reports by an agency or including a "sunset clause" that requires the program to be reauthorized by the legislature after a certain period of time.[135]

However, state legislatures do not oversee their executive branches very well or very often, for a number of reasons. First, the state executive branch is large and complex; by comparison, the state legislature is quite small. Even the best-staffed legislatures in the largest states do not have enough resources to examine every state agency closely all the time. Even if they had the resources, legislators are simply far more interested in lawmaking. Regardless of which is more important to a state's government and residents, most legislators get more electoral and professional payoff from introducing bills and working on legislation that their districts favor, even if those bills fail, than from spending countless hours trying to understand the intricacies of an executive agency and how well it is following legislative intent.

Representation

The third major duty of a state legislature is to represent the interests of the state's residents to its government.[136] Like electoral competition, we can think about representation at the macro or micro level. At the macro level, studies show that despite all the other forces on state government—especially those of interest

[132] Jennifer Dorroh, "Statehouse Exodus," *American Journalism Review* (April/May 2009), online edition; AJR Staff, "AJR's 2009 Count of Statehouse Reporters," *American Journalism Review* (April/May 2009), online edition.
[133] Brian J. Gerber, Cherie Maestas, and Nelson C. Dometrius, "State Legislative Influence over Agency Rulemaking: The Utility of ex Ante Review," *State Politics and Policy Quarterly* 5(2005):24–46.
[134] Edward M. Wheat, "The Activist Auditor: A New Player in State and Local Politics," *Public Administration Review* 51(1991):385–92.

[135] Carolyn Bourdeaux and Grace Chikoto, "Legislative Influences on Performance Management Reform," *Public Administration Review* 68(2008):253–65.
[136] Michael A. Smith, *Bringing Representation Home: State Legislators among Their Constituencies* (Columbia, MO: University of Missouri Press, 2003); Ronald E. Weber, "The Quality of State Legislative Representation: A Critical Assessment," *Journal of Politics* 61(1999):609–27; Malcolm E. Jewell, *Representation in State Legislatures* (Lexington, KY: University Press of Kentucky, 1982).

courtesy of Reuven Carlyle

Washington State Representative Reuven Carlyle uses this website and blog to develop two-way communication with his district. He wants to know what their concerns are so that he may represent them better in Olympia, and he wants them to know that he is doing this so that they will vote to reelect him.

groups, as you read about in Chapter 6—a state's overall public policy follows its residents' general values and ideology remarkably well.[137] This good representation is largely due to state legislatures, the institutions that make state law and strongly influence all other state policy. To understand how this good macro-level representation happens, we must look at micro-level representation, that is, how and why each state lawmaker represents his or her constituents. Because their districts are relatively small, because they spend most of their time living in their districts, and because they face reelection frequently, representing their districts comes as natural to state legislators as breathing, and they do it in a variety of ways.

First, legislators sponsor bills and vote on legislation to benefit the people and businesses residing in their districts. Sometimes, a legislator's personal ideology or party allegiance will have a small independent effect on how he or

she votes on a bill, but these usually overlap so closely with the district's interests (or at least with the legislator's perceptions of those interests) that these other effects are hard to see.[138] Indeed, a state legislator voting against his or her district's interests is among the rarest of political events, regardless of that lawmaker's ideology, party, district, or anything else. Legislative party leaders certainly don't want legislators to do this, even if it means voting against the party on a particular bill. Leaders know that voting against the district's interests imperils a member's reelection chances, thereby threatening the party's legislative influence. For example, a Democratic state senator from rural Georgia is certainly not going to support a gun control bill, even if it is one of her party's main agenda items. Gun control may be thought of as a public safety issue to Atlanta Democrats, but her constituents in the countryside see it as a threat to hunting and their traditional way of life.

State legislators also represent their constituents' interests by pursuing **pork barrel** projects for their districts.[139] These are specific public construction and economic development ventures whose benefits accrue largely to a specifically defined geographical area—like a legislative district or some subsection of it. Even conservative legislators who are ideologically opposed to most government spending often seek out projects for their districts. In addition to their commitment to representation, legislators "bring home the bacon" because they believe that it helps their reelection chances. Indeed, legislative leaders shower the districts of their electorally threatened co-partisans with such "worthy projects," as they are called in North Carolina, or "pet projects," as they

[137] Robert S. Erikson, Gerald C. Wright, and John P. McIver, "Public Opinion in the States: A Quarter Century of Change and Stability," in Jeffrey E. Cohen, ed., *Public Opinion in State Politics* (Stanford, CA: Stanford University Press, 2006); Robert S. Erikson, Gerald C. Wright, and John P. McIver, *Statehouse Democracy: Public Opinion and Policy in the American States* (New York: Cambridge University Press, 1993).

[138] Jenkins, 2008, op. cit.; Poggione, op. cit.; Shannon Jenkins, "The Impact of Party and Ideology on Roll-Call Voting in State Legislatures," *Legislative Studies Quarterly* 31(2006):235–57.

[139] Smith, 2003, op. cit.; Michael C. Herron and Brett A. Theodos, "Government Redistribution in the Shadow of Legislative Elections: A Study of the Illinois Member Initiative Grants Program," *Legislative Studies Quarterly* 39(2004):287–312.

are called in New York, in hopes of avoiding a party switch in those districts.[140]

Legislators also represent their constituents by doing casework and whatever else they can do to keep up communication with their voters. For example, in 2008, Pennsylvania lawmakers sent out nearly 300,000 calendars (with the lawmaker's name emblazoned on them) to constituents. Upon receiving a little political heat for what some saw as self-promotional fluff, the Senate majority leader said that the calendar was only "one of many informational materials made available to constituents."[141] Lawmakers never miss an opportunity to connect with the voters. This is why state legislators are so heavily involved in social media, despite their advanced average age (56). In 2009, as many as half of legislators in some states used Facebook, LinkedIn, and MySpace.[142] Many have their own well-designed websites and blogs, and some were among the first to embrace Twitter soon after its appearance in 2006. For example, at press time Missouri Senator Jolie Justus had 996 followers on Twitter (http://twitter.com/joliejustus), and she wasn't even the most followed legislative tweeter. These are all ways that lawmakers can reach out to their constituents to learn their needs, desires, and opinions, and given their strong reelection incentive to then give their constituents what they want, they help representation. Of course, these representation activities also advertise lawmakers, thus increasing incumbents' electoral advantages, for good or ill.

Finally, some state legislators feel a special responsibility to represent certain classes of people more broadly, regardless if they are constituents. This may be because a legislator is in a certain business or profession, such as farming or firefighting, and watches out for these interests in the state legislature. But this type of representation is especially conspicuous and felt by legislators who are women or of a minority racial or ethnic heritage. These lawmakers often assume a responsibility to watch out for other members of their group, regardless of where they live in the state.[143]

The Collective Action Problem

Lawmaking, oversight of the executive branch, and representation would be hard jobs to accomplish in the most efficient institution, but the unwieldy and complex legislative structure that our state constitutions establish for state legislatures make their three duties especially difficult. Imagine it. A state legislature populated by dozens of people from every part of the state, with a wide range of interests, ambitions, and goals, who come together at the capitol often for only a few months each year to try to solve the state's amazing array of complex problems. None of these people can be forced out by anyone in the group,[144] and they all have an equal say in any final decision. Two parallel groups (senators and representatives) work at the same time on the same problems, and both groups must agree in the end on the precise language of any decision. Plus, all these people work on very short-term contracts—contracts that most of them would like to see renewed—and all their deliberations and decisions occur in full public view (or at least in view of the media). The final kicker is that although they must work together to accomplish their job, they are held accountable in elections only as individuals. If you have ever worked on a group project for a class, you understand the tricky social dynamics involved with that sort of situation.

---

[140] Joel A. Thompson and Gary F. Moncrief, "Pursuing the Pork in a State Legislature: A Research Note," *Legislative Studies Quarterly* 13(1988):393–401; Ronald Smothers, "It's Pork. It's a Pet Project. It's a Christmas Tree," *The New York Times*, 5 March 2007, online edition.

[141] John L. Mick, "Lawmakers Spent $131,500 to Send Calendars to Constituents," *The Morning Call* (Allentown, PA), 9 January 2008, online edition.

[142] Pam Greenberg, "New Surveys Provide Snapshot of Legislators' Use of Social Media," *The Thicket at State Legislatures*, 23 October 2009, on-line edition.

---

[143] Camissa and Reingold, op. cit.; Haynie, op. cit.; Osborn, op. cit.

[144] Most legislatures have some method of expelling members, usually for malfeasance, but such expulsions are very rare.

This constitutional arrangement gives lawmakers a serious **collective action problem**.[145] That is, they have to figure out how to get their group to work together to accomplish common goals. You see these difficulties everywhere, from the local chapter of Delta Tau Delta trying to run a fundraiser to Ford trying to build and sell cars. Different kinds of organizations solve their problems in different ways. In a small group, like the fraternity, it can often be done by informal consensus building or a single person just doing all the work. But in a large operation such as Ford, institutions must be set up to accomplish its collective tasks. Businesses do this by establishing command-and-control structures and dividing the work among different units, such as product development, production, and sales. Because of its constitutional arrangements, however, a state legislature's job is unique. In particular, no one can order another person to perform a job; thus, state legislatures use a variety of techniques—both institutions and informal norms—to overcome their collective action problem. The resulting processes and systems are complex and rarely pretty, but they can work. Of course, there is always room for improvement, and the states continually tinker with their legislative institutions to improve their performance.

The basic strategy that legislatures use to solve their collective action problem is to divide themselves on two dimensions along which state policy varies—policy type and policy preference—and then assign some of its members the responsibility of organizing lawmakers in these subgroups. Three sets of institutions are used to do this—committees, party caucuses, and leaders. By distributing policy problems among their standing committees, giving representation to both parties at each stage of the process, and assigning leadership responsibilities to some of its members, state legislatures help solve their collective action problem and get their jobs done for the state.

Committees

From preventing birth defects to regulating cemeteries, legislatures deal with a vast range of public issues, and to do so, they must have access to information and expertise on all of them. Like Congress, each state legislature arranges its members into various committees to accomplish the tasks at hand. Each committee specializes in a policy area, such as agriculture, transportation, or K–12 education, so its members can gain knowledge and experience, becoming sort of a quasi-expert on that subject.[146] As we have seen, legislatures use these committees to screen and modify bills before they get to the chamber floor, and then on the floor, other legislators typically look to members of the bill's committee for guidance in roll call voting. Both parties are represented on each committee, so different policy perspectives are represented in the preliminary review of bills and a variety of members are available to help noncommittee members make decisions later in the process.[147]

In comparison to standing committees in the U.S. House of Representatives, state legislative committees tend to have much less control over bills relative to a chamber's leaders.[148] In the U.S. House, committees are the center of most policy-making activity, but in the typical state legislature, party caucuses, leaders' offices, and chamber floors also have considerable control. Furthermore, whether as a cause

[145] Lawrence Becker, *Doing the Right Thing: Collective Action and Procedural Choice in the New Legislative Process* (Columbus, OH: Ohio State University Press, 2005).

[146] Jesse Richman, "Uncertainty and the Prevalence of Committee Outliers," *Legislative Studies Quarterly* 33(2008): 323–47; Brian F. Schaffner, "Political Parties and the Representativeness of Legislative Committees," *Legislative Studies* Quarterly 32(2007):475–97; James Coleman Battista, "Re-Examining Legislative Committee Representativeness in the States," *State Politics and Policy Quarterly* 4(2004): 135–57; Nancy Martorano, "Balancing Power: Committee System Autonomy and Legislative Organization," *Legislative Studies Quarterly* 31(2006):205–34; Francis, op. cit.

[147] However, the majority party typically has a disproportionate share of seats on committees; see: Ronald D. Hedlund, Kevin Coombs, Nancy Martorano, and Keith E. Hamm, "Partisan Stacking on Legislative Committees," *Legislative Studies Quarterly* 34(2009):175–92.

[148] Richard Clucas, "Improving the Harvest of State Legislative Research," *State Politics and Policy Quarterly* 3(2003):387–419.

or an effect of this, most state legislatures don't have the seniority norm that automatically determines the chairs and continuing membership of congressional committees. As a result, state legislative committees are much less stable than those in Congress, frequently changing memberships and sometimes even forming and disbanding from session to session. All this combines to make committees in most state legislatures much weaker and less important as instruments of information gathering than those in Congress, especially the U.S. House, although this varies among the states.[149]

Party Caucuses

If committees are institutions that help legislatures develop at least some expertise in all the policy areas they must consider, then political parties are institutions that help legislatures consider at least most major points of view in every policy area. If these views are not represented, the legislature loses legitimacy as a policy-making institution. Democrats and Republicans have different perspectives in most of the areas of state policy, so organizing the legislature by party also organizes it by policy preference, even if in a general and imperfect way.

The importance of party as an organizing principle in state legislatures cannot be overstated. Besides those in Nebraska's nonpartisan unicameral body, 99.7 percent of today's state legislators were elected as either a Democrat or Republican, and that percentage has rarely been lower in modern times.[150] A **party caucus** is made up of all the members of a party in a chamber; thus, there are four party caucuses in each legislature (the Senate Democrats, the House Republicans, and so forth). Many party caucuses meet frequently to discuss strategy and policy; in some chambers, the most crucial policy decisions are made in the majority party caucus, rather than in committees

or on the chamber floor. Members of each party usually have their floor desks arranged together on the floor, with members of the other party on "the other side of the aisle," literally. Members of the same caucus may have their offices near one another, share staff, and even play softball on the same team against their chamber's other caucus. Certainly, all members of a party do not always agree on every policy—far from it, in some chambers. But a legislator's party affiliation is the single most important predictor of how he or she will vote on a bill, even more important than his or her general political ideology.[151] Their similarity in roll call voting is the result of shared policy preferences, a sense of common cause against the other party in the chamber, and caucus members taking voting cues from one another.

The party distribution of a state legislative chamber greatly affects the activity inside it, not only its policy output but also the way it does its work. The party that has a majority of the members of a chamber is said to "control" that chamber, and for good reason. A majority of members must vote in favor of a bill in committee and on the floor for it to pass, so the party in the majority can pretty much do whatever it wishes—if its members vote together.[152] A majority vote can often even change a chamber's institutions and rules, determine who gets power and who doesn't, stop the proceedings or move them in a different direction, and so forth. As a longtime staffer in the West Virginia legislature once stated, "If the majority wants to paint its chamber polky dot, you'd better buy the paint because we're going to paint it polky dot."[153] Recall also that, just as in elections, a majority can have influence far out of proportion to its representation in the chamber: the Matthew Effect 25:29.[154] In essence, a

---

[149] James Coleman Battista, "Why Information? Choosing Committee Informativeness in U.S. State Legislatures," *Legislative Studies Quarterly* 34(2009):375–398.

[150] National Conference of State Legislatures, "2008–09 (Post-Election) Partisan Composition of State Legislatures" (http://www.ncsl.org/default.aspx?TabId=19051).

[151] Jenkins, 2006, op. cit.; Jenkins, 2008, op. cit.

[152] This generalization is most often true. Sometimes votes require a supermajority, sometimes the result needed is in relation to those voting or those present or those elected, and so forth. But generally, if they stick together, majorities can control a chamber's behavior and decisions.

[153] This comment was made personally to one of the authors by this West Virginia legislative staffer.

[154] Hedlund et al., op. cit.

INSTITUTIONS MATTER

TIE-BREAKING INSTITUTIONS IN STATE LEGISLATURES

Most big decisions in state legislatures are determined by majority vote, but what happens when there is no majority? In countries where more than two parties have significant support, their legislatures frequently have more than two parties winning seats with none holding a majority. In such cases, their members routinely work to organize coalitions of parties to accumulate enough votes to get a majority.[1] A few years ago, the sole member of the Constitution Party in the Montana House, Representative Rick Jore, held the balance of power in that chamber when Democrats and Republicans were locked 49–50. Of course, this is highly unusual in U.S. state legislatures, because less than 1 percent of their members are typically anything except Democratic or Republican. Some chambers have an even number of seats, however, so an exact partisan tie is possible; and although unlikely, it has happened with surprising frequency in recent years. This is perhaps a reflection of the tendency of both parties in two-party systems to woo the median voter.[2] When this has occurred, state legislative chambers have used various institutional approaches to "untie" themselves and allow legislative business to proceed.

- In 26 states, the lieutenant governor presides over the Senate, and in all but one of those, the lieutenant governor gets to cast the deciding vote in any tie, including votes to organize the chamber. This approach was used to resolve tied chambers in Idaho in 1990 and Pennsylvania in 1992. The threat of lieutenant governor intervention may have forced a negotiated agreement in Virginia in 1995 (see below).
- Three states have passed specific laws to resolve such ties. The South Dakota and Montana senates require that, when tied, the presiding officer be drawn from the governor's party. Indiana's decision rule is similar, but a little more complicated.
- Some chambers' internal rules offer institutional options for resolving ties, such as for the possibility of co-leaders for the chamber and committees, one from each party. Such co-leaders alternate power daily, monthly, or on some other schedule, as determined by rule. This approach was used most recently in the Iowa Senate (2004) and the North Carolina House (2002).
- Some tied chambers have negotiated various ad hoc arrangements, drawing up contracts to divide power in various ways among the parties. For example, in 1995, Virginia let the lieutenant governor preside over the floor and then divided the committee chairs between the parties.
- Wyoming's unique approach may well be the fairest, even if it is the most arbitrary: In 1974, it broke a tie in its Senate with a coin toss.

Since 2007, the Alaska Senate has worked under a unique bipartisan arrangement. When Republicans won an 11–9 majority in the 2006 elections, factional disputes kept them from agreeing on a leader. As a result, six Republicans joined with some Democrats to organize the chamber, with a Republican president and Democrats chairing the key committees. They called this arrangement the bipartisan working group (BWG). The BWG worked so well that when the 2008 election yielded a tied chamber, the transition was much smoother than those in tied chambers with no such institution in place.

Do these institutions solve all the problems of partisan ties in chambers that are organized to be run by majorities? The National Conference of State Legislatures found that many lawmakers who went through these ties found that they definitely helped things go "better than expected," but it advises its members: "No matter how smooth the process seemed to go, most legislators experienced with chamber deadlock don't recommend that other legislatures try it."[3]

Notes

1 Daniela Giannetti and Kenneth Benoit, eds., *Intra-Party Politics and Coalition Governments* (New York: Routledge, 2008).
2 Anthony Downs, *An Economic Theory of Democracy* (Reading, MA: Addison-Wesley, 1977).
3 Quoted from: National Conference of State Legislatures, "In Case of a Tie . . . : Legislative Deadlock, Tied Chambers," http://www.ncsl.org/Default.aspx?TabId=17278; see also: Josh Goodman, "Yukon Truce," *Governing* (July 2008):20–21; William Claiborne, "Florida, Michigan Agonize over Power Charging in Deadlocked Legislatures," *The Washington Post*, 21 November 1992, online edition.

party that sticks together can win 100 percent of a chamber's decisions even if it has only one or two more members than the minority party. Because of this inordinate power, gaining a majority in a chamber is the Holy Grail of state legislative parties. (What happens if the parties are tied in a chamber? See the Institutions Matter box.)

Because a legislator's party affiliation is so much a part of his or her identity, changing it is a rare and serious step that none of them take lightly, even though it does happen on occasion. Sometimes ideological reasons cause a switch, as when Representative Rick Singleton of Rhode Island rejected his Republican Party membership in 2007 because he was so upset with then-President Bush and the national GOP.[155] More often, however, these party defections are strategic, showing the great power that a majority of votes represents. When a chamber has a close partisan split, as is common (see Table 7.2), if one or two members of the minority party can be enticed to cross the aisle, significant policy and power changes can happen. For example, after the 2008 election gave the Tennessee House Republicans a slim one-seat majority—their first majority in 40 years—the Democrats made a deal with Republican Representative Kent Williams to elect him Speaker, but to keep most of the other perks and power for the Democrats.[156] Montana Representative Rick Jore had the similar kingmaker role after the 2006 election, when he was the sole Constitution Party member in a chamber almost exactly evenly divided between the two major parties.[157] Probably the bloodiest and most complicated of these recent close-fought legislative party battles began with the 2008 election in New York,

when Democrats won a 32–30 majority in the Senate, the first time that caucus had a majority in almost 50 years. But in June 2009, after offering policy and pork barrel incentives, GOP leaders in the chamber managed to convince two Democrats to join them to vote again on leadership arrangements, resulting in two new leaders—a Republican and one of the defecting Democrats.[158] After considerable court battles and legislative shenanigans, including a month-long shutdown of the chamber, the party-switchers switched back, leaving the Democrats in charge again.[159] Because the political stakes are so high, any defection that affects policy or chamber leadership typically has extreme social and political repercussions for the defectors, as happened in 2009 in California and Minnesota, in addition to New York and Tennessee.[160]

While a close majority can sometimes be broken by a defector or two, perhaps surprisingly, the larger the majority a caucus has, the less its members tend to stick together and the less overt control the party can exert over legislative decision making.[161] When the difference between the number of seats the two parties have in a chamber is small—say, the

---

[155] Katherine Gregg, "Anger over Bush, D.C. Republicans Prompts Rep. Singleton to Bolt Party," *The Providence* (Rhode Island) *Journal*, 12 September 2007, online edition.

[156] Jeannie Naujeck, "Tennessee Legislature Opens Session with Surprise Vote," *Nashville Business Journal*, 13 January 2009, online edition.

[157] Associated Press, "Jore a Caucus of 1," *Billings* (MT) *Gazette*, 12 February 2007, online edition.

[158] Jeremy W. Peters and Danny Hakim, "Republicans Seize Control of State Senate," *The New York Times*, 8 June 2009, online edition; Fredric U. Dicker, "GOP Pols Dangling $6M to Lure Dems," *New York Post*, 25 November 2008, online edition.

[159] Alan Greenblatt, "A Call to Order," *Governing*, August 2009, p.12.

[160] Jordan Rau, Evan Halper, Patrick McGreevy, and Michael Rothfeld, "California Legislature Finally Approves New Budget," *Los Angeles Times*, 19 February 2009, online edition; Alan Greenblat, "Renegade Retribution: Minnesota Republicans Don't Have Much Use for Moderate Politics," *Governing* (May 2008):22.

[161] Hedlund et al., op. cit.; Nancy Martorano, "Cohesion or Reciprocity? Majority Party Strength and Minority Party Procedural Rights in the Legislative Process," *State Politics and Policy Quarterly* 4(2004):55–73; Aldrich and Battista, op. cit. On the other hand, California is a state where something like the opposite happened, with close partisan competition failing to yield strong parties, both in the legislature and out. This may have something to do with the extremism of the parties in the Golden State; see Seth E. Masket, *No Middle Ground: How Informal Party Organizations Control Nominations and Polarize Legislatures* (Ann Arbor, MI: University of Michigan Press, 2009).

five seats (out of 203) that divided the parties in the Pennsylvania House following the 2008 election—the majority party must work diligently to maintain control over legislation and to maintain their majority in the next election. The minority party smells success just a few votes away, so it scrambles to gain whatever advantage it can, whether to win passage of legislation or to position bills and votes to use as future campaign issues. When a minority party caucus faces a lopsided partisan split—like the Democrats' 20 percent of the seats in the Idaho Senate or the Republicans' 10 percent of the Massachusetts House—it knows the only way it will ever manage to pass a bill is with the help of many majority party members, so it tries to avoid partisan conflict. Because the majority party caucus is not threatened by the minority in such unbalanced chambers, they don't mind working with them from time to time. In fact, a majority party that isn't disciplined by the threat of a large minority often crumbles into regional, ethnic, or economic factions, making partisan conflict less relevant.[162] In such legislatures, political party is not a useful organizing principle, making the collective action problem more difficult to overcome.

Legislative Leadership

State legislatures have two fundamental problems of collective action that corporations and the executive branch of government lack: All members of the group (legislators) are constitutionally equal, and no one has responsibility for achieving its common goal. To address these problems, legislators select from their membership various leaders in whom they invest special powers and the responsibility to see that the groups' collective tasks are accomplished.

The two basic types of leaders reflect the organizing principles of a state legislative chamber: committee chairs and party leaders. Committee

In 2008, Rep. Karen Bass is sworn in as speaker of the California Assembly. Bass was the first African American women to serve as majority party leader and presiding officer in a state legislative chamber.

chairs call committee meetings, decide which legislation is to be heard and voted upon, and have what can often be significant procedural powers to organize and structure committee hearings and votes. These chairs are typically members of the majority party. While each committee usually has a minority party leadership position, that position has far less power than the chair. Of course, because most state legislative committees are less powerful than those of Congress, state committee chairs are correspondingly less powerful.

Conversely, party leaders are usually much more important in state legislatures than in Congress. Most party leadership in state legislatures is focused on a single office for each party in each chamber—the majority and minority party leaders. The majority party leader is the most powerful person in a chamber, serving as the presiding officer in all 49 state Houses[163] (usually called the "speaker") and in 24 state

---

[162] Matt Viser, "Democratic Infighting Escalates: Murray Calls Governor 'Irrelevant'," *Boston Globe*, 22 May 2009, online edition; V. O. Key, Jr., *Southern Politics* (New York: Vintage, 1949).

[163] There are only 49 state Houses of representatives, since the unicameral Nebraska legislature only has a Senate.
[164] Keith E. Hamm and Gary F. Moncrief, "Legislative Politics in the States," in Virginia Gray and Russell L. Hanson, eds., *Politics in the American State*, 9th ed. (Washington, DC: CQ Press, 2008). Note that in certain unusual political circumstances, a minority party member may become a chamber's presiding officer, as is currently the case in the Tennessee House, and was the case in 2008–2009 in the Louisiana House and in 2007–2008 in the Pennsylvania House. See Alan Greenblatt, "Austin's Surprise Speaker," *Governing* (March 2009):12–13.

Senates (usually called the "president").[164] The lieutenant governor presides over the Senate floor in 26 states, but in most of these, the real power still rests in the hands of the majority party's leader (usually called the "Senate president pro tempore" in these cases). Minority party leaders are important players in the legislative process, but most have far fewer formal powers and responsibilities than do majority leaders. Each party caucus also has several lower-level leadership positions, often appointed by the top leader, that as a group make up its leadership team.

State legislative party caucus leaders often dominate legislative proceedings, as suggested by the informal names they sometimes acquire, like the "Four Tops" in Illinois and the "Big Five" in California (including the governor).[165] In particular, state legislative majority party leaders have an especially strong hand in the process.[166] These leaders usually appoint committee chairs and members, and to the extent that they can do so, these leaders can have leverage over the output and proceedings of those committees and, therefore, the chamber as a whole.[167] Being a committee chair or on the party leadership team usually boosts a legislator's pay, power, and prestige, so these positions are coveted and those lawmakers holding them are beholden to the party leader who appointed them. Party leaders often negotiate among themselves and with the governor,

representing their caucuses on important bills, especially the budget. Party leaders may also control much of the legislature's staff, offices, parking spaces, and other resources. In short, party leaders, especially majority party leaders, typically run state legislatures.

These leaders cannot do whatever they wish, of course. Majorities still make decisions in legislatures, and these leaders do not constitute a majority by themselves—far from it. As a result, there is an interesting dynamic between leaders and **rank-and-file** legislators that is related to what political scientists call the "principal-agent problem."[168] A legislature's rank-and-file members (the principals) need their leaders (the agents) to help the rank and file meet their personal goals and the chamber meet its collective duties. Therefore, the rank-and-file members give their leaders considerable power. Without that power, not only couldn't a leader help the legislature overcome its collective action problem, but also no one would take the job of leader in the first place. Being leader is hard work, so legislators have to make the job both feasible and attractive to competent lawmakers. The appeal of these positions comes largely in the power that leaders have over legislative outcomes, personal aggrandizement, extra pay, and other perks. So the principle-agent *problem* is how legislators can get their leaders to meet their (the rank-and-file legislators') individual and collective goals without having to give leaders too much control over rank-and-file legislators and legislative output.

Typically, the harder the problems they need to solve, the more power that rank-and-file members must give their leaders, both to get the job done and to make the job attractive. As with legislative professionalism, since urban, diverse, and heavily populated states have more problems, they tend to have stronger legislative leaders.[169] Furthermore, where

[165] Kent D. Redfield, "What Keeps the 4 Tops on Top? Leadership Power in the Illinois General Assembly," in David A. Joens and Paul Kleppner, eds., *Almanac of Illinois Politics: 1998* (Springfield, IL: Institute of Public Affairs, 1998); and Andy Furillo, "'Big 5' Put a Range of Issues on the Table," *Sacramento Bee*, 25 August 2005, online edition.

[166] Richard A. Clucas, "The Contract with America and Conditional Party Government in State Legislatures," *Political Research Quarterly* 62(2009):317–28; Richard A. Clucas, "Legislative Professionalism and the Power of State House Leaders," *State Politics and Policy Quarterly* 7(2007):1–19.

[167] Kristin Kanthak, "U.S. State Legislative Committee Assignments and Encouragement of Party Loyalty: An Exploratory Analysis," *State Politics and Policy Quarterly* 9(2009):284–303.

[168] Richard A. Clucas, "Principal-Agent Theory and the Power of State House Speakers," *Legislative Studies Quarterly* 26(2001):319–39.

[169] Clucas, 2001, 2007, op. cit.

the parties are more ideologically polarized and/or partisan competition is greater, lawmakers give their leaders more power.[170] "The heathens are at the gates," so to speak, in these legislatures, so each party needs all the help it can get to hold the other one back. In terms of lawmakers' personal goals, where their salaries are higher and politics is more of a career for them (i.e., in professionalized legislatures), they care more deeply about getting reelected, so they need stronger leaders to help them do so. Table 7.5 shows the variation in the power of House Speakers across the states based on their formal appointment and procedural powers. For the most part, you can see that larger states with strong two-party competition and professional legislatures are near the top of the list and smaller states with one-party citizen-legislatures are near the bottom, despite a few exceptions (such as West Virginia, Rhode Island, Ohio).

Because leaders are elected by their caucuses, if they fail to help their co-partisans meet their goals, then they may not be reelected to their leadership positions in the next legislative session. This gives leaders strong incentive to help meet their colleagues' goals. On rare occasions, leaders can even be dumped midsession, as in Wisconsin in 2007, when Senate Democrats were so dissatisfied with the outcome of their state budget bill that they replaced Majority Leader Judy Robson with another member of their caucus whom they thought could do a better job for them.[171] Leaders can also lose their positions when a coalition of members of both parties is able to generate a majority of votes in the chamber and elect a new presiding officer. This is relatively rare, but it has occurred often enough recently to raise the question of whether some chambers are moving toward a "postpartisan politics."[172] In addition to the bipartisan coalition controlling the Alaska

---

[170] Clucas, 2009, op. cit.
[171] Steven Walters and Patrick Marley, "State Democrats Oust Robson, Pick Decker as Senate Majority Leader," *Milwaukee Journal Sentinel*, 25 October 2007, online edition.
[172] Greenblatt, 2009, op. cit.

Table 7.5

Legislative Leadership Strength—The Formal Powers of the Speakers of State Houses of Representatives

State	Index of Majority Leadership Strength
NY	4.75
IL	4.67
WV	4.50
FL	4.36
IA	4.25
MN	4.08
MD	4.05
GA	4.00
OK	3.86
CA	3.83
CT	3.83
RI	3.82
KS	3.75
NC	3.75
OR	3.75
PA	3.75
TN	3.75
VT	3.75
NH	3.67
AZ	3.58
ME	3.58
MI	3.50
NJ	3.50
CO	3.37
TX	3.33
AL	3.25
ID	3.25
IN	3.25
MO	3.25
UT	3.25
VA	3.25
MA	3.17
DE	3.00
MS	3.00

State	Index of Majority Leadership Strength
MT	3.00
NM	3.00
SC	3.00
LA	2.92
SD	2.75
WI	2.75
AR	2.33
WA	2.17
WY	2.08
AK	2.00
HI	1.75
ND	1.25
OH	1.25
NV	1.08
KY	0.25

Note: This is a summative scale of the formal powers of Speakers of state Houses of Representatives based on six equally weighted items: powers to appoint committee chairs, to appoint party leaders, to make committee assignments, to refer bills to committee, to control staff, and the amount of extra income a Speaker earns. These data are for the 2003–2004 sessions, the most recent data available. Nebraska is not included because it has no House.

Source: Christopher Z. Mooney, "Modeling Legislative Leadership Power: Principals, Agents, Tools, Influence, and Comparative Legislative Analysis in the U.S. States," presented at the 10th Annual State Politics and Policy Conference, Springfield, IL (June 2010).

Senate (see Institutions Matter box), since 2008, the New Mexico Senate and the Texas, Louisiana, and Tennessee Houses recently have had presiding officers elected with votes from each party.

Any overthrow of a top legislative party leader is quite rare, however, because most of them work very hard to help their caucuses meet their goals. First and foremost, this means that these leaders help their caucus members attain their primary personal goal—reelection.[173] This not only helps individual lawmakers, but it also helps the party's principle collective goal of gaining or retaining a majority, from which the policy and personal benefits of being in the majority flow to the caucus. Traditionally, legislative leaders have helped their caucus members' reelection efforts in a variety of ways, from making sure that they don't cast "bad" roll call votes that could be used against them by election opponents to helping them pass "good" bills and projects that they can tout in their campaigns. Leaders help train new members about constituent service and media relations, and they even work to draw legislative districts to the advantage of their caucus's members (as discussed earlier in the chapter).

In recent years, many caucus leaders have begun to take a more active role in their rank-and-file colleagues' actual campaigns, using a strategy of **electoral targeting**.[174] Through polling, social and election data, and long experience, legislative leaders identify perhaps half a dozen districts that are most likely to have close races in the general election. These races may lack an incumbent or have changing demographics or simply have an even distribution of party voters. In these races, and perhaps only these, extra campaign effort might be the difference between a win for either party. Unlike each rank-and-file lawmaker, caucus leaders' statewide perspective allows them to make the hard decisions about which candidates would and would not benefit from extra campaign help. By concentrating the party's resources in a few targeted districts, these leaders use them efficiently. Throughout the period since the previous election, and often over many years prior to this, these leaders will have used their powerful positions in the legislature to attract considerable campaign contributions from all

---

[173] The classic book on legislators' reelection goal was written about members of Congress, but the logic applies very well to state lawmakers; see: David Mayhew, *Congress: The Electoral Connection* (New Haven, CT: Yale University Press, 1974). The classic book on state legislative leadership is: Malcolm E. Jewell and Marcia Lynn Whicker, *Legislative Leadership in the American States* (Ann Arbor, MI: University of Michigan Press, 1994).

[174] Bill Boyarsky, *Big Daddy: Jesse Unruh and the Art of Power Politics* (Berkeley, CA: University of California Press, 2008); Richard A. Clucas, *The Speaker's Electoral Connection: Willie Brown and the California Assembly* (Berkeley, CA: IGS Press, 1995); Anthony Gierzynski, *Legislative Party Campaign Committees in the American States* (Lexington, KY: University Press of Kentucky, 1992); Loftus, op. cit.; and Wright, op. cit.

over the state (and the nation, sometimes), and they can use that money in these targeted races. They hire, train, and coordinate top-flight campaign personnel and inundate these races with massive campaign spending in an effort to swing them to their party.

Of course, both leaders of a chamber's two caucuses are more or less equally adept at this targeting strategy, which leads to legislative campaign activity that is very uneven across a state. As we have seen, most state legislative races are blowouts in general elections, and as such they generate a minimal amount of campaign activity and spending. Only a handful of targeted races scattered around the state will see intense campaign battles, with perhaps 10 times the amount of campaign spending as in nontargeted races. In effect, these targeted races for the legislature are proxy battlegrounds for the statewide parties, with the candidates themselves being almost irrelevant. Few of these candidates complain (at least very loudly), however, because the leaders are trying win these races for them. These targeted races will decide which party has a majority of legislators in the chamber in the next session. As such, they are too important to be left in the hands of mere candidates.

Thus, state legislators solve the collective action problem posed by their states' constitutions by using their internal rules and informal procedures to establish institutions: standing committees, party caucuses, and committee and party leaders. Without such institutions, state legislatures would not be able to accomplish any of their three jobs. The strength of these institutions varies among the states in relation to the level of the collective action problem in a state legislature.

Summary

American state legislatures are nuts and bolts institutions where democracy is up close and personal. Because of their small districts and more or less part-time responsibilities, these officials live, work, and play in and among their constituents on a regular basis. As a group, state lawmakers are demographically more like their constituents than any other group of state or federal elected officials, and their representativeness is getting better with every election. While redistricting, the homogeneity of their districts, and other forces have reduced the competitiveness of individual state legislative races, when taking the statewide or national view, we see that these elections are often very competitive or at least reflective of the partisan makeup of voters.

State legislatures are complex institutions charged by their states' constitution and traditions to do three major tasks: set the state's public policy, oversee its executive branch, and represent its citizens' values and interests before the government. However, by giving lawmakers equal power and electing them frequently, and by setting up a bicameral process and otherwise making lawmaking complicated, these constitutions make it difficult for legislatures to accomplish their duties. As a result, lawmakers have developed a variety of institutions and processes to help overcome these obstacles and serve the state. Standing committees, political parties, and legislative leaders help legislatures solve their collective action problem. Never content with these arrangements, the states continually tinker with their legislatures' institutions to improve their performance.

Key Terms

Administrative rules review committee

Amend

Bicameral

Bill

Bill sponsor

Casework

Chamber floor

Citizen-legislature

Collective action problem

Conference committee

Contiguous

Cracking

Divided government

Electoral targeting strategy

Ex post oversight

Gatekeeping

Gerrymander

Implementation

Incumbent

Incumbent-protection district

Legislative intent

Legislative professionalism

Malapportionment

Media market

Multimember district

Override

Packing

Party caucus

Pork barrel

Rank-and-file legislator

Redistricting

Roll call

Single-member district

Standing committee

State auditor

Supermajority

Swing seat

Term limits

Unicameral

Voting cue

Voting Rights Act of 1965

Discussion Questions

1. What are the major factors that influence voters' choices in state legislative elections? What barriers exist to voters receiving accurate information on these races?
2. Discuss the reapportionment revolution and the Supreme Court's role in changing legislative districts. What were the causes and effects of this "revolution"?
3. How well are women and racial and ethnic minorities represented in state legislatures? How and why does this representation vary among states? How has this changed—and continue to change—over time?
4. Discuss the role of parties, leaders, and committees in the legislative process. Why do they exist, and why and how do they vary among the states?

Suggested Readings

Hamm, Keith E., and Gary F. Moncrief. 2008. "Legislative Politics in the States," in Virginia Gray and Russell L. Hanson, eds., *Politics in the American States*, 9th ed. Washington, DC: CQ Press.

Haynie, Kerry L. 2001. *African American Legislators in the American States*. New York: Columbia University Press.

Kurtz, Karl T., Bruce Cain, and Richard G. Niemi, eds. 2007. *Institutional Change in American Politics: The Case of Term Limits*. Ann Arbor, MI: University of Michigan Press.

McDonald, Michael P., guest ed. 2004. "Special Issue: Electoral Redistricting," *State Politics and Policy Quarterly* 4:369–490.

Moncrief, Gary F., Peverill Squire, and Malcolm E. Jewell. 2001. *Who Runs for the Legislature?* Upper Saddle River, NJ: Prentice Hall.

Rosenthal, Alan. 2009. *Engines of Democracy: Politics and Policymaking in State Legislatures.* Washington, DC: CQ Press.

Rosenthal, Cindy Simon. 1998. *When Women Lead: Integrative Leadership in State Legislatures.* New York: Oxford University Press.

Squire, Peverill, and Gary Moncrief. 2009. *State Legislatures Today: Politics under the Domes.* Upper Saddle River, NJ: Prentice Hall.

Squire, Peverill, and Keith E. Hamm. 2005. *101 Chambers: Congress, State Legislatures, and the Future of State Legislative Studies.* Columbus, OH: Ohio State University Press.

Winburn, Jonathon. 2008. *The Realities of Redistricting: Following the Rules and Limiting Gerrymandering in State Legislative Redistricting.* Lanham, MD: Lexington.

Wright, Ralph G. 2005. *Inside the Statehouse: Lessons from the Speaker.* Washington, DC: CQ Press.

Suggested Media Resources

The Redistricting Game (http://www.redistrictinggame.org/): The Annenberg School for Communications has designed this online game "to educate, engage, and empower citizens around the issue of political redistricting." The game lets players act as redistricters trying to maximize various criteria and goals, and in the process shows them see how simply moving district lines can have big political impacts.

Wiseman, Frederick. 2007. *State Legislature: A Documentary*, Zipporah Films. This film (3 hours, 37 minutes) follows the Idaho legislature through its 2005 session. Directed by the famed documentarian and self-described "staunch social reformer," Frederick Wiseman, this critically acclaimed film is an unvarnished, unscripted, and unnarrated look at the complex world of lawmaking in the states.

Web Sites

American Legislative Exchange Council (http://www.alec.org): ALEC is a national association of conservative state legislators whose goal is to advance the Jeffersonian principles of free markets, limited government, federalism, and individual liberty.

Center for American Women and Politics (http://www.cawp.rutgers.edu): The CAWP is a unit of Rutgers University that conducts research and training about and for women in elective office in the United States. Women in state legislatures are a major focus of the CAWP.

National Black Caucus of State Legislators (http://www.nbcsl.org): The NBCSL is a bipartisan national organization that conducts research and training designed to enhance the effectiveness of its members, African American state legislators.

National Conference of State Legislatures (http://www.ncsl.org): The NCSL is a national, bipartisan organization that provides state legislators and their staff with research, technical assistance, and opportunities to exchange ideas on the most pressing state issues.

Progressive States Network (http://www.progressivestates.org): The PSN is a liberal organization website that conducts and publishes research, tracks state legislation, and coordinates and networks like-minded policy makers and citizens.

8

Governors and the State Executive Branch

BOBBY JINDAL IN THE GUBERNATORIAL FAST-LANE . . . WITH JUST A COUPLE OF POTHOLES

O n Saturday, October 20, 2007, Bobby Jindal was elected governor of Louisiana with 54 percent of the vote.[1] Yes, that's right—Saturday, October 20, 2007. Forty-five states elect their governors in even-numbered years, and almost all of them do so on a Tuesday in November, but this unusual election date was a harbinger of the many unusual things about Governor Jindal. First, at 36, he is the nation's youngest governor. Had he won the gubernatorial election of 2003, a race he barely lost to Kathleen Blanco, he would have been governor at 32, only two years older than the youngest state governor in U.S. history.[2] The second obviously unusual thing about Jindal is that he is Indian American; his parents immigrated to Baton Rouge from Khanpura in the Punjab the year before he was born. While non-Anglo governors are rare, Jindal's victory was made especially noteworthy by the fact that in 1991, only 16 years before his election, 671,009 (38.8 percent) Louisianans had voted for an avowed racist and former Ku Klux Klan leader for governor. Jindal is also a former Rhodes Scholar, an Ivy Leaguer, and a Republican—all pretty atypical for a Louisiana politician. From a policy perspective, what was most perhaps most unusual about Jindal was that he campaigned to clean up graft and corruption in Bayou State politics. What's more unusual—he meant it.

Jindal came into office with big plans, and he went to work immediately. He called two special sessions of the state legislature for early 2008 to deal with two general issues that were high on his campaign agenda—government ethics and reforming the state's tax system—perhaps the two toughest of issues in Louisiana politics. Recognizing that he had to take advantage of his postelection honeymoon, he moved quickly. To the surprise of many, he largely succeeded. Louisiana had long been the butt of jokes nationally about its corruption, vying regularly with states like Illinois for having the most former elected officials serving time in prison. Astutely riding the wave of voter disgust with the bungling and corruption surrounding the Hurricane Katrina recovery effort, in his first month in office, Jindal pushed through an ethics package comparable to that in the state of Washington, cited by the Center for Public Integrity as being the best in the nation. Legislators and governor's office officials were banned from having state contracts and lobbyists' wining and dining of lawmakers was limited, among other things. Not only relying on public opinion and arm-twisting, Jindal managed to push through his ethics package with finesse and an understanding of the legislative process, something he may have learned about in his three years in Congress and his time at the helm of the Louisiana Department of Health and Hospitals and as an Assistant Secretary of the U.S. Department of Health and Human Services in the Bush administration. He had to compromise a bit, but both he and the legislature could declare victory when the final package was passed. He then launched a statewide tour to publicize his success, preparing the way for his special session on taxes the following month. Jindal also demonstrated his political savvy when, after campaigning as a "true conservative," he backed only quietly such legislative measures as teaching evolution in school, a polarizing issue that could have generated enemies. On the other hand, conservative issues with broader appeal, like school vouchers, he supported forcefully and visibly. All this success did not go unnoticed outside his home state. Jindal was widely touted as a potential vice presidential candidate in 2008, spending time at Republican nominee Senator John McCain's Arizona ranch in the summer of that year, presumably interviewing for the slot. In the end, of course, McCain opted for another young, conservative, and nontraditional governor, Alaska's Sarah Palin.

But the job of governor is not an easy one, and Jindal has had his share of missteps. Even after his first successful legislative session in spring 2008, there were grumblings that his eye toward higher office had led to excessive caution, and not just among the staunch conservatives of his base. For example, following this session, he allowed over 100 bills to go into effect without his signature, more than the four previous Louisiana governors combined had done. And he had to backtrack on his early and prominent refusal to accept federal stimulus money in 2009. But perhaps Jindal's biggest pothole in his first year as governor was his handling of state legislative pay raises. In 2008, Louisiana lawmakers earned $16,800 per year, a figure set in 1980 and not changed since then. Not surprisingly, raising their own salary had long been on lawmakers' agenda, but that was very hard to do politically. On the campaign trail, Jindal himself had vowed to veto any such pay raise bill. But out of appreciation of the amount of work that lawmakers do, as a trade-off for gaining support on other areas of his policy agenda, or because he simply caved in to pressure from lawmakers, he waffled on this issue in June 2008, receiving considerable criticism for it in the media and among the public.

The event that perhaps best symbolizes all of Jindal's promise and problems was his selection in February 2009 to give the Republican response to President Barack Obama's first address to Congress. This was to be a sort of coming-out event, introducing to the nation the person whom some Republicans thought would be the face of their national party after its devastating losses in the 2008 elections. But his performance was less than stellar, to say the least, with conservative commentators being his most severe critics, calling his speech "animatronic" and "cheesy."[3]

But regardless of these problems, and especially because of the dearth of well-regarded Republican flag-bearers at the national level, it is clear that Bobby Jindal will be getting more chances to polish his presentation for a national audience. But more important than such set-piece speeches for his political future will be his trial-by-fire in the Louisiana governor's mansion over the next few years.

Louisiana Governor Bobby Jindal and his family on election night, 2007.

1   This vignette was developed using the following sources: Pamela M. Prah, "GOP Wins Louisiana Governorship," *Stateline.org*, 22 October 2007; Patrik Jonsson, "Coup in the Bayou: New Governor Jindal Promises Change in Louisiana," *Christian Science Monitor*, 15 January 2008, online ed.; Marsha Shuler and Mark Ballard, "Jindal Praises Session," *The Advocate (Baton Rouge)*, 27 February 2008, online ed.; Adam Nossiter, "Louisiana Governor Pierces Business as Usual," *The New York Times*, 28 February 2008, online ed.; Adam Nossiter, "In Louisiana, Inklings of a New (True) Champion of the Right," *The New York Times*, 2 June 2008, online ed.; Will Sentell, "Senate Sends Jindal Bill on Evolution," *The Advocate (Baton Rouge)*, 17 June 2008, online ed.; Adam Nossiter, "Legislators Raise Pay, and a Governor Pays the Price," *The New York Times*, 24 June 2008, online ed.; Jan Moller, "For Many Bills, Jindal Keeps Cap on Pen," *The (New Orleans) Times-Picayune*, 27 June 2008, online ed.; Robert Travis Scott, "Jindal Catches Flak for Rejecting Federal Cash," *The (New Orleans) Times-Picayune*, 24 February 2009, online ed.
2   California Governor James Neely Johnson was a mere 30 years old when he was elected in 1855.
3   Shaila Dewan, "Governor Jindal, Rising G.O.P. Star, Plummets after Speech," *The New York Times*, 26 February 2009, online ed.

Introduction

While Louisiana's history may suggest that Jindal is a curious person to be governing the state, as a young, energetic, capable, and experienced politician looking to make a difference in the world, he is of the very model of a modern American governor. As the eight-year administration of President George W. Bush moved to its denouement, with the country mired in two wars and a miserable economy, and the federal government's reputation at home and abroad at a low ebb, the allure of Washington was not strong.[1] And besides, there is only one chief executive job in Washington, and today, it is filled by someone very much like today's new breed of governors. Along with Jindal, the states are run by people like Minnesota's Tim Pawlenty, Michigan's Jennifer Granholm, California's Arnold Schwarzenegger, Arkansas's Mike Beebe, and Washington's Christine Gregoire, among many others, people with vision and energy who have shown that the very tough job of governing a state during bad economic times is the sort of challenge that brings out the very best in people.[2] A few such governors who showed early promise have failed to pan out, some—like Illinois's Rod Blagojevich and South Carolina's Mark Sanford—very publicly so. Many have said that being governor is the best job in American government today—and that it may also be the hardest. In particular, in these tough times, with people suffering and the states' budgets severely out of whack (see Chapter 10), a state's residents, businesses, and public officials look increasingly to the governor to solve their problems. Fortunately for Americans, the talent pool filling governors' offices around the country has never been deeper.

The governor is the single most-visible and powerful person in state government. As the official **head of state** (like the president of the United States or the queen of England), the governor is the symbol of the state to people, organizations, and other governments, in and out of the state. So when North Dakota Governor John Hoeven helped stack sandbags as the Red River rose in the spring of 2009, he demonstrated the concern of all North Dakotans for the plight of those affected, just as Michigan's Granholm's visits to automobile manufacturing plants and board rooms around her state are a way to show the state's deep interest in that faltering industry. On a more positive note, when Alabama Governor Bob Riley traveled to Australia, France, and Singapore in July 2009, he was singing the praises of the workers and business opportunities in the Heart of Dixie State, trying to drum up business for its aerospace and shipbuilding industries. Governors meet with schoolchildren and sports champions, business and community leaders, delegations of foreign dignitaries, and many others, showing these people their states' interest in them and the people they represent.

Also like the president, in addition to being the head of state, a governor is the state's chief executive officer and policy maker, taking a major role in formulating, enacting, and implementing a wide range of public policy. Given the size and complexity of state governments today, few administrative jobs in the world compare to being the governor of even the smallest state. Only a handful of countries are as big and complex as California or New York, and even medium-sized states, such as Wisconsin and Maryland, are about the size of smaller, but important, countries, such as Denmark and Sierra Leone. Governors are sometimes compared to the CEOs of Fortune 500 companies; but this comparison is not exactly apt. On the one hand, only about half of the states have budgets that would put them among the 500 largest corporations in the world. While California's $200+ billion annual budget would certainly place it among the 10 largest corporations, the budgets of about 20 percent of the states are under $10 billion, much smaller

---

[1] The hope engendered in the early days of the administration of Barack Obama seems to have put some luster back into federal government service.

[2] Louis Jacobson, "First-Term Govs Largely Successful," *Stateline.org*, 25 July 2008, online ed.

than even Nike or Amazon.com. On the other hand, the multiplicity of functions, and especially the public function, of state governments make them at least as great a managerial challenge as a multinational corporation, regardless of their size. But there is one place that governors and Fortune 500 CEOs certainly do not compare—their salaries. While California's Schwarzenegger's annual salary of $206,500 may sound lucrative, even companies on the bottom of the Fortune 500 list typically pay their CEO's much more than this. For example, Nike's William Perez earns a salary about 10 times that of Schwarzenegger, not to mention his benefits and stock options.

Thus, being governor is a big job with big responsibilities, and people are clearly not doing it for the money. So why do they do it? Why are there always candidates for these offices, candidates who spend millions of dollars and stake so much of their time, energy, and reputation to win them? Three reasons stand out. First, a governor has the ability to have a major impact on politics, policy, and people's lives in a state. In virtually no other job can a person have such a large effect. Second, the challenge of doing such a complex and visible job well draws highly motivated and skilled people to it. In this way, governing a state is like working on a massive Suduko puzzle—but one whose result is important to millions of people. Third, the governor's office is highly prestigious, and furthermore, those who do it well have used it as a stepping stone to other important and attractive jobs. For example, more presidents had previously been governor than any other type of office or position. In 50 of the 57 presidential elections in U.S. history, at least one of the major party candidates for president or vice president had been a governor; often, more than one governor was on the ballot. More generally, governors regularly go on to fill a wide variety of other positions that are among the most interesting and significant in the country, including key federal-level cabinet positions, seats in the U.S. Senate, and top executive positions in business, education, and the arts.

Gubernatorial Elections

Gubernatorial races are the most important elections on any state's political calendar, often drawing even more interest in a state than presidential elections. Forty-eight states hold gubernatorial elections every four years,[3] with 34 of these being held in the even-numbered year without a presidential election (for example, 2010, 2014, etc.).[4] Nine states elect their governors to four-year terms during presidential election years, and five states hold their gubernatorial elections in odd-numbered years (see Figure 8.1). While all governors are now elected directly by a state's voters this was not always the case. In the early days of the U.S., six state legislatures elected their governor; the last such election was in South Carolina in 1864. In fact, the Vermont and Mississippi constitutions still provide for legislative election of their governor if no candidate in the general election receives a majority of the vote. While rare, this last happened in 1999, in Mississippi.[5] Some states, mostly in the South, use a run-off election if no candidate gets a majority in the general election or, as in the case of Jindal in 2007, in a first-round election. In these states, a run-off is needed about one-third of the time. Surprisingly, the leader in the first round actually loses the run-off about one-third of the time.[6]

Unlike with state legislatures, term limits for governors have existed in most states for a long time, and they have rarely been controversial. There has long been a tradition of chief executives at the state and federal levels serving only for a relatively short period of time. Perhaps long-serving executives look too

[3] New Hampshire's and Vermont's governors still serve two-year terms, although there has been a push in the Granite State to move to a four-year gubernatorial term. See: Josh Goodman, "A Four-Year Term for New Hampshire Governors?" *Governing*, January 2009, p. 7.
[4] Audrey S. Wall, ed., *The Book of the States: 2008*, vol. 40 (Lexington, KY: Council of State Governments, 2008), Table 4.1.
[5] Michael J. Dubin, *Party Affiliations in State Legislatures* (Jefferson, NC: McFarland and Co., 2007).
[6] Richard L. Engstrom and Richard N. Engstrom, "The Majority Vote Rule and Runoff Primaries in the United States," *Electoral Studies* 27(2008): 407–16.

Figure 8.1

Gubernatorial Election Cycles

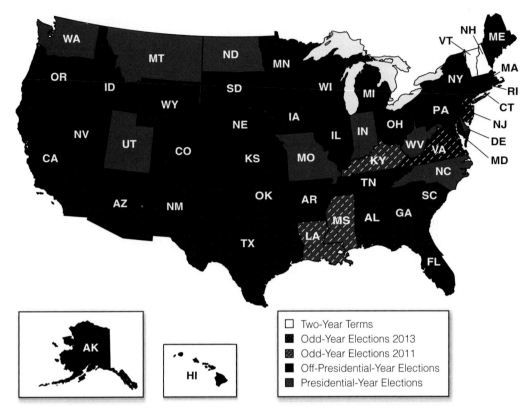

Two-Year Terms
Odd-Year Elections 2013
Odd-Year Elections 2011
Off-Presidential-Year Elections
Presidential-Year Elections

Source: Audrey S. Wall, ed., *The Book of the States: 2008,* vol. 40 (Lexington, KY: Council of State Governments, 2008), table 4.1.

much like despots to Americans. But for some reason this doesn't seem to be a problem for mayors, many of whom have served a succession of several terms. For example, while voters in the 15 states with legislative term limits have never repealed them, when New York Mayor Michael Bloomberg bumped up against a two-term limit in 2008, he was able to get it repealed with a minimum of fuss.[7] Table 8.1 shows that 37 governors are limited in the number of terms they can serve, with most being limited to two four-year terms. In the early days of the

country, many states limited their governors to a single term; today, Virginia is the last state to do so.[8] But even in those states without gubernatorial term limits, it is rare for a governor to serve more than two terms. For example, only one governor has done so in Illinois since its new constitution was adopted in 1970.[9] Much like the presidential norm established by George Washington (and codified in the 22nd

[7] Josh Goodman, "The Limits of Limits," *Governing*, April 2009, p. 14.

[8] As with New Hampshire's two-year term, there has been discussion in Virginia about allowing governors to serve more than a single term. See: Rob Gurwitt, "Gubernatorial Term Limits: The Last One-Term Governor," *Governing*, October 2005, pp. 17–19.

| Table 8.1 |

Gubernatorial Terms and Term Limits

State	Term Length (Years)	No Limits	Lifetime Limit of Two Terms	Lifetime Limit of Three Terms	Two Consecutive Terms[a]	One Consecutive Term[a]
AL	4		X			
AK	4		X			
AZ	4		X			
AR	4		X			
CA	4		X			
CO	4		X			
CT	4	X				
DE	4		X			
FL	4		X			
GA	4		X			
HI	4		X			
ID	4	X				
IL	4	X				
IN	4				X	
IA	4	X				
KS	4		X			
KY	4		X			
LA	4		X			
ME	4		X			
MD	4		X			
MA	4	X				
MI	4		X			
MN	4	X				
MS	4		X			
MO	4		X			
MT	4				X[b]	
NE	4				X	
NV	4		X			
NH	2	X				
NJ	4		X			
NM	4		X			
NY	4	X				
NC	4		X			
ND	4	X				
OH	4		X			
OK	4		X			

(continued)

| Table 8.1 |

Gubernatorial Terms and Term Limits continued

State	Term Length (Years)	No Limits	Lifetime Limit of Two Terms	Lifetime Limit of Three Terms	Two Consecutive Terms[a]	One Consecutive Term[a]
OR	4		X			
PA	4		X			
RI	4		X			
SC	4		X			
SD	4		X			
TN	4		X			
TX	4	X				
UT	4			X		
VT	2	X				
VA	4					X
WA	4	X				
WV	4		X			
WI	4	X				
WY	4		X			
Total		13	32	1	3	1

Source: Christopher Z. Mooney, "Term Limits for Governors and State Legislators," in *Challenges and Opportunities on the Road to Reform in Illinois* (Urbana, IL: Institute of Government and Public Affairs, 2009).

Amendment to the U.S. Constitution in 1951), eight years usually seems to be enough, both for governors and voters.

Voting for Governor

How do people make their choice when voting for governor? Think about our discussion of voting in state legislative races (Chapter 7), and then apply that logic to voting for governor. The central difference between voting for these offices is that, for a variety of reasons, voters have much more specific information about gubernatorial candidates than they do about legislative candidates.[10] Campaigning has economies of scale, allowing gubernatorial candidates to transmit more sophisticated messages to voters more frequently. Since the race is run statewide, gubernatorial candidates can also advertise on television and radio more cost effectively than can those running for the legislature. But most important, political parties, interest groups, and the general public all recognize the governor's office as a uniquely important position in the state. As a result, gubernatorial candidates can raise more money to get their messages out to the public, groups will make their preferences in the race

---

[9] Of course, the last two Illinois governors have been chased from office with corruption charges (and convictions), but the previous Illinois governor, Jim Edgar, served only two terms even though he left office in 1999 with one of the highest gubernatorial public opinion ratings in the country.

[10] Randall W. Partin, "Campaign Intensity and Voter Information: A Look at Gubernatorial Contests," *American Politics Research* 29(2001): 115–40; and E. Freedman and F. Fico, "Whither the Experts? Newspaper Use of Horse Race and Issue Experts in Coverage of Open Governors' Races in 2002," *Journalism and Mass Communication Quarterly* 81(2004): 498–510.

INSTITUTIONS MATTER

GUBERNATORIAL TERM LIMITS AND STATE SPENDING

The state legislative term limits movement of the 1990s ignited a dramatic set of reforms in 15 states that had a variety of major impacts on politics and policy (see Chapter 7).[1] But far more states limit the terms of their governors than their lawmakers (see Table 8.1). Unlike legislative term limits, gubernatorial term limits have rarely been controversial, nor are they as diverse in their structure. In fact, even in states without legal gubernatorial term limits there are often established norms about how long a governor should serve. The most common formal and informal limit parallels that of the 22nd Amendment for U.S. presidents—a maximum of two four-year terms.

Just because gubernatorial term limits are common and uncontroversial doesn't mean they have no impact. However, this lack of controversy may explain why it has been only recently that scholars have actually tried to study these institutions systematically. The first study of gubernatorial term limits looked for fiscal effects and found none, but those scholars looked only at recent years when there was little variation in these limits among the states.[2] This may have meant only that they had less leverage to find impacts, not that they didn't exist. More recently, political scientists James Alt, Ethan Bueno de Mesquita, and Shanna Rose took advantage of the greater diversity in gubernatorial term limits across a 50-year period.[3] Alt, de Mesquita, and Rose hypothesized three potential effects. First, term limits might reduce accountability by taking away governors' incentive to work hard since they wouldn't have to worry about reelection. As Alaska Governor Sarah Palin famously said when she announced her resignation in July 2009, lame duck governors might just "sort of milk it."[4] Second, term limits could reduce the ability of voters to keep good governors and reject bad ones. Specifically, term limits require the retirement of some governors that voters might have preferred to keep. And third, term limits could reduce the quality of gubernatorial performance by failing to take advantage of the experience of seasoned governors. If governors learn anything on the job, then restricting their ability to be reelected reduces the benefits of that experience. Using measures of taxing, spending, and economic growth, Alt, de Mesquita, and Rose found evidence supporting each of these hypotheses.

Of course, this is only one study, and the final word has not been written on the effects of this institution. Future studies will likely take up this question by measuring gubernatorial performance in other ways and examining other potential effects.

Notes

1. Karl T. Kurtz, Bruce Cain, and Richard G. Niemi, eds., *Institutional Change in American Politics: The Case of Term Limits* (Ann Arbor, MI: University of Michigan Press, 2007).
2. Timothy Besley and Anne Case, "Political Institutions and Policy Choices: Evidence from the United States," *Journal of Economic Literature* 41(2003):7–73.
3. James Alt, Ethan Bueno de Mesquito, and Shanna Rose, "Accountability, Selection, and Experience: Theory and Evidence from U.S. Term Limits." Presented at the annual meetings of the American Political Science Association. Chicago, 2007.
4. Wayne Lawson, "Palin's Resignation: The Edited Version," *Vanity Fair*, 20 July 2009, pp. 12–17.

widely known, and voters will simply spend more time and energy paying attention to the race than they do for virtually any lower-level office.

Not surprisingly, incumbency has a big impact on voting for governor. But unlike with state legislators, it is not an unmitigated blessing. But all else being equal, it is better to be the incumbent than the challenger in a gubernatorial election. Since their constituencies are so much larger, governors cannot generate goodwill by doing the sort of personal constituent service that lawmakers can do. But governors often have their names and faces associated with many positive things in the state, like

AP Photo/Al Behrman

As head of state, a governor represents the state to people, businesses, and governments, both in and outside of the state. Here, Ohio's Governor Ted Strickland, along with Lieutenant Governor Lee Fisher, welcomes drivers entering the state from West Virginia along Interstate 70, just across the Ohio River. This helps Strickland's reelection efforts by reinforcing name recognition in a positive way with voters.

on "Welcome to State X!" signs on highways and parks, on roadmaps, and so forth. They frequently attend ribbon-cutting ceremonies throughout the state for public works projects or for new factories or businesses that the state had a hand in attracting.[11] Like with legislators, a governor also has a sizable staff who work continually to make him or her look good, and these staff can easily switch from governing work to campaign work when reelection time comes. Governors can also be seen as having broad and positive impacts on public policy and on a state in general.

As a result of these advantages, governors win reelection more often than they lose. From 1970 to 2009, 321 incumbent governors sought reelection, and 76.9 percent were successful. Of the 36 incumbent governors who ran for reelection from 2005 to 2009, only three were defeated. In 2009, when New Jersey Governor Jon Corzine was defeated by Chris Christie in aclose, hardfought battle, his deep unpopularitywas in large part due to the severe recession and the anti-incumbent feeling

in the electoratenationwide that year. The two other incumbent governors to lose since 2005—Alaska's Frank Murkowski (2006) and Kentucky's Ernie Fletcher (2007)—were embroiled in scandal. In fact, governors who are seen as successful in their office can overcome big obstacles. Pennsylvania Governor Ed Rendell was so popular in 2006 that he was able to raise taxes significantly and still beat handily a well-loved Pittsburgh Steelers Hall of Famer (Lynn Swann) for reelection. A successful incumbent governor's goodwill can even rub off on the candidate of his or her party when he or she is not running for reelection.[12]

But while incumbency is helpful for governors, compared to the much higher rates of reelection for state legislators, members of the U.S. House, and state supreme court justices, incumbent governors are relatively vulnerable. U.S. senators have prestige and constituency that parallel governors', thus attracting equally strong challengers and dealing with equally tough electoral terrain, but even they have a higher reelection rate than governors. Much of this vulnerability is due to the fact that, as chief executives, governors are held accountable for a state's problems to a much greater degree than are legislators at any level.[13] In fact, the only major office with a worse reelection rate in recent decades is that other chief executive of a large and complex government—the president of the United States. As chief executives, governors have to make tough choices that can anger some of their constituents, such as when Michigan's Granholm was forced to get involved with the mayor of Detroit's legal trouble in 2008 or when Arizona Governor Jan Brewer had to fight for a tax hike and budget cuts to address her

[11] Robert C. Turner, "The Political Economy of Smokestack Chasing: Bad Policy and Bad Politics?" *State Politics and Policy Quarterly* 3(2003): 270–93.

[12] James D. King, "Incumbent Popularity and Vote Choice in Gubernatorial Elections," *Journal of Politics* 63 (2001): 585–97.
[13] Adam Brown and Gary C. Jacobson, "Party, Performance, and Strategic Politicians: The Dynamics of Elections for Senator and Governor in 2006," *State Politics and Policy Quarterly* 8(2008): 384–409; David R. Mayhew, *Congress: The Electoral Connection* (New Haven, CT: Yale University Press, 1974).

state's recent budget mess.[14] Indeed, the recession has caused most governors to make unpopular choices lately. As the chief executive and most visible policy maker in a state, voters tend to hold their governor responsible for their state's condition, even for things that he or she might not reasonably be expected to control.

Fair or not, governors get the blame when things are going poorly and the credit when things are going well. In particular, voters hold incumbent governors accountable for the state's economy.[15] But interestingly, the effect of a state's economy on gubernatorial voting is quite nuanced, suggesting that voters are more sophisticated in making their decisions than you might expect. For example, by studying many gubernatorial elections over many years, scholars have found that voters tend to hold a governor accountable for the state's economy only if the governor's party controls the legislature (when he or she could be expected to control policy making),[16] in election years (when campaigning makes getting information about the governor's performance easier),[17] and when voters know something about the structure of the state's economy (so that they understand what the governor can and cannot do regarding the economy).[18] All this shows the importance of information in the voting process. When voters know more, they use this information thoughtfully; since they know more about governors, voters evaluate governors more thoughtfully than other state-level elected officials. On the other hand, there is evidence that voters don't always use this increased information rationally. For example, one recent study found that, when the economy is good, voters tend only to give their governor credit if he or she is of the voters' party, but when the economy is bad, they tend only to blame those governors of the opposing party.[19] Furthermore, this public stage and informed voting gives governors the opportunity to slip up very visibly, such as when Missouri Governor Matt Blunt got into trouble for purging his email system or when Massachusetts Governor Deval Patrick was called to task by the media for pursuing a book deal in Las Vegas during a crucial legislative debate.[20] And of course the fact that he was governor made South Carolina's Sanford's secret rendezvous with his Argentinean lover national front page news rather than a private concern for his family.

Not surprisingly, while gubernatorial voting is affected more by information about candidates and issues than is voting for state legislator, it is not the only factor influencing gubernatorial elections. As with other races, voters use various shortcuts that allow them to make a reasoned vote with a minimum amount of effort. The most important of these shortcuts is political party; people tend to vote for the gubernatorial candidate of the party to which they feel closest. And unlike his or her public record and policy positions, in practice, a candidate has little control over his or her party affiliation. Gubernatorial candidates have even less control over certain other factors that affect voting in these races, such as national-level forces,

[14] Charlie Cain and Mark Hornbeck, "Ouster Request Called a No-Win for Governor," *The Detroit News*, 14 May 2008, online ed.; Scarpinato, "Redo Budget, Brewer Tells Lawmakers," *Arizona Daily Star (Tucson)*, 2 July 2009, online ed.

[15] John E. Chubb, "Institutions, the Economy, and the Dynamics of State Elections," *American Political Science Review* 82(1988): 133–54; and Lonna Rae Atkeson and Randall W. Partin, "Economic and Referendum Voting: A Comparison of Gubernatorial and Senatorial Elections," *American Political Science Review* 89(1995): 99–107.

[16] Kevin M. Leyden and Stephen A. Borrelli, "The Effect of State Economic Conditions on Gubernatorial Elections: Does a Unified Government Make a Difference?" *Western Political Quarterly* 48(1995): 275–90.

[17] Jason A. MacDonald and Lee Sigelman, "Public Assessments of Gubernatorial Performance," *American Politics Quarterly* 27(1999): 201–15.

[18] Michael Ebeid and Jonathan Rodden, "Economic Geography and Economic Voting: Evidence from the US States," *British Journal of Political Science* 36(2006): 527–47.

[19] Aaron Strauss, "Partisan Bias and Gubernatorial Approval: The Quest for Asymmetries," presented at the 8th Annual State Politics and Policy Conference, Temple University, 2008.

[20] Frank Phillips and Matt Viser, "Patrick Chased Book Deal during Vote," *The Boston Globe*, 28 March 2008, online ed.; Eric Kelderman, "Govs' E-mail Purges Raise Hackles," *Stateline.org*, 6 December 2007, online ed.

like the country's economy and the popularity of the president.[21] But as gubernatorial campaigns have become more costly, sophisticated, and personality-based, the link between gubernatorial voting and presidential approval has weakened, with people voting more on party, the issues in the state, and the candidates in the race.[22]

Strategic Behavior, Political Competition, and Gubernatorial Campaign Spending

The growing importance of governors and state government has caused gubernatorial campaigns to become increasingly costly and competitive.[23] For example, when Indiana Governor Robert Orr ran for reelection in 1980, he spent $4.2 million.[24] But in 2008, when Governor Mitch Daniels ran in a very comparable reelection race in the Hoosier State, he spent $27.7 million—and this is adjusted for inflation.[25] A serious gubernatorial campaign even in a small state now costs millions of dollars. For instance, North Dakota's Hoeven's 2008 cake-walk to reelection cost him $1.8 million, even though he had no primary opponent and ended up receiving almost three-quarters of the votes cast in the general election. Figure 8.2 shows that total spending on gubernatorial races almost doubled between the 1977–1980 and 2005–2008 election cycles, again, even controlling for inflation. The spending spike in the 2001–2004 election cycle seems to have been somewhat of an aberration, but it is an aberration that can tell us something about why gubernatorial campaign costs have risen and why they vary from race to race.

The main reason why gubernatorial campaign spending varies so dramatically from state to state is population. Gubernatorial races are more expensive in larger states because in those states, candidates must communicate their message to more people. In 2006, in California alone, candidates spent a total of $129.0 million running for governor, while those in Wyoming spent only $1.4 million. In other words, spending in the California race—which, while high, was not a record amount—was almost 100 times as high as that in the Wyoming race. While this sounds crazily high, remember the huge difference in the populations of these two states. But since California has nearly 70 times as many residents as Wyoming, population explains only some, but not all, of this variation.

In order to understand the other forces driving spending in gubernatorial races, you must realize that the behavior of candidates and donors in these contests, like that of candidates and donors in most other races, tends to be strategic.[26] That is, these candidates and donors act differently depending on the situation in which they find themselves. And the most general principle of strategic behavior here is that when a race is close, these actors will put in their greatest efforts to win it. As an analogy, think about a game of recreation league basketball. When one team is beating its opponent handily, the coach may send in the second-stringers and the players on both sides take it a little easy. It becomes a sort of Kabuki dance, where everyone knows the outcome, but they go through the motions for the sake of form. But if the score is close, and especially if the league title is on the line, everyone plays as hard as he or she can and no quarter is given, even if all that is at stake is a little plastic trophy and bragging rights. The same dynamic is at work in gubernatorial

---

[21] Chubb, op. cit.

[22] Kenneth Dautrich and David A. Yalof, "The State of State Elections," in Carl E. Van Horn, ed., *The State of the States*, 4th ed. (Washington, DC: CQ Press, 2006).

[23] Thad Beyle, "Gubernatorial Elections, Campaign Costs and Powers," in *The Book of the States: 2008*, vol. 80 (Lexington, KY: Council of State Governments, 2008).

[24] This figure is adjusted for inflation to make the comparison appropriate.

[25] Our source for these campaign spending figures is: Thad Beyle and Jennifer M. Jensen, "The Gubernatorial Campaign Finance Database," www.unc.edu/~beyle/guber.html.

[26] Jeffrey Lazarus, "Incumbent Vulnerability and Challenger Entry in Statewide Elections," *American Politics Research*, 36(2008): 108–29; Adam Brown, "Gubernatorial Elections Reconsidered: Challengers, Donors, and Governors in the 2006 Campaign," working paper, Brigham Young University, 2009; Brown and Jacobson, op. cit.

Figure 8.2

Campaign Spending in Gubernatorial Elections (by Election Cycle)

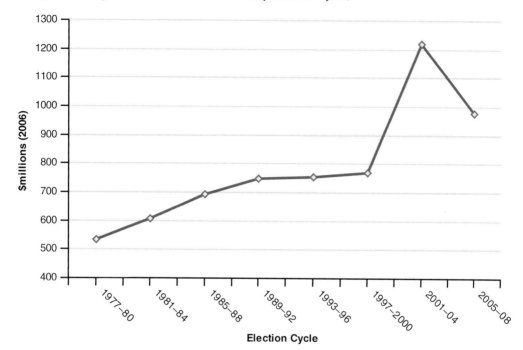

Note: These data are the total amount of campaign spending reported in the gubernatorial races in each election cycle, adjusted for inflation to 2006 dollars.

Source: Raw data from: Thad Beyle and Jennifer M. Jensen, "The Gubernatorial Campaign Finance Database," http://www.unc.edu/~beyle/guber.html.

campaigning. When polling or experience or simply a gut feeling makes it obvious to everyone who is likely to win a race, both sides continue to campaign, but they try not to break a sweat doing it. But when the race is tight, when either candidate could win, all parties and candidates spend every dollar they have and exert every bit of their energy. No one wants to lose an important race like that for governor for want of just one more public appearance or one more round of TV ads.

While unlike in basketball, where the coach controls the level of competition by bringing in the second-string or keeping in the starters, in elections, this is done largely through the strategic behavior of donors (how much money they are willing to contribute?) and challengers (are the best challengers willing to risk a run?). But the result is the same. In general, all things

equal, more money is spent in close races for governor than in blowouts.

So the next question is, What factors influence the level of competition in a gubernatorial race? Like with legislative races, the first thing to consider in this regard is whether an incumbent is running for reelection. While incumbent governors are more likely to lose than are incumbent state legislators, they still have a leg up in their races. They have run and won in the state before, they are well known, and they have the resources of their office to help their public image. Thus, the most important aspect of strategic behavior is whether the incumbent governor is going to run. If not, no single candidate usually has such a large head start in the race. As a result, an open race will attract more candidates.

Why are potential gubernatorial candidates so strategic in deciding whether to run? First, realize that running for any office is costly. Certainly, it takes time and money, but candidates also have to do unpleasant things like ask people for campaign contributions and speak to endless groups and events. And just as important, the potential of losing is always there. To lose a race is not only embarrassing, but it can also end a political career.[27] Most potential candidates for governor are elected officials currently in office, and they may need to choose between running for governor and running for reelection in a relatively safe race. This is especially true for state legislators, members of Congress, and other statewide elected executive officials, like lieutenant governors and attorneys general. Therefore, these highly qualified and experienced candidates are most likely to run for governor only when they have a good chance of winning. And again, the first consideration here is whether there is an incumbent in the race. Incumbents will usually only be challenged by quality opponents if they are especially unpopular and, therefore, seen as "beatable."

Unlike with state legislative races, where so many are uncontested, the opposing major party will almost always find someone to run against even a very popular incumbent governor, but occasionally that person is little more than a sacrificial lamb filling a place on the ballot. Such candidates are doing their duty for their party, and they may neither put much energy into the campaign nor get many campaign contributions to spend. In response, the popular incumbent needs to spend little to win the race. For instance, in 2008, when the West Virginia Republican Party needed someone to run against Governor Joe Machin, one of the country's most popular incumbents in a strongly Democratic state, the best they could come up with was a one-term former state senator and head of a right-to-life group. The result was not surprising, if you think about strategic political behavior—that GOP candidate's campaign managed to spend only $44,000 and get

25.7 percent of the general election votes. However, since the office of governor is so much more powerful and important in American politics these days than seats in the state legislature, the U.S. House, or, some might say, the U.S. Senate, there are fewer true sacrificial lambs in gubernatorial races than in these other races. But the principle still applies—the less competitive the race, especially when there is an incumbent running for reelection, the less money will be spent on both sides.

In addition to the presence of an incumbent in a race, potential candidates' strategic choices also hinge on the distribution of party voters in the state.[28] Why would a quality candidate who was successful in some other way risk losing a gubernatorial race where the state's partisan deck is stacked heavily against him or her? For example, while a Democrat may have a safe congressional seat in Alabama, the current statewide electorate is such that he or she would have a hard time being elected governor, even running in an open race. On the other hand, this strategic consideration is less important for potential gubernatorial candidates than it is for those for the legislature due to the difference in the level of information voters have about candidates for these two offices. Unlike legislative candidates, the extensive campaigning, news coverage, and advertising of gubernatorial candidates gives voters lots of specific information about them. So while legislative voting is often driven only by party, gubernatorial voting is less so. Therefore, it is not unusual for a "minority-party" gubernatorial candidate to win with a good campaign. For example, two of the most Democratic states in the country—Rhode Island and Connecticut—have not had a Democratic governor since 1995 and 1991, respectively.

The strategic behavior of gubernatorial candidates and donors leads to a circular situation whereby many strong candidates are attracted to races without a clear front runner, and with

[27] David L. Leal, *Electing America's Governors: The Politics of Executive Elections* (New York: Palgrave Macmillan, 2006).

[28] Peverill Squire, "Challenger Profile and Gubernatorial Elections," *Western Political Quarterly* 45(1992): 125–42.

more strong candidates in the race, the competition gets extremely fierce. And when conditions are right—when there is no incumbent in the race (or an unpopular one), when there is no one who is the obvious heir-apparent to the office, and when the statewide electorate is such that a candidate of either party could win—many well-qualified candidates may be attracted to the race. Because of their qualifications and expertise, such candidates are able to raise plenty of campaign money, and as the battle intensifies, more contributions come in on all sides, leading to a perfect storm of political spending. Thus, when competition is closest, no incumbent is running, and the partisan balance is even, gubernatorial campaign spending can be astronomical.

This discussion of strategic political behavior in gubernatorial elections helps explain the blip in campaign spending in the 2001–2005 election cycle seen in Figure 8.2. As it turns out, just five races in 2002 accounted for $544.2 million[29] of this spending, or 44.5 percent of the spending in all the 52 gubernatorial elections in that cycle. These five races were all in large states where both parties had won the governor's race in recent years. Four of these fit the profile for high competition and spending: two open seats (Illinois and New Jersey), an unpopular incumbent (California), and a seemingly weak incumbent who had succeeded to office after the resignation of the previous governor (Texas). The fifth of these expensive races in 2002 (New York), along with New Jersey's, offers an example of another, less predictable, factor that has often inflated gubernatorial campaign spending in recent years, the **self-financing candidate**.[30]

Certain multimillionaires appear to worry very little about spending $10 million or more pursuing a challenging and prestigious opportunity for public service. Two such men spent a total of over $75 million in the New Jersey governor's race in 2005. But in the 2002 New York race, Tom Golisano, the billionaire founder of Paychex, Inc., running on the Independence Party ticket, probably set the standard by single-handedly spending $76.3 million, almost all of it thought to be his own money.[31] Interestingly, self-financing candidates are not as strategic in choosing their races as are candidates who are more experienced politicians.[32] That is, their electability appears to have less influence on their choice to enter the race or spend money. For candidates who are not self-financed, strategic campaign contributors act as a reality check, so that even if the candidates themselves think they can win, when potential donors do not, their contributions will be small and infrequent and their resulting spending will be low. Self-financing candidates, undeterred by either internal or external strategic checks, tend to spend more than is "rational," as Golisano's race demonstrates dramatically. While he spent as much as has ever been spent on a gubernatorial campaign, he received only 654,016 votes, or 13.9 percent of those cast in his race. Put another way, he spent $116.33 per vote, not very strategic and certainly a record that will stand for some time to come.

Today's Governors: Who Are They?

Who are today's governors? What types of people are attracted to the governor's office, and more important, what types of people are successful in the tough election battles for these prestigious offices? Where do they come from and where are they going? Although each one has his or her own personal history,

---

[29] This is in 2006 dollars to make the comparison fair.
[30] Self-financing candidates have also been on the rise in congressional elections. See: Jennifer A. Steen, *Self-Financed Candidates in Congressional Elections* (Ann Arbor, MI: University of Michigan Press, 2006).

[31] Delen Goldberg and John O'Brien, "Meet Tom Golisano, the Man Who Flipped Control of the New York State Senate," *The (Syracuse, NY) Post-Standard*, 10 June 2009, online ed.
[32] Adam Brown, "What Money Can't Buy: Self-Financed Candidates in Gubernatorial Elections," presented at the 9th Annual State Politics and Policy Conference, University of North Carolina at Chapel Hill, 2009.

experiences, and background, we can make some generalizations about governors today.

First, as a group, they are a long way from the political hacks who often occupied governors' mansions before the 1960s.[33] Today's governors are younger and better educated than those in years gone by, and they have been highly successful in their chosen fields before becoming governor. Because they are young and successful when they enter the governor's office, they often move on to important and powerful careers after leaving office. Governors fight hard to win their jobs, and while in office, they pursue their vision of the state and its government energetically. In both their demographics and their professional experiences, today's governors are also a much more diverse group, although they are not nearly as diverse a group as are state legislators. It's hard to know whether it has been the increasing challenges of the governor's office that have attracted this new generation of governors or whether their skills, experience, and energy have caused the states and governors to come to the forefront of American politics and government. Probably some of both of these processes is at work. But regardless of the direction of causality here, governors are among the most competent and important political actors in the country today.

Governors and Their Careers

Prelude to the Governorship What does the résumé of the typical governor look like? As has long been the case, since the governorship is the top political job in a state, the most common career path is through considerable progressive experience in state and local government. They typically start their public service careers in the local or state legislature or in law enforcement, often as a local prosecutor. These days, governors have almost always been to college, and they usually have a

postgraduate education, especially in law. Specifically, the highest degree attained by the current crop of governors is: PhD—2, doctor of veterinary medicine—1; law degree—23, master's degree—8, bachelor's degree—14; and some college—2.[34] Most governors have been interested in politics, policy, and government from an early age, and their careers reflect this.

You can see the progressive nature of the state political career ladder by examining the positions held by the 50 current governors just before coming into office. Most commonly, these governors came from statewide elected positions, like lieutenant governor or secretary of state (see Table 8.2). As such, these governors had already faced

Table 8.2	
The "Last Job" of Current Governors	

Job	Number of Governors
Statewide Elected Official	
Lieutenant Governor	9
Attorney General	7
Secretary of State	3
Treasurer	2
State Legislature	
State Senate	3
State House	1
Congress	
U.S. House	7
Other	
Private Business	7
Mayor	3
Criminal Justice	4
Federal executive agency director	2
State executive agency director	1
State political party official	1

Note: These reflect job held by the current governors (as of January 2010) immediately before taking office, based on information on the governors' official websites and that of the National Governors Association.

[33] Larry Sabato, *Good-Bye to Good-Time Charlie: The American Governorship Transformed*, 2nd ed. (Washington, DC: CQ Press, 1983).

[34] This information was gathered by the authors and Pat McConnell at the University of Illinois at Springfield from these governors' professional web pages.

the same voters as in their gubernatorial race, and they had already served and were known among that constituency. Governors Jim Doyle (Wisconsin) and Bob McDonnell (Virginia) were attorneys general just before becoming governor, while Beverly Perdue (North Carolina) was lieutenant governor and Chet Culver (Iowa) was secretary of state. In fact, because of the movement of so many governors up (and out) in the middle of their terms recently, as we write this, six sitting governors are finishing out terms they succeeded to, mostly from lieutenant governor (such as Illinois's Pat Quinn and Alaska's Sean Parnell) but also from other offices in states without a lieutenant governor, such as Jan Brewer succeeding from the Arizona secretary of state's office. In addition, Connecticut's Jodi Rell, Nebraska's Dave Heineman, and Texas's Rick Perry succeeded from the lieutenant governorship before being elected in the own rights. Thus, the most recent previous job of fully 18 percent of sitting governors was lieutenant governor, for another 24 percent, it was some other elected statewide office.

Much further down the list, the next most common "last job" for governors in the public sector is as a member of the U.S. House of Representatives. This shows that being governor is a step up from the House on today's informal political career ladder.[35] Idaho's Butch Otter and Ohio's Ted Strickland recently took this route to the governor's mansion. In most states, congressional districts cover just a portion of the state, so members of Congress running for governor have the disadvantage of having to introduce themselves to new constituents. The same problem confronts local government officials trying to move into the governor's office, but three current governors have done so from big-city mayors' offices, like Tennessee's Phil

Bredesen (Nashville) and Pennsylvania's Ed Rendell (Philadelphia). But the mayoral path is less common than one might think (Sarah Palin's well-known path from Wasilla to Juneau notwithstanding), given the parallels between the two jobs. It seems that even popular mayors have a hard time appealing to voters outside of their home cities. For example, the last four mayors of Charlotte—the largest city in North Carolina—have run for statewide office and lost.[36] No mayor of New York, Chicago, or Los Angeles has become governor for more than a century, although not for want of trying.

Four governors, including South Dakota's Mike Rounds and Georgia's Sonny Perdue, have moved up straight from the state legislature. But as the governor's office has become more attractive in recent years, this path is less common than it used to be. Today, state lawmakers usually need to work their way up through more prominent positions, especially in large states where there are more business leaders, members of Congress, and big-city mayors to challenge for governor. A few current governors came straight from positions in the criminal justice system, such as Oregon's Ted Kulongoski, who was a state supreme court justice, and Colorado's Bill Ritter, who was Denver's district attorney. Other governors had been working in an assortment of jobs just prior to taking the state's helm, such as Hawaii's Linda Lingle's job as head of the state Republican Party and Indiana's Daniel's position as head of President George Bush's Office of Management and Budget.

The power and prestige of the governor's office also hold considerable cachet for those who have been successful in the private sector. While it seems more common today, outsiders have won governorships throughout our history, such as in 1911, when Woodrow Wilson moved from the presidency of Princeton University to New Jersey's governor's mansion (on his way to the White House). Running a state appears to many people to be quite

---

[35] Likewise, the fact that more members of the U.S. Senate are former governors (12) than governors who were previously a senator (0) seems to indicate that the Senate is seen as a step up from the governor's office on the political ladder. But this pattern of succession is also affected by the fact that many governors are term limited, and as such, are forced to move on to another position, should they decide to stay in politics.

[36] Alan Greenblatt, "Charlotte's Curse," *Governing*, March 2008, p. 18.

similar to managing a large private business, and extraordinarily successful businesspeople often take their first step into politics by running for the governor's office, some of them successfully (on the other hand, remember New York Governor-wannabe Golisano). Some of these business-to-governor stories are well known, like those of Governors George W. (Texas) and Jeb (Florida) Bush, California's Arnold Schwarzenegger, and Minnesota's Jesse Ventura.[37] Other governors with perhaps a lower national profile have also moved straight from the private sector, including North Dakota's Hoeven and Montana's Brian Schweitzer. But while business experience may help a governor, the differences between the public and private sectors can sometimes be baffling. For example, while Jon Corzine was a smashing success running the preeminent investment bank on Wall Street, governing New Jersey proved puzzling to him.[38] Several governors, such as New Hampshire's John Lynch and Delaware's Jack Markell, had successful business careers but went into the governor's office only after serving in another, less demanding, government position. Such a path can both weed out those unsuited to government service and give those who do become governor valuable public sector experience.

After the Governor's Mansion

If the governor's office is at the top of a state's political ladder, what can a governor do for an encore? This is an especially important question for those many people in recent years who have been elected governor in their 30s and 40s, giving them the prospect of a long career after leaving the governor's office. Table 8.3 shows the first "post-governor" job or activity for those most recently leaving the office in each state. As you can see, the most common thing for former governors to do today is what former governors have always done—put together a

---

Table 8.3

"First-Next Job" of Most Recent Former Governor in Each State

Type of Job	Number of former governors
Private Activities	
Business	21
Retired	10
Public Service	
President	1
Federal cabinet secretary/ Ambassador	5
U.S. Senate	2
U.S. House	1
State senate	1*
Other	
Federal prison	3
College professor	3
Presidential candidate	2
DNC chair	1

*As president of the New Jersey State Senate, when then-Governor James McGreevey resigned on November 15, 2004, Richard J. Codey succeeded to the governorship. At the end of McGreevey's term, Codey returned to the senate.

Note: These numbers represent our best understanding of the first job, profession, or activity the last governor in each state had after leaving office, based on the personal web sites of these former governors and media searches on LexisNexis. These are the governors who left office after the 2008 elections or before.

---

lucrative portfolio of business activities that can include legal work, lobbying, public speaking, corporate board service, and public relations work. Twenty-one of the 50 most recent former governors have done this. One might say that these governors are cashing in on their years of experience and many contacts made in state government. But who can blame them? Being governor is an extremely demanding job without an extremely high level of compensation, and as we have seen, it is often the pinnacle of a long career of public service. Former governors who work primarily in the private sector also often serve part-time on various important public commissions and

---

[37] Ventura had also served a stint as the mayor of a small Minneapolis suburb.

[38] Alan Greenblatt, "Tougher Work than Wall St," *Governing*, December 2007, pp. 32–38.

boards at the state and national levels, such as the National Commission on Terrorist Attacks Upon the United States, or the "9/11 Commission," 30 percent of whose membership was former governors, including its chair, New Jersey's Thomas Kean.

Many of today's former governors want to continue in public service full-time, and 10 of those in Table 8.3 found a way to do so. Of course, the position that is most clearly above the governorship in the American political pecking order is president of the United States. The fact that these two positions are more similar to one another than any other two positions also makes voters, political operatives, and governors themselves think of the states' chief executives as a natural talent pool for presidential candidates. This has been true throughout U.S. history, as former governors have served as president for 108 years of the nation's 222-year history under the U.S. Constitution—almost 50 percent of the time. While we often think of the U.S. Senate as a natural training ground for presidents, the 2008 election of Barack Obama was the first time a sitting senator was elected to the presidency since John F. Kennedy in 1960, and the last one before Kennedy was Warren G. Harding in 1920. Already, talk about 2012 challengers to Obama centers around governors and former governors, such as Florida's Charlie Crist, Minnesota's Pawlenty, and Louisiana's Jindal.

Of course, while only a small percentage of former governors actually become president, just as important is the idea that a governor *could* become president. When governors are thought of as "presidential timber" by the media, the political parties, and, just as importantly, by governors themselves, it burnishes the image both of governors and of their offices. This attracts higher-quality candidates to run for the office and gives sitting governors more influence, both within and outside of their states. And a governor's presidential aspirations may even be good for a state, as he or she strives to perform well to gain favorable publicity. For example, the performance of Massachusetts' Governor Mitt Romney in managing Boston's "Big Dig" highway

reconstruction in 2006 was seen by many as having implications for his 2008 presidential bid, giving him an incentive to do the job well.[39] Furthermore, running a state is a great way both to improve a future president's skills and to weed out those unfit or unwilling to do a good job as president. For example, Alaska's Palin, South Carolina's Sanford, and even Illinois's Blagojevich had at one time been touted as promising presidential aspirants, but their actions as governor demonstrated that perhaps they were best suited to other work. Without that test by fire, perhaps if they had served in a less demanding position, like in the U.S. Senate, their deficiencies might not have become apparent before they entered the Oval Office.

But far more commonly than either the presidency or the Senate, former governors fill many appointive public service jobs, primarily at the national level, especially on presidents' cabinets and as ambassadors to other countries. Currently, four of 14 members of President Obama's cabinet are former governors— Iowa's Tom Vilsack (Secretary of Agriculture); Washington's Gary Locke (Secretary of Commerce); Kansas's Kathleen Sebelius (Secretary of Health and Social Services); and Arizona's Janet Napolitano (Secretary of Homeland Security). Historically, this is not an unusual number. Several former governors have served on the U.S. Supreme Court in U.S. history, although none has done so since California Governor Earl Warren became chief justice in 1953. The vice presidency is another national position for which governors are routinely considered. But despite Alaska's Palin's highly visible candidacy in 2008, only two governors have actually served in the position in the past 90 years.[40] And regardless of the outcome, virtually any discussion of a presidential appointment for such high positions regularly includes the names of at least one governor, such as the

---

[39] Glen Johnson, "Gov. Romney's Future May Hinge on Big Dig," *Sacramento Bee*, 18 July 2006, online ed.

[40] These former governors were New York's Nelson Rockefeller (who was appointed, rather then elected, after President Richard Nixon's resignation) and Maryland's Spiro Agnew.

YOU DECIDE

WHEN ARE PERSONAL ISSUES THE STATE'S PROBLEMS?

Governors are human, of course. But sometimes the human failings of these very visible figures impinge on their ability to govern. In June 2009, South Carolina Governor Mark Stanford's trip to Argentina posed for South Carolinians, and for readers of this book, a question not only about what is right and wrong personally and morally, but also about what is professionally unacceptable.

The facts are pretty straightforward. Governor Sanford, a staunch family-values conservative and rising star in the Republican Party nationally, took a weeklong trip alone to relax after a tough legislative session. He apparently told no one precisely where he was going or how he could be contacted—not his cabinet, his lieutenant governor, his staff, or his wife and four children. As the days passed and his mysterious absence began to make national news, questions arose not only about his safety, but about the professional propriety of a governor being out of touch with state government for so long. What if there had been a natural disaster and the National Guard had been needed? What if a prison riot had broken out? What if important and immediate decisions were needed about legislation or government spending or the execution of a convict? Luckily for South Carolina, none of these crises arose, and the only real problems were for Sanford, his family, and his political future. But some people, including other governors,[1] raised questions about the irresponsibility of Sanford's actions and how they might affect his ability and competence to govern. In the end, Sanford rebuffed calls to resign and as yet, efforts to impeach him have been unsuccessful, so (at press time) he remained at the helm of the Palmetto State.

The Sanford case raises general questions about when a governor's personal behavior affects his or her ability to governor a state. The actions of several other governors in recent years have also raised this question. Nevada Governor Jim Gibbons was dogged by media reports of his marital disputes early in his term, including about his efforts to have his estranged wife legally ejected from the governor's mansion.[2] While Gibbons managed to weather those storms and serve out his term, in 2008, New York Governor Elliot Spitzer resigned following revelations that he patronized prostitutes.[3]

Why was Gibbons able to stay in office while Spitzer was not? How were these governors' transgressions and situations different? Was it because Spitzer committed a crime by buying sexual services? Did that make his removal from office a must? What about Sanford? Aside from being AWOL from duty, there was some question of his using state funds to visit his Argentinean lover.[4] Should that be enough to disqualify him from office?

Investigate these cases by reading legitimate news sources about them, and then think about the types of actions for which a governor should resign or be removed from office. When do a governor's action make it impossible or inappropriate for him or her to govern, and why?

Other cases to investigate and consider include:

- Impeachment of:
  - Illinois's Rod Blagojevich in 2009
- Resignations by:
  - New Jersey's James McGreevey in 2004
  - Connecticut's John Nowland in 2004
  - Arizona's Fife Symington in 1997
- Other cases involving:
  - Ohio's Bob Taft's 2006 conviction for failing to report lobbyist's gifts
  - The purging of emails by Missouri's Matt Blunt, Texas's Rick Perry, and Alaska's Sarah Palin
  - Problems alleged and/or confirmed with criminal pardons distributed by Kentucky's Ernie Fletcher and Paul Patton and Tennessee's Ray Blanton

Notes

1. Andy Sher, "Tennessee: Bredesen Says Governors 'Obligated to Be in Contact,'" *Chattanooga Times Free Press*, 27 June 2009, online ed.
2. David McGrath Schwartz, "Governor's Textual Misconduct: Gibbons Acknowledges 'Mistake,' Denies Affair," *Las Vegas Sun*, 12 June 2008, online ed.
3. Eric Kelderman, "Spitzer, 22nd Disgraced Gov to Leave Office," *Stateline.org*, 12 March 2008, online ed.
4. Jim Rutenberg and Robbie Brown, "Governor Used State's Money to Visit Lover," *The New York Times*, 27 June 2009, online ed.

buzz around Michigan's Granholm as a potential appointee to the Supreme Court in 2009 or the incessant media chatter about a whole list of governors as potential vice presidential candidates for both parties in 2008.[41]

Governors' appointments, and the talk leading up to them, often have as much to do with political considerations for the president as they do with the qualifications that governors bring to these positions. Traditionally, cabinets are formed by balancing the interests of various factions and parts of the country. For example, picking a governor from a farming state, like Iowa's Vilsack, to serve as Secretary of Agriculture is a tried and true way for a president to show he has concern for rural America. Sometimes more strategic, or some might say, Machiavellian, considerations may be at play. For example, President Obama was said to have co-opted a strong potential opponent for his 2012 reelection bid by appointing Utah Governor Jon Huntsman to the prestigious ambassadorship to China.[42] But politics aside, there is no doubt that the qualities that have caused governors to be elected and the experience they gained running their states make them a powerful and skilled talent pool for any high-level position.

Women and Minorities as Governor

Until 1975, almost every governor in U.S. history had been an Anglo man. But since then, especially in the past two decades, significant progress has been made in electing governors who, as a group, are more representative of Americans' sex and race,[43] just as progress has been made in electing more diverse state legislators (see Chapter 7).

The most sweeping change in American governors' demographics has been the election of 22 women to the post in the past third of a century. Only three women had ever served as governor before 1975, and these were spouses of former governors who had been term limited, banned from office for official malfeasance, or had died. These first women governors were clearly elected as surrogates for their husbands. One even ran under the slogan "Two governors for the price of one," and another used the slogan "Let George [her husband] do it."[44]

In 1974, Connecticut's Ella Grasso, a former state legislator, secretary of state, and member of the U.S. House, became the first woman elected governor on her own merits. Grasso's success and reelection, along with changing values about sexual roles in the American politics, helped Washington State's Dixy Lee Ray follow her in 1977. Three more women were elected to governorships in the 1980s, and six more in the 1990s. This exponential acceleration in women's gubernatorial representation continued with 11 women being elected governor in the 2000s (see Figure 8.3). Indeed, six women were elected or reelected in 2006 alone—fully 17 percent of those winning gubernatorial elections that year. And the trend shows no sign of stopping. For example, the top early prospects for the 2010 California governor's race were both women, former eBay CEO Meg Whitman and U.S. Senator Dianne Feinstein.[45] In addition to those women who have been elected governor, since 1982, eight women have succeeded to the governorship when the elected governor died, resigned, or was impeached, serving anywhere from several days to three years. Two of these, Jane Dee Hull of Arizona and Jodi Rell of Connecticut, were later elected to a full term as governor in their own right.

A total of 31 women have now served as governor (see Table 8.4). While most of them have been Democrats, the balance has not been overly

[41] Daniel C. Vock, "Govs Rarely Picked for VP Slot," *Stateline.org*, 20 August 2008, online ed.

[42] Charles Mahtesian, "Stealth War: Obama Sabotages GOP," *Politics.com*, 3 June 2009, online ed.

[43] As to sexual orientation, no openly gay person has ever been elected governor. In 2004, New Jersey's Governor Jim McGreevy came out as a gay man during his term.

[44] Quoted in Susan J. Carroll, "Women in State Government: Historical Overview and Current Trends," in *The State of the States*, vol. 36 (Lexington, KY: Council of State Governments, 2004).

[45] John Wildermuth, "Feinstein, Whitman Are Governor Race Favorites," *San Francisco Chronicle*, 12 November 2008, online ed.

Figure 8.3

The Exponential Growth of Elected Women Governors, Decade by Decade

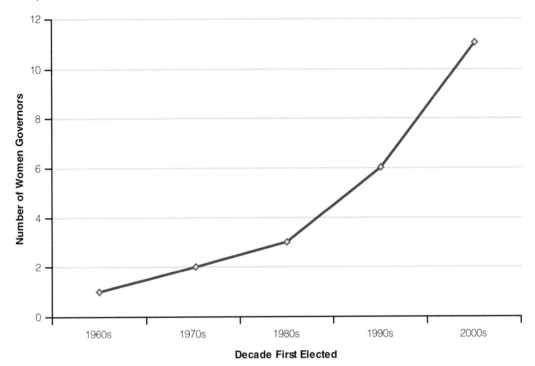

Note: These numbers do not include those women who succeeded to the governor's office due to death, impeachment, or resignation, unless they were later elected to the job.

lopsided (19 Democrats and 12 Republicans). Just as important, 23 different states have had a woman governor, and these states represent the country very broadly, from New Hampshire and New Jersey to Texas and Louisiana, from Alaska and Arizona to Michigan and North Carolina. Clearly, the rise of the woman governor is not a regional, partisan, or ideological phenomenon.[46] And as women continue to serve as governors and receive high marks for their performance,[47] Americans will become accustomed to seeing women in powerful executive positions in government, allowing candidates to be judged more

on their qualifications than their sex. This levels the playing field for female candidates and may lead to better sexual representation in all public offices. Just as the increasing numbers of women in state legislatures in the 1970s and 1980s encouraged the flourishing of women in the U.S. Senate in the 1990s and 2000s, Hillary Clinton's run for president in 2008 was probably helped significantly by the rise of woman governors in the 1990s and 2000s—or, more accurately, the old bias against electing women to executive office was likely reduced by these governors' success. It is very likely that first woman in the White House will get there through a governor's mansion.

Racial and ethnic gubernatorial representation has improved more slowly and unevenly in the states than has sexual representation. Studies continue to show that voter bias disadvantages

---

[46] Jason Windett, "State Effects and the Emergence and Success of Female Gubernatorial Candidates," presented at the 9th Annual State Politics and Policy Conference, University of North Carolina at Chapel Hill, 2009.

[47] Pamela M. Prah, "Report: Women Govs Get High Marks," *Stateline.org*, 30 November 2007, online ed.

Table 8.4

Woman Governors of the U.S. States

Name	State	Party	Dates of Service
Wives of Former Governors			
Nellie Taylor Ross	Wyoming	D	1925–1927
Miriam "Ma" Ferguson	Texas	D	1925–1927, 1933–1935
Lurleen Wallace	Alabama	D	1967–1968[a]
Elected in Their Own Right			
Ella Grasso	Connecticut	D	1975–1980[b]
Dixy Lee Ray	Washington	D	1977–1981
Martha Layne Collins	Kentucky	D	1983–1987
Madeleine M. Kunin	Vermont	D	1985–1991
Kay A. Orr	Nebraska	R	1987–1991
Joan Finney	Kansas	D	1991–1995
Barbara Roberts	Oregon	D	1991–1995
Ann Richards	Texas	D	1991–1995
Christine Todd Whitman	New Jersey	R	1994–2001
Jeanne Shaheen	New Hampshire	D	1997–2003
Jane Dee Hull[c]	Arizona	R	1997–2003
Judy Martz	Montana	R	2001–2005
Ruth Ann Minner	Delaware	D	2001–2009
Linda Lingle	Hawaii	R	2002–
Janet Napolitano	Arizona	D	2003–2009
Kathleen Sebelius	Kansas	D	2003–2009
Jennifer Granholm	Michigan	D	2003–
Kathleen Blanco	Louisiana	D	2004–2008
M. Jodi Rell[d]	Connecticut	R	2004–
Christine Gregoire	Washington	D	2005–
Sarah Palin	Alaska	R	2007–2009
Beverly Perdue	North Carolina	D	2009–
Successors			
Vesta M. Roy	New Hampshire	R	1982–1983
Rose Mofford	Arizona	D	1988–1991
Jane Dee Hull[c]	Arizona	R	1997–2003
Nancy P. Hollister	Ohio	R	1998–1999
Jane Swift	Massachusetts	R	2001–2003
Olene Walker	Utah	R	2003–2005
M. Jodi Rell[d]	Connecticut	R	2004–
Jan Brewer	Arizona	R	2009–

a   Died in office.
b   Resigned for health reasons.
c   Jane Dee Hull succeeded to office upon the resignation of Fife Symington in 1997 and then was elected to a full term in her own right in 1998.
d   M. Jodi Rell succeeded to office upon the resignation of John Rowland in 2004 and then was elected to a full term in her own right in 2006.

| Table 8.5 |

Governors with Minority Racial or Ethnic Heritages

Name	State	Party	Dates of Service	Racial or Ethnic Heritage
Ezequiel Cabeza De Baca	NM	D	1917[a]	Latino
Octaviano Ambrosio Larrazolo	NM	R	1919–1921	Latino
George Ryoichi Ariyoshi	HI	D	1974–1986	Asian American
Jerry Apodaca	NM	D	1975–1979	Latino
Raul H. Castro	AZ	D	1975–1977	Latino
Toney Anaya	NM	D	1983–1987	Latino
John Waihee	HI	D	1986–1994	Hawaiian
Robert Martinez	FL	R	1987–1991	Latino
L. Douglas Wilder	VA	D	1990–1994	African American
Benjamin J. Cayetano	HI	D	1994–2002	Asian American
Gary Locke	WA	D	1997–2005	Asian American
Bill Richardson	NM	D	2003–	Latino
Deval Patrick	MA	D	2007–	African American
Bobby Jindal	LA	R	2008–	Indian American
Successors				
Pinkney B. S. Pinchback	LA	R	1872–1873	African American
David A. Paterson	NY	D	2008–	African American

a   Died in office.

Source: We have identified these governors' heritages based on their biographies on the National Governors Association website, media reports, and other online sources. But like Americans generally, the racial and ethnic heritage of many politicians in this country is not clear cut or easy to identify from documentary sources.

non-Anglo candidates in gubernatorial races.[48] But some governors with minority heritages have been elected in recent years, especially in those states with smaller proportions of Anglos than the nation as a whole (see Table 8.5).[49] Hawaii,

[48] Gary M. Segura and Luis R. Fraga, "Race and the Recall: Racial and Ethnic Polarization in the California Recall Election," *American Journal of Political Science* 52(2008): 421–35; Christina Bejarano and Gary Segura, "What Goes Around, Comes Around: Race, Blowback, and the Louisiana Elections of 2002 and 2003," *Political Research Quarterly* 60(2007): 328–37.

[49] We have identified minority governors based on their biographies on the National Governors Association website, media reports, and other online sources. Of course, like Americans generally, the racial and ethnic heritage of many politicians in this country is not clear cut or easy to identify from documentary sources.

with its polyethnic society, has elected two Asian American governors and one of native Hawaiian ancestry. New Mexico has the country's highest proportion of Latinos, and it has elected five Latino governors, including its current head of state, former U.S. Energy Secretary and presidential candidate, Bill Richardson. New Mexico's neighbor, Arizona, also elected a Latino governor, as has Florida, two other states with sizable Latino populations. In 1990, Virginia's L. Douglas Wilder became the first African American to be elected a state governor. Since only 20 percent of Virginia's population at that time was African American, this clearly demonstrated that even in the South, significant numbers of white people will vote for a black person. While seven other states with higher proportions of black residents have never elected an African American governor, at least one poll suggested that even in Alabama, where gubernatorial candidates used to compete with one another by holding virulent racist positions, a black person could be elected governor in the near future.[50]

Especially promising in this regard is the fact that three non-Anglo men have been elected governor recently in states where people with their racial heritage made up only a very small proportion of voters. Washington State's Gary Locke, an Asian American, Massachusetts's Deval Patrick, an African American, and Louisiana's Jindal, an Indian American, were obviously elected with mostly white votes, since in none of these states did people of their heritage make up more than 7 percent of the population. In addition, in March 2008, New York Lieutenant Governor David Paterson succeeded to the governorship when Governor Eliot Spitzer resigned as a result of a prostitution scandal. Paterson is not only African American, but he is also legally blind. While no one has studied or even tracked the number of disabled governors, Paterson's succession to the governorship of the second largest state in the country was seen as an inspiration for blind people as well as African Americans.[51] Thus, while racial and ethnic minorities are much underrepresented in the ranks of the nation's governors, the recent elections of Locke, Patrick, and Jindal—and the elections of Paterson and many other non-Anglos to a other statewide offices—in states where people of their own heritage are in the distinct minority suggest that more governors of color may be elected in the coming years.

New York Governor David Paterson is the first legally blind governor in U.S. history, as well as being one of the few African-American governors.

The Duties of the Governor— Manager, Policy Maker, and Intergovernmental Liaison

Once in office, what does a governor do, and how? The answers to these questions are not as clear as you might think, nor are they as clear as they seem to be for officials of the other two branches of state government. Legislators pass laws, and judges interpret and enforce them in court, but what exactly do governors do? We see them in the media giving speeches, meeting with various officials and members of the public, touring disaster areas, and so forth, and we are vaguely aware that they somehow "run state government," but what does that mean?

In general, governors have three basic duties— managing the state government **bureaucracy**, helping make public policy for the state, and acting as the liaison for the state government with local governments, other state governments, the national government, businesses, and even foreign countries. Each of these is a demanding and complicated task that requires all of a governor's institutional and informal powers, as well as all of his or her personal knowledge, skills, and abilities. We will talk about the powers that

[50] Charles J. Dean, "Black Governor Now Possible in State, 53% Say in Survey," *Birmingham (Alabama) News*, 12 August 2008, online ed.

[51] Lisa W. Foderaro, "The New Governor Also Serves as an Inspiration for the Blind," *The New York Times*, 18 March 2008, online ed.; Verena Dobnik, "Black Pride Surges with Paterson's Rise to N.Y. Governor," *State Journal-Register* (Springfield, IL), 16 March 2008, p. 7.

governors can use to accomplish these tasks later in this chapter, but first, here is a brief outline of what their duties entail.

Chief Executive Officer: Managing the Bureaucracy

Although the republican values of our country's founders led many of them to value the legislative over the executive function of government, it was clear to those writing the early states' constitutions that at the very least, an administrator was needed to implement the policies passed by the legislature. Thus, the original job of the governor was simply to do this, supervising various agencies staffed by government workers to provide the minimal services that the states then provided their residents, collect taxes, and pay the state's bills. In this sense, the governor is like the chief executive officer of the state, trying to carry out the wishes of the legislature, which acts like a very hands-on board of directors. In the early years of the republic, these duties and workers were few; but as the nation and its needs for public services grew, so did the responsibilities of the executive branch of state government. Today, state government is the single largest employer in almost every state. At last count, 4.3 million people worked for state governments nationwide, including over 100,000 each in 11 states.[52] Even the states with the fewest state employees—Vermont, Wyoming, and the Dakotas—each has over 10,000 of them. All but a small percentage of these workers serve in the states' executive branches, and most of these are under the governor's control. As these state executive agencies have grown, so has the importance of the governor's job of managing them.

Given the importance of policy implementation and the size and complexity of the bureaucracy, it should not be surprising that most governors spend a good deal of time trying to impose their will on the executive branch. The state bureaucracy is a mammoth operation, and

the governor is but one person, perhaps with several dozen staff. The agencies are like battleships, moving along relatively smoothly in one direction, doing their duty as they have always done it. Despite common misperceptions and biases, the people who work in state agencies tend to be highly skilled and dedicated professionals who come to the job proud to do what they think of as important work. The generally high level of competence of these people helps governors tremendously by making the huge ship of state run smoothly on a daily basis.

A governor's management duties are much like those of a CEO of a large corporation or non-profit organization, with their problems typically consisting of two types. First, sometimes problems arise with an agency's standard operating procedures so that its ongoing tasks and goals are not being accomplished correctly. Whether it is a morale problem or a goal misplacement issue, governors and their staff need to keep an eye on the various agencies to anticipate and solve such problems. Second, and more problematic, sometimes governors want to change the goals and behaviors of an agency significantly. Inertia, professional pride, and perhaps even the policy preferences of these state workers can make it difficult for a governor to make quick and significant changes. Like a battleship, the agencies will turn, but they do so slowly. Sometimes, a governor just needs to communicate his or her preferences clearly; often, bureaucrats are happy to do what the governor wants, as long as they know what that is and if it fits with their professional norms. Sometimes more forceful actions must be taken, especially those involving a governor's budget powers or executive orders.

Chief Policy Maker: Charting the Course

The original idea of the governor simply as an errand boy for the policy-making legislature quickly gave way both to the realities of state government's daily duties and to Americans' disenchantment with an entirely legislature-driven

---

[52] Morgan and Morgan, op. cit., p. 359.

government.[53] In particular, as you read about in Chapter 7, lawmakers sometimes have a parochial view of public policy, focusing only on their respective districts and the next election coming up in a couple of years. The governor can take a broader view and, sometimes, a longer view. The governor is positioned as the single best person to understand the problems of the state overall and the competing interests at play. It's not that governors are perfect in these respects, it's just that, as an institution, no official is better placed to do so in state government. Today, the general public, the media, and the legislature all expect the governor to propose at least the broad parameters of state government policy. Of course, governors are no more policy dictators than they are dictators of the bureaucracy—less so, really. But the governor is expected to set the tone for state policy making.

In general, the governor's job as chief policy maker involves defining for the legislature and other relevant political actors which public problems are most important and which solutions are most feasible and effective. The state could address countless problems at any given time, but policy makers must ration its limited resources, choosing carefully which problems are most pressing and where the state can do the most good. Every state capital is swarming with people and organizations trying to interest policy makers in their pet problems, whether it is deteriorating highway bridges, ineffective pre-K education, overcrowded prisons, or what have you. The person who can define which issues are most important has tremendous power.[54] Wise governors use their powers judiciously to do just that.

Once the most important public problems have been identified, their potential solutions also need to be prioritized. Every public problem could be dealt with in many different ways. These various alternatives are not all likely to work equally well, and neither are they equally economically or politically feasible. As chief policy maker, the governor's job is to develop, weigh, and modify the various alternatives, and then to work for the adoption of the ones he or she thinks are best. As you know, the legislative process is so complex that it requires strong leadership to pass the laws that help determine state policy. But even though the governor has only a small formal role in this process (at the signing or vetoing stage), and even though lawmakers are sensitive about breaching the constitutional boundaries between the branches,[55] all those in and around the process expect the governor to use his or her powers to engage informally in the process at all stages. In addition, governors use their powers to set policy formally and informally in the administration of state government every day by establishing rules, plans, and norms in the bureaucracy.

Intergovernmental Relations Manager: Working Well with Others

An increasingly important job for governors has been acting as the point person for relationships between their states and other governments, including local governments, other state governments, the national government, and even foreign governments and Indian tribal governments.[56] The globalized economy, instant communications, and fast transportation mean that people, businesses, and governments interact with one another constantly and repeatedly, as you read about in Chapter 2. Commerce, social problems, and crime move freely across state borders, as they do, perhaps a little less freely, across international borders. Four states border Mexico, 10 border Canada, 16 others have ocean coastlines, 33 have federally recognized Native American tribes, and

[53] Nelson C. Dometrius, "Governors: Their Heritage and Future," in Ronald E. Weber and Paul Brace, eds., *American State and Local Politics: Directions for the 21st Century* (New York: Chatham House, 1999).
[54] John W. Kingdon, *Agendas, Alternatives, and Public Policies* (Glenview, IL: Scott, Foresman, 1984).

[55] Alan Rosenthal, *Heavy Lifting: The Job of the American Legislature* (Washington, DC: CQ Press, 2004), ch. 9.
[56] Thad Beyle, "Governors: The Middlemen and Women in Our Political System," in Virginia Gray and Herbert Jacob, eds., *Politics in the American States*, 6th ed. (Washington, DC: CQ Press, 1996).

every state has at least one international airport. In addition, each state has hundreds or thousands of local governments. As the central coordinating figure in state government, governors have by necessity taken on the role of intergovernmental relations (IGR) manager.

Many of these IGR interactions are financial, especially with so many federal grants coming to the states and state and federal grants going to local governments.[57] This net of financial transactions has drawn the three levels of American government so close that it is often hard to tell where one leaves off and another begins. Governors play an important role in coordinating these financial relationships, but their IGR duties go far beyond this. They work with representatives of other governments in negotiations over mutual and competing interests in much the same way that presidents do in international relations. Governors work with national governments to try to attract business to a state, as when Tennessee's Bredesen traveled to China, Japan, Switzerland, Germany, and Poland in the summer of 2009 to help bring jobs to a new mega-business park near Brownsville in western Tennessee, or when the governors of California, Texas, and New Mexico went to Mexico City in 2008 to discuss the explosion of drug violence in the borderlands with Mexican President Felipe Calderon.[58]

Governors regularly work with other governors to deal with mutual problems. Sometimes these are ad hoc issues between a small number of states, like when Missouri's Nixon and Illinois's Quinn worked together to promote building a high-speed rail corridor between Chicago and St. Louis.[59] More generally, the **National Governors Association (NGA)** is a 100-year-old nonpartisan institution that provides a vehicle for governors to consult one another about their common problems.[60] The NGA has significant staff resources and structured meetings and agendas through which governors both learn what other states are doing and how to work with them. Furthermore, the NGA works as an interest group for governors and the states, allowing them to speak with a single voice to Washington when they can agree to do so.

While it has become increasingly important in recent decades, the gubernatorial job of IGR manager is made more difficult by the fact that it is both newer and less well defined than the job of either chief policy maker or manager of the bureaucracy. Therefore, governors must use their powers creatively to be successful IGR managers.

The Powers of the Governor

How do governors accomplish the three jobs that we have just outlined? This is not an easy question to answer, perhaps since governors seem to work more idiosyncratically than other political actors in the states, such as legislators, judges, lobbyists, and so forth. Or perhaps the fact that there is only one governor per state at any given time makes their idiosyncrasies more obvious. The personal variations in their behavior sometimes make it hard for scholars to draw useful generalizations about gubernatorial behavior. Certainly scholars who study U.S. presidents have this problem in the extreme.[61] But those studying American governors have worked to deal with this by analyzing, comparing, and generalizing about various **gubernatorial powers**.[62] While it is true that, like

---

[57] Timothy J. Conlan and Paul L. Posner, eds., *Intergovernmental Management for the Twenty-First Century* (Washington, DC: Brookings Institution, 2008).

[58] Associated Press, "Tenn. Governor Plans Trade Mission to Japan, China," *Boston Globe*, 30 June 2009, online ed.; Juliet Williams, "Border Governors Head to Mexico as Violence Rises," *Arizona (Tucson) Daily Star*, 2 June 2008, online ed.

[59] Jake Wagman, "Jay Nixon, Pat Quinn on Board High-Speed Rail Plan," *St. Louis Post-Dispatch*, 27 June 2009.

[60] Pamela M. Prah, "Govs Celebrate Past, Look to '09," *Stateline.org*, 7 November 2008, online ed.; Pamela M. Prah, "Governors Hopeful after Obama Meeting," *Stateline.org*, 3 December 2008, online ed.

[61] Gary King and Lyn Ragsdale, *The Elusive Executive: Discovering Statistical Patterns in the Presidency* (Washington, DC: Congressional Quarterly Press, 1988).

[62] Thad Beyle and Margaret Ferguson, "Governors and the Executive Branch," in *Politics in the American States*, 9th ed. (Washington, DC: CQ Press, 2008).

with presidents, gubernatorial power is largely the power to persuade,[63] governors have a variety of tools—both formal and informal—that, when used skillfully, can make them more "persuasive." We talk here about governors' formal and informal "powers," but keep in mind that they each define a continuum of power or control over a given situation. These are tools that vary a great deal from state to state, so that the office of governor is more or less strong from state to state and even, especially in the case of informal powers, from governor to governor.

Formal Powers—A Governor's Institutional Tools

The formal powers that states give their governors, largely in their constitutions and statutes, are institutions available to any governor working under a given legal arrangement. These are powers that a state's policy makers have explicitly decided to give to their governors. In recent decades, the states have increased their governors' formal powers in each of these areas, but significant variation among the states remains.

Control over the Budget The number-one problem facing governors and states in recent years has been balancing their states' budgets. The current recession has hit the states with a double whammy—their expenses are up as more people and businesses need state government help and their revenues are down as their principle tax bases, income and sales, have declined or not grown normally.[64] But as you will see in Chapter 10, the budget is always the central concern of state policy makers because it is perhaps the most concrete expression of a state's public policy. Almost everything a state does, from providing needy children with health care to housing prisoners to building and maintaining roads, requires spending money, and the budget plans

and authorizes all the state's spending, as well as lays out the sources of its revenue.

Although the budget must pass through the regular legislative process each year,[65] all but a few states give the governor special institutional powers in the budget process that they do not have in regular lawmaking. To begin with, most governors have the responsibility to estimate the revenues for the coming year and to propose spending for most agencies. This gives them a great advantage over the legislature and bureaucracy in determining where and how state money will be spent.[66] A budget bill[67] is extremely technical, detailed, and complex, so the legislature often can only review and edit it around the edges, with most of the governor's proposal usually being adopted. On the other hand, special fees and taxes that are dedicated by statute for particular purposes limit governors' budget-making power by reducing the discretion with which they can target spending. For example, gasoline taxes that are statutorily committed to building new roads cannot be used to buy textbooks or even fund mass transit. Although **dedicated funds** are still a relatively small part of most states' budgets, many interest groups advocate them strongly for their pet programs so that they will be more immune to cuts in the future.

Of course, in bad economic times like we are in today, with revenues falling and expenses

---

[63] Richard E. Neustadt, *Presidential Power and the Modern Presidents* (New York: Free Press, 1990).

[64] Donald J. Boyd and Lucy Dadayan, "State Tax Decline in Early 2009 Was the Sharpest on Record," *State Revenue Report* 76(July 2009): 1–19.

[65] For those few states that still do biennial budgeting, the budget bill(s) must pass through the legislature every two years.

[66] William Ewell, "Measuring Institutional Political Power in the American States," presented at the 8th Annual State Politics and Policy Conference, Temple University, 2008; Doug Goodman, "Determinants of Perceived Gubernatorial Budgetary Influence among State Executive Budget Analysts and Legislative Fiscal Analysts," *Political Research Quarterly* 60(2007): 43–54; James W. Douglas and Kim U. Hoffman, "Impoundment at the State Level: Executive Power and Budget Impact," *American Review of Public Administration* 34(2004): 252–58; Dall W. Forsythe, *Memos to the Governor: An Introduction to State Budgeting*, 2nd ed. (Washington, DC: Georgetown University Press, 2004); Charles Barrilleaux and Michael Berkman, "Do Governors Matter? Budgeting and the Politics of State Policymaking," *Political Research Quarterly* 56(2003): 409–17.

[67] Some states use a series of bills for the budget, but the principle here is the same.

rising, having their special budget responsibility is a mixed blessing for governors, at best. Even Democrats like North Carolina's Perdue and Maryland's Patrick O'Malley are ordering massive budget cuts and Republicans like Arizona's Brewer and Utah's Huntsman are pushing for tax hikes.[68] In 2009, several Republican governors tried to make political hay by rejecting some of the federal stimulus money—the so-called "Obama Bucks"—that was being sent to the states to fight the recession. While these governors also had some legitimate policy concerns with this program,[69] their opposition to this seemingly "free" money during hard budget times became a public relations problem for most of them. South Carolina's Sanford was even sued successfully by a high school student to accept the money.[70] On the other hand, sometimes a smart governor can use budget crises to eliminate waste, cut old programs that have out-lived their usefulness, and otherwise craft government to bring public policy more in line with his or her vision for the state.[71]

Veto Powers As discussed in Chapter 7, a governor's only institutional role in the state's legislative process is after both chambers have passed a bill in identical form, when the governor must choose whether to sign it into law or to veto it, sending it back to the legislature for further consideration. Legislatures have the opportunity to override a veto by voting again in favor of the bill in both chambers, usually by a supermajority vote. But given the difficulty of mustering a supermajority on a controversial measure (and a bill is controversial by definition if it has been vetoed by the governor), vetoes are very difficult to override.[72] For example, during his 14-year tenure in Wisconsin in the 1980s and 1990s, Republican Governor Tommy Thompson made 1,937 legislative vetoes, and the Democrat-controlled Wisconsin legislature failed to override a single one of them.[73] However, conflict over tough questions of government cutbacks appears to have led to more veto overrides during the current period of economic hardship. For example, South Carolina's Sanford issued 243 vetoes in a recent budget bill—and the legislature overrode 228 of them; Connecticut's Rell was overridden on seven bills in a single day.[74]

Governors in different states have different levels of veto power. All governors can execute a full, or "package," veto on bills—the same veto power as the president. But in most states, the governor's veto power is even stronger than that of the president. First, 44 governors have the **line-item veto,** the ability to veto one or more specific lines in a bill while letting the rest of it pass into law.[75] In 30 of these states, the governor can only line-item veto **appropriations bills,** and these money bills are where governors most often use the item-veto. Indeed, the item veto is designed so that the legislature cannot hold an entire bill hostage for a single aspect of it that the governor finds objectionable. Twelve states also give their governors the **reduction veto** on appropriations bills, allowing them to reduce the amount that is authorized to be spent on a budget item. In addition, six states give their governors even greater

---

[68] Mark Binker, "Perdue Mandates Furlough for State Workers," *(Greensboro) News-Record,* 29 April 2009, online ed.; Daniel Scarpinato, "Brewer: Fix Deficit by Raising Sales Tax," *Arizona (Tucson) Daily Star,* 2 June 2009, online ed.; Robert Gehrke, "Huntsman Wants to Push Cigarette Tax to $3," *The Salt Lake Tribune,* 7 January 2009, online ed.; Laura Smitherman, "O'Malley Calls for 5% Cuts in State Agencies' Budgets," *Baltimore Sun,* 26 September 2008, online ed.

[69] Peter A. Harkness, "When the Well Runs Dry," *Governing,* May 2009, pp. 18–19.

[70] Rich Brundrett, "S.C. High Court Orders Sanford to Accept Money," *The State (Columbia, SC),* 7 June 2009, online ed.

[71] Raymond C. Scheppach, "The Economic Downturn: An Opportunity for Governors?" *Stateline.org,* 2 April 2008, online ed.

[72] Vicky M. Wilkins and Garry Young, "The Influence of Governors on Veto Override Attempts: A Test of Pivotal Politics," *Legislative Studies Quarterly* 27(2002): 557–76.

[73] Steven Walters, "Thompson's Legacy," *Milwaukee (WI) Journal-Sentinel,* 24 December 2000, pp. 1A, 10A.

[74] Andy Brack, "Policy Vetoes Go over Better Than Ideological Ones," *South Carolina Statehouse Report.com,* 1 July 2007; Christopher Keating. "Historic Day for Legislature as Seven Vetoes Are Overridden," *Hartford (CT) Courant,* 13 August 2009, on-line ed.

[75] For the details on which governors have which type of veto power, see: Wall op. cit., pp. 185–86.

power with the **amendatory veto,** which allows them to send a bill back to the legislature with a message asking for a specific change.[76] The legislature can then either override the veto by passing the original bill or item with a supermajority vote or pass the governor's suggested language with a simple majority vote. Because it is often much easier to generate a simple majority to agree with the governor than to generate a supermajority to oppose him or her, the amendatory veto can be a powerful tool.

These types of veto vary in their effectiveness and in allowing governors more or less surgical control in their response to legislation.[77] And they also vary in their power beyond just the obvious ability to stop a bill or item from becoming law. As we have seen, the legislative process is complex, and it is easy to derail a bill. So if a bill that he or she disapproves of gets to the governor's desk, that governor has missed many earlier opportunities. The implied threat of the veto is always an arrow in the governor's quiver, and it gives lawmakers strong incentive to craft bills with the governor's wishes in mind. Not surprisingly, governors issue more vetoes when they face a legislature controlled by the other party, whose policy preferences are more likely to differ from those of the governor.[78] Governors with strong institutional veto powers are also more likely to use this tool.

Appointment Powers Governors vary considerably in their ability to make appointments to positions in government. These include appointments to judgeships and various boards and commissions, but the most important powers of appointment tend to be those to top posts in the executive branch. Governors who can put their own people into most of the policy-making and upper-management positions in the executive branch can better control the bureaucracy and policy implementation.[79] This helps a governor get policies administered as he or she wants them to be, and it forces those who want to influence such an agency to deal with the governor or the governor's appointee. Governors can also reward their supporters with positions of prestige and power, and such appointments can even be used as bargaining chips for a governor in dealing with state legislators or others in the policy-making process. Democratic Strickland used some appointments in a creative—and very political—way in Ohio in 2008 when he appointed some Republican legislators from swing districts to administrative positions, thus giving his party a better chance of winning those seats in the next election.[80] On the other hand, when a governor's appointee does something embarrassing, the governor is often held responsible, at least politically. But overall, a governor is stronger if he or she appoints more rather than fewer state government officials.

Beyond merely the number of appointments governors get to make, their appointment powers vary in two important ways among the states. First, as we will talk more about later in this chapter, some states allow for the direct and independent election of various top-level executive branch officials, including the lieutenant governor, attorney general, secretary of state, treasurer, and others. The impact on gubernatorial power of this is that when these officials are elected independently, not only can governors not control them or their agencies

---

[76] In addition to Alabama, Illinois, Massachusetts, Montana, New Jersey, and Virginia, South Dakota gives its governor the amendatory veto when the legislature is in session, and Wisconsin does so only on budget bills; see: Daniel C. Vock, "Govs Enjoy Quirky Veto Power," *Stateline.org*, 24 April 2007, online ed.

[77] Thad Kousser and Justin H. Phillips, "Reevaluating the Item Veto," presented at the 8th Annual State Politics and Policy Conference, Temple University, 2008; J. A. Dearden and T. A. Husted, "Do Governors Get What They Want? An Alternative Examination of the Line-Item Veto," *Public Choice* 77(1993): 707–23.

[78] Carl E. Klarner and Andrew Karch, "Why Do Governors Issue Vetoes? The Impact of Individual and Institutional Influences," *Political Research Quarterly* 61(2008): 574–84.

[79] Thad Beyle, "Being Governor," in Carl E. Van Horn, ed., *The State of the States*, 4th ed. (Washington, DC: CQ Press, 2006).

[80] Jim Siegel, "Strickland to Hire GOP Incumbents," *The Columbus (OH) Dispatch*, 23 July 2008, online ed.

directly, but they may also actually be rivals for power. Remember that many governors held one of these positions themselves before moving up to the governor's mansion.

The states also vary in how far up into the managerial positions of the bureaucracy a state's **civil service system** reaches. At one time, some governors would gain political power from handing out as many as 20,000 **patronage jobs** to political supporters and their families. Although no one begrudges a governor the power to appoint the top managers of state government so as to hold the bureaucracy accountable and set public policy, many of these positions—such as workers on road construction crews and driver's license examiners—clearly

REFORM CAN HAPPEN

LIMITING GUBERNATORIAL INTERIM APPOINTMENT POWERS—TAKING SOME OF THE LUSTER OFF OF THESE "(BLEEPING) GOLDEN" THINGS

In the predawn Chicago hours of December 9, 2008, federal agents rousted Illinois Governor Rod Blagojevich out of a sound slumber, arresting him on charges of committing a series of corrupt acts. Perhaps the most startling of these alleged acts[1] was the federal prosecutors' claim that Blagojevich had offered to appoint the highest bidder as replacement for then-President-Elect Barack Obama in the U.S. Senate. Under Illinois state law, the governor could, without consultation or approval, make such an appointment. As Blagojevich was taped saying to an aide, that unilateral power made this "a (bleeping) golden" opportunity for corruption. This power was demonstrated when three weeks after his arrest, in the middle of the impeachment process that would force him from power in a few weeks, Blagojevich appointed former Illinois Attorney General Roland Burris to Obama's seat. The fact that Blagojevich could make that appointment in the face of the public outrage following his arrest further illustrates the unchecked power in his hands.

The Blagojevich-Burris affair was more than just another unseemly episode in a long series of unseemly episodes in Illinois political history. Obama administration appointments in 2009 led to Senate vacancies in New York, Delaware, and Colorado that caused related, if less dramatic and criminal, controversies.[2] The death of Senator Ted Kennedy in 2009 led the Democrat-dominated

AP Photo/Seth Wenig

Then-Governor Rod Blagojevich takes a "perp walk" on December 9, 2008, after being arrested on multiple charges of public corruption. Among other things, Blagojevich was charged with trying to sell the appointment to replace Barack Obama in the U.S. Senate after his election to the presidency.

Massachusetts legislature to reverse a policy it had established in 2004 for fear that then-Governor Mitt Romney, a Republican, could appoint a replacement in case Senator John Kerry defeated President George Bush. In 2002, Alaska Governor Frank Murkowski appointed his daughter, Lisa Murkowski, to a vacant seat in the Senate, leading to cries of nepotism, and the resulting uproar helped Sarah Palin beat him in the 2006 gubernatorial primary. In addition to Senate replacements, some states allow governors the unilateral power to appoint replacements for state court judgeships (see Chapter 9), some statewide elected officials, and others.

Most gubernatorial appointments to high-level positions require some sort of legislative or voter approval, but the appointment of interim officeholders is, in many states, an exception to this. As a matter of public policy, such appointments have a legitimate argument. Legislative approval for interim appointments can take time and special elections are expensive, but gubernatorial appointments are fast and cheap. So for some jobs that need to be filled quickly, the desire for frugality and alacrity, combined with faith in governors' goodwill and intentions, have informed public policy here. But these recent interim appointment controversies have put into stark relief the potential for corruption, or even just bias, that giving governors unchecked interim appointment power can yield, and this has led to reform efforts in many states. For example, the Murkowski controversy led to a 2004 ballot initiative that stripped Alaska governors of the power to appoint interim Senate replacements.[3] Other states have also taken this power from their governors for the Senate and other offices, while others have imposed restrictions on interim appointments, such as mandating special elections, that the appointee be a member of the same party as the person in the vacated position, and legislative approval.[4] As is often the case in public policy making, this is a case of demonstrated public problems leading to a reevaluation of values and the reform of public policy in response.

Notes

1. At press time, Blagojevich has not been convicted of, nor admitted to, any of these crimes.
2. Jim Abrams, "Renewed Demand to Change the Way Open Seats Filled," *The Boston Globe*, 28 August 2008, on-line ed.
3. John Gramlich, "Furor over Senate Seat Not Unique to Illinois," *Stateline.org*, 23 December 2008, online ed.
4. Kathleen Miller, "Lawmakers Push for Voters to Fill Senate Vacancies," *State Journal-Register* (*Springfield, IL*), 5 February 2009, p. 12.

had no policy-making power. Although state legislators might not be persuaded to vote for a governor's bill by the offer of a road crew job for themselves, they might be happy to get one of these jobs for a constituent or supporter. States with extensive civil service systems hire more workers through merit testing, giving governors less power over the bureaucracy and fewer political bargaining chips. But sometimes patronage appointments can be more trouble than they are worth. Not only does a strong, merit-based civil service system help the governor give the state high-quality public service, it also helps him or her avoid scandals in the bureaucracy that can be tied to back to the governor.

Term Length and Term Limits A governor is more powerful if those with whom he or she deals in the political process believe that he or she may be around for a long time. Governors who will soon be leaving office have less to threaten or offer those with whom they negotiate. State bureaucrats, interest groups, and legislators (at least where no legislative term limits are in place) may be able just to wait out a governor who will soon be replaced, giving them little incentive to compromise. Of course, how long a governor serves depends in large part on voters (and, in some cases, federal prosecutors), but two institutions also affect a governor's tenure potential: term length and term limits. Look back at Table 8.1 to see how these vary among the states.

Institutional reforms in recent decades seem to have been inconsistent with respect to gubernatorial tenure. First, many states lengthened their governors' terms in the 1960s and 1970s, changing from two-year to four-year terms. Today, only governors in Vermont and New Hampshire have two-year terms, and even these states continue to consider moving to four-year terms. On the other hand, the states are also moving quietly toward term-limiting their governors, with fully 37 states now doing so in some way. As a result of these diverging patterns, 32 states now allow only two consecutive four-year terms, just as the 22nd Amendment does for the U.S. president.

Executive Orders Governors, like presidents, can issue **executive orders**, official pronouncements that mandate certain government actions.[81] Executive orders are public documents, typically filed with the secretary of state or some other official for public access. They have the force of law, but their scope is usually limited and they can be overturned by future governors simply with another executive order. The power of governors to make executive orders varies as to whether they are authorized by statute, constitution, or simply tradition; by the areas of policy in which a governor is authorized to make such orders; and whether they can be reviewed by the legislature or are subject to any other restrictions.[82] Governors are typically authorized to make executive orders in four policy areas: to reorganize or control the bureaucracy; to call out the National Guard to respond to emergencies or crises; to set up commissions to study particularly vexing public problems; or to respond to federal rules, regulations, and initiatives. The stronger the legal basis for these executive orders, the broader the scope of their power, and the fewer restrictions or less oversight of them, the more potent a tool they become for a governor.

Tools to Influence the Legislative Agenda
Governors have two institutional powers that help them influence the legislature's **policy agenda**. First, at the beginning of each legislative session, governors give a **State of the State (SOS) address** to the legislature,[83] a major speech much like the president's annual State of the Union address. The SOS address provides an opportunity for governors to identify the public problems that they think their legislatures should tackle in the coming session and to offer a list of proposals to address those problems.[84] As the symbolic kickoff of the legislative session and an important set-piece event on a state's political calendar, governors imbue their SOS addresses with rhetoric that reflects the state's values and interests as well as their own personalities.[85] Of course, the legislature is not in any way bound to follow the agenda the governor lays out in the SOS address, but traditionally, these proposals receive serious consideration. Indeed, legislators will complain of a lack of leadership if the governor's SOS address does not offer them clear guidance.

The other institutional power that lets governors set the legislative agenda is their ability to call the state legislature into **special session** once its regular session has been adjourned. Just the threat of a special session can be a potent weapon against part-time legislatures because it would require these members to sacrifice extra time from their "regular" jobs. Lawmakers may quickly acquiesce to the governor's legislative demands to avoid this overtime work, for

---

[81] Margaret R. Ferguson and Cynthia J. Bowling, "Executive Orders and Administrative Control," *Public Administration Review* 68(2008): S20–S28.

[82] Wall, op. cit., pp. 187–88.

[83] In some states, this is called a budget address; in some states, governors will give both a SOS address and a budget address; sometimes during a governor's first term, his or her inaugural speech serves this function. Regardless of what it is called, all governors have some more or less official way to communicate at the beginning of a legislative session what they want lawmakers to consider during it.

[84] Margaret R. Ferguson, "Gubernatorial Policy Leadership in the Fifty States" (Ph.D. diss., University of North Carolina at Chapel Hill, 1996).

[85] Barbara Ferrara, "The Effect of Gender on a Governor's Policy Agenda" (D.P.A. diss., University of Illinois at Springfield, 2010); J. Cherie Strachan, "Citizenship, Leadership and Public Life in the Gubernatorial Phetoric from Three Distinct States," presented at the 8th Annual State Politics and Policy Conference, Temple University, 2008; Margaret R. Ferguson and Jay Barth, "Governors in the Legislative Arena: The Importance of Personality in Shaping Success," *Political Psychology* 23(2002): 787–808.

which they do not receive extra pay.[86] Special sessions are especially important tools in those six states where the legislature only holds a regular session once every two years and those many other states where the length of their regular sessions is otherwise severely limited by law. Special sessions allow legislatures to deal with policy problems as they arise rather than waiting perhaps many months to reconvene.

What can make this ability an effective tool is that, more than simply assembling legislators in a special session, governors are empowered to set a limited agenda for that session, in effect forcing lawmakers to consider specific issues. For example, in the summer and fall of 2009, governors in Indiana, California, West Virginia, and many other states called special

sessions to force their state legislatures to deal with recession-related budget crises. Calling a special session not only shows the legislature that the governor really cares about an issue, but it also puts the media's spotlight on their deliberations, increasing pressure on lawmakers to act. On the other hand, while the governor can force the legislature into special session on a particular issue, he or she cannot force it to pass anything. A recalcitrant legislature can simply adjourn a special session without taking any action. Occasionally, a battle royal ensues as the governor keeps calling the legislature into special session and the legislature keeps adjourning itself without acting.[87] But this sort of brouhaha is rare because the media, the public, and rank-and-file legislators

COMPARISONS HELP US UNDERSTAND

THE INSTITUTIONAL POWER OF THE GOVERNORS

Figure 8.4 shows how governors' formal, institutional powers vary around the country. This index of gubernatorial powers is made up of indicators based on the number of independently elected executives in a state and a governor's appointment power over leaders of state agencies, term length and term limits, budget control, veto strength, and executive order strength. These powers are all based on state laws and constitutional provisions that states have adopted primarily as a way of establishing a governorship with the level of power and control over the state bureaucracy and state policy making that their policy makers think appropriate. Like all indicators of social science concepts, this one is not perfect, but it does give us an idea about the types of states where citizens and policy makers think their governors should be more or less powerful.[1]

First, you see that some of the states in the South have weaker governorships. This is probably a legacy of the reaction to the strong **Reconstruction era** governors in the post–Civil War era. Another apparent pattern is that more populous and urban states tend to have more powerful governorships, whereas smaller, rural states tend to have weaker ones. This might be a case of states equipping their governors with just the level of power they need to deal with the forces at work in their states. Governors in large or urban states must contend both with more diverse public problems and with a broader range of actors in the policy-making arena, such as big-city mayors, strong unions, major industries and corporations, and so forth. Perhaps these governors need greater formal power just to do their jobs as well as those governors with less formal power do theirs in the small, rural states where they are big fish in a small pond. What other patterns do you detect in this figure? What state characteristics have you read about in earlier chapters that might be relevant here? For example, how might legislative professionalism factor in here? What other historical or institutional or demographic features might lead a state to want or need a stronger governor or a weaker one? Try both to develop hypotheses in this regard and to test those arguments by looking at the data in Figure 8.4

(continued)

---

[86] Legislators usually receive expense money for these special sessions to cover their meals, hotels, and so on, but they do not typically receive extra salary for them.

[87] Doug Finke, "Under Pressure: Groups Push Jones on Budget Cuts Vote," (*Springfield, Ill.*) *State Journal-Register*, 4 October 2007, p. 1.

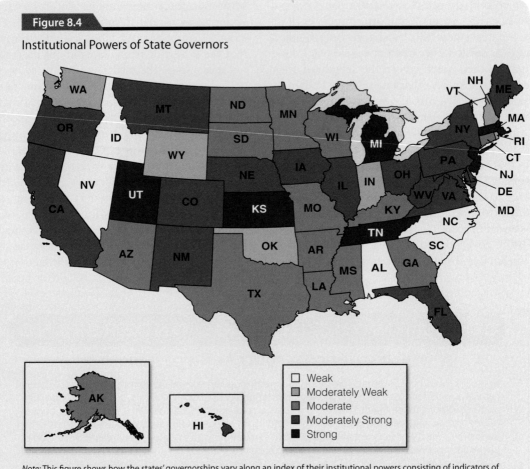

Figure 8.4

Institutional Powers of State Governors

Legend:
- ☐ Weak
- Moderately Weak
- Moderate
- Moderately Strong
- ■ Strong

Note: This figure shows how the states' governorships vary along an index of their institutional powers consisting of indicators of independently elected executives, appointment power over leaders of state agencies, term length and term limits, budget control, veto strength, and executive order power.

Source: Scale developed by the authors with data from: Thad Beyle and Margaret Ferguson, "Governors and the Executive Branch," in *Politics in the American States,* 9th ed. (Washington, DC: CQ Press, 2008), pp. 212–213; and Wall, op. cit., pp. 187–188.

Note
1. Beyle and Ferguson, op. cit.; Pamela M. Prah, "Massachusetts Gov Rated Most Powerful," *Stateline.org,* 9 March 2007, online ed.

quickly get fed up with the spectacle and the expense, giving both lawmakers and the governor strong incentive to settle their differences.[88]

---

[88] Greg Bluestein, "Special Sessions on Budgets Costly," *State Journal-Register (Springfield, IL),* 25 July 2009, p. 7.

Informal Powers—Unofficial, but Potent

In addition to the formal, institutional powers that states give their governors as a matter of official public policy, the circumstances surrounding the office, the state, and the incumbent himself or herself also help determine how effective a governor can be in running the state. These informal powers are not as easy to see or compare as are the institutional powers, but that does not make them any the less important in understanding how a given state's governors, or any given governor within a state, does the job. Like formal powers, their potency can vary among states, among governors within a state, and sometimes even over the term of a single governor. Certain informal powers are hard to study. For example, some governors are just more charismatic or intelligent than others. While these characteristics can certainly affect a governor's performance, assessing them systematically would be difficult. But several important dimensions of a governor's informal power are comparable across the states and across time and are based on the office itself rather than on the person holding it. Of course, just as with the institutional powers, the effectiveness of these informal powers in helping governors manage a state and achieve their policy agendas depends in large part on the skills of the governor in using them.

Head of State As mentioned earlier, the governor is a state's symbolic "head of state," representing the state to people both within and outside of the state, just as the queen of England does for her country and the president does for the United States as a whole. Using this symbolic role, governors can gain **political capital** by undertaking largely ceremonial duties that get them around the state in a positive way. Greeting school children, giving commencement speeches, cutting ribbons on public projects, and so forth allow people to see a governor in a positive, nonpolitical light. As head of state, governors also gain influence because modern-day Americans want executive leadership from our government. When we think about government acting to help us, we often think about the governor, the president, or the mayor rather than the state legislature, the Congress, or the city council. Governors can benefit from this attitude by stepping into the role forthrightly, pursuing an active policy agenda in the legislature and taking a strong hand with the executive agencies.

Acting in his head of state role, California Governor Arnold Schwarzenegger breaks ground on a new biotech manufacturer in Vacaville.

Although other actors in the political system may sometimes chafe under such an "imperial" governor, like the general public, they too expect the governor to lead and will complain if such leadership does not materialize. Indeed, one study found that even in a highly partisan state legislature, bills advocated by the governor were regularly supported even by members of the opposite party—except during election years.[89]

Besides the ceremonial duties that governors use to burnish their image, they often take symbolic actions as head of state to demonstrate sympathy with their constituents in a politically useful way. In 2009 and 2010, for example, governors frequently demonstrated that they were aware of and working to fix the economic recession and states' budget crises. Delaware's Markell was among many who cancelled their inaugural balls in January 2009 to show fiscal responsibility and concern. As an alternative, Markell led a "Weekend of Service" to help those in need.[90] Other governors, like Connecticut's Rell and Kentucky's Steve Beshear, very publicly took pay cuts

[89] Thad E. Hall, "Changes in Legislative Support for the Governor's Program over Time," *Legislative Studies Quarterly* 27(2002):107–22.
[90] Emily Bazar, "Many Governors Cut Glitz from Inaugurations," *USA Today*, 9 December 2008, online ed.

and furlough days right along with other state workers.[91]

Being the head of state can also backfire if things do not go well. A governor who is not a strong and visible leader may lose influence with the people and state officials. Some have argued that this, rather than reactions to specific objectionable actions, was in large part what led to California Governor Gray Davis's recall ouster in 2003.[92] Furthermore, governors are often blamed for state actions, even if they had little to do with them. A quaint example of this from the 1950s and 1960s was a reaction in many states to their initial adoption of the sales tax. Upset with the increased paperwork and expense, shopkeepers would often ring up the price of an item at the cash register, adding, ". . . and a penny for the governor."[93]

Public Opinion Related to the power of being head of state is the effect of public opinion on a governor's informal power. Governors have long used the argument that their statewide electoral mandate gives them the backing of the state's people for whatever they want to do. Since the advent of public opinion polling, a governor's support in the state can be assessed more finely and followed as it changes throughout the term.[94] A governor riding high in the polls will be quick to point out this fact to obstinate legislators, bureaucrats, or the media. Lawmakers, in particular, are much more susceptible to the blandishments of a popular governor's because they have to face the voters themselves. On the other hand, a governor's sliding poll numbers may embolden opposition lawmakers.

Governors monitor their ratings closely through their own private polls (sometimes run through their campaign offices to avoid any suggestion of impropriety) and do what they can to keep them high, such as using their head of state role to appear at popular, non-political functions like county fairs and state championship sporting events. Some governors go even further, like when California's Schwarzenegger executed an extensive and sophisticated public image "makeover" after his poll numbers began to drop in his first term.[95] But much of a governor's popularity is beyond his or her direct control. As a governor's term progresses, he or she will have to make choices that disappoint and anger some members of the public, causing his or her popularity to decline over time, just as it does for presidents. But one study found that while this leads to governors having lower popularity than, for example, U.S. senators when a reelection campaign begins, unlike senators, governors can use their other formal and informal powers to improve their popularity substantially during the campaign.[96]

Other factors beyond a governor's control can also affect his or her popularity. For example, governors of large states tend to have lower ratings than governors of less populated states. Larger and densely populated states tend to have more, bigger, and more complex public problems than other states, making the job of governor more difficult. The national economy is another strong influence on gubernatorial popularity that is largely out of a governor's hands.[97] On the other hand, the state economy also has an impact here, and governors probably have at least some control

[91] Mark Pazniokas, "Governor Takes Symbolic Step to Reduce State Deficit," *The (Hartford, CT) Courant*, 14 January 2009, online ed.; Jack Brammer, Jim Warren, and Beth Musgrave, "Beshear Takes 10% Pay Cut," Lexington Herald-Leader, 9 December 2008.

[92] Michael Lewis, "The Personal Is the Antipolitical," *New York Times Magazine* 153(2003): 40–130.

[93] Philip J. Roberts, *A Penny for the Governor, a Dollar for Uncle Sam: Income Taxation in Washington* (Seattle: University of Washington Press, 2002).

[94] Richard G. Niemi, Thad Beyle, and Lee Sigelman, "Gubernatorial, Senatorial, and State-Level Presidential Job Approval: The U.S. Officials Job Approval Ratings (JAR) Collection," *State Politics and Policy Quarterly* 2(2002): 215–29.

[95] Gary Delsohn, "Governor Embarks on Image Change," *Sacramento Bee*, 26 July 2005, online ed.

[96] Brown and Jacobson, op. cit.

[97] James D. King and Jeffrey E. Cohen, "What Determines a Governor's Popularity?" *State Politics and Policy Quarterly* 5(2005): 225–47.

over this.[98] Governors' actual or perceived handling of major state crises can also affect their popularity. West Virginia's Joe Manchin saw his popularity rise dramatically when he was seen as handling a coal-mining disaster effectively in 2006, whereas public approval of Louisiana's Kathleen Blanco went down fast after the Hurricane Katrina debacle. And, of course, a scandal, whether caused by a governor or his or her appointees, can reduce popularity quickly.[99]

Mass Media Attention Governors also try to influence their popularity through the skillful use of the mass media. The governor's office is especially well positioned to gain political capital from the effective use of print, broadcast, and online media, and the special attention they get from the media relative to other state policy makers is one of their primary informal powers.

Of course, the governor is clearly an important and well-known person whose actions are significant to a lot of people. But governors attract special media attention for a variety of other reasons, much of them having to do with the fact that it is just much easier to report on and understand state government by focusing on the governor. The governor is a single, authoritative news source. Who speaks authoritatively for the legislature, the courts, or the bureaucracy? No one. Who seems more reliable and unbiased on any given issue, the governor or an interest group spokesperson? Often, it is the former. Certainly, significant, thoughtful, and honest people work in all those other institutions, but in none is there a single, recognizable news source that a reporter can go to time and again for the final word on that institution's position on an issue.

Also, keep in mind that news organizations make money by attracting readers, viewers, or listeners. It is easier to do this by discussing a familiar person rather than a more obscure official—like the speaker of the state house—who, although important, would need to be introduced to the media consumer before getting to the heart of the story. Americans' attention span for political news is extremely short, especially for news about state politics.[100] The governor is just easier to understand than the legislature—both for media consumers and for reporters. The governor is like the boss of the state or the parent of the family; people are familiar with this role, even if it does distort reality. Legislatures are complex, mysterious, and unfamiliar, so it is harder to write a relatively short, understandable news story about them. It is also no accident that governors' power and prestige rose in the 1960s and 1970s just as television became the main source of political news for Americans.[101] Governors are particularly attractive for television news, where stories are much shorter than in newspapers and rely more on pictures. A governor speaking at a press conference or giving a speech makes pretty good television; a governor touring a disaster site makes great television. On the other hand, the state legislature in session makes bad television (except as a background shot while the reporter speaks); legislative negotiations and discussions are even worse.

Governors also work hard to make the job of reporters very easy. They hire professional media relations staff (many of whom are former statehouse reporters themselves) to develop effective press releases and manufacture television-friendly media events at times convenient for news deadlines. Some governors even send out prepackaged video clips of themselves making brief comments on current issues. This allows those TV stations without the resources to have their own

[98] Jeffrey E. Cohen and James D. King, "Relative Unemployment and Gubernatorial Popularity," *Journal of Politics* 66(2004): 167–82.
[99] Jay Barth and Margaret R. Ferguson, "American Governors and their Constituents: The Relationship between Gubernatorial Personality and Public Approval," *State Politics and Policy Quarterly* 2(2002): 268–82.
[100] G. Patrick Lynch, "The Media in State and Local Politics," in Mark J. Rozell, ed., *Media Power, Media Politics* (Lanham, MD: Rowman & Littlefield, 2003).
[101] Dometrius, op. cit.

statehouse reporter—which is most stations, these days—to air footage that looks like their own reporter actually interviewed the governor. Of course, governors are not likely to send out footage that makes themselves look bad, so while they help the station get good video for the nightly news, they present themselves in a good light without fear of any tough questions from reporters. Of course, while this can only help a governor's popularity, it does raise serious questions about the quality and ethics of journalism about state government.

Gubernatorial Staff Each governor employs a sizable body of personal staff who work directly for him or her in whatever way the governor wishes to arrange them.[102] Their staff includes press spokespeople, legislative liaisons, and deputy governors to coordinate policy areas that spread out over a variety of agencies, such as education or drug enforcement. Unlike cabinet secretaries and other official managerial appointees, these staff members are solely responsible to the governor and should have no mixed loyalties. They have no agencies or interest groups to appease, and their appointments typically are not subject to legislative approval. Their staff serves as the governor's extra eyes, ears, feet, and hands, greatly extending his or her reach and information-gathering ability and acting as a proxy for the governor.[103]

The size of a governor's staff varies dramatically across states, from a dozen close aides and secretaries to an extended office of well over 100 staffers in a variety of roles, with the largest governor's offices being found in the more populous states.[104] In some states, the budget office is considered part of

the governor's staff. This unit has the primary responsibility for developing the governor's budget proposal and monitoring the budget's execution throughout the fiscal year. As governors have gained more budget authority in recent decades, these offices have been increasingly shifted to governors' direct control rather than being independent units. For many governors, the state budget office now acts as one of the main tools for controlling the bureaucracy and guiding policy, much the same way that presidents now use the federal Office of Management and Budget.[105]

The Governor in the State's Political Environment

Although the governor is the head of state, chief executive, and the single most important political figure in most states most of the time, he or she is only one actor in a large and complex political system. Therefore, governors' effectiveness not only depends on their formal and informal powers, it is also affected by the political environment in which they find themselves. Elsewhere in this book, you read in detail about many of these other actors and aspects of the state political environment, but in this section, we discuss two aspects of the environment that have very special impacts on a governor's ability to govern: the partisan balance in the legislature and other rivals for power. Like governors' formal and informal powers, these vary among the states in relatively clear and observable ways.

Partisan Balance in the State Legislature

A governor's ability to make public policy, and the ways in which a governor goes about trying to make public policy, depends in large part on the partisan balance in the state legislature.

---

[102] National Governors Association, *Governor's Office Operations: The Many Roles of the Governor's Chief of Staff.* (Washington, DC: National Governors Association, 2006).

[103] Robert J. Dilger, "A Comparative Analysis of Gubernatorial Enabling Resources," *State and Local Government Review* 26(1995): 118–26.

[104] Margaret R. Ferguson, *The Executive Branch of State Government* (Santa Barbara, CA: ABC-CLIO, 2006), pp. 176–79.

[105] Forsythe, op. cit.

Lawmakers of the governor's party are often thought of, and often think of themselves, as loyal lieutenants of the governor. In particular, an important job of the legislative leaders of the governor's party is to marshal the party's members behind the governor's bills.[106] Therefore, governors whose party is in the majority in both legislative chambers, a situation known as **unified government**, can get their bills passed—if their party sticks together. Of course, this is not always as simple as it sounds, since the legislature is an independent branch with its own interests and great pride in its role in the policy-making process. For example, in 2007, when Massachusetts's Patrick became the first Democratic governor in the Bay State in 16 years, the dashed expectation for a less rancorous legislative-executive relationship left some longing for the good old days of **divided government**, when at least one chamber of the legislature is not controlled by the governor's party.[107]

But in reality, divided government usually makes it more difficult for a governor to pass his or her legislative agenda.[108] Governors are less aggressive in pursuing their legislative agendas, more conciliatory, and more open to compromise when facing a legislature controlled by the other party,[109] and this reduces his or her ability to set policy. In such cases, not only does the legislative majority have basic ideological differences with the governor, but the party also has an electoral incentive at least to offer alternative positions on key issues, if not to sabotage the governor's efforts actively. Of course, when the legislature and the governor are at loggerheads publicly, the governor's advantage with the media really helps in the battle over public opinion, if he or she handles the press skillfully. Sometimes the legislature can work against the governor so subtly that the public does not recognize its obstructionism. Divided government has become much more common in recent decades, encouraged by legislative professionalism and the personalization of gubernatorial campaigns.[110]

Rivals for Power

Finally, a governor can be more influential in state politics and government if a state has fewer other heavyweight political actors who can act as rivals. A major factor here is the number and importance of independently elected statewide executives in state government, and we'll discuss these at some length in the next section. But outside of state government, other potential gubernatorial rivals may exist. In states with large urban centers, major corporations, or a large federal government presence, state government can be pushed from the front page by mayors, business leaders, and federal officials who are significant actors in the political process. Governors with less competition for political attention and power in their state typically have more informal influence. Thus, the governors of New York and Illinois are often less well known and less influential in their states than are the mayors of New York City and Chicago. The same is somewhat true for California (except perhaps when the governor is a former movie star), but less so because neither Los Angeles nor San Francisco dominate that state the way that Chicago and New York City dominate theirs. In addition to mayors and other local

---

[106] Malcolm E. Jewell and Marcia Lynn Wicker, *Legislative Leadership in the American States* (Ann Arbor, MI: University of Michigan Press, 1994).

[107] Edward L. Glaeser, "Blessings of a Divided Government," *The Boston Globe*, 1 May 2009, online ed.

[108] Cynthia J. Bowling and Margaret R. Ferguson, "Divided Government, Interest Representation, and Policy Differences: Competing Explanations of Gridlock in the Fifty States," *Journal of Politics* 63(2001): 182–206; Ferguson, 2006, op. cit., pp. 195–96.

[109] Chad Murphy, Martin Johnson, and Shaun Bowler, "Executive Speeches and Divided Government: Is There Common Ground in a House Divided?" presented at the 8th Annual State Politics and Policy Conference, Temple University, 2008.

[110] Morris P. Fiorina, *Divided Government*, 2nd ed. (Boston: Allyn & Bacon, 1996).

Massachusetts Governor Deval Patrick speaks with a major rival for power and attention in Bay State politics, Boston Mayor Tom Menino. Having served since 1993, Menino is many years senior to Patrick in his position.

officials, leaders of major corporations and other institutions can also challenge a governor's place in the media and political spotlight. This is the case in Michigan, for example, with the heads of General Motors, Ford, and the United Auto Workers Union. On the other hand, the governors of Maine, West Virginia, and North Dakota, among others, have less competition of this sort and so can dominate state politics more easily.

The State Executive Branch beyond the Governor

The governor is the most visible member of the executive branch of state government, but there are thousands of other people working for the state every day to help him or her set and implement public policy in the state. Two components of the state executive branch that deserve special discussion are a state's independently elected statewide executives and its bureaucracy. In this section, we describe each of these briefly, and we refer to and discuss them in many other ways throughout this book.

Independently Elected Statewide Executives

Forty-seven states (all except Maine, New Hampshire, and Tennessee) elect statewide executive branch officials in addition to their governor. This is a remnant of **Jacksonian democracy** and the **Progressive era,** periods of American history when it was thought that the more control voters had over their leaders, the better. The idea behind them was that these independently elected statewide officials would provide checks and balances within the executive branch and that they would allow voters a direct voice to counteract the influence of interest groups and political parties in state government. These institutions are quite unlike those of the federal government, of course, where we elect only the president and vice-president, with the latter really being just an appointed team member of the former. Not surprisingly, the states vary dramatically in both the number of the executives they elect and the scope of their duties.

The states elect from one (the governor) to 13 statewide executives, with six being average.[111] Figure 8.5 shows how the numbers of these officials vary around the country. In addition, the powers and scope of control of these officials vary greatly among the states, even for officials with the same title. The secretary of state (SOS) may be the most widely varying job. In some states, the SOS is just a minor official whose main job is to keep records on elections, but in other places, they have a variety of other duties, some of which are very important. For instance, the Illinois SOS is in charge of issuing driver's licenses and motor vehicle license plates, making this official second only to the governor in political power and the size and scope of government operations that he or

---

[111] Wall, op. cit., pp. 197–202. But also note that the *Book of the States'* data on some of the more obscure of these offices is suspect. Those interested in independently elected statewide officials and their duties are advised to examine the websites of the states and their officers.

Figure 8.5

Independently Elected Statewide Executives

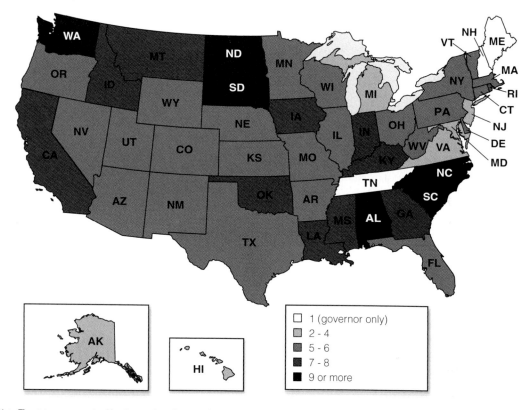

1 (governor only)
2 - 4
5 - 6
7 - 8
9 or more

Note: The states are organized by the number of statewide independent executives they elect.

Source: Data developed by the authors from: Audrey S. Wall, ed., *The Book of the States: 2008*, vol. 40 (Lexington, KY: Council of State Governments, 2008), pp. 197–202, and the websites of the various states and their officers.

she controls. Aside from the governor, here are the most common of these executives, along with the number of states that elect them[112] and their typical duties:

- Lieutenant governor (43 states)—The LG is sort of the vice-president of the state, doing whatever the governor asks. The LG's main responsibility is to succeed the governor in case of resignation, impeachment, or death, which is no nominal responsibility or rare

event. At press time, six sitting governors are former lieutenant governors filling out their predecessor's terms. In 2009, after the disruption of rocky transitions following two recent gubernatorial resignations, New Jersey elected its first LG, Kim Guadagno.[113] Another very important job of LGs in 26 states is to preside over the floor activities of the state senate. This duty is so important in Texas, for example, that some argue it makes the LG more powerful than

[112] Some states have these offices but do not elect them independently. For example, in Alaska, the attorney general is appointed by the governor and confirmed by the state senate.

[113] Cynthia Burton, "The Who, The What of Lieutenant Governor," *The Philadelphia Daily News*, 27 June 2009, online ed.

the governor in the Lone Star State. In some states, LGs run executive departments, serve on task forces, and do other duties, usually on an ad hoc basis at the bidding of the governor.

- Attorney general (43 states)—The AG is the chief legal officer of the state, representing the state in legal matters. The duties of these officials range among states where they are heavily involved in criminal prosecutions to the more common case of AGs focusing on civil law issues, often acting as consumer advocates. In recent years, AGs have been in the forefront of major class action lawsuits with significant impacts, such as against the big tobacco companies in the 1990s and more recently against automobile companies and banks during the current economic crisis.[114]

- Secretary of state (36 states)—As mentioned, the SOS does a range of different jobs in different states, but it is largely a record-keeping office, in many states focusing especially on elections.

- Treasurer (35 states), auditor (24 states), and comptroller (10 states)—These are officers who take care of the state's money in one way or another. Again, specific duties vary among the states, but generally, treasurers handle the state's borrowing and invest its savings, comptrollers hold the state's current checkbook and write checks as authorized, and auditors follow up after the fact to make sure that public money was spent as the legislature and related laws required. In 2003, Florida consolidated these functions into the office of chief financial officer, who is elected statewide.

- Secretaries of education (14 states), agriculture (12 states), and insurance regulation (10 states)—Some states feel that certain policy activities of the state are so important—and perhaps so prone to being controlled

by special interests in the legislature—that they have decided to elect the executives in charge of those agencies. Other such policy areas with their own statewide elected executive(s) include labor (four states), public utility regulation (three states), and public lands (one state). South Carolina even elects the adjutant general of its National Guard.

Some argue that these independently elected executives cause needless confusion among a state's residents about which official is responsible for what government function. Furthermore, the provision of public services may sometimes take a backseat to politics as agencies controlled by these officers fight for policy turf and public resources. Certainly, the more officers with whom the governor has to share state government, the less power and influence he or she has. In addition, since these officials are often looking to ascend the state's political ladder—and eventually sit in the governor's chair—there can often be conflict among them as the less-visible "statewides" work to gain public attention and support. This can be exacerbated when, as is often the case, these officers are not all of the same party. This type of executive branch divided government can cause friction, just as when different parties control the legislature and governor's office.[115] As we have seen, many governors once held one of these positions before taking the reins of power in the state, and sometimes the previous governor had not been quite ready to release them yet him or herself.

On the other hand, these offices give rising politicians a place to learn the trade of executive management and politics where the stakes are perhaps less high than they are in the governor's mansion. In this way, independently elected statewide offices act as a training ground for future governors, senators, and members of Congress. Notably, many of the women who have become governor in

---

[114] Tim Higgins, "Nebraska AG Presses GM," *The Detroit Free Press*, 27 June 2009, online ed.; Jonathan D. Glater and Vikas Bajaj, "Cuomo Seeks Recovery of Bonuses at A.I.G.," *The New York Times*, 16 October 2008, online ed.

[115] Fred Monardi, "'Divided Government' in State Executive Branches," *Politics & Policy* 31(2003): 232–50.

recent years came up through these offices, such as former attorneys general Granholm of Michigan and Gregoire of Washington and former lieutenant governor Perdue of North Carolina.[116] Indeed, the existence of these offices in a state tends to formalize the political career ladder, reducing confusion (and perhaps opportunity) in state elections, for good or ill.[117]

The State Bureaucracy

The bureaucracy of the executive branch is the quiet giant of state government. Although the media often report about the legislature, the governor, and even the courts, it is the bureaucracy that does most of the day-to-day jobs of state government, from teaching college students, to testing people for their driver's licenses, to guarding people convicted of crimes, to caring for patients in public hospitals, to regulating cemeteries and carnivals, and so much more. A generic term for the people who work in the executive branch agencies is "bureaucrat," but the disparaging connotations of that word do a disservice to the people who, with an incredible array of talent and great dedication to public service, bring you state government services every day. State workers are hired for their specific expertise to carry out the work that voters and policy makers want done. They are accountants, doctors, engineers, teachers, carpenters, social workers, police officers, and virtually every other profession and trade you can think of.

In high school civics, you learned that bureaucrats simply execute policy set by policy makers, and this certainly is mainly what they do. But because of their expertise and experience, and because of the realities of government in action, bureaucrats also determine, or at least influence, much public policy in the process of doing their work, both formally and informally. Formally, high-level administrators write **administrative rules** to implement state law. By necessity, legislation is written in general language. Legislators have neither the time nor the expertise to go into detail about, say, how a college engineering curriculum ought to be written or how deer hunting ought to be regulated. The agencies charged by the legislature with carrying out these general policies use their training and experience, and their highly skilled staff, to write these detailed rules and regulations. Formal administrative rules have the force of law, although the legislature has the power to countermand them before or after they go into effect.[118] But in practice, because those who write these rules generally try hard to follow legislative intent and because lawmakers simply don't have the time or expertise to scrutinize every proposed rule, most administrative rules go into effect without much oversight.

Bureaucrats, even **street-level bureaucrats**, also make policy informally through the decisions they make every day that have the power of the state behind them.[119] When Officer Caroline Tolbert of the Iowa State Patrol chooses between giving you a warning or writing you a ticket when she catches you driving five miles per hour over the speed limit on Interstate 80, it may matter a lot to you personally, but it isn't public policy. But when all the Iowa state troopers patrolling I-80 routinely make similar decisions over a period of time, they are in practice setting policy for the state, however informal it may be.

In fact, the speed limit serves as a good example of how bureaucrats set policy both formally and informally. First, the Hawkeye State's legislature charges the Iowa Department of Public Safety (IDPS) with setting speed limits

---

[116] Judith R. Saidel, Xiaolei Chen, and Alison C. Olin, "Women in State Policy Leadership, 1998–2005: An Analysis of Slow and Uneven Progress," a report of the Center for Women in Government and Civil Society, University at Albany, State University of New York (Winter 2006).

[117] Alan Ehrenhalt, "A Deep Bench," *Governing*, 9–10 July 2009.

[118] Brian J. Gerber, Cherie Maestas, and Nelson C. Dometrius, "State Legislative Influence over Agency Rulemaking: The Utility of Ex Ante Review," *State Politics and Policy Quarterly* 5(2005): 24–46.

[119] Norma M. Riccucci, *How Management Works: Street-Level Bureaucrats and Welfare Reform* (Washington, DC: Georgetown University Press, 2005).

on roads and highways. Lawmakers in Des Moines don't know where cars can go safely at certain speeds, so they leave it up to the traffic engineers at IDPS to make that determination. IDPS has the experts who are familiar with the up-to-date research, best practices, and most relevant laws on the subject. As a result of their deliberations, IDPS sets the speed limit at 70 miles per hour along certain stretches of I-80 by writing an administrative rule, and that rule is then posted on highway signs—"SPEED LIMIT 70 MPH."

However, through their years of experience, state troopers may have found that clever lawyers can challenge their radar guns' technology and make it hard to convict people for going just a little bit over the speed limit. And besides, in their professional judgment, the troopers may believe that it's more important for them to spend their limited time stopping people who drive especially fast or recklessly in other ways. If this is a common perception and experience among troopers, they may choose not to stop people until they are going, perhaps, 76 miles per hour on I-80. In essence, they are implementing a speed limit of 76 miles per hour simply by not giving anyone a ticket until they go faster than that. In this way, they are setting informal public policy. Of course, if you don't want a ticket, you should never go faster than the posted speed limit because you never know for sure what the informal limit is on a particular stretch of road. This sort of street-level policy making goes on in thousands of ways every day in every part of the state bureaucracy, and it has a major impact on the way government actually affects people's lives.

This discussion of bureaucratic policy making reflects a fundamental tension that informs government work every day, the tension between the values of **neutral competence** and **political accountability** in government. Street-level bureaucrats hold a strong ethic that they are experts in their field and, therefore, they should be allowed to do their jobs without undue political influence from above. This value of neutral competence is strong in government service, with roots in the Progressive era. The idea is that elected policy makers should set only broad parameters of policy based on values that should be applied fairly to all. It is the trained and experienced bureaucrat's job to translate those values into implemented policy actions in the agencies. Neutral competence is enhanced by the use of state employees who are hired and promoted through a civil service system process using tests and other indicators of professional proficiency.

On the other hand, elected officials want political accountability in the bureaucracy so that the "will of the people"—or, more accurately, the will of the elected officials in question—can be reflected in policy implementation. Governors work to encourage political accountability by appointing agency managers and controlling the state budget; legislators do so mainly by writing legislation, but they also use various techniques of bureaucratic oversight (see Chapter 7). From a policy perspective, this tension between neutral competence and political accountability largely plays out in decisions about how high up in an agency's organizational chart civil service hiring should go or, put another way, how far down into the bureaucracy a governor's appointment powers should go. Recent research suggests that a mix of gubernatorial appointees and merit-based employees in an agency's workforce enhances its efficiency,[120] but there is continual debate and reform about just what this mix ought to be.

Not surprisingly, governors and legislators appreciate political accountability in the bureaucracy, but bureaucratic neutral competence helps these policy makers tremendously by allowing the massive machinery of state government to run smoothly day to day. Judicious management of the state bureaucracy can also help governors control public policy, and many of their powers are useful in doing so. But typically, policy makers just need to communicate

---

[120] George A. Krause, David E. Lewis, and James W. Douglas, "Political Appointments, Civil Service Systems, and Bureaucratic Competence: Organizational Balancing and Executive Branch Revenue Forecasts in the American States," *American Journal of Political Science* 50(2006): 770–87.

their preferences clearly to state workers. Bureaucrats are usually happy to follow the lead of policy makers, as long as it is communicated clearly and fits with their professional norms and understanding of what the law allows and requires. Sometimes policy makers try to intervene inappropriately in the bureaucracy, which can cause trouble both for the proper administration of policy and, if it becomes publicized, for the policy makers, themselves. For example, when it was revealed recently that certain legislators and political appointees had tried to influence admissions decisions at the University of Illinois, both that very large agency and the policy makers involved were caused considerable embarrassment.[121] When the state is providing some limited good or service, having strong professional criteria for decisions about their allocation is imperative for achieving the ultimate policy goals, faith in government, and simple fairness. This is exactly the strength of a strong professional bureaucracy.

Summary

American state governors are among the most powerful and important public officials in the country today. The 50 governors are an impressive bunch, with extensive training and experience behind them and jobs as cabinet secretaries, ambassadors, corporate and not-for-profit CEOs, and perhaps even presidents in front of them. They are also a more diverse group than ever before. Because the office is so significant in American politics and government, it is much prized by ambitious political actors, which has led to skyrocketing campaign spending on governors' races. In state government, governors have three basic roles—manager of the bureaucracy, chief policy maker, and manager of intergovernmental relations. To do these jobs, the states provide their governors with more institutional power than at any other time in history, and their informal power can be tremendous if used skillfully. A state's political environment, including the partisan balance in the legislature and the existence of other centers of political power, also influences a governor's effectiveness. Besides governors, most states elect several other statewide executive officials independently, and the governor divides up the state's policy implementation duties with these officials. The state government's bureaucracy, those ten's of thousands of expert public servants who do the daily jobs of government, also has a major role both in policy implementation and in policy making.

Key Terms

Administrative rules	Dedicated funds	Line-item veto
Amendatory veto	Divided government	National Governors Association
Appropriations bill	Gubernatorial powers	
Bureaucracy	Head of state	Neutral competence
Civil service system	Jacksonian democracy	Patronage job

---

[121] Tara Malone, Stacy St. Clair, and Jodi S. Cohen, "Clout Goes to College," *Chicago Tribune*, 29 May 2009, pp. 1, 5–6.

Policy agenda   Reconstruction era   State of the State address

Political accountability   Reduction veto   Street-level bureaucrats

Political capital   Self-financing candidate   Unified government

Progressive era   Special session

Discussion Questions

1. What factors are responsible for the dramatic rise in the cost of gubernatorial campaigns?
2. What is the typical profile of a governor? What sorts of jobs do they have before and after serving as governor, and why do we see the patterns we do in a state's political career ladder?
3. How important is a governor's veto power? How do these powers vary among the states? What factors affect a state's need or desire for a strong governor?
4. How do the formal and informal powers of governors differ?
5. What effect does the partisan balance in a state's legislature have on gubernatorial power?
6. How do the values of neutral competence and political accountability influence the debate over a governor's and legislature's control over the bureaucracy? How might these values be prized differently for different policy areas?

Suggested Readings

Beyle, Thad, and Margaret Ferguson. 2008. "Governors and the Executive Branch." In Virginia Gray and Russell L. Hanson, eds., *Politics in the American States*, 9th ed. Washington, DC: CQ Press.

Carsey, Thomas M. 2000. *Campaign Dynamics: The Race for Governor.* Ann Arbor, MI: University of Michigan Press.

Ferguson, Margaret Robertson. 2003. "Chief Executive Success in the Legislative Arena." *State Politics and Policy Quarterly* 3:158–82.

Ferguson, Margaret R., ed. 2006. *The Executive Branch of State Government: People, Process, and Politics.* Santa Barbara, CA: ABC-CLIO.

Forsythe, Dall W. 2004. *Memos to the Governor: An Introduction to State Budgeting.* Washington, DC: Georgetown University Press.

Klarner, Carl E., and Andrew Karch. 2008. "Why Do Governors Issue Vetoes? The Impact of Individual and Institutional Influences." *Political Research Quarterly* 61(4):574–84.

Leal, David L. 2006. *Electing America's Governors: The Politics of Executive Elections.* New York: Palgrave Macmillan.

Merriner, James L. 2008. *The Man Who Emptied Death Row: Governor George Ryan and the Politics of Crime.* Carbondale, IL: University of Southern Illinois Press.

Morehouse, Sarah McCally. 1998. *The Governor as Party Leader: Campaigning and Governing.* Ann Arbor, MI: University of Michigan Press.

Niemi, Richard G., Thad Beyle, and Lee Sigelman, eds. 2002. "Special Issue: Approval Ratings of Public Officials in the American States: Causes and Effects." *State Politics and Policy Quarterly* 2:213–316.

Sabato, Larry. 1983. *Goodbye to Good-Time Charlie: The American Governorship Transformed*, 2nd ed. Washington, DC: Congressional Quarterly Press.

Sinclair, Upton. 1994 [1935]. *I, Candidate for Governor: And How I Got Licked*. Berkeley, CA: University of California Press.

Weintraub, Daniel. 2008. *Party of One: Arnold Schwarzenegger and the Rise of the Independent Voter*. Sausalito, CA: PoliPointPress.

Suggested Media Resources

American Governors (http://www.globalcomputing.com/GovernorsContent.htm): Private website that is conveniently linked to the website of each U.S. state governor.

State of the State speeches (http://www.stateline.org/live/ViewPage.action?siteNodeId=152&languageId=1&contentId=-1): Stateline.org has linked all governors' state of the state speeches since 2000 to this page.

Web Sites

Border Governors Conference (http://www.bordergovernorsconference.com/): The BGC is an example of groups of governors organized around a common interest. It is an annual meeting of the four U.S. governors whose states border the Mexican border and their six counterparts in Mexico. The BGC also conducts research and holds bimonthly discussion groups among gubernatorial staff.

Democratic Governors Association (http://www.democraticgovernors.org/) **and Republican Governors Association** (http://thegopcomeback.com/): The DGA and the RGA are voluntary political organizations designed to support the reelection of governors, and the election of new governors, of their respective parties. These organizations raise money, develop strategy, and develop press releases and some research to help shape the policy agenda and for partisan political purposes regarding U.S. governors' races. They are not affiliated with the nonpartisan National Governors Association.

National Governors Association (http://www.nga.org/portal/site/nga): The NGA is a bipartisan organization of the nation's governors, which shares best practices, conducts research, holds conferences, and lobbies Congress and the president for the common interests of the states and the governors. The NGA website has lots of information on individual governors and links to their sites.

9

The State Court System

JUDICIAL ELECTIONS AND JUDICIAL FAIRNESS IN THE MOUNTAIN STATE

Brent Benjamin is a justice on West Virginia's Supreme Court of Appeals (WVSCA), but in June 2009, five members of the Supreme Court of the United States (SCOTUS) decided that he should not make decisions on certain cases.[1] The problem that SCOTUS justices have with Benjamin has to do with campaign spending—not his, but spending that was done on behalf of him by another person. And the case in which the SCOTUS made this decision has had important implications for courts and campaigns across the country.

Benjamin was elected to the WVSCA in 2004 with the help of over $3 million of mostly independent spending by Don Blankenship, CEO of Massey Energy, the fourth largest coal company in the country. As it happens, Massey Energy, its subsidiary A.T. Massey Coal, and Blankenship frequently appear before the WVSCA, in large part because all appeals of trial decisions go directly to the WVSCA, since the state has no intermediate court of appeals. The case that the SCOTUS decision pertained to involved an appeal of a huge settlement against Massey that the WVSCA heard. A lower court judge had ordered Massey Coal to pay $50 million (now more like $80 million, with the interest) for predatory business practices relating to its battle with another coal company, run by Hugh Caperton. Caperton tried to force Benjamin to **recuse** himself from the case, that is, to step aside because of the potential of his being biased in favor of Massey. Benjamin refused to do so, claiming that Blankenship's campaign spending did not bias him. Blankenship himself claimed he spent the money not in an effort to help Benjamin, but to defeat Benjamin's opponent, incumbent WVSCA justice, Warren McGraw. Does this sound complicated enough to be the plot of a John Grisham story? In fact, it is. The biggest difference between this West Virginia saga and the plot of Grisham's 2008 novel, *The Appeal*, is that the book is set in Mississippi.

After bouncing around in the lower federal and state courts for several years, in June 2009, the SCOTUS ruled in *Caperton v. Massey Coal*[2] that Blankenship's spending was such an extreme factor in the McGraw-Benjamin race, such a high proportion of the total spending involved, that Benjamin should be recused for **conflict of interest**.

Caperton v. Massey Coal sent shock waves through the 37 states that elect judges in competitive elections, and its implications are just beginning to be realized. The SCOTUS held that even the *appearance* of undue bias caused by campaign contributions is enough to force a judge off a case, and this was a very new and serious ruling. Aside from its implications for the fair administration of justice and elections, the implementation of the decision may turn into a nightmare for the state courts. In particular, the Court left open the question of how much campaign spending is enough to induce bias. If $3 million is enough to cause the appearance of bias, then what about $1 million or $1,000 or $100? Is it a matter of degree only or of principle? Some people predict a flood of "*Caperton* motions" in civil cases, as lawyers routinely try to get judges thrown off their cases where almost any amount of campaign contributions were made by the other side in the case. Indeed, the four dissenters in the *Caperton* decision posed 40 questions that needed to be answered for any case to decide whether the decision is applicable. Furthermore, and potentially even more destabilizing to the judicial systems of these 37 states, *Caperton* and *Republican Party of Minnesota v. White* (2002), a decision that we talk about later in this chapter, show that the SCOTUS is willing and ready to intervene in judicial elections to an extent that it has never done before. Scholars and lawyers wonder aloud what the next major decision in the area will be.

West Virginia offers three other examples of potential questions that the SCOTUS could take up regarding the state courts and their elections, where the specter of judicial bias has been raised for different reasons. And it just so happens that each of these examples revolves around Massey's CEO Blankenship. First, in May 2008, WVSCA Chief Justice Elliot "Spike" Maynard lost his reelection bid following the publication of photos of him and Blankenship dining together in Monaco with two female companions. Maynard said he just happened to be in Europe at the same time as his old friend Blankenship, and so he dropped by to see him. But voters apparently didn't buy Maynard's story. Second, while now-retired WVSCA Justice Larry Starcher never had any electoral disputes with Blankenship, he sure made his opinion of him known, calling him "stupid," "evil," and a "clown" who was "trying to buy influence like buying candy for children."[3] But even though Blankenship's actions made him "want to puke," Starcher claimed that he could be fair to him and refused to recuse himself in cases where Blankenship was involved.[4] Third, remember former-Justice Warren McGraw? How impartial might he have been in Blankenship's case had he managed to beat Benjamin in 2004? In that case, would Blankenship have tried to force McGraw to recuse himself? What would the SCOTUS have said about that? Would the logic and outcome of the case have been any different?

AP Photo/Jeff Gentner

All of these questions about judicial elections and recusal involve a balancing of a person's right to a fair and impartial trial and another person's right to free speech. (According to an earlier SCOTUS decision,[5] campaign spending is treated as political speech.) These are issues that are at the heart of a variety of concerns about judicial elections and other forms of judicial selection in recent years. This is nothing new; the states have been struggling with how to select their judges for over 200 years, as we will see. The U.S. states are virtually the only place in the world where any judges are selected by voters. As should not surprise you by now, however, different states select their judges in different ways.

Beyond elections, these West Virginia cases raise a wide variety of issues that are important to the administration of justice in the American states, including the role of intermediate courts of appeal, bench trials and the relationships among judges working together, the role of the judiciary in policy making, and even the most general questions of what we want out of our judicial system. These are all important issues even for states that don't elect their judges, issues that Americans have been grappling with since the founding of the country.[6]

AP Photo/Bob Bird

1 This vignette draws on several sources: Richard A. Brisbin, Jr., and John C. Kilwein, "The Future of the West Virginia Judiciary: Problems and Policy Options," *The West Virginia Public Affairs Reporter* 24(2007):2–14; Richard A. Brisbin, Jr., "Judicial Elections on the Silver Screen," *Judicature* 89(July–August, 2005):44–47; Ian Urbina, "West Virginia's Top Judge Losses His Re-election Bid," *The New York Times* 15 May 2008, online edition; Adam Liptak, "West Virginia Judge Steps Out of Case Involving a Travel Companion," *The New York Times*, 19 January 2008, online edition; John Schwartz, "Uncertainty in Law Circles over New Rules for Judges," *The New York Times*, 10 June 2009, online edition; Joan Biskupic, "Supreme Court Case with the Feel of a Best Seller," *USA Today*, 18 February 2009, online edition; Jake Stump, "Lots of Questions Follow Supreme Court's Benjamin Decision," *Charleston (WV) Daily Mail*, 9 June 2009, online edition; Lawrence Messina, "Scandal Clouds W. Va. Court Race as 3 States Vote," *Herald-Dispatch (Huntington, WV)*, 12 May 2008, online edition.

2 *Caperton v. A.T. Massey Co., Inc* 556 U.S. XXX (2009).

3 Adam Liptak, "U.S. Supreme Court Is Asked to Fix Troubled West Virginia Justice System," *The New York Times*, 12 October 2008, online edition.

4 Adam Liptak, "Case Studies: West Virginia and Illinois," *The New York Times*, 1 October 2008, online edition. Starcher retired from the court at the end of his term in January 2009.

5 *Buckley vs. Valeo* 424 U.S. 1 (1976).

6 For recent scholarship on these issues, see: James L. Gibson and Gregory A. Caldeira, "Campaign Support, Conflicts of Interest, and Judicial Impartiality: Can the Legitimacy of Courts Be Rescued by Recusals?" Working paper, 2009. Department of Political Science, Washington University, St. Louis, MO; Chris W. Bonneau and Melinda Gann Hall, *In Defense of Judicial Elections* (New York: Routledge, 2009).

Introduction

As the opening vignette to this chapter demonstrates, big issues about the implementation of justice and the selection of judges are facing the states today, and around the country, there is plenty of variation and reform of the institutions involved. State court systems are so complex that most people don't even understand their own state's system well. In this chapter, we describe the wide variety of courts and judicial activity in the states and consider the effects of these differences. Understanding state courts and how they work can have a significant impact on your life—especially when it's your day in court. Beyond this, studying the state courts can tell us much about the states and the people and politics in them.

Some people think they know a good deal about the legal system, but these beliefs are often mistaken. Courtroom and law enforcement dramas have long been staples on television, and now we can even see the "real" criminal justice system in action on *Cops, Judge Joe Brown*, and the like. Americans have been fascinated by such shows since the earliest days of television.[1] As early as 1949, *The Black Robe* aired re-creations of New York City night court trials—sometimes with the real defendants playing themselves! The popularity and variety of these shows—dramas, comedies, "reality" shows—show Americans' interest in crime and the criminal justice system.

Perceptions of the judicial system acquired from television, however, often give a distorted view of this important branch of government. For example, dramatic courtroom battles are far less common than tedious negotiations; rather than sensational murder trials, the vast majority of criminal cases are for minor offenses, such as drug possession, simple assault, or drunk and disorderly conduct. Criminal cases themselves make up a minority of questions before the courts in this country, with disputes between people, businesses and governments

over damages, contract violations, and such being much more common. Importantly for this chapter, despite the extensive media coverage of the U.S. Supreme Court, state courts handle over 100 times more cases than federal courts. And notwithstanding urban legends and the occasional news story of multimillion-dollar jury awards for scalding hot coffee or whiplash, most lawsuits result in either no or a modest amount of money being awarded to the injured party.

The administration of justice has been an aspect of government with which people have been deeply concerned since time immemorial, because those who interpret and enforce the law—judges and the police—literally have life-and-death power over us and the force of the government behind them. Not surprisingly, the American states have spent considerable effort over the years trying to get their judicial systems right. As a result, the three themes of this book—institutions, reform, and comparison—become thoroughly intermingled when discussing the courts. The states have continually tinkered with their judicial institutions, and the history of these reforms reflects the history of Americans' values. Because it seems to be so much harder to get our judicial institutions right, because the social conditions surrounding the courts change so often, and because the courts must do so many different jobs, the institutions of the states' judicial branches vary far more than those of either their executive or legislative branches. In this chapter, we explore both the causes and the effects of this institutional variation in an attempt to understand the *real* reality of our state court systems.

The Dimensions of the American Legal System: Federal and State Courts and Civil and Criminal Law

There are two basic dimensions that characterize the American judicial system: state versus federal courts and criminal versus civil law.

---

[1] Michael Asimov, ed., *Lawyers in Your Living Room! Law on Television* (Chicago: American Bar Association, 2009).

Much of the complexity of the state court systems can be clarified by understanding these dimensions.

State Courts and Federal Courts

As you learned in Chapter 2, much of American politics and government is determined—and complicated—by federalism; the judicial system is no different. While most people can easily distinguish between their state legislature and Congress and between their governor and the president, however, the distinction between federal and state courts is often harder for people to understand.

Every state is served by parallel systems of state and federal courts. That is, each state has its own court system, and the federal court system also covers each state. The court system that a case goes into depends primarily on the nature of the crime or conflict involved. Most simply, if the crime or conflict is about a federal law, then the case goes into the federal court system; if it is about a state law, then it goes into the state court system. But whether a law is a state law or a federal law is somewhat idiosyncratic, depending on the actions of Congress and the state legislatures over the years. However, we can make some generalities.

First, it is important to understand that, by far, most legal cases in the United States are handled in state courts, including almost all civil cases (except bankruptcies, all of which are handled by the federal courts). For example, in 2006 (the last year for which these data are available), while 88,094 criminal cases went through federal courts, fully 9,312,716—over 100 times as many—went through the state courts.[2] Most of the crimes that you have heard of—assault, murder, robbery, and so forth—as well as almost all traffic infractions, are violations of state laws

or local ordinances. Federal crimes typically involve federal officials (like assassinating the president), interstate activity (like taking a stolen car across a state border), or activities that were outlawed by Congress for some historical reason (like bank robbery and kidnapping). The proportion of state versus federal cases is even more lopsided for civil cases (which we discuss in the next section), like lawsuits for injuries and divorce and child custody cases.

For some cases, it is not obvious whether state or federal law is at issue. For example, when a person is arrested for manufacturing and selling methamphetamine, he or she is violating both federal and state laws, and so could be charged in either system. In such cases, the state and federal prosecuting authorities usually negotiate which of them will pursue the charges, with the decision often being based on the resources and interests of the arresting authorities and, especially, who made the initial arrest. Sometimes, if a case is lost in one system, it can be brought again in the other system. Even more problematic is when state and local law come into conflict. The supremacy clause of the U.S. Constitution usually leads courts to find that federal law trumps any conflicting state law, but sometimes political considerations may lead informally to state law holding sway. For example, while federal drug laws ban the possession of marijuana under most circumstances, the Obama administration has chosen not to prosecute those people in the 13 states that allow people to use the drug for medicinal purposes.[3] In these ways, federalism can add both flexibility and complication to lawsuits and criminal cases.

---

[2] See the National Center for State Courts (http://www.ncsconline.org) and the Bureau of Justice Statistics (http://www.ojp.usdoj.gov/bjs/).

[3] These states are: Alaska, California, Colorado, Hawaii, Maine, Michigan, Montana, Nevada, New Mexico, Oregon, Rhode Island, Vermont, and Washington. See: *State-by-State Medical Marijuana Laws* (Washington, DC: Marijuana Policy Project, 2008).

TERRY SCHAMITT/UPI/Landov

When federal laws and state laws conflict, federal law is supreme. However, sometimes the federal government informally defers to state law in such circumstances, such as the Obama administration's decision not to prosecute people who possess medically prescribed marijuana in states that allow it.

Criminal Law and Civil Law

The distinction between criminal and civil law is also central to understanding the state court system, since state courts deal with both types of law.[4] Criminal cases involve the government prosecuting a person for violating a criminal statute. The person may be charged with doing something that is prohibited (like breaking into a house) or not doing something that is required (like paying taxes). The idea is that if a person (or corporation or some other entity) has violated a criminal statute, he or she or it has committed an offense against the people of a jurisdiction. Criminal complaints are therefore initiated by government prosecutors in the name of "the people," and in state court systems, the head prosecutors are typically elected at the county level.[5] These lead prosecutors have different titles in different states, usually something like "district attorney" or "state's attorney." These officials supervise

an office of sometimes dozens of assistant prosecutors, depending on the size of their jurisdiction. Their job is to follow up on the criminal investigations of the police, decide which cases are worth bringing to trial, negotiate with defense attorneys, and act as the people's lawyer in cases that go to trial.

Civil cases involve noncriminal legal conflicts between people, corporations, or even governments or governmental units. Such cases can arise out of a dispute over a contract, where one party to the contract feels that another party has not lived up to his or her obligations, or a dispute where one party claims to have been injured (whether bodily, psychologically, or monetarily) by another party, such as in an automobile accident. Civil cases are brought by the **plaintiff,** the party that feels he or she (or it, in the case of a corporation or governmental unit) has been injured, against the **defendant,** the party that allegedly has done the injury. The case is all about the plaintiff trying to get the defendant to redress the injury, usually by giving the plaintiff a certain amount of money. Lawyers in civil cases make arguments based on case law, or **common law,** a traditional legal system about disputes over contracts and injuries that has evolved case by case over the last 500 years or so, first in England and then in the United States.[6]

Thus, although civil and criminal cases differ from one another, they have one fundamental commonality: They both involve a conflict between two parties that is (or may be) brought before a judge for an authoritative resolution. The role of the courts regarding both civil and criminal law is to resolve specific disputes between specific people or groups by applying the law to the facts of the case as presented by the disputants. This role is the same whether the dispute is over an accusation of murder or an accusation that the landlord failed to fix a leaky faucet.

---

[4] Lawrence Baum, *American Courts: Process and Policy,* 6th ed. (Belmont, CA: Cengage, 2007), ch. 7.
[5] In a few states, these head prosecutors are appointed by the governor or another executive official.

[6] Lawrence M. Friedman, *A History of American Law* (New York: Touchstone, 2005).

The Organization of State Court Systems

Different states organize their court systems in different ways, and these institutional differences can affect the efficiency, and perhaps even the fairness, of the administration of justice. In general, however, most state court systems have the same basic hierarchical structure, with each level having its unique role in the process. Figure 9.1 shows this generic state court system structure. In very broad strokes, **trial courts** establish the facts of a case and apply the law, **intermediate courts of appeal**

evaluate questions of fairness about the trial, and the **supreme court** decides whether a law or legal procedure is allowable under the state's constitution. The pyramidal structure of Figure 9.1 reflects both the fact that these courts' authority flows hierarchically from the top to the bottom and the fact that the number of cases handled by these courts drops dramatically as you move up the pyramid.

Trial Courts

If you have ever seen *Law & Order*, *Judge Judy*, or almost any other courtroom drama or reality show, you have been watching a trial

---

Figure 9.1

The Structure of a Generic State Court System

Supreme Court
(.4%)

Intermediate
Courts of Appeal
(.8%)

Trial Courts (98.8% total)

General Jurisdiction Trial Courts (39.4%)
Specialty/Limited Jurisdiction Trial Courts (59.4%)

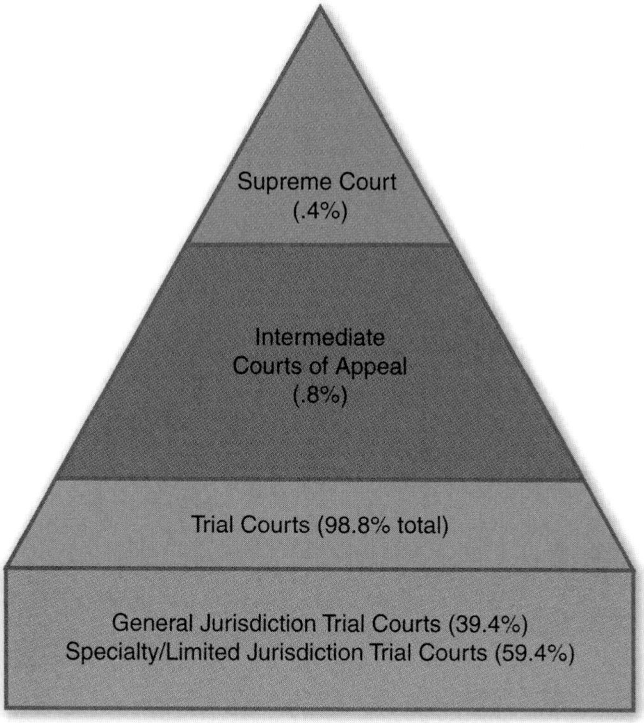

Note: The figures given were the percentage of the total number of cases disposed of in all state court systems across the country by each type of court in 2006, the most recent year for which these data are available.

Source: Shauna M. Strickland, Chantal G. Bromage, Sarah A. Gibson, and William Raftery, *State Court Caseload Statistics, 2007* (Williamsburg, VA: National Center for State Courts, 2008).

John Neubauer/PhotoEdit

Only trial courts use juries to resolve disputes, and even only relatively few trial courts use them.

court. Television shows focus on trial courts because that is really the only level of court that anyone would probably want to watch. The proceedings of intermediate courts of appeal and supreme courts are exciting only to those involved in the cases themselves and to legal scholars. It is also appropriate that trial courts get the most public attention because the vast majority of cases begin and end there. Indeed, virtually every case starts in a trial court, and only about 1 percent[7] of them get any farther than that (see Figure 9.1).

For both civil and criminal cases, trial courts have two basic functions: to establish the facts of the case, and to apply the relevant law to those facts. As straightforward as this may sound, this process contains considerable room for judgment—and sometimes, for error.

Procedures and Decision Making The fundamental job of any court system is to resolve disputes between parties and to back those resolutions with the authority of the state. Trial courts are the first—and usually the last—step in this conflict resolution process.

The first thing a trial court must do is determine the facts of the case. These facts are often the subject of dispute between the parties, making this no small task. For

example, a prosecutor claims that Nick Bodell stole a specific Nokia cell phone from a 2003 Ford Taurus with Kansas license plate number XCJ 420 in the early morning hours of August 21, 2009, in front of 5504 Joe Sayres Avenue. By pleading not guilty, Bodell disputes this claim of fact—he did not take that camera from that car on that day. In a civil suit example, Brittany Sing claims that she ate tainted coleslaw at Boone's Saloon on January 10, 2010, and it made her sick. If the owners of Boone's dispute this claim of fact, then they may go to court to get a definitive resolution of this question.

In addition to such factual disputes, the parties may also disagree about which specific statute or case law applies to these facts. So even if Sing got sick at Boone's, was the restaurant negligent in such a way that would require the owners to pay her damages? Even if Bodell indeed took that camera from that car on that night, should this action fall under the category of burglary or breaking and entering? These questions of the application of law are also debated and decided in trial court.

Trial courts resolve legal disputes between two parties through a process of **adversarial argument** and **adjudication** by a neutral third party. Both sides make their best argument in court, usually with the help of a trial lawyer, an attorney who specializes in working with clients going through trials. Each side makes its case through legal and logical analysis, by questioning witnesses to help establish the facts of the case, and by presenting any documents and physical evidence that supports their side of the disputed story. This process will sound familiar to viewers of courtroom dramas; but unlike on television, real trials have almost no surprises because both sides not only are pretty sure about what their witnesses will say, but typically, they also know who the opposition's witnesses are and what those witnesses are going to say.

The rationale behind this adversarial approach to judicial decision making is that it gives both sides a strong incentive to do their

[7] Shauna M. Strickland, Chantal G. Bromage, Sarah A. Gibson, and William Raftery, *State Court Caseload Statistics, 2007* (Williamsburg, VA: National Center for State Courts, 2008).

YOU DECISE

HOW SHOULD WE SELECT JURORS?

To assemble a trial jury, courts usually draw people randomly from a listing of residents of its jurisdiction. The hope is to get a cross section of the community to hear the case—a jury of one's peers. Random selection helps yield juries that are, on average, representative of the community—but only if the original list from which a jury pool is drawn is a fair representation of that community. Years ago, property tax rolls were used, but this meant that only landowners would serve on juries. A more recent tradition has been to use voter registration lists, since they are more broad based, but there are plenty of people living in a community who are not registered to vote (e.g., noncitizens and those who have no interest in politics). Some states have turned to driver's license lists as an alternative, or even a mix of voter and driver lists. Other options include lists of public utility customers and housing units.

What are the pros and cons of each of these types of lists? Remember, the goal is to get a group that is representative of a community's residents so as to yield a representative trial jury. What sort of biases might each of these types of lists have? That is, what sorts of people would be more or less likely to be included on each of these types of lists? Once we know what these biases are, we must consider whether each of these biases is necessarily a problem. For example, using voter lists keeps noncitizens off juries—is this necessary or even a good idea? Why or why not?

Another important issue for trial courts these days is simply getting enough jurors. The more restrictive the list from which a court draws its jurors, the smaller the number of people who are available, and so the more often each person might have to serve. Many people even work actively to get out of jury duty, whether by pleading hardship or illness, or even by not registering to vote. States are dealing with this problem both by getting tougher on such exemptions and by making jury duty less onerous (e.g., by shortening lengths of service and increasing jury pay). A court in North Carolina has even taken to tracking people down in the streets and forcing them into jury duty![1] How does this figure into your answers to the previous questions? How might you devise a juror list and system of selection that might avoid any of the problems you see?

Note

1. Denise LaVoie, "Courts Struggle to Find Jurors," *The State Journal-Register (Springfield, IL)*, 28 July 2007, p. 40.

best both to sharpen their own arguments and to counter those of the opposition. A neutral third party then resolves the conflict by deciding which version of the facts and the law to accept. Who is this neutral third party in U.S. state courts? In a trial court, there are two possibilities. First, a **jury** may make the decision. Trial juries consist of about a dozen people, selected randomly from a broad-based list of residents of the court's jurisdiction. The most commonly used lists are voter rolls and driver's license lists, but some places use lists of taxpayers or public utility customers (see You Decide! box).

The jury's job is to listen to the arguments of both sides in the trial and the presiding judge's instructions and then to render a verdict—an authoritative decision—about the dispute. In a jury trial, the judge is there to ensure that the trial is conducted fairly, in accordance with the relevant rules and laws. Of course, a judge can have considerable impact on the jury's verdict by how he or she runs the trial, decides on procedural questions, and instructs the jury before its deliberations. But the final decision making on the dispute, in terms of both the facts and the application of the law, is done by the jury.

Juries can be unpredictable. Judges have extensive legal training and experience, but juries are meant to represent a cross section of the community. For good or ill, they may be swayed by factors other than objective facts and a strict interpretation of the law. Trial lawyers may even appeal to jury members' emotions purposely, in addition to the law or facts. For instance, one might argue that a doctor's neglect may have caused a baby to carry a scar or disability for life or that the 80-year-old man who was killed in the car accident really didn't have long to live anyway. We have all seen media reports of runaway juries awarding seemingly outrageous sums in lawsuits or freeing "obviously guilty" defendants.[8]

Despite the potential for an appeal to a higher court in some circumstances, the fact that a trial yields an authoritative decision makes the parties in any case nervous. Think about it. Suppose a person ran their car into yours, causing $2,000 worth of damage, and you took him to court to get this money. The trial might result in you getting all that $2,000 or getting nothing. That could have quite an impact on your life, or at least it could have quite an impact on your budget for a few months. Criminal defendants have it much worse—they walk into the courtroom to hear a decision that could send them to prison for years or release them immediately. Despite the implication of TV dramas that every loser in every court case "is going to appeal," a trial court's decision is the final decision in a dispute almost every time. The magnitude of these consequences and the uncertainty of the outcomes encourage most defendants, plaintiffs, and prosecutors to minimize the unpredictability of their trial as much as possible. This leads to two common and important characteristics of state court trials.

First, again despite what you see on television, most trials do not use juries, but are **bench trials,** in which a single judge not only runs the trial but also makes the final decision on the facts and the law. Judges are far more predictable than juries because they usually follow standard legal practice and interpretation closely. Also, where discretion is possible, experienced trial court judges have long records that help the parties in the case evaluate how they are likely to rule. Although the assignment of judges to cases is typically done by a neutral court administrator, lawyers sometimes have some influence over who will hear their case. When they do, they try to get a sympathetic judge.

The second result of trial uncertainty is that the vast majority of legal disputes are settled between the parties before they even get to trial. By one estimate, only 1 percent of civil disputes filed in trial courts are finally decided at trial (i.e., they are informally settled before trial);[9] beyond this, a vast and unknown number of legal disputes get settled before they even get formally filed. In criminal cases, the uncertainty of conviction and sentencing frequently encourages the defense and prosecution to agree on a **plea bargain,** a reduction in charges or sentence in exchange for an admission of guilt from the defendant. For example, a prosecutor with shaky evidence of drunk driving might allow the defendant to plead guilty to reckless driving, a crime that carries far less penalty and social stigma. Plea bargaining assures the prosecutor of a conviction, while allowing the defendant to avoid the possibility of a more severe sentence.

Plea bargaining has pros and cons.[10] On one hand, it is an efficient way to administer justice. If all the cases filed in state trial courts had to be settled with a full trial (especially a jury trial), the cost to the state would be

---

[8] Eric Helland and Alexander Tabarrok, "Runaway Judges? Selection Effects and the Jury," *Journal of Law, Economics, and Organization* 16(2000):306–33.

[9] Henry R. Glick, "Courts: Politics and the Judicial Process," in Virginia Gray and Russell L. Hanson, eds., *Politics in the American States*, 8th ed. (Washington, DC: CQ Press, 2004).

[10] George Fisher, *Plea Bargaining's Triumph: A History of Plea Bargaining in America* (Stanford, CA: Stanford University Press, 2003).

astronomical and the already-slow progress of cases through the system would grind to a halt. On the other hand, people charged with a crime may be intimidated into pleading guilty even if they are innocent. This pressure may be especially difficult to withstand for defendants who are poor and poorly educated; and when a scared and desperate person is faced with having to choose between 2 years in prison or the possibility of 10 years, the 2 years might sound pretty good—until he or she has to serve them.

Prison is extremely difficult to live through, even under the best conditions, and once a person is out and labeled an "ex-con," his or her social and economic prospects drop dramatically.[11] In 14 states, they cannot even vote.[12] Routine plea bargaining may also have contributed to the massive increase in prison populations in the past 25 years, something that is strapping state budgets to the breaking point today.[13] In addition, plea bargaining may leave victims of crime feeling that they have not received justice. Thus, the efficiency of plea bargaining may come at the expense of fairness in the trial courts.

Uncertainty in trial courts also influences how civil cases are handled. Not every disagreement should be settled in court. Going to court is expensive, time-consuming, and uncertain, so often just the threat of a lawsuit gives the parties enough incentive to work out a deal, with the people on the two sides compromising more or less depending on their available resources and what they believe is the strength of their case. In difficult disputes, this can turn into a game of chicken, with both sides putting off a settlement until the very last minute. In fact, many civil suits are settled literally "on the courthouse steps," with the

parties resolving the dispute privately on or just before their court date.

As with plea bargaining, **out-of-court settlements** increase the efficiency of the civil justice system, but they also have their downside. Most obviously, this process benefits those with more experience in the judicial system and more resources—especially money.[14] In addition, some argue that the prevalence of out-of-court settlements encourages unscrupulous people to abuse the civil law system by suing big companies and wealthy individuals for damages that never occurred. A company may settle such a baseless case simply because of the uncertainty and cost of defending itself in court and the potential for the bad publicity from the suit. On the other hand, trial lawyers, victims' rights groups, and consumer groups argue that civil lawsuits are an important check on the rich and powerful, keeping them accountable for damages their actions may cause to even the poorest person. In this sense, this system offers for a way for average citizens to fight big companies and institutions—and even units of government.[15]

Although juries add considerable uncertainty to judicial decision making, trial court judges are certainly not legal robots who make decisions in a sort of "mechanical jurisprudence."[16] A case probably wouldn't even get to court if there was no uncertainty about the facts or the law, since a plea deal or

---

[11] Bruce Western, *Punishment and Inequality in America* (New York: Russell Sage Foundation, 2007).

[12] Elizabeth Hull, *The Disenfranchisement of Ex-Felons* (Philadelphia, PA: Temple University Press, 2006).

[13] K. Jack Riley, Nancy Rodriguez, Greg Ridgeway, and Dionne Barnes-Proby, *Just Cause or Just Because? Prosecution and Pleas-Bargaining Resulting in Prison Sentences on Low-Level Drug Charges in California and Arizona* (Santa Monica, CA: RAND, 2005).

[14] Joel B. Grossman, Herbert M. Kritzer, and S. Macauley, "Do the 'Haves' Still Come out Ahead?" *Law and Society Review* 33(1999):803–10; W. F. Samuelson, "Settlements out of Court: Efficiency and Equity," *Group Decision and Negotiation* 7(1998):157–77; Herbert M. Kritzer, "Contingent-Fee Lawyers and Their Clients: Settlement Expectations, Settlement Realities, and Issues of Control in the Lawyer-Client Relationship," *Law and Social Inquiry* 23(1998):795–821.

[15] Jeff Yates, Belinda Creel Davis, and Henry R. Glick, "The Politics of Torts: Explaining Litigation Rates in the American States," *State Politics and Policy Quarterly* 1(2001):127–43.

[16] Melinda Gann Hall, "State Courts: Politics and the Judicial Process," in Virginia Gray and Russell L. Hansen, eds., *Politics in the American States* (Washington, DC: CQ Press, 2008), p. 230.

out-of-court settlement would be in the best interests of the guilty or negligent party. Strong professional norms restrain judges from letting their personal preferences color their decisions, but political scientists have found evidence that judges' backgrounds and values can sometimes influence them. For example, one study found that trial court judges hand out somewhat longer prison sentences as they get closer to their reelection dates.[17] Such judges, like candidates for other offices, seem to be concerned with appearing "soft on crime" just before they face the voters. Other studies have found that female judges give longer sentences to rapists, that evangelical Protestant judges are more conservative in death penalty, obscenity, and gender discrimination cases, and that appointed judges are less likely to follow public opinion on school reform cases than elected judges.[18] Although judges—especially trial court judges—probably don't consciously let these factors color their decisions, unconscious bias may creep in when ambiguity about the facts and law in a case gives a judge discretion.

All of this demonstrates how different trial court decision making is from that in the legislative or executive branches. First, governors and legislators can consider a wide variety of information and points of view, but the only things a trial court judge or jury can consider comes through the formal adversarial process. In fact, any communication by either party in the case with the judge or jury outside of the regular courtroom procedures is both inappropriate and illegal. Second, the courts are passive decision makers. While a governor or legislator can identify a public problem and propose a solution for it, judges can make decisions only about questions that are brought to them in a formal case. Finally, judges decide on specific disputes about specific facts and law in specific cases. Legislatures (and, to a large degree, governors) make policy decisions that apply equally to everyone. Although state courts—especially supreme courts—sometimes make broader policy in an informal way (as we will see later), the main focus of judicial decision making is always on the individual case at hand.

Courts of Limited Jurisdiction Every state has **general jurisdiction** trial courts, that is, courts where virtually any type of criminal or civil case can be tried. At least 40 states also have various trial courts of **limited jurisdiction** specializing in particular types of cases (see Table 9.1). Such courts are an institutional way to increase the efficiency of the court system.

Some courts of limited jurisdiction simply handle minor matters. For example, traffic courts deal mainly with processing motor vehicle violations and assessing fines, with only the occasional dispute over a ticket. On the civil side, small claims courts handle suits claiming limited amounts of damages, with that limit ranging from $1,500 in Kentucky to $25,000 in Tennessee and averaging $5,000. For example, landlord–tenant disputes typically go to small claims courts. Small claims

[17] Gregory A. Huber and Sanford C. Gordon, "Accountability and Coercion: Is Justice Blind When It Runs for Office?" *American Journal of Political Science* 48(2004):247–63.

[18] Christine H. Roch and Robert M. Howard, "State Policy Innovation in Perspective: Courts, Legislatures, and Education Finance Reform," *Political Research Quarterly* 61(2008):333–44; Donald R. Songer and Kelly A. Crews-Meyer, "Does Gender Matter?" *Social Science Quarterly* 81(2000):750–62; Donald R. Songer and Susan J. Tabrizi, "The Religious Right on the Court," *Journal of Politics* 61(1999):506–26.

This is a "teen court" in action. These are courts where teenagers act as judge and jury to try other teens for minor offenses.

Table 9.1

Official Names of the States' Supreme Courts, Intermediate Courts of Appeals, and Trial Courts

State	Supreme Court	Intermediate Courts of Appeal	Trial Courts of General Jurisdiction	Trial Courts of Limited Jurisdiction
AL	Supreme Court	Court of Criminal Appeals Court of Civil Appeals	Circuit Court	Probate Court Municipal Court District Court
AK	Supreme Court	Court of Appeals	Superior Court	District Court
AZ	Supreme Court	Court of Appeals	Superior Court	Municipal Court Justice of the Peace Court Tax Court
AR	Supreme Court	Court of Appeals	Circuit Court	City Court District Court
CA	Supreme Court	Courts of Appeal	Superior Court	*
CO	Supreme Court	Court of Appeals	District Court	County Court Municipal Court Denver Probate Court Denver Juvenile Court Water Court
CT	Supreme Court	Appellate Court	Superior Court	Probate Court
DE	Supreme Court	*	Superior Court	Court of Common Pleas Family Court Justice of the Peace Court Alderman's Court Chancery Court
FL	Supreme Court	District Courts of Appeal	Circuit Court	County Court
GA	Supreme Court	Court of Appeals	Superior Court	Civil Court County Recorder's Court Municipal Court State Court Juvenile Court Magistrate Court Probate Court City Court of Atlanta
HI	Supreme Court	Intermediate Court of Appeals	Circuit Court	District Court Family Court
ID	Supreme Court	Court of Appeals	District Court	Magistrates Division
IL	Supreme Court	Appellate Court	Circuit Court	*

(continued)

Table 9.1

Official Names of the States' Supreme Courts, Intermediate Courts of Appeals, and Trial Courts continued

State	Supreme Court	Intermediate Courts of Appeal	Trial Courts of General Jurisdiction	Trial Courts of Limited Jurisdiction
IN	Supreme Court	Court of Appeals Tax Court	Superior Court Circuit Court	County Court City Court Town Court Probate Court Small Claims Court of Marion County
IA	Supreme Court	Court of Appeals	District Court	*
KS	Supreme Court	Court of Appeals	District Court	Municipal Court
KY	Supreme Court	Court of Appeals	Circuit Court	District Court
LA	Supreme Court	Courts of Appeal	District Court	Justice of the Peace Court Mayor's Court City and Parish Courts Juvenile Court Family Court
ME	Supreme Judicial Court Sitting as Law Court	*	Superior Court	District Court Probate Court
MD	Court of Appeals	Court of Special Appeals	Circuit Court	District Court Orphan's Court
MA	Supreme Judicial Court	Appeals Court	Superior Court	District Court Boston Municipal Court Juvenile Court Housing Court Land Court Probate & Family Court
MI	Supreme Court	Court of Appeals	Circuit Court Court of Claims	District Court Probate Court Municipal Court
MN	Supreme Court	Court of Appeals	District Court	*
MS	Supreme Court	Court of Appeals	Circuit Court	Chancery Court County Court Justice Court Municipal Court
MO	Supreme Court	Court of Appeals	Circuit Court	Municipal Court
MT	Supreme Court	*	District Court	Justice of the Peace Court Municipal Court City Court Water Court Workers' Compensation Court
NE	Supreme Court	Court of Appeals	District Court	Workers' Compensation Court County Court Separate Juvenile Court
NV	Supreme Court	*	District Court	Municipal Court Justice Court

State	Supreme Court	Intermediate Courts of Appeal	Trial Courts of General Jurisdiction	Trial Courts of Limited Jurisdiction
NH	Supreme Court	*	Superior Court	District Court Probate Court
NJ	Supreme Court	Appellate Division of Superior Court	Superior Court	Tax Court Municipal Court
NM	Supreme Court	Court of Appeals	District Court	Magistrate Court Municipal Court Probate Court Bernalillo County Metropolitan Court
NY	Court of Appeals	Appellate Division of Supreme Court Appellate Terms of Supreme Court	Supreme Court County Court	Court of Claims Surrogates' Court Family Court District Court City Court Civil Court of the City of New York Criminal Court of the City of New York Town and Village Justice Court
NC	Supreme Court	Court of Appeals	Superior Court	District Court
ND	Supreme Court	Temporary Court of Appeals**	District Court	Municipal Court
OH	Supreme Court	Courts of Appeal	Court of Common Pleas	Municipal Court County Court Mayors Court Court of Claims
OK	1. Supreme Court 2. Court of Criminal Appeals	Court of Civil Appeals	District Court	Court of Tax Review Municipal Court Not of Record Municipal Criminal Court of Record
OR	Supreme Court	Court of Appeals	Circuit Court	County Court Justice Court Municipal Court Tax Court
PA	Supreme Court	Superior Court Commonwealth Court	Court of Common Pleas	Philadelphia Municipal Court Philadelphia Traffic Court District Justice Court Pittsburgh City Magistrates

(continued)

Table 9.1

Official Names of the States' Supreme Courts, Intermediate Courts of Appeals, and Trial Courts continued

State	Supreme Court	Intermediate Courts of Appeal	Trial Courts of General Jurisdiction	Trial Courts of Limited Jurisdiction
RI	Supreme Court	*	Superior Court	Workers' Compensation Court District Court Traffic Tribunal Municipal Court Family Court Probate Court
SC	Supreme Court	Court of Appeals	Circuit Court	Magistrate Court Municipal Court Family Court Probate Court
SD	Supreme Court	*	Circuit Court	*
TN	Supreme Court	Court of Appeals Court of Criminal Appeals	Circuit Court Criminal Court	Juvenile Court Municipal Court General Sessions Court Probate Court Chancery Court
TX	1. Supreme Court 2. Court of Criminal Appeals	Courts of Appeals	District Court Criminal District Court	County Court at Law Justice of the Peace Court Constitutional County Court Municipal Court Probate Court
UT	Supreme Court	Court of Appeals	District Court	Juvenile Court Justice Court
VT	Supreme Court	*	Superior Court District Court	Environmental Court Probate Court Vermont Judicial Bureau Family Court
VA	Supreme Court	Court of Appeals	Circuit Court	District Court
WA	Supreme Court	Court of Appeals	Superior Court	Municipal Court District Court
WV	Supreme Court of Appeals	*	Circuit Court	Magistrate Court Municipal Court Family Court
WI	Supreme Court	Court of Appeals	Circuit Court	Municipal Court
WY	Supreme Court	*	District Court	Justice of the Peace Court Municipal Court Circuit Court

*State has no court of this type.
**In 1987, North Dakota established the Temporary Court of Appeals (TCA) on an experimental basis. Some years, no cases are assigned to the TCA, and so it does not meet.

Source: Audrey S. Wall, *The Book of the States 2008*, vol. 40 (Lexington, KY: Council of State Governments, 2008), pp. 277–80; National Center for State Courts, http://www.ncsconline.org/D_Research/Ct_Struct/Index.html.

court proceedings can be somewhat informal, often with the parties presenting their own arguments to an **adjudicator** without lawyers. The filing fee for bringing such a suit is kept low (perhaps $20), making these courts very accessible. However, the relatively small amounts of money involved and the informality of the proceedings do not mean that traffic and small claims courts can be treated lightly. Their decisions have the force of law, the same as for any other trial court decision. Landlords frequently win judgments, regardless of the merits of the case, by default in small claims court when the tenant ignores the summons to court. The lesson is that you should always show up to court when you are called, no matter how frivolous you think the matter is. Many states also use courts with very limited jurisdictions to deal with special populations or special crimes. Such **specialty courts** and **problem-solving courts** have become popular reforms in recent years, with the thinking being that judges and other professionals in the legal system may need to specialize to mete out justice fairly under some circumstances (see Reform Can Happen box).

Courts of limited jurisdiction are used heavily in the states that have them. In fact, in 2006, the last year for which these data were compiled, of all the cases taken up by a trial court, 67 percent came before a court of limited jurisdiction.[19] Traffic cases make up over half of the entire state court system caseload, and small claims court cases are the largest single category of civil cases.[20] This is not to say that these courts handle the most important cases; clearly, the opposite is true. But courts of limited jurisdiction are an institutional reform that does a very good job of helping implement justice fairly and efficiently in the states. Usually, if a party in a case is not satisfied with the decision of a court of limited jurisdiction, he or she can appeal to a trial court of general jurisdiction for a new

trial; but relative to the number of cases that these courts handle, this is done infrequently, further indicating the effectiveness of these courts.

Intermediate Courts of Appeal

Trial courts establish the facts of a case and apply the law to those facts, arriving at an authoritative decision about a dispute. Trial courts are not perfect, however, so American court systems establish procedures and institutions for people to "appeal" their cases. Appellate courts are the institutions that handle these appeals.

Perhaps surprisingly, the legitimate grounds for an appeal in either civil or criminal law have nothing to do with the facts of the case. An appeals court almost never deals with questions of facts; these are determined by the trial court. A person cannot appeal a trial court decision simply because he or she doesn't like the verdict. A case can be appealed based only on questions about either of two things: the fairness of the trial or the constitutionality of the law involved. Most state court systems have two levels of appellate courts designed to handle these issues: intermediate courts of appeal and the supreme court. Although it is overgeneralizing a bit to say so, it is not far off to say that intermediate courts of appeal decide questions about a trial's fairness and supreme courts decide questions of constitutionality.

The Role of the Intermediate Courts of Appeal Intermediate courts of appeal (ICAs) have jurisdiction over those cases that are appealed from trial courts of general jurisdiction. In essence, ICAs act as a check to ensure that trials are carried out fairly. Without this oversight, trial judges could act arbitrarily and tyrannically, something that the nation's founders feared. The Fifth Amendment to the U.S. Constitution gives Americans the right to a fair trial, and the ability to appeal a trial court's decision plays a large part in maintaining that right.

State supreme courts originally had the job of directly overseeing the fairness of state trial courts. By the mid-20th century,

---

[19] Richard C. LaFountain et al., eds., *Examining the Work of State Courts, 2007* (Williamsburg, VA: National Center for State Courts, 2008).
[20] Ibid.

REFORM CAN HAPPEN

SPECIALTY AND PROBLEM-SOLVING COURTS

Many states have recognized that judges and other legal professionals should not be expected to know everything about every type of law and legal situation. In response, they have reformed their judicial systems to allow for a bit of specialization, with the idea being that the administration of justice might be improved with some distribution of labor through the use of specialty courts.[1] For many years, many states have used such specialty courts as family courts (divorce and child custody issues), probate courts (wills and estates), juvenile courts, and tax courts. What these courts have in common is that they focus on technical areas of the law and/or they serve special populations with legal and social needs that are different than the average person accused of a crime or arguing a civil dispute.

Some states have also established additional specialty courts to address their states' particular needs. For example, Colorado and Montana have water courts to settle disputes over that precious commodity in those arid states, and Delaware (along with 13 other states) has business courts to deal with the many disputes that arise in that mecca of business incorporation. Many states recognize the special needs of justice in sparsely populated areas by designating rural courts. Tribal courts are often established on Native American reservations, although these are typically nested within the federal court system.

Recently, a whole new series of court reforms in various states and cities focus on special populations with unique and problematic justice needs, that is, problem-solving courts. In 1989, Florida established the first drug court. Those who commit either minor drug offenses and/or other minor offenses (such as prostitution or petty theft) while being addicted to drugs are often not well served in the regular criminal justice system. They may not be especially dangerous to themselves or others, but a few years in prison could transform them into a dangerous person. Drug courts focus on drug treatment and reintegration into the community as quickly as possible. By one count, there are some 2,100 drug courts around the country today, and they have been relatively successful at turning drug addicts' lives around.[2] Innovating further, in 1997, Florida established mental health courts to deal with the special criminal justice needs of those with mental illness. Buffalo, New York, was a leader in establishing veterans courts with the same idea in mind, and seven states now have these.[3] San Diego, California, innovated by establishing homeless courts for people with no permanent residence, and now many other cities and eight states have followed their lead.[4] Teen courts are another reform now used in all but one state that allows young adults to run entire court proceedings to deal with petty crimes committed by their peers. Overall, specialty courts, and especially problem-solving courts, are largely successful reforms that states and communities use to make an ever-more complicated legal environment more efficient, effective, and fair.

Notes

1. See the National Center for State Courts' website on these courts for further information: http://www.ncsconline.org/wc/courtopics/ResourceCenter.asp?id=17. Also see: Patrick McConnell, "Specialty Courts in America." Manuscript. University of Illinois at Springfield, 2010.
2. Erik Eckholm, "Courts Give Addicts a Chance to Straighten Out," *The New York Times*, 15 October 2008, online edition.
3. John Gramlich, "New Courts Tailored to War Veterans," *Stateline.org*, 18 June 2009; McConnell, op. cit.
4. Steven R. Binder, *The Homeless Court Program: Taking It to the Streets* (Washington, DC: American Bar Association, 2002); McConnell, op. cit.

however, as states' populations grew, many of their supreme courts became overloaded with relatively routine appeals, denying them the time they needed to consider the deeper issues of law raised only occasionally by certain important cases.

ICAs are an institutional reform designed to relieve this burden on state supreme courts.

ICAs decide on appeals that do not raise general points of law, allowing the supreme courts to consider only the most significant cases, as we will discuss later. Fifty years ago, only 13 states had ICAs; today, 40 states do. Those 10 states without ICAs tend to be small or lightly populated states with less complex economies. Among the 11 smallest states, only Hawaii and Alaska—states established after ICAs were an accepted institution—and North Dakota have them; and North Dakota's ICA is only set up as an experimental, "temporary" institution.

North Dakota's ICA provides an example of how and why these courts have been used. Founded in 1987, North Dakota's Temporary Court of Appeals (TCA) was explicitly established to take the load off its supreme court.[21] The North Dakota Supreme Court assigns various retired and active judges and attorneys to the TCA for one-year terms as needed to cover the caseload. In some years there are so few cases that no cases at all are assigned to the TCA. On the other hand, the supreme courts in West Virginia and Nevada, the two largest states without an ICA (although they are among the least populous states overall), routinely have problems with overload, resulting in perennial talk of judicial reform in those two states.

By relieving the supreme court of the burden of routine appeals, an ICA helps the state court system make fair, timely, and consistent decisions.[22] ICAs promote fairness by reviewing trials where proper procedures may not have been followed. They promote timeliness by reducing the backlog that an overworked supreme court can generate.[23] They promote

consistency by ensuring that trial judges and juries throughout the state apply legal procedures and law the same way.

Procedures and Decision Making The procedures and decision making of ICAs differ markedly from those of trial courts. First, all appeals are heard only by judges, never by a jury, and they are usually heard by more than one judge, perhaps three to five of them. No witnesses testify, and no physical evidence is presented. Witnesses and evidence are used in trials to determine the facts of the case, and these case facts are generally accepted as true in an appeal. This is why a person cannot appeal simply because he or she wanted the decision in the trial to go the other way; the facts that are established in the trial are the facts used by all levels of the court system. Rather than arguing the facts of the case, the parties to the case simply offer arguments about the trial's fairness. These arguments are made in **legal briefs,** documents in which the parties point out what they see as the problems with the trial and respond to the arguments made in the other party's brief. Thus, the primary "evidence" at an appeal is the **trial transcript,** the official record of events in the trial. Typically, the actual parties to the case don't even attend ICA hearings (whereas they almost always attend the trial). Instead, only their lawyers appear before the ICA to represent their interests, and these attorneys are usually specialists in appeals, not the same lawyers who argued the trial. Indeed, for some appeals, legal arguments are made completely through their legal briefs, with no public hearing.

ICAs also differ from trial courts in their decision making. After hearing or reading both sides' arguments, the panel of judges votes on the appeal, with the majority determining the verdict. Of course, this means that there can be disagreement among the panel of judges— that's why there is usually an odd number. The process by which the panel of judges on the U.S. and state supreme courts come to a decision has been studied at length, but very little

---

[21] "The North Dakota Judicial System" (Bismarck, ND: North Dakota Supreme Court, 2007).

[22] Roger A. Hanson, *Appellate Court Performance Standards and Measures* (Williamsburg, VA: National Center for State Courts, 1999).

[23] Megan Callahan, "Influences on the Cases of the State Courts of Last Resort." Presented at the annual meetings of the 2007 Midwest Political Science Association, Chicago, IL.

study has been done of ICAs' decision making, especially at the state level.[24] General models of judicial panel decision making suggest that it can be efficient and fair.[25] Typically, the panel hearing an appeal does not consist of all the state's ICA judges. The judges are divided, usually geographically, into panels to cover their large caseloads more efficiently. Only for certain especially important or controversial cases will all of a state's ICA judges sit together *en banc*, that is, as a whole.

The final decisions of trial courts and ICAs also have an important, fundamental difference. In a trial court, case facts are determined and the conflict is resolved through the application of law. That is, in criminal cases, people can be found guilty and sentenced to jail, and in civil cases, fault can be assigned and judgments awarded. But in ICAs, the judges' decision is about the original trial itself—was it fair or not? If the ICA decides that the trial was fair or, more specifically, if it fails to accept the exact arguments of unfairness brought in the appeal, the decision of the trial court is upheld. On the other hand, if the ICA accepts the argument that the trial was flawed, either it can order the lower court to correct the sentence or judgment or it can overturn the entire decision, necessitating a completely new trial. Sometimes, after a trial's verdict has been overturned on appeal, the prosecutor or the party to the lawsuit that won the original trial decides not to pursue a new trial. For example, in the example mentioned earlier in the chapter, the appeals court may decide that the stolen cell phone that police found in Nick

Bodell's possession on August 21, 2009, cannot be used as evidence because it was found during an illegal search. Without that piece of evidence, the prosecutor may decide that she cannot win a second trial and so she drops the case. That would be the prosecutor's decision, however; ICAs only make decisions about the procedures of the trial, not the facts of a case or its verdict.

Supreme Courts

Once upon a time, "things were so quiet on the . . . State Supreme Court that you could hear the justices' arteries clog,"[26] but that is anything but true today. In the 21st century, state supreme courts regularly make decisions that have momentous impacts on their states' residents, businesses, and local governments, and many of their decisions have significant impacts well beyond the borders of their states. On all matters of a state's law, its supreme court is the final arbiter, that is, it is the **court of last resort** in that state.[27] State supreme courts also have important administrative duties, usually running their states' entire court system and regulating their legal professions. Thus, a state's supreme court dominates its entire legal system.

Jurisdiction Trial courts have **original jurisdiction** over the vast majority of cases in a state's judicial system, and ICAs handle appeals of trial court decisions on issues of procedural fairness. So, what is a state supreme court's jurisdiction? In part, this depends on whether the state has an ICA. In the 10 states without an ICA, the supreme courts' **dockets** mostly consist of the same sort of routine fairness appeals

---

[24] For example, see: Thomas Hammond, Chris W. Bonneau, and Reginald Sheehan, *Strategic Behavior and Policy Choice on the U.S. Supreme Court* (Stanford, CA: Stanford University Press, 2005); Cornell W. Clayton and Howard Gillman, eds., *Supreme Court Decision-Making: New Institutionalist Approaches* (Chicago: University of Chicago Press, 1999). For a study of intermediate appeals court decision making in federal courts, see: Kevin M. Scott, "Understanding Judicial Hierarchy: Reversals and the Behavior of Intermediate Appellate Judges," *Law and Society Review* 40(2006):163–91.

[25] Jeffrey R. Lax, "Constructing Legal Rules on Appellate Courts," *American Political Science Review* 101(2007):591–604.

[26] Shirley S. Abrahamson, "Homegrown Justice: The State Constitutions," in Bradley D. McGraw, ed., *Developments in State Constitutional Law* (St. Paul, MN: West, 1985), p. 315.

[27] The U.S. Supreme Court may overturn a state supreme court's decision but only based on some aspect of the U.S. Constitution, not state law. In another example of institutional variation among the states, Texas and Oklahoma each have two supreme courts, one for civil cases and one for criminal cases, but each of these has the last word for the cases it hears.

Figure 9.2

State Court System Structures—Two Examples

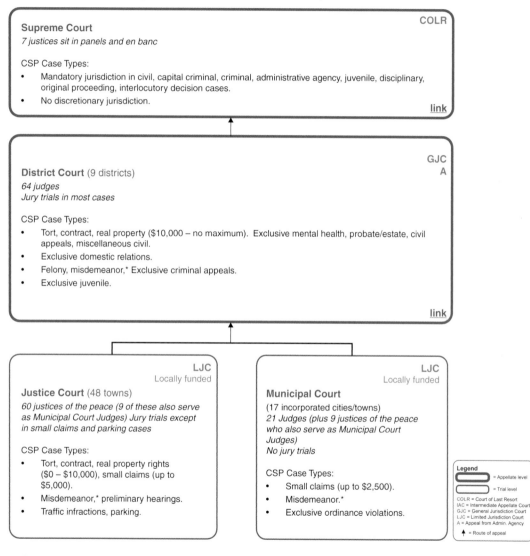

Nevada
(Court structure as of Fiscal Year 2007)

Supreme Court   COLR

7 justices sit in panels and en banc

CSP Case Types:
- Mandatory jurisdiction in civil, capital criminal, criminal, administrative agency, juvenile, disciplinary, original proceeding, interlocutory decision cases.
- No discretionary jurisdiction.

link

District Court (9 districts)   GJC
                                                                           A
64 judges
Jury trials in most cases

CSP Case Types:
- Tort, contract, real property ($10,000 – no maximum). Exclusive mental health, probate/estate, civil appeals, miscellaneous civil.
- Exclusive domestic relations.
- Felony, misdemeanor,* Exclusive criminal appeals.
- Exclusive juvenile.

link

LJC
Locally funded

Justice Court (48 towns)

60 justices of the peace (9 of these also serve as Municipal Court Judges) Jury trials except in small claims and parking cases

CSP Case Types:
- Tort, contract, real property rights ($0 – $10,000), small claims (up to $5,000).
- Misdemeanor,* preliminary hearings.
- Traffic infractions, parking.

LJC
Locally funded

Municipal Court

(17 incorporated cities/towns)
21 Judges (plus 9 justices of the peace who also serve as Municipal Court Judges)
No jury trials

CSP Case Types:
- Small claims (up to $2,500).
- Misdemeanor.*
- Exclusive ordinance violations.

Legend
⬭ = Appellate level
▭ = Trial level
COLR = Court of Last Resort
IAC = Intermediate Appellate Court
GJC = General Jurisdiction Court
LJC = Limited Jurisdiction Court
A = Appeal from Admin. Agency

↑ = Route of appeal

*District Court hears gross misdemeanor cases; Justice & Municipal Courts hear misdemeanors with fines under $1,000 and/or sentence of less than six months.

(continued)

Figure 9.2

State Court System Structures—Two Examples continued

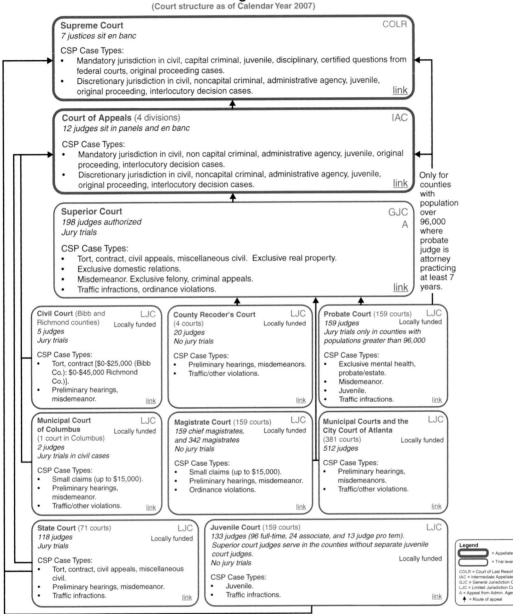

Georgia
(Court structure as of Calendar Year 2007)

Supreme Court   COLR
7 justices sit en banc

CSP Case Types:
- Mandatory jurisdiction in civil, capital criminal, juvenile, disciplinary, certified questions from federal courts, original proceeding cases.
- Discretionary jurisdiction in civil, noncapital criminal, administrative agency, juvenile, original proceeding, interlocutory decision cases.   link

Court of Appeals (4 divisions)   IAC
12 judges sit in panels and en banc

CSP Case Types:
- Mandatory jurisdiction in civil, non capital criminal, administrative agency, juvenile, original proceeding, interlocutory decision cases.
- Discretionary jurisdiction in civil, noncapital criminal, administrative agency, juvenile, original proceeding, interlocutory decision cases.   link

Superior Court   GJC
198 judges authorized   A
Jury trials

CSP Case Types:
- Tort, contract, civil appeals, miscellaneous civil. Exclusive real property.
- Exclusive domestic relations.
- Misdemeanor. Exclusive felony, criminal appeals.
- Traffic infractions, ordinance violations.   link

Only for counties with population over 96,000 where probate judge is attorney practicing at least 7 years.

Civil Court (Bibb and Richmond counties)   LJC   *Locally funded*
5 judges
Jury trials

CSP Case Types:
- Tort, contract [$0-$25,000 (Bibb Co.): $0-$45,000 Richmond Co.)].
- Preliminary hearings, misdemeanor.   link

County Recoder's Court   LJC   *Locally funded*
(4 courts)
20 judges
No jury trials

CSP Case Types:
- Preliminary hearings, misdemeanors.
- Traffic/other violations.   link

Probate Court (159 courts)   LJC   *Locally funded*
159 judges
Jury trials only in counties with populations greater than 96,000

CSP Case Types:
- Exclusive mental health, probate/estate.
- Misdemeanor.
- Juvenile.
- Traffic infractions.   link

Municipal Court of Columbus   LJC   *Locally funded*
(1 court in Columbus)
2 judges
Jury trials in civil cases

CSP Case Types:
- Small claims (up to $15,000).
- Preliminary hearings, misdemeanor.
- Traffic/other violations.   link

Magistrate Court (159 courts)   LJC   *Locally funded*
159 chief magistrates, and 342 magistrates
No jury trials

CSP Case Types:
- Small claims (up to $15,000).
- Preliminary hearings, misdemeanor.
- Ordinance violations.   link

Municipal Courts and the City Court of Atlanta   LJC   *Locally funded*
(381 courts)
512 judges

CSP Case Types:
- Preliminary hearings, misdemeanors.
- Traffic/other violations.   link

State Court (71 courts)   LJC   *Locally funded*
118 judges
Jury trials

CSP Case Types:
- Tort, contract, civil appeals, miscellaneous civil.
- Preliminary hearings, misdemeanor.
- Traffic infractions.   link

Juvenile Court (159 courts)   LJC
133 judges (96 full-time, 24 associate, and 13 judge pro tem).
Superior court judges serve in the counties without separate juvenile court judges.   *Locally funded*
No jury trials

CSP Case Types:
- Juvenile.
- Traffic infractions.   link

Legend
▭ = Appellate level
▭ = Trial level

COLR = Court of Last Resort
IAC = Intermediate Appellate Court
GJC = General Jurisdiction Court
LJC = Limited Jurisdiction Court
A = Appeal from Admin. Agency
↑ = Route of appeal

Note: Here are two examples of the wide variety of ways in which state court systems are structured. Notice that Nevada's system is relatively simple, without even an intermediate court of appeals. Georgia's system is more complex, having more specialty courts and an ICA. Also notice how the different types of courts can have different names in different states; for example, trial courts of general jurisdiction in Nevada are called district courts, whereas in Georgia they are called superior courts. Go to the National Center for State Courts' website (http://www.ncsconline.org/D_Research/Ct_Struct/) to see how these compare to the structure of the court system in your state.

The justices of the Michigan Supreme Court hear a case. State supreme courts not only have the last word on the interpretation of state law, they also have a strong hand in administering the judicial and legal systems in their respective states.

that occupy the time of ICAs. In states with the three-tiered system (as shown in Figure 9.1), however, supreme courts have significant discretion over which cases they hear, making them especially important actors in state government and policy.

In the 40 states with ICAs, the state supreme courts handle three types of cases. First, they hear cases about the balance of power in state government at the highest levels. These cases are few and far between, but their consequences can be the most extensive. In particular, when the state legislature and the governor have a conflict over their constitutional powers, the supreme court can be called on in its role as the final arbiter of the state's constitution. For example, South Carolina was among several states in 2009 where governors and legislatures battled over accepting federal economic stimulus funds and state supreme courts were called on to sort things out. The Palmetto State's high court ruled against Governor Mark Sanford, stating that "under the constitution and laws [of South Carolina], the General Assembly is the sole entity with the power to appropriate funds."[28] This was a case of a dispute over the institutional powers

of the legislative and executive branches; acting as a neutral third party, the judicial branch resolved it. Likewise, when the Ohio General Assembly complained that Governor Ted Strickland overstepped his veto powers, it was the Ohio Supreme Court that settled the matter.[29] The parties to these cases can bring suit directly in the supreme court because they usually don't involve disputes of fact and so no trial is needed. Everyone agreed about what Sanford and Strickland did; they just disagreed on whether their actions were constitutional.

Second, in some states, the supreme court is required to hear appeals of certain criminal convictions. For example, most trials resulting in a death sentence must be reviewed by the supreme court regardless of the facts of the case, what happened in the trial, or even the defendant's wishes. The states vary greatly on which other appeals their supreme courts are required to hear and the percentage of the supreme court's docket that is made up of such cases. For example, all of the cases handled by five state supreme courts (in Iowa, North Dakota, Nevada, Delaware, and Wyoming) are mandatory, while in two states (West Virginia and New Hampshire), none of them are.[30]

This leads naturally to the other category of cases that state supreme courts hear—discretionary cases. Most supreme courts, especially in those 40 states that use ICAs, get to choose to hear certain appeals of trial court and ICA decisions. That is, part of their dockets is discretionary. Why do these supreme courts decide to hear some appeals but not others? What are their decision criteria in selecting cases to hear? Simply put, these high courts pick cases to review, not because of any intrinsic issue of fairness or fact with the specific cases involved, but because of *their potential implications for public policy and state law more*

[28] Rick Brundrett, "S.C. High Court Orders Sanford to Accept Money," *The State (Columbia, SC)*, 5 June 2009, online edition.

[29] Reginald Fields, "Ohio Supreme Court Voids Strickland Veto of Liability Bill," *The (Cleveland) Plain Dealer*, 7 August 2007, online edition.

[30] Richard C. LaFountain et al., eds., *Examining the Work of State Courts, 2007* (Williamsburg, VA: National Center for State Courts, 2008), p. 63.

Figure 9.3

Discretionary Caseload of State Supreme Courts

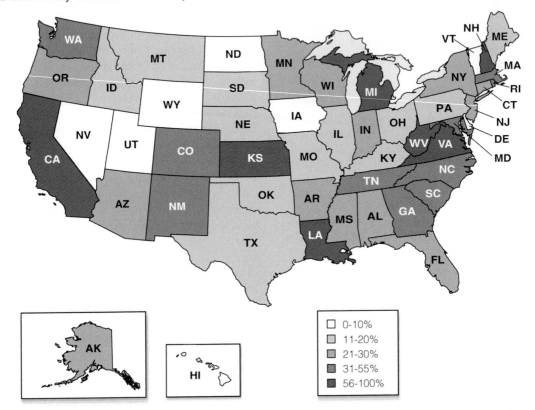

Source: Richard C. LaFountain et al., eds., *Examining the Work of State Courts, 2007* (Williamsburg, VA: National Center for State Courts, 2008), p. 63.

generally. Thus, where ICAs exist, the development of a state supreme court's docket is a significant decision-making process in itself, and one in which political scientists are quite interested. In this respect, state supreme courts are much like the U.S. Supreme Court. If a party in a case does not feel that the trial was fair and the ICA decision went against him or her anyway, or if the case involves a dispute over the state constitutionality of a law, then that party may officially request the supreme court to hear the case, even though most of these requests are denied. Nationwide, state supreme courts grant only 7 percent of these requests.[31]

In a recent year, an average of 29.2 percent of a state supreme court's caseload was discretionary across all states.[32] Figure 9.3 shows how the discretion of these courts' caseloads varies among the states.

State supreme courts grant these requests for discretionary hearings very carefully, with the aim of clarifying the interpretation of state law. Trial courts and ICAs follow the lead of their supreme court closely in applying state statutes and case law both because of judicial norms and because a supreme court can overturn lower court decisions. So, supreme courts choose to hear cases on which their

---

[31] National Center for State Courts, *Examining the Work of State Courts, 2003* (Williamsburg, VA: National Center for State Courts, 2004).

[32] LaFountain et al., op. cit.

decisions can be used as examples, or **precedents**, for lower courts facing similar cases.

Supreme courts try to identify cases that raise ambiguous legal questions that are common to a class of cases. This ambiguity often leads to inconsistency in trial court and ICA decisions. Without clear guidance on a point of law raised in cases facing them, lower court judges must use their own best legal reasoning in arriving at decisions. If different judges' reasonings vary, however, decisions on similar cases will not be consistent across judges. Because the consistent administration of justice is a hallmark of a fair legal system, and because the state supreme court has the responsibility to maintain a fair legal system in the state, supreme courts agree to hear cases that allow them to clear up these ambiguities.

State law on a subject may be ambiguous for at least two reasons. First, when a statute is new, its practical implications sometimes need to be worked out, and the supreme court may have to interpret it for judges, the police, lawyers, and the public. For example, in recent years, 12 states have passed statues banning or regulating aggressive driving, or "road rage," in response to the deaths, injuries, and property damage it can cause.[33] Because these statutes are the result of the legislative process, they typically do not define "aggressive driving" clearly. This leaves it up to police officers and trial court judges to decide whether a person's specific behavior in a case violates the law of a state. If conflict over, or inconsistency in, how these officials interpret such a state law arises, a representative aggressive-driving case will make its way to the state's supreme court for clarification. Because each state's statute and constitution are unique, such clarification needs to be done by each state's high court.

Legal ambiguity can also arise due to changes in society, the economy, or even technology. For example, suppose that state statutory and case law have traditionally given visitation rights to noncustodial parents in divorce cases.[34] Then, what if a nonmarried, live-in couple has a child and one of the partners moves out? Should that person be given visitation rights? This is so similar to the traditional divorce situation that trial judges have for many years ruled consistently that traditional divorce case law applies. What if a couple had a child but never lived together and simply stopped being romantically involved? Can the divorce analogy be applied here for child custody? Still pretty close, you say? What about a couple (married or not) who had a child using a sperm donor? Is the man entitled to visitation rights after a breakup? Looked at from another perspective, is that sperm donor (or egg donor) responsible to support the child financially? The Pennsylvania Supreme Court recently weighed in on this issue when a lower court muddied that water by requiring child support from a sperm donor.[35] What if a lesbian couple has a child through sperm donation? What about a couple who used both sperm and egg donation to produce a child? The Maryland Court of Appeals recently decided that a certain set of twins had no mother at all—they were conceived with their father's sperm from a donated egg and carried by a surrogate mother.[36]

When they see a murky area of the law, supreme courts do not shy away from even the most baffling new issue. It is a supreme court's duty to clarify the law for all the courts below it in its state. As the facts in these cases move further from those in established case law, the legal questions become more ambiguous and court decisions become less consistent.

---

[33] Governors' Highway Safety Association, "Aggressive Driving Laws," August 2009 (http://www.ghsa.org/html/stateinfo/laws/aggressivedriving_laws.html); Victor E. Flango and Ann L. Keith, "How Useful Is the New Aggressive Driving Legislation?" *Court Review* 40(3–4)(2004):34–43.

[34] Related to this example, consider the way the legal definition of "parent" evolved in the following cases before the California Supreme Court: *In re Nicholas H.* (6 June 2002) 28 Cal. 4th 56; *In re Jesusa V.* (16 April 2004) 97 Cal.App. 4th 878; and *Elisa B. v. Superior Court* (22 August 2005) 118 Cal.App. 4th 966.

[35] Mark Scolforo, "Pa. Sperm Donor Ruled Liable for Child Support," *The Philadelphia Inquirer*, 11 May 2007, online edition.

[36] Andrea F. Siegel, "Ruling Alters Idea of Mother," *The Baltimore Sun*, 17 May 2007, online edition.

By hearing a representative case of this type, a supreme court can make a definitive legal interpretation and bring consistency and fairness to them.

Procedures and Decision Making State supreme court decision making is similar to that of ICAs. There are no juries, witnesses, or physical evidence, only lawyers making oral arguments and filing detailed and lengthy legal briefs that describe and support the parties' arguments. Supreme courts are also made up of multiple judges (typically called "justices"), but unlike ICAs, supreme courts decide almost all cases en banc. Decisions are made with a majority vote; supreme courts have an odd number of justices (usually five to nine) to avoid ties.

Because a supreme court's decisions serve as precedents for its lower courts, they are usually supported by elaborate written opinions explaining the legal reasoning behind them, especially for its discretionary cases. The **majority opinion** is the official report giving the rationale behind the majority decision on the case. This is the ruling legal reasoning that stands as precedent for future cases of this type in the state.

Because supreme court justices have sharp legal minds and strong opinions, however, and because their discretionary cases are typically on debatable points of law, disagreement arises more often on supreme courts than it does on ICAs. When one or more justices dissent from a case's majority opinion, he or she can write a dissenting opinion. A dissenting opinion can establish the arguments for future legal debate on a point of law, perhaps even signaling that the court might change its mind in the future if it has a personnel change. Even if a justice agrees with the majority, he or she may do so for reasons other than those stated in the majority opinion. If so, and if the justice feels strongly enough to do so, he or she may write a concurring opinion, outlining alternative reasons for voting with the majority. In fact, sometimes even justices in the minority write multiple dissenting opinions, outlining their various reasons for voting against the majority. Thus, supreme courts are the most intellectual of state government institutions; a state supreme court sometimes seems more like an advanced seminar in a law school than a government agency—sometimes. From a public policy perspective, the more fractured a court's voice, the less clear guidance it gives to lower courts. State supreme courts are typically less fractious than the U.S. Supreme Court, with state justices more often deferring to one another's legal expertise than fighting tooth and nail along ideological lines.[37]

The Administrative Duties of the State Supreme Court In addition to making authoritative decisions on state law, most state supreme courts also administer the entire court system and regulate the legal profession in their state. These duties make supreme courts much more influential in state government and policy than they would be if they had only judicial powers. Often, the chief justice is especially involved in these administrative activities, but the entire court has a responsibility and an important role to play here.

The supreme court is responsible for the smooth operation of the entire state court system as an organization. This involves hiring and supervising clerks, court bailiffs, court reporters, and others; buying supplies; and dealing with the budget, among other duties. Even the court system's website is the responsibility of the supreme court.[38] Each supreme court employs a **director of state courts** to do most of this day-to-day administrative work. A court director is a major state administrator, on the same level as a secretary of a cabinet-level state executive agency (see Comparisons Help Us Understand box).

---

[37] Rick A. Swanson, "Judicial Perceptions of Voting Fluidity on State Supreme Courts," *Justice System Journal* 28(2007):199–218; Kevin T. Arceneaux, Chris W. Bonneau, and Paul Brace, "On Consensus in State Supreme Courts." Presented at the annual meetings of the 2007 Midwest Political Science Association, Chicago, IL.

[38] Reginald Fields, "Ohio Hoping to Link All Courts on One Web Site," *The Cleveland Plain Dealer*, 19 March 2007, online edition.

COMPARISONS HELP US UNDERSTAND

STATE SUPREME COURT PROFESSIONALISM

The institutional capacity of state and local government is a question that we have discussed throughout this book. Some governments have strong, professional institutions, and some are more part-time, "citizen" institutions. Americans have mixed emotions about the propriety of strong, professional government. On one hand, professionalized government institutions allow (at least in theory) for effective and efficient administration of policy; on the other hand, some people think that they can threaten our liberty. The way that states and communities balance these concerns and desires in developing their institutions can tell us a lot about the values of the people living there and what we think about the institutions involved.

For example, Peverill Squire, a political scientist who teaches at the University of Missouri at Columbia, recently developed an approach to evaluating the professionalism of state supreme courts.[1] Squire also studied the professionalism of state legislatures (see Figure 7.1),[2] and he based his courts measure on that earlier work. His basic idea was to identify indicators of the extent to which state supreme courts could attract qualified judges and make informed decisions, that is, "to generate and evaluate information" regarding cases,[3] using the U.S. Supreme Court as a baseline for comparison. He used data on judges' salaries, the control over their docket, and the amount of their staff to develop a scale of state supreme court professionalism, which we break down and display in Figure 9.4.[4]

We can think about comparisons here in two ways—comparing the states' supreme courts to one another and comparing these courts to other types of institutions. First, let's compare them across states, using Figure 9.4. What hypotheses can you develop about why a state would want to have a more or less professional supreme court? Start by thinking about what it is that a more professional supreme court would give a state, and then think about what type of state (or what type of people) would prefer more or less of that. Alternatively, you can think about what a professional supreme court would cost a state, and how that might factor in here. Might anything about the political ideology or economics of state have an impact here? What about a state's social or cultural characteristics—how might they come into play? Once you have thought about this a bit, check your hypotheses against the data in Figure 9.4. Do your hypotheses appear to be correct? Do you see any patterns that suggest any other forces that might be at work?

Next, consider how the professionalism of state supreme courts compares to that of other institutions. First, Squire's research makes it clear that the professionalism of state supreme courts is much more like that of the U.S. Supreme Court than the professionalism of state legislatures is like that of the U.S. Congress. The differences here are stark; many state supreme courts are almost as professional as the U.S. Supreme Court, while all state legislatures are far less professional than Congress. The most professional state legislature, California's, is far more professional than even the next state legislature on the list, but its professionalism relative to Congress is roughly only the average relative ranking for the state courts. In other words, the states are more than willing to put up with legislatures that are far less well staffed and paid, and that work far fewer days, than Congress, while they are much more likely to support supreme courts that are quite similar to the U.S. Supreme Court in their professionalism. Why does this difference exist? What does this tell you about these types of institutions, legislative and judicial, and about the jobs they do?

Finally, think about the impacts of state supreme court professionalism. As we have seen before, we can use the variation among the states on institutions like this to evaluate their impacts. What difference does it make if a state ranks higher or lower on supreme court professionalism? Is justice fairer or swifter? Or does professionalism simply vary in response to the requirements of a state? Scholars have begun to study this question and found a few impacts. For example, researchers have found that more professional courts seem to allot greater docket space to the have-nots in the legal system, have better reputations and be cited more often by other courts,[5] and break more new legal ground.[6] Why might supreme court professionalism have these impacts? What other impacts might it have?

(continued)

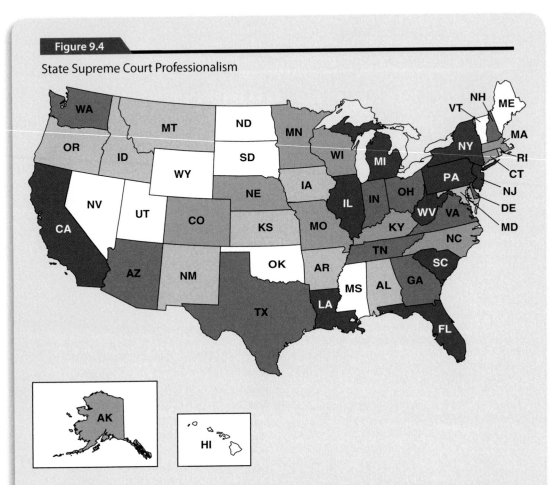

Figure 9.4

State Supreme Court Professionalism

Note: Peverill Squire developed a measure of state supreme court professionalism based on 2004 data on justices' salary, legal staff, and control over their own docket, all as compared to the U.S. Supreme Court. We developed the data for this figure by averaging Squire's four slightly different scales and then categorizing those raw professionalism values into quintiles. Note that *darker* states have *more* professional state supreme courts.

Source: Modified from: Peverill Squire, "Measuring the Professionalization of U.S. State Courts of Last Resort," *State Politics and Policy Quarterly* 8(2008):223–38.

Notes
1. Peverill Squire, "Measuring the Professionalization of U.S. State Courts of Last Resort," *State Politics and Policy Quarterly* 8(2008):223–38.
2. Peverill Squire, "Measuring Legislative Professionalism: The Squire Index Revisited," *State Politics and Policy Quarterly* 7(2007):211–27.
3. Squire, 2008, op. cit., p. 223.
4. Squire actually presents four highly correlated scales. We make a single scale by averaging these, and then we break that scale down into quintiles in the map in Figure 9.4.
5. Gregory A. Caldera, "The Transmission of Legal Precedent: A Study of State Supreme Courts," *American Political Science Review* 79(1985):178–94.
6. Bradley C. Canon, and Lawrence Baum, "Patterns of Adoption of Tort Law Innovation: An Application of Diffusion Theory to Judicial Doctrines," *American Journal of Political Science* 75(1981):975–87.

During the recent economic downturn, state governments have been cutting budgets significantly, and the courts are not immune from these actions. Supreme courts have had to institute systemwide hiring freezes for judges, replacing human court reporters with electronic recording devices and eliminating language interpreters, along with the furlough days and lay-offs the rest of state government is facing (see Chapter 10).[39] Also like many agencies in the executive branch of state government, the judicial branch actually sees an increase in work during bad economic times. As Chief Justice Margaret Marshall of Massachusetts's Supreme Judicial Court said in her annual address to the state's bar association recently, "The cruel irony is that in difficult economic times the demands on our courts intensify. More people file for divorce or to modify support obligations. The criminal docket swells; foreclosures, evictions, and debt collection matters escalate."[40] In Utah, it was estimated that civil filings were up 22 percent.[41] Even in less-stressful budget times, it is the supreme court's job to work with the executive and legislative branch to get the resources the court system needs. This has sometimes led to showdowns in court, with the supreme court (or its members) suing the governor or legislature over judges' salaries and other judicial branch resources.[42]

The state supreme court also regulates the legal and judicial professions in most states. In accord with state statutes, and often in collaboration with the state bar association, the court runs training courses for new judges, regulates the bar examinations that prospective lawyers must pass before being allowed to practice law, and establishes professional and ethical standards for the state's lawyers and judges. For example, the Illinois Supreme Court recently rewrote the Illinois Rules of Professional Conduct for lawyers, a 120-page document that covers everything from attorneys' relationships with clients and judges, their responsibilities to clients with diminished capacity, conflicts of interest, and safeguarding a client's property, to candor, fairness, and impartiality in the courtroom.[43]

The supreme court also establishes procedures for investigating and sanctioning judges and lawyers accused of unethical conduct. Charges of impropriety or incompetence against lawyers are common, largely because so many lawyers are in practice and they often deal with expensive and sensitive disputes. In most states, the supreme court, again often in collaboration with the state bar association, sets up a board to investigate and prosecute such charges in a quasi-judicial process. Supreme courts establish similar boards for judges. But because there are far fewer judges than lawyers and because judges, presumably, hold themselves to a higher ethical standard than lawyers, such judicial review and sanction are relatively rare. Such cases do arise, however, including recent cases in Texas and Wisconsin of state supreme court justices themselves being held to account, one for conflicts of interest and the other for failing to review a last-minute plea for a stay of execution because it came after she had left the office for the day.[44] Of course, lawyers and judges are

---

[39] E.g., see: Grant Schulte, "In Yearly Speech, Top Judge Warns of Furloughs," *The Des Moines Register*, 15 January 2009, online edition; Ben Winslow, "Utah's 1,000 Court Employees May Be Forced to Take Unpaid Leave," *Deseret News (Salt Lake City, UT)*, 29 January 2009, online edition.

[40] Anonymous, "Judge Says Justice Will Be Served Despite Cuts," *The Boston Globe*, 25 October 2008, online edition.

[41] Winslow, op. cit.

[42] Jay Gallagher, "State Judges Sue Governor, Lawmakers Over Salary Raises," *The Democrat and Chronicle (Rochester, NY)*, 11 April 2008, online edition; Jo Napolitano, "Ruling Grants 900 Illinois Judges Back Pay," *The New York Times*, 21 May 2004, online edition.

[43] Illinois Supreme Court Rules, Article VIII, "Illinois Rules of Professional Conduct" (http://www.state.il.us/court/SupremeCourt/Rules/Art_VIII/default_NEW.asp).

[44] Michael Brick, "Texas Judge Goes to Trial over Execution," *The New York Times*, 18 August 2009, online edition; Steven Elbow, "Update: State Supreme Court Reprimands Ziegler in Unprecedented Ruling," *Wisconsin State Journal (Madison)*, 2 June 2008, online edition.

subject to criminal and civil law like everyone else; these special review boards are designed to evaluate and sanction behavior that, although maybe not illegal, might violate professional standards and ethics. For example, although it may not be illegal for a judge to direct profanity at a defendant, it is not the sort of behavior that is conducive to the proper administration of justice and so a judicial review board might punish a judge for it.

Policy Making in the Courts

In your high school American government class, you learned that the legislative branch makes law, the executive branch implements it, and the judicial branch interprets it. But as you saw in the previous chapter, while the legislative branch certainly does make policy, the executive branch (especially the governor) does, too. Does the state judicial branch make policy as well? In the narrowest sense that legislatures and governors establish statutes and official rules and regulations, no, judges do not make policy; but if we think of policy making a little more broadly, then the state judicial branch—especially the supreme court—is very much involved in policy making.

Although the advisability and propriety of judicial policy making are debated,[45] the nature of law and the role the supreme court plays in the state legal system make it inevitable. In writing law, legislators cannot consider every eventuality, so statutes often have gray areas. As you have read about already, sometimes legislators even intentionally write bills in ambiguous language to help get them through the legislative process—vague wording may allow different legislators to believe different things about a bill and thus support it for different reasons. But the courts must enforce laws in specific cases based on specific factual circumstances. To do so, judges must decide on the exact meaning of the relevant law. State supreme courts have their clearest judicial policy-making power when they make the definitive interpretation of state law. Of course, this power is limited to ambiguously worded constitutional provisions, statutes, and rules, the decisions can be overturned if the legislature clarifies the law or changes the constitution, and the decisions can be made only on points of law that are brought before them in specific cases. In practice, however, the interpretation of state law by the supreme court frequently has a significant impact on public policy.

One way to look for judicial policy making is by identifying those factors that affect supreme court justices' votes on cases. Certainly, the facts of a case and legal precedent ought to have a tremendous impact on judicial decision making; if not, our entire system of justice would be illegitimate. Fortunately, study after study has shown that case facts and existing legal decisions play predominant roles in the decisions of state supreme court justices—but predominant is not exclusive. These same studies show that several other factors can also affect supreme court justices' voting on cases.[46] First, the ideology of both a justice and the state's population can affect judicial decision making, especially on highly polarizing and well-publicized issues, such

---

[45] For example, consider the different opinions of two groups over the Massachusetts Supreme Judicial Court's decision that the state cannot ban same-sex marriage: Andrea Lafferty, "Massachusetts Supreme Judicial Court Legalizes Same-Sex Marriage!" Traditional Values Coalition, 2004, http://www.traditionalvalues.org/modules.php?sid=1323; and National Organization for Women (NOW), "NOW Leaders Applaud Massachusetts Supreme Court Ruling Favoring Same-Sex Marriage Rights," 2004, http://www.now.org/issues/lgbi/020604marriage.html.

[46] Paul Brace and Melinda Gann Hall, "The Interplay of Preferences, Case Facts, Context, and Structure in the Politics of Judicial Choice," *Journal of Politics* 59(1997):1206–31.

as the death penalty and abortion.[47] Other studies have shown that a justice's political party,[48] gender,[49] race,[50] and even religion[51] may sometimes influence his or her voting. Because these factors influence judicial decision making systematically, over and above the effects of case facts and law, it is reasonable to say that the state supreme court is in the business of policy making.

If justices' votes are affected by things that are irrelevant to the case before them—like their party or gender—then is this not the very definition of biased judicial decision making? Perhaps, but judges are human, not legal machinery, so we cannot expect "robo-jurisprudence." Judges bring a lifetime of personal and professional experience to the bench, and it should not be surprising that this colors their thinking a bit once they put on their robes. These biases may be small, and justices may do their best to eliminate them, but they do exist.

In particular, these biases may come into play most often when state supreme court justices interpret statutes and case law in ambiguous areas of law, that is, when they are influencing public policy. When a supreme court determines the specific meaning of a statute in a category of legal situations (e.g., as in the parental rights cases discussed in this chapter), those biases—or values—are applied and reified in policy by becoming a legal precedent. All the lower courts in that state must then interpret that law similarly in that category of legal situation or risk getting their decisions overturned upon appeal. And some supreme court decisions can even influence legal decisions—and therefore, influence public policy—outside of the court's own state. While they would not be legally controlling precedent there, if lawyers and judges elsewhere find those legal arguments compelling and use them in supporting their own points, then the force of their own good thinking can affect public policy through other states' supreme court decisions. Figure 9.5 shows how the states' supreme courts' out-of-state impact varies. Do you see any patterns in this map that might help explain why a supreme court has more or less out-of-state influence on other courts? Do you see any social, economic, or political correlates of a state supreme court's citation rate? Do you see any relationship to supreme court professionalism (Figure 9.4) or judicial selection method (discussed below and seen in Figure 9.6)?

State supreme courts can also affect public policy through **judicial review.** Just as the U.S. Supreme Court assesses whether state and federal law jibes with the U.S. Constitution, state supreme courts have the power to judge whether a statute violates its state's constitution and, if so, to nullify that law.[52] For example, the power of judicial review is what allowed the Iowa Supreme Court to strike down that state's law limiting marriage to one man and one women in April 2009, effectively establishing same-sex marriage in the Hawkeye State (see Chapter 13).[53] In recent

[47] Richard P. Caldarone, Brandice Canes-Wrone, and Tom S. Clark, "Partisan Labels and Democratic Accountability: An Analysis of State Supreme Court Abortion Decisions," *Journal of Politics* 71(2009):560–73; Paul Brace and Brent D. Boyea, "State Public Opinion, the Death Penalty, and the Practice of Electing Judges," *American Journal of Political Science* 52(2008):360–72; Craig A. Traut and Carol F. Emmert, "Expanding the Integrated Model of Judicial Decision Making: The California Justices and Capital Punishment," *Journal of Politics* 60(1998):1166–80.

[48] Caldarone, Canes-Wrones, and Clark, op. cit.; Philip Dubois, *From Ballot to Bench* (Austin: University of Texas Press, 1980).

[49] Mahdavi McCall, "Structuring Gender's Impact: Judicial Voting across Criminal Justice Case," *American Research Review* 36(2008):264–96; Mahdavi McCall, "Gender, Judicial Dissent, and Issue Salience: The Voting Behavior of State Supreme Court Justices in Sexual Harassment Cases, 1980–1998," *Social Science Journal* 40(2003): 79–97; Songer and Crews-Meyers, op. cit.

[50] Chris W. Bonneau and Heather Marie Rice, "Impartial Judges? Race, Institutional Context, and U.S. State Supreme Courts," *State Politics and Policy Quarterly* 9(2009):381–404.

[51] Songer and Tabrizi, op. cit.

[52] Laura Langer, *Judicial Review in State Supreme Courts: A Comparative Study* (Albany: State University of New York Press, 1999).

[53] Monica Davey, "Iowa Court Voids Gay Marriage Ban," *The New York Times*, 4 April 2009, online edition.

State Supreme Courts' Impacts on Judicial Decisions in Other States

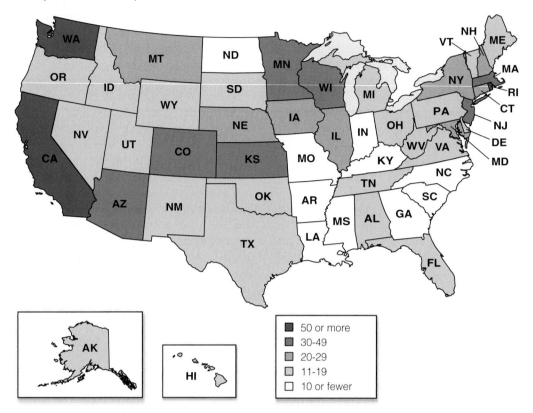

Legend:
- ■ 50 or more
- ■ 30-49
- ■ 20-29
- ■ 11-19
- □ 10 or fewer

Note: This map rates the states on the amount of their state supreme courts' decisions that were cited and followed at least three times by out-of-state courts from 1986 to 2005. Note that *darker* states have *more* decisions that are followed outside their own state.

Source: Jake Dear and Edward W. Jessen, "Measuring the Comparative Influence of State Supreme Courts: Comments on Our 'Followed Rates' Essay," *University of California, Davis Law Review* 42(2008):1665-70, graph 3.

decades, state supreme courts have been especially active in using judicial review, although their propensity to do so varies over time and among the states. One study examined over 3,000 judicial review cases heard by the 50 state supreme courts and found that almost 20 percent of the laws involved were overturned.[54] Another study found that the Washington State Supreme Court invalidated as many as one of every four laws it reviewed.[55] Of course, the influence of these decisions goes well beyond those directly involved in the case being reviewed, applying to everyone potentially affected by that law. This gives considerable staying power to this sort of court-made constitutional law.

Judicial review is a process that mixes the judicial branch and the legislative branch in

[54] Craig F. Emmert, "An Integrated Case-Related Model of Judicial Decisionmaking: Explaining State Supreme Court Decisions in Judicial Review Cases," *Journal of Politics* 54(1992):543–52.

[55] Charles H. Sheldon, "Judicial Review and the Supreme Court of Washington, 1890–1986," *Publius* 17(1987): 69–89.

Tim McQuillan, of Ames, Iowa, speaks to reporters in 2009 accompanied by his husband, Sean McQuillan, right, about their judicial review case before the Iowa Supreme Court that resulted in that court holding that the states ban on same-sex marriage was unconstitutional.

the policy-making process, sometimes in a very uncomfortable way. Remember that the state legislature (and usually the governor) have usually[56] approved of the law that the supreme court is then depositing in the legal trash can. The legislature can reverse such nullification by initiating a change in the state constitution and then passing the law again, but this process is much more difficult than simply amending a statute. Lawmakers don't like to be rebuked in this way, but sometimes they have political reasons for passing a law that they think will probably be thrown out by the courts. A legislator running for reelection can then say, "At least I *tried* to do something, but that bad old supreme court circumvented the will of the people!" (i.e., the will of the legislature). Consider Iowa's same-sex marriage law mentioned above in this respect. More often, lawmakers are interested in producing policy that is more than just symbolic, policy that they want to see pass constitutional muster and be implemented in the state. As such, legislators try to anticipate what their high court will and will not allow in a policy area and then craft

legislation to meet the court's constitutional standards, as recent studies have shown.[57]

Thus, the state judicial branch, especially the supreme court, has various ways of influencing public policy, but several factors work against the courts having a strong and direct policy-making role. Perhaps most important, the judicial branch has little policy-making legitimacy in popular American political culture.[58] Judges' values are not supposed to enter into their decisions; they are just supposed to apply the law to the facts of the case. Judges are also supposed to evaluate each case individually, while policy making is about setting general rules. So, by admitting to making policy, a judge would be violating professional and cultural norms. Furthermore, unlike legislatures and governors, courts are passive decision makers, simply deciding on those cases that have been brought before them. Consequently, even if judges wanted to make policy, their agenda would be set by events and outsiders to a much greater degree than are the policy agendas of legislatures and governors.

Thus, although the nature of the job obliges state judges—especially those on supreme courts—to influence public policy, norms and customs make the acknowledgment of that influence difficult. Indeed, if you ask a judge, even a state supreme court justice, if the courts make policy, he or she will likely deny it vehemently. In fact, it wasn't until recent decades that political scientists started studying whether even U.S. Supreme Court justices made decisions based on criteria other than case facts and the law.[59] The substantial evidence that the

---

[56] As you read about in Chapter 4, the supreme courts frequently thrown out laws passed through the initiative process.

[57] Teena Wilhelm, "Strange Bedfellows: The Policy Consequences of Legislative-Judicial Relations in the American States," *American Politics Research* 37(2009):3–29; Elizabeth A. Stiles and Lauren L. Bowen, "Legislative-Judicial Interaction: Do Court Ideologies Constrain Legislative Action?" *State and Local Government Review* 39(2007):96–106.

[58] Hall, 2008, op. cit.

[59] Glendon A. Schubert, *The Judicial Mind: The Attitudes and Ideologies of Supreme Court Justices, 1946–1963* (Evanston, IL: Northwestern University Press, 1965).

courts have a strong and pervasive influence on state and local public policy in the United States makes it important even for those of us who never see the inside of a courtroom to care about the institutions and performance of the judicial branch of state government.

Judicial Selection

Unique among major classes of American public officials, state judges are selected in a variety of ways, sometimes varying between different levels of the same state court system. Whereas all governors and state legislators are elected and all federal judges are appointed by the president, depending on the state and the level of the court, state judges may gain their judicial robes in any of five very different ways: appointment by the governor or state legislature, partisan or nonpartisan election, or a hybrid of election and appointment known as the **Merit Plan.** Another unique aspect of judicial selection in the states is that virtually no other judges in the world are selected by any type of election, while the great majority of state judges have to face the voters in some way at some point in their career. This variety of forms of judicial selection demonstrates Americans' evolving attitudes and ambivalence about the role of the judiciary in the political process. It also offers political scientists a unique opportunity to examine how the institutions by which officials gain office affect their behavior in office.

Judicial Selection Methods

Let's start with a basic description of these judicial selection methods. Figure 9.6 shows how the states select their supreme court justices, but some states use different selection methods for different courts. Indiana has the most diverse system, using three of the five selection methods for its trial courts alone. In addition, the details of some states' systems vary idiosyncratically. For example, in Illinois, Pennsylvania, and New Mexico (only its supreme court), judges are initially elected in

partisan elections, but they can run for reelection through a **retention election.** Although classifying judicial selection methods can be a little tricky, important distinctions can be drawn. Following are the five most commonly used categories of state judicial selection method.[60]

Legislative Appointment Under the earliest state constitutions, just after independence, most states' judges were appointed by their legislatures, reflecting the faith that the founders had in those representative assemblies. Today, only South Carolina and Virginia continue to select their judges this way. In these states, a legislative committee or commission screens candidates and reports its findings to the full legislature for a vote. These judges are appointed for a fixed term and subject to reappointment by the legislature.

Gubernatorial Appointment Three states—Hawaii, Maine, and New Jersey—continue to use the second-oldest method of selecting judges: gubernatorial appointment. In these states, the governor has almost unfettered discretion in appointing judges to a fixed term (with the caveats that judges can serve only until age 70 in New Jersey and legislative approval is needed for appointees in Maine and New Jersey).

Partisan Elections In 12 states, judges for at least some state courts are elected on partisan ballots. Just like governors and state legislators, those wishing to become a judge in these states must earn a party's nomination through a primary election, a party convention, or a party slating process and then face an opponent from the other party (or parties) in a general election. Among the six states that

---

[60] These five categories are the ones most commonly used by political scientists studying judicial selection. For more details, the best general source is the most recent edition of *The Book of the States* (Wall 2008, op. cit., pp. 286–93). The website of the National Center for State Courts (http://www.ncsconline.org/) is another good source. The best place to find the exact details of selection and retention for each class of judges in a given state is that state's supreme court own website.

Figure 9.6

State Supreme Court Selection Mechanisms

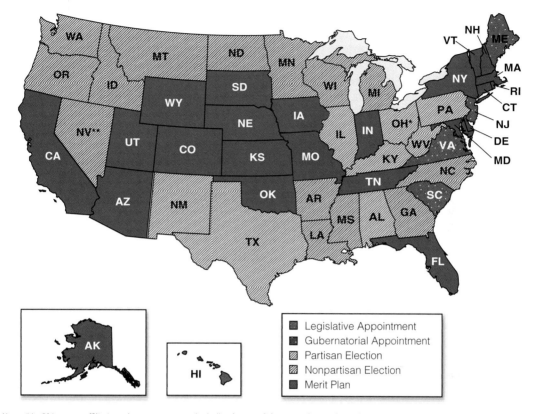

Legislative Appointment
Gubernatorial Appointment
Partisan Election
Nonpartisan Election
Merit Plan

Notes: * In Ohio, party affiliations do not appear on the ballot, but candidates are chosen through partisan primaries.
** In 2010, voters in Nevada will decide whether to change from a system of nonpartisan elections to the Merit Plan for selecting their state supreme court justices.
Source: Audrey S. Wall, *The Book of the States 2008*, vol. 40 (Lexington, KY: Council of State Governments, 2008), pp. 277–78. See the source for details.

use partisan elections for only some of their judges, all but New Mexico use them for trial courts, using other methods for judges on their supreme courts and ICAs.

Nonpartisan Elections The second-most common method of state judicial selection is nonpartisan election, with 21 states using this method for at least some of their courts. These elections are usually held in the spring, often coinciding with nonpartisan municipal elections, rather than during the November general election.

Merit Plan The Merit Plan (also called the Missouri Plan, after the first state to adopt it) is the most widely used judicial selection method, with 24 states using some variant of it for at least some of their courts. Three steps define this selection method. First, a nominating commission is formed to recruit and evaluate potential judges. The composition of this commission varies from state to state, but it generally includes representatives of key government institutions (such as the state legislature, governor, and state supreme court) and the legal establishment (perhaps leaders or appointees of the state bar association). When a specific judicial vacancy arises, the commission identifies a small number of qualified candidates (usually three) and sends their names to the governor. Next, the governor appoints one of the nominees to the vacancy for a short term, typically one to three years in length. Finally, once a new judge has served this probationary term, he or she faces the voters in a retention election. In a retention election, the question on the ballot is not which candidate the voter prefers, as in a regular election, but whether this judge should be allowed to be retained for another (usually much longer) term. In other words, only one name is on the retention ballot (that of the incumbent judge), and voters chose to retain him or her or not. This probationary term and retention election are the hallmarks of the Merit Plan.

To a political scientist, especially one who has learned the craft by studying the states, all this variation in these selection institutions raises two obvious questions: (1) Why have different states chosen different methods? and (2) How do the different methods of judicial selection affect the administration of justice (or anything else) differently? That is, what are the causes and effects of these institutions? We turn to these questions next.

Why Do States Select Their Judges Differently?

We establish institutions for selecting a class of public officials based on the functions that we believe these officials should perform and the values that we hold about these functions. So, for example, we want lawmakers to represent the values of a jurisdiction's residents,[61] so we elect them, and we want bureaucrats who have professional expertise, so we select them through a civil service system of tests and knowledge-based criteria. But since the colonial era, Americans have debated what we want out of our state judges, and the current

variation in judicial selection methods reflects in large degree the evolution of Americans' values about our courts.[62] While this debate is a subtle one, the current variation in state judicial selection roughly follows the historic and geographic distribution of Americans' beliefs about the proper role of the courts.

What is the proper role of judges in our representative democracy? This is not an easy question. Consider how you think judges should make decisions. As we have discussed, legal culture and norms hold that their decisions should be based only on the law and the facts of the case—this is the fair administration of justice that we prize. But what should be done when the fair administration of justice conflicts with public opinion? Such conflicts are more common than you might think, and simple, universal resolutions to them are sometimes illusive. For example, an angry mob might want to lynch a person who they think got a too-lenient sentence for a certain crime. Most Americans would agree that the judge was right to ignore the wishes of this community and apply the law as passed by the state legislature. But what about when a law is passed by a state legislature that conflicts with the fundamental rules of governance or human rights set out in the state's constitution? Should a state supreme court override the current will of the people (the statute) in favor of the constitution, which represents the will of the people at a previous time? In the federal court system, judges are appointed for life so that they can protect constitutional rights and values against the heat of current popular opinion. They have done this to protect the rights of minorities of all types, from African Americans trying to vote in the South to the Ku Klux Klan and neo-Nazi groups trying to hold rallies in predominantly Jewish neighborhoods,[63] but in the states, most judges must face the voters at some point, and they can be thrown out of office

---

[61] Of course, this is an oversimplification of our expectations of lawmakers, as we discussed in Chapter 7.

[62] Charles H. Sheldon and Linda S. Maule, *Choosing Justice: The Recruitment of State and Federal Judges* (Pullman: Washington State University Press, 1997).

[63] Donald A. Downs, *Nazis in Skokie: Freedom, Community and the First Amendment* (South Bend, IN: University of Notre Dame Press, 1985).

if voters don't like their decisions. This makes standing up for an unpopular minority dicier for state supreme court judges than those in the federal system (see Chapter 13 for more on this in morality policy issues).[64]

This issue becomes an especially pointed one when a supreme court rules that a law passed through the initiative process is unconstitutional. Supreme courts in several direct democracy states have recently come under attack for frustrating the "will of the people" in this way. For example, in 2008, the California Supreme Court held that a 2000 initiative banning same-sex marriage was unconstitutional. The public outcry was loud and swift, resulting in the narrow passage later in 2008 of a new initiative, Proposition 8, that actually changed the state's constitution in order to implement the ban. The retention of supreme court justices in California has been seen to be threatened by these actions,[65] but is this right?

Even if you agree that the judiciary should protect certain basic rights against popular opinion, consider other legal situations where the law and the facts are not clear-cut, giving a judge room for interpretation. To what extent should judges decide such cases using their professional judgment based on their years of legal training and experience, and maybe even their ideological and political values and biases, and to what extent should they reflect the values and preferences of the communities they serve? Another question about judicial selection that is not entirely unrelated is whether there is a difference between the ability of voters to understand the job of a judge, on one hand, versus the job of a governor or legislator, on the other, such that we can trust the average person to know who would make a good governor or legislator but not who would make a good judge.

These are difficult questions, and the debate surrounding them is reflected in the institutions the states use to select their judges.[66] The earliest state legislatures embodied what was seen as the only legitimate source of political power—the people. The British had used the colonial courts as instruments of oppression and thus the founders were suspicious of them, just as they were suspicious of governors. Thus, the first state governments subordinated their courts to their legislatures by giving the latter the power to appoint judges. As state legislatures fell out of favor in the early 19th century, states embraced executive leadership, including giving governors the power to appoint judges. Thus, in keeping with the strongly elitist tone of early American democracy, state judges were almost all appointed for the country's first half-century.

With the rise of Jacksonian democracy in pre–Civil War America, the states began electing many more of their officials directly, including judges. In 1832, Mississippi became the first to elect its judges, and by 1900, about 80 percent of the states did likewise. Like all officials in this era, judges were elected on partisan ballots, with the idea being that the party label would give voters an indication of the candidates' values and preferences. Thus, judges would reflect voters' values in the same way that legislators or governors would.

By the early 20th century, the good-government reformers of the Progressive Era advocated nonpartisan judicial elections. The Progressives valued judges who would decide cases fairly and impartially based on the law and the facts of the case. They felt that partisanship and political ideology should have nothing to do with the administration of justice, so it made no sense to select judges using those criteria. Nonpartisan elections would force

---

[64] Brian DiSarro, "Judicial Accountability or Majority Tyranny? Judicial Selection Methods and State Gay Rights Rulings." Presented at the 2007 State Politics and Policy Conference, Austin, TX.

[65] Bill Ainsworth, "Same-Sex Marriage: Law-and-Order Appointee Now Known for Greater Rights," *Union-Tribune (San Diego, CA)*, 13 June 2008, online edition.

[66] Chris W. Bonneau and Melinda Gann Hall, *In Defense of Judicial Elections* (New York: Routledge, 2009); F. Andrew Hanssen, "Learning about Judicial Independence: Institutional Change in the State Courts," *Journal of Legal Studies* 33(2004):431–73.

voters to select judges on more job-related criteria, like their training and experience. North Dakota established the first nonpartisan judicial elections in 1910, and by 1952, 15 other states had done so.

Finally, in 1940, Missouri adopted the first Merit Plan, that hybrid of appointment and election. The values reflected by this institution were also a hybrid. The first part is the notion that judicial selection is best made by experts (the selection committee and the governor) because the job is highly technical and voters know little about it. But the retention election reflects the democratic impulse to give voters a way to evaluate their judges once the latter are in office. In this way, the Merit Plan is a scientific management approach to good government, an effort to appoint a qualified person to the post based on technical merit and then letting voters review that person based on his or her subsequent performance on the job.

Thus, the diversity among the states in judicial selection reflects the diversity of our values about the role of judges over time and around the country. New states adopted the institution that reflected the values in vogue at the time of their statehood. For example, from 1846 to 1900, every state admitted to the union initially elected its judges on a partisan ballot.[67] Likewise, when states made major changes to their constitutions, they tended to adopt the method that better reflected the contemporary values about the judiciary. In recent decades, Rhode Island, Delaware, New Hampshire, New York, Tennessee, and South Dakota all changed to the Merit Plan; since 1992, Mississippi, Arkansas, and North Carolina all moved in this direction by changing from partisan to nonpartisan elections.

Often, these changes are instigated by a scandal or some other problem with their system. For example, in 2010, Nevada will vote on whether to change from a nonpartisan election system to the Merit Plan. The Silver State's legislature called for this referendum after an elected judge's "volatile, angry, paranoid and bizarre behavior" led the supreme court to assign her an armed security detail and question her competence.[68] The thinking was that someone as problematic as that judge could have risen to the bench only through elections—a Merit Plan would have screened her out very early on in the process. Although a state can—and often does—tolerate a rogue or incompetent state lawmaker, for example, the damage such a judge can do to the lives of those whose cases come before him or her could be intolerable.

Why have some states retained their older systems of judicial selection? This can often be explained simply by inertia and the difficulty of changing a state's constitution. For example, Article VI, Section 7 of Virginia's state constitution requires judges to be selected by the legislature; this provision has not been changed since the constitution was adopted in 1776. In other states, even when the opportunity to change their selection method arose, it was not taken because the existing system reflected the values of the state well. For example, even though Illinois adopted a completely new constitution in 1970, it continued to elect its judges on a partisan basis due to the highly partisan and individualistic political culture of the state. However, even in the Prairie State, recent high-priced and nasty election campaigns for the Illinois Supreme Court have raised calls for reform.[69]

---

[67] Kermit L. Hall, "Progressive Reform and the Decline of Democratic Accountability: The Popular Election of State Supreme Court Judges, 1850–1920," *American Bar Foundation Research Journal* 2(1984):345–63.

[68] Jeff German, "Lawmakers Pave Way for Vote on Appointing Judges," *The Las Vegas Sun*, 6 June 2009, online edition.

[69] Editorial, "Change Way Judicial Races Are Financed," *State Journal-Register (Springfield, IL)*, 10 June 2009, p. 6.

What Difference Does a Judicial Selection Method Make?

The variation in how states select their judges has given political scientists a unique opportunity to assess the impact of these selection methods and the impact of political institutions more generally. Before reviewing the results of recent research on this question, let's consider what effects reformers and their critics expected.

The original approach of appointing judges was criticized for reducing the independence of the courts and shifting political power to the appointing institution, whether the governor or legislature.[70] One of the central principles of American government is the separation of powers among the three branches, and elite appointment may upset that balance.[71] Appointments might also affect the type of person who rises to the bench. For example, in South Carolina, one of only two states still using legislative appointment, almost all judges are former state lawmakers.

Judicial elections also have critics, with the American Bar Association (ABA) being perhaps the most prominent among them.[72] Given the widespread use of judicial elections and the extensive debate about them over the past 100 years, these arguments are more extensive and multifaceted than those regarding judicial appointment.

First, judicial elections have long been criticized for being low-turnout, low-information events.[73] Few voters seem to know anything about candidates for state judgeships, especially below the supreme court level. Without such information, voters cannot form and express a coherent preference about who should be a judge. People tend either to skip judicial races on ballots or to fall back on voting cues that may be weakly related to their preferences, completely irrelevant, or even misleading. As a result, judges such as the problematic one in Nevada may get elected. In partisan elections, the party label may provide some information about a candidate's political values and policy preferences, but it says nothing about his or her fairness and judicial competence; and in nonpartisan elections and primaries, voters are not privy to even this limited information.

Traditionally, one of the reasons that voters have known so little about judicial candidates is the professional norm that these candidates should not use anything in their campaigns beyond basic résumé data. In essence, judicial candidates had been able to tell voters only where they went to law school and what jobs they held. This information may be useful to voters who are familiar with the legal profession, but not to the general public. For example, few voters would be able to rank the qualifications of two judicial candidates knowing only that one attended the University of Texas School of Law and served as a clerk in the U.S. Circuit Court of Appeals and that the other attended the Texas Tech University School of Law and was a partner in Gardner, Westbrook, and Pinckney, LLC.

In particular, the legal profession frowns on judicial candidates offering the sort of information that we expect from candidates for other offices—their opinions on the important issues that might face them. So perhaps surprisingly, no self-respecting judicial candidate would run a TV ad that said, "Emily Zimmer for Judge—No More Coddling Criminals" or "Reelect Judge Rachel Levine and Help Stop Runaway Lawsuits," even though we would not be surprised to see

[70] Kermit Hall, "The Judiciary on Trial: State Constitutional Reform and the Rise of the Elected Judiciary, 1846–1860," *The Historian*, 45(1983):337–54.

[71] Of course, because all federal judges are appointed by the president, the same argument could be made about the federal judiciary.

[72] James Sample, "Justice for Sale," *The Wall Street Journal*, 25 March 2008; American Bar Association, "Independence of the Judiciary: Judicial Elections Are Becoming More Politicized," 2006, http://www.abanet.org/publiced/lawday/talking/judicialelections.html.

[73] David Klein and Lawrence Baum, "Ballot Information and Voting Decisions in Judicial Elections," *Political Research Quarterly* 54(2001):709–28.

a state legislative candidate run such ads—in fact, we would expect it. This professional norm against policy-oriented information in judicial campaigns is a natural extension of the norm that judges should administer the law based only on the specific facts and the established law involved in each case. How would you like to be on trial on a charge of drunk and disorderly conduct—guilty or not—before the newly elected Judge Zimmer fresh off her "law-and-order" election campaign? Or suppose you were suing a negligent doctor for botching a surgical procedure. Would you want Judge Levine to hear your case? Governors and legislators are expected to have opinions on public policy and discuss them in their election campaigns; judges are expected to face all decisions before them with an unbiased mind. Some states have tried to embody these norms in law, with varying impacts (see Institutions Matter box);[74] but beginning with the important 2002 U.S. Supreme Court case, *Republican Party of Minnesota vs. White*, the federal courts have begun to strike down these regulations as unconstitutional infringements on free speech.[75]

Another important concern some people have with judicial elections arises from recent dramatic increases in campaign spending, especially in supreme court races.[76] As highlighted in the opening vignette of this chapter, some people are troubled by how and why judicial candidates receive their campaign contributions. One problem is that lawyers and law firms have long been the major donors in these races, raising concerns about judicial fairness when these donors subsequently appear in court. While judges certainly deny such bias, it may creep into the courtroom unconsciously, as at least one recent study suggests.[77] Perhaps even more worrisome is the recent trend of interest groups becoming involved in state supreme court races because of the broad judicial issues that are decided there.[78] These groups have been contributing money and airing independent TV ads for the judicial candidates they favor, with no feelings of constraint by judicial norms about the content of such ads. Nasty, independently funded commercials have been pivotal in some races, implying judges are soft on crime, in bed with certain economic interests, or even friendly to child molesters. One commercial in a 2008 Michigan Supreme Court race lambasted a candidate with "Probation for a terrorist sympathizer? We're at war with terrorists!"[79]

Certain states have been particularly hard hit with these expensive and bitter campaigns—Ohio, Alabama, Illinois, Texas, and West Virginia, in particular. This seems like an odd mix of states, doesn't it? These are states with no clear regional connection and with a variety of social and economic characteristics, but with one thing in common: partisan elections for their supreme courts. Even some nonpartisan election states (e.g., Mississippi, Michigan, Wisconsin) have begun having expensive and bitter races for their high

[74] C. Scott Peters, "Canons of Ethics and Accountability in State Supreme Court Elections," *State Politics and Policy Quarterly* 9(2009):24–55.

[75] *Republican Party of Minnesota v. White*, 536 US 765 (2002); U.S. Eighth Circuit Court, *Dimick v. Republican Party of Minnesota* (No. 05–566).

[76] Chris W. Bonneau, "What Price Justice(s)? Understanding Campaign Spending in State Supreme Court Elections," *State Politics and Policy Quarterly* 5(2005): 107–25; Brendan Kirby, "Alabama Had Costliest (But Not the Nastiest) Court Race," *The Press-Register (Birmingham, AL)*, 11 November 2008, online edition.

[77] Damon M. Cann, "Justice for Sale? Campaign Contributions and Judicial Decisionmaking," *State Politics and Policy Quarterly* 7(2007):281–97.

[78] Kathleen Hale, Ramona McNeal, and Jason Pierceson, "New Judicial Politics? Interest Groups in State Supreme Court Races." Presented at the 2008 meetings of the Midwest Political Science Association, Chicago, IL.

[79] John Gramlich, "Nasty Judicial Races Renew Complaints," *Stateline.org*, 8 December 2008, online edition.

INSTITUTIONS MATTER

THE IMPACT OF ETHICS REGULATIONS FOR JUDICIAL ELECTIONS

The authors of some state constitutions in the 19th century decided to elect their judges, hoping to make the judicial branch of state government independent of the legislative and executive branches. The unique role of judges in our political system, however, requires that they not only be independent of the other branches of government, but also independent of other pressures, some of which elections may actually increase. We want impartial judges who decide each case based on its merits and not based on their ideology or political predisposition. Although we don't mind legislators and chief executives espousing their policy positions and making promises on the campaign trail and collecting campaign contributions, we are leery about judges doing so. Making campaign promises suggests that perhaps something other than the facts of a case may affect a judge's decision; campaign contributions imply another sort of potential influence.

The states have developed a series of institutions to help shield judges from such electoral pressures—ethics regulations about what can and cannot happen in judicial elections. These laws have become increasingly important in recent years as judicial races, especially at the state supreme court level, have become more competitive, consequential, and expensive.

In 2002, however, the U.S. Supreme Court struck down one important type of these regulations. *Republican Party of Minnesota v. White* invalidated bans on judicial candidates announcing their views on legal or political issues that might come before their court. The Supreme Court said that such "announce clauses" violated candidates' 1st Amendment right to free speech. Other ethics regulations continue to exist in some states, such as bans against making promises or commitments about taking certain actions on the bench and against soliciting campaign contributions, but as a result of the *White* decision, the legal position of these regulations is in flux.

Like many institutions we have discussed in this book, the variation of these judicial campaign regulations among the states allows scholars to test their impacts. Northern Iowa University political scientist C. Scott Peters has done this recently, shedding considerable light on judicial elections in the process.[1] As you have read about in various chapters, state and local elections generally are typically low-information affairs, but this is a particular problem for judicial elections. If voters don't know much about the candidates in the race, it is difficult for them to make a rational judgment in the voting booth. Peters theorized that the ethics regulations on judicial campaigns would actually reduce the amount and quality of the information voters had to work with even further. While it is difficult to assess directly how these institutions affect the quality of voter decisions, Peters found that they do have the follow-on effect of both limiting the number of candidates challenging sitting judges and increasing the vote-share of those incumbents. In short, these ethics regulations tend to advantage incumbents. Why would this be? Perhaps it is because when challengers have a harder time getting out information about themselves, voters will just fall back on the default choice of voting for the incumbent. This is a good example of a government institution's unintended effect.

Do you think that this unexpected effect of judicial campaign regulations is good or bad for a state? If bad, is it worth suffering that price if these regulations are having their originally intended effect of making sure judges are more open-minded and independent in the courtroom (an open question, by the way)? If not, how might regulations be devised that meet the original goals of shielding judges' independence without giving incumbent judges that extra advantage? What other unintended consequences might these ethics regulations have and how might you adjust the regulations to eliminate them? How would you test any of your hypotheses?

Note

1. C. Scott Peters, "Canons of Ethics and Accountability in State Supreme Court Elections," *State Politics and Policy Quarterly* 9(2009):24–55.

courts.[80] Retention elections are also sometimes heated, as in California Supreme Court races following hot-button decisions involving the death penalty and same-sex marriage.[81]

Expensive and bitter campaigns raise two particular problems for reformers. First, conflict of interest can be a concern, especially when one side in a case is represented by a contributor and the other side is not. The West Virginia case that led off this chapter might be an extreme example of this, but even if there is no explicit quid pro quo on a case—which would be bribery and patently illegal—might a judge develop an unconscious bias on certain cases based on his or her campaign support? Even less directly, might not interest groups tend to support candidates who have a particular point of view, thereby stacking the judiciary in their favor? This happens all the time in other elections, so why not with judicial elections?

The second concern some have with expensive and bitter judicial campaigns is their potential effect on the legitimacy of the court system itself. If judges—or even just their surrogates—are involved in unseemly campaigns, will that reduce the appearance of fairness for the general public? One of the bedrocks of the justice system is that if people think it is fair, they are willing (if not happy) to accept judgments that they don't like. Some argue that this is even more important for the judicial branch than the executive and legislative branches, which after all can be replaced more frequently. Recent studies show that elections, especially bitter, expensive, and highly publicized battles, can reduce the

court's legitimacy in the public's eyes.[82] Political scientist James Gibson's new study has broken these campaign effects down in some detail and compared state legislatures and supreme courts on them.[83] Gibson finds that only large amounts of campaign contributions from interest groups reduce the public's opinion of these courts; candidates talking about policy positions and even running attack ads do not cause people to think less well of them. Especially interesting, he also finds that this pattern of effects on state supreme courts' legitimacy is no different than those regarding state legislatures. In other words, Gibson finds evidence that, at least on these characteristics of elections, the general public holds their judges to no different standard than their lawmakers. Furthermore, absent such costly and nasty races, other studies find that a court's legitimacy doesn't seem to be affected at all by how its judges rose to the bench.[84] That is, if the election campaigns are not too bitter and expensive, Americans do not seem especially troubled by selecting their judges like they select other state policymakers.

So, after considering some of these arguments against judicial election and elite appointment, the Merit Plan probably sounds like a pretty good alternative, right? After all, who could argue against picking judges based

[80] Steven Walters, Stacy Forster, and Patrick Marley, "After Bitter Race, Calls for Reform," *The Journal/Sentinel (Milwaukee, WI)*, 2 April 2008, online edition; Greg Giroux, "Negative Ad Trend in Judicial Campaigns Draws Objections," *Politics.com*, 24 May 2007, online edition.

[81] Traut and Emmert, op. cit.; "John H. Culver and John H. Wold, "Rose Bird and the Politics of Judicial Accountability in California," *Judicature* 70(1986):81–89.

[82] James L. Gibson, "Challenges to the Impartiality of State Supreme Courts: Legitimacy Theory and 'New-Style' Judicial Campaigns," *American Political Science Review* 102(2008):59–75; James L. Gibson, "Campaigning for the Bench: The Corrosive Effects of Campaign Speech? *Law and Society Review* 42(2008):899–928; Damon A. Cann and Jeff Yates, "Homegrown Institutional Legitimacy: Assessing Citizens' Diffuse Support for State Courts," *American Politics Research* 36(2008):297–329.

[83] James L. Gibson, "'New-Style' Judicial Campaigns and the Legitimacy of State High Courts," *The Journal of Politics* 71(2009):1285–304.

[84] James P. Wenzel, Shaun Bowler, and David J. Lanoue, "The Sources of Public Confidence in State Courts: Experience and Institutions," *American Politics Research* 31(2003):191–211; Sara C. Benesh, "Understanding Public Confidence in America Courts," *Journal of Politics* 68(2006):697–707.

on merit? Indeed, this hybrid of expert evaluation and voter double-checking through a retention election has been the most frequently selected approach by the states that have changed their judicial selection method since World War II. Most would agree that judges need certain technical expertise and training; not just anyone can be a judge. Going back to Thomas Jefferson, Americans have strongly believed that the average citizen could serve well as a legislator; even the executive skills needed of a governor are probably more evenly distributed in the population than those skills needed to be a judge. Furthermore, the average person probably cannot determine who has the specialized skills that a judge needs. Would you want your doctor or car mechanic to be selected by a popular vote or would you rather have them picked (or at least certified) by experts in their fields? The Merit Plan also reduces the temptation in appointment systems for judicial selection to be made on criteria other than pure technical merit, such as political party or returning a political favor.

On the other hand, as we have seen time and again in this book, all institutions have a variety of effects, not all of them good or even intended. We have to be careful not to take labels like "Merit Plan" at face value. If you stop to think about it, it sounds like the sort of marketing slogan that could have been cooked up over martinis on *Mad Men*.

What exactly does *merit* mean in this context? In practice, merit is defined for this reform based on the values of a state's legal establishment. Old, established law firms, the state bar association, and their political allies tend to dominate Merit Plan nomination committees. For example, Oklahoma's Judicial Nominating Commission is made up of six members of the Oklahoma Bar Association elected by their fellow bar members, six nonlawyers appointed by the governor, and one member elected by

This ad for attorneys Fetman and Garland may generate significant name recognition—and business—that could help them should they someday decide to run for an elective judgeship. However, it will not likely impress the legal establishment who control nominations in the Merit Plan judicial selection process.

the other 12.[85] These people know—and really care about—the difference between the University of Texas School of Law and the Texas Tech University School of Law. So they may well be the best people to evaluate judicial merit. Some states at least try to expand their pool of potential judges more broadly. For example, in 2009, New Hampshire's Judicial Selection Commission began its work in filling a Supreme Court vacancy by running an online ad for applicants;[86] but where the NHJSC placed this ad is telling—on the website of the New Hampshire Bar Association.

The informal social hierarchy that exists in the legal profession also suggests certain differences in the types of lawyers selected to be judges through the Merit Plan and through elections or appointment. Consider the "See a Lawyer for 10 Bucks" guy who advertises on afternoon television and on city buses. He is not likely to attain a judgeship through the Merit Plan because he likely does not impress the legal establishment. He might have a pretty good chance of winning a judicial election,

[85] Oklahoma Bar Association, "2009 Judicial Nominating Commissions Elections,." (http://www.okbar.org/news/news09/jnc/default.htm).

[86] Kathryn Marchhocki, "Online Ad Seeks NH Supreme Court Justice," *Union-Leader (Manchester, NH)*, 6 January 2009, online edition.

however, because of the name recognition that his TV and bus ads have generated, his money, and his self-promotional talent. The background, values, and clients of establishment lawyers can be quite different than those of lawyers who advertise on buses. Think about who gains and loses when these values are reflected in judicial decision making.

So far, we have mainly considered reformers' arguments about the effects of these different judicial selection methods, but what has objective research told us about them? In addition to the research judicial campaigns, scholars have used the institutional variation among the states in judicial selection method to test a variety of theories about their effects, both those espoused by reformers and others that reformers had not considered.

First, scholars have looked at the effect of selection method on the demographic characteristics of judges. This is difficult due to the homogeneity among judges; even compared to other public officials, state judges are overwhelmingly middle-aged, middle class, white, and male. However, this is changing, in particular with many more women coming to the bench, a reflection of the better gender balance in the legal profession in recent years.[87] Paralleling the rise of women in legislatures, whereas in 1980, only 3 percent of state supreme court justices were women, today that figure is 29 percent.[88] More people of minority heritages are becoming judges, too.[89] But both socially and educationally, the bench is a homogeneous place. Given the educational and training requirements for the job, it is probably not surprising that, more than any other class of public officials, judges' professional backgrounds are very similar.

Political scientists have found that elections lead to less racial and ethnic diversity among judges and that Merit Plans and appointment systems tend to increase it.[90] Why? First, because elections are decided on a majority-rule principle, if people tend to vote for those of their own racial or ethnic group (an arguable assumption, of course), only candidates from majority groups will win for each slot. On the other hand, with an appointment system or Merit Plan, the appointing officials may look at the totality of the bench and purposefully seek diversity, whether because they think that it is the right thing to do or as a way of rewarding various constituencies. If this is so, why do we find that women judicial candidates do worse in election systems, even though they constitute a slight majority in most states?[91] Attribute this to a lingering gender bias in the electorate, something that affects elections for almost all offices. As with the changing demographics of governors and legislators, this argument is supported by judges' increased gender diversity in recent years as norms about women's roles in our society have changed.

Most political scientists studying the effects of judicial selection have focused on judicial decision making because of its potential to affect the administration of justice and public policy. The general conclusion of these studies is that judicial selection does not affect judges'

[87] Jennifer M. Jensen and Wendy L. Martinek, "The Effects of Race and Gender on the Judicial Ambitions of State Trial Court Judges," *Political Research Quarterly* 62(2009):379–92; Margaret S. Williams, "Ambition, Gender, and the Judiciary," *Political Research Quarterly* 61(2008):68–78.

[88] McCall, 2008, op. cit.

[89] Kaitlyn L. Sill, "Judicial Selection and Racial Diversity: The Selection of African Americans to State Supreme Courts." Presented at the 2007 meetings of the Midwest Political Science Association, Chicago, IL.

[90] Barbara L. Graham, "Do Judicial Selection Systems Matter? A Study of Black Representation on State Courts," *American Politics Quarterly* 18(1990):316–36; Mark S. Hurwitz and Drew Noble Lanier, "Explaining Judicial Diversity: The Differential Ability of Women and Minorities to Attain Seats on State Supreme and Appellate Courts," *State Politics and Policy Quarterly* 3(2003):329–52; Sill, op. cit.

[91] Nicholas O. Alozie, "Selection Methods and the Recruitment of Women to State Courts of Last Resort," *Social Science Quarterly* 77(1996):110–26; Kathleen A. Bratton and Rorie L. Spill, "Existing Diversity and Judicial Selection: The Role of the Appointment Method in Establishing Gender Diversity in State Supreme Courts," *Social Science Quarterly* 83(2002):504–18; Hurwitz and Lanier, op. cit.

decisions much, if at all.[92] This is good—we hope that judges' decisions are driven by the law and the facts of the cases before them. The norm that judges should be impartial arbiters of justice appears largely to override any institutional differences among selection methods. But political scientists have found various marginal impacts of selection method on judicial decision making, primarily differences between elected judges on one hand and appointed and Merit Plan judges on the other, especially at the supreme court level.

First, as democratic theory suggests and as elections' critics fear, elected judges' decisions tend to reflect the ideology and values of their state's citizens, especially in competitive elections and on issues that are in the public eye, such as the death penalty.[93] Perhaps even more worrying for those critics, elected judges tend to adjust their decisions as elections approach (even retention elections), reflecting their state's ideology ever more closely and issuing harsher criminal sentences.[94] Elections also lead to more plea bargaining, fewer trials, fewer dissenting opinions on controversial issues decided by supreme courts, and closer adherence to U.S. Supreme Court precedent.[95] These effects suggest an effort by incumbent judges to reflect their constituents' values and reduce conflict, both of which might help their reelection chances. Partisan elections seem to result in judges who vote in ways that reflect their partisanship[96] and, in civil cases, who grant higher awards to injured parties.[97] Finally, as reformers suspected, two current studies have found that judges elected on nonpartisan ballots are more responsive to their constituents than those elected on partisan ballots.[98] At least on highly salient cases, like abortion questions in supreme courts, nonpartisan ballots give judges no cover from unpopular decisions.

While political scientists research the various causes and effects of judicial selection reform, for Americans and state policy makers, the question is a normative one—which method is best? Although researchers don't have a definitive answer to this question, they have done a good deal to focus it down to one of basic values. Most scholars working on this question, especially legal scholars, find themselves siding with the institution that emphasizes the value of the independence of experts, that is, the Merit Plan. Given the values of those who devote their lives to the academic study of the law, it should not be a surprise that this is the approach that appeals to them. In fact, the ABA believes there are so many problems with any kind of judicial election that it has recently eliminated its support even for the retention elections of the Merit Plan, favoring instead direct appointment by the governor.[99] Since the ABA is the epitome of the legal establishment

[92] Henry R. Glick and Craig F. Emmert, "Selection Systems and Judicial Characteristics: The Recruitment of State Supreme Court Justices," *Judicature* 70(1987):228–35.

[93] Paul Brace and Brent Boyea, "State Public Opinion, the Death Penalty, and the Practice of Electing Judges," *American Journal of Political Science* 52(2008):360–72; Traut and Emmert, op. cit.; Savchak and Barghotti, op. cit.; Brace and Hall, 1997, op. cit.

[94] Melinda Gann Hall, "Constituent Influence in State Supreme Courts: Conceptual Notes and a Case Study," *Journal of Politics* 49(1987):1117–24; and Melinda Gann Hall, "Electoral Politics and Strategic Voting in State Supreme Courts," *Journal of Politics* 54(1992):427–46; McCall, 2008, op. cit.; Huber and Gordon, op. cit.

[95] Scott A. Comparato and Scott D McClurg, "A Neo-Institutional Explanation of State Supreme Court Responses in Search and Seizure Cases," *American Politics Research* 35(2007):726–54; Melinda Gann Hall, "State Supreme Courts in American Democracy: Probing the Myths of Judicial Reform," *American Political Science Review* 95(2001):315–30; Harold W. Elder, "Property Rights Structures and Criminal Courts: An Analysis of State Criminal Courts," *International Review of Law and Economics* 7(1987):21–32.

[96] Paul Brace and Melinda Gann Hall, "Justices' Response to Case Facts," *American Politics Quarterly* 24(1996): 237–61; and Stuart S. Nagel, *Comparing Elected and Appointed Judicial Systems* (Beverly Hills, CA: Sage, 1973).

[97] Alexander Tabarrok and Eric Helland, "Court Politics: The Political Economy of Tort Awards," *Journal of Law and Economics* 42(1999):157–88.

[98] Caldarone, Canes-Wrone, and Clark, op. cit.; Brandice Canes-Wrone and Kenneth W. Shotts, "Do Elections Encourage Ideological Rigidity?" *American Political Science Review* 101(2007):273–88.

[99] American Bar Association Commission on the 21st-Century Judiciary, *Justice in Jeopardy* (Chicago: American Bar Association, 2003).

in this country, their interests would be maximized by this process.

Today's debate on judicial selection is not just between scholars advocating the Merit Plan (or direct appointment) and political party hacks advocating partisan elections. Some political scientists take the view of this normative question that highlights a different set of values than those of legal scholars. In particular, Michigan State University political scientist Melinda Gann Hall, often with her colleague, University of Pittsburgh's Chris Bonneau, has weighed into the debate about judicial elections as one of their strongest champions.[100] Mainly studying state supreme elections and decision making, Hall builds her argument by first demonstrating that judicial races are no less competitive than most other comparable races, like those for Congress and most statewide offices.[101] The information that voters have about judicial races, as reflected in the factors that influence their votes, is not much different than for those other races, either.[102] Hall and Bonneau also take a completely different tack on the issue of campaign spending, negative ads, and partisan labels than do the ABA and judicial elections' other critics.[103] They find that each of these increases the interest in, and the information available to, voters in judicial races, resulting in increased voter participation, a judicial branch that is more responsive to public values, and victories for better qualified candidates. Another set of studies of ICA elections finds largely supportive evidence.[104]

Hall and Bonneau have managed to focus the debate over judicial selection, demonstrating how competing values are at play, rather than simply a matter of which method is "best." One view considers judges to be public officials who, while following professional norms and rules and using their training and experience, should be thought of like any other public officials in a democracy, with *responsiveness* to the voters being a value we should prize. The other view considers judges to be a special type of public official, one whose *independence* from all forces not related to the case, the law, and their professional standards we should value. These values parallel those that we hold for legislators, governors, and mayors (responsiveness), on the one hand, and for bureaucrats (independence) on the other. If you hold the former view, Hall and Bonneau's research suggests that we should forgo all the middle-of-the-road reforms, like nonpartisan elections and Merit Plan retention elections, and use only partisan elections, since that is the selection method that generates the most interest and information in their elections and, thereby, are the most responsive to the public. If you hold the latter view, the ABA's advocacy of a pure appointment process makes sense, since it would guarantee the judiciary's independence from any influence of public opinion.

---

[100] Hall and Bonneau, 2009, op. cit.

[101] Melinda Gann Hall, "State Supreme Courts in American Democracy: Probing the Myths of Judicial Reform," *American Political Science Review* 95(2001):315–30.

[102] Melinda Gann Hall and Chris W. Bonneau, "Predicting Challengers in State Supreme Court Elections: Context and the Politics of Institutional Design," *Political Research Quarterly* 56(2003):337–49; Melinda Gann Hall and Chris W. Bonneau, "Does Quality Matter? Challengers in State Supreme Court Elections," *American Journal of Political Science* 50(2006):20–33.

[103] Bonneau and Hall, 2009, op. cit.; Melinda Gann Hall, "Voting in State Supreme Court Elections: Competition and Context as Democratic Incentives," *Journal of Politics* 69(2007):1147–59; Chris W. Bonneau, "The Effects of Campaign Spending in State Supreme Court Elections," *Political Research Quarterly* 60(2007):498–99; see also: Brent D. Boyea, Victoria Farrar-Myers, Chris Bonneau, and Damon M. Cann, "Contributor Decisions in Judicial Elections: Explaining the Impact of Partisan and Nonpartisan Election Formats." Presented at the 9th Annual State Politics and Policy Conference, Chapel Hill, NC.

[104] Matthew J. Streb, Brian Frederick, and Casey LaFrance, "Voter Rolloff in a Low-Information Context: Evidence from Intermediate Appellate Court Elections," *American Politics Research* 37(2009):644–69; Matthew J. Streb and Brian Frederick, "Conditions for Competition in Low-Information Judicial Elections: The Case of Intermediate Appellate Court Elections," *Political Research Quarterly* 62(2009):523–37; Brian Frederick and Matthew J. Streb, "Paying the Price for a Seat on the Bench: Campaign Spending in Contested State Intermediate Appellate Court Elections," *State Politics and Policy Quarterly* 8(2008):410–29.

So while scholars have recently learned a considerable amount about the impacts of judicial selection processes, two things continue to make designing the perfect system difficult: (1) Each approach involves trade-offs and requires value judgments, and (2) the values involved—responsiveness to the public and the independence of experts, or rather, democracy versus technocracy—are not easily resolved in our political culture. Is it any wonder, then, that these institutions continue to vary widely among the states and that calls for reform continue everywhere?

Reform and the State Courts

The history of American state courts and the civil and criminal justice systems has been one of institutional experimentation and reform. From partisan and nonpartisan elections to the Merit Plan, from intermediate courts of appeal to family and drug courts, from directors of state courts to boards that review attorney and judicial misconduct, the states have been trying to get the administration of justice right throughout our history. The lack of a clear vision about what we want from our courts makes this an especially difficult and continuing task. Certainly, we want fair and impartial adjudication of cases based on the facts and law, but we also want our courts to reflect the basic values and principles that our citizens hold dear. Furthermore, we want the courts to guard the basic rights of minorities because, besides being the right thing to do according to Americans' basic political values, we know that each of us will be in the minority sometimes, and we want our rights protected then.

Fulfilling all these needs is a tall order for the courts, so it should be no surprise that we never get them exactly right. Consider the following reforms that have been touted recently and how they speak to the values we want our courts to reflect.

- **Tort reform**—Bringing a civil suit against a person, government, or corporation that we feel has injured us is an old way of settling disputes in the Anglo-American tradition of common law. Such an injury is known as a **tort**. Some argue that tort actions are occasionally abused, whether through excessive awards for damages or outright fraud. Business groups, medical groups (because doctors are the target of many tort suits), and their political allies (often Republicans) have led the fight for reforms that limit the right to sue or the amount that can be awarded in a lawsuit.[105] Trial lawyers, consumer and victims' rights groups, and their political allies (often Democrats) oppose tort reform, arguing that the ability to sue for damages not only compensates those who have suffered such damages, but also encourages manufacturers and other businesses to avoid inflicting damage in the first place.

- **Criminal court reforms**—Criminal courts have also been the target of procedural reform efforts recently in an effort to make justice both fair and efficient there. Some of the most experimental of these reforms have struck at the oldest and most established traditions in Anglo-American courtrooms. For example, Oregon and Louisiana criminal trials tend to be shorter than in other states because they don't require a jury's unanimous agreement to convict.[106] As of 2008, judges in Florida can allow jurors to ask questions of

---

[105] Jefferey O'Connell and Christopher J. Robinette, *A Recipe for Balanced Tort Reform: Early Offers with Swift Settlements* (Durham, NC: Carolina Academic Press, 2008); Eric Helland and Alexander Taborrok, *Judge and Jury: American Tort Law on Trial* (Oakland, CA: The Independent Institute, 2005).

[106] Adam Liptak, "Guilty by a 10–2 Vote: Efficient or Unconstitutional?" *The New York Times*, 7 July 2009, online edition. The U.S. Supreme Court has recently agreed to hear a case (*Bowen v. Oregon* No. 08–1117) that challenges the constitutionality of non-unanimous juries, so this reform may not be an option soon.

witnesses, something that has never been allowed before in our legal tradition.[107] In another break from the past, the Virginia Court of Appeals (the Old Dominion's ICA) recently granted the first ever "Writ of Actual Innocence" after DNA evidence exonerated a person wrongly convicted of a crime.[108]

- **Prison reforms and alternatives**—The United States incarcerates a far greater proportion of its population than any other industrialized country. With a prison population of over 2 million, greater than 1 percent of adult Americans are imprisoned today, a record even for this country.[109] This prison population explosion has both strained state budgets and led many to question the efficacy, fairness, and humanity of our criminal justice system. Drug courts, mental health courts, and veterans courts are all, in part, meant to address this crisis. States have also tried other reforms, including the greater use of parole and probation for nonviolent offenders. By one estimate, it costs a state $79 per day to keep a person in prison, while it costs $3.50 per day to monitor that person on probation or parole.[110] Some reforms are aimed at reducing **recidivism** rates, which are both a cause and an effect of prison overcrowding. For example, a new law in Kansas gives prisoners a better shot at parole if they complete educational and drug-treatment programs.[111] Other

Educational programs for people incarcerated by the states, such as this classroom in a juvenile corrections facility in Nebraska, are meant to provide positive alternatives for prisoners, reduce their recidivism rates, and, in the end, reduce state prison costs.

reforms try to deal directly with the costs of prison, such as instituting telemedicine capacities in prisons, charging convicts for their medical care, and even, in one drastic and controversial move tried in Ohio and Georgia, cutting back on prisoners' meals.[112]

- **CourTools**—CourTools are a set of 10 performance measures developed by the National Center for State Courts in an effort to make courts more user friendly and efficient.[113] Aimed at evaluating court systems rather than specific judges, Cour-Tools use both objective court data and surveys of those who have participated in the judicial system as parties to a case, jurors, witnesses, and family members.

---

[107] Colleen Jenkins, "Change Lets Jurors Submit Questions for Trial Witnesses," *The St. Petersburg (FL) Times*, 4 January 2008, online edition.

[108] Maria Gold, "Va. Court Grants First-Ever Innocence Writ," *The Washington Post*, 13 August 2008, online edition.

[109] Jenifer Warren, *One in 100: Behind Bars in America* (Philadelphia, PA: Pew Center for the States, 2008).

[110] Keith B. Richburg, "State Seek Less Costly Substitutes for Prison," *The Washington Post*, 13 July 2009, online edition.

[111] John Gramlich, "States Seek Alternatives to More Prisons," *Stateline-org*, 18 June 2007, online edition.

[112] Kurt Erikson, "Illinois Prisons Seek Medical Cost Savings," *Quad-City (Rock Island, IL) Times*, 23 April 2009, online edition; Associated Press, "Perdue OKs Charging Inmates for Health Care," *The Atlanta Journal-Constitution*, 22 April 2009, online edition; Associated Press, "Prison Blues: States Slimming Down Inmate Meals," *The Atlanta Journal-Constitution*, 5 June 2009, online edition.

[113] See the National Center for State Courts' website for more details on CourTools: http://www.ncsconline.org/D_Research/CourTools/tcmp_courttools.htm.

Summary

State justice systems are both complex and diverse, and the central themes of this book—the importance of institutions, reform, and comparisons—become thoroughly intermingled when discussing them. Because a court can have a significant and direct impact on a person's life, and because we have ambiguous expectations for our courts, Americans have continuously reformed these institutions. This has led to the substantial state-to-state variation we see among them today. Despite this complexity, we can identify clear patterns and use this variation to understand how the states' institutions of justice work.

State courts settle civil and criminal disputes among people, corporations, and government entities. These courts work as a self-contained system within each state, working parallel to, rather than in competition with or as inferior to, the federal court system. State trial courts, intermediate courts of appeal (ICAs), and supreme courts each have an important and unique role in administering justice. Roughly speaking, trial courts see disputes first, determine the facts of the case, and apply the law. ICAs examine the appeals about the fairness of trial proceedings. The supreme court assesses the constitutionality of state laws and legal procedures; it is the final arbiter of disputes over the state's constitution and law. Although their explicit job is just to interpret and apply the law in specific disputes, by doing so, the courts have a major impact public policy.

Unlike most other American public officials, state judges gain their positions through a variety of methods, depending on the state and the level of the court. These judicial selection methods include appointment by the governor or legislature, partisan and nonpartisan election, and the Merit Plan. There is perpetual call for the reform of judicial selection, with different methods being touted by those who hold different values about the courts. Although scholars have found some significant impacts of the ways in which judges are selected, little evidence exists that judges selected in different ways behave radically differently from one another on the bench.

Key Terms

Adjudication

Adjudicator

Adversarial argument

Bench trial

Common law

Conflict of interest

Court of last resort

Defendant

Director of state courts

Docket

General jurisdiction

Intermediate courts of appeal

Judicial review

Jury

Legal brief

Limited jurisdiction

Majority opinion

Merit Plan

Original jurisdiction

Out-of-court settlement

Plaintiff

Plea bargain

Precedent

Problem-solving courts

Recidivism

Recuse

Retention election

Specialty court

Supreme court

Tort

Trial court

Trial transcript

Discussion Questions

1. Discuss the differences between criminal and civil law.
2. What is the difference between a jury trial and a bench trial? What are the advantages and disadvantages of each type of trial?
3. Why do states have intermediate courts of appeal, and what is their role in the judicial process?
4. How and why do state supreme courts influence public policy?
5. What are the different methods states use for selecting judges? Why is there such variance across the states?

Suggested Readings

Baum, Lawrence. 2007. *American Courts: Process and Policy*, 6th ed. Belmont, CA: Cengage.

Bonneau, Chris W., and Melinda Gann Hall. 2009. *In Defense of Judicial Elections*. New York: Routledge.

Hall, Melinda Gann. 2001. "State Supreme Courts in American Democracy: Probing the Myths of Judicial Reform." *American Political Science Review* 95:315–330.

Hall, Melinda Gann. 2008. "State Courts: Politics and the Judicial Process," in Virginia Gray and Russell L. Hanson, eds., *Politics in the American States*, 9th ed. Washington, DC: CQ Press.

James L. Gibson. 2009. "'New-Style' Judicial Campaigns and the Legitimacy of State High Courts." *The Journal of Politics* 71(4):1285–1304.

Langer, Laura. 2002. *Judicial Review in State Supreme Courts: A Comparative Study*. Albany, NY: SUNY Press.

Lessenger, James E., and Glade E. Roper, eds. 2007. *Drug Courts: A New Approach to Treatment and Rehabilitation*. New York: Springer.

Peters, C. Scott. 2009. "Canons of Ethics and Accountability in State Supreme Court Elections." *State Politics and Policy Quarterly* 9(1):24–55.

Sheldon, Charles H., and Linda S. Maule. 1997. *Choosing Justice: The Recruitment of State and Federal Judges*. Pullman, WA: Washington State University Press.

Squire, Peverill. 2008. "Measuring the Professionalization of U.S. State Courts of Last Resort." *State Politics and Policy Quarterly* 8(3):223–238.

Streb, Matthew J., ed. 2007. *Running for Judge: The Rising Political, Financial, and Legal Stakes of Judicial Elections*. New York: New York University Press.

Suggested Media Resources

CourTopics (http://www.ncsconline.org/WC/CourTopics/topiclisting.asp): This is an information database website run by the National Center for State Courts that provides in-depth information on court-related topics. CourTopics has links to resource guides, overviews, FAQs, state profiles, and other types of information.

Justice Case Files (http://www.ncsconline.org/D_Comm/OrderGrphNovel.asp): These are graphic novels developed by the National Center for State Courts to teach people about various issues facing the state courts.

Benched: The Corporate Takeover of the Judiciary, Wayne Ewing Films, Inc. This 2005 advocacy documentary tells the story of the 2004 Illinois State Supreme Court race between Lloyd Karmeier and Gordon Maag, in which advocacy groups on both sides of the "tort reform" issue spent millions of dollars in the most expensive judicial race in history. Directed and produced by Wayne Ewing. Running time: 75 minutes.

Web Sites

American Bar Association (http://www.abanet.org/): The ABA is the largest professional association of lawyers in the United States, whose activities include accrediting law schools, training lawyers and judges, and advocating for changes in the law and legal system that it feels necessary.

Association of Family and Conciliation Courts (http://www.afccnet.org/): The AFCC is a nonprofit association of all types of professionals who work in family courts and mediation processes. Its members include judges, lawyers, mediators, psychologists, researchers, social workers, court administrators, and others interested in improving this type of specialty court. Other types of specialty courts have similar associations, but since family courts are among the oldest of this type of court, this association is currently the most well developed.

National Association of Court Management (http://www.nacmnet.org/): The NACM is a professional association for those who manage courts and court systems in the United States. It provides state, local, and federal court administrators information about best practices in running courts efficiently and effectively, and it advocates on behalf of courts and court administrators to the legislative and executive branches of government.

National Center for State Courts (http://www.ncsconline.org/): The NCSC is a professional association for judges that provides them with training, conducts research about law and legal systems, and advocates for judges' interests in the political system.

10

AP Photo/Ross D. Franklin

Fiscal Policy

BOOM AND BUST BUDGETING

When the economy is booming, state and local revenues can exceed expectations and provide funds for more public services, for tax cuts, or both. When things go bust, as they did spectacularly in 2008, people stop investing, some lose their jobs, and people consume less. Tax revenues dry up. Consider Arizona. It was a low tax engine of economic growth since 2000. People moved there seeking jobs and housing. The construction boom generated thousands of jobs. Rising home values gave people equity they could borrow against, to purchase goods and services. Jobs and spending pumped revenue into state and local governments, and spending increased. The amount of funds that Arizona State University received from the state per student enrolled increased each budget year from $5,900 in 2002 to a record $8,000 per student in 2008.

Then it went bust. The world realized that home values in booming areas like Arizona were overvalued and purchased with far too much debt. Homeowners across the United States began defaulting on loans. In January 2008, the Swiss megabank UBS reported huge losses due the shaky U.S. real estate market. In spring of 2008, Bear Sterns, one of America's largest investment firms, collapsed. A large California mortgage bank failed in July. Banks quit lending, the real estate market dried up, and the consumer spending, construction jobs, and business investments that had provided tax revenues for Arizona, and other states, dried up. In September 2008, other major financial institutions failed or avoided failure via government take-over. Arizona's senior U.S. Senator and Republican presidential candidate, John McCain, briefly suspended his campaign so he could take part in the bailout negotiations.

The economy continued to decline, and it became clear that Arizona's budget for the 2008–09 fiscal year would end up in deficit. In January 2009, the legislature patched a $1 billion hole, and expected to have the budget balanced at the end of the fiscal year (June 30, 2009). State employees were furloughed. Pac 10 football coaches were given pay cuts. University budgets were cut 18 percent. By July 2009, however, the state faced a $2.5 billion deficit (in the 2008–09 budget), equal to 25 percent of the budget. Meanwhile, the state had to plan a 2009–10 budget, and revenue forecasts showed a $3 billion deficit for that budget.

A special session of the Republican-controlled legislature met in the summer of 2009, but failed to produce an agreement with the Democratic governor about how to close the 2009–10 gap. A voter-approved rule requiring a two-thirds majority of the legislature to raise taxes took that option off the table. The state used spending cuts, one-time federal stimulus funds, and proposed the sale of state House and state Senate buildings (pictured in the opening of this chapter) to close part of the deficit in September. Entire academic programs were cut at universities, and per student funding was set at the lowest level in years. Spending on social services was cut, and 10,000 families lost state health insurance. Despite this, the state's treasurer predicted Arizona would be out of money by November 2009 if the state did not take further action.

At least 34 other states faced double-digit deficits when planning their 2009–10 budgets. Such is fiscal politics when a recession eats away revenues. Unlike their federal counterparts, states and localities must eventually balance their budgets. State and local officials have less room to hide from tough budgeting choices. This chapter examines how and when states and cities make choices about taxation and spending, and what are possible consequences of these choices.

Sources: National Conference of State Legislatures, "State Budget Update, July 2009." Denver, CO: National Conference of State Legislatures, 2009; Casey Newton, "10,000 Working Parents in Arizona to Lose Health Insurance," *Arizona Republic,* 8 September 2009.

Introduction

State and local governments provide people with a wide array of services—literally from birth to death. States, counties, and cities run hospitals and health care systems, child care programs, elementary education, and colleges and universities. They provide for public safety by enforcing building codes, inspecting restaurants, maintaining drinking water systems, and operating police and fire-fighting services. Some jurisdictions even run cemeteries.

One of the most difficult tasks of governing is generating the revenue required to fund the wide range of public services that people expect and demand and then balancing limited revenues with those demands for services and programs. Matters are complicated by the fact that people do not agree on what the government's spending priorities should be and by disagreement over which taxes should be used to fund government. Fiscal politics involves policies and decisions relating to raising and spending public money. Fiscal policy—or budgeting—is how state and local elected officials figure out who gets what from government, at whose expense.

People generally do not like to pay taxes, but a fundamental trait of a sovereign government is that it has some ability to coerce citizens to pay their taxes. For example, it is very difficult, and typically illegal, to avoid paying taxes that you owe. Whether a tax applies to your income or the purchase of this book, the federal, state, county, or city governments that have the power to tax also have the power to penalize you if you are found to have avoided a tax you owed.

To some observers, the tax and spending powers of government are feared because they see governments as predatory **leviathans**, always seeking and finding new funding sources and collecting ever more revenue.[1] The leviathan theory of government proposes that politicians tax and spend without regard to how much citizens are actually willing to pay. The word *leviathan* refers to government as an ever-growing, predatory giant, but fiscal politics and policy aren't so simple. In democratic societies, governments at any level are in a weak position to simply rely on coercion or duplicity to collect the revenues they need. Voters are not easily tricked into paying taxes they don't like, and history shows that this nation was founded after a revolution against taxes that people found unreasonable. Some taxes are more unpopular than others (few taxes can be called popular), and some levels of taxation are not realistic. As we shall see in this chapter, perceptions of unreasonable taxation can still lead to public revolts that affect what state and local governments can do. In Chapter 12, we also see that taxation may affect whether businesses and people leave one place to locate in another.

Although government is constrained in regard to raising revenues, nearly all elected officials have a spending program they will fight to defend—largely in response to demands from their constituents. For elected representatives, the act of budgeting involves balancing demands for expensive government programs against practical limits on how much revenue a government can or should raise. Budgeting is an attempt to deal with scarcity: There's never enough money to fund every possible government program that people might want. As we

[1] William Niskanen, *Bureaucracy and Representative Government* (Chicago: Aldine-Atherton, 1971); "Revenue Structure, Fiscal Illusion and Budgetary Choice," *Public Choice* (1976):45–61; James Buchanan and Richard E. Wagner, *Democracy in Deficit* (New York: Academic Press, 1977); Robert Higgs, *Crisis and Leviathan: Critical Episodes in the Growth of American Government* (New York: Oxford, 1987).

shall see, states and communities deal with scarcity in different ways, and their ability to balance demands for programs against limits on resources depends on many factors. Demands for government spending vary widely across places due to differences in state populations. More children, for example, may mean more demand for education; more elderly may mean more spending on health care. Demand may never overlap with public willingness to pay because some people may be willing to support taxes to pay for services that assist them, but they may be reluctant to support funds for public goods and services they don't use.

Criteria for Evaluating Taxes

The public's willingness to pay a particular tax (or a fee or charge) is one criterion we will use in this chapter when evaluating the revenue sources that state and local governments use. Willingness to pay, as we will illustrate, may be a function of how visible a tax is. We also focus on additional features of taxes that are of interest to political scientists, economists, and perhaps most importantly, government officials. As we examine different taxes, we see they differ in terms of **tax equity**—or who bears the burden of paying them. With a **progressive tax**, the wealthier people pay a larger proportion of their total income to cover the tax than the less affluent pay of theirs, whereas a **regressive tax** will have the poor pay a larger proportion of their income than the wealthy do to cover the tax.

Some governments may also be positioned to use taxes that are exportable. **Exportable taxes** are those mostly paid by people from other places (such as hotel taxes and taxes on natural resources, such as oil). Taxes also differ in their **elasticity,** that is, in how stable (or volatile) revenues from the tax are in times of economic boom and bust. Furthermore, some taxes may be "neutral" in their ability to alter the economic behavior of people and businesses.

Others may create odd incentives that distort behavior. All these factors enter into the politics of which taxes governments use to fund public services.

Options for revenues also vary widely due to the economic structure of a state or community, institutional differences, and differences in popular support for taxation. Options for revenues that are available in California and New York, such as increasing the state personal income tax, are not available in, say, Florida or Texas. California and New York have established income taxes and have rather liberal public preferences for government spending. Florida and Texas, in contrast, have voters who may be less sympathetic to public spending, and neither state has adopted a personal income tax. States also vary considerably on what can be taxed. Alaska can rely heavily on revenue from oil extraction, whereas Ohio cannot.

Why Do Some Places Tax and Spend More Than Others?

State and local governments raise and spend about 10 percent of the nation's gross domestic product. When spending of federal money transferred to states and localities is added in, all state and local governments spend roughly the same amount as the federal government. This reflects that states and localities spend money they collect in taxes, in charges, and fees and also spend hundreds of billions of dollars that the federal government collects each year that is transferred to states and localities.[2] Federal funds, rather than replacing state

---

[2] The U.S. Census estimated that states raised and spent $1.45 trillion in 2007 (excluding transfers from the federal government), and local governments raised $1.34 trillion in 2007, (excluding transfers). That is a total of $2.32 trillion. Total federal spending in 2007 was $2.8 trillion. States and localities spent 3.06 trillion when transfers are included.

money, seem to correspond with greater state spending. States that receive more money from the federal government also spend more of their own funds for public services.[3]

Each level of government competes for revenue—sometimes applying the same kind of taxes to the same sources. This is why in some places, you may pay a state income tax in addition to your federal income tax or a local sales tax on top of your state's sales tax. However, the American fiscal environment has evolved such that the national government, the states, and local governments each have one particular revenue source, respectively, that they tend to rely upon for much of the resources they raise by taxation.

A paycheck lists the multiple levels of government that tax a person working in New York City.

Comstock/Getty Images

---

[3] Garand, "Explaining Government Growth in the United States."

States vary in terms of how much revenue they raise and how they raise it. Some rely heavily on traditional taxes, others raise revenue from resource extraction and gambling. This makes it difficult to clearly define which states have the highest taxes. It depends on how we rank the states. The first two columns in Table 10.1 rank states according to how much they tax residents relative to the amount of income in the state per person. This ranking only considers traditional tax revenue sources, not those from fees (e.g., tuition), gambling, and others. Ranked this way, New Jersey, New York, and Connecticut tax the most and Alaska, Nevada, and Wyoming tax the least.

The third column ranks states somewhat differently: according to the total tax dollars collected per resident. Again, this ranking gives priority to traditional tax sources (income, sales, and property), but the rankings express how much is raised regardless of how wealthy the state is. Rankings in columns 2 and 3 differ somewhat because relatively wealthy states like Massachusetts and Illinois, and resource-rich Wyoming, move up in the rankings. Although these states rank near the average in terms of tax levels as a percent of state income, they generate more revenue because there is more wealth being taxed—if even at a lower rate than in less affluent states. When states are ranked this way, less affluent states with average tax rates (e.g., West Virginia) and relatively affluent states with low taxation (e.g., Alaska) rank lowest.

Rankings in column 4 of Table 10.1 look quite different. States are ranked here according to how much total revenue (traditional tax and other sources) is generated per person. Ranked this way, Alaska and Wyoming, sparsely populated states that generate funds from natural resources, top the list. More populous places like Georgia and Arkansas drop in this ranking. These rankings are affected by the state's level of wealth and the size of its population, but they also reflect the political and economic circumstances that shape the mix of taxes used in a state. Big

Table 10.1

States Ranked by Tax Revenue and Total Revenue Received, 2008

State	State and local tax revenue as % of per capita income, 2008	Effort Ranked by tax revenues as % of per capita state income, 2008	Effort Ranked by **tax** revenue received per capita, 2008	Yield Ranked by **total** **revenue** received per capita, 2008	Capacity Ranked by income per capita, 2008
New Jersey	11.8%	1	2	9	3
New York	11.7%	2	3	3	4
Connecticut	11.1%	3	1	12	1
Maryland	10.8%	4	4	24	6
Hawaii	10.6%	5	7	15	14
California	10.5%	6	6	4	11
Ohio	10.4%	7	18	16	31
Vermont	10.3%	8	12	17	22
Wisconsin	10.2%	9	17	25	23
Rhode Island	10.2%	10	10	11	19
Pennsylvania	10.2%	11	11	21	20
Minnesota	10.2%	12	8	14	16
Idaho	10.1%	13	27	45	42
Arkansas	10.0%	14	37	47	48
Maine	10.0%	15	21	20	34
Georgia	9.9%	16	23	50	38
Nebraska	9.8%	17	19	10	25
Virginia	9.8%	18	9	34	12
Oklahoma	9.8%	19	22	44	33
North Carolina	9.8%	20	28	42	39
Kansas	9.6%	21	20	37	24
Utah	9.6%	22	35	32	45
Massachusetts	9.5%	23	5	5	2
Delaware	9.5%	24	16	6	17
Kentucky	9.4%	25	41	48	47
Oregon	9.4%	26	24	8	27
Michigan	9.4%	27	26	23	28
Indiana	9.4%	28	34	33	40
West Virginia	9.3%	29	48	39	49
Illinois	9.3%	30	14	27	13
Iowa	9.3%	31	31	29	32
Missouri	9.2%	32	33	43	37
North Dakota	9.2%	33	30	19	26
Colorado	9.0%	34	13	22	9

State	Effort State and local tax revenue as % of per capita income, 2008	Effort Ranked by tax revenues as % of per capita state income, 2008	Effort . Ranked by **tax** revenue received per capita, 2008	Yield Ranked by **total** **revenue** received per capita, 2008	Capacity Ranked by income per capita, 2008
Washington	8.9%	35	15	7	8
Mississippi	8.9%	36	50	31	50
S. Carolina	8.8%	37	45	35	46
Alabama	8.6%	38	44	36	43
New Mexico	8.6%	39	46	13	44
Montana	8.6%	40	43	26	41
Arizona	8.5%	41	40	46	35
Louisiana	8.4%	42	38	18	29
Texas	8.4%	43	32	40	21
Tennessee	8.3%	44	42	38	36
South Dakota	7.9%	45	47	41	30
N. Hampshire	7.6%	46	29	49	10
Florida	7.4%	47	36	28	15
Wyoming	7.0%	48	25	2	5
Nevada	6.6%	49	39	30	7
Alaska	6.4%	50	49	1	18

Source: Tax Foundation (2009).

states like New York and California have more wealth to tap *and* have relatively high taxes, so they rate high regardless of how the states are ranked.

It is well documented that wealthier states tax more (per person) than less affluent states.[4]

Wealthy states have a greater tax base, and they also have more complex economies that create demands for rules and regulations—the basic stuff of government.

As noted, the final column in Table 10.1 ranks states according to their level of per capita personal income, from the wealthiest (Connecticut) to the least affluent (Mississippi). When the first two columns are compared to the final column, we can see that wealthier states tend to tax more than less wealthy states. The relationship is much stronger than suggested in Table 10.1, because these rankings do not illustrate how dollars of tax revenue correspond with dollars of state income. Figure 10.1 illustrates a clear linear pattern: As state per capita (per person) income rises, so does tax revenue collected per person.

[4] Dye, *Politics, Economics, and the Public*; and Richard Hofferbert, "The Relationship Between Public Policy and Some Structural and Environmental Variables in the American States," *American Political Science Review* (1966):73–82; James Alt and Robert Lowry, "Divided Government, Fiscal Institutions, and Budget Deficits: Evidence from the States," *American Political Science Review* 88(1994):811–28; David Primo, "Stop Us Before We Spend Again: Institutional Constraints on Government Spending," *Economics and Politics* 18(2006):269–312; John Matsusaka, *For the Many or the Few* (Chicago: University of Chicago Press, 2004).

Figure 10.1

State and local taxes collected per capita, 2008, by state income per capita

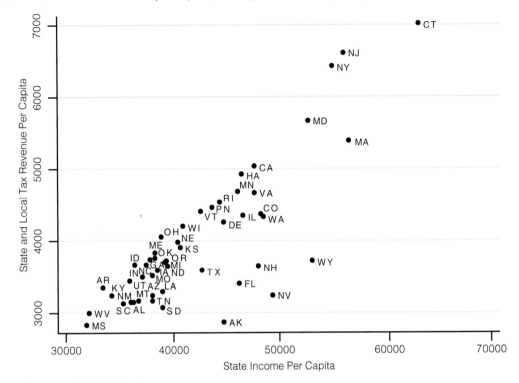

Source: U.S. Census of Governments, 2007.

Politics Matters

There are two key points to consider in Figure 10.1. First, state income appears to be a solid predictor of how much states tax. Why is this? Second, a few states don't fit the pattern. Some relatively wealthy states, such as New Hampshire, Florida, Nevada, and Wyoming, tax less (per capita) than their level of per capita income might predict.

Research suggests the answer to the first question is political. State income is strongly correlated with the political ideology of a state's residents.[5] Citizens in politically liberal states (e.g., Connecticut, Maryland, New York,

California) are more supportive of active government, so they tax themselves more. People in conservative states (e.g., Mississippi, Arkansas, Kentucky, Utah) are less sympathetic to government, so they tax less. In other words, poor states tend to be more conservative. This may seem to contradict the idea that less affluent people tend to be liberal Democrats, and that wealthier people tend to be conservative Republicans. That pattern actually holds. However, an influential study demonstrates that wealthy people in rich states like Connecticut and New York tend to be much more liberal than wealthy people in less affluent states like Mississippi.[6] As a result,

---

[5] Robert Erickson, Gerald Wright, and John McIver, *Statehouse Democracy: Public Opinion and Policy in the American States* (Cambridge, MA: Cambridge University Press, 1993).

[6] Andrew Gelman, *Red State Blue State Rich State Poor State: Why Americans Vote the Way They Do* (Princeton, NJ: Princeton University Press, 2008).

wealthy states have higher state and local taxes and more public services.

As for the second point, several of the states that deviate from the pattern plotted in Figure 10.1 generate much of their revenues from nontraditional revenue sources (tourism, gambling, natural resources) and thus rely less heavily on taxes.

One of the primary determinants of spending, however, is political. States where people have more liberal opinions tend to elect liberals, who spend more on public services. States where people have more conservative opinions tend to elect conservatives, who spend less. Even after accounting for a state's income, liberal states spend more per pupil on education and have more expansive Medicaid and welfare programs.[7] States also spend more on welfare when less affluent voters turn out in higher proportions in state elections.[8]

Next, we consider the various tools that state and local governments use to raise revenues from a variety of sources, and the political issues associated with some of these.

Where Does the Money Come From? Major Sources of Revenues

Income Tax

The first state began collecting income taxes in 1911, prior to the constitutional amendment that granted the federal government the power to tax income. The most recent state to adopt an income tax was Connecticut in 1991. Today, most of the revenue collected in the United States as income tax goes to fund the federal government. For most states, however, income taxes are a major part of their mix of revenue sources. Nearly all states (41) tax personal income, and two more states (Tennessee and New Hampshire) tax just personal income from investments. In addition, Alaska and Florida tax corporate income. This means that Wyoming, Washington, Nevada, Texas, and South Dakota are the only states that lack taxation of personal or corporate income.[9] A handful of states allow local governments to levy an income tax. The proportion of all states' total personal income collected in state income taxes has increased steadily since the 1960s.[10]

A few states have a **flat rate tax** for their income tax, where everyone pays the same rate, but most state income tax systems place people into one of several brackets defined by how much they earn. Tax rates increase for each bracket, with people in the highest income brackets paying the highest tax rate. Even for people in the top brackets, state income tax rates are far lower than those levied by the federal government. An average state has about five brackets, with the tax rate for people in the lowest income bracket averaging about 2.6 percent, and the rate for people in the highest bracket averaging about 6.8 percent. Hawaii and Oregon (11 percent), New Jersey (10.7 percent), California (10.5 percent), and Vermont (9.4 percent) have the highest rates for top income brackets.[11] In some states (California and New Jersey), the top bracket starts at $1,000,000 in income. In Oregon and Hawaii, an income of $175,000 is subject to the top bracket tax.

Evaluating the Income Tax Supporters of the income tax note several features they find attractive. Advocacy groups note that states making use of an income tax have the most

---

[7] Erikson, Wright, and McIver, *Statehouse Democracy*, p. 85.
[8] Kim Q. Hill and Jan Leighley, "The Policy Consequences of Class Bias in State Electorates," *American Journal of Political Science* (1992):351–65.

[9] South Dakota does levy a tax on bank income.
[10] James Garand and Kyle Baudoin, "Fiscal Policy in the American States," in V. Gray and R. Hanson, eds., *Politics in the American States: A Comparative Analysis,* 8th ed. (Washington, DC: CQ Press, 2004).
[11] http://www.taxadmin.org/fta/rate/ind_inc.html; http://www.taxfoundation.org

progressive revenue systems overall, whereas the poor pay a much larger proportion of their income in state and local taxes than the wealthy in states that lack an income tax (such as Washington, Florida, and Texas).[12] Income taxes are relatively easy for governments to collect (through payroll deduction), and revenues collected tend to be more stable in times of economic downturns when compared to sales taxes. Public opinion polls illustrate that voters find state income taxes more politically acceptable than federal taxes and property taxes, at least in states where the income tax already exists.[13] One study of the political consequences of adopting income taxes found that the party in control of the legislature that adopted the tax was usually re-elected. When voters did punish politicians for adopting a state income tax, Republicans were much more likely to suffer than Democrats.[14] This may be due to the fact that Republican voters expect more fiscal prudence from Republicans than Democratic voters expect from Democrats.

Critics point out that income is already taxed by the federal government, and that inflation can drive people who get **cost of living allowances (COLAs)** into higher tax brackets even though their real earning power does not increase. Income taxes may also distort the incentives that people have to work; and by taxing income that people save, it creates disincentives for savings, which makes less money available for investment and economic growth.

Sales Tax

If you travel overseas, you might find that you pay a form of a national sales tax—also known as a consumption tax, value-added tax, or goods and services tax. These are taxes on what people spend rather than on what they earn. In the United States, taxation on the sale of goods and services is largely the domain of states and local governments. States began taxing the purchase of goods during the Great Depression of the 1930s. At the time, federal social programs were in their infancy and states were searching for resources to deal with massive unemployment and poverty.

Mississippi first adopted the sales tax in 1932, and another 11 states had adopted it by 1933.[15] Today all but five states (Oregon, Alaska, Montana, New Hampshire, and Delaware) have a sales tax. About half of all tax revenue collected by state governments comes from the sales tax. California has the highest sales tax (8.25 percent), followed by Indiana, Mississippi, New Jersey, Tennessee, and Rhode Island (at 7 percent).[16] In addition, nearly all states grant their local governments the power to levy an additional increment on top of the state rate. This is the reason why you might pay a different rate as you move from one county to the next inside a state. When local sales taxes are considered, residents in parts of several high-sales-tax states pay over 9 or 10 percent in state and local sales tax on their purchases (e.g., residents of Seattle, Chicago, and parts of Tennessee).

Evaluating the Sales Tax One of the most noteworthy features of the sales tax is its relative political acceptability. Surveys of opinion

[12] 1996 Center for Tax Justice Report: Michael P. Ettlinger, John F. O'Hare, Robert S. McIntyre, Julie King, Neil Miransky, and Elizabeth A. Fray, "Who Pays? A Distributional Analysis of the Tax Systems of the 50 States," Citizens for Tax Justice, http://www.ctj.org/html/whopay.htm.
[13] Shaun Bowler and Todd Donovan, "Public Responsiveness to Taxation," *Political Research Quarterly* 48(1995):79–99.
[14] Susan Hansen, *The Politics of Taxation: Revenue without Representation* (New York: Praeger, 1983).

[15] Richard Winters, "The Politics of Taxing and Spending," in V. Gray and R. Hanson, eds., *Politics in the American States: A Comparative Analysis*, 7th ed. (Washington, DC: CQ Press, 1999).
[16] California's rate includes a 1 percent statewide local sales tax, http://www.taxadmin.org/fta/rate/sales.html.

demonstrate that when compared to other major revenue sources, state sales taxes are the most popular (or usually the least disliked). Taxes are collected at the point of sale on individual purchases, so they may not be as noticeable to the taxpayer as lump sum payments that can come due with property taxes and income taxes. For local governments, sales tax revenue can be particularly attractive because it offers the opportunity to get folks from out of town to bear some of the costs of funding services. As a tax on consumption, sales taxes may also create fewer distortions in people's incentives to work, save, and invest than an income tax does.

Susan Hansen's study suggests that most state governments that adopted a state sales tax between 1911 and 1977 survived the next election, but that they faced a slightly greater threat of defeat than governments that adopted the income tax. Again, Republican governments that adopted the tax were at a greater risk of defeat than Democratic governments.[17]

The sales tax has two clear weaknesses, however. The first is the elasticity or stability of it as a revenue source. The total amount collected depends on how much people are spending on "big-ticket" consumer goods. When the economy cools, and consumer confidence wanes, the demand for things such as new cars, boats, televisions, computers, and construction materials declines—and so does sales tax revenue. This problem is magnified when the sales tax applies only to goods and not to services.

The second issue is equity. People who earn less usually spend all their income, which means the sales tax applies to most of what they earn. People who earn more are able to save and invest some of what they earn, and the sales tax does not apply to that portion of their income. This means the poor pay much more of their overall income to sales taxes than the rich. It also means that states that rely heavily on sales taxes have the most regressive tax systems. Many states offset the regressive nature of this tax by exempting basic items such as food and medicine from the tax. The definition of basic needs is a political question and must be defined by the legislature. The California legislature's attempt to apply the sales tax to "non-essential luxury foods" (snacks) in California set various lobbyists scrambling to defend their particular products as essential, basic foods. They eventually launched a successful initiative (Proposition 163) to amend the state constitution in 1992 (the Don't Tax Food and Water Campaign) to prohibit the state from applying the sales tax to things like candy and bottled water.

Due to growing exemptions and shifts in the nature of the economy, the base of what the sales tax applies to has been eroding over time. Over the past several decades, spending has shifted from goods to services (lawyers, health care, advertising, consulting), and purchases are moving from the physical storefront to the virtual store online. Services are not always covered by state sales taxes (in part due to successful lobbying efforts by the affected groups), and states have particular difficulty collecting taxes from sales made via the internet (see Institutions Matter box). As the base of the tax erodes, states are under pressure to raise sales taxes on the remaining items subject to the tax.[18] If more exemptions are made for "basic" necessities, the remaining base of the sales tax becomes more dependent on big-ticket purchases, making revenues even more volatile.[19] Sales taxes may also distort behavior by creating incentives for people to travel to make purchases where taxes are lower or by encouraging them to shop online in order to avoid paying any sales tax.

---

[17] Hansen, *The Politics of Taxation.*

[18] Winters, "The Politics of Taxing and Spending."

[19] W. Duncombe, "Economic Change and the Evolving State Tax Structure: The Case of the Sales Tax," *National Tax Journal* (1992):308.

Property Tax

The property tax predates the income and sales taxes as the traditional source of public revenue and continues to serve as the primary revenue source for local governments. Some states collect state property taxes, but for most states, the property tax contributes less than 2 percent to total state taxes collected. However, property taxes are the main source of revenues for local governments. Property taxes are typically levied as a flat rate proportion (1 percent), for example, multiplied by the assessed value of property. These rates are often referred to as mill levies. A 1 percent mill levy is the same as saying the tax is $1 per $1,000 in assessed value of property, or the property value multiplied by .01. The amount one pays in tax is determined as much by the value of the property as by the tax rate. Most homeowners pay the same rate on residential property, with those having more valuable homes paying a higher tax amount overall. For example, a home assessed at $276,000 in Clark County, Washington, is subject to a 1.618 percent annual county property tax (or 0.00161 mill), a 2.766 percent state property tax (0.00276 mill), and various other

INSTITUTIONS MATTER

STATE AND LOCAL SALES TAX AND THE INTERNET

Traditional sales tax rules evolved in an era where goods were mostly sold to local people from local businesses. Today, what happens to the sales tax when more people make purchases via the internet from businesses in other states? If the vendor has a physical presence in your state (such as a shop or warehouse), it must charge sales tax for your state and local governments. If no "bricks and mortar" presence exists, however, it is not required to collect the tax. Some worry that this gives online retailers a major advantage over local businesses. As the internet now becomes a common shopping destination, large retailers such as Wal-Mart, Target, Toys "R" Us, and Barnes and Noble that have physical stores in nearly every state have attempted to avoid charging sales taxes by setting up separate legal dot-com entities that were, at least on paper, distinct from their traditional stores. Large online retailers such as Amazon.com also argue that the old rules are obsolete and that it is too complicated to collect taxes for 50 states and thousands of local governments. Complicated as it might be, Amazon is in the business of managing online sales and collecting sales taxes for clients such as Target.

Given the difficulty of administering and monitoring internet sales, states focus enforcement on a few "big-ticket" items, such as cars. Large-volume online sales of clothing, books, and music remain untaxed. A 2009 study estimated that states lost nearly $8 billion in revenue to online sales in 2008 alone.[1] States may lose $38 billion annually in sales tax revenue by 2011 as more consumers and retailers shift to the internet—with some states losing nearly 10 percent of their total tax collections.[2] States did band together to pressure retailers to voluntarily charge sales tax, and in 2003 some large, traditional retailers (Walmart.com and ToysRUs.com) began to do so. However, absent federal legislation, states cannot force online retailers to pay the tax, and the high-tech industry has lobbied successfully on Capitol Hill against giving states power to enforce their sales tax collections for purchases made online.[3] As of 2009, 41 states had adopted a standardized rule to make it easier for retailers to collect sales taxes from online sales, but unless Congress grants states the power to tax such sales, not much can change.

Notes

1. Donald Bruce and William F. Fox, "State and Local Sales Tax Revenue Losses from E-Commerce: Updated Estimates" (Chattanooga, TN: University of Tennessee, Center for Business and Economic Research, 2001).
2. Donald Bruce, William Fox, and LeAnn Luna, "State and Local Government Sales Tax Revenue Loss from Electronic Commerce" (Chattanooga, TN: University of Tennessee, 2009).
3. Brian Krebs, "Internet Sales Tax Effort on Hold Now," *Washington Post,* 17 December 2003, online edition.

property taxes. It would owe $446 a year in county property tax and $763 per year in state property tax (most state property tax rates are much lower than this).[20] All property taxes are usually collected on a single bill or two bills that arrive six months apart. This means that taxpayers are likely to be highly attentive to the total dollar amount they pay in property taxes (compared to what they pay

in sales taxes—imagine if you received one large bill each year for all that you owed in sales taxes rather than paying it at each individual purchase). Depending on where the property is located, the bill may include taxes for the county, the city, the school districts, the state, and other special service districts (that is, library districts, port districts, and water districts).

In the first half of the 20th century, property taxes accounted for nearly all of municipal revenues. Today, the local government revenue

---

[20] State laws also determine what percentage of the assessed value of property is subject to the tax.

CLARK COUNTY TREASURER 2007 REAL PROPERTY STATEMENT

Property Tax Questions	(360) 397-2252	**Doug Lasher**
Automated Tax Information	(360) 397-6054	**Clark County Treasurer**
Internet Address:	WWW.CLARK.WA.GOV/TREASURER	Post Office Box 9808
Property Value Questions	(360) 397-2391	Vancouver, WA 98666-8808
Property Account Number: 023456-789.0		8 am to 5 pm everyday except Wednesday which is 9 am to 5 pm

SHORT LEGAL	PROPERTY ADDRESS
COLUMBIA RIVER ESTATES - 1 LOT 1	1804 TRAILS END DRIVE VANCOUVER , WA 98682-1804

CLARK, WILLIAM
1804 TRAILS END DRIVE
VANCOUVER WA 98665-1804

29636
1/1

TAX PAYMENT OPTIONS

PAY	DUE	TAX	INT/PEN	TOTAL DUE
Full Tax	04/30/2007	2,781.89	.00	2,781.89
Half Tax	04/30/2007	1,390.95	.00	1,390.95
Delinquent	04/30/2007	.00	.00	.00

Code District: 037000

Property taxes are calculated by multiplying the total tax rate by the taxable value divided by 1,000

TAXING DISTRICT	% VOTER APPROVED	NON-VOTER APPROVED	TAX RATE	AMOUNT
STATE SCHOOL	0	100	2.17899	550.19
COUNTY	0	100	1.22492	309.29
LOCAL SCHOOL	100	0	3.93355	993.22
CITY	0	0	0.00000	.00
PORT	0	100	0.33713	85.13
FIRE	0	100	1.23072	310.76
NORTH COUNTRY EMS	0	100	0.00000	.00
LIBRARY	0	100	0.35747	90.26
CEMETERY	0	0	0.00000	.00
ROADS	0	100	1.52742	385.67
GREATER CLARK PARKS	0	100	0.22720	57.37
DNR FIRE PATROL				.00
TOTAL			**11.01740**	**2,781.89**

Total taxes paid in the calendar year 2006 $ 2,806.59 Interest/Penalty paid in the calendar year 2006 $ .00

ASSESSED VALUE		2006	2007
	LAND	0	97,500
	STRUCTURE	0	155,000
TOTAL:		220,200	252,500

OFFICIAL NOTICE

You are able to pay your current taxes at any branch of 1st Independent Bank.
You must provide your billing coupon when making your payment.
Go to www.firstindy.com for the nearest location.

THIS COUPON MUST ACCOMPANY PAYMENT

Property Account Number: 023456-789.0

For a mailing address change, please fill out the form on the back side of this coupon.

Due Date: April 30, 2007 **1st half**

OS0234567890RP

YEAR	TAX	DEL INT/PEN	TOTAL
07	2,781.89	.00	2,781.89

CLARK, WILLIAM
1804 TRAILS END DRIVE
VANCOUVER WA 98665-1804

$ ☐☐,☐☐☐,☐☐☐.☐☐

2007 HALF DUE	TOTAL DUE
1,390.95	2,781.89

MAKE CHECKS PAYABLE TO CLARK COUNTY TREASURER

P.O. BOX 9808
VANCOUVER, WA 98666-8808

0234567890110100002781890001390955

Clark County Treasurer

Property tax bills require a large lump sum payment. This example lists all the different local governments that tax a single property.

mix is quite different. Because cities, counties, and towns now use a wider range of taxes and fees to raise revenue while also receiving funds from the national government and their state governments, property taxes now contribute less overall to local budgets. Nonetheless, it is still the primary source of revenue for local governments. At the end of the 20th century, property taxes still generated 79 percent of all local tax revenues.[21] Cities, counties, school districts, and special districts (see Chapter 12) each levy their own property taxes.

The Property Tax Evaluated

One traditional rationale for the property tax is that it taxes people who benefit the most from local public services. Property values are increased by public services, such as fire, police protection, and quality schools, so property taxes target people who benefit from these services. Historically, real property (land, homes, and farms) was the place where most Americans held their wealth. When fewer people owned property and fewer people invested their wealth in stocks and bonds, the wealthy had a greater share of their assets in real property. This made a tax on property relatively progressive.

In the contemporary era, however, home-ownership is no longer something reserved for the wealthy. About two-thirds of American families now own a home. Moreover, for most middle-class families, a home is their primary investment and thus represents most of their wealth. In contrast, the wealthiest people today have much more of their wealth invested in paper assets. Property taxes—a flat rate—thus cost the poor (if they can buy a home) and the middle class a larger share of their wealth than they cost the wealthiest people. Some economists suggest contemporary property taxes are highly regressive.[22]

Property Taxes and Tax Rebellions

This may explain why property taxes are consistently rated as the most unpopular tax by Americans.[23] Voters are particularly sensitive to property taxes. With sales and income taxes, marginal changes in rates don't tend to translate into increased hostility to the tax. Unlike the sales tax, property tax payments are made in a lump sum (unless built into monthly mortgage bills), which may add to the sting of the tax. One of the biggest political liabilities of the tax is that inflation in home values can drive up a person's tax burden much faster than any increase in their income. In booming housing markets, home prices may increase 15 to 30 percent per year. Local governments are often required by law to reassess home values frequently, leading some homeowners to find steep increases in their property tax bills virtually overnight. Tax bills increased dramatically, not because elected officials raised the rates but because market demand increased home values.

This dynamic of rising home prices driving tax bills higher fueled a rebellion against property taxes in California (Proposition 13 in 1978) and Massachusetts (Proposition 2 1/2 in 1980) and led to an antitax movement[24] that has consequences to this day. Populist antitax advocates became fixtures in many states: Howard Jarvis (California), Bill Sizemore (Oregon), Tim Eyman (Washington), and Douglas Bruce (Colorado) rallied the public around antitax proposals they promoted via ballot measures. Policies that cut the property tax proved among their most popular proposals.

The success of ballot measures in several states and general demands for "tax relief" pressured legislatures across the nation to enact various laws that exempted property owners from

---

[21] National Council of State Legislators, *A Guide to Property Tax: Property Tax Relief* (Denver, CO: National Council of State Legislators, 2002).

[22] Daniel B. Suits, "Measurement of Tax Progressivity," *American Economic Review* 67(4)(1977):747.

[23] Bowler and Donovan, "Public Responsiveness to Taxation."

[24] David O. Sears and Jack Citrin, *Something for Nothing in California* (Berkeley, CA: University of California Press, 1982); David Lowery and Lee Sigelman, "Understanding the Tax Revolt: Eight Explanations," *American Political Science Review* (1981):963–74; Daniel A. Smith, *Tax Crusaders and the Politics of Direct Democracy* (New York: Routledge, 1999).

new tax burdens resulting from rapid increases in the value of their homes and land. Exemptions date back to the 1930s, when states allowed poor homesteaders protections from foreclosure during the Great Depression. Today, many states make various exemptions for low-income households, veterans, and the elderly. Exemptions for agricultural land allow owners to resist pressures of selling to developers in order to avoid a growing tax burden. Exemptions, although popular, come at a cost of lost tax revenues for each level of government that collects property tax. Some states, such as Ohio, reimburse local governments for property tax revenues lost due to exemptions granted by the state.

Property tax revolts are not limited to the nation's hottest real estate markets and persisted long beyond the 1980s. In 2006, activists in 20 states were pushing for new property tax limits. Becky and Don Fagg of Lexington, South Carolina, saw their property taxes double in just five years as out-of-state buyers drove up local real estate prices and property assessments. The increased tax burden threatened their retirement plans, motivating Mrs. Fagg to form a group dedicated to abolishing taxes on a person's primary residence.[25] South Carolina used higher than expected sales tax revenues to reduce what homeowners would pay in property taxes in 2008.

On the Olympic Peninsula in Washington, Shelly Taylor and Jill Wilnauer reacted to rapid increases in their property taxes—increases produced by the heated local real estate market—by forming a group to press their state legislature to limit increases in the assessed value of homes to 1 percent per year. Hundreds of people crammed into a hall to attend the group's meeting where they announced their proposed constitutional amendment. The Washington amendment did not advance through the legislature, but a ballot initiative promising rebates on property taxes was rejected by Washington voters in 2009.

Other Revenue Sources

Given the political difficulties of relying on traditional tax sources such as income, property, and general sales taxes, states and communities also generate revenues from taxes that are more narrowly targeted as well as direct charges for services. Over the last two decades, state and local governments are relying more heavily on some of these "other" sources of revenues and have been using them more than ever before.[26]

Selective Sales Taxes

General sales taxes, as discussed, apply to most common purchases. Additional sales taxes are often levied on select items, such as fuel, alcohol, tobacco products, and public utilities. Sometimes, these taxes are referred to as excise taxes, or **sin taxes,** because they target behavior—such as drinking or smoking—that many people believe should be discouraged. If higher taxes actually cause people to consume less of the targeted item, the state may benefit. If demand for the item is elastic and responds to increases in prices, higher taxation will lead to less consumption of the item targeted with the tax. But if the tax applies to something that has **inelastic demand**—that is, something people must have regardless of the cost—a higher sin tax might not lower consumption.

Motor Vehicle Fuel Most of the revenues collected in this category come from state taxes on gasoline and diesel. Gas taxes are charged per gallon, with a state rate added on top of the $0.18 per gallon in tax going to the federal government. Most states add about another $0.20 per gallon—Alaska has the lowest ($0.08 per gallon), with California ($0.399), Washington ($0.375), Connecticut ($0.364), and Florida ($0.345) the highest. Several other states have gas taxes over $0.30 per gallon.

[25] Rafel Gerena-Morales, "Across U.S., Rising Property Taxes Spark Revolts," *Wall Street Journal,* 1 February 2006, p. B4.

[26] Data in this section are from the Federation of Tax Administrators, http://www.taxadmin.org, and the 2009 report of the Tax Foundation, www.TaxFoundation.org.

The political acceptability of gas taxes may be enhanced by the fact that these funds are often dedicated to transportation expenses. Gas taxes, as a share of a state's personal income, were lower in 2000 than they were in the 1960s and 1970s.[27]

Tobacco Products The proportion of state revenues from cigarette and tobacco taxes has been increasing recently. In several states that experienced tax rebellions in recent decades, citizens have actually voted to raise their state taxes. Or, at least, they voted to raise taxes on people who smoke.

On average, cigarette taxes increased from $0.21 per pack in 1996 to $0.77 by 2006, and continued to climb. Cigarette taxes have proved popular in part because they target an unpopular minority (smokers), with increases often linked to spending on public health programs. Voters in Washington and California, for example, approved cigarette tax increases that earmarked funds for health care (and antitobacco education). As a result of these taxes, cigarette prices now vary substantially across states. As of 2010, Rhode Island charged the most: $3.46 tax per pack (on top of federal taxes of $1.01 per pack). In July 2011, Hawaii's tax will increase to $3.00 per pack. Hawaii charged $2.80 in state taxes per pack in 2010. New York ($2.75), New Jersey ($2.70), Wisconsin, ($2.52), Vermont ($2.24), and Washington ($2.02) were the next highest, respectively. It seems that proximity to Canada—where tobacco taxes are high—and U.S. neighbors with higher tobacco taxes gives states greater ability to raise these taxes without fear that residents can buy their smokes elsewhere. Smoking is a much more affordable habit in the South, particularly in tobacco-producing states. South Carolina ($0.07), Missouri ($0.17), Tennessee ($0.20), Virginia ($0.30), North Carolina ($0.35), Georgia

($0.37), and Kentucky ($0.60) have the nation's lowest cigarette taxes.[28]

Alcoholic Beverages On average, states charge about $0.25 in tax on a gallon of beer. Alaska, which has no neighboring state to buy from, has the highest rate ($1.07 per gallon) and some of the nation's most expensive beer. Alabama, Georgia, and Hawaii are not far behind. Some of the cheapest beer in the United States can be found in Missouri (the home of Anheuser-Busch/Budweiser—which controls 45 percent of U.S. beer sales), Colorado (the home of Coors—which controls 10 percent of U.S. beer sales), Oregon (center of the U.S. microbrewing industry), and Wisconsin (the home of many thirsty Green Bay Packer fans, Miller, Pabst, and Stroh's Brewing—the latter three control 33 percent of U.S. beer sales). Beer taxes in each of these states, and in Pennsylvania and Wyoming, are under $0.09 per gallon. The distribution of beer taxes suggests that industries are able to avoid sin taxes in states where the industry is a key part of the economy. Wine taxes are also lowest in California[29] ($0.20 per gallon), the nation's largest wine-producing state, and highest in Alaska, Florida, and Iowa—places where wine should probably not be produced.

Although Rhode Island may seem like a leviathan when it comes to taxing smokes, the state is relatively libertarian when it comes to beer, taxing it at just $0.11 per gallon. Conversely, some states with low cigarette taxes have relatively high alcohol taxes (e.g., South Carolina, Mississippi, Virginia). Overall, the tax bite on smoking and drinking appears to be hardest in Alaska, Florida, and Hawaii (where tourists bear much of the costs) and lowest in Missouri, Kentucky, and Colorado.[30]

---

[27] Garand and Baudoin, "Fiscal Policy in the American States."

[28] Cigarette tax information is from the Federation of Tax Administrators, http://www.taxfoundation.org. Rates are as of July 1, 2009, unless noted.

[29] In New Hampshire, Pennsylvania, Utah, and Wyoming, states control wine sales and apply different taxes.

[30] Based on ranking states in terms of the sum of their wine, spirits, beer, and cigarette taxes. This ranking excludes states with government-operated liquor stores.

Direct Charges

Some of what state and local governments do can be funded by direct charges to the people who use a service, also known as **user fees**. For every $4 that state and local governments collect in taxes, another $1 is collected in user charges and fees. States generate billions in revenue by charging users of hospitals, highways, higher education, and other services. User charges for hospitals, sewers, garbage collection, airports, and parks contribute tens of billions of dollars to local government revenues. For the most part, none of these services are fully funded by charges to users, but fees reduce the amount of revenue from general taxes that would otherwise be used as funding.

Despite the names, user fees and charges are a source of revenue, just like any other tax. States and local governments have come to rely more heavily on fees and charges in recent years because they make it possible to avoid increasing visible taxes, such as sales or income tax. Critics of direct charges and fees argue that they can be highly regressive because people at all income levels often pay the same flat fee.

Estate and Inheritance Taxes

Eleven states collect inheritance taxes,[31] and more states collect estate taxes (some collect both). Inheritance taxes are levied on what an heir (but not a spouse) receives after inheriting something. Estate taxes are levied on the estate of a deceased person before it is distributed. Critics of estate taxes argue that they force "family farms" to be broken up upon the death of a property owner and that they amount to double taxation because the property taxes are already paid by the person accumulating the wealth. Political opponents of estate taxes have successfully rebranded these as "death taxes," although they can be levied on the living person inheriting a person's wealth (rather than the dead person). Federal and state estate tax programs typically made exemptions for family farms, and as of 2010, the minimum value for an estate to owe the federal tax was $3.5 million. This meant that the vast majority of people inheriting money are not affected by the tax.[32] Advocates of the estate tax—including Bill Gates Sr., father of one of the world's richest men—note that the estate tax is fair because it taxes wealth that was not earned by the person receiving it. Estate taxes may also be a way to tax accumulated wealth that has avoided taxation during a person's lifetime. The estate tax is also one of the few instruments of progressive taxation available to government. Gates estimates that the repeal of the estate tax would largely benefit future heirs of the wealthiest estates in this country—several of whom have funded the successful anti-estate tax lobbying effort.[33]

In 2001, President George W. Bush signed a bill that phased down the federal estate tax, and had it disappear in 2010 and reappear in 2011. Until recently, most states didn't set their own estate tax rates but collected an amount based on the federal estate tax. Because most states' estate taxes were linked to the federal tax, these taxes would end with any repeal of the federal estate tax, costing states several billion dollars. As of 2009, 17 states had instituted their own independent estate taxes. It might not matter, because President Barack Obama has indicated he would retain the federal tax on estates valued over $3.5 million beyond 2011.

Lotteries

Lotteries are seen by some as a form of voluntary taxation and have been popular enough to be approved by voters in many states. Lotteries were common in the 19th century, and lottery

---

[31] These include: Connecticut, Indiana, Iowa, Kansas, Kentucky, Maryland, Nebraska, New Jersey, Oregon, Pennsylvania, and Tennessee.

[32] Elizabeth McNichol, Center for Budget and Policy Priorities, 2004, http://www.cbpp.org/2-18-04sfp.htm#_ftn1.

[33] William Gates Sr. and Chuck Collins, "Tax the Wealthy: Why America Needs the Estate Tax," *American Prospect,* 17 June 2002.

advocates point out they were used in 1776 to raise money for the Colonial Army.[34]

Widespread corruption and strong opposition on moral grounds led to the elimination of government lotteries. No states had public lotteries again until 1964, when New Hampshire adopted a state lottery. Seven more states had lotteries by the 1973, but the lottery swept the nation after the tax revolts of the late 1970s and 1980s. Modern lotteries were promoted to state legislators and voters (by a corporation that prints the tickets and sells lottery equipment) as a politically painless way to raise revenues that could be earmarked for public education.[35] Although they are classified as a regressive tax,[36] most tickets are purchased by middle- and upper-income people.[37]

Forty-two states now have lotteries, with North Carolina adopting a lottery in 2006. Most states have their lottery funds earmarked for education. North Carolina's gambling revenues—estimated at over $1 billion through 2010—are earmarked for education, but this allowed the state to reduce general revenues spent on education.[38] The North Carolina case suggests that lottery funds may simply replace general revenue funds spent on education, resulting in no net gain for schools. However, one national study found that earmarking rules matter. Every dollar of lottery profit earmarked for education increased state education spending by more than would be the case if the funds were not prededicated to education.[39]

In 2008, 18 states had lottery sales well over $1 billion each, with nearly $61 billion in sales nationally.[40] However, less than $18 billion of that was profit that contributed to state revenues. Most states dedicate their lottery revenues to education. Because only a fraction of sales end up as revenues, lotteries contribute a very small percentage to state funds, even to education budgets. One estimate is that states receive only 30 cents in revenue for every dollar wagered and that the yield has been in decline since the 1990s. In California, where profits are dedicated to education, the lottery provides less than 2 percent of all funds for the state's K–12 system.[41] Some evidence reveals that the market for the lottery is saturated: With so many states now running lotteries, and with competition from the growing tribal gambling industries, more places now exist for a limited number of gamblers to risk their money. States respond to declining sales by increasing payouts, which can result in modest revenues.

Gambling

All but two states (Hawaii and Utah) have dropped their prohibitions against all forms of gambling. The recent expansion of legal gambling facilities means that taxes on gross receipts from casino gambling are one of the faster-growing sources of state revenues. Indian nations are major players in expanding the American gambling industry (the industry prefers to refer to the business as gaming, not gambling). A tribe negotiates a compact with its state government about the scope of casino operations allowed in exchange for a certain share of the casino revenues. As tribes and states become more dependent on each other in this way, tribes have become some of the largest campaign donors for legislators in

[34] National Association of State and Provincial Lotteries, http://www.naspl.org/history.html.

[35] David Broder, *Democracy Derailed: Initiative Campaigns and the Power of Money* (San Diego, CA: Harcourt, 2000), pp. 83–84.

[36] John Mikesell and C. Kurt Zorn, "State Lotteries as Fiscal Saviors or Fiscal Fraud," *Public Administration Review* 46(1986):311–20.

[37] Daniel B. Suits, "Gambling Taxes: Regressivity and Revenue Potential," *National Tax Journal* 30(1977):25–33.

[38] Mosi Secret, "Lottery Will Replace $1B in State Money: Bill Was Changed after Passage," *Independent Weekly,* 8 February 2006, online edition.

[39] Neva Kerbeshian Novarro, "Does Earmarking Matter? The Case of State Lottery Profits and Educational Spending," Stanford Institute for Economic Policy Research Discussion Paper no. 02–19 (Stanford, CA: Stanford Institute for Economic Policy Research, 2002).

[40] http://www.naspl.org/.

[41] California Department of Education, *State Lottery Fact Book 2004* (Sacramento, CA: California Department of Education, 2004).

some states. For Nevada, gambling revenues are a method to export the state's tax burden to people from out of state.

Severance Taxes

Severance taxes are levied on resources "severed" from the earth or sea and are applied to resource extraction industries, such as fishing, mining, and coal, oil, and natural gas production. Most states lack the natural resources that make severance taxes a significant source of revenues; however, some are blessed with valuable natural resources that provide a major source of revenues. Severance taxes are levied on the volume of the resource extracted. When market prices for the resource are up, these revenues boom. If prices collapse, so do revenues.

The global price of oil spiked dramatically in 2007 and 2008, moving from $60 per barrel to nearly $130 by mid-2008. Revenues were booming in resource-rich states. Alaska generated over 80 percent of state revenues from severance taxes, Wyoming collected 40 percent, and North Dakota 34 percent. New

Mexico and Oklahoma also collected at least 14 percent of state revenues from severance taxes.[42] Texas collected more than twice as much as any state other than Alaska ($4.1 billion), but given Texas's diverse revenue system, this was only about 9 percent of the state's total tax collections. The economic collapse of late 2008 corresponded with a sharp decrease in demand for oil, and the price dropped to below $50 per barrel in early 2009. As a result, in a two-month period in 2009, Alaska went from a projected budget surplus to having one of the nation's largest projected deficits for 2010.

Tax and Expenditure Limits

Property tax revolts of the 1970s were followed by more antitax and spending-limit ballot measures in many states. Elected officials in still more states embraced various policies designed to curb the growth of taxation and government spending. Known

---

[42] 2008 data at http://www.census.gov/govs/www/statetax08.html. Accessed September 2009.

YOU DECIDE

SUPERMAJORITIES FOR TAX INCREASES?

Many fiscal conservatives argue that more needs to be done to constrain government's ability to tax. Sixteen states have rules that require a supermajority vote of the legislature to approve a tax increase. This means that 60 percent, 66 percent, or (in the case of Arkansas, Michigan, and Oklahoma) 75 percent of legislators must agree to the tax. Colorado and Missouri also require that voters approve tax increases that come out of the legislature. Three states (Arkansas, California, and Rhode Island) require a supermajority to pass a budget.

Supporters of such policies contend that, since taxes involve "taking" something from people, they are different than "regular" laws that legislatures consider. As such, decisions about taxes deserve special constitutional safeguards to ensure broad public consensus and thorough deliberation. Opponents of supermajority rules contend that they are inherently un-democratic. Such rules may give a relatively small minority in the legislature the ability to block a tax or an entire budget that may have broad majority support. Not every supermajority rule is the same. Some have more teeth to them than others, and legislatures can find nontax revenues to fund programs. As a result, scholars have some trouble reaching a consensus about how much supermajority rules might affect tax revenues available to a state. That begs a key question, however.

Assuming that such rules could make it harder for a state to raise taxes or pass a budget, would that be a good thing?

collectively as **tax and expenditure limitations (or TELs)**, these policies set formulas that determine by how much revenue and spending can grow. These formulas typically limit growth in spending or future revenues collected from existing sources to some level that keeps pace with inflation or population growth (or some combination). By 2009, 30 states had adopted some form of TELs: 23 had spending limits, 4 had tax revenue limits, and 3 had both.[43] Sixteen states also established the **supermajority vote requirement** in order to pass a tax increase (see You Decide box).

TELs are particularly attractive to people who accept the leviathan model of fiscal policy. However, substantial academic debate continues over whether TELs actually limit the growth of government expenditure over the long term. Several observers blame (or credit) California's Proposition 13 of 1978 with a dramatic reduction in revenue available for public services, particularly schools.[44] Others note that although property tax limits and spending limits affected which level of government raised revenues (shifting taxation from one level of government to another), overall spending was largely unaffected.[45] The first generation of TELs—particularly those enacted by legislators rather than via ballot initiatives—may not have had much effect on limiting the growth in taxation and spending.[46] It is difficult to evaluate the effects of these policies because the same formula limiting revenue growth (e.g., a limit tied to population growth) might have quite different effects in a state with rapid population growth than in a state with no population growth.[47] A second generation of TELs adopted in the 1990s and more recently may have more teeth than those adopted in the 1970s and 1980s.[48]

Colorado's Taxpayer Bill of Rights (or TABOR) serves as an example. In addition to strict formulas limiting revenue growth, TABOR required a public referendum to approve any tax increase proposed in the legislature (see Reform Can Happen box). One critical case study of TABOR suggests that it resulted in substantially reduced levels of government spending, with education and health care suffering.[49]

Effects of State Tax and Expenditure Limits

Although we noted that some debate ensues about whether TELs have systematic effects on reducing how much states tax and spend, it seems clear these policies do have effects—even some that may have been unintended. TELs may have adverse effects on a state's credit rating because they limit the government's discretion in raising funds needed to service debt. In particular, strict tax limits may lead to higher borrowing costs for states because limits can make it hard to raise revenue needed to make debt payments.[50] States may avoid TELs

[43] National Council of State Legislators, http://www.ncsl.org/Default.aspx?TabId=12633. Accessed September 2009.

[44] Peter Schrag, *Paradise Lost: California's Experience, America's Future* (Berkeley, CA: University of California Press, 2004).

[45] Elisabeth Gerber, Arthur Lupia, Mathew McCubbins, and D. R. Kiewiet, *Stealing the Initiative: How State Government Responds to Direct Democracy* (Upper Saddle River, NJ: Prentice Hall, 2001).

[46] Shaun Bowler and Todd Donovan, "Evolution in State Governance Structures," *Political Research Quarterly* (2004):189–96; James Alt and Robert Lowry, "Divided Government, Fiscal Institutions and Budget Deficits: Evidence from the States," *American Political Science Review* 88(1994):811–28.

[47] Ronald Shadbegian, "Do Tax and Expenditure Limitations Affect the Size and Growth of Government?" *Contemporary Economic Policy* (January 1996):22–35.

[48] Michael New, Limiting Government through Direct Democracy: The Case of State Tax and Expenditure Limitations, Cato Policy Analysis no. 420 (Washington, DC: Cato Institute, 2001).

[49] Bell Policy Center, "Ten Years of TABOR: A Study of Colorado's Taxpayer's Bill of Rights" (Denver, CO: Bell Policy Center, 2003).

[50] James Poterba and Kim Rueben, *Fiscal Rules and State Borrowing Costs* (San Francisco: Public Policy Institute of California, 1999).

REFORM CAN HAPPEN

COLORADO'S TABOR

In 1996, Colorado voters approved a constitutional amendment drafted by Douglas Bruce, known as the "Tax Payers' Bill of Rights," or TABOR. Whereas many state TELs attempt to limit the growth of government with rules about spending growth, Colorado's TABOR focuses on limiting revenue growth. When writing a new budget, revenues from all sources (other than the federal government) cannot exceed the previous year's revenues by more than the rate of population growth, plus inflation. If the state's economy is booming, and tax collections are higher than the growth rate, any excess revenues must be returned to voters unless voters vote to spend the money. If the state's economy is in recession and revenues decrease, funds for the next year's budget are based on the recession year revenues, plus the allowed rate of growth. TABOR thus prolonged the effects of recessions on Colorado's budget by ratcheting down revenues for future, nonrecession years.

Colorado voters have shown some willingness to tweak TABOR by approving "deBrucings"—proposals that allow the state or local governments to keep revenue collected above the TABOR limits. All but 4 of 178 school district deBrucings were approved by voters as of 2009, and over 400 were approved in cities.[1] In 2005, Colorado voters elected to suspend some of TABOR's provisions to allow the state to retain $3.7 billion in revenue growth that otherwise would be returned to taxpayers.[2] The suspension was temporary, and Governor Bill Ritter (D) was working to place an initiative on the 2011 state ballot to eliminate parts of Colorado's TABOR.[3]

Notes

1. Debbie Bell, "TABOR 101: Expert Explains City Ballot Question," *Canon City Daily Record*, 4 September 2009.
2. Tax Foundation, http://www.taxfoundation.org/research/show/283.html.
3. Peter Marcus, "Guv Wants TABOR Eased," *Denver Daily News*, 13 September 2009, online edition.

by shifting spending authority to new programs and different jurisdictions. One study found that TELs enacted via the initiative led to the formation of new "special service districts" that operate park, library, fire, and other services—a way to tax and spend "off budget" by jurisdictions beyond the reach of state TELs.[51] Special districts can also provide a more direct method to ensure that beneficiaries of a public service are the ones who pay taxes for it.

A comprehensive study of the general effects of direct democracy on state and local fiscal policy found that states with the ballot initiative process have more tax cuts, rely more on fees for revenues, and have shifted spending from the state to local levels. These state and local fiscal policies may reflect popular opinion in these states.[52]

Fiscal Federalism

State and local governments receive substantial money from the federal government to promote the federal government's goals in areas such as health care, urban renewal, education, and transportation. The relative power of the federal government and the states is often measured in dollars, with the efforts of federal and state governments to exert control over policies limited by their willingness to pay for such authority.

---

[51] Bowler and Donovan, "Evolution in State Governance Structures."

[52] John Matsusaka, *For the Many or the Few: The Initiative, Public Policy and American Democracy* (Chicago: University of Chicago Press, 2004).

During the 1960s, the expansive social welfare programs under the Lyndon B. Johnson administration's Great Society led the federal government to become involved in virtually every state and local governmental activity. Between 1960 and 1968 (during which time John F. Kennedy and Johnson, respectively, were president), the number of new federal grant programs available to state and local governments almost tripled, from 132 to 379, with federal aid to states and localities more than tripling, from $7 billion in 1960 to $24 billion in 1970.[53]

The federal role in financing state and local government activity abated after the election of Ronald Reagan in 1980. Reagan's annual budgets eliminated or reduced funding for many programs established in the 1960s and 1970s. Welfare reform legislation, passed by President Bill Clinton in August 1996, also changed the federal role in funding state spending. Federal funds made up roughly 40 percent of state and local expenditures in 1980, but by 2006, they made up roughly 34 percent.[54]

Federal transfers increased in 2009 as part of Barack Obama's $737 billion economic stimulus package. It included $140 billion that states and localities could use to maintain programs after the recession ate away at state and local revenues. These funds were one of the major sources many states relied upon to balance their 2008–09 budgets.[55] Since the 2009 stimulus was ostensibly a one-time boost of federal funds, some state and local governments faced tougher decisions about how to balance their budgets for 2010 and beyond.

The federal government's largess in aid to the states and their localities does not come free. The federal government uses a number of mechanisms to compel the states to spend the money according to the wishes of Congress. The federal government provides grant-in-aid to state and local governments. There are two general types of grants that the federal government uses to distribute funds to subnational governments.

Categorical grants limit how much discretion state and local governments have in using federal money. State and local governments apply for federal categorical grants that provide money for specific purposes, such as Head Start (a federally sponsored preschool program), urban forestry programs, flood mitigation assistance, or historic battlefield preservation. Some categorical grants have matching requirements, whereby the state or local government must pay part of the program's costs. Today, Congress provides about 600 different categorical grants to state and local governments. Since the 1980s, substantial federal dollars come to states and local governments through **block grants**. These were created to consolidate categorical grants, and are allocated by broad functional areas (such as community development) rather than specific purposes. Block grants allow state and local governments more discretion over how, where, and on whom to spend the grants.

General Funds Versus Non-General Funds

All of these various revenues may end up in different budgets before they are spent. Revenues collected from the general sales tax, income tax, and property tax often end up in a state or local government's general fund budget. Some states may also put their lottery revenues and other miscellaneous funds in their general budget. General fund revenues can typically be used for any purpose, so politicians have substantial discretion over how such revenues might be spent. Budget battles in the legislature, or between the legislature and the governor, largely center on what should be done with general fund revenues.

[53] Timothy Conlan, *New Federalism: Intergovernmental Reform from Nixon to Reagan* (Washington, DC: Brookings Institution, 1988), p. 6.

[54] U.S. Census Bureau, http://www.census.gov/prod/2004pubs/04statab/stlocgov.pdf.

[55] Center on Budget and Policy Priorities, 2009, http://www.cbpp.org/cms/index.cfm?fa=view&id=2831

Revenues that are collected for a specific purpose or transferred to a state or community for a specific program often end up in a non–general fund budget. For example, most money that comes as transfers from the federal government is allocated to fund health and welfare programs and cannot be spent on other things. Likewise, tuition and fees collected by universities are dedicated to fund universities and cannot be spent on other programs. Gas taxes are often dedicated to road construction and transportation only, and most states earmark their lottery funds for education. This means that budget writers often have very little discretion over how non–general fund revenues can be spent. Over half of a state's total revenues may end up in a non–general fund budget. In Virginia's 2009–10 budget, for example, 54 percent of all state revenues went into the non–general fund.

Adding It All Up: Variation in State Revenue Packages

Every state and local government has its own unique combination of revenue sources. When state revenue sources are displayed graphically, it's often in the form of a pie, with larger slices depicting the major revenue sources. Unfortunately, there's not one single pie to consider, as the overall mixture of state or local revenue can be expressed at least three ways. The first is to think in terms of the tax revenues a government generates on its own, but state and local taxes are only part of the story—governments also generate substantial revenues by charging for services. This means we must also consider these additional nontax revenues as part of a government's revenue package. Finally, much of what state and local governments spend comes from funds transferred from other, higher levels of government, so a third way to express a government's revenue mix is to include all "own-source" revenues (taxes and other sources) plus transfers from other levels of government.

The Mix of State Revenues

The 50 states combined had nearly $1.5 trillion in annual revenue in 2007. To put that amount in perspective, the federal government collected about $1.7 trillion in annual revenue the same year (excluding Social Security).[56] Figure 10.2 illustrates the sources of all funds available to state governments. Of the $1.45 trillion available, about $1 trillion was generated by states.

Figure 10.2

Sources of all state revenue, 2007

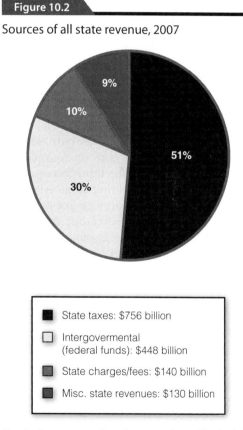

- State taxes: $756 billion
- Intergovermental (federal funds): $448 billion
- State charges/fees: $140 billion
- Misc. state revenues: $130 billion

Note: Total state revenues from all sources = $1.47 trillion (excludes $519 billion in insurance trust revenues).
Source: U.S. Census Bureau, State Government Finances, 2007, http://www2.census.gov/govs/estimate/0700ussl_1.txt

---

[56] http://www.usgovernmentrevenue.com/yearrev2007_0.html.

This includes about $749 billion collected via state taxes, $141 billion in direct charges and fees collected by states, and about $130 billion from miscellaneous state revenue sources. Federal funds and direct charges allow states to spend about twice what they collect in taxes. Direct charges apply to users of state services and include college tuition, road tolls, park fees, and the like. As noted in Chapter 2, the federal government redistributes substantial funds back to the states each year—over $430 billion, mostly to fund health and welfare expenses shared between the state and federal governments.

About 73 percent of all state-generated (or own-source) revenues come from taxation, with another 14 percent from direct charges for services and 13 percent from interest earned on investments and other miscellaneous sources. Most revenue from direct charges for public services (paid only by those who use the services) comes in the form of tuition for higher education. This is one of the fastest-growing sources of funds for state governments.

Figure 10.3 focuses more narrowly on what the average state's mix of tax revenues might look like: about one third coming from general sales tax (plus another 15 percent from "selective" sales taxes on things like gas, cigarettes, and alcohol), just over one third from individual income taxes (plus another 7 percent from corporate income taxes), 6 percent from license fees (mostly on vehicles), and the rest from miscellaneous taxes. Taxes bring in most, but by no means all, the revenues that states generate. The discussion of Rhode Island in the "Comparisons Help Us Understand" section illustrates that states vary substantially in how heavily they rely on different types of revenue.

States vary tremendously in the mix of revenues they use to fund public services. A balanced package of revenues—like a balanced stock portfolio—helps bring stability to a state's budget process through periods of economic recession. But can states thrive without having both an income and sales tax, the two main pillars of revenue systems? A few states endowed with natural resources or specialized

Figure 10.3

Sources of taxes generated by state governments, 2007

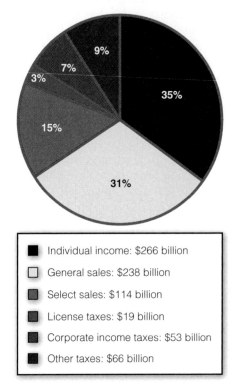

Individual income: $266 billion

General sales: $238 billion

Select sales: $114 billion

License taxes: $19 billion

Corporate income taxes: $53 billion

Other taxes: $66 billion

Note: Total state revenues generated from state taxes = $756 billion.
Source: U.S. Census Bureau, State Government Finances, 2007, http://www.census.gov/govs/state/0700usst.html.

industries avoid having to rely on one of the major taxes (income and sales). Alaska and Texas have generated tremendous revenue from oil and gas. Wyoming has profited from mining, Nevada from gambling, and Florida from tourism. These revenue sources export the burden of state taxes to people in other states, and allow these states to get by without income taxes. However, they may face budget crises when prices of their key commodity crash or if the tourist industry crashes (as Florida and Nevada learned after September 11, 2001).

Absent major tourism or natural resources, few states have the luxury of funding their operations without sales and income taxes—which, as mentioned, are the two main pillars of state revenue. Those that have only one must rely heavily on it. Oregon lacks a sales tax, so it collects over 70 percent of state tax revenues from the income tax. Washington lacks an income tax, so it must collect over 75 percent of its tax revenue from the sales tax. New Hampshire has neither a general sales nor a general income tax and manages to balance its budget via frugality and having local governments fund many services. Although no state is average, most have revenue packages that look less like Washington, Oregon, Alaska, or New Hampshire and more like what is shown in Figure 10.3.

The Mix of Local Revenues

When transfers from higher levels of government are factored in, local governments collect about $1.34 trillion in revenues (plus another $118 billion from utilities, and $75 billion from insurance funds). Local governments, including cities, counties, school districts, and other special districts, collect just over $830 billion in locally generated taxes and charges, with the majority of this coming from the property tax.

Figure 10.4 illustrates that local governments collect 39 percent of this $1.34 trillion from local taxes, with a similar proportion of funds coming from transfers (mostly from their states). Most of these transfers are state funds dedicated to school districts and to cities and counties to cover their costs of running health programs. Another 16 percent of local funds comes from direct charges, mostly for hospitals, airports, and sewerage.

When we focus only on the revenues that local governments collect themselves, we find that a local government's revenue package looks quite different from a state's revenues. Although most locally generated revenues come from local taxes, local governments rely much more on charges and fees than do states. Sixteen percent of locally generated revenues

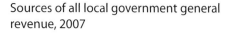

Figure 10.4

Sources of all local government general revenue, 2007

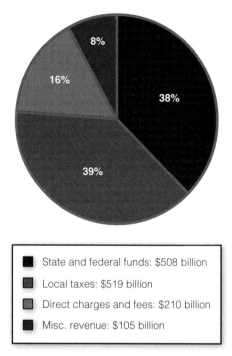

- State and federal funds: $508 billion
- Local taxes: $519 billion
- Direct charges and fees: $210 billion
- Misc. revenue: $105 billion

Note: Total local revenues = $1.34 trillion. Excludes $75 billion in revenues from insurance trusts and $118 billion from utilities.
Source: U.S. Census Bureau http://www2.census.gov/govs/estimate/0700ussl_1.txt

come from user fees and charges for services, compared to 10 percent for state-generated revenues.

Figure 10.5 breaks down the sources of the $519 billion in taxes generated by local governments. Again, we see a substantially different picture when we compare locally generated tax revenue (Figure 10.5) to tax revenue generated at the state level (Figure 10.3). Local governments have a much less diversified tax portfolio compared to states, and they rely heavily on the property tax. School districts and special districts (those that provide services such as fire protection or libraries) rely almost exclusively on property taxes.

COMPARISONS HELP US UNDERSTAND

RHODE ISLAND: A "SIN TAX" REVENUE MODEL TO EMULATE?

Concerns about social costs have limited the expansion of state-regulated gambling in some states. Others earn substantial revenues from gambling—from both Indian tribe operations and from other state-regulated games. Rhode Island collects a whopping $1,300 per capita in lottery and video lottery terminal (VLT) sales.[1] It is one of only six states that combines a lottery with fast-paced VLTs that allow people to bet a great deal in a short period. Revenues from gambling made the tiny state 12th overall in the United States for total lottery revenues. The state lottery program was established in 1974, and thousands of VLTs have been located at racetracks since 1995. Over 11 percent of the state's general revenues came from gambling one year, whereas the U.S. average for states with a lottery is just 2 percent of revenues. Delaware, South Dakota, and West Virginia, which also make heavy use of VLTs, are the only states that rival Rhode Island in how much lottery and VLT revenue is generated per capita. Rhode Island also collects another 4 percent of all revenues from cigarette taxes. Rhode Island collects more from smoking and gambling than it does from inheritance taxes and general business taxes combined. Of course, size and location matter. Hardly any place in Rhode Island is more than 10 miles from Connecticut or Massachusetts. Many people from other states pass through Rhode Island, which might make it easy for the state to export its tax burden by selling them lottery tickets and cigarettes.

Note
1. State of Rhode Island and Providence Plantations, Revenue Estimating Conference Memorandum, 2005 December 19.

Oregon Lottery official checks on a state gambling terminal in a Salem tavern. There are over 2000 video poker outlets that provide the state with revenue.

AP Photo/Rick Bowmer

Who Bears the Burden of State and Local Taxes?

Other than the income tax, most revenues that states and communities rely on are relatively regressive, compared to the federal tax structure. That is, those who earn less income pay more of their income in state and local taxes. At the same time, the wealthiest people, having far more income, pay more of the total dollars collected. Just as states and cities differ in the revenue packages they use, they also differ in terms of how regressive their

Figure 10.5

Local tax revenues by source, 2007

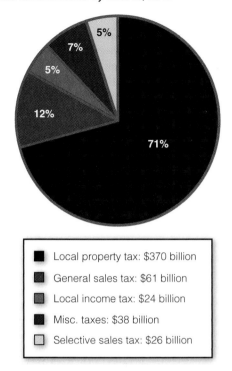

5%
7%
5%
12%
71%

■ Local property tax: $370 billion

◼ General sales tax: $61 billion

◼ Local income tax: $24 billion

■ Misc. taxes: $38 billion

☐ Selective sales tax: $26 billion

Note: Total Local Tax revenues = $519 billion.

Source: U.S. Census Bureau http://www2.census.gov/govs/estimate/0700ussl_1.txt

Table 10.2

The 10 Most Regressive State Tax Systems (Taxes as shares of income for nonelderly residents)

	Taxes as a % of Income		
	Poorest 20%	Middle	Top 1%
Washington	17.6%	11.2%	3.3%
Florida	14.4%	9.8%	3.0%
Tennessee	11.7%	8.9%	3.4%
South Dakota	10.0%	8.4%	2.3%
Texas	11.4%	8.4%	3.5%
Illinois	13.1%	10.5%	5.8%
Michigan	13.3%	11.2%	6.7%
Pennsylvania	11.4%	9.0%	4.8%
Nevada	8.3%	6.5%	2.0%
Alabama	10.6%	9.6%	4.9%

Note: States listed in bold have no income tax.

taxes are. As Table 10.2 illustrates, the poorest 20 percent of a state's population can pay 12 to 18 percent of their income in state and local taxes, whereas the richest residents in the same state pay as little as 2 or 3 percent of their income in state taxes. In some states (Delaware, Hawaii, Minnesota, and Montana), all income groups pay about the same share of their income in state taxes.

Why such differences? States that adopted the income tax early tend to rely on it more heavily, making their tax systems more progressive. A state's economy matters as well. States with larger manufacturing sectors and with wealthier people have more progressive revenue systems. Taxation may also be more progressive in states with strong competition between parties. A party out of power trying to win support from a broad base of voters may have an incentive to propose increased government spending for the poor and middle class, financed by taxes on the rich.[57] Economic growth and Democratic governors are also associated with more progressive taxation.[58] States that never adopted the income tax tend to have the most regressive overall revenue systems.

[57] David Lowery, "The Distribution of Tax Burdens in the American States: The Determinants of Fiscal Incidence," *Western Political Quarterly* (1986):137–58; V. O. Key, *Southern Politics in the State and Nation* (New York: Knopf, 1949). This effect may depend on the period being studied. See B. R. Fry and R. D. Winters, "The Politics of Redistribution," *American Political Science Review* 70(1970):508–22.

[58] Neil Berch, "Explaining the Changes in Tax Incidence in the States," *Political Research Quarterly* 48(1995):629–41.

Since the tax revolt of the late 1970s, states and local governments have begun to rely more heavily on user fees (particularly direct democracy states) and specific sales taxes, such as cigarette taxes—trends that may make revenues more regressive over time.

When Do Taxes Go Up or Down?

Tax "innovation," or the adoption of new taxes, is a function of need and political opportunity. Factors that increase the need for new revenues also increase the likelihood that a government might adopt a new tax or raise an old one. Perhaps the most important thing motivating a state to adopt new taxes is, not surprisingly, fiscal hardship. States have not typically adopted new sales and income taxes during prosperous years. Although such taxes are unpopular, a fiscal crisis may make tax increases more palatable for voters and reduce the risk elected officials face when they increase taxes.[59]

Some research suggests that politicians also wait until after an election year to raise unpopular taxes, but the frequency of tax increases the year after a general election also reflects that some states budget for two years (a biennial budget). Budget that might reflect promises from the previous election are drawn in the first year of the biennium, after a new governor and legislature may have been elected. Less unpopular revenue sources—like the lottery or targeted user fees—may be more likely to be adopted in an election year as politicians try to avoid highly unpopular tax increases. New taxes adopted in one state may also be more likely if a neighboring state has already adopted the tax.[60] Some studies suggest the scope of government spending

increases when the same party controls both the legislature and governor's office, particularly when Democrats have unified control outside of the South.[61] Others find evidence that party control of government may not correspond with tax increases.[62] Similarly, politicians are more likely to increase existing taxes when the political costs are lowest, that is, when the next election is far away and the economy is bad.[63]

Taxes also go down. States often implement tax cuts when the economy is strong and revenues are growing. During the boom of the mid- to late 1990s, 44 states enacted tax cuts. Tax cuts are often packaged as a means to stimulate a state's economy, although one think-tank report suggests that states with the largest tax cuts of the 1990s had the biggest fiscal problems and were more likely to have their credit rating downgraded in the next decade. Between 2001 and 2006, states with the largest tax cuts had weaker job growth.[64]

What Are the Effects of Taxes?

Do taxes help or hurt long-run economic development? This is one of the more contentious questions in politics as well as in the academic world of economists and political

---

[59] Hansen, *The Politics of Taxation*.

[60] Francis Berry and William D. Berry, "State Lottery Adoptions as Policy Innovations," *American Political Science Review* (1990):395–415.

[61] Hansen, *The Politics of Taxation*; James Alt and Robert Lowry, "Divided Government, Fiscal Institutions and Budget Deficits"; W. Robert Reed, "Democrats, Republicans and Taxes: Evidence that Political Parties Matter," *Journal of Public Economics* 90(2006):725–50.

[62] Francis Berry and William D. Berry, "Tax Innovation in the States: Capitalizing on Political Opportunity," *American Journal of Political Science* (1992):715–42; David Primo (2006).

[63] Francis Berry and William D. Berry, "The Politics of Tax Increases in the States," *American Journal of Political Science* (1994):855–99.

[64] Nicholas Johnson and Brian Filipowich, *Tax Cuts and Continued Consequences* (Washington, DC: Center for Budget and Policy Priorities, 2006).

scientists. Some economic theory assumes that growth depends on the development of physical and human capital; that is, on the amount that machines and people can produce. Human capital includes education, skill, and training. Physical capital can be seen in factories, tools, roads, and equipment. Traditional models of growth assume that taxes are just part of some equilibrium level of capital and that economic growth results from technical changes that increase productivity.

But things are more complex than this. There are different types of taxes—some might discourage the formation of human and physical capital, some might have fewer effects, and other taxes might actually encourage capital formation. Different taxes also have different effects on how people spend their money and invest. In other words, the relationship between taxes and economic growth depends on how the money is raised and varied expenditures. Taxes that are spent on education, for example, can generate positive effects on the formation of human capital—effects that a private market might not produce.[65] However, the personal income tax might also discourage entrepreneurial activity.[66] Taxes on corporate earnings, on the other hand, might discourage economic growth,[67] but when corporate taxes are low relative to high personal income taxes, entrepreneurial activity might be encouraging because people have greater incentives to incorporate businesses.[68]

Some studies show positive effects of state taxation on state economic growth, and some studies find negative effects.[69] Results are sensitive to the statistical methods used, the time period examined, and the tax or spending patterns that are examined. Studies of state taxing and spending from the 1950s found no relationship between taxes and growth.[70] Some studies from the 1970s and early 1980s found a negative relationship, with one noting that welfare spending harmed economic growth, whereas business taxes increased growth.[71] Further evidence shows that state tax increases used to fund welfare payments depress economic growth[72]; however, state taxes spent on education, highways, and public health and safety have been shown to have favorable impacts on the location decisions of businesses.[73] One overview of these studies concluded that most found "a weak or insignificant relationship between taxes and economic performance" because they failed to account for what taxes were spent on. Taxes dedicated to health, education, and highways

[65] Robert Lucas, "On the Mechanics of Economic Development," *Journal of Monetary Economics* (1988):3–42; Enrico Moretti, "Estimating the External Return to Higher Education," *Journal of Econometrics* (2003):175–202.

[66] William M. Gentry and R. Glenn Hubbard, "Tax Policy and Entrepreneurial Entry," *American Economic Review* (2000):283–87.

[67] Young Lee and Roger H. Gordon, "Tax Structure and Economic Growth," *Journal of Public Economics* (2005).

[68] J. B. Cullen and Robert H. Gordon, "Taxes and Entrepreneurial Activity: Theory and Evidence for the U.S.," NBER Working Paper No. 9015 (New York: National Bureau of Economic Research, 2002).

[69] James Heckman, "A Life-Cycle Model of Earnings, Learning, and Consumption," *Journal of Political Economy* 84(4)(1976):S11–S44; in contrast, see P. A. Trostel, "The Effect of Taxation on Human Capital," *Journal of Political Economy* (1993):327–50.

[70] Clark C. Bloom, *State and Local Tax Differentials and the Location of Manufacturing* (Iowa City, IA: Bureau of Business and Economic Research, 1955); Wilbur Thompson and John M. Mattilla, *An Econometric Model of Postwar State Economic Development* (Detroit:, MI: Wayne State University Press, 1959); Dennis W. Carlton, "Why New Firms Locate Where They Do," in W. Wheaton, ed., *Interregional Movements and Regional Growth* (Washington, DC: The Urban Institute, 1979).

[71] Thomas Romans and Ganti Subrahmanyam, "State and Local Taxes, Transfers, and Regional Economic Growth," *Southern Economic Journal* (1979):435–44; Robert J. Newman, "Industry Migration and Growth in the South," *Review of Economics and Statistics* (1983):76–86.

[72] Romans and Subrahmanyam, "State and Local Taxes"; L. Jay Helms, "The Effect of State and Local Taxes on Economic Growth: A Time Series–Cross Sectional Approach," *Review of Economics and Statistics* 67(1985):574–82.

[73] Helms, "The Effect of State and Local Taxes on Economic Growth."

were found to have a positive effect on private investment and employment in a state, but welfare spending had a negative effect. The authors concluded that their findings should not be interpreted as a prescription for curtailing welfare spending. They noted, rather, that states face a "vicious cycle" in a prolonged economic slump. They risk crowding out public investment in health, education, streets, and highways if they increase welfare spending alone, but raising taxes to fund public investment and welfare may further depress the economy.[74]

The Growth of State Governments

The size of government can be thought of in terms of the proportion of the total economy that is taxed and spent by government. Whatever the effects of taxing and spending, state governments are now much larger than they were 50 years ago. When the size of the economy is measured as the sum of everyone's personal income, state governments spent about $0.04 of each dollar of personal income in 1950. Today, they spend about $0.16 of each dollar.[75]

Nearly all of this growth in the size of state government occurred from 1950 to 1970. Growth was driven by massive state investments in education and highways during this period. Prior to the 1950s, the federal highway system was nonexistent, and states spent much less on infrastructure. This growth period was also when many states were building new public universities. California, for example, spent heavily on public investment in the 1950s and 1960s, building multibillion-dollar water projects, five new University of California campuses, eight new California State University campuses, and dozens of community colleges.

With highway construction on the wane by the late 1960s and the political revolts against taxation taking effect in the late 1970s, the size of state government peaked around 1978 and then declined through the 1980s. After the federal government shifted responsibility for welfare to the states in the 1990s, the size of state government began a steady increase back to levels seen in the late 1970s.[76]

Trends in State and Local Revenues

Governments have grown in size since the 1950s. With this growth and with changes in the economy, the mix of revenues that now fund state governments has changed. Federal revenues sent to the states increased sharply from 1955 through 1975 and now play a larger role in state budgets than they did 50 years ago. Then, states collected almost two thirds of their revenue via selective sales taxes, general sales taxes, and license taxes. As the scope of government grew, states came to rely less on selective sales taxes and license taxes, and now rely more heavily on income taxes, general sales taxes, and charges and fees (tuition).[77] Although states have increased their reliance on federal funds, income taxes, and fees, a much smaller proportion of state revenues is now generated by selective sales taxes on gasoline.[78]

As states struggled in 2009 to recover from the recession, they approved more new tax revenues than at any time in the past decade. Despite this, new tax revenues approved for fiscal year 2010 budgets still made up only about 17 percent of what states used to fill their budget gaps (the remainder came mostly from

---

[74] Alaeddin Mofidi and Joe A. Stone, "Do State and Local Taxes Affect Economic Growth?" *Review of Economics and Statistics* (1990):686–91.

[75] Garand and Baudoin, p. 293.

[76] Garand and Baudoin, "Fiscal Policy in the American States."

[77] Robert Lowry, "Fiscal Policy in the American States," in Virginia Gray and Russell Hanson, eds., *Politics in the American States: A Comparative Analysis*, 9th ed. (Washington, DC: CQ Press, 2008), pp. 296–97.

[78] Winters, "The Politics of Taxing and Spending."

cuts, and federal funds). Several states relied on higher personal income taxes. Eight states raised income tax rates on their top brackets, with increases in half of those states adopted as temporary or one-time measures. California and New York approved billions in new tax revenues for 2010. Two states (Vermont and North Dakota) reduced income tax rates. Florida raised its tobacco tax and approved $1 billion in new fees.[79]

Where Does the Money Go? Government Spending

Discussing state and local revenue sources before examining what government spends the money on is a bit like putting the cart before the horse. Revenues are generated in large measure to satisfy public demands for programs and services and to fund budget drivers—the major programs that state and local governments operate.

Figures 10.6 and 10.7 illustrate the major program spending areas for state and local governments, respectively. State and local governments combine to spend about $2.7 trillion: $1.4 trillion by the 50 states and $1.4 trillion by local governments.

Education

The largest area of direct state spending illustrated in Figure 10.6 is education—35 percent of total spending by the states. The amount of state funds spent on education is actually much larger than what is suggested by Figure 10.6, because states transfer hundreds of billions of dollars to local governments to fund K–12 schools. Local schools have their own revenue source (local property taxes), but state funds are used to supplement what schools raise in

local taxes. Because these funds are actually spent at the local level, they are included in our picture of the local government spending mix (Figure 10.7). If we had illustrated state spending just as a percentage of state-generated funds (excluding federal funds for social programs), education would be an even larger area of state expenditure. Figure 10.6 illustrates funds that are spent directly by the state, and omits state funds spent by local school districts.

Unlike local K–12 schools, state colleges and universities have no local tax revenues and are totally reliant on state funds and tuition they collect from students. The majority of direct state spending on education (80 percent) goes to operate universities, community colleges, and vocational schools. The National Association of State Budget Officials notes that "when the state fiscal picture darkens, higher education often is the first category of spending to cut." Colleges and universities are an easy target because they are one of the largest state services that allow costs, however painful, to be transferred to users (students or their parents). Many states responded to the 2002 fiscal crisis by accelerating the shift toward financing higher education with higher direct charges (fees and tuition), while reducing general fund revenues spent. Over the decade that ended in 2004, tuition and fees increased 47 percent at public four-year universities.[80] Several states proposed tuition increases of 10 percent or more in 2009.

Figure 10.7 illustrates that education is the largest component of local government spending—39 percent of all local expenditures, 94 percent of which is spent on elementary and secondary education (K–12 schools). Most of this money is raised by local property taxes or provided by the states and is spent by local school districts. The largest cost of education is labor: paying salaries for teachers, counselors, school administrators, technology staff, cooks, and so on.

[79] State Budget Update: July 2009, National Conference of State Legislatures; State Tax Update: July 2009, National Conference of State Legislatures.

[80] National Association of State Budget Officers, State Expenditure Report (Washington, DC: NASBO, 2003).

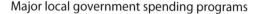

Figure 10.6

Major state government spending programs, 2007

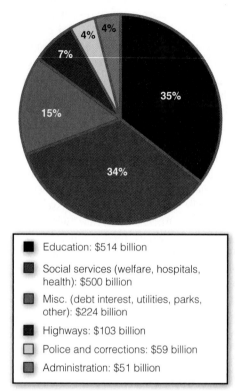

- Education: $514 billion
- Social services (welfare, hospitals, health): $500 billion
- Misc. (debt interest, utilities, parks, other): $224 billion
- Highways: $103 billion
- Police and corrections: $59 billion
- Administration: $51 billion

Note: Total expenditure = $1.45 trillion (excludes $182 billion in insurance benefits payments).
Source: U.S. Census Bureau, State Government Finances, 2007, http://www.census.gov/govs/state/0700usst.html.

Figure 10.7

Major local government spending programs

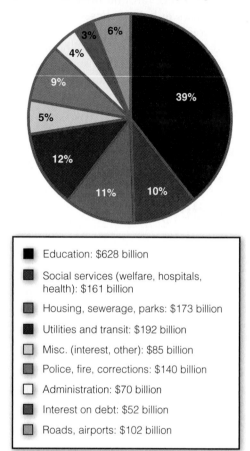

- Education: $628 billion
- Social services (welfare, hospitals, health): $161 billion
- Housing, sewerage, parks: $173 billion
- Utilities and transit: $192 billion
- Misc. (interest, other): $85 billion
- Police, fire, corrections: $140 billion
- Administration: $70 billion
- Interest on debt: $52 billion
- Roads, airports: $102 billion

Note: Total local government expenditure = $1.6 trillion. Excludes $31 billion in insurance trust expenditure.
Source: U.S. Census Bureau, http://www2.census.gov/govs/estimate/0700ussl_1.txt

Social Services: Health Care

Thirty-four percent of money spent by states funds social services. Social service spending, the second largest and fastest-growing component of state budgets, is dominated by health care. When looking at Figure 10.6, it is important to remember that a large part of overall state spending is financed by the federal government. Much of the federal dollars going to states are from the **Medicaid** program (see Chapter 14). Medicaid accounts for most of state social service spending—about 20 percent of all state expenditures.[81] Given the absence of national health care insurance and the high costs for private health insurance, states are left with much of the responsibility for providing health care to the millions of Americans who are uninsured. Federal funds come with

[81] Kenneth Feingold et al., "Social Program Spending and State Fiscal Crisis," Urban Institute Occasional Paper no. 70 (Washington, DC: Urban Institute, 2003).

standards that define minimal levels of service the states must provide, and federal dollars are given to match state spending on Medicaid. If states want to provide additional health care beyond the minimal standards—for example, offering prenatal care or providing basic health care insurance for the working poor—they must spend more. A growing proportion of social service spending is used to fund prescription drug purchases.

Because spending on hospitals, long-term care for the elderly, mental health, and other health care–related services comprise the single-largest part of a state's budget, health care spending is the largest target for cuts in times of economic downturn. Given the size of health care in the overall state budget, it is nearly impossible to reduce spending without rolling back reimbursement rates paid to health care providers (doctors, hospitals, and nursing homes), freezing reimbursement levels, or cutting back on the number of people eligible for benefits. In times of fiscal crunch, states will cut back on health care, even if it means losing federal Medicaid matching dollars.[82] Nonetheless, the proportion of state spending on health care has been growing. Local governments, in contrast, spend much less on social services, as these programs are largely administered by the states.

Social Services: Aid to the Poor

Assistance to the poor, or welfare programs, works in a similar manner as medical benefit programs. Federal government funds are sent to the states and topped up by a state if it expands services offered or people who are eligible. Cash assistance to the poor represents a much smaller proportion of state spending on social services than health care: less than 20 percent of all social service spending. Social welfare programs include transferring cash to

individuals and providing services. In 1996, Congress passed the Temporary Assistance to Needy Families (TANF) block grant program and shifted much of the responsibility for welfare assistance programs from the national government to the states. The TANF program also represented a contraction of total welfare benefits. By 1998, states and communities were spending 20 percent less on cash assistance to the poor than they were in 1992.[83]

Pensions and Unemployment

A major component of state expenditures is payments from insurance and trust funds. States spend about as much on these programs as on higher education, but they are considered "off budget" because they have their own funding sources. States maintain various trust funds to provide unemployment coverage for state residents or to provide compensation to residents who cannot work because they were injured on the job. States also maintain pension funds to cover their own employees' retirement payments, some of which provide rather generous benefits. In theory, these can be "pay as you go" programs. Workers pay weekly or monthly contributions into an unemployment insurance fund, for example, and are eligible for benefits if they lose work. Likewise, the state, as an employer, matches public employees' contributions to public pension funds to create a pool of money to cover future retirement benefit costs for state workers and public school teachers. Pension funds may be invested in order to increase their value.

In practice, things do not always work this way. When revenues are low, some states and cities forgo contributing to trust funds or borrow from the funds in order to make it appear that their budgets balance. If pension fund investments go bad, states may also have to make up for losses. States have full

---

[82] Feingold et al., "Social Program Spending and State Fiscal Crisis."

[83] Mark Rom, "Transforming State Health and Welfare Programs," in *Politics in the American States: A Comparative Analysis* (Washington, DC: CQ Press, 2004).

responsibility for workers' comp and unemployment programs, so these programs do not factor into the local spending mix. For many state governments and some local governments, obligations to fully fund public employee retirement pension accounts may be a looming crisis. It is easy to forgo collecting revenues to cover the costs of pension funds, but if the deficits in such accounts grow over time, it may be harder to make up lost ground. A 2004 survey of cities found 79 percent reporting that their pension funds' fiscal health was eroding. San Diego's public employee pension fund was nearly $2 billion in deficit in 2004. The city had been providing lavish benefits while reducing payments into the fund. When a stock market crash reduced the value of the fund, the city faced bankruptcy.[84] Many pension funds suffered from the market collapse of 2008. In New York, the state and local governments agreed to higher contributions to employee retirement funds as the state's fund lost 30 percent of its value. This required higher property taxes so governments could meet their pension obligations.[85]

Transportation and Highways

About 7 percent of state spending and 6 percent of local spending are for transportation. Localities also spend more than states on transit systems. Most state expenditures on transportation are funded by earmarked revenues placed in special non–general fund accounts, usually from gasoline taxes. Federal funds are also directed to the states for highway construction and cover about 30 percent of transportation spending. States also finance highways with bonds. Transportation

represents the largest part of state spending in capital budgets. States spend more on transportation infrastructure than they do on building prisons, universities, housing, and all other infrastructure combined.

Government Administration and Debt Interest

Four percent of state and 4 percent of local expenditure are used to operate public buildings, run court systems (including paying public defenders, judges, and prosecutors), and fund general administrative costs.

Public Safety, Police, and Prisons

Four percent of state spending and 9 percent of local spending finance public safety programs. At the state level, 66 percent of public safety costs fund corrections operations (mostly salaries for prison guards and other staff); most of the remainder pays for state troopers (highway patrols). The operation of prisons is a growing part of state budgets. At the local level, most spending in this area supports local police forces.

Do State and Local Spending Actually Reflect What People Want?

Much of governing involves responding to the popular demands for spending. Thus, if a state's population consistently tells politicians they want more spent on schools and playgrounds, we might expect more spent on schools and playgrounds. Likewise, if voters routinely approve taxes and bonds for parklands, we might expect legislators to interpret this as a signal to spend money on recreation amenities. Other factors, however, may drive spending away from what most voters (or the average voter) want. This raises at least two questions: How much do state and local

---

[84] John Ritter, "San Diego Now Enron by the Sea," *USA Today,* 24 October 2004.

[85] Adam Sichko, "Pension Fund Increase Could Lead to Local Tax Hikes," *The Business Review* (Albany), 3 September 2009.

spending reflect what people really want? and How much should they reflect what most people want?

In addition to trying to determine the preferences of the general public, elected officials hear from many different interest groups who each want some unique benefit just for themselves: a tax break here, a new road there, higher salaries for prison guards or professors, more spending on somebody's favorite program—public funds to help all sorts of relatively narrow concerns. In many legislative hearings, representatives of rather narrow constituencies may outnumber everyone else.

Governing involves the need to balance these demands and the ability to anticipate other things that also need to be done. These may include things the public might not be paying much attention to or that they might not want to spend much money on. Courts' interpretations of state and federal constitutions often force states to spend millions to reduce prison crowding. The business climate in part of a state may be threatened by traffic gridlock, forcing politicians to find ways to fund transportation options in that area. Even lightly used bridges, levees, and tunnels will eventually need maintenance or modernization to meet new safety or seismic standards. The fact that these matters may require public investment does not necessarily mean that the public supports such spending.

Part of writing a public budget, then, includes spending on some things many people do not want. Furthermore, critics of government spending suggest politicians and bureaucrats inflate public spending for their own purposes and that fiscal illusion allows them to hide much of what they spend from the public's eyes by using revenue sources that are hard to notice.[86] Finally, some (but not all) studies found that state spending levels had nothing to do with whether Democrats or Republicans were in office.[87] This has been used to argue that public opinion has little do with how much a government spends. Although partisan differences in spending are not always apparent in studies of the states, there is convincing evidence that states with more liberal electorates tax and spend more, and conservative states tax and spend less.[88]

Budgeting

Deficits and Balanced Budget Requirements

If the federal government decides it wants to spend more than it is collecting in taxes, it can. The federal government can finance its operations by selling long-term U.S. Treasury bonds. Investors buy the bonds and earn interest on their investment over time. This allows for long-term borrowing to finance the annual operations of the federal government. In recent decades the federal budget has been in deficit more years than not, which means a large percentage of each federal budget includes funds to pay interest on bonds that are outstanding. Critics of chronic federal deficits look to state **balanced budget rules** as a model for fiscal reform. In all but one state, these rules require that proposed budgets are projected to balance at the end of the fiscal year. Twenty-seven states also prohibit deficits from being carried into the next fiscal year.[89]

---

[86] Wagner, *Democracy in Deficit*.

[87] Thomas Dye, *Politics Economics, and the Public* (Chicago: Rand McNally, 1966); James Garand, "Explaining Government Growth in the US States," *American Political Science Review* (1988):837-49. See also notes 4 and 5 above.

[88] Robert S. Erikson, Gerald C. Wright, and John P. McIver, *Statehouse Democracy: Public Opinion and Policy in the American States* (Cambridge: Cambridge University Press, 1993), p. 85.

[89] Robert Lowry, 293–94.

Borrowing

State governments cannot run deficits—at least not in the same way the federal government does. Virtually all states—Vermont is the only exception—have constitutional rules that require annual (or biannual) spending to not exceed revenues. Many states actually write two budgets, with balanced budget rules applying to the state's **operating budget**. Operating budgets cover spending on services, salaries, and purchases of supplies. States might borrow funds in the short term to manage cash flow problems during the year (some tax collections peak in certain months, but government expenses, such as paying salaries, are more constant). Short-term debts are supposed to be repaid by the end of the budget cycle. **Capital budgets** can be a separate matter; states and local governments issue long-term bonds to finance capital investment in roads, bridges, buildings, and other infrastructure. Capital budgets may be funded with long-term borrowing, which is a form of deficit spending. Borrowing, rather than paying costs up front, can be seen as a fair way of paying for infrastructure that will be in use for years. Paying for a road, a bridge, or a sports arena all at once means that some of those who paid for it will die or move away before the project is completed and thus never benefit from it.

In addition to having balanced budget rules, some states require that voters approve the sale of any bonds that will be used to finance long-term borrowing. Some also require a supermajority vote in the legislature before the proposal can go to voters for approval.

Do Budgeting Rules Matter?

But do these budgeting rules really make any difference? Some balanced budget rules have weak provisions for enforcement. Most studies suggest that tough rules do work at preventing deficits when they are combined with limits on government borrowing, but weak rules do not.[90] Some rules simply require the governor to submit a balanced budget to the legislature or require the legislature to enact a balanced budget at the start of the fiscal year. But a state with such rules may still be allowed to run a deficit if revenue or spending estimates end up wrong.[91] Rules that simply require the budget to be balanced when written may be less effective than rules that require it to be balanced at the end of the year. Likewise, constitutional rules may be more effective than regular laws that politicians can easily amend. Finally, balanced budget rules may be more effective when enforced by an independently elected state supreme court than when enforcement depends on a court appointed by the politicians who write the budget.[92] One study noted that balanced budget rules were more effective when Republicans were in office.[93]

Some rules regulating long-term capital borrowing don't necessarily lead to less state indebtedness. Requiring a supermajority vote in the legislature for transportation infrastructure bills, for example, may create incentives to place a transportation project in every representative's district.[94] Even voters seem more likely to approve state-level borrowing if a project is proposed for their local area.[95]

---

[90] James Poterba, "Budget Institutions and Fiscal Policy in the U.S. States," *American Economic Review* 86(2) (1996):395–400.

[91] James Poterba, "Balanced Budget Rules and Fiscal Policy: Evidence from the States," *National Tax Journal* (1995):329–27.

[92] Hening Bohn and Robert P. Inman, "Balanced Budget Rules and Public Deficits: Evidence from the U.S. States," NBER Working Paper no. W5533, 1996, http://ssrn.com/abstract=4069.

[93] James Alt and Robert Lowry, "Divided Government, Fiscal Institutions, and Budget Deficits: Evidence from the States," *American Political Science Review* 88(1994):811–28.

[94] Kiewiet and Szakaly, "Constitutional Limitations of Borrowing."

[95] Shaun Bowler and Todd Donovan, *Demanding Choices: Opinion, Voting, and Direct Democracy* (Ann Arbor, MI: University of Michigan Press, 1998).

Budget Surpluses

Independent of whatever these balanced budget rules may produce, states have a fairly predictable record of not only balancing their budgets but also ending with a surplus. In many years, states maintain a surplus "rainy day fund" to be used in times of crisis. When 50 state budgets were considered across a 40-year period starting in 1961 (that is, 2,000 different budgets), 83 percent produced surpluses. Texas and New Mexico ran in the black every single year. Although Massachusetts (52 percent of budgets had a surplus), Hawaii (55 percent), and Rhode Island (60 percent) were least likely to run surpluses, they usually did.[96] With state governments usually running surpluses, they soften the effects that federal deficits might have on the national economy. States and communities run deficits at their own peril. Lenders charge states more in interest if they have more debt (relative to the size of their economies).[97]

There may be a political risk, however, in maintaining a large "rainy day fund." A large surplus can become a target for antitax activists, as it illustrates that government is collecting more revenue than it needs to spend. California's tax revolt of the 1970s occurred when the state was running a multibillion-dollar surplus. Washington voters also slashed their motor vehicle tax in the late 1990s when the state was running a surplus.

Boom to Bust Budgeting

After the national economy faced a crisis in 2008, most states had difficulty balancing their budgets. Budgeting in recession years, however, can encourage great creativity. In addition to cuts in spending and raising taxes, states have responded by delaying payments they owed, raising tuition, offering early retirement programs to lower salary costs, expanding gambling, raiding transportation and pension funds, mortgaging funds awarded in a settlement with tobacco companies, and borrowing money to fund operations. In 2009, eight states used rainy day funds to help balance their budget. Smokers helped some states balance their books by paying higher cigarette taxes.

The most dramatic case of boom to bust budgeting may be California, where income tax revenues exploded in the 1990s as people cashed in on stock options in the superheated tech industry. During the 1990s, the state increased spending on K–12 education, expanded medical care eligibility, froze tuition, and cut taxes while balancing its budget. A recession began in March 2001, the tech bubble burst, and tax revenues from stock options and capital gains taxes fell from $17 billion to $6 billion between 2001 and 2002. By 2003, California faced a $38 billion deficit if it was to maintain its previous year's spending—a deficit equal to 40 percent of projected spending.[98] To put that in perspective, the deficit was larger than the entire biennial (two-year) budget for Virginia. In 2004, California voters approved the sale of $15 billion in bonds to cover part of their deficit, but interest payments on these bonds were projected to consume 7.5 percent of general fund spending by 2009. Such gimmicks only worked in the short term. When the national economy went into a deep freeze in 2008, the state was facing another $40 billion deficit for 2009 and 2010. Before reaching a budget deal that included substantial spending cuts and tax increases, California briefly ran out of operating cash in 2009, and was paying people with IOUs.

---

[96] Garand and Baudoin, "Fiscal Policy in the American States."

[97] Tamim Bayoumi, Morris Goldstein, and Geoffrey Woglom, "Do Credit Markets Discipline Sovereign Borrowers?" *Journal of Money, Credit and Banking* 27(1995):1046–59.

[98] Reports from 2003 and 2005 place the deficits at $31 billion to $38 billion, respectively; see American Legislative Exchange Council, "Budget Deficit Chart," http://www.alec.org/meSWFiles/pdf/Deficits.pdf and Public Policy Institute of California, "Just the Facts: California's State Budget."

California's sustained fiscal crisis, although an extreme case, was not unique. The economic decline that began in 2007 and accelerated in 2008 was one of the most severe recessions since World War II. It came after a period when many states cut taxes, while maintaining spending via increased charges, fees, and delays in funding pension obligations. California was not alone in expanding spending while cutting taxes in the boom years of the 1990s and early 2000s.[99] The net tax revenues collected by all states combined, in dollar amounts, was cut every year from 1995 to 2002.[100] By 2010, boom had gone full bust. Forty-eight states forecast combined deficits of $166 billion for their fiscal year 2010 budgets, and $350 billion for 2011.[101] Many responded by cutting social services at a time when demand—for job training, education, unemployment insurance, health care—was peaking due to the poor economy.

Summary

In surveys of state and local fiscal politics from previous decades, the taxing and spending patterns of states and communities were often explained largely in terms of "environmental" factors. That is, wealthy states were said to spend more because they had more. Political factors, such as public opinion, budgeting rules, and other partisan and institutional forces, were largely dismissed because most studies found little effect of politics on fiscal policy.

The dismissal of political and institutional forces was probably a mistake resulting from flawed measures of political influence and from a lack of investigation. We now have detailed measures of state public opinion and decades of research examining the effects that taxing and spending limits (TELs), balanced budgeting rules, direct democracy, and popular opinion have on taxation and spending. Although some debate the magnitude of the effects of such rules, or of public opinion, it is clear that politics matters, perhaps more than anything else, in determining who gets what from government via fiscal policy.

Key Terms

Balanced budget rules

Block grants

Capital budget

Categorical grants

Cost of living allowances (COLAs)

Elasticity

Exportable tax

Flat rate tax

Inelastic demand

Leviathan

Medicaid

Operating budget

Progressive tax

Regressive tax

Sin tax

Supermajority vote requirement

Tax equity

Tax and expenditure limitations (TELs)

User fees

---

[99] Feingold et al., "Social Program Spending and State Fiscal Crisis."

[100] Elaine Magg and David Merriman, *Tax Policy Response to Revenue Shortfall* (Washington, DC: Urban Institute, 2003).

[101] Center for Budget Policy Priorities, "Press Release: New Fiscal Year Brings Painful Spending Cuts, Continued Budget Gaps in Almost Every State," 29 June 2009, http://www.cbpp.org/cms/index.cfm?fa=view&id=2853.

Discussion Questions

1. How does state income tax factor into a state's revenue mix? What are the benefits and critiques of state income taxes?
2. How do internet sales influence state and local sales tax collection?
3. What factors have fueled rebellion against property taxes? What reforms have resulted?
4. What are the positive and negative effects of state tax and expenditure limits?
5. How do local revenue mixes differ from state revenue mixes? What are the different key revenue sources for each of these?

Suggested Readings

Beamer, Glenn. 1999. *Creative Politics: Taxes and Public Goods in a Federal System*. Ann Arbor, MI: University of Michigan Press.

Briffault, Richard. 1996. *Balancing Acts: The Reality Behind State Balanced Budgets*. New York: Twentieth Century Fund Press.

Brunori, David. 2005. *State Tax Policy: A Political Perspective*, 2nd ed. Washington, DC: Urban Institute Press.

Crain, W. Mark. 2003. *Volatile States: Institutions, Policy, and State Economies*. Ann Arbor, MI: University of Michigan Press.

Forsythe, Dall W. 2004. *Memos to the Governor: An Introduction to State Budgeting*, 2nd ed. Washington, DC: Georgetown University Press.

Lowry, Robert C. 2008. "Fiscal Policy in the American States," in V. Gray and R. Hanson, eds., *Politics in the American States: A Comparative Introduction*. Washington, DC: CQ Press.

Smith, Daniel A. 1998. *Tax Crusaders and the Politics of Direct Democracy*. New York: Routledge.

Thurmaier, Kurt M., and Katherine G. Willoughby. 2001. *Policy and Politics in State Budgeting*. Armonk, NY: M. E. Sharpe.

Web Sites

Cato Institute (http://www.cato.org): A conservative organization that provides policy analysis "based on individual liberty, limited government, free markets and peaceful international relations."

Center for Budget Policy Priorities (http://www.cbpp.org): A liberal organization that conducts research on the needs of low-income families and the impact of policies on state budgets. Works with states and nonprofit groups to advocate for the needs of low-income families. Provides analysis of state fiscal policy.

Federation of Tax Administrators (http://www.taxadmin.org): Comparative information on state tax rates and state tax agencies.

National Association of State and Provincial Lotteries (http://www.naspl.org): Represents lottery organizations and provides reports about revenues from state lotteries.

National Association of State Budget Officers (http://www.nasbo.org): Professional organization for all state budget officers. An independent association with membership consisting of the heads of state budget offices and state finance departments. Provides reports on trends in the fiscal condition of the states.

National Council of State Legislators (http://www.ncsl.org): An organization that provides research, technical assistance, and other information to state legislators. Provides reports on state and federal relations and on key policy issues.

U.S. Census Bureau, Census of Governments (http://www.census.gov/govs/www/): Detailed data on state and local expenditures and revenues.

11

CITY HALL

The Structure of Local Governments

WHO IS IN CHARGE? WEAK AND STRONG MAYORS

In March 1991, the Los Angeles Police Department's brutal beating of African American motorist Rodney King was captured on video. The tape was played repeatedly on television news, leading many to view the LAPD as a racist organization. The LAPD already had a strained relationship with the black community in south Los Angeles after aggressive responses to gang violence in the area. The LAPD's chief, Daryl Gates, also had a reputation for being arrogant and racially insensitive. He had been quoted as saying that African American suspects occasionally died while in choke holds "because their veins or arteries don't open up like normal people" and for saying drug users should be "taken out and shot." After the King beating, local politicians, community organizations, and national figures, such as Jesse Jackson and Al Sharpton, called for Gates to be dismissed.

Mayor Tom Bradley, however, had no power to hire or fire his city's police chief. Those decisions were controlled by an independent, five-member police commission designed to function like a corporate board of directors. Although the mayor appointed the police commissioners, he could not control the commission's decisions. Political control of the police chief was further limited because the Los Angeles City Charter gave the police commission little power to discharge the chief. The charter granted the chief "substantial property right" to his job. The intent of the LA Charter, drafted in 1925, was to remove political control of city affairs from "politicians" and place it in the hands of professional managers. Architects of the city charter expected that city departments would be corrupted if politicians had direct control over them.[1]

Mayor Bradley asked Gates to resign on April 2, 1991, but Gates refused. The police commission also tried to suspend Gates but could not, due to Gates's status as a civil servant. Gates remained in office. On April 29, 1992, the officers involved in the beatings were acquitted of all charges by a California jury. Violent riots began in Los Angeles shortly after the verdict was announced. On the first evening of the rioting, Gates attended a fundraising dinner and announced that the situation would soon be under control. Rioting lasted for three days and left 53 dead. Gates remained in office until late June 1992, when he finally resigned.

Mayors in some other cities, in contrast, have far more power to hire and fire city employees. When New York City Mayor Michael Bloomberg saw a city employee playing solitaire on a city computer in 2006, he fired the man on the spot with no warning or severance pay. In 2001, the mayor of St. Petersburg, Florida, fired that city's chief of police for racial insensitivity after the chief compared a black motorist's appearance to that of an orangutan.[2] The mayor of Baltimore fired the head of the city's police force after the chief was accused of beating his girlfriend.[3] In this chapter, we learn why the powers of these local elected officials vary so widely and learn why some public employees are more insulated from political control than others. Politics in Los Angeles, and similar cities, is shaped heavily by institutional reforms designed to limit political control of municipal functions. Cities like Baltimore and New York City, in contrast, have traditions of unfettered political control of the administration of city departments.

Mayors of America's two largest cities differ in the powers they have to control city departments. New York's Charter grants Mayor Michael Bloomberg substantial power to hire and fire personnel. Former Los Angeles Mayor Tom Bradley is shown here with Chief Willie Williams in 1993. Williams was hired by the LA Police Commission after Chief Daryl Gates resigned.

1   Report of the Independent Commission on the Los Angeles Police Department (Los Angeles: Independent Commission on the Los Angeles Police Department, 1991), ch. 10.
2   National Briefing, "South Florida: Mayor Fires Police Chief," *The New York Times,* 20 December 2001.
3   National Briefing, "Mid Atlantic: Maryland: Mayor Fires Police Commissioner," *The New York Times,* 11 November 2004.

Introduction

The structure of American local governments today is the product of reforms that redesigned political institutions at the beginning of the 20th century. Some of these reforms have been discussed briefly in other parts of this book: non-partisan local elections and direct democracy, for example. These are part of a larger package of institutional changes that fundamentally redefined how state and local politics work in much of the United States. Local political party organizations, or "party machines" that controlled public offices in many American cities in the 19th century, were the primary target of these reforms. We begin with a brief description of the major forms of local governments in the United States today and then examine the "machine" origins of American cities in order to understand how these local institutions have evolved into what they are today.

Many Americans might take for granted—or resent—the vast array of local governments in the United States. Local governments, including municipalities, counties, school districts (these are discussed in Chapter 15), and numerous special service districts, provide a wide array of public services. Many Americans today reside in a town or city that is part of a larger county. Scattered across those two levels of government are school districts and various special districts that provide services to your place of residence. Given all these different types of local governments, your place of residence is likely located in several local governments simultaneously.

Forms of Local Government

Municipalities

Each state has its own unique rules about how municipal governments (cities, towns, and villages) are structured and how new municipalities are incorporated. Municipalities, like all local governments, are limited to doing only what their state says they may do. This concept, commonly known as **Dillon's rule,** means that a state legislature can make different rules about how various municipalities in a state might function. Many states have one set of rules for large cities (or special rules that affect only one city) and other rules for smaller municipalities. As we see below, these rules define what these places do and how they may do it. Larger, older cities often provide a wide range of general services—including police, fire protection, building inspections, water service, and many others. As we see in Chapter 12, new cities may provide fewer services.

Counties

States are divided into geographic areas that perform some of the same functions as municipalities. Most states refer to these as counties, although they are known as boroughs in Alaska and parishes in Louisiana. Municipalities exist within counties,[1] and counties provide general services to portions of the county that are unincorporated (that is, outside city or town boundaries). Some counties contract with smaller cities and towns to provide a service the municipality does not offer. The range of public services provided varies substantially across the 3,000 counties in the United States. Counties are, traditionally, administrative and record-keeping jurisdictions for their states. County governments are thus often responsible for recording property records, conducting property tax assessments, administering elections, law enforcement, running jails, running courts, maintaining roads, and processing birth and death records.

Modern county governments have assumed many of the same responsibilities as large municipalities. In some ways, counties do even more than many large cities. Much of the federal and state money for health programs is spent in county hospitals and through county-administered health programs. Some states rely heavily on counties to regulate land use and development.

---

[1] In Virginia, municipalities are jurisdictions independent from the counties they are located in. In Connecticut and Rhode Island, county governments play no functional role.

Special Districts

Special districts, or single-purpose governments, typically provide one particular service for an area. School districts may be the best-known single-purpose governments, but special districts supply dozens of different services (e.g., flood control, soil conservation, fire protection, and libraries). As of 2009, there were over 37,000 special districts in the United States. The geographic footprint of a special district may cut across city or county lines. As we see in the next chapter, a high density of special districts in an area can reduce the number of functions engaged by a municipality.

The Rise of the Urban United States

Despite the huge number of cities, counties, and special districts that exist today, the United States began as a largely rural nation with little need for the public services that local governments provide today. In 1787, just 5 percent of its population resided in cities. It was, according to Thomas Jefferson, "a mass of cultivators." The Jeffersonian vision of proper democracy was one of local government in small, rural communities centered on agriculture. Democracy would survive in the United States only if its citizens were able to govern themselves directly at the local level by participating in local affairs.[2] Jefferson promoted the **Land Ordinance of 1785** as a way for the new U.S. Congress to raise money and to guarantee room for agrarian growth. The Jeffersonian vision of local agrarianism was further institutionalized by his 1803 **Louisiana Purchase.** Ample land supply ensured that the United States remained largely a rural nation of small towns throughout the 19th century. As Figure 11.1 illustrates, few people lived in large, densely populated cities. As late as 1890,

barely one-third of Americans lived in places with a population greater than 2,500. Cities continued to be viewed by many as a threat to democracy, whereas agrarian communities were seen as the soul of pure democracy. Yet, despite Jefferson's misgivings, the United States became a nation of large cities as immigration and industrialization fueled their growth after the Civil War.

In 1850, there was only one U.S. city with a population over 500,000 (New York) and just five others with more than 100,000 residents: Baltimore, Boston, Philadelphia, New Orleans, and Cincinnati. Each of these had less than 200,000 inhabitants. By 1870—just 20 years later—there were 14 U.S. cities with over 100,000 people; seven had more than 250,000 people. Chicago grew tenfold between 1850 and 1870, to 299,000. By 1890, America had 28 cities with a population of 100,000 or more, with New York, Chicago, and Philadelphia each having over 1,000,000 people. By 1910, cities like Louisville, Minneapolis, Denver, Seattle, and Portland were all much larger than the second-largest American city was in 1850.[3]

Immigration

Although the United States largely remained a nation of small communities throughout the 19th century, its large cities were magnets for European immigrants. Immigrants were pushed from Europe by social transformations that moved peasants from their traditional lands by poverty and, for the Irish, by famine. They were pulled to the United States by the prospect of jobs associated with booming industrialization, by opportunities to farm, and by the prospect of political and religious liberties.

---

[2] Herbert Storing, *What the Antifederalists Were For* (Chicago: University of Chicago Press, 1981).

[3] Data from Campbell Gibson, "Population of the 100 Largest Cities and Other Urban Places in the United States: 1790–1990," U.S. Census Bureau. Population Division Working Paper no. 27, June (Washington, DC: U.S. Census Bureau. Population Division, 1998).

Figure 11.1

Percentage of Americans Living in Urban Places, 1790–2000

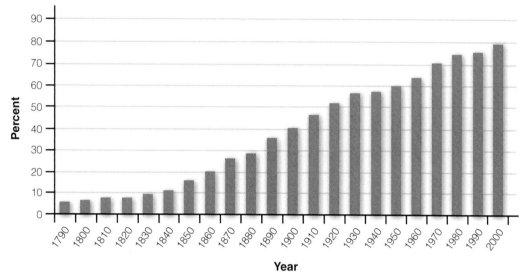

Source: U.S. Census Bureau data. Urban areas are defined as places with a population of over 2,500.

As Figure 11.2 illustrates, millions of Irish and Germans emigrated from their native counties to the United States from 1850 to 1910. In 1890, there were nearly 2 million foreign-born Irish living in the United States, primarily in cities (this was equal to more than half the population of Ireland at the time). The social transformation produced by this immigration was profound. Prior to the 1840s, there was a limited measure of ethnic and religious heterogeneity in the United States. There were few Catholics or Jews and a limited range of Protestant denominations, for example. In 1850, Catholics made up just 5 percent of the U.S. population. With mass emigration from Ireland, Germany, central Europe, Scandinavia, Russia, Italy, and elsewhere, ethnic and religious diversity increased dramatically. Millions of Catholics emigrated from Germany and Ireland from 1850 to 1910. Millions more emigrated from Italy, Russia, Poland, and Austria in the first decade of the 20th century. By 1906, 17 percent of Americans were Catholic, making Catholics the single-largest religious group

in the nation.[4] Millions of Jews also immigrated to American cities between 1880 and 1915—primarily from Eastern Europe (Poland, Latvia, Lithuania, and the Ukraine) and Russia. In 1910, there were 13.5 million people who were foreign born living in the United States, mostly in cities (see Figure 11.3).

The Need for Municipal Government

Multiple governments providing many public services are a relatively modern phenomenon. Governments played little role in providing social services or public services for much of the 19th century. No social security, no food stamps, no Medicaid, and no Environmental Protection Agency of the federal government existed at

---

[4] Julie Byrne, *Roman Catholics and Immigration in Nineteenth Century America* (Research Triangle Park, NC: National Humanities Center, 2000).

Figure 11.2

Immigration to the United States, in Millions, by Country of Origin

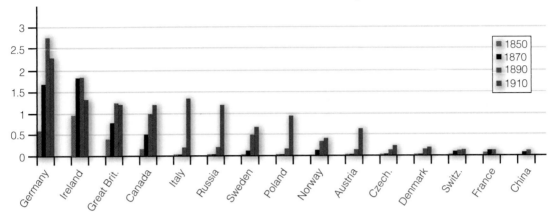

IMMIGRATION TO UNITED STATES, IN MILLIONS

Legend: 1850, 1870, 1890, 1910

Source: U.S. Census Bureau.
Note: Each bar represents the number of immigrants from a nation over the course of one decade.

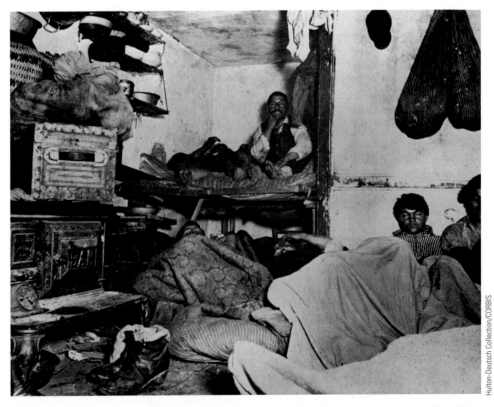

Hulton-Deutsch Collection/CORBIS

Dens of Death. New York City's crowded shanties and tenements, circa 1880s; photo by Jacob Riis. Riis's muckraking photography turned public attention toward the problems of crowded, unsanitary housing and urban poverty and helped drive support for reforming city governments.

Figure 11.3

Percentage Foreign Born: Large Cities and Rural Areas, 1870–2000

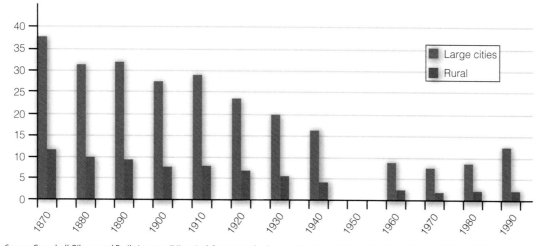

Source: Campbell Gibson and Emily Lennon, "Historical Census on the Foreign Born Population of the United States: 1850–1990," U.S. Census Bureau, Population Division Working Paper no. 29, February (Washington, DC: U.S. Census Bureau. Population Division, 1999).
Note: Bars represent the percentage of residents who are foreign born, for each decade. Large cities are defined as places over 100,000.

that time. The rapid **urbanization** of the United States largely outpaced the bare minimal levels of basic public services, such as sewerage, street lighting, and garbage collection, as well as any publicly provided social welfare. As cities grew, the need for basic services also grew. Urbanization meant increased fire risks. Cities required sanitation (for humans and horses alike). The growth of manufacturing industries meant more people were crowded into polluted cities.

The provision of public services in this context was minimal and haphazard. Public and private police forces patrolled cities simultaneously. Fire departments were largely organized by volunteer groups, which often operated as private entities. Although Boston employed paid firefighters as early as 1678, few other U.S. cities followed Boston's lead over the next 200 years. New York City did not have paid firefighters until 1865.[5] A large city could have had multiple

---

[5] Terry Golway, "Firefighters," *American Heritage Magazine* 56(6)(November/December 2005).

neighborhood-based fire brigades that did not cooperate with each other. Nineteenth-century local governments had developed with only minimal powers to regulate building standards, business practices, or public health. As there had never been much need for a public sector prior to the 1870s or for public employees, there were few regulations regarding who city officials could hire or fire. In short, the need for effective local government outpaced the urbanization and development of U.S. cities.

Origins of Urban Party Machines

Urbanization created new demands for public services and also created new forms of politics. As Figure 11.3 illustrates, immigration built U.S. cities. Many of the new immigrants settled in cities and raised their families in cities. By 1870, 44 percent of New York City's residents were born outside of the United States; 48 percent in Chicago were foreign born, as were 49 percent in San Francisco. The population of the 25 largest

Firefighting is one of the oldest and most dangerous services provided by local governments. In June 2007, nine firefighters were killed battling a warehouse fire in Charleston, South Carolina, the largest loss of life since the September 11, 2001, attacks. Charleston has one of the oldest professional fire departments in the United States.

U.S. cities outside the South was at least one-quarter to one-third foreign born in 1890.[6]

Growth of the Voting Population

At the same time, the use of elections was expanding, although to a much more limited extent than what exists today. In the early 1800s, states placed substantial limits on who could vote. The number of voters in the United States increased

dramatically after 1824. Several states began extending the right to vote to most white men in the 1820s, and all but one state moved to allow direct voting in presidential elections by 1832. By 1828, when Andrew Jackson was elected, the number of people voting tripled over what it had been in 1824. The size of the voting population continued to grow after the 1820s. Massachusetts and New York eliminated property requirements for voting in 1821, followed by Tennessee (in 1834), New Jersey (in 1844), and Virginia (in 1850). Connecticut removed the taxpaying requirement in 1845; Ohio did so in 1851.[7] In the spirit of **Jacksonian democracy,** states were also expanding the range of offices subject to popular election. The first mayor of Chicago was elected in 1837 (he served one year). The first popular election of a Philadelphia mayor was held in 1840. With mass participation in federal, state, and local elections just emerging in the 1830s, there was a need for new methods to recruit candidates, communicate with voters, and earn voter loyalties. Out of this context, modern political parties were born—as institutions designed to meet the challenges of mobilizing regular people who had never before been allowed to play a role in elections.[8]

Early Political Parties

A political group (in some cities, they were known as "clubs" before being called parties) seeking to control a city would need to organize support of enough people in enough neighborhoods so they could win elections. Volunteer firehouses provided one base for organizing, as they were distributed in various neighborhoods across a city. Firehouses served as a sort of social center, as did local pubs. By the 1850s, volunteer fire departments were becoming more Irish and more Catholic.[9] Political clubs found the firehouse

---

[6] Campbell Gibson and Emily Lennon, "Historical Census on the Foreign Born Population of the United States: 1850–1990," U.S. Census Bureau, Population Division Working Paper no. 29, February (Washington, DC: U.S. Census Bureau, Population Division, 1999).

[7] Alexander Keysar, *The Right to Vote: The Contested History of Democracy in the United States* (New York: Basic Books, 2000), table A.2

[8] Richard Gunther and Larry Diamond, "Species of Political Parties," *Party Politics* 9(2003):167–99.

[9] Golway, "Firefighters."

Harper's Weekly, August 19, 1871

Thomas Nast cartoon of Boss Tweed and Tammany Hall politicians. The upper panel refers to a *New York Times* story uncovering $5.6 million paid to a Tammany-controlled firm (Ingersoll's Co.) that supposedly supplied carpets for the county court house. The *Times* reported on numerous contracts that showed the city paid tens of millions of dollars to contractors selected by Tammany and to a firm owned by Tweed himself, with no evidence of any benefits for the city.

their ability."[10] Machine politicians in several large cities (see Table 11.1) came up through the ranks of firefighters, as did one of the nation's greatest political operatives, William "Boss" Tweed of New York City's **Tammany Hall** machine.[11]

Urban Party Machines

Urban political party organizations—known as **machines**—were born out of this 19th-century environment of industrialization, urbanization, rapid immigration, expanding democracy, and the absence of basic public services. These local party organizations gained and maintained control of cities by organizing neighborhoods to deliver votes for machine candidates on election day. One observer described machines as "quasi-feudal" because they were very hierarchical. At the top of the hierarchy sat the boss or the core group of leaders. The local boss and local party leaders might control the machine from the position of an elected office, but not every boss held local office. Below the boss and other organization leaders, a city was divided into districts (or **wards**), and each of these was divided into smaller units. Local neighborhoods, divided into **precincts,** were at the bottom of the hierarchy. Voters in neighborhoods remained loyal to the machine leaders when leaders

and pubs places to organize and recruit loyalists, and volunteer fire departments became political forces in large cities like New York, Baltimore, and St. Louis. Firehouses weren't simply a means that parties used to organize support but also provided "an arena in which those who wished to exercise political leadership could win men's loyalty by demonstrating

---

[10] Amy Bridges, *A City in the Republic: Antebellum New York and the Origins of Machine Politics* (Ithaca, NY: Cornell University Press, 1984).

[11] Amy Greenberg, *Cause for Alarm: The Volunteer Fire Department in the Nineteenth Century City* (Cambridge, MA: Harvard University Press, 1998).

Table 11.1

Great Party Machine Politician Names and Nicknames

Name	City and Position
James Michael "Mayor of the Poor" Curley	Boston Mayor, 4 terms between 1914 and 1949
John "Bathhouse" Coughlin	Chicago First Ward Alderman 1893–1938
Michael "Hinky Dink" Kenna	Chicago First Ward Alderman 1897–1923
"King" James McManes	Philadelphia Republican Machine, 1866–1880s
"Iz" Durham	Philadelphia Republican Machine, early 1900s
"Sunny Jim" McNichol	Philadelphia Republican Machine
William "Boss" Tweed	New York Tammany Hall Boss, 1860s–1872
Abraham "OK" Hall	New York Tammany Hall, 1870s
"Slippery Dick" Connolly	New York, City Comptroller, 1870s
George Washington Plunkitt	New York, State Senator; Tammany Hall, 1880s
"Silent" Charlie Murphy	New York Tammany Hall Boss, 1902–1924
John Francis "Red Mike" Hylan	New York Mayor, 1918–1925

Sources: Clarence Stone. 1996. "Urban Political Machines: Taking Stock" PS: Political Science and Politics, Vol 29, no. 3. pp 446–50; Peter McCaffery. 1993. *When Bosses Ruled Philadelphia*. Penn State University Press.

provided them with favors or services. In immigrant neighborhoods where few residents had any political power or English language skills, relatively small favors might be mutually beneficial to party leaders and machine supporters alike. Irish Catholics were the backbone of machines in several, but not all, cities.

Favors that a machine organization provided to supporters could include help with finding a place to live, or assistance with food (a turkey on Christmas), or help with home-heating fuel in winter. Services could include help with the police, help with finding a job, or help with making contacts in business.[12] Machines may have also helped immigrants obtain citizenship (so they could vote). Some machine organizations offered illicit businesses protection from law enforcement, thus earning the support of tavern owners, prostitution businesses, and gambling operations. A few city machines had reformist intentions, establishing municipally owned utilities to improve water, sewer, and street-lighting services.

These 19th-century urban party machines operated as **clientele parties;** that is, the party machine (acting as a sort of patron) served working-class and immigrant voters (the clients) by providing personal favors in exchange for votes. Machine politics was most notable in large cities, but this style of local politics also operated in small towns and rural areas.[13] Support for a party machine organization was not based on ideology but on the leaders' personalities, ethnic solidarity, and/or neighborhood loyalties.[14] This being the case, a machine could operate with a Democratic Party label or a Republican Party label. Most were Democrat, yet the Philadelphia machine of 1867–1933 was Republican.[15]

---

[12] Steven P. Erie, *Rainbow's End: Irish Americans and the Dilemmas of Urban Machine Politics, 1840–1985* (Berkeley: University of California Press, 1988).

[13] Erie, *Rainbow's End.*

[14] Gunther and Diamond, "Species of Political Parties."

[15] Peter McCaffery, *When Bosses Ruled Philadelphia* (University Park: Pennsylvania State University Press, 1993).

Patronage

Clientele politics involves providing something of value in exchange for political support. Prior to the late 19th century, appointment to most government jobs was controlled by elected officials. Winning politicians had the power to fire government employees and replace them with their supporters. For urban party machines, public sector jobs were one of the more lucrative perks that they could use to reward the people who helped keep the machine running. This **patronage** system occasionally had a high cost for politicians. Carter Harrison Sr., the mayor of Chicago, was assassinated in his home in 1893 by a "disappointed office seeker." Some cities such as Chicago retain elements of a patronage-based system to this day.

Precinct-Based Politics

A political machine's ability to organize a city politically depended on its ability to maintain support at the neighborhood level. Many precincts had workers loyal to the party—perhaps led by a **precinct captain**—who provided information about residents' needs and their voting habits to people higher up the party machine hierarchy. Voters might support the machine in response to the patronage and favors it provided or as the result of friendship with party loyalists in neighborhoods or some common social bond with a precinct worker. Party organizations maintained contacts in neighborhoods by sponsoring picnics, sporting events, dances, and other social events "to keep people in the orbit of the machine."[16] Service as a precinct captain was a potential means for career advancement within the party organization.

District Elections, Large Councils

Given the concentration of different ethnic groups in distinct parts of a city, and given neighborhood-based political loyalties that flowed from this, it was easier for a machine to organize a city on ethnic loyalties when representation on the city council was based on small geographic units. Local councils where each member was elected from a small geographic district helped to transfer ethnic-based neighborhood loyalties into political representation. City councils (or boards of aldermen) with a large number of districts allowed distinct, homogeneous neighborhoods to form the basis of an individual district. A smaller district would be more likely to be ethnically homogenous and thus be easier to organize on the basis of common social bonds or patronage. This helped machine organizations reach out to various ethnic groups concentrated in different parts of a city. As an example, in 1900, the Chicago City Council had 70 members, with two aldermen from each district, elected to two-year terms in partisan elections.

Partisan Elections, Party Ballot Machine control of a city required electing as many machine loyalists as possible to local councils and local offices. The "Democrat" or "Republican" name attached to a party organization provided a banner, or easily communicated brand label, under which the organization's local candidates sought office. Some parties also controlled a newspaper in a city to promote the organization and its candidates.[17] Early American elections were largely unregulated affairs, and secrecy was not always expected in voting. In some places, party organizations printed their own ballots to distribute to voters. Parties gave voters preprinted ballots listing the party's local candidates, with

---

[16] Clarence Stone, "Urban Political Machines: Taking Stock," *PS: Political Science and Politics* 29(3) (1996):446–50.

[17] Robert McChesney, *Corporate Media as a Threat to Democracy* (New York: Seven Stories Press, 1997).

ballots listing only candidates preferred by the local party organization leaders. This helped the machine control who sought office, and it allowed party poll watchers to observe who voters were supporting. Party ballots printed in party newspapers could be clipped by voters to be cast when they arrived at the polling place. Party-printed ballots meant that there was little secrecy in voting, but it also provided a means of voting for new immigrants and others who were not literate enough to read a ballot and fill in without assistance the names of candidates they preferred. With much of the electorate having limited literacy, party-printed ballots made it possible for parties to communicate easily with voters and made it easier for many voters to participate in elections.

Timing of Elections Local party machines could have substantial influence on state and federal races if local elections were held at the same time as state or national contests. Local party organizations had incentives to bring their supporters to the polls in order to maintain control of the city. When local elections were contested in conjunction with state and federal races using straight-ticket ballots, machine organizations could deliver votes for the party's candidates seeking state and congressional offices, and they could have influence over presidential elections. High-profile state and national races, combined on the ballot with local contests, made it easier for machine organizations to mobilize a larger number of voters. Voter turnout in local elections is higher when local elections are held at the same time as national elections.[18] A local party machine's influence in the state or national party organizations as well as in state capitols and Washington, D.C., was enhanced by the local organization's ability to demonstrate that it could deliver votes for the party's candidates for higher office.

Corruption

Machines maintained voter support with patronage and favors and by building social bonds with their supporters. But some machine organizations also paid their supporters to show up to vote, and in parts of a city where support was weak, they could boost their vote share through electoral fraud—hence the classic machine-inspired slogan "Vote early, and vote often." Stuffing ballot boxes and bribing people for votes were not uncommon, and they were not something limited to big cities.[19] Support at elections—whether earned or bought—was not always enough for a party machine to maintain control of a city. Kickback schemes required people who were given public jobs or awarded lucrative city contracts to pay back part of their salary or revenues to the machine organization. Bribes were offered to judges and other officials who needed to be brought on board. Bribes could also be used to control who won contracts to build city facilities. Alliances with business leaders were important to machine politicians, as business provided resources (money and jobs) for the machine, but machine politicians and machine loyalists also had personal financial interests in private real estate and development businesses and benefited from inside information about where their cities would need to buy land or build bridges and roads.

Who Benefited from the Machines?

It is clear that machines often aided illicit businesses and that many machine leaders enriched themselves personally through their corrupt political activities. Machines also operated cities

---

[18] Zoltan Hajnal and Paul Lewis, "Municipal Institutions and Voter Turnout in Local Elections," *Urban Affairs Quarterly* 5(2003):645–68.

[19] Loomis Mayfield, "Voting Fraud in Early Twentieth-Century Pittsburgh," *Journal of Interdisciplinary History* 24(1)(1993):59–84; and Genevive Gist, "Progressive Reform in a Rural Community: The Adams County Vote Fraud Case," *Mississippi Valley Historical Review* 48(1961):60–78.

inefficiently, as they needed an inflated number of public employees to boost their opportunities for handing out jobs as patronage. This inflated public sector came at a cost that was borne by taxpayers. When factors like these are considered, it might seem hard to conclude that urban machines provided benefits to anyone but the machine leaders. Machine bosses, like Tammany Hall's George Washington Plunkitt and Richard Croker, made it no secret that they got rich off of politics. As Plunkitt famously stated, "I seen my opportunities, and I took 'em."[20] Likewise, Croker claimed, "I work for my own pocket all of the time."[21]

Despite overt corruption and inefficiencies, however, some argue that machines acted as a humanizing force, making life better for masses of immigrants arriving to the United States.[22] For one thing, the level of corruption, although shocking by contemporary American standards, was not debilitating to local economies. As Chicago Mayor Carter Harrison Sr. noted in the late 1890s, the two major desires of machine politicians and regular Chicagoans were to make money and spend it. Machine corruption and graft—skimming from local contracts and insider trading in real estate markets—probably encouraged machine politicians to boost local economic development and pursue pro-growth strategies. More growth meant more graft, but it also meant more jobs. And because some key businesses could leave a city and move elsewhere if graft and corruption got too bad (see Chapter 12), there were limits to what machines could extract from businesses.[23]

Whatever their corrupt practices were, machines needed to win elections, and the greater the legitimate voter support they had, the better were their chances of winning. This meant they had to deliver something to voters—although contemporary studies suggest that machines had few decent-paying jobs to offer supporters.[24] Machines needed far more votes than they had city jobs to be filled. Machines were able to transfer real political power in many cities away from a minority of relatively affluent Protestants to the new Catholic majority. Others credit machines with contributing to the peaceful development of the United States by promoting personality-based and patronage-based politics rather than divisive ideological or radical class-based political divisions.[25] Although urban party machines championed "the little guy," workers, and the immigrant, they rarely flirted with socialist ideology. They also frequently opposed union efforts at organizing workers.[26]

But these latter points open urban party machines to further criticism. By emphasizing personal loyalties and patronage, and by opposing the emergence of organized labor (unions) in the late 19th century and early 20th century, machines may have hampered the upward mobility of the United States' less affluent urban immigrants.[27]

Demise of the Machines

Regardless of whether urban machines served their supporters well, the era of machines

[20] William L. Riordan, *Plunkitt of Tammany Hall: A Series of Very Plain Talks on Very Practical Politics* (1905; reprint, New York: Bedford Books, St. Martin's, 1993).

[21] Lincoln Steffens, *The Autobiography of Lincoln Steffens* (New York: Harcourt, 1968).

[22] Clarence Stone, "Urban Machines: Taking Stock," *PS: Political Science and Politics* 29(1996):450; Steffens, *The Autobiography of Lincoln Steffens.*

[23] Rebecca Menes, "Corruption in Cities: Graft and Politics in American Cities at the Turn of the Twentieth Century," NBER Working Paper no. 9990, September (New York: National Bureau of Economic Research, 2003).

[24] Erie, *Rainbow's End.*

[25] Edward Banfield and James Q. Wilson, *City Politics* (New York: Vintage, 1963).

[26] Dennis R. Judd and Todd Swanstrom, *City Politics: Private Power and Public Policy* (New York: Pearson Longman, 2004).

[27] Martin Sheffter, "The Emergence of the Political Machine," in W. Hawley and M. Lipsky, eds., *Theoretical Perspectives on Urban Politics* (Englewood Cliffs, NJ: Prentice Hall, 1976); Bridges, *A City in the Republic*; McCaffery, *When Bosses Ruled Philadelphia.*

REFORM CAN HAPPEN

TAMMANY HALL AND BOSS TWEED

Tammany Hall was a social organization that came to control New York City politics through much of the 19th century. In its early years, the Tammany Society was organized by Aaron Burr to build support for delivering New York's Electoral College votes to Thomas Jefferson in the 1800 presidential election. By the 1840s, Tammany was a de facto branch of the Democratic Party. Large numbers of Irish immigrants began arriving in New York in the late 1840s; Tammany sped their naturalization in exchange for vote support, and Irish Americans became the base of the Tammany organization. Tammany used its vote strength to dominate state and local elections. Around 1870, Tammany politicians defrauded the city of hundreds of millions of dollars in public funds. Boss William Marcy Tweed attempted to maintain popular support at the time with patronage and by diverting funds to buy coal for the city's poor during a severe winter in 1871. The *New York Times* and *Harper's Weekly* focused public attention on Tammany's corruption in the early 1870s. Both featured cartoons by Thomas Nast savagely lampooning Tweed and his cronies. This media scrutiny helped reformers defeat Tammany candidates in the election of 1871. Tweed fled to California but soon returned and was jailed for one year in 1874, then released. He was soon arrested again for his part in stealing public funds but fled to Spain. Someone there recognized him from a Nast cartoon, and he was arrested and returned to a New York jail, where he died in 1878. Nonetheless, the Tammany organization continued to play a strong role in New York long after Tweed's demise.[1]

Notes
1. Gustavus Myers, *History of Tammany Hall* (New York, 1917).

came to an end in the 20th century. Machines thrived when there were large masses of immigrants with limited language skills who lacked economic opportunities and political influence. As immigrants became more educated and affluent over time, the political base of urban machines weakened. Eventually, as immigrants earned better livings, the relative value of the favors provided by the machines declined. Changes in federal laws produced a dramatic decline in immigration after 1910, further eroding the machine's base of support. Organized labor also became more influential in the early decades of the 20th century and competed directly with machines for the loyalty (and votes) of working-class people. And as a result of the Great Depression of the 1930s, the federal government became much more active in providing for the basic needs of the poor. All these forces worked to dilute the influence of urban party machines.

Some big-city machines—but not all—can also be faulted for failing to respond adequately to the problems facing cities at the end of the 19th century. Many did a poor job of providing public services. Basic functions, such as streetcar service, street lighting, and sewers, were contracted to underfinanced private operators. Some party machines awarded lucrative utility monopolies to their business allies, instead of having the city provide the service or contracting with a firm best suited to providing a service. These private contractors often went bankrupt or defrauded local governments of their investments, leaving cities in debt and with inadequate public services.[28] Public health was also severely neglected. Basic services, such as municipal garbage removal, were sporadic.

---

[28] Amy Bridges, *Morning Glories*.

The Urban Reform Movement

One reason for the demise of the urban party machines, then, is functional. Machines functioned poorly on several levels. Some functions that they had performed well, such as maintaining personal, ethnic-based loyalties and providing token material rewards for their supporters, also became less important as society gradually changed. The shortcomings of urban life grew more apparent. Sporadic epidemics made thousands ill, and by the late 1880s, people had knowledge that germs were spread more rapidly in crowded places. **Muckraking journalists** rallied the public against the dangers of crowded, inadequate urban housing and the exploitation of child labor in urban factories and publicized the dangers of slaughterhouses and mass-produced food sources.

But a major reason for the demise of the machines is that rules defining how cities were governed were changed to make it far more difficult for popular political organizations to control city affairs. Industrialization and urbanization happened quite rapidly in the later part of the 19th century. By the early 1900s, several social movements were forming in both the United States and Canada to combat the ill effects of industrialization and urban life. In this environment, reformers of various stripes battled party machines to restructure the organization of city governments.

Many reform proposals were attempts to systematically change the rules about how cities could function—to replace the 19th-century personal-based style of clientelism with a more impersonal bureaucracy. Urban reformers believed that raw politics as a method for governing cities could be improved with efficient public administration.[29] Efficient administration included depersonalizing politics and replacing party loyalists in city departments with people who served because they had merit and specific job qualifications. Reformers wanted to insulate the functions of local governments from the influence of politicians who ruled because they could win elections.

Who Were the Reformers?

The various groups that worked to redefine local political institutions in the first two decades of the 20th century are loosely known as the **Progressive era** reformers. They should not be confused with the Populist reform movement discussed in previous chapters, although the goals of these groups often overlapped. The **Populist era** of the late 19th century was largely centered in rural and agricultural areas and in western mining regions. Populists believed that government and business were dominated by elites conspiring against common people—particularly against farmers. Populists emphasized reforms that broke up concentrations of political and economic power and favored new rules that nationalized ownership of key industries and empowered common citizens (see Chapter 4). Populists are characterized as having disdain for experts and elites[30] and believed in strengthening the power of popular majorities (voters).

Progressives, in contrast, recognized that the concentration of political and economic power could be dangerous. Their targets of concentrated economic and political power included monopolistic trusts that controlled major industries, including beef, sugar, and oil. Party machines were targeted as concentrations of political power that dominated politics in many cities. Progressives also had a different vision for reform than Populists. Many Progressives believed that society could be improved through scientific study and better administrative practices and by limiting the power that wealthy corporations had in politics. As Wisconsin

---

[29] Kenneth Feingold, *Experts and Politicians: Reform Challenges to Machine Politics in New York, Cleveland and Chicago* (Princeton, NJ: Princeton University Press, 1995).

[30] Richard Hofstadter, *The Age of Reform* (New York: Knopf, 1955).

governor Robert M. Lafollette Sr. said, "My goal is not to smash corporations, but to drive them out of politics."

Progressives, as their name suggests, embraced what they viewed as the positive aspects of progress associated with the modern era: science, technology, and efficiency. Progressives believed that efficiency in business and government could be improved if the proper information was available and the best people were charged with implementing policy.[31] For example, Progressives believed that federal government agencies were needed to regulate private business practices and that local public health agencies were needed to collect data, such as vital statistics, which could be used to improve living conditions. Many Progressives embraced the idea that scientific management practices and practical expertise could replace politics in the administration of local government. They were not antidemocratic, but some Progressives found that popular partisan control of local governments could be a barrier to efficient administration.

Many Different Reform Groups

Many different reform groups emerged in the early 20th century, with distinct agendas. Although they are now lumped together under the Progressive label, there was no single Progressive organization or overarching Progressive movement. There were Progressive, reformist wings in both the Republican and Democratic parties. While serving as the Democratic governor of New Jersey from 1911 to 1913, Woodrow Wilson fought local Democratic Party machines in his state by promoting direct primaries (see Chapter 3 and Chapter 5) and campaign finance regulations. At the same time, Teddy Roosevelt's wing of the Republican Party was promoting antitrust reforms to reign in the power of huge corporations. The Progressive era

also corresponded with the rise of the modern conservation movement, which was dedicated to preserving natural resources and establishing national forests and parks. During this time, numerous other reform groups advocated for expanding the scope of public education, regulating investments in stocks and bonds, passing food safety laws, eliminating the exploitation of child labor, and improving working conditions. Religious groups and others also promoted the prohibition of alcohol as a remedy to many of the era's social ills (see Chapter 14).

Women as a Force for Social Reform Women's groups were active in promoting Progressive reforms early in the 20th century. Lacking the power to vote, many politically engaged women sought to improve society and change policy by organizing groups that promoted reform goals.[32] In Chicago, the City Club and Women's City Club of Chicago conducted investigations of urban ills and published recommendations for reforms.[33] The Boston Women's Municipal League performed a similar role in that city. Influential women's clubs organized in most major cities. One study estimates that over 1 million women participated directly in the reform movement under the banner of "municipal housekeeping"—championing reforms that improved sanitation, education, and public health.[34] Women's clubs united under the General Federation of Women's Clubs. Ellen Swallow Richards, an MIT-educated scientist, demonstrated the need for food safety laws. Jane Addams worked with the City of Chicago to improve garbage cleanup, sewers, drinking water, medical care, and street lighting.[35] In the

---

[31] Samuel Haber, *Efficiency and Uplift: Scientific Management in the Progressive Era: 1885–1930* (Chicago: University of Chicago Press, 1964).

[32] Daphne Spain, *How Women Saved the City* (Minneapolis: University of Minnesota Press, 2000).
[33] Maureen A. Flanagan, "Gender and Urban Political Reform: The City Club and the Woman's City Club of Chicago in the Progressive Era," *American Historical Review* 95(1990):1032–50.
[34] Flanagan, "Gender and Urban Political Reform."
[35] Jane Addams, *Twenty Years at Hull House* (Chicago: The Phillips Publishing Company, 1910).

early years of the 20th century, women also organized the backbone of the women's suffrage movement, and women played a major role in promoting reforms to legalize birth control.

Changing the Design of Local Institutions

The urban reform movement was born in this environment as a reaction against party machine dominance of local government. Groups advocating for new political arrangements formed in many American cities in the early years of the 20th century, and national organizations, including the U.S. Chamber of Commerce and the National Municipal League, provided urban reformers with ideas for reshaping local politics and the administration of local government. Many of these reforms, detailed below, linked improvements in administration with weakening the power of local party machines and made it more difficult for elected officials to affect how cities work.

Class Conflict and Institutional Reform

One influential interpretation of the Progressive era is that reformers were motivated not so much by the goal of fixing the ills of industrialization and urbanization as they were by a reaction to the "status revolution" brought about by industrialism, immigration, and the expansion of mass democracy. Several studies suggest that reform advocates came from the ranks of the wealthy, educated, Protestant classes who had lost political influence to immigrant and working-class groups represented by the machines.[36] Historian Richard Hofstadter notes that industrialization created a new social class of superrich (e.g., Andrew Carnegie, John D. Rockefeller, and Leland Stanford) who dominated business and government with their wealth.[37] At the same

time, urban party machines increased the political clout of urban immigrants. Both of those trends shifted power away from the descendants of established, upper-class, patrician Protestant families. These upper-status people may have promoted reforms to reassert their social and political clout over the new superrich "robber barons" and the new, largely Catholic immigrant working class.[38]

Another interpretation argues that the Progressives were largely drawn from a new middle class that was emerging from industrialization: a class of managers, business professionals, and administrators who sought to apply new business models to local politics.[39] Observers have noted that attempts at getting the politics out of city administration with a business model of government meant gutting the representation of lower-status minorities.[40] Some Progressives promoted southern-style Jim Crow laws in order to limit the political influence of racial and ethnic minorities.[41]

How Did Local Institutions Change?

One prominent national advocacy group, the National Municipal League, offered reformers a blueprint for how to rebuild local political institutions so that the influence of mass-based political parties would be weakened and the influence of unelected experts would be increased. The National Municipal League publicized its ideas for reform in a **model city charter**. The first model charter was drafted after several years of conferencing among urban reform groups, including the City Club of New York and the Municipal League of Philadelphia.[42] The model

---

[36] Samuel P. Hays, *The Politics of Reform in Municipal Government in the Progressive Era* (Indianapolis, IN: Bobbs-Merrill, 1972).

[37] Hofstadter, *The Age of Reform*.

[38] David Morgan and Robert England, *Managing Urban America* (Chatham, NJ: Chatham House, 1999).

[39] Robert H. Weibe, *Businessmen and Reform: A Study of Progressive Movements* (Chicago: Quadrangle, 1968).

[40] Banfield and Wilson, *City Politics*, 170–71.

[41] Glenda Elizabeth Gilmore, ed., *Who Were the Progressives?* (New Haven, CT: Yale University Press, 2002).

[42] National Municipal League, *Municipal Program* (New York: Macmillan, 1900).

REFORM CAN HAPPEN

SEWER SOCIALISM

Not every city's politics was dominated by major party machines at the end of the 19th century. Milwaukee elected the first Socialist mayor in the United States in 1910, and Socialists briefly held a majority of seats on the city council.[1] Socialist Daniel Webster Hoan served as mayor from 1916 to 1940. Whereas Progressive reformers of the same era sought to improve living conditions and reduce corruption, Milwaukee Socialists also emphasized public ownership. Victor Berger, a Milwaukee newspaper editor, built the Socialists into a powerful local organization—a sort of political machine—by emphasizing reform goals. Milwaukee Socialists cleaned up neighborhoods with municipally owned sewage systems, street lighting, water systems, power systems, housing, bus system, and parks. As New York City Mayor Fiorello La Guardia once said, there is no Republican, no Democratic, no Socialist way to clean a street or build a sewer; there's merely a right way or a wrong way.[2] At least 18 Socialist mayors were elected during the Progressive era.

Notes

1. Wisconsin Historical Society, "Milwaukee Sewer Socialism" (Madison: Wisconsin Historical Society, 2006).
2. Kevin Baker, "Hizzoners," *The New York Times*, 2 May 1999.

charter was an attempt to bring national attention to how various local experiments with new political arrangements "worked" (or "failed") in various cities. Elements of the model city charter were (and continue to be) updated periodically, and the earliest model charters embodied the Progressive reformers' ideal of how local government should function.

Because state laws define how charters for local governments are to be drawn, reform advocates had to lobby state legislatures to change state rules about local government arrangements. Progressive reformers were also able to define (or redefine) rules shaping local charters by electing sympathetic candidates as state legislators and governors. Some states had Progressive wings in both the Democratic or Republican parties, but Progressives were more often associated with the liberal wing of the Republican Party.

In many parts of the United States, there was wide public support for Democrats and Republicans who promoted Progressive reforms. Candidates who adhered to the Progressive reform agenda were elected governor in several states, including Robert M. Lafollette Sr. of Wisconsin

(first elected as a Republican, 1901–1905, and latter as an Independent Progressive), John A. Johnson of Minnesota (a Democrat, 1905–1909), Edward Hoch of Kansas (a Republican, 1905–1909), Charles Evans Hughes of New York (a Republican, 1907–1910; Hughes defeated Tammany-linked Democrat William Randolph Hearst), Hiram Johnson of California (1910–1920, first elected as a Republican under the Lincoln–Roosevelt Party label, then as a Progressive), Simon Bamberger of Utah (a Democrat, 1917–1921), Charles Hillman Brough of Arkansas (a Democrat, 1917–1921), and Gifford Pinchot of Pennsylvania (a Republican, 1923–1927 and 1931–1935).

Although all these governors are often classified as Progressives, some emphasized social reforms (e.g., public health and improved public education) and economic reforms (e.g., regulating monopolies) when in office more than changes to political institutions. Reformers committed to changing the nature of local political institutions also lobbied state governments to grant cities **home rule charters.**

A Menu of Reforms

Prior to the Reform era (another name for the Progressive era), mayors in most large cities had few formal powers, with major decisions controlled by large city councils. Machine organizations exercised their influence over a city by controlling council elections. Some of these institutional arrangements were characterized as **weak mayor–council systems**. Voters elected the mayor and council separately, but weak mayors often had little formal influence over city budgets, city departments, or what the city council did. By the middle of the 1800s, most U.S. cities had a city council and mayor who shared legislative and administrative powers.[43]

This does not mean that American mayors had little influence over city affairs prior to the adoption of the reforms discussed below. Table 11.2 lists the results of a survey of historians that ranks the best and worst mayors in the United States from 1820 to 1990. The rankings here are probably biased toward overrepresenting better-known mayors, particularly from large eastern cities. There may have been several lesser-known mayors (terrible or excellent) from the South or West that these historians ignored. Nonetheless, most of the worst-rated mayors were machine operatives whose political influence stemmed not as much from the formal powers granted them in a city's charter but from their links with the party machine and their skill with clientele politics. At the top of the list of "worst" mayors is "Kaiser Bill" Thompson, who served three terms as mayor of Chicago. Thompson, a pro-German during World War I, fought against anticorruption reforms and allowed Chicago's gangsters to run unchecked (organized crime supplied the city with beer, wine, and liquor during the Prohibition era). After being defeated and investigated for fraud, he beat a reformist Prohibitionist incumbent to

win a third term by promising to reopen the city's taverns.[44] Thompson died a rich man.

Other notorious pre–Reform era mayors include Frank Hague of Jersey City, whose influence in the national Democratic Party helped Franklin D. Roosevelt win the Democratic Party's nomination for president in 1932. Hague started as a precinct captain, earned a job as a city janitor, and 10 years later was mayor. The Hague machine's skill at stuffing ballot boxes and other modes of voter fraud allowed Hague to dominate politics in his state for years. Hague also became a millionaire, despite a salary of $8,000 per year.[45] Conversely, the best-rated mayors are those who worked to reform city institutions.

It is important to consider that in the early decades of the 20th century, there were many ideas for changing how local political institutions operated and that these ideas have had a tremendous effect on defining how local governments work today.

Mayor–Council Government Progressives had conflicting views about how powerful a city's mayor should be and what the relationship between the mayor and council should be. Some early reformers believed that strong mayors were needed so that a reformist leader could take firm control of government and check the actions of the city council.[46] And by concentrating control of city administration in one institution (the mayor's office) and legislative and policy-making power in another institution (the city council), reformers hoped that the separation of powers would produce better governance. A mayor with strong powers who was directly elected by the voters could also be held accountable at the ballot box. This idea of a

---

[43] Charles Adrian, "Forms of City Government in American History," *Municipal Yearbook* (Washington, DC: International City Manager's Association, 1988).

[44] Melvin G. Holli, *The American Mayor: The Best and Worst Big City Leaders* (University Park: Pennsylvania State University Press, 1999).

[45] John Fund, "How to Steal an Election," *City Journal*, 2004, http://www.city-journal.org/printable.php?id=1701.

[46] Charles Adrian and Charles Press, *Governing Urban America* (New York: McGraw Hill, 1977), p. 160.

Table 11.2

Scholars' Rankings of the Best and Worst Mayors in American History

Worst	
1) William H. "Kaiser Bill" Thompson	Chicago, 1915–1923, 1927–1931
2) Frank Hauge	Jersey City, 1917–1947
3) James "Jimmy" Walker	New York, 1926–1932
4) James Michael Curly	Boston, 1914–1917; 1922–1925; 1930–1933; 1946–1949
5) Frank Rizzo	Philadelphia, 1972–1980
6) A Oakley Hall	New York, 1868–1872
7) Dennis Kucinich	Cleveland, 1977–1979
8) Fernando Wood	New York, 1855–1858; 1860–1862
9) Sam Yorty	Los Angeles, 1961–1973
10) Jane Byrne	Chicago, 1979–1983
Other "worst"	
"Diamond Joe" Quimby	Springfield, 1989–current
Michael Bilandic	Chicago, 1976–1979
Wilson Goode	Philadelphia, 1984–1992
John V. Lindsay	New York, 1966–1973
Best	
1) Fiorello La Guardia	New York, 1934–1945
2) Tom L. Johnson	Cleveland, 1901–1909
3) David Lawrence	Pittsburgh, 1946–1959
4) Hazen Pingree	Detroit, 1890–1897
5) Samuel "Golden Rule" Jones	Toledo, 1897–1904
6) Richard J. Daley	Chicago, 1955–1976
7) Frank Murphy	Detroit, 1930–1933
8) Daniel W. Hoan	Milwaukee, 1916–1940
9) Tom Bradley	Los Angeles, 1973–1993
10) Josiah "Great Mayor" Quincy	Boston, 1823–1828
Other best	
Andrew Young	Atlanta, 1982–1990

Source: Melvin G. Holli. 1999. *The American Mayor: The Best and the Worst Big City Leaders* (University Park, PA: Penn State University Press). From surveys of 120 experts about mayors of the largest U.S. cities between 1820 and 1990.

strong, accountable mayor also reflected a business model of government. In a business corporation, for example, shareholders and a board of directors give a chief executive strong authority over the day-to-day operations of a business, and shareholders or the board can remove an executive if they are dissatisfied with the performance of the corporation. At the end of the 1890s, a strong mayor was seen as a cure to municipal corruption.[47]

[47] Victor S. Desantis and Tari Renner, "City Government Structures: An Attempt at Clarification," *State and Local Government Review* 324(2002):95–104.

Figure 11.4

Weak Mayor–Council System

The National Municipal League's first Model City Charter (of 1900) recommended that mayors be given strong executive powers. Under a **strong mayor–council system,** mayors are directly elected by the voters at the same time that the city council is. Depending on how many powers a city grants its mayor, a strong mayor may interact with a city council in a manner similar to how a governor interacts with a state legislature. A strong mayor can be given executive powers that include hiring and firing heads of city departments (and other staff), drafting budgets, and vetoing acts of the city council. Mayors may have even stronger powers if they are elected to long terms (four years rather than two), if they are not limited in how often they can seek reelection, if they don't have to share budget powers with the council, and if they have control over city schools. Figures 11.4 and 11.5 illustrate two versions of mayor–council government.

The second edition of the Model City Charter, published in 1915, gave up on the strong mayor plan. Since then, subsequent Model City Charters in 1928, 1933, 1941, 1964, and 1989 advocated a council–manager system with an appointed city executive (see below). About one-third of U.S. cities had mayor–council forms of government as of 2002, but many have mayors who have limits on their formal executive powers. About 40 percent of mayor–council cities have mayors with strong powers to affect budgets and appointments of city staff.[48] Most American cities that have a mayor today, particularly in smaller cities, have mayors with weak executive powers. Just 12 percent of U.S. mayors have the responsibility for developing budgets, and just 17 percent of mayors have the power to appoint department heads. Less than 30 percent of U.S. mayors have the power to veto acts of their city's council. Eighty-five percent of American mayors' jobs are considered part-time positions.[49]

---

[48] International City Managers Association, "2001–2002 Survey" (Washington, DC: International City Managers Association, 2002).

[49] http://www.ncl.org/publications/index.html.

Figure 11.5

Strong Mayor–Council System

As Table 11.3 illustrates, many of the United States' largest cities have mayor–council systems of government today. These cities vary in how the mayor shares power with the city council.

Council–Manager Government After 1915, the National Municipal League began advocating for a **council–manager system** of government.[50] The council–manager system is the epitome of the business model of local government. Under this system, a small (five- to seven-member) council hires a professional administrator to implement its policies. The appointed executive is responsible for preparing the budget, directing day-to-day operations of city departments, overseeing personnel management, and serving as the council's chief policy advisor.[51] City managers supervise city staff, and they recruit, hire,

and fire city employees within the boundaries of civil service rules. Cities with a pure form of the council–manager system either have no mayor or have a very weak mayor who serves on the council. Most U.S. cities have council–manager governments.[52]

Under the council–manager arrangement illustrated in Figure 11.6, the city council may appoint one of its own members to serve as a part-time mayor, but the mayor's role is largely ceremonial (e.g., attending functions, presiding over meetings). About 37 percent of council–manager cities have no elected mayor. Another 47 percent have a mayor elected by voters, but the mayor has no veto power and little executive power. Mayors in council–manager systems may nonetheless act as spokespersons for their community and, despite their limited executive power, may be the most visible representative of the community.

[50] International City Managers Association, *The Council-Manager Form of Government* (Washington, DC: ICMA, 2006).

[51] International City Managers Association, *Form of Government Survey* (Washington, DC: ICMA, 2001).

[52] Robert Salisbury Source should be: David Morgan, Robert England, and John Pellissero, *Managing Urban America* (Washington, DC: CQ Press, 2006).

Table 11.3

Largest U.S. Cities with Mayor–Council Systems of Government

City	Population	Pop. Rank	Grade	Council Elections
New York, NY	8,214,000	1st	B	51 districts
Los Angeles, CA	3,849,000	2nd	C	15 districts
Chicago, IL	2,833,000	3rd	B−	50 districts (wards)
Houston, TX	2,144,000	4th	C+	9 districts, and 4 at-large
Philadelphia, PA	1,448,000	6th	B	10 districts, and 7 at-large
Detroit, MI	871,000	11th	B−	9 at-large
Jacksonville, FL	794,000	12th	B−	14 districts, and 5 at-large
Indianapolis, IN	785,000	13th	B+	25 districts, and 4 at-large
San Francisco, CA	739,000	14th	C	11 at-large
Columbus, OH	733,000	15th	C	7 at-large
Memphis, TN	670,000	17th	C+	13 districts
Baltimore, MD	631,000	19th	B−	18 districts
Boston, MA	591,000	22nd	B−	9 districts, and 4 at-large
Seattle, WA	582,000	23rd	B	9 at-large
Milwaukee, WI	573,000	25th	B	17 districts
Denver, CO	566,000	26th	B−	11 districts, and 2 at-large
Louisville, KY	554,000	27th	n/a	26 districts
Nashville, TN	552,000	29th	C+	35 districts, and 5 at-large
Albuquerque, NM	504,000	33rd	n/a	9 districts
Atlanta, GA	486,000	34th	C+	12 districts, and 3 at-large
Fresno, CA	466,000	36th	n/a	7 districts
Cleveland, OH	444,000	40th	C	21 districts (wards)
Omaha, NE	390,000	42nd	n/a	7 districts
Oakland, CA	397,300	44th	n/a	7 districts, and 1 at-large
Tulsa, OK	382,000	45th	n/a	9 districts
Honolulu, HI	377,000	46th	B	9 districts
Minneapolis, MN	372,000	47th	B+	13 districts (wards)

Note: Grade is the overall performance rating for the cities rated by The Government Performance Project. 2000. *Governing Magazine.* 2006 population figures.

A council–manager system gives executive powers and administrative control to the council-appointed administrator, known as a city manager (in some places, the position is called the city administrator, chief executive officer, or chief administrative officer). Executive powers, such as the authority to prepare a budget or hire department heads, are granted to the unelected, professional executive who serves at the pleasure of the city council. A majority vote is required to fire a manager. Managers are expected to stay clear of political disputes and should not engage in local political activity. Most city managers now have professional academic training (a master's degree), and most serve in their position for about five years and

Figure 11.6

Council–Manager System

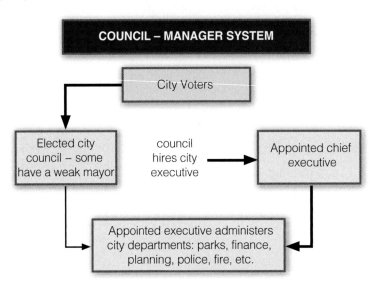

have about 17 years of job experience in public administration.[53] Many managers move from city to city during their careers, and city managers' salaries average over $160,000 in cities that have between 120,000 and 220,000 residents.[54]

Adoption of the council–manager reform was rapid and widespread. In 1908, Staunton, Virginia, became the first city to pass an ordinance that defined the authority of an appointed executive. In 1912, Sumter, South Carolina, was the first city to define a council–manager system in its charter, and Dayton, Ohio, became the first large city to adopt the council–manager system in 1913.[55] By 1915, 82 cities had adopted the system, and twice as many more had by 1920.[56] The council–manager plan was subsequently

adopted throughout the United States and is also used in Australia, Canada, the Netherlands, and New Zealand. Most U.S. cities and towns—particularly smaller places—now operate with some version of a council–manager system, often with the councils elected in nonpartisan elections. Of the 247 American cities with a population over 100,000, 144 (58 percent) use a council–manager system. Some of the largest cities using this system include Cincinnati, Dallas, Kansas City, Phoenix, and Las Vegas. Over 92 million Americans live in cities governed with a council–manager system.[57]

Table 11.4 lists the largest American cities that use the council–manager system of government today.

Council–Manager and Mayor–Council Blends

Cities continue to alter their charters to redefine the separation of powers between councils, mayors, and appointed city executives. Some mayor-councils adopted rules that borrowed features of

[53] ICMA salary survey Worcester Regional Research Board. *Oh Manager, Where Art Thou? Best Practices for Selecting a City Manager* (Worcester, MA: ICMA, 2004).
[54] International City Managers Association, *The Council-Manager Form of Government.*
[55] http://www.ncl.org/npp/charter/process.html.
[56] International City Managers Association, *The Council-Manager Form of Government.*

[57] Adrian, "Forms of City Government in American History."

Table 11.4				

Largest U.S. Cities with Council–Manager Systems of Government

City	Population	Pop. Rank	Grade	Council Elections
Phoenix, AZ	1,512,000	5th	A	8 districts
San Antonio, TX	1,296,000	7th	B	10 districts
San Diego, CA*	1,256,000	8th	B	8 districts
Dallas, TX	1,232,000	9th	C+	14 districts
San Jose, CA	929,000	10th	B−	10 districts
Austin, TX	709,000	16th	A−	6 at-large
Ft. Worth, TX	653,000	18th	n/a	9 districts
Charlotte, NC	611,000	20th	n/a	7 districts, and 4 at-large
El Paso, TX	609,000	21st	n/a	8 districts
Las Vegas, NV	552,147	28th	n/a	6 districts (wards)
Oklahoma City, OK	537,000	30th	n/a	8 districts (wards)
Tucson, AZ	518,000	32nd	n/a	7 at-large
Long Beach, CA	472,000	35th	B	9 districts
Sacramento, CA	453,000	37th	n/a	8 districts
Mesa, AZ	447,000	38th	n/a	6 districts
Kansas City, MO	447,000	39th	B−	6 districts, and 6 at-large
Virginia Beach, VA	435,000	41st	B+	7 districts, and 4 at-large
Colorado Springs, CO	369,000	49th	n/a	4 districts, and 5 at-large
Arlington, TX	362,000	50th	n/a	5 districts, and 4 at-large

Note: Grade is the overall performance rating for the cities rated by the Government Performance Project. 2000. *Governing Magazine.* 2006 population figures.

the council–manager system in order to increase the autonomy of professional administrators. As an example, San Francisco became the first mayor–council city to hire a professional administrator in 1931, yet it remained a relatively strong mayor–council system.[58]

More recently, some council–manager systems have adopted features from mayor–council systems to increase direct political control by voters.[59] Surveys of cities suggest that over the last 25 years, a large number of cities have been switching from mayor–council systems.[60] In larger cities, however, there may be greater public pressure to have political institutions that make it easier for citizens to hold elected officials directly accountable for how a city operates. This has led some council–manager cities to adopt some of the features of mayor–council systems, such as directly elected mayors, as well as mayors with veto powers over councils.

Mayors in several cities, including Sacramento's Kevin Johnson, have championed charter revisions that give the mayor new powers. Proponents argue strong mayors can be more effective leaders. In 2009, Johnson asked voters to grant him the

[58] H. George Frederickson, G. A. Johnson, and C. Wood, "The Changing Structure of American Cities," *Public Administration Review* 64(May 2004).
[59] Desantis and Renner, "City Government Structures."
[60] Frederickson, Johnson, and Wood, "The Changing Structure of American Cities."

AP Photo/Rich Pedroncelli

Sacramento Mayor Kevin Johnson

power to write the budget, appoint department heads, and veto acts of the city council. Dallas voters rejected a strong-mayor proposal in 2005.

Other council–manager cities have abandoned their council–manager systems. As examples, in 1999, Cincinnati voters approved a charter amendment that added a directly elected mayor to their council–manager system. The Cincinnati mayor has some elements of strong-mayor powers, can veto the council, and has a role in selecting the city manager, but a city manager remains in charge of administering Cincinnati's city departments and implementing policies approved by the council. Voters in San Diego, a council–manager city, approved a referendum in 2004 to have a four-year experiment with a strong mayor–council system. The experiment began in 2006. Oakland, California, voters approved a similar experiment in 1998 at the request of then-mayor Jerry Brown. Four years later,

they voted to make the strong-mayor system permanent. In 2009, Mayor Kevin Johnson, a former NBA star, sponsored and qualified a ballot measure asking voters to change from a council–manager to strong-mayor form of government.

Commission System The National Municipal League was initially enthusiastic about a third form of local government: the commission system. The commission system was another attempt to isolate the administration of government from politics. Under this system, voters would select people, rather than a city council, to run city departments. A commission of these elected administrators shared executive and legislative powers.

In some early versions of the commission system, voters elected commissioners who would head specific city departments—for example, a finance commissioner, a public works commissioner, and a public safety (police and fire) commissioner. These commissioners would meet together as a council to pass city budgets (a legislative function), but each individual would be in charge of administering his or her own city department (an executive function). Most of these commission systems soon proved unworkable, as commissioners would promote the interests of their own departments over the general needs of the city, and it was difficult for anyone to coordinate city policy across rival city departments. Portland, Oregon, the 32nd largest U.S. city, is the only remaining large city to use the commission form of government. In Portland, voters elect a nonpartisan mayor and four nonpartisan commissioners, who serve together as a council. The mayor is in charge of assigning the administration of various departments to the four commissioners. Tulsa, Oklahoma, was one of the last remaining commission systems in a large city. Tulsa abandoned its commission form of government in 1989, switching to a mayor–council system.

At-Large Elections In addition to altering the powers of mayors and city councils, many of the

Progressive reforms from the early 1900s were aimed at changing how councils represented a city and how local elections were conducted.

Councils elected by individual districts increase opportunities for a political group or candidate to win support based on the social or ethnic bonds of specific neighborhoods. In district elections, only voters in the district vote for their representative. This meant that various ethnic minority groups concentrated in distinct neighborhoods could win council seats. Racial and ethnic minorities are more likely to win seats via districts than under city-wide elections (known as at-large elections).[61]

In the early 1900s, Progressive reformers argued that at-large elections would make it more difficult for machines to organize cities from the precinct level up based on ethnic loyalties. In at-large elections, everyone in the city votes for each "position" on the city council. This allows a cohesive majority to sweep every council seat. At-large elections may also produce council representation with more of a citywide focus, whereas representatives elected by districts may have more parochial concerns. Most American cities now have at-large elections, although classic strong-mayor cities, and the 60 largest U.S. cities, are more likely to use district elections (see Tables 11.3 and 11.4). Some cities have representatives on their council elected partly by districts and partly citywide.

Since the 1970s, the U.S. Supreme Court has ruled that at-large elections may illegally dilute the influence of minority groups, and as a result, many larger cities (which have more minorities) have switched from at-large to district elections and other alternative election systems in recent decades (see Chapter 3).

Smaller Councils Large councils elected by district made it easier to organize a city on ethnic and neighborhood lines, as more seats on the council allowed the city to be divided into many distinc-

tive council districts. Reformers promoted smaller councils elected at large as a means to create governments that had a more "citywide" focus.

Nonpartisan Elections Party labels allowed the machines an easy way to inform their supporters whom they should vote for. All they needed to do was select the candidates nominated by the machine organization listed as a Democrat (or Republican) candidate (depending on the city). Progressives and the National Municipal League promoted the idea that elections for local offices did not require partisan labels. This made it more difficult for low-literacy voters to support a party organization's candidate. Most U.S. cities now have nonpartisan elections, especially cities with council–manager forms of government. Ninety percent of council manager cities have nonpartisan elections.[62]

Australian Ballot The urban party machine's ability to communicate with its supporters was also eroded with the introduction of the Australian ballot (also known as the secret ballot). Unofficial, party-printed ballots were favored by machines because they listed only one party's candidates (that of the machine organization). The government-printed Australian ballot, in contrast, listed candidates from all parties and required voters to pick and choose among them in a private voting booth without assistance. Australian ballots also allowed voters to "split their ticket" and vote for candidates from different political parties and weakened the influence of local precinct captains who had printed and distributed ballots.[63] New York adopted the Australian ballot throughout the state in 1890.[64]

---

[61] Richard Engstrom and Michael D. McDonald, "The Election of Blacks to City Councils," *American Political Science Review* 72(1981):344–54.

[62] Desantis and Renner, "City Government Structures."

[63] Some elite party officials may have allied with reformers in support of the Australian ballot to limit the influence of local precinct captains. John Reynolds and Richard McCormick, "Outlawing 'Treachery': Split Tickets and Ballot Laws in New York and New Jersey, 1880–1910," *Journal of American History* 72(1986):835–58.

[64] Gary Cox and Morgan Kousser, "Turnout and Rural Corruption: New York as a Test Case," *American Journal of Political Science* 25(1981):646.

In the southern and western regions of the United States, Australian ballots were adopted for different reasons. They made it difficult for third parties, such as the Populists, to win support from illiterate working-class voters who required party-printed, **straight-ticket ballots**.[65] Nonpartisan elections, contested with Australian ballots, likely made it much more difficult for party organizations to get their supporters to vote for machine candidates.

Off-Year Elections   Elections happen in cycles. When local elections are held on separate dates than other elections (presidential, congressional, or gubernatorial), fewer people are likely to take notice. A study of cities in California found that when local elections were held jointly with presidential elections, turnout was 36 percent higher than when elections were held at times when there were not any higher-level offices up for election. Local elections held in synch with a gubernatorial race had 21 percent higher turnout than a "local-only" election, and similar increases in turnout occur when local races are on the same ballot as candidates in a presidential primary.[66]

Voter Registration   Prior to the late 1890s, there was little regulation of who could vote. Before then, a voter who arrived at the polls was automatically registered for the next election,[67] and party machines are reported to have created ways to offer immigrants "instant citizenship" to make them eligible for voting.[68] Repeat voting also inflated vote totals. One New York City election produced a reported turnout of 8 percent more than the total city voting population.[69]

By the early 1900s, many states attempted to combat electoral fraud by requiring that voters personally apply for registration before each election. Many early registration statutes applied only to the state's largest cities.[70] In 1908, the New York state legislature passed regulations on voting, requiring that all voters in cities of over 1 million people produce personal identification when voting and sign in when voting. Signatures could be matched to registration applications, and poll workers could query voters. Districts in New York City suspected of fraud-inflated vote totals in 1906 had substantially less voting in 1908.[71] As voter registration spread to other states, voter turnout in American elections fell sharply.[72]

Civil Service–Merit System   Many federal government jobs became protected by civil service rules only after President James A. Garfield was assassinated in 1881 by a party activist who did not receive the patronage appointment he expected. The **Pendleton Act** of 1883 established a Civil Service Commission that began to depoliticize (or bureaucratize) the hiring and firing of many federal employees. The modern **civil service** system requires that public employees should be hired only on the basis of merit (that is, based on job-specific qualifications) and that they should not be fired unless employers can prove just cause for doing so. However, the federal civil service system does not apply to state and local governments. States and cities have adopted their own civil service systems, but differences exist across places in how many

---

[65] J. Morgan Kousser, *The Shaping of Southern Politics* (New Haven, CT: Yale University Press, 1974).

[66] Zoltan Hajnal, Paul Lewis, and Hugh Louch, *Municipal Elections in California: Turnout, Timing and Competition* (San Francisco: Public Policy Institute of California, 2002).

[67] Cox and Kousser, "Turnout and Rural Corruption."

[68] See Fund, "How to Steal an Election"; Kevin Phillips and Paul Blackman, *Electoral Reform and Voter Participation* (Washington, DC: AEI Press, 1975); Gist, "Progressive Reform in a Rural Community"; Mayfield, "Voting Fraud in Early Twentieth-Century Pittsburgh," for dates on introduction of these reforms across states.

[69] Fund, "How to Steal an Election."

[70] Walter Dean Burnham, *Critical Elections and the Mainsprings of American Politics* (New York: Norton, 1970), p. 81.

[71] John Lapp, "Election: Identification of Voters," *American Political Science Review* 3(1)(1909):62–63.

[72] Jerrod Rusk, "Communications," *American Political Science Review* 65(1971):1152–57; Jerrod Rusk, "Comment: The American Electoral Universe," *American Political Science Review* 68(1974):1028–49.

public jobs are classified as civil service and in terms of how many public employees serve at the pleasure of elected officials. Public jobs that do not fall under state or local civil service rules can still be awarded by political appointments.

Federal civil service rules did not apply to state and local government employees. Progressive reformers promoted the adoption of civil service rules on a city-by-city basis after 1900. By 1935, at least 450 U.S. cities had adopted some form of a civil service system. At least 200 more had adopted a civil service–merit system by 1938, including 80 percent of cities over 100,000.[73] This transferred the routine, day-to-day tasks of city governments from political loyalists to bureaucrats. By 1939, federal law required that states adopt some form of civil service for state workers, and in the 1960s, many states began requiring that their cities develop civil service–merit systems to depoliticize the hiring and firing of public employees. By the 1990s, most (but not all) states required their cities to adopt merit-based civil services.[74]

Today, cities vary in terms of how many city positions are classified as political appointments or civil service. In most places, only a few "policy advisor" positions are left for elected officials to appoint. In less-reformed cities, a strong mayor may still control numerous appointments to a wide range of city jobs and boards. A contemporary mayor of Chicago is estimated to control the appointment of 900 to 1,200 city positions.[75]

Although patronage-based cities are often linked with corruption, some studies suggest that they may be less expensive to run. Patronage allows local party officials more control over employee wages. In contrast, civil service unions may command higher wages. City workers may also be more accountable to voters in a patronage system than where they are protected by civil service rules.[76]

Corrupt Practices Acts After 1900, several states adopted laws to make it illegal to use bribes in elections and illegal to impersonate someone else when voting. An Oregon Corrupt Practices Act passed by voter initiative in 1908 designated as corrupt "the unlawful expenditure of money for election purposes; which covers the giving of cigars and tobacco; undue influence, including the threat of even a 'spiritual injury,' [im]personation; bribery; betting by a candidate on any pending election, or furnishing money therefore; seeking nomination for a venal motive, and not in good faith." Some states also attempted to regulate elections by limiting campaign expenditures.[77]

Strict Rules for Public Contracts Most states also now require cities to abide by strict rules when spending public money. These rules are designed to limit the ability of public officials to use public funds for their own benefit (or for the benefit of their supporters). These rules govern how public employees can make routine purchases and how contracts for public work shall be put to bid (most require sealed bids that conceal the identity of the firm bidding for the job). Other rules require detailed public records of expenditures and that city departments be subjected to external audits.

[73] Pamela Tolbert and Lynne Zucker, "Institutional Sources of Change in the Formal Structure of Organizations: The Diffusion of Civil Service Reform, 1880–1935," *Administrative Science Quarterly* 28(1983):22. Also see H. George Frederickson, Bret Logan, and Curtis Wood, "Municipal Reform: A Well Kept Secret," *State and Local Government Review* 35(1)(2003):7–14.

[74] Frederickson, Logan, and Wood, "Municipal Reform."

[75] Author's personal communication with Ron Michaelson, former executive director of the Illinois State Board of Elections.

[76] Ester Fuchs, *Mayors and Money: Fiscal Policy in New York and Chicago* (Chicago: University of Chicago Press, 20XX; Joseph Gyourko, "Looking Back to Look Forward: Learning from Philadelphia's 350 Years of Urban Development," *Brookings-Wharton Papers on Urban Affairs* (2005):1–58.

[77] Leon E. Aylsworth, "Corrupt Practices," *American Political Science Review* 65(1909):50–56.

Local Direct Democracy Many reform advocates also promoted the adoption of the direct initiative, referendum, and recall for use in cities and counties. We discussed these institutions in Chapter 4. Initiatives were seen as a way to advance reform goals that might not be approved by a city council. In 1893, California changed its law to allow the initiative in every county. Nebraska granted residents of all its cities the right to use initiatives in 1897. By 1911, state laws were changed to allow initiatives in cities in 11 states, mostly in the West.[78]

Municipal Reforms as a Continuum and Constant Process

Research suggests that municipal reform efforts had greater success in places where there were fewer working-class and immigrant voters, as these voters were the major supporters of the urban party machines. This means that some of the reforms discussed above were less likely to end up being adopted in older cities and were more likely to be adopted in smaller communities and in places outside the northeastern states.[79] Cities with high percentages of Irish immigrants were particularly resistant to adopting reforms during the Progressive era, as were northern cities that had a machine presence during the Reform era (e.g., Albany, New York; Baltimore; Boston; Chicago; Cleveland; Hartford, Connecticut; Jersey City, New Jersey; New Haven, Connecticut; Indianapolis; Philadelphia; Toledo, Ohio; and Youngstown, Ohio). Western cities, and cities without established machines, were more likely to adopt several of these reforms during the Progressive era (e.g., Colorado Springs, Colorado; Pasadena, Sacramento, and San Jose, California; and Wichita, Kansas).[80]

The structure of any city's political institutions today can be categorized in terms of

a continuum, with cities employing fewer of these reforms at one end of the continuum and many reforms at the other. Cities now show limited variation regarding whether or not they have corrupt practices rules, civil service systems, or strict rules about public spending. But a large amount of variation still exists across cities in terms of how these rules work and in who ultimately administers the city. These rules mean that cities also vary in terms of how much direct control elected officials ultimately have on how their city is administered.

This brings us back to the opening vignette of this chapter. The structure of political institutions that existed in Los Angeles when the Rodney King beating was videotaped placed that city much further toward the reform end of continuum than New York. Cities like Los Angeles that adopted their charters during or after the Progressive reforms employ a large number of the reforms listed above. Rigid civil service rules, and relatively weak executive authority granted to the mayor, meant that Chief Gates could not be fired, despite overwhelming political pressure to do so. A classic reformed city would likely have a council–manager system employing a professional city manager and a weak mayor (or no mayor). The council would be elected at large in nonpartisan elections scheduled when no higher-profile partisan races are being contested.

Larger cities, particularly those in eastern states where political institutions were more firmly established before the Progressive Reform era began, are more likely to be located on the less reformed end of the continuum: that is, they are more likely to have partisan elections, council elections by district, large city councils, and nearly all city affairs controlled by elected officials. This does not mean that former machine cities, such as Chicago and New York, have been insulated from the reform movement: both of these mayor–council cities now have some reform institutions (such as civil service). As Table 11.3 illustrates, cities with mayor–council systems are still "less reformed" in that they are more likely to have larger councils (even when population is accounted for),

---

[78] John Matsusaka, *For the Many or the Few* (Chicago: University of Chicago Press, 2004).

[79] James Weinstein, *Corporate Ideal in the Liberal State, 1900–1918* (Boston: Beacon Press, 1968).

[80] James Gimpel, "Reform Resistant and Reform Adopting Machines: The Electoral Foundations of Urban Politics," *Political Research Quarterly* 46(2)(1993):371–82.

with a high proportion of the council representing individual districts. Mayor–council cities listed in Table 11.3 average 15 seats in size, with 83 percent of seats elected from districts. In contrast, council–manager city councils listed in Table 11.4 average nine seats in size, with 68 percent elected by district.

It is important to remember that city institutions are flexible and change frequently in response to crises and public demands for reform. The reform of municipal institutions is a continuing process. After the Rodney King incident, Los Angeles went through a process of reevaluating its charter, and proposals for stronger mayoral power emerged. And, as noted above, larger council–manager cities, including some listed in Table 11.4, are also considering changing their institutions to provide for greater political accountability in the form of a strong, directly elected mayor. Many cities and counties periodically appoint or elect **charter review commissions** for the purpose proposing changes to city institutions that voters might accept or reject.

Consequences of Municipal Reforms

One thing that occurred after the Reform era was that reformed cities became more efficient and had less political corruption. The cumulative effect of many of these reforms may be efficient, professional, modern city administration that is more capable of managing the "housekeeping" functions of cities. Building codes and public health standards are now much more likely to be implemented and administered by civil servants following standard operating procedures. Business licenses and lucrative contracts to provide services to a city are more likely to be granted on the basis of standard operating procedures rather than political favoritism. Public works projects are now far more likely to be constructed by qualified contractors who offer the lowest bid. Well-regulated public utilities now provide many cities with water, power, street lighting, and sewerage. Police enforce laws

with greater objectivity, and politicians cannot easily enrich themselves by directing the police to "selectively" enforce laws. Of course, it is difficult to prove that reforms themselves made cites more efficient and less corrupt. Since the early 1900s, all U.S. cities, reformed and unreformed alike, are probably governed better today.

Nonpolitical Administration?

The discussion of party machines in this chapter suggests that patronage, corruption, and other inefficiencies may have inflated public spending in unreformed cities. We also might expect public spending to be higher in unreformed cities because classic machines were designed to be responsive to many different groups that might demand city services. Reforms such as at-large, nonpartisan elections and council–manager systems could insulate city officials from such demands. One influential study did find less taxing and spending in reformed cities,[81] but subsequent research found few differences in city finances in reformed versus unreformed cities.[82] Council–manager systems may limit how much direct influence elected officials have on how city money is spent, but this need not mean that these cities spend less or that their appointed managers are insulated from political pressures. Modern city managers face pressure from elected officials for changes in how (and to whom) services are delivered and for changes in how cities are managed.[83]

Efficiency–Accountability Trade-Off?

Some observers suggest that gains in administrative efficiency may come at the price of less direct control of city government by citizens.

---

[81] Robert Lineberry and Edmond Fowler "Reformism and Public Policies in American Cities," *American Political Science Review* (1967):701–16.
[82] David Morgan and John Pelissero, "Urban Policy: Does Political Structure Matter?" *American Political Science Review* 74(1980):999–1006.
[83] James H. Svara, "The Politics-Administration Dichotomy Model as Aberration," *Public Administration Review* 58(1998):51.

With so many administrative functions now supervised by appointed city managers and public employees protected against being fired for political reasons, it may be more difficult for a majority of voters to hold their government accountable at the ballot box for unpopular actions. Rigid bureaucratic rules, civil service protections, and "red tape" may make it difficult for elected officials to put political pressure on city administrators, but these rules ensure that politicians cannot use their position to enrich themselves and their friends. A study of non-partisan city council members also found that unlike machine politicians, nonpartisan elected officials may care little about getting reelected and thus have little regard for public opinion.[84]

Another side exists to the efficiency–accountability trade-off, however. Cross-national studies show that high levels of political corruption increase cynicism about politics and depress respect for the rule of law.[85] Public corruption causes people to retreat from conventional politics. In contrast, reforms that root out political corruption may increase public confidence in democracy.

Barriers to Mass Participation

Several studies find that the combined effects of reforms, such as off-year elections and nonpartisan elections, act to depress voter participation in reform cities.[86] These reforms make local elections less visible to many people and make it more difficult for many people to evaluate candidates. We provide more discussion of this in Chapter 3. For much of the 20th

century, turnout for local elections was higher in large machine cities than in large reform cities.[87] Lower turnout may lead to substantial reductions in the representation of Latinos and Asian Americans on city councils and in mayors' offices. African Americans win office less often when turnout is depressed by off-year elections.

Class and Racial Bias

Scholars also note that politics and elections in reform cities such as Houston and San Jose became dominated by powerful nonpartisan "slating groups" that promoted the election of white professionals, business owners, and land developers.[88] Some of these groups were just as dominant in local politics in reform cities as party organizations were in machine cities.[89] Class and racial bias in local politics may be affected by low turnout, itself a product of some reforms. Turnout can be lower than 10 percent in some off-year, nonpartisan local elections. Although there may not be large differences in who votes and who does not vote in high-turnout national elections, very low turnout in local elections may increase the class and racial differences between voters and nonvoters.[90] This may distort democracy because elected officials may be more attentive to the interests of voters than nonvoters. Low turnout rates also result in less representation of Latinos and Asian Americans as mayors and on city councils than they might receive when turnout is higher. At-large elections can further increase the influence of middle-class and upper-class groups in local politics by reducing opportunities for representation of African Americans and ethnic minorities (see Chapter 3). Maintaining lower levels of minority

[84] Kenneth Prewitt, "Political Ambitions, Volunteerism, and Electoral Accountability," *American Political Science Review* (1970):5–17.

[85] Todd Donovan, David Denemark, and Shaun Bowler, "Trust, Citizenship and Participation: Australia in Comparative Perspective," in David Denemark et al., eds., *Australian Social Attitudes: The 2nd Report* (Sydney: University of New South Wales Press, 2007).

[86] Albert Karing and B. Oliver Walter, "Decline in Municipal Voter Turnout: A Function of Changing Structure," *American Politics Quarterly* 11(1983):491–505; Hajnal and Lewis, "Municipal Institutions and Voter Turnout in Local Elections."

[87] Jessica Trounstine, "Dominant Regimes and the Demise of Urban Democracy," *Journal of Politics* (2006):879–93.

[88] Chandler Davidson and Luis Fraga, "Slating Groups as Parties in a 'Nonpartisan' Setting," *Western Political Quarterly* 41(1988):373–90; and Bridges, *Morning Glories.*

[89] Trounstine, "Dominant Regimes and the Demise of Urban Democracy."

[90] Albert Karing and B. Oliver Walter, "Decline in Municipal Voter Turnout: A Function of Changing Structure," *American Politics Quarterly* 11(1983):491–505.

INSTITUTIONS MATTER

HOME RULE CHARTER

The U.S. Constitution does not mention local governments or specify anything about the powers of local governments (the 10th Amendment does state that powers not delegated to the federal government via the U.S. Constitution are "reserved" to the states). After the American Revolution and after the ratification of the U.S. Constitution, the states assumed the role of defining what local governments would do, just as colonial governments had done before. Today, states and cities outline the powers of governments in **municipal charters**. A local government's charter defines how it will be governed by listing rules about the powers of local officials and the conduct of elections. Each state government may define the powers of local government as it sees fit. Within any one state, state law may allow large cities and counties different charter arrangements than smaller places. State constitutions and laws thus define what the role of towns, cities, villages, counties, and other local governments will be. One class of local government charter is the home rule charter. Home rule is when the state government delegates power about setting up local political arrangements to a local government. A home rule charter can give local governments—or a specific local government—substantial discretion to decide how it will arrange its government, how it will conduct elections, what services it will provide, how it will raise and spend revenues, and how it will hire and fire employees. Home rule charters could grant a local government the autonomy to decide how to operate across all these areas. A more limited home rule charter could let local governments make their own decisions in some areas but not others. If powers are not delegated to the local government, then state laws define how things will operate locally. During the Progressive Reform era, some reformers believed it was better to let each city have home rule to best identify how it should restructure its political institutions.

officeholders has consequences for who gets what from city government. Fewer minorities in offices mean fewer minority citizens holding city jobs.[91]

At-large elections may also change how council members do their jobs. One study concluded that districted, partisan elections were more likely to produce representation that mirrors the community and that partisan elections made it easier for voters to hold elected officials accountable.[92] At-large elections have also been found to be used, intentionally, to disenfranchise blacks in southern cities and counties.[93] Council–manager governments are also seen as being slower in their responsiveness to the demands of emerging political groups in a city.[94] Another study found that mayor–council cities were more responsive than council–manager cities in responding to social and racial cleavages in a city[95] and incorporating minorities into city jobs.[96] Minority mayors may have more ability to affect what government does, and serve their constituents, in mayor–council systems.[97]

[91] Peter K. Eisenger, "Black Employment in Municipal Jobs: The Impact of Black Political Power," *American Political Science Review* 76(1982):380–90; Lana Stein, "Representative Local Government: Minorities in the Municipal Workforce," *Journal of Politics* 48(1986): 694–713; Thomas Dye and James Renick, "Political Power and City Jobs: Determinants of Minority Employment," *Social Science Quarterly* 62(1981):457–86.

[92] Susan Welch and Timothy Bledsoe, *Urban Reform and Its Consequences* (Chicago: University of Chicago Press, 1988).

[93] Chandler Davidson and George Korbel, "At-Large Elections and Minority Group Representation: A Reexamination of Historical and Contemporary Evidence," *Journal of Politics* 43(1981):982.

[94] Charles H. Levine, Irene S. Rubin, and George Wolohojian, "Resource Scarcity and the Reform Model: The Management of Retrenchment in Cincinnati and Oakland," *Public Administration Review* 41 (1981):627.

[95] Lineberry and Fowler, "Reformism and Public Policies in American Cities."

[96] Stein, "Representative Local Government."

[97] Albert Karing and Susan Welch, *Black Representation and Urban Policy* (Chicago: University of Chicago Press, 1980).

YOU DECIDE

MORE POLITICAL JOBS, OR FEWER?

Civil service is one key feature of "reformed" local government. Reformers hoped to improve how places were governed by removing 'politics' from the administration of public services. Most of the people you interact with who work for a local government—people who issue building permits, police officers, county health department workers—are employed in a civil service system. Many are unionized. Strict personnel rules govern how (or if) they are hired, promoted, transferred across departments or fired, and rules define specific job duties. These rules emphasize standard operating procedures, in part to insure that elected officials can't meddle too much with how services are provided. Strict civil service systems thus make it difficult for elected officials to fix parking tickets or help their friends get building permits.

But is more politics needed in public employment? Beyond a few policy advisor jobs, civil service rules prevent most mayors, county executives, and other local elected officials from having any influence over how public employees do their jobs. People facing lines in government offices or long waits for permits often complain about "bureaucrats" and "red-tape," but standard operating procedures often limit the discretion public employees have in doing their jobs.

If public employees were hired and directed by elected officials, and potentially fired by them, there might be a closer link between voters and the people who do the business of governing. If a mayor who hired employees lost an election, the next mayor might decide to replace those workers with staff who are more likely to get the job done.

Would public employees work better to implement policies people wanted if their job depended on voters remaining satisfied with how well government was being run?

Summary

In this chapter, we examine how the United States began as a rural nation but experienced rapid urbanization in the mid-1800s. The growth of cities outpaced the growth of effective government, and urban machines emerged in this context with a style of politics that thrived for decades. The machine style emphasized personal bonds over substantive government services. The style is well-represented by a machine politician quoted as saying that he wanted to be sure that there has to be someone in every ward of his city that "any bloke can come to—no matter what he's done—and get help. Help, you understand; none of your law and justice, but help."[98]

The personal touch of machine politicians might have helped some people find jobs or fix problems with the law, but it could not ensure that all people were treated equally before the law. The absence of law, justice, and effective municipal services made machines a target for reforms that redesigned local political institutions. The modern bureaucratic city, for all its cold impersonal character, is designed to have routine standards that public employees must follow if everyone is going to be treated the same.

---

[98] Martin Lomansy, quoted in Steffens, *The Autobiography of Lincoln Steffens.*

This chapter also illustrates how changes in political institutions can affect who gets what from local government. The reforms adopted during the Progressive era altered how people become engaged with local politics. Some reforms were clearly designed to limit which sort of people would be mobilized. Many of these reforms survive to this day, but others, such as at-large elections, are often challenged and rejected. Overall, the municipal reforms discussed here may have subtle effects on how a modern city is governed. Elected officials in reformed cities have less direct influence over some administrative matters than their counterparts in cities that adopted few reforms. The opening vignette in this chapter provides a dramatic example of this. But for all their supposed separation of politics and administration, highly reformed cities may differ from contemporary "unreformed cities" not so much in how efficiently they are governed but in who governs. Institutions that increase participation, increase diversity in representation, and guarantee electoral competition—such as partisan local elections, local elections held during presidential contests, and representation by district—may create a more pluralist form of local politics. By pluralist, we mean a form of politics where more voices are heard and where it is difficult for any single group to consolidate power.

Key Terms

Charter review commission

Civil service

Clientele parties

Council–manager system

Dillon's rule

Home rule charters

Jacksonian democracy

Land Ordinance of 1785

Louisiana Purchase

Machines

Model city charter

Muckraking journalists

Municipal charters

Patronage

Pendleton Act

Populist era

Precinct

Precinct captain

Progressive era

Straight-ticket ballot

Strong mayor–council system

Tammany Hall

Urbanization

Ward

Weak mayor–council systems

Discussion Questions

1. What was Jefferson's vision for American communities? What caused this model to see drastic change?
2. How were cities governed during the 19th-century urbanization and industrialization boom?
3. What ended the urban party machine era?
4. How did the urban reform movement change the design of local governments?
5. Discuss the differences between the mayor–council and council–manager systems of government. What are the advantages and disadvantages of each?

Suggested Readings

Bridges, Amy. 1984. *A City in the Republic: Antebellum New York and the Origins of Machine Politics*. Ithaca, NY: Cornell University Press.

———. 1997. *Morning Glories: Municipal Reform in the Southwest*. Princeton, NJ: Princeton University Press.

Elkins, Steven. 1987. *City and Regime in the American Republic*. Chicago: University of Chicago Press.

Erie, Steven. *Rainbow's End: Irish Americans and the Dilemmas of Urban Machine Politics, 1840–1985*. Berkeley: University of California Press.

Riordan, William L. 1993. *Plunkitt of Tammany Hall: A Series of Very Plain Talks on Very Practical Politics*. New York: Bedford Books, St. Martin's (Originally published in 1905).

Spain, Daphne. 2000. *How Women Saved the City*. Minneapolis: University of Minnesota Press.

Web Sites

International City Manager Association (ICMA; http://www.icma.org): The professional and educational organization for appointed city managers, administrators, and assistants. ICMA provides technical assistance, training, and information resources to its members and the local governments. Also publishes the city manager code of ethics. Founded in 1914.

National Civic League (http://www.ncl.org): A nonprofit, nonpartisan group founded in 1894 by Teddy Roosevelt and others to promote municipal reform and community democracy. NCSL serves as a resource for anyone interested in cutting-edge community-building practices. The group was originally known as the National Municipal League and periodically publishes recommendations for government structures (the Model City Charter).

National League of Cities (http://www.nlc.org): Lobby groups for local government interests in Washington, D.C. The oldest and largest national organization representing municipal governments throughout the United States.

12

The Politics of Place

COMPETITION OVER GROWTH AND DEVELOPMENT

Vernon, California, was incorporated in 1905 just south of downtown Los Angeles by John B. Leonis, a savvy businessman, and two ranchers who owned land near railroad lines. Upon **incorporation**, they ensured that their five square miles of land would be zoned "exclusively industrial." That is the town's motto today. As of 2000, Vernon had a population of only 91 (with 60 registered voters), but it is also home to 1,200 businesses that employ 44,000 people. Given this sparse population and huge commercial and industrial base, Vernon generated over $300 million in annual revenues from taxes and by selling bonds and electricity. It generates large annual surpluses after funding infrastructure and public services.[1] Most residents are well-paid city employees or relatives of city workers who live in homes owned by the city (this helps city officials control who can vote in local elections—but elections are a rare event). Among other services Vernon funds (including police, fire, and many services for industries), the city spends about $164 per person each year on a library. Directly across the Los Angeles River, Vernon's neighbor, Commerce, is similarly situated. The City of Commerce was incorporated in 1960 to prevent Vernon and Los Angeles from annexing valuable commercial land. It generates substantial tax revenues from industry, trucking distribution businesses, shopping malls, and a casino. Commerce provides its 13,000 residents free bus service, pays Los Angeles County to provide them fire and police services, and spends $184 per person on libraries—four times the library funds for an average California city and not much less than what Beverly Hills spends.

Several cities were also established to the south and east of downtown Los Angeles and Vernon that would serve as residential suburbs for the families of people who worked in factories in other cities. Within a few miles of Commerce and Vernon are Huntington Park, Bell, Maywood, South Gate, and others. Working-class populations in these towns boomed during World War II to serve defense industries, and for much of the 20th century, racial segregation ensured the cities were overwhelmingly white. Times have changed. Race riots in nearby Watts in 1965, the collapse of high-wage manufacturing jobs, the demise of defense spending, and immigration contributed to a flight of white residents to more affluent communities during the 1970s and 1980s. These cities still serve as bedroom communities for people who work in Vernon and Commerce, but they cannot compete with their industrial and commercial neighbors when it comes to generating tax revenues needed to fund public services. Poverty rates are higher, and tax revenues and home values are lower in these immigrant bedroom cities. Whereas Vernon and Commerce spend rather lavishly on libraries, Bell, South Gate, and Maywood spend nothing. Huntington Park managed just $0.23 spending per person on books. This chapter discusses why life is different in these places. We demonstrate how and why communities use local land use powers to compete for businesses and residents that help them financially and how they have used rules to keep people out of places. These rules shaped U.S. metropolitan regions and continue to affect who gets what from government.

The power to incorporate as a city comes with the ability to control land use, and greater control over local revenues. The City of Vernon, California (population 90) earns millions of dollars per year from industries and a power plant located inside its border. These revenues allow Vernon to spend lavishly on public services.

1   Hector Becerra, "Vernon Shoo-Ins Shoo Outsiders," *Los Angeles Times* 12 February 2006, http://www.latimes.com/news/local/la-me-vernon12feb12,0,6053598, full.story? coll=la-home-headlines.

Introduction

As noted in the previous chapter, local governments are creatures of their state governments. They exist, in a sense, at the pleasure of their state. The range of services they provide, the discretion they have for making independent decisions, the range of powers granted to local elected officials, the jurisdiction of municipal courts, and the form of local elections—all these structural features of local governments are regulated by state laws.

We have also detailed the dominant role that states and the federal government have in setting the agenda for fiscal policy, health and welfare policy, transportation, and higher education. Local governments retain a key role in controlling much of primary and secondary education policy and financing (see Chapter 15), but this power mostly lies in the hands of school districts.

So, what is left for **general purpose local governments**? What are the primary political functions of cities and counties? What do they "do" that is distinct from the powers and functions of state governments and school districts? Our first thought might be of traditional local services: fire protection, police, and sanitation. These are important services that many cities and counties provide, but as we suggest below, this is far from what being a city or county is all about. Many cities and counties have no police force, no fire department, and no garbage collection, and they provide no water service. So, what, then, is the key feature of local politics?

Land Use: The Key Power of American Counties and Cities

Although cities and counties are formally legal creatures of their state governments, states have traditionally granted local governments (counties and cities) substantial power over land use decisions. Land use refers to a broad set of policies we discuss below. Some of these policies are often referred to as zoning. **Zoning** involves decisions about where different sorts of things are allowed to be built and how much of various things get to be built. Land use policy, defined more broadly, involves attempts to influence the character of development that occurs in a jurisdiction's borders. These policies might work to keep certain types of people and industries out, while making it easier for other types of people and businesses to move in.

We suggest that the politics of many American local governments, and the historical development of American communities, can be best understood in terms of land use politics. Much of the politics of American places involves conflicts inside communities over the uses of land and conflicts between communities over development. The importance of land is best understood when considered in the environment where American communities find themselves. First, we must understand that cities and counties keep much of the revenue they collect locally, and they need revenues to thrive. Second, we must recognize that the revenues they collect depend, in large part, on who (or what) ends up locating within the county or city's borders. Third, it is important to remember that people and businesses have some level of mobility.

Local Governments and Demands for Public Services

Consider how these three forces might interact. Any government needs revenues to provide services. Demands for local services, such as parks, roads, streetlights, libraries, police protection, or social services, depend in part on who (or what) locates in a city. Families with lots of kids produce demands for schools, parks, and children's libraries. A manufacturing plant might want a place that provides industrial infrastructure or cheap water and power. Land use policies can affect who locates in a place and thus affect demands for services. Zoning that allows one type of duplex, apartment buildings, or single-family housing might attract more kids. Zoning that allows only high-end condominiums or very few houses per acre might attract people with fewer kids. Zoning that allows for heavy manufacturing uses might yield demands for infrastructure such as water and power. Zoning that allows light industry might produce different service requirements for cities and counties. Zoning affects and reflects the services that a place needs to provide.

Land Use and Local Revenues

Just as different land uses are associated with different service needs, they also produce different revenues. Recall from Chapter 10 that local governments depend heavily on property and sales taxes for their locally generated revenues. Some forms of land use offer tremendous potential local revenues, whereas others do not. Expensive homes might generate more property tax revenues than less expensive homes or apartments. Charges and fees applied to each new home constructed in a jurisdiction are another potential source of revenues. Commercial activity generates sales tax revenues and jobs. Car dealerships may generate limited property tax revenues but add greatly to a community's share of sales tax collections.

Location Decisions of Businesses and Firms

At any point in time, people and businesses are trying to decide where to locate. Probably dozens of factors—many somewhat random—enter into their location decisions. People move where they can afford to live or move to be near their jobs or families. They move to get away from somewhere or someone or to enjoy a different lifestyle. But some people looking to buy homes might also make their location decision, in part, after considering the quality of local schools, parks, public safety, and other public services. At the same time, they might consider what their taxes would be if they locate in one city versus another or in an unincorporated part of a county.

The same goes for business firms. When moving operations or opening a new facility, a business likely has dozens of things to consider when choosing where to locate. Businesses need to consider the local labor pool, their access to people who supply them their raw materials, and their access to those who buy their goods. But the places they have to choose between may also offer different mixes of public services at different tax levels.

The Competitive Local Environment

This is the environment where American cities and counties find themselves. Cities and counties provide services, and the cost of providing these services requires that they generate revenues. They can try to affect both demands for services and the flow of revenue with land use decisions. One theory predicts that places will make land use decisions with an eye toward "net fiscal gain"; that is, by encouraging development that brings in more revenues than service cost while discouraging development that costs more to service than the revenues it generates.[1] Another theory proposes that residents and businesses keep a keen eye on their local tax costs and service benefits and that they pack up and move when their costs exceed the benefits they receive from their local government.[2] Local governments must compete, then, to keep spending efficient and taxes low if they are to retain the firms and residents who contribute the most revenues.

One way to think of the political environment of American local governments, then, is

---

[1] James M. Buchanan, "Principles of Urban Fiscal Strategy," *Public Choice* (1971).
[2] Charles Tiebout, "A Pure Theory of Municipal Expenditures," *Journal of Political Economy* (1956).

to think of cities and counties as businesses in a competitive marketplace. As a "business," one place might offer a unique mix of public services, maybe providing publicly owned water and power, plus its own unique location, its unique opportunities for access to nice areas, and some particular opportunities for access to transportation. All of this comes at a price: the taxes and fees charged by that jurisdiction. A neighboring community might offer a different mix of services, perhaps leaving water and power service to the private market. It might also have a different "price" (or tax level) for locating there. As general purpose local governments, cities and counties are somewhat like supermarkets, grocery stores, or a little corner shop from this perspective. Different stores cater to different types of customers. One store might emphasize bargain prices over service (and have you bag your own groceries). Another store down the road might charge more but offer more customer service and expensive gourmet items. If a store offers the wrong combination of things at too high a price, it loses customers.

In this market model of local politics, businesses and residents are like consumers in a marketplace. They are assumed to select places to locate just as they might select where they shop for groceries. If they don't like what they get for their money, they move. On its face, this assumption might seem unrealistic. Many—perhaps most—people cannot tell you how much they pay in taxes for local services or for such things as sewer, water, and schools, let alone know what some other local jurisdiction might be charging. Even if they could, people have roots in their communities; friends, family, jobs, and neighbors make them hesitant to move. The poor and racial minorities who are subject to continued housing discrimination, in particular, often have little choice about where they can locate; and most businesses probably have similar roots that prevent them from packing up, even if they were keenly aware of their local tax bills.

Although the pure market model of local politics is highly unrealistic, it is a useful analogy to help understand and explain much of what local governments do, why they do it, and what they don't do. In addition, the model is not as unrealistic as it might first seem. There is evidence that some homeowners pay attention to their mix of taxes and public services—at least for public schools—when they decide where to move.[3] There is also evidence that local taxes factor into the broad range of things businesses consider when they make their decisions about where to locate, although mainly after the range of location choices has been narrowed to a particular metropolitan area. Moreover, if enough local officials know (or just think) that a few key residents or businesses behave as the market model suggests, then many things may work as the model predicts.

Metropolitan Fragmentation

One reason why a market model is used to describe politics of local places in the United States is population growth occurs in highly fragmented metropolitan areas. Natural increases in population and immigration mean that the United States will add about 30 million new residents between 2000 and 2010—about the population of the State of New York. Millions of people will also move from one state to another. Table 12.1 lists America's 15 largest metropolitan areas and their rates of growth from 2000 to 2008. The greater Atlanta area added over 1.1 million residents during this period and the Dallas area over 1 million people. Estimated growth rates for the greater Houston and Phoenix areas also suggest each of these regions absorbed over 1 million additional

[3] Paul Teske, Mark Schneider, Michael Mintrom, and Samuel Best, "Establishing the Microfoundations of a Macro Theory," *American Political Science Review* (1993); and Stephen Percy and Brett Hawkins, "Further in Tests of the Individual-Level Propositions from the Tiebout Model," *Journal of Politics* 54(1992):1149–57.

Table 12.1			

The 15 Largest U.S. Metropolitan Areas, 2008

		Population	Growth since 2000
1	New York-Northern New Jersey-Long Island, NY-NJ-PA	19,006,798	4%
2	Los Angeles-Long Beach-Santa Ana, CA	12,872,808	4%
3	Chicago-Naperville-Joliet, IL-IN-WI	9,569,624	5%
4	Dallas-Fort Worth-Arlington, TX	6,300,006	22%
5	Philadelphia-Camden-Wilmington, PA-NJ-DE-MD	5,838,471	3%
6	Houston-Sugar Land-Baytown, TX	5,728,143	21%
7	Miami-Fort Lauderdale-Miami Beach, FL	5,414,772	8%
8	Atlanta-Sandy Springs-Marietta, GA	5,376,285	27%
9	Washington-Arlington-Alexandria, DC-VA-MD-WV	5,358,130	12%
10	Boston-Cambridge-Quincy, MA-NH	4,522,858	3%
11	Detroit-Warren-Livonia, MI	4,425,110	−1%
12	Phoenix-Mesa-Scottsdale, AZ	4,281,899	32%
13	San Francisco-Oakland-Fremont, CA	4,274,531	4%
14	Riverside-San Bernardino-Ontario, CA	4,115,871	26%
15	Seattle-Tacoma-Bellevue, WA	3,334,813	10%

Note: Growth rates from April 1, 2000, through July 1, 2008.

Source: U.S. Census Bureau.

residents. Table 12.2 illustrates fast growth rates in some of the nation's smaller and midsized metropolitan regions—in the West and the South.

Obviously, new residents in these areas must live somewhere. Over 80 percent of Americans reside in a **metropolitan area** that consists of a central city, suburbs, and unincorporated areas governed by a county. There are at least 300 metropolitan areas in the United States. A single metro area may consist of multiple central cities, several dozen other incorporated cities, and several counties. Each metropolitan area in the United States is thus fragmented into dozens of different general purpose local governments providing unique location options—cities, counties, and towns, in addition to school districts and special districts. As we see below, many of these governments compete against each other to attract growth that helps their place while competing to avoid growth that might not help.

| Table 12.2 | | | | |

Fastest Growing U.S. Metropolitan Areas (over 100,000), 2008

Rank	Metropolitan Area	Population in 2008	% Growth	Foreclosure Rank in 2009
1	St. George, UT	137,589	52%	14
2	Provo-Orem, UT	540,820	44%	31
3	Greeley, CO	249,775	38%	31
4	Bend, OR	158,456	37%	5
5	Raleigh-Cary, NC	1,088,765	37%	145
6	Las Vegas-Paradise, NV	1,865,746	36%	1
7	Cape Coral-Ft. Myers, FL	593,136	35%	2
8	Gainesville, GA	184,814	33%	n/a
9	Austin-Round Rock, TX	1,652,602	32%	31
10	Phoenix-Mesa-Scottsdale, AZ	4,281,899	32%	9
11	Myrtle Beach-N Myrtle Beach, SC	257,380	31%	85
12	Boise-Nampa, ID	599,753	29%	32
13	Prescott, AZ	215,503	29%	27
14	Fayetteville, AR-Rodgers, MO	443,976	28%	34
15	Charlotte-Gastonia, NC-Concord, SC	1,701,799	28%	112

Note: Growth rates from April 1, 2000, through July 1, 2008. Foreclosure ranking from Realty Trac Reports on 203 metropolitan areas with populations over 200. Ranks for Bend and St. George estimated from news reports.

Source: U.S. Census Bureau.

The Los Angeles area is one of the largest and most fragmented of all areas. Los Angeles County has 292 towns and cities, of which 88 are incorporated as legally recognized municipal governments (cities). The four counties that border Los Angeles County contain another 94 incorporated cities (34 in Orange County, 26 in Riverside County, 10 in Ventura County, and 24 in San Bernardino County).

Los Angeles is not unique. The Minneapolis–St. Paul area includes 10 different counties, each with many cities and districts. There are six counties surrounding Chicago, seven in the greater Kansas City area, seven in the Denver area, eight in Indianapolis, nine around New York City, and 11 around Dallas–Fort Worth. The top four most fragmented U.S. metropolitan areas—measured in terms of the number of local governments per person and the dispersion of people across cities—are the St. Louis (MO–IL), Allentown–Bethlehem (PA–NJ), Louisville (KY–IN), and Ann Arbor (MI) metropolitan areas.[4] Within any metropolitan area are also dozens of **special districts** that supply one specific public service, such as fire protection, parks, libraries, or hospitals, as well as school districts (see Chapter 15).

---

[4] Eran Razin and Mark Rosentraub, "Are Fragmentation and Sprawl Linked?" *Urban Affairs Quarterly* 35(2000):830.

Most American cities and counties exist in a sort of competitive arena, surrounded by dozens of other cities and counties that may have their own unique powers to tax, spend, and make decisions about land use inside their own borders. When people move from one metropolitan area to another, they face a range of choices about which specific place in the region they may locate. Likewise, assuming a resident or firm in a large traditional central city like Chicago can afford to move, there are dozens of choices about where to relocate within the greater Chicago area, including suburban cities and unincorporated, semirural places.

Location choices are obviously constrained by many factors, but the American local environment is unique when compared to much of the developed world. American cities and counties are also granted far more control over land use and zoning powers than other nations. The scope of these powers varies across the states; and American cities are far more dependent on locally generated revenues than cities in Canada or Europe, for example. This means that in the United States, location decisions of residents and firms have tremendous consequences for the places they move to as well as the places they leave. If a large firm exits a place, it takes its contribution to that jurisdiction's tax base with it. So, too, when wealthy residents move away. This, combined with the fragmentation of U.S. metropolitan regions, means that there are some places that win big and others that lose big when people and businesses move.

What's a City?

The discussion thus far begs two important questions: What's a city, and what are the differences between city and county control over land use? We typically think of a **metropolitan area** as having a central city, surrounded by suburbs. Los Angeles, New York, and Chicago are our traditional ideas of what cities are; but what about suburban places like Lawndale (near Los Angeles), Levittown

(near New York), and Lincolnshire (near Chicago)? Some of these are actual incorporated cities; some are not. Ninety-eight percent of incorporated American cities are relatively small places with populations of less than 100,000 people. Nearly two-thirds are places with less than 25,000 residents. Today, most Americans live in suburban cities that lack the scale, density, and social diversity of a larger, central city. A **suburb** is a city when, following state law, it incorporates as a municipality.

In most states, places often have strong incentives to become cities. If a place incorporates and becomes a formal city, it can have many or all the powers to tax, spend, and control land use as a traditional central city. If a place remains unincorporated, the larger county government where it is located may have substantial control over such matters. State laws determine the range of powers that incorporated cites have. Once incorporated, cities have some latitude in deciding what sort of services they will offer—or if they will offer any at all.

New Cities versus Traditional Cities

These newer suburban places where most Americans now live are much different than older, traditional American central cities, such as Detroit, Philadelphia, or San Francisco. Some observers use terms such as *exurbs* (for extra-urban) and *edge cities* to refer to newer, non–central city places that initially developed far from a central place. Edge cities can be viewed differently from standard suburbs because they include job opportunities in addition to housing and shopping. However, growth and sprawl may eventually fill in any space between central cities, suburbs, and edge cities. Furthermore, it is not always so easy to identity a central city. Houston, Phoenix, and Los Angeles are sprawling megacities surrounded by many suburbs, but they look and feel much different than traditional cities like Boston or Chicago. Regardless of what we call these places, more Americans now live in suburbs of all sorts than live in rural places or central cities. Many of these suburban places hardly existed 50 years ago. Consider the Washington, D.C.–Arlington, Virginia, region as an example. Arlington and Washington, D.C., are somewhat traditional, neighboring cities with a mix of residential neighborhoods, cultural precincts, and economic activity that employs more than just city residents. Many people who work in those cities now live in the booming suburbs of North Virginia's Fairfax County, some in incorporated cities, such as Falls Church and Fairfax, and many in unincorporated suburban places, like McLean and Annandale. More than twice as many people live in Fairfax County than Washington, D.C. Farther out from these Virginia suburbs, but within commuting distance of D.C., lie relatively isolated places with rapidly growing populations and their own economies (that is, exurbs or edge cities), such as Manassas or Tyson's Corner.

There is often much less that is public in newer cities than in older ones, as traditional cities typically do much more in the way of providing public utilities, public services, parks, and other amenities. Progressive reformers of the early 20th century (discussed in Chapter 11) sought to improve urban living conditions by granting cities monopoly powers to supply local services that were in short supply, including street lighting, drinking water, electricity, sewerage, and waste collection. Earlier in the 19th century, local governments had granted monopolies to private firms for such services or waited for the private market to supply them. But this often led to inadequate private investment in such services, bankruptcies, and political corruption in the awarding of contracts.[5]

The Progressives' idea was to use the authority of the city to do something that the free market was failing to do. Cities began to act as nonprofit organizations that amassed enough capital (by borrowing or taxing) to supply infrastructure and services at a fair price to residents. Many older, traditional cities still reflect this Progressive ideal and provide a wide range of public services.

The Lakewood Plan

The United States experienced dramatic changes in the 1950s because millions of families were suddenly able to purchase new homes in new communities. At least three forces interacted to create a booming market for single-family homes. First, after World War II, the federal government began expanding subsidies that lowered the cost of financing a home loan. Second, at the same time soldiers were returning from Europe and the Pacific to buy homes, innovations in mass production of homes by builders, such as William J. Levitt, lowered building costs. Third, massive federal subsidies built a highway system that made it possible to build on cheap land far from the traditional city at the center of a metropolitan area.

Many cities that incorporated after this suburban boom did so with no intention of offering the full range of public services that older cities did. The role that cities play in the provision of local public services profoundly changed in the later half of the 20th century as existing cities shifted away from the tradition of providing a broad mix of public services, while new cities formed that provided very little in the way of services.[6] Privatization of city services and **contracting for services** began to replace the tradition of cities being a single level of government that provided residents with local services, such as libraries, parks, health services, and fire protection.

In 1953, the community of Lakewood, California, developed a contract with Los Angeles County that became a model for how many new suburban cities would deal with providing

[5] Amy Bridges, *Morning Glories: Municipal Reform in the Southwest* (Princeton, NJ: Princeton University Press, 1997).

[6] David Lowery, "Consumer Sovereignty and Quasi Market Failure," *Journal of Public Administration Research and Theory* 8(1998).

NIRA Photo

Aerial photograph of Levittown, New York. Built in the 1950s, Levittown was one of the first modern U.S. suburbs. Prices for new homes were relatively low because developer William J. Levitt built on cheap land beyond the central city and standardized much of the construction process.

services. At the time, Lakewood was the largest private land development in the United States—a massive 17,500-home development 10 miles from Los Angeles. Developers and residents had little interest in collecting Lakewood city taxes to pay for police, firefighters, road maintenance, building inspections, sewer service, or libraries. When Lakewood was unincorporated, these services were supplied by the county. The Lakewood Plan involved a detailed contract with Los Angeles County that allowed municipal incorporation for Lakewood, with the county continuing to provide the new City of Lakewood with some of the services it received when it was an unincorporated area.

Lakewood, and similar places that incorporate like this, might not seem to get much out of the deal if we simply consider cities as places designed to provide services for residents. These newer cities can avoid providing traditional municipal services (and avoid the higher taxes needed to fund services) if they contract for services with other governments, with special districts, or with private firms (for such things as garbage collection). But these cities acquire two key powers when they incorporate: the power to control land use and the power to collect their own taxes. Control of these powers proved very popular for many places after the Lakewood plan innovation. Other places in Los Angeles County incorporated as cities with hardly any residents but with control over zoning and access to huge tax revenues. Local industries incorporated prime commercial land (as the City of Commerce) and prime industrial land (as the City of Industry).[7]

---

[7] Gary Miller, *Cities by Contract: The Politics of Municipal Incorporation* (Cambridge, MA: MIT Press, 1981).

Local governments have also been privatizing services more rapidly since the 1970s, as cities sell off publicly owned utilities and private firms have expanded their offerings of services, like garbage collection and sewage treatment.[8] A 1995 survey of the 100-largest cities in the United States found that only three had not privatized some of their services. But most larger cities "had not fully embraced the privatization approach in a broad-based manner." The most commonly privatized services were towing, garbage collection, building security, street repair, and ambulance services.[9]

The Lakewood model for cities spread across American metropolitan regions during the post–World War II suburbanization boom. Newer cities and unincorporated places can now choose to offer little in public services, but they have a wide range of options when it comes to contracting for services. As Table 12.3 illustrates, over 25,000 new special districts were formed since 1952 to provide a particular service for a specific geographic area. Their district boundaries can include many incorporated cities as well as unincorporated areas. These districts have their own appointed or elected boards that oversee operations. Many have the power to raise taxes, issue bonds, build facilities, and employ people who provide a service. Table 12.4 shows that the most common of these are

districts that manage natural resources (land management, soil conservation, water quality protection, and similar programs), fire protection, water supply, housing, and sewage treatment. The most rapidly growing categories of special districts are library districts (91 percent more since 1987), districts that provide multiple services (56 percent more), and districts designed to protect public health (53 percent more). The latter do everything from mosquito abatement to immunization and AIDS education outreach.

What Do Cities Do?

In addition to providing police, traditional city services may include water, public transit, sewers, nursing homes, libraries, hospitals, stadiums, natural gas, electricity, landfills, and airports. American cities that were formed in the 1800s provide many of these, with over 70 percent offering fire, water, and sewer service.[10] But special districts, contracting, and privatization have changed what it means to be a city. Over 10 percent of American cities do not provide a single municipal service other than police. Another 12 percent offer just one municipal service from the list above. Most cities formed after the 1950s don't provide fire protection, water service, sewerage, or public transit.[11]

Table 12.3								

Number of Local Governments in the United States

Year	2007	2002	1992	1982	1972	1962	1952	1942
County	3033	3034	3043	3041	3044	3043	3052	3050
City (municipality)	19492	19431	19296	19076	18517	17997	16807	16220
Town (unincorporated)	16519	16506	16666	16734	16991	17114	17202	18919
Special district	37381	35356	33131	28078	23885	18323	12340	8299

Source: US Census of Governments.

---

[8] E. S. Savas, *Privatization: The Key to Better Government* (Chatham, NJ: Chatham House, 1987).
[9] Robert Jay Dilger, Randolph R. Moffett, and Linda Struyk, "Privatization of Municipal Services in American's Largest Cities," *Public Administration Review* 57(1997):21.

[10] Nancy Burns, *The Formation of American Local Governments: Private Values in Public Institutions* (Oxford: Oxford University Press, 1994).
[11] Burns, *The Formation of American Local Governments*, p. 9.

Table 12.4

Special District Functions

	Number of Districts	% of All Districts	Change Since 1987
Natural resources	7026	(20%)	+10%
Fire protection	5743	(16%)	+13%
Water supply	3423	(10%)	+12%
Housing and community development	3413	(10%)	−1%
Sewerage	2020	(6%)	+26%
Cemeteries	1670	(5%)	+3%
Libraries	1582	(4%)	+91%
Parks and recreation	1314	(4%)	+31%
Highways	767	(2%)	+24%
Health	743	(2%)	+53%
Hospitals	735	(2%)	−6%
School building authorities	530	(2%)	−27%
Airports	512	(1%)	+39%
Other utilities	485	(1%)	n/a
Other	2194	(6%)	+47%
Multiple function districts	3199	(9%)	+56%

Source: U.S. Census of Governments.

With contracting and privatization, places can incorporate strategically and become cities that are very limited in what they do. What many do is use their public land use and tax powers to attract and assist private business. The example of Vernon, California, in the opening of this chapter may be a bit extreme, but it illuminates this fact. The strategy of forming cities for specialized economic purposes is not new. Oil companies incorporated an oil field as a city (Signal Hill) in Los Angeles County in the 1920s to prevent the City of Long Beach from annexing the area and gaining the tax revenues. Dennis Judd, a keen observer of American cities, demonstrates that through American history, cities were founded for economic purposes. The American colonies were chartered by England as mercantile corporations. Major American cities, such as Denver, Chicago, Pittsburgh, and Kansas City, developed because local boosters in those places were able to outcompete rival communities in recruiting residents and businesses and securing access to railways.[12]

The larger and older U.S. cities evolved before the spread of Lakewood-style suburbs, however. Over time, their metropolitan areas evolved—fragmenting as more and more places incorporate to assume control of their own land use and tax powers. Of course, traditional cities try to grow by annexing outlying areas that might add to their tax base. But annexation is often resisted by residents in the targeted area, and older central cities can run out of adjacent unincorporated places to annex. One major study of municipal incorporation concluded that most incorporation attempts were motivated by a desire to maintain control of taxation and by fears of annexation by another city.[13]

---

[12] Dennis R. Judd, *City Politics: Private Power and Public Policy* (Upper Saddle River, NJ: Pearson Longman, 2004).
[13] Miller, *Cities by Contract.*

YOU DECIDE

WHO IS TO BLAME FOR THE "HOUSING BUBBLE" THAT BURST?

Home prices collapsed in 2008 when lending in America seized up, with the effects being particularly pronounced in areas that had experienced rapid growth over the previous decade. The economic crisis had several sources, but one major problem was that the global financial sector became dependent on unregulated financial instruments that could only remain valuable if housing prices continued to rise. As the financial industry realized the true risk involved with financial instruments linked to inflated housing values, lending collapsed.[1] Trillions of dollars of wealth disappeared, the economy crashed into a severe recession, and home foreclosures spiked. As Table 12.2 illustrates, some of the most rapidly growing regions had the highest home foreclosure rates.

So, who is to blame for inflating home prices and the collapse that followed? While the U.S. population has shifted toward the West and the South, demand for housing in those areas increased. It is difficult to distinguish between the forces of demand and supply associated with the boom in home prices in the 2000s. Low interest rates made home purchases more affordable. Financial institutions began granting loans so people could buy homes without necessarily having enough income to make payments. Many people took advantage of these risky loans. Others purchased homes "on spec," overextending their ability to pay in the short term with the hope of selling at a higher price a couple years later. Local policies that subsidize some of the costs of housing development (paving roads, building parks and fire stations) also helped to facilitate the rapid expansion of the supply of housing in many regions.

It is a complicated story that reflects how local land use policies, home construction, and federal regulations of the financial industry are interrelated, and are critical elements of the global economy.

Notes
1. Michael Lewis, "The Man Who Crashed the World," *Vanity Fair* (August 2009).

Another study suggests that incorporation of new cities in Michigan, Texas, and Florida in the 1950s and 1960s was motivated by manufacturers and white residents seeking to form exclusive communities that walled themselves off from less-affluent African Americans.[14]

Race and the Rise of Suburbs

The rise of new suburban cities did not occur by accident. Homeownership started to become something accessible to average Americans in the 1930s, when the federal government began underwriting part of the cost of home loans.

In addition to the federal highway system, two public housing programs were instrumental in the creation of the suburbs: the Federal Housing Administration (FHA), created by the National Housing Act of 1934; and the Veterans Administration (VA) loan program, created by the Servicemen's Readjustment Act of 1944. Before the FHA program, a homebuyer would need a cash down payment of no less than 33 percent of a home's value in order to secure a home loan. The FHA insured the risk of the loan for a bank, which allowed banks to require a much lower down payment (10 percent of the home's value). The VA program worked in a similar manner for veterans.[15]

---

[14] Burns, *The Formation of American Local Governments.*

[15] Kenneth T. Jackson, *Crabgrass Frontier: The Suburbanization of the United States* (Oxford: Oxford University Press, 1985).

Figure 12.1

Percent of Homebuyers with FHA and/or VA Loans, 1950–2008

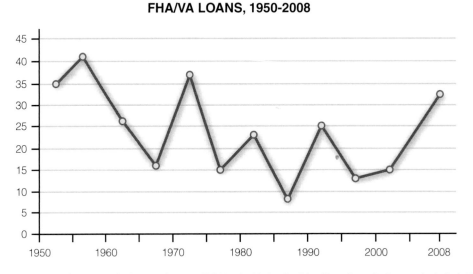

Sources: U.S. Department of Housing and Urban Development, "U.S. Housing Market Conditions," http://www.huduser.org/periodicals/USHMC/fall2001/summary-2.html; and Dennis R. Judd, *City Politics: Private Power and Public Policy* (Upper Saddle River, NJ: Pearson Longman, 2004).

As Figure 12.1 illustrates, during the period between 1950 and 1970, at some points, as much as 40 percent of all private new home construction was financed with FHA and VA loans. Figure 12.2 illustrates that the 1950s was a period of incredible levels of new home construction. More homes were built in 1950, for example, than in any year during the 1980s and 1990s. Millions of Americans were able to purchase their first home because of the FHA and VA programs, and the vast majority of these were new homes being built in new communities.[16]

The original FHA lending criteria relied on real estate and banking industry preferences for racially segregated neighborhoods. From 1946 to 1959, less than 2 percent of FHA loans went to African Americans.[17] The FHA removed race as a formal criterion for lending in 1950, but banks, developers, and real estate agencies continued to enforce de facto segregation of housing, legally, because mixed-race areas were perceived as a bad investment. The Federal Housing Act of 1968 finally made it illegal for banks, developers, and realtors to discriminate in the housing market on the basis of race. In the meantime, over 30 million new homes were constructed, mostly in all-white suburbs, and over 1,200 new American cities were incorporated (see Table 12.3).

Both the VA and FHA programs also used lending criteria that favored new, detached, single-family housing construction over the higher-density, multifamily housing more common in older cities.[18] As a result, some suggest that the FHA and VA programs should be seen as a massive federal subsidy that locked racial and ethnic minorities in older cities while moving middle-class whites out of established central cities and into new suburbs.[19] Kenneth Jackson estimates that suburban St. Louis received more than six

[16] Judd, *City Politics*, p. 147.
[17] Mark Gefland, *A Nation of Cities: The Federal Government and Urban America* (Oxford: Oxford University Press, 1975).
[18] Jackson, *Crabgrass Frontier*.
[19] Douglass Massey and Nancy Denton, *American Apartheid: Segregation and the Making of the Underclass* (Cambridge, MA: Harvard University Press, 1993).

Figure 12.2

Annual Construction of New Private Housing in the United States, 1950–2008 (thousands of units built per year)

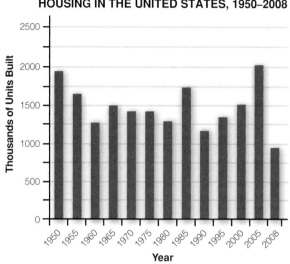

ANNUAL CONSTRUCTION OF NEW PRIVATE
HOUSING IN THE UNITED STATES, 1950–2008

Source: U.S. Census Bureau, Statistical Abstract of the United States: National Data Book, 723, table 1199, http://www.census.gov/indicator/www/newresconst.pdf.

times as much FHA money per capita than the city of St. Louis. Long Island (a suburban area adjacent to New York City) received 60 times more FHA money per resident than Bronx County (an older, urban part of New York City).[20]

The rise of the suburbs meant that older cities were locked into a spiral of decline, encouraged by federal housing policies.[21] Prior to the suburban boom, traditional cities became home to a growing portion of the U.S. African American population. African American migration from southern farms to northern cities increased in the early 1900s, as industrial jobs motivated hundreds of thousands to move north to find work in factories. This migration was accelerated by both world wars, when emigration from Europe slowed and demand for industrial labor increased. These events transformed the demographics of northern cities during the 20th century. Working-class blacks entered older cities

in large numbers (having few location options), whereas middle-class whites fled to newer suburbs—taking their tax revenues with them.

Regulating Land Use: Zoning and Eminent Domain

Land use powers—that is, the power to determine permissible and impermissible land uses—were originally given to state governments. Over time, however, local governments assumed more control of what went on inside their borders. There are at least four major legal powers that cities have to affect land use. Taxing and spending are two.[22] Our discussion

[20] Jackson, *Crabgrass Frontier*, p. 208.
[21] Massey and Denton, *American Apartheid*, p. 55.

[22] T. W. Patterson, *Land Use Planning: Techniques of Implementation* (Malbar, FL: Kreiger Publishing, 1988); Roger W. Caves, *Land Use Planning: The Ballot Box Revolution* (Beverly Hills, CA: Sage, 1992).

of the market model of the city introduced the idea that a city's mix of taxing and spending might affect who locates where. We will return to this idea in a moment. Zoning and eminent domain are two additional powers cities may use to affect who gets to locate where.

American cities have traditionally been granted the authority to regulate public health, safety, and welfare. These are known as a local government's **police powers**. When state legislatures charter cities and counties, they grant them wide authority to exercise police powers. The exercise of these powers extends far beyond maintaining a police force; it also includes the ability to regulate building design, the quality of food in restaurants, and what can be built in flood zones as well as the ability to operate immunization programs. The police powers are perhaps the most important tool cities have to affect land use.

City governments were relatively passive actors in the 1800s. By the late 1800s, after decades of industrialization and immigration, American cities were overcrowded, much of their housing was dangerous and unregulated, and sanitation was lacking. Use of local police powers to regulate public health and safety accelerated in the early 20th century, as Progressive reformers, muckraker journalists, and others targeted the dangerous living conditions of cities (see Chapter 9).

Zoning Powers

Land use zoning was one of the chief innovations of local police powers during the Progressive era. During the period of rapid industrialization, factories and housing in cities were at times built shoulder to shoulder. The development of cars and trucks suddenly allowed a more rapid dispersion of people and industries between 1910 to 1920, creating new conflicts over land use.[23] Zoning had its origins

in New York City, where wealthy Fifth Avenue residents organized to protect their exclusive residential and commercial shopping area from encroachment by the city's textile industry. The city passed the first zoning ordinance in the United States in 1916, specifying specific land uses that could be isolated in distinct areas: residential, commercial business, warehouse, and industrial. Many cities copied New York City's policy, and by the late 1920s, 60 percent of the nation's urban areas had zoning laws.[24]

Zoning was promoted as a way to prevent incompatible land uses from being in the same place. With zoning, slaughterhouses could be forced to locate far from schools or housing; factories and residential areas could be kept apart. Contemporary zoning plans often have land divided into agricultural, residential, and industrial areas.[25] Of course, someone's land may have more value if zoned one particular way. For example, vacant land near a growing city may have much more value if it is zoned to allow residential or commercial use rather than agricultural. If a local government zones land one particular way, then the landowner might not profit as much when selling or developing the land. This was the challenge to local zoning facing the U.S. Supreme Court in 1926. In a landmark case, *Village of Euclid v. Ambler Realty Company,* the Ambler Company argued that Euclid, Ohio, had unfairly devalued its land by "down zoning" its use from commercial to residential and that they had done so without due process or just compensation.

The Court sided with Euclid, ruling that zoning was a logical extension of the city's police powers that existed to protect public health and safety. Traditional police powers allow local governments to close unhealthy restaurants or require that building designs meet safety standards. These regulations create costs for property owners, but because they serve a public purpose, local governments are

---

[23] William A. Fishel, "An Economic History of Zoning and a Cure for Its Exclusionary Effects," *Urban Studies* 41(2004):317–40.

[24] Seymour Toll, *Zoned America* (New York: Crossman, 1969).

[25] Caves, *Land Use Planning.*

not required to compensate property owners for inconvenience or loss of profit. The Court ruled that cities can likewise use zoning, and affect the value of land, without having to require compensation. The Court went as far in the *Euclid* case as to state that zoning could be used to prevent incompatible residential developments from overlapping. The "residential character" of single-family home neighborhoods could be "utterly destroyed" by large apartment buildings, and, thus, it was legitimate to use zoning to separate such neighborhoods from high-density housing.[26]

Zoning powers are a powerful, popular, and often controversial tool to affect land use. It is "far and away the most widely employed land use control technique today."[27] It is powerful and popular because it allows communities to shape their character and destiny by defining land values, usually without having to compensate property owners for their losses when the permissible use of the land is changed.[28] When a new city takes shape in raw, undeveloped land, zoning is the tool that can be used to make a place "exclusively industrial," exclusively commercial, exclusively residential, or some mix of these.

Zoning allows a city to plan its development. Very-low-density zoning is used to control the pace of development by regulating when an area can be built up, and low-density zoning can be used to protect watersheds used for drinking supplies, to preserve agricultural lands, to force development out of erosion-prone areas, and to preserve scenic areas. Higher-density zoning can be used to encourage construction in specific areas. Zoning maps can also be used to exclude land uses that people don't want in their community—by requiring relatively large and uniform lot sizes and forbidding the construction of duplexes and apartments, zoning can be used to ensure that only expensive housing is available in a place.

Zoning: Taking or Regulating? Zoning is controversial for at least two reasons. First, local politics in most American cities centers around land use issues, and zoning determines how land will be used. Great profits are to be made if land is zoned to allow development; greater profits are to be made if the land is zoned for whatever use is in greatest demand. It is not surprising, then, to find developers, large landowners, building industry officials, and representatives of real estate firms attending planning commission meetings to lobby city officials for particular zoning policies. Pro-development forces may oppose some of the regulations that local governments employ to control land use. To some people denied unfettered use of their land, zoning is seen as an unfair regulatory taking.

Critics of land use regulations refer to them as **regulatory takings** because they lower property value, via regulation, without requiring any compensation to the owner. The 5th Amendment to the U.S. Constitution stipulates, "[N]or shall private property be taken for public use without just compensation." Historically, this was seen as limiting what the federal government could do, not states and their cities, because the original Bill of Rights was designed to limit the power of the federal government. In 1833, the Supreme Court ruled the 5th Amendment placed no overt requirements for compensation by state and local governments. In the landmark case *Barron vs. Baltimore*, the Court ruled that the 5th Amendment did not require the city of Baltimore to compensate the owner of a wharf for damages caused by a public project that lowered the wharf's value.[29] The Court began to use the 5th Amendment to require compensation by state and local governments in 1897.

How far can local governments go with regulations that lower the value of someone's

---

[26] *Village of Euclid v. Ambler Realty Co.*, 272 US 365 (1926); cited in Judd, *City Politics*.
[27] Caves, *Land Use Planning*, p. 30.
[28] J. R. Levy, *Contemporary Urban Planning* (Englewood Cliffs, NJ: Prentice Hall, 1988).
[29] *Barron v. Baltimore* (1833).

property? Generally, the regulation must forward some "public use" and should not cause a particular owner to bear the burden of the regulation's cost. But public use and burden have been interpreted broadly. In 1992, the Supreme Court let stand an Escondido, California, rent control ordinance that froze rents charged on the pads of land that mobile home owners rent to park their houses. Additional rules prevented landowners from raising land rents on mobile home pads when a mobile home was sold to a new owner and prevented them from evicting people who continued to pay their rent. Owners of mobile home parks argued this was an unfair taking. They claimed the rules prevented them from profiting from rising land values and that the rules forced them to subsidize low rents for mobile home residents. The Court said this was not an actual "taking" and required no compensation to landowners because the city did not physically occupy the land or force the landowners to rent mobile homes.[30]

In another case, David Lucas bought beachfront property in South Carolina, where he planned to build vacation homes. The state then passed the Beachfront Management Act, a law designed to protect the state's fragile barrier islands ecosystem. The law prevented Lucas from developing his barrier island property. Lucas argued the state law rendered his property valueless and hence was an unfair taking. The Supreme Court ruled in favor of Lucas in 1992 but held that compensation by governments would be required only if a law made a property totally valueless by depriving the owner of "all economically beneficial uses." Regulations that still allow at least some minimal economic use of land do not require compensation.[31] In earlier cases, however, the Court has required a local government to pay compensation for "partial takings," for example, when a county-built airport made it impossible to use neighboring land for residential (but not commercial) use.[32]

Eminent Domain

The 5th Amendment has been interpreted as granting state and local governments the power to take property for public use but requiring that government pay compensation. This is referred to as **eminent domain**. In general, if a state or local government acts to promote some clear public use (e.g., an airport, coastal preservation, or highway construction), compensation is usually required if land is physically taken from someone. In theory, governments cannot take land from one person just to give it to another.[33] In practice, however, there may be few limits on a local government's ability to forcibly seize private property that will remain in private hands, as long as it is willing to pay compensation.

In 1998, a private nonprofit redevelopment group was established in New London, Connecticut, to revitalize an industrial section of the city that contained several homes. The city hoped that new manufacturing firms and new businesses would generate more tax revenues than the existing homes. Using the power of eminent domain, the city told dozens of homeowners they had to sell in 2000 so the land underneath them could be transferred to the developer. Seven homeowners refused, arguing that it was unconstitutional for the city to take their property in order to promote private economic development.[34] Opponents of the New London action argued the city violated the "takings" clause of the 5th Amendment and worried that it opened the way for cities to boost their tax revenues by transferring any low-revenue-generating residential property to shopping-mall developers offering more in tax revenues. In 2005, the Supreme Court ruled 5–4 against the homeowners and allowed New London's redevelopment plans to move forward. The Court held (in *Kelo v.*

---

[30] *Yee v. City of Escondido* (1992).
[31] *Lucas v. South Carolina Coastal Commission* (1992).
[32] *Griggs v. Allegheny County* (1962).

[33] James G. Durhan, "Efficient Just Compensation as a Limit on Eminent Domain," *Minnesota Law Review* 69(1985).
[34] *Kelo v. City of New London* (2005).

City of New London) that taking private property from one owner to give to another private owner was a legitimate use of eminent domain because economic growth from the new development was a permissible "public use." The decision sparked a reaction across the nation. A number of states passed ballot initiatives barring "takings" for economic development, and several state legislatures considered similar legislation.

Much Is at Stake

In rapidly growing suburban areas, the stakes of local politics surrounding land use control issues, and the potential for conflict, can be quite high. If developers succeed in preventing regulations on local land use, residents may experience a major change in the pace of growth in their community. Open spaces can be lost, traffic may become unbearable, new housing may outstrip available services, and schools may become increasingly overcrowded.

Yet, if slow-growth forces succeed in promoting local regulations that prohibit building in certain areas, developers (and owners of rural, agricultural, or forestry land in the path of growth) stand to lose tremendous profits they hoped to realize. Landowners may be an easier target for regulations than businesses. Critics of local zoning rules suggest that the "fear of exit" limits how far local governments can regulate how businesses operate. If a city places too many costly rules on businesses, then businesses might move away. But landowners cannot take their property away when local governments regulate how it can be used.[35] Rather than exit, then, landowners must remain organized and active in the local political arena. Political controversy over land use regulations have fanned a "property rights" movement dedicated to limiting government's use of its police powers in land use control.

Zoning Controversy: Exclusion by Race and Income

Another major controversy surrounding zoning involves how it might be used to exclude people from a community. Zoning may be highly neutral in intent but nonetheless have unintended class and racial implications. It is clear that some forms of zoning can increase home prices. If rules require larger lots and bigger homes and exclude high-density apartment buildings, housing costs more. Some suggest that zoning had its origins in attempts to exclude minorities and the poor from newer suburban areas.[36] From this perspective, zoning is seen as a public tool used to exclude minorities and the less affluent, just as private sector lending and real estate practices once did (discussed above).[37]

A survey of the 25 largest metropolitan areas in the United States found that zoning rules that allow nothing but low-density zoning are associated with places that have fewer black and Hispanic residents.[38] Low-density zoning (allowing no more than eight homes per acre) means there is less rental housing, which likely squeezes out housing opportunities for the less affluent. About 15 percent of cities in the nation were found using low-density-only zoning that allowed nothing but expensive, low-density housing. Use of this policy varies widely by region. It occurred disproportionately in regions with the highest segregation between black and white

[35] William Fischel, *Regulatory Takings: Law, Economics and Politics* (Cambridge, MA: Harvard University Press, 1998).

[36] Michael N. Danielson, "The Politics of Exclusionary Zoning in Suburbia," *Political Science Quarterly* (1976).

[37] Richard F. Babcock and Fred Bosselman, *Exclusionary Zoning: Land Use Regulation and Housing in the 1970s* (New York: Praeger, 1973).

[38] Rolf Pendall, "Local Land Use Regulation and the Chain of Exclusion," *Journal of the American Planning Association* 66(2000):125–42.

populations: Boston, New York, Philadelphia, Pittsburgh, and Cleveland. Almost half of the suburban communities around Boston used low-density-only zoning.[39]

Minority populations may be shrinking in places using low-density-only zoning. In 1990, black and Hispanic populations were relatively smaller than in 1980 in such places, despite growing movement of minorities to the suburbs.[40] There is no question that blacks had greater access to suburbs after the 1980s than during the 1950s and 1960s, but there is evidence they were being channeled into relatively few suburbs.[41] Other commonly used local land use controls—requiring adequate public facilities where growth will occur or using "urban growth boundaries" to concentrate growth in designated areas—were not found to have racially exclusionary effects.[42] But cities have other tools that can be used to exclude less-affluent residents. Some states—including Illinois and California—give their cities the power to let local voters decide if publicly subsidized housing for low-income residents can be built in their jurisdiction.[43] It is difficult to convince affluent voters that they need low-income housing in their town.

Evidence of exclusionary effects of land use regulations has produced calls for limiting local control over zoning. In 1971, the National Committee Against Discrimination in Housing (NCADH), a civil rights group, stated that "there can be no effective progress in halting the trend toward predominantly black cities surrounded by almost entirely white suburbs . . . until local governments have been deprived of the power to exclude subsidized housing and to manipulate zoning and other controls to screen out families on the basis of income, and, implicitly, of race."[44] Although some progress has occurred in integrating U.S. suburbs, it has not resulted from limiting local power to control land use.

In fact, the federal courts continue to allow cities to ban the construction of rental housing, unless state laws say otherwise or there is clear evidence of the intent to discriminate on the basis of race. The NCADH critique against zoning came the same year that a case involving the city of Black Jack, Missouri, reached the U.S. Supreme Court. Black Jack, a suburb of St. Louis, incorporated in 1970 to take control of zoning from St. Louis County. Area residents moved to incorporate immediately after a nonprofit group announced plans to use federal subsidies to construct low-income housing in Black Jack. The new city of Black Jack quickly adopted zoning rules that banned apartment buildings before the subsidized housing was built. Some observers noted that there was evidence that the city founders' explicit intent was to keep less-affluent blacks out of Black Jack.[45]

For a brief period, a federal court ruling suggested that it would be unconstitutional for a city to ban apartments if the effect was exclusionary, regardless of what the intent of the ban was (in other words, zoning could be seen as de facto segregation). However, in 1977, the court upheld a Chicago suburb's ban on subsidized, racially integrated apartments for low- and moderate-income residents. The court ruled that the policy of Arlington Heights, Illinois (a city of 64,000 people with only 27 African Americans in 1970), could not be challenged

[39] Pendall, "Local Land Use Regulation," 138.

[40] Pendall, "Local Land Use Regulation."

[41] Mark Schneider and Thomas Phelan, "Black Suburbanization in the 1980s," *Demography* 30(1993):278.

[42] Pendall, "Local Land Use Regulation"; but see Todd Donovan and Max Neiman, "Local Growth Control Policies and Changes in Community Characteristics," *Social Science Quarterly* 76(1995):780–93.

[43] Normal D. Peel, Garthe E. Pickett, and Stephen T. Buehl, "Racial Discrimination in Public Housing Site Selection," *Stanford Law Review* 23(1970):63–147; *James v. Valtierra* 420 U.S. 137 (1971) upheld the constitutionality of such rules.

[44] Cited by Danielson, "The Politics of Exclusionary Zoning in Suburbia," 1.

[45] Judd, *City Politics*, p. 281; and Donald Kirby et al., *Residential Zoning and Equal Housing Opportunities* (Washington, DC: Urban Institute, 1972).

REFORM CAN HAPPEN

RACIAL SEGREGATION, INCOME, AND AFFORDABLE HOUSING

Westchester County, New York, is one of America's wealthiest counties. In 2006, the county was sued in federal court by the Anti-Discrimination Center. The center argued that because the county received federal community development funds that the Fair Housing Act required it "affirmatively further fair housing to the maximum extent possible."[1] The suit argued that Westchester County made no effort to evaluate racial discrimination and segregation in housing, and that it took no steps to overcome discriminatory barriers to housing associated with race and national origin stereotyping. In many of the wealthier communities in the county, blacks and Hispanics make up less than 3 percent of the population.

After a federal judge found in 2009 that the county had "utterly failed" to meet its fair housing obligations, the county agreed to a settlement with the federal Department of Housing and Urban Development (HUD). The county will spend $60 million of its own money over seven years to build or acquire 630 homes or apartments in towns where blacks make up less than 3 percent of the population and Hispanics constitute less than 7 percent. Efforts will be made to market the new housing to minority residents seeking housing in affluent, white communities. The county also acknowledged that local zoning rules such as minimum lot sizes and low-density housing can prevent construction of affordable housing, and that it could challenge cities that use such policies.

A Westchester County official said the settlement reflected a historic shift in the federal government's philosophy about fair access to housing. Deputy HUD Secretary Ron Simms said the agreement was "consistent with the President's desire to see a fully integrated society." The agreement may become a model for how the Obama administration evaluates local housing policies and zoning rules. Deputy Secretary Simms stated that from now on, HUD was "going to hold people's feet to the fire."[2]

Notes
1. http://www.antibiaslaw.com/westchester-false-claims-case. Accessed August 18, 2009.
2. Sam Roberts, "Westchester Adds Housing to Desegregation Pact," *The New York Times* 11 August 2009.

with evidence showing the policy effectively excluded African Americans.[46]

Typically challenges to such zoning must establish there was an intent to exclude based on race. Because it is nearly impossible to prove a racially motivated intent in courts, local zoning ordinances have been largely immune to challenges over their exclusionary effects.

---

[46] *Arlington Heights v. Metropolitan Housing Corp.*, 429 U.S. 252 (1977).

Land use policies that limit housing options to sprawling McMansions have been challenged for being racially exclusionary.

Look Photograph/Beateworks/Encyclopedia/Corbis

National Snow and Ice Data Center/Photo Researchers, Inc.

Population Density in the United States. Bright spots represent densely populated areas. Darkest regions are unpopulated.

The Enduring Role of Pro-Growth Forces in Local Politics

Whatever the exclusionary effects of zoning might be, much contemporary zoning is motivated by demands to regulate the pace and character of residential development rather than by intentional racism. Local regulations on land use emerge from local political processes that may pit pro-growth forces against "slow-growth" forces worried about traffic, sprawl, loss of open space, and rapid housing construction that outpaces the supply of schools and parks.

The Growth Machine

Popular concern about the consequences of suburbanization and sprawl has been growing

and may be greater now than in previous decades. One description of the internal politics of American cities suggests that political conflict centers on two groups who have rival visions about land use. Although the following portrait is overly simplistic, it is a decent characterization of the internal group politics of many rapidly developing suburban areas.[47] One key group that is active in local politics is made up of people who expect to profit from buying, selling, and developing land. Their orientation to land is based on how land can be improved and sold. This pro-development coalition might include not only developers and builders but also the owners of local businesses (e.g., banks, car dealers, or locally owned

[47] The following draws ideas from John Logan and Harvey Molotch, *The Political Economy of Place* (Berkeley, CA: University of California Press, 1987).

newspapers) who stand to grow their businesses if local population growth increases.

In most cities, over most of the 20th century, pro-growth forces have typically held the upper hand. Because land use rules directly affect their livelihoods, they have much more incentive than others to stay organized and engaged in politics. Furthermore, they have used a compelling nonpartisan political message that often enjoys widespread public support: "Growth brings jobs, so it's good for everyone." In places where the pace of development is slow (or where growth is lagging or absent), this message may be particularly resonant. Given the historic political success of this pro-growth group, the coalitions running many American cities have been referred to as "**growth machines**" that exist largely to facilitate development[48] rather than provide much in the way of services and amenities. Because the public often accepts that growth is good, pro-development policies are expected to generate little political controversy.[49] There is evidence that development generates significantly less community controversy in slower-growing places and in places with more unemployment.[50]

The Rise of Slow-Growth Politics

A second, rival group consists of residents whose orientation to a place is based not on the profit potential of their land but on the value they receive from living in their city. National surveys show that most suburban residents favor limits on local growth.[51] Surveys also show that perceptions of rapid growth are associated with negative attitudes about growth.[52] Many people perceive population growth and the intensification of land use as threats to their neighborhoods. Perceptions of declining local quality of life, increased traffic, or crowded schools are associated with support for slowing the pace of development.[53] People dissatisfied with growth organize to elect representatives who are committed to using zoning tools to restrict development. These people may be sensitive to their quality of life and to the bonds they have with friends and neighbors. They grow fond of amenities near their homes, such as wetlands, orange groves, open hillsides, woodlands, and farms.

Although the market model of city competition assumes dissatisfied residents might move away as amenities disappear or as they perceive their neighborhoods to deteriorate, exit is an extreme option for most people dissatisfied with trends in their community. Rather than exit, people join neighborhood associations to defend their neighborhood from traffic and crowding. Rapid residential development might also require tax increases to build more roads and schools and lead some residents to join anti-tax groups. Development that moves into sensitive scenic areas may also rally local environmentalists. Most neighborhood associations organize as a result of residents' concerns about development.[54]

At some point, in some places, these and other actors might coalesce to challenge the traditional pro-growth forces in a city and demand greater regulation of land use. The political coalition challenging the growth machine has alternately been referred to as favoring slow growth, growth control, smart growth, or managed growth. Slow-growth

[48] Harvey Molotch, "The City as a Growth Machine," *American Journal of Sociology* (1976).

[49] Paul Peterson, *City Limits* (Chicago: University of Chicago Press, 1981).

[50] Todd Donovan, "Community Controversy and Adoption of Local Economic Development Policies," *Social Science Quarterly* 74(1995):386.

[51] Mark Baldassare and Georgjeanna Wilson, "Changing Sources of Suburban Support for Local Growth Controls," *Urban Studies* 33(1996):459–71.

[52] Roland Anglin, "Diminishing Utility: The Effect of Citizen Preferences for Local Growth," *Urban Affairs Quarterly* 25(1990):684–96.

[53] Mark Baldassare, "Predicting Local Concern about Growth: The Roots of Citizen Discontent," *Journal of Urban Affairs* 6(1985):39–49; Scott Bollens, "Constituents for Regionalism: Approaches to Growth Management," *Urban Affairs Quarterly* 26(1990):46–67.

[54] John Logan and Gordana Rabrenovic, "Neighborhood Associations: Their Issues, Their Allies and Their Opponents," *Urban Affairs Quarterly* 26(1990):68–94.

politicians are more likely to emerge in places with rapid growth and in cities that use district elections (where it might be easier to organize neighborhoods).[55] Political mobilization against development in California was found to be higher in cities that had higher proportions of white-collar residents and a history of local initiative use. Such places also adopted the most restrictive controls on growth.[56] Prior to the 1970s, it was rare to see challenges to the pro-development policies of U.S. cities. However, during the 1970s, rapid residential growth precipitated successful challenges to pro-growth forces in places such as Palo Alto, Santa Barbara, and Petaluma, California (the latter is a suburb of San Francisco); Ann Arbor, Michigan; Boulder, Colorado; Ramapo, New York; and Boca Raton, Florida. By the mid-1970s, over 400 communities had adopted some forms of growth controls.[57]

By winning council seats, dislodging sitting council members, or using ballot initiatives, anti-development forces in many cities were able to pass policies that limited housing construction. These include ceilings on population growth and moratoriums on new building permits, water connections, or sewer hookups. Other growth control policies include requirements for environmental impact statements, requiring a public vote to approve new construction, zoning to preserve open space, limits on how many homes could be built per year, and requiring that developers build infrastructure and grant land to the public. By the 1980s, growth control policies were adopted by hundreds of additional jurisdictions in states, including California, Colorado, Florida, New Jersey, and New York. Several states adopted statewide growth management plans that attempted to regulate where suburban growth could occur.[58]

Slow-growth forces had their earliest influence in university communities and relatively affluent places where threats to scenic resources (e.g., beaches, coastal access, and mountainsides) mobilized residents against local development. As the public mood in more communities became less supportive of growth, the range of cities adopting growth controls expanded. Support for growth control policies did not appear to have a clear ideological or partisan color[59] nor were growth control policies more prevalent among higher-income, higher-social-status suburbs.[60] They were more likely to be found in middle-class suburban cities with higher proportions of residents who were white-collar professionals. Although born out of disaffection with growth, there may be a fairly long lag between when a city experiences rapid growth and when citizens finally mobilize against development.[61] This means that the public's reaction to the potential ill effects of growth, such as crowding and traffic, likely occurs after a place has already experienced substantial development.

Do Growth Controls Work?

Critics of growth controls argue that they restrict the supply of housing in the face of strong demand and thus increase the price of

---

[55] Mark Schneider and Paul Teske, "The Anti-Growth Entrepreneur: Challenging the Equilibrium of the Growth Machine," *Journal of Politics* 55(1993):720–36.

[56] Todd Donovan and Max Neiman, "Citizen Mobilization and the Adoption of Local Growth Control," *Western Political Quarterly* (1992):651–75.

[57] D. Dowall, *Suburban Squeeze* (Berkeley, CA: University of California Press, 1984).

[58] Scott Bollens, "State Growth Management Acts: Intergovernmental Frameworks and Policy Objectives," *Journal of the American Planning Association* 58(1992):454.

[59] Max Neiman and Mark Gottinder, "Characteristics of Support for Local Growth Control," *Urban Affairs Quarterly* (1981).

[60] Marc Baldassare and William Protash, "Growth Controls, Population Growth and Community Satisfaction," *American Sociological Review* 47(1982):339–46.

[61] Todd Donovan and Max Neiman, "Community Social Status, Suburban Growth and Restrictions on Residential Development," *Urban Affairs Quarterly* 28(1992):323–36. Another study found no relationship between growth rates and the adoption of regulations on development. John Logan and Min Zhou, "The Adoption of Growth Controls in Suburban Communities," *Social Science Quarterly* 71(1990):118–29.

housing. Others claim that growth controls are an "environmental protection hustle" that defends privileged homeowners[62] and reflects attempts by homeowner "cartels" to create housing scarcity in order to increase home values.[63] Some studies have found that restrictive local zoning led to less housing density and less multifamily housing. Economists point out that the cumulative effects of certain policies, such as zoning for low-density housing, requiring environmental impact statements, and requiring developers to pay infrastructure costs and fees for school construction, increase the cost of homes—but this effect may be limited to California and some eastern cities.[64] One California city requires fees of $45,000 per each new home. Courts generally require that **impact fees** be set to be roughly proportional to the impact that new development creates, and that there is some "essential nexus" of a relationship between the fee and how it is spent. School impact fees are thus spent on schools, and transportation fees on roads and transit.

Economists note that there may also be benefits to land use regulations that are built into higher home prices.[65] It is hard to isolate the effect of regulations on housing prices, as growth controls are common in areas that are quite desirable to live. San Diego and Cleveland, for example, have about the same amount of land available per household. San Diego has extensive land use regulations compared to Cleveland, and land and homes are much more expensive in San Diego.[66] San Diego's housing may be much more expensive as a result of regulations or the fact that there is greater demand to live near the warm Pacific Coast beaches than the frigid shores of Lake Erie. San Diego's regulations may also reflect greater political pressure to preserve highly valued scenic amenities. Housing costs in San Diego may also be driven up by people who value the scenic areas that growth regulations have preserved.

Land use regulations can have at least two major economic effects: they can attempt to restrict housing growth (supply) or they can attempt to make new growth pay for its true costs (on infrastructure, schools, parks, and the local environment). There is no clear evidence that local growth controls actually slow growth,[67] but there is evidence that growth controls may help cities better manage their finances.[68] This suggests these policies may be aiming more for making growth pay its own way than actually stopping new growth. One study found growth restrictions associated with faster population growth because many regulations don't actually limit housing supply, and those that do may trigger building booms before they take effect.[69] Local population ceilings and caps on housing permits have also been easily circumvented in many places.[70]

---

[62] Bernard Freiden, *The Environmental Protection Hustle* (Cambridge, MA: MIT Press, 1979).

[63] R. Ellickson, "Suburban Growth Controls: An Economic and Legal Analysis," *Yale Law Review* 86(1977):389–511.

[64] Edward Glaeser and Joseph Gyourko, "The Impact of Zoning on Housing Affordability," National Bureau of Economic Research Working Paper no. 8835 (New York: NBER, 2002).

[65] Glaeser and Gyourko, "The Impact of Zoning on Housing Affordability"; Henry O. Pallakowski and Susan Wachter, "Private Markets, Public Decisions: An Assessment of Local Land Use Controls for the 1990s," *Land Economics* 66(1990):315–24; J. Black and J. Hoblen, "Land Price Inflation and Affordable Housing," *Urban Geography* 6(1985):27–47; and Anne B. Shlay and Peter Rossi, "Keeping Up the Neighborhood: Estimating the Net Effects of Zoning," *American Sociological Review* 46(1981):703–19.

[66] Glaeser and Gyourko, "The Impact of Zoning on Housing Affordability," 23.

[67] John Logan and Min Zhou, "Do Suburban Growth Controls Control Growth?" *American Sociological Review* 54(1989):461–71; and John Landis, "Do Growth Controls Work? A New Assessment," *Journal of the American Planning Association* 58(1992):489.

[68] Landis, "Do Growth Controls Work?" 502.

[69] Todd Donovan and Max Neiman, "Local Growth Controls and Changes in Community Characteristics," *Social Science Quarterly* 76(1995):780.

[70] Landis, "Do Growth Controls Work?" 502.

INSTITUTIONS MATTER

REASONS FOR SPRAWL

The pace of growth of developed land in American metropolitan areas expands much faster than population growth. Why? (1) Federal, state, and local policies have subsidized the expansion of housing into undeveloped, raw land; (2) Americans like single-family homes with big backyards; (3) because families are getting smaller and there are fewer people per housing unit, we are building more homes per person than ever before; and (4) we also build much bigger homes than before.

Table 12.5 lists North American (U.S. and Canadian) metropolitan regions in terms of one indicator of **sprawl:** the number of people per square mile of developed land. Fewer people per square mile

Table 12.5

North America's 10 Least Densely Population Metropolitan Regions

Population per Square Kilometer	
Nashville, TN	457
Oklahoma City, OK	468
Mobile, AL	507
Knoxville, TN	537
Little Rock, AR	592
Tulsa, OK	602
Birmingham, AL	602
Kansas City, MO-KS	646
Greensville, SC	647
Youngstown, OH	834

North America's 10 Most Densely Population Metropolitan Regions

Toronto, Ont.	2469
Los Angeles, CA	2240
Miami, FL	2096
New York City - North New Jersey	2088
Montreal, Queb.	2061
Honolulu, HI	1761
Chicago, IL - Gary, IN	1655
San Francisco - Oakland, CA	1603
Ottawa, Ont. - Hull, Queb.	1572
Ft. Lauderdale, FL	1461

Source: Eran Razin and Mark Rosentraub, "Are Fragmentation and Sprawl Linked?" *Urban Affairs Quarterly* 35(2000):830.

suggests that single-family homes are being built on large lots. The least dense places are U.S. regions that experienced much of their development after the rise of modern freeway-oriented suburbs. The list of places with the greatest population densities includes older U.S. regions where substantial development took place before the 1950s and regions in states with longer-standing state growth management laws (Hawaii and Florida). Density in Honolulu, Miami, and Ft. Lauderdale may have as much to do with state rules as physical geography, however. The effect of land use rules can be seen in the number of Canadian metropolitan regions that have higher population density. These Canadian regions have room to sprawl, but provincial governments in Canada have more control of land use than municipal governments. Provincial or state-level planning may thus constrain some sprawl.

Table 12.6 provides another illustration of sprawl at the state level by ranking states in terms of growth in land used for development and the decline in population density. All these measures show that land use in the American South is growing fastest and that new growth there is more spread out than before.

There may be a positive side of sprawl, however. Sprawl can represent access to land that is cheaper to build and thus access to lower-cost housing. Low-density construction can mean more privacy than what exists in many cities. Lower-cost housing may also provide more opportunities for the less affluent to find quality housing. In this sense, there is something democratic and egalitarian about sprawl,[1] but it comes at a price. Access to cheap land requires freeways that must be paid for. New suburbs require new schools, roads, parks, and traffic lights and costly extensions of water mains and sewers. Developers won't usually pay for this unless rules force them to, but if they are forced to internalize the costs of sprawl, their new homes are less affordable.

Notes
1. Robert Bruegmann, *Sprawl: A Compact History* (Chicago: University of Chicago Press, 2005).

Table 12.6

The Most Rapidly Sprawling States with the Greatest Sprawl from 1982 to 1997

	Increase in	Decrease in
	Urban Land	**Population Density**
Georgia	+75%	−20%
North Carolina	+70%	−20%
Tennessee	+68%	−29%
New Hampshire	+66%	−28%
West Virginia	+65%	−45%
New Mexico	+64%	−17%
Florida	+63%	−7%
South Carolina	+63%	−25%
National average	+39%	−13%

Source: Jerry Anthony, "Do State Growth Management Regulations Reduce Sprawl?" *Urban Affairs Review* 39(2004):376-97.

Are We Better Off Without Zoning?

Advocates of the private market argue that land use regulations are more trouble than they are worth. Local, regional, and state rules limit how land can be used and require the "heavy hand" of government in planning. Market forces, they argue, will lead to more competition and the construction of what people really want, at a lower price.[71] If it were not for zoning and land use rules, low-cost mobile homes and high-density apartments might be more common in affluent areas. If land has scenic value, people will pay more to live there and free up space for others elsewhere. Taken further, the antiregulation argument might allow people to run businesses from their homes to help cover housing costs. In many places, zoning prevents this. Anti-zoning critics point to the relatively unregulated land markets of Houston, Texas, as a model. In Houston, commercial businesses, like gas stations and stores, are allowed to locate next to residences; and Houston has some of the nation's cheapest housing. Zoning, they might add, can be unfair, and if it allows only low-density housing, it can encourage sprawl.

Defenders of land use regulations argue that the private market fails to really deal with the true costs of growth and development. If there were no rules, they argue, wetlands would be paved and beaches would be closed off; and if developers built parks, they would have no incentives to open them to the public. There would be no guarantee that quiet residential neighborhoods would be spared the pressure of busy shops, crowded apartments, or access to adequate parking. A private market, furthermore, cannot plan ahead for the consequences of growth, including sprawl, traffic, and the need for school construction. Cities, furthermore, are in competition with each other. If a city opens itself up to any sort of development, residential property values might drop, residents may exit, and tax revenues decline. Zoning, they argue, may have costs, but it also has more in the way of benefits.

Regardless of who is correct in this argument, advocates of land use controls have the upper hand, as most people appear to support regulations on what can be built where,[72] and zoning is well established as a power of local governments.

The Local Land Use Dilemma

Rather than asking if zoning is good or bad, it might be better to consider which levels of government are best suited to deal with land use questions.

As we have illustrated in this chapter, land use policy is largely controlled by county and city governments, and land use policy can reflect the competition between localities. When considered at the local level, zoning and various land use regulations can be quite effective in helping a city's fiscal bottom line: Excluding multifamily units might lower service pressures on schools, encouraging large-lot single-family homes might bring in more tax revenues than apartments, and rules making developers "pay as they go" can keep taxes down. Without aggressive land use controls, a city may shoot itself in the foot.

But cities usually exist in a larger region, and many of the problems that citizens have to deal with—traffic, pollution, habitat loss, loss of open space, gross disparities in the quality of local schools, the segregation of the poor, and long distances between where people live and work—are problems of regional significance. These regional problems cannot be solved with local control of land use, and local control of land use might act to make some problems—such as segregation of the poor and separation of housing from employment—worse.

---

[71] William Fischel, *The Economics of Zoning Laws: A Property Rights Approach to American Land Use Controls* (Johns Hopkins University Press, 1985); B. Frieden, *The Environmental Hustle* (Cambridge, MA: MIT Press, 1979).

[72] Baldassare and Wilson, "Changing Sources."

State and Regional Planning Alternatives

Some states and regions have adopted policies that change their local government's control over land use. As of 2004, several states had adopted laws that mandate or place strong pressures on local governments to plan for growth with an eye toward some long-term comprehensive plan. Although many states have established commissions to study sprawl or enhanced incentives for developers to preserve open space, few actually mandate that local land use plans conform with regional or state goals, such as containing sprawl.

State Growth Management Laws

States with mandatory, comprehensive growth laws may require that local governments define fixed **urban growth areas** (UGAs) to concentrate development while also requiring that local land use plans be approved by a regional or state authority. Some require the state approve major changes in local zoning plans. Florida's law prohibits local governments from issuing building permits unless adequate public services (transportation, water, sewer, and parks) are available. Washington requires that counties adopt comprehensive plans with UGAs that preserve rural areas. Oregon's law also restricts development to areas inside UGAs.

There is evidence that Florida's state growth management plan slowed development in targeted areas.[73] Population density, an indicator of sprawl, declined in Florida by 7 percent and Oregon by 2 percent, much lower rates than the national average during a period of rapid housing growth; and population density increased under Washington's growth management law.[74]

---

[73] Richard Feiock, "The Political Economy of Growth Management," *American Politics Quarterly* 22(1994):208–20.
[74] Jerry Anthony, "Do State Growth Management Regulations Reduce Sprawl?" *Urban Affairs Review* 39(2004): 376–97.

Regional Revenue Sharing

Local control of land use and local control of tax revenues combine to create incentives for places to attract businesses or residents who produce a high tax yield. It also means that some cities enjoy a large share of the benefits of development without having to pay for the costs. As an extreme example, tens of thousands of people commute to jobs in cities like Vernon, Industry, and Commerce in southern California. Those cities generate huge tax revenues, but other cities with fewer resources have to provide the parks, libraries, neighborhoods, and schools for the people who work in tax-rich commercial cities.

Some regions have implemented regional tax base sharing to reduce competition among cities for development and to create a fairer distribution of tax benefits. The idea is most advanced in the Twin Cities region of Minnesota, where 60 percent of the tax base created by new commercial properties is taxed by the city it locates in, whereas the other 40 percent is placed in a pool that is shared by all communities. Since 1975, this tax base sharing has led to a large decrease in the disparities in tax bases across cities in the region. There are variants of this policy in the Rochester, New York; Dayton Ohio; and Hackensack, New Jersey regions.

Competition for Local Economic Development

Much of the discussion thus far centers on the politics surrounding residential development. We have shown that zoning and other land use policies may have effects on how a city develops and on who lives where.

Cities have another set of tools they use in the competition to attract business and industry, which we refer to broadly as economic development policies. Although some cities may actively use zoning and land use regulations to shape or limit residential development, nearly all make active use of economic development policy to attract businesses and firms. Many cities do both—they regulate residential growth while promoting economic development that brings jobs and tax revenues. One study found that most cities that make active use of residential growth controls also had moderate to active use of economic development policies at the same time. State governments are also active in working to attract business to their state, often partnering with cities and counties to do so.

States and cities compete against each other to attract businesses that might add a positive contribution to local revenues and bring local jobs. Sometimes, this competition is highly visible, for example, when a giant manufacturer like Saturn, Toyota, Intel, or Boeing announces that it is going to move thousands of jobs and billions of dollars in investment to a new location. These firms entertain competing offers from communities across the nation—offers that might include tax breaks, discounted utility service, subsidies for roads and other infrastructure, and worker training programs.

The Logic of State and Local Economic Development Policy

At some point, the location decisions of any business involve an assessment of costs: How much does it cost, say, to locate in Chicago, Dallas, or Seattle? The logic behind state and local economic development policies is to try to lower a firm's cost of locating in a particular place, thus making that place more attractive than rival locations.

There are many factors that might go into a firm's decision to move to a particular part of the country. These include climate, easy access to the people who buy their product, access to raw materials, access to a particular labor pool, transportation, availability of buildings and land, and many other factors. The decision about where to locate inside a particular region might be based on a different set of factors: the cost of property, taxes,

construction, room for expansion, and many other things.[75] Managers might also consider quality-of-life issues. Many things associated with location can affect a firm's cost of production (or what economists call the supply side of what drives their behavior). Some of the things associated with the cost of production, such as land prices, tax rates, the costs of buildings, the price of utilities, and even the cost of training workers, might be affected by state and local economic development policies. The logic of many state and local economic development policies, then, is to offer a firm an attractive mix of things that makes it cheaper (or more profitable) to locate in one place versus another.[76]

How Does It Work?

Competition to recruit and retain sports franchises and car manufacturers represents some of the most visible examples of the economic development policy game. By threatening, either subtly or explicitly, to move a team or a plant from one place to another or by dangling thousands of new manufacturing jobs in front of different communities, these businesses hope to extract something from a host city. A state or local government is motivated to pay something to attract or retain the business if it knows the business has real options about where to locate or if it values what the business contributes to the local economy.

For example, as much as New York officials might want to think George Steinbrenner could never take his Yankees baseball team out of New York City or the Empire State, he has a credible threat of exit. The current Los Angeles Dodgers and San Francisco Giants baseball teams moved away from New York in the 1950s. Both "New York" football teams, the Giants and the Jets, now play in New Jersey. Given this context, and Steinbrenner's threat

---

[75] Peter Eisinger, *The Rise of the Entrepreneurial State: State and Local Economic Development Policies* (Madison, WI: University of Wisconsin Press, 1988), p. 221.

[76] Eisinger, *The Rise of the Entrepreneurial State.*

State and local governments in Tennessee competed against other regions by providing GM with incentives to locate the Saturn assembly plant in Spring Hill. Saturn employed about 4,000 workers at the plant when GM put it on "standby" after emerging from bankruptcy in 2009.

of exit, New York officials opted to pay over $300 million in 2005 to help Steinbrenner to build a new Yankee Stadium in New York.[77]

Cities may work together with their county and state governments to craft a list of incentives to attract (or retain) a business, particularly with high-profile cases like sports teams and huge manufacturing plants. Although the Yankees or an automobile plant are some of the highest-profile cases in which communities compete for investment, this competition extends to smaller cities as well. Many cities, both large and small, have offices staffed with experts whose jobs are to attract business to the community. Suburban cities compete for economic development, as do rural places and big cities.

A survey of all U.S. cities with a population between 10,000 and 250,000 asked city planners about 64 different "development tactics" that places might use to attract and retain private investment. One striking finding was that only 13 of 938 cities reported doing nothing to attract economic development. On average, these small to midsized cities used about 18 different economic development policies. The most common included efforts at improving city infrastructure (78 percent of cities reported they improved their water, sewer, parking, and streets for businesses), promotional activities (79 percent reported advertising the community to prospective new businesses), land management (62 percent reported such activities as consolidating lots, condemning or acquiring land, or leasing or donating land to developers), and offering financial

[77] Allen Barra, "Stadium Cheating, Wild Pitch: Why Does George Steinbrenner Want to Tear Down the House That Ruth Built," *Village Voice* 9 May 2005.

incentives (52 percent reported using policies such as issuing tax-exempt bonds, giving cash contributions to projects, or deferring tax payments on projects).[78] Local governments can also issue industrial development revenue bonds to pay the cost of new buildings, industrial parks, and other facilities that might attract businesses.

Who Uses Local Economic Development Policies?

Not all cities are aggressively seeking economic development, but many do. Some places try to offer more to businesses than other places care to or need to. Several studies have found that cities with less affluent residents and higher poverty levels offer businesses more incentives to locate, probably because officials feel keen pressure to attract jobs to such cities. There is also evidence that places with greater fiscal stress tend to be most likely to offer businesses incentives to locate in their community, and newer suburban residential cities are less likely to.[79] It seems that cities most in need of extra tax revenues and jobs that might come with economic development give away the most cash to try to get it.[80] Competition also increases how much cities offer to attract development. Some cities appear to be locked in a sort of economic development policy arms race: A city offers more to attract firms when it is surrounded by other cities that are also active in offering incentives to business.[81]

Effects of Local Economic Development Policies

This raises two fundamental questions: Do these policies work to bring businesses and jobs to the cities that offer incentives, and do public giveaways to businesses generate more gains for the city than what they cost it? There is no easy answer to either question. There are success stories about state and local giveaways generating substantial benefits. In early 2006, the Korean manufacturer Hyundai was searching for a place in the southern United States to locate a new American assembly plant to build its Kia line of cars. Kia was reported to have offers from Meridian, Mississippi; Chattanooga, Tennessee; Decatur, Alabama; Aiken, South Carolina; and Hopkinsville, Kentucky, before settling on West Point, Georgia.[82] The Kia automobile plant is estimated to involve a $1.2 billion investment and the creation of 5,000 to 10,000 new jobs. If it stays in operation for several years, the state's investment is likely to be returned in the form of new jobs, new tax revenues generated by the facility, and taxes from well-paid workers. But there are also many attempts that yield questionable gains, particularly when a city fights to retain an existing business. There is substantial debate about whether concessions paid to retain sports franchises can ever pay for themselves.[83]

---

[78] Arnold Fleishman, Gary P. Green, and Tsz Man Kwong, "What's a City to Do? Explaining Differences in Local Economic Development Policies," *Western Political Quarterly* (1992):678–99.

[79] Todd Donovan, Max Neiman, and Susan Brumbaugh, "Two Dimensions of Local Growth Strategies," in Mark Baldassare, ed., *Studies in Community Sociology 4* (JJAI Press, 1992), pp. 153–69.

[80] Irene S. Rubin and Herbert J. Rubin, "Economic Development Incentives: The Poor (Cities) Pay More," *Urban Affairs Quarterly* 23(1987):37–62.

[81] Fleishmann, Green, and Kwong, "What's a City to Do?" See also Ann O'M. Bowman, "Competition for Economic Development among Southeastern Cities," *Urban Affairs Quarterly* 23(1988):511–27.

[82] Walter Woods, "Ga. Reported Front Runner for Kia Plant," *Atlanta Journal-Constitution* 27 February 2006.

[83] Charles C. Euchner, *Playing the Field: Why Sports Teams Move and Cities Fight to Keep Them* (Baltimore, MD: Johns Hopkins University Press, 1994).

There are also reasons to expect only modest effects of policies that lower the location costs of businesses. Things that local governments can actually affect are not the primary factors affecting a business's location decision because there are larger factors (climate, the local labor pool, and access to markets) that are largely beyond the control of state and local governments. Lower state-level taxation may attract more private investment, but if states cut taxes too low, they risk cutting public services (e.g., schools, roads, and public safety) that make the state attractive.[84] At the local level, there is evidence that giveaways to businesses will attract new investment and bring in new employers, but their new jobs don't go to residents of the city hosting the business.[85] It is difficult for the city paying to attract a business to force that business to hire people from the host city, particularly in a metropolitan region with many other cities nearby.

The worst-case scenario for the effects of competition for economic development is that it may create a sort of arms race, or a "beggar thy neighbor" race to the bottom, where local governments compete against each other and give away so much that they have little to show for it in the end. Consider the situation when a firm is certain to locate in a specific region. Regardless of whether cities in the region were in competition, one will get the firm. If there is no competition, a city might get the firm without having to give up much in subsidies and tax breaks. But if there is fierce competition, one city will get the firm but at a higher cost in incentives to the business. The business is better off with this sort of competition and maybe the city that wins the competition is also, but the region may be worse off. If the firm was going to locate there anyway, cities bid against each other to lower the public benefits of having the business. **Regional revenue-sharing** plans (discussed above) are attempts to allow all cities in the region to share in the benefits of business location and mute cutthroat competition among neighboring cities.

The Consequences of Metropolitan Fragmentation

By now, it should be clear that the fragmentation of U.S. metropolitan regions has a great effect on what cities do. Local control of land use and local tax powers create incentives for cities to compete. They utilize land use controls in attempts to affect who lives where, and they utilize economic development policies to try to affect which firms locate where.

Some argue that it is a good thing to have several dozen independent cities in the same area, locked into this sort of competition. To them, more fragmentation means residents and businesses have more location choices, which increases competition between places to keep them happy. Places compete because of the threat of exit or because residents in fragmented regions might know if someone else in the area is getting a better deal on services and thus pressure city hall for a similar deal.[86] One net result of this competition is supposed to be **efficiency gains**. But efficiency is a hard thing to define when talking about the places where people live and their reasons for living there. One benchmark for efficiency is the size of local government, measured in terms of municipal spending per resident. Cities in places with more competition—that is, with more surrounding suburbs and municipalities—spend less.[87] Competition

[84] Eisinger, *The Rise of the Entrepreneurial State*, p. 220.

[85] Richard Feiock, "The Effects of Economic Development Policy on Local Economic Development," *American Journal of Political Science* 35(1991):643–55.

[86] Roger Parks and Elinor Ostrum, "Complex Models of Urban Service Delivery Systems," *Urban Policy Analysis*.

[87] Mark Schneider, "Inter-Municipal Competition, Budget-Maximizing Bureaucrats, and the Level of Suburban Competition," *American Journal of Political Science* 33(3) (1989):612.

might make cities less likely to provide a wide range of services or to provide services at less cost than it would be otherwise.

The trade-off for these efficiency gains may be **intermunicipal inequality**. Suburbanization since the 1950s corresponded with a growing gap in income inequality between the U.S. central cities and their suburbs. A study of 55 metropolitan areas found suburbs growing wealthier, with inequality greater in regions having more reliance on local property taxes to pay for services. Local dependence on property taxes may increase the pressure on a city to exclude less-affluent residents (in order to boost the tax base) and thus increase income inequality in the region. A substantial minority presence in a region also corresponds with growing inequality, suggesting that the presence of racial minorities leads suburbs to adopt exclusionary land use policies.[88] Fragmentation is also associated with more sprawl.[89]

In addition to the efficiency and inequality consequences, fragmentation of metro areas may make it quite difficult for people to understand who is responsible for the services they receive (or don't receive). People living in areas where cities, counties, and special districts are all providing different services across traditional city boundaries find it difficult to identify who provides what.[90] This may make them less likely to be engaged with local politics. People may have stronger psychological attachments to a single political jurisdiction that provides a consolidated package of services— a traditional city—than they have to a place that receives services from several different types of local governments.[91]

Isolation of the Poor in Major U.S. Cities

For decades, growth in U.S. metropolitan regions has been defined by a patchwork of competition and policies that exclude the poor from sharing in the fruits of economic prosperity.[92] Some suggest that fragmented metropolitan regions are designed to ensure that resources are separated from needs.[93] The major U.S. cities, and many of its poorer suburbs, face a dilemma. Decades of incorporation leave large central cities, such as Los Angeles, Detroit, New York, Chicago, and Milwaukee, as well as older suburbs surrounded by neighboring communities that are rich in resources and in their tax base. Suburbs are by no means universally affluent. Many older, "inner-ring" suburbs closest to the center city have high poverty rates. Residents from newer suburbs, however, may enjoy suburban affluence and the amenities of their neighboring large city and may even work there, but they don't pay taxes as full-time city residents do. A history of racial segregation, federal subsidies, and rigid zoning laws in newer suburbs also leaves the older communities with a greater share of the region's poor residents— residents who have greater needs for public services. But metropolitan fragmentation

[88] John R. Logan and Mark Schneider, "Governmental Organization and City/Suburb Income Inequality, 1960–1970," *Urban Affairs Quarterly* 17(1982):303–18.

[89] E. Razin and M. Rosentraub, "Are Fragmentation and Sprawl Interlinked? North American Evidence," *Urban Affairs Review* 35(2000):821.

[90] William E. Lyons, David Lowery, and Ruth Hoogland DeHoog, "Institutional-Induced Attribution Errors: Their Composition and Impact of Citizen Satisfaction with Local Governmental Services," *American Politics Quarterly* 18(1990):169–96.

[91] David Lowery, William Lyons, and Ruth Hoogland DeHoog, "Citizenship and Community Attachment in the Empowered Locality," *Urban Affairs Quarterly* 28(1992):69–103.

[92] Downs, "The Real Problem with Suburban Anti-Growth Policies."

[93] Max Neiman, "Social Stratification and Governmental Inequality," *American Political Science Review* 53(1976): 474–93; Richard Child Hill, "Separate and Unequal: Governmental Inequality in the Metropolis," *American Political Science Review* 68(1974):1557–86.

means that many businesses and industries generating tax revenues are outside the traditional city's reach.

Big central cities are not the only losers in the competition among local governments. Suburban cities where the less affluent do reside spend more per person to serve their populations, but they have less valuable property to tax. This means people in poor suburbs have to pay much more in taxes per dollar value of property. Poor suburbs spend more per person than rich suburbs on health, hospitals, and public housing but less per person on police, fire, parks, and sanitation. They are also more heavily in debt.[94] With lots of valuable property, rich places generate more tax revenues per dollar value of property and thus can tax property at a lower rate. Wealthy suburbs can also provide their residents more total services at a lower tax rate. Commenting on the unfairness effects of U.S. suburbanization, Anthony Downs, a prominent critic, notes that "the non-poor majority has rigged the game so that the poor are not represented" in the suburbs. "The non poor cannot vote against . . . their own exclusion. This unjust situation is not likely to change until non-poor suburbanites suffer an intense shortage of under skilled labor that costs them much more dearly than it does now."[95]

Regional and Metropolitan Government?

Fragmentation of political authority over taxes and land use is the norm in U.S. metropolitan regions. But there have been proposals to deal with the effects of fragmentation by having

cities and counties share some of their local powers with regional governments. Early in the 20th century, Progressive reformers advocated the consolidation of local governments to create more efficient administration and **economies of scale** in the delivery of services. The assumption behind metropolitan government was that it would be cheaper and more efficient to provide services such as fire protection, sanitation, or public transportation from a large, centralized bureaucracy than from several competing jurisdictions.[96]

However, research suggests that consolidation does not necessarily lead to increased efficiencies for many public services.[97] Competition, it seems, generally produces more efficiency than consolidation. With some things that governments do, such as regional mass transit and air quality management, regional governments may have distinct advantages, however. Problems of sprawl and income inequality may be less severe when government is consolidated.[98] "Efficiency" gains may arise in regions where places compete to provide local services, but people living in fragmented regions who supposedly experience efficient service provision (or less service) are not happier about their public services than people who live in areas with consolidated government.[99]

---

[94] Mark Schneider and John Logan, "Fiscal Implications of Class Segregation: Inequalities in the Distribution of Public Good and Services in Suburban Municipalities," *Urban Affairs Quarterly* 17(1981):23–36.

[95] Downs, "The Real Problem with Suburban Anti-Growth Policies," 29.

[96] Nelson Wikstrom and G. Ross Stephens, *Metropolitan Government and Governance: Theoretical Perspectives, Empirical Analysis, and the Future* (Oxford: Oxford University Press, 1999).

[97] Gordon Tullock, "Federalism and Problems of Scale," in G. Brennan, R. L. Matthews and B. Grewal, eds., *The Economics of Federalism* (Canberra: Australian National University Press, 1981); David Lowery, "Answering the Public Choice Challenge to Progressive Reform Institutions: A Neoprogressive Research Agenda," *Governance* 12(1999):29–56.

[98] David Rusk, *Cities without Suburbs*; Anthony Downs, *New Visions for Metropolitan America* (Washington, DC: Brookings Institution, 1994).

[99] William E. Lyons and David Lowery, "Governmental Fragmentation versus Consolidation: Five Public Choice Myths about How to Create Informed, Happy Citizens," *Public Administration Review* 49(1989):533–43.

Summary

Even with the rise of statewide land use rules and attempts at regionalism with programs such as revenue sharing and metropolitan government, it is unlikely that local control over land use and taxes will change substantially in the next decade. The concept of home rule—where cities and counties have substantial political control over their affairs—is firmly rooted in American political institutions. Nonetheless, population growth will continue to create pressure for the development of more land and for local control over who gets to build and what they get to build. This has consequences for who lives where. Population growth will likely create further pressure on some communities to regulate growth. Competition among places under the current institutional structures—fragmented authority over land use and local control over tax revenues—will continue to create places that are winners and losers: cities and towns for the wealthy, cities and towns for the middle class, and cities and towns for the less affluent.

If sprawl continues to elicit popular discontent, however, and if future development is associated with growing social inequalities between places, many states may face decisions in years to come about whether local control of land use and tax authority may have to be limited in some ways. These institutional arrangements are fundamentally important to who gets what from government.

Key Terms

Contracting for services	Incorporation	Sprawl
Economies of scale	Intermunicipal inequality	Suburb
Efficiency gains	Metropolitan areas	Urban growth areas
Eminent domain	Police powers	Village of Euclid v. Ambler Realty Company
General purpose local government	Regional revenue sharing	Zoning
Growth machine	Special districts	
Impact fees		

Discussion Questions

1. Explain the market model of local politics. How is this model effective and how is it unrealistic?
2. How are contemporary cities different than older, traditional ones? How does the definition of "city" continue to change?
3. What are the effects of the special districts created by the Lakewood Plan model?
4. What factors have contributed to the rise of suburban cities? How are racial/economic demographics affected?
5. What are the benefits and drawbacks of current zoning policies?

Suggested Readings

Bruegmann, Robert. 2005. *Sprawl: A Compact History.* Chicago: University of Chicago Press.

Burcell, Robert, Anthony Downs, and Sahan Mukherji. 2005. *Sprawl Costs.* Washington, DC: Island Press.

Burns, Nancy. 1994. *The Formation of American Local Governments: Private Values in Public Institutions.* Oxford: Oxford University Press.

Downs, Anthony. 2004. *Still Stuck in Traffic.* Washington, DC: Brookings Institution.

Garreau, Joel. 1991. *Edge Cities: Life on the New American Frontier.* New York: Anchor.

Judd, Dennis R. 2004. *City Politics: Private Power and Public Policy.* Upper Saddle River, NJ: Pearson Longman.

Kemmis, Daniel. 1990. *Community and the Politics of Place.* Norman, OK: University of Oklahoma Press.

Logan, John, and Harvey Molotch. 1987. *Urban Fortunes: The Political Economy of Place.* Berkeley, CA: University of California Press.

McGinnis, Michael, ed. 1999. *Polycentric Governance and Development: Readings from the Workshop in Political Theory and Policy Analysis.* Ann Arbor, MI: University of Michigan Press.

Rusk, David. 1993. *Cities without Suburbs.* Baltimore, MD: Woodrow Wilson Center Special Studies, Johns Hopkins University Press.

Turner, Margery Austin, and Lynette Rawlings. 2005. *Overcoming Concentrated Poverty and Isolation.* Washington, DC: Urban Institute.

Websites

AnthonyDowns.com (http://www.anthonydowns.com): According to his website, Downs is "the world's leading authority on real estate and urban affairs." A senior fellow at the Brookings Institution, Downs is probably the world's leading authority on suburban sprawl in the United States.

Land Use Law Center (http://www.law.pace.edu/landuse): The Land Use Law Center is "dedicated to fostering the development of sustainable communities in New York State."

Smart Growth (http://www.smartgrowth.org): A group challenging policies that facilitate sprawl. Dedicated to a range of housing options, walkable neighborhoods, mixed land uses, preservation of critical areas and open space, attractive communities, and "a sense of place."

Urban Futures (http://www.urbanfutures.org): A program of the conservative Reason Foundation devoted to providing market-oriented analysis of land use and economic development issues.

Urban Institute (http://www.urban.org): Think tank that conducts and publishes studies on urban issues, including housing issues and poverty in urban communities, gentrification, and homelessness.

13

Reuters

Morality Policy

BLOODY KANSAS AND THE POLITICS OF MORALITY POLICY

O n May 31, 2009, the quiet of a Sunday morning service at the Reformation Lutheran Church in Wichita, Kansas, was shattered when one of the church's ushers was shot in the head at point-blank range.[1] A domestic dispute? A robbery? No, this was a political assassination, the most recent incident in the long—and sometimes violent—history of morality politics in Kansas.

Although extreme, the murder by an antiabortion extremist of one of the few doctors still performing late-term abortions in the United States, Dr. George Tiller, was by no means the only time that the Sunflower State had seen "politics by other means" in moral battles over public policy. The state's very birth was defined by bloody battles among activists who, driven by moral concerns, had streamed into the state to battle one another over slavery. Less murderous battles have also been fought over deeply moral issues. For example, in 1881, Kansas became the first state to write the prohibition of alcohol into its constitution, following a period of violent destruction of saloons by Carrie Nation and others, and it was among the last states to repeal statewide prohibition—in 1948. For the past two decades, the state has been a major front in the policy debates over morality issues in education. Advocates have included points about basic principles, God, and religious scripture in their arguments about sex education, educational financing, charter schools, and especially the teaching of evolution. The state has been whip-sawed between conservative and moderate science education policies since 1999, when the elected state school board set policy that allowed for the teaching of creationism or intelligent design for the first time. The board has flipped back and forth at least twice in membership ideology—and science policy—since then.

There is irony in Kansas's location at the geographical center of the country. Throughout its history, the state has either been at one extreme end of the spectrum on these especially volatile issues or its residents have reflected both extremes nationally, resulting in pitched political battles within the state. Certainly, Kansas has not been at the center of every morality issue. Its gambling policies have developed quite like the average state in recent years, and same-sex marriage has not been prominent on its political agenda. But the state seems to have had more than its share of these fights. In particular, its abortion politics, which for decades centered on George Tiller and his Wichita clinic, have made the state stand out recently.

Although he was no policy advocate, that May morning in the church vestibule was not Tiller's first encounter with morality politics, and his experiences serve as a good example of how tough morality policy battles can be, especially in Kansas. Tellingly, his killer shot him in the head because, as he had since 1998 at the suggestion of the FBI, Tiller wore a Kevlar vest. He had been a national lightening rod for antiabortion activism for decades, the recipient of many threats—and more—of violence. As the owner-operator of the Women's Care Clinic in Wichita since 1975, only two years after *Roe v. Wade* had made the procedure legal nationwide, Tiller performed abortions regularly as part of his practice. Abortion opponents abhorred the procedure, claiming that, while perhaps legal for the moment, it violated their interpretation of mandates in the Christian Bible[2] and, as such, was immoral. Their policy goal is to seek government restrictions on abortion, but sometimes they also work to stop abortions one pregnant woman at a time. It was through this direct-action politics that Tiller found himself a target. In 1986, his clinic was bombed, and in 1993, he was shot in both arms by an activist who was also convicted of setting fires and committing acid attacks at nine abortion clinics in Oregon, California, Idaho, and Nevada. Almost continuously since the early 1990s, Operation Rescue, a national group dedicated to stopping abortions, has held a vigil outside his clinic. These actions were, in part, the impetus behind the national Freedom of Access to Clinics Act of 1994. Indeed, Operation Rescue actually moved its headquarters from California to Wichita in 1999 to be closer to the action at Tiller's clinic.

Tiller had also been involved with somewhat more conventional politics in his career. He was repeatedly charged with violating a Kansas law requiring another doctor's approval before performing an abortion, a law he challenged in federal court as being overly restrictive on a woman's right to privacy. In 2006 and 2008, opponents worked to slow down his operation by dusting off a rarely used 1887 Kansas law allowing for voters to petition for a grand jury investigation. Tiller's handling even became a major issue in furious election battles for Kansas attorney general. The politics of abortion policy in Kansas even turned from the deadly serious to the absurd at one point, when an activist sued a state legislator for assault when that lawmaker tried to rip his bug-mask off when the activist protested him wearing a cockroach costume. Clearly, morality politics—especially in Kansas—is anything but boring and routine.

AP Photo/Charlie Riedel AP Photo/Orlin Wagner

1 This vignette is based on information gathered from the following sources: John Hanna, "Abortion Foes: Shooting Could Silence Debate," *State Journal-Register (Springfield, IL)*, 2 June 2009, p. 3; John Hanna, "Lawmaker Faces Suit for Assault," *Lawrence (KS) Journal-World and News*, 19 June 2007, online edition; Robert Smith Bader, *Prohibition in Kansas: A History* (Lawrence, KS: University Press of Kansas, 1986); Peter Slevin, "Battle on Teaching Evolution Sharpens," *The Washington Post*, 14 March 2005; John Hanna, "Analysis: Abortion Politics Made Ground Slippery for Morrison," *Lawrence (KS) Journal-World and News*, 17 December 2007, online edition; Monica Davey, "Grand Juries Become Latest Abortion Battlefield," *The New York Times*, 17 June 2008, online edition; Anonymous, "Kansas Court Blocks Abortion Grand Jury," *USA Today*, 6 February 2008, online edition; John Hanna, "Abortion Legal Challenge Iffy with New Supreme Court," *The Bismarck (ND) Tribune*, 9 July 2007, online edition; Roxana Hegeman, "Kan. Abortion Foes Use 1887 Law against Clinics," *The Boston Globe*, 18 January 2008, online edition; Ron Sylvester and Dion Lefler, "Morrison: 15 Tiller Charges Meritless," *The Kansas City (MO) Star*, 28 June 2007, online edition.
2 Most antiabortion advocates in the United States are Christian, and therefore base their opposition to it on the Christian Bible. Certain adherents of other religions, particularly Islam, and philosophies also oppose abortion on moral grounds.

Introduction

In the final three chapters of this book, we bring together our discussion of state and local government politics and institutions by discussing the end goal of government—public policy. Policy is all about what government does, why it does it, and how it does it. Throughout this book, we have talked about many types of policy in various contexts, but in these chapters, we deal with three broad categories of policy in more depth, exploring how institutions affect them, how and why policy reforms occur in them, and how comparisons of different policies across the states and communities can help us understand politics and government better.

The story of morality politics in Kansas in the opening vignette for this chapter is obviously full of unusual political events. Political assassination—especially of nonpoliticians—is rare in American politics, and lawsuits against state legislators by insect-costumed activists are even rarer. Certain policies, however, such as same-sex marriage and abortion regulation, in addition to evolution and sex education in the public schools, and government regulation of pornography, alcohol, and gambling, have inspired extraordinary political acts in the American states and communities, both in recent years and throughout our history. Most standard theories of political behavior and policy making suggest that people act politically in ways that enhance their own well-being, especially their economic well-being. These **morality policies**, on the other hand, generate debate over the basic values that define our personal identities rather than debate over such tawdry and transient values as political or economic advantage. These are debates about what is fundamentally right and wrong rather than about who gets what. Because of the unique debate that morality policy stirs up, the politics surrounding it have been thought to be quite different than that surrounding more run-of-the-mill policy, such as transportation or criminal justice policy.[1]

In this chapter, we examine morality policies in the states and communities, trying to understand how the institutions of government deal with them, how reform comes about on them, and how and why they differ throughout the country. Morality policies are very much in the news these days, even though they are probably much less significant in your daily life than are the policies we will discuss in the following two chapters: policies about health care, social welfare, and education. Unlike these other types of policy, morality policies are classified by the politics they generate rather than by their subject matter. Because of the unique nature of the debate surrounding these issues, their politics have unique characteristics that political scientists are just beginning to understand.

In a broad context, the politics of morality policy are not much different than those of other types of policy. The institutions of American state and local government restrict the form that politics can take within them. Morality policies have important differences from those policies that these institutions are accustomed to handling, but these institutions go a long way toward channeling them into the typical patterns of policy making and politics for which these institutions were designed. Indeed, in the end, the characteristic patterns of issue evolution and reform that state and local government institutions encourage are followed even for these unique policies—at least for the most part.

What Is Morality Policy?

Even during these times of economic upheaval, we continue to hear much about morality in politics—"culture wars," "sin taxes," religious

---

[1]Christopher Z. Mooney, ed., "The Public Clash of Private Values: The Politics of Morality Policy," in *The Public Clash of Private Values: The Politics of Morality Policy* (New York: Chatham House, 2001).

leaders making pronouncements on such public issues as school curriculum, abortion, same-sex marriage, and the like. Some pundits even claimed that President George W. Bush was reelected in 2004 because voters liked his stance on "moral issues."[2] Although economic hardship seems to have pushed these issues off most voters' front burner these days,[3] they are still an important factor in politics around the country in many ways. Before we can analyze these politics, however, we must first understand what makes a policy a "morality policy."

A deep streak of morality has run through American policy debate since the Pilgrims landed at Plymouth Rock in 1620 with the goal of establishing an ideal commonwealth, a "city on a hill"[4] that would serve as a model of good government for the world. To be sure, the Pilgrims had many traditional, nonmorality policy goals (e.g., that government should treat its citizens fairly and provide for their common good), but always lurking in the political thought of the Pilgrims and their genetic and philosophical descendants was the idea that public policy ought to reflect the basic moral values of their Protestant Christianity.[5] In particular, they believed that public policy ought to outlaw—or at least discourage—"sin," certain violations of their basic religious principles or values.

Astute foreign observers of American politics have long noted the importance of religion and morality in U.S. political life, for good or ill. In the early 1800s, the French commentator Alexis de Tocqueville wrote that although "religion never intervenes directly in the government of American society . . . it should be considered the first of their political institutions." Later in that century, the British writer G. K. Chesterton wrote that the United States was a nation "with the soul of a church." In the 20th century, the Swedish sociologist Gunnar Myrdal argued that this country was the most "moralistic and moral[ly] conscious . . . branch of Western Civilization."[6] In short, this country has long been a "hellfire nation,"[7] where moral arguments regularly find their way into political discourse.

Even today, religion often factors into morality policy debate. Politicians of both parties regularly appeal to God and religion—especially the predominant Christian religion—in their political rhetoric. For example, a few years ago, former Illinois Governor Rod Blagojevich (a Democrat) claimed that his fight for health insurance for the poor was "Armageddon, and we are on the side of the Lord," at the same time that his Missouri counterpart, former Governor Matt Blunt (a Republican), stood in the pulpit of a church and called for more faith-based organizations

---

[2]This is the sort of analysis you read in the newspapers just after the election; for example in: Anonymous, "ELECTION 2004: Religious Vote Fuels Victory for GOP," *Atlanta Journal-Constitution*, 4 November 2004, p. A19. Social scientists have studied morality politics and voting in this and other elections, coming to a somewhat mixed bag of conclusions. Most scholars seem to refute the impact of morals voting in 2004; for example, see: Morris P. Fiorina, *Culture War? The Myth of a Polarized America* (New York: Pearson Longman, 2005); D. Sunshine Hillygus and Todd G. Shields, "Moral Issues and Voter Decision Making in the 2004 Presidential Election," *PS: Political Science & Politics* 38(2005):201–09; Gary Langer and Jon Cohen, "Voters and Values in the 2004 Election," *Public Opinion Quarterly* 69(2005):744–61. On the other hand, some social scientists have found evidence of the impact of such voting in 2004; see: Laura R. Olson, Wendy Cadge, and James T. Harrison, "Religion and Public Opinion about Same-Sex Marriage," *Social Science Quarterly* 87(2006):340–60; Kenneth Mulligan, "The 'Myth' of Moral Values Voting in the 2004 Elections," *PS: Politics and Political Science* 49(2008):109–14.

[3]"Independents Take Center Stage in the Obama Era," Report for the Pew Research Center for the People and the Press, 21 May 2009, http://pewresearch.org/pubs/1229/political-values-core-attitudes-trends-2009.

[4]John Winthrop, "A Model of Christian Charity," in Robert C. Winthrop, ed., *Life and Letters of John Winthrop* (quoted in Bartleby.com, http://www.bartleby.com/73/1611.html, 1867[1630]).

[5]James A. Morone, *Hellfire Nation: The Politics of Sin in American History* (New Haven, CT: Yale University Press, 2003).

[6]All quoted in Morone, ibid., p.4.

[7]Ibid.

to get involved in politics.[8] Political scientists Brian Calfano and Paul Djupe recently found that Republican candidates, in particular, were adept at imbuing their political speech with "a type of religious code" that politically conservative voters would understand but that would be subtle enough not to offend those who do not share their social agenda.[9] Another scholar examined how rhetoric espousing "sacred values," those "nonnegotiable convictions grounded in transcendent authority rather than reasoned consequences," was used in American political debate.[10] He found that such talk did not change people's minds, but it did help shift the nature of the politics involved, increasing the intensity of debate and political participation levels, while at the same time reducing the ability of the opponents to compromise and come to an agreement. When such sacred political rhetoric becomes frequent and loud on one side of a political discussion, it is likely that a morality policy is at the center of that debate.

In the past 20 years, political scientists have begun to look systematically at American morality policy and its politics, focusing especially on the states and communities, which federalism has allowed to dominate in this area of policy.[11] An early student of morality policy in the states and communities, Texas A&M University scholar Kenneth Meier, argued that when "one segment of society attempts by governmental fiat to impose its values on the rest of society," the result is morality policy.[12] Although most law, especially criminal law, imposes values on society by defining right and wrong behavior, these values are usually not controversial. For example, most people agree that it is wrong to break into someone's house and steal a television, so banning this behavior does not generate much conflict. But, for example, when a state allows men to marry one another, some people's deep-seated moral values are offended. Some believe that homosexuality is morally wrong, and therefore that it is immoral for the state to support it, whether symbolically, by issuing a marriage license, or financially, by giving the couple the various rights, privileges, obligations, and duties accorded to married couples. Because of the clear consensus among Americans that the government ought to support heterosexual marriage in this way, no conflict of basic values is raised by doing so; but a significant number of Americans have a moral objection to same-sex marriage, and they do not want to support it, even if only through public policy.

This example highlights an important way that morality policy is different from nonmorality policy. Whereas most public policy is primarily about distributing economic costs and benefits, morality policy often has little economic impact, even on those arguing about it. Morality policy is about the government supporting one set of values at the expense of another set of values. For example, when a middle school in Portland, Maine, began providing condoms and birth control pills to its students, the moral outrage of some Mainers was not based on the cost of those items, but on the fact that the school seemed to be condoning premarital sex among very young teenagers.[13] When a state lawmaker from Chicago

---

[8]Mike Ramsey, "God & Rod: Reactions Mixed to Governor's Use of Religious Appeal," *State Journal-Register (Springfield, IL)*, 24 March 2007, p. 1; Matthew Franck, "Blunt Aims to Boost Role of Churches," *St. Louis Post-Dispatch*, 28 September 2007, online edition.

[9]Brian Robert Calfano and Paul A. Djupe, "God Talk: Religious Cues and Electoral Support," *Political Research Quarterly* 62(2009):329–39.

[10]Morgan Marietta, "From My Cold, Dead Hands: Democratic Consequences of Sacred Rhetoric," *Journal of Politics* 70(2008):767–79.

[11]Christopher Z. Mooney, "The Decline of Federalism and the Rise of Morality Policy Conflict in the United States," *Publius* 30(2000):171–88.

[12]Kenneth J. Meier, *The Politics of Sin* (Armonk, NY: M. E. Sharpe, 1994), p. 4. Meier is the godfather of morality policy scholarship, and *The Politics of Sin* is the place to start reading on this subject.

[13]David Hench, "School Birth Control Backed," *Portland (ME) Press Herald*, 2 November 2007, online edition.

shouted "It's dangerous for our children to even know that your philosophy exists!" at a witness during a legislative hearing on a proposed "moment of silence" law for public schools, there were no budgetary implications of the bill or his "philosophy."[14] The lawmaker's problem was that the witness's philosophy conflicted with her moral values.

Nonmorality policy is typically defined by the substance with which the policy deals, like health care policy or education policy. Morality policy, however, is defined by the debate surrounding it. One set of scholars makes the apt analogy that, just as science is defined by the application of the scientific method rather than the thing to which the method is applied, morality policy is defined by the terms of the debate, not by the subject that is debated.[15] *Thus, morality policies are those on which at least one significant side of the debate makes its arguments in morally based language.* That is, one side argues that its opponent's position is just morally wrong. Morality policies are those about which contentious normative questions of right and wrong are put on the table for the government to decide. A policy dealing with any topic could be a morality policy if one of the relevant voices in the debate uses moral arguments. This is why policies dealing with such a wide range of topics—intoxicating substances, homosexuality, reproduction, firearms, gambling, criminal justice, and so forth—can be lumped into the same category. Political scientists do this because the politics of this sort of policy share common characteristics that can be very different from those for most other types of policy. We study

these policies as a group to understand their common characteristics.

Moral arguments are assertions that a behavior is banned or required by some unquestionable ethical authority. The most common sources of such assertions are the basic religious documents that adherents believe to be the fonts of fundamental truth. The Christian Bible, the Islamic Koran, and the Jewish Talmud are examples of such documents. Although their interpretation is often disputed, people debating public policy sometimes find some basic moral arguments in these documents to be useful. Such arguments may also come from other sources, such as the U.S. Constitution or ideas about "natural rights," but the most common ones in American policy debates have a religious basis.

In practice, only one side of a morality policy debate usually makes moral arguments, with those on the other side making nonmorality-based claims. Conflicting moral arguments rarely have enough support in a state or community to make them equally useful in a policy debate. For example, while people who want to ban the death penalty may argue that it is morally wrong for the state to kill, the other side often makes the more instrumental claim that the threat of execution deters murder.

Although scholars have not yet determined how some advocates are able to make their moral arguments relevant in a policy debate while others are not, part of the explanation seems to be that successful advocates are able to convince enough people that the policy violates their basic values, thereby threatening their core identity.[16] For example, suppose a town's liquor board licenses a strip club to open. Its opponents may be able to convince (or simply remind) enough people that pornography denigrates and objectifies women and, therefore, violates their basic values, making the strip club's very

---

[14]Eric Zorn, "Rep. Monique Davis to Atheist Rob Sherman: 'It's Dangerous for Our Children to Even Know That Your Philosophy Exists!'" *Chicago Tribune*, 3 April 2008, online edition.

[15]David C. Leege, Kenneth D. Wald, Brian S. Krueger, and Paul D. Mueller, *The Politics of Cultural Differences: Social Change and Voter Mobilization in the Post-New Deal Period* (Princeton, NJ: Princeton University Press, 2002).

[16]Michael Lienesch, *In the Beginning: Fundamentalism, the Scopes Trial, and the Making of the Anti-evolution Movement* (Chapel Hill, NC: University of North Carolina Press, 2009).

Table 13.1

The Language of Anti-Same-Sex Marriage Initiatives in Arizona: Complex Failure and Simple Success

Year	Language of the Ballot Measure	Result
2006	"To preserve and protect marriage in this state, only a union between one man and one woman shall be valid or recognized as a marriage by this state or its political subdivisions and no legal status for unmarried persons shall be created or recognized by this state or its political subdivisions that is similar to that of marriage."	Failed
2008	"Only a union of one man and one woman shall be valid or recognized as a marriage in this state."	Passed

Note: The opponents of same-sex marriage in Arizona learned their lesson after the defeat of the 2006 (top) ballot measure—keep it simple. In 2008, they reduced their measure from 58 words with complicated sentences to a simpler 20-word sentence—and they won. Morality policy is best sold as a simple appeal to basic moral values.

existence immoral to them, even if they never set foot in it. The fact that their local government has sanctioned this immoral activity may be enough to motivate some people into political action. If an advocate can convince enough people to care about such a violation of their values, then that advocate's moral argument becomes relevant to the debate, and the policy will take on the qualities of a morality policy.

Morality policy has two other characteristics that help determine its unique politics.[17] First, it tends to be less technical than other policies, at least for the side making the moral argument. The question is not whether a policy will "work," but whether it is right or wrong based on the advocates' interpretation of a religious text, such as the Bible or the Koran, or some other text or belief system that they feel is morally authoritative. In fact, the simpler the argument the better, oftentimes. For example, from 1998 to 2008, 41 statewide initiatives were voted upon to define marriage as only a

union between a man and a woman,[18] and only one of them was rejected—in 2006 in Arizona. In response to their defeat, the Arizona initiative supporters simplified the language of the measure to focus on the basic issue—and they won in 2008 (see Table 13.1).

The simplicity of the argument and its clear relationship to a person's basic values lead to the final significant characteristic of morality policy—people can get very excited about it. Or, more precisely, interest groups can easily encourage a significant segment of the public to become very excited about it.[19] Public participation in state and local policy making is usually very limited; the average citizen is just too busy with work and family to know or care much about it. However, morality policy's simple arguments allow anyone to be well informed, and advocates can use the "attack on our basic values" argument as motivation for people to pay attention and even to become vocal and active on these issues. These characteristics have

---

[17]Meier, op. cit.; Donald P. Haider-Markel and Kenneth J. Meier, "The Politics of Gay and Lesbian Rights: Expanding the Scope of the Conflict," *Journal of Politics* 58(1996): 332–49; Mooney, op. cit.

[18]These initiatives were morality policies designed to ban same-sex marriage.

[19]Christopher Z. Mooney and Richard G. Schuldt, "Does Morality Policy Exist? Testing a Basic Assumption," *Policy Studies Journal* 36(2008):199–218.

YOU DECIDE

EVOLUTION, INTELLIGENT DESIGN, AND CREATIONISM: PUBLIC SCHOOL BIOLOGY AS MORALITY POLICY?

The mix of science and religion in the American public school curriculum has generated morality politics for at least 100 years. The terms of the debate appear to have changed in recent years, however, and those changes tell us something about morality policy politics. When biology teacher John Scopes was arrested for discussing the theory of evolution with his high school students in Dayton, Tennessee, in 1925, it set off a trial that highlighted the clash of cultures every bit as strongly as today's fights over same-sex marriage and abortion. That trial, memorialized in the play and movies, *Inherit the Wind,* showed how the acceptance of modern biology among scientists and the educated elite in the United States seemed to put them sharply at odds with those who took the story of a seven-day creation from the Bible's book of Genesis as literal truth. The climax of the play has Matthew Harrison Brady, the character representing the creationist view, mindlessly rattling off the books of the Bible and appearing to have had a mental and physical breakdown—the symbolic collapse of a rigid morality in the face of the inexorable advance of the more reasonable and thoughtful ideas of science.

Flash forward 85 years, and in today's morality politics about the public school biology curriculum, the roles appear reversed. By modifying their language and working in an incremental way within the political system, modern-day, fundamentalist evolution-doubters are on the outside looking in—but they appear to be making headway. Espousing a theory of "intelligent design" rather than pure creationism, and using rhetoric replete with such words as *theory, hypotheses, ideas,* and *skepticism,* rather than the stiff morality of Matthew Harrison Brady, these advocates are working within school boards in states and communities across the country, and they seem to have public opinion on their side.[1] A recent survey by the Pew Forum on Religion and Public Life found that only 26 percent of Americans believe that humans evolved through a process of natural selection; in fact, 42 percent think that the world has always existed in its current form.[2] On the other side of the debate, scientists and their supporters are all asputter from the attacks on their orthodoxy, and understandably so. Ideas revolving around evolution are the foundation of modern biology, a science that has made great strides. For example, in a recent decision on the subject, a U.S. federal judge said that a certain policy promoting nonevolution science in schools was "breath-taking inanity" and an "utter waste of monetary and personnel resources" by the local government involved.[3] This is strong language, indeed, from the federal bench.

What is the appropriate role of public opinion and moral values in public policies like this, where strong professional criteria often drive policy decisions? Should strong public values overrule even the values of science in such cases? Why or why not? In what other policy areas do you find clashes of moral values and professional values like we see in this school biology curriculum debate? Should public values determine policies regarding natural resources and agriculture, for example, where science has much to say about what government ought to be doing and where those scientific dictates can be at odds with what farmers, miners, or the general public would prefer? Think about the general role of science and other sorts of professional norms and values in public policy making. In a democracy, do or should these norms and values have a privileged place in public policy debates, and if so, under what conditions, and on which policies? Who gets to decide what these norms and values are? How do these sorts of values and norms differ from moral values in ways that are relevant to public policy?

Notes
1 Eric Plutzer and Michael Berkman, "Evolution, Creationism, and the Teaching of Human Origins in Schools," *Public Opinion Quarterly* 72(2008):540–53.
2 Report from the Pew Forum on Religion and Public Life, "Many Americans Uneasy with Mix of Religion and Politics," (Washington, DC: The Pew Research Center for the People and the Press, 2006).
3 Quoted in: Michael Berkman, Julianna Sandell Pacheco, and Eric Plutzer, "Evolution and Creationism in America's Classrooms: A National Portrait," *PLoS Biology* 6(2008):e124.

led to an increase in the use of initiatives and referendums on morality policies in the last quarter century, such as those 41 statewide votes on defining marriage mentioned earlier.[20] Recent research also shows that simply having a morality policy initiative on the ballot can both motivate more people to vote[21] and change how people think about the candidates in that election.[22] In other words, morality initiatives can change the nature of the entire election in which they are held.

Unique Features of Morality Policy Politics

The politics of morality policy hold a variety of unique characteristics regarding interest group activity, political frustration, and enforcement problems.

---

[20]T. Alexander Smith and Raymond Tatalovich, *Cultures at War: Moral Conflicts in Western Democracies* (Peterborough, ON: Broadview Press, 2003), ch. 7.

[21]John A. Grummel, "Morality Politics, Direct Democracy, and Turnout," *State Politics and Policy Quarterly* 8(2008):282–92.

[22]Todd Donovan, Caroline J. Tolbert, and Daniel A. Smith, "Priming Presidential Votes by Direct Democracy," *Journal of Politics* 70(2009):1217–31.

Interest Group Activity, Altruism, Grassroots, and Activism

Interest groups are central to morality policy making, and their activities differ in important ways from those groups working on nonmorality policy. First, as discussed in Chapter 6, most groups consist of people or businesses seeking economic benefits from public policy. Forming and maintaining a group require time and money, and the primary reason most people are willing to do so is that they expect some sort of financial gain from it. Many people who form and join groups that are working on morality policy, however, do so for noneconomic reasons. Of course, the liquor industry fights restrictions on alcohol sales for economic reasons, and companies that run casinos lobby legislatures and join groups to make their businesses more profitable, but these groups don't make moral arguments in the policy discussion. The groups working to ban abortion, gambling, or teaching evolution in schools will gain no economic benefit from the political victory of their causes. Perhaps these groups' leaders benefit economically from the political battle because it brings in donations and dues to pay their salaries, but the vast majority of these groups' members contribute their time and money solely to advance a moral cause for which they will neither gain nor lose a penny. These groups' members are motivated by a sense of **altruism,** a rare motive in American politics.

American Stock/Hulton Archive/Getty Images

Anti-alcohol crusader, Carrie Nation, here showing off the hatchet she used to smash up Kansas saloons in the late 19th century.

Who are these rare birds in American political life, these altruistic policy activists? Why are they so moved by their altruism to enter the political battle on morality issues? The answers to these questions can be found in understanding what these issues mean to these activists.

Certain people hold particular moral values so deeply that when these values are threatened, they are motivated to act, regardless of economic incentives. These people will even use their economic resources—time, money, and more—in the pursuit of what they believe to be an important moral cause. In American politics, such folks tend to hold a deep religious faith. Liberal or conservative, religious leaders and activists have been at the forefront of morality policy crusades from the beginning of the republic, fighting against slavery, the sale of alcohol, gambling, capital punishment, abortion, the use of embryonic stem cells in research, and more. As this list suggests, these groups tend to fight *against* things that currently exist. This is suggestive of the mechanism behind these groups' politics. They are not typically motivated for positive change; that is, they do not foresee an addition they could make to improve the world. Rather, they more often react to evils that arise in the world that irritate them mor-

ally. Their political goals tend to be to remove those irritants.

In recent years, people belonging to traditional, conservative religious denominations seem to be more easily motivated by such a threat to their values and faith than those whose religion is either less important to them or of a less dogmatic nature.[23] In particular, those who take their religious texts literally, believing them to be the direct word of God, can be motivated to act politically by a policy entrepreneur who interprets such a text to mean that their values are threatened by a government action. Compared to other industrialized countries, the United States is very religious,[24] and more people are motivated by a direct threat to their religious values here than by a threat to their political values.[25] Although religious people and groups are not the only ones active in morality policy making, they are often the only ones making moral arguments; those who define the debate in nonmoral terms tend not to be religious. For example, many anti-abortion groups are closely associated with fundamentalist Protestant denominations or the Roman Catholic Church, and they make morality arguments based on their interpretation of the Christian Bible. Their opponents who work to keep access to abortion open, such as Planned Parenthood, tend to be secular.[26] These activists make arguments

---

[23]Kimberley H. Conger, *The Christian Right in Republican State Politics* (New York: Palgrave, 2009); Christopher G. Ellison, Samuel Echevarria, and Brad Smith, "Religion and Abortion Attitudes among U.S. Hispanics: Findings from the 1990 Latino National Political Survey," *Social Science Quarterly* 86(2005):192–208; Geoffrey Layman, *The Great Divide: Religious and Cultural Conflict in American Party Politics* (New York: Columbia University Press, 2001).

[24]Pippa Norris and Ronald Inglehart, *Sacred and Secular: Religion and Politics Worldwide* (New York: Cambridge University Press, 2004).

[25]Still, a threat to a person's economic interests is probably a far more significant political motivator than either of these two altruistic motives.

[26]Deborah R. McFarlane and Kenneth J. Meier, *The Politics of Fertility Control: Family Planning and Abortion Policies in the American States* (Chatham, NJ: Chatham House, 2000).

about women's health care and control of their own bodies and the financial and psychological burden of unwanted pregnancies. That is, their arguments have medical, psychological, and economic bases rather than a moral basis.

Another characteristic of these politics is that due to the intense values-charged issues involved, morality policy making attracts many interest groups with a relatively narrow focus, sometimes called **single-issue groups**.[27] Groups like the National Right to Life Committee (advocating abortion restrictions), the Hemlock Society (advocating the right to die), and the People for the Ethical Treatment of Animals (advocating the rights of animals) usually start out with a highly constricted agenda, even if they expand it over time. Furthermore, to an extent not seen in most nonmorality policy making, morality-based interest groups tend to mobilize their highly motivated members to work directly in the political arena. Often, these are not simply groups whose members write checks and let their blue-suited lobbyists do the work. These groups often organize traditional **grassroots activities,** such as rallies and marches at the state capitol during the legislative session, letter-writing and telephone-calling campaigns, well-attended meetings and poster-making sessions, vigils, and boycotts. These group leaders can motivate their members to get involved in political activities by tapping into their shared deep commitment to the values reflected in their group's policy positions.

These morality policy groups and advocates engage in many activities and tactics that are quite unusual in American politics. For example, both liberal and conservative ministers and priests will energize their flocks and direct political action from the pulpit on morality policy, something you rarely see during debates over, for example, transportation

or education policy.[28] Morality policy groups are also adept at using new and alternative media to inform and activate group members and like-minded people, everything from Christian radio and television programs to websites devoted to their causes to social networking sites.[29] In addition, these highly motivated morality policy activists sometimes do extraordinary things in the pursuit of their policy goals. In the 1990s, for example, the antiabortion group Operation Rescue staged extensive, intensive, and long-term protests and vigils at abortion clinics in cities around the country.[30] These advocates sacrificed their social and family lives, and some of them even gave up their jobs, so that they could pursue this direct political action. This is extraordinary behavior in American politics.

Occasionally, political violence can also result as highly motivated (some might say unbalanced) morality policy activists take direct political action to an extreme.[31] The murder of Dr. George Tiller described in this chapter's opening vignette is an unusual, but not an isolated, example of this sort of political action. Other morality policy advocates have committed murder, blown up buildings, and committed other forms of political terrorism in various states and communities. The same moral and religious fervor that motivates an Islamic militant to strap dynamite to his

---

[27]Smith and Tatalovich, op. cit. pp. 78–80.

[28]Paul A. Djupe, Laura R. Olson, and Christopher P. Gilbert, "Whether to Adopt Statements on Homosexuality in Two Denominations," *Journal for the Scientific Study of* Religion 45(2006):609–21; Sara Diamond, *Spiritual Warfare: The Politics of the Christian Right* (Boston, MA: South End Press, 1999).

[29]Cynthia Burack, *Sin, Sex, and Democracy: Antigay Rhetoric and the Christian Right* (Albany, NY: SUNY Press, 2008).

[30]Susan E. Clarke, "Ideas, Interests, and Institutions: Shaping Abortion Politics in Denver," in Elaine B. Sharp, ed., *Culture Wars and Local Politics* (Lawrence, KS: The University Press of Kansas, 1999).

[31]James Davidson Hunter, *Before the Shooting Begins: Searching for Democracy in America's Culture Wars* (New York: Free Press, 1994).

body in Peshawar can motivate an American to plant a pipe bomb at a Planned Parenthood clinic or burn down a new subdivision that he or she feels has damaged the environment. When some people's deeply held moral values are sufficiently threatened, they may decide that even sacrificing their lives or freedom may be justified.

When extremists commit such acts, leaders of groups on their side of a morality policy debate will denounce them, although sometimes implying that they went only a little too far. Some of these leaders are lambasted for being disingenuous in these denials; their opponents, the media, and law enforcement officials sometimes claim that the often violent language that some leaders use incites such extreme behavior from unbalanced supporters. For example, in a press release issued after the killing of George Tiller, Randall Terry, founder of Operation Rescue, said:

> George Tiller was a mass-murderer. We grieve for him that he did not have time to properly prepare his soul to face God . . . Those men and women who slaughter the unborn are murderers according to the Law of God.[32]

Terry went on to compare Tiller's killer to Nat Turner, the leader of an 1831 slave uprising in Virginia, suggesting that although excessive, the ends of his act were laudable.[33]

Lawmaking: Political Frustration and Success

Of course, political violence is highly unusual in the United States, even in morality policy debates; but the source of this violence—frustration with the political process—is common in morality politics. Because morality policy activists typically espouse a black-and-white, right-or-wrong view of public policy, working within the normal state and local policy-making routine almost guarantees that they will be frustrated and angry with the process and the outcome. How can people who believe that their policy position is dictated by God listen calmly to someone arguing for a position that they feel is morally repugnant? How can they agree to a compromise or graciously accept losing in the legislative process on some arcane procedural maneuver that they don't understand? If *frustration* is defined as "needing to do something but being kept from doing it," then the regular policy-making process in the states and communities is simply a recipe for frustration for highly motivated morality policy activists.

This clash of perspectives, values, and cultures—even between policy makers and activists who are political allies—typically leaves morality policy advocates on the losing end of the process, at least at first. The Roman Catholic Church and the various Evangelical Protestant churches and ministers were equally outraged at the U.S. Supreme Court's *Roe vs. Wade* decision that struck down most state and local laws banning abortion in 1973. The Catholic Church was much more hierarchically organized, so it was able to become politically active and effective in the area by the late 1970s. It took the evangelicals, a less centralized group by the nature of their religious beliefs, well into the 1980s before becoming a political powerhouse on this issue.[34]

---

[32]"George Tiller Was a Mass-Murderer, Says Randall Terry—We Grieve That He Did Not Have Time to Properly Prepare His Soul to Face God," Christian Newswire press release, 31 May 2009, http://www.christiannewswire.com/news/8967610531.html.

[33]Alexandra Jaffe, "Randall Terry Compares Tiller's Killer to Nat Turner," *The Washington Independent*, 11 June 2009, online edition.

[34]Paul J. Fabrizio, "Evolving into Morality Politics: U.S. Catholic Bishops' Statements on U.S. Politics from 1792 to the Present," in Christopher Z. Mooney, ed., *The Public Clash of Private Values: The Politics of Morality Policy* (New York: Chatham House, 2001).

However, when such morality policy advocates can sustain their energy, interest, and motivation, once they can gather resources and learn both how the policy-making process works and the value of that process, and if their views actually reflect those of a significant segment of the state or community (not necessarily a majority), they can make an important impact on public policy. Policy makers really want to set policy that reflects their constituents' values, and if a group accurately represents those values, policy makers will agree to their proposals. Legislators, council members, governors, and mayors all have to face the electorate to keep their jobs, and they sure do not want to be on the wrong side of their constituents on these highly visible and relatively simple morality policy questions.[35]

Ironically, when the leaders of morality policy groups learn the traditional political process too well, with all its give and take, compromise, and thinking about the long run, it sometimes can frustrate and annoy their followers all the more, risking the leaders' credibility and clout. For example, in the 1990s, Pat Robertson's Christian Coalition and other conservative evangelical groups became so powerful that they began to look more like political insiders than moral crusaders, both to their members and to the political establishment.[36] They took over the Republican Party in many states and Robertson himself made a credible run for president in 1988. All this political success, however, failed to garner the policy goals for which their followers truly pined: the complete ban of abortions in the United States, among other things. This resulted in the frustration that led to many of the direct action politics of Operation Rescue and other more radical groups during the 1980s and 1990s.

Implementation: The Problem of "Unenforceable" Laws

When a strong morality policy becomes law, it is often difficult to enforce. This is especially true for **vice laws**, bans on activities some believe are sinful (see Reform Can Happen box). Over the course of American history, state and local governments have banned all sorts of "sins," such as alcohol, pornography, sodomy, prostitution, and even interracial marriage.[37] When morality policy advocates convince policy makers to accept their definition of an activity as sinful, such laws can be enacted with ease; as one morality policy scholar claimed about lawmakers, "No one is willing to stand up for sin."[38] However, the police or regulatory agency charged with implementing such bans often has a hard time enforcing them because—as the same scholar said—for some people, "sin is fun."[39]

One reason that morality policy is difficult to implement is that these laws are written to express basic moral values rather than to solve a public problem, so policy makers simply give

[35]Christine Pappas, Jeanette Mendez, and Rebekah Herrick, "The Negative Effects of Populism on Gay and Lesbian Rights," *Social Science Quarterly* 90(2009): 150–63; Christopher Z. Mooney and Mei-Hsien Lee, "Legislating Morality in the American States: The Case of Pre-Roe Abortion Regulation Reform," *American Journal of Political Science* 39(1995):599–627; Mooney and Lee, "The Influence of Values on Consensus and Contentious Morality Policy: U.S. Death Penalty Reform, 1956–82," *Journal of Politics* 62(2000):223–39.
[36]Conger, op. cit.

[37]In 1967, the U.S. Supreme Court found that banning interracial marriage violated the 14th Amendment to the U.S. Constitution, thus overturning such laws (*Loving v. Virginia*, 388 U.S. 1, 395 [1967]).
[38]Kenneth Meier, "Drugs, Sex, and Rock and Roll: A Theory of Morality Politics," in Christopher Z. Mooney, ed., *The Public Clash of Private Values: The Politics of Morality Policy* (New York: Chatham House, 2001).
[39]Ibid.

REFORM CAN HAPPEN

THE POLITICS OF DEMON RUM—PROHIBITION, REGULATION, AND REPEAL

The prohibition of alcohol was on the reform agenda of certain early Americans interested in morality since the Massachusetts Pilgrims of the 17th century, but widespread interest in pursuing the policy arose with the Second Great Awakening, a period of religious revival in the United States in the 1830s and 1840s.[1] These Protestant Christians argued that drinking liquor was sinful, causing men to neglect their families and women to take up a life of "bad virtue" (i.e., promiscuity and prostitution). This early antialcohol movement also had a strong xenophobic flavor to it, something that continued throughout its history in this country. Many Catholic immigrants from Germany and Ireland enjoyed their liquor (at least publicly) to a greater degree than did those Protestants whose ancestors had settled the United States from Britain and Scotland earlier in our history.[2] A "temperance movement" developed before the Civil War, with some success. Maine passed the first statewide ban on recreational alcohol in 1851, with several other states and cities adopting their own "Maine Laws" soon thereafter. These reforms were unpopular with working class people and immigrants, causing civil unrest and problems implementing them. In fact, Maine repealed its prohibition in 1856, following riots set off by the revelation that the main advocate of the reform, Portland mayor Neal Dow, had hoarded a large amount of alcohol for "medicinal purposes" for him and his friends.

The Civil War briefly took the steam out of the temperance movement, but it was soon revived, promoted by newly formed groups like the Women's Temperance Union, the Anti-Saloon League, and the Prohibition Party. Policy successes by these groups included the passage of laws like Kansas's constitutional ban on alcohol in 1881. The movement grew quickly, motivated again by the xenophobia and anti-Catholicism aroused by the mass immigration from southern and eastern Europe around the turn of the 20th century. The movement's biggest success was with the adoption of the 18th Amendment to the U.S. Constitution, banning the sale and manufacture of alcohol throughout the country. Prohibition was widely supported by popular Evangelical Protestant preachers of the day, like Billy Sunday, along with white supremacist groups, like the Ku Klux Klan.[3] But the 18th Amendment was widely credited with sparking a national crime wave in the 1920s and a widespread breakdown in the respect for law. The onset of the Great Depression added more pressure to repeal this reform, and it was one of President Franklin Roosevelt's top agenda items upon taking office in 1933. By the end of that year, the 21st Amendment had repealed the 18th Amendment.

Despite conventional wisdom, the prohibition story does not end in 1933. Many states took much longer to repeal their own alcohol bans than did the national government. In fact, it wasn't until 1966 that the last state to do so—Mississippi—went "wet." Even today, 261 counties in the United States are "dry," banning the sale of liquor entirely, and 374 additional counties are "moist," in that alcohol sales are only allowed in certain local jurisdictions there.[4] As Table 13.2 shows, most of these dry and moist counties are found in the bastions of Evangelical Protestantism, the southeastern U.S. states. In fact, every county in Tennessee is either dry or moist, restricting alcohol to some extent. Many states also have restrictions on selling alcohol on Sundays and by the drink, state control of

THE DEFENDER OF THE 18th AMENDMENT

This cartoon from the 1920s shows the KKK in a positive light— as "the defender of the 18th Amendment".

sales of alcohol, and other regulations. The direction of reform on this issue, overall, is toward fewer restrictions. In 2008, Colorado became the 35th state to allow the sale of liquor on Sunday. Eight of the remaining 15 states with the Sunday ban are those of the old Confederacy, and two others are Oklahoma and West Virginia, states with the same political culture.[5] Even Georgia, in the heart of the Bible Belt, is considering allowing Sunday sales, while Utah, a state whose politics are heavily influenced by the antialcohol Mormon church, liberalized its liquor regulations in 2009 in hopes of improving tourism.[6]

Table 13.2			

Prohibition of Alcohol: Wet, Dry, and Moist Counties in the States

State	Dry Counties	Moist Counties	Counties with Some Alcohol Prohibition	Number of Counties in the State
TX	35	181	216	254
TN	15	80	95	95
KY	53	37	90	120
AR	42	0	42	75
NC	4	33	37	100
MS	31	3	34	82
OK	31	0	31	77
KS	28	0	28	105
AL	14	12	26	67
VA	0	11	11	134
WV	0	8	8	55
GA	1	6	7	159
FL	5	0	5	67
NM	0	2	2	33
LA	1	0	1	64
SD	1	0	1	66
ID	0	1	1	44
TOTAL	261	374	635	

Source: Adapted from: John Frendries and Raymond Tatolovich, "'A Hundred Miles of Dry': Religion and the Persistence of Prohibition in the American States," *State Politics and Policy Quarterly.* Forthcoming.

Note: The third column is simply the sum of the first two. Note that the proportion of dry and moist counties in a state does not necessarily correlate with the proportion of a state's residence covered by these restrictions. Wet states tend to be more populated.

Notes

1 Morone, op. cit.

2 Joseph R. Gusfield, *Symbolic Crusade: Status Politics and the American Temperance Movement* (Urbana, IL: University of Illinois Press, 1963).

3 Michael Lewis, "Keeping Sin from Sacred Spaces: Southern Evangelicals and the Socio-Legal Control of Alcohol, 1865–1915," *Southern Cultures* 15(2009):40–60; Masatomo Ayabe, "Ku Kluxers in a Coal Mining Community: A Study of the Ku Klux Klan Movement in Williamson, County, Illinois, 1923–1926," *Journal of the Illinois State Historical Society* 102(2009):73–100.

4 John Frendries and Raymond Tatolovich, "'A Hundred Miles of Dry': Religion and the Persistence of Prohibition in the American States," *State Politics and Policy Quarterly.* Forthcoming.

5 John Gramlich, "States Revisit Prohibition-Era Booze Laws," *Stateline.org,* 7 July 2008, online edition.

6 Valerie Richardson, "Utah Relaxing Liquor Laws to Entice Tourists," *The Washington Times,* 22 June 2009, online edition.

less thought to how they will actually work.[40] Perhaps more fundamentally, the law may simply have little impact on changing these human behaviors. Think about these bans as attempts to discourage people from engaging in certain activities by increasing the cost of doing so.[41] Even without a ban, using recreational drugs or employing or being a prostitute has significant costs, including health risks and social stigma, as well as dollars and cents. Banning these activities increases these costs by adding fines, jail time, and even greater social stigma. Certainly, these additional costs will dissuade some people from participating in such activities; but for those people who really want to do them, the relatively minor cost increases state and local governments can impose—especially after factoring in the often small probabilities of getting caught—may not be enough to stop them from continuing to "sin."[42]

Just as important, those charged with enforcing these laws often do not share their advocates' zeal for them.[43] The police may not think that pursuing recreational drug users, illegal gamblers, or those in the sex trade is a good use of their time and energy; they might rather focus on enforcing laws against violent crime or improving traffic safety. In fact, the police may even have more compassion for those engaged in these activities because they encounter them so frequently.

Whether a morality policy is poorly crafted, too weak to discourage a behavior, or simply ignored by those enforcing it or engaged in the activity, the result is the same: Morality policies are often not implemented well. Although some may decry this situation and demand more stringent enforcement, in one important sense, implementation may be irrelevant to many morality policy advocates. Morality policy can be as much about symbolism and affirming values as it is about changing behavior.[44] State or local law asserts the official values of the government and its citizens, regardless of whether those values are always expressed in the behavior of those citizens. In the end, this may satisfy some of the most ardent morality policy advocates.

Issue Evolution: Morality Policy Making Over Time

Understanding the characteristics of morality policy allows us to explain better the politics surrounding it. Bizarre and inexplicable political behavior (like assassinating doctors in church vestibules) may become more understandable if we see it in the context of morality policy. As with other types of policy, we can also understand morality policy politics better by following its characteristic **issue evolution**, a fairly predictable pattern of how issues come onto the public agenda, how their politics develop, and how they then recede from active debate.[45] State and local government institutions largely define this process, and even though morality policy is quite distinct from run-of-the-mill nonmorality policy in some ways, these institutions

[40]Malcolm L. Goggin and Christopher Z. Mooney, "Congressional Use of Policy Information on Fact and Value Issues," in Christopher Z. Mooney, ed., *The Public Clash of Private Values: The Politics of Morality Policy* (New York: Chatham House, 2001); Meier, ibid.

[41]Meier, ibid.

[42]Ann-Marie E. Syzmanski, "Dry Compulsions: Prohibition and the Creation of State-Level Enforcement Agencies," *Journal of Policy History* 11(1999):115–46; Tom R. Tyler, *Why People Obey the Law* (New Haven, CT: Yale University Press, 1990).

[43]Smith and Tatalovich, op. cit.

[44]Murray Edelman, *The Symbolic Uses of Politics*, 2nd ed. (Urbana, IL: University of Illinois Press, 1985).

[45]Our discussion of morality policy evolution draws much from the more general pattern of punctuated equilibrium in policy development discussed in: Frank R. Baumgartner and Bryan D. Jones, *Agendas and Instability in American Politics* (Chicago: University of Chicago Press, 1993).

impel morality policy politics to follow some of the same basic patterns.

Policy Equilibrium: Reflecting the Values of the Majority

State and local public policy on the vast majority of potential moral questions are in sync with mainstream public opinion. As such, policy makers have little incentive to change it or even discuss it. This **policy equilibrium** exists because policy makers have a strong incentive to reflect their constituents' preferences on morality policy, as many studies have shown.[46] Because these issues affect people's basic values and are simple to understand, they make ideal material for campaign ads to attack incumbents. For example, suppose that a state legislator from a conservative rural district votes for a resolution to allow same-sex marriage. His or her opponent's campaign in the next election could highlight that single vote so much that it becomes the only thing that catches voters' attention and sticks in their minds on election day. As you know, most people know very little about their state legislators' voting records. If the one thing they do know is that their legislator voted for a bill that conflicts with their basic moral values, that legislator will not be reelected. Politicians understand this dynamic very well. Although they try to represent their constituents' interests whenever they can, policy makers make a special effort to do so on these simple, visible morality issues. Thus, it is not surprising that most potential morality policy issues are simply not on the active **political agenda** at any given time. Only when the values of a significant portion of the population are threatened do morality issues begin to generate political activity.[47]

Policy Shock: Let the Politics Begin

On occasion, something happens to change either public opinion or public policy, thus upsetting the happy equilibrium between them. Such a **policy shock** can be caused by a variety of things, such as a social change (perhaps a burst of immigration or a war), a technological innovation (such as when embryonic stem cell research became feasible), or even an unusual political event (such as a state or federal supreme court unilaterally changing morality policy by declaring a law unconstitutional).[48] By disrupting the policy-opinion equilibrium, a policy shock gives policy makers, interest groups, and other **policy entrepreneurs** the incentive and opportunity to place the morality policy in question on the active political agenda.[49] Whether from a deep concern for some moral value or through sheer political opportunism—or a little of both—a morality policy entrepreneur can stir up general public sentiment far more easily than someone advocating a nonmorality policy. To excite the public interest, the entrepreneur needs only point out the threat (in the entrepreneur's opinion) to the moral values of the state or community. Once a significant segment of the population thinks of the issue in moral terms, it is easy to get it on the political agenda, because policy makers

[46]Jeffrey R. Lax and Justin H. Phillips, "Gay Rights in the States: Public Opinion and Policy Responsiveness," *American Political Science Review* 103(2009):267–386; David L. Schecter, "Legislating Morality Outside of the Legislature," *Social Science Journal* 46(2009):89–110; Elizabeth Anne Oldmixon, "The Religious Dynamics of Decision Making on Gay Rights Issues in the U.S. House of Representatives, 1993–2002," *Journal for the Scientific Study of Religion* 46(2007):55–70; Pappas, Mendez, and Herrick, op. cit.; Mooney and Lee, op. cit., 1995 and 2000.

[47]Donley T. Studlar, "What Constitutes Morality Policy? A Cross-National Analysis," in Christopher Z. Mooney, ed., *The Public Clash of Private Values: The Politics of Morality Policy* (New York: Chatham House, 2001).
[48]Baumgartner and Jones, op. cit.
[49]John W. Kingdon, *Agendas, Alternatives, and Public Policies*, 2nd ed. (New York: Harper Collins, 1995); Mark Schneider and Paul Teske, "Toward a Theory of the Political Entrepreneur: Evidence from Local Government," *American Political Science Review* 36(1992):737–47.

always want to bring morality policy into balance with their constituents' values. When a state or community cannot reach a consensus on the moral value in question, however, the policy shock and ensuing political activity make this lack of consensus abundantly clear. In this situation, morality policy politics really kicks into high gear.

Return to Policy Equilibrium: Fitting a Square Peg into a Round Hole

If and when morality policy advocates come to understand that success in state and local policy making requires compromise and patience, they can chip away at the most egregious problems they see and move slowly toward their ideal policy goals. In the American policy-making process, advocates of any change—whether morality based or not—who demand everything at once usually achieve only failure. This characteristic of our political system can generate considerable frustration among morality policy advocates, in particular, due of the strident, urgent nature of their moral crusades. With patience, however, they often achieve small, incremental successes. The degree to which public opinion supports their ultimate policy goals determines how far they can proceed toward them in the long run.

For example, consider how opponents of capital punishment have been able to restrict its use over the course of U.S. history. Following the punitive and almost medieval English legal tradition of the time, America's first criminal justice systems executed criminals frequently. Indeed, in 18th-century New York, about 25 percent of those convicted of crimes—any crimes—were hanged.[50] Among other things, anti–death penalty reformers argued that it was immoral for a government to kill

a convict, regardless of the crime committed.[51] These reformers ran up against public opinion that distinctly favored execution as a form of punishment, at least for certain offenses. As a result, by 1880, executions were banned in only five states—all with predominantly moralistic political cultures (Michigan, Rhode Island, Wisconsin, Iowa, and Maine).

When these reformers shifted their efforts from trying to eliminate the death penalty altogether to just trying to limit it in certain specific ways, however, they had tremendous success. They began by arguing that executing innocent people was wrong. That was a moral argument, but it was certainly not a contentious one. Reformers then argued that fewer crimes merited the death penalty, with prison being a more appropriate punishment for many crimes. Again, that was reasonable enough. Next, they objected to public and painful executions as humiliating, inhumane, and unnecessary. Many people could buy those moral arguments, too—we are not barbarians, after all. For each of these arguments, death penalty reformers also suggested specific, incremental policy changes, reforms such as strict due process rules for trials, only executing those convicted of first-degree murder, and "humane" execution methods (e.g., banning public executions and using the electric chair and the gas chamber), all of which were widely adopted in the states. So, although these reformers have not succeeded in the clear, symbolic victory of banning capital punishment entirely in the United States, in practice, they have dramatically reduced the number of actual executions here (see Figure 13.1).

Thus, when morality policy advocates make their arguments less about absolute moral values and more about specific, relatively minor, step-by-step problems, they can be successful in reforming policy. Policy makers sympathetic

---

[50]Walter Berns, *For Capital Punishment: Crime and the Morality of the Death Penalty* (New York: Basic Books, 1979), pp. 43–4.

[51]Christopher Z. Mooney and Mei-Hsien Lee, "Morality Policy Re-Invention: State Death Penalties," *Annals of the American Academy of Political and Social Science* 566(1999):80–92.

Figure 13.1

Executions in the United States: The Incremental Success of Death Penalty Reformers

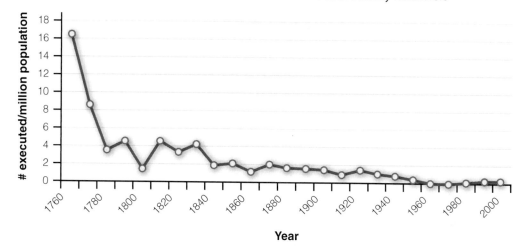

Note: This figure shows the sharp decline in the number of executions per million residents in the United States since 1770.

Sources: Death Penalty Information Center, http://deathpenaltyinfo.org/article.php?scid=8&did=269; U.S. Department of Justice, Office of Justice Programs, Bureau of Justice Statistics, http://www.ojp.usdoj.gov/bjs/glance/tables/exetab.htm; and Ken Park, ed., *World Almanac and Book of Facts 2006* (New York: World Almanac Books, 2005), p. 477.

to their cause encourage this change of tactics, because doing so changes the politics of morality policy into something more routine and familiar. Policy makers are much more comfortable when basic policy goals and values are agreed upon by all parties, with only the practical steps needed to reach these goals being debated. Such policy debate is less threatening to elected officials because it reduces the chances that opponents will use their positions on these highly visible and contentious issues against them in the next campaign. Incremental, instrumental policy change is also more comfortable for nonelected executive branch officials and legislative staff because it plays to their strengths and experience in policy analysis. Thus, all the institutions and actors in the regular policy-making system encourage morality policy reformers to work for incremental changes rather than major ones and to use instrumental arguments rather than moral ones. If these reformers conform to this more routine politics, they are rewarded by being able to move their policy goals forward (that

is, if they reflect the moral values of much of the population).

As morality policy reformers learn the institutions of the policy-making process and adjust their tactics accordingly, the terms of the debate change. Morality arguments are purged and replaced with less contentious ones. So the gambling policy debate shifts from being about gambling's immorality to being about its impacts on tax revenue and tourism and, perhaps, about how to help those few people who are gambling addicts.[52] Censorship is no longer about banning those films that no one should be allowed to see; instead, it is about labeling films so that adults can make an informed decision about just how much sex and violence they want to see.[53]

---

[52]Patrick A. Pierce and Donald E. Miller, *Gambling Politics: State Government and the Business of Betting* (Boulder, CO: Lynne Rienner, 2004).

[53]Richard A. Brisbin Jr., "From Censorship to Ratings: Substantive Rationality, Political Entrepreneurship, and Sex in the Movies," in Christopher Z. Mooney, ed., *The Public Clash of Private Values: The Politics of Morality Policy* (New York: Chatham House, 2001).

INSTITUTIONS MATTER

FEDERALISM AND MORALITY POLICY

One American political institution that helps reduce morality policy rhetoric and conflict is federalism. Americans share many basic values, but there are also regional differences among those who hold various traditional religious values and political ideologies, as well as differences among those who think that certain moral values ought to influence public policy.[1] Some people worry about the resulting patchwork of morality regulation that results from the various state and local laws,[2] but federalism allows states and communities to shape policy to reflect better the differences among their respective residents' moral views, allowing for a closer congruence of public opinion and policy than if we had a unitary system of government and, therefore, yielding less conflict on these issues.[3]

Consider two neighboring states—Nevada and Utah. In 1930, long before it became legal in any other state, Nevada embraced casino gambling as a way to generate state revenue and promote economic development. Utah, on the other hand, is one of only two states (along with Hawaii) that still have a blanket ban on gambling—not even church basement bingo is legal. Furthermore, the sale of alcohol is strictly regulated in Utah, whereas in Nevada, it flows much more freely. Even prostitution is legal (although heavily regulated) in some parts of Nevada—but certainly not in Utah. Clearly, Nevada is not Utah, and the institution of federalism allows these states to express the different values of their citizens on these and other morality policies.

The states also recognize the importance of allowing morality policy to reflect the variation of values within their own borders. For example, institutions like state home rule laws typically give communities the authority to set local decency laws, which is why the location and number of pornography outlets and strip clubs varies so much within states. Many states also allow for local units of government to ban alcohol sales. Some cities, even rough-and-tumble Chicago, also have ordinances that allow neighborhoods to vote themselves alcohol-free or ban adult bookstores if they violate the values of their residents. These institutions—federalism, home rule, local options, and neighborhood control—allow policy makers to fine-tune public policy to fit the values of citizens, thereby avoiding conflict and controversy on these visible and electorally dangerous morality issues.

Notes
1   Robert S. Erikson, Gerald C. Wright, and John P. McIver, *Statehouse Democracy* (New York: Cambridge University Press, 1993); Layman, op. cit.
2   Michael Mintrom, "Competitive Federalism and the Governance of Controversial Science," *Publius* 39(2009):606–31.
3   Mooney (2000), op. cit.

Prostitution is banned, not because it is sinful, but because of the sexually transmitted diseases, exploitation of women, and drug abuse associated with it. Even the terminology of the debate changes: "Gambling" is now called "gaming," "censorship" yields to talk of "parental advisories" via "ratings systems," and "prostitution" becomes the "sex trade."

Thus, the institutional and political forces of state and local government tend to force morality policy making into the mold of run-of-the-mill, nonmorality policy making. By doing so, they "de-moralize" it, discouraging the political discussion of moral values, focusing on minor changes rather than major ones, and closely matching policy to public opinion so as to reduce the aggravation that any discontinuity could cause. As this proceeds, a morality issue returns to equilibrium and again moves off the policy agenda—at least until the next external shock starts the entire process again.

Morality Policy Politics in the States and Communities: Two Examples

Now that you have read about the typical pattern of morality policy politics in American states and communities, let's consider two extended examples. Although neither of these issues has completed the full cycle by returning to an entirely stable equilibrium—both issues are very much on the political agenda today—they illustrate well how the policy-making process works when basic moral conflict enters into the political debate. First, we describe the politics of the morality policy that has figured most prominently in American politics in recent decades—abortion regulation. Abortion politics has arguably had an impact on the current American political system as deep and long lasting as that of the Cold War or the globalization of the economy. Second, we look at a relatively new morality issue—same-sex marriage. The intensity and fast-changing terms of this issue provide a good example of a policy debate at the height of moral controversy.

Abortion Regulation

Certain morality policies have generated some of the most important political battles in American history. Because morality issues are technically simple, highly visible, and touch on many people's basic values, they can motivate social movements with political impacts far beyond the immediate issue at hand. The fights to abolish slavery in the 19th century and to ban alcohol in the early 20th century were two such issues. As we begin the 21st century, we are living in a political environment shaped in large part by the debate over another such momentous morality policy—the regulation of abortion.

The battle over abortion policy at all levels of government is one of the most important factors determining the shape of American politics today, from our polarized political parties to the rise of the Christian Right to the importance and political respectability of arch-conservative political thought. In 1964, Republican Barry Goldwater lost the presidential race in one of the most lopsided landslides in history, a loss widely attributed to his "extreme" (his own word) conservative politics. At that time, Ronald Reagan was a Democrat, and many conservative Democrats and moderate—and even liberal—Republicans served in the U.S. Congress. The Catholic Church was not involved in politics (except on a few issues involving its own economic self-interest), and most television evangelists' talk focused exclusively on saving souls.[54] Today, Goldwater and Reagan are mainstream Republican icons, the congressional parties are almost ideologically pure (with liberal Republicans being among the rarest of political creatures), and the Catholic Church and Evangelical Protestant churches and church leaders are among the most powerful political forces in the country. What caused American politics to change so fundamentally in the last half century? Many would argue that a single word explains it: abortion. And much of the abortion politics that has changed this country during this period has occurred in the states and communities.

Equilibrium Prior to the Civil War, a lack of medical skill rendered moot most political questions about artificial abortion.[55] As advances in surgical technique made the

---

[54]But consider the Rev. Billie James Hargis, who in the 1940s and 1950s was the godfather of conservative radio and television evangelists. See: James Reichley and A. James Reichley, *Faith in Politics* (Washington, DC: Brookings Institution, 2002).

[55]James C. Mohr, *Abortion in America: The Origins and Evolution of National Policy, 1800–1900* (New York: Oxford University Press, 1979); Luker, op. cit.; Tribe, op. cit.

procedure practical in the late 19th century, the American Medical Association (AMA), a fledgling interest group and professional association of medical doctors, argued that, as a medical procedure, questions about when an abortion was appropriate should be settled by doctors. The AMA successfully fought for state and local laws banning abortions that were not "medically necessary," that is, those that were not ordered by a medical doctor. Thus, their advocacy was not morally based, but driven by professional and economic goals. These regulations kept those other than medical doctors (homeopaths, midwives, etc.) from performing abortions. So by the early 20th century, abortion policy was in equilibrium, and the little policy discussion that did arise was largely technical.

Cracks in this long abortion policy equilibrium began to appear in the 1960s. In 1962, Sherri Finkbine, a popular television personality in Phoenix, took Thalidomide for anxiety during her pregnancy.[56] The drug did severe and irreparable damage to the fetus she was carrying, and her doctor recommended an abortion. Finkbine's local hospital refused to perform the procedure, however, arguing that it was not medically necessary. She made a well-publicized appeal to change the hospital's decision, and when that appeal was denied, she traveled to Sweden for the abortion. Reports of thousands of "Thalidomide babies" born without arms or legs in Europe and outbreaks of severe birth defects caused by German measles in the United States at this time made Finkbine's case representative of a situation faced by many women, causing a heated and widespread controversy on the issue.

As a result of the Finkbine case and others like it, certain states began reforming their abortion laws in the 1960s. One of the first things they did was to codify that the

Table 13.3

State Abortion Regulation Reforms before Roe vs. Wade (1973)

State	Year of Reform
Mississippi	1966
California	1967
Colorado	1967
North Carolina	1967
Georgia	1968
Maryland	1968
Arkansas	1969
Delaware	1969
Kansas	1969
New Mexico	1969
Oregon	1969
Alaska	1970
Hawaii	1970
New York	1970
South Carolina	1970
Virginia	1970
Washington	1970
Florida	1972

Source: Christopher Z. Mooney and Mei-Hsien Lee, "Legislating Morality in the American States: The Case of Pre-*Roe* Abortion Regulation Reform," *American Journal of Political Science* 39(1995):599–627.

procedure was allowable when the life or the health of the pregnant woman was at risk (see Table 13.3). The advocates of the reform were primarily medical groups who argued that this was strictly a health issue. The reform had so little moral opposition that conservative standard-bearer Ronald Reagan, as the governor of California, signed one of the most liberal abortion regulations into law in 1967.[57]

---

[56]Raymond Tatalovich, *The Politics of Abortion in the United States and Canada* (Armonk, NY: M.E. Sharpe, 1997).

[57]John Culver and April Smailes, "Abortion Politics and Policies in California," Presented at the Annual Meeting of the Western Political Science Association, Seattle, WA, 1999.

Although they did not dominate the debate, rumblings of moral arguments had begun to appear around even these early reforms. The nascent women's movement, including groups such as the National Organization for Women (NOW), organized in 1966, picked up the mantle of abortion reform, and some Catholic and Evangelical Protestant leaders made moral arguments against it. The 18 states that loosened their abortion regulations between 1966 and 1972 tended to have fewer Catholics and fundamentalist Protestants and more educated and working women than states that did not adopt any of these reforms, a pattern foreshadowing the future morality politics on the issue.[58] In particular, moral concerns began to arise about whether abortions should be available *on demand*, for any reason, to a pregnant woman. As of January 1973, only four states (Alaska, Hawaii, New York, and Washington) allowed abortion on demand.

The Shock: Roe vs. Wade (1973) That month, January 1973, the U.S. Supreme Court shocked both proponents and opponents of abortion regulation reform by striking down all state abortion laws in *Roe vs. Wade*.[59] This decision thrust the question of abortion on demand squarely into public debate, with all its moral implications. Based on its earlier finding[60] that the federal Bill of Rights implied a right to privacy, the Court held that states could not limit a woman's right to abortion on demand in the **first trimester** of pregnancy, although they could regulate abortion in the second and third trimesters.

Few on either side of the issue felt that the Supreme Court would go this far in deregulating abortion.[61] Antiabortion groups had largely ignored the case, not even filing any **amicus curiae briefs** with the Court on it. Likewise, the emerging groups interested in deregulating abortion had focused their energies on incremental reforms in the states. In reaction to *Roe*, however, antiabortion groups were energized dramatically and organized permanently. On the other hand, those groups advocating for a woman's right to abortion on demand actually became less active immediately after the *Roe* decision. They thought they had won the argument, so they moved on to other issues—at least for the moment.

The Morality Politics of Abortion Regulation
Roe v. Wade's political shock cannot be overestimated. The decision set off a firestorm of morality politics that has helped define American politics ever since.[62] Those who felt that their basic moral values were threatened by legalizing abortion on demand got very busy in the political arena. The first major group to do so was the Roman Catholic Church, which had the advantages of having millions of active members, a well-developed hierarchical organizational structure, and a clear, long-standing doctrine opposing any artificial interference with conception and birth. Prior to *Roe*, the Catholic Church had been very wary of direct political involvement.[63] But abortion on demand threatened its basic values and teachings so deeply that the church stepped forthrightly into the political arena on a morality issue for the first time. Its antiabortion activities in the 1970s included directives from bishops to priests and from priests to parishioners to oppose abortion regulation reform, messages on the subject from the pulpit, posters

---

[58]Larry D. Barnett, "The Roots of Law," *Journal of Gender, Social Policy, and the Law* 15(2007):613–86; Mooney and Lee (1995), op. cit.

[59]*Roe vs. Wade* 410 U.S. 113 (1973).

[60]*Griswold v. Connecticut* 381 U.S. 479 (1965).

[61]Marian Faux, *Roe v. Wade* (New York: Macmillan, 1988).

[62]N. E. H. Hull and Peter Charles Hoffer, *Roe v. Wade: The Abortion Rights Controversy in American History* (Lawrence, KS: University Press of Kansas, 2001).

[63]Fabrizio, op. cit.

in church halls, and the use of existing church groups and organizations to organize rallies, send letters to politicians, compose **Op-Ed articles** for newspapers, and undertake other political actions. *Roe v. Wade* quickly transformed the American Catholic Church into a juggernaut of an interest group.

Legalized abortion on demand also threatened the basic moral values of many American Evangelical Protestants; but because their organizational structures were less rigid, these churches took longer to organize for political action than did the Catholics. By the early 1980s, however, conservative Protestants had established such interest groups as the American Christian Cause, Concerned Women for America, and the Moral Majority. These groups were both well organized and politically potent, working effectively through both grassroots political action and by taking over the Republican Party apparatus in many states.[64]

These antiabortion groups used basic moral arguments in their political rhetoric. Although they also raised some technical medical issues (such as when a fetus feels pain), their basic arguments focused on their fundamental belief that life begins at conception. Thus, they argued, anything that stops fetal development artificially is, effectively, murder. This logic naturally led these groups to the argument that legalized abortion amounted to mass murder, something with the moral equivalency of the Holocaust and other massive atrocities. Words such as *slaughter* and *genocide* are strongly evocative of emotion and moral outrage, making them very useful in changing minds, energizing activists, and gaining media attention. Because most of these antiabortion groups were religiously based, it was quite natural for them to back their arguments with religious authority, primarily the Christian Bible for Protestant groups and papal pronouncements for Catholic groups. These groups began calling themselves **"pro-life"**; the moral implication

that their opponents were somehow "anti-life" or "pro-death" was not accidental.

On the other side of the abortion regulation battle, interest groups that advocated the right of women to abortion on demand made no religiously based moral arguments. Rather, they focused mainly on the practical implications of unwanted pregnancies and the disproportionate burden that women bore for them. However, at root, they supported their position with philosophical—some might say moral[65]—arguments about women's civil right to control their own bodies. These groups tended not to be religiously based (although many liberal Protestant churches supported them), but rather were secular women's and medical groups. The positive name these groups adopted for themselves was **"pro-choice."** Perhaps unintentionally, this moniker reflects the nonmoral nature of their arguments. Certainly no "choice" could be involved if the issue was driven by a moral imperative.

Post-*Roe* abortion politics began with pro-life forces trying to ban the procedure outright in their state legislatures. Indeed, they were successful in getting anti-abortion legislation passed in many states, particularly where individuals' religious and ideological views matched those of these groups.[66] Legislators and governors in these states eagerly tried to bring public policy back into line with their constituents' views. Indeed, many states even passed new abortion bans, reaffirming their pre-*Roe* policies. These **expressive actions** allowed policy makers to demonstrate that they shared their constituents' views, but they had no practical effects because *Roe* made them clearly unconstitutional.

As the 1970s progressed, pro-life reformers grew less satisfied with symbolic victories, and they modified their strategies and policy

---

[64]Matthew Moen, *The Transformation of the Christian Right* (Tuscaloosa, AL: University of Alabama Press, 1993); Conger, op. cit.

[65]Some might argue that arguments based on an appeal to basic rights in the Constitution are themselves moral arguments. See Smith and Tatalovich, op. cit.

[66]Lee Epstein and Joseph F. Kobylka, *The Supreme Court and Legal Change* (Chapel Hill, NC: University of North Carolina Press, 1992); Glen Halva-Neubauer, "Abortion Policy in the Post-Webster Age," *Publius* 20(1990):27–44.

agenda to work better with state and local government institutions and policy-making processes. These highly motivated advocates not only continued to expand their political base by appealing to their supporters' sense of moral outrage about abortion, but they also learned how to use this political clout to influence policy makers through direct lobbying, campaign contributions, and political endorsements. More important, they shifted their short-term policy goals from the immediate banning of all abortions to chipping away incrementally at the availability of them. Their hope was that such reforms would reduce the number of abortions that were actually performed. Their basic strategy became to make getting an abortion as difficult as possible so that more women contemplating the procedure would be discouraged and choose another way to deal with their unwanted pregnancies.[67]

Pro-life groups took a scattershot approach to this incremental reform strategy, working to pass a variety of abortion restrictions in as many states and communities as possible, hoping that the federal courts would not strike them all down. In essence, they were testing the limits of what abortion restrictions the courts would allow. In an important decision in 1976,[68] the Supreme Court struck down four of seven restrictions in a Missouri law as unconstitutional. More important for the emerging incremental pro-life strategy, however, was that the Court let three of these restrictions stand. These restrictions were rather minor, requiring some medical recordkeeping, defining the "viability" of a fetus, and requiring a woman's "informed consent" before she could have an abortion. These successes encouraged other states to pass more restrictions, and as the 1970s and 1980s progressed, the federal courts responded more and more favorably to the pro-life legal arguments.[69] Reforms such as mandatory waiting periods, bans on public

funding of abortions for poor women, various regulations of facilities and doctors providing abortions, and spousal and parental consent passed in state after state. In their decisions in *Webster vs. Reproductive Health Services* (1989)[70] and *Planned Parenthood v. Casey* (1992),[71] the Supreme Court went about as far as it could in allowing the states to regulate abortion restrictively without overturning the basic right to a first trimester abortion that was enunciated in *Roe vs. Wade*.[72] In recent years, different states have passed a multitude of abortion restrictions and regulations, including mandatory reading of various statements about fetal development and adoption options, counseling about potential risks of abortion, fetal ultrasounds, and rules allowing medical professionals to object to certain duties on religious grounds.[73]

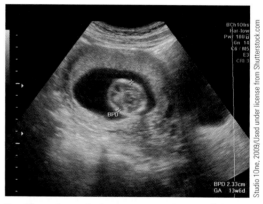

Pro-life and pro-choice groups continue to fight over incremental policy changes, such as requiring that a pregnant woman view an ultrasound of her fetus (above) before having an abortion.

[67]Epstein and Kobylka, ibid.

[68]*Planned Parenthood of Central Missouri v. Danforth* 428 U.S. 52 (1976).

[69]Epstein and Kobylka, op. cit.

[70]*Webster v. Reproductive Health Services* 492 U.S. 490 (1989).

[71]*Planned Parenthood v. Casey* 505 U.S. 833 (1992).

[72]Barbara Hinkson Craig and David M. O'Brien, *Abortion and American Politics* (Chatham, NJ: Chatham House, 1993).

[73]Christine Vestal, "Ultrasound at Center of State Abortion Wars," *Stateline.org*, 25 June 2008, online edition; David G. Savage, "Broader Medical Refusal Rule May Go Far Beyond Abortion," *The Los Angeles Times*, 2 December 2008, online edition.

Complementing their strategy of working incrementally through the legislative and judicial processes, ever since the 1980s, pro-life groups have tapped into their sympathizers' moral outrage by engaging extensively in direct political action, even if just to stop one abortion at a time. In particular, these groups routinely stage demonstrations outside abortion clinics, both to encourage group solidarity by allowing their members to express their opinions publicly and to try to influence the personal decisions of pregnant women entering the building. These clinic demonstrations range from loud events involving dozens of protesters (sometimes with pro-choice counter-demonstrators mixed in) to as few as one lone picketer. You see an example of the latter in a pivotal scene in the movie *Juno*, when a pregnant young woman is approached by such a protester—a girl from her high school—who tells her that "your baby has fingernails." The strong views of these pro-life advocates, the emotional state of the pregnant women, and the strong views of pro-choice advocates often make these situations very tense, resulting in much emotional trauma and sometimes physical and verbal violence and arrests. Local government officials—mayors, city councils, and police—are often reluctantly forced into morality policy politics when they have to weigh the free speech rights of advocates on both sides against public order ordinances.[74]

Even as pro-life groups succeed in their incremental policy-making strategy in most states, some pro-life activists, filled with the zeal of the morally righteous, feel intense frustration at not being able to ban abortion quickly and completely. This frustration has led to several well-publicized acts of violence, such as the one described at the beginning of this chapter.[75] Since the 1970s, there have been 40 documented bombings of clinics, over

160 arsons, thousands of acts of vandalism, and hundreds or thousands of threats of violent acts; in the 1990s alone, seven abortion clinic employees were killed and another 13 were wounded.[76] The abortion debate may be the only issue in American politics today that generates this level of political violence. But perhaps a more effective tool than actual violence in putting a chill into the abortion environment has been the pervasive use of political harassment by pro-life activists.[77] This is direct political action that targets individual people involved in providing abortions with the goal of forcing them out of the business. Following clinic employees home from work, picketing their houses and churches, sending postcards to their neighbors, and other actions are harassment that can cause not only annoyance, but fear among those targeted that they may be the next one to be physically attached.

Other pro-choice activists have used economic boycotts as a way to achieve their political goals. But even in this, the morality politics of the abortion issue have led to some extreme and aggressive tactics. For example, in 2003, when a pro-life activist and construction contractor discovered that Planned Parenthood was building a clinic in Austin, Texas, he organized the construction trades and contractors around the city to refuse to do work on the building.[78] When the boycott showed signs of cracking, his group barraged contractors—and their religious leaders and friends—with telephone calls, imploring them to support the boycott. Some contractors received up to 1,200 phone calls a day. Clearly, the motivation for all these extraordinary political actions goes beyond the economic or partisan or even

---

[74]Clarke, op. cit.

[75]Jennifer Gonnerman, "The Terrorist Campaign against Abortion," *The Village Voice*, 3–9 November 1998, online edition; Hunter, op. cit.

[76]"Incidents of Violence and Disruption against Abortion Providers" (Washington, DC: National Abortion Federation, 2006).

[77]Alesha E. Doan, *Opposition and Intimidation: The Abortion Wars and Strategies of Political Harassment*" (Ann Arbor, MI: University of Michigan Press, 2007).

[78]Doan, op. cit., pp. 2–5.

Abortion protest

AP Photo/Charles Dharapak

the ideological; the motivation is a perceived attack on these people's basic moral values, values that get to the heart of their very identity. When they believe that the normal political process is failing to support these values, they resort to extraordinary political actions.

Return to Equilibrium? Recently, the amount and intensity of grassroots political activity on abortion policy have waned in many places. Does this mean that political equilibrium on the issue has returned? Perhaps—but if so, probably only for a limited time. Pro-life groups continue to pursue their incremental strategy successfully in the states.[79] Today, although women continue to have the legal right to a first-trimester abortion on demand, the ability to exercise that right is severely limited in many states, especially by the availability of doctors willing to perform them. For example, only one abortion clinic is currently operating in the entire state of Mississippi.[80] Pro-life reformers also continue to adopt new tactics as they learn to work within the regular political institutions of the state and local

governments. For example, before staunch pro-life reformer Phillip Kline lost elections in 2006 and 2008, he used his powers as local prosecutor and Kansas attorney general to subpoena abortion clinic records extensively. While pro-choice activists claimed that this was harassment, Kline said he was just checking for violations of health and safety regulations and evidence to prosecute child rapists.[81] Pro-life reformers have even begun using various nonmorality-based arguments in their campaigns, claiming, for example, that abortion harms a woman's health.[82] Furthermore, some of the political power of the pro-life movement may have been dissipated by the split between those who wish to continue working incrementally within the system and those more frustrated activists who want to ban the procedure altogether.[83]

Further evidence of policy equilibrium is that while many abortion policy bills continue to be introduced every year in every state legislature, the only ones receiving serious attention tend to be those that make only small changes and have limited practical impacts. For example, in 2005, the Texas state legislature had heated debate over a bill to require parental *permission* for a minor to have an abortion—a significant, but still incremental, step from the existing law requiring only parental *notification*. In that same session, Texas lawmakers also gave considerable attention to a bill that would have just slightly strengthened restrictions on third-trimester abortions, even though fewer than 50 such abortions are performed in the state each year.[84]

[79]Kirk Johnson, "New Push Likely for Restrictions over Abortion," *The New York Times,* 20 April 2007, online edition.

[80]Peter Slevin, "Antiabortion Efforts Move to the State Level," *The Washington Post,* 8 June 2009, online edition.

[81]John Hanna, "Kan. AG Alarms Abortion-Rights Groups," *Sacramento Bee,* 27 September 2006, online edition.

[82]David Crary, "South Dakota Voters to Weigh Abortion Ban," *State Journal-Register,* 3 November 2006, p. 8.

[83]T. W. Farnam, "Antiabortion Initiatives Divide Movement," *The Wall Street Journal,* 21 April 2008, online edition.

[84]Michelle M. Marinez, "House Passes Abortion Measures," *Austin American-Statesman,* 17 May 2005, online edition.

Figure 13.2

Abortion Restrictions in the States, 2010

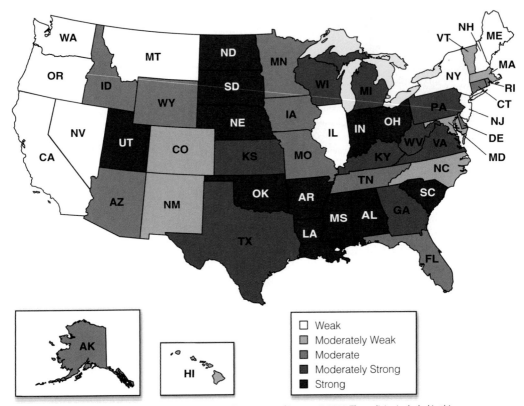

Note: This map shows restrictiveness of abortion regulations in the states as of January 1, 2010. The policies included in this measure are parental notification or consent for minors; reporting all abortions to a state authority; pre-abortion counseling requirements; pre-abortion waiting period requirements; "Choose Life" automobile license plates available; blocking abortion clinic entries prohibited (coded as less restrictive); and pre-abortion ultrasound required or counseling.

Source: Alan Guttmacher Institute, "State Policies in Brief: An Overview of Abortion Laws," 2009, http://www.guttmacher.org/statecenter/spibs/spib_OAL.pdf.

Currently, the restrictiveness of abortion regulation varies substantially from state to state (see Figure 13.2), and just like before *Roe,* a state's abortion regulations largely reflect the basic values of those who live there.[85] Abortion is more strictly regulated in conservative, rural states with many Evangelical

Protestants. In addition, the more Catholics who live in a state, the more restrictive its abortion policy is, all things being equal. That's why in Figure 13.2 you see some typically more liberal, urban states like Ohio, Michigan, Wisconsin, and Pennsylvania mixed in among the states with the toughest abortion regulations, along with rural states and those in the South (e.g., Mississippi, the Dakotas, and Georgia). In fact, a new study by political scientists John Camobreco and Michelle Barnello shows that as time has passed since *Roe,* a state's abortion regulations have reflected the

[85]Dana Patton, "The Supreme Court and Morality Policy Adoption in the American States: The Impact of Constitutional Context," *Political Research Quarterly* 60(2007):468–88; M. H. Medhoff, "The Determinants and Impact of State Abortion Restrictions," *American Journal of Economics and Sociology* 61(2002):481–93.

values of its citizens ever more closely.[86] Even members of the U.S. House, among the most electorally safe politicians in the country, vote to represent their constituents' values scrupulously on abortion issues.[87] This close correlation between values and abortion policy that federalism allows has helped to bring abortion policy into a greater degree of equilibrium than perhaps at any time since 1973 when the U.S. Supreme Court handed down the *Roe vs. Wade* decision.

Even if some measure of equilibrium has been reached on abortion regulation in this country, however, it certainly has a different tone than the policy equilibrium before *Roe*. At best, it is a very uneasy balance, more like an armed cease-fire than a settlement. The pro-life forces maintain their morality-based policy goals, still hoping to ban the procedure outright nationwide. Each sides is ever vigilant so that the other side does not gain even an inch of ground on the issue. Everyone involved knows that a single Supreme Court decision could shock the system again, starting another round of intense morality politics in the states and communities. This is why the abortion views of Samuel Alito figured so prominently in the U.S. Senate hearings for his Supreme Court nomination in 2005, while those of John Roberts (in 2005) and Sonia Sotomayor (in 2009) seemed somewhat less important. Alito was replacing Justice Sandra Day O'Connor, a swap that many thought would shift the balance on the Court significantly on abortion law. On the other hand, Chief Justice William Rehnquist's replacement by Roberts and Justice David Souter's replacement by Sotomayor were seen as less important because these pairs

of judges were thought to have similar positions on abortion.[88]

The first evidence of Alito's impact on the abortion debate was in *Gonzalez vs. Carhart* (2007), upholding a 2003 federal law banning "partial-birth abortion" (or "intact dilation and extraction" to the medical community and pro-choice forces).[89] In a challenge to a similar Nebraska statute in 2000,[90] O'Connor voted with the 5–4 majority that the law was unconstitutionally vague, but in *Gonzales*, Alito's vote created a majority that approved the ban. Activists in several states, including South Dakota, Louisiana, and Mississippi, have been working to pass laws completely banning abortion to set the stage for a challenge with which the newly aligned Supreme Court might completely reverse *Roe*.[91] Will some new decision soon become the shock that sends abortion policy making in the states and communities back into a morality policy frenzy? Only time will tell.

The overall impact of this generation-long morality policy struggle over abortion regulation has fundamentally changed the American political landscape. The debate caused religious conservatives to become an organized, active, powerful, and permanent political force in states and communities across the country for the first time since World War II. Catholic and fundamentalist Protestant groups have found their political voices and developed the institutions needed to ensure that they will be

---

[86]John F. Camobreco and Michelle A. Barnello, "Democratic Responsiveness and Policy Shock: The Case of Abortion," *State Politics and Policy Quarterly* 8(2008):48–65.

[87]Elizabeth A. Oldmixon, "Culture Wars in the Congressional Theater: How the U.S. House of Representatives Legislates Morality, 1993–1998," *Social Science Quarterly* 83(2002):775–88.

[88]Charlie Savage, "On Sotomayor, Some Abortion Rights Backers Are Uneasy," *The New York Times*, 28 May 2009; Jan Crawford Greenburg, "How Focus on Roe Pushes Aside Other Court Issues," *Chicago Tribune*, 29 December 2005, online edition.

[89]*Gonzales v. Carhart* 550 U.S. XXX (2007).

[90]*Stenberg v. Carhart* 530 U.S. 914 (2000).

[91]Associated Press, "Timeline of Abortion Developments in South Dakota," *Yankton (ND) Press*, 18 October 2008, online edition; Associated Press, "La. Senate Sends Abortion Ban to Gov.," *Sacramento Bee*, 6 June 2006, online edition; Associated Press, "Miss. House Advances Bill to Ban Abortion," *Chicago Tribune*, 1 March 2006, online edition.

a major factor in state and local politics for decades to come. The intensity and breadth of this morality policy debate has even realigned our political parties, causing greater ideological polarization in them than at any time since the Civil War.[92] As policy makers' and the public's views have sharpened and hardened, the relatively close division of public opinion on the issue suggests that there may be no long-term equilibrium on this morality policy in our lifetimes.

Same-Sex Marriage

Same-sex marriage has only recently exploded onto the states' and communities' policy agendas, but already it exhibits many of the key characteristics of morality policy. Although we cannot predict the progress of this issue in coming years—or even a few months from now—its progress so far suggests that it will generate active morality politics in the states and communities for the foreseeable future.

Equilibrium The legal and social status of American homosexuals has improved dramatically since the gay rights movement began in the late 1960s.[93] Even so, placing same-sex couples on an equal legal and social status as married heterosexual couples was virtually unthinkable until very recently—even among gay rights activists. In fact in 13 states, it was actually illegal for two men or two women to have sex with one another before the U.S. Supreme Court overturned all state and local **antisodomy** laws in 2003 (see Figure 13.3).[94] Although gay rights had been on many state and local government agendas since the 1970s, activists focused on such relatively incremental measures as eliminating discrimination against gays in employment, housing, adoption, and

the like. Gay rights groups made steady, but largely quiet, political headway by arguing that sexual orientation, like race and gender, is simply a condition of life into which people are born, and, therefore, it is unfair to discriminate against people on account of it.[95] Like with pre-*Roe* abortion regulation, by the early 1990s, gay rights laws in the states and communities typically reflected the ideology and values of their residents.[96]

The Shock: The Hawaii State Supreme Court and Same-Sex Marriage, 1993 As with abortion regulation, the shock of a court action set off the morality politics of same-sex marriage. But rather than a federal court decision, morality policy on this issue was set off by the Hawaii State Supreme Court. Before the Aloha State's high court actions in 1993, same-sex marriage was not even on the agenda of the Human Rights Campaign, the National Gay and Lesbian Task Force, or any of the other major gay rights advocacy groups. The leaders of these interest groups were taken as much by surprise as were their opponents by the events that thrust the issue into the limelight.[97]

While gay rights groups pursued steady, incremental change in state and local law, from time to time same-sex couples challenged the implicit ban on same-sex marriage simply by applying for a marriage license at their local

---

[92]Layman, op. cit.

[93]Eric Marcus, *Making Gay History: The Half-Century Fight for Gay and Lesbian Equal Rights* (New York: Harper, 2002).

[94]*Lawrence and Garner v. Texas* 539 U.S. 558 (2003).

[95]Martin Dupuis, *Same-Sex Marriage, Legal Mobilization, and the Politics of Rights* (New York: Peter Lang, 2002).

[96]Haider-Markel and Meier, ibid; S. A. Soule, "Going to the Chapel? Same-Sex Marriage Bans in the United States, 1973–2000," *Social Problems* 51(2004):453–77; Kenneth D. Wald, James W. Button, and Barbara A. Rienzo, "The Politics of Gay Rights in American Communities: Explaining Anti-Discrimination Ordinances and Policies," *American Journal of Political Science* 40(1996):1152–78.

[97]Patrick J. Egan and Kenneth Sherrill, "Marriage and the Shifting Priorities of a New Generation of Lesbians and Gays," *PS: Political Science and Politics* 38(2005):229–33.

Figure 13.3

States with Antisodomy Laws before *Lawrence vs. Texas* (2003)

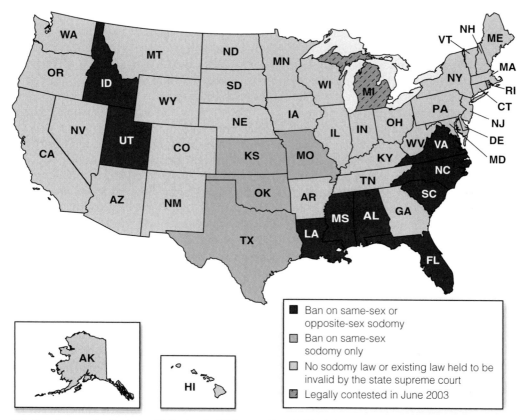

Ban on same-sex or opposite-sex sodomy
Ban on same-sex sodomy only
No sodomy law or existing law held to be invalid by the state supreme court
Legally contested in June 2003

Note: These laws were in effect in June 2003, when the U.S. Supreme Court decision in *Lawrence vs. Texas* invalidated all state antisodomy laws. Those states that are not marked had no law against sodomy (or any existing law had been invalidated by its supreme court).

Source: Policy Institute, National Gay and Lesbian Task Force, http://www.thetaskforce.org/downloads/sodomymap0603.pdf.

courthouse and suing the relevant local official when they were denied one.[98] These courts routinely failed to accept the couples' arguments about equal protection and equal rights under the state and federal constitutions, and they lost their cases. The establishment gay rights groups viewed this radical strategy as naïve, and discouraged it for fear of political backlash.[99]

In Hawaii in 1993, however, something unusual happened. Three same-sex couples sued the state for the right to marry—and they won. The Hawaii Supreme Court held that limiting marriage to heterosexual couples constituted sex discrimination, thereby violating the Hawaii Constitution.[100] This decision shocked people, policy makers, and interest groups across the country, those both in favor of and opposed to gay rights, instantly stirring the political pot on the issue.

---

[98]Daniel R. Pinello, *America's Struggle for Same-Sex Marriage* (New York: Cambridge University Press, 2006).

[99]Jason Pierceson, "Pushing for Equality within the Backlash: Same-Sex Marriage and Civil Unions in Three Midwestern States," Presented at the 2009 American Political Science Association meetings, Toronto, ON.

---

[100] *Baehr v. Lewin* 852 P.2d 44 (Hay Sup.Ct. 1993).

Why should someone in Florida or New York care whether Hawaii lets same-sex couples marry? Aside from people be threatened by same-sex marriage in general (see below), the reason for the nationwide interest in the Hawaii court decision was that a state's marriage laws have direct implications for other states. The **Full Faith and Credit Clause** of the U.S. Constitution encourages each state to recognize, honor, and enforce other states' actions, especially in the areas of civil and family law. Such reciprocity is what makes a couple's marriage in one state legally binding in another state. Thus, the reason both proponents and opponents of same-sex marriage became extraordinarily interested in the Hawaii case was the idea—although not a tested legal fact—that if one state allowed same-sex marriage, then every other state would have to recognize those same-sex marriages performed in that state. So, with this decision, the morality politics of same-sex marriage began in earnest.

The Morality Politics of Same-Sex Marriage In combination with the Constitution's Full Faith and Credit Clause, the 1993 Hawaii decision severely threatened certain people's deeply held moral values about family, sexuality, and natural law; this was especially the case for people who thought that homosexuality itself was morally wrong. Interest groups that took this view and became active in state politics tended to be associated with religious organizations, such as certain fundamentalist Protestant denominations and the Roman Catholic Church, that read the Christian Bible literally and interpreted it to say that homosexuality was an "abomination unto the Lord."[101] In fact, many of the most active groups opposing same-sex marriage—groups like Focus on the Family and the Christian Coalition—cut their political teeth fighting for stricter abortion regulation.[102] Their arguments against same-sex marriage, like their arguments against abortion, were morally based and supported by their interpretation of biblical passages. Grassroots veterans of the abortion wars were easily motivated by such arguments.

One lesson the leaders of these groups took from their abortion experiences was the importance of appealing in a straightforward way to certain people's basic values in defining the issue. However, because of the growing tolerance of homosexuality in the United States, as reflected in the various state and local gay rights laws in the 1970s and 1980s, arguing that homosexuals themselves were immoral would not likely attract the broad public support they needed.[103] Instead, they argued that same-sex marriage threatened that "sacred institution," traditional heterosexual marriage.[104] By threatening heterosexual marriage, same-sex marriage was said to threaten our entire society, undermining its moral foundation, leading to polygamy and incest, and destabilizing society in general.[105] To symbolize this argument, these groups assumed for themselves the positive moniker "pro-family." This was an excellent political choice—after all, who could be anti-family? Note the parallel to the anti-abortion label, "pro-life." This parallel was not accidental.

---

[101]Donald P. Haider-Markel, "Policy Diffusion as a Geographical Expansion of the Scope of Political Conflict: Same-Sex Marriage Bans in the 1990s," *State Politics and Policy Quarterly* 1(2001):5–26.

[102]John Russell, *Funding the Culture Wars: Philanthropy, Church and State* (Washington, DC: National Committee for Responsive Philanthropy, 2005).

[103]Frederick Liu and Stephen Macedo, "The Federal Marriage Amendment and the Strange Evolution of the Conservative Case against Gay Marriage," *PS: Political Science and Politics* 38(2005):211–17.

[104]Christian Worldview Concepts, "A Case against 'Gay Marriage.'" *Christian Worldview Concepts* 1(2004):1–4.

[105]Ronald L. Steiner, "A Commentary on the Old Saw that Same-Sex Marriage Threatens Civilization," in Gordon A. Babst, Emily R. Gill, and Jason Pierceson, eds., *Moral Argument, Religion, and Same-Sex Marriage* (Lanham, MD: Lexington Press, 2009).

On the other side of the debate, same-sex marriage advocates argued that the legal sanction of homosexuals' long-term, committed relationships was a civil rights and equal protection issue. These groups drew the analogy between their struggle and the racial civil rights groups of a generation earlier, which was perhaps the most successful social movement in American history and one that retains very broad positive associations among Americans to this day.[106] In this way, same-sex marriage supporters' argument was one of fairness rather than religious morality: Because homosexuality is a condition of nature, like being a woman or being black, rather than a moral failing, it is unfair to deny homosexuals the right to participate fully in society, including by getting married. Thus, pro-same-sex marriage arguments were based less on an appeal to basic moral values than on an appeal to justice.

After the Hawaii decision, advocates on both sides of the issue made their cases in the states and in Washington, D.C. In doing so, however, there were at least two significant differences between the politics of same-sex marriage and the politics of abortion regulation. First, the morality-based argument of the groups opposing same-sex marriage resonated well with a clear majority of people in the country.[107] Even though Americans were increasingly tolerant of homosexuals as the 20th century came to an end, same-sex marriage was just a step too far for most people. Second, the Hawaii Supreme Court (and later, courts in Massachusetts, Connecticut, Vermont, and Iowa) found that a ban on same-sex marriage violated the state's constitution rather than the federal constitution (as in *Roe v. Wade*), and most state constitutions are far easier to amend than the federal document. These two features—one regarding public opinion and one regarding an institution—of the political landscape caused the morality politics of same-sex marriage to take a very different path than that of abortion regulation.

Soon after the Hawaii decision, conservatives in Congress saw a disjuncture between public opinion and the potential legalization of same-sex marriage. To close that gap, they put the federal **Defense of Marriage Act (DOMA)** on a fast track, with President Bill Clinton signing it on September 21, 1996. DOMA supported the values of reformers opposing same-sex marriage in two ways. First, it explicitly allowed an exception to the Full Faith and Credit Clause, allowing states not to recognize same-sex marriages sanctioned in other states if they so chose. Second, it defined marriage for purposes of federal law (such as for determining eligibility for Social Security survivor's benefits) as being "a union of one man and one woman as husband and wife." By 2000, 34 states had adopted "little DOMAs," likewise defining marriage and banning the recognition of same-sex marriages from other states, and five more states have done so since then.[108] The unusual speed with which both the federal and state governments acted in response to the Hawaii case shows both how well anti-same-sex marriage groups were able to mobilize their members and sympathetic policy makers and how potent the moral threat that same-sex marriage represented to many Americans' basic values at this time. Just like with the politics of abortion regulation, this shows how closely politicians monitor and respond to

---

[106]Jason Pierceson, "Same-Sex Marriage and the American Political Tradition," in Gordon A. Babst, Emily R. Gill, and Jason Pierceson, eds., *Moral Argument, Religion, and Same-Sex Marriage* (Lanham, MD: Lexington Press, 2009).

[107]Donald P. Haider-Markel and Matthew S. Kaufman, "Public Opinion and Policy Making in the Culture Wars: Is There a Connection between Opinion and State Policy on Gay and Lesbian Issues?" in Jeffrey E. Cohen, ed., *Public Opinion in State Politics* (Stanford, CA: Stanford University Press, 2006).

[108]Karen Struening, "Looking for Liberty and Defining Marriage in Three Same-Sex Marriage Cases," in Gordon A. Babst, Emily R. Gill, and Jason Pierceson, eds., *Moral Argument, Religion, and Same-Sex Marriage* (Lanham, MD: Lexington Press, 2009).

public opinion on morality policies.[109] Hawaii's policy makers worked just as fast as did those elsewhere, putting a referendum before the voters in 1998 for a state constitutional amendment explicitly outlawing same-sex marriage. The state's voters then approved the ban before its supreme court could rule on an appeal in the original case.

By this time the genie was out of the bottle, however; same-sex marriage advocates had seen how the judicial route could bypass more majoritarian policy-making approaches.[110] In another landmark case, in 1999, a same-sex couple in Vermont won a marriage license lawsuit.[111] What made the Vermont case different from the Hawaii case was that Green Mountain State policy makers decided not to fight the decision. Rather, the legislature and governor embraced the idea, passing legislation in 2000 establishing **civil unions** in the state, an alternative to marriage into which same-sex or opposite-sex couples could enter. This was a legally binding and legally recognized relationship, but using the term "civil union" helped diffuse the moral objections that moderates had to same-sex marriage, per se. Because the state would still be recognizing and sanctioning homosexuality, however, conservative activists fought civil unions, too. In fact, as the terms of the debate have evolved quickly in recent years,

even some gay rights activists have also come to object to civil unions, seeing them as second-class alternatives to full marriage.[112]

Even in liberal Vermont, civil unions were not an easy sell in 1999. In the 2000 general election, just after the Democratic state legislature had passed the bill, 16 lawmakers who supported it lost their seats, the Republicans won a majority in the House and almost a majority in the Senate, and Governor Howard Dean had the toughest state race of his career. But the law was not repealed, which made Vermont the first state to establish an official relationship for same-sex couples with all the legal trappings of marriage, if not the name.

The next chapter in this story also starts with a court case, but it had the most wide-ranging effects. In decisions delivered in November 2003 and February 2004, the Massachusetts Supreme Judicial Court ruled not only that the state's constitution prohibited any marriage law that discriminated between same- and opposite-sex couples, but also that anything short of *true marriage* would establish an "unconstitutional, inferior, and discriminatory status for same-sex couples."[113] The court directed the state legislature to craft legislation allowing same-sex couples to marry, and on May 17, 2004, Massachusetts became the first state to issue regular marriage licenses to same-sex couples.

If the Hawaii case set off alarm bells for same-sex marriage opponents in 1993, the Massachusetts high court's actions showed that this was no longer a drill. By 2004, many states and communities allowed nonmarried couples (of the same or opposite sex) to establish legal relationships that allowed them some of the benefits of married couples, such as hospital visitation rights, inheritance rights, and the like. But here was the real thing—same-sex

[109]Elizabeth Anne Oldmixon and Brian Robert Calfano, "The Religious Dynamics of Decision Making on Gay Rights Issues in the U.S. House of Representatives, 1993–2002," *Journal for the Scientific Study of Religion* 46(2007):55–70; Lax and Phillips, op. cit.; Pappas, Mendez, and Herrick, op. cit.

[110]Susan Gluck Mezey, *Queers in Court: Gay Rights Law and Public Policy* (Lanham, MD: Rowan and Littlefield, 2007); Brian DiSarro, "Judicial Accountability or Majority Tyranny? Judicial Selection Methods and State Gay Rights Rulings," Presented at the 2007 State Politics and Policy Conference, Austin, TX; Melinda D. Kane, "Timing Matters: Shifts in the Causal Determinants of Sodomy Law Decriminalization, 1961–1998," *Social Problems* 54(2007):211–39.

[111]*Baker v. State* 744 A.2d 864 (Vt. 1999).

[112]Alison Leigh Cowan, "Gay Couples Say Civil Unions Aren't Enough," *The New York Times*, 17 March 2008, online edition. Indeed, in 2009, the Vermont General Assembly overrode Governor Jim Douglas's veto to allow gays and lesbians to marry.

[113]Pinello, op. cit.

marriage, plain and simple. And the Massachusetts decision set off a nationwide movement. In February and March 2004, same-sex couples across the country began asking their city, town, and county clerks for marriage licenses, and in several places, they got them.[114] San Francisco, California, and Multnomah County, Oregon, made front-page news nationwide for granting marriage licenses to thousands of same-sex couples; local officials in such places as New Paltz, New York; Asbury Park, New Jersey; and Sandoval County, New Mexico, also issued marriage licenses to same-sex couples during this heady period.

As it turned out, public opinion in most American states and communities would not stand for such a quick and significant change in this morality policy. Outside of Massachusetts, courts and governors quickly ruled that any same-sex marriage licenses issued by local governments were null and void and that no more would be forthcoming. Perhaps more important—and emblematic of morality politics—in a burst of energy that demonstrated the severity of the threat to their moral values, opposition groups qualified and won ballot measures outlawing same-sex marriage in 13 states in 2004, two more states in 2005, and another eight in 2006. The only same-sex marriage ban that was defeated was in Arizona, in 2006. As discussed earlier in this chapter, this outcome might be due to the complicated wording of the measure (see Table 13.1). A more simply worded measure in 2008 was approved by the Grand Canyon State's electorate by an eight-percentage-point margin. As Table 13.4 shows, almost one half of the states voted on and banned same-sex marriage within one election cycle of the Massachusetts court decision establishing same-sex marriage there. This was certainly one of the quickest reform movements ever to sweep the country, and it was clearly the result of morality politics.

Why was direct democracy used so extensively and successfully in this movement to oppose same-sex-marriage reform? One reason was that groups opposed to same-sex marriage sought changes to state constitutions, since the Hawaii, Vermont, and Massachusetts court decisions were based on those states' constitutions, and constitutional amendment requires a referendum or initiative in most states. But more important, the politics of this morality policy made ballot measures the preferred political tactic for these opposition groups. In the early and mid-2000s, opponents of same-sex marriage were able to explain their arguments to a shocked constituency in simple, morally based terms: Traditional marriage is important and same-sex marriage threatens it—just see your Bible.[115] Even though Americans had grown increasingly tolerant of homosexuals by this time, there was still some bias against sexual minorities.[116] Deep-seated prejudices die hard, and even socially unacceptable discrimination can be expressed discreetly in the ballot box. For example, in 1996, over 30 percent of Kentucky voters chose to keep an archaic state requirement that the Blue Grass State's schools be racially segregated; in 2000, over 40 percent of Alabama voters voted to keep a ban on interracial marriage.[117] Since it is likely that racial prejudice is far less socially acceptable in the United States today than is

---

[114]Ibid.

[115]Vincent Price, L. Nir, and Joseph N. Cappella, "Framing Public Discussion of Gay Unions," *Public Opinion Quarterly* 69(2005):179–212.

[116]A. S. Yang, "The Polls—Trends: Attitudes toward Homosexuality," *Public Opinion Quarterly* 61(1997):477–507.

[117]Voter error could explain a portion of this shocking level of support for these racist policies. One study estimated that only 6.4 percent of these Kentucky voters actually intended to vote for school segregation—but this still demonstrates substantial support for a policy that had been found unconstitutional over 40 years before the vote. See: D. Stephen Voss and Penny Miller, "Following a False Trail: The Hunt for Backlash in Kentucky's 1996 Desegregation Vote," *State Politics and Policy Quarterly* 1(2001):62–80.

Table 13.4

Voting Results for Anti-Same-Sex Marriage Ballot Measures, 1998–2008

State	Vote (% Yes–% No)
1998	
Alaska	68–32
Hawaii	69–29
Year average	**69–31**
2000	
Nebraska[1]	70–30
Year average	**70–30**
2002	
Nevada	67–33
Year average	**67–33**
2004	
Arkansas	75–25
Georgia	76–24
Kentucky	75–25
Louisiana	78–22
Michigan	59–41
Mississippi	86–14
Missouri	71–29
Montana	66–34
North Dakota	73–27
Ohio	62–38
Oklahoma	76–24
Oregon	57–43
Utah	66–34
Year average	**71–29**
2005	
Kansas	70–30
Texas	76–24
Year average	**73–27**
2006	
Alabama	81–19
Arizona[2]	48–52
Colorado	55–45
Idaho	63–37
South Carolina	78–22
South Dakota	52–48
Tennessee	84–16
Virginia	57–43
Wisconsin	59–41
Year average	**71–29**
2008	
Arizona	56–44
California	52–58
Florida	62–38
Year average	**57–43**
2009	
Maine	53–47
Year average	**53–47**
Overall Average	**67–33**

Note:
1   Nebraska's 2000 anti-same-sex marriage amendment was overturned by a federal district court in May 2005 for being too broad.
2   Arizona's 2006 vote was the only one of these 31 initiatives and referenda to fail. In 2008, Arizona passed a very similar same-sex marriage ban. See Table 13.1 to compare the language of these measures.

Source: Policy Institute, National Gay and Lesbian Task Force; National Conference of State Legislatures.

prejudice against homosexuals, it should not be surprising that measures seen as validating and favoring the latter should go down to defeat in the ballot box.

Return to Equilibrium? In a five-day period in April 2009, same-sex marriage became legal in Iowa when its supreme court ruled that its statutory ban was unconstitutional, the Vermont legislature overrode its governor's veto to legalize same-sex marriage there, and the Washington, D.C., city council voted to recognize same-sex marriages conducted in other states.[118] Over the next two months, policy makers in Maine and New Hampshire passed same-sex marriage reforms, leaving Rhode Island the only New England state still banning

[118]Anonymous, "Gay Rights: The Not-So-Lethal Issue," *Governing*, May 2009, p. 15.

the unions.[119] As a result, just as happened five years earlier following the Massachusetts supreme court decision, gay rights activists had a heady spring of hope for major reforms nationwide.

Then, on November 3, 2009, it was pro-family groups' turn to celebrate as a popular referendum, a "people's veto," in Maine rejected the legislation passed in spring.[120] Californians were likewise whipsawed the year before when their supreme court legalized same-sex marriage in May, only to have voters reject it in November.[121] Thus, as the first decade of the 21st century came to an end, policy makers were shown that voters even in liberal New England and California were not ready to accept this morality policy reform. On the other hand, on the same day that Maine voters rejected same-sex marriage, Washington State voters approved their "Everything but Marriage" civil union initiative, suggesting that the difference between same-sex marriage and civil unions is quite significant.[122] Indeed, in the space of the 10 years since they were introduced to the country as a radical demand from Vermont's supreme court, civil unions have come to be seen as the conservative alternative to same-sex marriage, with gay rights groups no longer being satisfied with anything less than full marriage equality. Even opponents' moral objections are evolving; for example, some have adopted the position that same-sex marriage violates their religious freedom.[123]

These many and divergent developments demonstrate that the politics of same-sex mar-

Advocates in California march to repeal Proposition 8, the ban on same-sex marriage passed in the Golden State in 2008.

riage and related gay rights issues have certainly not returned to equilibrium. In fact, this is one of the fastest changing issue areas in state and local politics. We should expect to see considerable political activity on it for the foreseeable future. No one can predict with certainty what will happen in this volatile issue area in the near term, but as political scientists, we can learn much about state and local government politics and policy from the course of these events.

As of January 2010, five states allow full same-sex marriage: Connecticut, Iowa, Massachusetts, New Hampshire, and Vermont (see Figure 13.4). Thinking about the characteristics of these states can tell us much about the politics of morality policy; it can even tell us something about policy making in the states and communities, in general. First, except for Iowa, these are all New England states, the region that tends to be the most liberal in the country and the one that has the fewest

[119]Abby Goodnough, "New Hampshire Legalizes Same-Sex Marriage," *The New York Times*, 4 June 2009, online edition; Abby Goodnough, "Maine Governor Signs Same-Sex Marriage Bill," *The New York Times*, 6 May 2009, online edition. In November 2008, Connecticut's supreme court had directed that same-sex marriage be allowed in the state.

[120]Abby Goodnough, "Gay Rights Rebuke May Change Approach," *The New York Times*, 5 November 2009, online edition.

[121]Daniel B. Wood, "The Court Must Rule in 90 Days on the Legality of Proposition 8, Which Bans Same-sex Marriage," *Christian Science Monitor*, 6 March 2009, online edition.

[122]Chris Grygiel and Monica Guzman, "New Gay Rights Law Being Approved by Voters," *Seattle Post-Intelligencer*, 4 November 2009.

[123]Jennifer Moroz, "Clerics Need Not Sanctify Gay Rites," *The Philadelphia Inquirer*, 12 January 2007, online edition.

[124]The Pew Forum on Religion and Public Life, "U.S. Religious Landscape Survey," 16 October 2009, http://religions.pewforum.org/.

Figure 13.4

Same-Sex Marriage Policy in the States, 2010

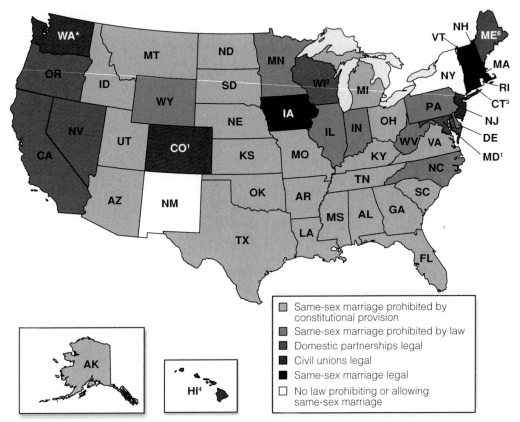

Legend:
- Same-sex marriage prohibited by constitutional provision
- Same-sex marriage prohibited by law
- Domestic partnerships legal
- Civil unions legal
- Same-sex marriage legal
- No law prohibiting or allowing same-sex marriage

1   Colorado's constitution bans same-sex marriage but civil unions for same-sex couples have been allowed by law since 2009; Maryland's constitution bans same-sex marriage, but domestic partnerships for same-sex couples have been allowed by law since 2008.

2   Wisconsin's constitution bans same-sex marriage and civil unions, but domestic partnerships for same-sex couples have been allowed by law since 2009.

3   In Connecticut, civil unions will be offered until October 1, 2010; after that date, couples in civil unions automatically will be converted to marriage.

4   In Hawaii, the constitutional amendment does not ban same-sex marriage, but stipulates that only the legislature, not the courts, can define marriage.

5   New Mexico, New York, and Rhode Island have taken no action on same-sex marriage, but New York Governors Elliot Spitzer and David Paterson have advocated for same-sex marriage (unsuccessfully) in the state legislature; in 2008, Paterson issued a directive to recognize same-sex marriages performed out-of-state, which the state courts have supported. In February 2007, Rhode Island Attorney General Patrick Lynch advised that the state recognize same-sex marriages from out-of-state, but the following December, the Rhode Island Supreme Court held that the state's family court had no jurisdiction to hear a divorce case for a same-sex marriage performed in Massachusetts.

6   In the spring of 2009, Maine's legislature and governor approved same-sex marriage, but on November 3, Pine Tree State voters rejected the statute in a popular referendum. In 2010, Maine policy makers could override this "people's veto" and reinstate same-sex marriage in the state. But until further action by policy makers, Maine allows only domestic partnerships.

Note: These data were valid at press time (November 15, 2009), but in this fast-changing policy area, you need to keep an eye on the newspaper for changes in these laws.

Source: Christine Vestal, "Gay Marriage Legal in Six States," Stateline.org, 4 June 2009, http://www.stateline.org/live/printable/story?contentId=347390, and updated by the authors.

Evangelical Protestants.[124] The only New England states without same-sex marriage are Maine and Rhode Island. Maine's voters are the only ones in New England who have had a direct say in policy making on this reform, and they have rejected it. The Catholic Church plays an important role in politics and public opinion in Rhode Island, but even there, Republican Governor Don Carcieri has indicated that he might be open to allowing domestic partnerships.[125] Thus, much of these same-sex marriage reforms can be explained by voter demography (or at least their religion) and ideology.

This regional pattern of policy adoption also reflects the sort of diffusion among neighboring states that we see in a variety of state policies, morality and otherwise.[126] Observing a neighboring state's experiences with a reform is a good way for policy makers and voters to assess how well it is working, to generate demand for it, and to ease it into people's consciousness. Then, if the reform is believed to be working well across the border, adopting it becomes much easier. This is the same dynamic of caution that we see in the incremental adoption of policy that is so prevalent in the states and communities.

The fact that policymakers have devised intermediate institutions short of marriage also demonstrates how they have tried to move incrementally on this morality policy just as they do on other types of policy. Civil unions allow policy makers to adjust their same-sex relationship policy in an effort to balance the needs and wishes of both sides of this debate among their constituents. Entering into a civil union allows a same-sex couple (or opposite-sex couple who does not wish to wed) the opportunity to enter into a marriage-like legal relationship in which they have certain specific obligations and rights regarding one another. The government establishing a civil union institution determines exactly what these obligations and rights are, but they can include such things as allowing a partner to make medical decisions for an incapacitated partner, to inherit property from a partner without a will, and to take custody of a partner's body after death. Colorado, Hawaii, New Jersey, and Washington currently allow civil unions. Another option farther down this policy scale is the **domestic partnership,** a legal relationship that is recognized to be somewhat weaker than a civil union; these are allowed in California, Maine, Maryland, Nevada, Oregon, and Wisconsin. On the other end of the scale, states can ban same-sex marriage in their constitutions or statutes in their little DOMAs. Figure 13.4 shows just how varied states' policies are on this morality policy.

Another characteristic of normal policy making in the states that same-sex marriage policy clearly reflects is the importance of federalism. Barring the unlikely event of a U.S. Supreme Court ruling in favor of or against same-sex marriage, the most important national institution that will define the path of these politics going forward is the 1996 federal DOMA law. Along with the little DOMAs that followed it in the states, that law patched the breach in the federalism firewall caused by the Constitution's Full Faith and Credit Clause. This isolates the direct effects of any state's actions on this morality policy, allowing each state the time and space to develop the policy that best reflects the values of its own citizens without threatening the values of people in other states and without being threatened by policy actions elsewhere. As a result, we will undoubtedly continue to see a nationwide patchwork of same-sex marriage policies, just as we see now with abortion regulation and many other types of domestic policy.

---

[125]Cynthia Needham, "Why Rhode Island Stands Alone in New England on Same-Sex Marriage," *The Providence (RI) Journal*, 9 May 2009, online edition; Katherine Gregg, "Carcieri Open to Domestic Partnership Law," *The Providence (Rhode Island) News*, 13 November 2009, online edition.

[126]Andrew Karch, *Democratic Laboratories: Policy Diffusion among the American States* (Ann Arbor, MI: University of Michigan Press, 2007).

AP Photo/Nati Harnik

"Going to the chapel …"— but only in Connecticut, Iowa, Massachusetts, New Hampshire, or Vermont.

Thus, while same-sex marriage is a morality policy that threatens the deep moral values of a good many Americans, while it is less an economic issue than a symbolic issue for most people, and even though it just burst upon political scene relatively recently, the political and governmental institutions that have long been in place in the states and communities are already forcing it into the mold of more routine politics. Federalism, incrementalism, regional diffusion, the influence of voters' demographics and ideology—these are all important in explaining the politics of same-sex marriage in the United States today. Interestingly, the politics of same-sex marriage has not yet generated the level of

COMPARISONS HELP US UNDERSTAND

PUBLIC OPINION ON SAME-SEX MARRIAGE—HAVE THE COURTS BROKEN THIS LINK?

In the past 20 years, few significant public policies have changed faster, more extensively, or more unexpectedly than state same-sex marriage policy. Along with these policies, public opinion on the subject has also changed a great deal. In 1990, few people even in the gay rights movement thought that same-sex marriage would be legal in the United States in their lifetimes. In fact, leaders of the movement actively worked against efforts to secure same-sex marriage fearing that it would cause a backlash, damaging their efforts at more incremental change, such as instituting antidiscrimination laws for homosexuals.[1] When a few activists pushed for their marriage rights in the courts, much to the surprise of almost everyone, they had some success—in Hawaii, Vermont, Massachusetts, Iowa, California, New Jersey, and elsewhere. These successes shocked the policy-making system dramatically, setting off a wave of pro- and anti-same-sex marriage initiatives and legislation throughout the country.

Morality policy typically hews closely to public opinion.[2] But clearly, the courts in this instance are having a strong influence on same-sex marriage policy, at least in some states, and judges often have different decision-making criteria than legislators, as you read about in Chapter 9. Some studies show, however, that public opinion sometimes influences the morality policy decisions of state supreme court justices;[3] furthermore, another recent study has shown that court decisions affect the morality policies passed in state legislatures.[4]

Notes
1. Ellen Ann Andersen, *Out of the Closet and into the Courts: Legal Opportunity Structure and Gay Rights Litigation* (Ann Arbor, MI: University of Michigan Press, 2005).
2. Patton, op. cit.; Camobreco and Barnello (2008), op. cit.; Mooney (2001), op. cit.; Mooney and Lee (2000), op. cit.
3 DiSarro, op. cit.; Hall (2001), op. cit.
4 Patton, op. cit.

With all these cross-cutting influences, how strong is the resulting relationship between public opinion and same-sex policy today? Figure 13.5 shows the distribution of public support for same-sex marriage in the states, based on polls taken from 1999 to 2008. We know that opinions on this issue have been changing (in no small part due to changes in public policy decisions in courts and legislatures), but these data probably give us a reasonably valid representation of at least the *comparative* support for same-sex marriage among the states. Compare this map to Figure 13.4, which shows how state same-sex marriage laws were distributed in January 2010. Do you see a relationship here? Are there many states in which law and opinion seem to be well out of line? What other institutional, demographic, economic, or political factors that you have read about in this book or the news might explain these discrepancies? How does the strength of the relationship between same-sex marriage policy and opinion compare with that of the state-level relationships you have seen elsewhere in the book?

Figure 13.5

Public Support for Same-Sex Marriage

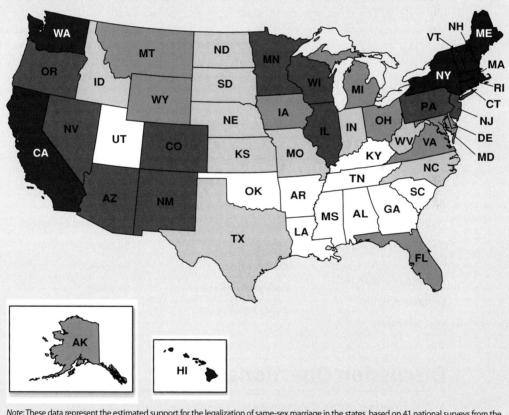

Note: These data represent the estimated support for the legalization of same-sex marriage in the states, based on 41 national surveys from the Roper Center's iPoll archive, dating from 1999 to 2008. The *darker* the state in this map, the *more* public support exists for same-sex marriage.

Source: Jeffrey R. Lax and Justin H. Phillips, "Gay Rights in the States: Public Opinion and Policy Responsiveness," *American Political Science Review* 103(2009):367-86. See the Appendix of this article for information on how they developed their scale.

moral outrage and frustration that has led to so much political violence on abortion policy. Perhaps it is simply too early in this process for such activity. Let's hope that this will be one morality policy that can be debated civilly, allowing us to avoid the tragic actions that have characterized other morality policies in recent years.

Summary

Morality policies invoke strong moral arguments from at least one side of the policy debate; at various times in the United States, alcohol prohibition, slavery, recreational drug use, gambling, censorship, and prostitution, among others, have been morality policies. People and groups advocate morality policy reforms because of a threat to their basic moral and religious values, rather than to seek some economic gain. Policy makers have great incentive to keep such policies in line with the values of their constituents, and they are usually successful at doing so. But sometimes a policy shock, such as a court decision or a technological breakthrough, upsets the morality policy equilibrium and instigates a cycle of morality policy politics. Because morality policies tend to be technically simple, highly visible, and hard to compromise on, their politics can be especially intense and bitter. The U.S. Constitution reserves the control over most such policies to the states, so that is where these battles are usually fought. The most important morality policy debate in the states and communities in recent decades has been over abortion regulation, while same-sex marriage has been an especially active issue in the 21st century. Morality policy debates that may become important in shaping our politics in the future include research with embryonic stem cells, animal rights, and the teaching of evolution and sex education in public schools.

Key Terms

Altruism	Full Faith and Credit Clause	Policy shock
Amicus curiae brief	Grassroots activities	Political agenda
Civil union	Issue evolution	Pro-life and pro-choice
Defense of Marriage Act (DOMA)	Morality policy	Single-issue groups
	Op-Ed article	Sodomy
Domestic partnership	Policy entrepreneur	Vice laws
Expressive action	Policy equilibrium	
First trimester		

Discussion Questions

1. Discuss the differences between morality and nonmorality policies. How do these differences lead to the differences we sees in the politics of these two types of policy?
2. What is political equilibrium and how is it maintained?
3. What are the unique characteristics of morality policy interest groups? Who are their members and how do they differ from the members of other types of interest groups?
4. Why is morality policy difficult to pass and implement?

5. What tactics did both pro-choice and pro-life advocates use in their battles over the issue of abortion? How has equilibrium been lost and regained in this battle?
6. How do the politics of abortion and same-sex marriage differ, and why?

Suggested Readings

Babst, Gordon A., Emily R. Gill, and Jason Pierceson, eds. 2009. *Moral Argument, Religion, and Same-Sex Marriage*. Lanham, MD: Lexington.

Cocca, Carolyn E. 2004. *Jailbait: The Politics of Statutory Rape Laws in the United States*. Albany, NY: State University of New York Press.

Conger, Kimberly H. 2009. *The Christian Right in Republican State Politics*. New York: Palgrave.

Epstein, Lee, and Joseph F. Kobylka. 1992. *The Supreme Court and Legal Change: Abortion and the Death Penalty*. Chapel Hill, NC: University of North Carolina Press.

Fiorina, Morris P. 2005. *Culture War? The Myth of a Polarized America*. New York: Pearson Longman.

Hunter, James Davison. 1991. *Culture Wars*. New York: Basic Books.

Meier, Kenneth J. 1994. *The Politics of Sin: Drugs, Alcohol, and Public Policy*. Armonk, NY: M. E. Sharpe.

Mooney, Christopher Z., ed. 2001. *The Public Clash of Private Values: The Politics of Morality Policy*. New York: Chatham House.

Morone, James A. 2003. *Hellfire Nation: The Politics of Sin in American History*. New Haven, CT: Yale University Press.

Mucciaroni, Gary. 2008. *Same Sex, Different Politics: Success and Failure in the Struggles over Gay Rights*. Chicago: University of Chicago Press.

Sharp, Elaine B., ed. 1999. *Culture Wars and Local Politics*. Lawrence, KS: University Press of Kansas.

Tatalovich, Raymond, and Buron W. Daynes, eds. 2004. *Moral Controversies in American Politics*. Armonk, NY: M. E. Sharpe.

Suggested Media Resources

Kaye, Tony. 2006. *Lake of Fire*, ThinkFilm. This 2-hour and 52-minute documentary graphically portrays the tactics and rhetoric of both sides of the intense abortion debate in the United States, going back to the 1973 *Roe vs. Wade* decision. This well-reviewed, black-and-white film includes interviews with such thinkers and activists on abortion and abortion politics as Noam Chomsky, Alan Dershowitz, Randall Terry, and Norma McCorvey.

Lawrence, Jerome, and Robert E. Lee. 1955. *Inherit the Wind*. This play is the fictionalized account of the trial of John Scopes, the Dayton, Tennessee, high school biology teacher tried in 1925 for violating state law by teaching evolution. Scopes was defended by Clarence Darrow, a well-known labor and civil liberties lawyer, and prosecuted by three-time presidential candidate and former U.S. Secretary of State William Jennings Bryan. The trial came to be seen as a battle between proponents of science and proponents of fundamentalist Protestant Christianity and as a test of these advocates' respective influences on public policy and American culture. The sparkling writing makes this play a perennial favorite in summer stock and high school theater. The 1960 movie (starring Gene Kelly, Fredric March, and Spencer Tracy) and 1999 made-for-television movie (starring Beau Bridges, George C. Scott, and Jack Lemmon) immortalized this courtroom drama with a decidedly pro-science slant.

Web Sites

Abortion Regulation

Alan Guttmacher Institute (http://www.guttmacher.org/): The Guttmacher Institute is a research and advocacy organization working in the field of sexual health and for the availability of abortion services for women.

American Family Association (http://www.afa.net): The AFA is a conservative Christian group dedicated to advocating public policy that reflects their interpretation of the Bible, including a complete ban on abortion.

Same-Sex Marriage

Focus on the Family (http://www.family.org): FOF is a leading conservative Christian group working on various morality policy issues, including advocating the legal definition of marriage as a relationship between one man and one woman.

National Gay and Lesbian Task Force (http://thetaskforce.org): The NGLTF is a research and advocacy group promoting gay rights, including same-sex marriage.

Teaching Evolution in the Public Schools

National Center for Science Education (http://ncseweb.org/): The NCSE is a not-for-profit, membership organization providing information and resources for schools, parents, and concerned citizens working to keep evolution in public school science education.

Intelligent Design Network (http://www.intelligentdesignnetwork.org/): The IDN is an advocacy group, networking platform, and provider of teaching and advocacy materials about teaching intelligent design. The IDN emphasizes what it calls "objectivity" in the comparison of intelligent design and evolution theories.

14

AP Photo/David Kohl

Social Welfare
and Health Care Policy

RUNNING AGAINST WELFARE

When running for president in 1980, Ronald Reagan enjoyed telling a story about a glitzy "welfare queen" who would cruise the streets of Chicago in her Cadillac. The woman, the affable Republican recounted, had some 80 aliases, 30 addresses, and a dozen Social Security cards. By gaming the system, Reagan claimed she was able to defraud Illinois and the federal government of some $150,000 in bogus claims. After some digging by the press, it was revealed that Reagan's story was really a figment of his imagination. No such woman existed. (Reporters did manage to find a Chicago woman who had four aliases and who had bilked Social Security out of $8,000 one year.) But the former governor of California wasn't hurt by his half-truths; rather, by demonizing welfare recipients, he tapped into a growing public sentiment against social welfare programs.

In the 1980s, an increasing number of people were viewing the U.S. welfare state as morally bankrupt. As journalist William Greider writes, Reagan's "famous metaphor—the 'welfare queen' who rode around in her Cadillac collecting Food Stamps—was perfectly pitched to the smoldering social resentments but also a clever fit with his broader economic objectives. Stop wasting our money on those lazy, shiftless (and, always unspoken, black) people. Get government off our backs, encourage the strong, forget the weak."[1]

Reagan's welfare queen trope also signaled a general return to the acceptance of states' rights. His administration stressed the need to defer judgments on matters of domestic policy to state and local governments. Although it took more than 15 years from the time he was first elected president, much of Reagan's vision of reducing the role of the federal government was realized in 1996 when President Bill Clinton, a Democrat, signed into law a bill "ending welfare as we know it." No longer would governors have to "go to Washington and kiss somebody's ring to do what everybody wants us to do and that is to change welfare in our society and give people jobs and hope and optimism," as Wisconsin Governor Tommy Thompson said in 1995 after abolishing his state's welfare department. The states would have broad discretion to determine how to run their welfare programs, but at a cost. In exchange for more autonomy, which still exists today, the states would also have to pick up a greater share of paying for their programs.[2]

1 William Greider, "The Gipper's Economy," *The Nation*, 28 June 2004; Ange-Marie Hancock, *The Politics of Disgust: The Public Identity of the Welfare Queen* (New York: New York University Press, 2004); Martin Gilens, *Why Americans Hate Welfare* (Chicago: University of Chicago Press, 1999); Saundra K. Schneider and William G. Jacoby, "Elite Discourse and American Public Opinion: The Case of Welfare Spending," *Political Research Quarterly* 58(2005):367–79.

2 Frances Fox Piven and Richard Cloward, *The New Class War: Reagan's Attack on the Welfare State and Its Consequences* (New York: Pantheon, 1982); R. Kent Weaver, *Ending Welfare as We Know It* (Washington, DC: Brookings Institution, 2000); and *United We Stand America, Preparing Our Country for the 21st Century: The Official Transcript of the United We Stand America Conference* (New York: HarperCollins, 1995), 207–08.

Introduction

Who controls social welfare and health care public policy in the United States, and who pays for it? Why is there such diversity across the states when it comes to these programs? Why are some states more innovative when it comes to reforming their health care and welfare systems? Underlying these questions is a deeper question: Why should states and communities provide any welfare or health care benefits to their citizens?

Although most of you are likely too young to remember President Reagan, the social welfare revolution he set into motion endures today, especially at the subnational level. At times coerced by the federal government and at other times proactive, states and local governments have proven themselves to be adept policy entrepreneurs. They have advanced and adopted competing policy solutions to an array of social welfare and health care problems, duplicating and discarding policies along the way. Due to their own tight budgets, and compiled by cuts in domestic spending by the federal government, state and local governments have often had to come up with creative solutions when dealing with health care and social welfare issues.

We begin our inquiry with some background on America's poor. We then ask who—the states or the federal government—should provide and pay for social welfare and health care policies. After providing an overview of the diffusion of public policies across the states, we conclude by discussing an array of social welfare and health care policies, some of which are financed and administered by, or jointly with, the federal government. As with morality politics, a variety of factors can cause states and localities to adopt new social welfare and health care policies, thereby disrupting the policy equilibrium. After the initial shock, politics and policy tend to return to equilibrium. Due to the number of public policies discussed, however, we do not provide detailed case studies of the policy equilibrium dynamic in play as we did with abortion and same-sex marriage in Chapter 13.

America's Poor

The overall poverty rate in the United States has been relatively stable since the early 1970s. In its most recent estimate, the U.S. Census Bureau reports that nearly 40 million Americans live below the poverty line, or roughly 13 percent of the country's total population. Yet, if you put 100 economists and sociologists in a room and asked each one to define poverty, you would likely hear 100 different answers. Defining who is poor and what constitutes poverty is not a science. Rather, it is impressionistic and contingent on changing economic conditions and social norms. As such, our official government measure of poverty has changed over time, depending on what standards and measurements are used in the calculation. According to the U.S. Census Bureau, the 2009 federal poverty guideline for a family of four is a household income of $20,050 or less.[1]

Who Are America's Poor?

As Table 14.1 shows in some detail, children, women, and minorities are disproportionately likely to be poor in this country. Of the roughly 40 million Americans living below the poverty line, more than 3 million are aged 65 and older, or nearly one of every 10 seniors. Although the proportion of elderly who are impoverished has been dropping over the past 30 years, the percentage of children living in poverty has increased steadily since 2000. Over 14 million

---

[1] U.S. Department of Health and Human Services, "The 2009 HHS Poverty Guidelines," http://aspe.hhs.gov/POVERTY/09poverty.shtml; Kathleen Short, John Iceland, and Joseph Dalaker, "Defining and Redefining Poverty" (paper presented at the annual meetings of the American Sociological Association of America, Chicago, 16–19 August 2002), http://www.census.gov/hhes/poverty/povmeas/papers/define.pdf; and U.S. Department of Health and Human Services, "Computations for the 2007 Annual Update of the HHS Poverty Guidelines," 2007, http://aspe.hhs.gov/poverty/07computations.shtml. Several other definitions of poverty exist: see U.S. Census Bureau, "American Community Survey 2004 Subject Definitions," http://www.census.gov/acs/www/Downloads/2004/usedata/Subject_Definitions.pdf.

Table 14.1

Who Are America's Poor?

Subject	Population (in millions)	Number Below Poverty Level (in millions)	% Below Poverty Level
Total Population	301.4	39.8	13.2
Age			
Under 18 years	74.2	14.1	19.0
18 to 64 years	189.3	22.1	11.7
65 years and over	37.9	3.7	9.7
Household			
Female-headed household (with related children under 18 years), no husband present	14.5	4.2	28.7
Race and Hispanic or Latino Origin			
White	240.5	27.0	11.2
Black or African American	38.0	9.4	24.7
American Indian and Alaska Native	2.3	.6	26.1
Asian	13.3	1.6	11.8
Native Hawaiian and Other Pacific Islander	.4	.07	16.7
Hispanic or Latino origin (of any race)	47.4	11.0	23.2
White, not Hispanic or Latino	196.9	17.0	8.6
Work Experience (16 years and over)			
Worked full time year-round in the past 12 months	104.0	2.8	2.6
Worked part time or part-year in the past 12 months	54.3	7.3	13.5
Did not work	77.7	17.1	22.0

Source: U.S. Census Bureau, "Income, Poverty, and Health Insurance Coverage in the United States: 2008," 2009, http://www.census.gov/prod/2009pubs/p60–236.pdf.

children under the age of 18, nearly one in five, live in poverty. Although millions of white, non-Hispanic children live in poverty, as a percentage, the rate is lower than it is for other racial and ethnic groups. One of every four African American and Native American children lives in impoverished households; one of every five Hispanic children resides in poverty.

Women, more so than men, bear the brunt of poverty in the United States. Of the 14.5 million female-headed households in 2008, nearly one in three fell below the poverty line. Roughly 6 million more single women than men live in poverty. Scholars have advanced several explanations for the **feminization of poverty,** a phrase coined by sociologists in the late 1970s. Some argue that the fragmented welfare state and paltry benefits have contributed to the rise in poverty of female-headed households. Others contend that it is changing family structures—including higher divorce rates and more children being born out of wedlock—that have led to more women being impoverished. Still others point to the significant wage gap and earning power between men and women.[2]

[2] Diana Pearce, "The Feminization of Poverty: Women, Work, and Welfare," *Urban and Social Change Review* 11(1978):28–36.

Figure 14.1

Where Are America's Poor? State Poverty Levels, 2008

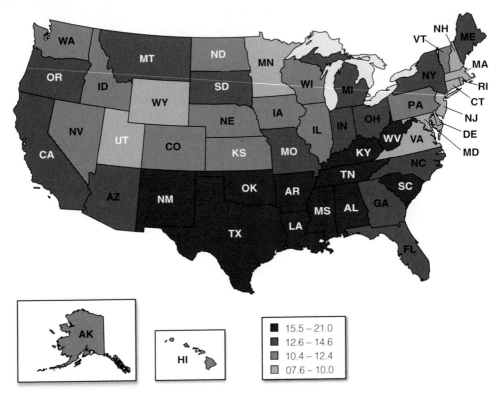

15.5 – 21.0
12.6 – 14.6
10.4 – 12.4
07.6 – 10.0

Source: U.S. Census Bureau, "Percent of People Below Poverty," 2008, http://factfinder.census.gov.

Where Are America's Poor?

Considerable variation exists across the states, and even within states, in terms of the level of poverty, as Figure 14.1 reveals. New Hampshire, with a rate of 7.7 percent in 2008, has the lowest poverty level of any state. Ten other states (Alaska, Hawaii, Massachusetts, Wyoming, Minnesota, Utah, Connecticut, New Jersey, Virginia, and Maryland) have poverty levels lower than 10 percent. Even in these relatively well-off states, though, pockets of acute poverty persist. At the other end of the spectrum, New Mexico, Arkansas, Louisiana, Mississippi, Kentucky, and West Virginia have poverty levels exceeding 17 percent. As it has in the past, Mississippi leads the way, with 21 percent of its population living below the poverty line. In Mississippi, New Mexico, and Louisiana, more than a quarter of all children live in impoverished homes.

Despite these figures, America's poor often remain hidden, out of plain sight of most Americans. Hurricane Katrina, which ravished the Gulf Coast in late August 2005, abruptly changed the situation. One of the most lasting images left in the wake of the Category 5 storm was the mass of impoverished people desperately trying to flee their city on foot. Kanye West, a Grammy-winning rapper appearing live in a concert for hurricane relief, criticized the federal government for not responding fast enough. Riffing on how the federal government is designed "to help the poor, the black people, the less well-off as slow as possible," West directly

Thousands of Hurricane Katrina survivors wait for relief outside the Superdome in New Orleans, 4 September 2005.

criticized former President George W. Bush, saying he "doesn't care about black people."[3] Bush's mother, former First Lady Barbara Bush, did herself little good when she unwittingly spoke callously of the Katrina refugees who had taken temporary shelter in the Houston Astrodome. "What I'm hearing, which is sort of scary, is they all want to stay in Texas," Mrs. Bush quipped. "Everyone is so overwhelmed by the hospitality," she continued, "and so many of the people in the arena here, you know, were underprivileged anyway, so this—this is working very well for them."[4]

Whatever one thinks of Katrina's victims— or the caustic comments of Kanye West or Barbara Bush—the hurricane exposed New Orleans' impoverished underbelly in graphic color. Televised images brought the plight of poor Americans, many of them minorities, into homes across the country. The destruction wrought by Katrina also stirred a national debate on the root causes of poverty in America.

Social commentators have long tapped into the tradition in America of blaming the victim. In his controversial 1971 book, The *Unheavenly City*, Edward Banfield, a political scientist and advisor to President Richard Nixon, once argued that America's urban poor were inculcated with a "lower-class culture." According to Banfield, youths who grow up in a lower-class culture are driven by a self-gratifying,

---

[3] "Kanye West Rips Bush during NBC Telethon," *Billboard*, 3 September 2005, http://www.billboard.com/bbcom/news/article_display.jsp?vnu_content_id=1001054572.

[4] "Houston, We May Have a Problem," *Marketplace*, 5 September 2005, http://marketplace.publicradio.org/shows/2005/09/05/PM200509051.html.

Michael Ainsworth /Dallas Morning News/Corbis News/Corbis

"live-in-the-moment" ethos, which destines many of them to remain poor.[5] Banfield's psychological analysis of the causes of urban poverty has been roundly criticized by social scientists who stress instead that the sometimes violent and even self-destructive behavior of some urban poor is in part an adaptive response to living in a stressful environment.

For many scholars, those belonging to America's **underclass,** a term popularized by sociologist William Julius Wilson, are seen largely as a product of their environment. Joblessness, social isolation, and impoverished neighborhoods are all symptoms of the urban underclass, which Wilson claims is caused by low levels of education, few economic opportunities, and lack of community safeguards and resources.[6] It is perhaps worth noting that America's underclass is not isolated only in cities; many rural areas are also plagued by high rates of unemployment and low levels of education and social capital.[7]

Domestic Policy Making in a Federal System

With the exception of "providing for the safety and welfare of citizens," you will have a hard time finding anything else concerning people's health or welfare in the U.S. Constitution. In theory, the crafting, implementation, and costs of our health care and social welfare policies are to be devolved to the states and their communities. It should not come as a surprise, then, that health care and welfare policies can be considerably different across the states. Indeed, we might expect such differentiation. Federalist systems of government inherently encourage policy experimentation among semiautonomous, subnational governments. The American states, U.S. Supreme Court Justice Louis Brandeis noted in 1932, should serve as "laboratories of democracy," as they can try "novel social and economic experiments without risk to the rest of the country."[8]

This experimentation often leads to competition among states and localities in the provision of public policy. Competition is often understood as a healthy process, as it can possibly lead to states and localities providing better services to their citizens at a lower cost.[9] Allowing states and localities to experiment with and compete in the provision of public policies can also help foster and develop a set of "best practices" for other jurisdictions to emulate.[10] But competition between the states combined with intermittent federal involvement may also lead to a confusing web of social services. Worse, it may lead to what some call a "race to the bottom." States and localities might cut social welfare and health care services in an effort to tighten their budgets and deter individuals seeking social services from migrating to a locale where benefits are higher.[11] Some, however, argue that the debate is moot, as the differences in social welfare benefits among the states are relatively insignificant.[12]

---

[5] Edward C. Banfield, *The Unheavenly City: The Nature and Future of Our Urban Crisis* (Boston: Little, Brown, 1970).

[6] William Julius Wilson, *The Truly Disadvantaged* (Chicago: University of Chicago Press, 1987).

[7] Sharon Austin, *The Transformation of Plantation Politics: Black Politics, Concentrated Poverty, and Social Capital in the Mississippi Delta* (Albany: State University of New York Press, 2006).

[8] Louis Brandeis, *New State Ice Company v. Liebmann*, 28 5 U.S. 262, 311 (1932).

[9] Charles Tiebout, "A Pure Theory of Local Expenditures," *Journal of Political Economy* 64(1956):416–24.

[10] David Osborne and Ted Gaebler, *Reinventing Government* (New York: Penguin, 1992).

[11] Paul Peterson and Mark Rom, *Welfare Magnets: A New Case for a National Welfare Standard* (Washington, DC: Brookings Institution, 1990); but see Craig Volden, "The Politics of Competitive Federalism: A Race to the Bottom in Welfare Benefits?" *American Journal of Political Science* 46(2002):352-63; and Mark Rom, Paul Peterson, and Kenneth Scheve, "Interstate Competition and Welfare Policy," *Publius* 28(1998):17–38.

[12] Sanford Schram and Joe Soss, "The Real Value of Welfare: Why There Is No Welfare Migration," *Politics & Society* 27(1998):39–66.

Sharing Responsibility for Policy Making

Most social welfare programs are administered in partnership by the federal government and the states through a system of grants-in-aid. As we discussed in Chapter 10, federal grant programs are available—most notably, categorical and block grants. Since the 1930s, Congress has used federal grants to influence and even control state and local social welfare programs. Martha Derthick, an astute observer of domestic policy making and federalism, argues that the federal grant system allows the national government to force state governments to enact policies they may not have otherwise, and in doing so, the state creates a constituency within the state that supports these federal programs.[13] At the same time, the federal government rarely implements social welfare programs itself. State and local governments, and increasingly nonprofit organizations and other agencies, serve as implementing organizations. This allows for some autonomy from the federal government when it comes to shaping programs at the "street-level."[14]

Compared with other advanced industrial countries, policy making in the United States is quite fragmented. Prior to the 1930s, states and communities were almost entirely responsible for providing their own health care and social welfare programs, with the federal government playing a limited role in all three domestic policy areas. During the New Deal, however, the federal government began to provide a safety net for people in need. During the height of the Great Depression, under the administration of Franklin D. Roosevelt, the country's growing indigent population overwhelmed many state governments. In 1933, the year Roosevelt took office, the national unemployment rate was nearly 25 percent; many states had considerably higher numbers of jobless people. Under the leadership of Roosevelt, the Democratic-controlled Congress passed the **Social Security Act** of 1935, which created several programs, including Social Security and what would become known as Aid to Families with Dependent Children (AFDC), or welfare. It would become the cornerstone of the federal government's effort to alleviate poverty among a growing underclass.

Since the 1930s, Congress has continued to exert its authority in domestic policy arenas traditionally left up to the states. During the Great Society programs of the 1960s, Congress greatly expanded America's welfare state, creating federal programs dealing with access to health care (Medicaid and Medicare), public housing, hunger and poverty relief, and local community action programs. In 2003, a Republican-led Congress preempted state programs by creating a prescription drug benefit program under Medicare (and requiring the states to pay for the benefit). As we discuss in more detail later on, in 2009 President Barack Obama signed into law an extension of the State Children's Health Insurance Program (SCHIP), which provides funding to states to insure children in low-income families not covered by Medicaid.[15] Thus, to characterize the making of health care and social welfare policy as a robust competition among the states and localities, with best practices rising to the top, would be a mistake. Despite its limited constitutional authority, the federal government plays a major role in the provision of an array of public policies. It often shares with the states the administration and costs of social welfare and health care programs. From income maintenance, to legal aid, to funds for family planning,

---

[13] Martha Derthick, "Ways of Achieving Federal Objectives," in Laurence O'Toole, ed., *American Intergovernmental Relations*, 3rd ed. (Washington, DC: Congressional Quarterly Press, 2000).

[14] Michael Lipsky, ed., *Street Level Bureaucrats* (New York: Russell Sage Foundation, 1980). See also Lael Keiser, "Street-Level Bureaucrats, Administrative Power and the Manipulation of Federal Social Security Disability Programs," *State Politics and Policy Quarterly* 1(2001):144–64.

[15] Daniel C. Vock, "States Suing Feds over Seniors' Rx Costs," *Stateline*, 20 May 2006, http://www.Stateline.org; National Conference of State Legislatures, "Children's Health Insurance Program," http://www.ncsl.org/programs/health/chiphome.htm.

to subsidized day care, to vouchers for food, to public housing, a host of federal agencies are heavily involved in policy making.

Paying for Programs

Despite the inherent bias of federalism favoring decentralized decision making, Congress frequently has flexed its muscle, often meddling in what have traditionally been state and local affairs. Although the federal government does not always foot the bill for its involvement in subnational policy matters, in the 2009–10 fiscal year, Congress authorized the spending of more than $450 billion to help defray the costs of health, welfare, and education policies in the states.[16]

This sizable sum flowing from the federal government is comparable to the tab picked up by state and local governments each year. According to one recent study, state and local governments also spend more than $300 billion a year on health care and welfare policies, to say nothing about the billions they spend for primary, secondary, and higher education (which we discuss in the following chapter).[17] Much of this spending by states and localities is mandated by the federal government. States, for instance, are required to provide cash assistance to needy individuals and make direct payments to health care vendors for medical assistance for the poor in accordance with federal guidelines. But state and local governments also spend billions on social welfare programs of their own design, such as providing for emergency medical and housing relief following natural disasters, refugee assistance, and constructing and maintaining nursing homes, orphanages, and hospitals.

Diffusion of Policies

Why do some states and localities adopt a set of policies, whereas others do not? The concept of **policy diffusion** has a rich tradition in political science. Diffusion of public policies occurs across time and space when one state or community adopts or emulates another jurisdiction's policies.[18] Jack Walker observed 40 years ago that "some states act as pioneers by adopting new programs more readily than others," and that once a few programs have been adopted, "new forms of service or regulation spread among the American states."[19] The political scientist characterized the diffusion of public policies in the states as an "S-curve," with adoption of new polices starting slowly with a few entrepreneurial pioneers, then rapidly taking off across the nation, and then slowing down once again as a few remaining states refuse to follow suit. Other political scientists have found that diffusion is often determined by such factors as the level of federal intervention in the policy area, the level of interparty competition, the economic prosperity of a community, and other time-specific factors.[20] Still others have found diffusion rates to be faster when federal incentives encourage the states to adopt the programs, and that elected

---

[16] U.S. Office of Management and Budget, "The Budget of the United States Government, Fiscal Year 2010, Historical Tables," http://www.gpoaccess.gov/USbudget/fy10/hist.html.

[17] Richard Toikka et al., "Spending on Social Welfare Programs in Rich and Poor States," U.S. Department of Health and Human Services, 30 June 2004, http://aspe.hhs.gov/hsp/social-welfare-spending04/.

[18] Jack Walker, "The Diffusion of Innovations among the American States," *American Political Science Review* 63(1969):880–99; Virginia Gray, "Innovation in the States: A Diffusion Study," *American Political Science Review* 67(1973):1174–85; Frances Stokes Berry and William Berry, "State Lottery Adoptions as Policy Innovations: An Event History Analysis," *American Political Science Review* 84(1990):395–415; Frances Stokes Berry and William Berry, "Innovation and Diffusion Models in Policy Research," in Paul Sabatier, ed., *Theories of the Policy Process* (Boulder, CO: Westview, 1999); Christopher Mooney and Mei-Hsien Lee, "Legislative Morality in the American States: The Case of Pre-Roe Abortion Regulation Reform," *American Journal of Political Science* 39(1995):599–627; and Donald Haider-Markel, "Policy Diffusion as a Geographical Expansion of the Scope of Political Conflict: Same-Sex Marriage Bans in the 1990s," *State Politics and Policy Quarterly* 1(2001):5–26.

[19] Jack Walker, "The Diffusion of Innovations among the American States," *American Political Science Review* 63(1969):880-99.

[20] Gray, "Innovation in the States."

officials often take electoral as well as racial politics into consideration when deciding whether to adopt a new health care or welfare policy reform.[21]

According to many observers, policy diffusion is influenced by geographic proximity, as "policymakers and citizens share the human cognitive bias of accept[ing] the familiar and being reassured by those things closest to them."[22] This perception is indeed often the case, although diffusion may also be influenced by policy entrepreneurs within bureaucratic agencies.[23] In their search to find solutions to their problems, policy makers often look first to their neighbors. Furthermore, because they are often found in competition with one another, states and localities in close proximity with one another have an economic incentive to emulate their next-door neighbors in an effort to not allow their citizens to exit. This logic can lead to programs that both enhance and harm the social welfare of a given state or community. For instance, a state may emulate its neighbor and adopt a lottery system of its own to bring in additional education dollars, doing so primarily to discourage its own residents from crossing over the border and playing a neighboring state's lottery. Conversely, a state may depress its level of assistance to welfare recipients so as to discourage poor people in a neighboring state from moving.

Adoption of Policies

Of course, although they are influenced by what kinds of policies are going on outside their borders, we should not expect states to blindly adopt their neighbors' policies without elected officials and policy makers in a state first assessing the economic and political conditions of their home state.[24] As we saw with morality policies, diffusion not only occurs due to a state's or community's proximity to its neighbors. With technological advances as well as policy clearinghouses, such as the National Conference of State Legislatures, the American Legislative Exchange Council, the Center for Budget Priorities, and the Urban Institute, state and local policy makers are exposed to an array of public policy options that have been adopted across the country. One recent study examining the diffusion of state-sponsored health insurance programs for children from 1998 to 2001 found that the diffusion of policy innovations was not limited to a geographic proximity; rather, states adopted the successful programs of other states because of their political, demographic, and budgetary similarities.[25] Another has found that the diffusion of policies—such as bans on smoking in public facilities—is able to percolate upward from local governments to state governments.[26]

Social welfare and health care policies also tend to map fairly closely with public opinion along a liberal–conservative spectrum in the states.[27] In other words, state and local policy makers tend to be fairly good at responding to what their citizens so desire. But many

[21] Susan Welch and Kay Thompson, "The Impact of Federal Incentives on State Policy Innovation," *American Journal of Political Science* 24(1980):715–26; Andrew Karch, *Democratic Laboratories: Policy Diffusion among the American States* (Ann Arbor, MI: University of Michigan Press, 2007). Robert Preuhs, "Descriptive Representation as a Mechanism to Mitigate Policy Backlash: Latino Incorporation and Welfare Policy in the American States," *Political Research Quarterly* 60(2007):277–92; Christopher Larimer, "The Impact of Multimember State Legislative Districts on Welfare Policy," *State Politics and Policy Quarterly* 5(2005):265–82.

[22] Christopher Mooney, "Modeling Regional Effects on State Policy Diffusion," *Political Research Quarterly* 54(2001):103–24.

[23] Manuel Teodoro, "Bureaucratic Job Mobility and the Diffusion of Innovations," American Journal of Political Science 53(2009):175–89.

[24] Berry and Berry, "State Lottery Adoptions as Policy Innovations"; and Lawrence J. Grossback, Sean Nicholson-Crotty, and David A. M. Peterson, "Ideology and Learning in Policy Diffusion," *American Politics Research* 32(2004):521–45.

[25] Craig Volden, "States as Policy Laboratories: Emulating Success in the Children's Health Insurance Program," *American Journal of Political Science* 50(2006):294–312.

[26] Charles Shipan and Craig Volden, "Bottom-Up Federalism: The Diffusion of Antismoking Policies from U.S. Cities to States," *American Journal of Political Science* 50(2006):294–312.

[27] Gerald Wright, Robert Erikson, and John McIver, "Public Opinion and Policy Liberalism in the American States," *American Journal of Political Science* 31(1987):980–1001.

REFORM CAN HAPPEN

WISCONSIN'S WELFARE EXPERIMENT

During the 1990s, many states requested waivers from the Department of Health and Human Services (DHHS) to experiment further with the provision of AFDC benefits. In Wisconsin, Tommy Thompson, the Republican governor of Wisconsin, led the charge to reform welfare. In the late 1980s, Thompson pushed through the state legislature a series of major changes to Wisconsin's AFDC program, placing increased responsibilities on welfare recipients. Hearing rumors that poor people were driving up Interstate 90 to Milwaukee to take advantage of Wisconsin's program, leaving Chicago in their rearview mirrors, Thompson's administration cracked down on Wisconsin's relatively generous welfare benefits.

Wisconsin's Learnfare program, which received a waiver from the DHHS in 1987, cut welfare payments made to parents of school-age children if their kids were found to be regularly truant. Thompson even went so far as to try to provide financial incentives for unmarried welfare moms to become married, a policy recommendation that was widely criticized by the Catholic Church, among others in the social welfare community. Despite the criticism, several other states considered similar proposals. In 1995, Wisconsin implemented Thompson's "Work Not Welfare" program, requiring welfare recipients to work in order to receive the remainder of their benefits. The program also placed time limits on how long recipients could receive benefits, previewing the changes adopted by Congress in 1996.[1] In part as recognition for his innovative approach to welfare reform, Thompson was appointed secretary of the DHHS by President George W. Bush in 2001, and served until 2005.

Note
1. Lawrence M. Mead, "The Politics of Welfare Reform in Wisconsin," *Polity* 32(2000):533–59.

other factors besides public attitudes lead to different social welfare and health care policies being adopted. A state's relative level of importance in the federalist system shapes how much federal aid the state will receive. Shifts in the amount of federal aid and federal intervention into policy domains often lie outside of the control of state and local governments. The dynamism, size, and diversity of a state's economy can affect the type of policies a state and its localities are likely to adopt, as can the relative strength of political parties and the density and diversity of interest groups in a state.[28]

Finally, there may be a class or racial bias in the provision of social welfare and health care services across the states. A state electorate with a disproportionate proportion of higher-class citizens tends to be rewarded with public policies that favor its economic interests, which come at the expense of lower-class citizens. Where the degree of economic and racial inequality is higher, social welfare spending in the states tends to be lower. Scholars have also shown that the generosity of a state's welfare policies is inversely related to the level of conservatism in the state as well as the caseload composition of racial minorities.[29]

[28] Thomas Dye, *Politics, Economics, and the Public: Policy Outcomes in the American States* (Chicago: Rand McNally, 1966); Frederick Boehmke and Richard Witmer, "Disentangling Diffusion: The Effects of Social Learning and Economic Competition on State Policy Innovation and Expansion," *Political Research Quarterly* 57(2004):39–51; and Toikka et al., "Spending on Social Welfare Programs in Rich and Poor States.; V. O. Key, *Southern Politics* (New York: Knopf, 1949); and Thad Kousser, "Politics, Economics, and State Policy: Discretionary Medicaid Spending, 1980–1993," *Journal of Health Politics, Policy and Law* 27(2002):639–71.

[29] Kim Quaile Hill and Jan Leighley, "The Policy Consequences of Class Bias in State Electorates," *American Journal of Political Science* 36(1992):351–65; Joe Soss, Richard Fording, and Sanford Schram, "The Color of Devolution: Race, Federalism, and the Politics of Social Control," *American Journal of Political Science* 52(2008):536–53; Nicholas Winter, "Beyond Welfare: Framing and the Racialization of White Opinion on Social Security," *American Journal of Political Science* 50(2006):400–20.

All these factors have been shown to help set the policy agenda in states and communities. As with morality policies, the stability of the policy equilibrium of health care and social welfare programs can abruptly change. More often than not, though, they tend to emerge sporadically, in a disjointed, incremental fashion, during "windows of opportunity."[30] Social changes and focusing events give policy entrepreneurs and other political actors the opportunity to alter the status quo. Disturbances such as the shift to a service sector, low-wage economy or rising health care costs can alter the political agenda of state and local governments. Yet, changing entrenched social welfare and health care programs often proves to be more difficult than preserving them.

Social Welfare Policy

What is welfare? When discussing social welfare programs, we often lump together two distinct types of programs: those providing social insurance and those providing public assistance. In the strict sense, **social insurance** is not welfare, as the programs are not means-tested. Rather, they are created by government to socialize risk. Social insurance programs provide economic assistance in the form of cash payments to the elderly, the disabled, and the unemployed—regardless of financial need—as long as the individual has financially contributed to the system. Social insurance programs are financed by compulsory contributions made by the beneficiaries and their employers. Although states do offer some social insurance programs, the federal government pays for and administers most of the programs in the United States.[31]

In contrast, **public assistance** programs provide aid—both cash and in-kind services— to the poor. The services and financial aid that government provides are **means-tested,** available only to individuals falling below the government's predetermined level of income or assets, and they are taxpayer financed. Assistance, sometimes provided in the form of cash and other times as services, is provided to those who are in need, which governments determine using a calculation of a person's income and assets. Public assistance programs are administered by either federal or state governments or, in some cases, jointly by both.

As you might suspect, the term **welfare** has many connotations. In the context of state and local government, it refers to a range of public assistance services provided by government to aid and protect the most vulnerable individuals in society. Social welfare policies in the United States are also often ad hoc (that is, piecemeal and without an overarching plan). The provision of social welfare in this country is provided through a patchwork of government programs at the national, state, and local levels, combined with services and aid provided by charities operating in the private sector. As we shall see, vulnerable populations are often eligible for public assistance as well as social insurance programs. Aged and disabled persons, children and their parents, and the unemployed are eligible for a variety of social welfare programs. It is fair to say, though, that public assistance programs— compared with those of other advanced industrial countries—are neither universal nor highly coordinated between the layers of government.[32]

Social Security

Social Security—formally known as the Old Age, Survivors and Disability Insurance (OASDI) program—is a social insurance program run

---

[30] John Kingdon, *Agendas, Alternatives and Public Policies* (Boston: Little, Brown, 1984), p. 76.

[31] See Christopher Howard, *The Hidden Welfare State: Tax Expenditures and Social Policy in the United States* (Princeton, NJ: Princeton University Press, 1997), for a discussion of how Americans define welfare and the implications that different definitions have for policy making and policy outcomes.

[32] Gøsta Esping-Andersen, *The Three Worlds of Welfare Capitalism* (Princeton, NJ: Princeton University Press, 1990); and Joe Soss and Lael Keiser, "The Political Roots of Disability Claims: How State Environments and Polices Shape Citizen Demands," *Political Research Quarterly* 59(2006):133–48.

by the federal government. Created during the Great Depression in the 1930s, Social Security provides a safety net to workers who do not have their own. Today, more than half the private sector workforce does not accrue a private pension. One of three workers has no dedicated retirement savings. Nearly three-quarters of the private sector workforce is without long-term disability insurance.

Social Security is an **entitlement** program. The New Deal program is self-financed, with workers contributing 7.65 percent of their gross paycheck (capped at $102,000) into the fund, which is then matched by their employers. Approximately 162 million workers in 2008, roughly 94 percent of the workforce, had Federal Insurance Contribution Act (FICA) withholdings deducted automatically from their paychecks—a mandated contribution into the Social Security trust fund. The Social Security Administration estimates that in 2010 it will provide upward of $650 billion to more than 51 million Americans eligible to collect their benefits. Most payments go to retirees. Nine of every 10 individuals aged 65 and over receive Social Security checks. These monthly payments, on average, account for nearly 40 percent of a recipient's income. For roughly one-fifth of the elderly, a Social Security check is their only source of income. Approximately 32 million beneficiaries are retired workers who receive an average of $1,153 in monthly benefits. Another 3 million recipients of Social Security are dependents of workers vested in the system. Payments to these beneficiaries amounted to roughly $1.6 billion in 2008.[33]

In addition to Social Security, the federal government funds a program jointly with the states that provides payments to some disabled workers. Social Security Disability Insurance (SSDI), which is funded by a payroll tax on all documented employees, provides benefits to individuals (and certain family members) vested in the program. State governments determine whether or not a claimant is disabled under the rules in the first stage of the disability determination process.[34] The purpose of the program is to provide income to people unable to work because of a disability. Every month, nearly 10 million beneficiaries, including disabled workers, their spouses, and their dependent children, receive SSDI payments.[35]

Unemployment Compensation and Workers' Compensation

Millions of Americans also benefit from two other social insurance programs. The Social Security Act of 1935 also established the Unemployment Insurance Program, which temporarily helps workers who have involuntarily lost their jobs. The federally funded program, which was modeled after Wisconsin's unemployment compensation legislation enacted three years earlier, is overseen by the Department of Labor but is administered and regulated by the states.[36] Qualifying employers are required to pay a federal tax based on the amount of wages they pay their workforce. The tax is deposited into a federal unemployment trust fund, with each state having its own account. Because states largely determine employer contribution requirements, eligibility, and benefit levels, the benefit packages available to unemployed workers vary considerably across the states. Today, the maximum allotted time a qualified beneficiary may receive unemployment payments is 26 weeks. In order

---

[33] Social Security Administration, "Social Security Basic Facts," 2 February 2006, http://www.ssa.gov/pressoffice/basicfact.htm. For several decades, questions have abounded over the entitlement program's solvency. Some economists have estimated that the Social Security Trust Fund will dry up by 2040, leaving many workers who are college-aged and younger high and dry come their retirement. In 2031, it is estimated that there will be 71 million eligible seniors over the age of 65, nearly twice the number today. More daunting is that by 2031, there will only be 2.1 workers for every Social Security beneficiary receiving payments; today, the ratio is a much healthier 3.3 workers for every beneficiary.

[34] Keiser, "Street-Level Bureaucrats, Administrative Power and the Manipulation of Federal Social Security Disability Programs."
[35] Social Security Administration, "Press Office," http://www.ssa.gov/pressoffice/factsfig.htm. The Social Security Administration also administers the Social Security Income (SSI) program, a public assistance program that uses general funds to provide monthly payments to impoverished elderly, blind, and disabled individuals on the basis of their financial need.
[36] Wisconsin Department of Workforce Development, "Timeline History: 1883–2004," http://www.dwd.state.wi.us/dwd/DWDHistory/default.htm.

to receive benefits, recipients must be seeking work; part-time earnings are deducted from unemployment benefits.[37]

Each state also administers its own Workers' Compensation program, which requires certain employers to pay into a fund that compensates employees who are injured or disabled on the job. Eligible beneficiaries are provided with monetary awards or health care coverage. If a worker is killed on the job, the fund compensates dependents of the deceased if he or she worked for a participating employer. The program also protects the liability of employers and employees, as it limits the amount a worker may be able to recover in a lawsuit over a work-related accident.[38] Many of the more industrial-based northeastern and midwestern states have created labor-management councils or commissions made up of business, labor, and state officials who work to reform and provide oversight of their workers' compensation and unemployment insurance programs.[39]

Public Assistance: From AFDC to TANF

A major change to social welfare policy in the American states occurred in 1996, when Congress passed the Personal Responsibility and Work Opportunity Reconciliation Act of 1996 (PRWORA), which created the **Temporary Assistance for Needy Families (TANF)** program. Although the primary goal of TANF was to move recipients off welfare and into the workforce, Congress included other goals, including caring for needy children; promoting preparation for jobs, work, and marriage; preventing and reducing out-of-wedlock pregnancies; and encouraging the formation and preservation of two-parent families.[40]

TANF is partially funded by the states and by the federal government through a series of block grants made to the states. It replaced a long-standing program also known for its acronym, AFDC, or Aid to Families with Dependent Children. Created in 1935 to provide financial assistance to widows, single mothers, and their children, AFDC was part of the Social Security Act. Originally, the joint federal-state categorical grant program was conceived as an income support program to provide cash payments to needy mothers with children. Over the years, though, its aim shifted to rehabilitating women, moving them from being dependent on welfare to having more self-sufficient lives sustained by work. Having to abide by federal guidelines, the states were required to provide financial assistance to eligible individuals but were able to craft their own definition of need, establish their own benefit levels, administer their own programs, and set their own income thresholds for eligibility. The states were then reimbursed, on a matching basis, for the benefits they paid to recipients.[41]

TANF has shifted the responsibility of providing welfare assistance to the poor from the federal government to the states. Not surprisingly, the increased flexibility among the states in regulating the eligibility requirements and administrating TANF has led to a variety of welfare assistance programs across the states. Instead of doling out direct cash assistance, as provided under AFDC, TANF allows the states to substitute noncash services, such as work preparation programs, vocational training, child care assistance, transportation credits, pregnancy counseling, and job training.

---

[37] Cornell University Law School, Legal Information Institute, "Unemployment Compensation," http://www.law.cornell.edu/wex/index.php/Unemployment_compensation; and Economic Policy Institute, "Workers Compensation," http://www.epinet.org/content.cfm/datazone_uicalc_index.

[38] Cornell University Law School, Legal Information Institute, "Workers Compensation," http://www.law.cornell.edu/wex/index.php/Workers_compensation.

[39] Daniel A. Smith, "Removing the Pluralist Blinders: Labor-Management Councils and Industrial Policy in the American States," *Economic Development Quarterly* 7(1993):373–89.

[40] Committee on Ways and Means, U.S. House of Representatives, 2005 Green Book, Government Printing Office, http://www.gpoaccess.gov/wmprints/green/2004.html.

[41] Jennifer Mittelstadt, *From Welfare to Workfare: The Unintended Consequences of Liberal Reform, 1945–1965* (Chapel Hill, NC: University of North Carolina Press, 2005).

For example, in 1997 Wisconsin adopted "Wisconsin Works" (known as W-2), which then Governor Thompson characterized as an "employment" program. W-2 continues to require all eligible recipients to work or further their education. Around the same time, Maine created its "Parents as Scholars" project, which provides tuition assistance to low-income parents to help them return to college. TANF also provides states with some flexibility in how they administer aid and services to recipients with special needs, including individuals with mental illness and physical disabilities as well as those with drug and alcohol dependencies. To help pay for these programs, in 1998, Congress authorized the Welfare-to-Work grants program, whereby the U.S. Department of Labor provides supplemental aid to state and local agencies to coordinate their TANF activities with employment-related services.

Cutting the Welfare Rolls under TANF To some who examine the raw number of individuals receiving aid under AFDC versus TANF, it appears that the program has been a success. In 1996, an average of 12.6 million women and children were receiving AFDC payments every month. In 2008, only 4.25 million women and children received TANF benefits, a two-thirds drop over the 12-year period. Nationally, less than 2 percent of the total population receives welfare assistance under TANF. It bears mentioning, of course, that although many have applauded the reduction in the number of recipients receiving welfare benefits, the income levels of many former recipients have not greatly improved.

The drop in welfare cases can be attributed to four factors. First, in the late 1990s, when the new TANF regulations were first being implemented, states were assisted in moving individuals off their welfare rolls by the booming economy. Second, TANF requires the states to clamp down on

serial welfare recipients—those who never left AFDC or those who were repeatedly on and off AFDC—forcing most recipients off welfare after two years. Third, the states are required to place most TANF recipients into work programs, pushing recipients to take jobs in the private sector, whatever the hourly wage. Finally, TANF's strict eligibility guidelines have led to lower participation rates: in 2000, only 50 percent of eligible families participated in TANF, compared to an 85 percent participation rate under AFDC in 1994. Today, despite more individuals in many states falling below the poverty line due to the poor economy, the total number of individuals who receive cash assistance is relatively low.[42]

Since TANF was adopted, there has been considerable variation across the states in the number of individuals who have been added or removed from the welfare rolls, as Table 14.2 shows. During the most recent economic downturn, several states including California, Florida, Maryland, New Mexico, Oregon, South Carolina, and Wyoming, have witnessed double-digit increases in the percentage of welfare recipients. More than 3 percent of California's population—over 1 million people—currently receive TANF benefits. Despite Florida's recent surge in TANF recipients, less than 0.5 percent of its population receives aid under the joint federal-state program. Sparsely populated Wyoming—which in 1996 was tied for the fewest number (13,000) of monthly AFDC recipients but which faced a 28 percent increase in its TANF case load between 2007 and 2008—had only 613 welfare recipients in 2008, by far the fewest number of any state. Other states, because of the stringency of their

---

[42] Olivia Golden, "Assessing the New Federalism: Eight Years Later," *Urban Institute*, 2005, http://www.urban.org/url.cfm?ID=311198; Jason DeParle, "Welfare Aid Isn't Growing as Economy Drops Off," *New York Times*, 1 February 2009, http://www.nytimes.com/2009/02/02/us/02welfare.html.

Table 14.2

State-by-State Welfare Assistance, 2008

State	Welfare Recipients, 2007	Welfare Recipients, 2008	% Change in Welfare Recipients	Total Population, 2008	% of Population Receiving Welfare Benefits
Alabama	42,920	41,849	−2.5	4,661,900	0.90
Alaska	7,974	7,316	−8.3	686,293	1.07
Arizona	88,235	88,781	0.6	6,500,180	1.37
Arkansas	21,075	19,689	−6.6	2,855,390	0.69
California	1,144,529	1,216,866	6.3	36,756,666	3.31
Colorado	24,720	24,453	−1.1	4,939,456	0.50
Connecticut	39,042	38,862	−0.5	3,501,252	1.11
District of Columbia	37,421	39,267	4.9	873,092	4.50
Delaware	9,244	10,049	8.7	591,833	1.70
Florida	74,994	87,632	16.9	18,328,340	0.48
Georgia	42,608	37,983	−10.9	9,685,744	0.39
Hawaii	10,617	10,890	2.6	1,288,198	0.85
Idaho	2,234	2,246	0.5	1,523,816	0.15
Illinois	68,001	62,525	−8.1	12,901,563	0.48
Indiana	117,097	113,572	−3	6,376,792	1.78
Iowa	42,174	38,500	−8.7	3,002,555	1.28
Kansas	34,391	31,215	−9.2	2,802,134	1.11
Kentucky	58,555	58,124	−0.7	4,269,245	1.36
Louisiana	21,841	19,545	−10.5	4,410,796	0.44
Maine	34,224	34,401	0.5	1,316,456	2.61
Maryland	52,084	57,601	10.6	5,633,597	1.02
Massachusetts	108,077	110,419	2.2	6,497,967	1.70
Michigan	226,520	196,775	−13.1	10,003,422	1.97
Minnesota	76,525	78,348	2.4	5,220,393	1.50
Mississippi	24,052	23,714	−1.4	2,938,618	0.81
Missouri	111,780	101,916	−8.8	5,911,605	1.72
Montana	7,836	8,091	3.3	967,440	0.84
Nebraska	23,790	23,067	−3	1,783,432	1.29
Nevada	21,062	21,796	3.5	2,600,167	0.84
New Hampshire	11,270	12,069	7.1	1,315,809	0.92
New Jersey	97,358	94,297	−3.1	8,682,661	1.09
New Mexico	34,346	38,219	11.3	1,984,356	1.93
New York	408,313	391,110	−4.2	19,490,297	2.01
North Carolina	47,898	49,653	3.7	9,222,414	0.54
North Dakota	6,700	7,295	8.9	641,481	1.14
Ohio	172,074	179,595	4.4	11,485,910	1.56

(continued)

Table 14.2

State-by-State Welfare Assistance, 2008 Continued

State	Welfare Recipients, 2007	Welfare Recipients, 2008	% Change in Welfare Recipients	Total Population, 2008	% of Population Receiving Welfare Benefits
Oklahoma	20,686	19,170	–7.3	3,642,361	0.53
Oregon	44,803	53,353	19.1	3,790,060	1.41
Pennsylvania	212,788	199,273	–6.4	12,448,279	1.60
Rhode Island	24,093	19,908	–17.4	1,050,788	1.89
South Carolina	32,886	38,050	15.7	4,479,800	0.85
South Dakota	5,929	6,172	4.1	804,194	0.77
Tennessee	151,843	144,705	–4.7	6,214,888	2.33
Texas	136,797	115,690	–15.4	24,326,974	0.48
Utah	11,218	12,324	9.9	2,736,424	0.45
Vermont	12,017	12,922	7.5	621,270	2.08
Virginia	62,715	65,546	4.5	7,769,089	0.84
Washington	112,583	124,937	11	6,549,224	1.91
West Virginia	21,223	22,927	8	1,814,468	1.26
Wisconsin	38,803	37,811	–2.6	5,627,967	0.67
Wyoming	478	613	28.2	532,668	0.12
United States	4,240,443	4,251,131	1.0	304,059,724	1.26

Source: Jason DeParle, "Welfare Aid Isn't Growing as Economy Drops Off," *New York Times*, 1 February 2009, http://www.nytimes.com/2009/02/02/us/02welfare.html.

requirements, have continued to slash the number of welfare recipients, even as more people become eligible due to the soured economy. Georgia, Louisiana, Michigan, Rhode Island, and Texas have led the way in discouraging new TANF recipients.[43]

Cutting Benefits under TANF In what came as a shock to many individuals and their families who were either receiving or who were eligible for welfare benefits under AFDC, TANF allows the states to reduce their expenditures on welfare benefits. With permission from the Department of Health and Human Services (DHHS), TANF also allows states to remove recipients from the welfare rolls sooner than the five-year maximum time limit. States may also petition the DHHS to extend welfare assistance beyond 60 months but for no more than 20 percent of their caseload. Just two years after President Clinton signed TANF into law, welfare spending by the states and communities was reduced by some 20 percent. Less than $1 in $5 spent by the states on social services is disbursed in the form of cash transfers;[44] and because TANF devolved much greater discretion to local case managers overseeing the transition from welfare-to-work, some

---

[43] U.S. Department of Health and Human Services, "Indicators of Welfare Dependence: Annual Report to Congress," 2005, http://aspe.hhs.gov/hsp/indicators05/index.htm.

[44] U.S. Department of Health and Human Services, "Fact Sheet," January 2010, http://www.acf.hhs.gov/opa/fact_sheets/tanf_factsheet.html.

have raised concerns that the prejudices of local-level administrators may lead to decisions over welfare assistance at the state and local level that may be racial tinged or biased against immigrants.[45]

By most standards, cash transfers to welfare beneficiaries are minimal. In 1996, the average monthly cash benefit to a single parent (usually a mother) with two dependent children was $428 a month; in 2008, it was only $465. Adjusted for inflation in real dollars, that's a decrease of 18.5 percent over the 12-year period. Table 14.3 documents cash benefits paid to a family of three (including the single parent) for the states for several years between 1996 and 2008.

Two-fifths of the states cap their temporary cash benefits, regardless of the size of the family. In Idaho, a TANF family—regardless of its size—received a maximum benefit of $309 a month in 2008, down 28 percent in inflation-adjusted dollars from the 1996 level. Wisconsin bases its monthly cash payments of $673 on the amount and type of work activity of the adult in the family. Southern states tend to provide much less in temporary welfare assistance under TANF than other states. All 10 states in 2008 that provided $280 or less a month to a mother with two dependent children were located in the South—Mississippi ($170), Tennessee ($185), Arkansas ($204), Alabama ($215), Louisiana ($240), Texas ($244), Kentucky ($262), South Carolina ($263), North Carolina ($272), and Georgia ($280). Annual TANF cash benefits in Tennessee and Mississippi amount to just over $2,000 a year, a paltry amount even by a third-world standard. In contrast, all nine states that provide temporary cash benefits in excess of $600 a month are located in the North (with the exceptions of California and Hawaii). Alaska leads the way,

providing $923 in monthly cash assistance to a family of three.[46]

In 2006, Congress reauthorized the funding for TANF for another five years. In doing so, the Republican-controlled Congress not only cut the amount of funding going to the states but also asserted its federal authority over the social welfare programs by imposing more rigorous work requirements for their welfare recipients. The states are now required to have a 90 percent work participation rate for all two-parent families and a 50 percent work participation rate for all single-parent families receiving aid. In 2004, all but 12 states failed to meet the 50 percent work participation cutoff. According to one close observer, Michael Bird of the National Conference of State Legislatures, the 2006 reauthorization of TANF "basically [took] the 'block' out of the block grant concept."[47]

The 1996 law had originally given the states considerable discretion to design programs to move poor families off welfare.[48] The federally imposed mandates in 2006 came with even sharper teeth. States failing to implement the work participation standards—which Michael Bird sees as "virtually guarantee[ing] that every state will incur penalties"—will be forced to forfeit roughly $23 million in federal penalties over a five-year period.[49] In addition, several innovative programs may be in jeopardy following Congress's 2006 reauthorization, as federal aid may not be used for educational programs that do not meet work participation requirements.

According to a study commissioned by the DHHS, cash assistance provided by the states

[45] Deborah E. Ward, *The White Welfare State: The Racialization of U.S. Welfare Policy* (Ann Arbor, MI: University of Michigan Press, 2005); Rodney Hero and Robert Preuhs, "Immigration and the Evolving American Welfare State: Examining Policies in the U.S. States," *American Journal of Political Science* 51(2007):498–517.

[46] Meridith Walters, Gene Falk, and Vee Burke, "CRS Report for Congress: TANF Cash Benefits as of January 1, 2004," updated 12 September 2005, http://www.nationalaglawcenter.org/assets/crs/RL32598.pdf; Liz Schott and Zachary Levinson, "TANF Benefits Are Low and Have Not Kept Pace with Inflation," Center on Budget and Policy Priorities, 24 November 2008, http://www.centeronbudget.org/pdf/11-24-08tanf.pdf.

[47] Christine Vestal, "Feds Pinch State Welfare Programs," *Stateline*, 3 February 2006, http://www.Stateline.org.

[48] Norma Riccucci, *How Management Matters: Street-Level Bureaucrats and Welfare Reform* (Washington, DC: Georgetown University Press, 2005).

[49] Vestal, "Feds Pinch State Welfare Programs."

Table 14.3

Maximum Monthly TANF Benefit Levels for a Single-Parent Family of Three, by State, 2008
(with comparative yearly data)

State	1996	2000	2002	2005	2008	Percent change in real (inflation adjusted) dollars, 1996–2008
Mississippi	$120	$170	$170	$170	$170	4.2%
Tennessee	185	185	185	185	185	−26.4
Arkansas	204	204	204	204	204	−26.4
Alabama	164	164	164	215	215	−3.5
Louisiana	190	190	240	240	240	−7.1
Texas	188	201	201	223	244	−4.5
Kentucky	262	262	262	262	262	−26.4
South Carolina	200	204	205	205	263	−3.2
North Carolina	272	272	272	272	272	−26.4
Georgia	280	280	280	280	280	−26.4
Indiana	288	288	288	288	288	−26.4
Missouri	292	292	292	292	292	−26.4
Oklahoma	307	292	292	292	292	−30.0
Florida	303	303	303	303	303	−26.4
Idaho	317	293	293	309	309	−28.3
Delaware	338	338	338	338	338	−24.1
West Virginia	253	328	453	340	340	−1.1
Arizona	347	347	347	347	347	−26.4
Colorado	356	356	356	356	356	−26.4
Nebraska	364	364	364	364	364	−26.4
Nevada	348	348	348	348	383	−19.0
Virginia	354	354	389	389	389	−19.1
Ohio	341	373	373	373	410	−11.5
Pennsylvania	421	421	421	421	421	−26.4
New Jersey	424	424	424	424	424	−26.4
Iowa	426	426	426	426	426	−26.4
D.C.	415	379	379	379	428	−26.4
Kansas	429	429	429	429	429	−26.4
Illinois	377	377	377	396	434	−15.3
New Mexico	389	439	389	389	447	−15.5
Montana	438	469	494	405	472	−20.7
North Dakota	431	457	477	477	477	−18.6
Maine	418	461	485	485	485	−14.6
Oregon	460	460	460	460	485	−22.4
Michigan	459	459	459	459	489	−21.6

State	1996	2000	2002	2005	2008	Percent change in real (inflation adjusted) dollars, 1996–2008
Utah	416	451	474	474	498	−11.9
Wyoming	360	340	340	340	506	3.4
Minnesota	532	532	532	532	532	−26.4
South Dakota	430	430	469	501	539	−7.8
Rhode Island	554	554	554	554	554	−26.4
Washington	546	546	546	546	562	−24.3
Maryland	373	417	472	482	565	11.5
Massachusetts	565	565	618	618	618	−19.5
New Hampshire	550	575	600	625	625	−16.4
Hawaii	712	570	570	570	636	−34.3
Wisconsin	517	673	673	673	673	−4.2
Connecticut	636	636	636	636	674	−22.0
New York	577	577	577	691	691	−11.9
Vermont	633	708	709	709	709	−17.6
California	596	626	679	723	723	−10.7
Alaska	923	923	923	923	923	−26.4
National Average	428	437	446	449	465	−18.5

Sources: U.S. Department of Health and Human Services, Administration for Children and Families, Office of Family Assistance, 2003 TANF Report to Congress, http://www.acf.hhs.gov/programs/ofa/annual report5/index.htm; Liz Schott and Zachary Levinson, "TANF Benefits are Low and Have Not Kept Pace with Inflation," Center on Budget and Policy Priorities, 24 November 2008, http://www.centeronbudget.org/pdf/11-24-08tanf.pdf.

declined in the mid-1990s, with expenditures on public assistance programs growing only slightly between 1997 and 2000 after TANF was enacted. When looking across states, those with weaker fiscal capacity spend less per capita on social welfare than wealthier states. Compounding this relative inequality, federal grants for social welfare programs were higher to states with greater fiscal capacity than to those with lower capacity, although the intergovernmental grants comprised a larger share of poorer states' social welfare budgets. The difference in spending between rich and poor states was most pronounced in the areas of nonhealth social services, including child welfare, energy assistance, child care, transportation assistance, and programs for the homeless.[50]

---

[50] Toikka et al., "Spending on Social Welfare Programs in Rich and Poor States."

Food Stamps

Try living on $3 a day in grocery money. In the spring of 2007, Oregon's Democratic governor, Theodore "Ted" Kulongoski, took a "Food Stamps Challenge" as a way to raise awareness about low-income people going hungry in his state and threats to cut Food Stamps benefits. The U.S. Food Stamps Program, now formally known as the Supplemental Nutrition Assistance Program (SNAP), is a federal program funded through the U.S. Department of Agriculture and jointly administered by the states. The states pick up roughly half the administrative costs of the program. Created in the 1930s during the Great Depression, in part as an agricultural price support system to keep food costs low, some 35 million Americans received Food Stamps in 2009. The program has been periodically revamped since the 1960s, but its main mission has been to augment the food-purchasing power of low-income households. In fiscal year 2009, the program cost the federal government nearly $38 billion to operate. On average, a Food Stamps recipient receives $101.53 a month, or roughly $1.13 a meal in benefits.[51]

The Food Stamps program imposes nationally uniform standards, so unlike TANF, little variation is seen across the states. It serves a diverse population, but all applicants are personally interviewed prior to becoming enrolled. Eligibility for the program is largely determined by income levels, and recipients do not have to have children or be disabled to qualify. Citizens, children who are legal immigrants, disabled legal immigrants, and legal immigrants who have lived in the country for at least five years are all eligible for the program. Applicants must register and search for work, and able-bodied adults under the age of 60 without dependents are only eligible for three months of assistance over a three-year period, unless a city receives a federal waiver because of high unemployment rates. Beneficiaries are issued electronic debit cards, which they may use to purchase food from participating retailers. Illegal immigrants are not eligible for Food Stamps nor are many legal immigrants who have resided in the country for less than five years. In addition, students, institutionalized individuals, and striking workers are not eligible for the program.[52]

Many people who otherwise are eligible for Food Stamps do not participate; many do not even realize they may be eligible for the benefits. As with other welfare programs, otherwise eligible individuals may shy away from receiving Food Stamps because of a negative stigma attached to the program. Still others may find

Governor Ted Kulongoski of Oregon shops for a week's worth of food on $21, the average for Oregonians receiving Food Stamps.

it difficult to navigate the bureaucratic maze that some states have created to apply for the program.[53] A few states have made it extremely difficult for eligible people living in their states to participate in the federally funded program. New York, for example, is one of four states that requires participants be fingerprinted. Along with a few other states, New York has been found to have illegally denied Food Stamps applications to eligible recipients. In 2009, roughly two-thirds

---

[51] U.S. Department of Agriculture, "A Short History of the Food Stamp Program," 2009, http://www.fns.usda.gov/fsp/rules/Legislation/history.htm.

[52] U.S. Department of Health and Human Services, "Indicators of Welfare Dependence"; and Food Research and Action Center, "Food Stamps Program," March 2006, http://www.frac.org/html/federal_food_programs/programs/fsp.html.

[53] Joe Soss, "Lessons of Welfare: Policy Design, Political Learning, and Political Action," *American Political Science Review* 93(1999):363–80; Sanford Schram, Joe Soss, and Richard Fording, eds., *Race and the Politics of Welfare Reform* (Ann Arbor, MI: University of Michigan Press, 2003); and Lael Keiser and Joe Soss, "With Good Cause: Bureaucratic Discretion and the Politics of Child Support Enforcement," *American Journal of Political Science* 42(1998):1133–56.

COMPARISONS HELP US UNDERSTAND

WHERE YOU LIVE DETERMINES YOUR ASSISTANCE

In 2009, the *New York* Times completed a thorough analysis of variations in government aid across the states. As discussed in the text, there are numerous hoops that individuals must jump through in order to be eligible for public assistance. Examining six different policy areas—welfare, unemployment insurance, housing assistance, Food Stamps, health insurance for poor adults, and health insurance for poor children—the *Times* documented how well the states were doing in terms of the coverage they provided for people in need. The study found that on average, only 21 percent of those eligible to receive cash welfare benefits, 44 percent of those eligible for unemployment benefits, and 30 percent of those eligible for housing benefits were receiving coverage. In contrast, 67 percent of those eligible to receive Food Stamps were covered.

The *Times* study highlighted the considerable variation across the states in terms of the percentage of those eligible to receive coverage who were actually receiving government aid. Averaging the scores across several policy categories, Vermont performed best, scoring above the national average in all policy areas, including ranking first in the coverage of those eligible to receive welfare benefits (49 percent covered). Maine, Massachusetts, Pennsylvania, and West Virginia rounded out the top states in terms of average coverage for those eligible across the six policies. Idaho and New Jersey covered a higher portion (67 percent) of those eligible for unemployment benefits than any other state, and South Dakota had the highest coverage (45 percent) of any state for those eligible to receive housing assistance. Nearly every Missourian (98 percent) eligible for Food Stamps received coverage, according to the study, with Maine a close second. Maine also led the nation (69 percent) in terms of the share of poor adults covered by government health program. Vermont and Massachusetts also topped the 60 percent rate.

Not all states received high marks in the study, however. Colorado ranked dead last among the states in terms of its coverage across the six policy areas. Only 8 percent of those eligible for cash welfare benefits were covered, and less than a third of those eligible for unemployment insurance and housing assistance received benefits. Texas, Utah, Florida, and Nevada rounded out the bottom five states in overall coverage.[1]

Note
1. Jason Deparle and Matthew Ericson, "Variations in Government Aid across the Nation," *The New York Times*, 9 May 2009, http://www.nytimes.com/interactive/2009/05/09/us/0509-safety-net.html.

of eligible individuals across the country actually participated in the program. However, nine states—California, Colorado, Idaho, Nevada, North Dakota, Rhode Island, South Dakota, Utah, Wyoming—had participation rates lower than 60 percent of the estimated population eligible to receive Food Stamps.[54]

---

[54] Jason Deparle and Matthew Ericson, "Variations in Government Aid across the Nation," *The New York Times*, 9 May 2009, http://www.nytimes.com/interactive/2009/05/09/us/0509-safety-net.html.

Housing Programs

Like Food Stamps, the federal government provides grants and aid to the states and localities to provide low-income housing. The Community Development Block Grant (CDBG) program, created by Congress in 1974, provides localities with funds to stimulate community development and improve housing. In the 1980s, under the Reagan administration, the program was decentralized, allowing states and communities to have broad discretion in determining what projects should be funded and how they should be implemented. Most CDBGs are allocated using a set of formulas and are made annually to eligible metropolitan areas and counties. Designated communities receive 70 percent of CDBG funds, with the states receiving the remaining 30 percent. In the 2009 fiscal year, the Department of Housing and Urban Development (HUD) transferred some $3 billion in CDBG funds.[55] Although municipalities and counties use CDBG funds for a wide variety of purposes, they must use them to benefit individuals with low or moderate incomes, prevent or eliminate slums or blighted areas, or meet the urgent needs of community development.

In addition to these entitlement CDBG funds, states also receive federal aid for housing and development projects. States may use the money to improve public facilities and housing that serve mostly low- and moderate-income persons, expand economic opportunities, and help eliminate hazardous conditions that may jeopardize the public health of a community. For example Kentucky receives additional nonentitlement CDBG funds to aid its small cities and communities. In 2005, the state received supplementary grants from HUD that totaled more than $26 million. Texas received more than $72 million in nonentitlement grants in 2008. Its state Office of Rural Community Affairs administers the grants, which serve more than 1,000 rural communities and 244 rural counties, helping some 365,000 low-income Texans each year.[56]

Recently, HUD oversaw more than $1 billion in federal aid to fund local projects under President Obama's American Recovery and Reinvestment Act of 2009. Priority went to local governments with "shovel-ready" projects that would create "suitable living environments, provide decent affordable housing, and create economic opportunities, primarily for persons of low and moderate income." Smaller cities—those with populations of less than 50,000—received CDBG stimulus dollars through their state. New York City received $48.3 million in CDBG stimulus aid, with Chicago and Los Angeles receiving roughly half as much. Albany, Georgia, received $309,660 in federal stimulus dollars, while Albany, New York, received $996,140; Alexandria, Louisiana, netted $177,284, and Alexandria, Virginia, brought home $335,003 in one-time CDBG aid.[57]

States and communities also receive annual federal assistance from the Federal Housing Administration (FHA), as we discussed in Chapter 12. The FHA also provides emergency assistance to cities and states. In 2005, after Hurricanes Katrina and Rita ravished the Gulf Coast, the FHA was thrust into the national spotlight. Responding to the needs of the millions of people living in the parts of Louisiana, Mississippi, Alabama, Florida, and Texas declared to be disaster areas by former President Bush, the FHA embarked on a program to guarantee mortgage financing with no down payment for any individual who was displaced during the storms. The new program applies equally to individuals who either owned or rented homes that were damaged or destroyed and allows victims of nature's wrath to buy homes anywhere in the country.[58]

Minimum Wage Laws

Critics of cutbacks to public assistance programs and the effort to downsize welfare dependency in the states often highlight the low wages that exist for many jobs in many states. Low wages can strain public assistance

---

[55] U.S. Department of Housing and Urban Development, "Fiscal Year 2009 Budget Summary," February 2008, http://www .hud.gov/about/budget/09/fy09budget.pdf.
[56] Governor's Office for Local Development, "Kentucky Small Cities Community Development Block Grant (CDBG) Program," http://www.gold.ky.gov/grants/cdbg.htm; Office of Rural Community Affairs, "Texas Community Development Block Grant Program," March 2006, http://www .orca.state.tx.us/index.php/Community+Development/ CDBG+General+Info.

[57] U.S. Department of Housing and Human Development, "Community Development Block Grants (Formula)," 2009, http://www.hud.gov/recovery/cdblock.cfm.
[58] U.S. Department of Housing and Urban Development, "HUD Announces No Down Payment Mortgages for Hurricane Disaster Victims," 2005, http://www.hud.gov/ news/release.cfm?content=pr05-143.cfm.

INSTITUTIONS MATTER

INITIATING THE MINIMUM WAGE

Are you working for minimum wage? If you are, there's a good chance you're making a different amount than someone working for minimum wage in another state. That's because states are permitted to set their own minimum wages—either higher or lower than the national rate. In addition to the District of Columbia, 27 states in 2009 had minimum wage laws requiring employers to pay their workers more than the federal minimum wage of $7.25 per hour. The State of Washington's minimum wage is the highest in the nation at $8.55 per hour. However, as Figure 14.2 shows, six states (Arkansas, Georgia, Kansas, Minnesota, Wisconsin, and Wyoming) have a minimum wage that is lower than the federal level, and five states (Alabama, Louisiana, Mississippi, South Carolina, and Tennessee) have no state minimum wage at all.

In Washington, as well as California, Oregon, Florida, Nevada, and Vermont, the state's minimum wage is indexed to the rate of inflation. This guarantees that the minimum wage will continue to increase even when the cost of living rises. It's no coincidence that every state (except Vermont) that has a minimum wage indexed to inflation passed their law at the ballot box using the initiative process. State legislatures are frequently under pressure from the business community to provide a "business-friendly" employment setting. Lawmakers tend to be reluctant to increase the minimum wage, fearing that it will increase the cost of doing business for employers. Taking matters into their own hands, citizen groups—led by the community associations such as ACORN and backed by the resources of organized labor—have successfully used the initiative process to not only raise the minimum wage, but also peg it to the rate of inflation.[1]

Note

1. U.S. Department of Labor, "Minimum Wage Laws in the States," June 2009, http://www.dol.gov/esa/minwage/america.htm; Mara Liasson, "Dems Back State Plans to Increase Minimum Wage," *National Public Radio*, 12 July 2006, http://www.npr.org/templates/story/story.php?storyId=5549264.

programs. Workers earning minimum wage, or even more, are known as the **working poor.** They often rely on public assistance—or the beneficence of charities—to make ends meet. Individuals who otherwise work hard and play by the rules must often rely on subsidized child care programs and housing, reduced or free school lunches for their children, Food Stamps and soup kitchens, and public health care to get by month to month. Increasingly, critics are making a moral argument that employers ought to pay a **living wage;** that is, a wage (and benefits package) that allows working members of a community to live decently.

Since 1938, Congress has mandated that certain employers pay their employees a minimum wage. The federal minimum wage in 1938 was $0.25 per hour. In 2007, the Democratic-controlled Congress voted to raise the federal minimum wage to $7.25 per hour by the summer of 2009, bumping it up incrementally from $5.25 per hour. It was the first raise in the federal minimum wage since 1997. In real dollars, the minimum wage in 2007 was the lowest it had been in the previous 50 years.[59] Some economists have estimated that over 7 million Americans, or 6 percent of the workforce, have benefited from the increase in the minimum wage. Who are minimum wage workers? Nearly three-quarters are

[59] Jared Bernstein, Elizabeth McNichol, and Karen Lyons, "Pulling Apart: A State-by-State Analysis of Income Trends," Center on Budget and Policy Priorities, April 2008, http://www.cbpp.org/files/4-9-08sfp.pdf; U.S. Department of Labor, "History of Changes to the Minimum Wage Law," 2009, http://www.dol.gov/whd/minwage/coverage.htm.

State Minimum Wage Laws, 2009

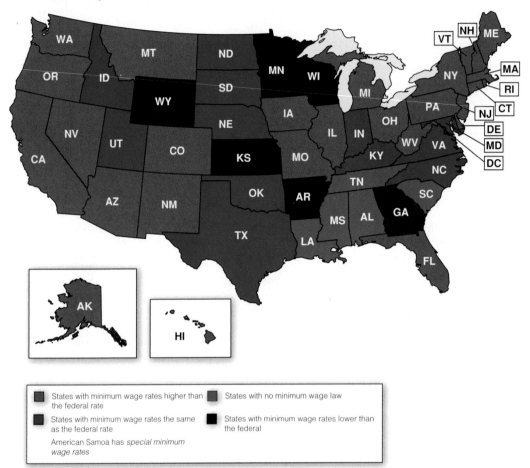

Source: U.S. Department of Labor, "Minimum Wage Laws in the States," June 2009, http://www.dol.gov/esa/minwage/america.htm.

adults, 61 percent are women, and almost half are full-time workers. Nearly 1 million are single mothers working to stay off welfare.[60]

Not all employees are covered by the minimum wage under the Fair Labor Standards Act, as Figure 14.2 reveals. Although companies with revenues of at least $500,000 a year must pay the federal minimum wage, the federal minimum wage does not apply to all jobs. Some agricultural workers, employees under the age of 20 during their first 90 calendar days of employment, some full-time students, apprentices, and some workers with disabilities are not covered. For these job classifications, employees are covered by state minimum wage laws.[61]

Undocumented Workers

Welfare reform has also been tied to the debate over immigration reform. Estimates

---

[60] Economic Policy Institute, "Minimum Wage Issue Guide," 2009, http://www.epi.org/publications/entry/issue_guide_on_minimum_wage/.

[61] U.S. Department of Labor, "Minimum Wage Laws in the States," June 2009, http://www.dol.gov/esa/minwage/america.htm.

place the number of undocumented immigrants living in the United States in 2008 at more than 11.9 million. Nearly one-third of all immigrants in the United States are likely in the country illegally, although recent reports indicate that the flow of

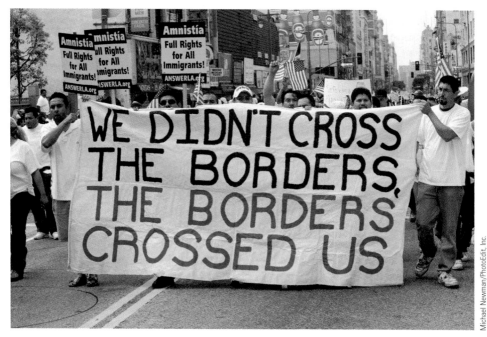

Immigration Supporters Rally in Los Angeles.

Counter Immigration Demonstration in Oklahoma City.

undocumented immigrants to the United States is slowing.[62]

According to a national household survey conducted in 2008, most illegal immigrants are from Latin America—particularly Mexico—which alone accounts for over half of all immigrants in the country without proper documentation. Many of these undocumented immigrants work in the service sector. Between one-fifth and one-third of all cooks, construction laborers, maids and housekeepers, grounds maintenance, and agricultural workers are estimated to be illegal aliens.[63]

The number and density of undocumented persons living across the states are uneven. As Figure 14.3 shows, some states—Maine, Vermont, West Virginia, Montana, Wyoming, Alaska, and the Dakotas—had less than 10,000 illegal immigrants in 2008. In contrast, California had an estimated 2.7 million illegal immigrants that year, and Texas had 1.45 million. Florida, New York, New Jersey and Arizona all had more than 0.5 million undocumented immigrants that year. As a proportion of its state's labor force, Nevada leads the nation, with an estimated 12.2 percent of its workers living in the state illegally. Other states with high proportions of workers who are in the country illegally are California, Texas, Arizona, Florida, and Colorado.

Critics of illegal immigration often claim that undocumented workers take low-paying jobs away from less-educated citizens and keep wages artificially depressed. The evidence for this claim, however, is mixed. Nationally, between 1980 and 2004, millions of illegal aliens migrated to California. In 2004, nearly 7 percent of the state's population was comprised of undocumented immigrants. The

wages for high school dropouts in the state fell 17 percent over the period. In Ohio, a state with only 1 percent illegal immigrants, the decline in wages for high school dropouts dropped 31 percent over the same time period. In Nevada, where 7.5 percent of the population is comprised of illegal immigrants, the median hourly wage is over $10 for high school dropouts, a dollar more than in Nebraska, Kentucky, and Ohio, three states with lower percentages of undocumented workers.[64]

Not surprisingly, states facing the largest influx of undocumented immigrants have gone the furthest in enacting public policies to crack down on the situation. Despite many in the business community who have praised the work ethic of illegal aliens and their willingness to work in low-paying or socially undesirable jobs, others have blamed them for the rising costs of public assistance and services. In 1994, for example, Californians passed a ballot initiative—Proposition 187—that effectively barred social welfare services to illegal immigrants and their children. Although the measure was subsequently nullified by a federal district court, other states have emulated the California measure, with some going even beyond it. In 2004, the citizens of Arizona passed Proposition 200, a statutory initiative requiring all public agencies to verify the immigration status of individuals seeking benefits by showing proof of citizenship. After the November election, a federal district judge in Tucson upheld the law. State and local public employees face possible criminal prosecution if they do not report undocumented immigrants or if they fail to verify the immigration status of those applying for public assistance.[65] Since 2004, several other states have followed suit with legislation similar to Arizona's.

[62] Jeffrey Passel and D'Vera Cohn, "Trends in Unauthorized Immigration Undocumented Inflow Now Trails Legal Inflow," Pew Research Center, 2 October 2008, http://pewhispanic.org/reports/report.php?ReportID=94.

[63] Jeffrey Passel and D'Vera Cohn, "A Portrait of Unauthorized Immigrants in the United States," *Pew Hispanic Center,* April 2009, http://pewhispanic.org/reports/report.php?ReportID=107.

[64] Eduardo Porter, "Cost of Illegal Immigration May Be Less Than Meets the Eye," *The New York Times,* 16 April 2006, p. BU3.

[65] Susan Carroll and Yvonne Wingett, "Prop. 200 Now Law in Arizona," (Phoenix) *Arizona Republic,* 23 December 2004, http://www.azcentral.com/specials/special29/articles/1223prop200hearing23.html.

Figure 14.3

Undocumented Immigrants

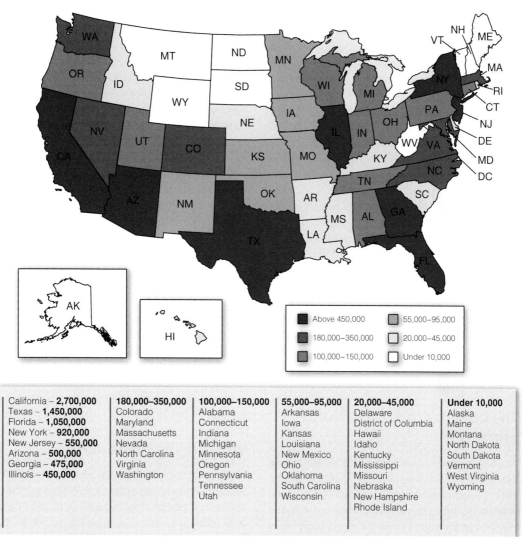

Above 450,000	55,000–95,000
180,000–350,000	20,000–45,000
100,000–150,000	Under 10,000

California – **2,700,000**	**180,000–350,000**	**100,000–150,000**	**55,000–95,000**	**20,000–45,000**	**Under 10,000**
Texas – **1,450,000**	Colorado	Alabama	Arkansas	Delaware	Alaska
Florida – **1,050,000**	Maryland	Connecticut	Iowa	District of Columbia	Maine
New York – **920,000**	Massachusetts	Indiana	Kansas	Hawaii	Montana
New Jersey – **550,000**	Nevada	Michigan	Louisiana	Idaho	North Dakota
Arizona – **500,000**	North Carolina	Minnesota	New Mexico	Kentucky	South Dakota
Georgia – **475,000**	Virginia	Oregon	Ohio	Mississippi	Vermont
Illinois – **450,000**	Washington	Pennsylvania	Oklahoma	Missouri	West Virginia
		Tennessee	South Carolina	Nebraska	Wyoming
		Utah	Wisconsin	New Hampshire	
				Rhode Island	

Source: Jeffrey Passel and D'Vera Cohn, "A Portrait of Unauthorized Immigrants in the United States," *Pew Hispanic Center,* April 2009, http://pewhispanic.org/reports/report.php?ReportID=107.

Health Care Policy

According to the U.S. Census, more than 46 million Americans (15.3 percent of the population) lack health insurance. Another 30 million are estimated to have inadequate health insurance. Over the past several years, millions of Americans have lost their health insurance.

The lack of health insurance and affordable health care has real costs for Americans. By one calculation, more than 18,000 people in the United States die prematurely each year because they don't have access to or cannot afford adequate health care. Medical bills are now the main reason for half of all personal bankruptcies. Also, the costs of health care are not only borne by those without insurance. Health care facilities spend nearly $100 billion in services and treatment each year caring for America's uninsured and underinsured. Covering their uncompensated costs, health care providers and insurance companies pass along nearly $40 billion a year to individuals who do have insurance—in the form of higher health care fees and insurance premiums.[66]

Unlike most advanced industrial countries, including neighboring Canada, the United States does not have a universal, **single-payer health care** system whereby doctors and other private health care professionals have their fees paid by the government at a fixed rate. Rather, health care in the United States is largely a private affair, regulated largely by market forces. Involvement in health care by the states and the federal government has been limited and largely piecemeal, although a few states and communities have expanded their health care programs. It also tends to be means-tested, whereby the government determines if recipients are eligible for benefits based on their income or assets. Those who fail to qualify for government programs—which is likely because they earn more than the federal poverty level—are left on their own.

Why Do Americans Lack Health Insurance?

The cost of health care in the United States has skyrocketed. Last year, over 17 percent of the country's gross domestic product (GDP) was spent on health care; in 1960, it was only 5 percent. Today, we spend more on health care than we do on food. Besides the escalating costs of health care, a major reason Americans do not have health insurance is that fewer employers include health coverage in their basic employment packages. Only three of every five workers have employer-based health coverage, leaving some 36 million working Americans who do not receive health care insurance from their employers. Others who remain in the ranks of the uninsured are largely unable to afford the cost of private health insurance premiums. A disproportionate number of those without employer-based coverage are minorities. Whereas 71 percent of white employees have health coverage included in their job package, only 51 percent of African Americans and 40 percent of Latinos have employer-based health insurance. Some states have tried to expand health care coverage by encouraging employers to provide health care benefits. In Maine, for instance, individuals and smaller companies are able to receive bulk discounts on insurance.[67]

Who lacks health insurance, and who should be responsible for providing it? Issues of public health, including both the protection of and improvement in the health of the public, have traditionally fallen to the states and their localities. In the 1960s the federal government ventured into the realm of public health, partnering with the states. But even today, states and their localities provide the bulk of health care assistance to citizens and noncitizens alike.

Who Are the Uninsured?

Most of the uninsured are elderly. Besides the elderly, who are by far the largest segment of the uninsured population, America's uninsured are low income (defined as earning below slightly less than $30,000, which is 200 percent of the

---

[66] U.S. Census Bureau, "Income, Poverty and Health Insurance Coverage in the United States: 2007," August 2008, http://www.census.gov/prod/2008pubs/p60–235.pdf; Institute of Medicine, "Hidden Costs, Value Lost: Uninsurance in America," National Academy of Sciences, 2003, http://www.iom.edu/CMS/3809/4660/12313.aspx; Families USA, "Health Care: Are You Better Off Today Than You Were Four Years Ago?" September 2004, http://www.familiesusa.org/assets/pdfs/Are_You_Better_Off_rev20053139.pdf; Institute of Medicine, "Hidden Costs, Value Lost."

[67] Paul Krugman and Robin Wells, "The Health Care Crisis and What to Do about It," *New York Review of Books*, 23 March 2006, http://www.nybooks.com/articles/18802; Sara Collins, Karen Davis, and Alice Ho, "A Shared Responsibility: U.S. Employers and the Provision of Health Insurance to Employees," *Inquiry* 41(2005):6–15; Kaiser Family Foundation/Health Research and Educational Trust, "Employer Health Benefits: 2005 Summary of Findings," 14 September 2005, http://www.kff.org/insurance/7315/sections/upload/7316.pdf; Bradley Shrunk and James Reschovsky, "Trends in U.S. Health Insurance Coverage, 2001–2003," Tracking Report no. 9, Center for Health Systems Change, August 2004, http://www.hschange.org/CONTENT/694/.

YOU DECIDE

SHOULD THE FEDERAL GOVERNMENT PROVIDE UNIVERSAL HEALTH CARE COVERAGE?

Jesse L. Jackson, the Democratic congressman from Illinois and son of the Reverend Jesse Jackson, is the sponsor of an Amendment to the U.S. Constitution that would guarantee "health care of equal high quality" and grant Congress the power to enforce and implement access to such care. With the number of Americans lacking health insurance climbing steadily, and with a growing number of underinsured Americans, is it time for the federal government to take over health care? If not, who should be responsible for providing health care coverage?[1]

Proponents of a universal, government-controlled health care system argue that health care is a human right. They argue that America's current system of health care—which depends on a mix of private insurance and joint federal–state programs—is broken. A federal health care system covering all Americans, they say, will reduce costs by encouraging patients to have regular checkups that are fully covered, and encourage preventative treatments, rather than having those who are sick and without insurance rely on emergency rooms for basic care. Centralizing the administration of health care, they contend, will reduce paper work, eliminate inefficiencies in claim approvals, and cut overhead costs. It will make health care more affordable, they say. And advocates contend that a centralized national database will make referrals easier for doctors, and medical professionals will be able to focus on practicing medicine, rather than filing with insurance companies and worrying about malpractice liabilities.

Opponents contend that a health care system administered by the federal government—including he so-called "Public Option" advanced by the Obama administration—won't be efficiently run, and that it will lead to increased taxes and government regulations. They argue that it will decrease flexibility for patients to choose their own doctors, and that government-mandated procedures will lead to poorer care. They also say that a universal health care system essentially socializes costs, which means that healthy individuals will end up subsidizing the medical care of those who are sick or injured. Critics of a single-payer system point to Canada, where patients who are frustrated by the long wait to receive routine treatments will travel to the United States to receive the care they want. They also point to cross-national public opinion surveys conducted in Germany, Canada, Australia, and Britain that show that a majority of respondents think their country's centralized health care system is broken.

What do you think? Does the current system of private, state, and federal health care coverage in the United States work? Are there gaps in coverage? If so, for whom? Does it make sense to centralize health care, creating a universal system of coverage? What are the potential advantages/costs of a single-payer system?

Note

1. Rep. Jesse L. Jackson, "Do We Have a Right to Health Care? *ABC News*, 13 October 2006, http://abcnews.go.com/WNT/PrescriptionForChange/Story?id=2563706&page=1.

---

federal poverty level for a family of three). Among this nonelderly population, low-income parents, their children, and low-income adults without children accounted for 65 percent of all the uninsured in 2003. The remaining 35 percent of the uninsured were workers (and their dependents) who earned at least twice the federal poverty level but were not covered by an employer's insurance or could not afford private insurance. In terms of race and ethnicity, minorities are considerably less likely to be covered by employer-provided health insurance than whites. According to the U.S. Census Bureau, a quarter of all African Americans do not have health care coverage, and 33 percent of Hispanics lack coverage.[68]

---

[68] Carmen DeNavas-Walt, Bernadette Proctor, and Cheryl Lee, "Income, Poverty, and Health Insurance Coverage in the United States: 2004," U.S. Bureau of the Census, August 2005, http://www.census.gov/prod/2005pubs/p60–229.pdf.

Considerable variation exists across the states when it comes to the percentage of nonelderly adults lacking health insurance. According to recent figures, Texas has the most dubious record, with 27 percent of its residents lacking coverage. Mississippi, California, and Florida all had rates topping 20 percent. At the other end of the spectrum, Minnesota (9 percent) and Wisconsin (10 percent) lead the nation with the fewest residents lacking health insurance.

Medicaid

The largest public health program in the United States is **Medicaid.** The program covers some 63 million low-income and disabled people and costs the federal and state governments more than $332 billion (in 2007) a year to run. A joint federal–state program created by Congress in 1965, Medicaid provides health care insurance to low-income individuals and their families. The federal agency that works with the states to administer the program is the Centers for Medicare and Medicaid Services (CMS), which has 10 regional offices spread across the country. Although most states have an agency that administers the program, some devolve the responsibility to their county or municipal governments.

Medicaid is means-tested; eligibility is determined by whether an individual (and his or her family) falls below a floor set by the federal government. The program requires the states to provide health care coverage to several categories of individuals, including those who qualify for welfare. States must also cover Supplemental Security Income (SSI) recipients—a federal cash assistance program for low-income aged, disabled, and blind persons—and all children born into families earning less than the poverty level. The states may also opt to provide additional health care for "medically needy" individuals and create programs assisting poor pregnant women and infants, institutionalized individuals, disabled children, and adopted children with special needs. In most cases, federal matching funds are available for these elective programs.[69]

Medicaid is jointly funded by the federal government and the states. The federal government provides the bulk of the funding, with the states picking the remainder of the tab, depending on their relative wealth. In 2009, the federal government provided 57 percent of the total cost of Medicaid, but the percentage of federal aid was higher in several states, including impoverished Mississippi, at 76 percent. State expenditures on Medicaid automatically increase or decrease each year according to formulas set by the federal government. Under a rule implemented by the Bush administration, states may require Medicaid recipients with household incomes greater than $24,900 (for a family of three) to make co-payments on doctor and hospital visits while giving patients more control over their health care options.[70] Still, Medicaid costs have increased with growth in state tax revenue lagging far behind program costs, especially in the nation's poorest states.[71] Costs have increased by nearly 10 percent every year since 2000, even though states are either freezing or reducing payments to health care providers, tightening eligibility requirements, restricting benefits, and increasing co-payments.

According to the most recent data available, the average expenditure on Medicaid by the federal government and the 50 states (and the District of Columbia) amounted to $4,575 a year per enrollee. As Table 14.4 reveals, the 14.4 million adults covered by Medicaid on the average monthly caseload, receive $2,142 in yearly benefits, with children receiving $1,708 annually. Year in and year out, the greatest cost

[69] Health Care Financing Administration, *The spDATA Book: Characteristics of Medicaid State Programs* (Washington, DC: Government Printing Office, 1993).

[70] Health Care Financing Administration, *The spDATA Book.*

[71] Toikka et al., "Spending on Social Welfare Programs in Rich and Poor States"; and Donald Boyd, "The State Fiscal Crisis and Its Aftermath," Kaiser Commission on Medicaid and the Uninsured, September 2003, http://www.kff.org/medicaid/loader.cfm?url=/commonspot/security/getfile.cfm&PageID=22130.

Table 14.4

Average Medicaid Payments per Enrollee by Enrollment Group, by State, 2006

	Children	Adults	Elderly	Blind or Disabled	Total
Arizona	$1,983	$1,533	$2,512	$5,575	$2,206
California	$1,228	$847	$8,369	$11,890	$2,740
Georgia	$1,435	$2,806	$7,295	$8,408	$3,296
Texas	$1,607	$2,510	$6,371	$10,615	$3,367
Louisiana	$1,003	$2,751	$7,007	$9,267	$3,563
Arkansas	$1,747	$1,108	$10,643	$10,031	$3,676
Tennessee	$1,681	$2,914	$7,214	$8,453	$3,975
Alabama	$1,799	$1,094	$7,404	$5,992	$4,015
Oklahoma	$1,879	$2,370	$8,872	$11,793	$4,063
Illinois	$1,400	$1,981	$5,037	$13,933	$4,129
Mississippi	$1,427	$2,111	$8,472	$7,540	$4,144
South Carolina	$1,691	$1,746	$4,844	$9,219	$4,165
Michigan	$1,134	$2,190	$10,423	$8,439	$4,199
Florida	$1,321	$2,275	$7,603	$10,233	$4,204
Oregon	$1,840	$3,381	$10,102	$10,218	$4,272
Missouri	$1,992	$2,057	$10,931	$10,775	$4,387
Washington	$1,490	$2,088	$11,180	$10,732	$4,388
Wisconsin	$1,234	$2,066	$8,804	$13,345	$4,440
Hawaii	$1,859	$2,832	$11,002	$12,956	$4,484
Nevada	$1,795	$2,274	$9,793	$13,409	$4,490
New Mexico	$2,091	$2,522	$11,271	$15,358	$4,521
Colorado	$1,762	$2,577	$12,730	$13,561	$4,759
Idaho	$1,598	$3,363	$12,115	$14,655	$4,799
Pennsylvania	$1,767	$2,576	$13,247	$8,585	$4,832
Virginia	$1,954	$2,990	$9,277	$12,154	$4,840
Kentucky	$2,074	$3,479	$8,841	$8,661	$4,870
Indiana	$1,868	$2,895	$14,628	$13,669	$4,907
North Carolina	$1,882	$3,133	$9,738	$12,673	$4,943
Utah	$1,508	$1,957	$9,742	$13,908	$5,005
Wyoming	$2,064	$3,424	$14,115	$18,120	$5,056
South Dakota	$2,145	$3,209	$12,066	$14,296	$5,072
Vermont	$2,523	$2,617	$9,089	$14,876	$5,096
Delaware	$2,255	$3,688	$12,760	$15,244	$5,152
Kansas	$2,071	$2,874	$13,350	$15,176	$5,578
Iowa	$1,769	$2,150	$13,863	$17,082	$5,600
Montana	$2,370	$3,376	$15,365	$12,067	$5,617
West Virginia	$2,014	$2,233	$11,430	$8,847	$5,682

(continued)

Table 14.4

Average Medicaid Payments per Enrollee by Enrollment Group, by State, 2006 (continued)

	Children	Adults	Elderly	Blind or Disabled	Total
Ohio	$1,696	$2,930	$18,034	$15,516	$5,768
Nebraska	$2,548	$2,587	$14,680	$16,940	$5,915
New Hampshire	$2,609	$2,784	$16,708	$15,100	$6,047
Maryland	$2,578	$3,003	$14,214	$18,434	$6,600
North Dakota	$1,931	$2,582	$18,652	$19,535	$6,925
Massachusetts	$3,565	$2,856	$14,878	$14,331	$6,961
Minnesota	$2,475	$2,927	$14,887	$23,131	$7,129
Connecticut	$2,363	$2,591	$23,124	$23,034	$7,598
Alaska	$4,078	$4,851	$19,809	$23,865	$7,644
Maine	$4,237	$4,389	$12,637	$19,928	$7,775
New Jersey	$2,086	$2,928	$16,668	$21,271	$7,869
New York	$2,140	$3,554	$20,819	$26,535	$7,927
Rhode Island	$3,199	$3,324	$16,750	$18,477	$8,082
District of Columbia	$2,908	$4,261	$16,919	$19,439	$8,484
National Average	$1,708	$2,142	$10,691	$12,874	$4,575

Sources: The Henry J. Kaiser Family Foundation, "Medicaid Payments per Enrollee, FY2006," 2009, http://www.statehealthfacts.org/comparetable. jsp?*ind*=183&cat=4.

per recipient is for the elderly and the blind and disabled who are covered under Medicaid. The combined federal and state costs in 2006 averaged $10,691 per elderly enrollee and $12,874 per blind or disabled enrollee.

Across the states, one can see a tremendous range in average Medicaid costs. Detailing federal and state payments for Medicaid, Table 14.4 shows the average level of payments in 2006 across all categories of Medicaid enrollees. In terms of overall Medicaid expenditures, nearly three-fifths of the states spend $5,000 or less a year per beneficiary, including Arizona and California, which pay well below $3,000 per Medicaid recipient. In contrast, six states spend more than $7,000 per recipient. Rhode Island leads the way among states, spending an average more than $8,000 on each Medicaid recipient, with New York, New Jersey, and Maine close behind. One study reveals that states with more "comprehensive"

health care programs tend to spend more per Medicaid recipients than those with piecemeal programs.[72]

In every state, many more Medicaid dollars are spent on the elderly than on impoverished children and nondisabled impoverished adults, but spending on these categories still vary widely across the states. On average, Alabama, Arizona, and Mississippi spent less than $6,400 a year on each blind and disabled Medicaid beneficiary, whereas Alaska, Minnesota, and New York spent in excess of $24,500 per recipient. In 2006, the average Medicaid expenditures for adults ranged from $847 a year in California to $4,851 a year in Alaska, and on children from a low of $1,003 in Louisiana to $4,237 in Maine. Although Maine is generous in its average payments to children, it

---

[72] Shruti Rajan, "Publicly Subsidized Health Insurance: A Typology of State Approaches," *Health Affairs* (May–June 1998):101–17.

is more miserly when it comes to elderly receiving Medicaid. Although still above the national average, in 2006, Maine's average Medicaid payment to the elderly was $12,637. By comparison, New York and Connecticut spent more than $20,000 per elderly recipient of Medicaid.[73] Spending on the elderly varies widely across the states due to the level of reimbursement a state opts to provide the owners of nursing homes that care for many Medicaid patients. In some states, nursing home owners constitute a powerful lobby and place tremendous pressure on state legislatures to reimburse them at a substantial rate.

Federal Medicaid Funding The ability of the states to provide their share of Medicaid funding tends to be predicated on the actions of the federal government. During the 2000s, rising Medicaid costs in the states were compounded by decisions in the nation's capital. Under the Bush administration, the federal government made sweeping cuts to Medicaid funding. Most of the cuts in federal spending were in the form of fewer dollars being transferred to the states to pay for and administer the joint program. In 2006, well before the economic meltdown, former President Bush's Health and Human Services secretary, Mike Leavitt, said that the federal government "is not in a position to help out states as much as before."[74] In an effort to make up for the decrease in federal funding, the Bush administration gave the states the option—if one can call it that—of reducing their own expenditures on Medicaid by either reducing the eligibility of those receiving Medicaid or reducing the range of benefits of the recipients. This put the states in an untenable position of having to either cut programs and benefits or increase taxes to offset their increased share for the program.

Under President Obama's 2009 American Recovery and Reinvestment Act, the federal government provided $15 billion in immediate stimulus dollars to the states for Medicaid relief. Because many states were having difficulty

meeting their financial obligations to fund Medicaid—putting at risk some 20 million Americans receiving Medicaid—the federal government temporarily increased its share of funding to all states by 6.2 percentage points, through the beginning of 2011. President Obama told the nation's governors that his plan will "help ensure that you don't need to make cuts to essential services Americans rely on now more than ever."[75]

Not surprisingly, none of these solutions sits well with the states, especially governors, most of whom have had severe budget problems on their plates. The rising costs of health care continue to comprise one of the most pressing issues facing governors and state policy makers. The Obama administration realizes this, but it faces daunting challenges to reform the health care system due to entrenched special interests and questions about what change would look like. Still, as more and more Americans lose or cannot afford health care coverage, the states are expected to pick up those who fall through the cracks. Despite budgetary constraints of their own, all states, including those with low fiscal capacity and high social needs, have had to increase their expenditures on Medicaid, at the same time they have had to make cuts in other health-related public assistance programs or make increases in premiums and co-payments for doctor visits. Bill Richardson, the Democratic governor of New Mexico, a persistent critic that the federal government has shortchanged the states on Medicaid funding, has said that the patchwork system of health care in the country places undue burdens on the states to provide health care to the poor. According to Richardson, "[S]tates will now become the true laboratories of innovation because the federal budget is not particularly helpful."[76]

State Experimentation with Medicaid States carry out their Medicaid programs in ways that vary tremendously. Over half of the

---

[73] Kaiser Family Foundation, "State Health Facts," 2006, http://www.statehealthfacts.org.
[74] Kathleen Hunter, "Bush Budget Short on State Aid," *Stateline*, 6 February 2006, http://www.Stateline.org.

[75] U.S. Department of Health and Human Services, "$15 Billion in Medicaid Relief Headed To States," 2009, http://www.hhs.gov/recovery/programs/medicaidfmap.html.
[76] Hunter, "Bush Budget Short on State Aid."

states require at least some of their Medicaid recipients to belong to managed care plans, and some spend more than four times as much as others on discretionary state Medicaid expenditures. Since 1974, Hawaii has used its federal Medicaid dollars, in tandem with a requirement that employers offer health care coverage for their regular employees, to offer universal access to health care. In 1994, Tennessee launched TennCare, an innovative managed care model of health insurance, but less than 10 years later, the state was forced to deny coverage to hundreds of thousands of recipients after operational costs threatened to bankrupt the state budget. Maine passed a law in 2003 providing a broad health care network financed jointly by Medicaid and employer contributions. Arizona, on the other hand, did not even implement its Medicaid program until 1982. Unfortunately, it is unclear why states have different types of health care coverage. Some scholars have found that state demographic and economic conditions help to explain cross-state variation in health-related expenditures, but others have found that political forces, such as party control of state legislatures and the power of interest groups, are the main determinants.[77]

From a partisan standpoint, Republican governors generally have pushed for market reforms to address the health care crisis. In Florida, for example, under former Governor Jeb Bush, the state drastically cut back on its Medicaid program by privatizing much of its health insurance program. Rather than providing a set menu of services under Medicaid, as other states do, in 2005 Bush quietly pushed through the state legislature a program that instead provides recipients with a lump sum of money with which they are expected to purchase their own private insurance. The Republican claimed that his program "empowers" low-income families by giving them more choice in obtaining health care coverage. Under his watch, Bush also allowed his state to cut Medicaid coverage for disabled and chronically ill children in need of nutritional supplements. Florida's administrative changes ended the financial assistance received by more than 1,000 children infected by AIDS and suffering from "wasting syndrome" as well as those unable to digest solid food because of cystic fibrosis.[78]

Several other states under the control of Republican governors have led the way in cutting Medicaid costs. In South Carolina, Governor Mark Sanford pushed for federal approval of a program that allows Medicaid recipients to establish health savings accounts. The tax-free accounts can be used by individuals to pay for their medical expenses or purchase health insurance. In Arkansas, former governor and 2008 GOP presidential candidate Mike Huckabee received federal approval for a plan subsidizing small businesses that provided minimal health care insurance for their employees and making patients more accountable for the costs of their own health care. "One of the reasons we have a healthcare crisis is because, as a consumer, I don't have that much skin in the game," Huckabee reasoned.[79] In 2005, Mississippi—under the leadership of Governor Haley Barbour—eliminated its Medicaid coverage of 65,000 elderly and disabled who had earnings between 100 percent and 133 percent of the federal poverty level, and Colorado passed a law in 2003 removing legal immigrants from Medicaid coverage. Georgia, in 2005 under the leadership of Governor Sonny Perdue—the first Republican elected governor of the state since Reconstruction—raised the eligibility income limit for low-income pregnant women and those with children, affecting some 7,500 people.[80]

[77] Mark Daniels, ed., *Medicaid Reform and the American States: Case Studies on the Politics of Managed Care* (Westport, CT: Greenwood, 1998); Charles Barrilleaux and M. E. Miller, "The Political Economy of State Medicaid Policy," *American Political Science Review* 82(1988): 1089–1106; Dye, *Politics, Economics, and the Public*; Richard Winters, "Party Control and Policy Change," *American Journal of Political Science* 20(1976):597–636; Kousser, "Politics, Economics, and State Policy."

[78] Carol Miller, "Policy Denies Nutrients to 1,000," *Miami Herald*, 24 March 2006, http://www.miami.com/mld/miamiherald/14173441.htm.

[79] Ronald Brownstein, "Governors on Divergent Paths to Control Health Costs," *Los Angeles Times*, 14 March 2006.

[80] Smith et al., "The Continuing Medicaid Budget Challenge."

Democratic governors and state legislatures, by contrast, have generally pushed for extending coverage under their state plans, even in times of tight budgetary constraints. Illinois, New Mexico, and California (under former Democrat governor Gray Davis) all made strides during the past 10 years to expand their health care coverage for children. In Illinois, the state in 2005 guaranteed that all children—regardless of their citizenship or income—would have access to health care coverage. After signing the legislation into law, former Governor Rod Blagojevich—who was impeached from office in 2009 amid charges of corruption—announced, "We have now done for kids what 40 years ago Medicare did for seniors." The Illinois state plan provides universal health care coverage using a sliding scale based on income to determine the premiums.[81]

There have also been some bipartisan reform successes. In Massachusetts, the Democratic-controlled state legislature—with support from former governor and GOP presidential candidate Mitt Romney—passed legislation in 2006 requiring all uninsured residents to purchase relatively inexpensive health insurance by July 1, 2007, or risk paying a fine. The innovative universal system of health care coverage requires the estimated 550,000 state residents without insurance to pay up to $250 a month for a basic policy. The program is underwritten in large part by some $385 million in federal Medicaid dollars (which the federal government threatened to eliminate if the state didn't reduce its number of uninsured), additional appropriations from the state, and an annual $295 per employee fee levied on businesses with 11 or more employees.[82]

State Children's Health Insurance Programs

In February 2009, in one of the first official acts of his administration, President Obama signed into law the Children's Health Insurance Reauthorization Act, which was established in 1997. With a stroke of his pen, Obama reversed President Bush's 2007 decision to veto a nearly identical bipartisan bill. The legislation increased federal funding for State Children's Health Insurance Programs (SCHIPs) by $35 billion over five years to cover an addition 4 million uninsured children. To pay for the increased coverage, Congress raised the federal tobacco tax from 39 cents to $1 per pack.[83] Earlier, in 1997, Congress initially provided over $24 billion in federal matching funds to the states over a period of five years to encourage them to create their own SCHIPs and expand their health care coverage for the millions of uninsured children whose parents do not qualify for Medicaid.

Following the passage of the federal law in 1997, there was widespread diffusion of SCHIPs across the states. Between 1998 and 2001, the programs in the states that were perceived as having successful SCHIPs—that is, the ones that were able to lower the rate of not having insurance among poor children at the same time they lowered costs—were emulated by other states. One study found that states adopting other states' successful SCHIPs were similar along both partisan and ideological lines and had similar budgetary constraints.[84]

The state-run SCHIP insurance programs, jointly funded by the federal and state governments and administered by the states, have been heralded as successes. Although the federal Department of Health and Human Services has final approval over the 50 state plans, the states have retained considerable discretion, operating within broad federal guidelines, to create their own health insurance programs for children, including eligibility requirements, the

[81] Brownstein, "Governors on Divergent Paths to Control Health Costs."

[82] David Fahrenthold, "Mass. Bill Requires Health Coverage," *The Washington Post,* 5 April 2006, p. A1; John Hechinger and David Armstrong, "Massachusetts Seeks to Mandate Health Coverage: Bill Would Penalize Citizens Who Don't Buy Insurance; Business Fears Higher Costs," *Wall Street Journal*, 5 April 2006, p. A1.

[83] "Cigarette Excise Tax," *State Legislatures* 35(April 2009):8.

[84] Volden, States as *Policy Laboratories*, p. 295.

package of benefits, the level of coverage, and how the programs are to be administrated. As a result, 73 percent of all children living in low-income families who are eligible receive SCHIP assistance, although some states do a much better job than others in covering those who are eligible.

Medicare

Medicare is a social insurance program wholly paid for and administered by the federal government. Signed into law in 1965 by President Lyndon B. Johnson, the program today serves approximately 43 million beneficiaries. The program, which serves primarily the elderly but also certain younger people with disabilities and those with chronic kidney disease, does not focus on the poor. Individuals are eligible for hospitalization coverage under Medicare if they (or their spouse) worked for at least 10 years and made required contributions paying into the Hospital Insurance Trust Fund. Employees and their employers pay a 1.45 percent payroll tax (along with Social Security) to fund the trust fund (commonly referred to as Medicare Part A). Medicare Part A generally covers all costs for the first 20 days of hospitalization (after an inpatient hospital deductible of $952 is met), and it is prorated thereafter. Those individuals who are eligible for hospital insurance may voluntarily apply for Supplementary Medical Insurance,

known widely as Medicare Part B. Part B covers 80 percent of the costs for a range of inpatient care, including physician bills, outpatient diagnoses, and physical therapy, after recipients have met the annual $124 deductible. The premium is $88.50 a month, and it is deducted directly from a recipient's Social Security, railroad retirement, or civil service retirement check.

In 2003, President Bush signed into law the Medicare Modernization Act, which was seen by many as a bonanza for pharmaceutical companies.[85] Americans spend more than $200 billion on prescription drugs annually, and the amount is growing by roughly 12 percent each year. The law provides a seemingly endless array of prescription drug plans from which eligible seniors are able to choose, to receive discounts on their medication. The drug coverage benefit, known as Part D of Medicare, immediately shifted more than 6 million poor Medicaid recipients over to the plan. The plan also covers seniors earning less than $19,000 a year, allowing these low-income seniors to purchase their prescription drugs with only $5 co-payments. By 2006, however, only 1.4 million of the 8 million eligible seniors had signed up for the drug coverage.[86] Seniors who are financially better off are also permitted to participate in the Medicare drug benefit plan, paying monthly premiums and standard co-payments for any prescription drugs they purchase.[87]

Summary

States and their local communities often face major challenges in the provision of social welfare and health care services. Compared to unitary systems of government, our federalist system demands a lot from our subnational levels of government. When it comes to social ills and inequalities, such as inadequate health care, poverty, unemployment, and homelessness, state and local governments are often the first (and in

---

[85] Marcia Angell, "The Truth about the Drug Companies," *New York Review of Books*, 15 July 2004, http://www.nybooks.com/articles/17244.

[86] Ceci Connolly, "Millions Not Joining Medicare Drug Plan," *The Washington Post*, 21 February 2006, p. A1.

[87] U.S. Department of Health and Human Services, "Prescription Drug Services," http://www.medicare.gov/pdphome.asp.

some cases, the only) line of defense. Time and again, state and local governments have shown their resilience and entrepreneurial spirit. Although frequently serving as "laboratories of democracy," competing with and learning from one another, states and communities do not always have the resources to meet the many societal problems at hand. At these times, there is an expectation that the federal government will step up to help out. When it does intervene, the federal government's heavy hand is often felt in its effort to reshape and standardize health and welfare policies across the states.

Some critics contend that it is possible that we're witnessing the gradual dismantling of America's welfare state,[88] and that the Obama administration's infusion of stimulus dollars into the states is just forestalling the inevitable. Fiscal constraints at both the state and federal levels have hampered the provision of social welfare and health care benefits to the most vulnerable members of society. In particular, the ever-expanding federal budget deficit and the weak economy have placed pressure on members of Congress and state lawmakers to reduce their financial commitment in funding many joint federal–state domestic programs. Many states have curtailed their experimentations with alternative health and welfare programs because of budgetary constraints or, alternatively, because of federal mandates directing them how to spend joint aid on TANF, Food Stamps, and Medicaid. It is likely that states and their communities will not be afraid to do battle with the federal government when trying to protect their social welfare and health care policies, but they will cooperate when it is to their advantage. What is certain is that states and local governments will continue to respond to policy shocks differently, drawing on a range of institutions to reform their policies to meet the demands of their diverse populations.

Key Terms

Entitlement	Policy diffusion	Temporary Assistance for Needy Families (TANF)
Feminization of poverty	Public assistance	
Living wage	Single-payer health care	Underclass
Means-tested	Social insurance	Welfare
Medicaid	Social Security Act	Working poor
Medicare		

Discussion Questions

1. What is policy diffusion, and how does the concept help to explain why some state and local governments adopt a set of policies, but others do not?
2. Who are America's poor, and how might the demographics of poverty affect what kinds of policies are adopted by the state and federal governments to address their needs?

---

[88] Neil Gilbert, *Transformation of the Welfare State: The Silent Surrender of Public Responsibility* (New York: Oxford University Press, 2002); Paul Pierson, *Dismantling the Welfare State: Reagan, Thatcher, and the Politics of Retrenchment* (New York: Cambridge University Press, 1994).

3. In 1932, U.S. Supreme Court Justice Louis Brandeis argued that in a federalist system, subnational governments should serve as "laboratories of democracy." Provide two recent examples of state governments taking Justice Brandeis's advice in the areas of health and welfare policy.

4. Discuss the transition from AFDC to TANF. What changed? What remained the same? More importantly, do you think poor individuals are better served under TANF, compared to AFDC?

5. Discuss state-level spending differences on Medicaid? Why do you think there is such variation in the spending on Medicaid across the states?

Suggested Readings

Daniels, Mark, ed. 1998. *Medicaid Reform and the American States: Case Studies on the Politics of Managed Care*. Westport, CT: Greenwood Press.

Karch, Andrew. 2007. *Democratic Laboratories: Policy Diffusion among the American States*. Ann Arbor, MI: University of Michigan Press.

Mittelstadt, Jennifer. 2005. *From Welfare to Workfare: The Unintended Consequences of Liberal Reform, 1945–1965*. Chapel Hill, NC: University of North Carolina Press.

Osborne, David, and Ted Gaebler. 1992. *Reinventing Government*. New York: Penguin.

Peterson, Paul, and Mark Rom. 1990. *Welfare Magnets: A New Case for a National Welfare Standard*. Washington, DC: Brookings Institution.

Pierson, Paul. 1994. *Dismantling the Welfare State: Reagan, Thatcher, and the Politics of Retrenchment*. New York: Cambridge University Press.

Riccucci, Norma. 2005. *How Management Matters: Street-Level Bureaucrats and Welfare Reform*. Washington, DC: Georgetown University Press.

Schram, Sanford, Joe Soss, and Richard Fording, eds. 2003. *Race and the Politics of Welfare Reform*. Ann Arbor, MI: University of Michigan Press.

Web Sites

Council of State Governments (http://www.csg.org): CSG provides policy information for all 50 states and publishes annually the indispensable Book of the States.

Governing (http://www.governing.com): This monthly magazine's primary audience is state and local government officials.

National Conference of State Legislatures (http://www.ncsl.org): NCSL provides a wealth of information to state legislators and the general public about state politics and policy.

National Governors' Association (http://www.nga.org): The NGA breaks down issues that are important to all 50 states, including welfare, education, health care, and budgets. It also contains the latest press releases and policy statements from various governors.

Stateline (http://www.stateline.org): Stateline, which is funded by the Pew Charitable Trusts, is staffed by professional journalists. In addition to original reporting on the news, Stateline provides links to other state and local news stories.

State Net (http://www.statenet.com): This full-service government relations firm provides data, legislative intelligence, regulations, and in-depth reporting to companies concerned about the actions of state government.

Stateside Associates (http://www.stateside.com): A government relations firm that provides information on policy issues, regulations, and legislative monitoring in the states.

Urban Institute (http://www.urban.org): The Urban Institute provides independent nonpartisan analysis on issues dealing with community development and economic and social policy.

15

White Packert/Getty Images

Education Policy

WHO'S GETTING SCHOOLED?

As public school systems go, they are worlds apart. First, consider the Chappaqua Central School District, located in tiny Westchester County, New York, home to Martha Stewart, Bill and Hillary Clinton, Vanessa Williams, and Kiss lead guitarist, Ace Frehley. Chappaqua has an exceptional system of public education, serving 4,000 kindergarten through high school students, 90 percent of whom are white. The district's total revenue for academic year 2009–2010 approached $90 million, the bulk of it generated from local property taxes, allowing the district to spend roughly $20,000 per student. Much of this expense was driven by its low 12:1 student–teacher ratio. And Chappaqua's heavy investment in education seems to be paying off: 97 percent of students attending its single high school, Horace Greeley, were proficient or better in math and reading in 2007, and its graduation rate was 99 percent.

In the other world, consider the Detroit City School District in Wayne County, Michigan. By most standards, the Detroit school system is an abysmal failure. This urban district, whose residents are mainly African American, serves approximately 150,000 students attending roughly 250 schools. In the 2008–2009 academic year, Detroit public schools averaged only one teacher for every 17 students, and less than $11,000 was spent on each child per year. Fewer than half of the system's high school students are proficient at math, and only two of three satisfy minimal requirements in reading. The school district's graduation rates are abysmal, the lowest in the country for urban public schools. Only one in four freshmen entering Detroit's high schools in 2004 received a diploma by 2008. According to guidelines set by the federal Department of Education, the Detroit school district has continually failed to make adequate yearly progress.

Some might say that the residents of the Chappaqua Central School District place a higher value on public education than those living in Detroit. But probably more to the point, those living in Chappaqua can more easily afford to pay for quality public schools. Median household income in the district nears $200,000, with the value of the median home over $1 million. Approximately 80 percent of Chappaqua residents aged 25 and older hold at least a bachelor's degree, and unemployment is low. Residents of Detroit probably value public education just as much as those of Chappaqua; the problem is that residents cannot afford to pay for it. Nearly three of four students are from economically disadvantaged families, qualifying them to receive a free lunch financed by the federal government. Nearly 50 percent of households in the district have annual incomes under $30,000, and only one in 10 adults has earned a bachelor's degree. Unemployment in Detroit is near the top in the country, roughly twice the national rate, and property values have plummeted, with the average home now worth less than $100,000. Resources for public education are scarce in the Motor City, and the educational results reflect that reality.[1]

Students at Guyton Elementary School in Detroit, Michigan

High School students graduating from Croton-on-Hudson, in Westchester County, New York

1   School district and demographic statistics for Chappaqua and Detroit are calculated from the National Center for Education Statistics (NCES), U.S. Department of Education, 2009, *http://nces.ed.gov/edfin/*; and City-Data.com, 2009, http://www.city-data.com.

Introduction

In contrast to our social welfare and health care systems, the United States does have a comprehensive, universal public education system—although many of the standards are set at the state and school district levels. Free, quality public education is a core societal value that is deeply held by most Americans. Starting in 1647, when English Calvinists passed a law in the Massachusetts Bay Colony requiring all townships to establish public schools funded through local property taxes, and spreading throughout the land in the 19th century, the concept of free-of-charge and universal public education has long been a hallmark of this country. Today, public education is viewed by many Americans as a fundamental right, although the U.S. Supreme Court has ruled otherwise.[1] In addition to providing students with the knowledge and skills to find a job or pursue their education and training in college or technical school, public schools—from kindergarten through college—inculcate students with civic responsibility. Public education also has many social side effects that can lead to better quality of life and economic development for everyone in a community, even beyond the students themselves.[2] Some states and communities have even explicitly emphasized delivering high-quality public education in order to cultivate a "creative class" of residents.[3]

And yet, as the opening vignette suggests, many of the nation's public schools are failing. Microsoft founder and social philanthropist Bill Gates has called America's high schools "obsolete." "By obsolete," Gates continued at a National Summit on High Schools, "I don't just mean they're broken, flawed or underfunded, though a case could be made for every one of those points. By obsolete, I mean our high schools—even when they're working as designed—cannot teach all of our students what they need to know today."[4] Although some students and education systems succeed, tens of thousands of students, especially those in urban America, are falling through the cracks of the educational system each year. Less than half of those students attending big-city high schools receive their diplomas. In addition to Detroit, high school graduation rates in Atlanta, Columbus, Dallas, Denver, Fort Lauderdale, Fort Worth, Houston, Kansas City, Los Angeles, Miami, Memphis, Milwaukee, Minneapolis, New York, Oakland, Oklahoma City, and St. Petersburg are below 50 percent; fewer than 40 percent of high school students living in Baltimore, Cleveland, and Indianapolis typically graduate on time. And for members of some racial and ethnic minority groups, the story is especially bad. Although there is considerable disagreement among experts on how to measure graduation rates, one study finds that roughly three-quarters of white and Asian American students graduate on time, but the rate is just over 50 percent for African Americans, Hispanics, and Native Americans.[5] Overall, roughly 70 percent of all high school students graduate on time. That means that of the estimated 4 million students who should graduate each year, about 1.2 million drop out annually. By one calculation, that's

---

[1] Loucas Petronicolos and William New, "Anti-Immigrant Legislation, Social Justice, and the Right to Equal Educational Opportunity," *American Educational Research Journal* 36(1999):373–408.

[2] Thomas Hungerford and Robert Wassmer, "K–12 Education in the U.S. Economy," National Education Association Research Working Paper, April 2004, http://www.nea.org/edstats/images/economy.pdf.

[3] Richard Florida, *The Rise of the Creative Class* (New York: Basic Books, 2002).

[4] Bill Gates, cofounder, Bill and Melinda Gates Foundation, prepared remarks, National Education Summit on High Schools, 26 February 2005, http://www.gatesfoundation.org/MediaCenter/Speeches/BillgSpeeches/BGSpeechNGA-050226.htm.

[5] Christopher B. Swanson, "Who Graduates? Who Doesn't? A Statistical Portrait of Public High School Graduation, Class of 2001," Urban Institute's Education Policy Center, 2004, http://www.urban.org/UploadedPDF/410934_WhoGraduates.pdf. See also Lawrence Michel and Joydeep Roy, "Rethinking High School Graduation Rates and Trends," Economic Policy Institute, 2006. http://www.epi.org/books/rethinking_hs_grad_rates/rethinking_hs_grad_rates-FULL_TEXT.pdf.

Public school children leaving a portable classroom in Florida.

approximately 7,000 students quitting school each day.[6]

Of course, as our opening vignette shows, educational outcomes vary dramatically across districts, but in many places, and for many students, the American public school system is failing. In this chapter, we look both at why and where American public schools are doing well and doing poorly. We use both a historical analysis of public education in this country and a comparison of institutional differences across the states and school districts to understand what works and what does not work and why. Although economics has much to do with today's problems in public education, educational institutions can impact these problems.

First, we examine how American education policy has evolved over time, highlighting what has become a regular crisis of confidence in public education each generation. These periodic crises—whether based in educational reality or calculated fear-mongering by politicians—disrupt the education policy equilibrium and lead to reform and policy change. Central to this discussion of American education policy evolution is a tension that exists between the states, their school districts, and the federal government that

is rooted in questions of federalism and public finance. This segues easily into our discussion of the ways states and school districts struggle to finance public education and our assessment of the equity and fairness of how school finances are allocated. Finally, we turn to questions concerning the organization and control of public education; that is, issues of educational institutions. In this section, we profile several innovations developed by states and school districts to deliver public education, including school vouchers, education management organizations, and charter schools.

Issue Evolution of Education Policy

For much of this country's history, local governments have taken the lead in providing elementary and secondary education to our nation's children. Left to their own devices to design, fund, and administer schools themselves, the local **school district** has traditionally had much autonomy from state government, to say nothing of the federal government. But states and the federal government are increasingly playing a considerable role in the provision of public education. Since 2001, the federal government has increased its involvement in

[6] "High School Dropouts in America," *Alliance for Excellent Education*, February 2009, http://www.all4ed.org/files/GraduationRates_FactSheet.pdf.

public education by tying federal funding to programmatic and outcome-based educational policies. Under President Barack Obama, the Department of Education has increased the level of funding for public education while relaxing some of the federal standards placed on states and local school districts by the Bush administration. At the same time, due to budgetary constraints as discussed in Chapter 10, many states as well as local school districts have had to make severe cuts to their educational programs, from pre-kindergarten to university systems.

Prior to the 1930s, states and their communities were almost entirely responsible for providing public education to schoolchildren, with the federal government playing a limited role. It made sense, then, that there would be considerable diversity in the type and quality of public education children received when attending public schools. Since the 1930s and the New Deal, however, Congress has at times exerted its authority—albeit much less than in health care and social welfare policies. During the Great Society programs of the 1960s, for example, Congress passed several laws providing more than $1 billion in federal aid for elementary and secondary public schools with high concentrations of low-income students, funds for summer programs, categorical grants to fund bilingual education for children with limited English, and scholarships and low-interest loans for college students. A generation later, President Bill Clinton signed into law a Democrat-sponsored bill in 1994, Goals 2000: Educate America Act, which reauthorized all federal education programs, developed a voluntary national system of skill standards and certifications, and created midnight basketball leagues in public housing projects.

Local and state control over public education became even more constrained in the 21st century, largely due to increasing national educational standards. There is considerable irony with respect to new federal standards concerning public education, as the increase in national constraints placed on states and local school districts transpired on the watch of a Republican

president, George W. Bush. Flying in the face of Ronald Reagan's 1980 campaign promise that he would abolish the Department of Education after being elected—he didn't—the federal government's presence in education policy is perhaps as great as in any time in American history. During the Bush administration, the federal government became much more heavily involved in overseeing K–12 public education. Thus, to characterize the making of education policy as a robust competition among the states and school districts, with little intervention from the federal government, would be a major mischaracterization. Despite its limited constitutional authority—and its minimal financial expenditures—the federal government plays a major role today in the formulation of education policy in the states and communities. From subsidized pre-K education, to vouchers for private school, to need-based school lunches, to testing children's educational progress, the federal government is heavily involved in education policy making.

Public Education in Crisis

The politicization of education policy is not new. With cyclical regularity, America's education system comes under a barrage of criticism every generation or so, at the federal, state, and local levels. Policy shocks have become a regular occurrence. In 1957, after the former Soviet Union successfully launched *Sputnik*, the first satellite to orbit Earth, federal officials decried the failure of the American education system to keep up with communist Russia. The following year, Congress passed the National Defense Education Act of 1958, which provided federal grants-in-aid to public and private schools (K–12 through universities) to stimulate the teaching of science, math, foreign languages, and area studies. It also provided low-interest loans to college students.[7]

A generation later, the policy equilibrium was again upset. State and federal officials—upon

---

[7] Barbara Clowse, *Brainpower for the Cold War: The Sputnik Crisis and National Defense Education Act of 1958* (Westport, CT: Greenwood, 1981).

hearing the distress of parents and teachers at the local level—once again pulled the education alarm bell. In 1983, President Reagan's blue ribbon panel, the National Commission on Excellence in Education, issued a devastating report, "A Nation at Risk." Among its other scandalous findings, the commission found that for the first time in American history, the average high school graduate was less well-educated than those who received their diplomas a generation earlier, and American public school students were not as well educated as their counterparts in other industrialized nations. In Cold War rhetoric matching that brought about by the *Sputnik* crisis, the commission claimed that American society was being eroded "by a rising tide of mediocrity that threatens our very future. . . . If an unfriendly foreign power had attempted to impose on America the mediocre educational performance that exists today, we might well have viewed it as an act of war. . . . We have, in effect, been committing an act of unthinking, unilateral educational disarmament."[8]

During the 2000 presidential campaign, the generational crisis in education was once again invoked, this time by George W. Bush. Highlighting the poor achievement of many children attending public schools, and the so-called **achievement gap** between rich and poor and white and minority students, Bush touted the free market as providing the solution for what ailed public schools. Downplaying issues of inadequate and inequitable funding of schools, the Texas governor pushed for greater school choice, including the privatization of public schools, the creation of charter schools unrestrained by state regulations, and school vouchers as possible solutions. His solution was to hold public schools accountable by withholding federal funds for schools that failed to perform. Soon after winning office, with much public fanfare and the bipartisan backing of Congress, Bush signed into law the **No Child**

U.S. Secretary of Education Arne Duncan, center left, and Maryland Gov. Martin O'Malley, speak to a class at Doswell Brooks Elementary School, after a news conference about education stimulus funding, in Capitol Heights, Maryland, 1 April, 2009.

Left Behind (NCLB) Act. As we discuss later in this chapter, the implementation of the 2002 law caused great consternation among both liberals and conservatives in numerous states and communities, forcing President Obama to direct the U.S. Department of Education to reevaluate many of the federal government's programs.

Growth in Public Education

America's system of public education continues to expand. Between 1985 and 2009, enrollment in K–12 public schools grew by more than 25 percent, with the fastest growth occurring at the elementary school level. Over the same period, private school growth, by comparison, grew by only 11 percent. Some 50 million children attend public elementary and secondary schools. An additional 18 million students matriculate at public postsecondary, degree-granting institutions (colleges, universities, and trade schools). Enrollment for grades K–12 is expected to continue to grow until 2016.[9]

---

[8] National Commission on Excellence in Education, "A Nation at Risk: The Imperative for Educational Reform," April 1983, http://www.ed.gov/pubs/NatAtRisk/index.

[9] U.S. Department of Education, National Center for Education Statistics, "Digest of Education Statistics, 2008," 2009, http://nces.ed.gov/programs/digest/d08/.

Every state requires children up to a certain age to be educated, either in public or private schools or through homeschooling. In 1852, Massachusetts became the first state to require children to attend school, and by 1918, every state had a compulsory education law on the books. Today, over half of the states require students to begin their schooling by age 6 years; others, such as Pennsylvania and Washington, allow students to begin school as late as age 8 years. Twenty-six states allow students to quit their studies at age 16, with the remaining requiring students to stay enrolled until they are at least 17 or 18 years of age.[10]

Accompanying the growth in K–12 enrollment has been an increase in the cost of public education. Expenditures by all K–12 institutions are roughly $1 trillion annually, with colleges and universities (public and private) expending close to $400 billion more. Nearly 5 percent of the country's gross domestic product (GDP) goes toward K–12 education alone. Adjusting for inflation, total spending on K–12 education has increased every year since 1955 in terms of total government spending or as a percentage of the national GDP. Back in 1955, total spending on primary and secondary education was $71 billion, only 2.6 percent of the GDP. Public elementary and secondary schools now employ more than 3.7 million teachers, up 17 percent from 1997. Although the average annual salary for public school teachers is roughly $50,000, it is only 1 percent higher than in 1995–1996, after controlling for inflation. There is also a tremendous range across the states when it comes to salaries for teachers. In 20 states, the starting salary for teachers averages less than $30,000 a year. The average salary for teachers tops $55,000 in Massachusetts, New York, New Jersey, Illinois, Connecticut, and California. By most accounts, the rising cost of public education is

not the result of escalating teachers' salaries. On average, teachers make up slightly more than half of all public school staff, but there is a wide deviation across the states. In South Carolina, teachers comprise 65 percent of all public school staff, but only 43 percent in Kentucky.[11]

Organizational Control and Responsiveness of Public Schools

There is a strong tradition of deferring to local school boards to carry out public education decisions. Yet, state governments ultimately exercise broad authority over school districts. As discussed in Chapter 11, local school districts are creations of state government. Not surprisingly, there is considerable variation across the states when it comes to how public school systems are organized.

Organizational Control of Public Schools

Nationwide, over 90 percent of all public schools are run by locally elected school boards. Three states—Hawaii, Alaska, and Maine—are outliers in that the state government has a heavier role in administering public schools. Hawaii is unique in that it has a unitary, state-run system for public education. In North Carolina and Virginia, counties are charged with running public schools. In some cases, mayors—including Boston's, Chicago's, and New York's—have taken over the administration of public schools that fall within their municipal jurisdiction. Although not going to the degree of state control over education as in Hawaii, Alaska, and Maine, some states have usurped local control over certain school

---

[10] National Conference of State Legislatures, "Compulsory Education," March 2006, http://www.ncsl.org/programs/educ/CompulsoryEd.htm.

[11] U.S. Department of Education, Center for Education Statistics, "Digest of Education Statistics, 2008."

districts. In the mid-1990s, for example, New Jersey's state Department of Education took over Newark's public schools because of failing schools. Since that time, though, the performance of the 42,000 students attending Newark's public schools has not improved much. In any given year, roughly half of all of Newark's 11th graders fail the comprehensive math test given by the state—twice the statewide failure rate. Two-thirds of Newark's eighth graders fail the state's math test and over half fail the language test.[12]

In most states, the local school board appoints a superintendent, hires staff and teachers, helps to determine the curriculum, and sets school calendars and attendance requirements. Perhaps most importantly, local school boards determine the annual tax levies for operating expenses and the capital construction budget of school districts. However, in most states, the rate of local tax levies to fund public schools as well as the ability to float school construction bonds are limited by the state constitution. By 1940, 27 states had placed constitutional limits on the bonding authority of local school districts, and 15 limited local tax levies of school districts.[13] Today, nearly all the states place these limits on school districts. In addition, most states now also require tax levy increases and bond measures to be put to a public vote via a referendum.

Some states even require a supermajority vote at the local level on such fiscal measures. Between 1942 and 2007, for example, local school levies in Washington had to receive a popular vote of at least 60 percent (and have at least 40 percent turnout of the last election) in order to be approved. Critics claimed that the

state's antimajoritarian requirement allowed a minority to thwart the building of a better education system by making it difficult for local school districts to fund new school programs and build new facilities. Although the success rate of local referendums is quite high (in part because they are placed on the ballot in desynchronized, off-year, and even special elections, all with very low turnout), the state legislature placed a successful constitutional amendment on the ballot in 2007 that lowered the threshold to a simple majority.[14] In Oregon, which has similar supermajority requirements for the passage of levy and bond measures, some school districts have had to close public schools early and issue layoff notices to teachers and administrators following the defeat of operating expense referendums. In 1986, the Estacada school district (southeast of Portland) shut down its schools twice after voters rejected requests to increase its budget.[15]

Local school boards are also legally constrained in all pedagogical and substantive areas set by the state legislature and state constitution. Every state has a secretary or commissioner who oversees the statewide Department of Education (or a similar agency, such as a Department of Public Instruction). Figure 15.1 displays an administrative flowchart for the Massachusetts public school system, which is typical for many states. The top public school administrator in 36 states is appointed; in the remaining 14 states, the education chief is elected statewide. These officials are in charge of supervising their state's public education system but usually work in tandem with a statewide board of education. All but two states (Minnesota and

---

[12] Damien Cave and Josh Benson, "Voucher Issue a Touchy Topic in Newark Race," *The New York Times*, 17 April 2006, p. A20.

[13] R. L. Johns, "Regulation and Limitation of Credit to Boards of Education," *Review of Educational Research* 11(1941):190–96.

[14] Eric Stevick, "New Legislature Brings New Hope for Levy Bill: Education Boosters See Good Prospects for a Bill to Let Levies Pass with a Simple Majority," (Everett, Wash.) *Daily Herald*, 5 January 2007, http://www.heraldnet.com/stories/07/01/05/100loc_a1levy001.

[15] Oregon Education Association, "150 Years of Public Service to Education," 2006, http://www.oregoned.org.

Figure 15.1

Administrative Flowchart for Massachusetts Public Schools

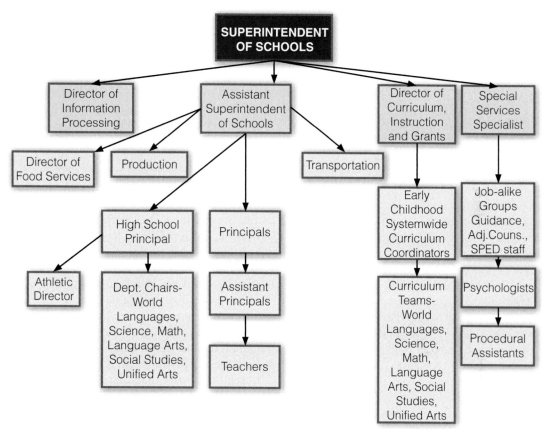

Source: http://www.walpole.ma.us/District_Home_page/OrgChart.html.

Wisconsin) have a state Board of Education. These semiautonomous bodies generally have six functions:

1. Establish certification standards for teachers and administrators.
2. Create standards for accreditation of school districts and teacher and administrator preparation programs.
3. Set high school graduation requirements.
4. Create state testing programs.
5. Review and approve the budget of the state education agency.
6. Develop rules and regulations for the administration of state education programs.

Currently, 32 states have statewide education boards that are appointed (usually by the governor), 11 have elected boards, and five states have boards that have both appointed and elected members. In the South, state control over education policy tends to be greater. In the North, especially in the New England region, local school districts tend to have more autonomy over their curriculum and other staffing decisions.[16]

Beginning in the 1950s, many states began drastically cutting their number of school districts. Taking advantage of economies of scale,

[16] Education Commission of the States, "State Boards/Chiefs/Agencies," 2006, http://ecs.org/html/issue.asp? issueID=192.

Table 15.1				

Number of School Districts and Distribution of the School-Age Population, 2000

School District Population	Number of School Districts	% of School Districts	Total School-Age Population	% of Total School-Age Population
Less than 5,000	6,252	43.7%	2,406,420	4.5%
5,000 to 9,999	2,550	17.8%	3,446,217	6.5%
10,000 to 19,999	2,377	16.6%	6,177,845	11.6%
20,000 to 39,999	1,637	11.4%	8,058,266	15.2%
40,000 or more	1,487	10.4%	33,007,255	62.2%
Total Population	14,310	100.0%	53,096,003	100.0%

Source: U.S. Census Bureau, Population Division, June 2004. Available: http://www.census.gov/population/www/documentation/twps0074/tab10.pdf.

proponents argued that by consolidating and centralizing districts, states could achieve increased cost savings in delivering educational programs. In 1932, there were over 127,000 independent school districts; today, there are roughly 14,000. As Table 15.1 shows, there are still thousands of very small school districts. Nearly 44 percent of all school districts serve populations of less than 5,000 people, amounting to 2.4 million school-age children. Only 1,487 school districts (10.4 percent) serve populations with greater than 40,000 people. Yet, large school districts account for 62.2 percent of the country's school-age population—some 33 million children under the age of 18.[17]

School District Responsiveness

Scholars are giving increased attention to how responsive school districts are to local public opinion. Although advocates of local control argue that school districts that devolve authority and decentralize decision making are more accountable, recent scholarship suggests this is not necessarily the case. Somewhat counterintuitively, a recent major study finds that of the more than "ten thousand democracies," appointed school boards tend to be at least as responsive as elected ones. The structure of school boards, it appears, does not necessarily impact the educational policies a school board adopts. School boards that are closest to the people—those run in New England–style town meetings, for example—tend not to reflect local public opinion any better than school boards appointed by other elected officials or even those folded within a city or county government. Local public opinion toward public education, especially of minorities, tends to be represented quite well by school boards that are unelected. This is perhaps due to the fact that other elected officials may be more apt to listen to and respond to public opinion and to place pressure on their appointees than school board members who are elected in low-information contests.[18]

More broadly, school boards generally do a good job reflecting local public opinion. Perhaps surprisingly, school boards that are integrated with other governmental bodies (such as counties or cities) have policies that are more reflective of the population being served. For example, a school district that is consolidated with a local government tends to have minority representation that is more reflective of the population being served. With respect to public support for school funding, as we discuss in

[17] U.S. Department of Education, Center for Education Statistics, "School District Demographics," June 2004, http://nces.ed.gov/surveys/sdds/.

[18] Michael B. Berkman and Eric Plutzer, *Ten Thousand Democracies: Politics and Public Opinion in America's School Districts* (Washington, DC: Georgetown University Press, 2005).

Table 15.2

Sources of Revenue for K-12 Public Schools, 1919–20 to 2006–07

School Year	Total (in thousands of dollars)	Federal (in thousands of dollars)	State (in thousands of dollars)	Local (in thousands of dollars)	Percent Federal	Percent State	Percent Local
1919–1920	$970,121	$2,475	$160,085	$807,561	0.3	16.5	83.2
1929–1930	$2,088,557	$7,334	$353,670	$1,727,553	0.4	16.9	82.7
1939–1940	$2,260,527	$39,810	$684,354	$1,536,363	1.8	30.3	68.0
1949–1950	$5,437,044	$155,848	$2,165,689	$3,115,507	2.9	39.8	57.3
1959–1960	$14,746,618	$651,639	$5,768,047	$8,326,932	4.4	39.1	56.5
1969–1970	$40,266,923	$3,219,557	$16,062,776	$20,984,589	8.0	39.9	52.1
1979–1980	$96,881,165	$9,503,537	$45,348,814	$42,028,813	9.8	46.8	43.4
1989-1990	$208,547,573	$12,700,784	$98,238,633	$97,608,157	6.1	47.1	46.8
1999–2000	$372,943,802	$27,097,866	$184,613,352	$161,232,584	7.3	49.5	43.2
2006–2007	$555,337,583	$47,041,419	$264,226,896	$244,069,269	8.5	47.6	43.9

Source: Lei Zhou and Frank Johnson, "Revenues and Expenditures for Public Elementary and Secondary Education: School Year 2006–07," U.S. Department of Education, National Center for Education Statistics, 2009, http://nces.ed.gov/pubs2009/2009337.pdf.

more detail in the following section, the level of school district financing also tends to map fairly closely to local public opinion. African American communities tend to support more spending on education than other racial and ethnic groups. Even communities with well-established elderly populations living on fixed incomes and with no school-aged children, who intuitively might seem likely to oppose the financing of public schools, generally support the use of property taxes to support quality public education.[19]

Financing Public Education

There are considerable differences across the states when it comes to the subsidization of higher education. There are also considerable differences across states and school districts regarding how much is spent per pupil on K–12 public education. Although some states

---

[19] Berkman and Plutzer, *Ten Thousand Democracies*; on the success of minority coalitions in school board elections, see: Rene R. Rocha, "Black-Brown Coalitions in Local School Board Elections," *Political Research Quarterly* 60 (2007): 315-27.

and school districts are striving to privatize public education, others are trying to bolster funding and enhance public schools.

Comparing K–12 Public Education Finance across the States

The financing of K–12 public education has undergone a major restructuring since the 1950s. Public financing of schools has been wholly reformed, with less reliance on local revenue sources to fund local schools. Public education has gradually become one of the largest budgetary items for state and local governments. On average, the states spend 21 percent of their annual budgets on K–12 education. As Table 15.2 shows, the total revenue needed to provide K–12 education has increased steadily over the years, even when factoring in inflation. In 1919–1920, local school districts provided 83.2 percent of the revenue for K–12 education, with the states providing 16.5 percent and the federal government less than 1 percent.

The states now play a major role in funding K–12 education. Since the 1920s, state governments have increasingly provided a greater proportion of the financing of public education.

Accordingly, the proportion financed by local government has decreased over time. The 1978 school year was the first in which state governments collectively provided more revenue than local governments for K–12 education. According to the most recent statistics provided by the U.S. Department of Education, state and local governments foot most of the bill for K–12 education: for every dollar spent on primary and secondary education, roughly 91 cents flow from state and local governments. State governments account for slightly less than half of total K–12 education revenue, and local governments account for slightly more than 40 percent. Despite the sizable number of mandates flowing from Washington, D.C., the federal government accounts for less than 10 percent of total revenues for K–12 public education.

When looking comparatively across the states, northeastern states tend to fund their public education systems to a far greater extent with local property taxes than do southern and western states. In northeastern states, well over 40 percent of all financing for public schools states is generated by local property taxes. Local property taxes account for roughly 35 percent of revenue in southern states and only 33 percent in western states. In midwestern states, local property taxes account for slightly less than 40 percent of total public school revenues. Western and southern states make up for the lack of property taxes by relying much more heavily on state funding. They also fund their systems of public education with a great share of federal dollars.

There are, of course, outliers to these general trends. In Illinois and Nevada, over 60 percent of K–12 funding flows from local revenue sources. In contrast, local property taxes account for less than 10 percent of K–12 funding in Vermont, and only 1.8 percent in Hawaii, not surprising because of its state-run education system. The federal government provides over 20 percent of K–12 funding in Mississippi, and 18.5 percent in Louisiana, but less than 5 percent in Connecticut and New Jersey. Table 15.3 provides the percentages of local,

Table 15.3

Percent of Total Public K–12 Revenues across Sources, by State, 2006

	Local	State	Federal
United States	44.4	46.5	9.1
Alabama	32.1	55.9	12.0
Alaska	24.3	58.7	17.0
Arizona	39.9	48.4	11.8
Arkansas	31.9	56.8	11.3
California	29.9	59.3	10.8
Colorado	50.2	42.5	7.3
Connecticut	56.7	38.5	4.8
Delaware	28.5	63.2	8.3
District of Columbia	87.8	*	12.2
Florida	50.4	39.5	10.1
Georgia	46.4	44.4	9.2
Hawaii	1.8	89.9	8.3
Idaho	33.0	56.2	10.8
Illinois	62.0	29.6	8.4
Indiana	44.0	49.1	6.9
Iowa	45.8	45.6	8.6
Kansas	36.4	54.6	9.0
Kentucky	31.1	57.3	11.7
Louisiana	38.1	43.4	18.5
Maine	47.8	42.4	9.9
Maryland	54.6	39.2	6.2
Massachusetts	47.4	47.0	5.6
Michigan	32.5	59.3	8.2
Minnesota	22.3	71.2	6.5
Mississippi	28.2	51.0	20.7
Missouri	57.6	33.5	8.9
Montana	39.8	46.2	14.0
Nebraska	58.1	31.9	10.0
Nevada	66.9	25.9	7.1
New Hampshire	55.3	39.2	5.5

	Local	State	Federal
New Jersey	53.3	42.3	4.4
New Mexico	14.3	71.2	14.5
New York	50.3	42.5	7.2
North Carolina	26.7	62.5	10.8
North Dakota	48.0	36.2	15.8
Ohio	48.7	43.7	7.6
Oklahoma	33.3	53.3	13.4
Oregon	39.8	50.4	9.8
Pennsylvania	56.5	35.4	8.1
Rhode Island	51.3	41.1	7.7
South Carolina	44.6	45.2	10.2
South Dakota	50.5	33.0	16.5
Tennessee	46.3	42.5	11.2
Texas	54.2	33.8	12.0
Utah	35.3	55.1	9.6
Vermont	6.8	85.6	7.6
Virginia	53.7	39.6	6.7
Washington	30.2	60.8	9.0
West Virginia	28.2	59.8	12.9
Wisconsin	41.7	52.3	6.0
Wyoming	45.8	44.1	10.1

Source: U.S. Department of Education, National Center for Education Statistics, Common Core of Data, Revenues and percentage distribution of revenues for public elementary and secondary education, by source and state or jurisdiction: Fiscal year 2006. http://nces.ed.gov/pubs2008/expenditures/tables.asp.

state, and federal funding for K–12 education for the 50 states and the District of Columbia.

The states have used several methods to ensure the funding of public schools. In the past, states would make fixed grants that went directly to school districts. These grants were usually based on the number of pupils per district, irrespective of the relative wealth of the district. Today, most states use a combination of two funding strategies to finance K–12 education. Some states use categorical grants, targeting revenue to support programs and facilities in property-poor districts that have maxed out

their local taxing revenues. The state is able to equalize school funding across school districts by using a formula that combines state dollars with local taxes as well as federal funds. Other states attempt to centralize school financing by using general funds to provide funding to all schools equally, avoiding inequalities across property-rich and property-poor districts. Figure 15.2 shows the complex system of funding public education in Colorado, which, among other sources, finances its schools with a mixture of property taxes, lottery funds, and school trust lands as well as income taxes, sales taxes, and other taxes that flow into its general fund.

There is considerable variation across states in terms of the amount of per pupil funding for K–12 public education. Per pupil spending has traditionally been the highest in northeastern states and the lowest in southern and western states, as Figure 15.3 shows. Vermont leads the nation in K–12 education spending per pupil. In 2006, the state spent an average of $15,139 on each elementary and secondary school student. Higher per pupil spending by a state, however, does not mean that students are guaranteed achieving higher academic performance. New York, which spent an average of $13,064 in 2006 to educate K–12 students, has one of the poorer graduation rates. Only 61 percent of New York State's ninth graders in 2003 graduated on time in 2007. In Alaska, where state spending is greater than $12,000 per pupil annually, only two-thirds of all students graduate on time, and in South Carolina, which spends more than $9,000 per student, only three of five entering freshman graduate in four years. By way of contrast, Utah, which allocates only $5,664 per K–12 pupil, has a graduation rate of 83 percent, the highest in the country.

Financing K–12 Public Education

Dissatisfied with the inequities in public education, many parents in the 1970s began pursuing legal avenues to challenge the reliance on local property taxes to fund public education. During the decade, numerous lawsuits were

| Figure 15.2 |

Colorado Sources of School Funding

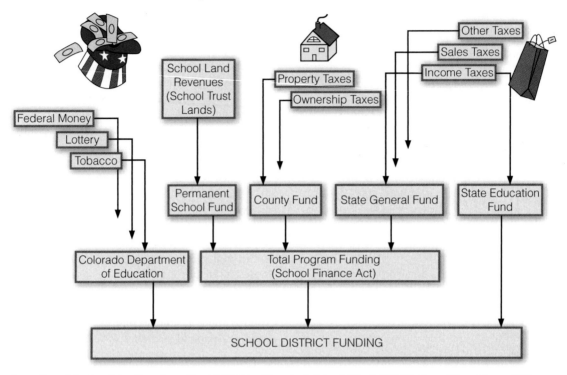

Source: Donnell-Kay Foundation, "Amendment 23 and Public School Financing in Colorado," March 2003, *http://www.dkfoundation.org/PDF/ Amendment23andPublicSchoolFinancingInColorado.pdf.*

filed by public interest groups that challenged the dependence on local property taxes to finance public school systems. The lawsuits were filed on behalf of poor school districts or minority children in poorly funded schools. They questioned the funding formulas for public education, claiming they violated the equity or adequacy of public education clauses found in most state constitutions. Between 1968 and 1998, hundreds of lawsuits were filed in state courts across the country. In more than 25 of the lawsuits, state supreme courts ruled that state funding formulas based on the property tax were unconstitutional.

California's Superior Court was the first in the country to find that its state's heavy reliance on local property taxes was unconstitutional because it caused gross disparities and inequities in the funding of public schools. Evidence introduced by the plaintiffs, the Western Center on Law and Poverty, showed wide disparities in funding existed across school districts, with districts raising over half of their revenue through local property taxes. The school funding in two Los Angeles County unified school districts— Baldwin Park and Beverly Hills—was particularly egregious, with the former spending only $577 per pupil in the 1968–1969 school year and the latter spending $1,232 per pupil. In its decision, the court found that the quality of public education for a child could not be a condition of his or her parents, or neighbors' property values. In its 1971 decision *Serrano v. Priest*, the court required the state to equalize local property tax bases by using statewide tax revenue and to provide poorer districts with

Figure 15.3

High School Graduation Rates and per Pupil Expenditures, 2007

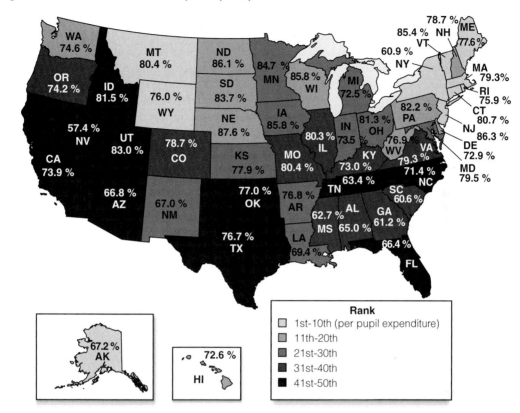

Sources: U.S. Department of Education, "The Averaged Freshman Graduation Rate for Public High Schools from the Common Core of Data," June 2007, http://nces.ed.gov/pubs2006/2006606rev.pdf; Hajime Mitani, "Per-pupil Expenditures Approaching $10,000," Editorial Projects in Education Research Center, 2009, http://www.edweek.org/rc/articles/2009/01/21/sow0121.h27.html.

funding to bring their per pupil spending up to the mean. Along with subsequent rulings, the state was forced to decouple school district expenditures from local property taxes, essentially making California's K–12 education system a unitary system, financed out of Sacramento.[20] California's system of financing

public education was further centralized with the passage of Proposition 13 in 1978, which directed property tax revenues to the state. In 1996, voters continued the centralization of school financing when they passed Proposition 98, which guaranteed a minimum level of state-funding for each school district.[21]

Advocates wanting to reform public school financing were dealt a blow in 1973 when the U.S. Supreme Court ruled that there was nothing in the U.S. Constitution guaranteeing citizens a

[20] Peter Schrag, *Final Test: The Battle for Adequacy in America's Schools* (New York: New Press, 2003); William Fischel, "How Serrano Caused Proposition 13," *Journal of Law and Politics* 12(1996):607–45; and D. Roderick Kiewiet, "Californians Can't Blame Everything on Proposition 13," *Public Affairs Report* 40(November 1999), http://www.igs.berkeley.edu/publications/par/Nov1999/Kiewiet.html.

[21] Jon Sonstelie, Eric Brunner, and Kenneth Ardon, "For Better or for Worse? School Finance Reform in California," *Public Policy Institute of California*, 2000, http://www.ppic.org/content/pubs/report/R_200JSR.pdf.

right to equal per pupil funding. In its 5–4 ruling, *San Antonio Independent School District v. Rodriguez* (1973), the court found that the 14th Amendment's Equal Protection Clause did not establish a right to equal per student funding. The court's decision left future questions of educational equity up to the states.

Notwithstanding the high court's ruling, many states were forced to alter their systems of school financing that were grounded in local property taxes after successful legal action. In the late 1980s, the school financing systems in Montana, Texas, and Kentucky—which were based solely on property tax revenues—were all struck down by state courts. The Texas legislature, for example, finally responded in 1994 with what became known as the "Robin Hood Plan." The plan, which set up regional taxing authorities and then shared local revenues across rich and poor districts, successfully reduced by $500 per pupil the gap in expenditures between property-poor and property-rich districts. However, it drastically reduced the total amount of property wealth that could be taxed to finance public schools.[22]

Financing Higher Education

State and local governments have invested considerable sums to build a world-class system of higher education. In fiscal year 2007, subnational governments spent some $83.5 billion on direct support for the general operating expenses of public and independent colleges and universities. This was up from just $21 billion in 1981. State sources fund roughly 90 percent of the higher education bill, with local appropriations filling in the balance. The funding of public colleges and universities, however, is largely contingent upon the state economy, and thus is highly unstable. Since 2001, many states have had weak economies, which has had long-term negative repercussions for the funding levels of higher education systems.[23]

Whether the recent increase in funding for higher education should be interpreted as a harbinger for better times for colleges and universities is not so clear, however. Future fiscal solvency of institutions of higher learning remains uneven across the states. Between 1991 and 2006, for example, nearly half of the states experienced enrollment growth that was above the national mean. Roughly one-third of those states—Arkansas, Georgia, Kentucky, Louisiana, Nevada, New Mexico, and Texas—increased per student state educational appropriations, with Georgia leading the way. In terms of state wealth (measured by the per capita total taxable resources of a state), 17 states exceed the national average for their per capita taxable resources. Of these states, only seven—Connecticut, California, Minnesota, New Jersey, New York, Rhode Island, and Wyoming—exceeded the national average for per capita spending on higher education. Nationally, support for higher education from state and local governments fell nearly 6 percent from 1995 to 2005, dropping to just $260 annually per capita. In 2006, the state of New Hampshire spent only $88 per capita to finance higher education.

A few states, relatively speaking, are pouring significant resources into higher education. Wyoming, not normally considered a leader in higher education, is at the top of the class, spending more than per capita than any other state on colleges and universities.[24] One of the reasons for Wyoming's relatively greater

[22] Caroline Hoxby and Ilyana Kuziemko, "Robin Hood and His Not-So-Merry Plan: Capitalization and the Self-Destruction of Texas' School Finance Equalization Plan," NBER Working Paper no. 10722, September (New York: National Bureau of Economic Research, 2004), http://www.nber.org/papers/w10722; and Ralph Blumenthal, "No Easy Solution as Texas Must Revisit School Financing," *The New York Times*, 28 March 2006, p. A15. See also, Christine H. Roch and Robert M. Howard, "State Policy Innovation in Perspective: Courts, Legislatures, and Education Finance Reform," *Political Research Quarterly* 61 (2008): 333–44.

[23] State Higher Education Executive Officers, "State Higher Education Finance, FY 2006," 2007, http://www.sheeo.org/Finance/shef_fy06.pdf.
[24] State Higher Education Executive Officers, "State Higher Education Finance, FY 2006."

commitment to funding higher education has to do with the fact that nearly 20 percent of its appropriations are generated through fees and lease agreements with oil and mineral extraction companies. Furthermore, in 2006, Wyoming voters approved the creation of a $500 million endowment paid for by state mineral taxes to create academic scholarships for all Wyoming students attending state universities and colleges as well as to pay for endowed chairs and research funds for state-school faculty.

Most other state systems of higher education are not fairing so well. When compared to the dwindling endowments of Harvard, Yale, Stanford, and other prestigious private universities, many state colleges and universities are hemorrhaging. In 2009, the president of Arizona State University announced that the school would cap freshman enrollment, close nearly 50 academic programs, eliminate more than 550 staff and 200 faculty positions, and require two-week furloughs for all employees, all in an effort to offset $88 million cuts in

state appropriations. Per-student funding from the state was reduced to $6,500, down from nearly $8,000 per student in the 2008 academic year.[25] Other state schools have felt the pinch. Florida State University has made substantial reductions in undergraduate admissions. "Something's got to give," former university President T. K. Wetherell said recently, noting that one of his secretaries pays almost $9,500 a year in day care, nearly three times the amount of FSU's annual tuition. "I don't think you can find anybody in America that can run a world-class university on one-third of what a day care center costs," the former Republican Speaker of the Florida House of Representatives lamented. "It can't be done."[26]

---

[25] "Fiscal Year 2009 state budget cuts force ASU to cap enrollment, freshman applications close March 1, five months early," Arizona State University, Press Release, February 2009, http://www.asu.edu/budgetcuts/.

[26] Brent Kallestad, "University President Announces Enrollment Freeze," *Daytona Beach* (Fla.) *News-Journal*, 15 June 2007.

COMPARISONS HELP US UNDERSTAND

GOT THE TUITION BLUES? WHAT A DIFFERENCE YOUR STATE MAKES

"Location, location, location"—it's not just the mantra of real estate agents. As you know all too well, where you live can have an enormous impact on how much money you pay for college. Even besides the issues of in-state versus out-of-state tuition and public versus private school tuition, students living in one state can pay a very different amount to go to a public school than those living in another state. For example, the best and the brightest Floridians pay next to nothing to attend the University of Florida, whereas Pennsylvanians pay more than $14,000 a year to go to Penn State. Why is there such an astounding difference? Pennsylvania and Florida are both large states, with major urban centers and extensive rural areas; both states tout diverse economies with a mix of industry, agriculture, and tourism. Penn State and the University of Florida are their state's flagship, land grant universities, and they consistently rank among the top 20 nationwide in undergraduate education. So why are the costs of attending these universities so different?

The answer to this question can be found in decisions made by policy makers in Florida and Pennsylvania and in the institutions and policies these policy makers have established. In 1997, the Florida legislature created the Bright Futures scholarship program, which until 2009 paid 100 percent of college tuition and fees for Florida high school graduates who earn at least a 3.5 grade point average (GPA) in high school and score over 1270 on the SAT. Those Florida students with lower scores get somewhat less tuition help, but it is still a considerable amount. Funded in part by the sales of lottery tickets, Florida's Bright Futures program costs the state almost $350 million a year—a sizable expenditure even for a big state. College tuition and fees for in-state residents remains under $5,000 per year, well below the national average for public universities.

Why did Florida policy makers establish this program to subsidize higher education so richly? They did so because Sunshine State lawmakers were worried about a "brain drain"—losing their top high school graduates to universities in other states. They feared that once gone, such students would not return to the state after college. Thus, Florida encourages its college-bound students to stay home by keeping tuition low. In addition, many of the Republican lawmakers—who controlled the state legislature—wanted to do away with need-based scholarships and replace them with merit-based ones like Bright Futures. So Florida policy makers had both economic and ideological reasons for making higher education extremely cheap.

Penn State (left) and the University of Florida (right) differ in many ways—besides those decided as a matter of public policy.

Why, then, is tuition so expensive at Penn State? The answer here also comes down to decisions made by state policy makers, but in Pennsylvania, these policy makers opted to subsidize private higher education more, and public higher education less, than do their counterparts in Florida. Although Pennsylvania spends nearly as much money per resident on higher education as Florida does, it has cut funding to public higher education in recent years while increasing both direct and indirect funding for private colleges and universities. In fact, some argue that the increasing privatization of higher education in Pennsylvania has virtually eliminated the distinction between public and private universities, just as it has in certain other states, like Colorado and Vermont. Such a public policy arises when policy makers see postsecondary education less as a public good that benefits the whole state and more as simply a private benefit for students who should, therefore, bear the brunt of its costs. Unlike Florida, Pennsylvania has many private colleges and universities for their high school graduates to choose from, so the possibility of a brain drain does not worry its policy makers. State appropriations now account for only about 20 percent of Penn State's total budget, forcing it to rely heavily on tuition and fees to pay its bills. This, in turn, leads to the high costs that Penn State students must pay.[1]

Note

1. Graham B. Spanier, "The Privatization of American Public Higher Education," Spring 2004, http://president. psu.edu/presentations/privatization_031604.pdf ; College Board, "2009–10 College Prices Keep Increases in Perspective," January 2010, http://www.collegeboard.com/student/pay/add-it-up/4494.html.

In an effort to keep tuition down but maintain the quality of their institutions of higher education, several states are relying on Americans' penchant for gambling to help. Nontax appropriations, such as proceeds generated from state lotteries, casinos, and other forms of gaming, have grown rapidly in some states since the 1990s. Revenue from these sources now accounts for nearly $2 billion of all state expenditures on higher education. In three states—Georgia, South Carolina, and West Virginia—more than 15 percent of state appropriations for higher education are derived from gaming revenues. Another 15 states generate at least some of their revenues through effective "sin taxes" on these activities.

Most of these states use revenues generated from these activities to provide need-based scholarships for higher education. Several states have modeled their programs after Georgia's HOPE (Helping Outstanding Pupils Educationally) Scholarship Program, which was established in 1993 and has awarded over $4 billion to over 1 million in-state students attending Georgia's universities, colleges, and technical schools. New Mexico's Student Success Scholarships, Oklahoma's Higher Learning Access Program, West Virginia's PROMISE Program, and South Carolina's HOPE Scholarship Program have all had notable success making higher education more affordable to qualified students. Georgia's HOPE Program is a merit-based program financed by state lottery revenues. Roughly 20 percent of the state's higher education budget was derived from funds generated by the lottery, and over 95 percent of in-state freshmen at the University of Georgia are scholarship recipients. The scholarship pays a student's full-time tuition and fees, plus additional money for books.[27]

Experimenting with Public Education

Embodying the entrepreneurial spirit, most states and school districts have experimented with new policies to try to reform the public school system and ensure that children receive a quality education. From public school choice within a school district, to vouchers for private education, to charter schools, to public–private partnerships, to tying teacher pay to student performance in the classroom or on state achievement tests, states and their respective school districts have pursued many market-oriented and outcome-based solutions to try to make students, teachers, and schools more accountable. Some programs have met with more favorable results than others.[28] We discuss five public elementary and secondary educational programs: school vouchers, educational management organizations, charter schools, homeschooling, and virtual schools.

School Vouchers

Many states and their school districts have turned to the private sector to try to revamp public education. The driving force behind the privatization of public education is the idea that the private sector, through competition and school choice, can be more efficient in providing a higher-quality education for students than existing public schools. The idea behind school vouchers, first floated by the late economist Milton Friedman in the 1950s, is to eliminate the education "monopoly" held by the public sector and teachers' unions, which some scholars claim have hampered academic achievement, especially for minority students.[29] By providing financial assistance in the form of **school vouchers** to

---

[27] Georgia Lottery, "HOPE Scholarships," 2007, http://www.galottery.com/gen/education/hopeScholarship.jsp.

[28] John F. Witte, "Private School versus Public School Achievement: Are There Findings That Should Affect the Educational Choice Debate?" *Economics of Education Review* 11(1992):371–94.

[29] Terry Moe, "Collective Bargaining and the Performance of the Public Schools," *American Journal of Political Science* 53(2009):156–74.

REFORM CAN HAPPEN

WASHINGTON, D.C.'S SCHOOL VOUCHER EXPERIMENT

Although Milwaukee's school voucher program—established in 1990—is the nation's longest-standing school choice program, Washington, D.C.'s school voucher experiment was perhaps the most extensive, but also the most short lived.

Established in 2003 by the Republican-controlled Congress and touted by President Bush, the federal Department of Education's school choice pilot program provided need-based vouchers of up to $7,500 annually to some 1,700 students selected in a lottery to participate. The parents of the mostly minority children received the taxpayer-funded vouchers, giving them the opportunity to attend 58 private (both secular and parochial) schools in the city. Supporters, such as former Mayor Anthony Williams, and D.C. Public Schools Chancellor Michelle Rhee, say the program gives poor parents the option of moving their children out of failing schools. "Part of my job is to make sure that all kids get a great education," Rhee argues, "and it doesn't matter whether that's in charter, parochial or public schools." According to Chancellor Rhee, who oversees the education system servicing the District's 58,000 students, vouchers are not "going to solve all the ills of public education, but parents who are zoned to schools that are failing kids should have the options to do better by their kids."[1]

Critics, such as the National Education Association, the largest teachers' union in the country, opposed the voucher program from the start. With Democrats taking over Congress in 2007, the NEA and other opponents of tax-payer funded vouchers marshaled their considerable clout to gut the D.C. program. The teachers' lobby argued that the program was mismanaged and that recipients of vouchers did no better on standardized tests than they did in their old schools. They argued that the creating of the voucher program in D.C. stemmed from Republicans exploiting "the frustration of these minority parents to push for a political agenda" that seeks to chip away at public schools. In 2009, the Democratic majority in Congress put the D.C. pilot program on ice, although due to pressure from the Obama administration, Congress voted to provide enough funding to allow students currently using vouchers to graduate from their private schools.[2]

Notes

1. Diana Jean Schemo, "Federal Program on Vouchers Draws Strong Minority Support," *The New York Times*, 6 April 2006, A1; Shailagh Murray, "Obama Offers D.C. Voucher Program Extension for Existing Students," *The Washington Post*, 6 May 2009, http://voices.washingtonpost.com/44/2009/05/06/obama_proposes_extending_dc_vo.html.
2. Sam Dillon, "Democrats Limit Future Financing for Washington Voucher Program," *The New York Times*, 28 February, 2009, p. A10.

parents who have children in poor- performing public schools, Friedman argued parents should be able to transfer their children to private schools, where—so the theory goes—incentives that drive the private sector will produce the same or better schools at a lower cost. Vouchers not only give parents more of a choice in their children's educational opportunities, supporters claim, but also force public schools to compete with private schools in order to retain students and public funding.[30] Critics charge that vouchers siphon funding from public schools, weakening them for the children who remain there and diverting dollars to schools that often do

---

[30] Milton Friedman, "The Role of Government in Education," in Robert A. Solo, ed., *Economics and the Public Interest* (New Brunswick, NJ: Rutgers University Press, 1955); and Alliance for School Choice, "School Choice around the Nation," 2006, http://www.allianceforschoolchoice.org/school_choice_states.aspx.

not have the same accountability standards that public schools must meet.[31]

Voucher programs—which, broadly defined, include not only tuition subsidies paid for by state (or federal) governments but also benefits through tax deductions—are permissible under the U.S. Constitution. In its 5–4 decision in *Zelman v. Simmons-Harris*, the U.S. Supreme Court in 2002 ruled that a Cleveland, Ohio, voucher program did not violate the establishment clause of the U.S. Constitution, even though vouchers could be used to send children to nonsectarian as well as religious private schools. A dozen states, as well as Washington, D.C., have adopted some form of voucher or tax credit school choice program, in which a total of 130,000 students participated in 2006. Milwaukee's Parental Choice Program, established in 1990, was the first voucher program of its kind.[32] Although the court's ruling upheld the city's school voucher program, school voucher programs have not been extensively replicated in other school districts or states, as some state constitutions expressly forbid the practice.

Many state educational voucher programs have run into legal roadblocks. Recently, voucher programs in Florida, Vermont, and Washington have been struck down by state courts. Florida's Opportunity Scholarship Program, touted by then governor Jeb Bush and enacted by the state legislature in 2000, provided tuition vouchers for students to attend private schools. But in 2006, the Florida Supreme Court nixed the program, ruling that it violated the state constitution's "uniform public education" clause. Similarly, the Colorado Supreme Court struck down a 2003 law passed by the state legislature that created a tax-funded voucher program that would have allowed students to attend private schools, including religious ones. The Colorado high court ruled that the law, which would have forced the state's 11 school districts to participate in the voucher program, violated a provision in the state constitution that local districts retain control over education funds that are raised locally.

Other states have faced not only legal barriers but also political ones when trying to create voucher programs. Voucher programs have faced stiff public opposition. Statewide public opinion is not particularly warm toward the programs (every voucher proposal placed on a statewide ballot via the initiative process has been defeated at the polls), and teachers unions have wielded considerable political clout to thwart the programs. Most recently, in a 2007 popular referendum, Utah voters soundly rejected the Republican state legislature's bid to permit school vouchers. The measure, which received only 38 percent support at the polls, would have allowed state dollars to be used to pay up to $3,000 for private tuition. After the defeat of the ballot measure, the president of the progressive Ballot Initiative Strategy Center, a nonprofit based in Washington, D.C., said, "It takes the wind out of the sails because no one wants to champion an issue that's a loser."[33]

Education Management Organizations

Other states have permitted their school districts to hire for-profit companies—called **education management organizations (EMOs)**—to

---

[31] National Education Association, "Privatization," 2006, http://www.nea.org/privatization/index.html.

[32] John F. Witte, *The Market Approach to Education: An Analysis of America's First Voucher Program* (Princeton, NJ: Princeton University Press, 2001); John F. Witte, "Who Benefits from the Milwaukee Choice Program?" in B. Fuller and R. Elmore, eds., *Who Chooses? Who Loses? Culture, Institutions and the Unequal Effects of School Choice* (New York: Teachers College Press, 1996); and National Conference of State Legislatures, "Vouchers, Tax Credits and Deductions," 2006, http://www.ncsl.org/programs/educ/VoucherMain.htm.

[33] National Education Association, "Privatization of Public Education: From Vouchers to Outsourcing," September 2004, http://www.nea.org/neatodayextra/0409extra.html; Barbara Miner, "Utah Voters Reject Voucher Plan," *Rethinking Schools* (Winter 2007/2008), http://www.rethinkingschools.org/archive/22_02/utah222.shtml.

INSTITUTIONS MATTER

"BABY BLAINE" AND THE PROHIBITION OF VOUCHERS IN SOME STATES

James Blaine, a Republican U.S. representative from Maine, advanced an amendment to the U.S. Constitution in 1875 that would have prohibited states from using any public funds or lands to support private schools "under the control of any religious sect." Nearly a century earlier, during the formative period of the nation, it was common for many communities, and even some states, to support with public funds religious institutions affiliated with the Protestant Church. Playing off the anti-Catholic sentiments and the nativist fear of "popery" that were quite prevalent among some Protestants in the 19th century, Blaine wanted to preempt efforts by immigrant communities to use their growing political clout to have public treasuries fund parochial schools tied to the Catholic Church. Although Blaine's effort proved unsuccessful at the national level, many states went on to adopt their own "Baby Blaine" constitutional amendments. Congress even passed a law requiring Blaine provisions to be included in the constitutions of all new states entering the union. Today, over 30 states have Blaine-like amendments in their constitutions, banning state aid to religious organizations, or private entities more generally. For example, in Nevada, "No public funds of any kind or character whatever, State, County, or Municipal, shall be used for a sectarian purpose." Alaska's constitution plainly states, "No money shall be paid from public funds for the direct benefit of any religious or other private educational institution." Arizona's is just as clear: "No tax shall be laid or appropriation of public money made in aid of any church, or private or sectarian school." Because of these institutional barriers, it is unlikely that education reformers will have much success pushing vouchers in these states. Blaine's legacy, questionable because of its bigoted underpinnings, continues to resonate in many of the states.[1]

Note

1. "Beware of the Ghost of James G. Blaine," *New York Sun*, 20 January 2006, http://www.nysun.com/article/26224; David Akerman, "Education Vouchers: Constitutional Issues and Cases," Report for Congress, Congressional Research Service, The Library of Congress, 20 May 2003, http://www.firstamendmentcenter.org/pdf/CRS.voucher1.pdf.

run some of their public schools. In 2001, the Pennsylvania Department of Education hired a private firm, Edison Schools, Inc., to assess Philadelphia's public schools, with some 200,000 students. The school district was in serious financial trouble, running up a $215 million debt. The state ended up taking over the district in December 2001, creating a five-member Philadelphia School Reform Commission to run the schools. The commission then contracted with seven different entities—Chancellor Beacon, Foundations, Inc., Universal Companies, Victory Schools, the University of Pennsylvania, Temple University, and Edison Schools—to administer 45 low-performing elementary and middle schools, with Edison receiving a five-year, $60 million contract to manage 20 schools. In 2005, the commission awarded Edison contracts to administer two more schools.[34]

Edison is the largest EMO in the country. In 2008–2009, it managed over 120 schools with over 350,000 students in 24 states as well as several schools in Washington, D.C. Although some have praised the revamping of public schools in Philadelphia and other school districts, there is substantial evidence that students attending these for-profit companies do not outperform those attending traditional

[34] Robert Strauss, "Edison Awarded 2 More Philadelphia Schools," *The Washington Post*, 16 May 2005, p. A3; Chris Whittle, *Crash Course: Imagining a Better Future for Public Education* (New York: Riverhead Hardcover, 2005).

public schools.[35] Citing dissatisfaction with results, school districts in Georgia, Kansas, and Texas recently terminated their contracts with Edison.[36]

Charter Schools

Publicly-funded and operated by a school district, **charter schools** are freed from many of the administrative, staffing, and pedagogical constraints facing traditional public schools. Charter schools usually have narrow missions, allowing them to focus on certain types of students and use alternative teaching and assessment methods. Because they have a semi-autonomous status and are not bound by district or statewide regulations, charter schools are able to utilize innovative pedagogies and creative methods of learning beyond what is being done in standard public schools. Charter schools are sometimes affiliated with a local business or institution of higher learning. Although exempt from many state and school district requirements, charter schools remain under the control of the local school board and may not promote a particular religious denomination, charge tuition, or use selective criteria for admissions.[37]

In 1991, Minnesota became the first state to allow school districts to establish charter schools, with California doing so the following year. Today, over 40 states have authorized local school districts to create charter schools. Hundreds of thousands of students in other school districts across the country—such as those attending public schools in Houston, New York City, Oakland, and Dayton, Ohio—have also opted for charter schools. Most public school charters are granted for three to five years. In 2006, over 3,600 charter schools were in operation, serving more than 1 million K–12 students.[38] Unlike school voucher and privatization programs, charter school programs tend to have bipartisan legislative support, although the diffusion of charter schools is likely as much driven by political factors as educational needs.[39] Indeed, the president of the American Federation of Teachers, a union representing thousands of public school teachers, called on school districts to create charter schools in the 1980s, partly as a way to stave off the push for private school vouchers and the creation of privately run EMOs.

Although supporters tout the flexibility charter schools provide public school educators, the schools have not been a universal success. Some critics charge that charter schools do not improve student achievement, whereas others decry the lack of information available to parents to make good choices regarding the merits of charter schools. An academic study conducted in Washington, D.C., finds that most parents initially like charter schools, but their support declines over time, due in part to the fact that their children's performance doesn't improve drastically.[40] Others criticize state governments for failing to provide adequate

---

[35] U.S. General Accounting Office, "Public Schools: Comparison of Achievement Results for Students Attending Privately Managed and Traditional Schools in Six Cities," October 2003, http://www.asu.edu/educ/epsl/EPRU/documents/EPRU-0310-45-OWI.pdf.

[36] "School Reform in Philadelphia," *Online Newshour,* 2005, http://www.pbs.org/newshour/bb/education/reform/schools.html.

[37] Ray Budde, "The Evolution of the Charter Concept," *Phi Delta Kappan* 78(1996):72–73; Michael Mintrom, *Policy Entrepreneurs and School Choice* (Washington, DC: Georgetown University Press, 2000); Michael Mintrom, "Policy Entrepreneurs and the Diffusion of Innovation," *American Journal of Political Science* 41(1997):738–65.

[38] Jonathon Christensen, "Charter School Data: What States Collect," National Charter School Research Project, 2006, http://www.ncsrp.org/downloads/hfr06/hfr06_briefweb.pdf.

[39] National Conference of State Legislatures, "Charter Schools," 2006, http://www.ncsl.org/programs/educ/CharterMain.htm; Yahong Zhang and Kaifeng Yang, "What Drives *Charter School Diffusion at the Local Level: Educational Needs or Political and Institutional Forces?" Policy Studies Journal* 36(2008):571–91 Thomas Holyoke, Jeffrey Henig, Heath Brown, and Natalie Lacireno-Paquet, "Institution Advocacy and the Political Behavior of Charter Schools," *Political Research Quarterly* 60 (2007): 202–14.

[40] Jack Buckley and Mark Schneider, *Charter Schools: Hope or Hype?* (Princeton, NJ: Princeton University Press, 2007).

oversight of charter schools. Some scholars complain that state education departments often do not collect enough student-level data from charter schools, making it impossible to gauge the individual progress of students. And many charter schools have been held up to public scrutiny for their curricula, such as integrating religious themes that are inappropriate for publicly funded schools.[41]

Homeschooling

One of the fastest growing reforms in K–12 education has been **home schooling**. Tracking the number of children being homeschooled is difficult; records on homeschooling kept by school districts and the states are often not complete, and many homeschooled children return to the ranks of the public schools. One scholar has estimated the number of children who were homeschooled in the 1960s at upward of 15,000.[42] As recently as a decade ago, national data on the number of children being homeschooled were still difficult to obtain. One estimate placed the figure at 850,000 nationwide in 1999, roughly 1.7 percent of all school-aged children in grades K–12. According to the DOE, over 1.5 million (or 2.9 percent of all school-aged children) were homeschooled in 2007, although others have put the figure closer to 2 million.[43] The main reason parents give for homeschooling their children is for moral or religious purposes.

Every state, as well as the District of Columbia, permits parents to homeschool their children, but a great degree of variation exists across the states concerning the laws regulating homeschooling. Most state legislatures passed statutes regulating homeschooling in the 1980s and 1990s, although Oklahoma has protected the right of parents to homeschool their children since statehood. Some states require the primary parent who is doing the homeschooling to have certain educational requirements, and others do not. A few states require certain subjects to be taught, but others have guidelines that are more vague. And some states mandate that homeschooled students be tested along the same lines as those educated in the public schools, whereas others do not require any formal assessments.[44]

The demographics of children who are homeschooled are quite different from those found in traditional public schools. Home-schooled children are disproportionately white and are members of lower- to middle-income families. Caucasian children are twice as likely as African American children to be homeschooled, and nearly four times as likely to be taught at home as Hispanic children. Children living in larger, two-parent families, with one parent not participating in the labor force, are far more likely to be homeschooled than other school-aged children. Most parents who opt out of the public school system cite concerns with the social environment of public schools and their desire to impart moral and religious teachings as reasons why they decided to engage in homeschooling. Voluminous pedagogical materials are available for parents of homeschoolers. According to a national survey conducted by the U.S. Department of Education in 2003, slightly less than half of all homeschooled children

[41] Robin Lake and Paul Hill, eds., *Hopes, Fears, and Reality: A Balanced Look at American Charter Schools in 2006* (Seattle, WA: National Charter School Research Project, 2006), http://www.ncsrp.org/cs/csr/download/csr_files/hfrdec1_web.pdf.

[42] Patricia Lines, "Homeschooling," ERIC Digest Series no. 151, 2001, http://eric.uoregon.edu/publications/digests/digest151.html.

[43] Stacey Bielick, "1.5 Million Homeschooled Students in the United States in 2007," U.S. Department of Education, National Center for Education Statistics, December 2008, http://nces.ed.gov/pubs2009/2009030.pdf; for alternative projections, see studies by the National Home Education Research Institute, http://www.nheri.org/.

[44] Peter Wielhouwer, Gregory Rathje, and Jamie Dye, "Before the Spelling Bee: Accounting for Variation in State Home School Regulations" (paper presented at the annual meeting of the State Politics and Policy Quarterly Conference, Austin, Texas, February 2007).

rely on some form of distance learning to supplement their studies. Over three-quarters of homeschooled students are instructed with curriculum materials obtained at a public library or from a private vendor. One-third of all homeschooling is done using materials obtained from a church, synagogue, or other religious organization.[45]

Critics of homeschooling have voiced numerous concerns. One of the chief complaints of homeschooling is whether the parent doing the teaching is qualified to do so and has the requisite skills necessary to educate his or her children. Their concerns have some empirical backing. Roughly one-quarter of all parents who teach their own children have a high school diploma or less, with only 20 percent having education beyond a bachelor's degree. Other critics cite the lack of socialization of homeschooled children with their peers and the diminished likelihood that children will be exposed to viewpoints differing from those of their parents, which can hinder the development of critical-thinking skills.[46] Despite these and other concerns, homeschooling is only likely to grow, as Americans have increasingly come to accept this alternative method of parents self-educating their children.

Virtual Schools

Taking advantage of advancements in technology to reach students who are failing to perform in the traditional classroom setting, many states have turned to online learning. All but 14 states have created statewide **virtual schools** to provide online, personalized course instruction. In the 2008 school year, roughly a million K–12 students were enrolled in online courses, which are administered by the states, school districts, or private companies contracted by states or school districts. Several of the states that have recently launched their virtual school programs, including Arkansas, Mississippi, and North Carolina, have witnessed exponential growth in their enrollments. One scholarly study estimates that half of all high school courses will be delivered online by 2019.[47]

Florida leads the nation in the number of students taking distance learning courses. It has some 64,000 students enrolled in its Florida Virtual School (FLVS). Created in 1997 by the state legislature as the nation's first statewide online public high school, the FLVS is a state-run program funded by pubic and private funding. The state's e-learning program employs more than 500 full-time credentialed teachers. It is open to both in-state and out-of-state students, providing an array of core subjects and electives for middle school and high school students, including numerous advanced placement courses. Florida residents (public school, private school, and homeschool students) may take online courses for free, but those who reside outside of Florida must pay $750 per credit hour. The state legislature permits FLVS to license and package its online lessons and sell them throughout the world. Recently, FLVS created a for-profit subdivision called Global Services which sells virtual lesson plans to other states as well as homeschool students who are not residents of Florida. Roughly two-thirds of the students enrolled in FLVS are from public and charter schools, and one quarter are homeschoolers. Six of 10 students are female, and one of five attends a low-performing public school.[48]

Critics of virtual schools, including the powerful accrediting agency the College

---

[45] Daniel Princiotta, Stacey Bielick, and Christopher Chapman, "Homeschooling in the United States: 2003," U.S. Department of Education, National Center for Education Statistics, 2003, http://nces.ed.gov/pubs2006/2006042.pdf.

[46] Rob Reich, "The Civic Perils of Homeschooling," *Educational Leadership* 59(2002).

[47] Ben Arnoldy, "Virtual Schools See Strong Growth, Calls for More Oversight," *Christian Science Monitor*, 14 May 2008, http://www.csmonitor.com/2008/0514/p03s08-usgn.html.

[48] Florida Virtual School, "Any Time, Any Place, Any Path, Any Pace," 2009, http://www.flvs.net/; Center for Digital Education, "Online Learning Policy and Practice Survey A Survey of the States," 2008, http://www.centerdigitaled.com/story.php?id=108006.

YOU DECIDE

SHOUD EDUCATION POLICY BE INITIATED?

Should voters be able to get something for nothing when it comes to public education? Over the past several election cycles, voters in states allowing the initiative have passed ballot measures increasing spending on public education. The ballot measures have not, however, earmarked dedicated revenue streams to fund these new programs. In 2002, voters in the state of Washington approved a class size reduction measure (Initiative 728) and a cost-of-living increase for teachers (Initiative 732) that did not create new revenue streams. That same year, voters in Florida passed their own class size reduction measure (Amendment 9). The ballot initiative was strongly opposed by former Republican Governor Jeb Bush, who was overheard saying he had "devious plans" to kill the measure because he thought it would cost the state too much. In 2000, Coloradoans passed a constitutional initiative (Amendment 23) providing increased funding for K–12 public education in the state. More than a decade earlier, Californians adopted Proposition 98, a constitutional amendment sponsored by the California Teachers Association mandating that K–14 education (which includes the first two years of college) receive roughly 35 percent of the budget from the state's annual general fund. All of these initiatives—which are still quite popular with the electorate—have effectively earmarked a portion of the state budget for public education.[1]

What do you think? Are opponents of these initiated education reform ballot measures correct? Should proponents be required to identify a dedicated revenue source—such as an increase to the sales tax, a tax on gaming, or a severance tax on the extraction of natural resources—when asking voters to approve these measures? Or should state governments be required to increase revenues or reallocate some of their general funds to pay for these voter-approved programs? More generally, do you think a quality public education should be a fundamental right?

Note
1. Washington Research Council, "Governor's Budget Sets Priorities, Lives within Means," Policy Brief 01–16, 20 December 2002, http://www.researchcouncil.org/Briefs/2002/PB02–16/BudgetLives.pdf; Mary Ellen Klas, "Class-Size Amendment May Finally Get Funding," *Miami Herald*, 17 April 2006, http://www.miami.com/mld/miamiherald/news/state/14358383.htm; Donnell-Kay Foundation, "Amendment 23 and Public School Financing in Colorado," March 2003, http://www.dkfoundation.org/PDF/Amendment23andPublicSchoolFinancing InColorado.pdf; Lisa Snell, "California's 2005 K-12 Education Primer," Policy Brief 40, *Reason*, May 2005, http://www.reason.org/pb40_california_education_reform.pdf.

Board, maintain that they cannot substitute for hands-on, in-class learning. This is especially true for natural science courses that tend to have a lab component. According to an official with the College Board, "You could have students going straight into second-year college science courses without ever having used a Bunsen burner." Skeptics of online learning also claim that virtual courses do not provide the kind of intellectual exchanges that are possible in classroom settings, and that students who are not self-disciplined may not be able to work independently to motivate themselves to do well online.[49] There is also concern that e-learning courses lack sufficient oversight, compared to in-class instruction, and that some states and school districts are pushing distance learning as a way to cut costs, as many states still provide the same amount of funding for students enrolled in virtual schools as those attending traditional schools. Proponents

---

[49] Lois Romano, "Online Degree Programs Take Off," *The Washington Post*, 16 May 2006, p. A06.

see this as a virtue. According to Cody Claver, who runs the Idaho Virtual Academy with some 2,000 students and 75 teachers and staff, "We are providing cost savings to the taxpayers because we are running 35 percent cheaper." But critics point to the potential for abuse. In California, for example, an accredited virtual school had fewer than 10 teachers for 1,500 students—a ratio that would equate 150 students in a traditional classroom. "There was virtually no overhead," one observer noted, but "the district got to keep the rest of the money." California state law now requires that virtual schools receive only a fraction of the per-pupil funding allocated to traditional schools.[50]

The Federal Role in Public Education

Even though it has no constitutional role, the federal government has increasingly become involved in the financing and administration of public education. Following the landmark 1954 decision *Brown v. Board of Education,* in which the U.S. Supreme Court used the equal protection under the laws language of the 14th Amendment to find segregation in public schools unconstitutional, the federal government frequently, if at times reluctantly, has intervened in the effort to desegregate public schools. In 1957, President Dwight D. Eisenhower went so far as to federalize the Arkansas National Guard to ensure the integration of Little Rock High School after Arkansas Governor Orval Faubus had used the troops to prevent nine African American students from entering the school. The 1964 Civil Rights Act solidified *Brown,* mandating that no federal funding could be used by schools if racial discrimination existed.

The following year, Congress enacted the Elementary and Secondary Education Act of 1965 (ESEA). ESEA provides federal funding in the form of categorical and block grants to the states and school districts with substantial levels of low-income families. Most of the federal government's aid for K–12 education goes directly to school districts. Title I of ESEA today provides more than $14 billion a year in aid to school districts with the aim of improving the academic achievement of students who come from families with substantial levels of poverty. Nearly every elementary school receives Title I funding, although only one-tenth of high schools receive such funding. Additional federal funding under ESEA goes toward incentive grants to the states to improve teacher quality, English language instruction, community learning centers, aid to schools that service children whose parents live on military bases, and after-school programs. The federal government also provides over $10 billion in aid through Part B of the Individuals with Disabilities Education Act (IDEA), which assists states and schools to educate children with disabilities. In the wake of Hurricane Katrina in 2005, which displaced thousands of public school students, the U.S. Department of Education provided vouchers amounting up to $7,500 per pupil that allowed students to attend private, sectarian schools.

The No Child Left Behind Act of 2002

Touted as the most significant piece of domestic legislation during his first term in office, President George W. Bush signed NCLB into law with much bipartisan fanfare in January 2002. Bush heralded the law as necessary for the nation's schools to narrow the educational achievement gap that separates students across the dimensions of race, ethnicity, income, English proficiency, and disability.[51] NCLB—the byproduct of libertarian, market-driven, school choice models of education reform—relies

---

[50] Arnoldy, "Virtual Schools See Strong Growth."

[51] National Conference of State Legislatures, "The No Child Left Behind Act and High School Reform," 2005, http://www.ncsl.org.

heavily on standardized testing of students in an effort to weed out and penalize poorly performing schools.[52] For some, it signaled a new era of "educational federalism."[53]

The federal law mandates that the states administer reading and math examinations to students in third through eighth grades as well as for high school students at least once. States are required to develop standards of proficiency and then track the progress toward proficiency of all their students. Students are then placed in eight subcategories—five are racial-ethnic (Caucasian, Asian, African American, Hispanic, and Native American) and three are based on need (special education, limited English proficiency, and free and reduced price meals). At least 95 percent of students in each subcategory must take the exams, and according to the legislation, students in every subcategory are expected to achieve 100 percent proficiency on the tests by 2014. Few educators think these expectations are realistic; indeed, nearly half of the states have "backloaded" their estimates of when they will achieve 100 percent proficiency, meaning they will need much steeper annual improvements as we approach the 2014 deadline.

The 2002 law, some 670 pages long and containing 588 federal mandates, is a mixed bag of carrots and sticks.[54] As for incentives, NCLB provides an array of federal resources to the states and their school districts. The law is intended to give increased flexibility to the states and school districts in allocating their federal dollars, provides grants for free tutoring to students in schools that are designated as "failing," and finances after-school learning programs. There are federal funds available for school districts to establish charter schools as well as grants to schools with heavy populations of American Indians, Alaska Natives, and students of migrant workers. NCLB assists parents who wish to transfer their children out of low-performing schools to other public schools, including charter schools. NCLB also provides funding for K–3 reading programs and grants for professional development as well as training for teachers and math and science curriculums.

In terms of sticks, NCLB packs a severe wallop for those school districts whose students fail to measure up to federal standards. Specifically, the law places harsh sanctions on states and school districts whose students do not meet certain achievement goals. If any one of a school's eight student subcategories fails to attain **adequate yearly progress** (**AYP**), which is based on its performances on annual achievement tests, the whole school receives a failing grade. The first time a school fails to meet AYP, the law stipulates that the school must notify parents that it is a "failing" school and allow students to transfer to a passing school in the district. If the school does not achieve AYP in all of the subcategories the following year, it must provide tutoring to students who performed poorly on the exam. If in the third year the school fails to meet AYP, it must introduce a new curriculum, extend the school day or year, or even replace school teachers and administrators. If after the fourth year the school still does not achieve AYP, the school may be closed down, taken over by the state, or transformed into an independent charter school.[55]

[52] See, for example, John Chubb and Terry Moe, *Politics, Markets and America's Schools* (Washington, DC: Brookings Institution, 1990; for a critique of this ideology, see Kevin Smith and Kenneth Meier, *The Case Against School Choice: Politics, Markets, and Fools* (Armonk, NY: M. E. Sharpe, 1995).

[53] Patrick McGuinn, *No Child Left Behind and the Transformation of Federal Education Policy, 1965–2005* (Lawrence, KS: University Press of Kansas, 2006); see also Paul Manna, *School's In: Federalism and the National Education Agenda* (Washington, DC: Georgetown University Press, 2006).

[54] Scott Abernathy, *No Child Left Behind and the Public Schools* (Ann Arbor, MI: University of Michigan Press, 2007); Paul Basken, "Parts of Education Law Are Ignored," *The Washington Post*, 11 April 2006, p. A4, http://www.washingtonpost.com/wp-dyn/content/article/2006/04/10/AR2006041001294.html.

[55] Jay Mathews, "No Reader Left Behind: A Guide to the Law," *The Washington Post*, 12 March 2006, p. B4.

Is NCLB Working?

Long overdue to be reauthorized by Congress, NCLB nevertheless has identified children in thousands of public schools who are not achieving the academic standards set by the U.S. Department of Education. In the 2004–2005 academic year alone, 24,470 public schools—some 27 percent of all schools—failed to meet AYP requirements. The state with the worse record of AYP improvement was Florida. Only 28 percent of all public schools in the Sunshine State improved their AYP scores in 2005 compared to the previous year, the worst percentage in the country. Two-thirds of Hawaii's public schools failed to show any improvement, as did over half in Washington, D.C., and Nevada.[56] In Minnesota, a state with a highly-regarded public education system, 358 out of the 672 schools in the seven-county Minneapolis/St. Paul metro area failed to achieve AYP in 2007.

Critics have charged that Congress has failed to adequately fund NCLB. In 2009, Title I federal appropriations for K–12 education exceeded $14 billion. Opponents of the law, however, counter that the federal government has been shortchanging the states and school districts. One estimate finds that between 2003 and 2009, Congress underfunded Title I appropriations by some $71 billion.[57] President Obama's 2009 stimulus package provided more than $100 billion for education programs, including $54 billion to help stabilize state budgets and maintain K–12 schools and higher education financing. But critics contend that this one-time infusion does not compensate for the continued underfunding of the program.

Other critics of the program, including Republican and Democratic governors and many state legislators and state education chiefs, argue that NCLB has usurped the power of locally controlled school districts to manage their own education programs. They argue that NCLB has mandated federal education standards, taking power away from state and local school officials. As such, they claim NCLB amounts to an unfunded federal mandate on states and school districts: they must abide by the various requirements of the federal legislation, but they also incur increased costs to carry out the federal programs. Some state and school officials claim that this is especially true regarding the standardized testing the NCLB requires for most elementary and secondary students attending public schools. In 2005, Connecticut sued the DOE for requiring the state to pay for more than $50 million in programs but not providing any financial assistance.[58]

Conservatives have charged that NCLB allows the federal government too much power to meddle in what should be the domain of state and local governments. In 2005, the Republican-dominated state legislature of Utah passed legislation to allow their school districts to opt out of NCLB provisions that differ with state guidelines, and allow the state to refuse to appropriate state funds to pay for programs mandated by the federal government, even if it means having federal funds withheld. In Virginia, concerned that the federal legislation intrudes on local control of education, Jim Dillard, the Republican chairman of the House Education Committee, said NCLB was a "massive federal intrusion" and was "simply unworkable" and "utopian nonsense." The liberal Vermont legislature passed a bill prohibiting the state to spend money to implement NCLB, and over 20 more states have requested that Congress appropriate more money to change or increase funding for the program.[59]

---

[56] Paul Basken, "States Have More Schools Falling Behind," *The Washington Post*, 29 March 2006, p. A17.
[57] National Education Association, "Funding Gap: ESEA Title I Grants to Local Educational Agencies," 2009, http://www.nea.org/assets/docs/title1gap.pdf.

[58] Kenneth Wong and Gail Sunderman, "Education Accountability as a Presidential Priority: No Child Left Behind and the Bush Presidency," *Publius* 37(2007):333–50.
[59] Greg Toppo, "States Fight No Child Left Behind, Calling It Intrusive," *USA Today*, 11 February 2004, http://www.usatoday.com/news/education/2004-02-11-no-child-usat_x.htm.

Other state and local education policy officials have criticized the law for not being stringent enough. The federal law exempts students in private K–12 schools from taking the annual standardized examinations, leading to less accountability for these schools. The law also allows the states to set their own benchmarks for AYP as well as the standards on the achievement tests and the formulas used to calculate AYP. Critics claim this allows states to manipulate actual progress levels of their schools. Oklahoma, for instance, showed improbable AYP improvement when the percentage of the state's "failing" schools fell from 25 percent to just 3 percent in one year. Diane Ravitch, an education professor at New York University and a former assistant secretary of education under President George H. W. Bush, claims that the "stats are meaningless in the absence of a common test and common standards."[60] Other critics of NCLB have argued that federally mandated tutoring programs for failing children, which cost upward of $1,800 per student, are of such poor quality that they are not worth the effort. Furthermore, the tutoring programs are not available in many of the poorest, and poorest-performing, schools.

Current Department of Education Secretary Arne Duncan, the former head of the Chicago public school system, is a cautious critic of NCLB. "I think we are lying to children and families when we tell children that they are meeting standards," Duncan said soon after being confirmed as secretary of education. "In fact, they are woefully unprepared to be successful in high school and have almost no chance of going to a good university and being successful."[61] For its part, the Department of Education claims that states do not have to participate in NCLB programs. Of course, if a state voluntarily opts out of the program the state is cut off from federal funding associated with the program, which in some cases is not an insignificant amount. Maryland, for example, risked losing millions of dollars in federal funding if it did not take over "failing" junior high and high schools in Baltimore. Wielding its stick, the federal agency has also threatened to withhold future funding earmarked to schools not meeting AYP if a state does not inform students in "failing" schools about their educational options. A 2006 report issued by the Department of Education found that over half of all school districts with subpar schools did not inform parents that their children attending "failing" schools could attend other public or private schools or that they could receive free tutoring. Only 17 percent of eligible students signed up for the free tutoring in 2005, and only 38,000 students transferred to other schools, less than 1 percent of the 4 million who were eligible.

Summary

The power of local school districts and even the states to determine education policy has eroded considerably over the past decade. Although the federal government has increased K–12 and higher education appropriations, Congress has attached many strings to these disbursements. The ability of states and school districts to be innovative and experimental has become circumscribed due to increased federal interven-

[60] Basken, "States Have More Schools Falling Behind."
[61] Eddy Ramirez and Kim Clark, "What Arne Duncan Thinks of No Child Left Behind," *US News and World Report*, 5 February, 2009, http://www.usnews.com/articles/education/2009/02/05/what-arne-duncan-thinks-of-no-child-left-behind.html.

tion in education policy. Specifically, states and their school districts have felt the heavy hand of the federal government since the passage in 2002 of NCLB. The multitude of federal standards and requirements that public schools and students must meet has preempted the authority of states and local school districts to devise their own strategies and solutions to deal with local educational problems. Furthermore, the implicit effort by the federal government to privatize public education—through the encouragement of school choice voucher programs, EMOs, charter schools, homeschooling, and virtual schools, combined with the closing of underperforming public schools—has limited the range of options traditionally left to state and local education officials.

Yet, you should not expect states and local school districts to take the recent federal usurpation of power over education policy lightly. As in past battles, they will swing back when the time and partisan alignments are right. Rest assured, education policy will continue to be one of the most hotly contested policy areas in the coming years and is likely to be a central hub of the perennial power struggle between state and local governments and the federal government.

Keywords

Achievement gap

Adequate yearly progress (AYP)

Charter school

Education management organizations (EMOs)

Homeschooling

No Child Left Behind Act (NCLB)

School districts

School vouchers

Virtual schools

Discussion Questions

1. What has been the traditional role of the federal government in education policy? How has that role evolved over time?
2. Discuss the politics of the No Child Left Behind Act (2002). Who initially supported the legislation, and who opposes it now, and why?
3. Who pays for public education? Are their differences across the states with regard to how much local and state support there is for financing public schools?
4. Discuss some of the recent innovations across the states with regard to "fixing" the educational crisis. What are the pros and cons regarding school vouchers, charter schools, education management organizations, and virtual schools?
5. Why do some states prohibit school vouchers to private schools? What does a 19th-century congressman from Maine have to do with this prohibition? Do you think states should have the ability to use tax dollars to finance private K–12 education?

Suggested Readings

Abernathy, Scott. 2007. *No Child Left Behind and the Public Schools*. Ann Arbor, MI: University of Michigan Press.

Berkman, Michael B., and Eric Plutzer. 2005. *Ten Thousand Democracies: Politics and Public Opinion in America's School Districts*. Washington, DC: Georgetown University Press.

Buckley, Jack, and Mark Schneider. 2007. *Charter Schools:* Hope or Hype? (Princeton, NJ: Princeton University Press).

Fiske, Edward, and Helen Ladd. 2000. *When Schools Compete: A Cautionary Tale*. Washington, DC: Brookings Institution.

Manna, Paul. 2006. *School's In: Federalism and the National Education Agenda*. Washington, DC: Georgetown University Press.

McGuinn, Patrick. 2006. *No Child Left Behind and the Transformation of Federal Education Policy, 1965–2005*. Lawrence, KS: University Press of Kansas.

Mintrom, Michael. 2000. *Policy Entrepreneurs and School Choice*. Washington, DC: Georgetown University Press.

Schrag, Peter. 2003. *Final Test: The Battle for Adequacy in America's Schools*. New York: New Press.

Whittle, Chris. 2005. *Crash Course: Imagining a Better Future for Public Education*. New York: Riverhead Hardcover.

Witte, John F. 2001. *The Market Approach to Education: An Analysis of America's First Voucher Program*. Princeton, NJ: Princeton University Press.

Web Sites

American Federation of Teachers (http://www.aft.org): With over 3,000 local affiliates, 43 state affiliates, and 1.3 million members, the AFT union provides a treasure trove of information advocating public education and its educators.

Friedman Foundation (http://www.friedmanfoundation.org): Founded to promote the ideals and theories of economists Milton and Rose Friedman, the foundation provides information on school choice and privatization efforts.

National Charter School Research Project (http://www.ncsrp.org): Based at the University of Washington, the NCSRP offers a wealth of scholarly research on the charter school debate.

National Conference of State Legislatures (http://www.ncsl.org): NCSL provides nonpartisan information on education legislation in the states, including data on education finance, voucher programs, and teacher quality.

National Education Association (http://www.nea.org): The NEA, with over 3.2 million members, offers a wealth of research and data on education reforms in the states and communities.

National Governors' Association (http://www.nga.org): The NGA provides nonpartisan information on education issues in the states.

U.S. Department of Education, National Center for Education Statistics (http://nces.ed.gov): The indispensable federal repository for data and analysis on education policy in the United States.

Achievement gap: The gulf in performance and educational attainment between rich and poor and white and minority students.

Adequate yearly progress (AYP): Mandated by the No Child Left Behind Act (NCLB) of 2002, it is a statewide accountability system requiring each state to ensure that every one of its schools and districts is meeting specified achievement goals.

Adjudication: To settle a dispute by judicial procedure.

Adjudicator: Legal professional trained in resolving disputes between parties outside of the courtroom.

Administrative rules: Regulations, restrictions, and requirements written by executive agencies and used to implement public policy enacted through the legislature, the courts, or the governor.

Administrative rules review committee: The state legislative committee whose job it is to check whether the thousands of rules that a state's executive agencies propose each year follow the intent of the legislation that authorized that agency to establish those rules.

Adversarial argument: As in a courtroom, when two parties to a dispute make their best arguments to a neutral third party, who then decides the dispute. This is as opposed to a negotiated settlement where the parties work back and forth between themselves to resolve the dispute.

Altruism: The motivation to act out of a desire to help others, rather than out of a desire for personal benefit.

Amend: To modify a bill in the lawmaking process.

Amendatory veto: The power of some states' governors to send a passed bill back to the legislature asking for specific changes in it before he or she will sign it.

Amicus curiae brief: Latin for a "friend of the court" brief, a legal argument offered by a person or group that is not a party to a case but would like to influence its outcome.

Annexation: The legal process of adding unincorporated land and/or residents beyond a political jurisdiction's boundary, to make it part of the incorporated jurisdiction. Annexation may be done to provide services to outlying areas, or to increase tax revenues for the jurisdiction annexing the land.

Appropriations bill: A bill that authorizes a state agency to spend money in specific ways.

Articles of Confederation: The country's first constitution, ratified in March 1781.

Astroturf campaign: An artificial campaign orchestrated by an interest group to appear as though it is growing naturally from the grassroots.

At-large elections: Many elections for local government such as city or county councils (or commissions) are often contested such that every voter in the jurisdiction votes on every council position up for election. Voters cast one vote per position being contested. Rather than representing a specific geographic area within the jurisdiction, elected officials represent the entire jurisdiction. At-large elections can allow a cohesive majority group to sweep every position.

Balanced budget rules: A requirement that a state's budget has revenues equal to spending. Rules may apply to projected revenues and spending, or to actual levels.

Bench trial: Trial with no jury, where the judge or judges alone decide the outcome.

Bicameral: Having two chambers, such as in 49 state legislatures and Congress, which have a house of representatives (called by another name in some states) and a senate.

Bill: A proposed law that is formally introduced by a legislator for consideration by his or her chamber.

Bill of Rights: Ratified in December 1791, the first 10 amendments to the U.S. Constitution ensure the protection of individuals and the states from the national government.

Bill sponsor: The legislator who proposes that a bill be considered by his or her chamber.

Bipartisan Campaign Reform Act of 2002: Also known as BCRA, this act not only banned federal political parties from using soft money for federal election activity but also restricted some activities of state and local parties.

Blanket primary: Primary elections nominate candidates for the general election. In a blanket primary election, candidates from all parties are listed on the same ballot. Voters participate regardless of their party affiliation, and are able to select candidates of different parties for different offices.

Block grants: Fixed-sum federal grants allocated by formula giving state and local governments broad leeway in designing and implementing designated programs.

Bureaucracy: The administrative structure of any large, complex organization, like a government, that is characterized by hierarchical control and fixed rules of procedure.

Campaign finance regulations: Rules and statutes regulating the ways in which money can be gathered and spent by political campaigns, defining what is required, permissible, and impermissible.

Capital budget: The portion of state spending on infrastructure such as buildings, bridges, and roads. Capital budgets may be exempt from balanced budget rules.

Casework: The activities of a legislator and his or her staff in helping constituents with specific problems, usually with state government. For example, a legislator may help a constituent solve a problem with getting a driver's license or adjusting a state tax bill.

Categorical grants: Grants from the federal government to states and cities that are for specific purposes defined by Congress.

Caucus: Used by parties to nominate candidates, with party members informally meeting, deliberating, and casting a vote for their preferred candidate.

Cause célèbre: French for a "famous legal case," denoting an issue causing heated controversy.

Centralization: Empowering a national governing authority with unitary control and authority.

Chamber floor: Where and when the members of one chamber (the house or senate) meet as a group to debate and vote on legislation.

Charter review commission: Commission appointed or elected by a city or county to propose changes to city institutions that voters might accept or reject.

Charter school: A public school that is operated by a school district, but is freed from the administrative, staffing, and pedagogical constraints of traditional public schools and usually has a narrow mission.

Citizen legislature: A state legislature that is largely a part-time body, whose members are paid a modest salary, have little staff, meet infrequently, and are expected to have careers and interests other than the state legislature.

Civil service: Appointed administrators and public employees. Civil service jobs are usually awarded based on merit exams and qualifications, rather than political connections.

Civil service system: A system of hiring, promoting, and firing government workers based on job-related criteria rather than on political connections or other biases.

Civil union: A relationship between two people (whether an opposite- or same-sex couple) with much of the legal rights and obligations of marriage, but without the title of *marriage*.

Class action lawsuit: A lawsuit brought by one party on behalf of a group of individuals all having the same grievance.

Clean money and public financing of campaigns: Some states provide public funds for candidates seeking political office if they agree to limits on the contributions they receive from private sources.

Clientele politics: A style of politics where the people in control of government provide something of value in exchange for political support. Support for clientele parties is based on what sort of favors a party can supply, or the personal contacts that the party builds with supporters.

Closed primary: A primary nomination election in which voters registered with a political party are permitted to vote only for candidates of the party with whom they are registered.

Coercive federalism: A federalist arrangement whereby the federal government spearheads and funds programs; also referred to as *creative federalism.*

Collective action problem: The problem of coordinating a group of people to achieve a common goal.

Commerce Clause: Gives Congress the power "to regulate Commerce with foreign Nations, and among the several States, and with the Indian Tribes." Used by Congress to expand its power vis-à-vis the states.

Committee jurisdiction: The policy area and bills that a legislative committee has the responsibility to consider in its deliberations.

Common law: The system of laws originated and developed in England, based on court decisions, the doctrines implicit in those decisions, and customs and usages rather than on codified written laws.

Commutation: The power of some governors unilaterally to reduce the sentence of a person convicted of a crime.

Comparative method: An approach to political analysis that entails comparing units of analysis (such as states or communities) on more than one characteristic to help understand the relationships among those characteristics.

Confederal system: Also known as a *confederacy*, a system of governance whereby the national government is subject to the control of subnational, autonomous governments.

Conference committee: A temporary legislative committee made up of equal members of the senate and house who meet to reconcile the differences between the versions of a bill passed by the two chambers and to propose a single version for both chambers to consider.

Conflict of interest: A situation in which a government decision maker may personally benefit from his or her official actions, or a judge has a personal interest in the outcome of a case that may bias his or her actions in that case.

Constitution: A document laying out the fundamental law defining the basic political institutions of a government and the fundamental values for which that government stands.

Constitutional initiative: An initiative measure that amends a state's constitution, or adds new language to a constitution. Constitutional measures can alter rules about a state's political process. If approved by voters, constitutional measures are typically more difficult for elected officials to amend or repeal than statutory initiatives.

Contiguous: Areas of land that touch (except for islands).

Contract lobbyist: A professional lobbyist who temporarily works on behalf of a client.

Contracting for services: A community or political jurisdiction entering a contract with another to provide services. Cities or unincorporated areas may contract with counties, other cities, or special districts for services such as fire, police, sanitation, and libraries.

Cooperative federalism: A federalism arrangement whereby responsibilities for most governmental functions are interdependent, shared between the federal and state governments.

Cost of living allowances (COLAs): A pay increase that matches the rate of inflation. COLAs maintain a fixed level of purchasing power, not an increase in purchasing power.

Council-manager system: Form of city government in which an elected council acts as a legislature, with no mayor. An appointed, professional city manager is hired to oversee executive functions. Some council-manager systems have one council member serve as a ceremonial mayor with no formal powers.

Court of last resort: Those courts whose decisions cannot be appealed to another court; these courts have the final word on a given set of laws. Typically called the *supreme court* (or something similar).

Cracking: Dispersing a party's voters among many districts so it will win fewer district races.

Cumulative voting: A form of voting in at-large elections for city councils and other bodies. Voters are given as many votes as positions up for election on the council. Rather than casting one vote per council position, voters can, if they want, give one candidate multiple votes. This makes it less likely that a cohesive majority will sweep all positions up for election.

Decentralization: Devolving to citizens or their elected representatives more power to make decisions, including the formation and implementation of public policies.

Dedicated funds: Special fees and taxes that are dedicated by statute for particular purposes and limit governors' budget-making power by reducing the discretion with which they can target spending.

Defendant: The person or institution against whom an action is brought in a court of law; the person being sued or accused of a crime.

Defense of Marriage Act (DOMA): Federal law enacted in 1996 that (1) defined *marriage* for the purposes of federal law as a relationship between one man and one woman, and (2) allowed the states not to recognize same-sex marriages sanctioned in other states.

Descriptive representation: The idea that a representative should reflect the characteristics of the people (the constituents) who she (or he) represents. Characteristics could include race, ethnicity, gender, and other traits related to the identity of the representative's constituents.

Devolution: The decentralization of power and authority from a central government to state or local governments.

Dillon's rule: Concept about the nature of local government powers (or "municipal corporations") from John F. Dillon, scholar and judge, circa 1872. Whereas states may be seen as having powers beyond those listed in the U.S. Constitution, local governments have only those powers explicitly granted to them by a state. Cities, counties, school districts, and "special districts" are thus legal entities created by their states.

Direct initiative: A measure proposed by a citizen or group. If the proposal qualifies with sufficient signatures, it is voted on directly by the public, and becomes law if approved.

Direct primary: An election in which voters select one candidate affiliated with a political party for each elected office; the party nominees later face one another in a general election.

Director of state courts: Administrator hired by a court system to handle the bureaucratic chores of the system, including personnel and budget issues.

District magnitude: The number of people elected to represent a political jurisdiction. In most American legislative races, district magnitude equals one. In at-large races, in multimember districts, and in most proportional representation systems, district magnitude is greater than one.

Disturbance theory: A macro-level theory that assumes groups emerge in response to societal changes.

Divided government: When two of the three legs of the legislative process (the governor, the house, and the senate) are controlled by different parties.

Docket: A calendar of the cases awaiting action in a court.

Domestic partnership: A relationship similar to a civil union, but usually with somewhat fewer legal rights and obligations.

Double jeopardy: The prosecution of a defendant for a criminal offense for which he or she has already been acquitted; this is prohibited by the Fifth Amendment to the U.S. Constitution.

Drug courts: Trial courts of limited jurisdiction used in some states and localities to prosecute certain minor drug and related offenses, with a focus on reducing recidivism and drug abuse treatment. Judges and lawyers working in these courts specialize in the issues surrounding drug abuse and addiction.

Dual federalism: A system of federalism whereby governmental functions are apportioned so that the national and subnational governments are accorded sovereign power within their respective spheres; sometimes referred to as "layer cake" federalism.

Earmark: In the context of government budgeting, the reservation of the revenue from a certain fee or tax into its own fund to be spent only for a specified purpose.

Earned media: Generating newsworthy events or stories for free publicity.

Economies of scale: Savings that may be achieved in the cost of production or service delivery by larger enterprises. Savings may be due to lower cost per unit of providing some service, or due to investment in expensive equipment that might be underutilized in a smaller setting.

Education management organizations (EMOs): For-profit companies hired to run some public schools.

Efficacy: The sense that one's effort at something can make a difference. *Personal efficacy* is the sense that you are able to understand politics.

External efficacy is the belief that public officials will respond to your political acts.

Efficiency gains: Providing services or goods at a lower cost per unit of service or per unit of the good supplied.

Elastic demand: Demand for something is said to be elastic if it responds to changes in price. If a tax raises the price of something that has elastic demand, such as travel or some luxury items, the tax may reduce consumption of the good.

Elasticity: The responsiveness of something to a change in price.

Electioneering: Explicitly supporting or opposing candidates or political parties, including recruiting and endorsing candidates, fundraising, phone banking, canvassing, and advertising.

Electoral targeting strategy: Caucus leaders taking a more active role in their rank-and-file colleagues' campaigns to help their party win close elections in particular districts.

Eminent domain: The power of the state and local governments to appropriate private property, typically for a public purpose. Some states also delegate this power to private entities, such as utility companies.

Entitlement: A government program guaranteeing a level of benefits to participating individuals or entities.

Ex post oversight: When the legislature investigates how well an agency is carrying out the intent of a law.

Executive budget: A reform of the Progressive era under which the first proposal of the budget for a government's next fiscal year is put together by the chief executive, whether it is the president, governor, or mayor.

Exportable tax: Taxes mostly paid by people from other places (such as hotel taxes and taxes on natural resources, such as oil).

Expressive act: Action taken for its symbolic meaning, rather than to have a practical effect.

Federal preemption: Federal government taking regulatory action that overrides state laws.

Federalism: The structural relationship between a national government and its constitutive states.

Feminization of poverty: The gap between women and men who are caught in the cycle of poverty, which is caused by occupational segregation, poor wages and lower pay than men, bearing the bulk of child care costs, and other structural conditions.

First trimester: The first three months of pregnancy, because a normal full pregnancy is nine months long.

Fiscal illusion: One explanation of government growth is fiscal illusion. The idea is that when states collect revenues by withholding taxes from paychecks or by taxing corporations, taxes are hidden. People might thus underestimate the true cost of public services, causing them to support more spending. James C. Garand, in "Explaining Government Growth in the U.S. States," contends that little empirical evidence supports this explanation.

Flat rate tax: A flat rate income tax applies the same tax rate to everyone, regardless of their income levels.

Free-rider problem: When the benefit of some valuable good or service cannot be restricted to those who pay for it.

Full Faith and Credit Clause: Article 4, Section 1, of the U.S. Constitution, which stipulates that the states must mutually accept one another's public acts, records, and judicial proceedings.

Full veto: The power of the chief executive to block the passage of an entire passed bill, subject to override by a supermajority vote of the legislature.

Functional party model: A theory that parties are pragmatic, self-interested organizations, striving to maximize votes in order to win elections and control political office.

Gatekeeping: Determining which questions and decisions will and will not be considered.

General jurisdiction: Referring to courts that deal with virtually any type of case.

General purpose local government: Cities and counties are general purpose governments, as they typically provide a range of services and functions; some provide much more than others.

General Revenue Sharing (GRS): A federal grant-in-aid program that provides financial aid to subnational units, but does not prescribe how those units are to allocate the funding.

Gerrymander: The process of drawing governmental district boundaries for political advantage.

Good-time Charlie: Some state governors in the mid-20th century who were less active in attacking public policy problems, less educated, older, and less qualified than most governors serving since that time; the term was coined by political scientist Larry Sabato.

Governmental watchdog: A group that monitors and publicizes the actions of government officials and agencies, and pulls a public alarm when something is awry.

Grandfather clause: Exemptions to post-Civil War rules granted to whites, based on the fact that they had a father or grandfather who was a citizen prior to the Civil War. As slaves (noncitizens), blacks were excluded by grandfather clauses.

Grassroots activities: Political activities undertaken by a group's members, rather than by its leaders, typically involving direct political action, like writing letters to policy makers and attending political rallies.

Growth controls: Various land use regulations that attempt to manage the pace and location of residential development.

Growth machine: A coalition of people active in local politics, united by a preference for policies that encourage population growth in their community.

Gubernatorial powers: Institutional and informal tools that a governor can use to develop and promote public policy, manage the state bureaucracy, and act as intergovernmental relations (IGR) manager, among other duties.

Head of state: The main public representative of a government.

Home rule: The delegation of power from a state government to local governments. Home rule charters define the boundaries of local government autonomy, and result in less state control over local government affairs.

Homeschooling: The education of children at home, typically by parents but sometimes by tutors, rather than in a formal setting of public or private school.

Hypothesis: A potential answer to a research question that is based on theory and that will be tested by observing data in the world.

Impact fee: Housing growth control fees set to be roughly proportional to the impact that new development creates.

Implementation: The execution by government agencies of laws passed by the legislature.

Incorporation: State laws define the process of municipal incorporation. This is required for a city or town to have greater autonomy from its county and state governments.

Incorporation of the Bill of Rights: A legal doctrine whereby parts of the U.S. Bill of Rights are applied to the states through the Fourteenth Amendment's Due Process Clause.

Incumbent: The person currently holding a position.

Incumbent-protection district: A governmental district drawn to give electoral advantage to the incumbent.

Indirect initiative: A measure proposed by a citizen or group. If the proposal qualifies, it is directed to the state legislature. The legislature can vote to approve the measure as written, or refer it to the voters for approval. The legislature may also refer an alternate proposal along with the initiative proposal.

Individualistic political culture: The general and informal set of beliefs and attitudes that politics in a state or community is a place where individuals can work to advance their personal economic and social interests largely the same as they would do in private business.

Industrial development revenue bonds: Debt issued by local governments on behalf of a private company for the purpose of building facilities or acquiring land. Interest payments on revenue bonds are financed by revenues from the project the bonds are issued for.

Inelastic demand: Demand for something is said to be inelastic if it does not respond to changes in price. If a tax raises the price of something that has inelastic demand, such as basic foods, medical care, or things that people are addicted to, the tax may not reduce consumption of the good.

In-house lobbyist: A professional lobbyist who is a permanent employee of an interest group.

Injunction: A court order prohibiting someone from taking some action.

Interest group: A formally organized body of individuals, organizations, or public or private enterprises sharing common goals and joining in a collective attempt to influence the electoral and policy-making processes.

Interest group system density: The number of functioning groups relative to the size of a state's economy.

Interest group system diversity: The spread of groups in a state across social and economic realms.

Intergovernmental relations: The interactions among the federal government, the states, and local governments.

Intermediate courts of appeal: Courts that hear appeals of trial decisions and are concerned with whether the trial was fair and conducted with proper procedures. ICAs were developed as a way to take the burden of routine appeals off of supreme courts so that supreme courts can focus on the most important cases.

Intermunicipal inequality: Differences between communities in the social status and wealth of community residents.

Issue advocacy: A form of political speech focusing on issues of public concern that mentions issues and the positions taken on those issues by elected officials or candidates, but stops short of expressly advocating the support or defeat of those elected officials or candidates.

Issue evolution: The process by which the definition and politics of a public policy issue change over time.

Jacksonian democracy: A broad philosophy of government, associated with the era when Andrew Jackson was president (1829-1837), that emphasized executive power, broad suffrage (for white males), the election of many public officials, laissez-faire economics, and patronage appointments for government employment.

Judicial review: The power of a supreme court to judge whether a law is in violation of the state constitution and, if so, to nullify that law.

Jurisdiction: Geographical or topical area over which a court, institution, or official has power and authority.

Jury: A randomly selected group of citizens who are sworn by a court to hear and render a verdict and/or set a penalty in a trial.

Lame duck: An elected official who will not or cannot run for his or her current office in the next election; also, any official who has been voted out of office and is serving in the last days of a term before the new official is sworn in.

Land Ordinance of 1785: An act of Congress that set a process to sell land west of the Appalachian Mountains, north of the Ohio River, and east of the Mississippi River for $1.00 per acre. The act set rules for the creation of townships in the area.

Legal brief: A document stating legal facts and arguments.

Legislative intent: What the legislature meant for a piece of legislation to do when it passed it.

Legislative professionalism: When a legislature is established to be largely a full-time body, with members who are paid a living wage, have plenty of staff, and believe that legislating is their primary job.

Legislative referendum: Legislation approved by the legislature, but referred to the voters for final approval. Some legislation, like constitutional amendments (in most states) or bond issues (in some states and communities), must be referred to voters for final approval.

Legislative turnover: The degree to which the membership of a legislature changes after an election.

Leviathan: The model of government as an entity that seeks to increase revenues beyond even what the public might demand.

Libertarianism: A political ideology that values freedom of individual action from government interference, control, or help.

Limited jurisdiction: Referring to courts that handle cases on only certain topics, such as traffic courts or probate courts.

Line-item veto: The power of some governors to block only parts of passed appropriations bills from becoming law, subject to override by a supermajority vote of the legislature.

Literacy tests: Post–Civil War rules that denied blacks the vote; literacy tests included tests designed to be too difficult for most people to pass. The test could ask people to interpret passages from the U.S. Constitution, and allowed local officials the discretion to judge if answers were right or wrong. Whites who would fail the tests could vote based on a grandfather clause.

Living wage: An area-specific level of income and benefits needed for working individuals to subsist at a basic or decent level that takes into consideration cost of living factors.

Lobbying: Communicating with elected officials in general, as well as the systematic effort to shape public policy by pressuring governmental officials to make decisions in line with the goals of an organized interest.

The term *lobbying* comes from the fact that representatives were often approached in the lobby of legislative buildings.

Local charter: In essence, a constitution for a local government, focusing primarily on the institutions of that government.

Louisiana Purchase: The purchase of the French Territory of Louisiana (more than 500 million acres of land) from France in 1803. The purchase included land that is now Arkansas, Kansas, Missouri, Iowa, Nebraska, and Oklahoma, as well as much of what is now Louisiana, Colorado, Minnesota, Montana, North and South Dakota, and Wyoming.

Machines: A term for local political party organizations that used patronage and clientele politics to control elections in many U.S. cities.

Majority-minority district: Legislative districts where district lines are drawn so that people from a specific minority group comprise a majority of voters in the district.

Majority opinion: The official report giving the rationale behind the majority decision on a case.

Malapportionment: When the districts in a legislative chamber are not equal in population.

Means-tested: The provision of need-based public assistance and financial aid by government that is available only to individuals falling below a predetermined level of income or assets.

Media market: Region where the population is exposed to the same (or similar) media offerings, including the same television and radio stations and newspapers.

Medicaid: Created by Congress in 1965, a joint federal- and state-financed public assistance program administered by the states that provides payments directly to health care providers for medical services rendered to means-tested low-income individuals and families.

Medicare: Created by Congress in 1965, a federally financed social insurance health care program for people 65 or older and people of all ages with certain disabilities.

Mental health courts: Trial courts of limited jurisdiction used in some states and localities to prosecute certain offenses by those who have a mental illness, with a focus on reducing recidivism by treating the mental illness. Judges and lawyers working in these courts specialize in the issues surrounding mental health.

Merit Plan: A method used to select at least some judges in 24 states whereby (1) a panel of experts recommends a few candidates for a judicial opening to the governor, (2) who then appoints one person to that position for a trial period, and (3) after which the judge faces a retention election to see whether he or she will earn a full term.

Metropolitan areas: Regions of mostly contiguous population centers, as defined by the U.S. Census Bureau. A large area, such as New York, can include several metropolitan areas (northern New Jersey, Long Island, and Connecticut) consolidated into a larger metropolitan area. Smaller regions, such as Pocatello, Idaho, may include cities and towns in a single county.

Meyer v. Grant: A 1988 U.S. Supreme Court ruling against a Colorado law that made it a felony to pay for the collection of signatures on initiative and referendum petitions. The Court ruled that spending to collect signatures was "core political speech" and that no state could ban campaign spending on signature collection. Since 2005, however, two federal appellate courts (the 8th Circuit and 9th Circuit) have permitted states to ban payment per signature, thus requiring that paid petitioners receive a salary or an hourly wage.

Mobilization of bias: The benefiting of private, organized interests in an interest group system.

Model city charter: Recommendations for how city political institutions should be arranged. Model charters published by the National Municipal League (now called the National Civic League) have been published since 1900.

Moralistic political culture: The general and informal set of beliefs and attitudes that politics in a state or community is intended to enhance the public good and for the uplifting of the have-nots of society.

Morality policy: A policy on which at least one side of the debate (and often only one side) bases its arguments on basic moral values, often supported by religious beliefs.

Muckraking journalists: Journalists and authors who exposed issues of political corruption, public health dangers, and child labor practices. The writing of muckrakers was featured in newspapers and magazines such as *Cosmopolitan*, *Harper's Weekly*, and *McClure's*. Some famous muckrakers included Thomas Nast, Lincoln Stephens, and Upton Sinclair.

Multimember district (MMD): Legislative districts that elect more than one representative. Some state legislative districts, and many local councils, have more than one representative elected per district.

Multiparty politics: Political systems where three or more parties are able to win office. The United States, in contrast, is dominated by two-party politics.

Municipal charters: The set of rules that define how cities are structured, what the powers of local officials are, and how local elections shall be conducted.

National Governors Association: Bipartisan association of the 55 state and territorial governors, supported by research and training staff, through which governors can consult one another about their common problems.

National Supremacy Clause: Stipulates that the U.S. Constitution and national laws and treaties "shall be the supreme law of the land."

Necessary and Proper Clause: Known also as the *Elastic Clause*, it grants Congress the power to make all laws that shall be "necessary and proper for carrying into execution the foregoing powers," that is, the other congressional powers listed in Article I, Section 8 of the Constitution.

Neutral competence: The value that a government agency should implement policy based only on original legislative intent and its workers' professional norms and training rather than by nonlegislative political pressure.

No Child Left Behind Act (NCLB): Signed into law by President George W. Bush in January 2002, the bipartisan act greatly expanded the role of the federal government in K-12 public education. The law requires annual assessments of student performance, requiring that children and schools attain adequate yearly progress (AYP).

Nonpartisan blanket primary: All candidates, regardless of their party, face off in the same primary election, with a candidate winning the election outright if he or she wins more than 50 percent of the vote.

Nonpartisan primary: An election to nominate candidates for the general election where candidates have no party labels, and all voters can participate. Used in many local elections, and at the state level in Nebraska.

Nullification: A constitutional theory, advanced most notably by John C. Calhoun and other advocates of states' rights, espousing the right of a state to declare null and void a law passed by the U.S. Congress that the state found to be unconstitutional or disagreeable.

Office-block ballot: Groups together all candidates running for a single political office by the political office rather than by their party.

OP-ED article: Newspaper article written to advocate a point of view, usually found opposite the editorial page (hence the name *OP-ED*).

Open primary: A primary nomination election. Any registered voter, including independents, can participate. Voters must decide which party's primary they will participate in, and can choose only among that party's candidates.

Operating budget: The part of a state's budget dedicated to paying for current operations, such as public services and public employee salaries.

Original jurisdiction: The right of a court to be the first to hear a case; where a case must begin its path through the judicial system.

Out-of-court settlement: An agreement made privately between the parties to a civil suit before a trial court decision.

Outsider gubernatorial candidates: Candidates for governor who are not traditional politicians but who have achieved success in other ways, such as in business or as entertainers.

Override: When the legislature passes a law despite a gubernatorial veto, usually by a supermajority vote in each chamber.

Packing: Concentrating one party's voters into a few districts so as to "waste" those votes over 50 percent, allowing the other party to win more district races.

Pardon: The power of some governors to throw out the conviction of a person convicted of a crime.

Participation bias: The difference between the general population of eligible voters and the people who actually participate in elections. Bias in participation exists if participants are substantially different than nonparticipants.

Partisan dealignment: The weakening of the attachment that voters have to a political party.

Partisan primary: A primary election to decide a party's nominee for the general election ballot.

Party boss: The head of an urban or state party machine who controls elections and the disbursement of patronage.

Party caucus: All the legislators in a given chamber from a given party, such as the house Democrats or the senate Republicans.

Party fusion: Permits two or more parties to nominate the same candidate for office,

with the candidate's name appearing on the ballot alongside the name of each party by which he or she is cross-endorsed.

Party identification: Also known as PID, it is the strength of an individual's attachment to a political party.

Party-column ballot: Groups together all candidates running for different political offices by their party affiliation, making straight-ticket voting possible.

Patronage: Favors and benefits that elected officials provide their supporters. Nineteenth-century party machines used city jobs as one source of patronage to reward loyal supporters.

Patronage appointments: The rewarding of government offices to loyal supporters in exchange for their political support.

Patronage job: A government job obtained at least in part through political connections rather than entirely by personal merit; used by elected officials to reward their political supporters and secure loyalty from the bureaucracy.

Pendleton Act: The Civil Service Reform Act of 1883, which created a modern civil service for the federal government. This made it more difficult for politicians to place their supporters in federal government jobs.

Petition: To make a formal request.

Plaintiff: The party that starts a lawsuit in a court of law.

Plea bargaining: A deal in which the defendant in a criminal case agrees to plead guilty to a lesser charge if the prosecutor agrees to drop a more serious charge.

Pluralism: A political theory that assumes conflict is at the heart of politics and that the diversity of interests will lead to consensual outcomes through discussion and debate.

Police powers: Local government power to provide for the common health, safety, and welfare of a community. The broad exercise of such power can be seen in setting public health, building, and food safety codes, and preventing construction in flood zones.

Policy agenda: The public problems and solutions that are discussed and addressed by policy makers at a given time.

Political culture: What people in a group or region generally believe about government and politics; what they think government ought to do and how people should act toward it.

Policy diffusion: The transfer or emulation of an idea, institution, or policy of one political jurisdiction by another.

Policy entrepreneur: A person who identifies a public need and works to motivate citizens and policy makers to change policy to satisfy that need.

Policy equilibrium: When policy-making forces (such as the current policy, interest group preferences, public opinion, and the issue environment) are balanced, so that little policy debate or change occurs.

Policy shock: An event that changes an issue's political environment, disrupts the policy equilibrium, and starts active policy making.

Political accountability: The value that government agencies should implement law following closely the wishes of current elected officials.

Political action committee (PAC): A legal entity that allows like-minded individuals who belong to a corporation, labor union, or virtually any other organization to bundle their contributions and give them to candidates or political parties.

Political agenda: The public problems and policy solutions under discussion by policy makers and the public at any given time.

Political capital: The intangible goodwill or support for an elected official that can be used to influence the actions of other officials informally.

Political ideology: A relatively coherent and consistent set of beliefs about who ought to rule, what principles ought to be used to govern, and what policies rulers ought to pursue.

Political institution: The rules, laws, and organizations through which and by which government functions.

Poll tax: A tax or fee that must be paid in order to secure the right to register or to vote.

Popular referendum: Legislation approved by the legislature (or a local government) that is put to a popular vote as a result of a successful petition for a referendum. It allows voters to have the final decision on legislation written by elected officials.

Populist era: The 1890s, during which time the Populist political movement was influential, particularly in the West. Populists advocated greater popular democracy, government control of key industries, and a national income tax.

Populist Party: A "third" American political party that had its greatest success in the 1890s. Populists were elected to state legislatures as well as to the U.S. House and Senate. The party called for political reforms including direct democracy, direct election of the U.S. Senate, and direct election of the president.

Pork barrel: A derogatory and subjective term referring to government spending that is focused on a single geographic area, such as a bridge or a park, suggesting that such spending is wasteful and politically motivated.

Potential interest: An interest that is yet to be organized but has some latent acceptance in society.

Precedent: A judicial decision that may be used as a standard in subsequent similar cases.

Precinct: One of the smallest geographic units in a town, city, or county. Precincts comprise several city blocks. A neighborhood might consist of several precincts.

Precinct captain: A party machine operative who worked to organize a city neighborhood on behalf of the party machine.

Primary election: An election to decide which candidates will be able to be listed on the general election (November) ballot.

Privatization: When a city transfers the authority to supply a service to a private firm.

Privileges and Immunities Clause: Ensures that residents of one state cannot be discriminated against by another state when it comes to fundamental matters, such as pursuing one's professional occupation or gaining access to the courts.

Problem-solving courts: Trial courts of limited jurisdiction whose focus is less on prosecuting crimes or settling lawsuits than on helping the parties in the case work out certain types of especially difficult problems; for example, family court, drug court, and mental health courts can be thought of as problem-solving courts.

Progressive era: A period of political change and reform during the early decades of the 20th century. Some Progressives hoped to reform politics by limiting the power of corporations and political parties.

Progressive Federalism: Rehashing of cooperative (or coercive) federalism, with the federal government calling most of the shots and setting the standards.

Progressive tax: A progressive tax has wealthier people pay a larger proportion of their income to cover the tax. The less affluent pay a lower share of their income toward the tax.

Progressives: Members of the political party and social movement of the early 20th century whose aim was to improve government and public policy through rationality and broadening political participation.

Pro-life and pro-choice: Positive, self-identifying labels for groups opposing abortion (pro-life) and supporting the availability of legal abortion (pro-choice).

Proposition 13: A constitutional initiative approved by California voters in 1978. One of the first major antitax initiatives, Proposition 13 froze property values at 1977 levels, limited future increases in property taxes, and is credited with setting an antitax mood that helped propel Ronald Reagan to the White House.

Public assistance: A means-tested program that provides aid—both cash and in-kind services—to the poor.

Public goods: Policies or actions providing broad benefits, rather than narrow benefits to a specific group.

Racial gerrymandering: Drawing boundaries for legislative districts on the basis of race.

Rank-and-file legislator: Legislator who does not hold a leadership position in his or her chamber.

Reapportionment revolution: The political upheaval in the states in the 1960s following the U.S. Supreme Court's mandate that they redraw their legislative and congressional districts to be equal in size in each chamber.

Recall: A vote to remove an elected official from public office. Recall proposals qualify if sufficient signatures are collected.

Recidivism: The tendency to relapse into a previous pattern of behavior, especially criminal behavior.

Reconstruction: The post-Civil War era (1865–1877) when government and public policy in the 11 states of the former Confederacy were dominated by the federal government, immigrants from the northern states ("carpetbaggers"), and freed slaves, and where those sympathetic with the Confederacy were shut out of the political process.

Recuse: To disqualify from participation in a decision on grounds such as prejudice, personal involvement, or conflict of interest.

Redistricting: The redrawing of political districts, as required after each census to keep them equal in population.

Reduction veto: The power of some state governors to reduce the level of spending authorized in an appropriations bill passed by the legislature, subject to an override by a supermajority vote of the legislature.

Reform: A word referring to a policy or institutional change that connotes a positive, purposeful change.

Regional-metropolitan government: Governing structures that united various local governments, often for a single purpose, such as managing airports, protecting air quality, running parks, or providing public transportation. A few large cities consolidated with their counties to form a single government (for example, Nashville and San Francisco).

Regional revenue sharing: Several local jurisdictions in an area can pool revenues from a tax source, or from new development, and then distribute the revenue across all jurisdictions.

Regressive tax: A regressive tax is one in which the less affluent pay a greater share of their income to cover the tax. The wealthy pay a lower share of their income toward the tax.

Regulatory takings: Government actions that deny a property owner fair use of property without adequate compensation.

Rent control: Local policies that attempt to limit the amount that landowners may increase rents each year on existing tenants.

Reserve Clause: The powers not delegated to the United States by the Constitution, nor prohibited by it to the States, are reserved to the States respectively, or to the people.

Responsible party model: A theory advanced by 18th-century Irish philosopher Edmund Burke that parties should be ideologically consistent, presenting voters with a clear platform and set of policies that are principled and distinctive. Elected officials are expected to be held responsible for implementing the party's program and policies.

Retention election: An election in which the issue on the ballot is whether an incumbent should be kept in office (yes or no), rather than one that offers a choice between two or more competing candidates.

Roll call: When legislators are required to cast a recorded vote on a bill or motion, whether in a committee or on the chamber floor.

Runaway jury: A subjective and pejorative term used to describe a jury whose verdict, in the judgment of the describer, goes against the obvious facts in the case.

School districts: A form of a special-purpose local government that operates public schools; differing in autonomy, their geographic boundaries, taxing authority, and policy recommendations are broadly set (and limited) by state officials.

School voucher: The use of public funds to cover the costs of private education, whereby financial aid in the form of a voucher is provided to parents to transfer their children from public schools to private schools.

Selective benefit: The provision by a group of some material, purposive, or solidarity incentive that can be enjoyed only by members of the group.

Self-financing candidates: Candidates for office who mainly use their own money for their campaign expenses.

Semiclosed primary: Voting in a party's primary is permitted for voters who are registered with the party or as independents.

Semiopen primary: Registered voters may vote in any party's primary, but they must publicly declare for which party's primary they choose to vote.

Sin tax: A tax on an item or behavior that is unpopular, or a tax on a product that the state seeks to reduce consumption of.

Single-issue groups: Interest groups with a relatively narrow focus.

Single-member district (SMD): Legislative district in which only one legislator from the same chamber serves.

Single-payer health care: A health system financed by one source—usually the federal government—in which doctors and other private health care professionals provide basic services to every person, with their fees paid by the government at a fixed rate.

Single-subject rule: Rules that require that an initiative address only one question or issue. Twelve states have such rules for their initiative process. The definition of a *single* subject varies widely, as does how courts interpret them. Some courts have become more assertive in rejecting initiatives on the grounds that this rule is violated.

Small claims courts: A trial court of limited jurisdiction that deals only with civil suits of less than a specified amount of claimed damages (e.g., $5,000) and in which the plaintiff and defendant are not represented by legal counsel.

Social capital: Networks of trust and reciprocity built from participation in voluntary social groups.

Social insurance: Rather than means-tested, a government-created program (such as Social Security) that socializes risk by forcing the compulsory contributions of participants.

Social Security Act: Technically known as the Old Age, Survivors and Disability Insurance program (OASDI), a federal social insurance program created in 1935 providing economic assistance mainly to retired workers and their families.

Sodomy: Any sexual act other than coitus between a man and a woman, often referring to homosexual activity.

Soft money: Campaign funds not regulated by federal election laws, originally intended to be used for party building and for state and local general electioneering activities.

Special districts: Local governments that are established (under state laws) for limited purposes, such as providing a single public service.

Special session: An extraordinary meeting of the legislature after its regular session has adjourned, usually called by the governor to consider a very limited policy agenda.

Specialty court: Courts with very limited jurisdictions to deal with special populations or special crimes.

Spoils system: An informal system in which political appointments are rewarded on the basis of political considerations, rather than fitness for office.

Sprawl: Sprawl is typically characterized by excessive land use. This includes low-density housing, limited options for transportation (other than cars), gaps between developed and undeveloped areas, high levels of pavement for parking spaces, and uniformity of housing type.

Standing committee: An at least semipermanent legislative committee that evaluates legislation in a particular area of policy.

State auditor: a high-ranking official who heads a unit that conducts financial and program evaluations of state agencies, both routinely and in response to legislative requests.

State of the State address: In most states, the annual address by the governor to the state legislature at the beginning of its session in which he or she describes the condition of the state and presents a policy agenda for the coming legislative session.

Statute: A law passed by a legislative body.

Statutory initiative: An initiative measure that amends a regular law, or adds a new law to the statute books. If approved by voters, statutory initiative measures have the status of laws passed through the regular legislative process. Statutory initiative laws are thus typically easier for elected officials to amend (or repeal) than constitutional initiative laws.

Stay of execution: The power of governors in most states with capital punishment to delay temporarily executing a condemned person.

Straight-ticket ballot: A type of ballot that allows (or requires) voters to cast their votes for candidates of a single political party.

Street-level bureaucrats: Government workers who have direct contact with the public, such as police officers, teachers, and driver's license examiners.

Strong mayor-council system: Form of city government where an elected mayor holds many executive functions, including influence over budgeting, appointment of department heads, and veto powers. Sometimes referred to as a mayor–council system.

Suburb: A community separate and distinct from an established central city. Suburbs can be incorporated cities or towns, as well as unincorporated places.

Super majority: A portion of a vote that is greater than one-half, such as two-thirds or three-fifths.

Supermajority vote requirement: A rule that requires more than a simple majority vote to approve a budget, for example, 60 percent or a two-thirds majority.

Supreme court: The highest court in a judicial system, with final appellate jurisdiction over cases of law in that system.

Swing seat: Legislative seats that are closely contested by the parties.

Tammany Hall: A machine that controlled New York City politics during the late 1800s.

Targeting electoral strategy: Focusing campaign resources where they will be most effective, especially by supplying more resources to close races and fewer to those in which a candidate will likely either lose or win.

Tax and expenditure limits (TELS): Rules that limit how much a state legislature may increase revenues or spending in an annual budget.

Tax equity: Tax equity refers to which income groups bear the burden of a tax.

Temporary Assistance for Needy Families (TANF): Created by Congress in 1996 to replace AFDC (Aid to Families with Dependent Children), a social welfare program that provides monthly cash assistance (up to four years) to means-tested poor families with children under the age of 18; it requires recipients to participate in a work activity.

Term limits: The requirement that a person can be elected to a certain office only for a specified number of terms or years.

Top-two primary: Allows eligible voters, irrespective of their party affiliation, to vote in a primary for any candidate running on any party ticket, with the top candidates from each political party squaring off in the general election.

Tort: Damage, injury, or a wrongful act to person or property—whether done willfully or negligently— for which a civil suit can be brought.

Traditionalistic political culture: The general and informal set of beliefs and attitudes that politics in a state or community is the domain of social and economic elites and that the have-nots ought not to get involved in politics.

Trial court: A court before which issues of fact and law are tried and determined for a legal case.

Trial transcript: The official, verbatim, and written record of what was said during a trial.

Two-party contestation: When both major parties have a general election nominee in a race for a given office.

Underclass: The least privileged social stratum, characterized by joblessness, social isolation, and impoverished and unsafe neighborhoods.

Unfunded mandate: A public policy that requires a subnational government to pay for an activity or project established by the federal government.

Unicameral: Having only one chamber, such as the Nebraska Legislature, which has a senate but no house.

Unified government: When all three legs of the legislative process (the governor, the house, and the senate) are controlled by the same party.

Unincorporated area: Areas of a county that have not formally incorporated as a municipality (city, town, and village). Unincorporated areas are typically administered by county governments, and may receive services from counties and special districts.

Unit of analysis: In scientific research, the generic person, place, or thing being studied.

Unitary system: A system of governance with a strong central government that controls virtually all aspects of its constitutive subnational governments.

Urban growth areas: Areas adjacent to existing development that is slated for future growth. Some state land use plans attempt to increase housing density within designated urban growth area boundaries before allowing development in outlying areas.

Urbanization: The sociologist Louis Wirth defined urbanization as a process where a city grows in size, density, and heterogeneity.

User fees: A direct charge for use of a service, charged to the user of the service. Examples include tuition and hospital charges.

Veto-proof majority: When the legislative majority party has a supermajority of members large enough to override a gubernatorial veto, if all majority party members vote to do so.

Vice laws: Laws banning certain activities thought to be sinful, particularly gambling, prostitution, pornography, sodomy, and drug use.

Village of Euclid v. Ambler Realty Company: A U.S. Supreme Court decision from 1926 that established that local government police powers include zoning power.

Virtual schools: Online, personalized course instruction.

Voting cue: A simple signal about how to vote, in lieu of more detailed information; for example, a candidate's political party.

Voting Rights Act: A law passed by Congress in 1965 designed to remove racial barriers to voting. The original law gave the federal government authority over local voter registration procedures in several southern states. It has been amended and reauthorized by Congress several times since 1965.

Voting-age population: All U.S. residents age 18 and over.

Voting-eligible population: All U.S. citizens age 18 and over who are not excluded from voter eligibility due to criminal status (felony convictions, incarceration, or parole) or due to being declared incompetent to vote.

Ward: Also known as a *district*. Districts and wards elect their own representatives to a city council.

Weak mayor–council systems: Form of city government where a mayor has limited formal power. In the machine era, a city council in weak mayor systems had influence over executive and administrative functions such as hiring and purchasing. Sometimes referred to as a council–mayor system.

Wedge issues: Controversial issues placed for a public vote via the initiative or referendum process by one political party or group, with the goal of dividing candidates and supporters of a rival party or group.

Welfare: A range of public assistance services provided by government to aid and protect the most vulnerable individuals in society; includes both social insurance and public assistance programs.

Winner-take-all: Also known as *plurality* election rules. When a single person represents a jurisdiction or just one person can win an elected position, the candidate with the most votes (the first to win, so to speak) is elected.

Working poor: A social stratum comprised of individuals who are gainfully employed, but who earn too little to subsist, thereby relying on public assistance and charities to make ends meet.

Writ of certiorari: The discretionary review of a lower court's ruling.

Zoning: The power of local governments to regulate land use. A zoning map divides a community into areas where specific types of land use are allowed (for example, residential, commercial, industrial, or agricultural). Zoning ordinances provide detailed standards for allowable building designs, lot sizes, building heights, landscaping requirements, and yard size, and how far buildings must be set back from the road.

Governors' Institutional Powers

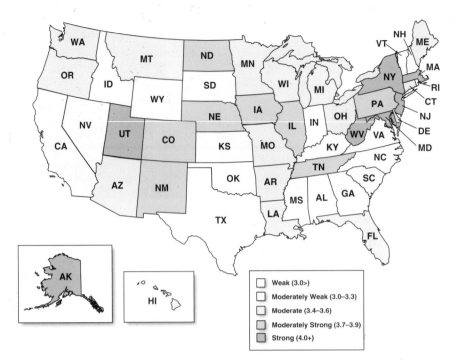

Note: This figure compares governorships' institutional power based on appointments, independently elected executives, tenure potential, the state budget, party control of the legislature, and the veto.
Source: A modification of an index developed in Thad Beyle and Margaret Ferguson, "Governors and the Executive Branch," in *Politics in the American States*, 9th ed., ed. Virginia Gray and Russell L. Hanson (Washington, D.C.: CQ Press, 2008).

★★

State Legislative Term Limits

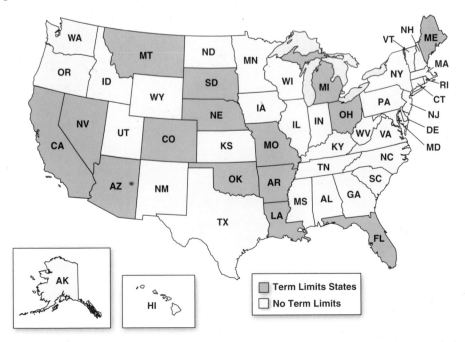